Communications in Computer and Information Science 1156

Commenced Publication in 2007
Founding and Former Series Editors:
Phoebe Chen, Alfredo Cuzzocrea, Xiaoyong Du, Orhun Kara, Ting Liu,
Krishna M. Sivalingam, Dominik Ślęzak, Takashi Washio, Xiaokang Yang,
and Junsong Yuan

More information about this series at http://www.springer.com/series/7899

Zibin Zheng · Hong-Ning Dai ·
Mingdong Tang · Xiangping Chen (Eds.)

Blockchain and Trustworthy Systems

First International Conference, BlockSys 2019
Guangzhou, China, December 7–8, 2019
Proceedings

Springer

Editors
Zibin Zheng ⓘ
Sun Yat-sen University
Guangzhou, China

Mingdong Tang ⓘ
Guangdong University of Foreign Studies
Guangzhou, China

Hong-Ning Dai ⓘ
Macau University of Science
and Technology
Macau, China

Xiangping Chen ⓘ
Sun Yat-sen University
Guangzhou, China

ISSN 1865-0929 ISSN 1865-0937 (electronic)
Communications in Computer and Information Science
ISBN 978-981-15-2776-0 ISBN 978-981-15-2777-7 (eBook)
https://doi.org/10.1007/978-981-15-2777-7

This Springer imprint is published by the registered company Springer Nature Singapore Pte Ltd.
The registered company address is: 152 Beach Road, #21-01/04 Gateway East, Singapore 189721, Singapore

Preface

Blockchain has become a hot research area in academia and industry. The blockchain technology is transforming industries by enabling anonymous and trustful transactions in decentralized and trustless environments. As a result, blockchain technology and other technologies for developing trustworthy systems can be used to reduce system risks, mitigate financial fraud, and cut down operational cost. Blockchain and trustworthy systems can be applied to many fields, such as financial services, social management, and supply chain management.

This volume contains the papers presented at the International Conference on Blockchain and Trustworthy Systems (BlockSys 2019), held in Guangzhou, China. This conference was held as the first in its series with an emphasis on state-of-the-art advances in blockchain and trustworthy systems. The main conference received 130 paper submissions, out of which 50 papers were accepted as regular papers and 19 as short papers. All papers underwent a rigorous peer review process – each paper was reviewed by three experts. The accepted papers together with our outstanding keynote and invited speeches led to a vibrant technical program. We are looking forward to future events in this conference series.

The conference would not have been successful without help from so many people. We would like to thank the Organizing Committee for their hard work in putting together the conference. First, we would like to express our sincere thanks to the guidance from Horary Chairs: Michael R. Lyu and Chunming Rong. We would like to express our deep gratitude to General Chairs: Zibin Zheng, Kuan-Ching Li, and Yan Zhang for their support and promotion of this event. We would also like to thank the Program Chairs: Patrick C. K. Hung, Hong-Ning Dai, and Mingdong Tang, who supervised the review process of the technical papers and compiled a high-quality technical program. We also extend our deep gratitude to the Program Committee members whose diligent work in reviewing the papers lead to the high quality of the accepted papers. We greatly appreciate the excellent support and hard work of Publicity Chairs: Daniel Xiapu Luo and Yong Ding; Publication Chairs: Jiajing Wu and Wei Liang; Local Organizing Committee Chairs: Xiangping Chen and Wuhui Chen; and Industry Chair: Jing Bian. Most importantly, we would like to thank the authors for submitting their papers to the BlockSys 2019 conference.

We believe that the BlockSys conference provides a good forum for both academic researchers and industrial practitioners to discuss all technical advances in blockchain and trustworthy systems. We also expect that future BlockSys conferences will be as successful as indicated by the contributions presented in this volume.

December 2019

Patrick C. K. Hung
Hong-Ning Dai
Mingdong Tang

Organization

Honorary Chairs

Chunming Rong   University of Stavanger, Norway
Michael R. Lyu   Chinese University of Hong Kong, Hong Kong, China

General Chairs

Zibin Zheng   Sun Yat-sen University, China
Kuan-Ching Li   Providence University, Taiwan, China
Yan Zhang   University of Oslo, Norway

Program Chairs

Patrick C. K. Hung   University of Ontario Institute of Technology, Canada
Hong-Ning Dai   Macau University of Science and Technology, Macau, China
Mingdong Tang   Guangdong University of Foreign Studies, China

Organizing Chairs

Xiangping Chen   Sun Yat-sen University, China
Wuhui Chen   Sun Yat-sen University, China

Publicity Chairs

Daniel Xiapu Luo   The Hong Kong Polytechnic University, Hong Kong, China
Yong Ding   Guilin University of Electronic Technology, China

Publication Chairs

Jiajing Wu   Sun Yat-sen University, China
Wei Liang   Xiamen University of Technology, China

Industry Chair

Jing Bian   Sun Yat-sen University, China

Special Track Chairs

Yong Ding	Guilin University of Electronic Technology, China
Yongjuan Wang	Henan Key Laboratory of Network Cryptography Technology, China
Chunxiang Gu	Strategic Support Force Information Engineering University, China
Ao Zhou	Beijing University of Posts and Telecommunications, China
Wei Liang	Xiamen University of Technology, China
Lijian Wei	Sun Yat-sen University, China
Yiwen Zhang	Anhui University, China

Program Committee

Alexander Chepurnoy	IOHK Research, Russia
Ali Vatankhah	Kennesaw State University, USA
Andreas Veneris	University of Toronto, Canada
Bahman Javadi	Western Sydney University, Australia
Bo Jiang	Beihang University, China
Buqing Cao	Hunan University of Science and Technology, China
Chang-Ai Sun	University of Science and Technology Beijing, China
Claudio Schifanella	University of Turin, Italy
Chunhua Su	Osaka University, Japan
Debiao He	Wuhan University, China
Fangguo Zhang	Sun Yat-sen University, China
Gerhard Hancke	City University of Hong Kong, Hong Kong, China
Guobing Zou	Shanghai University, China
Haibo Tian	Sun Yat-sen Univeristy, China
Han Liu	Tsinghua University, China
Jan Henrik Ziegeldorf	RWTH Aachen University, Germany
Jiwei Huang	China University of Petroleum, China
Kai Lei	Peking University, China
Kenneth Fletcher	University of Massachusetts Boston, USA
Kouichi Sakurai	Kyushu University, Japan
Laizhong Cui	Shenzhen University, China
Liehuang Zhu	Beijing Institute of Technology, China
Mario Larangeira	IOHK and Tokyo Institute of Technology, Japan
Muhammad Imran	King Saud University, Saudi Arabia
Omer Rana	Cardiff University, UK
Pengcheng Zhang	Hohai University, China
Qianhong Wu	Beihang University, China
Qinghua Lu	CSIRO, Australia
Raja Jurdak	CSIRO, Australia
Shangguang Wang	Beijing University of Posts and Telecommunications, China

Shijun Liu	Shandong University, China
Shiping Chen	CSIRO, Australia
Shizhan Chen	Tianjin University, China
Shuiguang Deng	Zhejiang University, China
Sude Qing	China Academy of Information and Communications Technology, China
Tao Xiang	Chongqing University, China
Ting Chen	University of Electronic Science and Technology of China, China
Tsuyoshi Ide	IBM, USA
Walter Li	Beijing University of Technology, China
Wei Luo	Zhejiang University, China
Wei Song	Nanjing University of Science and Technology, China
Weifeng Pan	Zhejiang Gongshang University, China
Xiaodong Fu	Kunming University of Science and Technology, China
Xiaoliang Fan	Xiamen University, China
Yu Jiang	Tsinghua University, China
Yucong Duan	Hainan University, China
Yutao Ma	Wuhan University, China
Zekeriya Erkin	Delft University of Technology, The Netherlands
Zhe Liu	Nanjing University of Aeronautics and Astronautics, China
Zhihui Lu	Fudan University, China
Zhiying Tu	Harbin Institute of Technology, China
Zoe L. Jiang	Harbin Institute of Technology (Shenzhen), China

Contents

Theories and Algorithms for Blockchain

A Group Signature Based Digital Currency System.................... 3
Haibo Tian, Peiran Luo, and Yinxue Su

RLWE Commitment-Based Linkable Ring Signature Scheme
and Its Application in Blockchain............................... 15
Qing Ye, Wenbo Wang, Yongli Tang, Xixi Yan, Jing Zhang,
Zongqu Zhao, and Panke Qin

A New Structure of Blockchain to Simplify the Verification............. 33
Jianjian Yu, Lei Fan, and Gongliang Chen

Improvement Research of PBFT Consensus Algorithm Based on Credit..... 47
Yong Wang, Zhe Song, and Tong Cheng

On Constructing Prime Order Elliptic Curves Suitable
for Pairing-Based Cryptography 60
Meng Zhang, Xuehong Chen, Maozhi Xu, and Jie Wang

A Global Clock Model for the Consortium Blockchains................. 71
Chao Zan and Hai-Chuan Xu

Histogram Publishing Algorithm Based on Sampling Sorting
and Greedy Clustering....................................... 81
Xiaonian Wu, Nian Tong, Zhibo Ye, and Yujue Wang

Aggregate Signature Consensus Scheme Based on FPGA............... 92
Jinhua Fu, Jiaheng Liu, Yongzhong Huang, Xueming Si,
Yongjuan Wang, and Bin Li

Information Encryption Mechanism Based on QR Code................ 101
Xiaohui Cheng, Tong Niu, and Qiong Gui

Performance Optimization of Blockchain

Lightweight Image Segmentation Based Consensus Mechanism 109
Jianquan Ouyang, Jiajun Yin, and Yuxiang Sun

BIT Problem: Is There a Trade-off in the Performances
of Blockchain Systems?...................................... 123
Shuangfeng Zhang, Yuan Liu, and Xingren Chen

A Novel Enhanced Lightweight Node for Blockchain   137
  Yulong Zhao, Baoning Niu, Peng Li, and Xing Fan

An Adaptive Modular-Based Compression Scheme for Address Data
in the Blockchain System.   150
  Zhen Gao, Zhaohui Guo, and Jinsheng Yang

Optimization Strategy of OpenFlow Flow Table Storage Based on the Idea
of "Betweenness Centrality".   161
  Zhaohui Ma and Yan Yang

Research and Implementation of Multi-chain Digital Wallet Based
on Hash TimeLock   175
  Zujian Li and Zhihong Zhang

Blockchain Security and Privacy

A Security Detection Model for Selfish Mining Attack   185
  Zhongxing Liu, Guoyu Yang, Xinying Yu, and Fengying Li

Scalable, On-Demand Secure Multiparty Computation
for Privacy-Aware Blockchains.   196
  Shantanu Sharma and Wee Keong Ng

Design and Analysis of an Effective Securing Consensus Scheme
for Decentralized Blockchain System.   212
  Jing Wang, Lingfu Wang, Wei-Chang Yeh, and Jinhai Wang

KCRS: A Blockchain-Based Key Compromise Resilient Signature System. . .   226
  Lei Xu, Lin Chen, Zhimin Gao, Xinxin Fan, Kimberly Doan,
  Shouhuai Xu, and Weidong Shi

Decentralized Access Control Encryption in Public Blockchain.   240
  Zhongyuan Yao, Heng Pan, Xueming Si, and Weihua Zhu

A Smart Grid Privacy Protection Scheme Based on Short
Fail-Stop Signature   258
  Shumei Xu, Ningbin Yang, and Quan Zhou

Decentralized Authorization and Authentication Based
on Consortium Blockchain   267
  Ao Zhang and Xiaoying Bai

Blockchain and Cloud Computing

Reduce the Energy Cost of Elastic Clusters by Queueing Workloads
with N-1 Queues.   275
   Cheng Hu and Mingdong Tang

An Anonymous Blockchain-Based Logging System for Cloud Computing . . .   288
   Ji-Yao Liu, Yun-Hua He, Chao Wang, Yan Hu, Hong Li, and Li-Min Sun

Blockchain and Internet of Things

An RFID Lightweight Authentication Technology Based on PUF-RFID
Structure Model   305
   Xiaodong Zheng, Songyou Xie, Chunmei Xie, and Wei Zhu

Enhancing User Privacy in IoT: Integration of GDPR and Blockchain   322
   Masoud Barati and Omer Rana

A Blockchain-Based Trustable Framework for IoT Data Storage
and Access.   336
   Jiangfeng Li, Shili Hu, Yang Shi, and Chenxi Zhang

A Hybrid Mutual Authentication Scheme Based on Blockchain Technology
for WBANs   350
   Jianbo Xu, Xiangwei Meng, Wei Liang, Li Peng, Zisang Xu,
   and Kuan-Ching Li

A Security Architecture for Internet of Things Based on Blockchain   363
   Wei Yang, Hao Wang, Yadong Wan, Yuanlong Cao, Zhiming Zhang,
   and Shaolong Chen

Blockchain and Mobile Edge Computing

Redundant Virtual Machine Placement in Mobile Edge Computing   371
   Siyi Gao, Ao Zhou, Xican Chen, and Qibo Sun

An Effective Resource Allocation Approach Based on Game Theory
in Mobile Edge Computing   385
   Bilian Wu, Xin Chen, Ying Chen, and Zhuo Li

A Cloudlet Placement Method Based on Birch in Wireless Metropolitan
Area Network.   397
   Kai Peng, Haodong Liang, Yiwen Zhang, Xingda Qian,
   and Hualong Huang

Blockchain-Empowered Content Cache System for Vehicle Edge
Computing Networks... 410
    Junjie Liu, Xuefei Zhang, Yijing Li, Qimei Cui, and Xiaofeng Tao

Optimal Computation Resource Allocation in Vehicular Edge Computing ... 422
    Shiyu Du, Qibo Sun, Jujuan Gu, and Yujiong Liu

Blockchain and Smart Contracts

Aplos: Smart Contracts Made Smart 431
    Eranga Bandara, Wee Keong Ng, Nalin Ranasinghe,
    and Kasun De Zoysa

A Trading Model Based on Legal Contracts Using Smart
Contract Templates 446
    Youqun Shi, Zihao Lu, Ran Tao, Ying Liu, and Zhaohui Zhang

Would the Patch Be Quickly Merged?.............................. 461
    Yuan Huang, Nan Jia, Xiaocong Zhou, Kai Hong, and Xiangping Chen

Manual Audit for BitUnits Contracts 476
    Siqi Lu, Haopeng Fan, Yongjuan Wang, Huizhe Mi, and Ling Qin

The Transformation from Traditional Application
to Blockchain-Based Application................................. 483
    Zhanghui Liu, Zhihao Huang, Xing Chen, and Yan Chen

Blockchain and Data Mining

A Survey on Blockchain Anomaly Detection Using Data
Mining Techniques 491
    Ji Li, Chunxiang Gu, Fushan Wei, and Xi Chen

Understanding Out of Gas Exceptions on Ethereum................... 505
    Chao Liu, Jianbo Gao, Yue Li, and Zhong Chen

Toward Detecting Illegal Transactions on Bitcoin Using
Machine-Learning Methods 520
    Chaehyeon Lee, Sajan Maharjan, Kyungchan Ko,
    and James Won-Ki Hong

RETRACTED CHAPTER: Urban Jobs-Housing Zone Division Based
on Mobile Phone Data... 534
    Xiaoming Liu, Luxi Dong, Meijie Jia, and Jiyuan Tan

Quantitative Analysis of Bitcoin Transferred in Bitcoin Exchange 549
    Yang Li, Zilu Liu, and Zibin Zheng

Image Clustering Based on Graph Regularized Robust Principal
Component Analysis 563
  Yan Jiang, Wei Liang, Mingdong Tang, Yong Xie, and Jintian Tang

Research on Marketing Data Analysis Based on Contour Curve
in Blockchain 574
  Yanjie Wang and Jianping Li

Knowledge Mapping and Scientometric Overview on Global
Blockchain Research 582
  Peng-Hui Lyu, Ran Tong, and Rui Yuan Wei

Prediction of Bitcoin Transactions Included in the Next Block 591
  Kyungchan Ko, Taeyeol Jeong, Sajan Maharjan, Chaehyeon Lee,
  and James Won-Ki Hong

Knowledge Distillation Based on Pruned Model 598
  Cailing Liu, Hongyi Zhang, and Deyi Chen

Blockchain Applications and Services

BTS-PD: A Blockchain Based Traceability System for P2P Distribution 607
  Xuecong Li, Qian He, Bingcheng Jiang, Xing Qin, and Kuangyu Qin

Blockchain-Based Credible and Privacy-Preserving QoS-Aware Web
Service Recommendation 621
  Xiaoli Li, Erxin Du, Chuan Chen, Zibin Zheng, Ting Cai, and Qiang Yan

A Blockchain-Based Data-Sharing Architecture. 636
  Yongkai Fan, Jinghan Wang, Zhenting Hong, Xia Lei, Fanglue Xia,
  Junjie Ma, Cong Peng, and Xiaofeng Sun

Hyper-FTT: A Food Supply-Chain Trading and Traceability System Based
on Hyperledger Fabric 648
  Kui Gao, Yang Liu, Heyang Xu, and Tingting Han

BBCPS: A Blockchain Based Open Source Contribution
Protection System 662
  Qiubing Zeng, Xunhui Zhang, Tao Wang, Peichang Shi, Xiang Fu,
  and Chenhui Feng

BCSolid: A Blockchain-Based Decentralized Data Storage
and Authentication Scheme for Solid. 676
  Ting Cai, Wuhui Chen, and Yang Yu

Research on Enterprise DNS Security Scheme Based
on Blockchain Technology. 690
  Jichuan Zhang, Jianhong Zhai, Ru Yang, and Shuyan Liu

A Dual-Chain Digital Copyright Registration and Transaction System
Based on Blockchain Technology   702
Wei Liang, Xia Lei, Kuan-Ching Li, Yongkai Fan, and Jiahong Cai

Nebula: A Blockchain Based Decentralized Sharing Computing Platform. . . .   715
Bin Yan, Pengfei Chen, Xiaoyun Li, and Yongfeng Wang

A Novel Vehicle Blockchain Model Based on Hyperledger Fabric
for Vehicle Supply Chain Management   732
Kun Wang, Mingzhe Liu, Xin Jiang, Chen Yang, and Hong Zhang

A Novel Exploration for Blockchain in Distributed File Storage   740
Zuoting Ning, Lu Li, Wei Liang, Yifeng Zhao, Qi Fu, and Hongjun Chen

Insurance Block: A Blockchain Credit Transaction Authentication
Scheme Based on Homomorphic Encryption   747
Lijun Xiao, Han Deng, Minfu Tan, and Weidong Xiao

Blockchain Electronic Voting System for Preventing One Vote
and Multiple Investment.   752
Jianquan Ouyang, Yifan Deng, and Huanrong Tang

Trustworthy System Development

An Authority Management Framework Based on Fabric and IPFS
in Traceability Systems   761
Jiangfeng Li, Yifan Yu, Shili Hu, and Chenxi Zhang

Deep Learning Based Dynamic Uplink Power Control for NOMA
Ultra-Dense Network System   774
Xu Liu, Xin Chen, Ying Chen, and Zhuo Li

Cooperative Traffic Signal Control Based on Multi-agent
Reinforcement Learning.   787
Ruowen Gao, Zhihan Liu, Jinglin Li, and Quan Yuan

A Trustworthiness-Based Time-Efficient V2I Authentication Scheme
for VANETs.   794
Chen Wang, Jian Shen, Jin-Feng Lai, and Jianwei Liu

Retraction Note to: Urban Jobs-Housing Zone Division Based on Mobile
Phone Data C1
Xiaoming Liu, Luxi Dong, Meijie Jia, and Jiyuan Tan

Author Index   801

Theories and Algorithms for Blockchain

A Group Signature Based Digital Currency System

Haibo Tian[✉], Peiran Luo, and Yinxue Su

Guangdong Key Laboratory of Information Security, School of Data and Computer
Science, Sun Yat-Sen University, Guangzhou 510006, Guangdong, China
tianhb@mail.sysu.edu.cn

Abstract. Digital currency regulation is a hot topic. Traditional privacy-enhanced digital currency system, like the CryptoNote, seeks to protect the privacy of senders and receivers. This paper presents a digital currency system based on the group signature scheme of Boneh et al. The system can protect users' privacy and enable regulations. The system uses the one-time address technology of the CryptoNote to achieve unlinkability. It uses the group signature in a ring style to achieve untraceability. The group manager in a group signature can open a problematic transaction, restore the real identity of the sender, and revoke the private key of the sender if needed, which makes the digital currency regulatable.

Keywords: Digital currency · Group signature · Regulation ·
Privacy · One-time address

1 Introduction

Although digital currencies such as Bitcoin have a profound impact on financial fields, they currently are not used as daily currencies. Many central banks try to follow the trend of digital currency to issue their fiat currencies. Facebook, as a company, proposes Libra, which binds legal currencies of several countries to achieve currency stability. They hope that their currency can be used in daily life, even to replace the fiat currencies of some countries. For fiat currencies of banks or currencies of companies, one of the core concerns of the government is the regulation of the currencies. The government has to prevent capital flight, enable anti-money laundering policies and so on. Some examples to show the importance of regulations are given in [2,8]. In contrast, users wish to keep their privacy. For citizens in a country, their consumption behaviors and other financial activities should be protected. Digital currencies used in daily life should not threaten privacy of users.

There are many privacy enhanced digital currency systems such as CryptoNote [16], ZCash [10], Dash [7] and Mimblewimble [15]. The CryptoNote system defines two properties of user privacy.

© Springer Nature Singapore Pte Ltd. 2020
Z. Zheng et al. (Eds.): BlockSys 2019, CCIS 1156, pp. 3–14, 2020.
https://doi.org/10.1007/978-981-15-2777-7_1

- Untraceability. For each incoming transaction all possible senders are equiprobable.
- Unlinkability. For any two outgoing transactions it is impossible to prove they were sent to the same person.

For the ring confidential transactions (RingCT) version of the CryptoNote, the amount of transactions are hidden too. Zcash and Dash achieve similar properties with different techniques. Mimblewimble is different since there are no addresses at all. Hinteregger and Haslhofer [9] give an analysis of Monero which is based on the CryptoNote. They show that Monero is currently mostly immune to known passive attack vectors and resistant to tracking and tracing methods applied to other cryptocurrencies. But on the other hand, their conclusion means that it is harder to regulate the XMR coins of Monero.

There are some proposals for digital currency regulations. A basic idea is to validate the legitimate of entities. In [2], a verified entity will have a certified address. In [8], an entity has an identity certificate. In [18], an entity has the membership of a group after it is registered. In [11], an entity should register their public keys. An other idea is to change the structure of a ledger. A ledger is divided into public part and private part. The public part is for user's privacy and the private part is just plain transactions, which could be regulated [13,17].

We try to balance the privacy and regulations in a scheme. We use group signatures so that all users of a digital currency system are members of a group. The group manager is an entry point of regulations. We integrate the one-time address technique and ring signature idea into the digital currency system so that user privacy is guaranteed. Comparing with other solutions, we propose the first digital currency system with enhanced privacy and regulations.

1.1 Related Works

Ateniese et al. [2] propose certified Bitcoins. They introduce an online third party to issue certified address for a user. If a user wants to spend coins in a certified address, it has to produce a signature for an embedded public key in a certified address. The identity of a user could be revealed by the third party if a certified address is used since the address is firstly generated by the third party. Qiping [11] proposes a patent to specify how to reveal the identity of a transaction sender by an revocation center. A user should register their public keys to the center. A transaction sender establishes a shared secret among a sender, a receiver and the revocation center. Then a receiver could receive coins and the revocation center could reveal the identity of a transaction sender. The two proposals provides an option for a user to be regulated. However dishonest users could close the option by traditional Bitcoin address or using an unregistered key pair.

Narula et al. [13] propose a privacy preserving auditing ledger for multiple banks. Basically, transactions are stored in different banks privately. The commitments values of a transaction are added to a public ledger. From the commitments and proofs, an auditor could extract some correct statistical information. Since plain transactions are stored in banks, the identity of a transaction sender could be revealed by banks if necessary. Tian et al. [17] propose a fiat coin framework where plain transactions are also stored in different commercial banks and a central bank. Their public ledger only stores hash values. A central bank could asks a commercial bank to reveal the identity of a transaction if needed. Lampkins and Defrawy [8] propose a digital currency system based on multiparty secure computation. They suppose a set of servers that share identity certificate and public key of a user. The servers could verify the identity certificate without knowing the identity. When an address is suspected, the servers collaborate to reveal the identity of an address. The three proposals should be implemented in their framework and are not compatible to the Bitcoin unspent transaction output (UTXO) model.

Wu et al. [18] propose a linkable group signature scheme based on the well-known ACJT group signature [1]. They embed trapdoor keys for an auditor and a supervisor. An auditor could link two group signatures and a supervisor could trace the identity of a transaction sender. They did not specify how to integrate their scheme into a digital currency system. And the traceability and likability in their paper are not totally the same as those in the CryptoNote.

1.2 Contributions

Basically, we propose a group signature based digital currency system that balances the privacy and regulation requirements. It could be implemented as an alternative of the CryptoNote and are compatible to the UTXO model.

- We show how to construct a digital system based on a group signature with unlinkability property and regulation entry points.
- We further use the group signature in a ring style to obtain untraceability.
- We show that the revocation procedure of Boneh et al. [5] is practical in the blockchain scenario.

Additionally, we show the consistency of our proposal with the CryptoNote so that techniques in the ring confidential transaction (RingCT) proposal could be integrated.

2 Preliminaries

This section defines a bilinear map, a q-strong Diffie-Hellman (q-SDH) problem and a decision linear problem. We adopt the descriptions defined in [5].

2.1 Bilinear Map

Let G_1, G_2 be two multiplicative cyclic groups of prime order p. g_1 is a generator of G_1 and g_2 is a generator of G_2. ϕ is a computable isomorphism from G_2 to G_1 with $\psi(g_2) = g_1$. e is a computable map $e : G_1 \times G_2 \to G_T$ with the following properties:

- Bilinearity: for all $u \in G_1$, $v \in G_2$ and $a, b \in \mathbb{Z}_p$, $e(u^a, v^b) = e(u, v)^{ab}$.
- Non-degeneracy: $e(g_1, g_2) \neq 1$.

2.2   q-SDH Problem

The q-SDH problem in (G_1, G_2) is defined as follows. Given a $(q + 2)$-tuple $(g_1, g_2, g_2^{\gamma}, g_2^{(\gamma^2)}, \ldots, g_2^{(\gamma^q)})$ as input where $\gamma \in \mathbb{Z}_p^*$, output a pair $(g_1^{1/(\gamma+x)}, x)$ where $x \in \mathbb{Z}_p^*$.

An adversary $\mathcal{A}$ has advantage ϵ in solving q-SDH in (G_1, G_2) if

$$Pr\left[\mathcal{A}(g_1, g_2, g_2^{\gamma}, g_2^{(\gamma^2)}, \ldots, g_2^{(\gamma^q)}) = (g_1^{1/(\gamma+x)}, x)\right] \geq \epsilon,$$

where the probability is over the random choice of γ in $\mathbb{Z}_p^*$ and the random bits of $\mathcal{A}$.

The (q, t, ϵ)-SDH assumption holds in (G_1, G_2) if no t-time adversary has advantage at least ϵ in solving the q-SDH problem in (G_1, G_2).

2.3   Decision Linear Problem

The decision linear problem in G_1 is defined as follows. Given $(u, v, h, u^a, v^b, h^c \in G_1)$ where $a, b \in \mathbb{Z}_p$ are randomly selected and $c \in \mathbb{Z}_p$, output 1 if $a + b = c$.

An adversary $\mathcal{A}$ has advantage ϵ in solving a decision linear problem in G_1 if

$$\left| \begin{matrix} Pr\left[\mathcal{A}(u, v, h, u^a, v^b, h^{a+b}) = 1 : u, v, h \leftarrow G_1, a, b \leftarrow \mathbb{Z}_p\right] \\ -Pr\left[\mathcal{A}(u, v, h, u^a, v^b, \eta) = 1 : u, v, h, \eta \leftarrow G_1, a, b \leftarrow \mathbb{Z}_p\right] \end{matrix} \right| \geq \epsilon,$$

where the probability is over the random choice of the parameters to $\mathcal{A}$ and the random bits of $\mathcal{A}$.

The (t, ϵ)-Decision Linear assumption holds in G_1 if no t-time algorithm has advantage at least ϵ in solving the decision linear problem in G_1.

2.4   Group Signature

Bellare et al. [3] give three properties that a group signature scheme must satisfy. Roughly, it should be correctly verified and traced. A group signature should not reveal identity of a signer. And all group signatures should be traced to a member of the group.

This paper uses the group signature of Boneh et al. [5]. They have proved that under the (q, t, ϵ)-SDH assumption and (t, ϵ)-Decision Linear assumption, their scheme is correct, full-anonymous and full-traceable.

3   The System

We show two systems in this section. The first system shows how to use a group signature in a digital currency system. The second system uses a group signature in a ring style to obtain untraceability.

3.1   System I

The system logically includes a group manager GM, many digital currency users DU_i, $1 \leq i \leq n$, many verification nodes of a blockchain VN_i, $i \in \mathbb{N}$.

System Setup. GM takes $(G_1, G_2, g_1, g_2, e, p)$ as system parameters. It then randomly selects $h \leftarrow G_1$ and $\xi_1, \xi_2, \lambda \leftarrow \mathbb{Z}_p$. GM computes $u = h^{\xi_1^{-1}}$, $v = h^{\xi_2^{-1}}$ and $\omega = g_2^{\lambda}$. It selects two secure hash functions $H_1 : \{0,1\}^* \to \mathbb{Z}_p$ and $H_2 : \{0,1\}^* \to G_1$. The group public key is $(G_1, G_2, g_1, g_2, e, p, h, u, v, \omega, H_1, H_2)$. The group private key is (ξ_1, ξ_2, λ). The GM could be further divided into two logical parts. One is a register center that holds λ. The other is a revocation center that holds (ξ_1, ξ_2). The value λ could further be shared by several entities as a secret so that revocation is an operation requiring authorization from multiple departments.

User Registration. DU_i registers to GM with his own identification information. After verification, GM produces a group private key as (A_i, x_i) where $x_i \leftarrow \mathbb{Z}_p$ is randomly selected and $A_i = g_1^{\frac{1}{(\lambda + x_i)}}$. GM stores the identity information and their private key in a locally private database.

One-Time Address. DU_i selects $\alpha' \leftarrow \mathbb{Z}_p$, sets his address as $T_1' = u^{\alpha'}$. DU_i stores α' locally in their wallet.

When DU_j wants to send coins to DU_i, it randomly selects $\beta' \leftarrow \mathbb{Z}_p$. DU_j computes $k_0 = H_1(T_1'^{\beta'})$, and computes an one-time address for DU_i as $(T_0 = u^{\beta'}, T_1 = T_1' u^{k_0})$. Figure 1 shows the one-time address in a transaction. As the value T_1 is finally part of the group signature in [5], we denote it as a group signature component directly.

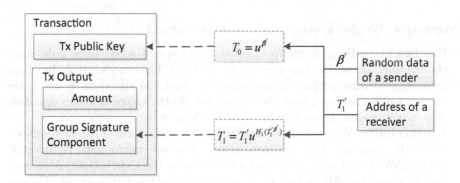

Fig. 1. Transactions with a group signature element

DU_i could check whether $T_1' = T_1 / u^{H_1(T_0^{\alpha'})}$. If the equation holds, the coins in the output belongs to DU_i.

Coin Spending. When DU_i wants to spend some coins in an address, it simply produces the other part of the group signature in [5].

- DU_i selects $\beta \leftarrow \mathbb{Z}_p$, computes $T_2 = v^\beta$ and $T_3 = A_i h^{\alpha+\beta}$ where $\alpha = \alpha' + H_1(T_0^{\alpha'})$.
- DU_i computes $\delta_1 = x_i\alpha$ and $\delta_2 = x_i\beta$. Then DU_i selects blind factors $r_\alpha, r_\beta, r_x, r_{\delta_1}, r_{\delta_2} \leftarrow \mathbb{Z}_q$ randomly.
- DU_i computes commitments $R_1 = u^{r_\alpha}$, $R_2 = v^{r_\beta}$, $R_4 = T_1^{r_x} \cdot u^{-r_{\delta_1}}$, $R_5 = T_2^{r_x} \cdot v^{-r_{\delta_2}}$ and

$$R_3 = e(T_3, g_2)^{r_x} \cdot e(h, \omega)^{-r_\alpha - r_\beta} \cdot e(h, g_2)^{-r_{\delta_1} - r_{\delta_2}}.$$

- DU_i then computes $c = H(T_0, T_1, T_2, T_3, R_1, R_2, R_3, R_4, R_5, M)$ where M is the other part of the transaction.
- DU_i then computes $s_\alpha = r_\alpha + c\alpha$, $s_\beta = r_\beta + c\beta$, $s_x = r_x + cx_i$, $s_{\delta_1} = r_{\delta_1} + c\delta_1$, $s_{\delta_2} = r_{\delta_2} + c\delta_2$.
- The group signature is $(T_2, T_3, c, s_\alpha, s_\beta, s_x, s_{\delta_1}, s_{\delta_2})$.

Node Verification. A verification node VN_i combines the value T_1 in the output of a transaction and the values $(T_2, T_3, c, s_\alpha, s_\beta, s_x, s_{\delta_1}, s_{\delta_2})$ in the input of a transaction to get a complete group signature and uses the group public key to verify the signature. If the group signature is valid, the transaction could be added to the blockchain. The group signature in [5] is verified as follows.

- A verifier computes $\tilde{R}_1 = u^{s_\alpha}/T_1^c$, $\tilde{R}_2 = v^{s_\beta}/T_2^c$, $\tilde{R}_4 = T_1^{s_x}/u^{s_{\delta_1}}$, $\tilde{R}_5 = T_2^{s_x}/v^{s_{\delta_2}}$, and

$$\tilde{R}_3 = e(T_3, g_2)^{s_x} \cdot e(h, w)^{-s_\alpha - s_\beta} \cdot e(h, g_2)^{-s_{\delta_1} - s_{\delta_2}} \cdot (e(T_3, w)/e(g_1, g_2))^c.$$

- The verifier checks whether $c = H(T_0, T_1, T_2, T_3, \tilde{R}_1, \tilde{R}_2, \tilde{R}_3, \tilde{R}_4, \tilde{R}_5, M)$. If the equation holds, the group signature is valid.

Properties. We give a simple analysis of the system I.

- **Double Spending.** A group member could spend some coins only when the member knows the exponent of T_1. In the UTXO model, if T_1 has been incorporated into a whole group signature, and the signature is valid, the output will be removed from the UTXO set. So the usage of group signature does not introduce more double spending chances.
- **Unlinkability.** We use a similar one-time address method as the CryptoNote. With the random value β', each group signature component is different. Futher, We do not require a standard address as the CryptoNote. A receiver could change its address frequently as specified by the BIP0044 [12]. For any two outgoing transactions, it is hard to prove they were sent to the same person. In fact, given T_1' of DU_i's address, $\tilde{T}_1'$ of DU_j's address, and T_0, T_1 in a transaction for DU_i or DU_j, an adversary has to judge whether an exponent is a hash output. In the random oracle model, if the discrete logarithm is hard, it is not easy to give an answer with non-negligible advantage.

- **Regulation.** The group manager or a revocation center or an alliance of revocation centers could open a group signature to reveal the identity of transaction sender. Suppose a group manager with a database storing users' information. It computes $A = \frac{T_3}{T_1^{\xi_1} \cdot T_2^{\xi_2}}$. Then it finds the user's private key and their identity in the local database. The identity is then revealed. If it is required to revoke the user, the group manager publishes (A, x) in the blockchain. We adopt the revocation procedure in a separate subsection.

Finally, we note that the system I only allows group members to spend coins. If a user does not register, it has no chance to participate in the system. This is different to the proposals in [2,11].

3.2 System II

The system I above does not provide untraceability. The system II uses a group signature in a ring style as the CryptoNote. The system I and II enjoy some same modules including system setup, user registration and one-time address generation. A new coin spending procedure and a node verification procedure are needed.

Ring Coin Spending. DU_i draws a set of addresses with the same amount coin to form an ordered list $\{T_0^l, T_1^l | 1 \leq l \leq m\}$ where $m \geq 2$ is the number of ring. We use i^* to denote DU_i's sequence in the list. DU_i produces the other part of their group signatures as follows.

- DU_i selects randomly $(T_2^l, T_3^l \in G_1)$ and $(c_l, s_\alpha^l, s_\beta^l, s_x^l, s_{\delta_1}^l, s_{\delta_2}^l \in \mathbb{Z}_p)$ for $1 \leq l \leq m$ and $l \neq i^*$.
- DU_i computes $g_l = e(H_2(T_0^l, T_1^l), g_2)$ for $1 \leq l \leq m$. It computes $I = g_{i^*}^\alpha$. Note that $\alpha = \alpha' + H_1(T_0^{i^* \alpha'})$.
- For $l \neq i^*$, DU_i computes $L_1^l = g_l^{s_\alpha^l} I^{-c_l}$, $R_1^l = u^{s_\alpha^l} T_1^{-c_l}$, $R_2^l = v^{s_\beta^l} T_2^{-c^l}$, $R_4^l = T_1^{s_x^l} u^{-s_{\delta_1}^l}$, $R_5^l = T_2^{s_x^l} v^{-s_{\delta_2}^l}$ and

$$R_3^l = e(T_3, g_2)^{s_x^l} \cdot e(h, w)^{-s_\alpha^l - s_\beta^l} \cdot e(h, g_2)^{-s_{\delta_1} - s_{\delta_2}} \cdot (e(T_3, w)/e(g_1, g_2))^{c_l}.$$

- For $l = i^*$, DU_i computes $L_1^{i^*} = g_{i^*}^{r_\alpha}$ and computes $(R_1^{i^*}, R_2^{i^*}, R_3^{i^*}, R_4^{i^*}, R_5^{i^*})$ as in the system I. Note that r_α is a blind factor selected by DU_i and $R_1^{i^*} = u^{r_\alpha}$.
- DU_i then computes

$$c = H \left(\begin{matrix} T_0^1, T_1^1, T_2^1, T_3^1, L_1^1, R_1^1, R_2^1, R_3^1, R_4^1, R_5^1, \ldots, T_0^m, \\ T_1^m, T_2^m, T_3^m, L_1^m, R_1^m, R_2^m, R_3^m, R_4^m, R_5^m, I, M \end{matrix} \right).$$

- DU_i then computes $c_{i^*} = c - c_1, \ldots, -c_{i-1}, -c_{i+1}, \ldots, -c_m \bmod p$.
- DU_i computes $s_\alpha^{i^*}, s_\beta^{i^*}, s_x^{i^*}, x_{\delta_1}^{i^*}, s_{\delta_2}^{i^*}$ as in the system I. Note that $s_\alpha^{i^*} = r_\alpha + c_{i^*} \alpha$
- The redeeming ring group signature is

$$(I, T_2^1, T_3^1, c_1, s_\alpha^1, s_\beta^1, s_x^1, s_{\delta_1}^1, s_{\delta_2}^1, \ldots, T_2^m, T_3^m, c_m, s_\alpha^m, s_\beta^m, s_x^m, s_{\delta_1}^m, s_{\delta_2}^m).$$

With the redeeming ring group signature, Fig. 2 shows a possible structure of multiple inputs. Each input should include m output indexes. For each input, there is a redeeming group signature. Note that an output index here includes a transaction identity and a output counter.

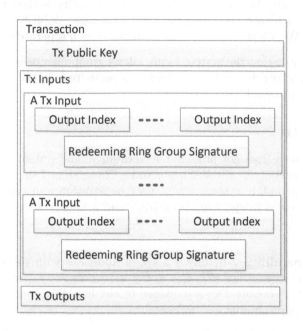

Fig. 2. An input in a transaction with ring group signature

Ring Node Verification. A verification node VN_i combines the value T_1^L in the output of a transaction and the values $(T_2^l, T_3^l, c_l, s_\alpha^l, s_\beta^l, s_x^l, s_{\delta_1}^l, s_{\delta_2}^l)$ in the input of a transaction to get m complete group signatures. VN_i uses the group public key to verify each group signature as in the system I. If all the group signatures are valid, the transaction could be added to the blockchain.

Properties. We give a simple analysis of the system II.

- **Double Spending.** Now even if an output is included in an input of a transaction, the output could not be removed from the UTXO set. In fact, the ledger is not easy to be divided into two sets now. Similar to the CryptoNote, the value I in a ring group signature has the same exponent as the value T_1. So if I appears more than one time, a double spending event happens.
- **Unlinkability.** The system II enjoys the same ont-time address generation procedure as the system I. So the system II has the unlinkability property.

- **Untraceability.** Since the group signature in [5] is based on a zero-knowledge protocol. The simulated group signatures are indistinguishable with a real signature. Then the only clue is the value I. Given two group signatures and a value I that tags one of them, if an adversary could distinguish which group signature is tagged, the untraceability does not hold. However, in a group signature, the values $s_\alpha^{i^*}, s_{\delta_1}^{i^*}$ and $T_3^{i^*}$ are computed by α and blind factors. The only useful value is $T_1^{i^*} = u^\alpha$ which is an element in G_1. Note that $I = g_i^{*\alpha}$ and $g_{i^*} = e(H_2(T_0^{i^*}, T_1^{i^*}), g_2)$ is an element in G_T. If the pairing implementation does not support multilinear pairing, it seems that it is hard to judge whether the two exponents of I and $T_1^{i^*}$ are the same. Roughly, an adversary faces a problem similar to the decisional Bilinear Diffie-Hellman problem. That is, given $(g_1, u, u^\alpha, H_2(T_0^{i^*}, T_1^{i^*}), \tilde{I})$, judge whether $\tilde{I} = e(H_2(T_0^{i^*}, T_1^{i^*}), g_2)^\alpha$.
- **Regulation.** We still suppose that a group manager with a database storing users' information. It computes $A^l = \frac{T_3^l}{T_1^{l\xi_1} \cdot T_2^{l\xi_2}}$ for $1 \leq l \leq m$. Since the values (T_2^l, T_3^l) are randomly selected when $l \neq i^*$, A^l is not included in the database with a probability at most n/p. Then with a probability at least $1 - mn/p$, the group manager could identify a user in the database.

3.3   RingCT Technique

It is not easy to find transactions with the same amount. So there is a RingCT proposal [14]. Their techniques could be trivially introduced to the system I or II. We give a simple example to show this fact.

In the coin spending face, suppose DU_j wants to transfer b_1 coins to DU_i from an address with coins a. Suppose the transaction fee is f. Then the value in the input address has a commitment $C_{in} = u^x v^a$ where x is a random value selected by the one who sends coins to DU_j. DU_j could obtain x by decrypt a ciphertext including x. The output to DU_i has a commitment $C_{o1} = u^{y_1} v^{b_1}$ where $y_1 \in \mathbb{Z}_p$ is a random value selected by DU_j. DU_j should encrypt y_1 for DU_j. For example, DU_j computes $H_1(T_1'^{\beta'} | \text{``EncKey''}) \oplus y_1$. An exchange address has a commitment $C_{o2} = u^{y_2} v^{b_2}$ where $y_2 \in \mathbb{Z}_p$ is a random value selected by DU_j. Then it is expected that $C_{in}/(C_{o1}C_{o2}v^f) = u^{x-y_1-y_2}$. Let $z = x - y_1 - y_2 \mod p$. Next put the input address T_1 of DU_j and the amount committed in the transaction together, one could make a value-address mixture $u^{\alpha+z}$. With the exponent value of the mixture, a ring group signature could be produced.

To further make the proposal practical, a range proof technique should be used to prove the range of committed value. We could not see any obstacles to apply the aggregate Schnorr non-linkable ring signature (ANSL) in [14] or the Bulletproofs technique in [4]. Any efficient range proof technique could be applied here. Figure 3 shows a full-fledged output with RingCT techniques. Note that in the range proof phase, the sender needs more random values except β' and y.

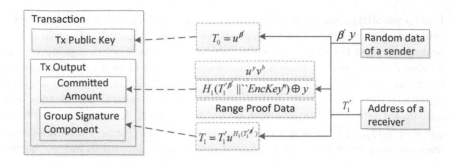

Fig. 3. An output in a transaction with RingCT technique

3.4 Revocation

As the system runs, users may be revoked from the system. We integrate the revocation method in [5] into the digital currency system.

Blockchain Revocation List. A group manager with the private key λ publishes the private keys information of a revoked user in the blockchain. That is, when a new block is produced, the block may include some transactions produced by the group manager where revoked key pairs are included. The revocation information in the blockchain forms a list

$$RL_{ht} = ((A_1^*, x_1), \ldots, (A_r^*, x_r))$$

where $A_i^* = g_2^{1/\lambda + x_i} \in G_2$ and the ht is a specified block height.

Group Public Key Update. Suppose the current block height is $1 \leq ht$, the current group public key includes (g_1, g_2, w). Now a new revoked private key information (A_1^*, x_1) is added to the block $ht + 1$. When the block $ht + 1$ is confirmed, any verifier should produce a new group public key. The new group key includes $\hat{g}_1, \hat{g}_2, \hat{w}$ where $\hat{g}_1 = \psi(A_1^*)$, $\hat{g}_2 = A_1^*$ and $\omega = g_2 \cdot (A_1^*)^{-x_1}$.

User Private Key Update. Suppose the private key of a user is (A, x) when the maximal block height is ht. When the block $ht + 1$ is confirmed, if the signer needs not spend coins, it could do nothing. However, if the signer wants to spend some coins, the signer should update their private key. The new private key of the user should be $(\hat{A}, x)$ where $\hat{A} = \psi(A_1^*)^{\frac{1}{x - x_1}} / A^{\frac{1}{x - x_1}}$. If the private key of a user is updated according to the RL_{ht-d}, and the user wants to spend some coins after block $ht + 1$ appears, then the user should update their private key according to the RL_{ht+1} where $d \in \mathbb{N}$.

When a verification node VN verifies a group signature, if should try the current group public key and its previous group public key for a block creation time to tolerate network delay. If a user is revoked at block ht, then after block $ht + 1$, the revoked user could not spend any coins.

Unfreeze Coins. If the coins the system are issued by a central organization, a revoked user may get back their coins after the user is inspected. To do this, the user should provide their private keys in the wallet so that the organization could make sure the total amount of revoked coins of the user. Then, the organization issue the same amount coins to the user with new address. The user certainly should apply new private keys from the group manager.

4 Performance Analysis

A group signature in the system I includes four elements of G_1 and six elements of $\mathbb{Z}_p$. When using the curves described in [6] one can take p to be a 170-bit prime and use a group G_1 where each element is 171 bits. Thus, the total group signature length is $171 \times 4 + 170 \times 6 = 1704$ bits. With these parameters, security is approximately the same as a standard 1024-bit RSA signature. In the system II, the total length is $(1704\,m + 1020)$ bits. In practise, for a higher security level, we recommend a 256-bit p and the total length of a group signature is 2564 bits for the system I.

To generate an address, a user needs an exponentiation. To send coins to an address, a user needs mainly two exponentiations. To spend coins in an address, a user needs about twelve exponentiations and three bilinear map computations. Two bilinear map computations could be precomputed. A user could also selects β and blind factors, computes eight exponentiations and store them in a table before the user spends some coins. When a user really wants to spend coins, it only needs to compute four exponentiations and one bilinear map with a table lookup. A verification node needs about twelve exponentiations and two bilinear map computations if three bilinear map computations is precomputed. The computation cost of the system II is roughly m times the computation cost of the system I at the coin spending phase.

5 Conclusion

We show group signature based digital currency systems. The system I has unlinkability and regulation property. The system II additionally has untraceability. The two systems could be enhanced by the ring confidential transaction techniques to make them practical. Our systems are suitable to the UTXO model. The group signature gives us an opportunity to reveal identity of a user and freeze coins of a user. If coins are issued by a central organization, there is a chance to unfreeze coins.

Acknowledgments. This work is supported by the National Key R&D Program of China (2017YFB0802500), Guangxi Key Laboratory of Cryptography and Information Security (No. GCIS201711), Natural Science Foundation of China (61672550), Fundamental Research Funds for the Central Universities (No. 17lgjc45). Natural Science Foundation of Guangdong Province of China (2018A0303130133).

References

1. Ateniese, G., Camenisch, J., Joye, M., Tsudik, G.: A practical and provably secure coalition-resistant group signature scheme. In: Bellare, M. (ed.) CRYPTO 2000. LNCS, vol. 1880, pp. 255–270. Springer, Heidelberg (2000). https://doi.org/10.1007/3-540-44598-6_16
2. Ateniese, G., Faonio, A., Magri, B., de Medeiros, B.: Certified bitcoins. IACR Cryptology ePrint Archive **2014**, 76 (2014)
3. Bellare, M., Micciancio, D., Warinschi, B.: Foundations of group signatures: formal definitions, simplified requirements, and a construction based on general assumptions. In: Biham, E. (ed.) EUROCRYPT 2003. LNCS, vol. 2656, pp. 614–629. Springer, Heidelberg (2003). https://doi.org/10.1007/3-540-39200-9_38
4. Bünz, B., Bootle, J., Boneh, D., Poelstra, A., Wuille, P., Maxwell, G.: Bulletproofs: short proofs for confidential transactions and more. In: 2018 IEEE Symposium on Security and Privacy (SP), pp. 315–334, May 2018
5. Boneh, D., Boyen, X., Shacham, H.: Short group signatures. In: Franklin, M. (ed.) CRYPTO 2004. LNCS, vol. 3152, pp. 41–55. Springer, Heidelberg (2004). https://doi.org/10.1007/978-3-540-28628-8_3
6. Boneh, D., Lynn, B., Shacham, H.: Short signatures from the weil pairing. J. Cryptol. **17**(4), 297–319 (2004)
7. Duffield, E., Hagan, K.: Darkcoin: peertopeer cryptocurrency with anonymous blockchain transactions and an improved proofofwork system (2014). https://docs.dash.org/en/stable/introduction/about.html. Accessed 2 Aug 2019
8. El Defrawy, K., Lampkins, J.: Founding digital currency on secure computation. In: Proceedings of the 2014 ACM SIGSAC Conference on Computer and Communications Security, CCS 2014, pp. 1–14. ACM, New York (2014)
9. Hinteregger, A., Haslhofer, B.: An empirical analysis of monero cross-chain traceability (2019). https://arxiv.org/abs/1812.02808. Accessed 2 Aug 2019
10. Hopwood, D., Bowe, S., Hornby, T., Wilcox, N.: Zcash protocol specification version 2019.0.4 (2019). https://zcash.readthedocs.io/en/latest/. Accessed 2 Aug 2019
11. Lin, Q.: An anonymous digital money trading supervision method with hidden center (2019). http://pss-system.cnipa.gov.cn/sipopublicsearch/portal/uiIndex.shtml
12. Marek, P., Pavol, R.: Multi-account hierarchy for deterministic wallets (2014). https://wiki.bitcoin.com/w/BIP_0044. Accessed 4 Aug 2019
13. Narula, N., Vasquez, W., Virza, M.: zkledger: privacy-preserving auditing for distributed ledgers. In: 15th USENIX Symposium on Networked Systems Design and Implementation (NSDI 2018), Renton, WA, USENIX Association, pp. 65–80, April 2018
14. Noether, S., Mackenzie, A., Team, M.C.: Ring confidential transactions (2016). https://www.researchgate.net/publication/311865049_Ring_Confidential_Transactions
15. Poelstra, A.: Mimblewimble (2016). http://mimblewimble.cash/20161006-WhitePaperUpdate-e9f45ec.pdf. Accessed 4 Aug 2019
16. Saberhagen, N.: Cryptonote v 2.0 (2013). https://www.mendeley.com/catalogue/cryptonote-v-20/. Accessed 1 Aug 2019
17. Tian, H., Chen, X., Ding, Y., Zhu, X., Zhang, F.: Afcoin: a framework for digital fiat currency of central banks based on account model. In: Guo, F., Huang, X., Yung, M. (eds.) Information Security and Cryptology, pp. 70–85. Springer, Cham (2019)
18. Zheng, H., Wu, Q., Qin, B., Zhong, L., He, S., Liu, J.: Linkable group signature for auditing anonymous communication. In: Susilo, W., Yang, G. (eds.) Information Security and Privacy, pp. 304–321. Springer, Cham (2018)

RLWE Commitment-Based Linkable Ring Signature Scheme and Its Application in Blockchain

Qing Ye, Wenbo Wang, Yongli Tang$^{(\boxtimes)}$, Xixi Yan, Jing Zhang, Zongqu Zhao, and Panke Qin

College of Computer Science and Technology, Henan Polytechnic University, Jiaozuo 454000, China
yltang@hpu.edu.cn

Abstract. Aiming at the problems of large key size and low computation efficiency of linkable ring signature (LRS) schemes from lattice, we construct a LRS scheme based on the RLWE (learning with errors from ring) commitment scheme and further apply the proposed LRS scheme to blockchain to construct an anonymous post-quantum cryptocurrency model. Concretely, we first prove through setting parameters reasonably, we can make a RLWE-based commitment scheme to have homomorphism; Then use the RLWE-based homomorphic commitment scheme, combined with the Σ-protocol and Fiat-Shamir heuristic to construct a LRS scheme; Finally, by combining the proposed LRS scheme with blockchain we present an anonymous post-quantum cryptocurrency model. Analysis shows that compared with the previous LRS schemes, since the proposed LRS scheme is constructed based on the intractability of RLWE problem which can be reduced to SVP (shortest vector problem) on lattice, it can both resist the quantum computer attacks and have smaller key size, signature size and higher computational efficiency. The proposed cryptocurrency model uses the proposed LRS scheme to ensure the sender's anonymity and the one-time stealth address to guarantee the recipient's anonymity, which can both protect users' identities and resist quantum attacks.

Keywords: RLWE · Blockchain · Ring signature · Quantum attack · Privacy · Cryptocurrency

1 Introduction

The blockchain is a new technology which is the underlying technology of Bitcoin. The earliest definition of blockchain comes from the paper published by Nakamoto in 2009 [1]. The two most important features of blockchain, that is, "decentralization" and "anonymity", make Bitcoin the most popular cryptocurrency. "Anonymity" means that the same user in blockchain have different addresses in different transactions. Outside users of a transaction can only see a certain amount of bitcoin was sent from one address to another, and do not know the specific user's identity corresponding to the address. However, the latest research shows that Bitcoin only partially solves the problem of

© Springer Nature Singapore Pte Ltd. 2020
Z. Zheng et al. (Eds.): BlockSys 2019, CCIS 1156, pp. 15–32, 2020.
https://doi.org/10.1007/978-981-15-2777-7_2

anonymity and unlinkability [2]. For example, when a user returns a change to himself, because two or more addresses of a single user will appear in the same transaction [3], multiple addresses of the same user are linked. Recently, there have been many discussions on the weak anonymity of Bitcoin [4, 5].

In this regard, researchers have proposed various privacy protection programs. Maxwell [6] proposed the Coinjoin technology, which combines multiple transactions of different users into one transaction, thus hiding the relationship between the input party and output party of the transaction. Mixcoin [7] uses a trusted third party to confuse bitcoin addresses, but this third party may violate the user's privacy and steal the user's bitcoin. Monero [8] uses ring signature and stealth address to protect user's privacy. It uses ring signature to hide the signer's identity and stealth address to hide the recipient's identity. Miers et al. [9] proposed Zerocoin based on zero-knowledge proof, which allows users to use their proof of ownership to spend coins instead of digital signatures, thus solving the problem of user transaction address disclosure. Sasson et al. [10] further proposed Zerocash based on the Zerocoin scheme, using a non-interactive zero-knowledge proof to realize a more anonymous electronic cash system to protect the privacy of users and transaction amount.

Ring signatures were proposed by Rivest et al. [11] in 2001, which allows a user to sign messages on behalf of a group of users. The verifier can be sure that the real signer is a member of a group of users, but he doesn't know which one is. The size of a traditional ring signature is usually $O(N)$, where N is the cardinality of the ring, and constructing a ring signature scheme whose signature size is $O(\log N)$ or $O(1)$ is an open problem. In 2015, Groth and Kohlweiss [12] proposed a ring signature scheme based on homomorphic commitment with a signature size of $O(\log N)$. First, literature [12] requires a homomorphic commitment scheme, such as Pedersen's [13] commitment scheme; Second, constructs a Σ_1-protocol for commitment to 0 or 1; Third, based on Σ_1-protocol, constructs a Σ_2-protocol for one out of N commitments containing 0; Finally, applying the Fiat-Shamir transform [14] on the Σ_2-protocol gives rise to a ring signature scheme. Considering the anonymity in the blockchain, ring signatures are obviously more appropriate than ordinary signatures. It is worth noting that if we simply replace the standard digital signature in the blockchain with a general ring signature, the spender may spend the same amount of money twice (that is, double-spending problem) or more without being noticed, due to the anonymity of ring signature. In order to solve this problem, it is necessary to enable the public to determine whether two or more ring signatures are generated by the same signer. The traceable ring signature [15] provides the ability to track key pairs that are used to sign different messages, and has been modified to one-time signature used in the Monero. The linkable ring signature (LRS) proposed by Liu et al. [16] not only can protect the signer's anonymity, but also can make anyone judge whether two signatures are generated by the same group member (linkability). In general, in order to solve the "double-spending" problem of blockchain, LRS is enough to meet the requirements.

At present, the cryptographic techniques in blockchain are mostly based on classical number theory problems (for example, large integer factorization and discrete logarithm problems). Once the quantum computer is applied, these cryptographic schemes will be broken in polynomial time. The new lattice-based cryptosystem has become a research hotspot in the post-quantum cryptography because of its advantages of simple operation, anti-quantum attack and there being worst-case random instances. The researchers also did some research on lattice-based ring signature schemes [17–19]. Literature [20], based on the weak Pseudo Random Function (wPRF), the accumulator and zero-knowledge proof, constructs the first lattice-based LRS scheme, whose security is based on the intractability of Short Integer Solution (SIS) problem. Literature [21], based on the ideal lattice-based homomorphic commitment scheme and the Σ_2-protocol [12], constructs an ideal lattice-based LRS scheme whose security is based on the Shortest Vector Problem (SVP) and applies the LRS scheme to the blockchain to construct a cryptocurrency model. In literature [22], a lattice-based LRS is constructed based on the lattice-based hash function, whose security is based on the Module-SIS problem (a variant of SIS problem) and the Module-LWE problem (a variant of learning with error problem). Recently, literature [23] constructed an unconditionally anonymous LRS scheme based on the BLISS signature scheme, whose security is based on the Ring Short Integer Solution (RSIS) problem. In general, the difficult problems commonly used in lattice-based cryptographic schemes are SIS and LWE, but the cryptographic schemes based on SIS and LWE problems usually have a large key size, ciphertext size and low computation efficiency. RSIS and RLWE (learning with error from ring) [24] problems (proposed by Lyubaskevsky et al. in 2010) are two improved variants in polynomial ring of SIS and LWE problems, respectively, and under the same level of security, the cryptographic schemes based on RSIS and RLWE problems usually have smaller key size and higher calculation efficiency.

In order to solve the problems of the large key size and low efficiency computation of LRS schemes from lattice, this paper reconstructs a lattice-based LRS scheme based on the RLWE commitment scheme [25] and further applies the proposed LRS scheme to blockchain to construct an anonymous anti-quantum attack cryptocurrency model. Specifically, the work of this paper includes the following three aspects: (1) Analyzing the RLWE commitment scheme [25] to prove through setting parameters reasonably it also has additive homomorphism besides hiddenness and binding; (2) Using the RLWE commitment scheme, combined with the Σ_2-protocol [12] and Fiat-Shamir heuristic to construct a LRS scheme based on RLWE problem. Compared with the previous LRS schemes, since the proposed scheme is constructed based on RLWE problem, and the keys are picked from the ring of polynomials, it not only can resist the quantum computer attack, but also has smaller key size and higher computational efficiency, and the description of the proposed scheme is simpler; (3) Combine the proposed LRS scheme with blockchain to give an anonymous post-quantum cryptocurrency model, which uses the LRS scheme to ensure the sender's anonymity, uses one-time stealth address to guarantee the recipient's anonymity, and can both resist quantum attacks and protect users' identities.

2 Preliminaries

2.1 Notations

Table 1 gives a description of the symbols commonly used in this paper.

Table 1. Notations

$a, b, \ldots$	Lowercase italic letters indicate polynomials over ring
$\boldsymbol{a}, \boldsymbol{b}, \ldots$	Lowercase bold letters indicate vectors
$\mathbb{R}$	Set of real numbers
$\mathbb{Z}$	Set of integers
$\|\cdot\|_\infty$	Infinite norm
$\|\cdot\|$	Euclidean norm
$\mathbb{Z}[x]$	Set of integer polynomials
$[n]$	Indicates from 1 to n
$a \cdot s$ or as	Multiplication of two polynomials over a ring
$\lceil x \rceil$	The smallest integer that is not smaller than x
$E(x)$	The mean of random variable x
$D(x)$	The variance of random variable x
$\|$	Concatenation of strings

2.2 Lattices and Hard Problems

Definition 1 (Lattices). Given n linearly independent vectors $\boldsymbol{b}_1, \ldots, \boldsymbol{b}_n \in \mathbb{R}^m$, the lattice they generate is defined as $\Lambda = \{\sum_{i=1}^{n} x_i \boldsymbol{b}_i : x_i \in \mathbb{Z}, 1 \leq i \leq n\}, \boldsymbol{b}_1, \ldots, \boldsymbol{b}_n$ is called a basis of the lattice, m, n are called the dimension and rank of the lattice respectively.

Definition 2 (Discrete Gaussian distribution). For arbitrary $\sigma > 0$, define a discrete Gaussian distribution centered at c on the lattice Λ as $D_{\Lambda,\sigma,c}(\boldsymbol{y}) = \frac{\rho_{\sigma,c}(\boldsymbol{y})}{\rho_{\sigma,c}(\Lambda)} = \frac{\rho_{\sigma,c}(\boldsymbol{y})}{\sum_{\boldsymbol{y} \in \Lambda} \rho_{\sigma,c}(\boldsymbol{y})}$, where $\boldsymbol{y} \in \Lambda$, $\rho_{\sigma,c}(\boldsymbol{y}) = \exp(-\pi \|\boldsymbol{y} - c\|^2 / \sigma^2)$.

Lyubaskevsky et al. [24] proposed the RLWE problem in 2010, and showed the search and decision versions of RLWE are polynomially related, and that there exists a quantum reduction from the worst-case approximate shortest vector problem (aSVP) on ideal lattices to RLWE problem.

Suppose $R = \mathbb{Z}[x] / < x^m + 1 >$ is a polynomial ring of degree m over $\mathbb{Z}$, where m be a power of 2, $f(x) = x^m + 1 \in \mathbb{Z}[x]$ is a monic irreducible polynomial. Let $R_q = R/qR = \mathbb{Z}_q[x]/ < f(x) >$ be a quotient ring with modulus q, where q is a positive integer. Let $\mathbb{Z}_q$ denotes $\{-\frac{q-1}{2}, \ldots, \frac{q-1}{2}\}$. χ_α represents a Gaussian distribution over R with a mean of 0 and a standard deviation of α.

Definition 3 (RLWE assumption). The decisional ring learning with errors assumption (denoted by $\text{RLWE}_{q,\chi}$) states that: Given multiple independent samples $(u, v) \in R_q \times R_q$, for any PPT algorithm, the advantage of distinguishing whether the samples are taken from $(a, b = a \cdot s + e)$ or $R_q \times R_q$ is negligible, where $a \leftarrow R_q, b \leftarrow R_q, e \leftarrow \chi$, $s \leftarrow R_q$ is secret.

2.3 RLWE Commitment Scheme

The non-interactive commitment scheme allows the sender to make a commitment c to a message a, and the sender hides a and sends c to the recipient. The sender will reveal the value of a and open the commitment c later, and the recipient can verify if c is indeed the commitment of message a. A non-interactive commitment scheme is a tuple of two polynomial time algorithms (G, Com). On input the security parameter λ, G sets the message space $\mathcal{M}$, the random number space $\mathcal{R}$ and the commitment space $\mathcal{C}$, and outputs a commitment key ck, where ck contains the public parameters used by the commitment algorithm Com. On input commitment key ck, a message $m \in \mathcal{M}$, Com randomly chooses $r \in \mathcal{R}$, and computes $c = Com_{ck}(m; r) \in \mathcal{C}$.

A non-interactive commitment scheme must satisfy the hiding and binding properties. The hiding property means that the commitment c will not leak the committed message a; The binding property means that one cannot make the same commitment c for different messages $a \neq a'$. A homomorphic commitment scheme requires the commitment scheme to satisfy homomorphism (i.e. additive homomorphism or multiplicative homomorphism) besides hiding and binding properties, that is, given commitment key ck, m_0, $m_1 \in \mathcal{M}$, r_0, $r_1 \in \mathcal{R}$, there is

$$Com_{ck}(m_0, r_0) \circ Com_{ck}(m_1, r_1) = Com_{ck}(m_0 \circ m_1, r_0 \circ r_1),$$

where "$\circ$" represents an addition or a multiplication operation.

In 2015, Benhamouda et al. [25] proposed a commitment scheme based on the RLWE assumption and proved it is hiding and binding. The specific algorithms are as follows:

G: Randomly picks $\boldsymbol{a}, \boldsymbol{b} \leftarrow (\mathbb{Z}_q[x]/ < x^n + 1 >)^k$ which are two polynomial vectors over ring, where n is the degree of polynomials and equals to the power of 2, $q \equiv 3 \bmod 8$ is a prime number, k is the multiplicative overhead of commitment size. $ck = (\boldsymbol{a}, \boldsymbol{b})$.

Com: Given a message $m \in \mathbb{Z}_q[x]/ < x^n + 1 >$, samples $r \leftarrow \mathbb{Z}_q[x]/ < x^n + 1 >$ and $\boldsymbol{e} \leftarrow \chi_{\sigma_e}^k$ conditioned $\|\boldsymbol{e}\|_\infty \leq n$, where $\sigma_e = \tilde{O}(n^{3/4})$, outputs $c = \boldsymbol{a}m + \boldsymbol{b}r + \boldsymbol{e}$.

Vfy: Given a commitment c, a message m', random number r', as well as $\boldsymbol{e}'$ and f', (Benhamouda et al. [25] allow for the additional small polynomial f' in openings, while an honest party can always set $f' = 1$). The algorithm accepts if and only if

$$\boldsymbol{a}m' + \boldsymbol{b}r' + f'^{-1}\boldsymbol{e}' = c \wedge \|\boldsymbol{e}'\|_\infty < \left\lfloor \frac{n^{4/3}}{2} \right\rfloor \wedge \|f'\|_\infty \leq 1 \wedge \deg f' < \frac{n}{2}.$$

Theorem 1 [25]. Let $\gamma > 6$ and q, k be polynomial in n conditioned

$$q \geq n^\gamma \geq n^6 \text{ and } k > \frac{18\gamma}{3\gamma - 16},$$

then under the RLWE-assumption, the above commitment scheme is computationally hiding and perfectly binding with overwhelming probability.

2.4 UTXO Ledger Model

UTXO (Unspent Transaction Output) model: Each transaction consists of transaction input and transaction output. There can be multiple transaction inputs and transaction outputs, which means that one transaction can merge the bitcoins in the previous multiple accounts and transfer them to another one or more accounts. The balance for each account is derived from the sum of all UTXOs under that account. Figure 1 shows how UTXO model works, where Transaction 1 contains one input and two outputs, and Transaction 2 contains three inputs and two outputs.

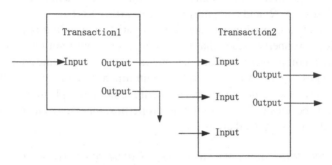

Fig. 1. UTXO ledger model

3 Analysis of the RLWE Commitment Scheme

For the RLWE commitment scheme [25], after analysis, we get the following lemma and theorem:

Lemma 1: For the RLWE commitment scheme, especially when $||e||_\infty \leq n/2$, given two different commitments $c_0 = Com(m_0, r_0, e_0)$, $c_1 = Com(m_1, r_1, e_1)$, there is $c_0 + c_1 = Com(m_0, r_0, e_0) + Com(m_1, r_1, e_1) = Com(m_0 + m_1, r_0 + r_1, e_0 + e_1)$.

Proof. Since

$$c_0 + c_1 = Com(m_0, r_0, e_0) + Com(m_1, r_1, e_0)$$
$$= am_0 + br_0 + e_0 + am_1 + br_1 + e_1$$
$$= a(m_0 + m_1) + b(r_0 + r_1) + e_0 + e_1,$$

and since $m_0, m_1 \in R_q, r_0, r_1 \in R_q$, we have $m_0 + m_1 \in R_q, r_0 + r_1 \in R_q$.

Now we analysis the case for $e_0 + e_1$. Since e_0, e_1 are independently chosen from $\chi_{\sigma_e}^k$, $E(e_0 + e_1) = E(e_0) + E(e_1) = 0$, $D(e_0 + e_1) = D(e_0) + D(e_1) = 2(\sigma_e)^2$. Since $\sigma_e = \tilde{O}(n^{3/4})$, $\sqrt{2}\sigma_e = \sqrt{2}\tilde{O}(n^{3/4}) = \tilde{O}(n^{3/4})$. Since $||e||_\infty \leq n/2$, $||e_0 + e_1||_\infty \leq ||e_0||_\infty + ||e_1||_\infty < n$. So $e_0 + e_1$ is also a random vector which obeys the Gaussian distribution $\chi_{\sigma_e}^k$ conditioned $||e_0 + e_1||_\infty < n$. Then we have $c_0 + c_1 = Com(m_0, r_0, e_0) + Com(m_1, r_1, e_1) = Com(m_0 + m_1, r_0 + r_1, e_0 + e_1)$.

Now we extend the above lemma to a more general case:

Theorem 2: For the RLWE commitment scheme, especially when $k < n^2$, $\|e\|_\infty \leq n/k$, there is $kc = Com(km, kr, ke)$.

Proof. The proof is similar to the proof of Lemma2. Here we omit it.

4   Linkable Ring Signature Scheme Based on RLWE Commitment

4.1   Linkable Ring Signature Definition
Definition 4: A LRS scheme is a tuple of five algorithms ($Setup$, $KGen$, $Sign$, $Verify$, $Link$) as follows:

- $pp \leftarrow Setup(1^\lambda)$ is a probabilistic polynomial time (PPT) algorithm which, on input a security parameter n, outputs the set of public parameters pp which can be used for all users.
- $(vk, sk) \leftarrow KGen(pp)$ is a PPT algorithm which, on input public parameters pp, outputs a public/private key pair (vk, sk).
- $\sigma \leftarrow Sign(pp, sk, \mu, U)$ which, on input public parameters pp, private key sk, a message μ, a set of public keys $U = \{vk_1, vk_2, \ldots, vk_N\}$, outputs a signature σ. We require that there is a $vk \in U$ such that (vk, sk) is a valid key pair output by $KGen(pp)$.
- accept/reject $\leftarrow Verify(pp, U, \mu, \sigma)$ which, on input public parameters pp, a set of public keys $U = \{vk_1, vk_2, \ldots, vk_N\}$, a message-signature pair (μ, σ), returns accept or reject. If accept, the message-signature pair is valid.
- linked/unlinked $\leftarrow Link(pp, \sigma, \sigma')$ which, on input two signatures (σ, σ'), returns linked or unlinked. If linked, the two signatures are linked which means they are generated by the same user.

4.2   Security Model

A LRS scheme should satisfy four essential properties [12, 26]: Correctness, unforgeability, anonymity and linkability. They are defined as follows:

Correctness. A LRS scheme should satisfy both verification and linking correctness. Verification correctness means signatures generated according to specification will be accepted by the *Verify* algorithm; Linking correctness means if two signatures are signed according to specification, then they are linked if and only if two signatures are generated by a common signer.

Before giving the definitions of unforgeability, anonymity and linkability, we consider the following oracles which simulate the ability of the adversaries in breaking the security of the LRS schemes:

- $(vk_i, sk_i) \leftarrow KO(pp, r_i)$. The KeyGen Oracle, on the ith query, picks randomness r_i, returns a public/private key pair (vk_i, sk_i).
- $\sigma \leftarrow SO(pp, sk_i, \mu, U)$. The Signing Oracle, on input private key sk_i, a message μ, a set of public keys $U = \{vk_1, vk_2, \ldots, vk_N\}$, returns a signature σ. Provided (vk_i, sk_i) has been generated by KO and $vk_i \in U$.
- $sk_i \leftarrow CO(vk_i)$. The Corruption Oracle, on input public key vk_i, returns the corresponding private key sk_i, provided (vk_i, sk_i) has been generated by KO.

In addition, in the random oracle model, there is also a random oracle HO provided for user's queries.

Unforgeability. Unforgeability for LRS schemes is defined by the game between a simulator S and an adversary A as follows:

(1) S generates and give the public parameters pp to A.
(2) A may query the above oracles adaptively.
(3) A give S a tuple of (U, μ, σ).

A wins the game if

(1) $Verify(pp, U, \mu, \sigma) = \text{accept}$;
(2) all of the vk_i in U are query outputs of KO;
(3) σ is not a query output of SO;
(4) all of the vk_i in U have not been input to CO.

We denote by

$$Adv_A^{unf}(\lambda) = \Pr[\text{A wins the game}];$$

Definition 5 (Unforgeability). If for any PPT adversary A, $Adv_A^{unf}(\lambda)$ is negligible, then a LRS scheme is unforgeable.

Anonymity. If a signature on a message μ under a ring U and key vk_i looks exactly the same as a signature on the message μ under the ring U and key vk_j, then a ring signature scheme is anonymous. Anonymity for LRS schemes is defined by the game between a simulator S and an adversary A as follows:

(1) S generates and give the public parameters pp to A;
(2) A may query KO adaptively;
(3) A chooses (i_0, i_1) such that (vk_{i_0}, sk_{i_0}), (vk_{i_1}, sk_{i_1}) have been generated by KO and $vk_{i_0}, vk_{i_1} \in U$;
(4) S chooses a random b from $\{0, 1\}$ and gives $\sigma \leftarrow SO(pp, sk_{i_b}, \mu, U)$ to A;
(5) A gives S the guess b'.

We denote by

$$Adv_A^{ano}(\lambda) = \left| \Pr[b' = b] - \frac{1}{2} \right|;$$

Definition 6 (Anonymity). If for any PPT adversary A, $Adv_A^{ano}(\lambda)$ is 0, then a LRS scheme is anonymous.

Linkability. Linkability for LRS schemes means it is infeasible for a signer to generate two valid signatures which are determined to be unlinked by algorithm Link. Linkability for LRS schemes is defined by the game between a simulator S and an adversary A as follows:

(1) S generates and give the public parameters pp to A;
(2) A may query the oracles adaptively;
(3) A give S two message-signature pairs $(\mu_1, \sigma_1), (\mu_2, \sigma_2)$ with two public key sets U_1, U_2.

A wins the game if

(1) All of the vk_i in $U_1 \cup U_2$ are query outputs of KO;
(2) $Verify(pp, U_i, \mu_i, \sigma_i)$ = accept for $i = 1, 2$ and σ_1, σ_2 are not query outputs of SO.
(3) A has queried CO less than two times (that is, A only have at most one user private key);
4) $Link(pp, \sigma_1, \sigma_2)$ = unlinked.

We denote by $Adv_A^{lin}(\lambda) = \Pr[\text{A wins the game}]$.

Definition 7 (Linkability). If for any PPT adversary A, $Adv_A^{lin}(\lambda)$ is negligible, then a LRS scheme is linkable.

4.3 RLWE Commitment-Based Linkable Ring Signature Scheme

Groth and Kohlweiss [12] show that if we have a homomorphic commitment scheme, we can construct a zero-knowledge proof system- a Σ_2-protocol for one out of N commitments containing 0, and then use the Fiat-Shamir heuristic to transform the interactive Σ_2-protocol to a non-interactive ring signature scheme. In this section, we apply the method of "commitment scheme-Σ_2-protocol- Fiat-Shamir heuristic" [12] to construct a RLWE commitment-based LRS scheme. The ring signature size based on this method is $O(\log N)$.

In our ring scheme, we set the user's private key as $sk_i = (r_i, e_i)$ where $r_i \leftarrow R_q$, $e_i \leftarrow \chi_{\sigma_e}^k$ and the corresponding public key as $vk_i = y_i = Com(0, r_i, e_i) = br_i + e_i$. δ_{il} is Kronercker's delta, i.e., $\delta_{ll} = 1$, $\delta_{il} = 0$ for $i \neq l$. Suppose there are at most N members in the ring, and without loss of generality, assume $N = 2^n$, and write $i = i_1 \ldots i_n$ and $l = l_1 \ldots l_n$ in binary. Let $f_j = l_j x + a_j$, $f_{j,1} = f_j = l_j x + a_j = \delta_{1l_j} x + a_j$, and $f_{j,0} = x - f_j = (1 - l_j)x - a_j = \delta_{0l_j} x - a_j$ for $l_j \in \{0, 1\}$, then we have for each i that the product $\prod_{j=1}^{n} f_{j,i_j}$ is a polynomial of the form

$$p_i(x) = \prod_{j=1}^{n} (\delta_{i_j l_j} x) + \sum_{k=0}^{n-1} p_{i,k} x^k = \delta_{il} x^n + \sum_{k=0}^{n-1} p_{i,k} x^k,$$

where $p_{i,k}$ is the coefficient of item of degree k.

Our LRS scheme is described as follows:

- *Setup*(1^λ): On input the security parameter λ, picks a positive integer $\gamma > 6$ and a positive integer m which is a power of 2, and picks a prime number $q \equiv 3 \bmod 8$ conditioned $q \geq m^\gamma \geq m^6$, sets $R_q = \mathbb{Z}_q[x]/ < x^m + 1 >$, selects two polynomial vectors $\boldsymbol{a}$, $\boldsymbol{b} \leftarrow R_q^k$ where $k > \frac{18\gamma}{3\gamma - 16}$, sets commitment space $C_{ck} = R_q^k$ selects a hash function $H : \{0, 1\}^* \rightarrow \{-1, 0, 1\}^\lambda$, supposes $N = 2^n$ is the cardinality of the ring and outputs public parameter $pp = \{\lambda, q, m, k, \boldsymbol{a}, \boldsymbol{b}, H\}$.

$KGen(pp)$: On input the public parameter pp, randomly chooses $r_i \leftarrow R_q$, $e_i \leftarrow \chi_{\sigma_e}^k$, returns user's public key $vk_i = y_i = br_i + e_i$, and keeps user's private key $sk_i = (r_i, e_i)$ secret.

$Sign(pp, sk_l, \mu, U)$: On input a private key $sk_l = (r_l, e_l)$, a message μ, and the public key set $U = \{y_1, y_2, \ldots, y_N\}$:

(1) Computes $I_l = ar_l + e_l$ as the link key.

For j from 1 to n,

- Ranomly chooses $u_j, w_j, s_j, t_j, \rho_k \leftarrow R_q$,
- Computes $C_{l_j} = al_j + bu_j + e_l$, $C_{w_j} = aw_j + bs_j + e_l$, $C_{v_j} = aw_jl_j + bt_j + e_l$,
- Computes $C_{d_k} = (\sum_{i=1}^{N-1} p_{i.k}y_i) + b\rho_k + e_l$, $C'_{d_k} = a\rho_k + e_l$, where $k = j - 1$,
- Sets $S_1 = \{C_{l_j}, C_{w_j}, C_{v_j}, C_{d_{j-1}}, C'_{d_{j-1}}\}_{j=1}^n$,

(2) Computes $x = H(pp, \mu, U, S_1, I_l)$,

For j form 1 to n,

- Computes $f_j = xl_j + w_j$,
- Computes $z_{w_j} = xu_j + s_j$,
- Computes $z_{v_j} = (x - f_j)u_j + t_j$,

(3) Computes $z_d = r_lx^n - \sum_{k=0}^{n-1} x^k \rho_k$,

- Sets $S_2 = \{f_j, z_{w_j}, z_{v_j}\}_{j=1}^n$,
- Outputs $\sigma = \{S_1, S_2, z_d, I_l, U\}$ as the signature.

$Verify(pp, \mu, \sigma, U)$: Checks if $C_{\ell_1}, \ldots, C_{d_{n-1}} \in C_{ck}$, and $f_1, \ldots, z_d \in R_q$, Computes $x = H(pp, \mu, U, S_1, I_l)$,
For j from 1 to n, computes and checks if

$$xC_{l_j} + C_{w_j} = Com(f_j, z_{w_j}, x + 1)$$

$$C_{l_j}(x - f_j) + C_{v_j} = Com(0, z_{v_j}, x - f_j + 1)$$

$$I_l x^n + \sum_{k=0}^{n-1} C'_{d_k}(-x^k) = Com(z_d, 0, x^n - \sum_{k=0}^{n-1} x^k)$$

$$\sum_{i=0}^{N-1} (y_i \prod_{j=1}^{n} f_{j.i_j}) + \sum_{k=0}^{n-1} C_{d_k}(-x^k) = Com(0, z_d, x^n - \sum_{k=0}^{n-1} x^k)$$

If all above equations hold, then outputs accept; Otherwise reject.

$Link(pp, \sigma_1, \sigma_2)$: On input two signatures $\sigma_1 = (\ldots, I_1, U_1)$ and $\sigma_2 = (\ldots, I_2, U_2)$, it checks if $I_1 = I_2$. If it holds, outputs linked; Otherwise, outputs unlinked.

5 Security Analysis

Theorem 3 (Correctness). Our LRS scheme is correct.

Proof. Since

$$xC_{l_j} + C_{w_j}$$
$$= x(al_j + bu_j + e_l) + aw_j + bs_j + e_l$$
$$= a(xl_j + w_j) + b(xu_j + s_j) + e_l(x + 1)$$
$$= Com(f_j, z_{w_j}, x + 1),$$

$$C_{l_j}(x - f_j) + C_{v_j}$$
$$= (al_j + bu_j + e_l)(x - f_j) + aw_j l_j + bt_j + e_l$$
$$= b(x - f_j)u_j + bt_j + a(x - f_j)l_j + aw_j l_j + e(x - f_j + 1)$$
$$= b(x - f_j)u_j + bt_j + a(x - (xl_j + w_j))l_j + aw_j l_j + e(x - f_j + 1)$$
$$= b(x - f_j)u_j + bt_j + axl_j(1 - l_j) + e(x - f_j + 1)$$
$$= b((x - f_j)u_j + t_j) + e(x - f_j + 1)$$
$$= Com(0, z_{v_j}, x - f_j + 1),$$

$$I_l x^n + \sum_{k=0}^{n-1} C'_{d_k}(-x^k)$$
$$= (ar_l + e_l)x^n + \sum_{k=0}^{n-1} (a\rho_k + e_l)(-x^k)$$
$$= a(r_l x^n - \sum_{k=0}^{n-1} \rho_k x^k) + e_l(x^n - \sum_{k=0}^{n-1} x^k)$$
$$= Com(z_d, 0, x^n - \sum_{k=0}^{n-1} x^k),$$

$$\sum_{i=0}^{N-1} y_i(\prod_{j=1}^{n} f_{j.i_j}) + \sum_{k=0}^{n-1} C_{d_k}(-x^k)$$
$$= \sum_{i=0}^{N-1} y_i(\delta_{i\ell} x^n + \sum_{k=0}^{n-1} P_{i,k} x^k) + \sum_{k=0}^{n-1} ((\sum_{i=1}^{N-1} y_i P_{i.k}) + b\rho_k + e_l)(-x^k)$$

$$= \sum_{i=0}^{N-1} \sum_{k=0}^{n-1} (y_i p_{i,k} x^k - y_i p_{i,k} x^k) + y_l(\delta_{\ell\ell} x^n) + \sum_{k=0}^{n-1} b\rho_k(-x^k) + e_l \sum_{k=0}^{n-1} (-x^k)$$

$$= y_l x^n - \sum_{k=0}^{n-1} b\rho_k x^k + e_l \sum_{k=0}^{n-1} (-x^k)$$

$$= (br_l + e_l)x^n - \sum_{k=0}^{n-1} b\rho_k x^k + e_l \sum_{k=0}^{n-1} (-x^k)$$

$$= b(r_l x^n - \sum_{k=0}^{n-1} \rho_k x^k) + e_l(x^n - \sum_{k=0}^{n-1} x^k)$$

$$= Com(0, z_d, x^n - \sum_{k=0}^{n-1} x^k),$$

our LRS scheme satisfy verification correctness. And if a signer use his private key to compute two signatures, we have $I_l = ar_l + e_l = ar_l' + e_l' = I_l'$ satisfying linking correctness.

Theorem 4 (Unforgeability). Our LRS scheme is unforgeable in the random oracle model if the RLWE commitment scheme is binding.

Proof. The unforgeability of our LRS scheme relies on the $(n + 1)$-special soundness (refer to Theorem 3 in [12]) of the Σ_2-protocol and simulates the hash function H as a random oracle. Consider a polynomial time adversary A that makes Q_K, Q_C, Q_S, and Q_H queries to the key generating oracle KO, corrupting oracle CO, signing oracle SO and random oracle HO, respectively, with at least unnegligible ε probability, winning the unforgeability game. We will show that we can use A to construct a polynomial time attack that breaks the binding property of the commitment scheme with unnegligible probability. We suppose A successfully forges a signature under public key vk_j.

Let us now give more details of how the attack works:

KO: when A queries KO, we answers honestly except on the jth (random $j \in \{1, \ldots, Q_K\}$) query where we choose random $r_j \leftarrow R_q, e_j \leftarrow \chi_{\sigma_e}^k$ and set $vk_j = Com(1, r_j, e_j)$, and return vk_j.

CO: when A queries CO, we answers honestly except when A queries vk_j, we abort.

SO: If A queries (pp, sk_j, μ, U), we sign honestly to generate S_1, I_l, and pick $x \leftarrow \{-1, 0, 1\}^\lambda$ at random. We then perform the random oracle HO to have $H(pp, \mu, U, S_1, I_l) = x$, except when (pp, μ, U, S_1, I_l) has already been queried before, we abort.

HO: All the queries and its corresponding outputs are saved in a list called H-list. When A queries (pp, μ, U, S_1, I_l), we first look for if there is a record about (pp, μ, U, S_1, I_l) in the H-list, if no, we pick $x \leftarrow \{-1, 0, 1\}^\lambda$ at random, add a record as $(pp, \mu, U, S_1, I_l)||x$ to H-list and return x; if there is, we return x.

Since suppose A with unnegligible probability forges a signature about (pp, μ, U) under public key vk_j, which is not a query output of SO and all of the vk_i in U have not been input to CO, we can suppose that A has queried $HO(pp, \mu, U, S_1, I_l)$ with unnegligible probability. Suppose at the point that the adversary call the random oracle HO on a query (pp, μ, U, S_1, I_l) used to get a challenge $x^{(0)}$, then we can rewind the adversary to the point where it made the query $HO(pp, \mu, U, S_1, I_l)$ used in the forged signature and give it random answers $x^{(1)}, \ldots, x^{(n)}$. Now the adversary may forge another n distinct signatures $(S_1, S_2^1, z_d^1, I_l, U)$, $(S_1, S_2^2, z_d^2, I_l, U)$, ..., $(S_1, S_2^n, z_d^n, I_l, U)$ on message μ and ring U. Now the $(n+1)$-soundness of the Σ_2 − protocol (refer to Theorem 3 in [12]) may permit extraction of an opening of some vk_i to $(0, r_i, e_i)$. Notice we set $vk_j = Com_{ck}(1, r_j, e_j)$, so with probability $\frac{1}{Q_K}$ we have $i = j$, which gives us a breach of the commitment scheme's binding property.

Theorem 5 (Anonymity). Our LRS scheme is anonymous, if the commitment scheme is hiding.

Proof. The technical approach of our LRS scheme is similar to [12, 21]: first construct a RLWE commitment based Σ-protocol for one out of N commitments containing 0 and then make the Σ-protocol non-interactive by using the Fiat-Shamir heuristic. Thus, the ring signature scheme inherits the properties of the Σ-protocol. The anonymity of our LRS scheme follows the special honest verifier zero-knowledge property of the Σ-protocol (refer to Theorem 3 in [12]), so it is anonymous if the underlying commitment scheme (RLWE-based commitment scheme) is hiding.

Theorem 6 (Linkability). Our LRS scheme is linkable if the LRS scheme is unforgeable.

Proof. Suppose A with unnegligible probability outputs two message-signature pairs (μ_1, σ_1), (μ_2, σ_2) with two public key sets U_1, U_2, where $Verify(pp, \mu_i, \sigma_i, U_i) =$ accept for $i = 1, 2$. Since the LRS scheme satisfies unforgeability, the two signatures can pass the verification if and only if A generates the two signatures according to the specification honestly, that is, $I_1 = ar_1 + e_1$ and $I_2 = ar_2 + e_2$. Since A only has one secret key, therefore $r_1 = r_2$, $e_1 = e_2$ and $I_1 = I_2$. which means σ_1, σ_2 can be linked by algorithm *Link*. It is contradict to the assumption.

6 Performance Analysis

The efficiency of the ring signature scheme mainly depends on the signature generation and verification time, and the size of keys and signature. Tables 2 and 3 compares the efficiency of our scheme with other lattice-based ring schemes in time and space. In Tables 2 and 3, l denotes the cardinality of the ring, q is a large prime number, positive integer k is the multiplicative overhead of commitment size. Literature [17–19] use matrix $A \in \mathbb{Z}_q^{n \times m}$, where $m \geq 5n \log q$, while literature [21] uses matrix $A \in \mathbb{Z}_q^{m \times m}$, where $m = \Theta(1)$. Our ring scheme does not use a matrix, but the polynomials of degree n from a polynomial ring. d denotes the number of independent random matrices used in the lattice-based cryptography schemes. T_{SP} and T_{EB} respectively represent the time when algorithms SamplePre and ExtBasis run once, T_{Mul} represents the time cost of the n scalar-multiplication operations, and $T_{EB} >> T_{Mul}$. Since Hash, polynomial and matrix addition operations take less time, their time overhead is ignored. We mainly consider time-consuming operations, i.e., matrix-vector multiplication, polynomial-polynomial multiplication.

The specific comparison results are shown in Tables 2 and 3:

Table 2. Comparison of time costs and difficult assumption

Scheme	Signature cost	Verification cost	Difficult assumption
[17]	$m(l+d)T_{EB} + m(l+d+1)T_{SP}$	$m(l+d+1)T_{Mul}$	SIS
[18]	$mT_{SP} + m(l+1)T_{Mul}$	$m(l+2)T_{Mul}$	SIS
[19]	$m(l+1)T_{Mul}$	$m(l+1)T_{Mul}$	SIS
[21]	$(7+m^2)T_{Mul}\log l$	$6mT_{Mul}\log l$	Ideal-SVP
Our scheme	$(8k+2)T_{Mul}\log l$	$7kT_{Mul}\log l$	RLWE

Table 3. Comparison of communication cost

Scheme	Public key size	Private key size	Signature size
[17]	$n(lm_1 + km_2)\log q$	$m_1^2 \log q$	$(l+d+1)m\log q$
[18]	$mn\log q$	$m^2 \log q$	$m(l+2)\log q$
[19]	$mn\log q$	$mk\log q$	$(lm+k)\log q$
[21]	$mn\log q$	$m^2 n\log q$	$(4m^2+6m+lm)n\log q$
Our scheme	$kn\log q$	$(k+1)n\log q$	$((6+l)k+4)n\log q$

As shown in Tables 2 and 3, in terms of time overhead, since in our scheme the main operations are polynomial-polynomial multiplication in the ring, and the multiplication of two polynomials in the ring is equivalent to performing n vector-vector inner product in parallel, and since $m > k > 54$, our signature generation verification time is shorter than that of [17–19, 21]. In terms of key size, our scheme's public key size, private key size and signature size are shorter than literature [17–19, 21]. In addition, the literature [17–19] and the literature [21] are based on the SIS assumption and the SVP assumption on the ideal lattice, respectively, while our scheme is based on the RLWE assumption, which not only can be reduced to the SVP assumption on ideal lattice, but also have a feature of simple description.

In addition, so many polynomial-polynomial multiplication operations in ring in our scheme can be realized by fast Fourier transform, which will greatly improve the computational efficiency. In a comprehensive comparison, our LRS scheme has a relatively small signature and key size, and the signature and verification time is also short.

7 Anonymous Post-Quantum Cryptocurrency Model Based on Linkable Ring Signature

Based on the proposed LRS scheme, we propose a more secure and efficient cryptocurrency model. This section gives a description of the cryptocurrency model.

In the transaction process, the sender's anonymity is protected by the proposed LRS scheme, and the receiver's anonymity is protected by the stealth address technology. Unlike other schemes, our cryptocurrency model can resist quantum attacks and use the linkability of LRS to prevent double spending of a user.

We assume that users Alice and Bob trade through APQB and Alice transfers the money to Bob.

(1) On input the security parameters λ, the system chooses an asymmetric encryption algorithm ES_1 and a symmetric encryption algorithm ES_2, runs $LRS.Setup(1^\lambda)$, and publishes the public parameters $pp = (\lambda, m, q, \boldsymbol{a}, \boldsymbol{b}, N, H)$.

(2) Alice runs $LRS.KGen(pp)$ to generate a key pair $(y_A,(r_A,\boldsymbol{e}_A))$, where $y_A = \boldsymbol{b}r_A + \boldsymbol{e}_A$, and Bob generates a key pair $(y_B,(r_B,\boldsymbol{e}_B))$ similarly. In addition, Alice and Bob generate another public/private key pairs $(pk_A, sk_A)(pk_B, sk_B)$ for algorithm ES_1.

(3) Alice randomly selects $r_p \leftarrow R_q$, $\boldsymbol{e}_p \leftarrow \chi_{\sigma_e}^k$, and generates a one-time address $y_d = \boldsymbol{b}r_p + \boldsymbol{e}_p + y_B$ for Bob, where $y_B = \boldsymbol{b}r_B + \boldsymbol{e}_B$, $(r_p, \boldsymbol{e}_p)$ is the partial signature key for the one-time address. Since only Bob holds $(r_B, \boldsymbol{e}_B)$, no one other than Bob (including Alice) can recover the full signature key corresponding to y_d. Further, Alice selects the key k for algorithm ES_2, and calculates $au_1 = ES_1.Enc_{pk_B}(k)$, $au_2 = ES_2.Enc_k(hash(pk_B)\|r_p\|\boldsymbol{e}_p)$.

(4) Alice selects the N-1 addresses $(y_1, \ldots, y_{Aj-1}, y_{Aj+1}, \ldots, y_{AN})$ which have the equivalent amount of currency to A, and set $U = (y_1, \ldots, y_{Aj-1}, y_A, y_{Aj+1}, \ldots, y_{AN})$. Then Alice inputs all his previous transactions into a hash function and obtains a hash value h, and computes $\sigma_A \leftarrow LRS.Sign(pp, (r_A, \boldsymbol{e}_A), h, U)$. Finally, Alice generates a transaction Tx which includes y_d, σ_A, h, U, transaction amount, au_1, au_2, and broadcasts Tx throughout the P2P network.

(5) Once received Tx, Bob first computes $k = ES_1.Dec_{sk_B}(au_1)$, then computes $hash(pk_B)\|r_p\|\boldsymbol{e}_p = ES_2.Dec_k(au_2)$, finally computes $r_d = r_p + r_B$, $\boldsymbol{e}_d = \boldsymbol{e}_p + \boldsymbol{e}_B$, and $y'_d = \boldsymbol{b}r_d + \boldsymbol{e}_d$. If $y'_d = y_d$, then it is a valid one-time address for Bob, where $(r_d, \boldsymbol{e}_d)$ is the valid signature key corresponding to y_d, and he saves $y_d, (r_d, \boldsymbol{e}_d)$ to his wallet.

(6) Once received Tx, miners first verify if the message-signature pair (h, σ_A) is valid by running $LRS.Verify(pp, h, \sigma_A, U)$, and then they look up the ledger to verify whether the signature is a double-spending by runs $LRS.Link$. If the signature can't be linked and can pass the $Verify$ check, miners pack the transaction Tx; Otherwise, they give up packing the transaction Tx.

(7) Bob can then use the corresponding signature private key $(r_d, \boldsymbol{e}_d)$ to spend the currency stored in the address y_d (Fig. 2).

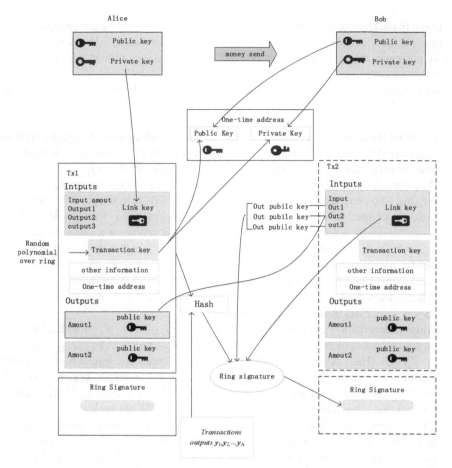

Fig. 2. Trading schematics in blockchain

8   Conclusion

In order to solve the problems of large key size and low computation efficiency of linkable ring signature (LRS) schemes from lattice, based on RLWE (learning with errors from ring) commitment scheme, combined with the Σ-protocol and Fiat-Shamir transformation method, this paper reconstructs a LRS scheme, and further applies the proposed LRS scheme to blockchain to provide an anonymous post-quantum cryptocurrency model. The security of the proposed LRS scheme is proved under the random oracle model, and a detailed efficiency analysis is given. Compared with previous lattice-based (linkable) ring signature schemes, since the proposed scheme is constructed based on the RLWE assumption, and uses a large number of small polynomials from ring, the scheme has smaller key and signature size and higher computational efficiency, and the description of the scheme is simpler. The cryptocurrency model uses the LRS scheme to ensure the sender's anonymity, uses one-time stealth address to guarantee the recipient's anonymity, and can both resist quantum attacks and protect users' identities.

Acknowledgments. This work was supported by the National Natural Science Foundation of China (61802117), the '13th Five-Year' National Crypto Development Foundation (MMJJ20170122), the Projects of Henan Provincial Department of Science and Technology under Grant (182102310923,192102210280), Key Research Projects of Henan Higher Education Institutions (18A413001,19A520025), Natural Science Foundation of Henan Polytechnic University (T2018-1), Young Backbone Teacher Funded Project of Henan Polytechnic University (2018XQG-10).

References

1. Nakamoto, S.: Bitcoin: A Peer-to-Peer Electronic Cash System (2008)
2. Barber, S., Boyen, X., Shi, E., Uzun, E.: Bitter to better—how to make bitcoin a better currency. In: Keromytis, A.D. (ed.) FC 2012. LNCS, vol. 7397, pp. 399–414. Springer, Heidelberg (2012). https://doi.org/10.1007/978-3-642-32946-3_29
3. Reid, F., Harrigan, M.: An analysis of anonymity in the bitcoin system. In: Altshuler, Y., Elovici, Y., Cremers, A., Aharony, N., Pentland, A. (eds.) Security and Privacy in Social Networks, pp. 197–223. Springer, New York (2013). https://doi.org/10.1007/978-1-4614-4139-7_10
4. Ober, M., Katzenbeisser, S., Hamacher, K.: Structure and anonymity of the bitcoin transaction graph. Fut. Internet 5(2), 237–250 (2013)
5. Ron, D., Shamir, A.: Quantitative analysis of the full bitcoin transaction graph. In: Sadeghi, A.-R. (ed.) FC 2013. LNCS, vol. 7859, pp. 6–24. Springer, Heidelberg (2013). https://doi.org/10.1007/978-3-642-39884-1_2
6. Maxwell, G.: CoinJoin: bitcoin privacy for the real world (2013). https://bitcointalk.org/index.php?topic=279249.0
7. Bonneau, J., Narayanan, A., Miller, A., et al.: Mixcoin: anonymity for bitcoin with accountable mixes. In: International Conference on Financial Cryptography and Data Security (FC 2014), pp. 486–504 (2014)
8. Bergan, T., Anderson, O., Devietti, J., et al.: CryptoNote v 2.0 (2013). https://cryptonote.org/whitepaper.pdf
9. Miers, I., Garman, C., Green, M., Rubin, A.D.: Zerocoin: anonymous distributede-cash from bitcoin. In: Symposium on Security and Privacy SP2013, pp. 397–411, May 2013. https://doi.org/10.1109/sp.2013.34
10. Sasson, E.B., Chiesa, A., Garman, C., et al.: Zerocash: decentralized anonymous payments from Bitcoin. In: Security and Privacy (SP 2014), pp. 459–474 (2014)
11. Rivest, R.L., Shamir, A., Tauman, Y.: How to leak a secret. In: Boyd, C. (ed.) ASIACRYPT 2001. LNCS, vol. 2248, pp. 552–565. Springer, Heidelberg (2001). https://doi.org/10.1007/3-540-45682-1_32
12. Groth, J., Kohlweiss, M.: One-Out-of-Many proofs: or how to leak a secret and spend a coin. In: Oswald, E., Fischlin, M. (eds.) EUROCRYPT 2015. LNCS, vol. 9057, pp. 253–280. Springer, Heidelberg (2015). https://doi.org/10.1007/978-3-662-46803-6_9
13. Pedersen, T.P.: Non-interactive and information-theoretic secure verifiable secret sharing. In: CRYPTO. Lecture Notes in Computer Science, vol. 576, pp. 129–140 (1991)
14. Fiat, A., Shamir, A.: How to prove yourself: practical solutions to identification and signature problems. In: CRYPTO. Lecture Notes in Computer Science, vol. 263, pp. 186–194 (1986)
15. Fujisaki, E., Suzuki, K.: Traceable ring signature. In: Okamoto, T., Wang, X. (eds.) PKC 2007. LNCS, vol. 4450, pp. 181–200. Springer, Heidelberg (2007). https://doi.org/10.1007/978-3-540-71677-8_13

16. Liu, J.K., Wong, D.S.: Linkable ring signatures: security models and new schemes. In: Gervasi, O., et al. (eds.) ICCSA 2005. LNCS, vol. 3481, pp. 614–623. Springer, Heidelberg (2005). https://doi.org/10.1007/11424826_65
17. Wang, F.H., Hu, Y.P., Wang, C.X.: A lattice-based ring signature scheme from bonsai trees. J. Electron. Inf. Technol. **32**(2), 2400–2403 (2010)
18. Tian, M.M., Huang, L.S., Yang, W.: Efficient lattice-based ring signature scheme. Jisuanji Xuebao (Chin. J. Comput.) **35**(4), 712–718 (2012)
19. Wang, S., Zhao, R.: Lattice-Based Ring Signature Scheme under the Random Oracle Model. Eprint Arxiv (2014)
20. Yang, R., Au, M.H., Lai, J., et al.: Lattice-based techniques for accountable anonymity: composition of abstract stern's protocols and weak PRF with efficient protocols from LWR. IACR Cryptology ePrint Archive, p. 781 (2017)
21. Zhang, H., Zhang, F., Tian, H., Au, M.H.: Anonymous post-quantum cryptocash. In: Meiklejohn, S., Sako, K. (eds.) FC 2018. LNCS, vol. 10957, pp. 461–479. Springer, Heidelberg (2018). https://doi.org/10.1007/978-3-662-58387-6_25
22. Baum, C., Lin, H., Oechsner, S.: Towards practical lattice-based one-time linkable ring signatures. In: Naccache, D., et al. (eds.) ICICS 2018. LNCS, vol. 11149, pp. 303–322. Springer, Cham (2018). https://doi.org/10.1007/978-3-030-01950-1_18
23. Alberto Torres, W.A., et al.: Post-Quantum one-time linkable ring signature and application to ring confidential transactions in blockchain (lattice ringCT v1.0). In: Susilo, W., Yang, G. (eds.) ACISP 2018. LNCS, vol. 10946, pp. 558–576. Springer, Cham (2018). https://doi.org/10.1007/978-3-319-93638-3_32
24. Lyubashevsky, V., Peikert, C., Regev, O.: On ideal lattices and learning with errors over rings. In: Gilbert, H. (ed.) EUROCRYPT 2010. LNCS, vol. 6110, pp. 1–23. Springer, Heidelberg (2010). https://doi.org/10.1007/978-3-642-13190-5_1
25. Benhamouda, F., Krenn, S., Lyubashevsky, V., Pietrzak, K.: Efficient zero-knowledge proofs for commitments from learning with errors over rings. In: Pernul, G., Ryan, P.Y.A., Weippl, E. (eds.) ESORICS 2015. LNCS, vol. 9326, pp. 1–14. Springer, Cham (2015). https://doi.org/10.1007/978-3-319-24174-6_16
26. Liu, J.K., Au, M.H., Susilo, W., et al.: Linkable ring signature with unconditional anonymity. IEEE Trans. Knowl. Data Eng. **26**(1), 157–165 (2013)

A New Structure of Blockchain to Simplify the Verification

Jianjian Yu[(⊠)], Lei Fan, and Gongliang Chen

School of Cyber Science and Engineering,
Shanghai Jiaotong University, Shanghai 200240, China
{oj01ol,fanlei,chengl}@sjtu.edu.cn

Abstract. Blockchain is first introduced in Bitcoin and has good performance in cryptocurrencies. With the growth of chain, the height of blockchain in Bitcoin has reached five hundred thousand, and the entire capacity of chain is more than 500 GB. If a light node wants to verify a transaction, it has to spend nearly one week to download the data of whole chain with download rate of 1 MB/s, which seriously hinders the usage of blockchain. In order to resolve this problem, checkpoint is used to reduce the capacity of data, but this centralized scheme obviously violates the decentralization of blockchain. Other schemes are proposed will change the structure of blockchain may suffer the risk that adversary can fork a blockchain to cheat the light nodes. In this paper, we propose a novel blockchain architecture, which simplifies the verification in blockchain and is compatible with most consensus mechanism. We append backlinks in some blocks, such that blocks not only look like a chain but also like a binary tree. We also introduce a challenge mechanism for against the forking attack on light nodes.

Keywords: Blockchain verification · Light node · Binary tree · Forking attack · Challenge mechanism

1 Introduction

Bitcoin [1] uses the blockchain, combined with proof-of-work consensus and appropriate incentive to achieve a cryptocurrency which is resistant to "double-spending". Over the years, blockchain technology has gained increasing recognition and attention. However, as the length of the blockchain continues to increase, the cost of light nodes entering the blockchain network increases, and cumbersome verification issues are highlighted.

According to the data from blockchain browser, the height of blockchain in Bitcoin has exceeded five hundred thousand. If each block stores 1 MB data, the full chain data of Bitcoin is over 500 GB. If the light node holds 1 MB/s download rate, it will cost the node six days to accomplish the transmission of all data in traditional way, which is intolerable.

1.1 Blockchain Verification Model and Terminology

Our research built on the core assumption of proof-of-work consensus, that there exist hash functions which are one-way and resistant-collision. Moreover, we assume the

© Springer Nature Singapore Pte Ltd. 2020
Z. Zheng et al. (Eds.): BlockSys 2019, CCIS 1156, pp. 33–46, 2020.
https://doi.org/10.1007/978-981-15-2777-7_3

calculation power of the whole network is N, and the attacker is αN, in which $\alpha < 50\%$ against the majority attack [2]. The calculation power mentioned here is not just the hashrate [3] in the Bitcoin, but represents the ability directly related to generating blocks in different consensus mechanisms, such as the product of hashrate and the coin-days in proof-of-stake [4]. Besides, we assume that the network is normal with no "eclipse" [5], ensuring that each node could connect to at least one honest node. Since these assumptions are the most basic requirements in blockchain, our structure can be applied to any type of existing blockchain implementation.

When a new node gets into the network and requests the latest block, it follows only two principles that the determinate foundation block (the first block in the blockchain) and the longest chain principle. Thus, its primary work is to test the connectivity between the foundation block and the latest block. Secondly, it is required to verify connectivity between the latest block and the blocks contains the transactions it cares. We call the former work "forward verification", and the second one "backward verification".

1.2 Related Work

In order to resolve the verification problem, checkpoint is used to summarize all previous block information and simplify the verification method. But the usual method to generate a checkpoint and make the light node trust is introducing a trusted-third-party, which is clearly contrary to the idea of decentralization.

Skipchain [6] proposes that each block records the hash of previous block with a height distance of b^i, in which $0 \leq i \leq \lceil \log_b n \rceil$, n represent the height of blockchain and b usually takes a value of 2. However, with the growth of chain, it takes increasing space to record backlinks. Otherwise it provides limited upgrade in verification. Aside from the problem of space consumption, the amount of block used for verification in Skipchain with the height of n is O(lg$n$).

The primitive called Non-Interactive-Proofs-of-Proof-of-Work (NIPoPoWs) [7] divides blocks of different heights into different levels. Each block only needs to record the hash of the previous block in every lower level in addition to the hash of the previous block in the current level. Compared with the Skip chain, NIPoPoWs saves the space in low level blocks.

LeapChain [8] proposed that the i-th block records the hash of previous block with a height distance of W(i), where

$$W(i) = \begin{cases} b^b & if\ i\ mod\ b = 0 \\ b^{i\ mod\ b} & otherwise \end{cases} \tag{1}$$

It reduces the space to store backlinks and maintains the amount of block used for verification at O(lg$n$), in which n represents the height of blockchain.

Whether it is Skipchain, NIPoPows or LeapChain, it is designed for the situation that the light node retains the necessary blocks already and wants to verify a transaction in previous blocks, which we call it "backward verification". They do not realize that the fixed structure reduces the cost of attack when a new light node enters the network and requests the latest block, the situation we call it "forward verification", and they do not provide a secure verification mechanism against this forking attack which we will explain detailly in Sect. 4.1.

1.3 Contributions

In this paper, we present a new tree-like blockchain structure, called "block-tree". In an ideal situation, the amount of block used for verification in our structure is $O(\lg n)$, and the extra space cost to store backlinks is at most the size of one block hash. Considering the forking attack on our structure, we introduce the challenge mechanism in the verification process. Such that, the attacker who mines the less blocks than it declared responses to the challenge successfully with a small probability. By increasing challenges, the probability of successful attack will be significantly reduced. And our structure is compatible with most current consensus mechanism researches and maintains resistant to the traditional attacks.

The remainder of this paper is organized as follows. Section 2 presents our proposed new structure and the rule to implement it. The new verification methodologies are given in Sect. 3. Then, the evaluation is included in Sect. 4. Finally, we conclude our work in Sect. 5.

2 Blockchain Structure

After the blockchain being proposed in Bitcoin, it has been applied to most cryptocurrencies like the Ethereum and EOS. But there was no significant change in the structure of blockchain. In this section, we will introduce the traditional structure of blockchain and our new structure.

2.1 Traditional Structure

Blockchain uses a hash function to join the blocks one by one into a chain. As long as users keep the latest block unchanged, all blocks before it can be uniquely determined, based on the hash function hypothesis in mathematic. Figure 1 shows the traditional block structure implemented in most blockchain projects.

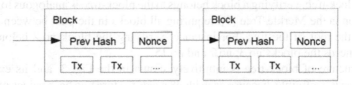

Fig. 1. Block structure in Bitcoin [1]

As shown in the Fig. 1, each block contains the hash of previous block. Therefore, the blocks are finally arranged in the form shown in the Fig. 2.

Fig. 2. Traditional blockchain structure

In this structure, user who wants to verify the latest block without any block data except the foundation block, must download all blocks between the foundation block and the latest block. Obviously, the complexity of verification in traditional structure is O(n).

2.2 New Structure

Adding backlinks makes that the verification method could jump from one block to further back block rather than just direct predecessor. In fact, we add backlinks based on the architecture of the binary tree. As shown in the Fig. 3, the solid lines link the blocks in the traditional way. By adding the dotted lines as the additional backlinks, the blockchain is folded into a tree-like structure, and we call it "block-tree", though actually it is not a tree in graph theory.

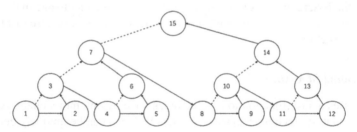

Fig. 3. Tree-like blockchain structure

In the block-tree, verifying a block belongs to the block-tree is analogous to verifying a transaction in the Merkle Tree [9], requiring all blocks in the path between the target block and the root of the tree. For instance, verifying the block no.2 belongs to the block-tree needs the blocks no.3, no.7 and no.15.

The structure of block-tree is intuitively shown in the Fig. 3, and its extra space consumption is negligible, because each block needs to store two hash values of previous block at most. The ideal situation is that the latest block happens to be the root of tree, where the verification complexity is $O(\lg n)$. When the blocks cannot form a full binary tree, scilicet the latest block is not the root of entire tree, the verification will become more complicated. For instance, verifying the connectivity between the block no.2 and the no.13 needs the blocks no.3, no.7, no.8, no.10, no.11 and no.13. Even in the worst situation, the complexity of verification is $O(\lg^2 n)$ and better than the traditional process.

2.3 Block-Tree Approach

Firstly, we use S_k denote the number of nodes in a binary tree with a height of k. Of course, we know that

$$S_k = 2^k - 1 \tag{2}$$

and

$$S_{k+1} = 2 * S_k + 1 \tag{3}$$

are always satisfied for any positive integer k.

Then we define a decomposition $\mathcal{D}(n)$ for any positive integer n, let

$$\mathcal{D}(n) = n = a_k * S_k + a_{k-1} * S_{k-1} + \cdots + a_2 * S_2 + a_1 * S_1 \tag{4}$$

in which, $a_i \in \{0, 1, 2\}$, $1 \leq i \leq k$, $a_k \neq 0$, and if there exists an a_j that satisfied $a_j = 2$, $1 \leq j \leq k$, then for each integer $i < j$, we have $a_i = 0$. We call this the tree-decomposition of n. And we can prove that for any positive integer n, the expression $\mathcal{D}(n)$ exists and is unique. The proof is given in the **Theorems** 2.1 and 2.2.

The $\mathcal{D}(n)$ represents the position of the block with a height of n in block-tree. Based on the tree-decomposition, we give the rules for the generation of block-tree:

(1) For each block except the foundation block, the hash of the previous block must be included.
(2) If the tree-decomposition of the height of the previous block contains an item with a coefficient of 2, then add an additional block hash to the current block as a backlink. The height of added block has the same tree-decomposition with the height of the previous block except the last non-zero coefficient, which is 2 in the previous block and is 1 in the added block.

The additional backlink appended to block is determined by Algorithm 1, where Tree_Decomposition(n) returns the array represents the coefficients in $\mathcal{D}(n)$, and the Tree_Composition(*Array*) returns the integer m that Tree_Decomposition(m) is *Array*. The position of the added block in the block-tree is shown in the Fig. 4.

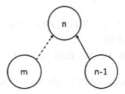

Fig. 4. Position of the added block m

Algorithm 1. Additional backlink appended to block n.

Algorithm 1 Additional backlink appended to block n.

Input: Height of block, n;

Output: Height of additional block, m;

1: **function** LEFTNODE(n)
2:     $m \leftarrow 0$
3:     **if** $n < 2$ **then return** m
4:     **end if**
5:     $Array \leftarrow$ Tree_Decomposition($n - 1$)
6:     **for** $i = 0$ to len($Array$)-1 **do**
7:         **if** $Array[i] = 2$ **then**
8:             $Array[i] \leftarrow 1$
9:             $m \leftarrow$ Tree_Composition($Array$)
10:             **return** m
11:         **end if**
12:     **end for**
13:     **return** m
14: **end function**

Theorem 2.1. For any positive integer n, $\mathcal{D}(n)$ exists.

Proof: For $i = 1, \forall n \le 2^i - 1$, we have $\mathcal{D}(n) = 1 = S_1$, exists.

Now we assume that for $i = k, \forall n \le 2^i - 1$, $\mathcal{D}(n)$ exists, then when $i = k + 1$, $\forall n \le 2^i - 1$,

(1) If $n = 2^i - 1$, then $\mathcal{D}(n) = S_{k+1}$, exists;
(2) If $n \le 2^{i-1} - 1$, which means $n \le 2^k - 1$, such that $\mathcal{D}(n)$ exists known by the induction hypothesis;
(3) If $2^{i-1} - 1 < n < 2^i - 1$, let $n' = n - S_k$, such that $1 \le n' < 2^k$, equivalently, $1 \le n' \le 2^k - 1$. Using the induction hypothesis, we find that the tree-decomposition of n' exists and we assume the result is as following

$$\mathcal{D}(n') = a_j * S_j + a_{j-1} * S_{j-1} + \cdots + a_2 * S_2 + a_1 * S_1, a_j \neq 0 \qquad (5)$$

Since $n' \le 2^k - 1 = S_k$, if $n' = S_k$, then $\mathcal{D}(n) = n' + S_k = 2 * S_k$. Otherwise, $n' < S_k$, we have that $j < k$ and

$$\mathcal{D}(n) = \mathcal{D}(n') + S_k = S_k + a_j * S_j + a_{j-1} * S_{j-1} + \cdots + a_2 * S_2 + a_1 * S_1 \qquad (6)$$

Thus, for $i = k + 1, \forall n \le 2^i - 1$, $\mathcal{D}(n)$ exists, and the general result follows by the Principle of Mathematical Induction.

Before we prove the Theorem 2.2, we first prove the following lemma.

Lemma 1. Suppose a positive integer m has the tree-decomposition $\mathcal{D}(m)$ as following

$$\mathcal{D}(m) = m = c_k * S_k + c_{k-1} * S_{k-1} + \cdots + c_2 * S_2 + c_1 * S_1 \qquad (7)$$

then the following inequality is satisfied.

$$c_k * S_k + c_{k-1} * S_{k-1} + \cdots + c_2 * S_2 + c_1 * S_1 < S_{k+1} \qquad (8)$$

Proof: For $k = 1$, $c_1 * S_1 \leq 2 * S_1 = S_2 - 1 < S_2$.

Now we assume that for $k = t$, inequality (8) is satisfied. When $k = t + 1$,

(1) If $c_k = 2$, then $c_{k-1} = c_{k-2} = \cdots = c_2 = c_1 = 0$, hence

$$c_k * S_k + c_{k-1} * S_{k-1} + \cdots + c_2 * S_2 + c_1 * S_1 = 2 * S_k < S_{k+1} \qquad (9)$$

(2) If $c_k \leq 1$, according to the induction hypothesis, we could know that

$$c_k * S_k + c_{k-1} * S_{k-1} + \cdots + c_2 * S_2 + c_1 * S_1 < c_k * S_k + S_k \leq 2 * S_k < S_{k+1}$$
$$\qquad (10)$$

Thus, for $k = t + 1$, inequality (8) is satisfied and the general result follows by the Principle of Mathematical Induction. In other words, the Lemma is proved.

Theorem 2.2. For any positive integer n, if $\mathcal{D}(n)$ exists, the expression is unique.

Proof: Suppose $\mathcal{D}(n)$ have different expressions, and may wish to set as follows

$$n = \mathcal{D}_1(n) = a_i * S_i + a_{i-1} * S_{i-1} + \cdots + a_2 * S_2 + a_1 * S_1$$
$$= \mathcal{D}_2(n) = b_j * S_j + b_{j-1} * S_{j-1} + \cdots + b_2 * S_2 + b_1 * S_1 \qquad (11)$$

in which $a_i, b_j \neq 0$.

if $i \neq j$, and we might as well assume $i > j$, then according to the Lemma 1, we know that

$$n = b_j * S_j + b_{j-1} * S_{j-1} + \cdots + b_1 * S_1 < S_{j+1} \leq S_i \leq a_i * S_i \leq n \qquad (12)$$

is a contradiction with the known! Hence, i is equals to j.

Let t be the biggest integer that makes $a_t \neq b_t$, we might as well assume that $a_t > b_t$. then

$$n = b_j * S_j + \cdots + b_t * S_t + \cdots + b_1 * S_1$$

$$< b_j * S_j + b_{j-1} * S_{j-1} + \cdots + b_t * S_t + S_t$$

$$\leq a_j * S_j + a_{j-1} * S_{j-1} + \cdots + a_t * S_t \leq n \qquad (13)$$

is a contradiction with the known! Hence there is no integer t that makes $a_t \neq b_t$, which means that the different expressions in Eq. (11) is same tree-decomposition of n. That is the unique $\mathcal{D}(n)$.

In this section, we introduce the traditional blockchain structure, propose our new structure, and give the rules for the formation of new structures. In the next section, we will introduce the verification process of the blocks under the new structure.

3 Verification Methodologies

In this section, we propose the verification methodologies in block-tree against the forking attack, including cases "backward verification", "forward verification" and "further forward verification".

3.1 Backward Verification

Backward verification refers to the situation that the light node holding the credible latest block requests the target block and verifies the connectivity between the target block and the latest block.

The latest block records the hash of the previous block which determines the previous block. If the attacker prepared different blocks of the same hash value, it is conflicted to the hash function hypothesis that the attacker undermined the resistant collision of hash function. Thus, the forward verification focusses on the balance between efficiency and space consumption.

The extra space cost in block-tree is less than the size of two block hashes. The verification method is also obvious that as long as the left child node of current block is higher than target, assign it as the current block and append it to the evidence chain, otherwise, assign the right child node as the current block and append it to the evidence chain. Repeat this until the current block is the target. The evidence blocks are determined by Algorithm 2. In an ideal situation, the amount of evidence blocks is $O(\lg n)$. Even in the worst situation, the complexity of verification is $O(\lg^2 n)$ and better than the traditional process.

Algorithm 2. The path from block m to block n.

Algorithm 2 The path from block m to block n.

Input: Height of target block, m; Height of the latest block, n;

Output: The blocks on the path from block m to block n, $path$;

1: **function** EVIDENCE(m, n)
2:     $path \leftarrow \{\}$
3:     **if** $m > n$ **then return** $path$
4:     **end if**
5:     $path.push\_back(n)$
6:     **if** $m = n$ **then return** $path$
7:     **end if**
8:     $left\_n \leftarrow$ LEFTNODE(n)
9:     **if** $left\_n > m$ **then** $path \leftarrow path+$ EVIDENCE($m, left\_n$)
10:    **else** $path \leftarrow path+$EVIDENCE($m, n-1$)
11:    **end if**
12:    **return** $path$
13: **end function**

3.2 Forward Verification

Forward verification refers to the situation that the light node holding the foundation block requests the latest block and verifies the connectivity between the foundation block and the latest block.

Verifying connectivity between the foundation block and the latest block in forward verification requires the same evidence blocks in backward verification. However, in a block-tree, the attacker may follow some honest blocks as the left subtree and mine the forking blocks as the right subtree. Thus, we propose that the light node chooses a leaf block in the right subtree as a challenge against the forking attack. Since the exact size of the right subtree that the attacker intends to fork is unknown, the light node must choose the leaf nodes from all possible right subtree as challenges. More specifically, starting from the rightmost leaf node, the consecutive 2^i leaf nodes to the left is the range to select challenges, where $i = 1, 2, 3, \cdots, \lceil \log_2 H \rceil$ and H denotes the height of blockchain. Unify all these challenges into one combination, we call it a complete challenge. The complete challenge in forward verification is determined by Algorithm 3, where the function LEAF(n) returns the last leafnode of block n. The function Leaforder($node$) and Leafnode($order$) are a pair of inverse functions that returns the order of the leafnode and the leafnode corresponding to the order. In forward verification, the trusted block is the foundation block. When the light node requests the latest block and the evidence blocks of the foundation block, it also requests the evidence blocks of all blocks in complete challenge.

Algorithm 1. A complete challenge between block m and block n.

Algorithm 3 A complete challenge between block m and block n.

Input: Height of trusted block, m; Height of the latest block, n;

Output: The blocks as challenges, c_blocks;

```
1:  function CHALLENGE(m, n)
2:      c_blocks ← {}
3:      if m > n then return c_blocks
4:      end if
5:      right_n ← Leaforder(LEAF(n))
6:      right_m ← Leaforder(LEAF(m))
7:      i ← 0
8:      while right_n − 2^i + 1 > right_m do
9:          c_blocks.push_back(random(right_n − 2^i + 1, right_n))
10:         i + +
11:     end while
12:     c_blocks.push_back(random(right_m, right_n))
13:     for j = 0 to len(c_blocks)-1 do
14:         c_blocks[j] = Leafnode(c_block[j])
15:     end for
16:     return c_blocks
17: end function
18:
19: function LEAF(n)
20:     Array ← Tree_Decomposition(n)
21:     for i = 0 to len(Array)-1 do
22:         if Array[i] ≠ 0 then return n − i
23:         end if
24:     end for
25:     return n − i
26: end function
```

3.3 Further Forward Verification

Further Forward verification refers to the situation that the light node holding a trusted past block requests the latest block and verifies the connectivity between the past block and the latest block. A practical example is the situation that the light node holds a verified past block and wants to catch up with the latest block.

Further forward verification can be regarded as the generalized situation of forward verification and there are two ways to catch up with the latest block based on the traditional structure or our block-tree. Depending on different security and efficiency requirements, there are different thresholds to choose the verification method. Our suggestion is that depending on the difference between the LEAF(n) and LEAF(m), if the difference is less than 128 choose the traditional structure, otherwise choose the block-tree and repeat ten rounds of complete challenge.

4   Evaluation

In this section, we first analyze the security of our approach. Afterwards, we simulate the verification method to show the efficiency of block-tree in verification.

4.1   Security

Correctness
The honest nodes gathering the majority hashrate of the full network generate the blocks faster than the attacker. And the honest nodes hold the full chain data, in which the blocks are organized according to the structure determined by block-tree. Hence, when the light node requests the evidence blocks, the honest nodes can response to the challenges with a series of connected blocks.

Forking Attack
Double spending and unfair mining income being the most critical issues on blockchain. The selfish mining [10, 11] helps the attacker to fork the chain with no need for 51% calculation power which undermines the fairness of mining. But the forking attack we mentioned here is for the situation that a light node enters the network and requests the latest block. When a light node enters the network, it holds only the foundation block or a past block and must request and verify the latest block. The new structure streamlines the verification, such that the light node requests less block data. However, depending on the fixed architecture, the attacker could predict the blocks that the light node will require. Then, the attacker can mine less fork blocks and provide it as the evidence of the latest block to the light node. The worse thing is that the attacker can provide blocks mined by honest nodes in the front combined with forking blocks in the back. This is exactly what called forking attack.

Soundness
We analyze security based on the assumptions in Sect. 1.1. If the attacker wants to fork the blockchain. Let n denote the number of blocks mined by honest nodes, then the attacker mined αn at the same time. There are at least $n/2$ leaf nodes in a block-tree with n nodes. If the light node chooses a leaf node randomly as a challenge, the attacker responses to the challenge successfully with a probability P_n. Because the evidence chain of two detached leaf nodes is longer than the evidence chain of a pair of brother leaf

nodes. The αn blocks could cover at most $\alpha n/2$ leaf nodes. It means that the probability the attacker responses to the challenge successfully is less than $\frac{\alpha n}{2}/\frac{n}{2}$, in other words,

$$P_n < \frac{\alpha n}{2}/\frac{n}{2} = \alpha < \frac{1}{2} \qquad (14)$$

We assume that the amount of leaf nodes the attacker intends to fork is n_l, and $2^k < n_l \le 2^{k+1}$. Thus, the amount of leaf nodes the attacker mined is αn_l at most. When the light node selects the challenge within the consecutive 2^k leaf nodes, the probability of the attacker responses to the challenge successfully is

$$P_k \le \alpha n_l / 2^k \qquad (15)$$

When the light node selects the challenge within the consecutive 2^{k+1} leaf nodes (if total number of leaf nodes is less than 2^{k+1}, then use the total number of leaf nodes to replace the 2^{k+1} can get the same conclusion), the probability of successful response is

$$P_{k+1} = \left(2^{k+1} - n_l + \alpha n_l\right)/2^{k+1} \qquad (16)$$

Obviously, the attacker responses to the complete challenge with a probability of P_c, and it is satisfied that

$$P_c < P_k * P_{k+1} \le \frac{\alpha(\alpha - 1)n_l^2 + 2^{k+1}\alpha n_l}{2^{2k+1}} = \frac{\alpha(\alpha - 1)\left(n_l + \frac{2^k}{\alpha - 1}\right)^2 - \frac{2^{2k}\alpha}{\alpha - 1}}{2^{2k+1}} \qquad (17)$$

Recalling that $\alpha < 0.5$ and $2^k < n_l \le 2^{k+1}$, we then have

$$P_c < \frac{\alpha}{2(1 - \alpha)} < \frac{1}{2} \qquad (18)$$

This means that the attacker responses correctly to a complete challenge with a probability less than 50%. Let t denote the rounds of complete challenge, the probability of the attacker responses to all these independent complete challenges is

$$P_{attack} = P_c^t < \frac{1}{2^t} \qquad (19)$$

When $\alpha = 0.5$ and $t = 10$, it yields a probability of no more than 0.1%, which is safe in most scenarios. However, the number of challenges we request is $t * \lceil \log_2 n \rceil$, and each challenge needs $O(\lg n)$ blocks as evidence. Thus, the entire security forward verification needs $O(\lg^2 n)$ blocks. It is still a good improvement to the traditional method. And our structure does not rely on specific cryptographic algorithms and inherits the traditional structure, thus it maintains resistant to the traditional attacks.

4.2 Simulation

Because what we change is the structure of blockchain, and it has nothing to do with the consensus. Thus, it is not necessary to generate the full block, and we will only simulate the number of blocks we need in the verification method. We then simulate the efficiency of the verifications in block-tree.

Forward Verification
We first simulate the forward verification without challenge, as the height of latest block increases until 10000, the number of required evidence blocks is shown in the left figure of Fig. 5. Forward verification without challenge is same as the backward verification. As shown in the Fig. 5, block-tree significantly simplified the verification, though it is not always good. And it is considerably better when the height is a power of 2.

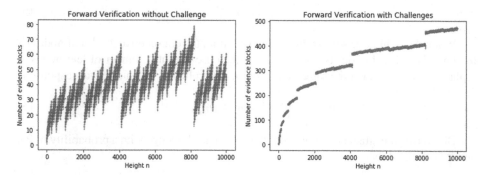

Fig. 5. Forward verification

We next simulate the forward verification with ten rounds of complete challenges. The number of required evidence blocks is shown in the right figure of Fig. 5. For each height we take one hundred times to simulate the forward verification with ten rounds of complete challenge and get the average number of evidence blocks. As shown in the Fig. 5, after adding challenges, the number of evidence blocks in block-tree is much increased. However, it is still significantly better than the traditional structure.

The performance of forward verification with different rounds of complete challenge is listed in Table 1. We simulate it at a height of 1000000 and repeat one thousand times for getting the average value. We could see that ten or fifteen rounds of complete challenge already meet the security needs of most situations.

Backward Verification
We randomly generate two numbers between 1 and 10000 represent the height of target block and the latest block. Repeating one million times, the number of evidence blocks group by distance is shown in the Fig. 6. The backward verification in block-tree is shown in the left picture and the LeapChain with $b = 8$ is shown in the right. In the ideal situation that the height is power of 2, the backward verification is significantly simplified in block-tree. And the time complexity of block-tree is close to the LeapChain compared to the size of the distance. Users can even use a combination of two structures without considering space consumption.

Table 1. Forward verification with different rounds of complete challenge

Rounds t	Number of evidence blocks	P_{attack}
0	102	100%
5	757	≈3.1%
10	1279	≈0.1%
15	1752	≈$3.1*10^{-5}$
20	2193	≈$9.5*10^{-7}$
30	3010	≈$9.3*10^{-10}$

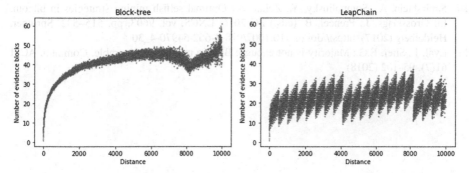

Fig. 6. Backward verification group by distance

5 Conclusion

In this paper, we propose a new structure of blockchain called block-tree to simplify the verification. For against the forking attack on the light nodes, we introduce the challenge mechanism. In the simulation results, our structure shows the advantage in verification, that we implement secure verification with only $O(\lg^2 n)$ chain data.

In the future, we plan to improve our architecture by adding some backlinks, which simplifies the verification in the situation that the latest block is not the root of the full chain.

Acknowledgments. This project was supported by National Key Research and Development Program of China "Research on new algorithms and new principles of electronic currency" (No. 2017YFB0802505).

References

1. Nakomoto, S.: Bitcoin: A Peer-to-Peer Electronic Cash System (2008). https://bitcoin.org/bitcoin.pdf
2. Majority attack. Bitcoin wiki. https://en.bitcoin.it/wiki/Majority_attack
3. Hashrate. Bitcoin wiki. https://en.bitcoin.it/wiki/Hash_per_second

4. King, S., Nadal, S.: Ppcoin: Peer-to-peer crypto-currency with proof-of-stake. Self-published paper (2012)
5. Heilman, E., Kendler, A., Zohar, A., et al.: Eclipse attacks on bitcoin's peer-to-peer network. In: 24th Security Symposium (Security 15), pp. 129–144 (2015)
6. Nikitin, K., Kokoris-Kogias, E., Jovanovic, P., et al.: CHAINIAC: proactive software-update transparency via collectively signed skipchains and verified builds. In: 26th Security Symposium (Security 17) (2017)
7. Kiayias, A., Andrew, M., Dionysis, Z.: Non-interactive proofs of proof-of-work. IACR Cryptology ePrint Archive **2017**(963), 1–42 (2017)
8. Regnath, E., Sebastian S.: LeapChain: efficient blockchain verification for embedded IoT. In: Proceedings of the International Conference on Computer-Aided Design, ACM (2018)
9. Merkle, R.C.: Protocols for public key cryptosystems. In: 1980 IEEE Symposium on Security and Privacy, pp. 122–122. IEEE (1980)
10. Sapirshtein, A., Sompolinsky, Y., Zohar, A.: Optimal selfish mining strategies in bitcoin. In: Grossklags, J., Preneel, B. (eds.) FC 2016. LNCS, vol. 9603, pp. 515–532. Springer, Heidelberg (2017). https://doi.org/10.1007/978-3-662-54970-4_30
11. Eyal, I., Sirer, E.G.: Majority is not enough: Bitcoin mining is vulnerable. Commun. ACM **61**(7), 95–102 (2018)

Improvement Research of PBFT Consensus Algorithm Based on Credit

Yong Wang[1,2], Zhe Song[1,2(✉)], and Tong Cheng[1,2]

[1] School of Computer Science and Information Security,
Guilin University of Electronic Technology, Guilin 541004, China
975415260qq.com
[2] Guangxi Key Laboratory of Cryptography and Information Security,
Guilin University of Electronic Technology, Guilin 541004, China

Abstract. This paper analyzes the advantages and disadvantages of the PBFT consensus algorithm and proposes an improved credit-based PBFT consensus algorithm(CPBFT). CPBFT changes the original C/S architecture to P2P architecture, reduces the consensus steps, and uses the voting method to elect the master node. In the election process, credit levels and credit coefficient are introduced, so that the probability that each node is elected as the master node is affected by the past behavior, and a reliable master node is elected more probably. Experiments show that compared with the PBFT algorithm, the CPBFT algorithm reduces the amount of data transmission on the network and increases the throughput.

Keywords: Practical Byzantine Fault Tolerance (PBFT) · P2P · Election · Credit levels · Credit coefficient

1 Introduction

In recent years, with the rapid development of Bitcoin, its underlying technology blockchain has gradually entered the public's view. Blockchain is a large distributed digital database (or ledger) that stores records of transactions [1]. Blockchain technology features decentralization, time series data, collective maintenance,programmability, and security [2]. It provides a solution to complete the transaction without the trust of both parties.

1.1 Related Work

The first time blockchain appeared in the public view was in the paper "Bitcoin: A peer-to-peer Electronic Cash System" [3] published by a scholar with the pseudonym "satoshi nakamoto". A consensus algorithm based on Proof of Work (POW) was proposed for the first time. The Proof of Work algorithm essentially requires the node to perform a series of operations, and the node that solves the problem can first have the right to generate blocks. Although the requirement for actual resources (computing power, electricity, time) is a strong point

© Springer Nature Singapore Pte Ltd. 2020
Z. Zheng et al. (Eds.): BlockSys 2019, CCIS 1156, pp. 47–59, 2020.
https://doi.org/10.1007/978-981-15-2777-7_4

for PoW protocols to guarantee efficiency in deterring adversaries, it is also the weak point for efficiency since it involves a constant expenditure and resources to work normally [4]. To solve this problem, the blockchain community began to propose new algorithms, King et al. [5] proposed a consensus mechanism of PoS (Proof-of-Stake) to alleviate the waste of resources caused by computing competition, it offers qualitative efficiency advantages over blockchains based on proof of work [6], but still did not get rid of the mining process. Larimer [7] proposed a consensus mechanism of DPoS (Delegated-Proof-of-Stake), DPoS uses the voting mechanism to concentrate the rights of all users in the hands of a few people. DPoS greatly speeds up the confirmation of transactions, but once the rights are concentrated in the hands of a few people, it may damage the interests of users [8]. Schwartz [9] proposed the RPCA (Ripple Protocol Consensue Algorithm) consensus mechanism, which combines the Byzantine failures problem and gets rid of the limitation of reaching consensus through mining, but Ripple has less research on decentralization applications. The PBFT algorithm was first proposed by Castro [10] and used to solve the problem of Byzantine failures problem. The algorithm guarantees that the blockchain will still function properly when no more than one-third of the nodes have Byzantine Fault.

In recent years, research on the improvement of the PBFT algorithm has increased significantly. The first is to optimize the scenario in which the system is assumed to have no Byzantine Fault. Lamport [11] proposes a consensus mechanism of Paxos. Ongaro, et al. [12] proposed a consensus mechanism of Raft. Raft is simplified by Paxos and has been improved and simplified. Raft is easy to implement. Cowling [13] proposed a consensus mechanism of HQ. The HQ references and optimizes PBFT to simplify communication for non-competitive situations. If there is competition, HQ performance also degenerates to be similar to PBFT.

In addition, it is optimized for Byzantine Fault scenarios. This type of optimization is basically improved on the basis of PBFT. Copeland [14] proposed a consensus mechanism of Tangaroa. Tangaroa has the advantage of Raft's easy-to-understand and both Byzantine fault tolerance. Kadena [15] proposed a consensus mechanism of ScalableBFT, ScalableBFT is able to achieve better performance than Tangaroa.

2   PBFT Algorithm Analysis

2.1   PBFT Algorithm Execution Process

As a classic distributed algorithm, PBFT is essentially a state machine replication algorithm, which models the service as a state machine, and the state machine completes the replica copy of different nodes in the distributed system. In this way, the state machine implements the operation of the service while preserving the state of the service. All nodes in the blockchain rotate in a view. In one view, there are three types of roles, client, master, and slave. Both the master node and the slave node are used as backup nodes to complete data backup. PBFT has specific requirements for the number of nodes, f represents the number of Byzantine nodes, R represents the total number of nodes, and 0 to $|R| - 1$ epresents each replica node number in the set. The ideal number of nodes is $|R| = 3f + 1$. The number of nodes R can be greater than this number, but this will only increase the system performance burden and will not improve the reliability of the system. The master node is selected using the following formula.

$$P = V \bmod |R| \tag{1}$$

where P is the replica number and V is the view number. When the master node fails to complete the consensus, the view change mechanism is used to continue the selection of the new master node. The PBFT consensus process includes five stages: request, pre-prepare, prepare, commit, and reply. As shown in Fig. 1.

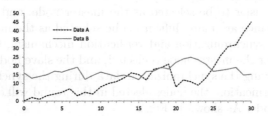

Fig. 1. Algorithm flow diagram of PBFT

2.2 PBFT Disadvantages Analysis

(1) The consistency protocol needs to be broadcast three times, and the number of broadcasts is too large, which consumes a lot of resources and reduces transaction efficiency. We use Z to define the number of messages to complete a consensus process.

$$Z = 2N^2 - 2N \tag{2}$$

(2) The selection of the master node has security risks. If the malicious node is selected multiple times, the consensus efficiency will be significantly reduced, the system resources will be wasted, and the system risk will be brought.

(3) The client can only send messages to the master node. When there are too many messages, it will bring too much burden to the master node, which is not suitable for the p2p network environment of the blockchain.

2.3 PBFT Improvement Plan

PBFT is a consensus algorithm applied in Alliance chain. This paper combines PBFT with improved Delegated Proof of Stake consensus algorithm, introduces the voting mechanism and the rating mechanism, and scores the behavior of the primary node. The nodes with poor historical performance are difficult to be elected. As the master node, the specific improvement plan is divided into the following points:

(1) Change the PBFT from the C/S response mode to the peer-to-peer network topology. Remove the client and divide all nodes into master and slave.
(2) Change the five steps of the traditional PBFT consensus into two steps. It includes two stages: consensus request and consensus confirmation. In the consensus request phase, the master node broadcasts transactions to each node.
(3) Each slave node elects the master node, and the master node is responsible for the production block.
(4) To improve the reliability of the master node, refer to the performance of each block in the current round of consensus, giving rewards or punishments, rewards or punishments through the integration. For nodes with different integration intervals, the nodes with different ratings have different weights in the calculation of voting. The purpose is to make the nodes with excellent performance easier to be selected as the master node, and the nodes with poor performance are more difficult to be selected as the master nodes.
(5) For the data synchronization and verification mechanism, the data is synchronized after the master node is elected, and the slave node is also responsible for verifying the synchronization data during the synchronization process. After verification, the nodes elected in this round will officially become the master node. As shown in Fig. 2.

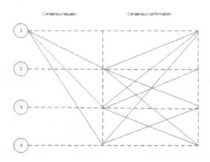

Fig. 2. Algorithm flow diagram of CPBFT

3 CPBFT Algorithm Design and Implementation

3.1 Algorithm Symbol

(1) The algorithm contains a total of n nodes, represented by R, including p master nodes and s slave nodes, each node is represented by the number[0,1,2,...,R-1].
(2) In all nodes, there are f Byzantine nodes and the total number of nodes is greater than or equal to 3f+1. In general, it is equal to 3f+1, because more nodes will not increase the reliability of the system and will increase the system load.

(3) In the system, v represents the view number, n represents the request number, and v and n are integers, and v and n are incremented by one each time the view changes or there is a new request. Also, the size of n must satisfy: H ≥ n ≥ h, We call H and h the upper and lower limits of the waterline respectively. The meaning of the waterline is to prevent a failed node from using a large serial number to consume the sequence space.

(4) We define the two steps of the consistency algorithm as consensus request and consensus confirmation.

(5) The initial score of each node is 50 points, A-level credit [100–60], B-level credit (60–40), C-level credit (40–0), and the master node of each round successfully generates a block plus 1 point. If the block is failed, the score is reduced by 20 points.

3.2 Algorithm Process

(1) Any node in the whole network can generate transaction data, and the generated transaction information is uniformly placed in the transaction data pool.

(2) The master node numbered m takes the transaction data from the data pool, packs the transaction data into blocks, and the master node also assigns a number n to the block. If the master node numbered m produces a genesis block, the master node is randomly selected.

(3) The master node m issues a consensus request message for the generated block, the consensus request message number is set to n, v represents the view number, S_i and D_i respectively represent the signature and the digest, and then the message is broadcast to all the slave nodes, and the consensus request message format is $<<$ CONSENSUS-REQUEST,v, S_i, D_i $>$, Block $>$, the slave node checks the message after receiving the consensus request message, and if it agrees to receive the request message, it will enter the consensus confirmation step, if it does not agree to request, broadcast the change view message, apply to overthrow the master node, change the view.

(4) After the node releases the consensus confirmation message, the node writes the consensus confirmation message to the message log and sends a consensus confirmation message to the node other than itself. The format of the consensus confirmation message is $<$ CONSENSUS-CONFIRMATION, v, n, S_i, D_i, i $>$ i indicates the node number. When the node receives 2f+1 consensus confirmation messages sent from the remaining nodes, and the consensus confirmation message is consistent with the consensus request message, it can be regarded as the consensus confirmation completion, and if it is not received after the timeout 2f+1 consensus confirmation messages are considered as system timeouts, and the consensus confirmation is not completed, and the block is discarded.

(5) After the consensus confirmation is completed, the consensus node will submit the request, save the block, and then add the block to the end of the blockchain.

3.3   Master Node Election

The master node election is to select the high-relief master node to produce the block. To improve the reliability of the master node, the scoring mechanism and credit coefficient will be introduced. The historical behaviour of the master node will affect the possibility of being elected as the master node in the future. We define the node that receives the voting information and calculates the number of votes as a computing node, and defines the node that receives the voting as the target node.

(1) The master node will produce n blocks during the term of the master node, of which n-1 blocks are transaction blocks, which store transaction information, and the last block stores the voting information. The voting format is $< VOTE, p, x, i >$ where r represents the target node number, x represents the level of the target node, i represents the node's number, and then broadcasts information to each node.

(2) After receiving the voting information of the computing nodes, Calculate the final number of votes for each node by the following formula

$$\text{Point} = P_i * X_i \tag{3}$$

Point indicates the final number of votes for the target node, P_i represents the number of votes received of the target node, and X_i represents the credit coefficient of the level of the target node. If the target node is an A-level node, the credit coefficient is 1.00. If the target node is a B-level node, the credit coefficient is 0.75. If the target node is a C-level node, the credit coefficient is 0.50. As shown in Table 1.

Table 1. Credit coefficient diagram

credit levels	Score interval	Credit coefficient
A	[100,60]	1.00
B	(60,40)	0.75
C	[40,0]	0.55

The node number with the highest number of votes is broadcasted. If there are multiple node votes in the first row, the one with the smallest number i is elected as the master node.

(3) After each node receives the final voting information of the remaining 2f+1 nodes, if f+1 nodes have the same voting information, the node on the voting information will be the next master node. And the block generated by the current master node to the voting information is saved to the end of the blockchain. The voting information broadcasted by each node includes the voting result of the node. As shown in Fig. 3.

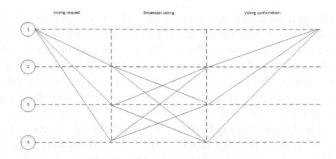

Fig. 3. Algorithm flow diagram of voting

3.4 Transaction Legality Judgment

After the slave node receives the transaction information from the current master node, it is mainly determined that the transaction is legal:

(1) It is determined whether the hash summary of the block is duplicated with the block hash summary already stored in the blockchain.
(2) Determine whether the transaction information format included in the block is legal.
(3) Determine whether the blockchain forks. The main criterion is whether the previous block of the current block is the last in the chain. If it is, there is no fork. Otherwise, the blockchain is forked.
(4) If the transaction script contained in the block can be executed correctly, then the transaction in the block is legal. Otherwise, the transaction information in the block is illegal. Only if all of the above are legal can it be determined that the transactions contained in the block are legal.

3.5 Data Synchronization and Data Validation

After the system selects the master node, it is accurate to say that the master node at this time is only the quasi-master node, and the quasi-master node cannot perform the function of the master node. It must be verified and confirmed in the following stages, and the quasi-master node can formally become the master node. This phase requires synchronization and validation of the data held by each node to ensure data consistency and to ensure the reliability of the master node.

Data Synchronization: After the system elects the master node, the slave node issues a data synchronization request message to the master node. The message format is $<$ DATA-REQUEST, t, v, m, S_i, i $>$, where v represents the view number and m represents the master node number, Si represents signature information, and i represents a node number. After receiving the message, the master node sequentially checks the view number and the master node number. If it is legal, it sends a synchronous success message to the slave node. The message format is $<$SUCCESSFUL-SYNCHRONIZATION, v, S_i, i$>$. If not, the master node sends the synchronization message and the corresponding backup data block to the slave node, and the message format is <<SYNCHRONIZATION-FAILED, v, S_i, i>, block>, where block is the corresponding backup data block.

Data Confirmation: After receiving the backup data block of the master node, the slave node verifies the legality of the received backup data block. If it is legal, it will broadcast the authenticated message to the other slave nodes. The message format is <VERIFICATION-PASSED, v, i, S_i, d> where v is the view number, i is the node number, Si is the signature information, and d is the summary information of the last block in the received backup data block. If it is not legal, the backup data block sent by the master node is discarded, and the received verification result message from other slave nodes is saved. After the slave node receives 2f+1 pass messages sent from other slave nodes, it can be confirmed that the backup data blocks sent by the quasi-master node to each slave node are consistent, and then the slave node will send the quasi-master node Feedback message, the message format is <PASS, v, S_i, i>. Otherwise, the quasi-primary node is considered to be a malicious node, broadcast view switch request, and request to replace the master node.

Verification Confirmation: If the quasi-master node receives 2f+1 completion synchronization messages, the quasi-master node will formally become the master node and complete the master node task.

The flow chart is as shown:

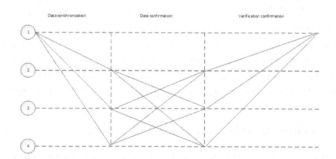

Fig. 4. Data synchronization and data verification flow chart

View Switching:
To ensure the reliability of the master node, we give the slave node the right to apply for switching views after discovering that the master node is not trusted. Re-select the master node by changing the view. The specific process is as follows:

(1) After the master node times out or does not generate a block or the slave node suspects that the master node is a malicious node, the slave node can broadcast a message requesting a replacement view. The message format is <CHANGE-VIEW, V_o, V_n, i, S_i> where V_o is the current view. V_n is the new view number, $V_n = V_o+1$, i is the current node number, and S_i is the signature information.

(2) After receiving the request message of the replacement view, the remaining slave nodes will verify the current master node, and correctly generate the block in time. If the slave node also has doubts about the master node, the broadcast confirmation request message is sent, and the message format is <CONFIRMATION-REQUEST,V_n,V_o,i,S_i>

(3) After the slave node receives 2f+1 different nodes to send an acknowledgement request message, it will prepare to re-elect the master node according to the election algorithm.

4   Experiment Analysis

4.1   System Design

In this paper, a blockchain system is designed. The consensus algorithm used is CPBFT. The system includes four module transaction modules, consensus modules, election modules and storage modules. The transaction module mainly collects the transaction data and encapsulates it into blocks, and then the consensus module performs consensus. The consensus module is responsible for broadcasting the consensus generated by the block generated by the master node. The consensus step includes two steps after the improvement, and the consensus module needs all nodes to participate. The election module elects the trusted master node through the election algorithm. The elected node will be responsible for generating the block during the term of office. The storage module is responsible for storing the blocks through which the consensus passes, and each backup node will save the block. The chain data structure is used to store the relevant data, and the elliptic curve asymmetric encryption algorithm is used to encrypt the data. The whole system has the decentralization property of the blockchain.

4.2   Performance Analysis

This paper proposes an improved credit-based PBFT consensus algorithm(CPBFT), which changes the C/S architecture of the traditional Byzantine fault-tolerant algorithm to the peer-to-peer architecture, and changes the consistency algorithm from three steps to two steps, making it more suitable for the blockchain. The peer-to-peer architecture of the chain introduces a scoring mechanism and a credit coefficient mechanism in the election of the master node, so that the elected master node is more reliable. This experiment will analyze the performance in terms of throughput, latency, communication overhead and fault tolerance. According to the PBFT consensus algorithm, if there are f Byzantine nodes, the total number of nodes is not less than 3f+1 nodes, so this experimental node contains 1 Byzantine node, and the total number of nodes is 4, 5, 6 respectively.

(1) Throughput

In general, throughput refers to the amount of transactions a system processes a request within a unit of time. High throughput systems can handle more transactions in a period of time. TPS (Transaction Per Second) is generally used in the blockchain system, and the formula is as follows:

$$\text{TPS}_{\Delta t} = \text{Transactions}_{\Delta t}/\triangle t \tag{4}$$

Where $\triangle t$ indicates the time from the issuance of the transaction information to the completion of the storage of the block, that is, the block time is generated, and the $\text{Transactions}_{\Delta t}$ indicates the number of transactions solved by the system within the time interval of the block. The system throughput is affected by the block size and the network environment. The larger the block, the more transactions it contains, and the corresponding network load will also increase.

We calculate the number of blocks in one second by counting the number of different nodes and average the results for all the results. The final result is shown below.

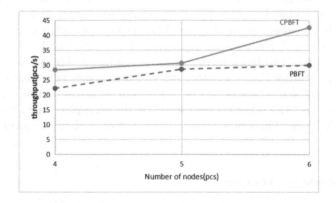

Fig. 5. Comparison of throughput between the two algorithms

By comparing with the traditional PBFT algorithm, the improved PBFT is tested to have a significant improvement in throughput.

(2) Delay

The throughput of the blockchain is mostly affected by the delay. Under the premise of consistency in other aspects, the smaller the delay, the higher the throughput of the blockchain system. In addition, the lower latency can also improve the zone. The blockchain consensus confirms the speed and effectively enhances the security of the blockchain system. The delay described in this article refers to the time taken by a block to complete the consensus process.

$$\text{Delay}_{\text{block}} = T_c - T_R \tag{5}$$

T_C represents the consensus confirmation completion time, T_R represents the consensus request time, and the improved PBFT algorithm performs multiple tests to take the average value. The result is shown in the following figure:

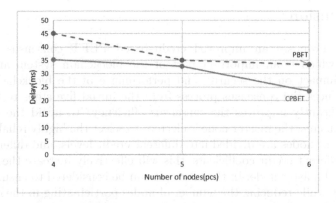

Fig. 6. Consistency delay comparison of two algorithms

(3) Low power consumption:
Compared with PBFT:
The primary consensus process of the PBFT algorithm consists of five steps, namely request, pre-prepare, prepare, commit, and reply. If there are a total of n replica nodes, the number of communication needs to be $2n^2 - 2n + 1$. The CPBFT proposed in this paper. There are two main steps in the consensus process of the solution, including consensus request and consensus confirmation. If there are n replica nodes, the number of communication needs to be $n^2 - n$. It can be seen that the CPBFT consensus algorithm has a more significant advantage in communication times than the traditional PBFT consensus algorithm.

(4) Algorithm fault tolerance
We know that the traditional PBFT can tolerate up to f Byzantine nodes. We use 4, 5, and 6 nodes as the consensus nodes for experimental verification. When there is a Byzantine node, the block can be generated normally. When more than one Byzantine node is used, the block cannot be generated normally, and TPS = 0.
If the master node is a Byzantine node, the master node fails to issue a consensus request message within a specified period, and the remaining slave nodes can issue a replacement view request, overthrow the master node, and re-select the trusted master node according to the election rule. If the master node is found to be overthrown, the new view will be switched again, the view number will be increased, and the block that completed the consensus in the previous stage will be saved. The block that has not completed the consensus will be discarded, and after the new master node is selected,

Blocks that were discarded in the previous phase will re-con the consensus. At the beginning of the new view, the synchronization and verification of the global nodes are performed to ensure the integrity and consistency of the global node data. The next round of consensus will be opened.

5   Conclusion

This paper proposes an improved credit-based PBFT consensus algorithm (CPBFT), which is an important part of the blockchain system and has an important impact on the security and performance of the blockchain system. CPBFT reduces the consensus process from the initial five steps to two steps, which significantly improves the consensus efficiency. To avoid the additional security problems, the master node is elected, to select the highly reliable master node, different nodes are divided into different credit levels, and different credit levels set different credit coefficients, this will effectively increase the reliability of the elected master node. In the future, it can be considered to ensure the system security while reducing the number of nodes participating in the consensus, which will effectively improve the performance of the blockchain system.

Acknowledgments. This research was supported by Guangxi Ministry of Education (No:2017KY0211), Guangxi Colleges and Universities Key Laboratory of Cloud Computing and Complex System(YF17105), Guangxi Key Laboratory of Cryptography and Information Security (No: GCIS201617) and Guangxi Key Laboratory of Trusted Software (No: KX201625).

References

1. Marc, P.: Blockchain technology: principles and applications. In: Xavier Olleros, F., Zhegu, M. (eds.) Handbook of Research on Digital Transformations. Edward Elgar, Cheltenham (2016)
2. Yuan, Y., Wang, F.-Y.: Blockchain: The state of the art and future trends. Acta Automatica Sinica **42**(4), 481–494 (2016)
3. Nakamoto, S.: Bitcoin: a peer-to-peer electronic cash system (2008). http://bitcoin.org/bitcoin.pdf
4. Ouattara, H.F., Ahmat, D., Ouédraogo, F.T., et al.: Blockchain Consensus Protocols (2017)
5. King, S., Nadal, S.: PPCoin: Peer-to-Peer Crypto-Currency with Proof-of-Stake, August 2012
6. Kiayias, A., Russell, A., David, B., Oliynykov, R.: Ouroboros: a provably secure proof-of-stake blockchain protocol. In: Katz, J., Shacham, H. (eds.) CRYPTO 2017. LNCS, vol. 10401, pp. 357–388. Springer, Cham (2017). https://doi.org/10.1007/978-3-319-63688-7_12
7. Larimer D.: Delegated proof-of-stake white paper (2014) http://www.bts.hk/dpos-baipishu.html
8. Xia, Q., Zhang, F., Zuo, C.: Review for consensus mechanism of cryptocurrency system. Comput. Syst. Appl. **26**(4), 1–8 (2017)

9. Schwartz, D., Youngs, N., Britto, A.: The ripple protocol consensus algorithm (2014). https://ripple.com/files/ripple_consensus_whitepaper.pdf. Accessed 15 Dec 2016
10. Castro, M., Liskov, B.: Practical byzantine fault tolerance and proactive recovery. ACM Trans. Comput. Syst. **20**(4), 398–461 (2002)
11. Lamport, L.: The part-time parliament. ACM Trans. Comput. Syst. (TOCS) **16**(2), 133–169 (1998)
12. Ongaro, D., Ousterhout, J.: In search of an understandable consensus algorithm. In: Proceedings of the 2014 USENIX Conference on USENIX Annual Technical Conference, USENIX ATC 2014, pp. 305–320. USENIX Association (2014)
13. Cowling, J., Myers, D., Liskov, B., Rodrigues, R., Shrira, L.: HQ replication: a hybrid quorum protocol for Byzantine fault tolerance. In: OSDI 2006: Proceedings of the 7th Symposium on Operating Systems Design and Implementation, pp. 177–190. USENIX Association, Berkeley (2006)
14. Copeland, C., Zhong, H.: Tangaroa: a Byzantine Fault Tolerant Raft. Class project in Distributed Systems, Stanford University (2014)
15. Kadena, M.W.: The first scalable, high performance private blockchain (2018)

On Constructing Prime Order Elliptic Curves Suitable for Pairing-Based Cryptography

Meng Zhang[1,2(✉)], Xuehong Chen[3], Maozhi Xu[1], and Jie Wang[1]

[1] School of Mathematical Sciences Peking University, Beijing 100871, China
menglucky@pku.edu.cn
[2] Aisino Corporation, Beijing 100195, China
[3] Industrial Control Systems Cyber Emergency Response Team,
Beijing 100040, China

Abstract. Since Boneh and Franklin implemented the Identity Based Encryption in 2001, a number of novel schemes have been proposed based on bilinear pairings, which have been widely used in the scenario of blockchain. The elliptic curves with low embedding degree and large prime-order subgroup (a.k.a pairing-friendly elliptic curves) are the basic components for such schemes, where prime order elliptic curves are most frequently used in practice. In this paper, a systematic method is utilized to find all the possible prime order families, then it is shown that all the existing constructions can be explained via our method. We further give the evidence that it's unlikely to produce extra families.

Keywords: Elliptic curves · Pairing-based cryptography · Blockchain · Data security · Privacy protection

1 Introduction

Pairing-based cryptographic schemes [1] have been widely used in a great amount of applications, from the key agreement to Identity Based Encryption, Attribute Based Encryption and Searchable Encryption, from short signature to a variety of signatures, which are especially suitable for identity authentication, data security and privacy protection in blockchain system. Suggested schemes include the well known one-round three-way key exchange [2] by Joux, Identity Based Encryption [3] by Boneh and SM9 [4] published by State Cryptography Administration of China.

In practice, the cryptographic pairings used to construct these systems are based on the Weil and Tate pairings on elliptic curves over finite fields, where the using of pairing friendly elliptic curves has become a standardized approach. Efficient constructions of such curves have been studied in several literatures, which can be referred to [5–9]. As shown in [10], the pairing friendly curves are very rare. The focus of this paper is to construct pairing-friendly elliptic curves of prime order, as such curves are most valuable in blockchain system.

© Springer Nature Singapore Pte Ltd. 2020
Z. Zheng et al. (Eds.): BlockSys 2019, CCIS 1156, pp. 60–70, 2020.
https://doi.org/10.1007/978-981-15-2777-7_5

Our contribution in this regard is that a systematic method is utilized to find such curves. By introducing a more generalized concept "parameterized families", we convert the problem to solving equation systems instead of exhaustive searching. We firstly apply it to the case of $\phi(k) = 2$ and show all quadratic families of elliptic curves of prime order can be obtained from parameterized families, then find several parameterized families for the case of $\phi(k) = 4$ and indicate quartic families of such curves are very rare, including only Freeman curves and B-N curves.

The paper is organized as follows: In Sect. 2, the concept of pairing-friendly curves is introduced. We describe the strategy and algorithm for searching parameterized families of pairing-friendly elliptic curves in Sect. 3 and apply it in Sects. 4 and 5 respectively. Finally, we conclude the paper in Sect. 6.

2   Pairing-Friendly Elliptic Curves

In this section, we briefly review basic knowledge about pairing friendly elliptic curves. As defined in [5], an elliptic curve E over $\mathbb{F}_q$ is said to be *pairing friendly* if there is a prime r with $r|\#E(\mathbb{F}_q)$ and the ratio $\rho = \frac{\log q}{\log r} \leq 2$, while the embedding degree k with respect to r satisfies $k \leq \frac{\log r}{8}$.

We also use the same notations as [5] to define a family of curves. An irreducible polynomial $f(x) \in \mathbb{Q}(x)$ is said to be *prime representative* if $f(x)$ has positive leading coefficient, and the set $S(f) = \{f(x) \in \mathbb{Z} : x \in \mathbb{Z}\}$ satisfies that $|S(f)| > 1$ and $\gcd(S(f)) = 1$. Based on the complex multiplication (a.k.a. CM) method for generating elliptic curves, we now introduce families of pairing-friendly elliptic curves.

Definition 1 (Families of pairing-friendly elliptic curves). *Let the triple* $(q(x), t(x), r(x))$ *be nonzero polynomials with rational coefficients.*

(1) $q(x) = p(x)^d$ for some $d \geq 1$ and $q(x)$ is irreducible and prime representative;
(2) $r(x) = c \cdot r'(x)$ with $c \in Z, c \geq 1$ and $r'(x)$ is irreducible and prime representative;
(3) $q(x) + 1 - t(x) = h(x)r(x)$ for some $h(x) \in \mathbb{Q}(x)$;
(4) $r(x)|\phi_k(q(x))$, where ϕ_k is the k-th cyclotomic polynomial;
(5) The CM equation $Dy^2 = 4q(x) - t(x)^2$ has infinitely many integer solutions (x, y).

If these conditions are satisfied, we refer to $(q(x), t(x), r(x))$ as a family of elliptic curves with the embedding degree k and the CM discriminant D.

For a family $(q(x), t(x), r(x))$, we can also use the definition of the ratio ρ in [5] as

$$\rho(q, t, r) = \lim_{x \to \infty} \frac{\log q}{\log r} = \frac{\deg q(x)}{\deg r(x)}.$$

Remark 1. A family of elliptic curves has prime order if $\rho(q, t, r) = 1$.

If the CM equation in (5) has a set of integer solutions (x_0, y_0) with both of $q(x_0)$ and $r'(x_0)$ are primes, then we are able to construct curves E over $\mathbb{F}_{q(x_0)}$ via the CM method, where $E(\mathbb{F}_{q(x_0)})$ has a subgroup of order $r'(x_0)$ and the embedding degree k with respect to $r'(x_0)$.

3   The Strategy for Constructing Pairing-Friendly Elliptic Curves of Prime Order

Our method is based on the parameterized families introduced in [11,12], which can be regarded as a generalization of Definition 1.

Definition 2 (parameterized families). *Let the denotations and conditions be the same as those in Definition 1, parameterized family of pairing-friendly elliptic curves is given by the following triple*

$$(q(x, a_0, a_1, ..., a_n), t(x, a_0, a_1, ..., a_n), r(x, a_0, a_1, ..., a_n))$$

where $a_0, a_1, ..., a_n \in \mathbb{Q}$.

For convenience, give the following definition.

Definition 3 (degree $\phi(k)$ family). *Let the triple $(q(x), r(x), t(x))$ represent a family of elliptic curves with embedding degree k, we refer to it as a degree $\phi(k)$ family when $q(x)$ and $r(x)$ are both degree $\phi(k)$ polynomials.*

By Definition 3, the construction of families of prime order for embedding degree k can be focus on degree $\phi(k)$ families.

The algorithm of generating prime order families can be modified by the method in [12], which is summarized in Algorithm 1.

Parameterized families in Algorithm 1 are a further generalization for families of pairing-friendly curves of prime order. However, it should be noted that not every concrete rational value set $(q_{\phi(k)}, a_0, ..., a_{\phi(k)-1})$ for parameterized family (q, r, t) gives rise to a degree $\phi(k)$ family. The process of converting a rational value set to a degree $\phi(k)$ family may fail for any of the following reasons:

1. There may not exist an x such that both q, r are primes as well as t is an integer.
2. Hasse Bound: the degree of x in t may be greater than half the degree of x in q.
3. CM Condition: denote $f = 4q - t^2$ as the CM polynomial, the degree of x in the square-free part of f may be greater than 2.

Remark 2 (A note for CM Condition). Freeman et al. in [5] concluded that if CM polynomial $f(x)$ is a square-free polynomial of degree at least 3, then there will be only a finite number of integer solutions to the equation $Dy^2 = f(x)$. Hence it violates the CM Condition once the degree of $f(x)$ is greater than 2.

Algorithm 1. Generating parameterized families with $\rho = 1$

Input: Embedding degree k.

Output: Parameterized family (q, r, t) with $\rho = 1$.

1. Let $q = q_{\phi(k)} x^{\phi(k)} + \sum_{i=0}^{\phi(k)-1} q_i' x^i$

2. Construct the equation system as equation system (4) in [12]

3. If $\mathrm{Det}(V_1) \neq 0$, solve equation system and get the unique solution expressed by $q_i' = q_i(q_{\phi(k)}, a_0, ..., a_{\phi(k)-1})$ where $i = 0, ..., (\phi(k) - 1)$, then q can be written as the form

$$q = q_{\phi(k)} x^{\phi(k)} + \sum_{i=0}^{\phi(k)-1} q_i(q_{\phi(k)}, a_0, ..., a_{\phi(k)-1}) x^i$$

4. Factor $\Phi_k(q)$ by x and get the irreducible factor r of degree $\phi(k)$. Multiplied by a constant, r can be written as

$$r = q_{\phi(k)} x^{\phi(k)} + \sum_{i=0}^{\phi(k)-1} r_i(q_{\phi(k)}, a_0, ..., a_{\phi(k)-1}) x^i$$

5. Compute trace polynomial as

$$t = q + 1 - r = \sum_{i=0}^{\phi(k)-1} t_i(q_{\phi(k)}, a_0, ..., a_{\phi(k)-1}) x^i$$

6. Output parameterized family (q, r, t)

The advantage of parameterized family (q, r, t) is that for a fixed embedding degree k, it contains all the possible forms of degree $\phi(k)$ families, which makes it possible to find all the families of prime order just by analyzing the coefficients of (q, r, t).

We show how to deal with restrictions of Hasse Bound and CM Condition.

- For Hasse Bound
  We list the equation as

$$t_i(q_{\phi(k)}, a_0, ..., a_{\phi(k)-1}) = 0, \tag{1}$$

where $i = \frac{\phi(k)}{2} + 1, ..., (\phi(k) - 1)$, then Hasse Bound can be satisfied as long as equation system (1) has solutions over $\mathbb{Q}$.

- For CM Condition
  We write CM polynomial as the form

$$f = 4q - t^2 = \sum_{i=0}^{2\phi(k)-2} f_i(q_{\phi(k)}, a_0, ..., a_{\phi(k)-1}) x^i, \tag{2}$$

f is typically square free and has degree $2\phi(k) - 2$ in x, so it is extremely unlikely that f is quadratic when $\phi(k) > 2$.

There are only two possibilities to achieve it.

(1) the high-order terms of $4q$ and t^2 cancel out
(2) f contains square factors
They are both very lucky cases. However, it is possible to find them by solving equation systems concerning coefficients of parameterized family.
For (1), we can solve equation system

$$f_i(q_{\phi(k)}, a_0, ..., a_{\phi(k)-1}) = 0 \tag{3}$$

where $i = 3, ..., (2\phi(k) - 2)$.

For (2), we may solve equations listed by the resultant of f and the first derivative of f with respect to x.

$$res(f, \frac{d_f}{d_x}, x) = 0. \tag{4}$$

If we are able to get a common solution for equation system (1) and (3) or (4), then we obtain a potential degree $\phi(k)$ family, thus it is possible to achieve a family of elliptic curves of prime order.

4 The Case $\phi(k) = 2$

We first survey pairing-friendly elliptic curves with $\phi(k) = 2$. In this case, $q(x)$ and $r(x)$ are typically quadratic polynomials, so we consider degree 2 families. MNT curves [13] are the first degree 2 families of prime orders, then several generalizations and extensions (a.k.a extended MNT curves) have been proposed in [6] by allowing group order with small co-factors.

Our work is to construct parameterized families for $k = 3, 4, 6$, and show they are more general families covering all the former work related to MNT curves and extended MNT curves.

From Algorithm 1, we see in the case $\phi(k) = 2$, the degree of x in t is 1, thus q and t satisfy Hasse Bound directly. Moreover, $f = 4q - t^2$ is quadratic with regard to x, so it naturally satisfies CM Condition as well. Thus we can simply compute parameterized families for $k = 3, 4$ and 6.

We derive the following three propositions.

Proposition 1. *The parameterized families (q, r, t) of (extended) MNT curves for $k = 3$ must have the form as*

$$q = q_2 x^2 - \frac{2q_2 a_1 a_0 - q_2 a_1^2 - 1}{a_1} x + \frac{q_2 a_1 a_0^2 - a_0 q_2 a_1^2 + q_2 a_1^3 - a_0}{a_1},$$
$$r = q_2 x^2 - q_2(2a_0 - a_1)x + q_2(a_0^2 - a_0 a_1 + a_1^2),$$
$$t = \frac{1}{a_1} x - \frac{a_0}{a_1} + 1.$$

Proposition 2. *The parameterized families (q, r, t) of (extended) MNT curves for $k = 4$ must have the form as*

$$q = q_2 x^2 - \frac{2q_2 a_1 a_0 - 1}{a_1} x + \frac{q_2 a_1 a_0^2 + q_2 a_1^3 - a_0}{a_1},$$

$$r = q_2 x^2 - 2q_2 a_0 x + q_2(a_0^2 + a_1^2),$$

$$t = \frac{1}{a_1} x - \frac{a_0}{a_1} + 1.$$

Proposition 3. *The parameterized families (q, r, t) of (extended) MNT curves for $k = 6$ must have the form as*

$$q = q_2 x^2 - \frac{2q_2 a_1 a_0 + q_2 a_1^2 - 1}{a_1} x + \frac{q_2 a_1 a_0^2 + a_0 q_2 a_1^2 - a_0 + q_2 a_1^3}{a_1},$$

$$r = q_2 x^2 - q_2(2a_0 + a_1)x + q_2(a_0^2 + a_0 a_1 + a_1^2),$$

$$t = \frac{1}{a_1} x - \frac{a_0}{a_1} + 1.$$

All the possible degree 2 families can be represented by enumerating values of q_2, a_0, a_1 and a_2 over $\mathbb{Q}$.

We list two examples for the case $k = 6$.

- Substituting $\{q_2 = 4, a_0 = 0, a_1 = \frac{1}{2}\}$ and $\{q_2 = 4, a_0 = 0, a_1 = -\frac{1}{2}\}$ to parameterized families (q, r, t) in Proposition 3 separately, we obtain the families

$$\begin{cases} q(x) = 4x^2 + 1, \\ r(x) = 4x^2 \pm 2x + 1, \\ t(x) = \mp 2x + 1. \end{cases}$$

They are just MNT curves for $k = 6$ [13].
- Substituting $\{q_2 = 16, a_1 = \frac{1}{2}, a_0 = -\frac{1}{2}\}$ to (q, r, t), we get a family

$$\begin{cases} q(x) = 16x^2 + 10x + 5, \\ r(x) = 4(4x^2 + 2x + 1), \\ t(x) = 2x + 2. \end{cases}$$

It's an extended MNT curve for $k = 6$ with a small co-factor 4.

5   The Case $\Phi(k) = 4$

In this section, we construct degree 4 families by parameterized families, in addition, we give the evidence that it is not likely to have any other degree 4 family except for Freeman Curves and B-N Curves.

According to Algorithm 1, the degree of x in t is 3 and the CM polynomial $f = 4q - t^2$ typically is square free and has degree 6 with respect to x, thus Eq. (1) and equation system (3) or (4) need to be solved after computing parameterized families.

We consider the case in terms of CM Condition. As discussed in Sect. 3, there are 2 possibilities to achieve it.

5.1   Square-Free CM Polynomial

We first survey the condition that CM polynomial f is square-free but the high-order terms of $4q$ and t^2 cancel out, which can be converted to solve equation system (3).

1. $k = 5$

   Compute parameterized family (q, r, t) for $k = 5$, then solve the Eqs. (1) and (3). We get only one non-trivial solution set $\{a_1 = \frac{1}{2}a_2, a_3 = 0, q_4 = \frac{16}{25a_2^2}\}$ over $\mathbb{Q}$. Substituting it to (q, r, t), a potential degree 4 family is obtained:

$$q = \frac{1}{25a_2^4}[16x^4 + (24a_2 - 64a_0)x^3 + (-4a_2^2 - 72a_2a_0 + 96a_0^2)x^2$$
$$+ (-16a_2^3 + 72a_2a_0^2 + 8a_2^2a_0 - 64a_0^3)x$$
$$+ (16a_0^4 - 24a_2a_0^3 - 4a_2^2a_0^2 + 16a_2^3a_0 - 29a_2^4)],$$

$$r = \frac{1}{25a_2^4}[16x^4 + (24a_2 - 64a_0)x^3 + (36a_2^2 + 96a_0^2 - 72a_2a_0)x^2$$
$$+ (14a_2^3 + 72a_2a_0^2 - 72a_2^2a_0 - 64a_0^3)x$$
$$+ (16a_0^4 - 14a_23a_0 + 11a_2^4 - 24a_2a_0^3 + 18a_2^2a_0^2)],$$

$$t = \frac{1}{5a_2^2}[8x^2 + (-16a_0 + 6a_2)x + (-6a_2a_0 + 8a_0^2 + 3a_2^2)].$$

It can be checked that CM polynomial $f = 4q - t^2$ is always negative, so (q, r, t) fails to be a degree 4 family. Therefore, for embedding degree $k = 5$, there exist no degree 4 families when f is square-free.

2. $k = 10$

   Compute corresponding parameterized family (q, r, t), then solve the Eqs. (1) and (3). We get only one non-trivial solution set $\{a_1 = -\frac{1}{2}a_2, a_3 = 0, q_4 = \frac{16}{25a_2^2}\}$ over $\mathbb{Q}$. Substitute it to (q, r, t), then get a potential degree 4 family:

$$q = \frac{1}{25a_2^4}[16x^4 + (24a_2 - 64a_0)x^3 + (76a_2^2 - 72a_2a_0 + 96a_0^2)x^2$$
$$+ (44a_2^3 + 72a_2a_0^2 - 152a_2^2a_0 - 64a_0^3)x$$
$$+ (16a_0^4 - 24a_2a_0^3 + 76a_2^2a_0^2 - 44a_2^3a_0 + 51a_2^4)],$$

$$r = \frac{1}{25a_2^4}[16x^4 + (24a_2 - 64a_0)x^3 + (36a_2^2 + 96a_0^2 - 72a_2a_0)x^2$$
$$+ (14a_2^3 + 72a_2a_0^2 - 72a_2^2a_0 - 64a_0^3)x$$
$$+ (16a_0^4 - 14a_23a_0 + 11a_2^4 - 24a_2a_0^3 + 18a_2^2a_0^2)],$$

$$t = \frac{1}{5a_2^2}[8x^2 + (-16a_0 + 6a_2)x + (-6a_2a_0 + 8a_0^2 + 13a_2^2)].$$

It is easy to check that all conditions of Definition 1 hold. Moreover, we observe parameterized family (q, r, t) for $k = 10$ is essentially equivalent to Freeman curves.

Freeman curves can be derived by taking $a_0 = a_2 = -\frac{2}{5}$:

$$q(x) = 25x^4 + 25x^3 + 25x^2 + 10x + 3,$$
$$r(x) = 25x^4 + 25x^3 + 15x^2 + 5x + 1,$$
$$t(x) = 10x^2 + 5x + 3.$$

Consequently, it can be concluded that for embedding degree $k = 10$, Freeman curves are the only degree 4 family when f is square-free.

3. $k = 8$ and $k = 12$

We compute parameterized family (q, r, t) for $k = 8$ and $k = 12$ separately, but find no common solution for equation system (1) and (3) over $\mathbb{Q}$. Therefore, there exist no degree 4 families in such case.

5.2   CM Polynomial Having Square Factors

An alternative to achieve CM condition is that CM polynomial has square factors, but it should be noted that even if f contains square factors, it's not necessarily to satisfy CM Condition when the degree of x is high.

However in the case $\phi(k) = 4$, we can obtain a quartic CM polynomial. Once it contains square factors, CM Condition must be satisfied since the degree of square-free part could only be $0, 1$ or 2.

1. $k = 5$

List equation system (1) as

$$-a_2^3 + a_3 a_2^2 + 2a_1 a_2^2 - a_1^2 a_3 + 2a_1 a_3^2 - 2a_1 a_3 a_2 = 0. \tag{5}$$

It can be seen that Eq. (5) defines an elliptic curve, so solving equation system (1) is equivalent to find rational points of Eq. (5). This curve has rank 1, thus we have infinite rational points. We enumerate all the points up to the bound 20 on the projective plane over $\mathbb{Q}$ by Sage.

$$
\begin{array}{lll}
(-1/16 : -3/8 : 1) & (0 : 0 : 1) & (0 : 1 : 1) \\
(2/9 : 4/3 : 1) & (1/2 : 1 : 0) & (1 : 0 : 0) \\
(18/11 : 3/11 : 1) & (2 : 0 : 1) & (2 : 1 : 1) \\
(2 : 4 : 1) & (8/3 : 4/3 : 1) &
\end{array}
$$

We substitute each of these points to equation system (4) by turn, but get no non-trivial solutions over $\mathbb{Q}$ in each case. Then we perform more experiments by extending the bound to 50 and 100, and observe it's more unlikely to achieve non-trivial solutions over $\mathbb{Q}$ because of the rapid expansion of coefficients.

2. $k = 8$

List equation system (1) and get the elliptic curve

$$2a_2^2 a_1 + a_3^3 - a_3 a_1^2 = 0. \tag{6}$$

This curve has rank 0 and just four points: $(-1:0:1)$, $(1:0:0)$, $(0:1:0)$ and $(1:0:1)$. We consider each of these points in turn, but get no non-trivial solutions over $\mathbb{Q}$ for equation system (4) in each case.

3. $k = 10$

List equation system (1) and get the elliptic curve

$$a_2^2 a_3 - a_3 a_1^2 + 2a_3^2 a_1 + 2a_2 a_3 a_1 + a_2^3 + 2a_2^2 a_1 = 0. \tag{7}$$

This curve has rank 1, thus we have infinite rational points. We compute all the points up to the bound 20 on the projective plane over $\mathbb{Q}$ by Sage.

$$
\begin{array}{lll}
(-1/16 : 3/8 : 1) & (0:0:1) & (0:-1:1) \\
(2/9 : -4/3 : 1) & (-1/2 : 1 : 0) & (1:0:0) \\
(18/11 : -3/11 : 1) & (2:0:1) & (2:-1:1) \\
(2:-4:1) & (8/3 : -4/3 : 1)
\end{array}
$$

Substituting each point to equation system (4), we find only the point $(0 : 0 : 1)$ gives non-trivial solutions $\{q_4 = \frac{1}{a_3^4}\}$ and $\{q_4 = \frac{1}{5a_3^4}\}$, so we get 2 potential degree 4 families. We check each family in turn, and produce either a reducible q, or a f being negative. We then perform more experiments by extending the bound to 50 and 100, and similarly with the case $k = 5$, it's more unlikely to achieve non-trivial solutions over $\mathbb{Q}$.

4. $k = 12$

List equation system (1) and get the elliptic curve

$$a_3 a_1^2 - a_3 a_2^2 - 2a_2^2 a_1 + 2a_3^2 a_1 = 0. \tag{8}$$

This elliptic curve has rank 0 and torsion group of order 8, with torsion points: $(-2:0:1)$, $(-1:-1:1)$, $(-1:1:1)$, $(0:0:1)$, $(0:1:0)$, $(1:-1:1)$, $(1:0:0)$ and $(1:1:1)$.

We consider each of these points in turn, and find most of them have non-trivial solutions over $\mathbb{Q}$ for equation system (4), but almost every solution produces contradiction at last such that q cannot be an integer or q is negative.

Finally, only the point $(1 : -1 : 1)$ generates a real degree 4 family. It corresponds to the relation $\{a_3 = a_1, a_2 = -a_1\}$. Substituting the relation to equation system (4) and choosing solution $\{q_4 = \frac{1}{36a_1^4}\}$, we get a parameterized family (q, r, t) as

$$
\begin{aligned}
q = \frac{1}{36a_1^4} \big[& x^4 + (2a_1 - 4a_0)x^3 + (-6a_0 a_1 + 12a_1^2 + 6a_0^2)x^2 \\
& + (6a_0^2 a_1 + 20a_1^3 - 24a_0 a_1^2 - 4a_0^3)x \\
& + (a_0^4 + 12a_1^2 a_0^2 + 28a_1^4 - 20a_0 a_1^3 - 2a_0^3 a_1) \big],
\end{aligned}
$$

$$r = \frac{1}{36a_1^4}[x^4 + (2a_1 - 4a_0)x^3 + (6a_1^2 - 6a_0a_1 + 6a_0^2)x^2$$
$$+ (6a_0^2a_1 - 4a_1^3 - 12a_0a_1^2 - 4a_0^3)x$$
$$+ (a_0^4 + 6a_1^2a_0^2 + 4a_1^4 + 4a_0a_1^3 - 2a_0^3a_1)],$$
$$t = \frac{1}{6a_1^2}[x^2 + (4a_1 - 2a_0)x + (10a_1^2 - 4a_0a_1 + a_0^2)].$$

The CM polynomial is

$$f = 4q - t^2 = \frac{1}{12a_1^4}(x^2 - 2a_0x + 2a_1^2 + a_0^2)^2.$$

It can be checked that all conditions of Definition 1 hold. We observe this family is essentially equivalent to B-N curves. If taking $\{a_1 = -\frac{1}{6}, a_0 = -\frac{1}{3}\}$, we can get exactly the same form as B-N curves, that is

$$q(x) = 36x^4 + 36x^3 + 24x^2 + 6x + 3,$$
$$r(x) = 36x^4 + 36x^3 + 18x^2 + 6x + 1,$$
$$t(x) = 6x^2 + 1.$$

6   Conclusion

In this work, we present a systematic strategy to construct pairing-friendly elliptic curves of prime order, then show that all the existing constructions of families of elliptic curves of prime order can be explained via our method, and it's much more impossible to find families of prime order with higher $\phi(k)$. The result can be served as a guideline when choosing curves to construct pairing-based cryptography for blockchain system.

Acknowledgments. The authors would like to thank the anonymous reviewers for insightful comments and helpful suggestions. Meng Zhang, Maozhi Xu and Jie Wang were partially supported by the National Key R&D Program of China, 2017YFB0802000 and Natural Science Foundation of China, 61672059. Xuehong Chen was partially supported by the National Key R&D Program of China, 2018YFB2100400.

References

1. Sakai, R., Ohgishi, K., Kasahara, M.: Cryptosystems based on pairing. In: Symposium on Cryptography and Information Security, pp. 135–148 (2000)
2. Joux, A.: A one round protocol for tripartite Diffie-Hellman. J. Cryptol. **17**(4), 385–393 (2004)
3. Boneh, D., Franklin, M.K.: Identity-based encryption from the Weil pairing. In: International Cryptology Conference on Advances in Cryptology, pp. 213–229. Springer (2001)

4. GM/T 0044.1-2016 Identity-based cryptographic algorithms SM9
5. Freeman, D., Scott, M., Teske, E.: A taxonomy of pairing-friendly elliptic curves. J. Cryptol. **23**(2), 224–280 (2010)
6. Le, D.P., Mrabet, N.E., Tan, C.H.: On near prime-order elliptic curves with small embedding degrees. In: Algebraic Informatics, pp. 140–151. Springer (2015)
7. Lee, H.S., Lee, P.R.: Families of pairing-friendly elliptic curves from a polynomial modification of the Dupont-Enge-Morain method. Appl. Math. Inf. Sci. **10**(2), 571–580 (2016). https://doi.org/10.18576/amis/100218
8. Okano, K.: Note on families of pairing-friendly elliptic curves with small embedding degree. JSIAM Lett. 61–64 (2016). https://doi.org/10.14495/jsiaml.8.61
9. Li, L.: Generating pairing-friendly elliptic curves with fixed embedding degrees. Sci. China Inf. Sci. **60**(11), 119101 (2017). https://doi.org/10.1007/s11432-016-0412-0
10. Urroz, J.J., Shparlinski, I.E.: On the number of isogeny classes of pairing-friendly elliptic curves and statistics of MNT curves. Math. Comput. **81**(278), 1093–1110 (2012)
11. Zhang, M., Hu, Z., Xu, M.: On constructing parameterized families of pairing-friendly elliptic curves with $\rho = 1$. In: Chen, K., Lin, D., Yung, M. (eds.) Inscrypt 2016. LNCS, vol. 10143, pp. 403–415. Springer, Cham (2017). https://doi.org/10.1007/978-3-319-54705-3_25
12. Zhang, M., Xu, M.: Generating pairing-friendly elliptic curves using parameterized families. IEICE Trans. Fundam. Electron. Commun. Comput. Sci. **101**(1), 279–282 (2018)
13. Miyaji, A., Nakabayashi, M., Takano, S.: New explicit conditions of elliptic curve traces for FR-reductions. IEICE Trans. Fundam. Electron. Commun. Comput. Sci. **84**(5), 1234–1243 (2001)

A Global Clock Model
for the Consortium Blockchains

Chao Zan[1] and Hai-Chuan Xu[2,3]($\boxtimes$)

[1] IT Department, Head Office of Bank of China LTD., Beijing 100818, China
zanchao_hq@mail.notes.bank-of-china.com
[2] Department of Finance, East China University of Science and Technology,
Shanghai 200237, China
hcxu@ecust.edu.cn
[3] Research Center for Econophysics, East China University of Science
and Technology, Shanghai 200237, China

Abstract. We propose a global clock model to achieve time synchronization for consortium blockchains. Based on the existing consortium blockchain framework, a global clock service node is added. We use the Byzantine fault-tolerant algorithm to ensure the stability of the global clock node services. In addition, Cristian and Berkeley time synchronization algorithms are used to improve the confirmation of timestamp information, so as to achieve strong consistency of consensus time. This method can strike a balance between the transaction performance and the timestamp consistency requirements. This method meets the time accuracy requirements of practical business applications, and effectively benefits the promotion of blockchain technology in time-sensitive business scenarios.

Keywords: Consortium blockchains · Global clock · Time synchronization

1 Introduction

Blockchains have recently attracted the interest of both academics and practitioners across a wide span of industries: from finance to healthcare, utilities, real estate and government sector [4]. In practical business applications, time is a crucial parameter. Business applications require the accuracy of transaction execution time at the level of minutes or even seconds, and all transactions must be precisely marked with timestamps [10]. Under the traditional centralized architecture, each party can rely on the authoritative credit of the central node and trust the transaction initiation time recorded by the central node. However, in a distributed system, such as a blockchain, the accuracy of the time stamping of each node cannot be verified due to a lack of a global clock and a sound verification mechanism [5]. The mainstream consensus algorithms such as proof-of-work (POW) [19], proof-of-stake (POS) [2], and practical Byzantine

© Springer Nature Singapore Pte Ltd. 2020
Z. Zheng et al. (Eds.): BlockSys 2019, CCIS 1156, pp. 71–80, 2020.
https://doi.org/10.1007/978-981-15-2777-7_6

fault tolerance (PBFT) [3] do not incorporate the timestamp information into the consensus process. Actually, the consensus result of a certain state of the global ledger is achieved on the premise of sacrificing the consistency requirement of the timestamp information.

For public blockchains, there is a 51% attack vulnerability problem. When an organization has mastered 51% of the networks computing power, it can recalculate the confirmed blocks and make profits by branching the block chain and reduplicating bitcoins. The 51% attack vulnerability also exists in the timestamp service of the public blockchains, where 51% refers to the number of nodes, rather than computational power. When an organization masters 51% of the nodes in the whole network, it can uniformly modify the local time of the node, thereby gradually affecting the timestamp of the global ledger [14]. Since the 51% attack of the timestamp service does not change the counterparty and the transaction amount, it will not form a recurring cost [8]. Its attack cost is too high and basically with no profit. Therefore, 51% attack vulnerability of the time stamp service is often ignored by the public blockchain users. For private blockchains which is established within enterprises, it doesn't need to design an additional timestamp service, because the nodes are highly trusted. It can utilize Network Time Protocol (NTP) clock synchronization system built by the enterprise to guarantee the accuracy of system time of each node [11,18]. For consortium blockchains, there exist 2 serious problems that will be detailed discussed in the next section: reliability of the third party time and Byzantine node timestamp attack. Concerning above analyses, we will solve these two problems for consortium blockchains in this paper.

The rest of this paper is organized as follows: In Sect. 2, we review the timestamp service of consortium blockchains and problem statement about time synchronization. The detailed design of our global clock model for consortium blockchains is presented in Sect. 3. Finally, Sect. 4 concludes the paper.

2   Timestamp Service and Problem Statement

In this section, we review the timestamp service of consortium blockchains and summarize existing problems.

2.1   Timestamp Service of Consortium Blockchains

There exists an "Impossible trinity" among decentralization, security and scalability in blockchain technology [9]. In order to meet the requirements of commercial security and high concurrency, consortium blockchains generally divide the functions of nodes. It weakens the decentralization to multi-centralization and seek improvements in security and scalability by strengthening authentication technology and efficient consensus algorithm. Different with the Bitcoin blockchain, Fabric model divides the functions of endorsement, ordering and verification undertaken by a single Bitcoin node into three categories, Peers (Endorsers) for endorsement, Peers (Comitters) for validation and Orderers for sorting [15] (see Fig. 1)[1]. It realizes the increase of transaction speed and a great reduction of transaction cost by retaining the "centralization" of some nodes [1].

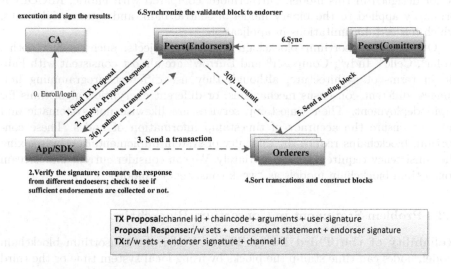

Fig. 1. Hyperledger Fabric architecture and transaction flow [15,20].

Fabric model does not establish a unified clock service. In addition to using the local system time, the nodes can also use the time service provided by Google's protobuf library [12]. In order to meet the demands of business transaction, Fabric model adds the transaction timestamp fields in block data structure (see Fig. 2).

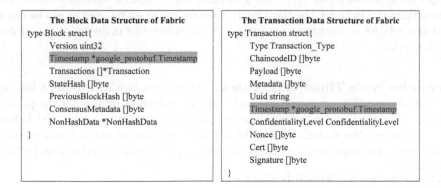

The Block Data Structure of Fabric	The Transaction Data Structure of Fabric
type Block struct{	type Transaction struct{
Version uint32	Type Transaction_Type
Timestamp *google_protobuf.Timestamp	ChaincodeID []byte
Transactions []*Transaction	Payload []byte
StateHash []byte	Metadata []byte
PreviousBlockHash []byte	Uuid string
ConsensusMetadata []byte	Timestamp *google_protobuf.Timestamp
NonHashData *NonHashData	ConfidentialityLevel ConfidentialityLevel
}	Nonce []byte
	Cert []byte
	Signature []byte
	}

Fig. 2. Hyperledger Fabric data structure.

---

[1] The CA node is used for customer authentication and don't participate in the consensus process. So we don't give a particular emphasis here.

The famous British legal digital currency, RSCOIN [7], also follows the same solution, classifying nodes based on the functions of endorsement, sorting and verification. However, RSCOIN is more primitive and the timestamp mechanism is not designed in this model. Furthermore, compared with Fabric, RSCOIN is primarily applied to the binary model of central bank and commercial banks, which has certain limitations in application.

Other top consortium blockchain platform projects, such as Sawtooth[2], Iroha[3], Cello[4], Indy[5], Composer[6] and Burrow[7] are almost consistent with Fabric in terms of architecture, although they use different programming languages, different consensus mechanisms, or different encryption algorithms for rapid deployment. Their timestamp services are likewise not systematic and can not ensure the accuracy of timestamp information of nodes. These consortium blockchains reduce the difficulty of system implementation by relaxing the consistency requirement appropriately. We can consider current mainstream consortium blockchain models as "weak consistency" models.

2.2   Problem Statement in Consortium Blockchains

Reliability of the Third Party Time. Under the consortium blockchain model, nodes can time stamp the blocks by using local system time or the third party time. If the local system time is selected, the verification node (Comitter) cannot judge the accuracy of timestamp information in the block due to the lack of global clock and time benchmark in the model. If the third party time service is selected as the global clock to time stamp the blocks and transactions, the reliability of third party time service cannot be verified due to the lack of third party time guarantee mechanism in the model, which will also generates security risks [14]. If the third-party time service is hacked, for example, Google's protobuf suddenly stops serving, or is hacked to provide the wrong time information to the node, Fabric will lose the trusted time source, which will cause the global ledger to be out of order [10]. When running time-sensitive transactions on the consortium blockchains, the third party time source must be used as global clock and the related mechanisms are necessary to ensure the stability of the global clock service.

Byzantine Node Timestamp Attack. Consortium blockchains are a kind of blockchains requiring registration and licensing, which is limited to the participation of consortium members. The nodes need to be fully authorized before they can access the system. Due to high trustworthiness of nodes in consortium blockchains, the mainstream consortium blockchains are designed to assume that

---

[2] https://github.com/hyperledger/sawtooth-core.
[3] https://github.com/hyperledger/iroha.
[4] https://github.com/hyperledger/cello.
[5] https://github.com/hyperledger/indy-sdk.
[6] https://github.com/hyperledger/composer.
[7] https://github.com/hyperledger/burrow.

there are no Byzantine nodes [16]. They assume that all nodes can accurately time stamp the blocks and no relevant mechanism is set to verify the accuracy of the timestamps of the nodes. However, if a node of the consortium blockchain is attacked by hackers, or the local system time is not updated timely due to hardware errors, such node will stamp the blocks or transactions with a wrong timestamp. Due to the lack of corresponding protection mechanism in the consortium blockchain model, this kind of behaviors will not be identified and be prevented in reaching consensus. Eventually, the timestamp information disorder will occur in global ledger [17].

3   A Global Clock Model for Consortium Blockchains

It is very difficult to find out the global state of distributed system. The essence of the problem is the lack of global clock, so it is difficult to guarantee that all nodes record the state information in uniform time. The consortium chain model ignores the requirements that the specific application scenario has for time accuracy. Without the guarantee mechanism of global clock and timestamp accuracy, it is impossible to make business decisions in real life.

Now, we propose a kind of global clock model for consortium blockchains. Based on the existing consortium blockchain framework, the global clock service node is added. We use the Byzantine fault-tolerant algorithm to ensure the stability of the global clock node services. In addition, Cristian and Berkeley time synchronization algorithms [6,13] are used to improve the confirmation of timestamp information, so as to achieve strong consistency of consensus time. The architecture and transaction flow of our global clock consortium blockchain model (hereafter GCCB) are show in Fig. 3.

3.1   Timer: Ensuring the Reliability of Clock Sources

We add a new global clock node to dock with multiple clock sources and use the Byzantine fault-tolerant algorithm to ensure the reliability of clock sources.

The clock sources are mainly obtained by three ways. The first way is to get by satellite, such as the global standard time provided by BeiDou Navigation Satellite System (BDS) or by GPS. The second way is to get by international atomic time (IAT), defined by the ultra-fine transition radiation frequency. The third way is to get by the Internet public service, such as the time source service provided by Google, Microsoft and National Time Service Center in China. Generally speaking, each node in the consortium chain will choose different clock source services. Therefore, to prevent a clock source from being attacked by hackers, the global clock node needs to dock with all clock sources used by the consortium chain node, and run detecting algorithm to check the accuracy of the clock source regularly. Here we choose to use the Byzantine fault-tolerant algorithm. As long as less than 1/3 of clock sources are not attacked by hackers at the same time, the algorithm can guarantee the stable global clock node service. The steps of the global clock node are as follows.

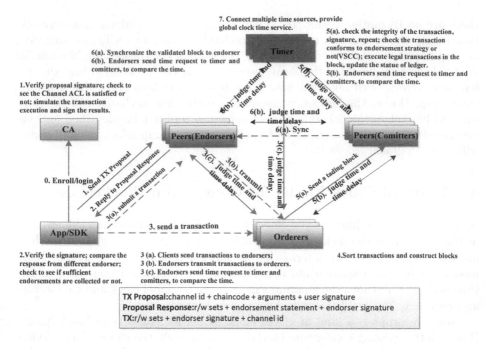

Fig. 3. GCCB architecture and transaction flow.

Step 1: we use T_i to represent the clock source, and t_i is the time obtained through the time source. Then, summarize various clock sources docked with the consortium chain nodes to form the clock source list $[T_1, T_2, T_3, ...]$. The global clock node docks with all time sources in the list, and sets up rotation threads $[P_1, P_2, P_3, ...]$ for each time source. The rotation threads run regularly, or get time list $[t_1, t_2, t_3, ...]$ from all clock sources when consortium chain nodes submit time requests to the global clock node.

Step 2: After obtaining $[t_1, t_2, t_3, ...]$, the global clock node runs the Byzantine fault-tolerant algorithm, that is, in the case that less than $1/3$ of the nodes are not attacked by hackers at the same time, $[t_1, t_2, t_3, ...]$ reach a consensus on global time t_c. The global clock node can perform rotation training and judge the stability of time sources by the consensus global time t_c.

3.2 Endorsers: Judging the Time Accuracy of the Local System and Stamping the Time

The endorsers use the Cristian time synchronization algorithm to judge the time accuracy of the local system, and stamp the times for transactions.

Step 1: If the threads $[P_1, P_2, P_3, ...]$ are triggered by the visiting of consortium chain nodes, the global clock node calculates the time t'_c of reaching a consensus, and then feedback $t_{Timer} = t_c + t'_c$ to the visiting nodes.

Step 2: After the endorser receives the global clock feedback t_{Timer}, it calculates the round-trip time t_{E2T} to the global clock node, and obtains adjusted time $t'_{Timer} = t'_{Timer} + t_{E2T}/2$.

Step 3: Compared t'_{Timer} with the local system time $t_{Endorser}$, if $|t'_{Timer} - t_{Endorser}| > \varepsilon$, then the endorser synchronizes the local system time $t_{Endorser}$, and repeat steps 1 to 3 until $|t'_{Timer} - t_{Endorser}| < \varepsilon$. Here ε indicates the upper limit of tolerance. According to the experience of Cristian and Berkeley time synchronization algorithms, it is recommended to set ε to $20\,\text{ms} < \varepsilon < 25\,\text{ms}$.

Step 4: When $|t'_{Timer} - t_{Endorser}| < \varepsilon$, the endorser uses $t_{Endorser}$ to adds the timestamp for the transaction, denoted as t_{Trans}, and sends the transaction to the orderer.

3.3 Orderers: Ensuring that the System Time of the Endorser Is Synchronized with the Global Clock Node

After the endorser submits the transaction, the orderer uses the Berkeley time synchronization algorithm to verify the system time of the endorser and the timestamp accuracy of the transaction. The detailed steps are as follows.

Step 1: After the endorser stamps the timestamp t_{Trans} for the transaction, it sends the transaction to the orderer for sorting.

Step 2: Using Berkeley time synchronization algorithm, the orderer sends time request to the global clock node and the endorser, and get the feedback t_{Timer} from the global clock node and $t_{Endorser}$ from the endorser. Considering round-trip times t_{O2T} and t_{O2E}, we can get $t'_{Timer} = t_{Timer} + t_{O2T}/2$ and $t'_{Endorser} = t_{Endorser} + t_{O2E}/2$.

Step 3: Compared t'_{Timer} with the local system time $t_{Orderer}$, if $|t'_{Timer} - t_{Orderer}| > \varepsilon$, then the orderer synchronizes the local system time $t_{Orderer}$.

Step 4: If $|t'_{Timer} - t'_{Endorser}| > \varepsilon$ or $|t'_{Timer} - t_{Trans} - (t_{O2T} + t_{O2E}/2)| > \varepsilon$, the orderer rejects the transaction submitted by the endorser and notifies the endorser to update the local system time and initiate the transaction again.

Step 5: If $|t'_{Timer} - t'_{Endorser}| < \varepsilon$, the orderer accepts the transaction, packages the transaction and forms a block, then uses the local system time $t_{Orderer}$ to stamp the block which is denoted as t_{Block}, and finally sends the block to the comitter.

3.4 Comitters: Ensuring that the System Time of the Orderer Is Synchronized with the Global Clock Node

After the orderer releases the block, the comitter uses the Berkeley time synchronization algorithm to verify the system time of the orderer and the timestamp accuracy of the block. The detailed steps are as follows.

Step 1: After the orderer stamps the timestamp t_{Block} on the block, it sends the block to the comitter for verification.

Step 2: Using Berkeley time synchronization algorithm, the comitter sends time request to the global clock node and the orderer, and get the feedback t_{Timer} from the global clock node and $t_{Orderer}$ from the orderer. Considering round-trip times t_{C2T} and t_{C2O}, we can get $t'_{Timer} = t_{Timer} + t_{C2T}/2$ and $t'_{Orderer} = t_{Orderer} + t_{C2O}/2$.

Step 3: Compared t'_{Timer} with the local system time $t_{Comitter}$, if $|t'_{Timer} - t_{Comitter}| > \varepsilon$, then the comitter synchronizes the local system time $t_{Comitter}$.

Step 4: If $|t'_{Timer} - t'_{Orderer}| > \varepsilon$ or $|t'_{Timer} - t_{Block} - (t_{C2T} + t_{C2O}/2)| > \varepsilon$, the comitter rejects the transaction submitted by the orderer and notifies the orderer to update the local system time and rebuild the block.

Step 5: If $|t'_{Timer} - t'_{Orderer}| < \varepsilon$, the comitter accepts the block packaged by the orderer and starts synchronizing the block to the endorser.

3.5 Endorsers: Ensuring that the System Time of the Comitter Is Synchronized with the Global Clock Node

After the comitter publishes the block, the endorser uses Berkeley time synchronization algorithm to verify the system time of the comitter. The detailed steps are as follows.

Step 1: After the comitter completes the block validation, it sends the block to the endorser.

Step 2: Using Berkeley time synchronization algorithm, the endorser sends time request to the global clock node and the comitter, and get the feedback t_{Timer} from the global clock node and $t_{Comitter}$ from the comitter. Considering round-trip times t_{E2T} and t_{E2C}, we can get $t'_{Timer} = t_{Timer} + t_{E2T}/2$ and $t'_{Comitter} = t_{Comitter} + t_{E2C}/2$.

Step 3: If $|t'_{Timer} - t'_{Comitter}| > \varepsilon$, then the endorser refuses to accept the block that the comitter sends, and notifies the comitter to update the local system time and initiate the transaction again.

Step 4: If $|t'_{Timer} - t'_{Comitter}| < \varepsilon$, the endorser accepts the block and completes the block synchronization.

4   Conclusion

In this paper, we propose a global clock model to achieve time synchronization for consortium blockchains. It can achieve strong consistency of block timestamp and transaction timestamp when reaching a consensus, so as to improve the information value of global ledger timestamp. This method can strike a balance between the transaction performance and the timestamp consistency requirements, meet the time accuracy requirements of practical applications, and effectively solve the application and promotion of blockchain technology in time-sensitive business scenarios.

Our model is of great significance in the following aspects. First, our model makes clear the roles of block timestamp and transaction timestamp in blockchain data structure: the transaction timestamp is stamped by the endorser to confirm the time at which the transaction is sent, while the block timestamp is stamped by the orderer to confirm the time when the transaction takes effect. In addition, since the system time of the user device is not used for timestamp, it is not necessary to synchronize the time through the consortium chain nodes.

Second, our model makes it clear that, in order to obtain accurate global time in the consortium chain system, the global clock node must be constructed to provide global clock service. Only when there is a uniform time standard, can each node of the consortium chain correctly record the ledger status. The global clock node can use Byzantine fault-tolerant algorithm to ensure the stability of clock service. The algorithm can ensure the stability of global clock node service on the premise that less than 1/3 of the time sources are attacked.

Finally, our model provides the solution to achieve the block chain consensus with strong time consistency. This method improves the accuracy of timestamp information in the consensus mechanism through a set of rigorous global clock synchronization methods, thereby enhancing the credibility of block and transaction timestamp information. All other blockchain models cannot achieve the strong consistency of the consensus time. For example, the Libra model[8] does not design time synchronization, and their transactions in the block are sorted by the sequence value. The accuracy of the transaction timestamp is determined by the tolerance upper limit. Within the tolerance upper limit, the libra model believes that the time stamped by the node is effective. Obviously, the Libra model cannot achieve the strong consistency of consensus time, by judging the value of timestamp within a certain time upper limit.

Acknowledgments. This work was partially supported by the National Natural Science Foundation of China (U1811462 and 71971081) and the Fundamental Research Funds for the Central Universities.

References

1. Androulaki, E., Barger, A., Bortnikov, V., Cachin, C., Christidis, K., De Caro, A., Enyeart, D., Ferris, C., Laventman, G., Manevich, Y.: Hyperledger fabric: a distributed operating system for permissioned blockchains. In: Proceedings of the Thirteenth EuroSys Conference, p. 30. ACM (2018)
2. Buterin, V.: Slasher ghost, and other developments in proof of stake (2014). https://blog.ethereum.org/2014/10/03/slasherghost-developments-proof-stake/
3. Castro, M., Liskov, B.: Practical Byzantine fault tolerance. In: OSDI, vol. 99, pp. 173–186 (1999)
4. Christidis, K., Devetsikiotis, M.: Blockchains and smart contracts for the Internet of Things. IEEE Access **4**, 2292–2303 (2016)
5. Conoscenti, M., Vetro, A., De Martin, J.: Blockchain for the Internet of Things: a systematic literature review. In: 2016 IEEE/ACS 13th International Conference of Computer Systems and Applications (AICCSA), pp. 1–6. IEEE (2016)

---

[8] https://github.com/libra/libra.

6. Cristian, F.: Probabilistic clock synchronization. Distrib. Comput. **3**(3), 146–158 (1989)
7. Danezis, G., Meiklejohn, S.: Centrally banked cryptocurrencies. arXiv preprint arXiv:1505.06895 (2015)
8. Dong, W., Liu, X.: Robust and secure time-synchronization against sybil attacks for sensor networks. IEEE Trans. Ind. Inform. **11**(6), 1482–1491 (2015)
9. Fischer, M., Lynch, N., Paterson, M.: Impossibility of distributed consensus with one faulty process. Technical report, Massachusetts Inst of Tech Cambridge lab for Computer Science (1982)
10. Freris, N., Graham, S., Kumar, P.: Fundamental limits on synchronizing clocks over networks. IEEE Trans. Autom. Control. **56**(6), 1352–1364 (2010)
11. Ganeriwal, S., Kumar, R., Srivastava, M.: Timing-sync protocol for sensor networks. In: Proceedings of the 1st International Conference on Embedded Networked Sensor Systems, pp. 138–149. ACM (2003)
12. Google: Protocol buffers - google code (2012). http://code.google.com/apis/protocolbuffers/
13. Gusella, R., Zatti, S.: An election algorithm for a distributed clock synchronization program. Technical report, University of California Berkeley, Department of Electrical Engineering and Computer Sciences (1985)
14. He, J., Chen, J., Cheng, P., Cao, X.: Secure time synchronization in wirelesssensor networks: a maximum consensus-based approach. IEEE Trans. Parallel Distrib. Syst. **25**(4), 1055–1065 (2013)
15. IBM: Hyperledger/fabric: Blockchain fabric incubator code (2016). https://github.com/hyperledger/fabric
16. Lamport, L., Shostak, R., Pease, M.: The Byzantine generals problem. ACM Trans. Program. Lang. Syst. **4**(3), 382–401 (1982)
17. Li, G., Niu, M., Chai, Y., Chen, X., Ren, Y.: A novel method of clock synchronization in distributed systems. Chin. Astron. Astrophys. **41**(2), 263–281 (2017)
18. Mills, D.: Internet time synchronization: the network time protocol. IEEE Trans. Commun. **39**(10), 1482–1493 (1991)
19. Nakamoto, S.: Bitcoin: a peer-to-peer electronic cash system (2008). https://bitcoin.org/bitcoin.pdf
20. Yang, B., Chen, C.: Principle, Design and Applications of Blockchains. China Mechine Press, Beijing (2018). (in Chinese)

Histogram Publishing Algorithm Based on Sampling Sorting and Greedy Clustering

Xiaonian Wu[✉], Nian Tong, Zhibo Ye, and Yujue Wang

Guangxi Key Laboratory of Cryptography and Information Security,
Guilin University of Electronic Technology, Guilin 541004, China
xnwu@guet.edu.cn

Abstract. The data produced by differential privacy histogram publishing algorithm based on grouping has low usability due to large approximation error and Laplace error. To solve this problem, a histogram publishing algorithm based on roulette sampling sort and greedy partition is proposed. Our algorithm combines the exponential mechanism with the roulette sampling sorting method, arranges the similar histogram bins together with a larger probability by the utility function and the restriction on the number of sampled entity. The greedy clustering algorithm is used to partition the sorted histogram bins into groups, and the error among histogram bins in each group is reduced by optimizing the lower bound error of the grouping. Extensive experimental results show that the proposed algorithm can effectively improve the usability of published data under the premise of satisfying differential privacy.

Keywords: Differential privacy · Histogram publishing · Roulette sampling · Greedy clustering · Grouping error

1 Introduction

Data publishing and privacy protection are two important mechanisms in data processing. However, data publishing is to effectively use the available information in the data, whereas privacy protection is to hide sensitive information in the data. It is challenging to make balance between these two mechanisms in data processing. Differential privacy [1] is considered to be an effective way to solve the above problems, since it has rigorous statistical model and can provide quantifiable privacy guarantees. Histogram publishing is an effective data publishing method in differential privacy, however, it also has some weaknesses such as high complexity and accumulated noise of long-range query error, which usually lead to low data usability and accuracy.

To reduce the error caused by adding too much noise in the histogram, Xu et al. [2] partitioned data based on the mean square error of the minimized query function. Xiao, Wang and Gehrke [3] processed data using the wavelet transform to reduce the error of long-range query. Hay et al. [4] made constrained reasoning on the histogram based on the least square method and the consistency constraint. Lee et al. [5] processed the noised data of histogram by the constrained maximum likelihood estimation. For reducing noise

© Springer Nature Singapore Pte Ltd. 2020
Z. Zheng et al. (Eds.): BlockSys 2019, CCIS 1156, pp. 81–91, 2020.
https://doi.org/10.1007/978-981-15-2777-7_7

accumulation and balance noise distribution, Ge et al. [6] first preprocessed the data using the density-based clustering algorithm, and then divided data via differential privacy, finally added noise. Zhang et al. [7] proposed the graph degree histogram publishing method with node-differential privacy to suppress the sensitivity of the publication mechanism and reduce the error.

Sorting and grouping the histogram is an effective way to improve the accuracy and reduce the noise. Sorting can arrange the similar data together and can improve the accuracy of the grouping, grouping the sorted histograms can overcome the accumulated error of the long range query in publishing histogram, however it also introduces approximation error. To addresses these issues, Zhang et al. [8] first added Laplace noise to the original histogram, and then sorted and grouped them according to the size of histogram bins. In [9], the histogram was sorted based on the Metropolis-Hastings and the exponential mechanism, and then an adaptive greedy clustering method based on the lazy group lower bound was employed to group the ordered histogram to reduce the error. Li et al. [10] combined the exponential mechanism and the hierarchical partition to balance the Laplace error and approximation error occurred in histogram grouping. Tang and Long [11] used a structure priority algorithm and a hybrid mechanism to reduce the sensitivity and the noise addition and structural error. Tang, Yang and Bai [12] adopted an adaptive privacy budget allocation strategy to balance the noise error and recombination error.

The histogram is also used in dynamic data publishing. In [13], Zhang and Meng proposed a flow histogram publishing method based on sliding window. In [14], Yan et al. used the fractal dimension differential privacy histogram publishing method to divide the dynamic data and add Laplace noise to improve data usability and efficiency.

To address the issues of data similarity and cumulative error in histogram sorting and grouping, this paper proposes a histogram publishing algorithm based on sampling sorting and greedy clustering (HPSSGC). With HPSSGC, the roulette sampling sorting is first employed to sample and sort on the original histogram, so that the similar histogram bins can be arranged together with a larger probability. Then, the sorted histograms are grouped by the greedy clustering algorithm. Finally, the Laplace noise is added to the grouped histogram bins and the data is published.

The remainder of this paper is organized as follows. In Sect. 2, we introduces some notations and preliminaries in privacy-preserving histogram publishing. Section 3 presents our method including the sorting algorithm and grouping method at the histogram, and provides secure analysis on the publishing algorithm. In Sect. 4, we empirically evaluate our method on three different real-world datasets. Finally, Sect. 5 concludes the paper.

2 Preliminaries

Differential privacy is an important tool in protecting data privacy during publishing, and it provides a theoretical privacy preservation for any background knowledge attacks. In this section, we briefly review some related definitions.

Definition 1. Neighboring datasets [1]. Suppose two datasets D and D' have the same structure and attributes. If D and D' differ in only one record, they are called neighboring datasets.

Definition 2. ε-Differential Privacy [1]. If there is a random algorithm M with the output set P, for all neighboring datasets D and D', any output $S \subseteq P$, M satisfies:

$$Pr[M(D) \in S] \leq exp(\varepsilon) \times Pr[M(D') \in S] \tag{1}$$

then the algorithm M satisfies the ε-differential privacy, where ε denotes the privacy preservation budget and $0 \leq \varepsilon \leq 1$. The smaller the ε, the higher the level of privacy preservation of M.

The Laplace mechanism is a widely used mechanism in protecting the differential privacy of numeric data by adding Laplace noise to the algorithm outcomes. The exponential mechanism is another mechanism, which can protect differential privacy of non-numeric data by using random sampling that satisfied a specific distribution instead of adding noise. Note that both mechanisms rely on the global sensitivity of the query function.

Definition 3. Global Sensitivity [1]. For a query functions f and a pair of neighboring datasets D and D', the global sensitivity of f is defined as follows:

$$\Delta f = \max_{(D,D')} \| f(D) - f(D')) \|_1 \tag{2}$$

where $\| f(D) - f(D') \|_1$ is the L_1 norm between the outcomes of the query functions $f(D)$ and $f(D')$.

The global sensitivity only depends on the query function f, and it has no relation with the dataset D, since it represents the range that the query function f makes a query over a pair of neighboring datasets.

Theorem 1. Laplace Mechanism [15]. For a given dataset D and a query function f : $D \to R^d$, the random algorithm $M(D) = f(D) + Y^d$ satisfies ε-differential privacy, where $Y^d = (Y_1, \ldots, Y_i, \ldots, Y_d)$, Δf denotes the global sensitivity of f over D, and $Y_i \sim Lap(\Delta f / \varepsilon)$ is a random noise, which subjects to Laplace distribution of the scale parameter $\Delta f / \varepsilon$.

Theorem 2. Exponential Mechanism [16]. For a given dataset D, let u be the utility function of all outcomes over D. If the random algorithm M satisfies the linear relationship between the probability of outputting r and $exp\left(\frac{\varepsilon \times u(D,r)}{2 \times \Delta u}\right)$, then M satisfies the ε-differential privacy, where $u(D, r)$ is the utility function of outcome r, and $\Delta u = \max_{(D,D'),r} \| u(D,r) - f(D',r) \|_1$ is the sensitivity of $u(D, r)$. The larger value of the utility function, the greater probability it would be selected.

3 Our HPSSGC Method

For a pair of neighboring datasets D and D', they are statistically divided according to some attribute to obtain histograms H and H', respectively, then these two histogram bins would differ in only one record.

In this paper, the histogram will be sampled and sorted using the roulette sampling technique. The ordered histograms are grouped with the greedy clustering algorithm, where each group is added Laplace noise to obtain the pending publishing histograms. The privacy budget ε is divided into two parts, where ε_1 for sorting the original histograms, ε_2 for the groupings, and $\varepsilon = \varepsilon_1 + \varepsilon_2$.

3.1 Roulette-Based Sample Sorting Method

The roulette selection algorithm [17] is a common selection operator in genetic algorithms, which divides the proportion on the roulette according to the entity fitness value. The principle of roulette can be described as follows. Assuming there are n values in set N, and the fitness value of entity i is f_i, then the probability that entity i is selected is $p_i = f_i/(\sum f_i), i = 1, 2, \ldots, n$.

The probability of selecting entity in roulette is positively correlated with the fitness value of the entity. The greater entity fitness, the higher probability the entity will be selected, which can avoid the local optimal problem caused by blind selection and greedy choice.

Suppose there is an original histogram $H = \{h_1, \ldots, h_i, \ldots, h_n\}$, where h_i is the histogram bin. If H is regarded as a population, h_i is regarded as an entity in H, and the roulette selection algorithm is used to select the entity, then the histogram bin with a larger fitness value would be extracted with a larger probability. Here, an exponential mechanism is used for sampling selection to satisfy differential privacy. Let $P(H, r_i)$ denotes the probability that an outcome r_i is sampled from H, and $r_i \in H$, then we have:

$$P(H, r_i) = \frac{exp(\frac{\varepsilon_1 \times u(H, r_i)}{2 \times \Delta u})}{\sum\limits_{j=1}^{n} exp(\frac{\varepsilon_1 \times u(H, r_j)}{2 \times \Delta u})} \tag{3}$$

where $exp\left(\frac{\varepsilon_1 \times u(H, r_i)}{2 \times \Delta u}\right)$ is the fitness function of entity r_i in H, $u(H, r_i)$ is the utility function, H is the histogram of the input dataset, ε_1 is the sampling privacy budget, and Δu is the global sensitivity of the utility function.

To rank the data with similar sampling results, a sampling sorting algorithm is designed to sort the data. Suppose H denotes the original histogram, and H_s is the sorted histogram. The underlying idea of the sample sorting algorithm are as follows:

(1) In the process of sorting, the histogram bin h' that newly added to H_s, will be the condition to select the next histogram bin from the H, which makes the results of each sample have greater similarity.

(2) If there are more bins in the histogram and more pending sample entities, then after the entity fitness values are normalized, the entity sampling probability will be lower and the similarity of the sample outcomes will be reduced. To arrange the similar data together as much as possible, it is necessary to increase the sampling probability of the similar histogram bins. Specifically, a threshold θ_1 is set to limit the number of pending sample entities, so that θ_1 entities with the largest fitness value in H are selected to constitute a sampling set H', which would reduce the

number of sampling histogram bins. Note that the threshold θ_1 can be dynamically adjusted according to the number of histogram bins.

(3) To put the similar data together, a more similar histogram bin needs to be selected from H' to make the fitness value larger when selecting the conditional histogram bin h' from H'. To make the fitness function to satisfy this requirement, an utility function based on the inverse of the distance between h' and h_i can be constructed as follows:

$$u(H, r_i) = -\left|h' - h_i\right| \qquad (4)$$

The outcomes of the utility function $u(H, r_i)$ over the histograms of two neighboring datasets differ in only one record, that is, $\Delta u = 1$. By substituting $u(H, r_i)$ and Δu into the sampling probability of formula (3), if the distance between h_i and h' gets closer, then the sampling probability becomes larger as the fitness value becomes larger, that is, the probability that the similar data are sampled and lined up together is greater.

Now, we present our roulette-based sampling sorting algorithm as follows:

Algorithm 1. The sampling sorting algorithm based on roulette.
Input: The original histogram $H=\{h_1,h_2,\ldots,h_i,\ldots,h_n\}$, privacy budget ε_1;
Output: The sorted histogram H_s;
  1) $h'=\min(H)$;   /* Find the minimum value of H as the initial condition histogram bin*/
  2) H_s.add(h');   /* Add the initial entity to the sorted set */
  3) H.remove(h');   /* Remove h' from H */
  4)   while $H\,!=$NULL do
  5) $F =$ Null;   /* Define the fitness value set */
  6)   for i=1 to $|H|$ do
  7) $F[i]=\exp((\varepsilon_1 \times u(H, h_i))/(2 \times \Delta u))$;   /*Calculate the fitness value $F[i]$ of the pending sample histogram bin h_i */
  8)   end for
  9)   sort(H, F);   /*Sort H in descending order according to the fitness value */
  10) $H_{select} =$ Null;   /* Define the sampling set */
  11)   if $|H|>\theta_1$ then   /* Restraint the number of sampling set */
  12)   for i=1 to θ_1 do
  13) H_{select}.add(h_i);
  14)   else
  15)   for i=1 to $|H|$ do
  16) H_{select}.add(h_i);
  17)   end if
  18) $h'=$ select(H_{select},F); /* Use the roulette sampling algorithm to select the next bin from the sample set H_{select} */
  19) H_s.add(h');
  20) H.remove(h');   /*Remove h' from the remaining histogram bins */
  21) end while

3.2 Grouping Method Based on Greedy Clustering

Grouping the sorted histograms can overcome the error accumulation of publishing histograms in long range query, however, the grouping process would also introduce approximate errors. Suppose the grouping on H_s as $G = \{C_1, \ldots, C_m, \ldots, C_k\}$, where $C_m = (l_m, r_m, c_m)$ denotes a group, $[l_m, r_m] \subseteq [1, n]$, n is the number of histogram bins,

l_m, r_m respectively represent the start and end coordinate of group C_m, the coordinates represent the places where bins are in the histograms, and c_m is the average value of bins in the group, $c_m = \frac{\sum_{i=l_m}^{r_m} h_i}{r_m - l_m + 1}$, $h_i \in C_m$. According to [9], the grouping error of C_m is defined as follows:

$$Error(C_m) = \sum_{i=l_m}^{r_m} (h_i - c_m)^2 + \frac{2}{(r_m - l_m + 1) \times \varepsilon_2} \tag{5}$$

where $\sum_{i=l_m}^{r_m} (h_i - c_m)^2$ is the approximate error and $\frac{2}{(r_m - l_m + 1) \times \varepsilon_2}$ is the Laplace error. Usually, the longer the grouping length, the larger the approximate error and the smaller the Laplacian error. It is a NP-hard problem to construct the best grouping scheme to minimize all errors.

Greedy clustering algorithm [9] adopts an adaptive clustering method to divide histogram bins in order. For a grouping scheme $G = \{C_1, \ldots, C_m\}$, adding a histogram bin h_{r_m+1} to the grouping C_m depends on the following conditions: if the error of C_m can be reduced when the bin h_{r_m+1} is added into grouping C_m, then it would be added into C_m; otherwise, it would be put into the next group.

Let $Error * (h_{r_m+1})$ be the low bound of grouping error in judging whether h_{r_m+1} can reduce the error of C_m, it can be defined as follows [9]:

$$Error * (h_{r_m+1}) \geq \frac{2}{(n - r_m)^2 \times (\varepsilon_2)^2} \tag{6}$$

In real-world applications, it is difficult for the grouping error of the histogram bins to reach the lower bound in formula (6). To improve the grouping accuracy, the low bound error of greedy clustering will be adjusted in the following section.

According to the grouping scheme $G = \{C_1, \ldots, C_m\}$, for the histogram bin h_{r_m+1}, there are two types of errors when it is combined with the later $n - r_m - 1$ histogram bins, i.e., the approximate error (AE) and Laplace error (LE). As described above, the longer the grouping length, the larger AE and the smaller LE. For $Error * (h_{r_m+1})$, we consider two extreme cases:

(1) h_{r_m+1} is put into a group independently. Thus, AE is 0, and LE reaches the maximum $2/\varepsilon_2^2$.
(2) h_{r_m+1} is inserted into a group along with the later $n - r_m - 1$ histogram bins. In this case, AE reaches the maximum $\sum_{h_j \in C_i} (h_j - c_i)^2$, where $c_i = \frac{\sum_{i=r_m+1}^{n} h_i}{n - r_m}$, and LE reaches the minimum $\frac{2}{(n-r_m) \times \varepsilon_2^2}$.

Thus, we have:

$$Error * (h_{r_m+1}) \geq \min(AE + LE)$$
$$\geq \min(AE) + \min(LE)$$
$$\geq \frac{2}{(n - r_m) \times \varepsilon_2^2} \tag{7}$$

Accordingly, the grouping low bound error of the greedy clustering algorithm is set as follows:

$$Error * (h_{r_m+1}) \geq \frac{2}{(n - r_m) \times \varepsilon_2^2} \tag{8}$$

With the new grouping low bound error, the sorted histogram H_s is grouped according to the greedy clustering method [9]. Then the grouping set $G = \{C_1, \ldots, C_m, \ldots, C_k\}$ is generated, and k independent Laplace noise $Lap(1/\varepsilon_2)$ are created and further injected into the corresponding groupings respectively. Specifically, for the group C_m, all histogram bins in the group become $c_m + \frac{Lap(1/\varepsilon_2)}{r_m-l_m+1}$, and finally the histogram $H_s' = \{h_1', h_2', \ldots, h_n'\}$ can be obtained. After H_s' is restored in the order of original histogram, the publishing histogram $H_p = \{h_{p1}, h_{p2}, \ldots, h_{pn}\}$ would be obtained. According to the above method, the cumulative error can be reduced.

3.3 Privacy Analysis

An algorithm can provide quantifiable privacy assurance if it satisfies differential privacy. In this paper, data can be published after performing sorting and grouping and adding Laplace noise. For the differential privacy of combinatorial algorithm, McSherry [18] presented the following combinatorial properties of differential privacy.

Theorem 3. Suppose there are n random algorithms $M_i (1 \leq i \leq n)$ satisfying ε_i-differential privacy, the combinatorial algorithms $\{M_i\}$ $(1 \leq i \leq n)$ over the same dataset D satisfy ε-differential privacy, where $\varepsilon = \sum_{i=1}^{n} \varepsilon_i$ [18].

Theorem 3 shows that a combinatorial algorithm composed of multiple algorithms satisfying differential privacy also satisfies differential privacy. In this paper, let the sample sorting algorithm be M_1 and the Greedy clustering algorithm be M_2.

For M_1, h_i is sampled from the sample set H_{selset} as the next histogram bin with a probability proportional to $exp\left(\frac{\varepsilon_1 \times u(H, h_i)}{2 \times \Delta u}\right)$, where H_{selset} is sorted by fitness value. According to Theorem 1, the algorithm M_1 satisfies the ε_1-differential privacy.

For M_2, it is grouped and added Laplace noise by following [9], and it satisfies ε_2-differential privacy according to Theorem 2.

Suppose the algorithms M_1 and M_2 act at the same dataset D and $\varepsilon = \varepsilon_1 + \varepsilon_2$, the algorithm in this paper satisfies ε-differential privacy according to the combinatorial properties of differential privacy.

4 Experimental Analysis

In our experiments, three real-world datasets that commonly used in the current histogram publishing studies are used, that is, waitakere, search_logs and social_network. Waitakere is the New Zealand's population data in 2006; Search_logs synthesizes search logs with keywords "Obama" from Google Trends and American Online between 2004 and 2010; Social_network contains 11k user information including user's relationships in the social network website. For these three datasets, we respectively implement our algorithm, AHP algorithm [8], IPHP algorithm [10] and structure priority algorithm (SPA) [11] in Java language, and compare data usability of the published histograms with these four algorithms, where the range query mean square error (MSE) is used as evaluation index. Note that the smaller MSE, the higher the data usability of published data.

For our algorithm, the threshold is set as $\theta_1 = 10$ based on the empirical data and the multiple evaluation results for the existing data. If the threshold is too small, the number of iterations will increase, and its cost will increase. Conversely, the threshold that is too large will result in a lower probability of similarity data being aligned. And which was confirmed by the experimental results. For testing, the privacy budget is set as ln2, 0.1, and 0.01, respectively, and the query range is chosen from 1 to 7000.

Experiment 1. Privacy budget allocation experiment of the HPSSGC algorithm

To test the effect on the outcomes using different privacy budget allocations in our algorithm, for the waitakere dataset, we set the ratios of ε_1 and ε_2 as 1:9, 3:7, 5:5, 7:3 and 9:1, and obtain the tested results about MSE as shown Fig. 1.

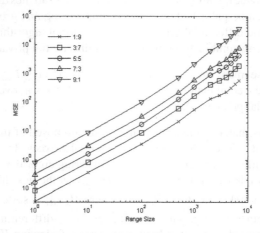

Fig. 1. MSE under different privacy budget allocations over the waitakere dataset.

In Fig. 1, the MSE error of the published data decreases as increasing the privacy budget allocation ratio of the grouping algorithm. One reason lies in that the privacy budget in the sampling sorting algorithm is mainly used to disturb the sampling output when the next bin is sampled. Our algorithm realizes the exponential mechanism by employing roulette sampling, which weakens the impact of the privacy budget. Another reason is that the privacy budget in the Greedy clustering grouping algorithm is mainly used to add Laplace noise. The larger the privacy budget, the smaller the added noise and the smaller the final data error. Thus, the privacy budget allocation ratio $\varepsilon1:\varepsilon2$ in our algorithm is set to 1:9 in subsequent experiments.

Experiment 2. Comparison of data usability of the published data with different algorithms

We test MSE of the published data using our HPSSGC algorithm, the AHP algorithm [8], the IPHP algorithm [10] and the structure priority algorithm (SPA) [11] over the above-mentioned three datasets, respectively. To ensure the stability of the test results, the four algorithms are running on three datasets for 30 times, and the final average MSE are shown in Figs. 2, 3 and 4.

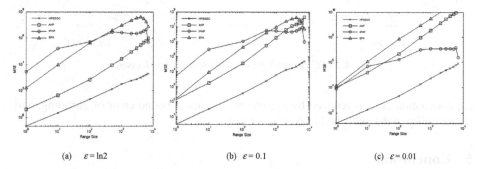

(a) $\varepsilon = \ln 2$ (b) $\varepsilon = 0.1$ (c) $\varepsilon = 0.01$

Fig. 2. MSE comparison over the waitakere dataset.

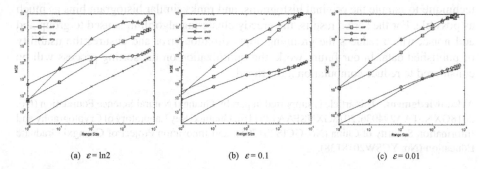

(a) $\varepsilon = \ln 2$ (b) $\varepsilon = 0.1$ (c) $\varepsilon = 0.01$

Fig. 3. MSE comparison over the social network dataset.

It can be seen from Figs. 2, 3 and 4 that for the same dataset and the same conditions, the smaller ε, the larger MSE and the higher degree of privacy protection. For the case of the same query scope and privacy budget, the structure priority algorithm employs V-optimization and exponential mechanism to directly divide the original histogram, which leads to low division accuracy and large query error. The IPHP algorithm directly uses the hierarchical partitioning algorithm to divide the original data, it provides low accuracy for the datasets with similar data but discrete distribution. The AHP algorithm sorts the original histogram and then groups, although the histogram global similarity is considered, the error is increased since additional noise is introduced during sorting. Our HPSSGC algorithm first uses the sample sorting algorithm to rank similar data with a large probability, and then employs the greedy clustering algorithm to group the sorted data. Since the sorting can improve the accuracy of grouping, the grouping

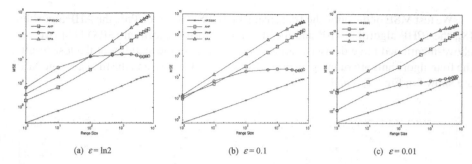

(a) $\varepsilon = \ln 2$ (b) $\varepsilon = 0.1$ (c) $\varepsilon = 0.01$

Fig. 4. MSE comparison over the search logs dataset.

approximation error is reduced by optimizing the lower bound error of grouping, and the usability of the published data is improved.

5 Conclusion

This paper proposed a histogram publishing algorithm based on roulette sample sorting and greedy clustering, to improve data usability under the premise of satisfying differential privacy. Our algorithm combines the exponential mechanism with roulette sampling technique to sample the original histograms, and ranks similar histogram bins as much as possible. For the sorted results, the greedy clustering algorithm is used to group and add noise, which reduces the grouping approximation error and ensures the usability of published data. In our future work, the optimization on the sorting process will be considered to reduce computational overhead.

Acknowledgment. This article is supported in part by Guangxi Natural Science Foundation (No. 2018GXNSFAA294036, 2018GXNSFAA138116), Guangxi Key Laboratory of Cryptography and Information Security of China (No. GCIS201705), and Innovation Project of Guangxi Graduate Education (No. YCSW2018138).

References

1. Dwork, C.: Differential privacy. In: Bugliesi, M., Preneel, B., Sassone, V., Wegener, I. (eds.) ICALP 2006. LNCS, vol. 4052, pp. 1–12. Springer, Heidelberg (2006). https://doi.org/10.1007/11787006_1
2. Xu, J., Zhang, Z.J., Xiao, X.K., et al.: Differentially private histogram publication. VLDB J. **22**(6), 797–822 (2013)
3. Xiao, X.K., Wang, G.Z., Gehrke, J.G.: Differential privacy via wavelet transforms. IEEE Trans. Knowl. Data Eng. **23**(8), 1200–1214 (2011)
4. Hay, M., Rastogi, V., Miklau, G., et al.: Boosting the accuracy of differentially private histograms through consistency. In: Proceedings of the 36th Conference of Very Large Databases, pp. 1021–1032. ACM, New York (2010)
5. Lee, J., Wang, Y., Kifer, D.: Maximum likelihood postprocessing for differential privacy under consistency constraints. In: Proceedings of the 21st ACM SIGKDD International Conference on Knowledge Discovery and Data Mining, pp. 635–644. ACM, New York (2015)

6. Ge, L., Hu, Y., Wang, H., He, Z., Meng, H., Tang, X., Wu, L.: IDP - OPTICS: improvement of differential privacy algorithm in data histogram publishing based on density clustering. In: Huang, D.-S., Jo, K.-H., Huang, Z.-K. (eds.) ICIC 2019. LNCS, vol. 11644, pp. 770–781. Springer, Cham (2019). https://doi.org/10.1007/978-3-030-26969-2_73

7. Zhang, Y.X., Wei, J.H., Li, J., Liu, W.F., Hu, X.X.: Graph degree histogram publication method with node-differential privacy. J. Comput. Res. Dev. 56(03), 508–520 (2019)

8. Zhang, X.J., Chen, R., Xu, J.L., et al.: Towards accurate histogram publication under differential privacy. In: Proceedings of the 14th SIAM International Conference on Data Mining, pp. 587–595. SIAM, Philadelphia (2014)

9. Zhang, X.J., Shao, C., Meng, X.F.: Accurate histogram release under differential privacy. J. Comput. Res. Dev. 53(5), 1106–1117 (2016)

10. Li, H., Cui, J.T., Lin, X.B., et al.: Improving the utility in differential private histogram publishing: theoretical study and practice. In: 2016 IEEE International Conference on Big Data, HangZhou, China, pp. 1100–1109. IEEE (2016)

11. Tang, Z.L., Long, S.G.: Differential privacy histogram publishing based on hybrid mechanism. J. Guizhou Univ. Nat. Sci. 35(4), 32–36 (2018)

12. Tang, H.X., Yang, G., Bai, Y.L.: Histogram publishing algorithm based on adaptive privacy budget allocation strategy under differential privacy. Appl. Res. Comput. https://doi.org/10.19734/j.issn.1001-3695.2018.11.0925

13. Zhang, X.J., Meng, X.F.: Streaming histogram publication method with differential privacy. J. Softw. 27(2), 381–393 (2016)

14. Yan, F., Zhang, X., Li, C., et al.: Differentially private histogram publishing through fractal dimension for dynamic datasets. In: 2018 13th IEEE Conference on Industrial Electronics and Applications, WuHan, China, pp. 1542–1546. IEEE (2018)

15. Dwork, C., McSherry, F., Nissim, K., Smith, A.: Calibrating noise to sensitivity in private data analysis. In: Halevi, S., Rabin, T. (eds.) TCC 2006. LNCS, vol. 3876, pp. 265–284. Springer, Heidelberg (2006). https://doi.org/10.1007/11681878_14

16. McSherry, F., Talwar, K.: Mechanism design via differential privacy. In: Proceedings of the 48th Annual IEEE Symposium on Foundations of Computer Science, Piscataway, NJ, pp. 94–103. IEEE (2007)

17. Holland, J.H.: Adaptation in Natural and Artificial Systems. MIT Press, Cambridge (1992)

18. McSherry, F.: Privacy integrated queries: an extensible platform for privacy-preserving data analysis. In: Proceedings of the ACM SIGMOD International Conference on Management of Data, pp. 19–30. ACM, New York (2009)

Aggregate Signature Consensus Scheme Based on FPGA

Jinhua Fu[1,2], Jiaheng Liu[2], Yongzhong Huang[1,3], Xueming Si[1,4],
Yongjuan Wang[1(✉)], and Bin Li[1]

[1] State Key Laboratory of Mathematical Engineering and Advanced Computing, Zhengzhou
450001, China
pinkywyj@163.com
[2] School of Computer and Communication Engineering, Zhengzhou University of Light
Industry, Zhengzhou 450002, China
[3] School of Computer Science and Information Security, Guilin University of Electronic
Technology, Guilin 541004, China
[4] School of Computer Science, Fudan University, Shanghai 201203, China

Abstract. With the rapid development of cryptocurrency, such as the Bitcoin,
block chain technology, as the bottom technology of Bitcoin, has been widely
concerned by researchers. Block chain has the characteristics of decentralization,
anonymity and non-tampering, which realizes the transformation from social trust
to machine trust. As an important part of block chain system, digital signature is
relatively inefficient. For this reason, this paper proposes an aggregation signature
scheme based on FPGA, which combines the aggregation signature technology
with the reconfiguration of FPGA, realizes the aggregation of multiple user signatures into one signature, and has multiple ECC acceleration modules in FPGA.
The efficiency of digital signature calculation is improved. Through experimental
analysis and comparison, the scheme uses FPGA reconstruction and aggregate
signature technology, which not only improves the computational efficiency of
ECC, but also improves the efficiency of signature verification and improves the
performance of block chain system.

Keywords: Aggregate signature · FPGA · Bitcoin · Blockchain · Digital
signature

1 Introduction

With the development of cryptocurrency such as Bitcoin, blockchain [1], as the underlying technology of Bitcoin, has been widely concerned by governments and financial
institutions all over the world. However, the development of blockchain is facing many
challenges, the most important challenge is to improve the performance of block chain
system. The performance optimization of block chain is still in the early research stage,
and there are still many problems to be solved. Aviv et al. introduced a directed acyclic
graph into the block chain system. A block can reference multiple ancestral blocks, so
that multiple blocks can be packaged in parallel in the network to accommodate more

© Springer Nature Singapore Pte Ltd. 2020
Z. Zheng et al. (Eds.): BlockSys 2019, CCIS 1156, pp. 92–100, 2020.
https://doi.org/10.1007/978-981-15-2777-7_8

transactions. And the transaction confirmation time will be shortened as more and more users join [2]. In order to solve the performance of block chain, Cai et al. proposed a double-chain model, that is, account block chain and transaction block chain [3].

In order to improve the efficiency of signature verification and improve the speed of transaction verification on the block chain and then optimize the performance of the block chain system, an aggregate signature consensus scheme based on FPGA is proposed. In this scheme, multiple signature messages are aggregated into one signature [4]. When the behavior of verifying signature occurs, the simple use of cpu to complete this task can not meet the performance requirements. In order to improve the computational performance, we make use of the characteristics of FPGA [5] parallelism and multiple registers to accelerate the signature verification operation. A number of parameters are input into the register by the PCIE interface, and the control points are added, doubled and coordinates converted by the main control state machine. Because of the large amount of calculation of point addition and doubling point, it is mainly realized by Barrett and KOA algorithm. On the other hand, the coordinate transformation is only calculated once, which is realized by serial modular multiplication, modular inversion and modular addition and subtraction. Therefore, the scheme not only reduces the storage space of the signature and saves the bandwidth resources of the bitcoin network, but also reduces the workload of signature verification. At the same time, the efficiency of signature verification is improved by using the reconfigurable characteristic of PFGA, and the performance of block chain system is improved.

2   The Achievement of the Plan

2.1   The Plan's Structure and Process

At present, the speed of Bitcoin transaction is relatively slow, and it can not meet the needs of industrialization. As the basic technology of Bitcoin, Blockchain has some problems, such as block capacity, throughput and scalability. These urgent problems must be solved in the development of Bitcoin and even of Blockchain technology. If these problems are not solved in time, people will challenge the development of Blockchain technology, which will lead to the decline of Bitcoin. Once these problems are solved, the value of Bitcoin will increase, and projects related to block chain will gradually fall to the ground. We propose an aggregate signature scheme based on FPGA, which uses the reconfigurability of the FPGA to design the elliptic curve acceleration module in the FPGA for parallel operation and optimize the elliptic curve digital signature algorithm. When multiple users initiate multiple bitcoin transaction requests, the CPU receives multiple users' digital signatures and public and private keys, then sends them to the FPGA for accelerated operation of signature aggregation, and finally generates aggregate signatures and returns them to the CPU for verification of aggregate signatures.

The public key and signature in the Bitcoin Block Chain System use the Elliptic Curve-based Digital Signature Algorithms (ECDSA) [6] (Fig. 1).

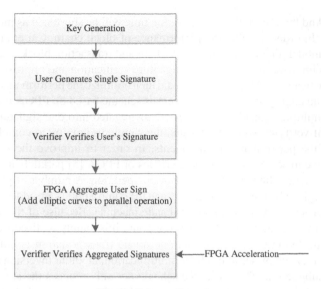

Fig. 1. Schema flow chart

The aggregate signature consensus scheme based on FPGA includes six parts: key generation algorithm, single signature generation algorithm, single signature verification algorithm, multiple signature aggregation algorithm, aggregate signature verification algorithm and acceleration module of FPGA. The specific scheme is as follows:

Parameter definition: elliptic digital signature D = (p, a, b, G, n, h). G is the base point on the elliptic curve, n is the order of the base point G, and h is the cofactor. Key generation: The user randomly chooses the signature private key d (0 < d < n), Q = dG as the signature public key.

Algorithm 1   Elliptic Curve Digital Signature Generation: The signature of message m is (r, s). The signer sends the message and signature (m, r, s) to the verifier to verify the digital signature.

Input: Message m of the signing user, key pair (d, Q)
Output: Signature (r, s)
1.   Generate a random number k, $1<=k<=n-1$
2. $KG=(x_1,y_1)$ and $r=x_1 \bmod n$
3.   If r=0 return 1.
4.   e=Hash(m)
5. $s=k^{-1}(e+rd) \bmod n$
6.   If s=0 return 1.

Algorithm 2 Elliptic Curve Signature Verification: Verifier receives the signature, and verifies whether (r, s) is the signer's signature of message m.

Input: Signature user's message m, signature = (r, s)

Output: Accept signature or reject signature

1. If (r, s) is the integer execution of interval [1, n-1]. Else refuses to sign
2. $e=Hash(m)$
3. $w =s^{-1} \bmod n$
4. $u_1=ew \bmod n$ and $u_2=rw \bmod n$
5. $X=u_1G + u_2Q = (x_2,y_2)$
6. IF X=0 Reject signature Else $v=x_2 \bmod n$
7. If v=r Accept signature Else Reject signature

Multiple signatures aggregation: Before signature aggregation, signature verification is needed for each user's aggregated signature. Otherwise, if any one of the signatures has problems, the aggregated signature will not be validated by the aggregated signature. The CPU submits N-group digital signatures to the FPGA at one time. The FPGA has several ECC acceleration modules. After receiving the data, the CPU performs parallel operations and outputs the aggregated signatures.

The acceleration module of FPGA: The acceleration module of FPGA consists of several acceleration modules of ECC. An acceleration module of ECC includes PCIE parameter input interface, register, master state machine and so on. Montgomery point multiplication algorithm is used to make full use of the reconfigurable characteristics of the FPGA, and point addition and point multiplication are calculated at the same time. Secondly, the fast modular multiplication of KOA and Barrett is realized by using the DSP of the FPGA, which speeds up the modular operation after multiplication with the largest amount of computation. Finally, multi-module parallelism makes full use of the spatial parallelism of the FPGA and improves the computational performance of ECC.

Algorithm 3 Aggregate Signature Verification Algorithms

Input:ID of identity list corresponding to user ui={ID_1,... ID_n}, public key list p={p_1,... P_n}, message list m={m_1,... m_n} and signature list

Output: Validation passes or validation does not pass

$Q_i=H_1(ID_i\|p_i)$ and $T=H_2(P_v)$

If $c(V,P)=e(\sum nQ_i,P_v)e(T,R)e(Q,\sum nP_i)$ Validation passed Else validation failed

---

3 Optimization of FPGA ECDSA

3.1 Point Multiplication in Montgomery

Since key operations are point multiplication of Elliptic Curve, and point multiplication is composed of point doubling and point addition which is concerned a large amount of modular arithmetic. Therefore, the choice of scalar multiplication, point addition and point doubling affect calculational efficiency over the Elliptic Curve directly. At present, Point Multiplication in Montgomery [7] is an algorithm in the highest efficiency and SPA-resistant capability. Algorithm4 show the specific process. K displays with the binary and l is the length of k, k[i] indicates k's i digit.

Algorithm 4 of point multiplication in Montgomery
Input: G,k
Output:Q=kG
Initialize P_0=G;P_1=2G;
1. for(i=l-2;i≥0;i--)
2. if(k[i]==0) $P_1 = P_0 + P_1$; $P_0 = 2P_0$;
3. else if(k[i]==1) $P_0 = P_0 + P_1$; $P_1 = 2P_1$;
4. end for
5. $Q = P_0$;

3.2 The Modular Multiplication of KOA and Barrett

Large Integer Multiplier of KOA

KOA decompose a complicated multiply operation into some simple ones by recursive. For Large Number A and B could decompose into two parts and could be indicated that

$$A(2) = 2^{|\bar{m}/2|}\left(2^{|\bar{m}/2|-1}a_{m-1} + \ldots + a_{\bar{m}/2}\right) + \left(2^{|\bar{m}/2|-1}a_{|\bar{m}/2|-1} + \ldots + a_0\right)$$

$$= 2^{|\bar{m}/2|}A_1 + A_0 \tag{1}$$

$$B(2) = 2^{|\bar{m}/2|}\left(2^{|\bar{m}/2|-1}b_{m-1} + \ldots + b_{|\bar{m}/2|}\right) + \left(2^{|\bar{m}/2|-1}b_{|\bar{m}/2|-1} + \ldots + b_0\right)$$

$$= 2^{|\bar{m}/2|}B + B_0 \tag{2}$$

For multiply operation of 256 digits $C = A \times B$ could be decompose into as below:

$$C = A \times B = (2^{128}A_1 + A_0)(2^{128}B_1 + B_0)$$

$$= 2^{256}A_1B_1 + 2^{128}[(A_1 + A_0)(B_1 + B_0) + A_1B_1 + A_0B_0]$$

$$+ A_0B_0 \tag{3}$$

Thus it can be seen, we should calculate that A_1B_1, $(A_1 + A_0)(B_1 + B_0)$, A_0B_0, in this way, we could obtain C. For FPGA, we use multiply operation through DSP sources which is supported of 64 digits. In this way, multiply operation of 256 digits can be decomposed into 128 digits and then 64 one, we can finish all the KOA by 3 recursive.

The Barrett use modulo reduction instead of a high-cost division. Because, $0 \leq A < P, 0 \leq B < P$ we know that AB $< P^2$, in order to calculate C = AB mod P, $0 \leq C < P$. We make X = AB, if there is Q, we make X $= Q \times P + C$; so C = X $- Q \times P$. The algorithm 5 shows the specific process.

Algorithm 5 modular multiplication algorithm of Barrett
Input: G,k
Output: C = A × B mod P
1. $M_1 = KOA(A, B)$;
2. $M_2 = KOA(\mu, \lfloor M_1/2^n \rfloor)$;
3. $M_3 = KOA(P, \lfloor M_2/2^n \rfloor)$;
4. $C = M_1 - M_3$;
5.   If(C > 2P) C = C - 2P;
6.   If(C > P) C = C - P;

The Whole Composition of FPGA

We control the point addition, point doubling and coordinate transformation by main controller. We use algorithm of Barrett and KOA to achieve it since the amount of point addition and point doubling is getting larger. We use serial modular, modular inverse and modular multiplication to achieve it over coordinate transformation at the last calculation. The modular multiplication make it possible under 2 digits and modular inverse use euclidean algorithm. We will not discuss those because those are simple with diversity.

4 Experiment

The FPGA chip model tested in this paper is xcku-060-ffva1156-2-i and the software is Vivado 2018.2.

4.1 Algorithm Performance

The clock frequency, resource occupation and calculation period of each module of ECC are shown in Table 1.

Table 1. Implementation of ECC modules

	Clock frequency	LUTs	REGs	DSP	Calculation period
Modular multiplication	45 MHz	5340	3494	144	11
Modular addition	45 MHz	9469	6582	144	112
Point doubling	45 MHz	8727	6583	144	108
Point multiplication	45 MHz	20100	18045	288	29578

As can be seen from Table 1, ECC modules occupy moderate resources and make full use of FPGA look-up tables, registers, DSP and other resources. At 45 MHz, the dot multiplication calculation cycle is 29578, which can calculate 1521.4 times per second.

In addition, 8 modules are instantiated inside the FPGA, and the overall calculation card is composed of 4 FPGA. The comparison of the speed of the entire FPGA and the CPU is shown in Table 2.

Table 2. Comparison of FPGA speed and CPU

Computing unit	Velocity (times/sec)	Increase multiple
CPU(i5-)	819.67	–
FPGA	48684.8	59.4

As can be seen from Table 2, compared with CPU, FPGA has improved 59.4 times. This is mainly due to the Montgomery point multiplication algorithm, which makes full use of the reconfigurable characteristics of FPGA and calculates point addition and point multiplication. Secondly, the fast modular multiplication of KOA and Barrett is realized by using DSP of FPGA, which accelerates the modular operation after multiplication with the largest amount of computation. Finally, multi-module parallelism makes full use of FPGA's spatial parallelism and improves ECC's computing performance.

4.2 Signature Verification Performance

From Figs. 2 and 3, it can be seen that the storage and time overhead of a common signature increase linearly with the number of signature messages. Using aggregate signature technology to optimize Bitcoin, the storage volume of a signature will become 1/n of that of a common signature, and since there is only one aggregate signature in a block, the block verification time will be reduced by 50%. Therefore, the scheme can not only reduce the storage space of signatures and save Bitcoin network bandwidth resources, but also cut down the workload of signature verification. At the same time, it can improve the aggregation of multiple signatures and the efficiency of signature verification, thus improving the performance of the block chain system.

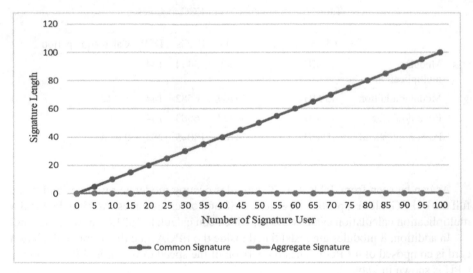

Fig. 2. Comparison of space occupancy between common signature and aggregate signature

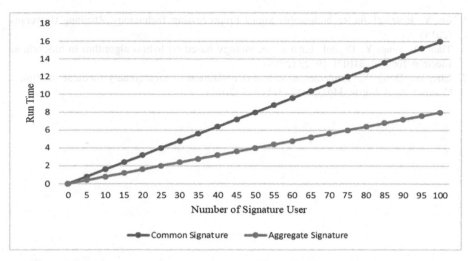

Fig. 3. Comparison of running time between common signature and aggregate signature

5 Conclusion

In order to reduce the block size and improve the Bitcoin block utilization rate and block chain digital signature calculation efficiency. This paper proposes a new idea of aggregation signature based on FPGA. The method combines the aggregation signature technology with FPGA reconstruction, and accelerates the elliptic curve by utilizing the characteristics of FPGA parallelism and many registers to improve the operation performance of the block chain system. Aggregation signature starts from the data structure of Bitcoin transaction, and on the basis of not affecting Bitcoin security and transaction integrity, it relies on cryptography technology to compress the volume of data, thus improving transaction processing and block verification speed. In a word, there are still many problems waiting for experts and scholars to study and solve in the block chain. The research we have done is only the tip of the iceberg in the block chain. For this reason, the follow-up work still starts from optimizing the performance of the block chain system to promote the healthy development of the block chain.

References

1. Yuan, Y., Wang, F.: The status quo and prospect of blockchain technology development. J. Autom. **42**(04), 481–494 (2016)
2. Lewenberg, Y., Sompolinsky, Y., Zohar, A.: Inclusive block chain protocols. In: Böhme, R., Okamoto, T. (eds.) FC 2015. LNCS, vol. 8975, pp. 528–547. Springer, Heidelberg (2015). https://doi.org/10.1007/978-3-662-47854-7_33
3. Cai, W., Yu, L., Wang, R., Liu, N., Deng, E.: Research on application system development method based on blockchain. J. Softw. **28**(06), 1474–1487 (2017)
4. Yuan, C., Xu, M., Si, X.: Consensus algorithm optimization scheme based on aggregate signature. Comput. Sci. **45**(02), 53–56+83 (2018)

5. Lu, Y.: Research on Reconfigurable Signal Preprocessing Technology. Zhejiang University (2018)
6. Tian, D., Peng, Y.: Digital signature technology based on hybrid algorithm in blockchain. Electron Technol. **31**(07), 19–23 (2018)
7. Che, W., Dong, X.: Implementation and optimization of montgomery modular multiplier. Comput. Appl. Softw. **34**(03), 312–315+333 (2017)

Information Encryption Mechanism Based on QR Code

Xiaohui Cheng[1,2], Tong Niu[1], and Qiong Gui[1(✉)]

[1] College of Information Science and Engineering,
Guilin University of Technology, Guilin 541000, China
cxiaohui@glut.edu.cn, niu5512@qq.com, guilucky@163.com
[2] Guangxi Key Laboratory of Embedded Technology and Intelligent System,
Jiangan Road No. 12, Guilin 541000, China

Abstract. With the rapid development of Internet of things technology, more and more attention has been paid to the security protection of personal information. This paper proposes an information encryption mechanism based on QR code to solve the problem of information leakage in data communication. The error correction mechanism of the QR code allows it to record information normally even if it is partially damaged. Taking advantage of this feature, this paper records secret information by changing limited data bits without destroying the original QR code. In addition, the secret sharing algorithm is introduced in this paper to divide the secret information into multiple parts for storage and transmission, and the original secret information can only be reproduced when all the information fragments are collected, further enhancing the security of information transmission. By combining the error correction mechanism of the QR code with the secret sharing algorithm, the secret information can be transmitted safely. The encryption mechanism can effectively reduce the suspicion of the attacker on the secret information, and has the advantages of large storage capacity and flexible storage.

Keywords: QR code · Information security · Secret sharing

1 Introduction

At present, the QR code as the information carrier of the Internet of Things perception layer has been widely used in the fields of payment and identity authentication with the development of the Internet of Things [1]. Considering the advantages of wide application of QR codes, low production cost, and simple production, it has begun to be used in the information security field. Long [2] and others analyzed the current attack methods related to QR codes, and proposed an encryption algorithm based on asymmetric cryptosystem to ensure the security of the QR code. Tao Sunjie [3] and others proposed an information transmission system based on QR code, which uses the QR code to encode the transmitted data to ensure the security of the transmitted information. Wu [4] Proposed a QR code information transmission mechanism based on information hiding technology, which uses information hiding technology to realize the secret transmission of information. Lin [5] then proposed that the information and

© Springer Nature Singapore Pte Ltd. 2020
Z. Zheng et al. (Eds.): BlockSys 2019, CCIS 1156, pp. 101–106, 2020.
https://doi.org/10.1007/978-981-15-2777-7_9

secret data can be split and transmitted through the QR code to ensure information security through the distributed system. Chow [6] further improved the secret sharing algorithm based on QR code through research.

Based on the current research, this paper proposes an information encryption transmission mechanism based on QR code. By combining the error correction mechanism of the QR code with the secret sharing algorithm, the encrypted information is hidden and transmitted securely without attracting the attention of the attacker.

2   Data Encryption Mechanism

The QR code has an error correction mechanism, which can effectively identify the QR code when it is damaged to a certain extent. Using this mechanism, some information bits of the QR code can be deliberately modified to hide secret information. Due to the protection of the error correction mechanism, the QR code containing the secret message is identical to the original QR code, thereby effectively protecting the secret information.

The secret sharing algorithm is an information transmission algorithm in the field of information security. By randomly dividing the secret information into n shares for transmission, each of the shares has no meaning and cannot restore the original secret information, and the original secret information can be restored only after having all the n pieces of information.

The QR code secret sharing mechanism proposed in this paper divides the secret message by segmenting it, then records it into the original meaningful QR code, and finally restores the information in the entire QR code. The basic steps are as follows:

- Step one: Give a secret message S
- Step two: Generate original QR code Cs1, Cs2, ..., Csn
- Step three: Divide the message S into S1, S2, ..., Sn
- Step four: Encode S1, S2, ..., Sn into Cs1, Cs2, ..., Csn, and generate a new QR code as Ch_1, Ch_2, ..., Chn
- Step five: Scan Ch_1, Ch_2, ..., Chn to determine whether the content is the same as Cs_1, Cs_2, ..., Csn
- Step six: Restore secret information

Among them, Csx and Chx are meaningful QR codes that can be recognized by the scanner normally, and the scanned information is the same.

3   Experimental Results and Analysis

This section will test the secret sharing mechanism proposed in the previous section, including the feasibility of the information mechanism and security. Through the experimental evaluation, the performance analysis of the mechanism in the above three aspects is obtained. This section will test the secret sharing mechanism proposed in the previous section, including the feasibility of the information mechanism, the amount of information carried, and security. Through the experimental evaluation, the performance analysis of the mechanism in the above three aspects is obtained.

3.1   Implementation of Information Confidentiality Mechanism

Figure 1 is an encryption process diagram through a QR code encryption mechanism, in which the experimental result is when the encrypted information is 7 bits.

Fig. 1. Experimental results comparison chart of 7 bit

In Fig. 1, (a)–(d) are original meaningful QR codes, (e)–(h) are corresponding to the secret coded QR code, and (i)–(l) are the difference between (a) and (e), (b) and (f), (c) and (g), (d) and (h), they are the result of the XOR. Taking (i) as an example, the white in (a) in which the white block indicates the same position in (i) becomes black in (e), and the opposite grey block indicates that it changes from black to white.

Scanning the QR code before and after encryption by the scanner can be found that the content before and after encryption is the same, indicating that the error correction mechanism is normal and not damaged. It realizes the shared transmission of secret messages without destroying the original normal QR code. The (i)–(l) is processed by the designed function, and the encrypted information G' is decrypted. By comparison, $G' = G$, the encryption and decryption is successful.

3.2   Information Quantity Experiment

In order to further enhance the security of the QR code, the changed QR code blocks are randomized during the experiment, that is, the encoded QR codes generated each time are different. Therefore, when the amount of encoded information is large, the changed blocks are increased, and the process of randomly distributing may cause some generated QR codes to be unreadable by the scanner. After experiments, it is possible that the amount of information generated by the randomness of the QR code is less than the theoretical value, and it may not be read. Figure 2 is an effect diagram in the case of different amounts of information.

In Fig. 2, in the case of 28 bit and 56 bit, there is no case where the QR code cannot be read. In the case of 84 bit and 112 bit, there is a probability of error. In the case of

Fig. 2. Different information volume renderings

120 bit, all the QR codes cannot be used. It is read normally. The experimental situation of 84 bit and 112 bit is shown in Fig. 3.

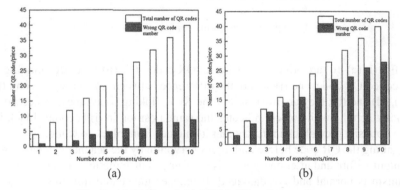

Fig. 3. (a) 84 bit and (b) 112 bit QR code encoding

Figure 3(a) is a diagram showing a case where a QR code is generated when the amount of data is 84 bits. As can be seen from the figure, due to the randomness of the encoding position, about one-quarter of the QR code cannot be scanned by the scanner after encoding. Read normally. Figure 3(b) shows that when the amount of data reaches 112 bits, it can be seen that nearly three-quarters of the QR code cannot be read normally.

Therefore, in order to guarantee the quality of the generated QR code, when the amount of secret information is large, the value of n should be considered, that is, the secret message is divided into more shares, and the amount of information allocated to each QR code is reduced. Or you can consider increasing the version of the encrypted QR code so that each QR code can encode more information. After the encryption and encoding are completed, the generated QR code should be scanned to ensure that it can be scanned normally.

3.3 Security Analysis

If the attacker has the relevant knowledge of the QR code and obtains it before and after the encoding, the version number of the QR code and the number of copies of the information are known by finding the difference between the two. In this case, the attacker can calculate the difference between the two. However, due to the randomness of the coding location, the attacker cannot know the order and meaning of these differences. Only brute force can be used. It is assumed that the version number of the encrypted QR code is 1, the number of copies is n, and the encrypted information is G bit. Then the amount of information allocated to each QR code is G/n, because the position information is not known, the possible ranking order is the full arrangement of the information amount, and the final crack is because the change of each position is not known to represent 1 or 0. The difficulty is 2 times the difficulty of the full arrangement. The final difficulty of deciphering is shown in Eq. (1).

$$p = \frac{1}{2^{\left(\frac{G}{n}+1\right)} \times n!} \tag{1}$$

It can be known from the Eq. (1) that when n is increased or G is increased, the deciphering probability can be lowered. When n and G take the minimum value, that is, $n = 1$, $G = 24$ bit, the deciphering probability p is 2.97×10^{-8}. This is the difficulty of fully arranging 24 bits, and it is also the stage with the highest probability of deciphering. In addition, when n is greater than or equal to 5 and G is greater than 50 bits, the probability of deciphering is almost zero. So even if the attacker obtains the version number of the QR code and n, it is impossible to decipher the encrypted message.

The number of information that can be corrected by the error correction mechanism of the QR code is limited. Since the encryption mechanism has modified a part of the information of the QR code, when the QR code is damaged again, it may not be completely repaired. Figure 4 is a result of adding salt and pepper noise and Gaussian noise to the encrypted QR code.

(a) Gaussian 0.3   (b) Gaussian 0.5   (c) Gaussian 0.8   (d) Gaussian 0.9   (e) Gaussian 1.0

(f) Salt and Pepper 5000   (g) Salt and Pepper 10000   (h) Salt and Pepper 20000   (i) Salt and Pepper 30000   (j) Salt and Pepper 40000

Fig. 4. Encrypted noise figure

The first line in the figure is Gaussian white noise, and the second line is salt and pepper noise. Experiments show that when the Gaussian white noise reaches the level of 1.0, the QR code cannot be recognized by the scanner and when the concentration of salt and pepper noise reaches 2000, the QR code also cannot be recognized normally. Experiments show that the information encryption mechanism has a certain influence on the error correction ability of the QR code, but it is enough to resist the wear and tear that the two-dimensional code may be subjected to during transmission.

4 Summary

This paper proposes a secure secret information encryption mechanism by combining the error correction mechanism of QR code with the secret sharing algorithm. This encryption mechanism utilizes the characteristics that the QR code changes part of the data and can still be read normally by the scanner, and the secret information is decomposed and hidden in the QR code. Because it is hidden in the normal QR code, this encryption mechanism is not easy to cause the suspicion of the attacker, and can effectively protect the secret information. It is confirmed by experiments that the encryption mechanism provided in this paper can flexibly store secret information, and it is very difficult to crack, and has the characteristics of large storage capacity and high security.

Acknowledgments. The research of this paper is supported by Natural Science Foundation of China (No: 61662017, No: 61262075, No: 61862019), Guangxi special fund project for innovation-driven development (Guangxi science AA1811009) and Guangxi key research and development plan (Guangxi science AB17195042), Guangxi Natural Science Foundation (Grantno: 2017GXNSFAA198223), we would like to extend our sincere gratitude to them.

References

1. Li, T., Liu Y., Tian Y.: A storage solution for massive IoT data based on NoSQL. In: 2012 IEEE International Conference on Green Computing and Communications (GreenCom), San Diego (2012)
2. Long, Q., Liu, X.H.: QR code encryption algorithm based on asymmetric cryptography. J. Chongqing Norm. Univ. (Nat. Sci.) **34**(03), 97–101 (2017)
3. Tao, S.J., Yu, T.: Design of data transmission system based on 2D code. Comput. Sci. **45**(S2), 597–600 (2018)
4. Wu, C.X., Wang, S.Y.: Two-dimensional code transfer system based on information hiding technology. Cyberspace Secur. **8**(06-07), 16–22 (2017)
5. Lin, P.Y.: Distributed secret sharing approach with cheater prevention based on QR code. IEEE Trans. Ind. Inform. **12**(1), 384–392 (2016)
6. Chow, Y.W., Susilo, W., Yang, G., Phillips, J.G., Pranata, I., Barmawi, A.M.: Exploiting the error correction mechanism in QR codes for secret sharing. In: Liu, J., Steinfeld, R. (eds.) ACISP 2016. LNCS, vol. 9722, pp. 409–425. Springer, Cham (2016). https://doi.org/10.1007/978-3-319-40253-6_25

Performance Optimization of Blockchain

Lightweight Image Segmentation Based Consensus Mechanism

Jianquan Ouyang[1,2](✉), Jiajun Yin[1,2], and Yuxiang Sun[1,2]

[1] College of Information Engineering, Xiangtan University, Xiangtan 411105, China
oyjq@xtu.edu.cn
[2] Key Laboratory of Intelligent Computing and Information Processing,
Ministry of Education, College of Information Engineering, Xiangtan University,
Xiangtan 411105, China

Abstract. Consensus mechanism is a fundamental technology of blockchain, ensuring the stability. The most popular consensus mechanism is proof-of-work mechanism. It attracts massive nodes through the distributed network and requires the nodes to generate nonces and hash them to accumulate workload. However, most of the generated nonces and hash values are meaningless and discarded. Such massive quantity of computational power are dedicated for nothing, which proves that the power are not used in an effective way. Thus, this paper proposes a neoteric MDL criterion of image segmentation based on an efficient chain code with Huffman coding and a novel consensus mechanism for blockchain using image segmentation with the proposed MDL criterion as the procedure of accumulating workload and generating nonces. The innovation points of this paper are: (a) it proposes a novel minimum description length model of pictures, which is applied to filtering the best segmentation of a picture; (b) it consummates the consensus mechanism with an image segmentation technology to replace the workload accumulating process, allowing nodes to segment images while mining blocks. The experimental results verified that blockchain nodes can segment images while mining blocks with this novel consensus mechanism, which makes full use of computational power.

Keywords: Consensus mechanism · Proof of work · Image segmentation · Minimum description length

1 Introduction

Recently, image process is quite popular, where image segmentation is required urgently by many other fields. Many industries demand the absence of image segmentation, such as analysis of medical images and satellite images. After collecting images, they should be accurately segmented and analyzed. Since the amount of the pictures is large and the contents of the pictures are complex, a lot of computational power should be devoted to this work. If there's a source to provide computational power, it will be helpful and beneficial and be of great significance to those fields which need image segmentation.

© Springer Nature Singapore Pte Ltd. 2020
Z. Zheng et al. (Eds.): BlockSys 2019, CCIS 1156, pp. 109–122, 2020.
https://doi.org/10.1007/978-981-15-2777-7_10

Therefore, we can combine the consensus mechanism with image segmentation, enable the nodes to segment images while mining blocks. A typical application scenario is as follow, the consensus mechanism offers an interface, which are connected to original image database and segmented image database. Clients who require the service of image segmentation are supposed to upload their images to the original image database. During the process of mining blocks, miners withdraw a random image from the original image database and segment it. After segmentation, the segmented image will be added to segmented image database. Clients are accessible to the segmented images with corresponding numbers or other vouchers. Under this application scenario, the gathered computational power are made full use, while the requirements of users are satisfied.

2 Related Work

2.1 State of the Art of Consensus Mechanism

Most of the consensus mechanisms currently used are based on the Proof of Work mechanism and the Proof of Stake mechanism. Proof of work can achieve block consistency [3], but its large amount of computational power is almost all used to do useless work, which leads to the waste of computing power. Billings proposed a proof of work mechanism based on the image of interest [4], which detects whether the image is a meaningless image while generating the block. The mechanism replaces the nonce generation part. In this process, nodes read the images and calculate their second degree entropies. For the images whose second degree entropies satisfy the specific requirements, the mechanism judges that it as an interesting image and reads the image content for encoding to generate a nonce. The workload proof mechanism utilizes computational resources to some extent, but its application scenarios are rare and simple.

In addition to the method of proof of work, there is a consensus mechanism based on proof of stake. Different from the proof of work, it allows nodes to participate in elections by investing in virtual resources, thus obtaining consensus from distributed networks [10]. It requires the node to invest a certain amount of digital currency on the new block as a voucher to participate in the generated block. The consensus mechanism will randomly assign the qualifications for verifying transactions and generating blocks based on the proportion of funds invested by each node. This approach to some extent stops the node from verifying fraudulent transactions, which will result in the loss of funds it invests. However, since the precondition of this method is that the node already has a certain wealth when it participates in the generation of the block, this method cannot be used at the beginning of the blockchain generation. Most consensus mechanisms that use the proof of stake approach also use the method of proof of work.

2.2 State of the Art of Image Segmentation

Region-based image segmentation is an important method of image segmentation. Lee proposed an image segmentation process based on the minimum description length [5]. The process uses a three-direction Freeman chain code [2] to describe the region boundaries. The picture is then encoded by region and the code length of the entire picture is calculated. Therefore, the minimum description length of the obtained image is different when the segmentation pattern is different. Then the segmentation pattern with the smallest minimum description length is selected as the optimal segmentation pattern. This image segmentation method is relatively mature, however, the model for calculating the minimum description length needs to be improved. It uses a three-direction Freeman chain code to describe the region boundary. This chain code uses one side of a pixel as the unit length, so the direction required to describe a single pixel at the boundary is 1–3. The use of such a chain code results in extra-long boundary direction chain and that the region of the same size are defined by direction chains of different length, which may affect the accuracy of the segmentation.

In addition, there are image segmentation methods based on deep learning. R-CNN is a typical deep learning framework. At first, an image is used as input, and regions of interest will be generated with certain proposal method. After that, every single region will be reshaped and passed to ConvNet. Convelutional Neural Network then extract the features of the regions before they are classified with SVMs. Eventually, the bounding boxes for each identified region will be predicted by using a bounding box regression [9]. As an improvement of traditional deep learning segmentation methods, Ronneberger proposed U-Net [8], a convolutional network for biomedical image segmentation. However, this method has strong specificity, which means a single model can only be used to segment a single type of image. If it is used in consensus mechanism, it will narrow the scope of application of consensus mechanism. In addition, the generation of a model involves a set of similar sample images for training, and the sample images need to be annotated in advance, that is to say, the segmentations of the images have to be given. In that case, the generation of the model still needs the participation of other segmentation algorithms.

3   Design of Image Segmentation Based Consensus Mechanism

3.1   Design of Procedure of Consensus Mechanism

Image segmentation based consensus mechanism are evolved from the proof of work mechanism. The difference is that nodes running this consensus mechanism accumulates workload by image segmentation process.

In order to apply the process of image segmentation to the process of Nonce generation, this paper replaces it with image filtering, image segmentation and image mapping.

Image segmentation consists of two parts: pre-segmentation and region merging. In pre-segmentation, the image will be split as much as possible into small regions. These areas will then be merged within several rounds until an optimal segmentation pattern that satisfies the requirement is generated.

After generating the segmentation image, the consensus mechanism will map the segmentation image to the data type required by the blockchain by formula computation or coding, and this value will participate as a nonce in the subsequent stages. The segmentation image is the result of pre-segmentation and region merging, and has the uniqueness and complexity of the source. Therefore, the nonce generated by the segmentation image map has the same characteristics. In this case, the cost of the attacker acquiring the same nonce is greatly increased, thereby enhancing the security of the blockchain.

An improved flowchart of the image segmentation based consensus mechanism is shown in Fig. 1:

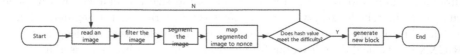

Fig. 1. Process of image segmentation based consensus mechanism

3.2 Image Segmentation

Minimum Description Length of Image. Image segmentation aims to finds the optimal segmentation pattern of an image, so we need an objective and accurate model to help us determine whether the current segmentation is the optimal segmentation. Lee proposed an image segmentation procedure based on minimum description length (MDL) [5], which belongs to the region-based image segmentation method. The minimum description length of the image is a result of calculating the required coding length according to the manner of dividing the region in the segmented image.

The calculation of the minimum description length of an image is as follows: The segmentation image contains a plurality of regions, each of which is defined as the average gray value of the pixels in its region and its boundary. The boundary is represented by a chain code, which includes a starting point and a direction chain. The minimum description length of an image can be defined as the sum of the code lengths of the four parts: the number of regions and the starting pixels, the chain codes, the average gray values of the regions, and the difference between the real data and the current model data, which can be expressed as a formula [5]:

$$L(y) = L(\hat{k}, startingpixels) + L(chains|\hat{k}, startingpixels)$$
$$+ L(\hat{\mu}|\hat{k}, startingpixels, chains) + L(y|\hat{k}, startingpixels, chains, \hat{\mu}) \tag{1}$$

where y is the gray value set of the original image (real data), $\hat{k}$ is an estimate of the total amount of regions, and $\hat{\mu}$ is an estimate of the regional average gray value. The same image is segmented in different ways, and the minimum description length is also different. By comparing the minimum description length of the images obtained by segmentation of these images, we can find an image segmentation pattern in which the minimum description length is the smallest, that is, optimal.

A Huffman Encoding Based Effective Chain Code. Chain code is a common method for describing shapes that can help reduce the amount of data needed to describe an image. Freeman chain code is a widely used chain code. Based on the Freeman chain code, Liu proposed an effective chain code based on Huffman coding [6], which defines eight directions, which are represented by C0–C7, representing eight angle (in the second column of Table 1 [6]).

The uniqueness of this chain code is that after each angle change, it re-determines the x-axis in the direction it is currently pointing. The advantage of this chain code is that the frequency of occurrence at large angles is significantly reduced (Fig. 2).

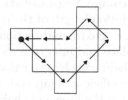

Fig. 2. Chain code Huffman encoding based

Table 1. Directions and corresponding angle movements

Direction	Angle movement
C_0	0°
C_1	45°
C_2	−45°
C_3	90°
C_4	−90°
C_5	135°
C_6	−135°
C_7	180°

By using the above-mentioned chain code to represent the regions of the segmented image, we derive the formula for calculating the total code length required for the chain codes of all regions in the segmented image:

We use $\{d_i = C_x\}$ to indicate the proposition: the i-th direction on the chain code is C_x. If this proposition is true, then $H_{\{d_i=C_x\}} = 1$; otherwise, $H_{\{d_i=C_x\}} = 0$.

Using r_j to represent the chain code length of region j, then the code length required for the chain codes of all regions in the image is:

$$NFCH = \sum_{j=1}^{\hat{k}} \sum_{i=1}^{r_j} (H_{\{d_i=C_0\}} + 2H_{\{d_i=C_1\}} + 3H_{\{d_i=C_2\}} + 4H_{\{d_i=C_3\}} \tag{2}$$
$$+ 5H_{\{d_i=C_4\}} + 6H_{\{d_i=C_5\}} + 7H_{\{d_i=C_6\}} + 7H_{\{d_i=C_7\}})$$

Considering the efficiency of the actual operation, we calculate the average length of codes required for a single direction based on the occurrence probabilities of the angle transformation to be 1.97, so the formula can be simplified as:

$$NFCH = 1.97 \sum_{j=1}^{\hat{k}} r_j \tag{3}$$

A Novel MDL Model of Image Segmentation. In [5], Lee obtained the formula of the minimum description length of the image by using the calculation formula of the encoding length of the three-direction Freeman chain code and the formula of Rissanen [7] to replace and integrate the four parts of the formula 1.

In this paper, we use the chain code length calculation formula (Eq. 3) which has just been derived from the efficient chain code based on Huffman coding to replace the calculation formula of the Freeman chain code length. The new MDL calculation model is as follow:

$$MDL(\hat{k}, \hat{\Omega}) = \hat{k} \log n + 1.97 \sum_{j=1}^{\hat{k}} r_j + \frac{1}{2} \sum_{j=1}^{\hat{k}} \log area_j + \frac{n}{2} \log(\frac{RSS_{\hat{k}}}{n}) \tag{4}$$

In this equation, n represents the total number of pixels; $\hat{\Omega}$ represents a set of regions; a_j represents the area (number of pixels) of the region j, $RSS_{\hat{k}}$ is the sum of squared residuals, $RSS_{\hat{k}} = \sum_{i=1}^{n}(y_i - \hat{f}_i)$ [5], where y_i is the gray value of the pixel i, $\hat{f}_i$ is the average gray value of the region where the pixel i is located.

Pre-segmentation. In order to find the optimal segmentation pattern of the image, it is necessary to find all possible segmentation patterns of the image as much as possible to ensure that the optimal segmentation is not missed. To this end, we should first divide the image into many regions within a reasonable range, which is pre-segmentation. The prototype of the pre-segmentation algorithm used in this paper is the seed growth algorithm [11].

However, since the seed growth algorithm sets the seed according to the fixed distance instead of setting it according to the size of the region, too many seeds are often set in the same region, resulting in the same region being divided into multiple sub-regions, which burdens the merging. Therefore, on the basis of the original algorithm, in order to improve the efficiency of image segmentation, this paper has improved the seed growth algorithm: remove the homogenous seeds in the stage of setting seeds. If the difference of the average gray values between a seed and its neighbor is less than the threshold, then the seed is a homogeneous seed and should be removed. To remove a homogeneous seed is to remove the seed from the seed list and releases the pixels it occupies.

The procedure of pre-segmentation is as follows:

(1) converting an image into a grayscale image;
(2) setting seeds (pixel blocks) at regular intervals in the image;
(3) marking seeds whose grey value difference between its maximum gray value pixel and minimum gray value pixel greater than a threshold as an invalid seed;
(4) traverse each valid seed, take the nearest non-homogeneous seed above and seed left, calculate the difference of the average gray value between the current seed and these two seeds, if one of the average gray values is less than the threshold, mark the current Seeds are homogenous seeds. It is worth noting that if the non-homogeneous seed closest to the current seed is an invalid seed, the process of finding homogenous seed of the current seed is skipped;
(5) remove all irrational seeds and homogenous seeds;
(6) traverse all the seeds, calculate the difference between the gray values of the pixels around the seed and its average gray value. If the difference is less than the threshold we set, the pixel will be added to the seed. The traversal of the seed will loop until no more pixels can be allocated. At this point, the seed grows into a region.
(7) pre-segmentation is generated by allocating all the remaining pixels to the region of the adjacent regions whose difference between the gray values is the smallest.

Merging. After the pre-segmentation is complete, we need to merge the regions one by one and generate all possible segmentation patterns to find the optimal segmentation pattern.

The selection of the optimal segmentation requires the minimum description length (MDL) model established in above. The MDL values are calculated after each round of merging until a smaller MDL value is not generated. Then, the segmentation pattern with the smallest MDL value is the optimal segmentation pattern.

The process of merging is as follows:

(1) use the pre-segmentation result as the initial segmentation;
(2) calculate the MDL value of the initial segmentation;
(3) generate an array of adjacent regions;
(4) according to the adjacent region table, all adjacent regions are pre-merged, and the MDL value is calculated basing on the segmentation pattern obtained after each time of pre-merging. If the current MDL value is the smallest at present, the regions pre-merged will be recorded;

(5) after pre-merging, the recorded pre-merged regions with which the minimum MDL value is obtained will be merged practically to generate a new segmentation pattern as the next initial segmentation. The whole process will be re-executed from (2) with the new initial segmentation. This process do not end until that a segmentation pattern with a smaller MDL value is not generated.
(6) get the optimal segmentation.

3.3 Mapping

After getting the segmented image, we need to convert it into a nonce of the data type required by the blockchain. For the blockchains like bitcoin whose consensus mechanism uses the string form nonce, the content of the segmented image is directly encoded as a nonce.

For the consensus mechanism using the integer type of nonce, the segmented images will be mapped as follows: calculate the MDL value of the segmented image;

> sum the gray values of all pixels of the segmented image;
> multiply the MDL value by the sum of the gray values;
> add current time stamp to the result above.

Formulated as:

$$Nonce = MDL \ of \ thesegmentedimage$$
$$* \ sum \ of \ the \ grey \ values \ of \ the \ segmented \ image \quad (5)$$
$$+ \ timestamp$$

3.4 Filtering

In order to prevent the system from being attacked by identical images, we need to filter the images we collect. In the image segmentation based consensus mechanism, if an attacker wants to attack the system, it is necessary to use a nonce generated by a certain image to repeatedly generate a block, thereby colliding with other blocks that use the same image to generate the same nonce to replace it. However, in general, two identical images are almost impossible to exist. But there is an exception that may make this type of attack a success, and that is blank images. The possibility of acquiring a blank image due to human or system factors cannot be excluded when the image is acquired, and the blank image is not unique, and the gray values of each pixel are completely the same, which gives the attacker an opportunity to take advantage of. Therefore, the image segmentation based consensus mechanism will filter the images before pre-segmentation, and exclude blank images in the library to avoid security risks.

This article uses the gray level co-occurrence matrix to solve this problem. The gray level co-occurrence matrix is used to judge the texture features of the image by counting the joint distribution of two pixels in the image separated by a certain distance on the same picture [1]. Through the gray level co-occurrence matrix, the angular second moment, contrast, correlation and entropy of the image can be calculated separately. In this paper, image suspiciousness is defined as the sum of angular second moment, contrast, correlation and entropy.

First, any blank image can be used to calculate the suspiciousness through the gray level co-occurrence matrix, which is then used as a criterion for judging the blank image. After each image is read, the consensus mechanism based on image segmentation will calculate the suspiciousness of the image. If the suspiciousness of the image is consistent with the standard, the image will be removed and the next image will be read.

4 Experimental Results

4.1 Pre-segmentation Experiment

The experimental object of the pre-segmentation experiment is the image of color patch shown in Fig. 3, and the seed growth algorithm before and after the improvement proposed in above are used for comparative experiments. The experimental parameters are configured as follows:

Fig. 3. Image of color patch

1. The image parameters are shown in Table 2:
2. The seed parameters are shown in Table 3:

Figure 4 shows the experimental results of the pre-segmentation.

Table 2. Image parameters

Image size	Image settings	Image type	Gray value range
80 * 80	ANTIALIAS	L-shaped grayscale image	0–255

Table 3. Seed parameters

Seed size	Seed interval	Seed distribution	Seed growth threshold
2 * 2	4	Horizontal and vertical	10

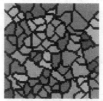

(a) Seed growth algorithm before improvement

(b) Improved seed growth algorithm

Fig. 4. Pre-segmentations of color patch image

It can be seen that the number of regions in the pre-segmentation obtained by using the not improved algorithm in Fig. 4(a) is much more than the improved algorithm in Fig. 4(b).

We conducted a merging test on the two pre-segmentation results, and the optimal segmentation results are the same. From this we can draw two conclusions: (1) the removal of homogenous seeds does not affect the results of optimal segmentation; (2) the extra segmented regions of Fig. 4(a) need to be merged.

From this we can judge that the rounds of merging required will increase for pre-segmentation generated by the not improved seed growth algorithm, which will increase the burden of region merging and drag down the efficiency of the entire system. Figure 4(b) is generated by the improved seed growth algorithm. Since the homogenous seeds are removed, the growth space for each seed is expanded, so that more homogeneous pixels can be added to the same region. In that case, the burden of region merging is reduced while ensuring that the optimal segmentation results are not affected.

Table 4 shows the length of time required to find the optimal segmentation pattern using the pre-segmentation results shown in Fig. 4(a) and (b), respectively. It can be clearly seen that the length of time required to perform the region merging with the pre-segmentation result in Fig. 4(b) to generate the optimal segmentation is less than one-seventh of that in Fig. 4(a), and the efficiency is significantly improved.

Table 4. Length of time required to find the optimal segmentation with pre-segmentation results obtained by two algorithms

Method	Seed growth algorithm	Improved seed growth algorithm
Length of time (minutes)	112	15

4.2 Mining with Image Segmentation Based Consensus Mechanism

This section will apply the image segmentation based consensus mechanism on the simplified Bitcoin blockchain and the simplified Ethereum.

Process and Parameters. The simplified version of Ethereum is modified from Jake Billings' simplified version of the Bitcoin blockchain [4]. The simplified Bitcoin blockchain we used in experiments is also modified from Jake Billings' simplified Bitcoin blockchain [4]. Because the interesting image based consensus mechanism is simple, the speed of generating nonce is faster than the image segmentation based consensus mechanism, so the difficulty for the image segmentation based consensus mechanism and the interesting image based consensus mechanism is set to 0 and 1 respectively to balance the speed of generating blocks (Table 5).

Table 5. Difficulty settings

Consensus mechanism	Difficulty
Image segmentation consensus mechanism	0
Interesting image based consensus mechanism	1

Function Test. Table 6 shows the results of the consensus mechanism based on image segmentation and the generation of blocks on the simplified Bitcoin blockchain based on the consensus mechanism of the image of interest. It can be seen that the consensus mechanism based on image segmentation can generate blocks on the simplified bitcoin blockchain as well as the consensus mechanism based on the image of interest.

Table 6. The results of two consensus mechanisms mining blocks on the simplified version of Bitcoin blockchain

Image	Generated Block
	Interesting image based consensus mechanism: ————Block 0———— Nonce 0x40_1VBORw0KGgoAAAANSUhEUgAAAAFAAAABQCAIAAABc2X6AAAgXU1EQVR4nF2cyW8b6dHGe2M32dwpLiJ1bbYYke9YYSBAkgyTIKZcAOeSefzY. prev None Data ———— genesis ———— Hash 0x20_dxcm2scSvhwyngy2omsyayx5jo4iyalnqxvzdl7hwhj2wdmrrikkp7x2xb6byytueu3ca4qbni3uiej6ok6swmrfwmbuksamdjwuhaa= ————End Block———— **Image segmentation based consensus mechanism:** ————Block 0———— Nonce 0x40_1VBORw0KGgoAAAANSUhEUgAAAAFAAAABQCAIAAABc2X6AAAf/U1EQVR4nJ1caXBWZ/U/d7/vlg0Cpi1U1gH9onWUIiFASEIWAiEJYV/Ko1xhSUI prev None Data ———— genesis ———— Hash 0x20_u316ac22fleetssg2rlkoy3h36pixz737dz4dgsgw3333bq1wlwx3aygopki43yqstpbnl2hiwzrgpkmhazlcitwhagk267ervscnqi= ————End Block———— chain start:<blockchain.Block instance at 0x11134f2d8>chain end

Table 6 and Fig. 5 show the performance of mining blocks with image segmentation based consensus mechanism and the interesting image based consensus mechanism on the simplified Bitcoin blockchain. The performance of the image segmentation based consensus mechanism on the simplified version of Bitcoin is similar to that on the simplified version of Ethereum. In contrast, for the interesting image based consensus mechanism, (1) the time of generating the blocks is irregular and contingent; (2) (on the same difficulty) the difference between the shortest generation time (0.3 min) and the longest generation time in the test (16 min) is more than 50 times. In this case, it is not accurate to estimate the nodes' workload by difficulty.

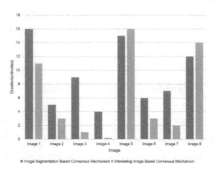

Fig. 5. Length of Block generation (simplified version of Ethereum)

4.3 Discussion

The following is a discussion of the advantages and the disadvantages of the image segmentation and consensus mechanism:

(1) In terms of image segmentation:
  (a) The image segmentation method based on region segmentation is used to expand the application scenario of the consensus mechanism; an improved seed growth algorithm is used, which comparing with the traditional seed growth algorithm, in the early stage of seeds setting, removed the homogenous seeds, which reduces the burden of merging and improves the efficiency of the image segmentation.
  (b) Using a new minimum description length calculation model, compared to Thomas's minimum description length model, which uses a high-efficiency chain code based on Huffman coding, which is more accurate when calculating the minimum description length of the segmented image to help finding a better image segmentation pattern;
(2) In terms of consensus mechanism:
  (a) Combining image segmentation with consensus mechanism to make up for the deficiencies of the proof of work mechanism, making rational use of the lost computational power to provide assistance in fields where there is a need for image segmentation;

(b) Compared with Jake Billings' consensus mechanism, the consensus mechanism uses the segmented images instead of the original images for nonce mapping. Due to the uniqueness and complexity of the segmented image source, the attack cost is greatly improved, thus improving the safety of consensus mechanism.

5 Conclusion

This paper proposes a novel consensus mechanism based on image segmentation. The consensus mechanism will make rational use of the computational power that the distributed network attracts, and replace the meaningless work during mining with a meaningful image segmentation process. The standard model for screening the optimal segmentation in this paper is the MDL model, which uses a chain code based on Huffman coding. In the experimental part, the consensus mechanism is applied to the simplified versions of the blockchain. The experimental results show that the blockchains based on this consensus mechanism perform effectively. The contrast experiment shows that this consensus mechanism can accurately segment the images. In addition, the consensus mechanism ensures the security of the blockchain and is able to contribute to the image processing field.

Acknowledgments. This research was supported by Key Projects of the Ministry of Science and Technology of the People's Republic of China (2018AAA0102301), CERNET Innovation Project (NGII20170715), Project of Hunan Provincial Science and Technology Department (2017SK2405).

References

1. Feng, J.H., Yang, Y.J.: A research on extracting texture characteristics basing on grey level co-occurrence matrix, vol. 2007, no. 3, pp. 19–22 (2007)
2. Freeman, H.: Computer processing of line-drawing images. PACM Comput. Surv. **6**(1), 57–97 (1974)
3. Han, X., Liu, Y.M.: A research on consensus mechanism in blockchain. Inf. Internet Secur. **2017**(9), 147–152 (2017)
4. Billings, J.: Image-based proof of work algorithm for the incentivization of blockchain archival of interesting images (2017)
5. Lee, T.M.: A minimum description length-based image segmentation procedure, and its comparison with a cross-validation-based segmentation procedure. J. Am. Stat. Assoc. **95**(449), 12 (2000)
6. Liu, Y.K., Zalik, B.: An efficient chain code with Huffman coding. Pattern Recognit. **38**(4), 553–557 (2005)
7. Rissanen, J.: Stochastic Complexity in Statistical Inquiry, p. 188. World Scientific, Singapore (1989)
8. Ronneberger, O., Fischer, P., Brox, T.: U-Net: convolutional networks for biomedical image segmentation (2015)
9. Sharma, P.: DA Step-by-Step Introduction to the Basic Object Detection Algorithms (Part 1) (2018)

10. Li, W., Andreina, S., Bohli, J.-M., Karame, G.: Securing proof-of-stake blockchain protocols. In: Garcia-Alfaro, J., Navarro-Arribas, G., Hartenstein, H., Herrera-Joancomartí, J. (eds.) ESORICS/DPM/CBT -2017. LNCS, vol. 10436, pp. 297–315. Springer, Cham (2017). https://doi.org/10.1007/978-3-319-67816-0_17
11. Wang, Y.H.: Tutorial: image segmentation. Graduate Institute of Communication Engineering (2010)

BIT Problem: Is There a Trade-off in the Performances of Blockchain Systems?

Shuangfeng Zhang, Yuan Liu$^{(\boxtimes)}$, and Xingren Chen

Software College, Northeastern University, Shenyang 110169, China
liuyuan@swc.neu.edu.cn

Abstract. Blockchain technology, as a revolutionary concept, born with Bitcoin, is triggering the start of a new era on information. It is generally recognized that the blockchain-based systems achieve high security in the process of information sharing in a distributed network, at the cost of low efficiency in terms of data throughput or high costs in consuming computational resources. A natural question we are interested in is whether there exists a trade-off principle between different performances of a blockchain system, which is also regarded as *blockchain impossibility triangle* (BIT) problem. In this paper, we propose an analysis method which can be used to verify the existence of the BIT. Our analysis method is composed of two layers. In the first layer the basic and core attributes are abstracted by building a consensus model, and in the second layer the analysis approach is designed to verify the existence of a BIT. Specifically, in the first layer, we firstly define a leaderless consensus model to quantitatively abstract the basic parameters in the process of system consensus, then three core attributes are justified to serve as the three vertices of the discussed triangle problem, namely security, cost, and efficiency. Based on the core attributes, we propose the credibility metric which measures the difficulty of achieving credible consensus for a given blockchain system. In the second layer, we analyze the existence of BIT, where we have demonstrated the conditions that a BIT exists and the conditions that the triangle does not exist. Finally, the proposed analysis method is applied in analyzing PoW based blockchain systems, where we have shown that there is no BIT problem in PoW based systems. Furthermore, the proposed analysis method can also help the blockchain developers in finding the promising directions of a new blockchain consensus mechanism.

Keywords: Blockchain · Impossibility triangle · Analysis method · Consensus mechanism · Security

1 Introduction

Blockchain is a secured and distributed ledger to record and track information without a centralized authority or a trusted third party. With its promising

© Springer Nature Singapore Pte Ltd. 2020
Z. Zheng et al. (Eds.): BlockSys 2019, CCIS 1156, pp. 123–136, 2020.
https://doi.org/10.1007/978-981-15-2777-7_11

features, including decentralization, traceability, non-temperability, and transparency, the blockchain technology has attracted tremendous attentions in various fields, such as finance [19], healthcare [12], security services [14], Internet of things [1,4] and so on.

Although blockchain technology seems to have unlimited prospects in the last decade (since 2008), blockchain-based applications have been imposed with many challenging concerns in realistic environments. These concerns focus on the system performance on the aspects of transaction confirmation efficiency (or transaction per second TPS), security against complex adversary attacks [6], costs in energy and incentives, and scalability in large-scaled distributed systems. Researchers have studied and tried to improve every aspect, but there still no well accepted and satisfactory evaluation metric to analyze and verify the performance of a blockchain-based system. Meanwhile, in a generalized distributed data storage system, the CAP theorem [2] has been proved to be consistent with the FLP impossibility triangle, implying that there exists a balance or trade-off between consistency(C) and availability(A) in the presence of a network partition tolerance(P). Regarding any blockchain-based system, the FLP or CAP principle should be applicable, and there is a trade-off among security (logically corresponding with consistency), scalability (logically corresponding with consistency availability), and decentralization (logically corresponding with consistency partition-tolerant). In this paper, instead of breaking through the impossible triangles, we aim to discuss the most three concerned performances of a blockchain consensus protocol instead of the whole blockchain system, namely efficiency, security, and cost, to study whether there always exists conflicts in improving each aspect. We propose an evaluation method to study the relationship of these three performance aspects, which is also referred to as blockchain impossibility triangle problem (BIT). We have made the following contributions to the state-of-the-art.

- A two-layer evaluation framework is proposed to formalize, abstract, and analysis the attributes of blockchain consensus protocols.
- We have proposed an analytical metric to justify the existence of the typical and special BIT.
- The existence of BIT in PoW based blockchain systems has been studied to demonstrate the effectiveness of the proposed evaluation method, which indicates the future improvement directions in developing a new PoW consensus mechanism.
- Three typical consensus mechanisms are comparatively analyzed based on the proposed analysis method.

The rest of this paper is organized as follows. We briefly introduce the background of this work in Sect. 2. In Sect. 3, we describe the proposed analysis method. The demonstration and application of the proposed method is presented in Sect. 4, followed by the conclusions in Sect. 5.

2   Related Work

In the past decade, there have been many studies on the performance analysis of blockchain systems. These studies are mainly focusing on security, efficiency, and cost.

2.1   Security of Blockchain

Byzantine Fault-Tolerance in Blockchain. Byzantine fault-tolerant algorithms have been studied for several decades in synchronous and asynchronous systems. Especially, the latter case satisfies the practical applications [3], e.g. Internet of the things (IoT), blockchain-based p2p systems. In a blockchain system, the consensus achieved among the untrustworthy entities is also called as the Byzantine general problem [7]. This problem describes a scenario of information transmission and confirmation. During the period of the Eastern Roman Empire, several confederate generals who could only rely on messengers to convey information among castles needed to make unified attacks or withdrawal orders. Meanwhile, they also need to prevent themselves from being deceived and confused by traitors. In this scenario, whether the correct instructions can be achieved depends on the proportion of traitors among generals, and this proportion is also used to evaluate the security level of a system towards tolerating Byzantine faults. For blockchain systems, malicious or invalid nodes are the betrayers and the ratio of these nodes over the total number of nodes reflects the tolerance of the system against malicious and invalid nodes. If the number of malicious nodes in the blockchain system exceeds this ratio, the blockchain system may not work properly. The typical consensus algorithms against Byzantine fault-tolerance have been analyzed in [18], where their Byzantine fault-tolerance are quantitatively compared.

Other Security Issues in Blockchain. There are other types of security issues in blockchain [8,18], for example, selfish mining attack [5,15], long delay attack [17], balance attack [11], etc.

2.2   Efficiency in BlockChain

The efficiency of a blockchain system is often discussed with the scalability issue [16,19]. The core function of the system is to generate consensus blocks to record information exchanges among the distributed nodes. For different blockchain systems, the ways of achieving consensus blocks are different. However, the basic data unit is generally same, i.e. transactions. Therefore, in order to measure the data throughput of a blockchain system, transactions per second (TPS) is usually utilized. Bitcoin is restricted to 7 transactions per second, which is incapable of dealing with most of the realistic trading environments [10].

2.3   Cost in BlockChain

Cost in a blockchain system refers to the resources consumed in executing consensus mining algorithms. The typical representative is proof of work (PoW) [10] in Bitcoin, where the process of mining is to calculate a hash with a guessed nonce as input and the winner is the node whose hash value satisfies a difficulty condition (e.g. started with a certain number of zeros). The motivation of utilizing the hash algorithm is that a hash function is difficult to calculate but easy to be verified. Another popular consensus algorithm applies stakes instead of computational resources to achieve the consensus, such as Proof of stake (PoS). Some other algorithms consume other kinds of resources instead of computing power or stakes, such as proof of space (PoSpc) [13].

Apart from the cost consumed by the blockchain consensus algorithm, new nodes in the blockchain system are also imposed on additional burdens to join the network, which is referred as the extensiveness cost. For consensus algorithms such as PoS, due to the high complexity of consensus validation time, the extensiveness cost increase rapidly when the node number reaches a certain threshold.

3   Analysis Method

The analysis method will be divided into two layers. In the first layer, we will abstract the basic attributes and core attributes to describe the performance of a blockchain system. To well understand each attribute, we design a consensus model based consensus process, where the attributes impacting the consensus process are defined and quantified. In the second layer, the abstracted core attributes are analyzed to verify the existence of general impossibility triangle (BIT) and special triangles.

3.1   The First Layer: Consensus Model and Attribute Abstraction

First of all, a blockchain system can be theoretically described as a multi-agent system model, where each agent communicates with its neighbors and is controlled in a distributed manner to achieve a collective group decision. It is also regarded as a leaderless consensus problem [9]. Specifically, suppose there are n distributed agents, and they are in a leaderless model. Each agent has a replica which is an order of transaction records. The network composed by these agents can be described as a directed graph $\mathcal{G}: (\mathcal{V}, \mathcal{E})$, where $\mathcal{V} = \{1, ..., n\}$ denotes the agent set and $\mathcal{E} = \{(i, j)\}$ is the directed link among the agents. If agent j can obtain information from agent i(but not necessarily vice verse), then $(i, j) \in \mathcal{E}$, and we also call that agent i is a neighbor of agent j. We use $\mathcal{N}_j$ to denote the neighbor set of agent j. A directed path is a serial of connected edges in form of $(1, 2), (2, 3), \dots (n - 1, n)$. A directed graph has a directed spanning tree if there exists at least an agent that has directed paths to all other agents.

Consensus Process Model. All the agents have a chance to meet at the end of each predefined period T, where the agents can exchange their opinions or information with their neighbors, targeting at reaching an agreement on the replica state $D = [d_0, d_1, ..., d_m]$ on the transaction order. By the end of each period, their replicas are updated according to their final decision. The decision of these agents can be achieved in two ways. In the first way, a leader is elected and all the other agents follow to the leader, and the leader proposes an order which will be updated to all the agents, e.g. PoW, PoS. In the second way, each agent communicates with other agents by proposing and voting for the final decision, e.g. BFT.

Remark 1. A consensus decision can be achievable only when the majority is reliable.

The decision result of the meet can be achieved through voting or any deterministic algorithm. Usually, the result is determined by the principle of the majority. For less than 50% of the selection standards, there may be more than two reasonable results happening at the same time. Therefore the necessary condition of a consensus decision to be achieved is that the majority (>50% in proportion) is reliable, indicating that the upper bound of (Byzantine) fault tolerance is 50%.

Actually, the meeting model is an abstraction of the consensus process of the blockchain system. We further divide the operation process into three stages: preparation, execution, and confirmation, as shown in Fig. 1. Firstly, in the stage of preparation, for security reasons, the system needs to collect the proof of the node validity. Only the nodes having submitted the "proof" and passing the *credibility standard* verification, can executive the consensus step. In the second stage, the consensus results are achieved, and in the third stage, the consensus results are to be *propagation* to all other nodes in the network for confirmation.

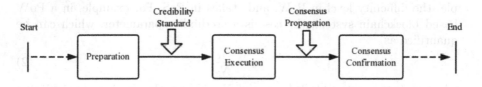

Fig. 1. The description of a general consensus process

Definition 1 (Credibility Standard). *A verifiable standard, which has been accepted by all the distributed and leaderless nodes, is regarded as a credibility standard. If a node(s) has achieved this standard, the node (nodes) is able to lead the consensus process.*

For example, the credibility standard in Bitcoin is the guessed nonce that satisfies the difficulty requirement. In reality, the distributed nodes need to consume a certain amount of resources (e.g. time, effort) to obtain the credibility standard. For a blockchain system, the credibility standard should be achieved within a certain time bound which determines the efficiency of transaction confirmation, which further determines the data throughput per unit time. Therefore, the difficulty of obtaining credibility directly affects the performance of blockchain systems.

In our model, the throughput of a system is quantitatively measured as follows.

$$e_b = \frac{N_b}{P + E + C} \tag{1}$$

where N_b is the transaction numbers in a block, and P, E, C are the required time of the consensus process taking in preparation, execution, and confirmation stages, respectively.

Basic Attributes of Blockchain. Based on the analysis above, we have abstractly describe the consensus process into three steps. To evaluate the performance of blockchain systems, some parameters impacting the process should be analyzed, for example, network status, consensus reach rate, and consensus confirmation rate, etc. We further classify all these parameters into three categories: credibility parameters, consensus parameters, and network parameters. Since all these parameters directly influence the performance of a blockchain system, we call them as the basic attributes of a blockchain system.

- **Credibility Parameters**: In the process of analyzing the credibility standard, we find that for different algorithms, the meaning of the credibility standard could be different. For PoW, for example, the difficulty of obtaining credibility is related to the difficulty of guessing a nonce. For POS, credibility is related to its stake. These parameters refer to the necessary factors of obtaining credibility standard in blockchain consensus algorithm, for example, the difficulty level in PoW, and stakes in PoS. For example, in a PoW based blockchain system, the cost is a credibility parameter, which can be quantified as

$$c_b = \frac{N_c}{N_b} \tag{2}$$

where c_b is the cost of blockchain, and N_c, N_b, are the number of calculation operations to generate a block and the number of transactions contained in a block.

- **Consensus Parameters**: The parameters set in the stage of the consensus execution, such as the false tolerance. For the blockchain system, there is a limit on the number of untrusted nodes that the consensus process operates normally. Once beyond this limit, the blockchain system will collapse. We define this attribute as Byzantine tolerance as the ratio of the number of failed nodes to the total number of nodes.

$$s_b = \frac{N_f}{N_a} \tag{3}$$

where s_b is the security of blockchain, and N_f, N_a, are the number of faulty nodes and the total number of nodes.

- **Network Parameters**: These parameters are usually related to real physical conditions such as the number of the nodes, bandwidth, transmission delay, etc. We usually set them as a constant in the analysis process.
- **Block Parameters**: These parameters refer to the settings for the block, such as block size, block rewards.

The basic parameters of blockchain will affect data throughput, security, and cost of blockchain, which are to be abstracted as the core attributes of a blockchain system.

Core Attributes of Blockchain. Core attributes are referred to as sets of basic attributes of blockchains. The core attributes in our model include security, efficiency, and cost. These attributes are the most concerned blockchain performance attributes, which are to be discussed in the triangle impossibility analysis in the next layer of our model.

(1) Security **S**

In a blockchain system, the construction of trust and cooperation are commonly happening among the distributed nodes. Initially, nodes in the blockchain systems are in an uncertain state instead of a trusted state. It is hard to justify whether a node will maliciously publish messages (DDOS) or maliciously use accounting rights (double spending) or cannot reply messages timely (unavailability). This is a more common status rather than the ideal cooperative state in distributed systems. Therefore, the security threats should be considered in the security attribute. We then denote a subset of basic parameters as the first core attribute: security.

$$\mathbf{S} = \{S_p, S_e, S_c, S_b\} \tag{4}$$

where S_p, S_e, S_c, S_b are credibility, consensus, network, and block parameters which affect security. It is worthy to note that $s_b \in S_e$.

(2) Cost **C**

Similarly, we also denote the cost core attribute **C** as a set of basic attributes in credibility, consensus, network, and block aspects.

$$\mathbf{C} = \{C_p, C_e, C_c, C_b\} \tag{5}$$

where the above-defined $c_c \in C_p$.

(3) Efficiency **E**

Furthermore, we denote the third core attribute **E** as a set of basic attributes in credibility, consensus, network and block aspects.

$$E = \{E_p, E_e, E_c, E_b\} \tag{6}$$

where $e_b \in E_b$.

The relationships of the credibility standard and the three core attributes are described as in Fig. 2. The three core attributes serve to reach the credibility standard. The three core attributes may have strong relationships as the three sets intersect with each other.

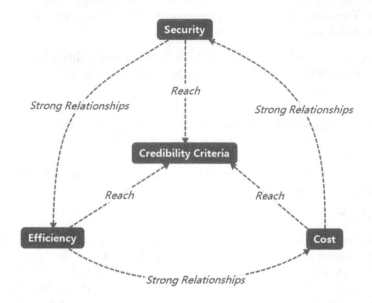

Fig. 2. The relationships among three attributes and credibility criteria

3.2   Second Layer: BIT Analysis

In the first layer of the analysis method, we have formalized the core attributes which are composed of the corresponding basic parameters. In the second layer, we will use these concepts to analyze the blockchain impossibility triangle problem. The analysis is based on determining the intersection of these core attributes.

If the impossibility triangle does exist, there is a certain displacement relationship between the three core attributes. Based on the analysis above, we know the three attributes are determined by one or more basic attributes. If the displacement relationship exists, it will extend to the displacement between basic attributes. On the contrary, if there is no intersection between the three sets, there is no impossibility triangle.

The intersected elements in the core attributes are not enough to determine the specific relationships among the core attributes. It is also necessary to quantitatively justify the improvement or deduction influence of these intersected elements to the three core attributes. The improvements of three core attributes are represented by **S+**, **E+**, **C+**, and the deductions of core attributes are represented by **S−**, **E−**, **C−**, respectively.

There is an obvious problem to use addition and subtraction signs to represent the improvement or deduction of core attributes. Usually, the impossibility triangles in a blockchain system refers to the condition that there are conflicts in promoting all the three attributes simultaneously. We then further refine the meaning of promotion when it comes to the discussed core attributes. For security, improving security means improving the performance of the system against attacks, denoted as a positive improvement. For efficiency, improving efficiency usually means increased data throughput. Therefore, improving efficiency also means improving the performance of the system in executing data storage, which is a positive change. For the aspect of cost, it is a common sense that improving costs means reducing cost value rather than increasing the value. Therefore, to avoid confusion, we define the element $\mathbf{C}+$ as the deduction of cost. Similarly, $\mathbf{C}-$ represents increased cost effect.

Impossibility Triangle Does Not Exist. There are two kinds of situations where the impossibility triangle cannot exist.

(1) BIT Not Existence Condition 1

The first case is that there is no intersection between the three core attributes of blockchain. In this case, the promotion or deduction of one core attribute alone will not have any impacts on the other two core attributes.

Remark 2. The impossibility triangle does not exist, when the following condition is true:

$$\mathbf{S} \cap \mathbf{E} \cap \mathbf{C} = \emptyset \tag{7}$$

(2) BIT Not Existence Condition 2

The second case is that although the core attribute sets of blockchain intersect $\mathbf{S} \cap \mathbf{E} \cap \mathbf{C} = \mathbf{X} \neq \emptyset$. However, when improving the basic attribute in the intersected set, the three core attributes rise or fall at the same time. This is the most ideal case, that is, only optimizing some basic attributes of blockchain can improve the overall performance of the blockchain system.

Remark 3. The impossibility triangle does not exist, when the elements in the intersected set $\mathbf{X} = \mathbf{S} \cap \mathbf{E} \cap \mathbf{C} \neq \emptyset$ lead consistent improvement or deduction effect to the three core attributes.

Special Impossibility Triangle. In a general blockchain system, there may be cases where a basic parameter is in two of the three core attributes. For this special case, which cannot be triangulated, we call it a *special impossibility triangle*.

This situation refers to

$$\mathbf{S} \cap \mathbf{E} \neq \emptyset \vee \mathbf{S} \cap \mathbf{C} \neq \emptyset \vee \mathbf{E} \cap \mathbf{C} \neq \emptyset \tag{8}$$

Referring to the previous analysis, when promoting the basic attributes in the intersection, there will be a special impossible triangle if the two core attributes are not elevated or decreased simultaneously. The above Remarks 2 and 3 still applicable in analyzing the existence of the special impossibility triangle.

4   Application

To present the validity of this analysis method, we demonstrate the applications in this section. Firstly, we select PoW algorithms to be analyzed, and then we show that our method can also guide the development of new blockchain consensus mechanisms.

4.1   Performance Evaluation of PoW Consensus Mechanism

According to the analysis above, we need to confirm the basic parameters of a blockchain system in the three core attribute sets so as to analyze whether there is an impossibility triangle in the blockchain system.

This section takes the PoW algorithm as an example. PoW consumes significant computational cost in achieving the credibility standard. We consider six basic parameters, including consensus type, block reward, block size, etc. The three core attributes are composed of these basic parameters as in Table 1.

Table 1. Elements in the sets of three attributes

	Security	Efficiency	Cost
Block size	*		
Consensus validation time	*	*	*
Network consensus time		*	
Computational difficulty		*	*
Network condition		*	
Number of nodes in the system			*

From Table 1, we can observe that the three core attributes have one intersected basic parameter which is the consensus validation time.

Take the impact of the consensus validation time on the security, cost and efficiency as s_1, e_1 and c_1. Suppose the consensus validation time is decreased, we discuss the change of s_1, e_1 and c_1

- s_1+: Reducing consensus time will lead to a relative increased speed of new block generation, reducing the possibility of attackers catching up with the main chain, and increasing the security of the blockchain for selfish mining.
- e_1+: According to Eq. (1), reducing the confirmation time can improve throughput of the system, indicating an improvement in efficiency.

- c_1+: According to the impact of scalability cost on a blockchain system, reducing consensus validation time can reduce the burden of joining nodes on the system, reducing the cost.

Therefore, we can draw a conclusion that there is no standard impossibility triangle in PoW based on Remark 3.

As we also observe that the efficiency and cost attributes intersects, and the elements of intersection are the consensus validation time and the computational difficulty. We then analyze the possibility of special impossibility triangle. The computational difficulty impacting in efficiency and cost is denoted by e_2 and c_2. Increasing of the computational difficulty will result in e_2- and c_2-, as explained as follows.

- e_2-: According to Eq. (1), the improvement of computational difficulty will lead to the higher difficulty of reaching the credibility criteria, that is, increasing W, which has a negative impact on efficiency.
- c_2-: The improved computational difficulty directly results in the increased cost consumed by each transaction.

According to the analysis above, we can also conclude that there is no special impossibility triangle in PoW.

Therefore, in our analysis, on the condition of evaluating a PoW blockchain system by considering the six basic parameters, there is no standard or special impossibility triangle.

4.2   Guiding Consensus Mechanism Design

Our analysis method is helpful in qualitatively justify the feasibility of a consensus mechanism especially in a given application scenario. We have observed that different consensus mechanisms have different credibility standard, and in turn, the feasibility analysis should be different. To apply our analysis method, we should construct the three core attributes and then analyze the feasibility of a consensus mechanism design. For example, when evaluating PoW in a IOT scenario, the computational power will be decreased and we may analyze the effects of this parameter to other core attributes, and then verify the its feasibility.

Furthermore, our analysis method can also assist in investigating new directions in improving an existing consensus mechanism. By abstracting an existing consensus process, we are able to analyze their core attribute relationships and then analyze each possible basic attribute influence to the core attributes. The attributes with consistent positive effects serve potential directions in improving the mechanism.

4.3   Comparisons of the Existing Consensus Mechanisms

In this section, we aim to quantitatively measure the three core attributes and compare these attribute values in the existing consensus mechanisms. We choose PoW in Bitcoin, PoS in Etherum, and PBFT in our comparison, and the result is shown as in Fig. 3.

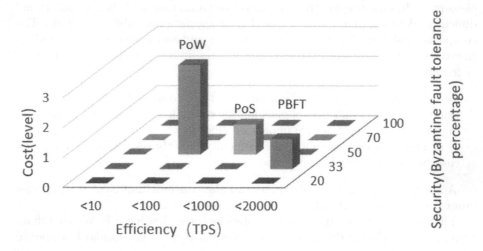

Fig. 3. Comparison of three consensus mechanisms in 3D

In Fig. 3, X-axis represents the security attribute which contains only Byzantine fault tolerance for simplicity. The Y-axis is efficiency which is represented by TPS, and Z-axis is the cost. The cost here only covers the computational cost, and we use cost levels to reflect the cost consumption of the three consensus mechanisms, specifically, 1 for low cost, 2 for medium cost, and 3 for a high cost. According to Fig. 3, we can observe that there is no dominant consensus mechanism with all the three attributes outperforming other mechanisms.

5   Conclusion

In this paper, we first abstract the consensus process of a blockchain system, then develop a method in analyzing the existence of BIT problem. The proposed analysis method is composed of two layers. In the first layer, the basic attributes and core attributes are formalized based on the abstracted consensus process. Moreover, the credibility standard is defined to connect the attributes with the system consensus requirements. In the second layer, the impacts of the attribute values to the three core attributes are captured in the form of improving or deduction signs, and the conditions for the BIT existence are studied. To evaluate the proposed method, we analyze PoW as an example, demonstrating that there does not exist blockchain impossibility triangles. We also indicate the possibility of our mechanism in guiding the development of consensus mechanisms. Furthermore, based on the proposed method, we compare the three typical consensus mechanism, showing that there is no dominant mechanism.

Acknowledgments. This work is supported in part by the National Natural Science Foundation for Young Scientists of China under Grant No. 61702090 and No. 61702084.

References

1. Biswas, S., Sharif, K., Li, F., Nour, B., Wang, Y.: A scalable blockchain framework for secure transactions in IoT. IEEE Internet Things J. **6**(3), 4650–4659 (2019)
2. Brewer, E.: Cap twelve years later: how the "rules" have changed. Computer **45**, 23–29 (2012)
3. Castro, M., Liskov, B., et al.: Practical Byzantine fault tolerance. In: Proceedings of the Third Symposium on Operating Systems Design and Implementation, pp. 173–186 (1999)
4. Christidis, K., Devetsikiotis, M.: Blockchains and smart contracts for the Internet of Things. IEEE Access **4**, 2292–2303 (2016)
5. Courtois, N.T., Bahack, L.: On subversive miner strategies and block withholding attack in bitcoin digital currency. arXiv preprint arXiv:1402.1718 (2014)
6. Gervais, A., Karame, G.O., Wüst, K., Glykantzis, V., Ritzdorf, H., Capkun, S.: On the security and performance of proof of work blockchains. In: Proceedings of the ACM SIGSAC Conference on Computer and Communications Security, pp. 3–16 (2016)
7. Lamport, L., Shostak, R., Pease, M.: The Byzantine generals problem. ACM Trans. Program. Lang. Syst. (TOPLAS) **4**(3), 382–401 (1982)
8. Liu, Z., Luong, N.C., Wang, W., Niyato, D., Wang, P., Liang, Y.C., Kim, D.I.: A survey on blockchain: a game theoretical perspective. IEEE Access **7**, 47615–47643 (2019)
9. Meng, Z., Ren, W., Cao, Y., You, Z.: Leaderless and leader-following consensus with communication and input delays under a directed network topology. IEEE Trans. Syst. Man Cybern. Part B (Cybern.) **41**, 75–88 (2011)
10. Nakamoto, S., et al.: Bitcoin: a peer-to-peer electronic cash system (2008). https://bitcoin.org/bitcoin.pdf
11. Natoli, C., Gramoli, V.: The balance attack against proof-of-work blockchains: the R3 testbed as an example. CoRR abs/1612.09426 (2016). http://arxiv.org/abs/1612.09426
12. Prokofieva, M., Miah, S.J.: Blockchain in healthcare. Australas. J. Inf. Syst. **23**, 1–22 (2019)
13. Ren, L., Devadas, S.: Proof of space from stacked expanders. In: Hirt, M., Smith, A. (eds.) TCC 2016. LNCS, vol. 9985, pp. 262–285. Springer, Heidelberg (2016). https://doi.org/10.1007/978-3-662-53641-4_11
14. Salman, T., Zolanvari, M., Erbad, A., Jain, R., Samaka, M.: Security services using blockchains: a state of the art survey. IEEE Commun. Surv. Tutor. **21**(1), 858–880 (2019)
15. Sapirshtein, A., Sompolinsky, Y., Zohar, A.: Optimal selfish mining strategies in bitcoin. In: Grossklags, J., Preneel, B. (eds.) FC 2016. LNCS, vol. 9603, pp. 515–532. Springer, Heidelberg (2017). https://doi.org/10.1007/978-3-662-54970-4_30

16. Vukolić, M.: The quest for scalable blockchain fabric: proof-of-work vs. BFT replication. In: Camenisch, J., Kesdoğan, D. (eds.) iNetSec 2015. LNCS, vol. 9591, pp. 112–125. Springer, Cham (2016). https://doi.org/10.1007/978-3-319-39028-4_9
17. Wei, P., Yuan, Q., Zheng, Y.: Security of the blockchain against long delay attack. In: Peyrin, T., Galbraith, S. (eds.) ASIACRYPT 2018, Part III. LNCS, vol. 11274, pp. 250–275. Springer, Cham (2018). https://doi.org/10.1007/978-3-030-03332-3_10
18. Zheng, Z., Xie, S., Dai, H.N., Chen, X., Wang, H.: Blockchain challenges and opportunities: a survey. Int. J. Web Grid Serv. 14(4), 352–375 (2018)
19. Zhong, L., Wu, Q., Xie, J., Guan, Z., Qin, B.: A secure large-scale instant payment system based on blockchain. Comput. Secur. 84, 349–364 (2019)

A Novel Enhanced Lightweight Node for Blockchain

Yulong Zhao, Baoning Niu$^{(\boxtimes)}$, Peng Li, and Xing Fan

Taiyuan University of Technology, Taiyuan, Shanxi, China
zyl34389@gmail.com, niubaoning@tyut.edu.cn, imleep@163.com,
fanxing0045@link.tyut.edu.cn

Abstract. Blockchain is a single linked list and its data volume grows endlessly. Each node in the Blockchain network keeps the entire data, which not only waste storage, but also requires a vast amount of computation which is wasteful and scales poorly. The SPV (simplified payment verification) node simplifies node storage, but decentralization, the most important feature of Blockchain, is compromised. To address the issue, this paper proposes a novel enhanced lightweight node called ESPV (Enhanced SPV) based on the analysis of the characteristics of Blockchain data. ESPV nodes label blocks as new and old, and keep all the new blocks while storing partial old blocks according their capacity. A hierarchical block partition routing table is established to ensure data availability when ESPV nodes access old blocks they do not have. An ESPV node has all the functions of a full node to ensure the decentralization and stability of a Blockchain system.

Keywords: Blockchain · Data management · Data analysis · Slice storage · Lightweight · Bitcoin

1 Introduction

Blockchain technology has gradually gained widespread attention due to its characteristics of tamper-proof, traceability, and decentralization. It originated from Nakamoto's Bitcoin white paper [1], and has been applied in many fields, such as digital cryptocurrency [1], supply chain finance [2], data notarization [3], and resource sharing [4]. Blockchain uses a chain structure and a consensus protocol to ensure that Blockchain data is tamper-proof and traceable. The endless monotonic increase of data puts increasingly large pressure on majority nodes with limited storage and computation capacity. A data storage method that uses a full copy (one copy per node) is not necessary and waste of storage space.

Taking Bitcoin as an example, up to March 27, 2019, 569,001 blocks were generated, with 395,438,152 transactions, 49,245,944 certified addresses, and volume of data is 196.15 GB [5]. According to bitnodes [6] statistics, the entire network uses the 7001 protocol (>=Satoshi: 0.8.x) and there are nearly 10,000 full nodes online. A full node requires nearly 200 GB of disk space to store the entire Blockchain data. It is conservatively estimated that all the participating nodes needs 2 PB of storage capacity to store the ledger, and it still grows linearly every year.

© Springer Nature Singapore Pte Ltd. 2020
Z. Zheng et al. (Eds.): BlockSys 2019, CCIS 1156, pp. 137–149, 2020.
https://doi.org/10.1007/978-981-15-2777-7_12

Full nodes keep the entire Blockchain data in their database, which mains that they have complete node functions, including verifying transactions (mining), transmitting data with other nodes. On the contrary, in order to reduce storage pressure greatly SPV node [1] maintains blockheader which need only 4.2 MB per. The storage space required for such a lightweight node is only linear with the block height, regardless of the block size. Although SPV nodes can alleviate storage pressure, they have to rely on the full nodes to verify transactions, which may result in security issues such as denial of service attacks [7] and witch attacks [8]. As the amount of Blockchain data increases, the number of SPV nodes also increase, while the number of full nodes, the degree of decentralization of the Blockchain system, data security as well as system stability decreases. From the perspective of data storage and data sharing, SPV node do not make contributions to Blockchain. For the simplified explain in this paper, we take the most popular public Blockchain platform, Bitcoin, as an example, though other Blockchain platforms adopt similar concepts and techniques.

This paper proposes a novel enhanced lightweight node called ESPV, which save the new blocks (the most recently generated blocks) with a full copy, allowing the lightweight node to perform transaction verification. Old blocks (blocks before the new block) are divided into slices to reduce data redundancy. Then we create a hierarchical block partition routing table to speed up data retrieval and ensure data availability.

The main contributions of this paper are as follows:

(1) A novel enhanced lightweight node named ESPV is proposed, which enable lightweight nodes to verify transactions, complete node functions, enhance peer-to-peer relationships, and ensure decentralization, stability and security of Blockchain systems.
(2) The old blocks are sliced and stored under the premise of ensuring the reliability and availability of the Blockchain data, thereby it can reduces the waste of storage space and enhances the scalability of the system. The complete block header data of Blockchain are saved to ensure the authenticity of the Blockchain data in the system.
(3) A routing table suitable for ESPV storage features is proposed, which not only increases the efficiency of Blockchain data search, but also achieves load balancing, and alleviates the problem of excessive pressure on the full node.

2   Related Work

The node in the Bitcoin network mainly includes full node and SPV node, which have different functions and mechanisms. The full node [1] is the first node that ensures the validity of the Blockchain by downloading and verifying the blocks from the genesis block to the most recently discovered block. It can share data and verify transactions independently. The SPV node merely saves the block header, so that only the payment can be verified. When verifying the payment, it is necessary to rely on pulling the MerkleBlock message [9] from the full node to meet the Bloom filter condition, and judging whether the target transaction is in the block through the hash authentication path of the Merkle tree. At the same time, the block header is used to check whether the block has been pushed into the chain enough depth to confirm whether the transaction is successful. Delgado-Segura et al. [10] analyzed the UTXO (unspent transaction output) data of Bitcoin and found that most UTXOs were generated in a few recent blocks.

In simplifying single-node data storage, there are mainly solutions such as block pruning, copy strategy, erasure code technology, and consensus unit. Bitcoin-core [11] proposes a block pruning strategy. The downloaded Blockchain data can be deleted after the UTXO set is built, which greatly reduces the storage space required by the node. However, with the popularity of the pruning strategy, the number of full nodes will decrease, and the reliability of the Blockchain data in the system will also decrease. Jia et al. [12] proposes a storage scalability model to store Blockchain data in a Blockchain by a certain proportion of network nodes, adding two additional chains. However increases system complexity while reducing storage space. Dai et al. [13] proposes a Blockchain storage framework with low storage requirements. Using the erasure code technique [14] to store the Blockchain data as chunks, reducing the storage and bandwidth pressure of the single node, and increasing the node's calculations. Xu [15] et al. proposes a consensus unit method, which allows nodes to form a community, and autonomous fragmentation stores Blockchain data in the community, but only for the private chain, the public chain has a problem of too much query overhead.

Nodes in P2P [16] networks have different types and data storage conditions. In order to speed up the retrieval of time, researchers present to establish a centralized or DHT-based [17] decentralized routing table. The centralized routing table is suitable for the case of a small number of network nodes [18]. When searching for data, the node in the network first requests the location of the data from the routing center, and it contacts the target node separately after obtaining the location of the target node. The system has a short response time and strong data availability, but the central server is under heavy pressure and remains the single point of failure. The performance of the routing table lookup algorithm based on DHT technology is $O(\log N)$ [19], and the load balancing is applied to a large-scale node network, so that the single point of failure is not exist. The DHT-based decentralized routing table is a content-based search method, which can directly find the location of each small data fragment, while it also needs to maintain an index data which would result in a large index table, high cost of data update and maintenance.

3   Enhanced Lightweight Node

From the discussions above, complete node functions include transaction verification, data storage and data sharing. The SPV node does not save the complete Blockchain data for reducing the data storage, nor can it mine, seriously dependence on the full node. In order to make the enhanced lightweight node has complete functions as the full node, the design of the ESPV also starts from three aspects.

Blockchain is a sequence of blocks, which holds a complete list of transaction records like conventional public ledger. All legal transactions can be traced back to the output of one or more transactions, the source of which is the mining reward, called coinbase (Fig. 2).

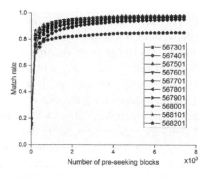

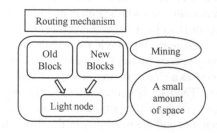

Fig. 1. Transaction matching ratio   **Fig. 2.** Enhanced lightweight node model

As shown in Fig. 1, the fixed interval sampling is performed on the blocks with the height of 567301 to 568201. The verification rate of the transaction gradually becomes flatter as the number of blocks looking forward increases. What's more, most of the transaction inputs are concentrated in the blocks generated later. So the authors conceived whether it is possible to verify most of the transactions by saving the most recently generated partial Blockchain data (new blocks), making it has mining capabilities. For old blocks which have fewer requests and no changes, the main purpose of them is to build a complete UTXO set. Therefore, we propose a novel enhanced lightweight node for the transaction characteristics of Bitcoin and the existing node model. The core idea is to treat new and old blocks differently. Instead of all redundant storage, data fragmentation technology can be adopted to reduce data redundancy and reduce storage space waste. Different storage strategies are adopted to increase the transaction verification function for lightweight node, improve the scalability of the system in terms of storage, maintain the equivalence between nodes, and ensure the degree of decentralization and stability of the system. In order to ensure data availability, data retrieval speed can be accelerated by designing an appropriate routing mechanism.

The rest of this paper is organized as follows: Sect. 3.1 introduces the new blocks storage strategy, Sect. 3.2 describes the old block storage mode, Sect. 3.3 elaborates the hierarchical block partition routing table and chain information, and Sect. 3.4 summarize the overall ESPV node architecture; Sect. 4 describes the experimental results and analysis; Sect. 5 summarizes the content of this article.

3.1 New Blocks Storage Strategy

The nodes in the network have a large amount of requests for new blocks, and it will consume a lot of bandwidth resources. The full nodes in the network need to synchronize the latest Blockchain data to participate in the mining, who want to get the latest Blockchain data as early as possible, and start mining on it to obtain the block reward with greater probability. The SPV nodes need to synchronize its block headers to complete payment verification. This is because Bitcoin uses a chained append mode, and the success of each transaction needs to ensure that it is packaged in the block, connected to the chain, and there is more than 6 new block acknowledgments above the block.

Based on the network characteristics of the new blocks, ESPV uses a fully redundant storage strategy to store new blocks data. The new blocks maintains a fixed window size. Each time a new block is obtained, the first block is deleted, and the UTXO of the block is deleted in the UTXO library. This can provide data sharing services for other nodes, reducing the bandwidth pressure of the full node and increasing the stability of the system.

When the node initializes, it first queries the latest block height h, and then downloads the Blockchain data with the block height from h-3000 to h from the network, and builds the UTXO library. If the transaction input is not found in the UTXO library during transaction verification, the transaction is forwarded to the full node. It can be seen from Fig. 1 that most of the transactions can be verified. When the number of verified transactions is sufficient, the corresponding block size will reach the maximum threshold set by the system and then they can be packaged into block to start mining calculation.

As can be seen from Fig. 3, the current number of block transactions is increasing at a linear rate, and a dynamic adjustment strategy is designed to ensure the availability of the system. Same as the mining difficulty adjustment cycle, ESPV is also adjusted every 2 weeks. The Bitcoin system generates a block on average for 10 min, and each 2016 block needs to be adjusted once. The node needs to record the last adjusted block height and use this as a starting point until the 2016 Blockchain data is generated. Randomly sample 40 blocks in this 2016 block. If the number of blocks in these blocks that have no more than 80% verifiable transactions in the first 3000 blocks is greater than 4, then the number of blocks in the new blocks is n plus 32. If the number of blocks with a verifiable ratio exceeding 95% is greater than 32, then n is reduced by 32, otherwise n does not change. As can be seen from Fig. 1, saving over 3,000 new blocks can verify more than 80% of transactions. According to the number of existing blocks and the number of new blocks to be saved, combined with the growth rate of the block, the number of changes in each cycle of the appropriate new block is estimated to be 32. So we set them as default values. Specific parameters can be custom configured to suit the hardware environment and needs of different nodes.

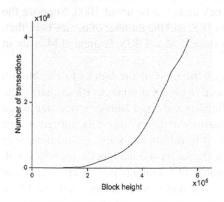

Fig. 3. Block transactions

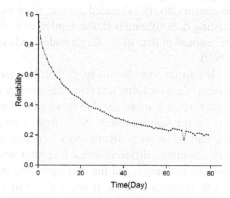

Fig. 4. Node reliability

3.2 Old Block Storage Strategy

The system has a small amount of requests for old blocks and it don't need bandwidth resources too much. They need to be pulled only when new full nodes join or rebuild the full node in the network. This is because it uses a log-like form that, once generated, becomes historical data that does not change, and nodes do not have to acquire them repeatedly. When verifying transactions at full nodes, a complete set of UTXOs needs to be built from the creation block to the new generated block. From the search for the input of the transaction, to ensure that it is not spent, the balance is greater than or equal to the expenditure, and the verification signature confirms the ownership of the asset, so the reliability and availability of the old blocks are very important for the entire system.

Considering the access characteristics of the old blocks, ESPV adopts the method of fragment storage, that is, each node saves part of the historical Blockchain data. This makes the storage pressure of each node smaller, reduces the waste of the storage space of the system, and increases the scalability of the system.

This paper uses the open source project bitnodes [20] to perform statistical analysis of the full node data in the Bitcoin network. As of April 10, 2019, the maximum number of simultaneous online connections of Bitcoin using the 7001 version of the protocol in the past two years was 12,770, the minimum value was 6,671, and 9,931 average [6]. It can be seen that the number of nodes simultaneously online has a certain stability. Therefore, the reliability of the node is statistically analyzed in this paper. Figure 4 is available. In a P2P system, the reliability relationship is:

$$a = \sum_{i=m}^{n} C_n^i p^i (1 - p)^{n-i} \ [21] \tag{1}$$

a: system reliability p: node reliability r: number of copies
Solvable: $r = \frac{\log(1-a)}{\log(1-p)}$

It is impossible to define a probability lower than $1/10^{50}$ according to Borel's law [22]. So set up $a = 1 - (1/10^{50})$ According to Fig. 4, the node reliability $p = 0.1$ can be conservatively estimated, so that r can be calculated to be about 1000. Suppose the existing data volume is D, the number of nodes is S, and the number of copies is R, then the amount of data that a single node needs to store is $M = DR/S$. Estimated M is about 20 GB.

It can be seen from Fig. 5 that the size distribution of the blocks in the bitcoin system is not uniform, and the nodes usually need to obtain continuous Blockchain data. Therefore, it is more suitable to adopt a continuous and fixed storage space size when performing fragmentation. According to the analysis of the existing data storage, a slice size can be set to 5 GB. In order to better adapt to different storage space differences between nodes, different initial fragment sizes are set for the old blocks, namely small, medium and large, and the corresponding number of fragments is 4, 8, and 12. When a node receives a block, it needs to count its size, and record the start and end block heights of the system block fragments. These height values are added to an array, defined as the slice anchor height set. These values will not change. Each node is bounded by these fixed block heights when joining a P2P network or performing data expansion and deletion. When a node joins the network, the node generates a random number from 0

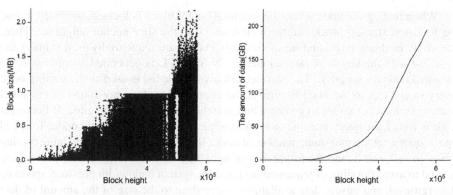

Fig. 5. Block size distribution   **Fig. 6.** Blockchain data volume

to the latest block height, and the height of the slice is anchored to the height closest to the random number as the starting height of its data storage, according to the size of its available space. Save the number of shards at the corresponding level.

The authors assume that the nodes with good performance, sufficient storage space, and strong stability in the whole system run full node, and other hardware-constrained nodes run ESPV node. In this way, the reliability and availability of Blockchain data in the system have a basic guarantee. As can be seen from Fig. 6, the current Blockchain data volume increases linearly, with an annual growth of 50 GB. To ensure the availability of the system, the initial fragment size needs to be increased by one each year, and the added nodes are extended one slice backward. In order to encourage the node to save the Blockchain data as much as possible, the ESPV sets different priorities for the nodes with different storage amounts, and the node that stores more data preferentially obtains the request reply. The node needs to provide some random block trading Merkle trees within a certain period of time. Checking is performed, which reduces the possibility of malicious nodes masquerading to store a lot of data.

3.3   Hierarchical Block Partition Routing Table and Chain Information

Combined with the storage strategy of the old blocks, ESPV designed a new routing mechanism: Hierarchical block partition routing table. According to the size of the node storage fragment, four block partition routing tables are constructed, which are small, medium, large, and full node routing tables. The routing table is stored in the form of a map. The key is the starting block number of the slice, the value is the array of nodes, and each node is an ip:port.

```
Map {
  Key: blocknumber,
  Value: [ip: port,…]
}
```

When finding the node where the specified height block is located, you need to find the fragment starting block number h closest to it in the slice anchor height set. Then, the small, medium, large, and full-node routing tables are sequentially used to query the node list with the key h. A random number N from 0-L is generated according to the obtained node list length L. The Nth element in the node list is used as the starting node to try to connect to the node in turn. If the connected node is not found in the small routing table, it continues to go down and searches from the routing table. If the target node is found, the query is terminated and a request is made to the target node. To speed up the query, set the maximum number of nodes in the small, medium, and large routing tables to 8, 4, and 2, and the full node routing table is not restricted. Direct positioning is used to avoid flooding of requested data, reduce system bandwidth pressure, speed up data retrieval, and ensure data availability. According to the size of the amount of data stored by the node, the nodes are accessed in a hierarchical manner from small to large. The unstable nodes can be utilized as much as possible, and the bandwidth pressure of the nodes with more nodes and more data is reduced, load balancing is performed, and local hotspots are avoided. ESPV sets an auditing mechanism when a node joins the routing table. Its continuous online duration takes more than 30 min. The resulting node is relatively stable, preventing frequent data updates from putting pressure on the system network bandwidth. As shown in Fig. 7, the statistics of the continuous online 30 min node show that the probability of being online within one month is about 70%, which can meet the system requirements. There is a jitter point in the Fig. 7 because the lab network failed for a while. The number of nodes that result in statistics is a little less. Does not affect the overall experiment.

To verify the authenticity of the data, ESPV saves all block header data. Each time the node obtains the Blockchain data from the network, the block hash value on the chain is compared with the calculated block hash value to verify the authenticity of the Blockchain data and maintain the security of the system data. Since the block head forms a chain, the POW (Proof of Work) is accumulated, and its security is the same as that of the full node. The amount of data in the block header is small and does not put pressure on the storage of the node. The corresponding ip will put into the blacklisted if the node provides the error block data.

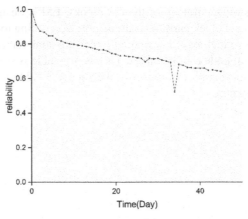

Fig. 7. Node reliability

3.4 ESPV Node Architecture

ESPV uses different ports for data sharing with nodes in the network. Accept and forward transactions using port 1. Port 2 performs the request and transmission of the block. Port 3 acquires and shares routing information. Port 4 sends and receives the block header.

Each module has its own function. The acquisition of new and old blocks requires the target node address to be retrieved from the block partition routing table to quickly pull data from the network. The UTXO library is built from the resulting new blocks for verification of the transaction. To speed up the retrieval process, build a caching mechanism for UTXO and load a portion of the recently generated UTXO into memory. Old blocks provide data services to other nodes in the system. The block header information can verify the authenticity of the blocks obtained from other nodes and ensure system security (Fig. 8).

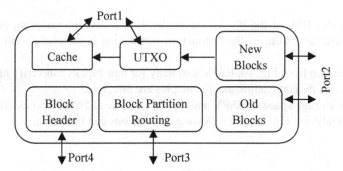

Fig. 8. ESPV module architecture

4   Experimental Results

The experimental development environment was an Intel(R) Xeon(R) E5-2609 v4 1.70 GHz CPU and a 16 GB memory server. Simulation experiments were performed using Bitcoin's existing Blockchain data.

In order to obtain experimental data, we built a Bitcoin node and used the Bitcoin-ETL [23] open source tool to process the Blockchain data. Then manually filter the data again, leaving only the fields we need, so that only one tenth of the data amount is needed, with about 300 GB of structured text data in json.

First, take 100,000 blocks as a group, randomly extract 100 blocks from them, and calculate the first 3000 blocks to verify the ratio of transactions in this block. The average value can be obtained in Fig. 9.

As can be seen from Fig. 9, ESPV is applicable to the entire life cycle of Bitcoin. The overall trading characteristics of Bitcoin are similar, and it is likely to be traded in the near future after getting the digital currency.

Second, test the ESPV transaction verification function using the latest Blockchain data. The experiment starts from the height of 568201 blocks, and each time the 2016

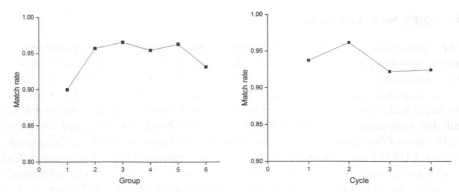

Fig. 9. Overall transaction verification rate distribution

Fig. 10. Transaction verification rate

block is a cycle, 10% of the blocks are randomly selected for sampling processing, and the average ratio value of the transaction verification is calculated, and Fig. 10 is obtained.

As can be seen from Fig. 10, ESPV's strategy for new blocks can verify higher ratio transactions, and dynamic adjustment strategies are effective.

Then, the storage space of ESPV and the whole node at 568201 blocks is shown in Fig. 11. By analyzing Fig. 11, the following conclusions can be drawn.

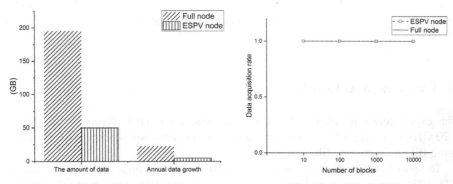

Fig. 11. Storage space comparison

Fig. 12. Data reliability

(1) The ESPV node has significantly less storage space than the full node.
(2) The data volume growth rate of ESPV is much smaller than that of the full node, which can meet the hardware conditions of ordinary PCs and increase the scalability of the system.

Assuming that 70% of the nodes in the whole network use ESPV, 30% are full nodes, and about 10,000 online nodes, it is conservatively estimated that the entire system can save about 1 PB of data storage space.

Finally, test the reliability and availability of ESPV. This paper uses the JAVA language to design a node object with node type, reliability, IP, port, block segment and network bandwidth attributes. A hierarchical block partition routing table is established by creating 10,000 node objects to simulate P2P nodes.

```
Class Node {
    String type;
    Double reliability;
    String ipPort;
    Int[] blockSegment;
    Double bandwidth;
}
```

Set node properties based on the distribution and reliability of existing network nodes. 200 seed nodes (full node) with a reliability of 0.9 and a network bandwidth of 10MBps (download speed, equivalent to 100 Mbps); the remaining 30% are full nodes, 70% are ESPV nodes, the reliability is 0.1, and the network bandwidth is 0.2–5 MBps random number. When creating a node object, the block segment attribute is randomly assigned a value of the tile anchor height concentration obtained from the real bitcoin data, and the block size uses the size data of the block in the existing bitcoin. Each trial and error requires a delay of 10 ms. Traverse the node and establish a routing table for the node. At the same time, 10,000 simulated full nodes are created, and the bandwidth and reliability are the same as above. A routing table is established and a comparative experiment is performed. Blockchain data of lengths of 10, 100, 1000, and 10000 are randomly obtained therefrom, also record the number of blocks they get from the full node, Figs. 12, 13 and 14 can be obtained.

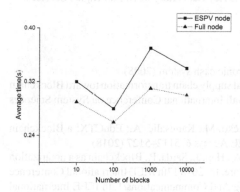

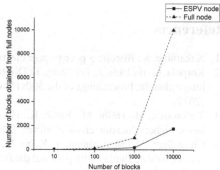

Fig. 13. Data availability

Fig. 14. Comparison of the number of blocks obtained from the full node

It can be seen from the experimental results that the ESPV node and the data availability of the entire node are both 100%, and the reliability is guaranteed. The ESPV node is slightly higher than the full node when obtaining the average time of the Blockchain data. This is because the system uses the unstable nodes as much as possible to cause delays, but it can also meet the application requirements and can be applied in the actual production environment. What's more, the number of blocks obtained from the full node is significantly reduced, reducing the pressure on the full node.

5 Conclusion

The amount of data in the Blockchain grows linearly, putting a lot of pressure on the storage of a single node. The SPV node solves the storage problem, but they rely entirely on the full node, making the pressure on the full node increase and the decentralization of the system weakened. This paper proposes a novel and well-functioning enhanced lightweight node. By analyzing the Blockchain data, it is found that a small amount of data can be saved to verify a certain amount of transactions, and the node has a mining function. Through statistical analysis of the total node data in the network, the random block storage of the old block is performed on the premise of ensuring data reliability and availability. Reduce storage pressure on a single node and increase system storage scalability, security, and stability. In order to speed up the data search speed, a hierarchical block partition routing table is designed to prevent flooding of data requests and put pressure on network bandwidth. Use chain information to ensure the authenticity of the data. In order to adapt to the mode of linear growth of Blockchain data, a dynamic adjustment strategy is proposed to ensure the availability of the enhanced lightweight node.

The enhanced lightweight node compromises between data storage space and transaction validation. UTXO support for early old blocks is poor, and it needs to be verified and packaged by all nodes. Further optimization is needed in the future.

Acknowledgments. This work was supported in part by the National Key R&D Program of China under Grant 2017YFB1401000, and in part by the Key Laboratory of Digital Rights Services.

References

1. Nakamoto, S.: Bitcoin: a peer-to-peer electronic cash system (2008)
2. Korpela, K., Hallikas, J., Dahlberg, T.: Digital supply chain transformation toward Blockchain integration. In: Proceedings of the 50th Hawaii International Conference on System Sciences (2017)
3. Turkanović, M., Hölbl, M., Košič, K., Heričko, M., Kamišalić, A.: EduCTX: a Blockchain based higher education credit platform. IEEE Access **6**, 5112–5127 (2018)
4. Chowdhury, M.J.M., Colman, A., Kabir, M.A., Han, J., Sarda, P.: Blockchain as a notarization service for data sharing with personal data store. In: 2018 17th IEEE International Conference on Trust, Security and Privacy in Computing And Communications/12th IEEE International Conference on Big Data Science And Engineering (Trust Com/BigDataSE), pp. 1330–1335. IEEE (2018)
5. Bitaps. https://bitaps.com/. Accessed 27 Mar 2019
6. Bitnodes. https://bitnodes.earn.com/dashboard/?days=730#nodes. Accessed 10 Apr 2019
7. Lau, F., Rubin, S.H., Smith, M.H., Trajkovic, L.: Distributed denial of service attacks. In: SMC 2000 Conference Proceedings. 2000 IEEE International Conference on Systems, Man and Cybernetics, "Cybernetics Evolving to Systems, Humans, Organizations, and Their Complex Interactions", cat no. 0, vol. 3, pp. 2275–2280. IEEE (2000)

8. Wang, L.H.: Research on security of P2P technology. Appl. Mech. Mater. **644**, 2826–2829 (2014)
9. Bitcoin-s-spv-node. https://github.com/bitcoin-s/bitcoin-s-spv-node/blob/master/src/main/scala/org/bitcoins/spvnode/networking/PaymentActor.scala. Accessed 37 Mar 2019
10. Delgado-Segura, S., Pérez-Solà, C., Navarro-Arribas, G., Herrera-Joancomartí, J.: Analysis of the bitcoin UTXO set. In: Zohar, A., et al. (eds.) FC 2018. LNCS, vol. 10958, pp. 78–91. Springer, Heidelberg (2019). https://doi.org/10.1007/978-3-662-58820-8_6
11. Bitcoin. https://github.com/bitcoin/bitcoin/blob/v0.11.0/doc/release-notes.md#block-f. Accessed 27 Mar 2019
12. Jia, D., Xin, J., Wang, Z., Guo, W., Wang, G.: ElasticChain: support very large blockchain by reducing data redundancy. In: Cai, Y., Ishikawa, Y., Xu, J. (eds.) APWeb-WAIM 2018. LNCS, vol. 10988, pp. 440–454. Springer, Cham (2018). https://doi.org/10.1007/978-3-319-96893-3_33
13. Dai, M., Zhang, S., Wang, H., Jin, S.: A low storage room requirement framework for distributed ledger in Blockchain. IEEE Access **6**, 22970–22975 (2018)
14. Lin, W. K., Chiu, D. M., Lee, Y. B.: Erasure code replication revisited. In: Proceedings of Fourth International Conference on Peer-to-Peer Computing, pp. 90–97. IEEE (2004)
15. Xu, Z., Han, S., Chen, L.: CUB, a consensus unit-based storage scheme for Blockchain system. In: 2018 IEEE 34th International Conference on Data Engineering (ICDE), pp. 173–184. IEEE (2018)
16. Amalarethinam, D.G., Balakrishnan, C., Charles, A.: An improved methodology for fragment re-allocation in peer-to-peer distributed databases (2012)
17. Hassanzadeh-Nazarabadi, Y., Küpçü, A., Özkasap, Ö.: Decentralized and locality aware replication method for DHT-based P2P storage systems. Future Gener. Comput. Syst. **84**, 32–46 (2018)
18. Li, Z.: Research on Key Technologies of High Availability P2P File Sharing System. H. Uni. Sci. Tech. (2009)
19. Liu J.: P2P distributed storage authentication system for DHT. N. Univ. (2010)
20. Bitnodes. https://github.com/ayeowch/bitnodes. Accessed 10 Apr 2019
21. Xu, J.: Research on Data Reliability of P2P Network Storage System. H. Eng. Univ. (2011)
22. Borel, E.: Probabilities and life, Vol. 121. D. Publ. (1962)
23. Bitcoin-ETL. https://github.com/blockchain-etl/bitcoin-etl. Accessed 27 Mar 2019

An Adaptive Modular-Based Compression Scheme for Address Data in the Blockchain System

Zhen Gao$^{(\boxtimes)}$, Zhaohui Guo, and Jinsheng Yang

Tianjin University, Tianjin 300072, China
zgao@tju.edu.cn

Abstract. Blockchain has broad development potential and application prospects. At present, the huge storage volume on each node becomes one of the main bottlenecks that restrict the expansibility of the blockchain system, so optimization for storage mechanism becomes an important issue. In this paper, a modular-based compression scheme is proposed to dramatically reduce the storage volume of the account addresses on each node in the blockchain system. The scheme could achieve optimal compression ratio for the different number of accounts by adaptively select the bit-width of the module for each account. Theoretical analysis and simulation experiments are performed to show the effectiveness of the proposed mechanism.

Keywords: Blockchain · Address · Storage · Optimization · Compression · Modular

1 Introduction

Blockchain is the underlying technology of cryptocurrencies such as Bitcoin and Ethereum [1] and provides a new way to solve the problems of poor reliability, low security and high trust cost in the current centralized model on the strength of decentralization, trustlessness, and traceability [2]. The blockchain has been widely researched and applied in the fields of finance, medical, education, and food safety in combination with IoT [3–7] and 5G [8].

With the increment of accounts and transactions in the blockchain system, the huge storage volume on each node becomes one of the primary bottlenecks [9]. By the end of 2018, the amount of data stored in Ethereum exceeded 110 GB meanwhile exceeded 190 GB in Bitcoin [10]. The current solutions for this problem can only release the storage burden to a limited extent, and the price is that the decentralization property of the blockchain system is weakened [11–14]. In [15], a new storage mechanism based on redundant residual number system (RRNS) has been proposed to reduce the storage volume of account balances on each node without destroying the decentralization property. The account (generally refers to address in the blockchain) is the unique identifier to the corresponding balance and also occupies huge storage volume. It makes sense that

© Springer Nature Singapore Pte Ltd. 2020
Z. Zheng et al. (Eds.): BlockSys 2019, CCIS 1156, pp. 150–160, 2020.
https://doi.org/10.1007/978-981-15-2777-7_13

the storage volume on each node will be reduced further if the addresses could also be compressed properly.

This paper proposes a modular-based address compression scheme to reduce the storage volume of the addresses on each node, in which each address is re-expressed by its remainder to one of the selected modules. To reduce the total volume as much as possible without destroying the uniqueness of each account on the node, the bit-width of the module is selected adaptively for each account according to the storage of other accounts. In addition, a query procedure for the balance corresponding to a specific address is designed to ensure the availability of the account information.

The remaining part of this paper is organized as follows. In Sect. 2, the traditional storage structure and the optimized storage mechanism based on RRNS for balance are introduced. The modular-based address compression scheme is introduced in Sect. 3, and the performance is analyzed theoretically and verified by simulations in Sects. 4 and 5, respectively. Finally, this paper is concluded in Sect. 6.

2 The Storage Mechanism in the Blockchain System

In this section, we will introduce the storage mechanism in the blockchain system, including the traditional storage structure and the optimized one based on RRNS.

2.1 The Traditional Storage Mechanism

Blockchain is a distributed database. The data stored in the blockchain can be divided into two parts, one is the transaction record and the other is the account information. The latter is essential for blockchain. The account information consists of the addresses and the balances, and the address is the unique identifier of the corresponding balance. In Ethereum, the account information is stored in a specialized database called "world state" in the form of key-value pairs. So the balance information can be indexed directly by addresses. Differently, there is no such "world state" database in the Bitcoin system. The balance information corresponding to an address is recorded in the transactions in the form of unspent transaction outputs (UTXO) and could be recovered through the traversal of the UTXO set.

In the traditional storage mechanism, the stored data on each node is just a copy of the complete blockchain and both of the addresses and the balance have fixed bit-width. The traditional storage mechanism is shown in Fig. 1, in which k_1 and k_2 are the bit-width of the address and the balance, respectively. The storage volume of account information would be huge for a large number of accounts. Taking the Ethereum as an example, the address is a 20-bytes number ($k_1 = 160$) and the balance is a 32-bytes number ($k_2 = 256$). By the end of June 2019, there are more than 73 million accounts registered in the Ethereum system [16]. It means that the storage volume of more than 3.6 GB is required just to store the account information. The 3.6 GB addresses are necessary for most basic functions in the blockchain, such as transfer and simple payment verification (SPV). So the compression of the account information is very valuable for light applications on an embedded platform with limited computation and storage resources.

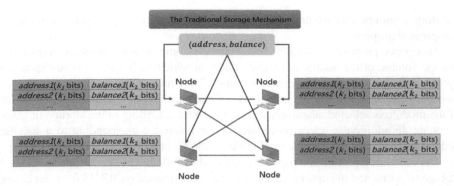

Fig. 1. Traditional storage of account information in the blockchain

2.2 The Storage Mechanism Based on RRNS

To compress the storage volume of balance information, a new storage mechanism based on RRNS is proposed in [15]. The balance of each address is partly stored on each node after performing modular arithmetic on the selected modules. With this design, the balances update on each node could be performed independently based on the algorithm attributes of the residual number system (RNS), and redundant remainders could be used for fault tolerance during the recovery of the balance. The structure of the storage mechanism based on RRNS is shown in Fig. 2, in which a b-bits number m_i is used to denote the module selected by the i-th node, and x_i, y_i denote the remainders of the balances to m_i on each node. Since b is set to be much smaller than the balance bit-width (k_2), the storage volume of the balances on each node is reduced dramatically.

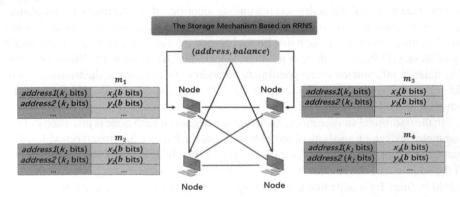

Fig. 2. The storage mechanism of balance information based on RRNS

3 Modular-Based Address Compression

Based on the description in Sect. 2, the storage volume of the balances on each node could be reduced dramatically by applying the RRNS-based scheme. However, the address and the balance are always corresponding one by one, and the storage volume on each node would be reduced further if the addresses could be compressed properly. In this section, an address compression based on the modular algorithm is proposed to reduce the storage volume of the address on each node. Besides, query rule is designed to ensure that users can always index the required balances by the compressed results under the proposed compression structure. It should be noted that this address compression scheme could be combined with the RRNS-based balance compression scheme [15], and it could be also applied independently for addresses compression in the normal blockchain system.

3.1 Address Compression Based on Modular Algorithm in the Blockchain

The basic idea is to compress the bit-width of address data on each node based on the modular algorithm. However, different from the balance, the address must be a unique identifier. So the key point of the address compression based on the modular algorithm is to avoid the presence of coresidual (or collision) on each node, which means the remainders of two different addresses to the same module may be equal. To achieve a high compression rate without collision, the Adaptive Bit-width growth Compression scheme (ABC) is proposed as follows.

(1) A set of N modules $\psi_N = \{m_1, m_2, m_3 \ldots m_N\}$ is preset as the common module set for all nodes, where m_i is a prime number among $(2^{ib-1} \sim 2^{ib}]$ with bit-width of ib. b is a number that is much smaller than the bit-width of complete address data (k_1). For the convenience of calculation and storage, b should be times of 8, so that the remainders are represented as bytes.

(2) For the i-th address (A_i) on a node, its remainder on m_1 is calculated firstly and expressed as r_i. If r_i is unique among all previous i remainders to m_1, r_i will be stored into a list corresponding to m_1 (named L_1) to represent A_i. But if the r_i already exists in L_1, the remainders of A_i on m_2 to m_N would be calculated in sequence, until r_i is unique in L_t $(2 \leq t \leq N)$. Based on the property of the modular algorithm, the volume of L_i is m_i.

Based on the ABC scheme, the key idea is to represent the address with bits as few as possible. When the number of accounts (N_a) is small, one or two lists $(L_1$ and $L_2)$ may be enough to store all the addresses without collision. When N_a becomes larger, it is more likely that the remainders of an address to small modules have collisions in the corresponding lists, then a value with larger bit-width is adaptively applied to represent the address.

An example of the ABC scheme for five addresses is shown in Fig. 3. The first two addresses are represented by their remainders to m_1 and store in L_1. The 3rd address is represented by its remainder to m_2 and store in L_2. The 4th and 5th addresses are represented by their remainders to m_3 and store in L_3. In this case, if $b = 16$, the compression ratio is $\{1 - [2 \times 16 + 1 \times 32 + 2 \times 48]/(160 * 5)\} * 100\% = 75\%$. In general, case, if the number of elements in L_i is l_i, the storage volume of the address data on a node before and after the compression could be expressed as $V_1 = k_1 N_a$ and

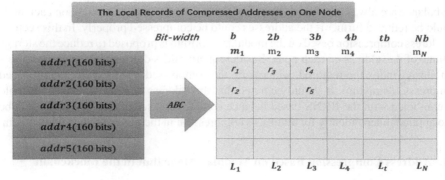

Fig. 3. The storage of compressed address data on one node

$V_2 = b \sum_{i=1}^{N} i l_i$, respectively, so the compression ratio could be expressed as

$$\beta = 1 - \frac{V_2}{V_1} = 1 - \frac{b \sum_{i=1}^{N} i l_i}{k_1 N_a} \tag{1}$$

In theory, for extremely large N_a, the number of modules or lists needed is $N_{max} = k_1/b$. And in practice, we may need to reserve space for each list ($m_i = l_i$). But we will show later in Sect. 4 that the number of necessary lists could be predicted for a specific N_a, and N would be much smaller than N_{max} for practical N_a, which means a large compression ratio could be achieved.

3.2 Query Rule for the Specific Address

With the ABC scheme, the compressed address is still the unique identifier for the corresponding balance, but the query rule is different. If an address is finally represented by its remainder to m_i and stored in L_i, it means its remainder to m_{i-1} already exists in L_{i-1}. For this reason, a reverse order query process is designed as following. After a node receiving a query transaction with a complete and specific address, the remainder of the address to m_N is calculated first. If the remainder exists in L_N, the corresponding balance would be replied to the user. If the remainder does not exist in L_N, the remainder of m_{N-1} will be calculated and checked again for existence. This process will be repeated on the next smaller module until the remainder is found in a list.

Based on this query principle, several lists may be checked, but the number of comparisons is the same as that in the normal blockchain system. The only overhead is that we need to calculate at most N modular operation over different modules. Considering that each comparison in the ABC scheme is between numbers with much smaller bit-width, the query complexity should be also much lower than that in the normal blockchain system.

4   Theoretical Analysis of the ABC Scheme

According to Eq. (1), the compression ratio β is determined by l_i and N_a, and it is obvious that l_i would increase for larger N_a. In this section, the relationship between l_i and N_a is analyzed firstly, then we can predict the compression ratio β for a specific N_a.

4.1   Expected Number of Remainders in Single List

Assuming that we have N_a accounts, and try to fill list L_i, the expected number of accounts that could be put in L_i can be expressed as

$$E_i(N_a) = \sum_{n=1}^{m_i} n p_n^i(N_a) \tag{2}$$

in which n is the possible number of the filled elements after N_a addresses are compressed, and $p_n^i(N_a)$ is the corresponding probability. Next, a recursive approach is applied to obtain $p_n^i(N_a)$ for a specific module m_i ($1 \le i \le N$). In the deduction, the remainders of addresses to m_i are assumed to be uniformly distributed among $[0, m_i - 1]$, which is verified in [17].

Let's consider the case that each address is compressed one by one. For the first address (A_1), L_i is empty, so $r_1 = \mod(A_1, m_i)$ would be stored in L_i, and $p_1^i(1) = 1$. For the second address (A_2), we have $r_2 = \mod(A_2, m_i)$, and the probability for $r_1 = r_2$ and $r_1 \ne r_2$ are $1/m_i$ and $(m_i - 1)/m_i = (1 - 1/m_i)$, respectively. For former case, we would have 1 elements in L_i ($n = 1$), and the probability is $p_1^i(2) = 1/m_i$. For the latter case, we would have 2 elements in L_i ($n = 1$), and the probability is $p_2^i(2) = (1 - 1/m_i)$. For the third account (A_3), we have $r_3 = \mod(A_3, m_i)$, and there are 3 possible cases ($n = 1, 2$ or 3). The probability for $n = 1$ is $p_1^i(3) = p_1^i(2) * 1/m_i = 1/m_i^2$. For $n = 2$, there are 2 subcases. One is that $r_1 \ne r_2$, but r_3 collides with r_1 or r_2, and the probability is $2/m_i$. The other is $r_1 = r_2 \ne r_3$, and the probability is $(m_i - 1)/m_i = 1 - 1/m_i$. So we could have $p_2^i(3) = p_2^i(2) * 2/m_i + p_1^i(2) * 1/(m_i - 1)$. For $n = 3$, there is only one case that $r_1, r_2,$ and r_3 are all different, and the probability is $p_3^i(3) = p_2^i(2) * (1 - 2/m_i)$. Following the same procedure, we can obtain $p_n^i(q)$ for all possible n after q addresses are compressed and tried to be filled in L_i. The basic operation for $q \le m_i$ includes 3 steps:

(1) $n = 1$: $p_1^i(q) = p_1^i(q - 1) * 1/m_i$

(2) $1 < n < q$: $p_n^i(q) = p_n^i(q - 1) * n/m_i + p_{n-1}^i(q - 1) * (1 - (n - 1)/m_i)$

(3) $n = q$: $p_q^i(q) = p_{q-1}^i(q - 1) * (1 - (q - 1)/m_i)$

When $q > m_i$, only steps (1) and (2) are needed. After all, N_a addressed are compressed ($q = N_a$), we can get $p_n^i(N_a)$ for $n = 1, 2, ..., m_i$, and the expected number of elements in L_i could be calculated according to Eq. (2).

4.2 Number of Remainders in Each List

Following the procedures in the last subsection, we can get the expected number of remainders in each list $E_i(N_a)$ $(i = 1, 2, ..., N)$ if we try to fill all the N_a compressed addresses in a single list. Then according to the proposed ABC scheme, the expected value of l_i $(i > 1)$ could be estimated as

$$l_i = E_i(N_a) - E_{i-1}(N_a) \tag{3}$$

and $l_1 = E_1(N_a)$. Then the data volume after compression could be estimated based on l_i $(i = 1, 2, ..., N)$, and the final compression ratio could be predicted according to Eq. (1).

5 Simulation Analysis of the ABC Scheme

The key performance indicator for the ABC scheme is the compression ratio. According to Eq. (1), this ratio is related to the total number of accounts (N_a), and the bit-width of each module. Since the bit-width for the i-th module (m_i) is ib, the value of b is also an important parameter. In this section, we will study the influence of N_a and b to the compression ratio β by simulations, and the results are also used to verify the correctness of the theoretical analysis.

5.1 Influence of Accounts Number on Compression Ratio

A simulation platform is established using Python 2.7. The program runs on a PC with Windows 10 operation system, Inter(R) Core(TM) i7-7700HQ CPU @ 2.8 GHz, and 8 GB memory. In order to simplify the simulation model, we take the Ethereum as an example, so the bit-width of addresses is 160 ($k_1 = 160$). To study the influence of the accounts number on the compression ratio, the value of b is fixed to be 16, and 10 modules are selected. The i-th module m_i is the largest prime number smaller than 2^{ib}. In the simulation, the first three modules are $m_1 = 65521$ (16 bits), $m_2 = 4294967291$ (32 bits) and $m_3 = 281474976710597$ (48 bits).

The simulation procedure is shown as pseudocode in Table 1, in which N_a is the total number of addresses, R is the number of runs for average, N is the number of modules and ψ_N is the set with N fixed modules. The addresses list $Addr$ includes N_a randomly generated 160-bit integers. The function 'getRemainder' returns the remainders of all addresses in $Addr$ to a module. The function 'unique' returns the unique elements within the input sequence (r) and the corresponding index. So the length of the index is actually the number of remainders in the current list (l_i). Then the function 'delete' removes all the addresses that already recorded in the current list according to the index, and the remaining addresses would be tried to be filled in the next remainder list. This process is repeated until the address list $Addr$ is empty. Then the compression ratio for the current run could be calculated according to Eq. (1). The whole process would be repeated R times, then the expected compression ratio is calculated by averaging the R results in the list of *comp_ratio*. This simulation is repeated for the accounts number of 10000 to 100000, and the expected compression ratio for each N_a is plotted in Fig. 4. For

Table 1. Simulation pseudocode for compression ratio of N_a addresses

Begin:
1. $b = 16$; $\psi_N = \{m_1, m_2, m_3 \dots m_N\}$ % b and N modules
2. $R = 1000$ % number of runs for average
3.   comp_ratio = zeros(1, R)   % compression ratio for each run
4.   list_len = zeros(1, N)   % number of elements in each list (l_i)
5.   **for** (j = 1: R)
6.   Addr=$\{a_1, a_2, a_3 \dots a_{N_a}\}$ % Na 160-bit addresses to be compressed
7.   **for** (i =1:N)
8.   remainders = getRemainder(Addr, m_i)
9.   [r, index] = unique(remainders)
10.   unique_num(i) =   len(index)
11.   Addr = delete(Addr, index)
12.   **if** (len(Addr==0))
13.   break
14.   **end if**
15.   **end for**
16.   comp_ratio(j) = $((b \sum_{i=1}^{N} il_i)/(160*Na)$
17. **end for**
18. expected compression ratio = mean(comp_ratio)
End

comparison, the theoretical results based on the recursive approach introduced in Sect. 4 are also plotted in the same figure.

From Fig. 4, we can see that the simulation results match the theoretical results very well, which verified the correctness of the recursive analysis approach. As expected the compression ratio decreases with the increment of the number of addresses. For a small number of accounts, e.g. $N_a < 10000$, the compression ratio is close to 90%, which means most of the addresses are recorded in L_1. This is because if all compressed addresses are represented by a 16-bits integer, the compression ratio would be $1 - 16/160 = 0.9$. When N_a increases to 100000, most compressed addresses are still stored in L_1 because it can store up to 65521 remainders, but more addresses are represented by 32-bit integers, so the compression ratio decreases gradually to 87.6%. Since the volume of L_2 is about 4.3 billion, almost all of the addresses would be compressed to 16 bits or 32 bits when N_a is smaller than 1 billion, and L_3 is almost empty. So for the most practical blockchain system, e.g. N_a equals to 73 million in Ethereum, $N = 3$ is enough, and the compression ratio would be larger than $(1 - 32/160) = 80\%$, which is a huge reduction of the storage.

5.2 Influence of Different Values of B

In this subsection, the effect of the value of b is studied. As mentioned in Sect. 3.1, b is should be times of 8 for convenience of storage. Here we make $b = 8$, then the first five modules are $m_1 = 251$ (8 bits), $m_2 = 65521$ (16 bits), $m_3 = 16777213$ (24 bits), $m_4 = 4294967291$ (32 bits) and $m_5 = 1099511627689$ (40 bits). With these new parameters

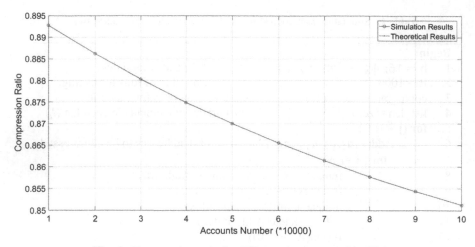

Fig. 4. Compression ratio for different accounts number (N_a)

($b = 8$, and $N = 5$), the same simulation code is used to calculate the compression ratio for address number N_a from 20000 to 200000, and the results are plotted in Fig. 5. For comparison, the results for $b = 16$, and $N = 3$ are also plotted. From the figure, we can see that the compression ratios for $b = 8$ are higher than that for $b = 16$. The improvement is about 0.7% for N_a around 20000, and it increases to about 3.5% for N_a = 200000. This is because a large part of addresses is represented by 24-bits integers for the case of $b = 8$ when is much larger than N_a. However, since the compression ratio for the case of $b = 16$ would be larger than 80% for reasonable large N_a, the improvement by $b = 8$ should be limited within 5% in the practical blockchain system.

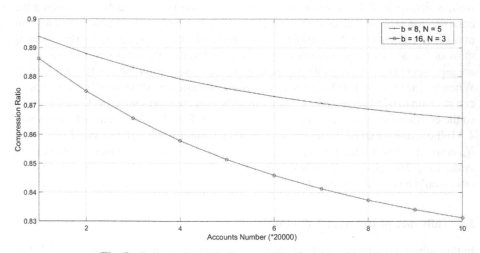

Fig. 5. Compression ratio for two cases ($b = 8$ vs. $b = 16$)

In addition, we also compare the simulation time for the two cases ($b = 16$ and $b = 8$), and the results are shown in Fig. 6. From the figure, we can see that the time for both cases increases linearly with the accounts number and that for the case of $b = 8$ is about 50% longer than that for $b = 16$. The reason for this phenomenon is that for the case of $b = 8$ more collisions would happen when we try to fill a compressed address into smaller list that is almost full, which will bring more comparison. However, the total time for both cases would be around several seconds even for millions of accounts, which would not be a big problem in the practical blockchain system.

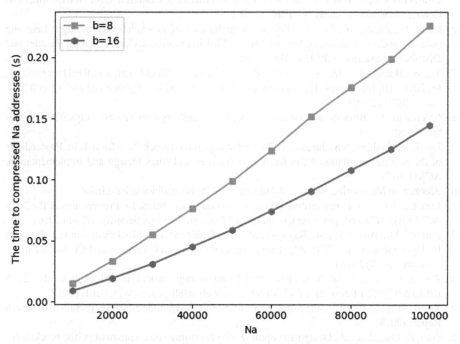

Fig. 6. Operational Time for two cases ($b = 8$ vs. $b = 16$)

6 Conclusion

In this paper, a modular-based compression scheme is proposed to reduce the volume of address data on a node in the blockchain system. In this scheme, the bit-width of the compressed address is adaptively selected according to the account number, so that the address would be represented with an integer with as small bit-width as possible. By both theoretical analysis and simulation experiments, we prove that the proposed scheme could provide a compression ratio of over 80% for the practical number of accounts, which is a huge reduction of storage for each node.

For the current stage, the theoretical analysis is performed using a recursive approach. In future work, we will try to optimize the approach and provide a closed form for the compression ratio for a specific account number.

References

1. Crosby, M., et al.: Blockchain technology: beyond bitcoin. Appl. Innov. **2**(6–10), 71 (2016)
2. Zyskind, G., Nathan, O.: Decentralizing privacy: using blockchain to protect personal data. In: 2015 IEEE Security and Privacy Workshops. IEEE (2015)
3. Iansiti, M., Lakhani, K.R.: The truth about blockchain. Harvard Bus. Rev. **95**(1), 118–127 (2017)
4. Swan, M.: Blockchain: Blueprint for a New Economy. O'Reilly Media Inc, Sebastopol (2015)
5. Tang, H., Ning, T., Ouyang, J.: Medical images sharing system based on blockchain and smart contract of credit scores. In: 2018 1st IEEE International Conference on Hot Information-Centric Networking (HotICN). IEEE (2018)
6. Duan, B., Zhong, Y., Liu, D.: Education application of blockchain technology: Learning outcome and meta-diploma. In: 2017 IEEE 23rd International Conference on Parallel and Distributed Systems (ICPADS). IEEE (2017)
7. Yu, W., Huang, S.: Traceability of food safety based on BlockChain and RFID technology. In: 2018 11th International Symposium on Computational Intelligence and Design (ISCID), vol. 1. IEEE (2019)
8. Nakamoto, S.: Bitcoin: a peer-to-peer electronic cash system (2009). https://bitcoin.org/bitcoin.pdf
9. Dorri, A., Kanhere, S.S., Jurdak, R.: Towards an optimized blockchain for IoT. In: Proceedings of the Second International Conference on Internet-of-Things Design and Implementation. ACM (2017)
10. Blockchain Monitoring Website, 8 December 2018. https://blockchain.info/
11. Luu, L., et al.: A secure sharding protocol for open blockchains. In: Proceedings of the 2016 ACM SIGSAC Conference on Computer and Communications Security. ACM (2016)
12. Zamani, M., Movahedi, M., Raykova, M.: Rapidchain: scaling blockchain via full sharding. In: Proceedings of the 2018 ACM SIGSAC Conference on Computer and Communications Security. ACM (2018)
13. Zheng, Q., et al.: An innovative IPFS-based storage model for blockchain. In: 2018 IEEE/WIC/ACM International Conference on Web Intelligence (WI). IEEE (2018)
14. Xu, B., et al.: EOS: an architectural, performance, and economic analysis. Technical Research Report (2018)
15. Guo, Z., Gao, Z., et al.: Design and optimization for storage mechanism of public blockchain-based on redundant residual number system. IEEE Access **7**, 98546–98554 (2019)
16. EtherscanWebsite. https://etherscan.io/chart/address
17. Gao, Z., Yang, W., Chen, X., et al.: Fault missing rate analysis of the arithmetic residue codes based fault-tolerant FIR filter design. In: Proceedings of the 2012 International On-Line Testing Symposium (2012)

Optimization Strategy of OpenFlow Flow Table Storage Based on the Idea of "Betweenness Centrality"

Zhaohui Ma[1,2] and Yan Yang[1](✉)

[1] School of Information Science and Technology, Guangdong University of Foreign Studies, Guangzhou 510006, China
mazhaohui@gdufs.edu.cn, 26593978@qq.com
[2] School of Computer Science, South China Normal University, Guangzhou 510631, China

Abstract. Since the advent of the Internet, its scale has expanded rapidly. Traditional network architecture is increasingly difficult to support this huge business. At this time, the clean slate team at Stanford University in the United States defined a new network architecture, SDN (Software Defined Network). The introduction of this network architecture has brought about tremendous changes in the development of today's networks. The separation of control layer from data layer through SDN enables network administrators to plan the network programmatically without changing network devices, realizing flexible configuration of network devices and fast forwarding of data flows. The controller sends the flow table down to the switch, and the data flow is forwarded through matching flow table items. However, the current flow table resources of the SDN switch are very limited. Therefore, this paper studies the technology of the latest SDN Flow table optimization at home and abroad, proposes an efficient optimization scheme of Flow table item on the betweenness centrality through the main road selection algorithm, and realizes related applications by setting up experimental topology.

Experiments show that this scheme can greatly reduce the number of flow table items of switches, especially the more hosts there are in the topology, the more obvious the experimental effect is. The experiments prove that the optimization success rate is over 85%.

Keywords: Software defined networking · Flow table · Betweenness centrality · Main road · Flow table optimization

1 Introduction

1.1 Background and Research Significance

In recent years, the arrival of the era of big data [1], artificial intelligence, mobile Internet and cloud computing [2] has changed people's way of life and brought great convenience to people's life. Nowadays, the business demand is increasingly complex and the number of users is increasing rapidly. However, the original network architecture is rigid.

© Springer Nature Singapore Pte Ltd. 2020
Z. Zheng et al. (Eds.): BlockSys 2019, CCIS 1156, pp. 161–174, 2020.
https://doi.org/10.1007/978-981-15-2777-7_14

Therefore, there is an urgent need for a new innovative network architecture that supports dynamic extensible and open free programming. In 2008, scholars at Stanford university firstly presented the concept of OpenFlow and expounded its basic theory, working principle and scenarios. The proposal of this technology solved the crisis of the traditional network architecture at that time, and also aroused the attention of the society and academia, which also opened the prelude for the emergence of SDN.

Software defined network [3, 4] is not a specific technology or protocol, but it is a network design idea and a network architecture. The core of SDN is OpenFlow [5] protocol, which is the Open interface protocol advocated by ONF (Open Networking Foundation), and the first standard southbound interface conforming to SDN specification. There are three layers in SDN architecture, including application layer, control layer and infrastructure layer from top to bottom. SDN is based on flow granularity control [6], and packets between switches are forwarded in the form of flow. For packets arriving at the switch, the switch will match each flow table item in the local flow table according to priority order. After a certain flow table item is successfully matched, the corresponding actions of the flow table item will be executed [7] to complete the processing of packets. If the match fails, the switch will build a Packet_in packet and send it to the controller. The controller will generate a new forwarding rule and send it to the switch, which will process the packet according to this new rule. However, the current flow table storage resources of switches are too limited to store all the flow table items in the network. Therefore, it is very necessary to study the flow table optimization of SDN.

1.2 The Related Research on SDN Flow Table Optimization

When a large number of data flows arrive at the switch and many packets do not have corresponding matching flow table items in the flow table of the switch, the switch will construct Packet_in packets to send to the controller. At present, most of the flow table hardware components of OpenFlow switches are TCAM three-state content addressing memory [8], which has a fast lookup speed and mature technology. However, TCAM has high cost, high power consumption and very limited storage capacity, which can only load 1k-2k stream items. Therefore, in order to widely popularize and apply SDN, it is urgent to solve the optimization problem of flow table in switch.

At present, the SDN flow table optimization can be divided into three categories: optimization based on flow table resource reuse, optimization based on multilevel flow table and optimization based on flow table item stagnation timeout.

An optimization based on flow table resource reuse is to compress a flow table item with the same matching fields into one flow table item. Li et al. defined a new flow table structure, proposed an algorithm of correlation degree between flow tables, and designed a process to update flow tables to store more flow tables [9].

Optimization based on multilevel flow tables is to divide the flow table into several sub-flow tables according to the matching fields to meet the storage of flow table items. Liu proposed multilevel flow table optimization of FPGA, which processed resources by adding table management module and resource pool module, so as to improve the scalability and flexibility of multilevel flow table [10].

Optimization based on flow table item stagnation timeout studies and analyzes the related information of real-time data flow, mainly focusing on the soft timeout and hard timeout of data flow.

In the first scheme, a single flow table item can manage multiple data flows, so as to make more precise and efficient use of the limited flow table space [11]. However, this scheme can only compress the flow table items according to the correlation degree, which is not extensible. In the second scheme, the multilevel flow table structure itself saves a lot of resource space, and the sub-flow table is under unified management and resource invocation in the table management module, which improves the extendibility and flexibility of the multilevel flow table. However, in the optimization process, delay is not considered comprehensively. The third scheme can improve switch performance and avoid congestion in control channel. However, without considering the characteristics of each stream, more frequently used stream items cannot be processed separately. Therefore, this paper proposes a flow table optimization strategy based on "betweenness centrality". Simulation results show that this method is simple and feasible, and can greatly reduce the number of flow table items in SDN switches.

1.3 Main Content and Structure of the Paper

This paper mainly introduces the related theory and technology of SDN, the platform and tools of simulation experiment. On this platform, we carried out an experiment on the optimization strategy of flow table storage based on "betweenness centrality", analyzed the experimental results, and drew a conclusion. Section 1 introduces the background of the current topic and the significance of studying SDN. Section 2 introduces some theoretical knowledge and related technologies of SDN. Section 3 introduces the implementation of flow table storage optimization strategy based on "betweenness centrality". Section 4 builds the topology, conducts simulation, and conduct comparative analysis of experimental results to draw conclusions. Section 5 is the summary and prospect of future research. It summarizes the experiment of this paper, proposes the shortcomings of this experiment and the future research direction.

2 SDN Related Knowledge and Technology

This section first introduces the composition of SDN architecture, and then analyzes the key technologies involved. The OpenFlow protocol is detailed described in the paper.

2.1 The Composition and Workflow of SDN Architecture

The SDN architecture defined by ONF is shown in Fig. 1. From top to bottom, there are application layer, control layer and infrastructure layer respectively.

The application layer has all kinds of programmable software. The open northbound interface provides a channel for users of the application layer, through which users can program the network abstract view provided by the control layer to realize corresponding network services and meet business requirements. The control layer is also known as

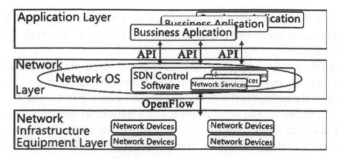

Fig. 1. SDN architecture

network control operating system (NOS). Different from traditional networks, it separates hardware devices from network control functions. The control layer consists of a programmable logic controller that handles the data at the infrastructure layer. The basic equipment layer, also known as the data forwarding layer, is composed of switches with data forwarding function, which are responsible for data collecting, data forwarding and data processing.

The workflow of SDN is that when the OpenFlow switch receives the packet, it first looks for the flow table item in the local flow table to match, and if the match is successful, it performs the action of matching the flow table item. If the match is unsuccessful, the data packet will be sent to the controller which decides where the packet goes. The control layer updates the flow table of the OpenFlow switch through the OpenFlow protocol, so as to realize centralized control of network data [12].

2.2 Overview of SDN Key Technologies and Betweenness Centrality

OpenFlow Protocol
OpenFlow protocol is the first southbound interface protocol and the most standard interface protocol. Now there are six versions of OpenFlow protocol, including OpenFlow1.0, OpenFlow1.1, OpenFlow1.2, OpenFlow1.3, OpenFlow1.4 and OpenFlow1.5, among which the most widely used and the most compatible ones are OpenFlow1.0 and OpenFlow1.3 (Fig. 2).

Ingress port	Ether Source	Ether Dst	Ether Type	Vlan id	Vlan Priority	IP src	IP dst	IP proto	IP TOS bits	TCP/UDP Src Port	TCP/UGP Des Port

Fig. 2. Header domain field of OpenFlow1.0 version

In OpenFlow1.0, its flow table items are composed of Header Fields, Counters and Actions, while in 1.3, they are composed of Match Fields, Priority, Counters, Instructions, Timeouts, and cookies. It can be seen that OpenFlow1.3 has several more fields for flow table items than the 1.0 version.

Figure 3 shows the related components of an OpenFlow1.3 flow table item:

Match Fields	Priority	Counters	Instructions	Timeouts	Cookie

Fig. 3. The components of flow table items

SDN Switch and Southward Interface Technology

Currently, the most well-known southbound interface technology is the OpenFlow protocol advocated by ONF. As an open protocol, OpenFlow breaks through the barrier of traditional network equipment manufacturers to the device capability interface. After years of development, with the joint efforts of the industry, it has been gradually improved and can comprehensively solve various problems in SDN network. Currently, OpenFlow has been widely supported by the industry and has become the de facto standard in the field of SDN. For example, OVS switches can support OpenFlow protocol.

SDN Controller and Northbound Interface Technology

Controller is an application program with control function of SDN, which is the core of the whole network. The controller interacts with the application layer and infrastructure layer respectively through the northbound interface and southbound interface, decouples the control function from the traditional network equipment, and is responsible for centralized management of the whole network, which is the spiritual hub for the normal operation of SDN network.

Different from existing international standards such as OpenFlow for southbound interface, northbound interface still lacks standards recognized by the industry, so the protocol formulation of northbound interface will become the focus of current competition in SDN field.

Ryu is an open source SDN controller designed and developed by Japanese NTT company. It is completely based on Python environment programming. Its simple code style, clear modules and good extendibility makes it very friendly to beginners. Ryu provides many developed interfaces, rich components, and a large number of library functions for developers to develop new control programs. Ryu also supports all versions of OpenFlow protocol and other southbound protocols such as Netconf and f-config. Ryu uses Apache license open source protocol standard and supports the combination with OpenStack in the field of cloud computing. Therefore, the controller is used in the simulation experiment.

Betweenness Centrality

In network science, it is very important to find the key nodes in the network. Network link prediction and other problems can be solved by analyzing the flow rate and node location of key nodes. In graph theory and network analysis, centrality is the index to determine the importance of nodes in the network, and the quantification of the importance of nodes. The method of determination has degree centrality, proximity centrality and betweenness centrality. Here we use betweenness centrality.

Betweenness centrality, shortened as betweenness, is the number of times that this node is in the shortest path between any two nodes. The higher the betweenness value is, the more times the node acts as a bridge, the more flow rate it passes through, and the more important role it plays in the network [13]. By calculating the betweenness value, we can accurately find the nodes with high flow rate in the network, but this is not applicable to large networks, because the time complexity of the algorithm to calculate the betweenness value is O(N3), which is too inefficient.

The formula of betweenness centrality is shown as follows, where N represents the number of nodes, gst represents the number of shortest paths from node s to node t, and nist represents the number of shortest paths from node s to node t of node I.

$$BC_i = \frac{1}{N^2 - 3N + 2} \sum_{s \neq i \neq t} \frac{n_{st}^i}{g_{st}} \tag{1}$$

In this experiment, the above formula 1 is used to calculate the betweenness value.

2.3 Summary

This section mainly introduces the basic theory of SDN, work flow, related technology and betweenness centrality formula. Firstly, the architecture and workflow of SDN are introduced, and the functions of each layer of SDN are briefly introduced. Then, the OpenFlow technology, controller and experimental platform Mininet of SDN are introduced. Finally, the basic theory and formula of betweenness centrality, the core idea of this experiment, are expounded.

3   Concrete Implementation of Flow Table Optimization Based on "Betweenness Centrality" Strategy

This paper presents a flow table optimization strategy based on betweenness centrality. By calculating the betweenness value of each switch in the network and comparing it with the pre-calculated threshold value, the qualified switch is selected as the main node to form a main road for flow table optimization. In this process, the selected main node may form a main road with a loop or produce multiple main road. It might even appear isolated nodes (the main node does not connect to other main nodes). Therefore, it is firstly needed to realize automatic threshold selection through the threshold selection algorithm according to different topology, and secondly to remove the loop of the main road by the ring algorithm, and to remove isolated nodes, etc., so as to find out an optimal main road.

Later, we specify the data in the network to be forwarded through this main road, which makes part of the flow rate concentrated on the main road and reduces the flow rate in other areas. Then, the flow table items distributed to this main road are optimized to greatly reduce the total number of flow table items in the network and achieve the purpose of optimizing the storage resources of flow table.

To verify the correctness of the "betweenness centrality" strategy, under the condition of unchanged simulation platform, the network topology and other experimental environment, on Ryu controller we in turn run the script file of two different algorithm, which are selecting the main road respectively based on the shortest path algorithm and based on "betweenness centrality". Then use the ping command in the mininet, ensure the whole network ping realization. Eventually both cases will produce different number of flow table items in switch. Compare and analyze the total quantity of flow table items. In addition to the horizontal comparison with the results produced by the script file based on the "shortest path" algorithm, we also did the vertical comparison. Under the same network topology, each access layer switch accesses 4 hosts (16 hosts in total) and 10 hosts (40 hosts in total), respectively, runs the script file of "shortest path" algorithm and the script file of "betweenness centrality", compares and analyzes the number of flow table items generated, and draws the conclusion.

3.1 The Selection of Threshold

The threshold value determines which switches can become main nodes. In the actual situation, different thresholds should be selected for different topologies, so as to select the main road that can achieve the optimal effect of flow table item quantity optimization. The specific selection process is shown in the following Fig. 4:

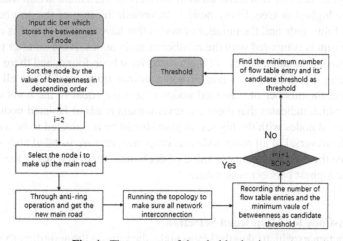

Fig. 4. The process of threshold selection

① Get the betweenness value of all nodes, and sort them in descending order according to the betweenness value.
② Choose the node with the top two betweenness values as the main node.
③ Select the largest total betweenness value as the main road among the selected main node and conduct anti-ring operation to get the new main road.
④ Take the main node of this main road with the minimum betweenness value as the candidate threshold, run the topology, ensure the whole network connection, and record the number of flow table items generated under the candidate threshold.
⑤ Choose the node that is not the main node but with the largest value (value must be greater than 0) and add it into the main node, and perform ③ ④ operation on the selected main node.

⑥ When all nodes are selected, compare the number of each candidate threshold flow table items, select the minimum number of candidate threshold flow table items as the threshold of this design.

After the above steps, the threshold that can produce the minimum number of flow table items can be selected.

3.2 The Process to Realize the Main Road Selection and Loop Removal

The Overview of Main Road Selection Process

The steps to select the main road are divided into three steps:

(1) First, select the threshold value with the best optimization effect according to a certain process, and then select the switch whose betweenness value is greater than or equal to the threshold value as the main node.
(2) Through the breadth-first traversal method, traverse each node in turn from the node with the highest degree. Every node is traversed, the sum of the number of child nodes of this node and the number of nodes that have been traversed is calculated, and the sum is compared with the number of main nodes. If the number is the same as the number of main nodes, all main roads have been found, and there is no need to traverse the child nodes again. If not, continue traversing. When all nodes are traversed, the number of traversed nodes is still not equal to the number of main nodes, which indicates that there are several main roads or isolated nodes, and the untraversed nodes with the highest degree should be re-selected to be traversed.
(3) After the traversal of all main nodes is completed, remove isolated nodes, and then calculate the total betweenness value of each main road, and select the main road with the highest betweenness value.

The Pseudo-Code for Main Road Selection

Link is the dictionary which takes the key as node, the value as the node directly connected to the other node. Road is the dictionary which takes the key as the root node, the value as the root node and its descendants. The node refers to the traversing nodes, main_node refers to the set of main rodes, y_node refers to the collection of known node (possible traversed nodes and non-traversed nodes), child_node refers to the collection of all child nodes of this layer, n_child_node refers to the collection of all child nodes of the next layer, and c_flag is used to determine whether there is the main road.

Input : link, main_node
1 : Link is sorted in descending order by number of values
2 : while (len(y_node)!=len(main_node))
3 :   if(len(y_node) == 0 or c_flag)
4 :   Select the first link key as the root for traversal, and add y_node,c_flag=0
5 :   y_node.append(child_node)
6 :   update "road"
7 :   delete link[node]
8 :   if (len(y_node)==len(main_node))
9 :   break
10 :   end if
11 :   for c ∈ child_node
12 :   repeat 5-10
13 :   add node's children to n_child_node
14 :   end for
15 :   if(len(n_child_node)>0)
16 :   continue
17 :   else:c_flag=1
18 : end while
19 : Remove isolated nodes in road, calculate the total number of betweenness of
        the roads, and select the road with the highest value as the main road
20 : end

Advantages and Disadvantages of the Algorithm
Advantages: in the case of only one main road or only one left main road, priority traversal of high nodes, can quickly find more child nodes. In addition, the number of its children is added to the number of traversed nodes for each node traversed, and then judged with the number of primary nodes. If the same is true, no other nodes need to be traversed (indicates that only this node has children, and other nodes are leaf nodes).

Disadvantages: when there are still several main roads, each node still needs to be traversed.

Overview of Main Road De-loop
The de-loop algorithm designed in this paper is based on depth-first traversal. First, the main nodes are sorted in descending order according to the size of the betweenness number, and the first two main nodes are added directly (the two main nodes must be loop-free). From the third main node, the third main node is used as the starting point for deep traversal (traversing the joined node). If the starting point are being traversed, directly traverse the untraversed nodes in the child nodes of the starting point. If it is not the starting point traversed, traverse each node. Then gather the nodes which are directly connected to this node and gather the child nodes of the starting point. Next find out the intersection. If no value exists in the intersection, continue traversing the next node. If the intersection has a value, the starting point is connected to the determined main node in a loop. It is needed to delete the starting point, terminate the traversal, and then add the next undetermined main node as the starting point for deep traversal. When all the main nodes are judged, the de-loop algorithm ends.

In general, this algorithm is to add main nodes in order of large betweenness number to form a new undirected graph G2 when all main nodes are known as undirected graph G1. The first two main nodes join directly without traversing. Starting from the third main node, each main node is added as a starting point and deep traversal is performed according to the newly formed undirected graph G2. When a loop is found, delete the starting point, update G1 and G2, and terminate the traversal. Then add the next undetermined main node as the starting point for deep traversal until all main nodes are judged.

The Pseudo-Code for Main Road Loop Prevention
Main_node is the set of main node, n_main_node is the set of undetermined main node, node represents the node being traversed, start is the starting point of deep traversal, child is the child node, index is the index of child node and stack simulates stack for backtracking. The stack stores nodes and index information and the bottom of the stack consists of the starting point and the index. Stack = [[node, index]]]. G1 represents the undirected graph formed by all main nodes. G1 = {m1: set([m1, m2...]), m2: set([m3, m4...]), ..., mn: set([m1, m2...])}. G1' key is the main node, and the value is other main nodes directly connected with the main node. G2 represents the undirected graph formed after adding main nodes in sequence according to G1, and the structure is consistent with G1.

```
Input: G1, main_node
 1: for start in main_node
 2: n_main_node.remove[start], update G2
 3: e_link=G2[start]
 4: if(len(e_link)==1)
 5:     continue
 6: end if
 7: stack=[[start,0]]
 8: while(stack)
 9:     (node,index)=stack[-1]
10:     if(index>=len(G2[node])
11:         stack.pop()
12:         continue
13:     end if
14:     if node !=start
15:         result=G2[node]&e_link
16:     if(len(result)>0)
17:         main_node.remove(start)
18:         update G1
19:         break
20:     end if
21:     child=G2[node][index]
22:     if node in G2[child]
23:         G2[child].remove(node)
24:     end if
25:     stack[-1][1]+=1
26:     stack.append([child,0])
27: end while
```

4 Simulation Experiment Process and Result Analysis

4.1 Experimental Environment Description

In this experiment, the operating system is Windows7 and the virtual machine is Ubuntu14.04. Mininet and Ryu controllers are installed in the virtual machine.

4.2 Experimental Topology

Firstly, the network topology required by the experiment was set up in the visual operation interface miniedit, as shown in Fig. 5. Among them, network segment 10.0.1.0/24 has host h1, h5, h9 and h13; network segment 100.0.2.0/24 has host h2, h6, h10 and h14; network segment 192.168.3.0/24 has host h3, h7, h11 and h15; network segment 200.0.4.0/24 has host h4, h8, h12 and h16. Switches s1 to s11 are connected to controller c0 respectively.

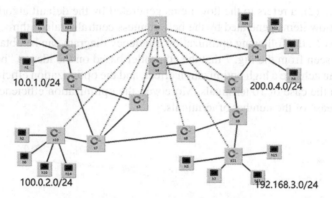

Fig. 5. Experimental topology

4.3 Analysis of Experimental Results

Experimental operation: Firstly, on the basis of the topology in Fig. 5, modify six topological scripts with different numbers of terminals, including 10, 16, 22, 28, 34 and 40. Then run the two algorithm scripts respectively, and record the number of corresponding flow table items after the whole network ping is realized. The final experimental results are shown in Fig. 6.

It can be clearly seen from the figure above that the number of terminals is an incremental arithmetic sequence with a tolerance of 6. When 6 terminals are added, only 12 more flow table items will be generated by the controller based on the idea of "betweenness centrality", while many more flow table items will be generated by the shortest path forwarding controller.

The statistical formula of optimization efficiency F is as follows:

$$F = \frac{a - b}{a} \times 100\% \tag{2}$$

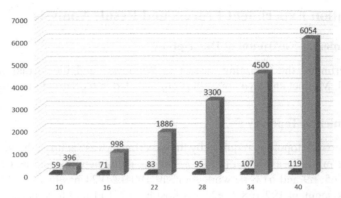

Fig. 6. A comparison chart of the number of flow table items generated by different number of terminals

In formula (2), a refers to the flow items generated by the default algorithm, and b refers to the flow items generated by the betweenness centrality algorithm

Based on (2), the following optimization efficiency diagram can be obtained.

It can be seen from the Fig. 7 that the controller based on the idea of "betweenness centrality" can achieve a high optimization effect, and the optimization efficiency can be up to 85% in the case of 10 terminals. Moreover, the optimization efficiency increases with the increase of the number of terminals.

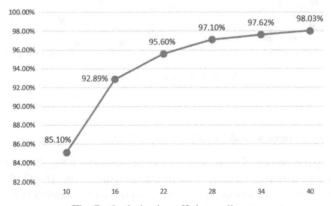

Fig. 7. Optimization efficiency diagram

The forwarding logic of the controller based on the idea of "betweenness centrality" in the topology center is certain, so for every additional terminal A, when two flow table items are added in the access layer switch S, the full network interconnection can be realized. A flow generated by A can go out from S. After going out, the flow table item issued before can be directly used to realize the forwarding of the flow. The other flow, which goes to destination A, goes to S and ends up in A. And for the shortest path forward controller, every time adding a terminal A, two flow table items are distributed to the nodes passing through the shortest path from A to any other node B in the network in order to achieve full network connectivity. If the shortest path from A to B passes through 6 nodes (including A and B themselves), 12 flow table items will be issued, which can only realize the interworking between A and B. By contrast, the number of terminals has a very small effect on the number of flow table items generated by the controller based on the idea of "betweenness centrality".

5 Summary and Prospect

5.1 Summary of the Paper

SDN realizes the separation of control function and forwarding function, so that hardware manufacturers no longer need to design and install the corresponding software system for each hardware, and the hardware is generalized. SDN can also carry out unified management of flow rate and realize centralized control, greatly reducing the difficulty of network maintenance. The network deployment of SDN network architecture is more convenient. The time of network deployment has been shortened and the cost of network operation and maintenance has been reduced. SDN can also achieve dynamic monitoring of flow rate and meet business requirements better and faster. With the advent of the era of great wisdom cloud, the huge network data and complex business require an increasing performance and service quality of today's network. The traditional network architecture cannot meet the needs of users. The emergence of SDN also points out a clear way for the bottleneck of the current network. Although SDN looks very powerful now, it is still in the development stage and many technologies are not mature yet. However, the open network architecture represented by SDN is still the development trend of the network in the future. At present, the research on the limited resources of SDN flow table is still a hot topic in academia and society.

To solve this problem, this paper proposes a flow table optimization strategy based on betweenness centrality. Betweenness centrality was proposed by professor Lyndon freeman, an American sociologist. It can be used to quantify the importance of a node in the network. In a network, the node with higher betweenness value act acts a bridge for other nodes and is more capable of promoting the communication between other nodes, which has a great influence. This node is located in the area of large flow, the need to carry the larger flow. Therefore, compared with other paths, the flow rate through the main road composed of betweenness centrality is the largest. Then, the flow table items on this main road are optimized by corresponding algorithm, which can greatly reduce the flow table items in the network and relieve the pressure of switches in other zone at the same time. Experimental results show that the flow table optimization method based on "betweenness centrality" can reduce the number of flow table items in the network.

5.2 Research Prospects

Although this experiment has achieved the expected effect, there are still some shortcomings in the following aspects:

(1) when selecting the main road according to the total value of the betweenness number, the design takes insufficient consideration of various situation, such as whether the main road has ring or not. It may be the case that the total value of the betweenness number of the main road after ring removal is not the maximum, which still needs to be improved.

(2) The flow table items issued by this experiment only take into account the network topology. However, the actual network environment is more complex, and there may be transmission failure of switch or host on the link, or connection of different switches to the host in the same network segment, etc., so the flow table items need to be considered more. There may be different topologies with different results. Therefore, in order to adapt to more topologies and more network situations, this strategy still needs to be further studied.

References

1. Manyika, J., Chui, M., Brown, B., et al.: Big Data: The Next Frontier For Innovation, Competition, and Productivity. McKinsey Global Institute, Washington, DC (2011). J. Analytics
2. Pallis, G.: Cloud computing: the new frontier of internet computing. J. IEEE Internet Comput. **5**, 70–73 (2010)
3. Open Networking Foundation. Software-Defined Networking: The New Norm for Networks. ONF White Paper (2012)
4. Zuo, Q.Y., Chen, M., Zhao, G.S., et al.: Research on SDN technology based on Open Flow. J. Softw. **24**(5), 1078–1097 (2013)
5. McKeown N., et al.: Open flow: enabling innovation in campus networks. ACM SIGCOMM CCR **38**(2), 69–74 (2008)
6. Fu, Y.H.: Research on SDN-based multipath load balancing algorithm and flow table allocation optimization algorithm. Anhui University (2017)
7. Xie, L.: Research on optimization technology of OpenFlow switch flow table in software-defined network. Zhejiang University (2015)
8. Zhang, S.J., Lan, J.L., Hu, Y.X., Jiang, Y.M.: Research progress on scalability of software defined network control plane. J. Softw. **29**(01), 160–175 (2018)
9. Li, X.W., Ji, M., Cao, M., Dai, J.Y.: Openflow storage optimization scheme based on resource reuse. J. Opt. Commun. Res. **02**, 8–11 (2014)
10. Liu, Y.: Research and design of optimization strategy for flow table in SDN switch. Beijing University of Posts and Telecommunications (2017)
11. Shi, S.P.: Research on OpenFlow flow table optimization technology. Zhengzhou University (2016)
12. Chen, L.Y., Zhang, X.Y.: Design and implementation of SDN performance measurement system. J. Chengdu Univ. Inf. Eng. **33**(01), 18–22 (2018)
13. Wang, X.J., Wang, B., Xia, Y.D., Lu, L.P., Liu, H., Xiong, X.: Evaluation method of core node of brain network based on mesoclization and k-shell. J. Comput. Eng. Appl. **53**(11), 44–49 (2017)

Research and Implementation of Multi-chain Digital Wallet Based on Hash TimeLock

Zujian Li and Zhihong Zhang[⊠]

School of Information Engineering, ZhengZhou University, ZhengZhou 45001, China
854686728@qq.com, iezhzhang@zzu.edu.cn

Abstract. In terms of interoperability between different blockchains issue and achieving value exchange between different blockchains, a convertible multi-chain digital wallet solution is proposed. The wallet realizes the exchange of different digital currency assets by hash timelock technology. In traditional blockchain projects, each blockchain is a closed island. Users need to exchange different digital currencies through centralized Exchanges, this is contrary to the idea of decentralization and non-tamperability of blockchains, safety and reliability depend entirely on Exchanges. By introducing hash timelock technology, multi-chain digital wallet can realize the exchange of digital assets in different blockchains without third-party intermediary, ensure its de-centralization characteristics, safety and reliability.

Keywords: Blockchain · Digital wallet · Hash timelock · Smart contract

1 Introduction

Blockchain [1] is considered as one of the revolutionary emerging technologies in recent years. The essence of blockchain is distributed ledger. By combining with traditional computer technology such as point-to-point transmission, consensus mechanism, encryption algorithm, it forms an innovative application mode in the Internet era. Blockchain have been fully used in the financial field with the characteristics of decentralization, traceability and non-tamperability.

With the continuous development of blockchain, many attention has been paid to digital wallet. As an important tool for custody of user's assets, digital wallet is the entrance to blockchain for ordinary users, and plays an indispensable role in blockchain technology. But in existing blockchain projects, most digital wallets are special wallets, which can only serve specific blockchains, they can not realize the transfer and conversion of digital currency. Although there are some digital wallets supporting multiple currencies, the underlying technical principles are in the form of centralized exchanges, which is contrary to the idea of decentralization and non-tamperability of blockchains.

2 Relevant Technology Research

2.1 Research on Cross-chain Technology

To solve the problem of value exchange between blockchains, it is generally acknowledged that the mainstream solution is to use cross-chain technology of blockchains.

© Springer Nature Singapore Pte Ltd. 2020
Z. Zheng et al. (Eds.): BlockSys 2019, CCIS 1156, pp. 175–182, 2020.
https://doi.org/10.1007/978-981-15-2777-7_15

Cross-chain technologies fall into three main categories, notary or multiple signature schemes, side chain/relay chain and hash timelock. Table 1 describes the principles of cross-chain technology.

Table 1. Cross-chain technology comparison

Cross-chain technology	Algorithmic principle	Shortcoming
Notary	Transfer of assets to notary accounts	Weak centralization
Side chain	Read the data in the side chain	Verification difficulties
Relay chain	Establishing relay chain	Data redundancy

Notary or multi-signature scheme is a weak centralized solution, transfer digital assets by locking assets in the main chain to multiple specific addresses and requiring signatures from multiple notaries. Ripple of Interledger protocol [2] enables assets of different blockchains to be transferred across chains through trusted third parties. Notary or multi-signature scheme is the simplest way to realize cross-chain asset transfer, but the security of asset transfer depends on the honesty of notaries.

Side chain technology transfers digital assets by reading the data in the main chain to verify the authenticity of transaction payments. BTC Relay project is to realize cross-chain payment by verifying Bitcoin SPV payment path to trigger the execution of ETH smart contract [3].

Relay technology is to link existing blockchain projects by building a relay chain to realize asset transfer of different blockchains. COSMOS [4] and Polkadot [5] projects are to build cross-chain platform of blockchain through the combination of notary and relay technology.

2.2 Research on Hash Timelock Algorithms

The emergence of hash locking technology is mainly to solve the transaction processing capacity of blockchains, by setting specific conditions and given hash value to achieve cross-chain transfer of digital Assets. Herlihy [6] proves the atomic nature of hash locking technology, which can ensure that both transfers occur or do not occur, and determines the security and reliability of blockchain asset exchange. This paper proposes a hash timelock algorithm based on hash locking technology. After improving the original algorithm, two different block chain assets are transferred. As shown in Fig. 1, the hash timelock algorithm flows as follows.

Step1. User A generates random ciphers s and gets the hash value H = hash (s) by hashing operation, which sends H to User B.
Step2. User A and user B lock their assets into specific smart contracts. User A smart contract logic is that if passwords are provided within 2X time, the assets are transferred to user B or returned to user A. User B smart contract logic is that if passwords are provided within X time, the assets are transferred to user A or returned to user B.

Step3. In order to get the assets of User B, user A provides passwords to user B's smart contract in X time.

Step4. Because of the passwords provided by user A, user B provided the passwords to user A's smart contract in 2X time and got user A's assets.

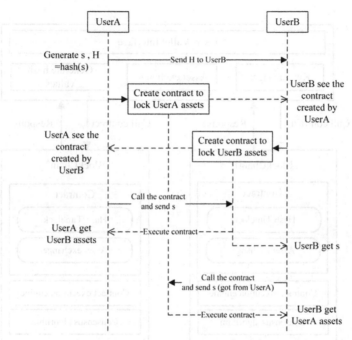

Fig. 1. Hash timelock algorithm process

3 Overall Design

The multi-chain digital wallet mainly satisfies the exchange of assets between any two different blockchains. The two blockchains are independent of each other, and each has its own consensus mechanism, smart contract execution engine and block data structure. The hash timelock smart contracts are deployed on different blockchains, and digital wallets exchange assets by calling hash timelock smart contracts on block chains. The overall structure of the digital wallet system is shown in Fig. 2.

(1) User Layer: It mainly includes wallet interface and related functions provided by wallet, such as key management, asset exchange and generating hash value.

(2) Block and Contract Layer: It mainly includes two different block chain networks. Each block chain network has its own smart contract execution engine, consensus mechanism and network broadcasting mechanism. Deploy corresponding smart contracts according to different block chain networks. Two different smart contracts realize the exchange logic of different user assets. Smart contracts include the logical

implementation of hash timelock. After deploying the smart contracts, Users call smart contracts through wallets and trigger asset exchange transactions.

(3) Physical Layer: Block chain physical layer stores data. Users call smart contracts and broadcast transactions in their respective block chain networks. Finally, transaction data is written in the blocks.

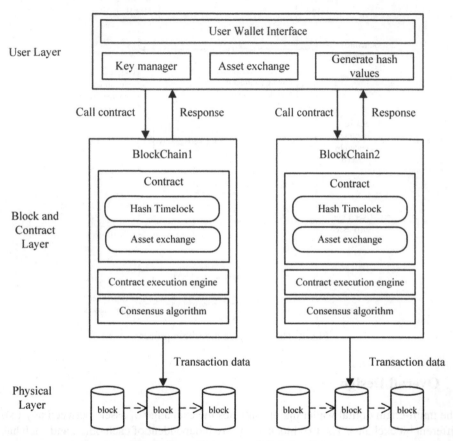

Fig. 2. Overall structure of digital wallet

4   Algorithmic Implementation

Cross-chain asset exchange process should satisfy atomicity and the operation of asset exchange is uninterruptible. In the case of successful operation, assets should be transferred smoothly to the other party's account. In case of operational failure, assets should be returned to the respective accounts of both parties. In the hash timelock algorithm, it should be considered that in case of overtime, the transfer fails and the assets are returned to their respective accounts.

Based on hash timelock asset exchange is mainly achieved through smart contract. Smart contract allow transactions to be conducted without a third party. Once smart contracts are executed, the execution process is irreversible. Thus, using smart contract to implement hash timelock algorithm can ensure the atomicity, security and immutability of asset exchange. The user calls the smart contract process through the digital wallet as shown in Fig. 3.

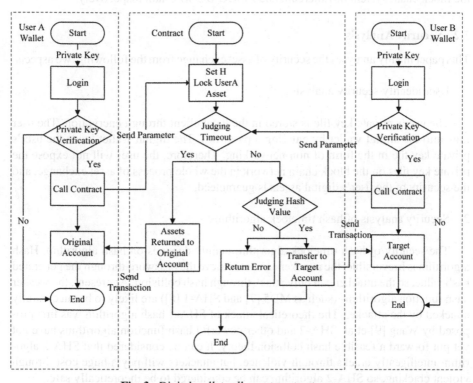

Fig. 3. Digital wallet call smart contract process

Figure 3 shows a one-way exchange of assets (for example, the assets of User A are transferred to User B), exchange of assets in another direction (for example, the assets of User B are transferred to Use A) is consistent with Fig. 3. Users interact with smart contract through digital wallets. Smart contract are responsible for executing the asset exchange process, user wallet is responsible for transferring parameter values to smart contract such as hash value, time setting and digital asset management.

Smart contract algorithm first determines whether the time-out occurs. If the time-out occurs, the asset exchange process will terminate and the locked digital assets will be returned to the original account. Otherwise, the hash value will be judged. If the password is correct, the digital assets will be exchanged, or the password error information will be returned.

5 Experiment and Result Analysis

5.1 Experiment Environment

In order to validate the asset exchange function of digital wallet, this paper simulates the asset exchange between blockchains by building private blockchain in the environment of Ethereum and FISCO BCOS. In this experiment, two server hosts were used to construct the block chain system of Ethereum and FISCO BCOS Chain respectively.

5.2 Security Analysis

This paper mainly analyses the security of asset exchange from the following two aspects.

1. User identity security analysis

    The user's private key file is stored in the local client through encryption. The user logs into the digital wallet by entering a password. The digital wallet loads the user's private key file in the form of non-networking. Therefore, the user will not expose the private key files on the block chain network in the whole process of asset exchange, and the security of the user's digital assets is guaranteed.

2. Security analysis of hash timelock algorithms

    The security of hash timelock algorithm mainly depends on hash algorithm. Hash algorithm is irreversible, the attacker can not retrieve the password through the generated hash value, so the attacker can only attack through hash collision. At present, the weaker hash function algorithms (such as MD5 [7] and SHA-1 [8]) are likely to be successfully attacked by the attacker. The theoretical attack of SHA-1 hash algorithm was first proposed by Wang [9] et al. SHA-2 and other powerful hash function algorithms have not yet put forward a feasible hash collision theory. It can be considered that SHA-2 algorithm intelligently cracks through violence, but attackers will pay a huge cost through violent cracking, so SHA-2 algorithm can be considered to be theoretically safe.

5.3 Delay Analysis

Assume that the asset exchange time is block chain out time plus hash lock time.

Firstly, we get the time of block generation rate, conduct one or more asset exchange transactions, record the start and end time of each transaction, and then compare it with the time of block generation rate. If the transaction time of asset exchange is related to the block chain generation rate plus hash locking time, it proves that the delay of asset exchange is related to the set hash locking time value. Because FISCO BCOS of consensus algorithm is PBFT, the block generation rate can not be predicted, so the delay analysis experiment is based on the block generation rate of Ethereum. The block generation rate of Ethereum and asset exchange test is shown in Fig. 4.

As shown in Fig. 4, the difference between the asset exchange time and the Ethereum block generation rate is equal to the hash timelock set by the experiment. The experimental results are consistent with the expected hypothesis.

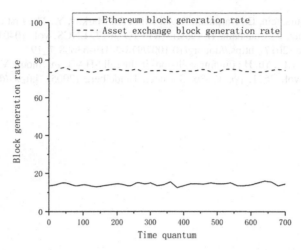

Fig. 4. Block generation rate of Ethereum and asset exchange

6 Conclusion

This paper mainly research the exchangeability of blockchain assets and the analysis and comparison of cross-chain technology. At the same time, the implementation of hash timelock technology is proposed. The logic of hash timelock technology is realized through smart contract, and the exchange of blockchain assets is completed by the interaction of digital wallet and smart contract. Based on hash timelock digital wallet solves the problem of simplification of wallet supporting assets, and proposes a technical idea of de-centralized exchange of digital assets. Users can complete asset exchange through the wallet without the help of a third party. The wallet uses hash timelock technology to ensure the security and reliability of digital asset exchange.

References

1. Nakamoto, S.: Bitcoin: a peer-to-peer electronic cash system (2008)
2. Hope-Bailie, A., Thomas, S.: Interledger: creating a standard for payments. In: Proceedings of the 25th International Conference Companion on World Wide Web, pp. 281–282. International World Wide Web Conferences Steering Committee (2016)
3. Buterin, V.: A next-generation smart contract and decentralized application platform. White paper (2014)
4. Kwon, J., Buchman, E.: Cosmos: a network of distributed ledgers (2016). https://cosmos. network/whitepaper
5. Wood, G.: Polkadot: vision for a heterogeneous multi-chain framework. White Paper (2016)
6. Herlihy, M.: Atomic cross-chain swaps. In: Proceedings of the 2018 ACM Symposium on Principles of Distributed Computing, pp. 245–254. ACM (2018)
7. Wang, X., Feng, D., Lai, X., et al.: Collisions for Hash Functions MD4, MD5, HAVAL-128 and RIPEMD. IACR Cryptology ePrint Archive 2004, 199 (2004)

8. Stevens, M., Bursztein, E., Karpman, P., Albertini, A., Markov, Y.: The first collision for full SHA-1. In: Katz, J., Shacham, H. (eds.) CRYPTO 2017. LNCS, vol. 10401, pp. 570–596. Springer, Cham (2017). https://doi.org/10.1007/978-3-319-63688-7_19
9. Wang, X., Yin, Y.L., Yu, H.: Finding collisions in the full SHA-1. In: Shoup, V. (ed.) CRYPTO 2005. LNCS, vol. 3621, pp. 17–36. Springer, Heidelberg (2005). https://doi.org/10.1007/11535218_2

Blockchain Security and Privacy

A Security Detection Model for Selfish Mining Attack

Zhongxing Liu, Guoyu Yang, Xinying Yu, and Fengying Li[✉]

School of Information Science and Engineering, Qufu Normal University,
Rizhao 276826, China
lfyin318@126.com

Abstract. As a new technology, the "decentralization" of blockchain
has been paid more and more attention. With the increasingly wide range
of applications of blockchain technology, its security has become a bottleneck restricting the development. In order to solve the problem, the
blockchain structure characteristic can be used to build a security detection model. Taking 51% attack detection as an example, the relationship
among attack state, attack intensity and attack time was analyzed. However, because of the variety of blockchain attacks, the test of only one
attack cannot verify the effectiveness of the detection model. On the
basis of the existing work, this paper studies the security of selfish mining attack under the existing detection model and compares it with 51%
attack, and finds that the attack block and honest block are related to
the ability of the attacker. When the attacker's ability exceeds half of the
total ability, the attack block is more than the honest block. However, for
the number of system states, there is a big difference between 51% attack
and selfish mining attack. Specifically, in selfish mining attack, when the
attacker's ability exceeds 25%, the number of states tends to stabilize.
While in 51% attack, the attacker's ability needs to exceed 50% in order
to stabilize. This shows that the detection model can well distinguish
51% attack and selfish mining attack. According to this characteristic,
we can further construct an effective alarm mechanism.

Keywords: 51% attack · Selfish mining · Security detection model ·
Blockchain · Contrast of attack

1 Introduction

1.1 Research Background

Blockchain technology is a distributed technology, which has the characteristic of
"decentralization". It can provide a secure and trusted method to maintain distributed database without using any trusted third party. Since it was proposed,
blockchain has attracted much attention and has been used in various fields,
including finance and the Internet of things. In a way, blockchain can bring huge
economic benefits. Therefore, it is difficult to avoid attacks by various hackers.

© Springer Nature Singapore Pte Ltd. 2020
Z. Zheng et al. (Eds.): BlockSys 2019, CCIS 1156, pp. 185–195, 2020.
https://doi.org/10.1007/978-981-15-2777-7_16

Because of the characteristics of blockchain technology itself, attacks specifically targeted at blockchain include 51% attack, selfish mining attack, eclipse attack, and physical attack. How to detect these attacks effectively, and on this basis, put forward some defensive measures, is a major problem. At present, the evaluation of blockchain security is mostly focused on the use of strict mathematical methods, but this method is more suitable for the analysis of a single attack, not for the analysis of the whole system.

Subsequent work also proposed a security model detection method based on the whole system state of block chain [4]. Specifically, first define the definition of the success state and the attack state in the blockchain system, and then different system states are recorded by changing different environmental parameters under different attack models. Once the system is found to be in an attack state, a message is send to the user to avoid further attacks. In this way, we can effectively resist the attack of blockchain system. Literature [1] proposed a security model detection method, but they just discussed the relationship between the total number of states and the number of attacks under 51% attacks. Therefore, on the basis of their work, this paper extends blockchain attack to selfish mining attack, and studies the influence of security model detection method on the security of blockchain system, and compares the security of selfish mining attack and 51% attack in terms of system parameters, number of states and attack intensity.

1.2   Related Work

Vasek et al gave an empirical analysis of Denial of Service Attacks (DDoS) in bitcoin system [8]. DDoS is a common attack in the bitcoin system, which is difficult to track the damage caused by such attack systematically. Vasek et al collected data from Bitcointalk.org, Bitcoincharts.org, Blockchain.info/pools and Bitcoin.it/wiki/Trade, and analyzed the DDoS attacks in Mining Pools and Currency Exchange. Heilman et al. discussed the impact of the eclipse attack on the bitcoin network [6]. The eclipse attack can attack the system mining and consensus process by controlling the IP addresses of the victim nodes, thereby destroying the links between them. They used the Probabilistic analysis he Monte Carlo to simulate the attack. At the end of this paper, we proposed a protective measure on the basis of botnet architecture: If each node stores enough valid addresses, it cannot be attacked, and the defense is implemented on bitcoind v0.10.1. Because it is closely associated with the financial industry, the blockchain system is also vulnerable to attacks similar to the Ponzi scheme. Chen et al proposed a classification model to discover the Ponzi scheme in Smart Contracts [3]. The experimental results show that at least 400 Ponzi schemes are running in Ethereum. The model they proposed can effectively detect and warn Ponzi schemes. Casado-Vara et al also proposed a new system of Wireless Sensor Network (WSN) [2], which can detect fraudulent attacks in the blockchain. Their data storage structure is in the form of DAG (Directed Acyclic Graph), in which the data is more secure. Meng pointed out that block chain technology can protect data integrity and ensure transparency in the processing process [7].

Therefore, block chain technology can be used to detect attacks in computer systems, but they did not point out how to detect attacks in the block chain system itself. Ye et al., started from the attack against the blockchain itself [4], analyzed the attack in the blockchain by analyzing the attack intensity, attack state and other parameters. The detection method can effectively detect attacks in the blockchain and put forward early warning in time. However, they only discussed the detection of 51% attacks in the model and did not involve other attack types.

1.3 Structure of Articles

Section 2 introduces some basic knowledge, including 51% attack and selfish mining attacks. In Sect. 3, first briefly introduces the security detection model of literature [1], then extends the model to selfish mining attack, and gives the pseudo code of selfish mining attack. Section 3.2 presents the test method and results, comparing 51% attack with selfish mining attack. Section 4 summarizes the whole paper and looks forward to the future work.

2 Basic Knowledge

2.1 51% Attack

As a typical "decentralized" distributed system, blockchain technology reaches an agreement on a certain problem through consensus mechanism jointly maintained by distributed nodes. Different systems use different consensus mechanisms, for example, the Bitcoin systems and Ethereum use proof of work consensus mechanism, EoS uses Delegated proof of stake consensus mechanism, and different consensus mechanisms use different password protection mechanisms. The 51% attack [1] and selfish mining attack [8] involved in this paper are mainly aimed at attack in PoW. In simple terms, in the PoW consensus mechanism, the greater the workload of a node, the greater the probability that it will get the accounting right in the blockchain. 51% attack is a kind of double spending attack, which modifies the accounting record in the blockchain by controlling more than 50% of the computing power in the network, so that a transaction can be spent repeatedly.

In order to ensure the consistency of the later analysis, this paper still uses the formula of 51% attack probability given in literature [1].

$$q_z = \begin{cases} 1, & p \leqslant q \\ \left(\dfrac{q}{p}\right)^z, & p > q \end{cases} \tag{1}$$

And q_z denotes the probability that the zth block is changed by an attacker, p denotes the probability that an honest miner gets the accounting right of the next block, and q denotes the probability that an attacker gets the accounting right of the next block. We can see that when the probability of an attacker is greater than that of an honest miner, the block accounting right can certainly be modified by the attacker. That's to say, when the probability of an attacker getting the accounting right is 51%, the probability of an honest miner is 49%, so the attacker can change the block content arbitrarily and perform a double spending attack. Therefore, effective measures must be taken to prevent this from happening.

2.2 Selfish Mining Attacks

Although 51% attack is very destructive, in general, it is very difficult to get more than 51% of the computing power of the whole network. So, 51% attack is difficult to realize in real system. However, Eyal et al proposed a selfish mining attack [5], which does not need to control 51% of the computing power, but only 25%. Selfish mining allows attackers to arbitrarily modify blocks by controlling only 25% of the computing power or 25% of the miners on the network conspired to obtain accounting rights.

The miners are divided into honest miners and selfish miners. The former mines on the public chain according to the mining strategy, while the latter can form a conspiracy to hide the blocks that have been dug. And the selfish miners consume the computing power of honest miners by building a private chain and strategically releasing blocks on the private chain, increasing their own computing power. In 51% attack, honest miners and attackers mine on the same public chain, and when they digs the block, they release the block directly onto the public chain. However, selfish miners conspire to establish a private chain, and when certain conditions are met, some information on the private chain can be made public. This is the difference between selfish mining attack and 51% attack.

Suppose the computing power of selfish miners is p and that of the honest miners is q. The selfish miners always link blocks to private chain after they find them, while honest miners always link the blocks to the longest chain. If there are two chains of the same length in the system at the same time, honest miners will link their blocks to the private chain with the probability of γ, and the probability of $(1-\gamma)$ to the public chain. The basic idea of selfish mining is as follows:

A. If the selfish miner finds a block and links the block to the private chain, and if the length of the public chain and the private chain is the same and the length of the private chain is 2, all blocks in the private chain will be exposed. At this time, there is a bifurcation in the system, honest miners do not know which is public chain and which is the private chain.
B. If the honest miner finds a block, the selfish miner first calculates the difference δ between the length of the private chain and the public chain. Assuming that there is only a public chain at this time, the honest miner links the block to the public chain and then updates the length difference δ' between the private chain and the public chain. (1) When $\delta = 0$, because honest miners link the new block to the public chain, causing the public chain length is increased

by 1, that is, $\delta' = -1$, and the public chain length exceeds the private chain length, so selfish miners combine the private chain to the public chain and dig mines on the public chain. (2) When $\delta = 1$, the selfish miner only releases the newly dug block in the private chain, in which case the length of the public chain is the same as that of the private chain, that is, the length of the public chain and the private chain is the same. (3) When $\delta = 2$, the selfish miner releases the private chain, in which case the private chain length has one block advantage over the public chain length, that is, $\delta' = 1$. Once honest miners dig a new block, they will link to the private chain. (4) When $\delta > 2$, the first unexposed block in the private chain is released.

3   Security Detection Model

3.1   51% Security Detection Model

In literature [1], the security of the whole blockchain system is detected by the attack intensity and the number of states. The attack intensity refers to the ability of the attacker, that is, the ratio p of computing power mastered by the attacker, while the number of states refers to the different states of the system. Here's a detailed description of the concept of state. In general, the structure of the block chain is a chain structure, but due to the existence of a fork, it may eventually appear as a tree structure. The state of a system refers to the structure of the whole tree, including the number of nodes, the depth and width of the tree, etc. If these are all the same, say that the two states are the same. The security state refers to an honest node connected to 6 blocks, and the attack state refers to the 6 nodes behind the attack node.

This section briefly describes the basic idea of the security monitoring model in literature [1]:

A. Initialize an honest node as the root node of the blockchain.
B. Generate a block based on the computing power p: (1) If the block is a block generated by an honest node, select a block for connection according to the weight of different nodes in the existing blockchain. (2) If the block is a block generated by an attack node, the block is divided into two cases: (a) If there are other attack nodes in the blockchain, link to the chain where the attack node is located (even if the chain is not the longest chain); (b) If there are no blocks generated by other attack nodes in the current block chain, select the leaf node on the longest chain to connect.
C. Record all different block states and re-initialize the block chain if there is a security state or an attack state.
D. Loop until no new state appears.

The safety monitoring model can effectively detect the relationship between the number of cycles and the number of occurrences of the attack block. In addition, the relationship between the computing power ratio and the total blockchain state can also be detected. It can effectively find out the rules of the attack block, even if it makes an early warning to the system.

3.2   Detection of Selfish Mining Attack

The difference between selfish mining attack and 51% attack is that there is only one public chain in 51% attack, the block structure on the chain is public knowledge, and the attack block information is the private information between attackers. In other words, honest miners can see the structure of the entire block, but do not know which block is the honest block and which block is the attack block. In selfish mining attacks, selfish miners not only share attack block information with each other, but also create a private chain to link all attack blocks to the private chain in order to improve the success rate of the attack, and release the private chain at the right opportunity. This method can effectively use the computing power of attack miners, so that their attack blocks are not scattered on the public chain, thereby increasing the ability of selfish mining attacks. Therefore, selfish mining can achieve the effect of 51% attack without controlling 51% computing power. However, whether the security detection model in literature [1] has the same detection effect on selfish mining has not been involved. Therefore, this paper embeds selfish mining attack into the security detection model of literature [1], and studies the relationship between the number of attacks and the attack state.

Through the analysis, it can be found that the strategy of honest miners is similar in selfish mining attack and 51% attack. The difference lies in how to deal with the private chain in selfish mining after the blockchain status is updated. In the 51% attack, there is no private chain, so when the state of the blockchain changes, miners only need to select different blocks according to the honest strategy or attack strategy to connect to enter the next round. However, in selfish mining, whether it produces an honest block or an attack block, it will have an impact on δ. Therefore, after the new block has selected the blocks that need to be connected, the δ should also be updated to prepare the selfish miners for the next round of strategic choices.

Pseudo code for selfish mining algorithm:

(1) Construct two chains: one public chain, one private chain plus hidden chain, and distinguish them by type identification;
(2) Generate an attack block by inputting the attack intensity p, and $(1-p)$ generate an honest block;
(3) Put the block in the chain (that is, put the value of type into the chain);
  (3.1) If an attack block is generated
      a. Calculate δ equal to the length of the private chain minus the length of the public chain;
      b. Add the block directly to the hidden chain;
      c. Hidden chain length++;
      d. If $\delta = 0$ and the hidden chain length is 2; turn the hidden chain into a private chain (modify the value of type); the hidden chain length becomes 0;
      e. Restore the attack intensity to the initial value;
  (3.2) If an honest block is generated

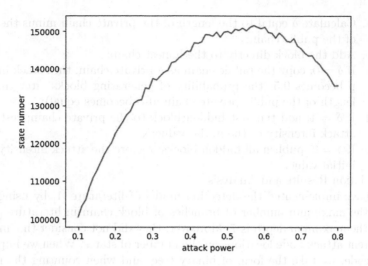

Fig. 1. With 51% attack, the number of states changes under different attack intensity

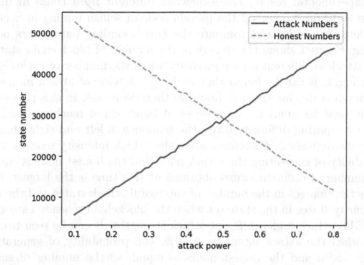

Fig. 2. With 51% attack, the changes in the number of successful attack states and security states under different attack intensity

    a. Calculate δ equal to the length of the private chain minus the length of the public chain;

    b. Add the block directly to the honest chain;

    c. If $\delta = 0$; copy the public chain as a private chain; the attack intensity p becomes 0.5 (the probability of generating blocks after the equal length of the public-private chain also becomes equal);

    d. If $\delta = 1$; add the first hidden block to the private chain; restore the attack intensity to the initial value;

    e. If $\delta = 2$; publish all hidden blocks; restore the attack intensity to the initial value.

(4) Simulation Results and Analysis

We have implemented the detection model of literature [1] by using C++, but the maximum number of branches of block chain in literature [1] is 5, and the maximum depth is 7. Moreover, they did not consider the impact of different attack node locations on the number of states. When we implement the code, we take the form of binary tree, and when counting the number of states, we consider not only the topological structure of the whole binary tree, but also the different states caused by different node types. Therefore, our experimental results are somewhat different from those in literature [1]. In addition, we embed the pseudo code of selfish mining in Sect. 3 into our detection code, and compare the corresponding parameters of selfish mining. Figure 1 shows the change in the number of block chain states with 51% attack at different attack intensity when the number of cycles is 30000. From Fig. 1, it can be found that with the increase of attack intensity, the number of states increases at first and then decreases. In this paper, binary tree is used to simulate the process of block chain reaching stable state. When comparing different states, the sequence of left and right child nodes is not distinguished. Therefore, when the attack intensity reaches 50%, the probability of generating the attack node and the honest node is equal, and the number of different states obtained at this time is the largest. Figure 2 shows the changes in the number of successful attack states and the number of security states in the state set when the blockchain reaches a steady state with 51% attack under different attack strengths. It can be seen from Fig. 2 that when the attack intensity is 50%, the probability of generating the attack nodes and the honest nodes is equal, so the number of successful attack states and security states is equal. As the attack intensity increases, the probability of generating attack nodes is also gradually increasing, so the number of successful attack states is gradually increasing, but the number of security states is gradually decreasing. When the attack intensity exceeds 50%, the number of successful attack states is greater than the number of security states. Figure 3 uses selfish mining as the attack mode, showing the changing trend of the number of states under different attack intensity. As can be seen from Fig. 3, when the attack intensity is greater than 20%, the number of states tends to a certain value. Compared with Fig. 1, it can be found that the number of states generated by the 51% attack is much larger than the number of states generated by the selfish mining. In selfish mining,

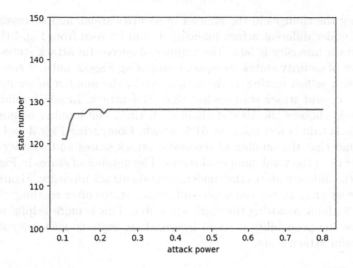

Fig. 3. With selfish mining attack, the number of states changes under different attack intensity

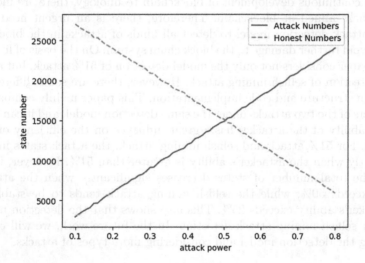

Fig. 4. With selfish mining attack, the changes in the number of successful attack states and security states under different attack intensity

both honest nodes and attack nodes give priority to finding the longest chain. In 51% attack, both the honest nodes and the attack nodes randomly select a branch chain according to the probability. The greater the depth of the node, the greater the probability of being selected. Therefore, the number of intermediate states of selfish mining in the blockchain is small and will soon reach a steady state. Figure 4 uses selfish mining as the attack mode, showing the changes in the number of security states and successful attack states under different attack intensity. It can be seen from Fig. 4 that when the attack intensity is 50%, the number of successful attack states and the number of security states are equal. Comparing Figs. 2 and 4, it can be found that with selfish mining as the attack mode, the number of security states and successful attack states is less than 51% attack. In selfish mining, since the node chooses the longest chain each time, the number of branches in the blockchain is less than the 51% attack. Comparing Figs. 3 and 4, it can be found that the number of successful attack states and security states is greater than the total number of states. The number of states in Fig. 3 refers to all the different states that under a certain attack intensity. Figure 4 shows all the security states and successful attack states after reaching the stable state, without removing the duplicate states. This is more helpful to further analyze the probability from an intermediate state to a security state or a successful attack state.

4   Conclusions

With the continuous development of blockchain technology, there are more and more attacks aimed at blockchain. Therefore, there is an urgent need for an efficient attack detection model to detect all kinds of attacks in the blockchain, so as to avoid further damage to the block chain system. On the basis of literature [1], this paper considers not only the model detection of 51% attack, but also the model detection of selfish mining attack. However, there are some differences in blockchain structure and code implementation. This paper mainly compares the parameters of the two attacks under the same detection model, and it can be seen that the ability of the attacker has a great influence on the efficiency of model detection. For 51% attack and selfish mining attack, the attack states increases significantly when the attacker's ability is greater than 51%. However, for 51% attack, the total number of states decreases significantly when the attacker's ability exceeds 50%; while the selfish mining attack tends to be stable after the attacker's ability exceeds 25%. This also shows that the detection model is better for selfish mining attack detection. In the future work, we will consider improving the detection model and considering more types of attacks.

References

1. Bastiaan, M.: Preventing the 51 proof of work in bitcoin (2015). http://referaat.cs.utwente.nl/conference/22/paper/7473/preventingthe-51-attack-a-stochasticanalysis-oftwo-phase-proof-of-work-in-bitcoin.pdf
2. Casado-Vara, R., Prieto, J., Corchado, J.M.: How blockchain could improve fraud detection in power distribution grid. In: Graña, M., López-Guede, J.M., Etxaniz, O., Herrero, Á., Sáez, J.A., Quintián, H., Corchado, E. (eds.) SOCO'18-CISIS'18-ICEUTE'18 2018. AISC, vol. 771, pp. 67–76. Springer, Cham (2019). https://doi.org/10.1007/978-3-319-94120-2_7

3. Chen, W., Zheng, Z., Cui, J., Ngai, E., Zheng, P., Zhou, Y.: Detecting Ponzi schemes on Ethereum: towards healthier blockchain technology, pp. 1409–1418, April 2018
4. Cong-Cong, Y.E., Guo-Qiang, L.I., Hong-Ming, C., Yong-Gen, G.U., Software, School of and University, Shanghai Jiaotong and School, Information Engineering and University, Huzhou: Security detection model of blockchain. J. Softw. (2018)
5. Eyal, I., Sirer, E.G.: Majority is not enough: bitcoin mining is vulnerable. In: Christin, N., Safavi-Naini, R. (eds.) FC 2014. LNCS, vol. 8437, pp. 436–454. Springer, Heidelberg (2014). https://doi.org/10.1007/978-3-662-45472-5_28
6. Heilman, E., Kendler, A., Zohar, A., Goldberg, S.: Eclipse attacks on bitcoin's peer-to-peer network. IACR Cryptology ePrint Archive 2015, 263 (2015). https://eprint.iacr.org/2015/263
7. Meng, W., Tischhauser, E., Wang, Q., Yu, W., Han, J.: When intrusion detection meets blockchain technology: a review. IEEE Access **6**(1), 10179–10188 (2018)
8. Vasek, M., Thornton, M., Moore, T.: Empirical analysis of denial-of-service attacks in the bitcoin ecosystem. In: Böhme, R., Brenner, M., Moore, T., Smith, M. (eds.) FC 2014. LNCS, vol. 8438, pp. 57–71. Springer, Heidelberg (2014). https://doi.org/10.1007/978-3-662-44774-1_5

Scalable, On-Demand Secure Multiparty Computation for Privacy-Aware Blockchains

Shantanu Sharma and Wee Keong Ng[(✉)] [iD]

School of Computer Science and Engineering, Nanyang Technological University,
Singapore, Singapore
shantanu005@e.ntu.edu.sg, awkng@ntu.edu.sg

Abstract. In private, permissioned blockchains, organizations desire to transact with one another in a privacy-aware manner. For instance, when Alice sends X crypto-tokens to Bob at time t, it is desirable for Alice and Bob to perform double-spending check without revealing each other's token balance. This also illustrates the fact that some input data from individual party is needed for secure computation in order to produce result data forming transaction details. In this paper, we consider secure computations in a blockchain involving multiple parties: Whenever a party has sensitive data to be computed with other parties, there is a need to exercise secure multiparty data sharing and computation (SMPC) among the parties (where parties may be *malicious*) to yield the result. Conventional SMPC is not scalable for a blockchain that has thousands of parties (blockchain nodes), and where secure computations may not always involve *all* blockchain nodes *all the time*, and the practical need for secure computation may range from sporadic to frequent. In this paper, we address these issues by designing a scheme that allows SMPC to be conveniently launched on-demand by any number of k-clique subsets of blockchain nodes. We show that our scheme is secure against any input data leakage and output leakage before, during, and after SMPC.

Keywords: Secure multiparty computation · Blockchain · SPDZ · Double Spending Problem · SPDZ2 · TopGear · Overdrive

1 Introduction

Public blockchains such as Bitcoin and Ethereum have fulfilled the promise of sustaining an open and transparent decentralized ledger where any member of the blockchain may check and verify the transactions in the ledger. Although member identity is pseudo-anonymous, transaction details are in public view. Such level of openness is not desirable when blockchain members have conflict of interests among themselves, as in a private, permissioned blockchain setting. For instance, what Alice bought from (and paid to) Bob should not be privy to Carol when Bob and Carol are competitors vying for sales from Alice. The aforementioned privacy-preserving double-spending check is another example.

© Springer Nature Singapore Pte Ltd. 2020
Z. Zheng et al. (Eds.): BlockSys 2019, CCIS 1156, pp. 196–211, 2020.
https://doi.org/10.1007/978-981-15-2777-7_17

Introducing privacy protection into blockchain is an active area of research. Much work has converged on the incorporation of Secure Multiparty Computation (SMPC) techniques into blockchains. In SMPC, n clients jointly compute a function securely on input data, without revealing the inputs to one another and only by exchanging messages among themselves. The security guarantee is that even if an adversary corrupts a subset of parties, the inputs of other parties are never revealed to the adversary.

To the best of our knowledge, the SPDZ protocol [7], along with its many improvements [5,6,9] is the most efficient method to date that enables SMPC within a system that scales with the number of parties as well as to provide a guarantee against malicious players. The core idea of SPDZ is that, instead of encrypting the parties' inputs, it is easier to work with random data, conduct some checks at the end of the protocol, and abort if malicious behavior is detected.

A straightforward way to incorporate conventional SMPC into blockchain is to have all blockchain nodes to be SPDZ nodes as well, so that all blockchain/ SPDZ nodes are in stand-by mode to perform SMPC anytime. This arrangement is costly and not practical for several reasons. First, with numbers of blockchain nodes possibly ranging to several thousands, all nodes can't be guaranteed to be online all the time. Second, SMPC may only be needed by some subset (k-clique) of blockchain nodes. Third, the need for secure computation may not be consistently high across all blockchain nodes.

We address these problems by proposing a way to perform on-demand SMPC by any k-clique of blockchain nodes. On-demand SMPC requires the ability to switch between conventional SMPC and SMPC involving only a subset of nodes. Existing SMPC protocols are incapable of handling on-demand k-clique SMPC: All parties in an SMPC network need to participate in every round to compute the result; if a subset of parties want to do SMPC among themselves, the tedious pre-processing phase has to be re-done.

In our proposed method, we have a Worker-network consisting of n nodes, pre-setup'ed to perform secure computations. Whenever any k-clique of blockchain nodes needs to perform SMPC, they securely transfer their input data to the Worker-network to perform the computations. In a way, the k-clique (*Client* nodes) outsourced SMPC to the Worker-network (*Worker* nodes doing SMPC). However, secure outsourcing of input (from Clients to Workers) is not defined in the original SMPC protocols. The transfer of input to a node in Worker-network can result in data leakage since the SMPC node receiving the input can be corrupt itself. In this paper, we propose a novel protocol to address this security issue.

Our Contributions in this paper is a scalable secure protocol for blockchain nodes to outsource computations to a Worker-network in a way that satisfies various security measures: (1) The proposed protocol is Universally Composable (UC)-secure up to $n - 1$ dishonest nodes. That is, we allow *all but one Worker* and *all but one Client* (providing the inputs) to be controlled by a malicious adversary; even in such unlikely scenario, we guarantee security of input as well as output and correctness of the output. (2) The protocol does not assume that a Client node has a network connection with every Worker node; we only need a Client to be connected to at least one Worker. (3) The protocol is scalable because we do not require all blockchain nodes to be SMPC nodes. Our protocol is built over SPDZ [7] and can be extended to other SPDZ-like protocols that are being already used in current systems such as SCALE-MAMBA [1].

The organization of the paper is as follows. We review related works in Sect. 2. Section 3 describes preliminaries required to understand the paper. In Sect. 4 we present our new approach of on-demand SMPC using SPDZ. Section 5 illustrates how the proposed protocol is used to securely check for double-spending in a blockchain. Section 6 concludes our findings and discusses future scope of our project.

2   Related Work

Confidentiality and privacy in the context of blockchain generally refer to the protection of blockchain transaction data and transaction counterparty identity from unauthorized parties. As such, much work [12] in this area investigated techniques to protect user identities and transaction details. Li *et al.* [11] proposed the use of side chains to allow blockchain nodes to join in order to transact with confidence. Each side chain is a private decentralized ledger where those members who joined are assumed to trust one another; thus, transaction details can be shared with the members. This approach breaks down whenever a member of a side chain is compromised and becomes malicious. Zyskind *et al.* [13] proposed to combine blockchain and off-blockchain storage to construct a personal data management platform focused on privacy. The blockchain became an access-control system to ensure that users own and control their personal data. They used a distributed private key-value data store for personal data. This work does not indicate how computations among nodes can be securely computed. Hawk [10] is proposed to protect transactional privacy. This is achieved by sending "encrypted" information to the blockchain, and relying on zero-knowledge proofs to enforce the correctness of contract execution and money conservation. However, Hawk relies on a *manager* which see the users' inputs and is *trusted* not to disclose users' private data. We feel that this security premise is too strong. In addition to identity and transaction detail protection, we feel that blockchain confidentiality and privacy should also be extended to the protection of input data during pre-transaction computation, the computation itself, and computation result, which will be used for transaction details.

Groundwork for efficient protocols for SMPC was laid down by BDOZ [2] which introduced the idea of using Homomorphic Encryption (HE) and bifurcation into Online and Pre-processing phase. The seminal work SPDZ [7] heavily optimized [2] by upgrading linearly HE to limited form of SwHE based on BV [3]. This change allowed a global MAC and permitted reduction of expensive ZKPoPK (Zero Knowledge Proof of Plaintext Knowledge) by a factor of n. Further optimization like Smart-Vercauteren SIMD packing allowed single

ZKPoPK to prove statements thousands of multiplication triple simultaneously. Introduction to Overdrive [9] suite of Pre-processing protocols reestablished significance of SPDZ by making SMPC implementation for large-scale solutions. It batched ZKPoPK across all parties to prove a joint-statement for secret input and accumulated ciphertexts, and improved computational efficiency by a factor of n. Recently in 2019, TopGear [5] was constructed as further improvement on HighGear of Overdrive by amortizing ZKPoPK and producing smaller slack providing more security for same parameters without additional computational cost. TopGear is currently being used in practical implementation like SCALE-MAMBA (as of v1.5 in July 2019) [1]. Despite years of research, existing SMPC protocols rely on participation of *every* node. Such strong assumptions prevents its disposal in practical systems. It also raises issues of scalability and addition of new nodes into an already established network. Hence, despite the obvious connection of Blockchain and SMPC, use of SMPC stemming from existing solution appears to be infeasible at first glance. We provide a solution to enable on-demand SMPC and integrate into a scalable blockchain built upon already existing premium solutions in SMPC literature.

3 Preliminaries

The proposed Worker SMPC network, like any conventional SMPC, works for dishonest majority (and static corruptions): As long as there is one honest party we can guarantee privacy of the inputs and correctness of the results, but we can neither guarantee termination nor fairness (SMPC assumption). We use SPDZ [7] and SPDZ-like protocols. Rather than operating on encrypted data, SPDZ works with randomness generated and conducts check for malicious behavior (if malicious behavior is encountered, the protocol aborts). For spawning legitimate randomness used in computation, Oblivious Transfer or Somewhat Homomorphic Encryption (SwHE) is used. SPDZ relies on SwHE, which allows computation of circuits of multiplicative depth one. To combat the problem of dealing with expensive public key encryption, SPDZ-like protocols follow a pre-processing model for more effective run-time while adhering to UC-security. In the pre-processing model, SPDZ is split into two phases: A Pre-processing phase and an Online Phase [2,5–7,9].

3.1 Pre-processing Phase

SPDZ is fast because laborious public-key tools to generate randomness are pushed to the pre-processing phase. This randomness is consumed to compute arithmetic circuit in the Online Phase. The correlated randomness to be generated is independent of the input for computation and the function to be computed. The bifurcation and independence of Online and Pre-processing phase implies that the Pre-processing phase can be run anytime, even months before computation of the function in Online Phase. Raw data produced in pre-processing is primarily *triples*, which are used for multiplication of two secret shared numbers in the Online phase, using Beaver's Trick.

3.2   Online Phase

The function to be securely computed by multiple parties is represented as an arithmetic circuit consisting of two operations: addition and multiplication. The multiplication of secret numbers during the computation is at the heart of many secret sharing-based MPC protocols because linear secret sharing schemes make addition easy, and the two operations together are complete[1]. Addition of two secret shared numbers can be done locally, and is done as natural component-wise addition of representations. Multiplication of two secret shared numbers require interaction between the parties and is done using Beaver's Trick and consumption of a *triple* per multiplication as stated earlier.

3.3   Security Concerns in Outsourcing to Worker SMPC Network

As certain subset of parties can be controlled by an adversary, it is vital to keep the inputs provided by blockchain nodes secret. We also have to ensure that the output of our calculation is correct and no extraneous error has been introduced by malicious party while computing the output. Privacy is guaranteed in the Online Phase by additively secret-sharing the inputs and outputs of each gate of the arithmetic circuit. Correctness of the output is guaranteed by authentication of the secret shares using information-theoretic MACs (Message Authentication Codes). However, rather than authenticating shares of secret values [2], SPDZ authenticates the shared value itself. More concretely, it uses a global MAC key α chosen randomly in message space $\mathcal{M}$, and for each secret value a, it will share a additively among the players, and also secret-share a MAC $\gamma(a) = \alpha a$. $\gamma(a)$ represents the MAC authenticating a under global MAC key α.

In the Online Phase, each to-be-authenticated secret-shared value $a \in \mathcal{M}$ is represented as follows:

$$\langle a \rangle := \left(\delta_a, (a_1, \ldots, a_n), (\gamma(a)_1, \ldots, \gamma(a)_n) \right)$$

where $a = \sum_n a_i$, $\gamma(a) = \alpha \cdot (a + \delta_a) \leftarrow \sum_n \gamma(a)_i$, and δ_a is public, also referred to as *public modifier* of a. Player P_i holds the tuple $(a_i, \gamma(a)_i)$.

Pre-processing and secret sharing of α is done in a slightly different manner:

$$[\![\alpha]\!] := \left((\alpha_1, \ldots, \alpha_n), (\beta_i, \theta(\alpha)_1^i, \theta(\alpha)_2^i, \ldots, \theta(\alpha)_n^i)_{i=1,\ldots,n} \right)$$

where $\alpha_i \in \mathcal{M}$ represents share of global MAC key with $\alpha = \sum_i \alpha_i$ and $\gamma(\alpha_i) \leftarrow \sum_j \theta(\alpha)_i^j = \alpha\beta_i$. $\gamma(\alpha_i)$ is supposed to represent MAC authenticating α under P_i's private key β_i. Player P_i holds the tuple $(\alpha_i, \beta_i, \theta(\alpha)_1^i, \theta(\alpha)_2^i, \ldots, \theta(\alpha)_n^i)$.

To carry out computations in the Online Phase, the parties need to know value of secret-shared addition or multiplication of two numbers. To facilitate that, SPDZ does "partial opening"; i.e., to obtain a, the associated values a_i are revealed but not the associated shares of the MAC. Unlike [2], SPDZ postpones the check on the MACs (of opened values) to the output phase. This is to avoid revealing of MAC key for every share and forging of MAC values. During the

---

[1] This fact is mirrored in the world of garbled circuits, where the free-XOR technique only requires to garble AND gates, which compute the product of two bits.

output phase, players generate a random linear combination of both the opened values and their shares of the corresponding MACs; they commit to the results and only then open α. The intuition is that, because of the commitments, when α is revealed, it is too late for corrupt players to exploit knowledge of the key. Therefore, if the MAC checks out, all opened values were correct with high probability, so we can trust that the output values we computed are correct and can safely open them. Opening of $\langle \cdot \rangle$-shared value is slightly different from opening of $[\![\cdot]\!]$-shared value. For concrete instantiation of Online Phase, the reader is referred to [7].

3.4   Protocols in SPDZ

Overview of some of the protocols that we are using from SPDZ is described below:

Protocol Reshare($e_{\mathbf{m}}$,enc ={NoNewCiphertext,NewCiphertext}):

- Upon input of public ciphertext $e_{\mathbf{m}}$, the protocol generates a new secret sharing $\langle m \rangle$ within the SMPC network.
- If enc = NewCiphertext, a "fresh" ciphertext $e'_{\mathbf{m}}$ is generated such that $\sum_i \mathbf{m}_i$ is the value contained in $e'_{\mathbf{m}}$. Else, pass.

Protocol PBracket($e_{\mathbf{v}}, \mathbf{v}_1, \ldots, \mathbf{v}_n$): If there exist secret sharing of a message $\mathbf{v}$ where $\mathbf{v}_i$ is privately held by player P_i and public ciphertext $e_{\mathbf{v}}$, the protocol generates $[\![\mathbf{v}]\!]$.

Protocol PAngle($e_{\mathbf{v}}, \mathbf{v}_1, \ldots, \mathbf{v}_n$): If there exist secret sharing of a message $\mathbf{v}$ where $\mathbf{v}_i$ is privately held by player P_i and public ciphertext $e_{\mathbf{v}}$, the protocol generates $\langle \mathbf{v} \rangle$.

4   Proposed Protocol

In this section, we describe our proposed protocol for securely transferring input data from Client nodes to Worker SMPC nodes and after secure computation, for securely transferring result data back to the Client nodes, under the strong security assumption that all but one Worker nodes are malicious.

4.1   Enabling On-Demand SMPC Through SPDZ

Operating any existing SMPC protocols for general functionalities between large number of parties have some practical hurdles. It requires all parties to be online at the same time, and the communication overhead of every practical protocol for dishonest majority quadratically scales with the number of parties. Real-world adaptions of secure computation delegates the computation $f(x_1, x_2, \ldots, x_n)$ to a set of untrusted Workers in a way that the work required to verify the correctness of the result is much less than the work needed to compute the function itself (while also protecting the privacy of inputs). Nevertheless, these solutions have limitations: They require honest majority and only guarantee security against passive corruptions.

To overcome this practical hurdle, we consider a setup where *Clients* want to delegate the computation to a set of untrusted *Workers* in a way such, that as long as there is one honest Worker, the followings hold: **(a)** Privacy of input is preserved, **(b)** output of the computation is preserved, and **(c)** work performed by the Clients is minimal and independent of the size of the function to be computed. A Client has to trust that at least one Worker is honest. Certainly, due to the SMPC assumption, a corrupted Worker may force the protocol to abort and prevent termination, but this is unavoidable in the dishonest majority case. The solution to this problem is addressed using *auditable SMPC* and is discussed later.

In this paper, we do not try to improve the efficiency of any SMPC protocol, rather we consider only the problem of how to let Clients securely provide inputs to the Worker-network and also securely obtain back the output of the computation. This *modular approach* is useful, both from a conceptual point of view, and also from a practical point of view. One can imagine that improvements on the underlying MPC protocols for the Workers would not require one to update the software on the Client side, such can be achieved via our method. Our proposed approach is addendum to already existing protocols and functionalities of SPDZ-type protocols. This allows seamless integration in existing solutions like SCALE-MAMBA [1]. TopGear, Overdrive, and SPDZ-2 [5,6,9] all employ similar functionalities, SwHE scheme, and MAC authentication scheme, which is marginally deviating from ones used in SPDZ. We first illustrate our procedure by providing the protocols Π_{InpDist} and Π_{OutNet} solely for SPDZ-1 and then extending it to $\Pi_{\mathsf{OutNet\_2}}$ which operates on SPDZ-2-like encryption scheme.

Compared to [8], our solution does not assume that a Client has a connection with every Worker. We give a method to resolve more stringent constraints and hence our protocol is more general and applicable to real world scenarios. Our set-up consists of a blockchain network of machines (called **SuperNetwork**) encompassing several clusters and cliques of *Clients* (All Clients may not be fully connected to one another in the *SuperNetwork*). Assuming that one of the cliques of size k wants to perform SMPC of a function; the k *Clients* providing the inputs. Every party wants to keep its input confidential but want to acquire the outcome of the function. The computation required is consigned to a network of Worker-network dedicated to do SMPC. We assume the general case where a Client is connected to only *one* Worker (instead of all the Workers like [8]).

For the remainder of the paper, the Worker-network, consisting of interconnected n computers, executes computations to be referred to as $\mathcal{W}$. The clique of Clients will be referred to as **k-Clique**.

The following assumptions are made about the setup:
- Every Client providing inputs is connected to at least one Worker in $\mathcal{W}$. The size of the clique can be larger than the Worker-network.
- At most *k-1* Clients in *k-Clique* are corrupt.
- At most *n-1* Workers in $\mathcal{W}$ are corrupt.
- SPDZ functionalities are accessible to all Workers and Clients in the *SuperNetwork* (blockchain) and $\mathcal{W}$.

Protocol $\Pi_{\mathsf{KeyGenArr}}$

Initialize:

Worker X will invoke $\mathcal{F}_{\mathsf{KeyGen}}$ to generate public key $\mathbf{pk}_{\mathsf{MPC}} \leftarrow (\mathbf{a}, \mathbf{b}_{\mathsf{MPC}})$ and each Worker W_i in $\mathcal{W}$ will obtain a secret share $\mathbf{sk}_{\mathsf{MPC}i} = (\mathsf{s}_{\mathsf{MPC}_{i,1}}, \mathsf{s}_{\mathsf{MPC}_{i,2}})$ of $\mathbf{sk}_{\mathsf{MPC}}$ where $\sum_n \mathsf{s}_{\mathsf{MPC}_{i,1}} = \mathsf{s}_{\mathsf{MPC}}, \sum_n \mathsf{s}_{\mathsf{MPC}_{i,2}} = \mathsf{s}_{\mathsf{MPC}} \cdot \mathsf{s}_{\mathsf{MPC}}$ *and* $\mathbf{b}_{\mathsf{MPC}} \leftarrow \mathbf{a} \cdot \mathsf{s}_{\mathsf{MPC}} + p \cdot \mathbf{e}_1$ (steps to generate $\mathsf{s}_{\mathsf{MPC}}$, $\mathbf{e}_1$ and $\mathbf{a}$ specified in $\mathcal{F}_{\mathsf{KeyGen}}$ implementation.)

Output:

New public key and secret key(distributed) from already existing public key and secret key(distributed) set up by $\mathcal{W}$.

KeyGenArr($\mathbf{pk}_{\mathsf{MPC}}, \mathbf{sk}_{\mathsf{MPC}}$):

1. $\mathbf{a}$ and $\mathbf{b}_{\mathsf{MPC}}$ are made public.
2. Client A generates s_A *and* $\mathbf{e}_2$ using $\mathcal{F}_{\mathsf{KeyGen}}$. It computes $\mathbf{b} \leftarrow \mathbf{b}_{\mathsf{MPC}} + \mathbf{a} \cdot \mathsf{s}_A + p \cdot \mathbf{e}_2$
3. New public key $\mathbf{pk}=(\mathbf{a},\mathbf{b})$ is made public and can be used for encryption while the new secret key is $\mathbf{sk}=\mathsf{s}_{\mathsf{MPC}} + \mathsf{s}_A$.

Protocol Π_{DecNet}

Initialize:

1. Given secret key distribution in the MPC network already exist such that Worker W_i holds $\mathsf{s}_{\mathsf{MPC}_{i,1}}$ and Client has another share s_A such that $\sum_n \mathsf{s}_{\mathsf{MPC}_{i,1}} = \mathsf{s}_{\mathsf{MPC}}$ and $\mathsf{sk} = \mathsf{s}_{\mathsf{MPC}} + \mathsf{s}_A$. Decryption is done in a similar way as Π_{DDec}.
2. W_i given $\mathbf{c} = (\mathbf{c}_0, \mathbf{c}_1, 0)$ and upper bound B on $\|\mathbf{t}\|_\infty$, computes-
   - $\mathbf{v}_1 \leftarrow \mathbf{c}_0 - (\mathsf{s}_{\mathsf{MPC}_{1,1}} \cdot \mathbf{c}_1)$
   - $\mathbf{v}_i \leftarrow -(\mathsf{s}_{\mathsf{MPC}_{i,1}} \cdot \mathbf{c}_1)$ *for* $i \neq 1$.
   And $\mathbf{t}_i \leftarrow \mathbf{v}_i + p \cdot \mathbf{r}_i$ where $\|\mathbf{r}_i\|_\infty \leq 2^{\mathsf{sec}} \cdot B/(n \cdot p)$.

Decryption:

1. Each Worker W_j in $\mathcal{W}$ sends $\mathbf{t}_j$ to Worker X.
2. Worker X computes $\mathbf{t}'_{\mathsf{MPC}} \leftarrow \sum_n \mathbf{t}_i$ and sends $\mathbf{t}'_{\mathsf{MPC}}$ to Client A.
3. Client A computes $\mathbf{t}' \leftarrow \mathbf{t}'_{\mathsf{MPC}} - \mathsf{s}_A \cdot \mathbf{c}_1$ and obtains message $m' \leftarrow$ decode($\mathbf{t}' mod p$).

- Sufficient data (triples, pair of random numbers, single random numbers and, shared bits and squares) have been generated in the pre-processing phase by $\mathcal{W}$ and k-*Clique*.
- Connections between Client-Worker and Worker-Worker are secure.
- All corrupt Clients and Workers can be controlled by a single adversary or multiple adversaries.
- A broadcast channel is available at unit cost in $\mathcal{W}$. Broadcast functionality and point-to-point channels, for single or multiple inputs and outputs, is available from SPDZ protocol (Appendix A.3 of [7]).

4.2   Securely Sharing Input Data with Worker SMPC Network

For simplicity, we first deal with the case when one Client transfers a single input data to the $\mathcal{W}$-network and a single result output is generated after the computation and is received by the same Client.

Procedure Π_{InpDist}

Input: Value m held by Client in *Super-Network* which will serve as input to Online phase.

Output: $\langle m \rangle$ with secret shares distributed among all the parties in Worker $\mathcal{W}$.

InpDist(m):

1. Worker X will invoke $\mathcal{F}_{\mathsf{KeyGenArr}}$ to get secure key distribution among the parties involved (All Workers in $\mathcal{W}$ and Client providing the input) and generate (pk, sk).

2. Client A generates $e_m \leftarrow \mathsf{Enc}_{\mathsf{pk}}(m)$ and transfer e_m to Worker X. e_m is made public (secure due to homomorphic encryption).

3. Workers in $\mathcal{W}$ set $(m_1, m_2, \ldots m_n) \leftarrow \mathsf{Reshare}_{\mathsf{Net}}(e_m, \mathsf{NoNewCiphertext})$ where each W_i holds m_i.

4. Generate $\langle m \rangle \leftarrow \mathsf{PAngle}(m_1, m_2, \ldots, m_n, e_m)$.

SubProtocol $\mathsf{Reshare}_{\mathsf{Net}}$

Input: $e_m = \mathsf{Enc}_{\mathsf{pk}}(m)$ which is a public ciphertext.

Output: Sharing m_i of m to each Worker W_i (additive sharing).

$\mathsf{Reshare}_{\mathsf{Net}}(e_m, \mathsf{enc})$:

1. $f \leftarrow \sum_n f_i$ where each f_i is sampled uniformly , $f \in (\mathbb{F}_{p^k})^s$ by each W_i

2. Each W_i computes and broadcasts $e_{f_i} \leftarrow \mathsf{Enc}_{\mathsf{pk}}(f_i)$.

3. Each W_i runs Π_{ZKPoPK} acting as prover of e_{f_i}.

4. Each Worker computes $e_{m+f} \leftarrow e_m \boxplus e_{f_1} \ldots \boxplus e_{f_n}$.

5. Workers invoke $\mathcal{F}_{\mathsf{DecNet}}$, Client A decrypts e_{m+f} to get $m + f$.

6. Client A makes $m + f$ public.

7. W_1 sets $m_1 \leftarrow m + f - f_1, rest\ m_i \leftarrow -f_i\ \forall i \neq 1$

Secure transfer of input data from Client to Worker is contingent upon the Worker being honest. If the Worker is not honest, the adversary will acquire absolute knowledge about the input. We introduce Procedure Π_{InpDist} for secure transfer of input from Client A to Worker X followed by verifiable secret sharing of the input in $\mathcal{W}$. As the Client is not connected to all the Workers, the use of only MAC authenticated input would not provide the required security as Worker X can be corrupt itself. Thus, the input to be provided by Client A is first encrypted and then sent to Worker X.

The encryption of input data is done using a key-pair which is secret shared among Client A and all Workers in $\mathcal{W}$. Such key sharing prevents absolute decryption by the adversary and also provides control over the encryption of input to both Workers as well as Client providing the input. We introduce $\Pi_{\mathsf{KeyGenArr}}$ to achieve such a key distribution. The protocol $\Pi_{\mathsf{KeyGenArr}}$ implements the ideal functionality $\mathcal{F}_{\mathsf{KeyGenArr}}$. We generate a new set of keys (pk,sk) by building on top of existing key-share required for SPDZ. After execution of protocol $\Pi_{\mathsf{KeyGenArr}}$, every Worker in $\mathcal{W}$ will have secret share of two secret keys: sk and $\mathsf{sk}_{\mathsf{MPC}}$ and access to two pubic keys: pk and $\mathsf{pk}_{\mathsf{MPC}}$ (although every Worker's share of sk is the same as its share of $\mathsf{sk}_{\mathsf{MPC}}$ and also its share of pk is the same as its share of $\mathsf{pk}_{\mathsf{MPC}}$). The only time the key-pair (pk,sk) is used for

---

SubProcedure Π_{OutNet}

Output:

1. Let $s_1, \ldots, s_T$ be all values publicly opened so far.
   Where $\langle s_k \rangle = \left(\delta_{s_k}, (s_{k_1}, \ldots, s_{k_n}), (\gamma(s_k)_1, \ldots, \gamma(s_k)_n) \right)$ for $k = 1, \ldots n$.
   (a) $[\![x]\!]$ is opened
   (b) Workers set $x_t = x^t$ for t= 1,2,...,T
   (c) Workers compute $\Psi \leftarrow \sum_T x_t s_t$
2. Each W_i calls $\mathcal{F}_{COM}$ to commit to $\Gamma_i \leftarrow \sum_T x_t \gamma(s_t)_i$
3. Committing y and $\gamma(y)$ based on $\mathcal{F}_{PREP}$ and encryption- Random values $[\![r_1]\!]$
   and $[\![r_2]\!]$ generated in the pre-processing phase is used for commitments of
   y_i and $\gamma(y_i)$.
   (a) Every W_i computes $e_{y'_i} \leftarrow \text{Enc}_{\text{pk}}(y_i + r_{1_i})$ and $e_{\gamma(y)'_i} \leftarrow \text{Enc}_{\text{pk}}(\gamma(y)_i + r_{2_i})$
       where r_{1_i} and r_{2_i} are shares of $[\![r_1]\!]$ and $[\![r_2]\!]$ held by W_i. W_i sends
       $e_{\gamma(y)'_i}, e_{y'_i}$ to Worker X.
   (b) Worker X computes $e_{y'} \leftarrow e_{y'_1} \boxplus e_{y'_2} \ldots \boxplus e_{y'_n}$ and $e_{\gamma(y)'} \leftarrow e_{\gamma(y)'_1} \boxplus$
       $e_{\gamma(y)'_2} \ldots \boxplus e_{\gamma(y)'_n}$. Worker X sends $e_{y'}$, $e_{\gamma(y)'}$ and δ_y to Client A.
   (c) $\mathcal{F}_{DecNet}$ is invoked to decrypt $e_{y'}$, $e_{\gamma(y)'}$. Client A obtains $y', \gamma(y)'$
   (d) $[\![r_1]\!]$ and $[\![r_2]\!]$ are opened in public.
4. Open $[\![\alpha]\!]$
5. – Each W_i asks $\mathcal{F}_{COM}$ to open Γ_i, all Workers check if $\alpha \cdot (\Psi + \sum_T x_t \delta_t) = \sum_n \Gamma_i$.
   – If okay, then output is correctly computed (The output itself may be
     wrong, but the calculations are done correctly). Else, abort.
6. Client A computes if $\alpha \cdot (y' + \delta_y - r_1) = \gamma(y)' - r_2$. If okay, then set output as
   y. Else, broadcast Incorrect_Output in k-Clique.

---

encryption/decryption is when we are executing Protocols Π_{InpDist} and Π_{OutNet}.
Elsewhere, while using SPDZ functionalities for computation in the Online phase
and Pre-processing phase, the key-pair $(\text{pk}_{\text{MPC}}, \text{sk}_{\text{MPC}})$ is used. Unless otherwise
stated, Enc_{pk} will refer to the encryption function using pk as key.

Any ciphertext spawned by Enc_{pk} requires decryption by sk. As sk has a
secret share held by Client A who is outside $\mathcal{W}$, Π_{DDec} of [7] cannot be used.
Motivated by a private variant of Π_{DDec} in [7], a modified secure implementation
of $\mathcal{F}_{\text{KeyGenDec}}$, as ideal functionality $\mathcal{F}_{\text{DecNet}}$ (specified in Appendix B), is proposed
for decryption in the given setup. The schematics of the protocol are similar to
Π_{DDec} but the realization of $\mathcal{F}_{\text{DecNet}}$: Π_{DecNet}, only decrypts "fresh" ciphertext,
that is ciphertext having the third component of the ciphertext under SwHE (as
described in [7]) as zero[2].

In the $\mathcal{F}_{\text{KeyGen}}$-hybrid model, the protocol Π_{DecNet} implements $\mathcal{F}_{\text{DecNet}}$ with
statistical security against any static, active adversary corrupting up to $n - 1$
computers in the Worker-network, if $B + 2^{\text{sec}} \cdot B < q/2$. Note that the bounds are
similar to [7] despite the number of parties involved in the new protocol being
$n + 1$ instead of n. The similarity of bounds help us to integrate our protocols

---

[2] The third component of the ciphertext is non-zero only if the ciphertext has under-
gone homomorphic multiplication.

with SPDZ seamlessly without changing the pre-processing phase, online phase security parameters, and bounds.

We present Procedure Π_{InpDist}, which in the presence of functionality $\mathcal{F}_{\mathsf{KeyGenArr}}$ and $\mathcal{F}_{\mathsf{DecNet}}$, securely distributes the input data in $\mathcal{W}$. Note it is not intended to implement any functionality, it is just a procedure.

$\mathsf{Reshare_{Net}}$ is similar to $\mathsf{Reshare}$ sub-protocol in [7]. The only difference is that instead of invoking $\mathcal{F}_{\mathsf{KeyGenDec}}$ like in $\mathsf{Reshare}$, it invokes $\mathcal{F}_{\mathsf{DecNet}}$. $\mathsf{Reshare_{Net}}$ is secure as the values are made public; i.e., $e_{\mathbf{m}}$ and $\mathbf{m}+\mathbf{f}$ have the same statistical distribution as $\mathsf{Enc}_{\mathsf{pk}}(0)$ and $\mathbf{m}$. Hence it is statistically impossible to derive the message or any information about the input provided by any party. Note that we do not require ZKPoPK for the transfer of encrypted data from Client A to Worker X as input provided will be correct if any computation needs to be done successfully (SMPC assumption).

4.3 Securely Sharing Output Result Data with Client

After successful input data dissemination, the computation that follows in Online phase is akin to SPDZ Online computation where addition and multiplication of shared data is done using Π_{Online}. The output procedure is slightly different from the original SPDZ's output procedure. To account for security over the $\mathcal{W}$ network and k-$Clique$, the output should not be revealed to anyone except Client A. Hence we again rely on encryption scheme to provide the security. $\mathcal{F}_{\mathsf{COM}}$, commitments based on $\mathcal{F}_{\mathsf{PREP}}$, is implemented using HE. SubProcedure Π_{OutNet} defined is the modified output functionality of the Online phase. We assume that shared secret MAC key $[\![\alpha]\!]$, sufficient number of multiplication triples ($\langle a \rangle, \langle b \rangle, \langle c \rangle$), and pairs of random values $\langle r \rangle, [\![r]\!]$, as well as single random values $[\![t]\!]$, $[\![x]\!]$ have been generated in the pre-processing phase.

SubProcedure $\Pi_{\mathsf{OutNet\_2}}$

Output:

1. The Workers call MACCheck protocol on input: all opened values so far. If fails, output $\varnothing$ and abort. $\varnothing$ represents the fact to the corrupted Workers remain undetected in this case.
2. Committing y and $\gamma(y)$ based on $\mathcal{F}_{\mathsf{PREP}}$ and encryption-
   (a) The MPC network generates $[\![y]\!] \leftarrow \mathsf{PBracket}(y_1, y_2, \ldots, y_n, e_y)$ with $\beta_i = \alpha_i$ (α is already secret shared in $\mathcal{W}$).
   (b) Workers set $[\![y + r]\!] \leftarrow [\![y]\!] + [\![r]\!]$ where $[\![r]\!]$ is random value generated in Π_{PREP}.
   (c) W_i sends signal to every W_j, to send part of it's MAC $\gamma(y + r)_i^j$ to W_i.
   W_i computes $(y + r) \cdot \alpha_i \leftarrow \sum_j \gamma(y + r)_i^j$.
   (d) W_i sets $\sigma_i \leftarrow \gamma(y + r)_i - (y + r) \cdot \alpha_i$
3. Worker W_i asks $\mathcal{F}_{\mathsf{COMMIT}}$ to broadcast $\tau_i^\sigma \leftarrow \mathsf{Commit}(\sigma_i)$.
4. Every Worker calls $\mathcal{F}_{\mathsf{COMMIT}}$ with $\mathsf{Open}(\tau_i^\sigma)$, and all Workers obtain $\sigma_j \; \forall j$.
5. If $\sigma_1 + \ldots + \sigma_n \neq 0$, the Workers output $\varnothing$ and abort. Else y is accepted as valid output.
6. $\mathcal{F}_{\mathsf{DecNet}}$ is invoked to decrypt e_y. Client A obtains the output y.

4.4 Generalization

As modern SPDZ-like protocol use slightly different implementation of SwHE and MAC-checks, we propose another procedure to cater to this. Since the onset of [6], modern protocols support *reactive computation* which opens up possibility of complex functions to be implemented for SMPC. To share the input from Client A to MPC network, we still use Π_{InpDist}[3]. The new MAC checking method and MAC distribution is different from original SPDZ protocol, hence verification of the final output using MACs needs to be changed in Π_{OutNet} to $\Pi_{\mathsf{OutNet\_2}}$. It is still similar but the values being encrypted and transferred are different. There is a change from [5,6] where the output of SMPC calculation was revealed to everyone or one-party in the SMPC network but in our case as any party in the SMPC network can be corrupt, we don't want to share the output with any party in the SMPC network.

Combined with ZKPoPK of [5] and efficient pre-processing phase, our procedure is useful for practical applications. Unlike traditional SPDZ bounds, using $\Pi_{\mathsf{OutNet\_2}}$ will require bounds corresponding to $n+1$ parties while handling encryption/decryption using (pk,sk) to accommodate for extra share of key sk. Calculations in the Pre-processing phase and Online phase can be carried out using bounds for n parties and will be unaffected by our procedure due to modularity.

Addendum: Efficiency of MPC computation can be increased by using Π_{DistDec} (introduced in [9]) instead of Reshare for Online Phase and Preprocessing phase. This switch helps us avoid costly encryption, decryption and ZKPoPK and reduce futile communication within the network. Π_{DistDec} can't be applied to $\mathsf{Reshare}_{\mathsf{Net}}$ as part of secret is key held outside the network with Client A. We can further improve the security of above stated procedures. Efficiency is not always enough for real-world applications. If the result we compute securely has severe economical and political consequences, such as in voting or auction applications, it may be required that correctness of the result can be verified later. Ideally, we would want that this can done even if all parties involved in the computation are corrupted, and even if the party who wants to verify the result was not involved in the computation. We can incorporate *Publicly Auditable MPC protocol* erected over SPDZ in [4] with our approach to construct a secure and auditable SMPC. This is possible due to modularity of our approach. Furthermore, to ensure correctness and security of input, after Π_{InpDist}, we can verify if the input distributed in $\mathcal{W}$ is correct or not by calling $\mathcal{F}_{\mathsf{DecNet}}$. Client providing the input can deliberate further if it wants to continue with the calculation or not. In scenarios where we are sure of rampant cheating and considerable compromise in the network, such technique will prevent frivolous calculation and wasteful use of data from Pre-processing phase.

---

[3] Instead of $\mathcal{F}_{\mathsf{KeyGen}}$ (which is used in $\Pi_{\mathsf{KeyGenArr}}$), we can use the covertly secure key generation protocol Π_{KeyGen} of [6]. The covertly secure key-generation is favorable for real-world application development.

5   Double Spending Problem in Blockchain

We illustrate how the proposed protocols can be used to perform privacy- preserving double-spending check in a blockchain. Consider the general case where node B agreed to pay p tokens to node R; B is the sender and R is the recipient. At any point in the blockchain, there are many senders (B's) and recipients (R's). We implement transaction processing in two phases. The *Agreement Phase* occurs in the beginning where all deals between the R and B are authorized. This is followed by the *Payment Phase* where the verification of legitimacy of transaction takes place and the wallets are updated accordingly. The separation of the two phases prevents double-spending. Protocol $\Pi_{\text{DoubleSpendCheck}}$ processes transactions in batches. The two phases of $\Pi_{\text{DoubleSpendCheck}}$ are run one after another in a sequential manner perpetually. This allows multiple transactions to take place at once and give enough time to update wallets of senders and recipients periodically. As we assume that parties are providing legitimate wallet value for multiple transactions, authorization and verification during transaction-batch processing prevents cheating, a party is not able to cheat during processing of a batch and as wallets are updated before *Payment Phase* of next batch, double spending is prevented. Our procedure allows a sender and recipient to be involved in multiple transactions concurrently. In the Payment Phase, if the sender is found to possess less funds than necessary to perform all transactions (involving that particular sender in that particular batch), the transactions are aborted and the recipients are notified (other parties can be notified also) of sender's attempt to cheat. As incriminating notification is sent throughout the blockchain, the cheater's credibility and trading capability is tarnished hence providing incentive for honesty.

After the onset of reactive computation after [6] (implemented Protocol $\Pi_{\text{OutNet\_2}}$), complex operations like comparison[4] can be performed in the Online Phase of SMPC protocols.

Addendum: For high-stake and high-value deals, additional checks like unique-ID verification of a product, identity affidavit of sender/receiver can be implemented in Agreement Phase. To provide additional security and authenticity we can use *auditable MPC* specified in [4] for computation combined with our approach, this mirrors real-world mining operation in a blockchain.

Raising Efficiency: As minimal complex operation takes place during $\Pi_{\text{DoubleSpendCheck}}$, computation power can be delegated to Π_{PREP} to generate pre-processing data on-the-run concurrently and frequently, and also promote generation of feasible amount of triples making the protocol practically deployable. Additionally, as Agreement Phase and Payment Phase are somewhat independent, Agreement Phase of the next batch can take place while Payment Phase of one batch is running/being processed, further decreasing run-time for a transaction.

---

[4] Practical implementation of comparison operation is provided in [1].

Procedure $\Pi_{\mathsf{DoubleSpendCheck}}$

Agreement Phase:

1. $R_1, \ldots, R_i$ and $B_1, \ldots, B_j$ sends the negotiated price of a commodity to $\mathcal{W}$ by invoking Π_{InpDist}. For a transaction between **sender** B_m and **receiver** R_n, the price sent by B_m is P_{B_m, R_n} and the price sent by R_n is P_{R_n, B_m}.

2. **Sender** B_m has transactions with multiple receivers where transaction between **sender** B_m and **receiver** R_n is denoted by $\mathcal{T}_{B_m, R_n}$. $\mathcal{W}$ computes $(P_{B_i, R_j} == P_{R_j B_i})?1 : 0$ for every $\mathcal{T}_{B_i, R_j}$ and the output is sent to B_i and R_j by invoking Π_{OutNet}.

3. If for $\mathcal{T}_{B_m, R_n}$ output is 0, the transaction is aborted, else continue to the transaction is authorized.

4. Multiple transactions are bundled into a batch and sent to Payment Phase.

Payment Phase: $\mathcal{W}$ pings all sender B_i in the transaction-batch to send B_m's wallet balance W_{B_m} via Π_{InpDist}. For every sender B_m-

1. $\mathcal{W}$ performs comparison $(W_{B_m} > \sum_{S_m} P_{B_m, R_{B_m^i}})?\ 1 : 0$ and sends the *output* to $\mathcal{R}_m$ using Π_{DecNet} where B_m performs authorized transaction with $\mathcal{R}_m = \{R_{B_m^1}, \ldots, R_{B_m^v}\}$. If *output* $== 0$, transaction is aborted and the blockchain is notified about B_m's attempt at cheating.

2. If *output* $== 1$, $\mathcal{W}$ pings all receivers $R_{B_m^i}$ in $\mathcal{R}_m$ to send $R_{B_m^i}$'s wallet balance (if not already in $\mathcal{W}$): $W_{R_{B_m^i}}$ via Π_{InpDist}.

3. $\mathcal{W}$ computes $W_{R_{B_m^i}} \leftarrow W_{R_{B_m^i}} + P_{B_m, R_{B_m^i}}$ and $W_{B_m} \leftarrow W_{B_m} - P_{B_m, R_{B_m^i}} \ \forall R_{B_m^i} \in \mathcal{R}_m$. The wallet values are overwritten using Π_{OutNet}.

6 Conclusions and Future Work

SMPC is an established way to preserve the confidentiality of individual party's input data while performing computation on the data among a number of parties. It seems natural to incorporate this into blockchain so that privacy concerns can be addressed. As we have noted in the paper, there are a number of practical and cost concerns with a straightforward adaptation.

In this paper, we propose a secure and scalable method to allow any number of blockchain nodes to engage in SMPC without comprising their data confidentiality before, during and after the SMPC. We have shown how it can be used for secure double-spending check in blockchain.

For future work, we will investigate the case of multiple concurrent blockchain nodes securely giving their input data to the Worker SMPC nodes for secure computation and getting multiple result data back in a secure manner.

A KeyGenArr

Following the set up assumptions from SPDZ, we assume $\mathcal{F}_{\mathsf{KeyGen}}$ implementation is available. $\mathcal{F}_{\mathsf{KeyGenArr}}$ ideal functionality is almost similar to $\mathcal{F}_{\mathsf{KeyGenArr}}$, the difference being that instead of n share of secret key, we will be generating n+1 secret shares, the additional share is for Client A party providing the input. Unlike $\mathcal{F}_{\mathsf{KeyGen}}$ where the maximal unqualified sets must be all sets of n-1 players to allow corruption of all but one player, here the maximal qualified sets are still all sets of n-1

Functionality $\mathcal{F}_{\mathsf{KeyGenArr}}$

1. After receiving "start" from all honest players and "start" from node providing the input, run $P \leftarrow \mathsf{ParamGen}(1^\kappa, M)$, and then, using the parameters generated run $(\mathsf{pk}, \mathsf{sk}) \leftarrow \mathsf{KeyGen}()$. Send pk to adversary.

2. We assume a secret sharing scheme is given with which sk can be secret-shared. Receive from the adversary a set of shares s_j or each corrupted player P_j.

3. Construct a complete set of shares $(s_1, \ldots, s_n, s_{n+1})$ consistent with the adversary's choices and sk. Note that this is always possible since the the corrupted players form an unqualified set. Send pk to all players and s_i to each honest P_i (s_{n+1} is s_A in implementation with rest of the n shares belonging to $\mathcal{W}$)

Functionality $\mathcal{F}_{\mathsf{DecNet}}$

1. After receiving "start" from all honest players and "start" from node providing the input, run $P \leftarrow \mathit{ParamGen}(1^\kappa, M)$, and then, using the parameters generated run $(\mathsf{pk}, \mathsf{sk}) \leftarrow \mathsf{KeyGen}()$. Send pk to adversary and to all players, and store sk.

2. On receiving "decrypt c to node" ($\mathsf{node} \in k\text{-}Clique$) for (B_{plain}, B_{rand}, C)-admissible c from all honest players, send c to adversary.

3. On receiving δ from the adversary, if $\delta \notin M$, send $\perp$ to node, $\delta \in M$, send $\mathsf{Dec}_{\mathsf{sk}}(c) + \delta$ to node.

---

players but these players belong to $\mathcal{W}$. Out of n+1 players here, at least 2 are assumed to be honest- one player in $\mathcal{W}$ and the other being Client A.

B   DecNet

$\mathcal{F}_{\mathsf{DecNet}}$ is just privatized version of the ideal functionality $\mathcal{F}_{\mathsf{KeyGenDec}}$. In [7], the cryptosystem is assumed to implement the ideal functionality $\mathcal{F}_{\mathsf{KeyGenDec}}$. We assume that only (B_{plain}, B_{rand}, C)-admissible ciphertexts are to be decrypted, this constraint is guaranteed by SPDZ's main protocol. $\mathcal{F}_{\mathsf{DecNet}}$ also specifies that players can cooperate to decrypt a (B_{plain}, B_{rand}, C)-admissible ciphertext.

The party getting the result of decryption in our setup through $\mathcal{F}_{\mathsf{DecNet}}$ is only furnished to node providing the input in $k\text{-}Clique$. Hence the functionality, unlike $\mathcal{F}_{\mathsf{KeyGenDec}}$, is actively secure and not passive secure as the adversary never learns the decryption result.

References

1. Aly, A., Cozzo, D., Keller, M., Orsini, E., Rotaru, D., Scholl, P., Wood, T.: SCALE-MAMBA v1.5: Documentation (2019). https://homes.esat.kuleuven.be/nsmart/SCALE/Documentation.pdf

2. Bendlin, R., Damgård, I., Orlandi, C., Zakarias, S.: Semi-homomorphic encryption and multiparty computation. In: EUROCRYPT 2011, Tallinn, Estonia, May 2011
3. Brakerski, Z., Vaikuntanathan, V.: Fully homomorphic encryption from ring-LWE and security for key dependent messages. In: CRYPTO 2011, pp. 505–524, Santa Barbara, CA, August 2011
4. Carsten, B., Damgård, I., Orlandi, C.: Publicly auditable secure multi-party computation. In: 9th International Conference on Security and Cryptography for Networks, Amalfi, Italy, September 2014
5. Cozzo, D., Smart, N.: Using TopGear in Overdrive: A more efficient ZKPoK for SPDZ. Cryptology ePrint Archive, Report 2019/035 (2019)
6. Damgård, I., Keller, M., Larraia, E., Pastro, V., Scholl, P., Smart, N.P.: Practical covertly secure MPC for dishonest majority – or: breaking the SPDZ limits. In: Crampton, J., Jajodia, S., Mayes, K. (eds.) ESORICS 2013. LNCS, vol. 8134, pp. 1–18. Springer, Heidelberg (2013). https://doi.org/10.1007/978-3-642-40203-6_1
7. Damgård, I., Pastro, V., Smart, N., Zakarias, S.: Multiparty computation from somewhat homomorphic encryption. In: Safavi-Naini, R., Canetti, R. (eds.) CRYPTO 2012. LNCS, vol. 7417, pp. 643–662. Springer, Heidelberg (2012). https://doi.org/10.1007/978-3-642-32009-5_38
8. Jakobsen, T., Nielsen, J., Orlandi, C.: A framework for outsourcing of secure computation. In: ACM 2014, Scottsdale, AZ, November 2014
9. Keller, M., Pastro, V., Rotaru, D.: Overdrive: making SPDZ great again. In: Nielsen, J.B., Rijmen, V. (eds.) EUROCRYPT 2018. LNCS, vol. 10822, pp. 158–189. Springer, Cham (2018). https://doi.org/10.1007/978-3-319-78372-7_6
10. Kosba, A., Miller, A., Shi, E., Wen, Z., Papamanthou, C.: Hawk: the blockchain model of cryptography and privacy-preserving smart contracts. In: IEEE Symposium on Security and Privacy, pp. 839–858, San Jose, CA (2016)
11. Li, W., Sforzin, A., Fedorov, S., Karame, G.O.: Towards scalable and private industrial blockchains. In: ACM Workshop on Blockchain, Cryptocurrencies and Contracts, pp. 9–14, New York, NY, USA (2017)
12. Yang, D., Gavigan, J., Wilcox-O'Hearn, Z.: Survey of confidentiality and privacy preserving technologies for blockchains. https://www.r3.com/reports/survey-of-confidentiality-and-privacy-preserving-technologies-for-blockchains/
13. Zyskind, G., Nathan, O.: Decentralizing privacy: using blockchain to protect personal data. In: 2015 IEEE Security and Privacy Workshops. IEEE (2015)

Design and Analysis of an Effective Securing Consensus Scheme for Decentralized Blockchain System

Jing Wang[1(✉)], Lingfu Wang[1], Wei-Chang Yeh[2], and Jinhai Wang[3]

[1] School of Computer Science and Information Security,
Guilin University of Electronic Technology, 541004 Guilin, China
wjing@guet.edu.cn
[2] Department of Industrial Engineering and Engineering Management,
College of Engineering, National Tsing Hua University, 30071 Hsinchu, Taiwan
[3] College of Electronic and Information Engineering, Foshan University,
582000 Foshan, China

Abstract. Blockchain, as a decentralized network system, has been attracting increasing attention in recent years. In a blockchain system, there must be a consensus mechanism to ensure the distributed consensus among all parties. Such consensus mechanism may also be applied to guarantee fairness, correctness, and sustainability of such decentralized systems. In this paper, we propose a novel consensus mechanism, named Proof-of-Credibility (PoC), which is an improved version of Proof-of-Work (PoW). Compared with existing consensus mechanisms, PoC provides strong resistance to resource centralization and other malicious attacks. First, we present the Serial Mining Puzzle (SMP) to resist collusive mining. SMP guarantees that participants only get negligible advantage by parallel solving. Second, PoC considers the influence of participant credibility, which is reflected by the mining behaviour of a participant. Thus, credible participants get higher probability of winning the mining competition than incredible ones. Finally, the performance of PoC is analyzed in terms of common prefix, chain quality and power cost. Our analysis indicates that PoC is security and incentive compatible with suitable security parameter settings.

Keywords: Decentralized system · Blockchain · Consensus mechanism · Proof-of-credibility

1 Introduction

Distributed and decentralized network systems are gaining popularity nowadays. More and more businesses and individuals have started to access application services from the Internet, which can provide a distributed and decentralized platform for deploying and hosting application of all kinds. Compared with the traditional application platforms, it offers a number of key advantages, including scalability, flexibility, and low cost. However, the security and manageability of

© Springer Nature Singapore Pte Ltd. 2020
Z. Zheng et al. (Eds.): BlockSys 2019, CCIS 1156, pp. 212–225, 2020.
https://doi.org/10.1007/978-981-15-2777-7_18

decentralized platforms arise as a central challenge. *Bitcoin*, as one of the most famous cryptocurrencies systems, provides an efficient way to maintain a decentralized network system. The core of *Bitcoin*-like systems, called *blockchain*, can be viewed as a decentralized public ledger [1]. The decentralized nature implies that the system can be maintained entirely by participants instead of an appointed Trusted Third Party (TTP). Thus, a consensus mechanism, such as Proof-of-Work (PoW), Proof-of-Stake (PoS) and so on, is needed for blockchain to prevent the double-spending attack [2]. Furthermore, the consensus mechanism provides a promising direction to guarantee the security and robustness of more generalized decentralized systems.

The consensus mechanism follows a fundamental assumption, named *honest majority*, where adversaries can break the mechanism with negligible probability since it is difficult to control the majority of the mining resource [3]. However, the presence of resource coalitions may violate the honest majority assumption and incurs a large lurking threat against blockchain security [4–6]. For instance, the largest mining pool, Ghash.IO, has controlled more than 50% mining capacity of the *Bitcoin* network [7]. In fact, the presence of resource colition is inevitable in the *Bitcoin*-like systems [8]. On the one hand, it is a large incentive of solo participants colluding to hedge mining risks and obtain more stable reward [9]. On the other hand, there is a built-in design limitation of the *mining puzzle*, which admits an effective coalition enforcement mechanism [8]. Thus, a significant challenge of blockchain security is to prevent malicious participants from centralizing resource to successfully implement 51% *attack* [10] and *selfish strategy attack* [8].

Recently, in order to prevent resource centralization, two kinds of solutions are proposed, which involve increasing either the risk or the cost of resource coalition. For the former, Miller et al. proposed a notion named *nonoutsourceable puzzle* [8], which allows participants of a coalition to steal reward of the coalition without producing any evidence to implicate itself. Thus, it effectively creates a disincentive for participants to join the coalition, which may incur a high risk of reward lost. For increasing the cost of coalition, Duong et al. [11] and Bentov et al. [12] proposed combined mechanisms of PoW and PoS, where malicious attacks can hold advantage in mining competition by controlling the majority of both computation power and coin stake. Thus, the cost of attack is greatly increased and the security threat can be mitigated. However, while such solutions mitigate the collusion incentives, blockchain still requires a consensus mechanism that essentially resists resource coalition, which strictly maintains the fairness of the blockchain.

In this paper, we propose an improved PoW mechanism, named Proof-of-Credibility (PoC). PoC consists of two core components: the Serial Mining Puzzle (SMP) and the Mining Credibility System (MCS). First, the SMP is a novel mining puzzle that resists to resource coalition. Different from nonoutsourceable puzzles, the serial puzzle prevents not only outsource mining but also parallel mining. Thus, computation resource coalition (e.g. mining pool) presents little advantage in the mining competition. Second, for avoiding the influence of malicious participants, the MCS is introduced into PoC to provide personalized mining difficulty for participants. The MCS evaluates credibility of each participant and quantifies the credibility-based mining difficulty. Ideally, the mining difficulty should monotonically decrease with the participant credibility. As a result, PoC tends to accept *next block* created by participants with a high credibility. Thus, the proposed PoC provides an efficient way to deploy secure blockchain. The contributions of this paper can be summarized as follows:

(1) We propose the *Serial Mining Puzzle* (SMP) to resist parallel mining, avoid resource centralization.
(2) We provide quantified *Participant Credibility*, which is evaluated by the mining events recorded in blockchain.
(3) We develop the *Personalized Mining Difficulty* to promote competitive advantage of credible participants during mining.

2   Related Work

Blockchain Based Decentralized Systems. Decentralized systems provide an effective means to develop large-scale applications with loosely coupled operation and management of individual systems [13]. The decentralized nature of such system also brings novel requirements and functions [14]. The most prominent example of decentralized systems is *Bitcoin*, which was built by Nakamoto in 2009 [15]. Soon after that, extending the distributed mechanism of *Bitcoin* beyond cryptocurrency has been gaining momentum [16]. Such blockchain based decentralized systems are being rapidly developed that will play a major role in the software engineering community and beyond [17,18].

Computational Puzzles. The consensus protocol of blockchain provides an efficient mean to avoid double-spending (i.e. a bitcoin is spent more than once) for *Bitcoin*-like systems [19]. Nakamoto first proposed the Nakamoto consensus using the Proof-of-Work (PoW) computational puzzle in *Bitcoin* [15]. Following the Nakamoto consensus, the blockchain may generate several temporary forks. But one of these forks will eventually surpass others and bring the eventual consensus [3,15,20]. Furthermore, several modified computational puzzles are proposed to solve some specific problems with the Nakamoto consensus. In order to increase the mining revenue, participants use customized hardware to improve mining efficiency. Recently, an Application Specific Integrated Circuit (ASIC) has achieved orders of magnitude better performance than common chips in terms of mining [21]. Thus, an ASIC-resistant mining puzzle is proposed to keep the competitiveness of commodity hardware in mining competition [22]. Meanwhile, a useful puzzle is provided to avoid the energy and resource waste during mining. Kroll indicated that any useful puzzle must produce a pure public good [9]. For protecting the decentralization of Bitcoin-like systems, Miller first proposed the notion of non-outsource-able puzzle to prevent participant coalition [8]. The non-outsource-able puzzle allows a participant of mining pool to steal the mining reward without producing any evidence that can potentially implicate itself.

Virtual Mining Proposal. Different from computational puzzles, Proof-of-Stake (PoS) is provided as a virtual mining proposal of blockchain [23]. Instead of costing external computing resources, it costs virtual resources to extend blockchain. Thus, PoS effectively avoids the waste of real resources. Recently, there are several versions of PoS proposed to acquire better performance, such as Proof-of-coin-age [23], pure Proof-of-Stake [24], Proof-of-activity [12] and so on. However, the stability and security of virtual mining systems is still an open problem, which needs to be formally addressed. King et al. believe that, in a virtual mining system, it may be more difficult for an attacker to acquire a sufficiently large amount of digital currency than to acquire a sufficiently powerful computing equipment [23]. However, Poelstra claims that external resource consuming is necessary for blockchain security [25]. The core argument is that virtual mining is susceptible to cost-less simulation attacks. These attacks cost nothing to construct an alternate view of history, in which the allocation of currency evolves differently [10].

Security and Performance Analyzation of Blockchain Consensus Protocol. A core concern of blockchain is the security and stability of its consensus protocol. The security has initially been proven (informally) in the *honest majority* model [3,15,20]. However, the model is unsatisfying since it does not provide sufficient guarantee of the *honest majority* assumption. Several researches deem that the mining reward of *Bitcoin*-like systems provides the incentive for participants to participate and maintain the system [15,26]. However, an economic analysis shows that a bitcoin-like system is not fixed, rule-driven, and incentive-compatible as some advocates claim [27]. In fact, a participant (or coalition) may deviate from the incentive compatible consensus protocol by using a selfish mining strategy when it controls more than a third of total computation power [28]. Furthermore, an optimal selfish mining strategy is provided as the best response to the honest behaviour [29]. It offers a lower bound of the resource amount (less than 25% of the total resources) needed for a profitable selfish mining strategy. This result highlights the importance of preventing the formation of participant coalitions [16]. To evaluate the blockchain performance, several researches attempt to formulate fundamental metrics of the blockchain [30]. Garay et al. provided two quantifiable properties named *common prefix* and *chain quality*, which describe the *liveness* and *persistence* of blockchain, respectively. In this paper, we also present the superiority of our PoC mechanism by these fundamental metrics.

3   The Credibility Based Consensus Mechanism

3.1   System Model and Definitions

Nakamoto proposed the detailed model of PoW based blockchain [15]. As shown in Fig. 1, blockchain consists of a set of *sequential* blocks, where each block is associated with a pre-block except for the *genesis block*[15]. Furthermore, each block includes two parts: block header and transaction records. Block header

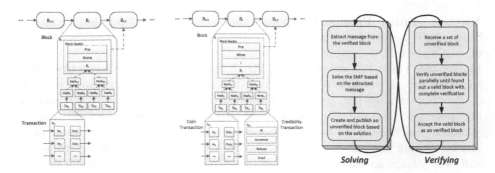

Fig. 1. PoW blockchain   **Fig. 2.** PoC blockchain   **Fig. 3.** Serial mining puzzle

contains three parameters: Pre that denotes the hash of pre-block, $Nonce$ that denotes a PoW solution of B_i, and R_i that denotes the root of a *Merkle tree* [15] formed by transactions. Finally, each transaction record includes a set of inputs $In_1, In_2, \ldots$ (i.e. the unspent coins of the *Bitcoin* system) and a set of outputs $Out_1, Out_2, \ldots$ (i.e. the new unspent coins of the *Bitcoin* system). In such PoW-based blockchain, the block creator named *miner* persistently searches the PoW solution to generate the next block. The participant will gain monetary award when its block is confirmed by blockchain.

3.2 Proof of Credibility

PoC improves PoW by providing the capability to resist to resource centralization and collusion. There are two core functional modules of PoC: SMP and MCS. First, SMP encourages participants to mine independently because collusive mining is no longer useful. Then, MCS is proposed to quantify personalized mining difficulty based on participant credibility. It increases the success probability for credible participants during mining and provide sufficient protection against decentralization to ensure security of PoC.

Figure 2 shows the overview of PoC blockchain. There are two key differences between the PoC and PoW blockchains. First, the block header parameter $Nonce$ is replaced by mining information $Mine$ and block height i. Different from $Nonce$, $Mine$ includes two parts: *serial mining puzzle solution* and the corresponding *verification* provided by multiple participants. $Mine$ carries detailed information of mining events and reflects the credibility of block creator. Second, *credibility transaction* is introduced to quantify participant credibility. However, credibility can not be transacted. Instead, it can only be updated by specific *mining-event* with an increment. Specifically, the credibility transaction includes four parts: *ID*, *Increment*, *Balance*, and *Proof*: *ID* denotes a credibility account of a participant, *Increment* denotes the credibility increment caused by the mining-event, *Balance* denotes the updated credibility balance, and *Proof* denotes the corresponding proof of occurrence of a mining-event.

3.3 Serial Mining Puzzle

SMP is a core module of PoC, which deters resource centralization, because it provides strong guarantee against parallel mining. In the PoC blockchain, participants persistently search the SMP solution instead of the PoW solution. Different from PoW puzzle, the proposed SMP require to solve in serial and verify in parallel. Intuitively, as shown in Fig. 3, the mining process of SMP is a cycle of two phases: solving and verifying. In the solving phase, participants serially search for the solution of a SMP with the last verified block message and publishes an unverified block with the solution. In the verifying phase, participants verify the unverified block in parallel to obtain a complete verification of a valid block.

Solving Phase. Firstly, the pre-block message is extracted as

$$M = S_{sk_{i-1}}(pre_{i-1}||hash(R_{i-1}||V_{i-1})), \tag{1}$$

where S denotes a digital signature algorithm, sk_{i-1} denotes a signing key of the pre-block creator, pre_{i-1} denotes the hash value of the pre-block B_{i-1}, R_{i-1} denotes the root of the Merkel tree of accepted transactions in the pre-block, and V_{i-1} denotes the complete verification set of B_{i-1} (The explanation of complete verification is given in **Verifying Phase**). Then, the initial mining message of current block is given as $msg = S_{sk_i}(M)||I$, where I denotes the height of current block. Finally, a mining series $\{a_n\}$ is defined as follows:

$$a_j = \begin{cases} null & j = 0 \\ a_{j-1}||b_{j-1} & j > 0 \end{cases}, \qquad b_j = Bit(hash(msg||a_j)),$$

where Bit denotes a random function which inputs a equal-length string (i.e. $hash(msg||a_j)$) and outputs a bit $b_j \in \{0,1\}$. Essentially, solving the SMP is to find the first valid a_l where $hash(msg||a_l)$ less than the specified difficulty D (see in Algorithm 1). It is clear that a_j can not be determined unless a_{j-1} has been determined. Thus, Algorithm 1 must be a serial algorithm instead of a parallel algorithm.

Algorithm 1. Serial Solving $\mathcal{S}(msg, D)$

Input: Block Message msg; Difficulty D
Output: Puzzle Solution: s
1: $s \leftarrow null$
2: $tmp \leftarrow hash(msg)$
3: **while** $tmp \geq D$ **do**
4:     $b \leftarrow Bit(tmp)$
5:     $s \leftarrow s||b$
6:     $tmp \leftarrow hash(msg||s)$
7: **end while**
8: **return** s

Verifying Phase. A weakness of SMP is the heavy computation cost by verifying which is close to the solving cost. However, verifying can be performed in parallel. Specifically, a block B_i is verified as a valid block if and only if it satisfies the following criteria: (1) $hash(B_i.s) < B_i.D$ where $B_i.s$ denotes the SMP solution of block B_i and $B_i.D$ denotes the mining difficulty; (2) each bit of $B_i.s$ is verified as a valid bit. Note that, the jth bit b_j of $B.s$ is *valid* iff $b_j = Bit(hash(msg\|a_j))$ where msg is the initial mining message and $a_j = b_0\| \cdots \|b_{j-1}$ is a part of $B_i.s$. The parallel multi-party verifying process is given in Algorithm 2. The participant continuously chooses an unverified block to verify until a complete verification set of a block is achieved.

Algorithm 2. Parallel Verifying $\mathcal{V}(\mathcal{S}_{ID})$

Input: A Unverified Block Set $\mathcal{S}_{ID}$
Output: Accepted Block $B_i \in \mathcal{S}_{ID}$, Verification set V_i
1: $v \leftarrow 0$
2: **while** $\mathcal{S}_{ID} \neq \emptyset \wedge v = 0$ **do**
3:     Choose a block $B_i \in \mathcal{S}_{ID}$
4:     **if** $hash(msg\|B_i.s) < B_i.D$ **then** $//B_i.s$ denote the mining message of B_i, $B_i.D$ denotes the mining difficulty of B_i
5:         Extract verifying bit from B_i: $bstr_{i,ID} = Extract(B_i.s, U_{ID})$ $// U_{ID}$ denotes the identity of verifier
6:         Verify the bit of $B_i.s$ indicated in $bstr_{i,ID}$
7:         **if** each verified bit is valid **then**
8:             Generate a successful verification and broadcast it:
9:             $V_{i,ID}^+ = (\mathcal{S}_{ID}(bstr_{i,ID}), B.s)$, $ORbstr_i \leftarrow bstr_{i,ID}$, $V_i \leftarrow \{V_{i,ID}^+\}$
10:            **while** $ORbstr \neq 111\ldots1$ **do**
11:                Receive verification of B_i broadcasted by others
12:                **if** receive a unsuccessful verification V_{i,ID_K}^- of B_i **then**
13:                    $\mathcal{S}_{ID} \leftarrow \mathcal{S}_{ID} - \{B_i\}$
14:                    **break**
15:                **else**
16:                    **if** receive a successful verification V_{i,ID_K}^+ of B_i **then**
17:                        $ORbstr_i \leftarrow ORbstr_i|bstr_{i,ID_K}$, $V_i \leftarrow V_i \cup \{V_{i,ID_K}^+\}$
18:                        **if** $ORbstr_i = 111\ldots1$ **then** $//$The complete verification set is achieved
19:                            $v \leftarrow 1$
20:                        **end if**
21:                    **end if**
22:                **end if**
23:            **end while**
24:        **end if**
25:    **else**
26:        Generate   a   unsuccessful   verification   and   broadcast: $V_{i,ID}^-$ $=$ $(\mathcal{S}_{ID}(estr_{i,ID}), B_i.s)$ $//estr_{i,ID}$ indicates invalid bit
27:        $\mathcal{S}_{ID} \leftarrow \mathcal{S}_{ID} - \{B\}$
28:    **end if**
29: **end while**
30: **return** B_i, V_i

3.4   The Mining Credibility System

In the blockchain, each block includes not only direct *transaction records* but also indirect *credibility records*. It implies that each block indirectly records the mining events, which actually reflect the credibility of participants. Thus, MCS is developed to evaluate participant credibility and quantifies credibility-based mining difficulty.

Credibility Account. Different from a coin account, acquiring a credibility account is more strict. The credibility account can be viewed as a coin account bounded with a unique global IP address. Specifically, a credibility account can validly gain block award when an IP binding certificate of the account has been confirmed by the blockchain. In this way, a credibility account is uniquely identified by a global IP address, which can also mitigate the witch attack in the PoC based blockchain. Note that, in the MCS of PoC blockchain, the credibility accounts sacrifice the anonymity for their credibility while the coin accounts keeping their anonymity without credibility.

Credibility Quantification. First of all, an ideal MCS requires that the participant credibility accurately reflects the mining behaviour of the participant.

In MCS, each cridibility participant $C_\mathfrak{p}$ of each participant $\mathfrak{p}$ is initialized to be 0 and the following mining-events are specified to affect $C_\mathfrak{p}$:

(1) $\mathcal{E}_i$, inserting a block into the chain. The credibility increment caused by $\mathcal{E}_i$ is calculated as $\Delta_i = \alpha(1 - e^{-\lambda_i A(\mathcal{E}_i)})$, where α is a positive constant that denotes the upper bound of the increment, λ_i is a positive constant that describes the rising tendency of increment, and $A(\mathcal{E}_i)$ denotes the transaction amount confirmed while $\mathcal{E}_i$ is occurring.

(2) $\mathcal{E}_s$, contributing a verification of inserted blocks. If participant $\mathfrak{p}$ successful submits a verification to block-chain, the increment of $C_\mathfrak{p}$ can be calculated as $\Delta_s = \beta(1-e^{-\lambda_s L_b(\mathcal{E}_s)})$, where $\beta > 0$ denotes the upper bound of increment Δ_s, $\lambda_s > 0$ controls the rising tendency of Δ_s and $L_b(\mathcal{E}_s)$ denotes the number of verified bits indicated in the verification.

(3) $\mathcal{E}_d$, detecting a forged block includes invalid bit. Let Δ_d be the increment of $C_\mathfrak{p}$ while $\mathfrak{p}$ detects a forged block that includes an invalid bit. Thus, $\Delta_d = \gamma(1 - e^{-\lambda_d L_v(\mathcal{E}_d)})$, where $\gamma > 0$ denotes the upper bound of Δ_d, λ_d denotes the rising tendency of Δ_d, and $L_v(\mathcal{E}_d)$ denotes the length of mining information of the detected block.

(4) $\mathcal{E}_c$, creating a forged block. The increment Δ_c of $C_\mathfrak{p}$ is produced while a block published by $\mathfrak{p}$ is verified as a forged block. Furthermore, $\Delta_c = min\{-\eta e^{\lambda_c C_p}, T\}$, where $T < 0$ denotes the upper bound of Δ_c, η and λ_c denotes two positive parameters influence increment Δ_c.

(5) $\mathcal{E}_a$, accepting a forged block. The event $\mathcal{E}_a$ represents that participant p has published a block with a forged pre-block. It implies that p accepts an incomplete or forged verification. Thus, the increment $\Delta_a = -\rho e^{-\lambda_a L_v(\mathcal{E}_a)}$, where $-\rho < 0$ denotes the lower bound of Δ_a, $-\lambda_a$ denotes the constant that controls the rising tendency of Δ_a, and $L_v(\mathcal{E}_a)$ denotes the length of the mining information of the pre-block.

(6) $\mathcal{E}_p$, publishing two blocks or verification with a close block height in different forks. It will produce a serious forking issue when a participant performs mining with different forks in parallel. Thus, such a dishonest behaviour will result in the following credibility increment $\Delta_p = -\tau e^{\lambda_p L_\mathfrak{p}(\mathcal{E}_p)}$, where τ denotes a positive constant coefficient, λ_a denotes the constant that controls the rising tendency, and $L_\mathfrak{p}(\mathcal{E}_p)$ denotes the total length of such blocks or verification published by $\mathfrak{p}$ with close block height.

Additionally, the influence of mining-event will decay with time. Thus, it is reasonable for each credibility increment to multiply a *exponential time-decay factor* $e^{-\lambda_t T}$, where $-\lambda_t < 0$ denotes an assigned constant and T denotes the height difference between the block when the mining-event occurs and the current block.

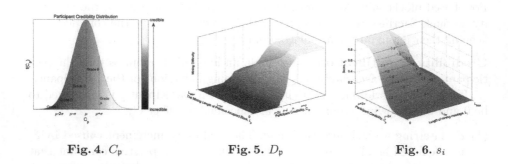

Fig. 4. $C_\mathfrak{p}$ **Fig. 5.** $D_\mathfrak{p}$ **Fig. 6.** s_i

Credibility Grading. Let credibility increments of a participant be a sequence of independent random variables $\Delta_1, \Delta_2, \ldots \Delta_n$ and each Δ_k. Assume that, following the Lyapunov central limit theorem [31], the distribution of $C_\mathfrak{p} = \sum_{k=1}^n \Delta_k$ tends to be normally distributed $N(\mu, \sigma^2)$, where $\mu = \sum_{k=1}^n \mu_k$ and $\sigma^2 = \sum_{k=1}^n \sigma_k^2$. Then, $C_\mathfrak{p}$ is graded based on its probability density function, as shown in Fig. 4: (1) Grade A, $C_\mathfrak{p} \in (\mu + \sigma, +\infty)$; (2) Grade B, $C_\mathfrak{p} \in (\mu, \mu + \sigma]$; (3) Grade C, $C_\mathfrak{p} \in (\mu - \sigma, \mu]$; (4) Grade D, $C_\mathfrak{p} \in (\mu - 2\sigma, \mu - \sigma]$; (5) Grade E, $C_\mathfrak{p} \in (-\infty, \mu - 2\sigma]$.

Credibility Based Mining Difficulty. Credibility grade represents the historical mining behaviour of a participant. Thus, it is reasonable to evaluate the current or future mining behaviour of a participant via its credibility grade. To encourage credible participants and penalize discredited participants, PoC introduces personalized mining difficulty for a participant based on its credibility. Let $D_\mathfrak{p}$ calculated by following piecewise function:

$$D_\mathfrak{p} = \begin{cases} 2^{\lfloor(\theta_a + \delta_a F(C_\mathfrak{p})) - \lambda \Delta_L \rfloor}, & C_\mathfrak{p} \in (\mu + \sigma, +\infty) \\ 2^{\lfloor(\theta_b + \delta_b F(C_\mathfrak{p})) - \lambda \Delta_L \rfloor}, & C_\mathfrak{p} \in (\mu, \mu + \sigma] \\ 2^{\lfloor(\theta_c + \delta_c F(C_\mathfrak{p})) - \lambda \Delta_L \rfloor}, & C_\mathfrak{p} \in (\mu - \sigma, \mu] \\ 2^{\lfloor(\theta_d + \delta_d F(C_\mathfrak{p})) - \lambda \Delta_L \rfloor}, & C_\mathfrak{p} \in (\mu - 2\sigma, \mu - \sigma] \\ 0, & C_\mathfrak{p} \in (-\infty, \mu - 2\sigma] \end{cases} \qquad (2)$$

where $F(C_\mathfrak{p})$ denotes the cumulative probability function of $C_\mathfrak{p}$, $\Delta_L = \max\{L_\mathfrak{p} - L_{Thr}, 0\}$ with $L_\mathfrak{p}$ denoting the length of the pre-block mining information produced by $\mathfrak{p}$, and L_{Thr} denotes a threshold. Furthermore, it is set $\theta_a = \theta_b + F(\mu + \sigma)(\delta_b - \delta_a)$, $\theta_b = \theta_c + F(\mu)(\delta_c - \delta_b)$, $\theta_c = \theta_d + F(\mu - \sigma)(\delta_d - \delta_c)$, $\theta_d = -\delta_d F(\mu - 2\sigma)$ and $0 < \delta_a < \delta_b \leq 1 < \delta_c < \delta_d$. Figure 5 shows how the personalized mining difficulty increases with $C_\mathfrak{p}$ and $L_\mathfrak{p}$.

3.5 Fork Selecting Strategy

There is a strategy for a participant to select a fork to extend from multiple received forks. First, each block B_i is assigned with a score s_i calculated as $s_i = F(C_\mathfrak{p})e^{-\max\{0, L_i - L_{Thr}\}}$, where $F(\cdot)$ denotes the cumulative probability function of participant credibility, $C_\mathfrak{p}$ denotes the credibility of $\mathfrak{p}$ that generates block B_i, L_i denotes the length of mining information of B_i, and L_{Thr} denotes a specified threshold. Figure 6 shows that $s_i \in (0, 1)$ and parameters $C_\mathfrak{p}, L_i$ incur different influences on s_i. Then, the chain score of a fork can be defined as $s_\mathcal{C} = \sum_{B_i \in \mathcal{C}} s_i$. Because the largest chain score implies the best chain quality, a participant accepts the fork with the largest score instead of the longest fork.

3.6 PoC Based Blockchain Protocol

Algorithm 3. PoC Protocol Π

1: Initialize: $\mathcal{C} \leftarrow B_0$ //$\mathcal{C}$ denotes the current chain and B_0 denotes the genesis block of the chain
2: **while** True **do**
3:    Upon receiving chain set $\mathcal{S}_\mathcal{C}$ and unrecorded information
4:    Extracting unverified block set $\mathcal{S}_{ID}$ which includes all current $\mathcal{B}_i$ of the chain $\mathcal{C}_i \in \mathcal{S}_\mathcal{C}$
5:    verifying the block $B_i \in \mathcal{S}_{ID}$ following the chain score s_i descending order
6:    $(B_i, V_i) \leftarrow \mathcal{V}(\mathcal{S}_{ID})$
7:    $\mathcal{C} \leftarrow \mathcal{C}_i$
8:    Updating the mining difficulty D following the current chain $\mathcal{C}$
9:    Calculated the initial mining message msg
10:   Solving the current mining puzzle
11:   $s_k \leftarrow \mathcal{S}(msg, D)$
12:   Generating new block B_k of $\mathcal{C}$
13:   $\mathcal{C} \leftarrow \mathcal{C}||B_k$
14:   Broadcast the current chain $\mathcal{C}$
15: **end while**

The overview of PoC based blockchain protocol is presented as Algorithm 3. Firstly, the chain $\mathcal{C}$ is initialized with the genesis block. Then, in each round, participants receive a set of chain $\mathcal{S}_\mathcal{C}$ from the whole network. The chain in $\mathcal{S}_\mathcal{C}$ is sorted by chain score. Thirdly, participants invoke the Algorithm 2 to verify

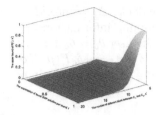 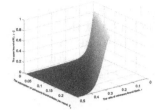 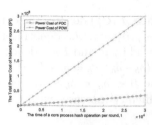

Fig. 7. Upper bound of probability $P[l^* \geq k^*]$

Fig. 8. Upper bound of probability $P[\gamma \geq \epsilon]$

Fig. 9. Power cost of PoC and PoW

the validity of current block B_i and get the corresponding verification set V_i. Finally, the participants invoke the Algorithm 1 to mine new block B_k of current chain with updated information. The new block B_k is broadcast to the network, which implies the current round of the PoC Protocol is finished.

4   Security Analysis and Performance Evaluation

Common Prefix Property. In PoC, a participant is punished with decreased credibility when it publishes blocks or verification of different forks with a similar height. Thus, it is reasonable to assume that the honest participant will only mine on one fork and the adversary only publishes blocks/verification on one fork in a temporal interval. Let C_1 and C_2 be the chains of two honest participants at a given round, k^* be the minimum integer such that $C_1^{\lceil k^*} \preceq C_2$ and $C_2^{\lceil k^*} \preceq C_1$[1]. Assume that all the last k^* blocks of C_1 and C_2 are produced in l rounds. The total length $2k^*$ of the sub-chains cannot be greater than the solution number X obtained by all participants in l rounds. Furthermore, let l also denote the minimum number of rounds that a participant is allowed to mine for different forks without punishment, $\mathcal{H}$ and $\mathcal{A}$ denote the sets of honest participants and adversaries, respectively. Let $X_{i,k}$ denote a Boolean random variable, where $X_{i,k} = 1$ iff there is a solution produced for C_1 or C_2 by participant i in the last $(l-k)^{th}$ round, the probability $P[X_{i,k} = 1]$ is calculated as follows:

$$P[X_{i,k} = 1] = \begin{cases} p_i, & i \in \mathcal{H} \\ \bar{p}_i^{2(k-1)}(1 - \bar{p}_i^2) + (1 - \bar{p}_i^{2(k-1)})p_i, & i \in \mathcal{A}, k < l \\ \bar{p}_i^{2(l-1)}(1 - \bar{p}_i^2) + (1 - \bar{p}_i^{2(l-1)})p_i, & i \in \mathcal{A}, k \geq l \end{cases} \tag{3}$$

where $\bar{p}_i = (1 - D_{\mathbf{p}_i}/N)^q$, $p_i = 1 - \bar{p}_i$ and q denotes the maximum times a participant processes the hash function in a round. Thus, the expectation of random variable $X = \sum_{i \in \mathcal{H} \cup \mathcal{A}} \sum_{k=1}^{l} X_{i,k}$ is calculated as follows:

$$\mu_1 = \sum_{i \in \mathcal{H} \cup \mathcal{A}} \sum_{k=1}^{l} E(X_{i,k}) \geq lf, \tag{4}$$

---

[1] The equantion is defined in [3]: $C_i^{\lceil k^*}$ denotes the sub-chain of C_i remove the latest k blocks, $* \preceq **$ denotes chain $**$ is contained in chain $*$.

where $f = S_a + S_h$, $S_h = \sum_{i \in \mathcal{H}} p_i$ and $S_a = \sum_{i \in \mathcal{A}} p_i$ are the expected number of solutions that may be found for a chain per round by all participants, honest participants and adversary participants, respectively. The length of chains l^* cannot be greater than the number of solutions X obtained in l rounds. Thus, $P[l^* \geq k^*] \leq P[X \geq 2k^*]$. By the Chernoff bound,

$$\begin{cases} P[l^* \geq k^*] \leq P[X \geq (1+\delta)\mu_1] \leq e^{-\frac{\delta^2 \mu_1}{3}}, & 0 < \delta \leq 1 \\ P[l^* \geq k^*] \leq P[X \geq (1+\delta)\mu_1] \leq e^{-\frac{\delta \mu_1}{3}}, & 1 < \delta \end{cases} \tag{5}$$

where $(1+\delta)\mu_1 \geq (1+\delta)lf = 2k^*$. Figure 7 shows the upper bound of $P[l^* \geq k^*]$ for $l = 10$, $f \in (0,1)$ and $k^* \in [5,20]$. It is clear that the probability $P[l^* \geq k^*]$ drops exponentially with k^*.

Chain Quality Property. Let random variable $Y = \sum_{i \in \mathcal{A}} \sum_{k=1}^{L} X_{i,k}$ be the number of solutions of a chain $\mathcal{C}$ found by adversary participants in L rounds and the expectation of Y can be calculated as $\mu_2 = \sum_{i \in \mathcal{A}} \sum_{k=1}^{L} E(X_{i,k}) = \sum_{j \in \mathcal{A}} Lp_j = LS_a$. Furthermore, let γ be the ratio of adversary-provided block to continuous blocks of chain $\mathcal{C}$ produced in L rounds. It is clear that $P[\gamma \geq \epsilon] \leq P[Y \geq \epsilon Lf]$. Following the Chernoff bound,

$$\begin{cases} P[\gamma \geq \epsilon] \leq P[Y > (1+\delta_a)\mu_2] \leq e^{-\frac{\delta^2 \mu_2}{3}}, & 0 < \delta \leq 1 \\ P[\gamma \geq \epsilon] \leq P[Y > (1+\delta_a)\mu_2] \leq e^{-\frac{\delta \mu_2}{3}}, & 1 < \delta \end{cases} \tag{6}$$

where $(1+\delta)\mu_2 = (1+\delta)LS_a = \epsilon Lf$. Figure 8 shows the upper bound of $P[\gamma \geq \epsilon]$ where $L = 100$, $f = 1$, $\gamma \in (0, 0.5]$ and $S_a \in (0, 0.25]$.

It is implies that, the chain quality of PoC mechanism is high enough while S_a is small enough. However, S_a must be small when the credibility of an adversary is lower than grade C. The condition is easy to obtain when participant credibility is accurately reflected by the credit rating.

Power Cost. Let n be the number of active participants, m be the average number of computing core per active participant, P be the average power cost that a core processes a hash operation, t be the times that a core runs a hash function per round and λ be the ratio of verified times to a round. Thus, the power cost of PoC mechanism of the whole network can be calculated as $\mathcal{P}_{PoC} = (1 - \lambda)ntP + \lambda mntP$. Let $(1 - \lambda)t \to q$ and $\lambda mt \to \alpha q$ where q denotes the maximum length of mining information and αq denotes the maximum length of verification. Thus, $\lambda \to \alpha/(m + \alpha)$, it can be simplified as $\lambda \to \alpha/m$ while $m >> \alpha$. Similarly, the power cost of PoW can be calculated as $\mathcal{P}_{PoW} = (t - 1)mnP + nP$. Let $\alpha = 0.2$, $m = 10$ and $n = 1000$, Fig. 9 shows the power cost of PoC and PoW increase with parameter t. However, PoC cost more power than PoW during verifying, the total power cost is much lower during mining.

5   Conclusions

In this paper, we propose a novel consensus mechanism named PoC. Compared with traditional consensus mechanisms, PoC provides strong resistance to resource centralization and malicious participant attacks. First, resource coalition gets negligible advantage in mining competition, because SMP is introduced in PoC. Second, in PoC, each participant is provided with personalized mining difficulty which depends on the participant credibility. Furthermore, the credibility of each participant is quantified by its mining behaviour, which guarantees that the more credible participants get the higher successful mining probability. Finally, the performance of PoC is thoroughly analyzed in terms of common prefix, chain quality and power cost. The analysis justifies that PoC is security and incentive compatible when suitable parameters are set, It also can provide strong security and robustness for blockchain based system.

Acknowledgment. This work was supported by the National Science Foundation of China (No. 61802083, 61862011), the Natural Science Foundation of Guangxi (2018GXNSFBA281164, 2018GXNSFAA138116).

References

1. Evans, D.S.: Economic aspects of Bitcoin and other decentralized public-ledger currency platforms. University of Chicago Coase-Sandor Institute for Law & Economics Research Paper No. 685 (2014)
2. Kwon, J.: Tendermint: consensus without mining (2014). http://tendermint.com/docs/tendermint_v04.pdf
3. Garay, J., Kiayias, A., Leonardos, N.: The Bitcoin backbone protocol: analysis and applications. In: Oswald, E., Fischlin, M. (eds.) EUROCRYPT 2015. LNCS, vol. 9057, pp. 281–310. Springer, Heidelberg (2015). https://doi.org/10.1007/978-3-662-46803-6_10
4. Laszka, A., Johnson, B., Grossklags, J.: When Bitcoin mining pools run dry. In: Brenner, M., Christin, N., Johnson, B., Rohloff, K. (eds.) FC 2015. LNCS, vol. 8976, pp. 63–77. Springer, Heidelberg (2015). https://doi.org/10.1007/978-3-662-48051-9_5
5. Gervais, A., Karame, G., Capkun, S., Capkun, V.: Is Bitcoin a decentralized currency? IEEE Secur. Priv. **12**(3), 54–60 (2014)
6. Bradbury, D.: The problem with Bitcoin. Comput. Fraud Secur. **2013**(11), 5–8 (2013)
7. Matonis, J.: The Bitcoin mining arms race: Ghash. IO and the 51% issue (2014)
8. Miller, A., Kosba, A., Katz, J., Shi, E.: Nonoutsourceable scratch-off puzzles to discourage Bitcoin mining coalitions. In: Proceedings of the 22nd ACM SIGSAC Conference on Computer and Communications Security, pp. 680–691. ACM (2015)
9. Kroll, J.A., Davey, I.C., Felten, E.W.: The economics of Bitcoin mining, or Bitcoin in the presence of adversaries. In: Proceedings of WEIS (2013)
10. Houy, N.: It will cost you nothing to "kill" a proof-of-stake crypto-currency (2014). http://papers.ssrn.com/sol3/papers.cfm
11. Duong, T., Fan, L., Zhou, H.-S.: 2-hop blockchain: combining proof-of-work and proof-of-stake securely (2016). https://eprint.iacr.org/2016/716
12. Bentov, I., Lee, C., Mizrahi, A., Rosenfeld, M.: Proof of activity: extending bitcoin's proof of work via proof of stake [extended abstract] y. ACM SIGMETRICS Perform. Eval. Rev. **42**(3), 34–37 (2014)

13. Vierhauser, M., Rabiser, R., Grünbacher, P.: A case study on testing, commissioning, and operation of very-large-scale software systems. In: Companion Proceedings of the 36th International Conference on Software Engineering, pp. 125–134. ACM (2014)
14. Dubois, S., Guerraoui, R., Kuznetsov, P., Petit, F., Sens, P.: The weakest failure detector for eventual consistency. In: Proceedings of the 2015 ACM Symposium on Principles of Distributed Computing, pp. 375–384. ACM (2015)
15. Nakamoto, S.: Bitcoin: a peer-to-peer electronic cash system. Manubot (2019)
16. Pass, R., Shi, E.: Fruitchains: a fair blockchain. In: Proceedings of the ACM Symposium on Principles of Distributed Computing, pp. 315–324. ACM (2017)
17. Talukder, A.K., Chaitanya, M., Arnold, D., Sakurai, K.: Proof of disease: a Blockchain consensus protocol for accurate medical decisions and reducing the disease burden. In: 2018 IEEE SmartWorld, Ubiquitous Intelligence & Computing, Advanced & Trusted Computing, Scalable Computing & Communications, Cloud & Big Data Computing, Internet of People and Smart City Innovation (SmartWorld/SCALCOM/UIC/ATC/CBDCom/IOP/SCI), pp. 257–262. IEEE (2018)
18. Dong, Z., Lee, Y.C., Zomaya, A.Y.: Proofware: proof of useful work blockchain consensus protocol for decentralized applications. arXiv preprint arXiv:1903.09276 (2019)
19. Bonneau, J., Miller, A., Clark, J., Narayanan, A., Kroll, J.A., Felten, E.W.: Research perspectives on Bitcoin and second-generation cryptocurrencies. In: IEEE Symposium on Security and Privacy (2015)
20. Miller, A., LaViola Jr., J.J.: Anonymous byzantine consensus from moderately-hard puzzles: a model for Bitcoin (2014). http://nakamotoinstitute.org/research/anonymous-byzantine-consensus
21. Bedford Taylor, M.: Bitcoin and the age of bespoke silicon. In: International Conference on Compilers, Architecture and Synthesis for Embedded Systems (CASES), pp. 1–10 (2013)
22. Tromp, J.: Cuckoo cycle: a memory-hard proof-of-work system. IACR Cryptology ePrint Archive, 59 (2014)
23. King, S., Nadal, S.: Ppcoin: peer-to-peer crypto-currency with proof-of-stake. Self-published paper, 19 August 2012
24. Vasin, P.: Blackcoin's proof-of-stake protocol v2 (2014). http://blackcoin.co/blackcoin-pos-protocol-v2-whitepaper.pdf
25. Poelstra, A.: Distributed consensus from proof of stake is impossible. Self-published Paper (2014)
26. Barber, S., Boyen, X., Shi, E., Uzun, E.: Bitter to better how to make Bitcoin a better currency. In: Keromytis, A.D. (ed.) FC 2012. LNCS, vol. 7397, pp. 399–414. Springer, Heidelberg (2012). https://doi.org/10.1007/978-3-642-32946-3_29
27. Kroll, J.A., Davey, I.C., Felten, E.W.: The economics of Bitcoin mining, or Bitcoin in the presence of adversaries. In: Proceedings of WEIS. Citeseer (2013)
28. Eyal, I., Sirer, E.G.: Majority is not enough: Bitcoin mining is vulnerable. In: Christin, N., Safavi-Naini, R. (eds.) FC 2014. LNCS, vol. 8437, pp. 436–454. Springer, Heidelberg (2014). https://doi.org/10.1007/978-3-662-45472-5_28
29. Sapirshtein, A., Sompolinsky, Y., Zohar, A.: Optimal selfish mining strategies in Bitcoin. In: Grossklags, J., Preneel, B. (eds.) FC 2016. LNCS, vol. 9603, pp. 515–532. Springer, Heidelberg (2017). https://doi.org/10.1007/978-3-662-54970-4_30
30. Garay, J.A.: Basic properties of the Blockchain: (invited talk). In: Proceedings of the ACM Workshop on Blockchain, Cryptocurrencies and Contracts, p. 1. ACM (2017)
31. Billingsley, P.: Convergence of Probability Measures. Wiley (2013)

KCRS: A Blockchain-Based Key Compromise Resilient Signature System

Lei Xu[1(✉)], Lin Chen[2], Zhimin Gao[3], Xinxin Fan[5], Kimberly Doan[6], Shouhuai Xu[6], and Weidong Shi[4]

[1] University of Texas Rio Grande Valley, Brownsville 78520, USA
lei.xu@utrgv.edu
[2] Texas Tech University, Lubbock 79409, USA
[3] Auburn University at Montgomery, Montgomery 36117, USA
[4] University of Houston, Houston 77004, USA
[5] IoTeX, Menlo Park 94025, USA
[6] University of Texas at San Antonio, San Antonio 78249, USA

Abstract. Digital signatures are widely used to assure authenticity and integrity of messages (including blockchain transactions). This assurance is based on assumption that the private signing key is kept secret, which may be exposed or compromised without being detected in the real world. Many schemes have been proposed to mitigate this problem, but most schemes are not compatible with widely used digital signature standards and do not help detect private key exposures. In this paper, we propose a Key Compromise Resilient Signature (KCRS) system, which leverages blockchain to detect key compromises and mitigate the consequences. Our solution keeps a log of valid certificates and digital signatures that have been issued on the blockchain, which can deter the abuse of compromised private keys. Since the blockchain is an open system, KCRS also provides a privacy protection mechanism to prevent the public from learning the relationship between signatures. We present a theoretical framework for the security of the system and a provably-secure construction. We also implement a prototype of KCRS and conduct experiments to demonstrate its practicability.

Keywords: Digital signature · Key Compromise Resilient · Blockchain · Privacy · Exposure detection

1 Introduction

Digital signatures can assure the authenticity and integrity of messages and play a critical role in many applications, while assuming that the private signing key is kept secret. In the real world, it is difficult to assure the security of private signing keys because the system storing the private signing key can be compromised. This has motivated a sequence of studies on mitigating the damages of key compromises, such as [1,4,6,7,9–11,13,16,18–20,26–30]. Even if a private signing key is not compromised, an attacker still can exploit its service to obtain

© Springer Nature Singapore Pte Ltd. 2020
Z. Zheng et al. (Eds.): BlockSys 2019, CCIS 1156, pp. 226–239, 2020.
https://doi.org/10.1007/978-981-15-2777-7_19

legitimate digital signatures [24,31]. Advanced cryptographic mechanisms, such as forward secure digital signatures [1,4,20], key-insulated public key cryptosystems [12–14], and intrusion-resilient schemes [19], can mitigate the damages of private signing key compromises. However, they are not compatible with existing digital signature standards and cannot detect key compromises.

On the other hand, the Certificate Transparency (CT) framework [22] has been proposed for monitoring and auditing TLS/SSL certificates with a cryptographically assured, publicly auditable, append-only certificate log. Although this approach is compatible to existing standards and can detect key compromises, it lacks the recovery capability for the compromised certificates. Recent work [2,25] has resorted to blockchain for addressing the aforementioned challenges, due to its salient features such as immutability and tamper detection. This approach is reminiscent of earlier studies on managing digital signatures [17,31]. However, these digital signature management systems expose users' behavior to the public, thereby raising privacy concerns.

In this paper, we propose a privacy-enhanced Key Compromise Resilient Signature framework, or KCRS for short, by leveraging a blockchain to enable privacy-preserving key compromise detection, invalid signature revocation, and key update. KCRS supports standardized digital signature schemes and utilizes a dual key strategy with a "signing" key pair for message authentication and a "master" key pair for signature linkage. In KCRS, both valid public keys and generated signatures are stored on the blockchain, which allows a user to easily detect a compromised signing key by monitoring blockchain records and act promptly. One-time signature and encryption are employed to protect users' privacy, such as the messages they signed and the pattern of their signature generations. A prototype implementation of KCRS using Hyperledger Fabric [3] demonstrates its effectiveness and efficiency in practice.

This paper is organized as follows. Section 2 describes the KCRS framework and its security model. Section 3 presents a concrete construction of KCRS and its security analysis. Section 4 describes the integration of KCRS with blockchain. Section 5 discusses the implementation of KCRS and evaluates its performance. Section 6 concludes the paper.

2   The KCRS Framework and Security Model

2.1   The KCRS Framework

A KCRS scheme consists of the following six algorithms:

Initialization. The following algorithm is used to initialize KCRS.

– *Setup* $(\lambda) \rightarrow pp$. The algorithm *Setup* takes the security parameter λ as input, and outputs the public parameters that are used by other algorithms.

Master Key Initialization. The following algorithm is used by a user (signer or verifier) to get his/her first key pair and register to KCRS.

- $MKGen\,(pp) \rightarrow (pk_M, sk_M)$. $MKGen$ takes the public parameters pp as input, and outputs a master public/private key pair (pk_M, sk_M), where pk_M also serves as the identity of its owner.

Signing Key Pair Generation. The following algorithms are used by a signer to select a signing public/private key pair.

- $SPKGen\,(pp, pk_M) \rightarrow (pk_S, aux)$. Given a master public key pk_M and the public parameters pp, the algorithm $SKGen$ returns a randomly selected signing public key pk_S and related auxiliary information aux.
- $SSKGen\,(pp, pk_S, aux, sk_M, pk_M) \rightarrow sk_S$. The algorithm is deterministic and takes the public parameters pp, the generated signing public key pk_S with auxiliary information aux, and master public/private key pair (sk_M, pk_M) as inputs. It returns a signing private key sk_S, which is used to generate signatures that can be verified by pk_S.

Signing Key Pair Detection. The following deterministic algorithm is used by a signer to check whether a given signing public key is generated using his/her master public/private key pairing information.

- $SKDetect\,(pp, sk_M, pk_M, pk_S) \rightarrow \delta$. If pk_S is generated using sk_M and pk_M, the algorithm returns 1; otherwise, it returns 0.

Signature Algorithm. The following two algorithms are used to generate/verify digital signatures.

- $SigGen\,(pp, sk_S, m) \rightarrow \sigma_{m,pk_S}$. The function $SigGen$ generates signature of m using signing private key sk_S.
- $SigVerify\,(pp, \sigma_{m,pk_S}, m, pk_S) \rightarrow \delta$. The algorithm $SigVerify$ returns $\delta = 1$ if the signature sig_{m,pk_S} is valid with respect to message m and public key pk_S; otherwise, it returns $\delta = 0$.

Link Verification. The following algorithm is used for one to establish the connection between a signature and its signer.

- $LNK\,(pp, \sigma, m, pk_M) \rightarrow \delta$. This is a deterministic algorithm that allows one to check whether the signer of σ is the owner of pk_M.

For a signature scheme, we usually assume both the message and the signature are in public. As a result, everyone can use LNK to recover the signer's identity. In the concrete construction of KCRS, we demonstrate how to limit this linking capability to the designated signature verifier via encryption.

2.2   Security Definitions of KCRS

Correctness. This means that a KCRS scheme works normally when the signer and verifier are honest. Specifically, (i) the signer can generate signing key pairs and sign messages that can be accepted by a verifier; (ii) if the signer sees a public signing key that is derived from her/his master public key, he/she can detect it; and (iii) for a targeted signature verifier, he/she can check whether a signature is related to a master public key or not.

Signature Unforgeability. This means that only the one who knows the signing private key can generate a valid signature, dubbed existential unforgeability under adaptive chosen-message attacks (EUF-CMA).

Definition 1 (EUF-CMA [15]**).** *A KCRS scheme is EUF-CMA secure if the probability attacker $\mathcal{A}$ wins the following game is negligible in security parameter λ:*

1. *The challenger $\mathcal{C}$ generates a pair of public/private key pair (pk_S, sk_S) using the public parameter pp, and gives pk to the adversary $\mathcal{A}$.*
2. *$\mathcal{A}$ queries $\mathcal{C}$ for signatures $\sigma_1, \ldots, \sigma_q$ on adaptively chosen messages $m_1, \ldots, m_q$, respectively.*
3. *$\mathcal{A}$ produces a pair of message and signature (m^*, σ^*). If m^* is not queried in a previous step and σ^* is a valid signature of m^*, then $\mathcal{A}$ succeeds.*

Note that KCRS has two pairs of public/private keys, but only the signing key pair is used for digital signature operations.

Signing Private Key Unforgeability. Unforgeability of signing private key (UF-SSK) assures that only the user who has the master private key can generate a signing private key, as formulated in Definition 2.

Definition 2 (UF-SSK) . *A KCRS scheme is UF-SSK secure if the probability that the adversary wins the following game is negligible in security parameter λ:*

1. *The challenger $\mathcal{C}$ generates a pair of master public/private key pair (pk_M, sk_M) using the public parameters pp. The master public key is given to adversary $\mathcal{A}$.*
2. *$\mathcal{A}$ queries $\mathcal{C}$ to obtain a sequence responses, e.g., signing public/private key pairs derived from (pk_M, sk_M) and other related information.*
3. *$\mathcal{A}$ generates a signing public/private key pair (pk_S^*, sk_S^*), which is different from any of the ones obtained in the previous queries.*
4. *If pk_S^* is derived from pk_M and matches with sk_S^*, then $\mathcal{A}$ succeeds.*

Signing Public Key Indistinguishability. Signing public key indistinguishability (IND-SPK) means that one cannot distinguish signing public keys generated from different master keys, thereby protecting the privacy of the signer.

Definition 3 (IND-SPK) . *A KCRS scheme is IND-SPK secure if the probability that an adversary wins the following game is negligibly greater than $1/2$ (with respect to security parameter λ).*

1. *The challenger $\mathcal{C}$ generates a master public/private key pair (pk_M, sk_M) using the public parameters pp, and gives pk_M to attacker $\mathcal{A}$.*
2. *$\mathcal{A}$ queries $\mathcal{C}$ with selected auxiliary information for signing public keys derived from pk_M.*

3. When $\mathcal{A}$ finishes the query phase, $\mathcal{C}$ runs SPKGen on pk_M to generate $pk_S^{(0)}$ and corresponding auxiliary information aux. $\mathcal{C}$ also randomly selects another key $pk_S^{(1)}$

4. $\mathcal{C}$ randomly selects $b \in \{0, 1\}$, and sends $(pk_S^{(b)}, aux)$ to $\mathcal{A}$.

5. $\mathcal{A}$ guesses the value of b and outputs $\hat{b}$.

6. If $b = \hat{b}$, $\mathcal{A}$ succeeds and the game returns 1; otherwise $\mathcal{A}$ fails and the game returns 0.

3 A KCRS Construction and Its Security Analysis

3.1 An ECDSA-Based KCRS Construction

Suppose two parties (i.e., the signer and the targeted verifier) share a secrete key dk securely. This can be achieved through an offline channel (e.g., using public key encryption/key encapsulation [8]).

- $Setup$ (λ) $\rightarrow pp$, where λ is the security parameter and $pp = (E(\mathbb{F}), P)$, where $E(\mathbb{F})$ is a selected elliptic curve on finite field $\mathbb{F}$, and P is a point on $E(\mathbb{F})$ with order about λ bits.
- $MKGen$ (pp) $\rightarrow (pk_M, sk_M)$, where $pp = (E(\mathbb{F}), P)$. This algorithm randomly selects a positive integer $s \xleftarrow{\$} (0, |P|)$ and sets $(pk_M, sk_M) = (sP, s)$.
- $SPKGen$ (pp, pk_M) $\rightarrow (pk_S, aux)$. This algorithm randomly selects an integer $r \xleftarrow{\$} (0, |P|)$ and calculates $(pk_S, aux) = (h(r \cdot pk_M)P + pk_M, rP)$, where $h() : E(\mathbb{F}) \rightarrow \mathbb{Z}_{ord(P)}$ is a hash function which works as a random oracle. In practice, $h(\cdot)$ can be implemented using SHA512 mod $ord(P)$ when $\lambda < 512$.
- $SSKGen$ ($pp, pk_S, aux, pk_M, sk_M$) $\rightarrow sk_S$. This algorithm first checks $pk_S \overset{?}{=} h(sk_M \cdot aux)P + pk_M$, where aux is a point on $E(\mathbb{F})$. If it passes the test, the algorithm computes and returns $sk_S = h(sk_M \cdot aux) + sk_M$; otherwise, it returns $sk_S = \perp$.
- $SKDetect$ ($pp, sk_M, pk_M, pk_S, aux$) $\rightarrow \delta$. This algorithm calculates $pk'_S \leftarrow h(sk_M \cdot aux)P + pk_M$. If $pk_S = pk'_S$, it sets $\delta \leftarrow 1$; otherwise, it sets $\delta \leftarrow 0$.
- $SigGen$ (pp, sk_S, m, dk) $\rightarrow \sigma_{m',pk_S}$. This algorithm pre-processes the message m before signing. Specifically, it calculates $m' \leftarrow Enc(m||r, dk)$ and generates $\sigma_{m',pk_S} \leftarrow Sign_{ECDSA}(sk_S, m')$, where $Enc()$ is a secure symmetric encryption scheme, dk is the secret key shared between the signer and the targeted verifier, and r is the random number selected by the signer in $SPKGen()$. m' is released to the public together with the signature σ_{m',pk_S}.
- $SigVerify$ ($pp, \sigma_{m',pk_S}, m', pk_S$) $\rightarrow \delta$. This algorithm is the same as the ECDSA signature verification algorithm $Verify_{ECDSA}$. If the signature σ_{m',pk_S} matches m' and pk_S, it returns $\delta \leftarrow 1$; otherwise, it returns $\delta \leftarrow 0$.
- LNK ($pp, \sigma_{m',pk_S}, m', pk_M, dk$). This algorithm first checks that σ_{m',pk_S} is a valid signature of m', and runs $Dec(m', dk)$ to recover r. The algorithm then computes $pk'_S \leftarrow h(r \cdot pk_M)P + pk_M$. If $pk'_S = pk_S$, it sets $\delta \leftarrow 1$ (i.e., signature σ_{m',pk_S} is linked to pk_M); otherwise, it sets $\delta \leftarrow 0$.

3.2 Security Analysis

Correctness of the KCRS construction can be verified by observation. Signature unforgeability is based on the security of ECDSA, which has been proved to be UF-CMA secure [23].

Signing Private Key Unforgeability (UF-SSK). This property is based on the Elliptic Curve Discrete Logarithm Problem (ECDLP): Given a generator P of an elliptic curve E, and a random point $Q \in \langle P \rangle$, find r such that $Q = rP$. In what follows, we first describe a simulation algorithm S that leverages A to solve an ECDLP instance and then prove the success probability of S. In order for A to produce a signing public/private key pair, s/he may need to see a sequence of signing public/private key pairs derived from the same master public/private key pair. During this procedure, we allow A to learn $h(\cdot) \cdot P$ based on his/her selection of random number r. However, we do not allow A to query hash function $h(\cdot)$ directly because it will disclose the master private key when A can query both the signing private key and the hash value. S maintains four tables corresponding to A's queries with selected random numbers: $R[i]$, which stores the random number A selected for the ith query of signing key pair; $H[i]$, which stores the scalar multiplication of the hash value and the base point for the ith query; $P[i]$, which stores the signing public key for the ith query; and $S[i]$, which stores the signing private key for the ith query. Because A is a probabilistic polynomial-time algorithm, it can make at most N queries before it outputs the fake signing key pair, where N is bounded by a polynomial of λ. S randomly selects an opportunity to feed the ECDLP instance to A and hopes it will generate the fake signing key pair based on the input. Algorithm 1 describes the simulator S.

Theorem 1. *The KCRS construction is UF-SSK secure under the ECDLP assumption in the random oracle model.*

Proof (sketch). In the random oracle model, A cannot distinguish the values S provided from the values in the real system. Thus, A will produce the fake signing key pair in Algorithm 1. Since A makes at most N queries and S randomly picks an opportunity in this process to leverage A to solve the target ECDLP instance, the probability that A decides to produce a fake signing key pair at the same time is at least $1/N$. If the target instance has been queried before, D will terminate and fail. However, the probability of such an event is negligible in λ because the space of r_i's is exponential in λ. Denote by E_0 the event that A successfully fakes a signing key pair after querying the oracle, and E_1 the event that S successfully solves the ECDLP instance. We have

$$\Pr[E_1] \geq \frac{1}{N} \Pr[E_0] - negl,$$

where $negl$ is the negligible probability that A queries the target ECDLP instance. If A can compromise the UF-SSK feature with a non-negligible probability, then $\frac{1}{N} \Pr[E_0] - negl$ is non-negligible and $negl$ is negligible. Therefore, $\Pr[E_1]$ is non-negligible, which contradicts with the ECDLP assumption.   □

Algorithm 1. ECDLP solver $\mathcal{S}$ using UF-SSK adversary $\mathcal{A}$.

Input: The base point P on $E(\mathbb{F})$; a random point $Q \leftarrow sP$ on $E(\mathbb{F})$, which is the ECDLP instance $\mathcal{S}$ wants to solve; the master public key pk_M, a point on $E(\mathbb{F})$; the maximum number of oracle queries N.

Output: An integer s or $\perp$.

$R[\ ] \leftarrow \emptyset; T[\ ] \leftarrow \emptyset; H[\ ] \leftarrow \emptyset; P[\ ] \leftarrow \emptyset; S[\ ] \leftarrow \emptyset; j \overset{\$}{\leftarrow} [1, N];$

for $i = 1$ to N do

    $\mathcal{A}$ selects a random number $r_i \in Z_{|P|}$; $R[i] \leftarrow r_i$; $idx \leftarrow \text{FIND}(R[\ ], r_i)$;

    if $i = j$ and $\mathcal{A}$ decides to generate the fake signing key pair then

        if $idx = 0$ then

            $H[i] \leftarrow Q - pk_M$, $P[i] \leftarrow Q$, which are shared with $\mathcal{A}$;

            $\mathcal{A}$ outputs a fake s;

            return s;

        else

            return $\perp$;

        end if

    end if

    if $idx = 0$ then

        $S[i] \overset{\$}{\leftarrow} (0, |P|)$; $P[i] \leftarrow S[i] \cdot P$; $H[i] \leftarrow P[i] - pk_M$;

    else

        $S[i] \leftarrow S[idx]$; $P[i] \leftarrow P[idx]$; $H[i] \leftarrow P[idx]$;

    end if

    If $\mathcal{A}$ queries the scalar multiplication of the hash value and the base point, return $H[i]$;

    If $\mathcal{A}$ queries the derived signing public/private key pair, return $(P[i], S[i])$;

end for

Signing Public Key Indistinguishability (IND-SPK). The IND-SPK security of the KCRS construction is based on the hardness of the following variant hashed decision Diffie-Hellman (VH-DDH) assumption, which has not been studied in the literature.

Definition 4 (VH-DDH on elliptic curve). *Given a generator P of an elliptic curve E, and three random integers $u, v, z \in (0, ord(P))$, VH-DDH assumption says that $(uP, vP, H(uvP)P)$ and $(uP, vP, H(zP)P)$ are computationally indistinguishable; i.e., for any probabilistic polynomial-time algorithm $\mathcal{D}$, $|\Pr[\mathcal{D}(uP, vP, H(uvP)P) = 1] - \Pr[\mathcal{D}(uP, vP, H(zP)P)] = 1|$ is negligible in the size of $ord(P)$, where H is a cryptography hash function works as a random oracle.*

The standard DDH assumption assumes (uP, vP, uvP) and (uP, vP, zP) are computationally indistinguishable. If f is a one-to-one mapping, it is easy to see that distinguishing $(uP, vP, f(uvP)P)$ and $(uP, vP, f(zP)P)$ is at least as hard as corresponding standard DDH problem; otherwise, an attacker can apply f to the DDH instance to solve it. For the variant hashed decisional Diffie-Hellman problem, the mapping function is a composition of a hash function and a scalar multiplication on the elliptic curve. The scalar multiplication is a one-to-one mapping when the scalar belongs to $(0, ord(P))$, which is true when the output size of the hash function is less than $ord(P)$. When the scalar multiplication is composed with the cryptography hash function that works as a random oracle, the result function is not one-to-one any more as the hash function can have collisions. However, the likelihood of collision is negligible, and one can still apply the composed function to a DDH instance and solve it with high probability if the variant hashed DDH is easy. Therefore, the variant hashed DDH problem is at least as hard as the standard DDH problem.

Theorem 2. *The KCRS construction is IND-SPK secure under the VH-DDH assumption in the random oracle model.*

Proof (sketch). The proof is to show that given an IND-SPK adversary $\mathcal{A}$, one can build an algorithm $\mathcal{D}$ to solve the VH-DDH problem as described in Algorithm 2.

Algorithm 2. VH-DDH solver $\mathcal{D}$ leveraging IND-SPK adversary $\mathcal{A}$.

Input: Point P on $E(\mathbb{F})$; VH-DDH instance $(uP, vP, H(zP)P)$; master public key $pk_M = uP$; the maximum number of oracle queries N
Output: A bit b where $b = 1$ if $uvP = H(zP)P$ and $b = 0$ otherwise
  $i \leftarrow 1$; $R[\ ] \leftarrow \emptyset$; $H[\ ] \leftarrow \emptyset$;
  while $\mathcal{A}$ wants to query for new signing public keys **do**
    $\mathcal{A}$ selects and send a random point $r_i P$ to $\mathcal{D}$; $R[i] \leftarrow r_i P$; $idx \leftarrow$ FIND$(R[\ ], r_i)$;
    if $R[i] = vP$ **then**
      return $\perp$;
    end if
    if $idx = 0$ **then**
      $H[i] \xleftarrow{\$} (0, ord(P))$; Sending $H[i]P + uP$ to $\mathcal{A}$;
    else
      Sending $H[idx]P + uP$ to $\mathcal{A}$;
    end if
    $i \leftarrow i + 1$;
  end while
  $Q \xleftarrow{\$} \langle P \rangle$; $\hat{b} \leftarrow \mathcal{C}(uP, (H(zP)P + uP, H(Q)P + uP), vP)$;
  if $b = \hat{b}$ **then**
    return 1;
  else
    return 0;
  end if

Denote by E_0 the event that the game given in Definition 3 returns 1 and E_1 the event that the game returns 1. If the input to Algorithm 2 is a valid VH-DDH instance, we have

$$\Pr[\mathcal{D}(uP, vP, H(uvP)P) = 1] = \Pr[E_0] - negl,$$

where *negl* is the probability that $\mathcal{A}$ queries with vP in the challenging phase. If the input instance is randomly generated, we have

$$\Pr[\mathcal{D}(uP, vP, H(zP)P) = 1] = \Pr[E_1] - negl.$$

We observe that $\Pr[E_1] = 1/2$ because the two signing public keys are independently and uniformly generated and follow the same distribution. Therefore, we have $Adv(\mathcal{D}) = |(\Pr[E_1] - negl) - (\Pr[E_0] - negl)| = |\Pr[S_0] - 1/2|$, which is equivalent to the advantage of $\mathcal{A}$ against the IND-SPK.   □

4   KCRS on Blockchain

KCRS uses the blockchain as a unified information sharing and storage platform for transactions related to digital signatures, messages/signatures, and other kinds of relevant information. Assuming the blockchain is not controlled by the attacker, the use of blockchain prevents an adversary from altering existing transactions while allowing all participants to verify transaction validity. KCRS on blockchain has four types of participants:

- *Signer*: A signer owns a private key and uses the private key to produce digital signatures.
- *Verifier*: A verifier receives and verifies digital signatures generated by a signer. The verifier needs to be convinced that a certain signer has signed a specific message to determine his/her next step.
- *Certificate Authority* (CA): A CA is responsible for setting up the initial public key certificates for the signers and verifiers.
- *Miner*: Miners participate in transaction verification and blockchain maintenance by producing/verifying blocks.

A signer needs to generate a public/private key pair and obtain a certificate of the public key from the CA when he/she joins the system. This key pair serves as the master key pair and identity of the signer, but is not used for daily signature generation and verification. When a verifier needs a signer to sign a message, he/she first contacts the signer through an off-chain channel to exchange information including a symmetric key that will be used to encrypt the message in question. The signer then generates a signing public/private key pair and signs the encrypted message as described in the algorithm *SigGen* and submits the signature to the blockchain as transactions. All miners verify the validity of the signature before embedding it into a block and storing on the blockchain. Figure 1 summarizes the workflow of KCRS.

4.1   Data Management for KCRS on Blockchain

The blockchain stores four types of transactions: (i) certificate of master public key pk_M, which is generated by the CA and will not change frequently; (ii) signing public key pk_S, which is generated by the signer based on the master private

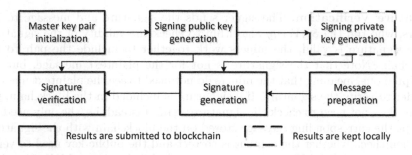

Fig. 1. The workflow of KCRS on blockchain. The output of each step is stored on the blockchain except the signing private key, and miners are responsible for validating outputs and maintaining the blockchain.

key; (iii) transformed message, which is the ciphertext of the original message plus the random number used to derive the signing key pair; (iv) signature, which is generated by the signer using signing private key.

Master public key certificate, signing public key, and signature have fixed sizes and are easy to be embedded into a block and included in the blockchain. However, the size of a message can vary greatly, so we let KCRS on blockchain stores the hash value of the message in a block while the message can be kept on another storage system that is more efficient and flexible. Logically, blocks are organized in a linear structure with a total order. In practice, a node can use a database with a dedicated field of order information to organize all transactions, and a user can search signatures or public keys by querying the database.

4.2 Operations of KCRS on Blockchain

Master Key Pair Initialization. We use permissioned blockchain, where each miner knows the CA's public key in advance. When a new user registers with the system, he/she submits his/her master public key together with a certificate of the public key. Each miner checks the certificate and the master public key, and runs a consensus protocol to include the registration information in the blockchain if it is valid.

Signing Key Pair Generation. According to the design of KCRS, a signing key pair is only used for a single message. The signer can either pre-generate a set of signing key pairs or wait until there is a need to sign a message. The signing public key is submitted to miners, and they run a consensus protocol to include it in the blockchain. The signer does not submit the random value used in the signing key pair generation to miners but keeps it secret.

Message Preparation. The verifier and signer communicate off-chain to exchange the message that needs to be signed and a symmetric key for encrypting the message. The signer adds information about the public key to the message and encrypts the result using the symmetric key. The prepared message does not need to be sent to the miners immediately.

Signature Verification. The signer sends the signature and message to the miners, who run the *SigVerify* algorithm to check the validity of the signature. If the signature is valid, the miners work together to include the pair to the blockchain. Note that the signature is not for the plaintext message, but the encrypted one, meaning that the miners do not need to see the plaintext message in order to verify the signature. If a signature is included in the blockchain, the verifier does not need to check the signature again. Instead, he/she only needs to decrypt the corresponding message stored on the blockchain with the signature, and then check whether the content is correct and the public key used to verify the signature is derived from the correct master public key using *LNK* algorithm.

5   Implementation and Performance Evaluation of KCRS

We implement KCRS using Hyperledger Fabric [3]. Since Fabric has its own PKI system, we use it to issue certificates to signers. Fabric divides the block construction into two steps: *endorsing* and *ordering*. In the process of endorsing, a group of endorsers check each transaction and endorse the valid ones by attaching their signatures. In the process of ordering, a group of orderers work together to determine the order of the endorsed transactions and put them on the blockchain. The default ordering in Fabric is implemented using Kafka [21], which is very efficient when the number of orderers is relatively small. To simply the implementation, we use a single node for the ordering service, and focus on the effect of different endorser configurations when measuring performance. Verifiers passively listen to KCRS and can retrieve signatures from the blockchain.

We deploy a KCRS prototype in Amazon Web Service (AWS). Nodes, including endorser nodes, are configured to utilize the t2.medium instance type, which has 2 processing cores and 4 GB memory. We distribute the nodes in different instances in order to reduce the bottleneck of computing resource. In this deployment, all endorser nodes join in a same channel. We also use different endorsement policies to manage the total number of signatures required by a transaction. For instance, policy *"AND('Org1.peer', 'Org2.peer')"* indicates that a transaction requires signatures from both organizations *Org1* and *Org2*.

Latency and Throughput. We evaluate the latency and throughput of the prototype with different parameters. Latency and throughput are mainly affected by to factors, the performance of the underlying blockchain system itself and the performance of the cryptographic operations. We fix the number of orderer node to one and measure the latency of per transaction. Figure 2 shows the results of changing the number of endorser nodes. We observe that the latency increases significantly when the number of endorsers changes from 1 to 3. This is because compared to a single-endorsement transaction, the orderer node need more time to process multiple endorsements. Both latency and throughput tend to level off when the number of endorsers is greater than 5.

Storage Cost. One of the major concerns of blockchain-based applications is the storage cost because the system has multiple copies of the blockchain and

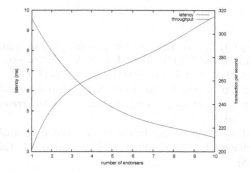

Fig. 2. KCRS performance: Latency is computed between the start time and the finish time with respect to a submitting a transaction; throughput is calculated by sending 1,000 transaction simultaneously and then collecting the start time and the finish time of the last block (if there are multiple blocks).

each of them keeps increasing. For blockchain-based KCRS, the storage cost of master public key certificates is negligible since they are relatively stable. Most transactions come from signatures and the generation of their signing public keys. When KCRS uses ECDSA with 256-bit keys, the size of a signature is 512 bits. The message size varies but we can keep its hash value (instead of the message itself) on the blockchain, the size of which is 256 bits when SHA256 is used. The auxiliary information attached to each signing public key is also an elliptic curve point, which is 512 bits. In summary, each signature request needs a storage of 192 bytes, and a modern computer can easily store hundreds of billions of such transactions. When elliptic curve compressing technologies are applied [5], the storage cost can be further reduced.

6   Conclusion

Private key exposure is one of the most devastating attacks against digital signatures. Although a variety of digital signature schemes have been proposed to mitigate the consequences of private key exposure, the detection of private signing key exposure has not been paid the due amount of attention. We have presented a new digital signature management framework, dubbed KCRS, which incorporates the capability of key exposure detection by leveraging the blockchain technology. We have described the formal security definition of KCRS: (i) only the legitimate user can update key information when key exposure is detected; (ii) only the relevant users can discover the relation between a signature and the signer. We have evaluated the performance of KCRS on blockchain and conducted experiments on Hyperledger Fabric. Experimental results show that KCRS on blockchain can handle a large number of users at a reasonable cost.

Acknowledgment. This work is supported in part by AFRL Grant #FA8750-19-1-0019 and NSF CREST Grant #1736209.

References

1. Abdalla, M., Reyzin, L.: A new forward-secure digital signature scheme. In: Okamoto, T. (ed.) ASIACRYPT 2000. LNCS, vol. 1976, pp. 116–129. Springer, Heidelberg (2000). https://doi.org/10.1007/3-540-44448-3_10
2. Al-Bassam, M.: Scpki: a smart contract-based PKI and identity system. In: Proceedings of the ACM Workshop on Blockchain, Cryptocurrencies and Contracts, pp. 35–40. ACM (2017)
3. Androulaki, E., et al.: Hyperledger fabric: a distributed operating system for permissioned blockchains. In: Proceedings of the Thirteenth EuroSys Conference, p. 30. ACM (2018)
4. Bellare, M., Miner, S.K.: A forward-secure digital signature scheme. In: Wiener, M. (ed.) CRYPTO 1999. LNCS, vol. 1666, pp. 431–448. Springer, Heidelberg (1999). https://doi.org/10.1007/3-540-48405-1_28
5. Blake-Wilson, S., Bolyard, N., Gupta, V., Hawk, C., Möller, B.: Elliptic curve cryptography (ecc) cipher suites for transport layer security (tls). Technical report (2006)
6. Chow, J., Pfaff, B., Garfinkel, T., Christopher, K., Rosenblum, M.: Understanding data lifetime via whole system simulation. In: Proceedings of Usenix Security Symposium 2004 (2004)
7. Chow, J., Pfaff, B., Garfinkel, T., Rosenblum, M.: Shredding your garbage: reducing data lifetime. In: Proceedings 14th USENIX Security Symposium, August 2005
8. Cramer, R., Shoup, V.: Design and analysis of practical public-key encryption schemes secure against adaptive chosen ciphertext attack. SIAM J. Comput. **33**(1), 167–226 (2003)
9. Dai, W., Parker, T.P., Jin, H., Xu, S.: Enhancing data trustworthiness via assured digital signing. IEEE Trans. Dependable Secure Comput. **9**(6), 838–851 (2012)
10. Ding, X., Tsudik, G., Xu, S.: Leak-free group signatures with immediate revocation. In: 24th International Conference on Distributed Computing Systems (ICDCS 2004), pp. 608–615. IEEE Computer Society (2004)
11. Ding, X., Tsudik, G., Xu, S.: Leak-free mediated group signatures. J. Comput. Secur. **17**(4), 489–514 (2009)
12. Dodis, Y., Katz, J., Xu, S., Yung, M.: Key-insulated public key cryptosystems. In: Knudsen, L.R. (ed.) EUROCRYPT 2002. LNCS, vol. 2332, pp. 65–82. Springer, Heidelberg (2002). https://doi.org/10.1007/3-540-46035-7_5
13. Dodis, Y., Katz, J., Xu, S., Yung, M.: Strong key-insulated signature schemes. In: Desmedt, Y.G. (ed.) PKC 2003. LNCS, vol. 2567, pp. 130–144. Springer, Heidelberg (2003). https://doi.org/10.1007/3-540-36288-6_10
14. Dodis, Y., Luo, W., Xu, S., Yung, M.: Key-insulated symmetric key cryptography and mitigating attacks against cryptographic cloud software. In: Proceedings ASIACCS 2012, pp. 57–58 (2012)
15. Goldwasser, S., Micali, S., Rivest, R.L.: A digital signature scheme secure against adaptive chosen-message attacks. SIAM J. Comput. **17**(2), 281–308 (1988)
16. Guan, L., Lin, J., Luo, B., Jing, J., Wang, J.: Protecting private keys against memory disclosure attacks using hardware transactional memory. In: Proceedings of the 2015 IEEE Symposium on Security and Privacy, SP 2015, pp. 3–19 (2015)
17. Haber, S., Stornetta, W.S.: How to time-stamp a digital document. In: Menezes, A.J., Vanstone, S.A. (eds.) CRYPTO 1990. LNCS, vol. 537, pp. 437–455. Springer, Heidelberg (1991). https://doi.org/10.1007/3-540-38424-3_32

18. Harrison, K., Xu, S.: Protecting cryptographic keys from memory disclosure attacks. In: The 37th Annual IEEE/IFIP International Conference on Dependable Systems and Networks, DSN 2007, 25–28 June 2007, Edinburgh, UK, Proceedings, pp. 137–143 (2007)

19. Itkis, G., Reyzin, L.: SiBIR: signer-base intrusion-resilient signatures. In: Yung, M. (ed.) CRYPTO 2002. LNCS, vol. 2442, pp. 499–514. Springer, Heidelberg (2002). https://doi.org/10.1007/3-540-45708-9_32

20. Krawczyk, H.: Simple forward-secure signatures from any signature scheme. In: ACM Conference on Computer and Communications Security, pp. 108–115 (2000)

21. Kreps, J., Narkhede, N., Rao, J., et al.: Kafka: a distributed messaging system for log processing. In: Proceedings of the NetDB, pp. 1–7 (2011)

22. Laurie, B., Langley, A., Kasper, E.: Certificate transparency. Technical report (2013)

23. Locke, G., Gallagher, P.: Fips pub 186–3: digital signature standard (dss). Federal Information Processing Standards Publication 3, 186–3 (2009)

24. Loscocco, P., Smalley, S., Muckelbauer, P., Taylor, R., Turner, S., Farrell, J.: The inevitability of failure: the flawed assumption of security in modern computing environments. In: Proceedings 21st National Information Systems Security Conference (NISSC 1998) (1998)

25. Orman, H.: Blockchain: the emperors new PKI? IEEE Internet Comput. **22**(2), 23–28 (2018)

26. Parker, T.P., Xu, S.: A method for safekeeping cryptographic keys from memory disclosure attacks. In: First International Conference on Trusted Systems (INTRUST 2009), pp. 39–59 (2009)

27. Shamir, A., van Someren, N.: Playing 'Hide and Seek' with stored keys. In: Franklin, M. (ed.) FC 1999. LNCS, vol. 1648, pp. 118–124. Springer, Heidelberg (1999). https://doi.org/10.1007/3-540-48390-X_9

28. Xu, S., Li, X., Parker, T.P.: Exploiting social networks for threshold signing: attack-resilience vs. availability. In: Proceedings of ASIACCS 2008, pp. 325–336 (2008)

29. Xu, S., Li, X., Parker, T.P., Wang, X.: Exploiting trust-based social networks for distributed protection of sensitive data. IEEE Trans. Inf. Forensics Secur. **6**(1), 39–52 (2011)

30. Xu, S., Sandhu, R.: A scalable and secure cryptographic service. In: Barker, S., Ahn, G.-J. (eds.) DBSec 2007. LNCS, vol. 4602, pp. 144–160. Springer, Heidelberg (2007). https://doi.org/10.1007/978-3-540-73538-0_12

31. Xu, S., Yung, M.: Expecting the unexpected: towards robust credential infrastructure. In: Dingledine, R., Golle, P. (eds.) FC 2009. LNCS, vol. 5628, pp. 201–221. Springer, Heidelberg (2009). https://doi.org/10.1007/978-3-642-03549-4_12

Decentralized Access Control Encryption in Public Blockchain

Zhongyuan Yao[1,2(✉)], Heng Pan[2], Xueming Si[2,3], and Weihua Zhu[2]

[1] The Henan Key Laboratory on Public Opinion Intelligent Analysis,
Zhengzhou 450001, Henan, China
zy454@uowmail.edu.au
[2] Zhongyuan University of Technology, Zhengzhou 450001, Henan, China
[3] Fudan University, Shanghai 200433, China

Abstract. Since its invention, the public blockchain has attracted more attention from both the academia and industry because of its fully decentralization and persistency features. However, the privacy issue in public blockchain is still challengeable. While there exists privacy preservation mechanisms proposed for the public blockchain, almost all of them can only solve partial of the privacy issue, either user privacy or data privacy indeed, in it. In this work, we present a decentralized access control encryption scheme which ensures user and data privacy simultaneously in public blockchain. With our cryptographic solution, the validity of one specific transaction can be publicly verified, while its content can only be retrieved by its intended receivers. Moreover, the origin of this transaction cannot be identified by any participant except the receivers in the network. Our analysis shows that our solution is really suitable to deploy in public blockchain and is proven secure under mathematical assumptions.

Keywords: Public blockchain · User privacy · Data privacy · Access control encryption · Decentralized sanitizers

1 Introduction

1.1 Background

Since it was first introduced in the seminal work [29] in 2008, the blockchain technology has received great interests and world-wide recognition from both the industry and academia. Generally, a blockchain can be valued as a chain of blocks in which all committed transactions are stored. The chain grows continuously when new blocks are generated and appended to it. As a perfect combination of several technologies including cryptographic hash, digital signature and distributed consensus mechanism, the blockchain enjoys desirable characteristics such as decentralization, tamper-resistance, auditability. Although the blockchain technology is initially served as the core mechanism for the Bitcoin, it can also be applied into various scenarios apart from cryptocurrencies.

© Springer Nature Singapore Pte Ltd. 2020
Z. Zheng et al. (Eds.): BlockSys 2019, CCIS 1156, pp. 240–257, 2020.
https://doi.org/10.1007/978-981-15-2777-7_20

For example, blockchain enables a transaction to be taken place in a decentralized environment and thus allows financial activities to be processed without any intermediary such as bank [21]. Moreover, with the blockchain technology, the transparency and traceability of ownership of the supply chain management system can be enhanced [16,45]. Additionally, the blockchain technology has witnessed its application in internet of things (IoT) [32], security services [38] and public services [26], etc.

According to the degree of centralization of the blockchain network, the blockchain can be categorized into three types: the public blockchain, the consortium blockchain and the private blockchain [10]. In a public blockchain network, anyone and everyone can join or leave it freely. Moreover, the participant is enabled to perform all core functionalities of the public blockchain including reading, writing and auditing the ongoing activities on the network. Obviously, the public blockchain is "fully decentralized". One example of the public blockchain is the blockchain used in the Bitcoin. Unlike the public blockchain where all nodes need to participate in the consensus process, the consortium blockchain requires a pre-selected set of nodes to control that process. Furthermore, The right to read the consortium blockchain may be public, or restricted to the participants. There may also exist hybrid routes where the root hashes of the blocks is public in consortium blockchain, it allows the public to make a limited number of queries to know the knowledge of partial of the blockchain state. Thus, the consortium is considered "partially decentralized". One popular consortium blockchain framework implementation is the Hyperledger Fabric project hosted by the Linux Foundation. A private blockchain, as its name suggests, is a blockchain where there exists a central trusted party which is in charge of the task of writing to the chain and granting selected parties the right to read the chain. The private blockchain seems more like a traditional centralized system empowered with a certain degree of cryptographic auditability. Therefore, it is still debatable that whether such a private system can be called a "blockchain". In fact, both the consortium blockchain and the private blockchain still require one or some trusted authorities in the system, which is contradict to the untrustworthy feature of the blockchain proposed in Bitcoin. Thus, they can hardly realize the full decentralization purpose introduced in [29].

1.2 Research Problem

Although the blockchain technology has developed rapidly over the past 10 years, it still has insufficiencies. Among them, the most fatal one is the privacy issue, which prevents it from being used in more potential applications where privacy is their first security concern. Indeed, the privacy issue in blockchain contains two sub-problems, the user and transaction privacy respectively. The user privacy says that it is impossible to trace the original issuer of a transaction form the script. While the transaction privacy ensures that the contents included in one transaction can only be accessed by specified users, and is confidential to the blockchain network. We find there are privacy preserving mechanisms which alleviate the privacy threat to the consortium and private blockchain, and some cryptographic tools are introduced to the public blockchain to ensure either user privacy or transaction privacy. However, there exists no thorough solution which enables the public blockchain to preserve both the user and transaction privacy. Since it is the public blockchain that achieves the goal of full decentralization and living in environment with no trust, and it is this two unique properties which make the public blockchain that attractive, we argue that the problem solving the privacy issue in public blockchain is meaningful and extremely urgent. Thus, we value it as our research problem.

1.3   Existed Works

The privacy problem in blockchain has been studied intensively since its invention. In the private blockchain, as it can be treated as a centralized system, many classical cryptographic primitives can be directly deployed to solve the privacy problem. Apart from cryptographic algorithms, some special privacy preserving methods are used in the consortium blockchain. For example, in the Enigma blockchain system [48], data is torn into pieces and then covered using ingenious mathematical technique, this method makes it impossible to recover the related origin data from one piece or a part of the pieces of the data. And in the Hyperledger Fabric project [41], multiple channels are built to separate different ledgers from different organizations and thus force a user to access to the only ledger generated cooperatively by users of its organization. However, since the public blockchain is fully decentralized and there exists no trusted party comparing to the private and consortium blockchain, the aforementioned mechanisms are not applicable to it.

There are some techniques used in the public blockchain to solve either the user or data privacy problem. For example, to hide the user privacy information leaked from the transaction of the public blockchain, the mixing mechanism, first proposed in [11], is introduced to obfuscate the transactions' relationships and thus makes it unlinkable between the sender and receiver of a transaction. There are multiple mixing service providers [1–3] available at present and some of them use centralized mixing mechanism. However, this centralized service imposes new security threat on the blockchain. That is, the mixing service provider must be always honest and highly reliable, which is a rather unrealistic assumption. To relieve the service subscribers of this security concern, the decentralized mixing mechanism is presented in [19,37]. Moreover, there are two approaches to realize this decentralized mixing mechanism. The first one is based on the CoinJion technique described in the Bitcoin Forum [27], and the main idea of it is "When you want to make a payment, find some one else who also wants to and make a joint one together.". The other way is the multi-party computation technique, first presented in [46]. With this method, all parties can only learn knowledge from the output and their own input after the computation. Thus, it is suitable for decentralized tasks where the computation is executed without a trusted party. Although those mixing mechanisms enjoy several benefit when providing user privacy in public blockchain, they still suffer from several limitations such as high mixing service fee, high delay waiting for the service and the risk of being blocked by Sybil attack.

Another tool to preserve the user privacy in public blockchain is the ring signature invented in [36]. With this primitive, a user can produce a valid signature on behalf of a set of possible signers chosen by itself, and no one can tell the real signer form the "ring" of users given only the transcript. One modified version of the ring signature is the traceable ring signature proposed in [18]. It empowers participants with the capability to link two signatures if they are signed by the same signer using the same message and tag and to reveal the anonymity of the signer of two signatures if they are produced with the same tag. The desirable properties, such as anonymity and linkability, provided by the ring signature have cultivated several ring-based privacy preservation mechanisms for the public blockchain, such example can be found in the Monero project [30] and also in [31, 42]. The ring signature provides strong user anonymity in public blockchain, however, it also incurs several problems to it. For example, the size of transactions and the signature itself could be very large if too many participants are involved in the "ring".

There are two main approaches to preserve data privacy in the public blockchain, i.e., NIZK proof and homomorphic cryptosystem. First proposed in [39], the non-interactive zero-knowledge proof (NIZK), which does not need the interaction phase between the prover and verifier, is a variant of the zero-knowledge proof (ZKP). The ability to independently prove the correctness of an assertion without leaking extra knowledge makes NIZK poof well suited for creating message privacy preserving protocols. The NIZK proof provides three desirable properties, the completeness, soundness and zero-knowledge. One example of the application of the NIZK proof in blockchain is the Zerocash project issued in [28]. In Zerocash, one special edition of the NIZK proof called zero-knowledge succinct non-interactive arguments of knowledge (zk-SNARKs) proofs [25] is used to hide a payment's address. Furthermore, the coin value is added in the commitment and zero-knowledge proof so that it is arbitrary and publicly verifiable. The zk-SNARKs proof achieves high level of user and data privacy in public blockchain, however, the expense of generating the transaction proofs is hardly affordable in such type of blockchain. The homomorphic cryptosystem supports a cryptographic methodology that satisfies homomorphism, it enables any participant to perform computation on the ciphertexts while preserving the data privacy. In general, homomorphic cryptography performs as black box, when given n ciphertexts and operations, it outputs the encrypted result of the same operations on the corresponding original data. This attractive feature makes homomorphic cryptography well suited for hiding and performing update of the amount and other metadata of a transaction. Typical implementations of homomorphic cryptographic systems which aim to protect data privacy of the public blockchain include the Pedersen commitment scheme [34] and the Paillier cryptosystem [33].

1.4   Our Contribution

In this paper, we present a decentralized access control encryption (DACE) scheme to tackle both the user privacy and data privacy problem in public blockchain simultaneously. With our DACE scheme, the content of one specific transaction can only be retrieved by its intended receivers, and also, the receiver can not identify the exact issuer of that transaction. This work contributes to the development of solving privacy issues in public blockchain in the following two aspects.

Firstly, we first introduce the access control encryption to public blockchain and give the first DACE scheme construction with compact size ciphertext. Our construction borrows idea from the primitive anonymous broadcast encryption [9,24,47], the resulted scheme keeps not only the ciphertext size compact but also the key size of each users in the DACE compact. Which makes our scheme possible to be deployed in the public blockchain considering the resource-constraint characteristic of it.

The main contribution of this paper is giving a decentralized implementation of the ACE scheme and further increasing its reliability in public blockchain. In our paper, we allow the sanitizing key to be shared among n sanitizers, while each node joining the public blockchain can be a sanitizer if it wants to. Only exact t of those nodes can collaboratively transform a ciphertext into a valid sanitized ciphertext which can be correctly decrypted by its receivers. In our construction, each of the n sanitizers is installed with an unique sanitizing key, and it would execute the same sanitizing algorithm on the ciphertext, either not or partially sanitized, received. One ciphertext can only be viewed as a partially sanitized ciphertext and cannot be decrypted by its intended receivers until it is processed by t sanitizers. Unlike previous scheme with only one sanitizer, our construction distributes the sanitizing functionality of the origin ACE among n sanitizers, it is impossible for one of sanitizers in our construction to produce a new access policy, so our construction imposes restriction on the capability of the sanitizer. Besides, as one message sender in our DACE construction can choose the t sanitizers itself to collaboratively produce a valid sanitized ciphertext, even some of the n sanitizers cannot provide service or off-line, our DACE system can never encounter the single-point-failure problem, so our DACE improves the reliability of the sanitizer and even the robustness of original ACE system.

1.5   Paper Organization

The rest of our paper is organized as follows. Section 2 presents useful notations and security assumptions used throughout our paper. We also formally give the definition of the decentralized access control encryption (DACE) scheme and two security models to cover the no-read rule and no-write rule property predefined in previous work in this section. In Sect. 3, in order to make the description of our scheme more easy to understand, we first present a new notion "sanitizing pipeline", then we give concrete construction of our DACE. We give security proofs in Sect. 4 and conclude this paper in Sect. 5.

2 Preliminaries and Definitions

2.1 Notations

Here, for the benefit of consistency, we give the notations used throughout the whole paper. Let $\mathbb{Z}_p$ denote a additive group where p is a large prime, let $\mathbb{G} \subset \mathbb{Z}_p$ be a multiplicative group with large prime order q and generator g, here we have $q|p-1$. For simplicity, we use $[u]$ to represent the successive list $\{0, 1, \cdots, u\}$. There are always three types of users involved in the ACE scheme, we denote them the message sender Se, the message sanitizer San and the message receiver Re separately. For a specific user, he can play the role of both Se and Re, we use ke, kd to represent this user's encryption and decryption key respectively. Assuming there are l layers in the ACE system, when a user in layer $\alpha \in [l]$ can send messages to a receiver in layer $\beta \in [l]$, we use the notation $\alpha \times \beta \to 1$ to denote such access policy, otherwise $\alpha \times \beta \to 0$. We use the access policy set $P : [l] \times [l] \to \{0, 1\}$ to cover the collection of all the access polices defined in the ACE system. When there exists n message sanitizers in our ACE definition, we assume each of them holds a unique secret sanitizing key ks. In order to keep the consistency of the description of our ACE system, we use [u+1,u+n] to denote the list $\{u + 1, u + 2, \cdots, u + n\}$ and also to represent identities of the n sanitizers, for simplicity, we use the notation $[u + n]$ to represent all identities of users involved in the ACE definition.

2.2 Hard Problems

Definition 1 (K-CCA problem). *For an integer k, and one element x randomly chosen from $\mathbb{Z}_q$, $g \in \mathbb{G}$, given $g, g^x, h_1, h_2, \cdots, h_k \in \mathbb{Z}_q, g^{\frac{1}{x+h_1}}, g^{\frac{1}{x+h_2}}, \cdots, g^{\frac{1}{x+h_k}}$ as inputs, the problem solver needs to output element $g^{\frac{1}{x+h}}$ for some $h \notin \{h_1, h_2, \cdots, h_k\}$. We say an algorithm $\mathcal{B}$ has advantage ϵ within time t in solving the K-CCA problem in $\mathbb{G}$ if*

$$\Pr[\mathcal{B}(g, g^x, h_1, h_2, \cdots, h_k \in \mathbb{Z}_q, g^{\frac{1}{x+h_1}}, g^{\frac{1}{x+h_2}}, \cdots, g^{\frac{1}{x+h_k}}) = g^{\frac{1}{x+h}}] \geq \epsilon,$$

where $h \notin \{h_1, h_2, \cdots, h_k\}$ and the probability is over the random choice of the generator g in $\mathbb{G}$, the random choice of $h_1, h_2, \cdots, h_k \in \mathbb{Z}_q$ and the random bits consumed by $\mathcal{B}$.

Definition 2 ((f, g, F)-GDDHE [13]). *Let $\mathcal{B} = (p, \mathbb{G}_1, \mathbb{G}_2, \mathbb{G}_T, e(\cdot, \cdot))$ be a bilinear map group system and let f, g be two co-prime polynomials with pairwise distinct roots, of respective orders t and n. Let g_0, h_0 be one generator of $\mathbb{G}_1$ and $\mathbb{G}_2$ respectively. the (f, g, F)-GDDHE problem is, given the tuple*

$$(g_0, g_0^\gamma, g_0^{\gamma^2}, \cdots, g_0^{\gamma^{t-1}}, \quad g_0^{\gamma \cdot f(\gamma)}, \quad g_0^{k \cdot \gamma \cdot f(\gamma)}) \in \mathbb{G}_1,$$
$$(h_0, h_0^\gamma, h_0^{\gamma^2}, \cdots, h_0^{\gamma^{2n}}, \quad h_0^{k \cdot g(\gamma)}) \in \mathbb{G}_2 \quad and$$
$$T \in \mathbb{G}_T$$

to decide whether T is equal to $e(g_0, h_0)^{k \cdot f(\gamma)} \in \mathbb{G}_T$ or is a random element in $\mathbb{G}_T$.

Theorem 1 (Generic security of (f, g, F)-GDDHE [13]). *For any probabilistic algorithm $\mathcal{A}$ that totalizes of at most q queries to the oracles performing the group operations in $\mathbb{G}_1, \mathbb{G}_2, \mathbb{G}_T$ and the bilinear map $e(\cdot, \cdot)$, let $\mathsf{Adv}^{gddhe}(f, g, F, \mathcal{A})$ denote the advantage that $\mathcal{A}$ can solve the (f, g, F)-GDDHE, then*

$$\mathsf{Adv}^{gddhe}(f, g, F, \mathcal{A}) \leq \frac{(q + 2(n + t + 4) + 2)^2 \cdot d}{2p}$$

with $d = 2 \cdot \mathsf{max}(n, t + 1)$.

2.3 Defining Our ACE

An ACE scheme with decentralized sanitizers is defined by the following polynomial time algorithms:

Setup(P, λ). On input the security parameter λ and an access policy set P : $[u] \times [u] \rightarrow \{0, 1\}$, the Setup algorithm outputs a master secret key msk and the public parameter pp, which include the description of the message space $\mathcal{M}$, the ciphertext space $\mathcal{C}$ and the sanitized ciphertext space $\mathcal{C}'$.

KeyGen(msk, i, t). On input msk, an identity $i \in [u + n]$ and a user type $t \in \{Se, Re, San\}$, the key generation algorithm KeyGen produces the following different types of keys accordingly:

- $ke_i = \mathsf{KeyGen}(msk, i, Se)$ when the user with identity i is a message sender, that is $t = Se$. ke_i is called the encryption key for that user.
- $kd_i = \mathsf{KeyGen}(msk, i, Re)$ when the user with identity i acts as a message receiver, that is $t = Re$. kd_i is called the decryption key for that user.
- $ks_i = \mathsf{KeyGen}(msk, i, San)$ when the user with identity i plays the role of a message sanitizer, that is $t = San$. ks_i is called the sanitizing key for that user.

Enc(ke_i, m). The encryption algorithm Enc, on input an encryption key ke_i and a message $m \in \mathcal{M}$, outputs a ciphertext $c \in \mathcal{C}$.

Sanit(c, SP_l). For one incoming ciphertext $c \in \mathcal{C}$, a sanitizer in one chosen sanitizing pipeline SP_l would process it using this sanitation algorithm Sanit with its own sanitizing key, and then relay the result to another sanitizer in the same path, and the next sanitizer would do the same as its predecessor. Our ACE scheme with decentralized sanitizers requires that c should be processed by all t sanitizers in the sanitizing pipeline SP_l collaboratively before becoming a valid sanitized ciphertext $c' \in \mathcal{C}'$.

Dec(c', kd_j). On input a sanitized ciphertext $c' \in \mathcal{C}'$ and a decryption key kd_j, the decryption algorithm Dec recovers the message $m' \in \mathcal{M} \cup \{\perp\}$.

2.4 Security Notions for Our DACE

Our DACE scheme must satisfy requirements formalized below:

Definition 3 (Correctness). *For all $m \in \mathcal{M}, i, j \in [u]$ such that $P(i, j) = 1$:*

$$\Pr[\mathsf{Dec}(kd_j, \underbrace{\mathsf{Sanit}(ks_t, \cdots, \mathsf{Sanit}(ks_l, \mathsf{Enc}(ke_i, m))))}_{t} \neq m] \leq negl(\lambda)$$

with $(pp, msk) \leftarrow \mathsf{Setup}(1^\lambda, P), ke_i \leftarrow \mathsf{KeyGen}(msk, i, Se), kd_j \leftarrow \mathsf{KeyGen}(msk, j, Re)$ and $ks_l \leftarrow \mathsf{KeyGen}(msk, l, San)$, where $l \in [u + 1, u + n]$. The above notation denotes that the encrypted message should be processed by exact t different sanitizers in the same sanitizing pipeline before becoming a valid sanitized ciphertext and then being decrypted to a valid plaintext, otherwise, the probability of a correct decryption should be negligible. The probability is taken over the random coins of all involved algorithms.

Definition 4 (No-Read Rule). *To define the No-Read Rule in our DACE scheme, we consider the following game played between a challenger $\mathcal{C}$ and a stateful adversary $\mathcal{A}$:*

No-Read Rule	
Game Definition	Oracle Definition
1. $(pp, msk) \leftarrow \mathsf{Setup}(1^\lambda, P)$;	$\mathcal{O}_G(i, t)$:
2. $(m_0, m_1, i) \leftarrow \mathcal{A}^{\mathcal{O}_G(\cdot), \mathcal{O}_E(\cdot)}(pp)$;	1. $k_i \leftarrow \mathsf{KeyGen}(msk, i, t)$
3. $b \leftarrow \{0, 1\}$	
4. $c \leftarrow \mathsf{Enc}(\mathsf{KeyGen}(msk, i, Se), m_b)$	$\mathcal{O}_E(i, m)$:
5. $c' \leftarrow \underbrace{\mathsf{Sanit}^{\mathcal{O}_G()}(\cdots, \mathsf{Sanit}^{\mathcal{O}_G()}(ks_1, c))}_{t}$	1. $ke_i \leftarrow \mathsf{KeyGen}(msk, i, Se)$;
6. $b' \leftarrow \mathcal{A}^{\mathcal{O}_G(\cdot), \mathcal{O}_E(\cdot)}(c')$	2. $c \leftarrow \mathsf{Enc}(ke_i, m)$
	3. $c' \leftarrow \underbrace{\mathsf{Sanit}^{\mathcal{O}_G()}(\cdots, \mathsf{Sanit}^{\mathcal{O}_G()}(ks_1, c))}_{t}$

Where $P : [u] \times [u] \rightarrow \{0, 1\}$ is the given access policy set and $t \in \{Se, Re, San\}$. When $|m_0| = |m_1|$, $i \in [u]$ and for all queries q to $\mathcal{O}_G$ with $q = (j, Re)$, it holds

$$P(i, j) = 0,$$

we say that the adversary $\mathcal{A}$ wins the No-Read game if its output $b' = b$.
Let $\Pr[\mathcal{A}$ wins the No-Read game] denote the probability the $\mathcal{A}$ wins the predefined game and $\mathsf{Adv}^{\mathcal{A}}_{No-Read}(ACE)$ its advantage to win the game, then an ACE scheme is said to satisfy the No-Read Rule if for all probabilistic polynomial time(PPT) algorithm $\mathcal{A}$

$$\mathsf{Adv}^{\mathcal{A}}_{No-Read}(ACE) = 2|\Pr[\mathcal{A} \text{ wins the game}] - \frac{1}{2}| \leq negl(\lambda).$$

Remark. The No-Read Rule model in [12] also covers the sender anonymity, or key-privacy, property when the second, fourth step of our game definition is changed to

$$(m_0, m_1, i_0, i_1) \leftarrow \mathcal{A}^{\mathcal{O}_G(\cdot), \mathcal{O}_E(\cdot)}(pp), c \leftarrow \mathsf{Enc}(\mathsf{KeyGen}(msk, i_b, Se), m_b)$$

accordingly and the requirement $P(i, j) = 0$ is changed to

$$m_0 = m_1, P(i_0, j) = P(i_1, j).$$

It is easy to find that our model can be extended to guarantee the sender anonymity with the above minimal modification, and the corresponding security proof would not be changed a lot indeed. Here, for simplicity, we first concentrate on the basic No-Read property.

Definition 5 (Extended No-Write Rule). *To define a model capturing the security of the sanitizers, we consider the following game played between a challenger $\mathcal{C}$ and an adversary $\mathcal{A}$:*

Extended No-Write Rule	
Game Definition	Oracle Definition
1. $(pp, msk) \leftarrow \mathsf{Setup}(1^\lambda, P)$;	$\mathcal{O}_S(i, Se)$:
2. $(m_0, m_1, j) \leftarrow \mathcal{A}^{\mathcal{O}_S(\cdot), \mathcal{O}_E(\cdot)}(pp)$;	1. $ke_i \leftarrow \mathsf{KeyGen}(msk, i, Se)$
3. $kd_j \leftarrow KeyGen(msk, j, Re)$	
4. $ke'_i \leftarrow \mathcal{A}^{\mathcal{O}_{San}(\cdot), \mathcal{O}_S(\cdot)}(pp)$	$\mathcal{O}_\mathcal{R}(j, Re)$:
5. $b \leftarrow \{0, 1\}$	1. $kd_j \leftarrow \mathsf{KeyGen}(msk, j, Re)$
6. $c \leftarrow \mathsf{Enc}(ke_i', m_b)$	$\mathcal{O}_{San}(l, San)$:
7. $c' \leftarrow \underbrace{\mathsf{Sanit}(\cdots, \mathsf{Sanit}(ks_1, c))}_{t}$	1. $ks_l \leftarrow \mathsf{KeyGen}(msk, l, San)$
8. $b' \leftarrow \mathcal{A}^{\mathcal{O}_{San}(\cdot), \mathcal{O}_E(\cdot)}(c')$	$\mathcal{O}_E(i, msg)$:
	1. $ke_i \leftarrow \mathsf{KeyGen}(msk, i, Se)$;
	2. $c \leftarrow \mathsf{Enc}(ke_i, msg)$

Let Q_S, Q_R and Q_{San} be the set of queries issued by $\mathcal{A}$ to $\mathcal{O}_S, \mathcal{O}_R$ and $\mathcal{O}_{San}$ respectively. Let I_S be all the identities $i \in [u]$ such that $(i, Se) \in \mathcal{Q}_S$, J_R be the set of all identities $j \in [u]$ such that $(j, Re) \in Q_R$ and L_{San} be all identities $l \in [u + 1, u + n]$ such that $(l, San) \in Q_{San}$ respectively. We have

- $\forall i \in I_S, j \in J, P(i, j) = 0$,
- There exists no "sanitizing pipeline" whose users are all included in L_{San}.

If the adversary's final output $b' = b$, we say that $\mathcal{A}$ wins the Extended No-Write Rule game defined above. Let $\Pr[\mathcal{A}$ wins the game] denote the probability that $b' = b$ and $\mathsf{Adv}^{\mathcal{A}}_{Ex-No-Write}(ACE)$ denote $\mathcal{A}$'s advantage when $\mathcal{A}$ wins this *game, then we say an ACE scheme satisfies the Extended No-Write Rule if for all PPT $\mathcal{A}$*

$$\mathsf{Adv}^{\mathcal{A}}_{Ex-No-Write}(ACE) = 2|\Pr[\mathcal{A} \text{ wins the game}] - \frac{1}{2}| \leq negl(\lambda)$$

In fact, we find the above two security models, the simplified no-write rule and the extended no-write rule, are considering the same security issue with only minimal differences. Namely, the former model defines one user i's no-write property in such a manner that i cannot send messages to another user j when the access policy $P(i,j) = 0$ even i,j are all corrupted or i gets help from users who also cannot send messages to j, while in the extended no-write rule model, user i's no-write property is defined similarly but with the exception that i can also gets help from at most $t-1$ sanitizers in one sanitizing pipeline rather than just from other users. Intuitively, the extended no-write rule model defined here should have already covered the simplified no-write rule model and is thus stronger than it.

3 The DACE

In this section, we firs illustrate how to construct a sanitizing cluster and how a new "sanitizing pipeline" with t sanitizers is formed when there are n sanitizers existed in the cluster, we also show you that the whole number of sanitizing pipelines and sanitizers in the sanitizing cluster can be increased in an on-demand manner. After that, we give a description of our ACE scheme with compact ciphertext size and decentralized sanitizers in detail.

3.1 The Sanitizing Cluster and Sanitizing Pipelines

We assume all sanitizers in our DACE system constitute a sanitizing clusters. Our DACE requires that only t sanitizers can collaboratively fulfill the sanitizing algorithm properly and converts one incoming ciphertext into a valid sanitized ciphertext which can then be decrypted by the intended receiver. To save the computational cost of the sanitizers in the sanitizing cluster when they do sanitization, we introduce the notion sanitizing pipeline. A sanitizing pipeline can be valued as a path predefined by the system authority containing a collection of exact t sanitizers chosen by it from the sanitizer cluster. one ciphertext can never be transformed into a valid sanitized ciphertext until it is processed by every nodes in the pipeline chosen in advance by the message sender. The system authority can actually produce as many sanitizing pipelines as it wants, and the collection of all the pipelines is represented as $\{SP\}$ which should be known by all the nodes in the ACE system. Given a polynomial $F(x)$ with degree $t-1$ such that $F(0) = y$, which is the secret to be shared. When one user with identity j wants to join the sanitizing cluster as a sanitizer, the system authority chooses $x_j \in \mathbb{Z}_p$ and computes $y_j = F(x_j)$, then y_j is allocated to this user as one of its secret, then the system authority would also produce a new sanitizing pipeline

sp_l and add this user as one member of this pipeline. Furthermore, as the authority knows all the t sanitizers in sp_l, another secret value $f_j = g^{-\prod_{i \neq j \wedge i \in sp_l} \frac{x_i}{x_i - x_j}}$ is computed by the authority in advance and then distributed to that sanitizer j. When one user with identifier j gets its own secret share (y_j, f_j) and the sanitizing pipeline identifier sp_l, it can work as a valid sanitizer member in the sanitizer cluster.

3.2   Our DACE Scheme

Our ACE scheme is defined by the following algorithms:

Setup(λ): This DACE system setup algorithm is executed by the system authority. Given the security parameter λ, a bilinear map group system $\mathcal{BM} = (p, g, \mathbb{G}, \mathbb{G}_1, e : \mathbb{G} \times \mathbb{G} \to \mathbb{G}_1)$ is generated such that $|p| = \lambda$, $g, h \in \mathbb{G}$ are two randomly selected generators of $\mathbb{G}$ and a secret value $\gamma \in \mathbb{Z}_p$ is chosen, sets $w = g^\gamma$. The authority also chooses a cryptographic hash function $\mathcal{H} : \{0,1\}^\lambda \to \mathbb{Z}_p$ which will be viewed as the random oracle in the security analysis. The authority also initializes the sanitizing clusters and sanitizing pipelines using the initialization algorithm defined above, after that, assuming there are n sanitizers and $|\{SP\}|$ sanitizing pipelines in the ACE system, notice that each element in $\{SP\}$ contains a list of sanitizers' identities and represents a unique sanitizing pipeline. Assuming there are u users which can play the role of the message sender and the message receiver, and each of them lays in one specific layer, supposing there are μ layers at most in the ACE system, let S_{L_β} denote the collection of identities of users laying in the β-th layer where $1 \leq \beta \leq \mu$, only the authority knows $\mathcal{AC} = (S_{L_1}, S_{L_2}, \cdots, S_{L_\alpha}, \cdot, S_{L_\mu})$, that is, only the authority has the knowledge of which user lays in which layer for all the u users. The authority also knows the whole sanitizing key $y \in \mathbb{Z}_p^*$. The authority defines the key space $\mathcal{KM} = \mathbb{G}_1$, the ciphertext space $\mathcal{C} = \mathbb{G}^6$, the sanitized ciphertext space $\mathcal{C}' = \mathbb{G}^6$ respectively. The public parameter $pp = (\mathcal{BM}, w, \mathcal{H}, \{SP\}, \mathcal{KM}, \mathcal{C}, \mathcal{C}')$, the master secret key $msk = (\mathcal{AC}, \gamma, y)$.

KeyGen(msk, pp, i, L_β, ty): When given pp, msk, one specific users' identity i, the layer L_β this user lays in and its user type $ty \in \{Se, Re, San\}$, the key generation algorithm is executed by the authority as follows;

- When $ty = Se$, that is, the authority needs to generate an encryption key ke_i for the user with identity i. The authority chooses $x_i \xleftarrow{R} \mathbb{Z}_p^*$ for this user with identity i and sets ke_i as;

$$ke_i = (h^{\prod_{i \in S_{L_\beta} \cup \cdots \cup S_{L_\mu}} (\gamma + H(i))}, h^{x_i \prod_{i \in S_{L_\beta} \cup \cdots \cup S_{L_\mu}} (\gamma + H(i))}, g^{-x_i \gamma}, e(g, h)^{x_i}, g^y)$$

- When $ty = Re$, that is, the authority needs to generate a decryption key kd_i for that user. When user with identity i lays in layer L_β, he can receiver messages sent from layers below its own, that is, his decryption key should be able to decrypt messages sent from layers from L_1 to L_β. Here the authority construct the decryption key of this user in such a manner that kd_i contains β

components and each component is response for decrypting ciphertexts from one specific layer;

$$kd_i = (kd_{i0} = g^{\frac{1}{\gamma+H(i)}}, kd_{i1} = h^{\frac{\Pi_{l\neq i\wedge l\in S_{L_1}\cup\cdots\cup S_{L_\mu}}(\gamma+H(l))-1}{\gamma}},$$

$$kd_{i2} = h^{\frac{\Pi_{l\neq i\wedge l\in S_{L_2}\cup\cdots\cup S_{L_\mu}}(\gamma+H(l))-1}{\gamma}}, \cdots, kd_{i\beta} = h^{\frac{\Pi_{l\neq i\wedge l\in S_{L_\beta}\cup\cdots\cup S_{L_\mu}}(\gamma+H(l))-1}{\gamma}})$$

- When $ty = San$, that is, the authority needs to generate a sanitizing key ks_i for that user. To do this, the authority chooses a $m-1$ degree function $F(x)$ such that $F(0) = y$. For each sanitizer j in the specific sanitizing pipeline, denoted by spl, the authority allocate a $x_j \xleftarrow{R} \mathbb{Z}_p^*$ to it and computes $y_j = F(x_j)$, the sanitizing key ks_i of the sanitizer with identity i should be;

$$ks_i = g^{-y_i \Pi_{j\neq i\wedge j\in SP_l}\frac{x_j}{x_j-x_i}}$$

Enc(m, ke_i, pp): Our ACE scheme borrows idea from the hybrid encryption scheme, that is, the asymmetric encryption scheme actually encrypts a symmetric encryption key, the real ciphertext is an encryption of the origin message using a symmetric key encryption scheme with the symmetric key encrypted by the previous asymmetric encryption scheme. Here, we only focus on the asymmetric part of our whole ACE and just use $SE_{sk}(m)$ to represent the symmetric encryption part. When given a message $m \in \mathcal{M}$, one message sender with identity i in layer L_β encrypts it as follows;

$$k_0, k_1, r_s \xleftarrow{R} \mathbb{Z}_p^*$$
$$C_1 = g^{-x_i\gamma k_1}, C_2 = g^{-x_i\gamma k_1 r_s}g^{-k_0\gamma}g^y,$$
$$C_3 = h^{k_1 x_i \Pi_{i\in S_{L_\beta}\cup\cdots\cup S_{L_\mu}}(\gamma+H(i))},$$
$$C_4 = h^{k_1 x_i r_s \Pi_{i\in S_{L_\beta}\cup\cdots\cup S_{L_\mu}}(\gamma+H(i))}h^{k_0 \Pi_{i\in S_{L_\beta}\cup\cdots\cup S_{L_\mu}}(\gamma+H(i))}$$
$$C_5 = e(g,h)^{x_i k_1}, C_6 = e(g,h)^{x_i k_1 r_s}$$

The symmetric key should be $sk = e(g,h)^{k_0}$, the real ciphertext should be $C_7 = SE_{sk}(m)$. So, the whole ciphertext of our ACE is the tuple $CT = (L_\beta, C_1, C_2, C_3, C_4, C_5, C_6, C_7)$. The message sender then chooses one sanitizing pipeline SP_l from all pipelines which are hard-wired with this sender.

Sanit(CT^v, pp, ks_{lv+1}): Given a ciphertext $CT^v = (L_\beta, C_1^v, C_2^v, C_3^v, C_4^v, C_5^v, C_6^v, Ci^v)$, no matter whether it is received from the message sender or from a sanitizer's predecessor, this sanitizer does as follows;

$$r_{v+1} \xleftarrow{R} \mathbb{Z}_p^*, C_1^{v+1} = g^{-x_i\gamma k_1}, C_2^{v+1} = g^{-x_i\gamma k_1 r_s}g^{-k_0\gamma}g^y ks_{lv+1}(C_1^v)^{r_{v+1}},$$
$$C_3^{v+1} = h^{k_1 x_i \Pi_{i\in S_{L_\beta}\cup\cdots\cup S_{L_\mu}}(\gamma+H(i))},$$
$$C_4^{v+1} = h^{k_1 x_i r_s \Pi_{i\in S_{L_\beta}\cup\cdots\cup S_{L_\mu}}(\gamma+H(i))}h^{k_0 \Pi_{i\in S_{L_\beta}\cup\cdots\cup S_{L_\mu}}(\gamma+H(i))}(C_4^v)^{r_{v+1}}$$
$$C_5^{v+1} = e(g,h)^{x_i k_1}, C_6^{v+1} = e(g,h)^{x_i k_1 r_s}(C_5^v)^{r_{v+1}}, C_7^{v+1} = C_7^v$$

After this sanitizer proceeds the incoming ciphertext as above properly, it would relay the partially sanitized ciphertext to the next sanitizer laying in the same sanitizing pipeline as itself if it is not the final sanitizer in this pipeline, otherwise, this sanitizer would relay the sanitized ciphertext to the intended receiver.

Notice that all sanitizers in SP_l will do the same as what we described above. When one ciphertext tuple $CT = (L_\beta, C_1, C_2, C_3, C_4, C_5, C_6)$ goes through the sanitizing pipeline SP_l and is processed by each of the t sanitizers in SP_l, the finally sanitized ciphertext should be represent as:

$$C_1^t = C_1 = g^{-x_i \gamma k_1}, C_2^t = g^{-x_i \gamma k_1 r_s} g^{-k_0 \gamma} g^y (C_1)^{r_1 + r_2 + \cdots + r_t} ks_{l1} ks_{l2} \cdots ks_{lt},$$

$$C_3^t = C_3 = h^{k_1 x_i \prod_{i \in S_{L_\beta} \cup \cdots \cup S_{L_\mu}} (\gamma + H(i))},$$

$$C_4^t = h^{k_1 x_i r_s \prod_{i \in S_{L_\beta} \cup \cdots \cup S_{L_\mu}} (\gamma + H(i))} h^{k_0 \prod_{i \in S_{L_\beta} \cup \cdots \cup S_{L_\mu}} (\gamma + H(i))} (C_3)^{r_1 + r_2 + \cdots + r_t}$$

$$C_5^t = C_5 = e(g, h)^{x_i k_1}, C_6^t = e(g, h)^{x_i k_1 r_s} (C_5)^{r_1 + r_2 + \cdots + r_t}, C_7^t = C_7$$

As we can see,

$$ks_{l1} ks_{l2} \cdots ks_{lt}$$

$$= g^{-y_{l1} \prod_{j \neq l1 \wedge j \in SP_l} \frac{x_j}{x_j - x_{l1}}} g^{-y_{l2} \prod_{j \neq l2 \wedge j \in SP_l} \frac{x_j}{x_j - x_{l2}}} \cdots g^{-y_{lt} \prod_{j \neq lt \wedge j \in SP_l} \frac{x_j}{x_j - x_{lt}}}$$

$$= g^{-F(0)} = g^{-y}$$

When the last sanitizer in SP_l has executed its sanitizing algorithm on one incoming partially sanitized ciphertext, he can just send $CT' = (L_\beta, C_1', C_2', C_3', C_4')$ to the intended receivers, where

$$C_1' = C_2^t = g^{-x_i \gamma k_1 r_s} g^{-k_0 \gamma} g^y (C_1)^{r_1 + r_2 + \cdots + r_t} ks_{l1} ks_{l2} \cdots ks_{lt}$$

$$= g^{-(x_i k_1 (r_s + r_1 + \cdots + r_t) + k_0) \gamma}$$

$$C_2' = C_4^t = h^{k_1 x_i r_s \prod_{i \in S_{L_\beta} \cup \cdots \cup S_{L_\mu}} (\gamma + H(i))} h^{k_0 \prod_{i \in S_{L_\beta} \cup \cdots \cup S_{L_\mu}} (\gamma + H(i))} (C_3)^{r_1 + r_2 + \cdots + r_t}$$

$$= h^{(k_1 x_i (r_s + r_1 + \cdots + r_t) + k_0) \prod_{i \in S_{L_\beta} \cup \cdots \cup S_{L_\mu}} (\gamma + H(i))}$$

$$C_3' = C_6^t = e(g, h)^{x_i k_1 (r_s + r_1 + r_2 + \cdots + r_t)}$$

$$C_4' = SE_{sk}(m) \text{ where } sk = e(g, h)^{k_0}$$

and L_β denotes the layer this message sender lays in.

Dec(kd_j, CT', pp): When given a properly sanitized ciphertext CT' and one user's decryption key kd_j, this user would first judge whether he is able to recover the origin message of the received ciphertext by checking whether the layer the receiver lays in is higher than that of the message sender. If the receiver can decrypt the ciphertext, he does as follows;

$$sk' = \frac{e(C_1', kd_{j\beta})e(C_2', kd_{j0})}{C_3'}, \text{ sets } K = (x_i k_1(r_s + r_1 + \cdots + r_t) + k_0)$$

$$= \frac{e(g^{-K\gamma}, h^{\frac{\prod_{l \neq i \wedge l \in S_{L_\beta} \cup \cdots \cup S_{L_\mu}}(\gamma + H(l)) - 1}{\gamma}})e(h^{K\prod_{i \in S_{L_\beta} \cup \cdots \cup S_{L_\mu}}(\gamma + H(i))}, g^{\frac{1}{\gamma + H(i)}})}{e(g, h)^{K - k_0}}$$

$$= \frac{e(g, h)^{K(1 - \prod_{l \neq i \wedge l \in S_{L_\beta} \cup \cdots \cup S_{L_\mu}}(\gamma + H(l)))}e(g, h)^{K\prod_{l \neq i \wedge l \in S_{L_\beta} \cup \cdots \cup S_{L_\mu}}(\gamma + H(l))}}{e(g, h)^{K - k_0}}$$

$$= e(g, h)^{k_0}$$

$$m' = DE_{sk'}(C_4')$$

4   Security Proofs

Theorem 2. *Our DACE scheme holds the No-Read Rule property assuming the $(f, g, F) - GDDHE$ problem is hard in the group system $\mathcal{BM} = (p, g_0, h_0, \mathbb{G}_1, \mathbb{G}_T, e(\cdot, \cdot))$ when the hash function H is modeled as random oracle. Concretely, if there is an adversary $\mathcal{A}$ which can break our scheme with non-negligible probability ϵ, supposing $\mathcal{A}$ makes at most q_H, q_{ke}, q_{kd} queries to the H hash oracle, encryption key query oracle and decryption key query oracle respectively, then we can construct another algorithm $\mathcal{B}$ that solves the (f, g, F)-GDDHE problem in the given group system with advantage at least $\frac{1}{2} \cdot (\frac{q_H - 1}{q_H})^{q_{kd}} \cdot \frac{1}{q_H} \cdot \epsilon$, where q_H, q_{kd} are defined above.*

Theorem 3. *Our DACE scheme holds the Extended No-Write Rule property assuming the $(f, g, F) - GDDHE$ problem is hard in the group system $\mathcal{BM} = (p, g_0, h_0, \mathbb{G}_1, \mathbb{G}_T, e(\cdot, \cdot))$ when the hash function H is modeled as random oracle. Concretely, if there is an adversary $\mathcal{A}$ which can break our scheme with non-negligible probability ϵ, supposing $\mathcal{A}$ makes at most q_H, q_{ke} queries to the H hash oracle, encryption key query oracle respectively, then we can construct another algorithm S that solves the (f, g, F)-GDDHE problem in the given group system with advantage at least $\frac{1}{2} \cdot \frac{1}{q_H} \cdot \epsilon$, where q_H, q_{kd} are defined above.*

We omit the details of our two formal proofs there because of the page limitation.

5   Conclusion

In this paper, we present a DACE scheme to solve the privacy issues in the public blockchain. Our construction is also believed to be the first one considering using multiple sanitizers rather than one to enforce the ACE. Our extended no-write rule model and the given corresponding proof show that our DACE is more secure and reliable because of the utilization of decentralized sanitizers. We find our scheme is really suitable to be deployed in such a fully decentralized environment, for example in the public blockchain. We prove the security of our scheme under non-standard assumptions with the help of the random oracle, thus our next work focuses on presenting DACE with constant ciphertext size and decentralized sanitizers secure without random oracle and under standard assumptions.

Acknowledgement. This work is supported by the Henan Key Laboratory of Network Cryptography Technology and the Henan High Education Key Project Foundational Research Plan, the project name is "The research on access control model of cloud-based medical data", the project No. 19A520047.

References

1. Bitblender. https://bitblender.io
2. Bitlaundry. http://app.bitlaundry.com
3. Bitmixer. https://bitccointalk.org/index.php?topic=415396.160
4. Bellare, M., Boldyreva, A., Desai, A., Pointcheval, D.: Key-privacy in public-key encryption. In: Boyd, C. (ed.) ASIACRYPT 2001. LNCS, vol. 2248, pp. 566–582. Springer, Heidelberg (2001). https://doi.org/10.1007/3-540-45682-1_33
5. Benaloh, J., Leichter, J.: Generalized secret sharing and monotone functions. In: Goldwasser, S. (ed.) CRYPTO 1988. LNCS, vol. 403, pp. 27–35. Springer, New York (1990). https://doi.org/10.1007/0-387-34799-2_3
6. Bertilsson, M., Ingemarsson, I.: A construction of practical secret sharing schemes using linear block codes. In: Seberry, J., Zheng, Y. (eds.) AUSCRYPT 1992. LNCS, vol. 718, pp. 67–79. Springer, Heidelberg (1993). https://doi.org/10.1007/3-540-57220-1_53
7. Boneh, D., Gentry, C., Waters, B.: Collusion resistant broadcast encryption with short ciphertexts and private keys. In: Shoup, V. (ed.) CRYPTO 2005. LNCS, vol. 3621, pp. 258–275. Springer, Heidelberg (2005). https://doi.org/10.1007/11535218_16
8. Boneh, D., Hamburg, M.: Generalized identity based and broadcast encryption schemes. In: Pieprzyk, J. (ed.) ASIACRYPT 2008. LNCS, vol. 5350, pp. 455–470. Springer, Heidelberg (2008). https://doi.org/10.1007/978-3-540-89255-7_28
9. Boneh, D., Waters, B., Zhandry, M.: Low overhead broadcast encryption from multilinear maps. In: Garay, J.A., Gennaro, R. (eds.) CRYPTO 2014. LNCS, vol. 8616, pp. 206–223. Springer, Heidelberg (2014). https://doi.org/10.1007/978-3-662-44371-2_12
10. Buterin, V.: On public and private blockchains (2015). https://blog.ethereum.org/2015/08/07/on-public-and-private-blockchains/
11. Chaum, D.: Untraceable electronic mail, return addresses, and digital pseudonyms. Commun. ACM **24**(2), 84–88 (1981)
12. Damgård, I., Haagh, H., Orlandi, C.: Access control encryption: enforcing information flow with cryptography. In: Hirt, M., Smith, A. (eds.) TCC 2016. LNCS, vol. 9986, pp. 547–576. Springer, Heidelberg (2016). https://doi.org/10.1007/978-3-662-53644-5_21

13. Delerablée, C.: Identity-based broadcast encryption with constant size ciphertexts and private keys. In: Kurosawa, K. (ed.) ASIACRYPT 2007. LNCS, vol. 4833, pp. 200–215. Springer, Heidelberg (2007). https://doi.org/10.1007/978-3-540-76900-2_12

14. Delerablée, C., Paillier, P., Pointcheval, D.: Fully collusion secure dynamic broadcast encryption with constant-size ciphertexts or decryption keys. In: Takagi, T., Okamoto, E., Okamoto, T., Okamoto, T. (eds.) Pairing 2007. LNCS, vol. 4575, pp. 39–59. Springer, Heidelberg (2007). https://doi.org/10.1007/978-3-540-73489-5_4

15. Fazio, N., Perera, I.M.: Outsider-anonymous broadcast encryption with sublinear ciphertexts. In: Fischlin, M., Buchmann, J., Manulis, M. (eds.) PKC 2012. LNCS, vol. 7293, pp. 225–242. Springer, Heidelberg (2012). https://doi.org/10.1007/978-3-642-30057-8_14

16. Fernández-Caramés, T.M., Blanco-Novoa, Ó., Froiz-Míguez, I., Fraga-Lamas, P.: Towards an autonomous industry 4.0 warehouse: a UAV and blockchain-based system for inventory and traceability applications in big data-driven supply chain management. Sensors 19(10), 2394 (2019)

17. Fiat, A., Naor, M.: Broadcast encryption. In: Stinson, D.R. (ed.) CRYPTO 1993. LNCS, vol. 773, pp. 480–491. Springer, Heidelberg (1994). https://doi.org/10.1007/3-540-48329-2_40

18. Fujisaki, E.: Sub-linear size traceable ring signatures without random oracles. In: Kiayias, A. (ed.) CT-RSA 2011. LNCS, vol. 6558, pp. 393–415. Springer, Heidelberg (2011). https://doi.org/10.1007/978-3-642-19074-2_25

19. Genkin, D., Papadopoulos, D., Papamanthou, C.: Privacy in decentralized cryptocurrencies. Commun. ACM 61(6), 78–88 (2018)

20. Gentry, C., Waters, B.: Adaptive security in broadcast encryption systems (with short ciphertexts). In: Joux, A. (ed.) EUROCRYPT 2009. LNCS, vol. 5479, pp. 171–188. Springer, Heidelberg (2009). https://doi.org/10.1007/978-3-642-01001-9_10

21. Jaoude, J.A., Saadé, R.G.: Blockchain applications - usage in different domains. IEEE Access 7, 45360–45381 (2019)

22. Kim, J., Susilo, W., Au, M.H., Seberry, J.: Adaptively secure identity-based broadcast encryption with a constant-sized ciphertext. IEEE Trans. Inf. Forensics Secur. 10(3), 679–693 (2015)

23. Lai, J., Mu, Y., Guo, F., Susilo, W., Chen, R.: Fully privacy-preserving and revocable id-based broadcast encryption for data access control in smart city. Pers. Ubiquit. Comput. 21(5), 855–868 (2017)

24. Libert, B., Paterson, K.G., Quaglia, E.A.: Anonymous broadcast encryption: adaptive security and efficient constructions in the standard model. In: Fischlin, M., Buchmann, J., Manulis, M. (eds.) PKC 2012. LNCS, vol. 7293, pp. 206–224. Springer, Heidelberg (2012). https://doi.org/10.1007/978-3-642-30057-8_13

25. Lipmaa, H.: Succinct non-interactive zero knowledge arguments from span programs and linear error-correcting codes. In: Sako, K., Sarkar, P. (eds.) ASIACRYPT 2013. LNCS, vol. 8269, pp. 41–60. Springer, Heidelberg (2013). https://doi.org/10.1007/978-3-642-42033-7_3

26. Lu, H., Huang, K., Azimi, M., Guo, L.: Blockchain technology in the oil and gas industry: a review of applications, opportunities, challenges, and risks. IEEE Access **7**, 41426–41444 (2019)
27. Maxwell, G.: Coinjoin: Bitcoin pricacy for the real world (2013). https://en.bitcoin.it/wiki/CoinJoin
28. Miers, I., Garman, C., Green, M., Rubin, A.D.: Zerocoin: anonymous distributed e-cash from bitcoin. In: 2013 IEEE Symposium on Security and Privacy, SP 2013, Berkeley, CA, USA, 19–22 May 2013, pp. 397–411 (2013)
29. Nakamoto, S.: Bitcoin: A peer-to-peer electronic cash system (2008). https://bitcoin.org/en/bitcoin-paper
30. Noether, S.: Ring signature confidential transactions for monero. IACR Cryptology ePrint Archive 2015, 1098 (2015)
31. Noether, S., Mackenzie, A.: Ring confidential transactions. Ledger **1**, 1–18 (2016)
32. Novo, O.: Scalable access management in iot using blockchain: a performance evaluation. IEEE Internet Things J. **6**(3), 4694–4701 (2019)
33. Paillier, P.: Public-key cryptosystems based on composite degree residuosity classes. In: Stern, J. (ed.) EUROCRYPT 1999. LNCS, vol. 1592, pp. 223–238. Springer, Heidelberg (1999). https://doi.org/10.1007/3-540-48910-X_16
34. Pedersen, T.P.: Non-interactive and information-theoretic secure verifiable secret sharing. In: Feigenbaum, J. (ed.) CRYPTO 1991. LNCS, vol. 576, pp. 129–140. Springer, Heidelberg (1992). https://doi.org/10.1007/3-540-46766-1_9
35. Phan, D.H., Pointcheval, D., Shahandashti, S.F., Strefler, M.: Adaptive CCA broadcast encryption with constant-size secret keys and ciphertexts. Int. J. Inf. Secur. **12**(4), 251–265 (2013)
36. Rivest, R.L., Shamir, A., Tauman, Y.: How to leak a secret. In: Boyd, C. (ed.) ASIACRYPT 2001. LNCS, vol. 2248, pp. 552–565. Springer, Heidelberg (2001). https://doi.org/10.1007/3-540-45682-1_32
37. Ruffing, T., Moreno-Sanchez, P., Kate, A.: CoinShuffle: practical decentralized coin mixing for bitcoin. In: Kutyłowski, M., Vaidya, J. (eds.) ESORICS 2014. LNCS, vol. 8713, pp. 345–364. Springer, Cham (2014). https://doi.org/10.1007/978-3-319-11212-1_20
38. Salman, T., Zolanvari, M., Erbad, A., Jain, R., Samaka, M.: Security services using blockchains: a state of the art survey. IEEE Commun. Surv. Tutorials **21**(1), 858–880 (2019)
39. De Santis, A., Micali, S., Persiano, G.: Non-interactive zero-knowledge proof systems. In: Pomerance, C. (ed.) CRYPTO 1987. LNCS, vol. 293, pp. 52–72. Springer, Heidelberg (1988). https://doi.org/10.1007/3-540-48184-2_5
40. Shamir, A.: How to share a secret. Commun. ACM **22**(11), 612–613 (1979)
41. Shen, C., Pena-Mora, F.: Blockchain for cities-a systematic literature review. IEEE Access **PP**(99), 1 (2018)
42. Sun, S.-F., Au, M.H., Liu, J.K., Yuen, T.H.: RingCT 2.0: a compact accumulator-based (linkable ring signature) protocol for blockchain cryptocurrency monero. In: Foley, S.N., Gollmann, D., Snekkenes, E. (eds.) ESORICS 2017. LNCS, vol. 10493, pp. 456–474. Springer, Cham (2017). https://doi.org/10.1007/978-3-319-66399-9_25
43. Susilo, W., Chen, R., Guo, F., Yang, G., Mu, Y., Chow, Y.: Recipient revocable identity-based broadcast encryption: How to revoke some recipients in IBBE without knowledge of the plaintext. In: Proceedings of the 11th ACM on Asia Conference on Computer and Communications Security, AsiaCCS 2016, Xi'an, China, 30 May - 3 June 2016, pp. 201–210 (2016)

44. Tassa, T.: Generalized oblivious transfer by secret sharing. Des. Codes Crypt. **58**(1), 11–21 (2011)
45. Toyoda, K., Mathiopoulos, P.T., Sasase, I., Ohtsuki, T.: A novel blockchain-based product ownership management system (POMS) for anti-counterfeits in the post supply chain. IEEE Access **5**, 17465–17477 (2017)
46. Yao, A.C.: Protocols for secure computations (extended abstract). In: 23rd Annual Symposium on Foundations of Computer Science, Chicago, Illinois, USA, 3–5 November 1982, pp. 160–164 (1982)
47. Zhang, L., Wu, Q., Mu, Y.: Anonymous identity-based broadcast encryption with adaptive security. In: Wang, G., Ray, I., Feng, D., Rajarajan, M. (eds.) CSS 2013. LNCS, vol. 8300, pp. 258–271. Springer, Cham (2013). https://doi.org/10.1007/978-3-319-03584-0_19
48. Zyskind, G., Nathan, O., Pentland, A.: Enigma: Decentralized computation platform with guaranteed privacy. Computer Science (2015)

A Smart Grid Privacy Protection Scheme Based on Short Fail-Stop Signature

Shumei Xu, Ningbin Yang, and Quan Zhou$^{(\boxtimes)}$

School of Mathematics and Information Science,
Guangzhou University, Guangzhou 510006, China
764061064@qq.com, yorknb@126.com, zhouqq@gzhu.edu.cn

Abstract. In promoting the development of intelligent and distributed power transmission systems, smart grid has attracted extensive attention. However, the data transmitted over smart grids are not protected, and then suffer from several types of security threats and attacks. How to provide an efficient security protocol to enhance the privacy protection of smart grid network and prevent information leakage has become a hot research topic of smart grid privacy protection. In this paper, a short fail-stop signature scheme based on factorization and discrete logarithm assumption is designed to protect the information privacy of smart grid. The proposed scheme can not only protect the privacy of smart devices in the smart grid, but also prevent the forgery of payment credentials, and ensure the trusted center to effectively manage and maintain smart grid users and payment credentials.

Keywords: Smart grid · Short fail-stop signature · Payment credential

1 Introduction

Smart grid has become a buzzword in recent years, attracting the attention of engineers and researchers in the fields of electricity and communications. Smart grid can not only replace traditional grid to become a new generation of grid, but also realize the informatization, digitalization, automation and interaction of smart grid. Through advanced technology, smart grid achieves the goal of reliable, security, economic, efficient, environmentally friendly and security use of power grid, that is, to provide power to smart devices in a more stable and reliable way [1]. The emergence of smart grid has changed the situation of queuing to buy electricity, plug-in card power and so on, and has brought great convenience to people's lives in combination with the latest online payment methods. These include: the use of distributed photovoltaic power generation to implement "self-use, surplus electricity sonline"; Electric cars and electric bicycles are charged using charging piles. Smart meters read the total power of household appliances and so on. Then, for users in smart grid, they hope to protect their privacy as if they were using cash in the process of using, and payment credential that can protect users' privacy can meet this requirement.

In order to protect users' privacy information in the user process, many scholars have done a lot of research in this field. Chen et al. [2] uses zero-knowledge proof to run a

© Springer Nature Singapore Pte Ltd. 2020
Z. Zheng et al. (Eds.): BlockSys 2019, CCIS 1156, pp. 258–266, 2020.
https://doi.org/10.1007/978-981-15-2777-7_21

blind signature protocol between the user and the store. This method can guarantee the unlinkability and protect the privacy of the user, but it is limited by the complexity of zero-knowledge proof. The protocol [3] proposed by Dimitriou et al. is based on [4] that allows the utility provider to anonymously authenticate smart grid. However, If some special case happened, TC will not be able to trace the user's identity. Zhao et al. [5] uses ring signature technology to construct a privacy protection scheme. Although this technology can hide the identity of the user, it cannot exclude the attacker who has a strong attack ability and can crack users' identities. Yang et al. [6] proposed a new authentication encryption scheme and a payment system based on authentication encryption scheme. The scheme claims to be able to realize sender authenticity, confidentiality and user anonymity, but the scheme is vulnerable to counterfeiting attacks. A privacy-preserving scheme [7] was proposed by Jeske et al. in smart grid based on the group signature. It can prevent replay attacks, However, the scheme cannot get the any users' formation.

In this paper, we propose a short fail-stop signature based on factorization and discrete logarithm hypothesis [8] is applied to construct a privacy protection scheme for smart grid. The scheme can realize secure one-way authentication and effective secure payment. More importantly, the validity period is attached to the payment credential so that the trusted center can manage its database more effectively. The TC authenticates the user's identity. After passing the authentication, the user applies to the TC for a face value, which is signed by the TC and issued to the user. When paying the fee, the user sends the payment voucher to the access point, and the payment can be completed as long as the access point verifies that the payment voucher is authentic and that the payment voucher is not reused. At the same time, the scheme has the advantages of transferability and unforgeability.

2   System Model and Security Requirements

2.1   Structural Model of Smart Grid

The smart grid structure model [9] mainly includes three layers: user (U), access point (AP) and smart grid trusted center (TC), as shown in Fig. 1.

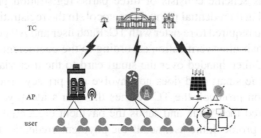

Fig. 1. Smart grid model

User (Us): including electric vehicles, electric bicycles, household appliances, photovoltaic power generation devices and other electrical equipment, which are embodied in smart IC cards, MAC codes, etc.

Access Point (APs): including smart meters, Charging pile, etc., which are directly connected to smart grid with users to provide services for users and smart grid trusted centers.

Smart Grid Trusted Center (TC): Smart Grid Trusted Center is the core part of the model and the dispatching and command center of the whole smart grid, which manages certificates, keys, users and access points.

2.2 Security Requirement

In order to protect the privacy of information and security during the use of smart grid, smart grid systems need to meet the security requirements of identity authentication, privacy protection, uniqueness of credential, unforgeability and transferability. These security requirements are described as follows:

(1) Identity Authentication: when all users and AP establish connection with smart grid trusted center, TC shall verify the signature information of users and AP to ensure that the received signature information has not been maliciously forged or modified.
(2) Privacy Protection: The user's identity information should remain anonymous, and no third party can track the user's identity except TC.
(3) Credential Uniqueness: During the use of smart grid system, users can only use the same payment credential once and cannot reuse it.
(4) Non-forgeability: Only TC can generate legal payment credentials, and users can only use legal payment credential to make payment.
(5) Transferability: Users can transfer payment credential to other users like ordinary cash and will not be tracked.

3 Privacy Protection Scheme Base on Short Fail-Stop Signature

In this paper, a short fail-stop signature is applied to construct a privacy protection scheme for smart grid. This scheme consists of three parts: registration protocol, credential production protocol and credential payment protocol. In the registration protocol phase, all users and APs are required to register with TC. Each user and AP generate themselves public/private key pair after verification according to the coefficients generated one by one by TC. The TC then handed over the smart card to the user via a secure channel. It is assumed that the smart card does not involve any privacy security issues. In the credential production protocol, the TC verifies the user's identity. After passing, the TC signs the required face value and sends the payment credential to the user. In the credential payment protocol, the user sends the payment credential to the AP. As long as the AP verifies that the payment credential is valid and is used for the first time, the scheme is completed. In order to ensure the anonymity of users in the payment process, this paper uses the payment credential when users pay fees to AP.

The scheme involves relevant symbols, as shown in Table 1:

Table 1. Symbol description

Symbol	Description
ID_i	The i-th user identity $(i = 1, \cdots, n)$
ID_{AP_ρ}	The ρ-th AP identity $(\rho = 1, \cdots, s)$
$\gcd(a, b)$	greatest common divisor of (a, b)
$\phi(\cdot)$	Euler function
$\lambda(\cdot)$	find the lowest common multiple
Z_n	The ring of integers modulo a number n
$H(\cdot)$	secure hash function, $H : \{0, 1\}^* \rightarrow Z_\beta$

Definition 1 (Payment Credential). Certain amount and validity period, issued by TC for users, credentials used for payment.

3.1 Registration Protocol

In this phase, each user and AP generate themselves public/private key pair after verification according to the coefficients generated one by one by TC.

Step1. Registered users i/AP_ρ send themselves packet $\langle ID_i/ID_{AP_\rho}, ID_{TC}, T_1 \rangle$ to TC.

Step2. After receiving the packet $\langle ID_i/ID_{AP_\rho}, ID_{TC}, T_1 \rangle$, according to the difference between the current time and the timestamp T_1, TC checks the freshness of packet. TC chooses two large primes p and q, where $p = c_1 \beta p' + 1$ and $q = c_2 \beta q' + 1$, p', q', β are also prime, $(c_1, c_2) \in Z$ and $\gcd(c_1, c_2) = 2$. To guarantee security, β is a prime that is difficult to deal with for a discrete logarithm problem on Z_n, α is an element with order β. TC computes $n = pq$, and $\gcd(\alpha, c_1 c_2 \beta^2 p' q') = 1$. Note that $\phi(n) = c_1 c_2 \beta^2 p' q'$ and $\lambda(n) = c_1 c_2 \beta p' q'$.

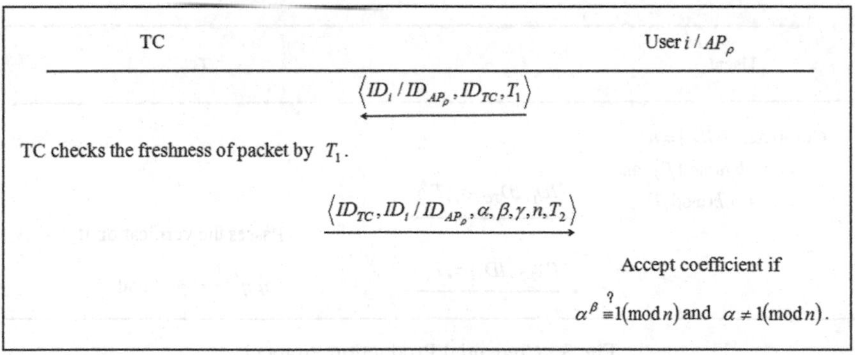

Fig. 2. Registration Protocol

Step3. Let N_β denote the subgroup of Z_n^* generated by α. TC continues to select a secret random number $x_i, a \in N_\beta$ and computes $\gamma = \alpha^a \pmod n$. Then TC send packet that contains parameters $\langle ID_{TC}, ID_i/ID_{AP_\rho}, \alpha, \beta, \gamma, n, T_2 \rangle$ to users i/AP_ρ, and $(p, q, x_i/y_\rho, a)$ is kept secret.

Step4. Upon receiving TC packet $\langle ID_{TC}, ID_i/ID_{AP_\rho}, \alpha, \beta, \gamma, n, T_2 \rangle$, according to the difference between the current time and the timestamp T_2, users i/AP_ρ checks the freshness of packet. And the $\alpha^\beta \equiv 1 \pmod n$ and $\alpha \neq 1 \pmod n$ will be verified by theusers i/AP_ρ. A coefficient is good if the above equation holds.

Step5. Users i/AP_ρ selects $a_1, a_2, b_1, b_2 \in Z_\beta$ as his secret key and computes $\eta_1 = \alpha^{a_1} \gamma^{a_2} \pmod n$ and $\eta_2 = \alpha^{b_1} \gamma^{b_2} \pmod n$. The public key is (η_1, η_2) (Fig. 2).

3.2 Credential Production Protocol

In this phase, the user i contacts TC, apply for θ face value. TC requires proof of identity (i.e. signature of user i). After verification, TC will issue a payment credential with θ face value to the user i.

Step1. User i computes $H(ID_i) = h$. To sign a message h, user computes $s_1 = a_1 + b_1 h \pmod \beta$ and $s_2 = a_2 + b_2 h \pmod \beta$. Let $\sigma_i = (s = (s_1, s_2), h, \theta)$, and take packet $\langle ID_i, ID_{TC}, \sigma_i, T_3 \rangle$ send to TC.

Step2. After receiving the packet $\langle ID_i, ID_{TC}, \sigma_i, T_3 \rangle$, according to the difference between the current time and the timestamp T_3, TC checks the freshness of packet. Then, TC verifies $\langle ID_i, ID_{TC}, \sigma_i, T_3 \rangle$ to ensure the packets, authenticity according to the following equation: $\eta_1 \eta_2^h \equiv \alpha^{s_1} \gamma^{s_2} \pmod n$.

Step3. If it does hold, according to the face value θ applied by the user, TC signs the face value θ. TC Arbitrary select $a_0 \in N_\beta$, $\varphi = \alpha^{a_0} \pmod n$, and a_0 is kept secret.

Step4. TC chooses $a_3, a_4, b_3, b_4 \in Z_\beta$ as secret key and computes $\psi_1 = \alpha^{a_3} \varphi^{a_4} \pmod n$ and $\psi_2 = \alpha^{b_3} \varphi^{b_4} \pmod n$. The public key is (ψ_1, ψ_2). Set $K = (\psi_1, \psi_2, a_3, a_4, b_3, b_4)$, to sign a message θ, TC computes $sig_K(\theta) = (m_1, m_2)$ (among them $m_1 = a_3 + \theta b_3 \pmod \beta$ and $m_2 = a_4 + \theta b_4 \pmod \beta$).

$m = (sig_K(\theta))^{x_i}$, Set $\sigma = (\alpha, \varphi, \theta, sig_K(\theta), T_{indate}, m)$, and TC take packet $\langle ID_{TC}, ID_i, \sigma, T_4 \rangle$ send to user i[10] (Fig. 3).

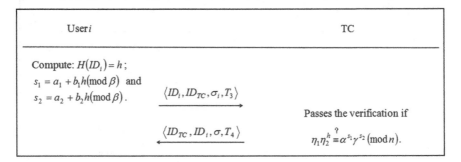

Fig. 3. Credential Production Protocol

3.3 Credential Payment Protocol

In this phase, the user i sends the payment credential σ to the AP_ρ. As long as the AP_ρ verifies that the payment credential is valid and is used for the first time, the scheme is completed.

Step1. After receiving the packet $\langle ID_i, ID_{AP_\rho}, \sigma, T_5 \rangle$, according to the difference between the current time and the timestamp T_5, AP_ρ checks the freshness of packet. And AP_ρ distinguish whether T_{indate} is within the validity period.

Step2. If T_{indate} is valid, then, AP_ρ verifies the payment credential by computing if $\psi_1 \psi_2^\theta \equiv \alpha^{m_1} \varphi^{m_2} (\bmod\, n)$ holds.

Step3. AP_ρ searches TC's database offline for m and rejects the payment credential if m exists, otherwise it is stored in TC's database to complete payment (Fig. 4).

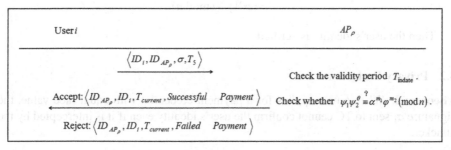

Fig. 4. Credential Payment Protocol

Of course, In addition to the payment to TC by users, e-payment can also be made between users and users. For example, in distributed photovoltaic power generation, "self-use, surplus power online" is implemented. Users ID_i can transfer the surplus power to the smart grid and sell it at the local price. User ID_j uses $\sigma = (\alpha, \varphi, \theta, sig_K(\theta), T_{\text{indate}}, m)$ to purchase power supply with equal face value θ at user ID_i.

Step1. User ID_i distinguish whether T_{indate} is within the validity period.

Step2. User ID_i continues to verify if T_{indate} is valid. Then, the payment credential passes the verification if $\psi_1 \psi_2^\theta \equiv \alpha^{m_1} \varphi^{m_2} (\bmod\, n)$.

Step3. User ID_i searches TC's database offline for m and rejects the payment credential if m exists, otherwise the payment process is completed, but m is not stored in the database. Such e-payment do not require any verification by TC, thus reducing the amount of computation and protecting the privacy of users.

4 Security Analysis

In this section, we will analyze the security of the proposed privacy protection scheme for short signatures. In order to protect the data privacy of smart grid, smart grid systems need to meet security requirements such as identity authentication, privacy protection, credential uniqueness and unforgeability.

4.1 Correctness

When all users and AP establish connection with smart grid TC, TC shall verify the signatures of users and AP (taking verification of user signatures as an example) to ensure that the received signature information has not been maliciously forged or modified.

Theorem 1. If $\eta_1 \eta_2^h \equiv \alpha^{s_1} \gamma^{s_2}$ equation holds, Then the user can pass the verification of TC.

Proof. Because of

$$
\begin{aligned}
\eta_1 \eta_2^h (\bmod n) &= \alpha^{a_1} \gamma^{a_2} \left\{ \alpha^{b_1} \gamma^{b_2} \right\} (\bmod n) \\
&= \alpha^{a_1 + b_1 m} \gamma^{a_2 + b_2 m} (\bmod n) \\
&= \alpha^{s_1} \gamma^{s_2} (\bmod n).
\end{aligned}
$$

Then the user's identity is verified.

4.2 Privacy Protection

Theorem 2. When a user applies for a payment credential with equal face value, the signature σ_i sent to TC cannot confirm the user's identity even if it is intercepted by the attacker.

Proof. The Hash function is required to be secure. For a given message h, ID_i cannot be found to make $H(ID_i) = h$. In this way, even if the attacker intercepts σ_i, the attacker cannot know which user sent it, thus protecting the privacy of the user.

Theorem 3. When the user uses the payment credential, no third party can track the user's identity except TC.

Proof. Because the payment credential is signed by TC, the information it contains has face value, TC's signature and the validity period of the credential, and there is no relevant information about the user. Even if σ is obtained, the third party can only confirm that the payment credential is valid after verifying $\psi_1 \psi_2^\theta \equiv \alpha^{m_1} \varphi^{m_2}$. The attacker cannot determine the user's real identity, which helps to protect the user's privacy.

4.3 Credential Uniqueness

Theorem 4. After ensuring the validity and validity of the payment credential, if m is not in TC's database, it can be ensured that the credential is unreusability.

Proof. Because of m is calculated by TC and will be stored in TC database after users use it. If the user uses the payment credential again, the AP first confirms the validity of the payment credential, then searches the TC database for the existence of m, and rejects the payment credential if it exists. Therefore, the credential payment protocol in this paper can ensure the non-reusability of the payment credential.

4.4 Unforgeability

Theorem 5. If someone forges TC's signature as (m'_1, m'_2) and passes the verification. Under the same face value θ, assume that the signature generated by TC is (m_1, m_2). By evaluating a_0, it can be proved that the signature is forged.

Proof. Because of $\psi_1 \psi_2^{\theta'} \equiv \alpha^{m'_1} \varphi^{m'_2} (\bmod\, n)$, $\psi_1 \psi_2^{\theta} \equiv \alpha^{m_1} \varphi^{m_2} (\bmod\, n)$

there are $\alpha^{m_1} \varphi^{m_2} = \alpha^{m'_1} \varphi^{m'_2} (\bmod\, n)$
set $\varphi = \alpha^{a_0} (\bmod\, n)$, then $\alpha^{m_1 + a_0 m_2} = \alpha^{m'_1 + a_0 m'_2} (\bmod\, n)$
that is $m_1 + a_0 m_2 = m'_1 + a'_0 m'_2 (\bmod\, \beta)$
$(m_1 - m'_1) = a_0 (m_2 - m'_2)(\bmod\, \beta)$
because (m'_1, m'_2) is forged, in other words $(m_2 - m'_2)^{-1}$ exist.

$$a_0 = (m_1 - m'_1)(m_2 - m'_2)^{-1}(\bmod\, \beta)$$

Since a_0 is only known by TC, if the results are equal through TC inquiry, (m'_1, m'_2) is a forged signature.

5 Conclusion

In this paper, a smart grid privacy protection scheme is proposed. Through the above description, we can see that the security analysis meets the security requirements. This scheme uses a short fail-stop signature based on factorization and discrete logarithm assumption, which has higher security and practicability. The security analysis shows that the proposed scheme can verify the user's identity and protect privacy at the same time, and illustrates the non-reusability of payment credential. The advantage of short fail-stop signature is that even if a very strong third-party attacker forges a signature, it can also detect whether it is forged or not, and at the same time it will no longer use the signature mechanism [11], but ignores a possibility that the third party with malicious intent may be TC itself. In the future work, I will consider privacy protection from a decentralized perspective in combination with blockchain technology.

Acknowledgments. This paper is supported by the R&D Project Plan in Key Field of Guangdong Province with Project No. 2019B020215004, National Key R&D Plan, Project No. 2018YFB0803600.

References

1. Zhang, W., Liu, Z., Wang, M., et al.: Research status and development trend of smart grid. Power Syst. Technol. **13**(4) (2009)
2. Chen, L., Enzmann, M., Sadeghi, A.-R., Schneider, M., Steiner, M.: A privacy-protecting coupon system. In: Patrick, A.S., Yung, M. (eds.) FC 2005. LNCS, vol. 3570, pp. 93–108. Springer, Heidelberg (2005). https://doi.org/10.1007/11507840_12

3. Dimitriou, T., Karame, K.: Enabling anonymous authorization and rewarding in the smart grid. IEEE Trans. Dependable Secure Comput. **14**(5), 565–572 (2017)
4. Dimitriou, T., Karame, K.: Privacy-friendly tasking and trading of energy in smart grids. ACM Symp. Appl. Comput. **21**(6), 652–659 (2013)
5. Zhao, J., Liu, J., Qin, Z., et al.: Privacy protection scheme based on remote anonymous attestation for trusted smart meters. IEEE Trans. Smart Grid **9**(4), 3313–3320 (2016)
6. Yang, J.H., Chang, Y.F., Chen, Y.H.: An efficient authenticated encryption scheme based on ECC and its application for electronic payment. Inf. Technol. Control **42**(4), 315–324 (2013)
7. Jeske, T.: Privacy-preserving smart metering without a trusted-thirdparty. In: Proceedings of the International Conference on Security and Cryptography, vol. 6585, no. 1, pp. 114–123 (2014)
8. Susilo, W.: Short fail-stop signature scheme based on factorization and discrete logarithm assumptions. Theoret. Comput. Sci. **410**(8–10), 736–744 (2009)
9. Yuan, Z., Xu, H., Han, H., et al.: Research of smart charging management system for electric vehicles based on wireless communication networks. In: 2012 IEEE 6th International Conference on Information and Automation for Sustainability (ICIAfS), pp. 242–247. IEEE (2012)
10. Stinson, D.R.: Cryptography Theory and Practice. CRC Press, London (1995)
11. Susilo, W., Safavi-Naini, R., Gysin, M., et al.: A new and efficient fail-stop signature scheme. Comput. J. **43**(5), 430–437 (2018)

Decentralized Authorization and Authentication Based on Consortium Blockchain

Ao Zhang$^{(\boxtimes)}$ and Xiaoying Bai$^{(\boxtimes)}$

Department of Computer Science and Technology, Tsinghua university,
Beijing, China
za17@mails.tsinghua.edu.cn, baixy@mail.tsinghua.edu.cn

Abstract. With the development of digital society, the number of Internet platforms increases rapidly and a huge amount of personal information is stored online. It is convenient for users to log in to all platforms with a common account. Third-party authorization protocols like OAuth 2.0 allow the delegation of access control to dedicated service providers. However, OAuth protocol follows the centralized approach to manage authorization and authentication information, which relies on a centralized party and makes it a target under attack. In practice, it is vulnerable to attacks like replay attack, cross-site request forgery (CSRF) attack, and so on. Also, the centralized party cannot provide customized access control for other platforms. To solve these problems, the paper proposes a consortium blockchain architecture and designs protocols for account management and distributed consensus. The paper discusses the potentials of the proposed approach to effectively address certain vulnerabilities in current OAuth-like authorization and authentication services with tolerable performance.

Keywords: Decentralized authorization and authentication ·
Consortium blockchain · Attribute-based access control model ·
Adapted PBFT protocol · OAuth-like protocol

1 Introduction

As technologies reshaping our life, more and more social activities are moving into the Internet. The number of Internet platforms increases rapidly and a large amount of personal data are collected and managed by large platforms, thus the access control system is extremely important to protect the security and privacy of user data. Traditional access control models can manage authorization and authentication in a standalone system. However, for the platforms, cross-platform data interaction becomes more frequent. For the users, a single account to manage data across all platforms is needed. OAuth protocol [4] was proposed to allow the delegation of access control to third-party platforms, which has been widely used in many platforms such as Google and Facebook. For example, we

© Springer Nature Singapore Pte Ltd. 2020
Z. Zheng et al. (Eds.): BlockSys 2019, CCIS 1156, pp. 267–272, 2020.
https://doi.org/10.1007/978-981-15-2777-7_22

can log in to other platforms using Google account and provide our avatar and nickname stored in Google. However, the third-party services are usually built on centralized authorization and authentication systems that are vulnerable to security risks from both internal and external attacks. First, the access control of a third-party platform depends on the large platform like Google, which means Google can pretend to be user and access data stored in the third-party platform. Second, insecure implementations of OAuth 2.0 may lead to replay attacks, impersonation attacks, CSRF attacks, and so on.

As the underlying technology of Bitcoin [6], Blockchain introduced a decentralized architecture so that every node in the network participates in the maintenance of a consensus ledger. Transactions recorded on the shared ledger are transparent to and validated by, every participant. In recent years, there are some attempts to build access control systems based on blockchain technology in various fields such as mobile phone [7], medical data protection [1], and IoT [3].

In counter to the vulnerabilities of a centralized authorization protocol, this paper proposes a blockchain-based authorization and authentication framework, using a consortium blockchain to replace the centralized database and to enhance system defensive capabilities with a consensus protocol for identity and authentication validation. The system follows the attribute-based access control (ABAC) model [5] and bases on the consortium blockchain architecture. The permitted nodes participating in the federation can: (1) share a ledger of user identities and privileges; (2) share the ledger for tracing authorization transactions; and (3) vote for the validation of users' identities and operation privileges. Compared with a traditional database, it strengthens data security with asymmetric cryptography and provides trust among different platforms. A consortium blockchain allows only licensed alliance members to participate in the network and consensus process. Because of the enhanced credibility of the participating nodes, it can take advantage of more efficient consensus algorithms and peer-to-peer data sharing mechanisms.

The main contributions of this paper are as follows: First, a consortium blockchain architecture designed for access control is proposed, which can provide security and trust between different platforms. Second, an adapted implementation for the attribute-based access control model is designed to be used in blockchain. Third, a prototype system is implemented and the preliminary experiment for performance and latency is evaluated.

2   Architecture Overview

Based on blockchain technology and the ABAC model, we propose a consortium blockchain architecture among federated nodes for third-party authorization and authentication. Figure 1 gives an overview of architecture design and workflow. Three roles are involved in the system. The client is the resource requester. It asks the resource owner for authorization and eventually requests the blockchain node to access the resource. The resource owner grants permission to access protected resources stored on the blockchain node. The proposed approach replaces

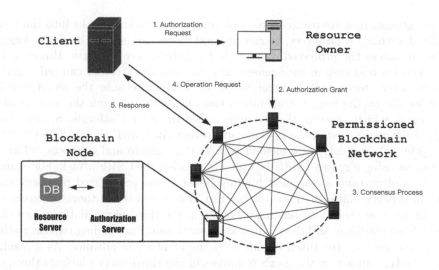

Fig. 1. The architecture of decentralized authorization and authentication

the centralized authentication server and resource server in the OAuth protocol with a consortium network. Each node in the network has equal status and participates in the storage of user authorization and authentication. The node is composed of a resource server and an authorization server. The resource server stores user resource with attributes and access control policy list, when the operation request received, the server can authenticate the attributes in the request using the access control policy list. The authorization servers manage the blockchain which stores the authorizations between users rather than transactions in cryptocurrency blockchain, and it can provide the attributes of each account for authentication in the resource server according to the blockchain. The whole process is mainly divided into five steps corresponding to the workflow in Fig. 1 and more details of each step are described in Sect. 3. The steps are as follows:

1. The client sends the *AuthorizationRequest* to the resource owner, which mainly contains the address of the client and the attributes to be authorized.
2. The resource owner verifies the *AuthorizationRequest* and sends the corresponding *AuthorizationGrant* to any blockchain node if it agrees.
3. If the received *AuthorizationGrant* is valid, the blockchain node will accept it and broadcast it in the network. After the consensus process, the authorization will be packaged into a new block and logged on the blockchain.
4. The client sends the *OperationRequest* with signature to the blockchain node which stores the resource it needs.
5. The resource server verifies the *OperationRequest* according to the attribute-based access control policy and replies to the client.

The system improves the security in centralized protocols like OAuth in several aspects. First, decentralized architecture can effectively reduce the severity of the attack. In a centralized protocol, once the attacker breaks into the centralized authorization server, he can pretend to be any user by issuing a forged token to access the protected resource in the third-party platform. However, in the decentralized system with consensus protocols, the attacker can only access the resource stored in the server which is broken. Because the secret key is kept locally by the user, the operation and authorization from the user cannot be forged, which protects the resource stored in other platforms. Second, the digital signature used in the system can prevent the CSRF attack. The OAuth-like protocol is widely implemented behind the website and connects different platforms using a redirected URL, which may bring the CSRF attack. For example, it is often used for account binding between the centralized platform and the third-party platform. The attacker can first access the authorized server to obtain an access token for binding accounts in the third-party platform and the centralized platform, and then induce the user to send the binding request to the client and provide the token obtained by the attacker in advance. As a result, the attacker can access the user's resources in the third-party platform through the account of the centralized platform. In our system, all authorizations and operations sent from the user need to be digitally signed, which can guarantee the source of the authorization. Third, the third-party platform sends the client secret to the centralized platform and retrieves the access token which makes it possible for the attacker to listen and replay the request to get the access token. In our system, there is no centralized platform to manage secret values for other platforms and every platform can get authorization directly from the user.

3   Protocol Design

This part describes the details in the system including the data structures in the blockchain, the attribute-based access control policy and the adapted PBFT protocol in the consensus process.

3.1   Blockchain Related Data Structure

In this system, we adopt the account state model from Ethereum rather than the UTXO model in Bitcoin, because the account state model is more suitable for the ABAC model. An account owns an address, a nonce value and several attributes. Each attribute has a name and a validity period. Once necessary, an account can authorize any of the attributes to another account, while the validity period of attributes authorized cannot exceed the original one. The authorization from an account to another contains the addresses of two accounts and the attributes authorized. Blockchain is the fundamental data structure used in our system to store authorizations. According to the authorizations stored in the blockchain, we can calculate the state of each account containing the address, the nonce, and the attributes under the account. The state is saved in memory and can be used to validate authorizations or operations from this account. As for the nonce value in the account state, it inits as 0 and increases by one when one authorization from the account is recorded on the blockchain. Any authorization with mismatched nonce value will be rejected. This can prevent the replay attack because once the authorization recorded on the blockchain, it cannot be accepted again due to the increased nonce value.

3.2   Attribute-Based Access Control Policy

This system is based on the Attribute-Based Access Control (ABAC) model, which defines four kinds of attributes: object attributes, subject attributes, operation attributes, and environment attributes. The resource server authenticates operation with these attributes according to the ABAC policy list. Each policy in the list contains four kinds of attributes and if the operation matches any one of them, it can pass the authentication. The object attributes are the attributes of the resource stored in the resource server. The subject attributes are attributes of account derived from the blockchain among authorization servers. The operation attributes are the operation type defined by the node. The environment attribute is the timestamp in the operation.

3.3   Adapted PBFT Algorithm

In the traditional distributed consensus domain such as database, researchers have proposed various consensus algorithms to ensure the consistency of data among distributed nodes and provide Byzantine Fault Tolerance (BFT) feature. The widely used BFT protocol is Practical Byzantine Fault Tolerance (PBFT) [2] proposed in 1999. We use an adapted PBFT algorithm in the access control system to help nodes maintain the same authorization ledger. The differences are as follows. The primary node in the PBFT protocol starts a new consensus process when it receives a request from the client. In our system, it starts a new consensus process in a solid interval and packages authorizations into a new block. In PBFT, view change happens when backup nodes find that the primary node seems to break down or be hacked. Beyond that, when it is long enough, nodes in our system also carry out a view change. This can prevent the malicious primary node to exclude some valid authorizations.

4   Prototype Implementation and Preliminary Experiment

We implement a prototype system to verify the feasibility of the designed framework and protocol and evaluate its performance and latency. The system is coded in the Go programming language. The resource server stores protected resources in MongoDB. In the blockchain network, communication among nodes is implemented using HTTP. The system mainly contains the client and the blockchain node. The client is used for users to manage their accounts, authorizations, and operations. The client interacts with the blockchain node after generating the operations and authorizations. The blockchain node contains an authorization server and a resource server: The authorization servers among nodes in the network maintain the same blockchain storing authorizations between clients with PBFT protocol. The resource manages the database according to the local ABAC policy list and consensus result from the authorization server. The authorization state of accounts among all nodes are the same while the databases are different.

To evaluate the performance of this system, we implement the prototype system and deploy 4 blockchain nodes on the Microsoft Azure cloud platform. Each server is a standard D2s v3 machine, with 2 vCPU, 2G memory, and 1,000 MBps bandwidth. A new block is generated every 2 s, and each block contains at most 1000 authorizations. In the test cases, 1000 pairs of keys are generated to simulate 1000 users with different attributes, then 10000 random authorizations are generated and sent to the four blockchain nodes at the speed of 500 authorizations per second, and the servers successfully process these requests in about 21 s. The result shows that the system reached the performance of about 500 TPS (transactions per second) and the latency is 1.2 s on average.

5 Summary and Conclusion

The paper proposes a decentralized access control framework based on a consortium blockchain, following the attribute-based access control model. The framework uses the asymmetric cryptosystem, which aims to enhance the security of OAuth-like protocols in many aspects, such as data transmission and storage. The authorization server in OAuth protocol is replaced by the decentralized consortium blockchain system, where authorizations are maintained by multiple nodes using PBFT consensus protocol. A preliminary experiment on the prototype system shows that it provides a promising solution with acceptable performance for access control.

References

1. Azaria, A., Ekblaw, A., Vieira, T., Lippman, A.: Medrec: using blockchain for medical data access and permission management. In: 2016 2nd International Conference on Open and Big Data (OBD), pp. 25–30. IEEE (2016)
2. Castro, M., Liskov, B., et al.: Practical byzantine fault tolerance. In: OSDI, vol. 99, pp. 173–186 (1999)
3. Ding, S., Cao, J., Li, C., Fan, K., Li, H.: A novel attribute-based access control scheme using blockchain for IoT. IEEE Access 7, 38431–38441 (2019)
4. Hardt, D.: The OAuth 2.0 Authorization Framework. RFC 6749, October 2012. https://doi.org/10.17487/RFC6749. https://rfc-editor.org/rfc/rfc6749.txt
5. Hu, V.C., et al.: Guide to attribute based access control (ABAC) definition and considerations (Draft). NIST Special Publication 800–162 (2013)
6. Nakamoto, S., et al.: Bitcoin: a peer-to-peer electronic cash system (2008). https://bitcoin.org/bitcoin.pdf
7. Zyskind, G., Nathan, O., et al.: Decentralizing privacy: using blockchain to protect personal data. In: 2015 IEEE Security and Privacy Workshops, pp. 180–184. IEEE (2015)

Blockchain and Cloud Computing

Reduce the Energy Cost of Elastic Clusters by Queueing Workloads with N-1 Queues

Cheng Hu[✉] and Mingdong Tang

School of Information Science and Technology, Guangdong University of Foreign Studies, Guangzhou 510006, China
huchengcs@gdufs.edu.cn, mdtang@gdufs.edu.cn

Abstract. In Data Centers (DCs), elastic clusters are introduced to cut down the huge energy cost. In elastic clusters, the number of working nodes can be manipulated based on the intensity of workloads. However, affected by the way of distributing workloads to working nodes, the required number of working nodes is different to meet the Service Level Agreement (SLA) of workloads. Workloads consist of several requests which come from clients. In general, workloads are queued and served with N-N queues. The first N means that multiple requests can be queued in the service queue maintained by cluster managers. In addition, the second N means that the service queue of each working node can also queue multiple requests. With N-N queues, requests are first received to the service queue maintained by cluster managers, and then are distributed to appropriate service queues of working nodes. According to queueing theory, a fact is that the service efficiency of N-N queues is lower than that of N-1 queues. Here, N-1 queues mean that the service queue maintained by cluster managers can queue multiple requests, while no request is allowed to be queued in working nodes. Motivated by this fact, we propose an N-1 queueing method to make all service queues work in the form of N-1 queues. Thus under same workloads, fewer working nodes are required to meet a same SLA. As a result, without suffering performance degradation, the energy cost of an elastic cluster can be significantly reduced.

Keywords: Elastic clusters · Energy saving · Service efficiency promotion · System performance promotion · Service queues

1 Introduction

In contemporary DCs, the expensive energy cost has become a big challenge. Not only a massive capital is consumed for electricity supply, but also the high electricity usage brings serious environmental pollution [9,20]. To cut down the huge energy cost of DCs, elastic clusters are introduced. An elastic cluster allows the number of working nodes to be dynamically geared. Thus, only partial nodes

© Springer Nature Singapore Pte Ltd. 2020
Z. Zheng et al. (Eds.): BlockSys 2019, CCIS 1156, pp. 275–287, 2020.
https://doi.org/10.1007/978-981-15-2777-7_23

keep working, and other nodes are maintained at a low power state for energy saving.

In general, a traditional cluster system [1, 3, 4] can be considered as a two-tier structure, where the first tier is a manager (or several managers for large-scale systems), and the second tier are working nodes. Because the manager and the working nodes can both maintain a queue to accumulate requests which form system workloads, the requests are generally queued and served with N-N queues. N-N queues mean that requests can be accumulated in both of the tiers. However, according to queueing theory, the service efficiency of N-N queues is lower than that of N-1 queues. Different from N-N queues, N-1 queues only allow requests to be accumulated in the first tier, and requests can not be accumulated (only can be directly executed) in the second tier.

In this paper, we propose an N-1 queueing method to make the queues of the manager and working nodes follow the form of N-1 queues. Thus, the service efficiency can be promoted, and fewer working nodes are required to maintain a same SLA. Ultimately, the energy consumption can be further reduced with our method, while not incur performance degradation.

The main contributions of this paper are as follows:

1. We analyze the process of queueing and serving requests in elastic clusters. From the analysis, we show that the queueing structure of a traditional elastic cluster is two-tier N-N queues.
2. Leveraging queueing theory, we discuss the response time of requests in a traditional cluster system, by modeling the cluster as a queueing system. Then, we reveal that the service efficiency of N-N queues is lower than that of N-1 queues.
3. We propose the N-1 queueing method to make the queues of the manager and working nodes follow the form of N-1 queues. In addition, we integrate a Quality of Service (QoS) perceptible module into the method, in an effort to timely re-gear the number of working nodes thus fitting workloads.
4. To attest the effectiveness of our method, we perform comparison experiments in a simulated traditional elastic cluster. In the experiments, three other hand-picked methods along with our method are tested for comparison.

The rest of this paper is structured as follows. Section 2 discusses the related work. Section 3 introduces a traditional elastic cluster, and carries out an analysis on the process of queueing and serving requests in the cluster. In addition, leveraging queueing theory, this section reveals that the service efficiency can be promoted by replacing N-N queues with N-1 queues. Section 4 proposes the N-1 queueing method, so as to promote the service efficiency and further reduce the energy cost of traditional elastic clusters. Section 5 carries out the experimental evaluation to attest the effectiveness of our method. Finally, Sect. 6 concludes this paper.

2   Related Work

Elastic clusters are proposed by many researchers to dynamically gear the number of working nodes, thus cutting down the energy cost of DCs. Considering elastic computing resources in the form of virtual machine (VM) instances to run jobs, Xu et al. [19] propose a heterogeneity and interference-aware VM provisioning framework, Heifer, to provision fitting VM instances for achieving predictable performance for tenant applications. Heifer can predict the performance of MapReduce applications by a lightweight performance model which regards both the online-measured resource utilization and VM interference. With extensive prototype experiments, they show that Heifer can guarantee the job performance while saving the job budget for tenants. In other words, the computing resources, i.e., the energy cost for a same workload is saved. Smart et al. [17] focus on reducing storage drive energy consumption in DCs. They optimise drive energy consumption within a custom built storage cluster which contains multiple drives, using multi-objective goal attainment algorithm to optimally assign individual commands to drives in order to achieve minimal command energy usage at the storage cluster level. Because the power of storage drives is low when drives are idle, no extra operation is needed to gear the number of working drives. How many and which drives should work depend on how many and which drives are assigned commands. Hameed et al. [6] refer several resource allocation studies and point out that a scalable design to support on-demand resource allocation is an efficient way to improve system energy efficiency and save system energy cost. They show that no matter adopting what manner, the goal is to provide suitable resources which match the demand of workloads. To achieve the goal, many methods can be used, such as resource allocation adaption policy, objective function and so on.

In elastic clusters, the fewer service resources are provided, the more energy is saved. However, a premise should be satisfied is that the provided service resources should meet the demand of workload, thus the quality of service can be guaranteed. Therefore, if the service efficiency can be promoted, more energy can be saved due to the reduction of the workload requirement on service resources. To promote the service efficiency, lots of efforts are made by several researchers. Lu et al. [13,14] notice that the bursts of workloads can greatly increase the system burden, so they propose a method to deal with the bursts and promote the system service efficiency on the bursts. In their method, the workloads in the bursts are first decomposed, by extracting the I/O requests which are out of the service limit from the workloads. Then, the extracted requests are postponed, and finally recombined into later workloads when slack exist. However, their method does nothing for normal workloads, in other words, the service efficiency on normal workloads is still the same with no promotion. Mardukhi et al. [15] use a genetic algorithm to select the optimal service for each task. Their algorithm can decompose the global constraints into the local constraints, and finally can select the optimal service through a simple linear search. As a result, the computation time can be greatly reduced. Because each task is optimally assigned, this work can promote the service efficiency for all tasks.

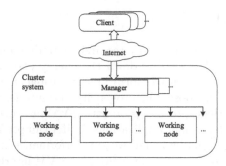

Fig. 1. The two-tier structure of a traditional cluster.

Zhang et al. [22] propose a service curve-based QoS algorithm to support three types of applications at a same storage system. Specifically, three scheduling queues with different priorities are adopted to schedule the I/O requests in latency guarantee applications, IOPS guarantee applications and best-effort applications. By using a service curve-based QoS algorithm, the scheduling can take account of the urgency status of I/O requests. Besides, to avoid failures of QoS targets, their algorithm can reschedule certain requests in the fairness queue, by migrating them to other appropriate queue.

3   System Architecture and Analysis

A traditional cluster system can be considered as a two-tier structure. As shown in Fig. 1, the first tier contains several managers, and the second tier contains plenty of working nodes. The system workloads are formed by the requests sent from clients via Internet. The system workloads are first received and accumulated by the managers, at the same time, the managers distribute the workloads to appropriate working nodes with specific mode, for example, a round-robin mode. In general, the requests are queued in a First In First Out (FIFO) way when they are accumulated, and they are evenly distributed to working nodes. Therefore, no matter how many managers a cluster system has, we can regard that only one queue is maintained by the managers.

The procedure of receiving requests and serving requests can be modeled as a queueing system, which works with the fashion of multiple single-server queues, i.e., the N-N queues as previously mentioned. To give an intuitive analysis, we assume that the arrival rate (λ) of requests is 400 per second, the mean service time (T_s) of a request is 2 ms. In addition there are 4 working nodes, each of which works follow an M/M/1 single-server queue (refer the study [10] for details). With this assumption, we can theoretically calculate the mean waiting time of requests by leveraging queueing theory, and the result is 5×10^{-4} s.

While, if the working nodes are not allowed to accumulate requests, the procedure can be modeled as another queueing system. This queueing system

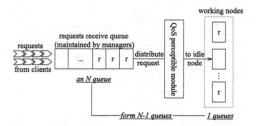

Fig. 2. The diagram of the N-1 queueing method.

works in the form of the N-1 queues, which belong to a fashion of M/M/N multi-server queues (refer the online chapters—Chapter 20 of the literature [18] for details). We can also theoretically calculate the mean waiting time of requests, and the result is 8.85×10^{-6} s. Even the number of working nodes is reduced to 2, the result is 3.8×10^{-4} s. Therefore, with the same hardware conditions and the same workloads, the service efficiency of N-1 queues is much higher than that of N-N queues. In other words, with N-1 queues, fewer working nodes are required to maintain a same SLA.

4   Method Implementation

Inspired by the above analysis, we propose an N-1 queueing method to make the involved queues follow the form of N-1 queues, expecting to further reduce the energy cost of elastic clusters. The key of changing N-N queues to N-1 queues is to restrict the working nodes to directly execute requests without accumulating. Therefore, for an elastic cluster, the N-1 queueing method is implemented in managers. Specifically, requests are first received by managers, and managers each time distribute a request to a working node which is idle (that is no request is being executed in the node). If all the working nodes are not idle, managers accumulate new arrival requests and keep tracing the state of working nodes. In this way, the traditional N-N queues of an elastic clusters are transformed to N-1 queues.

We present a diagram in Fig. 2 to clarify the process of the method. As shown, a restriction is made to forbid the working nodes from accumulating requests (the letter 'r' in the figure denotes a request), thus the N queue maintained by managers and the 1 queues of the working nodes together constitute a form of N-1 queues. In addition, a QoS perceptible module is integrated, which is used to monitor the QoS of the cluster. Because waiting time is a customary criterion of system QoS [2,7,12], we set an SLA that the maximum waiting time of a request can not be higher than a expected value WT_E. If the QoS tends to be lower or much higher than such SLA, the QoS perceptible module notifies managers to re-gear the number of working nodes thus fitting the coming workloads.

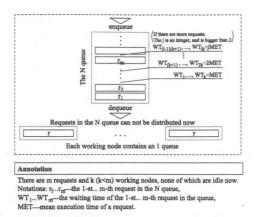

Fig. 3. The implementation of the QoS perceptible module.

To clarify how the QoS perceptible module is implemented, an illustration is provided in Fig. 3. The module is activated when the requests in the N queue can not be distributed, due to the reason that none of working nodes are idle. As shown in the figure, if the mean execution time of a request is MET, after approximately a time span of MET, all requests in the working nodes are finished. Then, the next k requests in the N queue can be distributed, and are executed immediately. Therefore, the waiting times of the 1-st to the k-th requests in the N queue are the same, and are approximately equal to MET, i.e.,

$$WT_1, ..., WT_k \approx MET.$$

Similarly,

$$WT_{(k+1)}, ..., WT_{2k} \approx 2MET,$$

and if there are more requests,

$$WT_{(j-1)(k+1)}, ..., WT_{jk} \approx jMET,$$

where j is an integer which is bigger than 2. Consequently, the waiting time of the last request in the N queue (it is the m-th request in the figure) can be approximately calculated, that is

$$WT_m = \lceil m/k \rceil \times MET.$$

If $WT_m > WT_E$ or $WT_m < 20\% \times WT_E$, it means that the QoS tends to be poorer than or much superior to the expected SLA. The former case indicates that the provided working nodes are insufficient to fulfill the SLA, the latter case indicates that surplus working nodes are provided. Accordingly, the QoS perceptible module notifies managers to re-gear (increase or decrease) the number of working nodes thus fitting the coming workloads.

5   Experimental Evaluation

5.1   Experiment Setup

The analysis made in Sect. 3 is based on queueing theory, and assumes that the distributions of the inter-arrival times and service times follow a negative exponential distribution. In practical situations, the distributions may be more complicated, but our N-1 queueing method can still play a role in promoting system performance and reducing system energy cost. The effectiveness of our method is tested with a simulator which simulates a traditional elastic cluster. The involved simulation parameters of the cluster are set according to the real results measured by Zhang et al. [21] on a typical cluster node. Concretely, these parameters include the power of a working node in different states, the time delay and energy consumption of switching a working node to a low power state (or vice versa). If necessary, please refer our previous work [8] for the details of these parameters.

The system workloads are produced by replaying a real-world network file system trace—deasna2[1], and only the daytime record in weekdays are used. In addition, the number of working nodes is manipulated in a reactive gradually adjusting way, i.e., adding or reducing one working node a time when detecting that the system performance is deficient or surplus. In addition, the frequency of manipulating the number of working nodes is limited in the EN-N method introduced below, thus reducing the time and energy penalty [8] from resource adjustment. An SLA is set that the maximum waiting time of a request no larger than $0.1\,s$ which are a widely used value [9], such as online games [16]. Accordingly, if any of the actual waiting times exceeds $0.1\,s$, the current system performance is considered to be deficient. Otherwise, if the mean value of all response times is lower than $0.1 \times 20\%$, namely $0.02\,s$, the system performance is considered to be surplus.

For comparison, besides our method, three other hand-picked methods are also tested. All the methods including ours are summarized as follows.

- **Baseline**: The baseline method works in the traditional way with N-N queues. To sufficiently utilize the capacity working nodes, each time a request is distributed to the working node whose queue length is the shortest. In addition, considering that it is hard to maintain the response time of each request meet the SLA, if the SLA of more than 98% requests can be maintained, the system will not be considered to be deficient. When current system performance is considered to be deficient or surplus as we discussed in the previous paragraph, this method immediately re-gear the number of working nodes.
- **EN-N**: The Energy-saving N-N queueing (EN-N) method works like the baseline method, but the timing for it re-gearing the number of working nodes is different. In order to restrain the energy penalty brought by resource scaling [8], EN-N performs a resource scaling operation every $30\,s$, and $30\,s$ are a practical value adopted in the studies [5,11]. Specifically, every time span of

---

[1] Please visit http://iotta.snia.org/traces/3378 for the details of deasna2.

30 s, EN-N calculates the mean waiting time of the requests which are finished during the time span. If the mean waiting time is higher than 0.1 s or lower than 0.02 s, this method re-gears the number of working nodes. Due to the use of the mean waiting time, a small number of violations of the SLA are allowed in this method. As a result, this method can save more energy than the baseline method.

- **N-N²**: In this method [13,14], each working node maintains two-level N queues. Between the two queues, the high level queue's priority is higher than that of the low level one. In normality that the waiting time of accumulated requests will not violate the SLA, only the high level queue is used. Otherwise, the length of the high level queue is limited to $\lfloor WT_E/MET \rfloor$, and the low level queue is used to receive the excess requests. Because there are two N queues in each node, this method is abbreviated as N-N². The N-N² method can mitigate the service congestion, and to some extent promote the system QoS under heavy workloads. Its timing when to re-gear the number of working nodes is the same as that of the baseline method.

- **N-1**: This method is the N-1 queueing (abbreviated as N-1) method we proposed in this paper. Due to the form of N-1 queues to handle requests, N-1 in theory can achieve a better efficiency than other methods. As a consequence, compared with other methods, N-1 tends to meet a same SLA with fewer working nodes. Actually, the following experimental results indicate that the reality is consistent with the theoretic inference.

To perform experiments efficiently, the above three methods along with our method, N-1, are concurrently tested, using an arbitrarily sliced one-hour trace segment. In addition, such test is repeated 10 times, and each time another arbitrarily sliced one-hour trace segment is used. Finally, a comprehensive experimental data are presented. In fact, similar results are observed for these concurrent tests.

5.2 Experimental Results

Request Waiting Time. Considering the huge number of requests, we present the mean waiting time of the requests finished in each time period. The time length of each time period is 10 s. As shown in Fig. 4, there are four subfigures, each of which corresponds to one method. In each subfigure, the lower diagram use the large scale to show a entire result. While the WT_E set in the SLA is 0.1 s, so we also present the upper diagram with an enlarged scale. In addition, in the top right corner, the average response time of all requests (overall average value) is shown with a rectangular border.

As shown in the figure, the mean waiting times greatly fluctuate for all the methods, and it is hard to find out which method is better. An intuitive observation is that the overall fluctuation for our method (N-1) is the smallest. According to the overall average values, N-N² achieves the lowest value. This is because N-N² can, to a certain extent, moderate the workload jam [13,14]. The second best is our method, and the third is the Baseline. But the overall average values

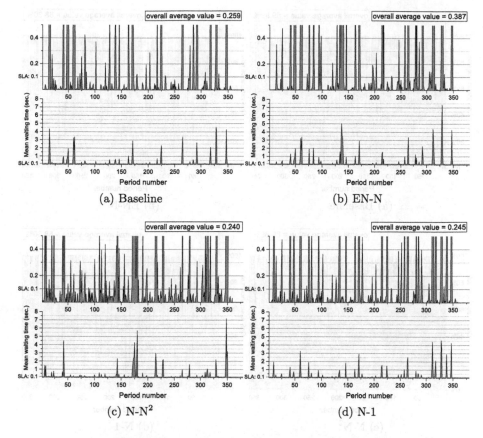

Fig. 4. Experimental results of waiting times.

of the three methods are very close. This indicates that all the three method can maintain a acceptable system QoS. However, the value for EN-N is about 54% higher than the other methods. For each method, there are several time periods in which the SLA is not satisfied. The reason is that, a time delay is needed to scale resources [8], and the resource demand of requests cannot be timely met. The situation of EN-N is the worst, for it uses a mean waiting time to reflect current QoS, and the time span of calculating the mean value and scaling resources is long.

QoS Assurance Rate. To further explore the service efficiency of each method, we present Fig. 5 to show the QoS assurance rates. The QoS assurance shows the percentage of requests whose response time satisfies the SLA. The diagrams are also plotted with the X axis represent the sequence number of each time period. As shown, for all the methods, the rate is higher than 90% in most time periods. While, for the N-N, EN-N and N-1 methods, the rate can drop below 40% in few time periods. This is caused by the sudden burst of workloads,

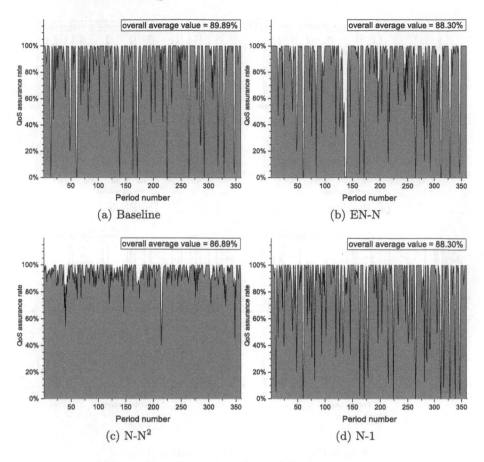

Fig. 5. Experimental results of QoS assurance rate.

and in the burst cannot be timely handled due to the time delay of scaling resources. By comparison, the N-N^2 method maintains a superior rate, that the rate is always higher than 40%. The reason is that, N-N^2 [13,14] can promote the service efficiency on busty workloads, by leveraging the two-level N queues in servers. As a result, N-N^2 provides a good QoS for majority requests, rather than drawing down the overall QoS. The overall average QoS assurance rates of all the methods are similar. Specifically, the baseline achieves the best result 89.89%, that values of N-1 and EN-N are the same at 88.3%, that value of N-N^2 is the lowest 86.89%. The reason for the worst result of N-N^2 is that, N-N^2 delays partial requests to maintain a good QoS for majority requests. This is useful in some scenarios, that N-N^2 can be used to guarantee the QoS of critical requests.

Energy-Saving Efficiency. The experimental results of energy consumption for each method are shown in Fig. 6. Each subfigure corresponds to one method, and the results are also shown for each time period. Besides, the total energy

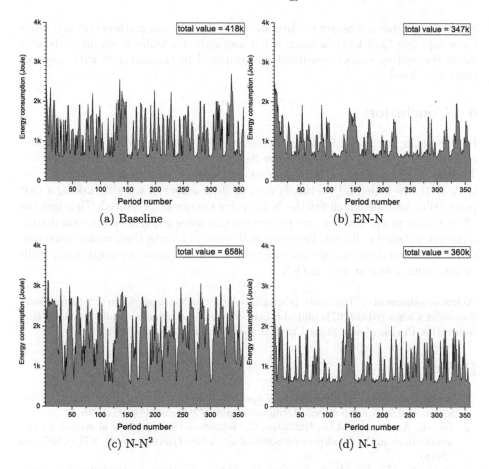

Fig. 6. Experimental results of system energy consumption.

consumption is shown in the top right corner with a rectangular border. As shown, the energy consumption greatly fluctuate with the variation of workload intensity. According to the total value, N-N^2 consumes the most energy. This reveals that more resources are needed to mitigate the influence of workload burst. While, other methods is indifferent to the workload burst, except scaling service resources. Accordingly, compared with N-N^2, the energy consumption of the other three methods are much lower, and the values are about 50% that of N-N^2. The energy consumption of EN-N is the lowest, on account of that EN-N uses a long time span to scale resources. In such way, EN-N restrains the energy penalty brought by resource scaling. Our method, N-1, consumes the second lowest energy, and the value is very close to that of EN-N. In addition, compared with the baseline, our method further reduced the energy cost by 13.88%.

With a comprehensive consideration on both the QoS and energy consumption, the experimental results indicate that, in contrast with other methods, our method can achieve a better performance. Specifically, our method still maintains an acceptable QoS level as some other methods do, while it significantly cuts down the system energy consumption compared to the methods with approximate QoS level.

6 Conclusion

In this paper, we reveal that the service efficiency of traditional elastic clusters can be improved by transforming the N-N service queues to N-1 service queues. Therefore, we propose an N-1 queueing method to implement this transformation. In the N-1 method, to timely re-gear the number of working nodes, a QoS perceptible module which fits the N-1 service queues is integrated. To attest the effectiveness of our method, we performed extensive experiments by simulating a traditional elastic cluster. Experimental results indicate that, under same conditions, our method can significantly cut down the system energy cost, while maintaining a similar system QoS.

Acknowledgments. This work is supported by the National Natural Science Foundation of China (61976061), and the School-level Characteristics and Technological Innovation Project, Guangdong University of Foreign Studies (18TS21).

References

1. Anagnostopoulos, I., Zeadally, S., Exposito, E.: Handling big data: research challenges and future directions. J. Supercomput. **72**(4), 1494–1516 (2016)
2. Biondi, A., Natale, M.D., Buttazzo, G.: Response-time analysis of engine control applications under fixed-priority scheduling. IEEE Trans. Comput. **67**(5), 687–703 (2018)
3. Deng, Y., Hu, Y., Meng, X., Zhu, Y., Zhang, Z., Han, J.: Predictively booting nodes to minimize performance degradation of a power-aware web cluster. Cluster Comput. **17**(4), 1309–1322 (2014)
4. Detti, A., Bracciale, L., Loreti, P., Rossi, G., Melazzi, N.B.: A cluster-based scalable router for information centric networks. Comput. Netw. **142**, 24–32 (2018)
5. Entrialgo, J., Medrano, R., García, D.F., García, J.: Autonomic power management with self-healing in server clusters under qos constraints. Computing **98**(9), 871–894 (2016)
6. Hameed, A., Khoshkbarforoushha, A., Ranjan, R., Jayaraman, P.P., Kolodziej, J., Balaji, P., Zeadally, S., Malluhi, Q.M., Tziritas, N., Vishnu, A., Khan, S.U., Zomaya, A.: A survey and taxonomy on energy efficient resource allocation techniques for cloud computing systems. Computing **98**(7), 751–774 (2016)
7. Hu, C., Deng, Y.: Fast resource scaling in elastic clusters with an agile method for demand estimation. Sustain. Comput. Inf. Syst. **19**, 165–173 (2018)
8. Hu, C., Deng, Y.: Aggregating correlated cold data to minimize the performance degradation and power consumption of cold storage nodes. J. Supercomput. **75**(2), 662–687 (2019)
9. Hu, C., Deng, Y., Min, G., Huang, P., Qin, X.: Qos promotion in energy-efficient datacenters through peak load scheduling. IEEE Trans. Cloud Comput. (2018). https://doi.org/10.1109/TCC.2018.2886187,

10. Hu, C., Deng, Y., Yang, L.T., Zhao, Y.: Estimating the resource demand in power-aware clusters by regressing a linearly dependent relation. IEEE Trans. Sustain. Comput. (2019). https://doi.org/10.1109/TSUSC.2019.2894708
11. Iritani, M., Yokota, H.: Effects on performance and energy reduction by file relocation based on file-access correlations. In: Proceedings of the 2012 Joint EDBT/ICDT Workshops, EDBT-ICDT 2012, pp. 79–86. ACM (2012)
12. Krioukov, A., Mohan, P., Alspaugh, S., Keys, L., Culler, D., Katz, R.: NapSAC: design and implementation of a power-proportional web cluster. ACM SIGCOMM Comput. Commun. Rev. **41**(1), 102–108 (2011)
13. Lu, L., Varman, P., Doshi, K.: Graduated QoS by decomposing bursts: don't let the tail wag your server. In: Proceedings of the 2009 29th IEEE International Conference on Distributed Computing Systems, ICDCS 2009, pp. 12–21. IEEE Computer Society, Washington, DC (2009)
14. Lu, L., Varman, P.J., Doshi, K.: Decomposing workload bursts for efficient storage resource management. IEEE Trans. Parallel Distrib. Syst. **22**(5), 860–873 (2011)
15. Mardukhi, F., NematBakhsh, N., Zamanifar, K., Barati, A.: Qos decomposition for service composition using genetic algorithm. Appl. Soft Comput. **13**(7), 3409–3421 (2013)
16. Messaoudi, F., Ksentini, A., Simon, G., Bertin, P.: Performance analysis of game engines on mobile and fixed devices. ACM Trans. Multimedia Comput. Commun. Appl. **13**(4), 57:1–57:28 (2017)
17. Smart, E., Brown, D.D.J., Borges, K.T., Granger-Brown, N.: Reducing energy usage in drive storage clusters through intelligent allocation of incoming commands. Appl. Soft Comput. **52**, 673–686 (2017)
18. Stallings, W.: Operating Systems: Internals and Design Principles, 9th edn. Pearson, Upper Saddle River (2017)
19. Xu, F., Liu, F., Jin, H.: Heterogeneity and interference-aware virtual machine provisioning for predictable performance in the cloud. IEEE Trans. Comput. **65**(8), 2470–2483 (2016)
20. Yang, L., Deng, Y., Yang, L.T., Lin, R.: Reducing the cooling power of data centers by intelligently assigning tasks. IEEE Internet Things J. **5**(3), 1667–1678 (2018)
21. Zhang, L., Deng, Y., Zhu, W., Zhou, J., Wang, F.: Skewly replicating hot data to construct a power-efficient storage cluster. J. Netw. Comput. Appl. **50**, 168–179 (2015)
22. Zhang, Y., Wei, Q., Chen, C., Xue, M., Yuan, X., Wang, C.: Dynamic scheduling with service curve for qos guarantee of large-scale cloud storage. IEEE Trans. Comput. **67**(4), 457–468 (2018)

An Anonymous Blockchain-Based Logging System for Cloud Computing

Ji-Yao Liu[1], Yun-Hua He[1,2(✉)], Chao Wang[1], Yan Hu[2,3], Hong Li[2], and Li-Min Sun[2]

[1] School of Information Science and Technology, North China University of Technology,
Beijing 100144, China
heyunhua610@163.com
[2] Beijing Key Laboratory of Internet of Things Security, Institute of Information Engineering,
CAS, Beijing 100093, China
[3] School of Computer and Communication Engineering, University of Science and Technology
Beijing, Beijing 100091, China

Abstract. Cloud computing has been in increasing concentration these years. Nevertheless, recently, it suffers the ambiguity in discerning responsibilities for unexpected incapable services. At this time, people refer to the logs. However, since logs may judge the fault, they are susceptible to malicious modification. Thus, their integrity is vital. Existing solutions leverage blockchain technology to tackle this problem, but few of them take the pseudo-anonymous nature of blockchain into considerations. This risks users' privacy when they anchor their logs onto the blockchain. Some solutions try to be anonymous, but they are not general enough to be practical. In this paper, we propose a blockchain-based anonymous logging system for cloud environment. Our system introduces zero-knowledge proof to realize anonymous authentication, which can ensure undeniability in auditing while doing no harm to anonymity. Through experimental evaluation, we evaluate the feasibility and anonymity of the proposed system.

Keywords: Log · Cloud computing · Blockchain · Zk-SNARKs · Anonymity

1 Introduction

These years, an increasing number of companies tend to utilize cloud computing, but the adoption towards it encounters some problems [1]. Cloud computing scheme offers less expense and easier maintenance compared with traditional solutions, but some issues occur due to users' indirect control over physical assets. One of them is the ambiguity in responsibilities for the discrepancy between agreements and actual performances. When such problems emerge, people refer to the logs. By analyzing the logs, they can find which of them, the user, or the Cloud Service Provider (CSP), is to blame. As the logs may decide the responsibility, persons who are guilty and have access to the logs, such as the CSPs in some situations, may tamper them to prevent lawsuits.

Present solutions use blockchain technology to help because of its tamper-proofing character [2–5]. Blockchain is a distributed ledger shared by a peer-to-peer (P2P) network, each node in which keeps a complete copy of it. According to some mechanisms,

© Springer Nature Singapore Pte Ltd. 2020
Z. Zheng et al. (Eds.): BlockSys 2019, CCIS 1156, pp. 288–301, 2020.
https://doi.org/10.1007/978-981-15-2777-7_24

usually the Proof of Work (PoW) scheme, all nodes may acquire the right to append a block to it. Thus, anyone who attempts to alter transactions written on it must control more than half of the computational ability in this P2P network, which is deemed quite challenging to achieve. Therefore, blockchain can help to construct tamper-resistant logging in many areas.

For logging in cloud computing, hashed logs stored on a blockchain prevent modification to them, but the deficiency of blockchain in anonymity potentially incurs privacy leakage. An invariant public-key can link all transactions of a user, leading to the unmasking of his access pattern, such as the distribution of requests at different times of a day. Attacks of de-anonymization aimed at such public-keys are not rare [6, 7]. Many researchers [2–4] ignore this problem while taking advantage of blockchain. Some researchers [5] realize this issue, but their solution is limited. They anonymize users by the group signature technology. However, choosing such a group is usually not practical among companies, which means there is no anonymity at the company level. Furthermore, it needs three Trusted Third Parties (TTPs), including a Certification Authority (CA), a Provenance Auditor (PA), and a Group Manager (GM). Thus, present solutions are still not satisfactory in privacy.

There is an apt tool to counter this problem—zk-SNARK [8, 9]. It is a kind of zero-knowledge proof with two useful characters. Firstly, anyone who holds both a proof and the corresponding verifying key generated by it can examine zero-knowledge statements announced by a prover without any interaction to him. Besides, both the verifying key and the proof are short enough to be published onto blockchain. With these two advantages, users can prove their identities with variant identifiers so that they can publish transactions anonymously. The only question is that it depends on a public parameter for security. Nonetheless, as demonstrated by ZeroCash [10], it may disturb in other applications, but is not a problem for blockchain. The reason is that blockchain itself is an ideal generator for such parameters.

Zk-SNARKs have been wildly used and proven powerful since it was designed. In the field of blockchain, crypto-currencies and smart contracts utilize it to enhance anonymity, such as ZeroCash and PrC [11]. In cloud computing, they are adopted to verifiable computing, like CCZK [12]. Nevertheless, there is currently no exploration of its usage of enhancing privacy in logging systems for cloud computing. However, there are two obstacles to apply it to logging systems in cloud environment. Firstly, if we directly apply the scheme proposed by crypto-currencies, CSPs may be able to deny logs recorded by them. Then, zk-SNARKs can be time-consuming. For instance, ZeroCash requires more than 5 min to generate a proof. As a slight modification in zero-knowledge statements can significantly change the whole workflow of our system, including the security of undeniability and the way users and CSPs interact, these two problems require an elaborated systematical design to integrate zk-SNARKs, on which we spend a lot of time. Except for applying zk-SNARKs, eliminating TTPs can also fundamentally remolds our design. To counter the three difficulties, we orchestrate the components and workflow in our system.

In this paper, we propose an anonymous logging system for cloud environment. We leverage zk-SNARKs to modify the traditional logging system so that we can realize undeniability while achieving anonymity. To make our system efficient, we employ a systematical design to reduce both computational and storage consumption brought by zk-SNARKs. For one thing, to reduce computation, we limit the zero-knowledge statements so as to reduce the generation time of the proof key in zk-SNARKs. For another thing, we replace validation transactions by digital signatures to alleviate the storage burden on blockchain. Besides, we delete TTPs from our system and redesign the way users and CSPs interact in order to relieve the risk of privacy leakage. We summarize our contributions in three aspects:

- We systematically design a logging system incorporating zk-SNAKRs for cloud environment, which achieves anonymity for such systems.
- We compose efficient zero-knowledge statements in zk-SNARKs and change the workflow of our system to ensure undeniability in auditing while doing no harm to anonymity.
- We evaluate our system in terms of anonymity, computation and storage consumption, and analyze the reason for the discrepancy among the anonymity performances of current systems and our system.

We organize our paper as follows. Section 2 reviews the present model and shows its shortage of anonymity. Then, we introduce the workflow of our system in Sect. 3. Detailed discussions about the realization of anonymity and undeniability are in part 4. Evaluations of the feasibility of our system and anonymity in three systems, including ours, are available in Sect. 5. Finally, in Sect. 6, we draw our conclusions.

2 Current Systems and Threat Model

In this section, we review the current system model and present the threat model. In the first part, we examine the current model of logging systems that ignores anonymity while incorporating blockchain. After that, we show how attackers undermine users' privacy in current systems.

2.1 Logging System Model in Cloud Environment

As shown in Fig. 1, in the current model, designers do not take anonymity into considerations, so they use the ordinary public chain. In such systems, users and CSPs record transactions directly on the blockchain via constant public-keys, leading to potential threats in privacy. Concretely, when a CSP sends a transaction to the blockchain that contains a hash of logs together with his public-key, the network accepts this transaction, seals it, and adds a timestamp. Then, the user validates that transaction in the same way. In this process, public-keys, timestamps, and transaction types are all in plaintext, so analyzers can categorize them easily. ProvChain1 is a typical system that follows this model.

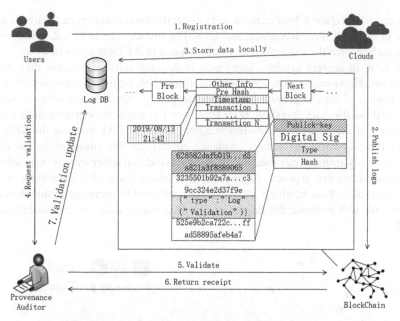

Fig. 1. Traditional logging system in cloud environment.

2.2 Threat Model

Attackers can learn a bundle of information in the current model by simply collecting public-keys on the blockchains [16], such as those shown in Table 1. Through experiments, we find that more than 55% of information is leaked when there is no anonymity method in the blockchains, such as ProvChain.

Table 1. Information Extracted from Blockchain

Public-key	Cloud	Timestamp of records	Timestamp of validations
k1	c1	2019/08/08 11:14	20190/8/08 11:16
k1	c1	2019/08/08 11:16	2019/08/08 11:18
k1	c1	2019/08/08 11:24	2019/08/08 11:30
k1	c2	2019/08/09 10:18	2019/08/09 10:22
k2	c2	2019/08/13 22:16	2019/08/13 22:18
k2	c3	2019/08/15 23:44	2019/08/15 23:46
k3	c1	2019/08/10 16:36	2019/08/10 16:40

An attacker can build the topology of services by utilizing the information published on a blockchain [6, 7], as shown in Fig. 2. Each line between a user and a CSP represents their user-server relation. Furthermore, as to a specific user, attackers can learn his access pattern in terms of time, frequency, and CPS. For instance, as in Fig. 2, attackers may learn which service the example user would request at different times of a day.

Till now, in current systems, users may leak some information, but they are still anonymous. However, in practice, they absolutely risk being de-anonymized. People record hashes of logs to prevent them from tampering. Nevertheless, once it happens, people will use them for litigation. If so, they have to submit those transactions together with their real identities to a Law-Enforcement Agent (LEA), because the LEA must connect their identities with those evidence strictly. In this situation, in the current model, not only transactions used are de-anonymized, but other transactions using the same public-keys are exposed. Finally, attackers may learn all transactions of a de-anonymized user. That is, all his activities are published to everyone in the blockchain network. We will evaluate the impact of revealed transactions on unrevealed ones in Sect. 5.

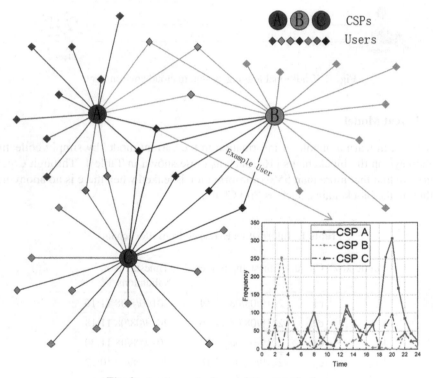

Fig. 2. Access analysis and de-anonymization

3 System Design

In this part, after introducing basic notions and tools, we build our system by four phases, where we answer the three questions mentioned in the Introduction briefly. More details about anonymity and undeniability are available in the next section.

3.1 Notions and Tools

If not explicitly mentioned, we use 256-bits long keys and hash function (SHA-256). We implement DSA for digital signatures and AES-256 for symmetric encryption.

Table 2. Basic notions

Basic notions	Meanings
PK_U SK_U	Key pair for registration. Under the DH scheme
op	User's operation
$sig_{PK_U}(op)$	User's digital signature for an op
h	The hash value of hashed entries in the Log DB
log	Contents of Logs
PK_C	Key pair of a CSP
SK_C	Meanings

In Table 2, we list the basic notions appearing in Fig. 3. Except PK_U and SK_U, we do not choose the Diffie-Hellman (DH) scheme for public key pairs because we do not use them to encrypt or decrypt, but for zero-knowledge proof. To generate such a key pair, a user randomly chooses a secret key first, then derives the public key via the hash function: $PK = Hash(SK)$. Besides, let H denotes a hash function customized from SHA-256. It accepts four parameters, each of which lengths 256 bits. Both the two processes above inherit the irreversible and collision-resistant characters from SHA-256. Besides, hash value h is generated by two steps: firstly, all logs are hashed individually; then, these hashes are hashed again into the final hash value, which is h. In this paper, when we talk about hash value h of some logs, we mean hash values generated by the two steps.

3.2 Architecture Design

Our system includes four phases in a typical circumstance: log generation, blockchain writing, validation, and audit. In this scenario, users not only record logs but also recover them. If the logs are modified, users can prove the modification to the LEA.

Log Generation. This phase includes steps 1, 2, 3, and 4, as shown in Fig. 3. Step 1, 2, and 4 describe the main steps of this phase. Firstly, the user logs-in and send operations with his signature. After finishing the operations, the CSP returns the hashed logs h and the random number r used for validation as soon as he stores the logs and their adjunctive information in his logging database (Log DB). However, one more step, i.e., step 3, is needed to eliminate the provenance auditor, which is necessary for traditional systems. Step 3 includes two sub-procedures. Firstly, the user requires all individual hashes of original logs and some randomly selected logs, and the CSP sends them back. Then, the user checks if the logs honestly reflect the status of cloud services and whether their hashes are included while the CSP computing h. If both verifications succeed, the user can believe that the logs are not modified at some probabilities, which will be further discussed in Sect. 5.

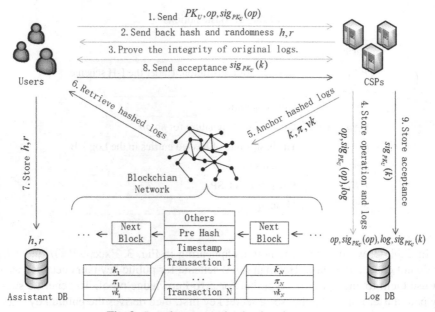

Fig. 3. Logging system in cloud environment.

Blockchain Writing. This phase involves only the CSP, as shown by step 5. In this phase, the CSP generates the transaction and anchors it onto the blockchain. To generate a transaction, the CSP computes k, π, vk as:

$$k = H(PK_C, PK_U, h, r) \tag{1}$$

π is a zk-SNARK proof for the following statements:

1. Know the SK_C corresponding to PK_C.
2. PK_C is included while computing (1).

vk is the verifying key corresponding to π.

Validation. Validation is necessary to ensure that the CSP anchors logs on the blockchain honestly. This phase includes all remnant steps, i.e., step 6, 7, 8, and 9, while step 7 and 9 are trivial.

Firstly, the user recomputes k according to formula (1). If he finds the same k paired with a correct proof π on the blockchain, he accepts the transaction. Then, he stores parameters used to compute k locally, which are indispensable when he wants to reconstruct the corresponding logs. After that, he signs the k to show that he has checked this transaction. Finally, to finish one logging, the CSP adds the receipt to the adjunctive information.

Audit. When a user checks his logs offered by his CSP, if he finds the logs not matching with the hash value he stored, he can prove the modification to the LEA with the following steps. First, he shows his and his CSP's public-keys that contained in k and locates it on the blockchain. Then, by showing r and h such that $k = H(PK_C, PK_U, h, r)$, he proves that his CSP wrote logs whose hash value is h, so naturally, he can ask his CSP to offer the original logs. Here we laconically describe what he should do, detailed demonstrations are in the next section.

4 Anonymity and Undeniability

In this part, we show how we achieve anonymity and undeniability in our system in detail. For anonymity, as both phase log generation and audit only involve communications between the user and the CSP, they do no harm to anonymity. Thus, we focus on phase blockchain writing and audit. After that, we analyze how we achieve undeniability.

4.1 Anonymity in Blockchain Writing

In this phase, the transaction sent to the blockchain network contains two parts: k and a pair of zk-SNARK proving components, i.e., π and vk.

In this phase, nodes in the blockchain network can only see a proving pair and a hash value. For the proof, they can verify the zero-knowledge statements as well, but know nothing about the identities of the user and his CSP. That is, they learn nothing about PK_C and PK_U via π and vk, due to the attribute of zero-knowledge of zk-SNARKs. For the hash value k, preimage resistance of the hash function ensures that no one can recover the original message, which prevents the identities from leakage. Thus, both users and CSPs are anonymous in this phase.

4.2 Anonymity in Audit

In this phase, the user reveals his and his CSP's identities in some transactions to the LEA for litigation. It means that these transactions are not anonymous anymore. This is inevitable because the LEA needs to match their identities in the real world with public-keys strictly. We consider it a kind of leakage.

We will show that the current models do not perform well in this situation in Sect. 5: transactions that should have been anonymous are not private any longer. Besides, the more transactions are used, the less anonymity the remnant ones have.

In contrast, in our system, identities of both users and CSPs are still strictly anonymized in all other transactions, despite revealed ones. That is because the r is still secret, the avalanche effect of hush functions ensures that even someone knows a specific pair of PK_C and PK_U, he cannot figure out whether a k on the blockchain indicates them. Therefore, in our system, in audit, no additional transaction is exposed except inevitable ones.

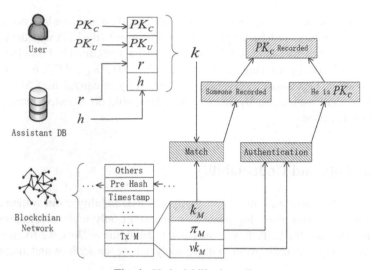

Fig. 4. Undeniability in audit.

4.3   Undeniability in Audit

In this part, we show how a user persuades an LEA when logs are modified. When a user wants to check his logs, at first, he refers to those offered by his CSP. He compares their hash values with those in his assistant database. If they do not match, he may conduct a lawsuit. For that, he should prove to the LEA that his CSP lies. If he succeeds, the LEA can enforce the CSP to show the original logs. To narrate how the user persuades the LEA, we cut what he should do logically into three statements:

1. He (the user) is the owner of PK_U.
2. Someone anchored the aimed transaction, admitting the User-CSP relation between PK_U and PK_C.
3. That someone is the CSP.

For step 1, the user proves his possession of the SK_U, i.e., the pre-image of PK_U. It is quite simple, so we do not talk about it. After that, the LEA accepts the statement 1.

Then, the user shows a group of parameters for formula (1) such that $k = H(PK_C, PK_U, h, r)$ to the LEA, which is the same as the k on the blockchain. After recomputing k, the LEA verifies the zk-SNARK proof to check whether the recorder is the owner of PK_C. If the verification succeeds, the LEA accepts the statement 2. We list all the information needed in statement 2 in Fig. 4, together with their source and aims. Finally, according to the service level agreement (SLA), the LEA ensures that PK_C belongs to the CSP. By these three steps, the LEA verifies that the CSP's possession of the original logs, so he can force the CSP to show them. If the CSP cannot, he is guilty.

5 Evaluations of Performance and Anonymity

In this section, we evaluate our system in two aspects: feasibility and anonymity. Firstly, we demonstrate the feasibility of our system. Then, after introducing *the degree of anonymity* to quantify anonymity in different systems, we compare our system's performance in privacy preservation, i.e., anonymity, with two previous systems.

5.1 Feasibility

In this part, firstly, we analyze the rates of CSP's successful cheatings in phase operation, step 3. In this step, the CSP may modify the original logs without being noticed by his user. When there are 1000 logs, if a user expects to notice any modification at the rate of 99%, the number of logs he should check relies on the number of modified logs. If only 1% logs are modified, the user needs to check 20.5% of all logs. Similarly, 2% corresponds to 10.8%, 5% to 4.4%, and 10% to 2.2%.

Then, we demonstrate that our system is feasible by showing that both its consumptions in computation and storage are acceptable. Firstly, neither of the two sources of computational overhead, blockchain and zk-SNARKs, is costly. For blockchain, we simply employ classic public blockchain in our system, which is the same as those in previous systems. That is, we do not change the structure of blockchain, but only change the contents of transactions. Therefore, the performance of blockchain is not a key point for our system.

Table 3. Time Consumption of zk-SNARKs

Configuration	Compile	Setup	Proof	Total
1C1T	3.81 s	38.75 s	4.22 s	46.77 s
2C2T	3.60 s	21.77 s	3.28 s	28.65 s
4C4T	3.81 s	14.84 s	2.79 s	24.72 s
4C8T	3.78 s	12.81 s	2.64 s	19.24 s

As to zk-SNARKs, we code the zero-knowledge statements by ZoKrates 错误!未找到引用源。. We conduct all experiments on virtual machines, with OS Ubuntu 16.04

LTS, 1 GB RAM. The host is a laptop, with CPU i7-6700HQ @ 2.60 GHz, RAM 8 GB @ 2133 MHz, OS Windows 10.

In Table 3, C and T represent the number of cores and threads, respectively. Considering the performance loss due to virtualization, it would be much better on a real machine. Besides, this is the consumption of one record, instead of one log. CSPs can simply pack logs generated in a period together in one transaction. Consequently, the cryptographic computation would not be a bottleneck of our system.

Table 4. Storage consumption

System	User/PA	Cloud	Blockchain
ProvChain	0B	74B	64B
BPPCF	1024B	200B	2048B
Our system	64B	182B	1669B

Then, in Table 4, we compare the storage consumption among three logging systems designed for cloud computing environment: ProvChain, BPPCF5, and our system. First of all, we can see that the amount of required storage of our system is acceptable. Then, compared with previous ones, as the ProvChain ignores anonymity, its advantage in storage is not surprising; however, our system exceeds BPPCF, which also considers the issue of anonymity.

5.2 Definition of Anonymity

In the current model, the service pattern on the company level is evident on the blockchain, such as access time, access frequency, and user-CSP pairs. We unify the quantifications of those aspects. We use the degree of anonymity d for a private system defined in [12]:

$$d = \frac{H(X)}{H_M} = \frac{-\sum(p_i * \log_2 p_i)}{-\sum(\frac{1}{N} * \log_2 \frac{1}{N})} = -\frac{\sum p_i * \log_2 p_i}{\log_2 N} \tag{2}$$

It bases on the amount of information defined by Shannon14. In this paper, p_i indicates the probability of discerning a user-CSP pair from all others. When all pairs are hidden, the probability is $1/N$ for all of them, which achieves the max entropy. Since H_M is the max entropy for any system and $H(X)$ is the remnant entropy, in our system, d shows the proportion of those still concealed pairs in all pairs.

Here we use a simple case to demonstrate this concept in our logging system: if there are 500 users, 5 CSPs engaged by each user, and 10000 transactions recorded on blockchain for each user-CSP pair, for an analyzer, there are only 500*5 different pairs in ProvChain, so the entropy is: $H(X) = \log_2(500 * 5) \approx 11.29$. Nevertheless, the max amount of entropy should be: $H_M = \log_2(500 * 5 * 10000) \approx 24.58$ when all users are fully anonymized. Thus, the degree of anonymity of ProvChain in this sample is: $d = H(X)/H_M = \frac{11.29}{24.58} \approx 0.46$.

The reason for such a discrepancy is that if an analyzer cannot learn whom a transaction belongs to, he must assume that these anonymous (500 ∗ 5 ∗ 10000) transactions belong to (500 ∗ 5 ∗ 10000) users. Contrarily, in current systems, users and CSPs use invariant addresses for all their transactions so that attackers know there are only (500 ∗ 5) user-CSP pairs, leading to a lower entropy in the system. As shown above, an attacker can get more than 54% $(1 - d)$ of complete information in ProvChain by simply collecting transactions.

5.3 Anonymity

In this part, we evaluate three systems, i.e., ProvChain, BPPCF, and ours, in three conditions. Details of these conditions are shown in Table 5. They represent three scales of implements: small, medium, and large. Multi-Cloud means the number of CSPs that a user may use simultaneously.

Table 5. Testing conditions

Condition No.	User number	Multi-cloud	Log number
1	1000	1	5000–10000
2	10000	5	5000–10000
3	100000	10	5000–10000

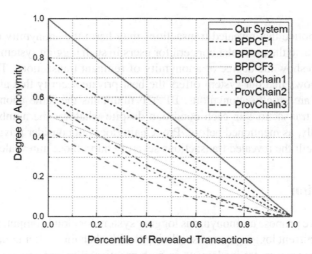

Fig. 5. Degree of anonymity in three systems.

In Fig. 5, the horizontal axis means the percentage of transactions exposed, such as those used in litigation. Our system hides all unrevealed transactions, so under all conditions, the degree of anonymity decreases linearly, which is the theoretical optimal performance. In BPPCF, it decreases linearly as well, but it is always lower than ours, which means that this solution does not realize the max anonymity. According to the linear decreases, we can conclude that in the process where more and more transactions are exposed, the entropy in BPPCF generally distributes evenly. Contrarily, in ProvChain, transactions exposed earlier contain more information than the later ones. That is because the foremost transaction leaks all information of those which have the same public-key, so the later ones, though not used, contain no information.

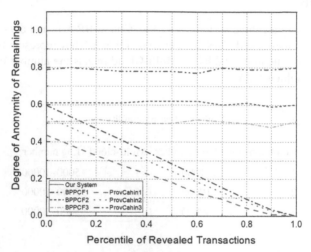

Fig. 6. Degree of anonymity in three systems for remnant transactions.

Since we notice that revealed transactions may harm the anonymity of unrevealed ones, which is also the particular concern for users in such logging systems, we conduct experiments to show the degree of anonymity of remnant transactions. The results are in Fig. 6. It shows that our system offers the best private security that all transactions not published are strictly anonymous. BPPCF maintains the same anonymity degree for remaining transactions in each condition despite whatever the number of them is exposed. Finally, as mentioned before, ProvChain does not consider privacy, so it does not perform well: the revealed transactions severely harm those unrevealed ones.

6 Conclusion

In this paper, we propose an anonymous logging system for cloud computing. Firstly, we point out that current logging systems utilizing the blockchain to offer tamper-resistance either ignore privacy or are inadequate in both practicability and anonymity. Then, we construct our system in four phases leveraging zk-SNARKs. After that, we explain how our system achieves anonymity and undeniability in detail. Finally, we implement experiments to illustrate our system in two aspects: for overhead, it is efficient in both computation and storage; for privacy (anonymity), it exceeds current systems.

References

1. Chunqiang, H., Li, W., Cheng, X., Jiguo, Yu., Wang, S., Bie, R.: A secure and verifiable access control scheme for big data storage in clouds. IEEE Trans. Big Data **4**(3), 341–355 (2018)
2. Liang, X., Shetty, S., Tosh, D., et al.: ProvChain: a blockchain-based data provenance architecture in cloud environment with enhanced privacy and availability. In: IEEE/ACM International Symposium on Cluster (2017)
3. Ramachandran, A., Kantarcioglu, M.: SmartProvenance: a distributed, Blockchain based data provenance system. In: CODASPY (2018)
4. Pourmajidi, W., Miranskyy, A.: Logchain: blockchain-assisted log storage. In: 2018 IEEE 11th International Conference on Cloud Computing (CLOUD), San Francisco, CA, pp. 978–982 (2018)
5. Zhang, Y., Wu, S., Jin, B.: Du, J.: A blockchain-based process provenance for cloud forensics. In: 2017 3rd IEEE International Conference on Computer and Communications (ICCC), Chengdu, pp. 2470–2473 (2017)
6. Reid, F., Harrigan, M.: An analysis of anonymity in the Bitcoin system (2011)
7. Ermilov, D., Panov, M., Yanovich, Y.: Automatic bitcoin address clustering. In: 2017 16th IEEE International Conference on Machine Learning and Applications (ICMLA), Cancun, pp. 461–464 (2017)
8. Groth, J.: Short pairing-based non-interactive zero-knowledge arguments. In: Abe, M. (ed.) ASIACRYPT 2010. LNCS, vol. 6477, pp. 321–340. Springer, Heidelberg (2010). https://doi.org/10.1007/978-3-642-17373-8_19
9. Lipmaa, H.: Progression-free sets and sublinear pairing-based non-interactive zero-knowledge arguments. In: Cramer, R. (ed.) TCC 2012. LNCS, vol. 7194, pp. 169–189. Springer, Heidelberg (2012). https://doi.org/10.1007/978-3-642-28914-9_10
10. Sasson, E.B., Chiesa, A., Garman, C., et al.: Zerocash: decentralized anonymous payments from Bitcoin. In: Security & Privacy (2014)
11. Lei, X., Shah, N., Lin, C., et al.: Enabling the sharing economy: privacy respecting contract based on public blockchain. In: ACM Workshop on Blockchain (2017)
12. Chiesa, A., et al.: Cluster computing in zero knowledge. IACR Cryptology ePrint Archive (2015)
13. Díaz, C., Seys, S., Claessens, J., et al.: Towards measuring anonymity. In: International Conference on Privacy Enhancing Technologies (2002)
14. Shannon, C.E.: A mathematical theory of communication. Bell Labs Tech. J. **27**(4), 379–423 (1948)
15. Eberhardt, J., Tai, S.: ZoKrates - scalable privacy-preserving off-chain computations. In: 2018 IEEE International Conference on Internet of Things (iThings), Halifax, NS, Canada, pp. 1084–1091 (2018)
16. Wang, J., Li, M., He, Y., Li, H., Xiao, K.: A blockchain based privacy-preserving incentive mechanism in crowdsensing applications. IEEE Access **6**, 17545–17556 (2018)

Blockchain and Internet of Things

An RFID Lightweight Authentication Technology Based on PUF-RFID Structure Model

Xiaodong Zheng[1], Songyou Xie[2(✉)], Chunmei Xie[3], and Wei Zhu[1]

[1] School of Software Engineering,
Xiamen University of Technology, Xiamen, China
{zxd, zhw}@xmut.edu.cn
[2] School of Computer Science and Engineering,
Hunan University of Science and Technology, Xiangtan, China
syou720@163.com
[3] School of Electrical Engineering and Automation,
Anhui University, Hefei, China
1225161700@qq.com

Abstract. With the rapid development of radio frequency identification (RFID) technology, RFID devices are beginning to exist widely in our daily lives, and people are paying more and more attention to RFID security. Traditional RFID-based encryption algorithms rely on expensive Hash function. Therefore, this paper proposes a lightweight RFID authentication protocol based on Physically Unclonable Functions (PUF), which uses the machine learning algorithm and string-matching algorithm, and presents a new mechanism of PUF challenge generation, which does not require expensive error correction code and fuzzy extractor. The implementation cost is lower. Through our security analysis, our identity authentication protocol can provide reliable security for low-cost RFID systems.

Keywords: PUF · RFID · Information security · Authentication protocol

1 Introduction

Traditional RFID systems consist of tags, readers, and back-end databases. Tags are used to store key information for authentication. The reader generates energy for the tag work by generating a magnetic field and can verify the identity of the tag [1]. The back-end database is the information storage and processing center of the RFID system the reader and the tag obtain the relevant authentication and data information by the wireless radio frequency. The reader will form a magnetic field within a certain range around the work [2]. When the tag enters the read/write area of the reader, the tag can obtain the energy required for the internal working of the circuit. The tag sends the information to the reader after processing (calculating and storing) and modulating the internal data, and the reader achieves the purpose of the authentication tag by demodulating and verifying the received information [3].

© Springer Nature Singapore Pte Ltd. 2020
Z. Zheng et al. (Eds.): BlockSys 2019, CCIS 1156, pp. 305–321, 2020.
https://doi.org/10.1007/978-981-15-2777-7_25

Typically, RFID devices work in an insecure environment where readers and tags exchange data through public channels and are vulnerable to theft and tampering by Attackers [4]. Therefore, in the RFID system how to secure each entity accurate authentication is particularly critical, and the limited space storage capacity and computing capacity of the RFID system has a huge challenge to the security mechanism, traditional encryption algorithms, such as hashing algorithm, will greatly improve the cost of the tag, is not conducive to low-cost RFID system implementation, and traditional tags can be cloned, and attackers spoof the reader by cloning tags to fake legitimate tags, making the reader falsely authenticate the malicious tag [5].

The Physically Unclonable Functions (PUF) is a new hardware-based security identification technology, which takes advantage of the random difference in manufacturing of integrated circuits, the response generated in the challenge input to PUF is unique [6], the PUF application in the security field can also reduce the cost loss of the system [7], such as the current PUF has been widely used in RFID authentication scheme, key generation and storage areas [8].

The traditional PUF-based RFID authentication scheme requires the manufacturer to integrate PUF into the RFID tag, and then RFID stores a large number of challenge-response pairs (CRPs) in the reader (database) during the registration phase, during the authentication phase, the reader sends an challenge message to the tag, the tag generates the response information R' according to PUF, then sends the R' to the reader (database), the reader (database) extracts the pre-stored R, and determines the legitimacy of the tag by judging whether R and R' are equal. However, this type of scheme has several drawbacks:

(a) This type of RFID authentication scheme requires the reader (database) to have a large storage space, which will increase the cost of manufacturing RFID Systems.
(b) PUF's CRPs information has been known beforehand, in the certification requires a fixed CRPs information, rather than randomly generated CRPs information, so that the overall security of the RFID system will be reduced.
(c) PUF in some harsh conditions (such as noise, device aging, etc.) will output an unstable response, so in order to make the legitimate R' and pre-stored R value equal, in this type of scheme will often require expensive error correcting code mechanism, which will greatly increase the cost of the system, and the error correcting code mechanism itself also has certain uncertainty, is not suitable for the widespread use.

2   Related Work

2.1   Related Background

The inherent random difference of PUF is represented by the random difference of input and output behavior. Inputting a challenge to PUF can map unpredictable response information.

Challenge: C

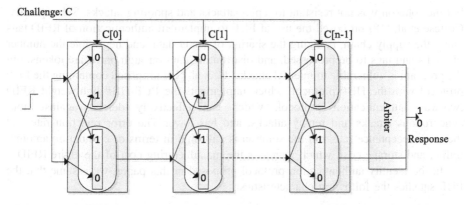

Fig. 1. Arbiter PUF

Arbiter PUF circuit structure is a type of PUF, as shown in Fig. 1, the arbiter PUF is composed of n multiplexers (MUX) and an arbiter (Arbiter). The MUX has two inputs and two outputs, and there are two internal terminals. Transmission lines (00, 11), due to the difference in manufacturing process, the line delay of each MUX is different, so when the signal passes through different lines, there will be different delays, which means that the transmission speed of the two signals is different. When the challenge signal C[n] at the MUX is 0, the signal passes directly in the MUX, corresponding to the two lines of the MUX internal connection (00). When C[n] is 1, the signal crosses, corresponding to the MUX internal connection (11) Two lines, the arbiter determines the output bit by arbitrating the transmission speed of the top and bottom signals. If the top signal arrives first, the arbiter outputs a bit 1. If the bottom signal is reached first to the arbiter, the arbiter outputs a bit 0.

The PUF technology is superior to the traditional digital cryptography encryption technology, because the PUF utilizes the hardware's own cryptographic primitives to implement the security protection function, and the manufacturing cost is low, and only a few hundred gates are required to implement a simple PUF structure. PUF technology can better resist attackers' physical attacks and memory read attacks [9].

At present, RFID-based identity authentication protocols mainly include: Hash function protocol [10], HB series protocol [11] and improved LMAP+ protocol [12]. These protocols have obvious security vulnerabilities and high cost, among which Hash The function requires a large amount of hardware resource overhead to support of approximately 7,350 to 10,868 gates such as SHA-256 [13]. Traditional cryptography-based RFID certification protocols are difficult to meet demand for manufacturing costs [14].

Since the input and output behavior of PUF is unique, we can utilize PUF to RFID device identity authentication [15]. First, Bolotnyy et al. [16] proposed a PUF-based RFID authentication scheme that uses hardware support to protect information security. The advantage of this scheme is that it requires only a small amount of hardware resources, but the scheme is vulnerable to replay attacks. Devadas et al. [17] applied PUF to small passive RFID tags to achieve anti-counterfeiting and secure access, but the solution was not resistant to replay attacks and spoofing attacks. Subsequently, Cortese et al. [18] proposed the use of PUF to implement authentication of RFID tags along the supply chain, realizing the sharing of secret data, and negligible the number of CRPs and tags to be processed, and distributing data through hardware tokens, but the program is vulnerable to internal attacks. Li et al. [19] proposed combining the PUF protocol with the HB# protocol, which implements the PUF-HB# lightweight RFID two-way authentication protocol, which can effectively defend against non-synchronous attacks and replay attacks, and has lower The error rejection rate and the error acceptance rate, but the solution is still high in terms of calculation amount, traffic, and storage cost, which increases the manufacturing cost of the entire RFID.

In the identity authentication protocol proposed in this paper, we assume that the PUF satisfies the following characteristics:

(a) Physical unclonability. The input and output behavior of PUF is formed by random differences in the internal structure of the hardware. This difference cannot be artificially controlled. The attacker cannot clone the circuit PUF structure with the same behavior through hardware modeling,

(b) Uniqueness. Because of the different line delay and logic gate in the PUF structure, when different challenge (input) information is input the PUF, the response (output) behavior of PUF is also different, that is, a challenge corresponds to a response,

(c) Unpredictability. Unable to predict PUF other CRPs based on collected CRPs information.

(d) Robustness. When a challenge message is repeatedly input to the same PUF, the response information of the PUF remains substantially the same ϖ ϖ'.

2.2 Machine Learning Attack

From the above we can know that the output input behavior of the PUF is determined by its internal delay vector ϖ. If the delay vector ϖ is acquired by the attacker, the attacker can use the acquired ϖ to attack the PUF. Ruhrmair [20] first proposed the use of ES and LR machine learning algorithms to attack PUF, based on ES (Evolution Strategies) machine learning attack idea: by generating a random PUF (i.e. PUF model of random delay vector ϖ'), and check which the ϖ' of the PUF model is closest to the ϖ of the original PUF, which can be found by entering the challenge training. The PUF model will be saved as a parent, while other PUF models will be discarded. In the next generation, the delay vector ϖ' of the parent PUF model is randomly mutated to produce multiple progeny, in which the PUF model closest to the original PUF will be preserved. This process is repeated many times, the behavior of the PUF model will be closer to the original PUF, and the attacker can use this PUF model to maliciously attack the system integrated with the PUF structure.

It should be noted that the machine learning attack PUF in this section adopts the software modeling method. By training the delay vector ϖ' closest to the ϖ of the original PUF, the behavior of the PUF is simulated by the Chameleon simulator to generate the simulated PUF. Hardware modeling PUF is still not achievable, because the random variation inside the hardware in the manufacturing process is uncontrollable, so it is impossible to manufacture a PUF with the same structure. The simulated PUF has similar behavior to the original PUF, so it can be used in identity authentication.

3 The Proposed Scheme

In this section we will use machine learning to improve the security of the system. Mehrdad et al. proposed a double PUF-based identity authentication protocol [21], which used an original PUF and an analog PUF in their double PUF authentication protocol. The PUF in server is the analog PUF, and the tag is the original PUF. Analog PUF is obtained by legal manufacturers through machine learning. The double PUF structure does not require ultra-precise and ultra-high frequency time stamping modules, and the implementation cost is also low.

In this section, we will propose a more secure and reliable RFID authentication protocol, and use double PUF structure and string-matching algorithms in the protocol. In this section, the Reader and Database in RFID are represented by the Server. Our scheme has two phases, the registration phase and the certification phase.

3.1 Registration Phase

We assume that G is a p-order multiplicative cyclic group whose generator is g. Both p and q are a large prime number, where $q = 2p + 1$, all elements in G belong to Z_q^*, the element type is $g^a \bmod q$, and $a \in Z_q^*$ is a random number. In this agreement, g^a is used to denote $g^a \bmod q$. In the registration phase, the registration center assigns a unique identity ID_i, and ID_j to each tag and server, and randomly selects two random numbers x_i and x_j as the private key of the tag and server, and then calculates their public keys $G_1 = g^{x_i}$, $G_2 = g^{x_j}$, and publishes them to the public communication environment, in addition, the tag selects a master key z_i, and the server saves the key $k_i = 1/(g^{x_i} + z_i)$. The manufacturer integrates a unique hardware PUF structure for each tag. The registration center sends the delay vector of each PUF structure to the server in the registration phase. The server stores these delay vectors according to the ID_i of each tag, and the analog PUF constructed based on the delay vector is represented by PUFM.

3.2 Certification Phase

When the tag is in the working range of the server, the RFID protocol certification phase will be started, including the server authentication tag phase, the tag authentication server phase, and the shared session key phase. The protocol certification step is shown in Fig. 3:

(A) Server authentication tag phase

> Step 1: Tag get public key g^{x_i} from public environment, calculates $A_1 = g^{x_j x_i}$ and $R_i = PUF(A_1)$, Then the tag generates a random number a and computes $A_2 = g^{x_j x_i + a} \oplus R_i, A_3 = g^{a(g x_i + z_i)}$, At the same time, the tag generates a random number b to update the key data, $x_{inew} = x_i b, g_{new}^{x_i} = g^{x_i b}$, At last, the tag sends the message $ID_i, A_2, A_3, g_{new}^{x_i}$ to the server for verification.

Step 2: After the server receives the authentication information ID_i, A_2, A_3, $g_{new}^{x_i}$, the server first obtains the public key information g^{x_i} corresponding to the tag ID_i in the public channel, and computes $A_4 = g^{x_i x_j}$, $R_j = PUFM(g^{x_i x_j})$, $A_5 = A_3^k = g^a$, $A_6 = A_2 \cdot A_3 = g^{x_i x_j + a}$ and $R_i = A_6 \oplus A_2$, and, through the string matching algorithm (as shown in Fig. 2) compares the strings of R_i and R_j bit by bit. If the unmatched bit is within the error threshold, the server authentication tag succeeds.

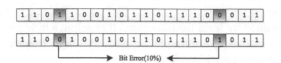

Fig. 2. String matching algorithm

(B) Tag authentication server phase

Step 3: Server selects a random number c, and calculates $A_7 = g^c$, $g_{new}^{x_j} = g^{x_j c}$, $x_{jnew} = x_j c$, $k_{inew} = 1/(g_{new}^{x_i} + z_i)$, $SKB = R_i \oplus g_{new}^{x_i x_{jnew}}$, $R_j' = PUFM(g_{new}^{x_i x_{jnew}} \oplus R_i)$, $A_8 = g_{new}^{x_i c} \oplus R_j'$. And message A_7 and A_8 is then sent to tag.

Step 4: After the tag receives information A_7 and A_8, calculates $A_9 = A_7^{x_{inew}} = g^{c x_{inew}}$, $R_j' = g^{c x_{inew}} \oplus A_8$, The tag calculates $R_i' = PUF(g_{new}^{x_i x_{jnew}} \oplus R_i)$ with its own PUF, then by determining the number of unmatched bits of R_i' and R_j', it is determined whether the server passes the authentication. When the error bits of R_i' and R_j' are lower than the error threshold, the tag authentication server succeeds.

(C) Shared session key phase

Step 5: Tag calculates $SKA = R_i \oplus g_{new}^{x_j x_{inew}}$ and $A_{10} = g_{new}^{x_j x_{inew}} \oplus R_i \oplus R_j' \oplus SKA$, the message A_{10} is transmitted to the server.

Step 6: After receives the A_{10}, the server calculates $A_{11} = g_{new}^{x_i x_{jnew}} \oplus R_i \oplus R_j' \oplus SKB$, and check if A_{11} and A_{10} are equal, if yes, the server and tag sharing session key $SK = R_i \oplus g_{new}^{x_i x_{jnew}}$.

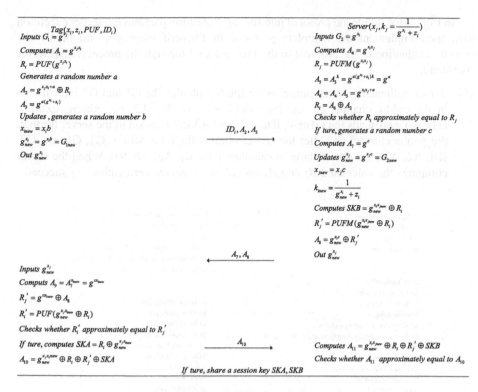

Fig. 3. Certification phase

4 Protocol Analysis

4.1 Proverif Security Verification

Proverif is a protocol security verification tool that allows us to check the correctness of the protocol and whether the security meets the requirements of the system [22]. In this section, we formalize the protocol of this article into the Proverif language, and verify the security of the session key and the correctness of the two-way verification in the Proverif tool.

First, we define the parameters, functions, regions, events, and queries of the protocol. Parameters define parameters (ch, sch, SKA, SKB, g, IDi, IDj, xi, xj, zi), where (sch, SKA, SKB, IDi, IDj, xi, xj, zi) are private parameters. In functions we define the functions used (PUF, PUFM, exp(exponent), xor, add, inv(inversion), mul (multiplication)). In the equations we define the execution rules of some functions, such as (xor, inv, exp). Event defines four events, including TagStart and TagAuth events and ServerStart and ServerAuth events. Queries asks about the security of the session keys SKA and SKB, and asks if the server has correctly verified the tag, and whether the tag verifies the server. Proverif checks the security of the entire protocol according to the queries and outputs the result.

In Fig. 4, we divide the protocol into the tag execution part and the server execution part, then implement the complete protocol in Proverif language, and finally the security evaluation of the protocol in the Proverif tool through the process!Tag||!Server command.

(1) Server authentication tag phase. After the tag obtains the G1 and G2 information in the public channel ch, the tag calculates (A1, Ri, A2, A3, xinew, gxinew, G1new), and sends the G1new, IDi, A2, and A3 information to the server through the public channel ch. After the server obtains the information (G1, G1new, G2, IDi, A2, A3), the server starts to calculate (A4, Rj, A5, A6, Ri). When the server compares the calculated Rj and Ri successfully, server verification tag succeeds.

```
(*Tag code*)let Tag=                              (*Server code*)let Server=
let G1=exp(g,xi) in                               let G2=exp(g,xj) in
out (ch,G1);                                      out (ch,G2);
in(ch,G2:bitstring);                              in (ch,(G1:bitstring,G1new:bitstring));
!                                                 in (ch,(IDi:bitstring,A2:bitstring,A3:bitstring));
(                                                 let ki=inv(add(exp(g,xi),zi)) in
event TagStart(IDi);                              !
let A1=exp(G2,xi) in                              (
let Ri=PUF(A1)in                                  event ServerStart(IDj);
new a:bitstring;                                  let A4=exp(G1,xj) in
let A2=xor(mul(A1,exp(g,a)),Ri) in                let Rj=PUFM(A4) in
let A3=mul(exp(exp(g,a),exp(g,xi)),exp(exp(g,a),zi))in    let A5=exp(A3,ki) in
new b:bitstring;                                  let A6=mul(A2,A3) in
let xinew=mul(xi,b) in                            let Ri=xor(A4,A2) in
let gxinew=exp(exp(g,xi),b) in                    if Ri=Rj then
let G1new=gxinew in                               new c:bitstring;
out (ch,G1new);                                   let A7=exp(g,c) in
out (ch,(IDi,A2,A3));                             let G2new=exp(G1,c) in
in (ch,(A7:bitstring,A8:bitstring,G2new:bitstring));    let xjnew=mul(xj,c) in
let A9=exp(A7,xinew) in                           let Rj1=PUF(xor(exp(exp(G1new,xjnew),Ri)) in
let Rj1=xor(A9,A8) in                             let A8=xor(exp(G1new,c),Rj1) in
let Ri1=PUF(xor(exp(exp(G2new,xinew),Ri)) in      let SKB=xor(Ri,exp(exp(G1new,xjnew)) in
if Ri1=Rj1 then                                   let kinew=inv(add(G1new,zi)) in
let SKA=xor(Ri,exp(G2new,xinew)) in               out (ch,(A7,A8,G2new));
let A10= xor(xor(xor(exp(G2new,xinew),Ri),Rj1),SKA) in    in(ch,A10:bitstring);
out (ch,A10);                                     let A11= xor(xor(xor(G1new,Ri),Rj1),SKB) in
event ServerAuth(IDj);                            if A11=A10 then
0                                                 event TagAuth(IDi);
).                                                0
                                                  ).
```

Fig. 4. Certification phase

(2) Tag authentication server phase. After the verification tag is successful, the server generates a random number c, starts the calculation (A7, G2new, xjnew, Rj1, A8, SKB, kinew) and sends the information (A7, A8, G2new) to the tag. After the tag receives the information (A7, A8, G2new), it starts counting (A9, Rj1, Ri1). If Rj1 is equal to Ri1, the tag verification server succeeds.

(3) Shared session key phase. The tag continues to calculate (SKA, A10), and sends A10 to the server through ch, the server calculates A11 after receiving the information A10, and if A11 is equal to A10, it will determine that the keys SKA and SKB are the session keys of both parties. The information interaction behind the two parties will be encrypted and decrypted by SKA or SKB.

```
(*results*) Completing equations...
Completing equations...
-- Query not attacker(SKA[])
Completing...
Starting query not attacker(SKA[])
RESULT not attacker(SKA[]) is true.
-- Query not attacker(SKB[])
Completing...
Starting query not attacker(SKB[])
RESULT not attacker(SKB[]) is true.
-- Query inj-event(ServerAuth(id)) ==> inj-event(TagStart(id))
Completing...
Starting query inj-event(ServerAuth(id)) ==> inj-event(TagStart(id))
RESULT inj-event(ServerAuth(id)) ==> inj-event(TagStart(id)) is true.
-- Query inj-event(TagAuth(id_44)) ==> inj-event(ServerStart(id_44))
Completing...
Starting query inj-event(TagAuth(id_44)) ==> inj-event(ServerStart(id_44))
RESULT inj-event(TagAuth(id_44)) ==> inj-event(ServerStart(id_44)) is true.
```

Fig. 5. Result phase

The execution results of the Proverif security verification tool are shown in Fig. 5. Four queries were successfully executed. From the result graph we can see the session key SKA, SKB is secure, the tag and the server also perform two-way authentication, and the protocol has successfully passed Proverif verification.

4.2 BAN Logic Analysis

4.2.1 Symbol and Rule Description

BAN logic [23] is a widely used protocol security analysis method that plays a very important role in the process of authentication and session key generation. The symbols and rules of the BAN logic are as follows (Table 1):

Table 1. BAN logic symbol description

Symbols	Description	Symbols	Description
$P|\sim X$	P sends information X	$P \triangleleft X$	P receives information X
$P \equiv \# X$	P believes that X is new	$P|\equiv X$	P believes in information X
(X, Y)	X or Y composition information (X, Y)	$(X, Y)_K$	(X, Y) encrypted by key K
$P \overset{K}{\leftrightarrow} Q$	K is the shared key of P and Q	$P \Rightarrow X$	P can control information X

Rule 1: Message meaning rule: $\frac{P|P\overset{K}{\leftrightarrow}Q,P\triangleleft\{X\}_K}{P|\equiv Q|\sim X}$, if P believes that it shares the key K with Q, and P receives the encrypted information $\{X\}_K$, then P believes that Q has sent message X.

Rule 2: Nonce verification rule: $\frac{P|\equiv\#(X),P|\equiv Q|\sim X}{P|\equiv Q|\equiv X}$, if P believes that X is new and P believes that Q has sent message X, then P believes that Q believes X.

Rule 3: Jurisdiction rule: $\frac{P|Q\Rightarrow X,P|\equiv Q|\equiv X}{P|\equiv X}$, if P believes that Q can control X and believes that Q believes X, then P believes X.

Rule 4: Freshness conjuncatenation rule: $\frac{P|\equiv\#(X)}{P|\equiv\#(X,Y)}$, if P believes that X is new, then P believes that (X, Y) is new.

Rule 5: Belief rule: $\frac{P|\equiv Q|\equiv(X,Y)}{P|\equiv Q|\equiv(X)}$, if P believes that Q believes in information (X, Y), then P believes that Q believes in information (X).

Rule 6: Seeing rule: $\frac{P\triangleleft(X,Y)}{P\triangleleft X}$, if P receives the information (X, Y), then P also receives (X).

BAN logic analysis is widely used for the correctness of key agreement authentication protocols. Ideally, only if the protocol meets specific target requirements, the agreement can be considered logical and secure. The following goals should be met in the authentication protocol proposed in this paper:

(1) $Tag| \equiv Tag \overset{SK}{\leftrightarrow} Server$

(2) $Tag| \equiv Server| \equiv Tag \overset{SK}{\leftrightarrow} Server$

(3) $Server| \equiv Tag \overset{SK}{\leftrightarrow} Server$

(4) $Server| \equiv Tag| \equiv Tag \overset{SK}{\leftrightarrow} Server$

4.2.2 Formalization of Agreement

First, the protocol proposed in this paper is converted into BAN logical symbols in the order of message delivery, as shown below:

Message 1:

$$Tag \rightarrow Server : ID_i, (g^{x_j x_i + a}, a)_{R_i}, A_3$$

Message 2:

$$Server \rightarrow Tag : A_7, (g_{new}^{x_i x_{jnew}}, g_{new}^{x_i c}, Tag \overset{SK}{\leftrightarrow} Server)_{R_i}$$

Message 3:

$$Tag \rightarrow Server : (g_{new}^{x_j x_{inew}}, R'_j, Tag \overset{SK}{\leftrightarrow} Server)_{R_i}$$

Message 1 means that the tag sending information of $ID_i, (g^{x_j x_i + a}, a)_{R_i}, A_3$ to the server, wherein $g^{x_j x_i + a}, a$ information is encrypted by R_i, and message 2 means that the server sends message $A_7, (g_{new}^{x_i x_{jnew}}, g_{new}^{x_i c}, Tag \overset{SK}{\leftrightarrow} Server)_{R_i}$ to the tag, where $g_{new}^{x_i x_{jnew}}, g_{new}^{x_i c}$, $Tag \overset{SK}{\leftrightarrow} Server$ is obtained by R_i through PUF calculation, so the information is also encrypted by R_i, and SK indicate SKB or SKA. Message 3 is that the tag sends the message $(g_{new}^{x_j x_{inew}}, R'_j, Tag \overset{SK}{\leftrightarrow} Server)_{R_i}$ encrypted by the R_i to the server.

4.2.3 Protocol Hypothesis

Before performing the Ban logic analysis, we also make some assumptions about the protocol, as shown in Table 2:

A_1 and A_2 indicate that tag and server believe that a, b and c are new, because a, b and c are randomly generated by tag and server respectively, so the assumption is established, A_3 and A_4 indicate that tag and server believe that $(g_{new}^{x_i x_{jnew}}, g_{new}^{x_i c})$ and $(g_{new}^{x_j x_{inew}}, R_j')$ are new respectively, this is because $(g_{new}^{x_i x_{jnew}}, g_{new}^{x_i c})$ and $(g_{new}^{x_j x_{inew}}, R_j')$ are calculated from random numbers a, b and c, so A_3 and A_4 are also true.

A_5 and A_7 indicate that the tag believes the key R_i shared with the server, and the tag believes that the server can control the session key SK. This is because R_i can be calculated by the PUF of the tag, and SK is also determined by the random number c of the server, so A_5 and A_7 were established. Because the server can extract the information of R_i by calculation and compare the R_j generated by itself, if the approximation is equal, the server considers that R_i is trusted, and the SK information is also calculated by the random number b of the tag, so A_6 and A_8 were established.

Table 2. Protocol hypothesis

Assumptions	Assumptions
$A_1 : Tag \mid\equiv \#(a, b)$	$A_2 : Server \mid\equiv \#(c)$
$A_3 : Tag \mid\equiv \#(g_{new}^{x_i x_{jnew}}, g_{new}^{x_i c})$	$A_4 : Server \mid\equiv \#(g_{new}^{x_j x_{inew}}, R_j')$
$A_5 : Tag \mid\equiv \# Tag \overset{R_i}{\leftrightarrow} Server$	$A_6 : Server \mid\equiv \# Tag \overset{R_i}{\leftrightarrow} Server$
$A_7 : Tag \mid\equiv \# Server \Rightarrow (Tag \overset{SK}{\leftrightarrow} Server)$	$A_8 : Server \mid\equiv Tag \Rightarrow (Tag \overset{SK}{\leftrightarrow} Server)$

4.2.4 BAN Logic Proof Process

Next, according to the BAN logic rules, we prove that our protocol scheme can be achieved with the initial assumptions, and the proof process of Goal (1) and Goal (2) is as follows:

(1) According to message 2, we can know:

$$p1 : Tag \vartriangleleft (g_{new}^{x_i x_{jnew}}, g_{new}^{x_i c}, Tag \leftrightarrow Server)_{R_i}, A_5$$

(2) According to $p1$, we apply the seeking rule to get:

$$p2 : Tag \vartriangleleft (g_{new}^{x_i x_{jnew}}, g_{new}^{x_i c}, Tag \overset{SK}{\leftrightarrow} Server)_{R_i}$$

(3) After getting $p2$ and A_5, we can get according to the meaning-message rule:

$$p3 : Tag \mid Server \mid \sim (g_{new}^{x_i x_{jnew}}, g_{new}^{x_i c}, Tag \overset{SK}{\leftrightarrow} Server)$$

(4) According to hypothesis A_3, we can confirm with the freshness conjuncatenation rule:

$$p4 : Tag|\equiv \#(g_{new}^{x_i x_{jnew}}, g_{new}^{x_i C}, Tag \overset{SK}{\leftrightarrow} Server)$$

(5) After getting $p3$ and $p4$, we apply the nonce-verification rule to get:

$$p5 : Tag\big| \equiv Server|\equiv (g_{new}^{x_i x_{jnew}}, g_{new}^{x_i C}, Tag \overset{SK}{\leftrightarrow} Server)$$

(6) Calculated according to $p5$ and the belief rule:

$$p6 : Tag\big| \equiv Server\big| \equiv (Tag \overset{SK}{\leftrightarrow} Server)$$

(7) According to A_7 and $p6$, the jurisdiction rule can be used to obtain:

$$p7 : Tag|\equiv (Tag \overset{SK}{\leftrightarrow} Server)$$

$p6$ and $p7$ implement goal (2) and goal (1), and the remaining goal (3) and goal (4) implementations are as follows:

(8) According to message 3, we can get:

$$p8 : Server \lhd (g_{new}^{x_j x_{inew}}, R_j', Tag \overset{SK}{\leftrightarrow} Server)_{R_i}$$

(9) According to $p8$ and A_6, we can use the message-meaning rule to get:

$$p9 : Server|\equiv Tag| \sim (g_{new}^{x_j x_{inew}}, R_j', Tag \overset{SK}{\leftrightarrow} Server)$$

(10) Obtained according to A_4 and freshness-conjuncatenation rule:

$$p10 : Server|\equiv \#(g_{new}^{x_j x_{inew}}, R_j', Tag \overset{SK}{\leftrightarrow} Server)$$

(11) According to $p9$, $p10$ and nonce verification rule

$$p11 : Server\big| \equiv Tag\big| \equiv (g_{new}^{x_j x_{inew}}, R_j', Tag \overset{SK}{\leftrightarrow} Server)$$

(12) According to $p11$, we can use the belief rule to get:

$$p12 : Server\big| \equiv Tag\big| \equiv (Server \overset{SK}{\leftrightarrow} Tag)$$

(13)   According to A_8 and $p12$, we can use the jurisdiction rule to get:

$$p13 : Server \Big| \equiv (Tag \overset{SK}{\leftrightarrow} Server)$$

Goal (4) and goal (3) are implemented in p12 and p13. The BAN logic analysis process ends here. We have achieved all the goals and proved that our protocol is in line with BAN logic. In the ideal working environment, our agreement can meet the logical needs of the system.

4.3   Safety Analysis and Comparison

Our protocol uses two computational difficulty problems: (1) Discrete Logarithm Problem: Even if the attacker knows the value of g^a, the attacker cannot calculate a in the polynomial time. (2) Computational Diffie-Hellman Problem: Even if the attacker knows g^a, g^b and the attacker can't calculate the value of g^{ab} in polynomial time. In this section, we will specifically analyze the performance of this article in the face of some major malicious attacks.

(A)   Machine learning attack

In order to implement machine learning attacks, the attacker needs at least the number of challenge-response pairs (CRPs) of N_{min} to achieve the purpose of software modeling of PUF. The number of N_{min} is mainly determined by the error threshold e and the structure of PUF [16]. In the protocol proposed in this paper, the PUF challenge information is composed of the private keys x_i, x_j and the public keys g^{x_i}, g^{x_j}. The malicious attacker cannot completely control the $g^{x_i x_j}$ information of the PUF. In the worst case, the malicious attacker can pretend to be a malicious tag or server to control g^{x_i}, or g^{x_j}. Due to the unpredictable nature of PUF, when different challenge information is input the PUF, the response information of the PUF will be very different, if not fully controlled $g^{x_i x_j}$, the attacker can't attack the PUF by controlling the challenge information. The first PUF response information R_i is encrypted with the key $g^{x_i x_j + a}$, i.e. $A_2 = g^{x_j x_i + a} \oplus R_i$, the second PUFM response information R'_j, R'_j is encrypted by $g^{x_i c}_{new}$, i.e. $A_8 = g^{x_i c}_{new} \oplus R'_j$, due to the elliptic curve problem And the discrete logarithm problem, the attacker cannot calculate the $g^{x_i c}_{new}$ value in the polynomial time, and since a and c are random numbers, the attacker cannot calculate the delay vector of the PUF by analyzing A_2 and A_8 information, so the protocol in this paper is face machine learning attacks are safe.

(B)   Man-in-the-MiddleAttack

Man-in-the-MiddleAttack refers to the attacker's multiple intercepted information and analyzes the key parameter values required for authentication, and then falsifies these key parameters to make illegal tags or readers pass certification. In the protocol of this paper, each key information is corresponding, such as x_i corresponding to g^{x_i}, x_j corresponding to g^{x_j}, z_i and x_i together determine the key k_i, in the calculation of the tag will get g^{x_j} information from the public channel the calculation of g^{x_j} and its own x_i generates the key $A_1 = g^{x_j x_i}$. After the server acquires g^{x_i}, it calculates and generates $A_4 = g^{x_i x_j}$ with its own x_j, and the generated key information $g^{x_i x_j}$ and $g^{x_j x_i}$ are equal and are input the PUF as the challenge information of the PUF. If one of the two key information is forged, it will directly affect the output information of the PUF, and the generated R_i and R_j will not be equal. After each successful authentication, the key information (x_i, x_j, g^{x_i}, g^{x_j}, k_i) is synchronously updated by the generated random numbers b and c. If the attacker forges one of the information, the key inconsistency will occur. In the case, the verification was unsuccessful, so our protocol is also very safe in the face of Man-in-the-MiddleAttack.

(C) Counterfeit attack

Counterfeit attack refers to an attacker impersonating a legitimate tag and attempt to trick the server into authenticating. We assume that the attacker can obtain the key information stored in the NVM (non-volatile memory), namely (x_i, z_i, PUF, ID_i), and the public key information g^{x_j}, and can be intercepted on the common channel (ID_i, A_2, A_3) information, when the tag enters the working area of the server, the tag calculates $A_1 = g^{x_j x_i}$, and randomly generates a random number a, calculates R_i, $A_2 = g^{x_j x_i + a} \oplus R_i$, $A_3 = g^{a(gx_i + z_i)}$, and generates a random number b to update the internal key information, i.e. $x_{inew} = x_i b$, $g_{new}^{x_i} = g^{x_i b}$, Then, the request authentication information (ID_i, A_2, A_3) is sent to the server. After receiving the information and obtaining the public key g^{x_i}, the server calculates $A_4 = g^{x_i x_j}$, $R_j = PUFM(g^{x_i x_j})$, $A_5 = A_3^k = g^a$, $R_i = A_6 \oplus A_2$, where the server will compare the information of R_j and R_i. It is obvious that R_j and R_i are not equal here. This is because R_i is not generated by PUF. Due to the physical unclonability of PUF, the attacker cannot physically model the PUF structure and our protocols can also block machine learning attacks, and attackers cannot train PUF models by collecting PUF CRPs, so our protocol is resistant to Counterfeit attack.

(D) Replay attack

In a replay attack, an attacker usually intercepts a successful authentication message of a legitimate tag, and then uses these messages to initiate an authentication request to deceive a legitimate tag or server for successful authentication. In this protocol, an attacker can intercept information (ID_i, A_2, A_3, A_7, A_8, A_{10}), and the attacker wants to achieve the purpose of malicious authentication by replaying the (ID_i, A_2, A_3), (A_7, A_8), and (A_{10}) information. The purpose of malicious authentication is unachievable. This is because before each round of information transmission, the tag or server will update its own key information by random number, i.e. $x_{inew} = x_i b$, $g_{new}^{x_i} = g^{x_i b}$, $x_{jnew} = x_j c$, $g_{new}^{x_j} = g^{x_j c}$, if the previous round is also played back, can make the key information will be inconsistent. For example, $g_{new}^{x_i x_{jnew}}$ is not equal to $g^{x_i x}$. If the key information is not equal, it will cause $R_i = PUF(g^{x_j x_i})$ not equal to $R_j = PUFM(g_{new}^{x_i x_{jnew}})$, $R_j' = PUFM(g^{x_i x_j} \oplus R_i)$ is not equal to $R_j' = PUF(g_{new}^{x_j x_{inew}} \oplus R_i)$, and authentication fails. When the replay attack is launched, the security of the RFID system can also be guaranteed.

(E) Forward security

Forward security refers to the loss of the session key used in the previous communication when the current session key is lost. In our agreement, the session key

$SKA = R_i \oplus g_{new}^{x_j x_{inew}}$, $SKB = R_i \oplus g_{new}^{x_i x_{jnew}}$, $SKA = SKB$, It can be seen that our session keys SKA and SKB both contain two random numbers b and c, which means that the current session key is almost not equal to the previous session key, and R_i is generated by the PUF. Due to the unpredictability of the PUF, the attacker cannot determine the information of the output R_i of the PUF, so our protocol has forward security, even if the current key is compromised, will not reveal the session key of the previous communication, and will not reveal the content of the previous communication.

(F) Tracking attack

In a tracking attack, if the value of a parameter in a system remains the same, the attacker can intercept the information value and replay the information value to achieve the purpose of attacking the system. There are two key update phases in this protocol, namely, the tag updates the keys $x_{inew} = x_i b$, $g_{new}^{x_i} = g^{x_i b}$ and the server through the random number c to update the keys $x_{jnew} = x_j c$, $g_{new}^{x_j} = g^{x_j c}$, $k_{inew} = 1/(g_{new}^{x_i} + z_i)$ through the random number b. In this protocol, since there is no direct connection between each session key due to the existence of random numbers, even if some session keys are exposed to the attacker under special circumstances, it will not affect the security of other session keys, so the protocol can resist tracking attacks.

In recent years, the attack methods for RFID systems have emerged in an endless stream. It is a key step in the development of RFID to propose a more secure authentication protocol to ensure the security of RFID systems. Table 3 lists the security performance comparisons between this and other protocols. From the above figure, we can see that the protocol proposed in this paper can resist multiple attacks including machine learning attacks, and the security performance is better than other protocols.

Table 3. Comparison of security performance of different authentication protocols

Attack attribute	[24]	[25]	[26]	Proposed protocol
Machine learning attack	Yes	Yes	Yes	Yes
Replay attack	No	No	No	Yes
Tracking attack	No	No	Yes	Yes
Side channel attack	Yes	Yes	Yes	Yes
Counterfeit attack	No	Yes	No	Yes

5 Summary and Outlook

Due to the limitation of system power and resource consumption by low-cost RFID system, this paper proposes a dual-PUF-based RFID two-way identity authentication protocol, which can be implemented with limited hardware resources. In our protocol, a double PUF circuit structure and string-matching authentication method is proposed to implement two-way identity authentication. The server does not need to store the PUF

CRPs, which effectively saves the cost of the system, and the authentication parties can jointly generate the PUF challenge information. The generated response information is encrypted by the key and then transmitted. Through the analysis of this paper, we believe that the proposed protocol can meet the security requirements of low-cost RFID systems and can solve the security threats faced by today's low-cost RFID systems.

At present, there are still many problems that PUF technology needs to solve, such as the impact of environment on PUF system and unstable output. PUF technology is very worthy of scholars to study and research. The next step is to study the improvement of PUF stability in low-cost error correction codes and identity protocols.

Acknowledgement. This research is funded by the National Natural Science Foundation of China (Grant 61572188), Scientific Research Program of New Century Excellent Talents in Fujian Province University, Industrial Robot Application of Fujian University Engineering Research Center, Minjiang University (MJUKF-IRA201802), Fujian Provincial Natural Science Foundation of China (Grant 2018J01570), the CERNET Innovation Project (Grant NGII20170411) and the young teacher's education scientific research project of Fujian province (Grant no. JT180455), Educational and teaching reform and construction project of Xiamen University of Technology (Grant JG2019048).

References

1. Liang, W., Xie, S., Long, J., et al.: A double PUF-based RFID identity authentication protocol in service-centric internet of things environments. Inf. Sci. **503**, 129–147 (2019)
2. Xian, X., Chen, F., Wang, J.: An insight into campus network user behaviour analysis decision system. Int. J. Embedded Syst. **9**(1), 3 (2017)
3. Yl, L.: RFID zero knowledge certification protocol research. Tianjin University (2013)
4. Quwaider, M., Jararweh, Y.: Cloud-assisted data management in wireless body area networks. Int. J. Comput. Sci. Eng. **14**(1), 16 (2017)
5. Zanetti, D.: RFID authentication (2012)
6. Liang, W., Xie, S., Li, X., Long, J., Xie, Y., Li, K.-C.: A novel lightweight PUF-based RFID mutual authentication protocol. In: Hung, J.C., Yen, N.Y., Hui, L. (eds.) FC 2017. LNEE, vol. 464, pp. 345–355. Springer, Singapore (2018). https://doi.org/10.1007/978-981-10-7398-4_36
7. Alzubaidi, M.A.: A new strategy for bridging the semantic gap in image retrieval. Int. J. Comput. Sci. Eng. **14**(1), 27 (2017)
8. Liang, W., Liao, B., Long, J., et al.: Study on PUF based secure protection for IC design. Microprocess. Microsyst. **45**, 56–66 (2016)
9. Igier, M., Vaudenay, S.: Distance bounding based on PUF. In: Foresti, S., Persiano, G. (eds.) CANS 2016. LNCS, vol. 10052, pp. 701–710. Springer, Cham (2016). https://doi.org/10.1007/978-3-319-48965-0_48
10. Katz, J.: Analysis of a proposed hash-based signature standard. In: Chen, L., McGrew, D., Mitchell, C. (eds.) SSR 2016. LNCS, vol. 10074, pp. 261–273. Springer, Cham (2016). https://doi.org/10.1007/978-3-319-49100-4_12
11. Avoine, G., Bingöl, M.A., Carpent, X., et al.: Privacy-friendly authentication in RFID systems: on sublinear protocols based on symmetric-key cryptography. IEEE Trans. Mob. Comput. **12**(10), 2037–2049 (2013)

12. Gurubani, J.B., Thakkar, H., Patel, D.R.: Improvements over extended LMAP+: RFID authentication protocol. In: Dimitrakos, T., Moona, R., Patel, D., McKnight, D.H. (eds.) IFIPTM 2012. IAICT, vol. 374, pp. 225–231. Springer, Heidelberg (2012). https://doi.org/10.1007/978-3-642-29852-3_17
13. Xie, S., Liang, W., Xu, J., et al.: A novel bidirectional RFID identity authentication protocol. In: 2018 IEEE SmartWorld, Ubiquitous Intelligence & Computing, Advanced & Trusted Computing, Scalable Computing & Communications, Cloud & Big Data Computing, Internet of People and Smart City Innovation, pp. 301–307. IEEE (2018)
14. He, D., Zeadally, S.: An analysis of RFID authentication schemes for internet of things in healthcare environment using elliptic curve cryptography. IEEE Internet Things J. 2(1), 72–83 (2015)
15. Gao, Y., Ranasinghe, D.C., Al-Sarawi, S.F., et al.: Emerging physical unclonable functions with nanotechnology. IEEE Access 4, 61–80 (2016)
16. Gao, Y., Ranasinghe, D.C., Al-Sarawi, S.F., et al.: Memristive crypto primitive for building highly secure physical unclonable functions. Sci. Rep. 5, 12785 (2015)
17. Strohmeier, M., Lenders, V., Martinovic, I.: On the security of the automatic dependent surveillance-broadcast protocol. IEEE Commun. Surv. Tutor. 17(2), 1066–1087 (2015)
18. Delvaux, J., Peeters, R., Gu, D., et al.: A survey on lightweight entity authentication with strong PUFs. ACM Comput. Surv. (CSUR) 48(2), 26 (2015)
19. Li, H.: PUF-HB#: lightweight bidirectional RFID authentication protocol. J. Beijing Univ. Posts Telecommun. 36(6), 13–17 (2013)
20. Rührmair, U., Sehnke, F., Sölter, J., Dror, G., Devadas, S., Schmidhuber, J.: Modeling attacks on physical unclonable functions. In: Proceedings of the 17th ACM Conference on Computer and Communications Security, pp. 237–249 (2010)
21. Rostami, M., Majzoobi, M., Koushanfar, F., et al.: Robust and reverse-engineering resilient PUF authentication and key-exchange by substring matching. IEEE Trans. Emerg. Top. Comput. 2(1), 37–49 (2014)
22. Blanchet, B., Smyth, B.: ProVerif 1.85: automatic cryptographic protocol verifier. User Manual and Tutorial (2013)
23. Burrows, M., Abadi, M., Needham, R.M.: A logic of authentication. Proc. R. Soc. Lond. A - Math. Phys. Sci. 1989(426), 233–271 (1871)
24. Brisbanne, O.M., Bossuet, L.: Restoration protocol: lightweight and secure devices authentication based on PUF (2017)
25. Idriss, T., Bayoumi, M.: Lightweight highly secure PUF protocol for mutual authentication and secret message exchange. In: 2017 IEEE International Conference on RFID Technology and Application (RFID-TA), pp. 214–219. IEEE (2017)
26. Huang, H.H., Yeh, L.Y., Tsaur, W.J.: Ultra-lightweight mutual authentication and ownership transfer protocol with PUF for Gen2 V2 RFID systems. In: Proceedings of the International Multiconference of Engineers and Computer Scientists (2016)

Enhancing User Privacy in IoT: Integration of GDPR and Blockchain

Masoud Barati[✉] and Omer Rana[✉]

School of Computer Science and Informatics, Cardiff University,
Cardiff CF24 3AA, UK
{BaratiM,RanaOF}@Cardiff.ac.uk

Abstract. The development of Internet of Things (IoT) industries has raised significant questions in terms of accountability of smart devices and user privacy. The advent of European General Data Protection Regulation (GDPR) in such industries enabled users to control their collected data and be informed about the collecting devices. This paper by using blockchain technology provides the audit trail of IoT devices under GDPR rules. It translates a set of such rules into smart contracts to protect personal data in a transparent and automatic way. By proposing an abstract model and designing some business processes, the paper shows how the integration of GDPR and blockchain can appear in the design patterns of IoT devices to achieve a greater transparency of privacy.

Keywords: Internet of Things · User privacy · Blockchain · Smart contracts · General Data Protection Regulation

1 Introduction

IoT devices are expected to reach over 25 billion by 2025, being much more than the number of human population projected to be nearly 8 billion [1]. Such devices are found in military and civilian domains that range from smart cities to Internet of battlefield things. The development of IoT recently raises a main challenge for the protection of personal data, since security breaches in such environment can involve substantial privacy risks for the users whose data are processed by smart objects. In fact, users are surrounded by plenty of devices, collecting their data and possibly transmitting them to unknown third parties. Some IoT users may set their wearable devices in broadcast mode and when they are within discoverable range, any other node can access their personal data by sending an unsafe request. In order to address this, the potential of using blockchain technology for enhancing user privacy and trust in IoT-based applications has been studied [2–5]. Furthermore, the General Data Protection Regulation (GDPR), providing the control of users over their personal data, is another promising solution that has recently been suggested for the improvement of user privacy in IoT [6–8].

The key roles defined in GDPR are a data subject, a controller or joint controller, and a processor. The data subject is directly or indirectly identified

© Springer Nature Singapore Pte Ltd. 2020
Z. Zheng et al. (Eds.): BlockSys 2019, CCIS 1156, pp. 322–335, 2020.
https://doi.org/10.1007/978-981-15-2777-7_26

through an identifier (e.g., name and IP address). The controller is a person or organization determining what operations will be executed on user data. The notion of joint controller is introduced where two or more controllers jointly identify the purpose of data processing. Finally, the processor is responsible for processing personal data on behalf of a controller or joint controller [6]. GDPR gives the responsibility of any violation in data processing to controllers or joint controllers, but also gives a shared responsibility to processors when data subject has no direct control on the processing steps of personal data. Given some recent approaches integrating GDPR into IoT environments, a framework was proposed whereby the GDPR-compliant processing of personal data was realized [9]. Through the framework, data controllers were be able to notify IoT users in a transparent and unambiguous manner about the status of their personal data. In [10], an IoT Databox model making devices accountable to users was designed. The proposed model met the GDPR requirements to enhance the user privacy and trust. The author of [11] examined what role the major upgrade of data privacy regulations under the GDPR can play in addressing the user data protection implications posed by the IoT environment.

Blockchain is a public ledger comprising of a distributed, shared database, and a set of connected nodes [12]. It has lately exploited in IoT to improve transparency, trust, and privacy. For instance, a blockchain-based trust framework for collaborative IoT was proposed in [13]. The framework by defining a set of smart contracts enforced IoT platforms to follow some specific rules in order to build trust in their communications. In [14], a blockchain-based technique providing secure management of healthcare big data in IoT was proposed. The technique combined the advantages of the private key, public key, and smart contracts to promote user privacy and make a patient-centric access control for electronic medical records. A privacy-preserving blockchain based publish/subscribe model for IoT systems was proposed in [15]. The model protected data privacy and interests of subscribers and enabled publishers to control any data access.

Although aforementioned approaches took advantages of novel privacy-aware solutions (i.e., GDPR and blockchain) to safely protect user data, none of them proposed a combination approach to automatically verify GDPR rules over data processing units by monitoring a blockchain network. Moreover, they did not consider the GDPR compliance of operations handled by IoT devices at design time before accessing or manipulating user data. This paper by representing an illustrative example shows how the integration of GDPR and blockchain can appear as sub business processes in the design patterns of IoT devices to protect EU citizens from privacy breaches. It translates some GDPR rules into smart contracts to facilitate the automatic verification of smart objects whose roles are data controller or processor. The paper also presents an abstract model to demonstrate how users and IoT devices are connected to a blockchain network to access our GDPR-based smart contracts. Finally, the contracts are implemented and deployed in a global test network to evaluate their transaction costs and mining time.

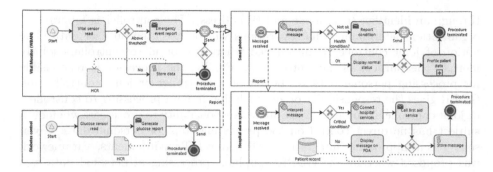

Fig. 1. The process model of IoT-based e-health monitoring system.

The rest of the paper is structured as follows. Section 2 describes an e-health monitoring system and examines the GDPR compliance of operations carried out by its smart devices. Section 3 gives some clues about the translation of GDPR rules into smart contracts. Section 4 provides the experimental results, and finally Sect. 5 concludes the paper and gives some indications about future work.

2   An IoT-Based e-Health Monitoring System Scenario

Imagine that a patient is monitored by a vital monitor device which is a body sensor and transfers the patient's health information via Wireless Body Area Network (WBAN). The patient activates the device to be informed about his general health conditions by measuring heart beat rate, breathing rate, and so on. As a part of the vital monitor device, the patient is equipped with a smart diabetes control device that automatically measures the blood glucose level. Moreover, the patient has a smart phone involving built-in IoT communicators, which enable communication with any wireless network interface. As seen from the design pattern of e-health monitoring system depicted in Fig. 1, both diabetes control and vital monitor devices interact with the smart phone to transfer health relevant information. In case of an abnormal health condition, the smart phone connects to the nearest emergency centre and sends a report containing current status of patient. The centre has a smart alarm system that can automatically call first aid services when the patient requires an emergency assistance. The alarm system also maintains the health condition of patient in its local storage that can be accessed by physicians.

Given the design patterns demonstrated in Fig. 1, the healthcare information, categorized as sensitive data in GDPR, is produced by both vital monitor and diabetes control devices. Such data are stored in the Health Care Record (HCR) databases making it easy to provide all helpful information for patient and physicians in advance. When the patient suffers from diabetes or any chronic diseases, the devices immediately send healthcare information to the smart phone to be interpreted and forwarded to the closest hospital.

From the GDPR perspective, the secure protection of such information is an obligation. For instance, the smart alarm system should support an encryption technique for accessing or storing healthcare information. Basically, a question that can be raised here is how GDPR rules can be integrated into the design patterns of such smart devices to ensure the protection of patient data.

2.1 Data Processing Purposes in e-Health Monitoring System and GDPR Compliance

Each IoT device in Fig. 1 deals with or handles a part of patient information. The vital monitoring device generates vital parameters of patient measured through a number of sensors. It stores the parameters (data) in the HCR database and transfers them to the smart phone when a measured parameter is beyond threshold. The diabetes control device gets the blood sugar of patient and maintains it in the HCR. In case of a high glucose level, the device provides the smart phone the measured information. Subsequently, the smart phone accesses the data produced by devices and delivers it to the alarm device embedded in the nearest hospital. The phone also performs some profiling activities such as statistical calculations on data to evaluate the medical status of patient during a day. Finally, the smart alarm device receives the patient data and keeps it in its local database. It also displays the data in a legible format to be readily observed by doctors.

The purposes of data processing of these devices (actors) can be expressed by some typical operations: *access*, *store*, *profiling*, and *transfer*. More precisely, the operations of vital monitoring, diabetes control, smart phone, and smart alarm devices on patient data are {*store, transfer*}, {*store, transfer*}, and {*access, store, profiling*}, and {*access, store*}, respectively.

Given the operations, several GDPR rules in the forms of legal questions such as those already presented in [16] can be assigned to each operation. Figure 2 represents the questions.

Access: The Art. 32(1)(a) of GDPR requires actors who access sensitive data to have an encryption for preventing unauthorized access to the data. To this end, two legal questions can be proposed for the operation. The first question asks about the personal data whether it is sensitive or not. In the case of sensitive data, the second question is related to the protection of personal data. For instance, the healthcare information that are accessed by both smart phone and alarm device can be considered as sensitive data in GDPR standard.

Store: The Art. 17 of GDPR requires actors who store personal data to provide a capability for their user to erase their personal data at anytime. Moreover, the Art. 5(1)(e) of GDPR does not allow actors to store personal data longer than the time which is necessary for data processing. The first legal question is related to the Art. 17. The two last questions are raised based on the Art. 5(1)(e).

Profiling: The Art. 22 of GDPR states that any profiling operation on users who are under 18 or whose personal data are in the category of sensitive data is risky and an encryption mechanism is required. The first legal question

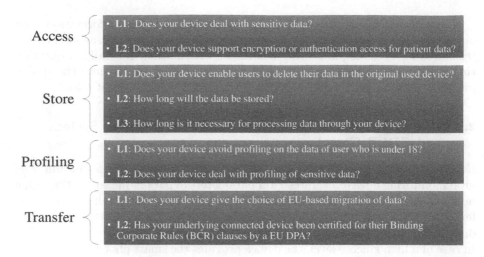

Fig. 2. GDPR legal questions assigned to operations

asks about the filtration of profiling operations such as analysis or prediction on personal data of underage users. The second one asks actors whether their devices deal with profiling of sensitive data or not.

Transfer: The Art. 44–47 of GDPR restrict actors to transfer personal data only inside Europe or the countries holding Binding Corporate Rules (BCR) certifications. The BCR is internal rules (e.g. code of conduct) which are adopted by a community of multinational companies that want to move personal data internationally across various jurisdictions [16]. The first and second legal questions are, respectively, related to the geographical location of actors receiving personal data and the BCR status of data receiver.

Regarding the roles defined in GDPR, all aforementioned IoT devices play as data processors. Except smart alarm device, the rest can also have the role of data controller when they transfer the generated or interpreted data to other devices.

3   Verification of GDPR Rules Through Blockchain

IoT networks contains heterogeneous digital devices with various hardware configurations. Plenty of IoT devices, called as lightweight nodes, are only able to collect or transmit data [17]. Some devices, called as full nodes, are also have powerful calculation chips able to process collected data (e.g., smart phones). Since lightweight nodes have computation and storage limitations, they cannot directly interact with a blockchain network. To address this, lightweight nodes should be served by full nodes to connect blockchain. For instance, both diabetes control and vital monitor devices, classified as lightweight nodes, should be accessed or controlled via a user-friendly platform installed on the smart phone to communicate with a blockchain.

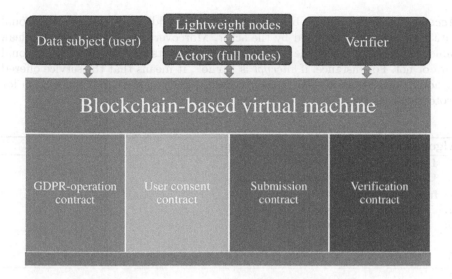

Fig. 3. An abstract model for user privacy using blockchain

An abstract model of our blockchain-based technique is demonstrated in Fig. 3. The user, verifier, and each IoT device should get a unique identity that refers to a blockchain wallet ID such as an Ethereum [18] account to be registered in the blockchain network.[1] Upon the registration, they can access the smart contracts implemented to protect user data with respect to GDPR rules. The actors (controllers/processors) can be full nodes, manufacturers of lightweight nodes, or even the platforms of lightweight nodes normally installed on some full nodes. The verifier is a third party connected to the blockchain-based virtual machine in order to take part in the verification of blockchain. It can also report the actors whose operations do not comply with GDPR requirements. The details about the smart contracts applied in the model are provided as follows.

3.1 GDPR-Operation Contract

It checks the GDPR compliance of actors' operations. Through the contract, actors can claim what operations will be executed on user data. The contract defines a function for each operation activated by actor. Some clues for the implementation of the contract are provided as follows.

Assuming that *compliance* is a Boolean variable that its value shows whether the execution of an operation will comply with its designated GDPR rules or not. For each type of operation, the function's outputs are: the actor address, the personal data processed by the operation, and the value of *compliance*. The outputs are recorded in a blockchain for the aim of verification.

---

[1] If device is a lightweight node, it is indirectly registered in the blockchain via the full node communicating with.

***Access*()**: Let add_a and D_r be, respectively, actor address and the set of personal data that must be processed by the actor. Moreover, let *encrypt* be a Boolean value that shows whether the service of actor supports the encryption of personal data or not. For instance, if *encrypt* is "`true`", it means that the service offered by actor provides an authentication technique such as a secure login system for protecting sensitive data.

Algorithm 1. The function of access operation

    Input: add_a, D_r, *encrypt*
    Output: add_a, D_r, *compliance*

1: **function** ACCESS
2:    *compliance* = `true`;
3:    **if** *encrypt* == `false` **then**
4:        *compliance* = `false`;
5:    **return**(add_a, D_r, *compliance*);

Algorithm 1 presents the function. If the value of *encrypt* is "`false`", the execution of operation violates the GDPR rule legislated in Art. 32(1)(a).

***Store*()**: Let add_a, D_w, T_t, and T_s be actor address, required personal data, the time totally taken for data processing, and the period of time during which personal data will be kept in the storage of actor, respectively. Moreover, let *erase* be a Boolean value that clarifies whether the service of actor enables users to erase their data at any time or not. For example, if the value is "`true`", it means that the service or device has an option for users to delete their data from the local storage of actor.

Algorithm 2. The function of store operation

    Input: add_a, D_w, *erase*, T_t, T_s
    Output: add_a, D_w, *compliance*

1: **function** STORE
2:    *compliance* = `true`;
3:    **if** *erase* == `false` or $T_t < T_s$ **then**
4:        *compliance* = `false`;
5:    **return**(add_a, D_w, *compliance*);

As represented in Algorithm 2, the execution of *store* operation complies with GDPR, if *erase* is "`true`" and $T_s \leq T_t$.

***Profiling*()**: Let add_a, D_p, and *encrypt* be, respectively, actor address, the personal data that must be processed, and a Boolean value representing whether the encryption of sensitive data is supported or not. Furthermore, let *isadult* be a Boolean value so that if the service of actor performs only profiling operation on user over 18, *isadult* is "`true`".

Algorithm 3. The function of profiling operation

Input: add_a, D_p, $isadult$, $encrypt$
Output: add_a, D_p, $compliance$

1: **function** PROFILING
2:     $compliance =$ **true**;
3:     **if** $isadult ==$ **false** or $encrypt ==$ **false then**
4:         $compliance =$ **false**;
5:     **return**(add_a, D_p, $compliance$);

Given Algorithm 3, the execution of operation violates GDPR rule (Art. 22) if $encrypt$ is "**false**" or $isadult$ is "**false**".

***Transfer*()**: Let add_a, D_t, and loc be actor address, the personal data that must be transferred, and the country name of data receiver, receptively. Assuming that BCR is a set containing the list of countries holding BCR certification and EU is a set involving the names of European countries.

Algorithm 4. The function of transfer operation

Input: add_a, D_t, loc
Output: add_a, D_t, $compliance$

1: **function** TRANSFER
2:     $compliance =$ **true**;
3:     **if** $loc \notin EU$ **then**
4:         **if** $loc \notin BCR$ **then**
5:             $compliance =$ **false**;
6:     **return**(add_a, D_t, $compliance$);

As seen from Algorithm 4, if personal data is sent outside Europe and the country of data receiver has not been certified by BCR, the value of *compliance* is "false".

3.2   User Consent Contract

The smart contract enables data subject to give a vote as a consent or negation for the execution of operations already claimed through GDPR-operation contract. In fact, after specifying the GDPR compliance status of an operation, which was calculated and stored in a blockchain by GDPR-operation contract, data subject retrieves the records of blockchain and accepts or rejects the execution of operation. Figure 4 represents the business process in which actor stores its claim in a blockchain and data subject gives a vote to the actor's operations on personal data. In the business process of e-health monitoring system, the pattern (Fig. 4) can be added as a sub process just before the typical operations (access, transfer, etc.) executed by devices. For instance, in the smart phone, the pattern is appended just before "message received", "profile patient data", and "send" activities.

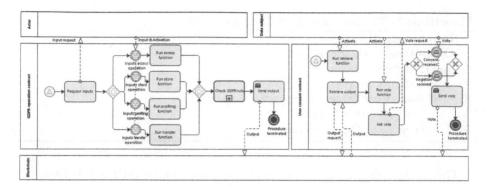

Fig. 4. Business process of activities in GDPR-operation and user consent contracts

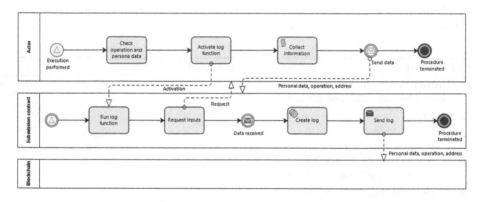

Fig. 5. Business process of activities performed through submission contract

3.3 Submission Contract

Figure 5 demonstrates a design pattern for interactions between actor and submission smart contract. The actor deploys submission contract to store its address, executed operation, and the personal data processed by the operation in a blockchain. The contract uses a function, called *log*, to submit such information in the blockchain. In the business process of e-health monitoring system, the pattern (Fig. 5) can be added as a sub process after the operations executed by devices. For example, in the vital monitor device, the pattern should appear just after "**send**" and "**store data**" activities.

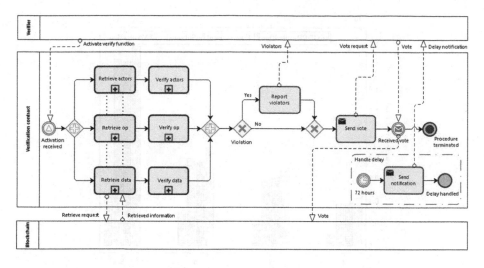

Fig. 6. Business process of interactions performed through verification contract

3.4   Verification Contract

Figure 6 shows the business process through which the verification of actors is accomplished. Once the function of the verification contract, called *verify*, has been activated, the list of actors, their operations, and the processed personal data are retrieved from the blockchain. A violation is clarified by verification contract if the executed operation of actor did not get the user consent or some personal data processed by the operation are different with those already claimed by actor via the GDPR-operation contract. The verifier gives a vote after detecting any violation, and the vote is stored in the blockchain for future references. Notably, the sub process *handle delay* is considered to notify verifier about any violation or breach before 72 h referring to Art. 33 of GDPR. In our blockchain-based model, the duty of notifying violations is, however, delegated to the verifier instead of actors.

After completing the procedures represented in the business processes of devices existing in e-health monitoring system, the pattern depicted in Fig. 6 can individually be executed through verifier.

4   Experimental Results

An initial prototype was built through Ropsten [19], which is a public blockchain test network. We implemented our proposed smart contracts on Ethereum using Solidity [20]. The smart contracts were written with the concern of minimum gas consumption per each function or transaction. They were tested using Remix, which is an online IDE for Solidity running deployed contracts. The smart contracts *User consent*, *GDPR-operation*, *Submission*, and *Verification* were deployed in Ropsten. The amount of gas used for the contracts deployment in

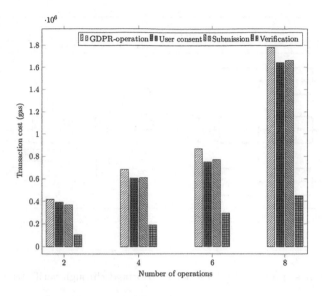

Fig. 7. The relationship between the number of operations and gas consumption

the network was 1156961 for *User consent*, 1494786 for *GDPR-operation*, 527497 for *Submission*, and 1246963 for *Verification*.

4.1 The Impact of Number of Operations on Consumed Gas

This experiment by changing the number of operations evaluates the amount of gas used for the activation of functions or transactions in our proposed smart contracts. The assumption is that we have only one IoT device and the number of operations executed by the device varies from 2 to 6. Moreover, each operation deals with some personal data (healthcare information). The number of personal data is randomly selected between 1 and 5 per each times of execution. Our proposed smart contracts were deployed in the Ropsten environment and each function with different parameters was activated five times to calculate the average used gas results.[2] Figure 7 illustrates the results of the experiment. The x-axis shows the number of operations and the y-axis indicates the average rate of gas consumption for the transactions of each smart contract. As seen from the bar chart, when the number of operations increases, the amount of used gas increases gradually. For instance, the rate of gas consumed for user consent contract is around 390673 with two operations and reaches nearly 1641859 when we have eight operations. The most portion of cost should be paid for the transactions implemented in GDPR-operation contract, since they had the greatest number of opcodes compared with the transactions of other contracts.

---

[2] For each times of execution, an operation is randomly selected among *access*, *store*, *profiling*, and *transfer*.

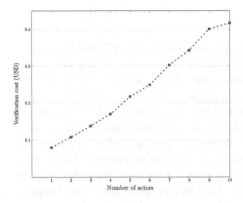

Fig. 8. The relationship between number of actors and verification cost

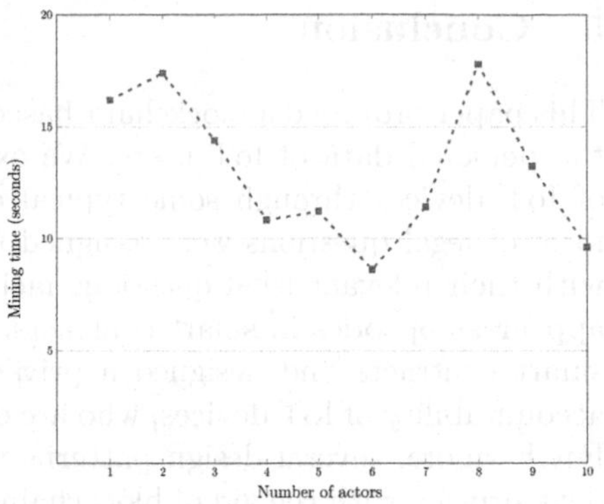

Fig. 9. The relationship between number of actors and mining time

4.2 The Impact of Number of Actors on Verification Cost and Mining Time

It is assumed that the number of actors (devices) varies from 1 to 10 and each actor executes only one operation. Furthermore, the number of personal data processed by the operation is randomly selected between 1 and 5. For a given number of actors, one actor is supposed to violate user consent. Figure 8 shows the relationship between the number of actors and the cost that should be paid for detecting the violation through verification contract. In the experiment, the contract was deployed in Ropsten and the gas price was 3.3 (gwei). Moreover, the average cost spent on activating the *verify* function was calculated after five times execution of smart contracts.[3] As seen from the graph, when the number of actors increases, the verification cost rises constantly. In fact, the complexity of verification process goes up and more storage space is required when the number of actors increases.

Another experiment evaluates the relationship between the number of actors and the mining time taking for executing the transactions of verification contract, which was also tested by Ropsten.[4] Figure 9 represents the amount of time taking in seconds for the verify function to be successfully mined by a miner since its activation time. As seen from the figure, there is a fluctuation in the trend of the graph with the increase of the number of actors. The results show that the time depends on the interest of miners for mining the verify function and does not depend on the number of actors or function parameters. As a result, the miners can usually take an arbitrary time for the mining process.

---

[3] The verify function, implemented in the verification contract, checks whether operations of actors on personal data conform to user consent or not.

[4] The assumptions of the experiment are the same with previous experiment, namely the investigation of cost by changing the number of actors.

5   Conclusion

This paper proposed a blockchain-based approach, supporting GDPR, to protect the personal data of IoT users. We expressed the purposes of data processing of IoT devices through some typical operations. A set of GDPR rules in the form of legal questions were assigned to each operation. Such operations along with their relevant legal questions facilitated the translation of GDPR rules to appear as opcodes in smart contracts. The paper proposed some GDPR-based smart contracts and designed a privacy-aware abstract model to improve the accountability of IoT devices, who are data controllers or processors of user data. Furthermore, several design patterns were presented to show how the right to data privacy with the aid of blockchain and GDPR can be added to the business processes of IoT devices at design time. Such patterns enforced devices to carry out any operation on personal data under the user consent. Otherwise, they were classified to be violators. Notably, the integration of GDPR and blockchain in our approach is not only limited for improving privacy in IoT environment. It can also be prescribed for any kind of service-based environments such as SOA and cloud computing. Our proposed smart contracts were deployed in Ropsten test network and the results indicated that there is a direct relation between the number of operations executed on personal data and the cost spent on the verification of operations in accordance with GDPR rules. The mining time was, however, independent of the complexity of proposed smart contracts.

The future work will focus on the implementation of our approach in an IoT testbed with a heterogeneous group of devices. Moreover, we will try to define more typical operations and take into consideration more GDPR rules based on the functionalities of IoT devices. The implementation of our designed abstract model in a permissioned or private blockchain such as Hyperledger Fabric is also another potential research avenue for future investigation.

References

1. Patsioura, C.: Blockchain and distributed ledger technologies: what's the value for IoT? Technical report, GSMA Intelligence (2018)
2. Boudguiga, A., et al.: Towards better availability and accountability for IoT updates by means of a Blockchain. In: IEEE European Symposium on Security and Privacy Workshops, Paris, France, pp. 50–58 (2017)
3. Panarello, A., Tapas, N., Merlino, G., Longo, F., Puliafito, A.: Blockchain and IoT integration: a systematic survey. Sensors 18(8), 2575 (2018)
4. Hassan, M.U., Rehmani, M.H., Chen, J.: Privacy preservation in blockchain based IoT systems: integration issues, prospects, challenges, and future research directions. Futur. Gener. Comput. Syst. 97, 512–529 (2019)
5. Casino, F., Dasaklis, T.K., Patsakis, C.: A systematic literature review of blockchain-based applications: current status, classification and open issues. Telemat. Inform. 36, 55–81 (2019)
6. Virvou, M., Mougiakou, E.: Based on GDPR privacy in UML: case of e-learning program. In: 8th International Conference on Information, Intelligence, Systems and Applications, Larnaca, Cyprus (2017)

7. Wachter, S.: Normative challenges of identification in the Internet of Things: privacy, profiling, discrimination, and the GDPR. Comput. Law Secur. Rev. **34**(3), 436–449 (2018)
8. Castelluccia, C., Cunche, M., Metayer, D.L., Morel, V.: Enhancing transparency and consent in the IoT. In: IEEE European Symposium on Security and Privacy Workshops, London, UK, pp. 116–119 (2018)
9. Rantos, K., Drosatos, G., Demertzis, K., Ilioudis, C., Papanikolaou, A.: Blockchain-based consents management for personal data processing in the IoT ecosystem. In: 15th International Joint Conference on e-Business and Telecommunications, Porto, Portugal, pp. 572–577 (2018)
10. Crabtree, A., et al.: Building accountability into the Internet of Things: the IoT Databox mode. J. Reliab. Intell. Environ. **4**(1), 39–55 (2018)
11. Loideain, N.N.: A port in the data-sharing storm: the GDPR and the Internet of Things. J. Cyber Policy **4**(2), 178–196 (2019)
12. Zheng, Z., Xie, S., Dai, H., Chen, X., Wang, H.: An overview of blockchain technology: architecture, consensus, and future trends. In: IEEE 6th International Congress on Big Data, Honolulu, USA, pp. 557–564 (2017)
13. Tang, B., Kang, H., Fan, J., Li, Q., Sandhu, R.: IoT passport: a blockchain-based trust framework for collaborative Internet-of-Things. In: 24th ACM Symposium on Access Control Models and Technologies, Toronto, Canada, pp. 83–92 (2019)
14. Dwivedi, A.D., Srivastava, G., Dhar, S., Singh, R.: A decentralized privacy-preserving healthcare blockchain for IoT. Sensors **19**(2), 326 (2019)
15. Lv, P., Wang, L., Zhu, H., Deng, W., Gu, L.: An IoT-oriented privacy-preserving publish/subscribe model over blockchains. IEEE Access **7**, 41309–41314 (2019)
16. Corrales, M., Jurčys, P., Kousiouris, G.: Smart contracts and smart disclosure: coding a GDPR compliance framework. In: Corrales, M., Fenwick, M., Haapio, H. (eds.) Legal Tech, Smart Contracts and Blockchain. PLBI, pp. 189–220. Springer, Singapore (2019). https://doi.org/10.1007/978-981-13-6086-2_8
17. Qiu, H., Qiu, M., Memmi, G., Ming, Z., Liu, M.: A dynamic scalable blockchain based communication architecture for IoT. In: Qiu, M. (ed.) SmartBlock 2018. LNCS, vol. 11373, pp. 159–166. Springer, Cham (2018). https://doi.org/10.1007/978-3-030-05764-0_17
18. Ethereum. https://www.ethereum.org/. Accessed 10 Sept 2019
19. Ropsten testnet PoW chain. https://github.com/ethereum/ropsten. Accessed 7 Sept 2019
20. Solidity. https://solidity.readthedocs.io/en/v0.5.3. Accessed 5 Sept 2019

A Blockchain-Based Trustable Framework for IoT Data Storage and Access

Jiangfeng Li, Shili Hu, Yang Shi, and Chenxi Zhang$^{(\boxtimes)}$

School of Software Engineering, Tongji University, Shanghai 201804, China
{lijf,1931530,shiyang,xzhang2000}@tongji.edu.cn

Abstract. As the use of Internet of Things (IoT) devices is increasing dramatically, it is necessary to provide a trustable framework when IoT data are stored and used inside or outside IoT devices. Blockchains and smart contracts provide solutions to construct trustable environments in data storage and access. Unfortunately, current blockchain technology only suits for situations that a small or medium amount of data is stored and used, but it has a very low performance when a large amount of data gathered by IoT devices needs to be stored and accessed. This paper proposes a three-layer blockchain-based trustable framework for IoT data storage and access. In the framework, users, roles, permissions, data objects, and their relationships are formally defined. Based on these definitions, smart contracts with role-based access control (RBAC) model are developed. Additionally, a snapshot mechanism is designed to collect IoT data in order of time stamps and put it into files stored in the inter-planetary file system (IPFS). We developed a prototype of supply chain tracing system on Ethereum and IPFS for feasibility verification and performance evaluation of the proposed framework. The framework not only guarantees data integrity in storing IoT data, but also ensures data confidentiality when the IoT data is used. Moreover, simulation results illustrate that the prototype system has high performances in time, space, and gas consumption.

Keywords: Blockchain · Trustable framework · Smart contract · IPFS · IoT data

1 Introduction

Last decade has witnessed the boom of applications of the Internet of Things (IoT) in various areas of our society, such as agriculture [1], industry [2], and smart home [3]. Under the circumstance, a large number of IoT devices have been used in IoT systems. Those well-connected IoT devices in a system compose an IoT network. Data is collected by the devices and transmitted in the IoT network. In this case, there is a large amount of available data generated in an IoT network. However, it is a big challenge that how to manage the data securely [4]. That means a trustable environment has to be provided to keep the privacy and security of data in data storage and transmission. Moreover, as the amount of IoT data grows, requirements of large-scale data analysis are gradually increasing. An efficient solution for large-scale data transmission and aggregation is urgently needed.

© Springer Nature Singapore Pte Ltd. 2020
Z. Zheng et al. (Eds.): BlockSys 2019, CCIS 1156, pp. 336–349, 2020.
https://doi.org/10.1007/978-981-15-2777-7_27

Blockchain is a technology that provides a public ledge which only accepts transactions signed by specific addresses and private keys [5]. This ledge can record IoT data by packing them into transactions and blocks. Nodes or IoT devices can pack the data locally and upload them into the ledge permanently. With smart contracts, we can deploy decentralized applications (DApps) which are trustful for every IoT devices in the network. DApps can execute some logic business automatically like traditional applications. However, comparing with the traditional applications and systems, DApps cost gas for execution and storage, which is related to digital currencies [6]. Besides, as blockchain is not designed to store large amounts of data, its storage capacity and scalability still limit its integration with IoT [7]. As a consequence, traditional blockchain implementations cannot satisfy the requirements of IoT application.

To address these issues, this paper proposes a trustable framework using blockchain technology for IoT data storage and access. The main contributions of the paper are listed as follows:

1. A blockchain-based trustable framework is proposed to guarantee data integrity when IoT data is stored or transmitted in an IoT network.
2. A blockchain-based RBAC model is presented. In the model, we define four entities and three rules. Under the model, smart contracts are designed to keep the data confidentiality when the data is accessed and used by various users. We proposed a mechanism to aggregate the IoT data in the storage process by specific rules, which reduces the burden of blockchain on transaction processing and the space occupation of data.
3. A prototype system based on the trustable framework is developed and deployed in a private Ethereum network. The prototype system is used to perform experiments and evaluate the performances of the trustable framework.

This paper is organized as follows. Section 2 introduces related works about data storage and access control in IoT based on blockchain. The trustable framework is described in Sect. 3. Section 4 designs RBAC smart contracts and Sect. 5 explains details of snapshot mechanism. Section 6 provides a prototype system to evaluate performances of the trustable framework. The paper is concluded in Sect. 7.

2 Related Works

The blockchain-based IoT system has already been widely used. For example, the system proposed by Xu et al. [8] is designed to ensure the authenticity of electronic devices and systems during their lifecycles. Mondal et al. [9] used RFID and blockchain to realize the traceability of food in supply chain. But the problems of IoT data storage must be solved, or we have to pack all the data into blocks at a high cost.

Actually, it is better to store the raw data off-chain and record the corresponding receipt on the blockchain. Ayoade et al. [10] proposed approaches to store the heterogeneous IoT data in Trustable Execution Environment (TEE), and use smart contracts to manage data access on blockchain. This solution provides a blockchain-based trustable architecture for IoT data storage, but its permission model and TEE is only suitable for private network.

Role-based Access Control (RBAC) is a permission model, in which users are associated with roles and roles are associated with different permissions to services [11]. With this model, it is easy to manage the permissions of IoT devices on data access control. The security of this model has greatly improved after being realized on blockchain with smart contracts. Zhang et al. proposed SCBAC [12] to manage IoT devices which used smart contracts and local servers to realize a data access control on IoT devices. Cruz et al. proposed RBAC-SC [13], which involved the Role concept to realize a trans-organizational management on IoT devices. It was combined with a role-issuing organization to control the Roles out of the blockchain. But both local servers and role-issuing organizations are centralized, and the data authenticity and service availability cannot be guaranteed. So, a decentralized storage method is needed.

Inter-Planetary File System (IPFS) is a decentralized P2P file system [14]. It can provide a much cheap service on file storage and costs less space than traditional blockchain, which uses a hash string to represent a file uniquely while storing and keeps the file in data blocks. Ali et al. [15] shows that by recording a file hash on blockchain, the unique data file on IPFS can be identified. And they regard IPFS as an ideal file storage platform for developing a decentralized access control model for IoT. But the framework they proposed limits the data storage of one device in one file, which is not suitable for RBAC and produces a space wasting while insertion. Therefore, we replace the private servers in SCBAC and storage service providers in RBAC-SC with IPFS to protect the authenticity and verifiability of IoT data. But we need another algorithm to allow RBAC and save more on IPFS.

Several researches show that the IoT data are produced in chronological order and can be aggregated by time and categories in many cases [16, 17]. Because it is space-wasting to store light files on IPFS [14], a data aggregation mechanism is needed to merge light records into data files in a proper size. In this paper, a snapshot mechanism is proposed for this requirement, which aggregates data into data files based on specific rules and provides version control.

Our framework in this paper realizes a trustable and decentralized data storage on IPFS by protecting the data authenticity with a reliable access control based on blockchain. With the integration of RBAC smart contracts and snapshot mechanism, this framework can provide a low cost, high efficiency, and practical management service for chronological IoT data.

3   Blockchain-Based Trustable Framework

A blockchain-based trustable framework is proposed to provide a trustful environment for data storage and data access. The framework has two characters. Data integrity is one of these two characters. That means, the framework prevents data stored in it from being changed. Role-based data access is the other. It ensures that the framework offers different data access permissions to various users and IoT devices.

The framework contains three layers, which are Infrastructure Layer, Middleware Layer, and Application Layer. In the Infrastructure Layer, the data generated by IoT devices are stored in a decentralized environment, which consists of blockchain node and IPFS node. Permission Management and Storage Management are two main functional components in the Middleware Layer. Permission Management contains several kinds of smart contracts and provides a reliable RBAC service. Storage Management manages the storage of data and maintains the rules of data aggregation. In the Application Layer, application interfaces are provided. The framework offers services of data storage and data access through the interfaces, such as web UI and mobile APPs. Figure 1 shows the structure of the trustable framework.

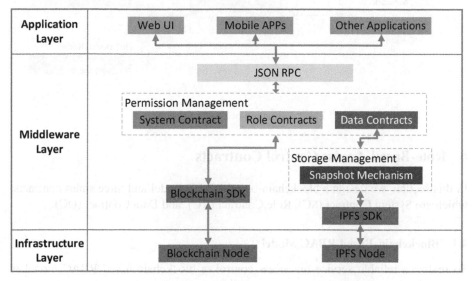

Fig. 1. Structure of blockchain-based trustable framework

As far as most of the IoT devices cannot afford to run a blockchain node or an IPFS node independently, we defined two kinds of nodes in the network, Data Hub Node and IoT Device Node. The former works on high-performance computers and the later works on IoT devices. Different jobs are assigned to the two types of nodes according to their capabilities in calculation and storage. The Data Hub Node is designed to store files for IPFS, work as a miner for blockchain and provide services for applications, so it runs all three layers' components. The IoT Device Node is responsible for data aggregation, and it only runs the middleware layer of our framework.

Therefore, we divide the network into several units called Unit Network. As it is displayed in Fig. 2, a Unit Network contains a Data Hub Node and some IoT Device Nodes. These IoT Device Nodes communicate with the Data Hub Node directly through the Infrastructure Layer by sending encrypted transactions and data files.

After reading the data stream from IoT hardware, an IoT Device Node can upload a data file to IPFS and receive a file hash as the receipt. By recording the file hash to the blockchain with encrypted transactions, every piece of the data will be stored permanently. The Data Hub Node can only analyze the transactions from its Infrastructure Layer, so the risk of data tampering is the lowest. If the Data Hub Node is no longer available, IoT Device Nodes can find a replacement easily because all the Data Hub Nodes in the network share the same ledge and file blocks.

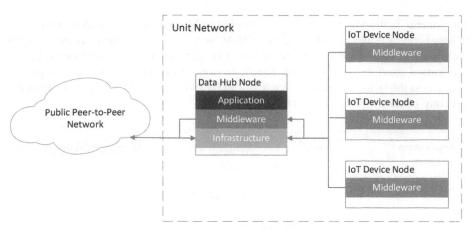

Fig. 2. Structure of a Unit Network

4 Role-Based Access Control Contracts

In this section, we design a blockchain-based RBAC model and three smart contracts, which are System Contract (SC), Role Contract (RC), and Data Contract (DC).

4.1 Blockchain-Based RBAC Model

To realize a reliable service on access control, a blockchain-based RBAC model is proposed.

Firstly, four entities are defined in our blockchain-based RBAC model: *user*, *role*, *permission*, and *object*.

- **Definition 1 (Operation):** Operation is access activity that a system owns. Operation *read* and *write* are the only two operations in the system. Let OP be the set of operations.

$$OP = \{read, write\}$$

- **Definition 2 (Object):** Object is a data entity, which is an atomic entity and cannot be divided any more. Let ob and OB be object and the set of objects respectively.

$$ob = \langle obID, obAddress, obName \rangle$$
$$OB = \{ob_1, ob_2, \ldots, ob_k\}$$

where $obID$ is the unique ID of ob, $obAddress$ is the address of ob on the blockchain, $obName$ is the name of ob, and $ob_i (1 \leqslant i \leqslant k)$ is the i-th object in OB.
- **Definition 3 (Permission):** Permission is a vector that contains object and operation. Let p and P be permission and the set of permissions.

$$p = \langle pID, pObject, pOperation \rangle$$
$$P = \{p_1, p_2, \ldots, p_l\}$$

where pID is the unique ID of permission p, $pObject$ is an object of p, $pOperation$ is the permitted operation of p, and $p_i (1 \leqslant i \leqslant l)$ is the i-th permission of P.

- **Definition 4 (Role):** Role is a vector that contains a finite set of permissions. Let r and R be role and the set of roles.

$$r = \langle rID, rAddress, rName, \bigcup_{k=1}^{l_k} rPermission \rangle$$

$$R = \{r_1, r_2, \ldots, r_m\}$$

where rID is the unique ID of role r, $rAddress$ is the address of r on the blockchain, $rName$ is the name of r, $\bigcup_{k=1}^{l_k} rPermission$ is the set of permissions of r, and $r_i (1 \leqslant i \leqslant m)$ is the i-th role of R.

- **Definition 5 (User):** User is an entity that uses objects. Let u and U be a user and the set of users.

$$u = \langle uID, uAddress, uName, uRole \rangle$$

$$U = \{u_1, u_2, \ldots, u_n\}$$

where uID is the unique ID of user u, $uAddress$ is the address of u on the blockchain, $uName$ is the name of u, $uRole$ is the role of u, and $u_i (1 \leqslant i \leqslant n)$ is the i-th user of U.

Then, several functions are defined as follows.

1. $assignRole(u \in U, r \in R)$ assigns role r to user u.
2. $assignPms(r \in R, p \in P)$ assigns permission p to role r.
3. $access(u \in U, ob \in O, op \in OP)$ returns $true$ if user u operates op on object o.
4. $getRole(u \in U)$ returns the assigned role of user u.
5. $getPms(r \in R)$ returns the set of permissions which belongs to role r.
6. $getObj(p \in P)$ returns the target object of permission p.
7. $getOp(p \in P)$ returns the permitted operation of permission p.

Therefore, we define several rules for this permission model.

- **Rule 1 (Rule of Role Uniqueness)** A user can only own one role, which means two or more roles cannot be related to a user at the same time.
  Under the Rule 1, function of role assignment is defined as,

$$\forall u_i \in U, r_j \in R, 1 \leqslant i \leqslant n, 1 \leqslant j \leqslant m, getRole(u_i) = \emptyset,$$
$$assignRole(u_i, r_i) \Rightarrow r_j \leftarrow u_i.uRole$$

The Rule 1 gives constraint that a role is assigned to a user only when the user is not related to any role. If the user has been related to a role already, a new role cannot be assigned to the user unless the old role is removed.

- **Rule 2 (Rule of Permission Upgrade)** A role updates its permission only in the situation that the new permission has a higher grade than the old one.

Under the Rule 2, function of permission assignment is defined as,

$$\forall r_i \in R, p_j \in P, p_x \in getPms(r_i), 1 \leqslant i \leqslant m, 1 \leqslant j, x \leqslant l, i \neq j,$$
$$getObj(p_j) = getObj(p_x) \wedge (getOp(p_j) > getOp(p_x)),$$
$$assignPms(r_i, p_j) \Rightarrow r_i.rPermissions \leftarrow r_i.rPermissions \cup p_j$$

The Rule 2 gives constraint that a new permission can be assigned if none of the existed permissions of the role has a higher grade than the new one.

- **Rule 3 (Rule of Access Relevance)** A user can access an object if there is a consistent relationship among user, role, permission, operation, and object.

Under the Rule 3, function of access permission verification is defined as,

$$\forall u_i \in U, o_j \in O, op_x \in OP, 1 \leqslant i \leqslant n, 1 \leqslant j \leqslant k, 1 \leqslant x \leqslant 2,$$
$$\exists r_y \in R, p_z \in P, 1 \leqslant y \leqslant m, 1 \leqslant z \leqslant l,$$
$$access(u_i, o_j, op_x) \Rightarrow (u_i \in getMembers(r_y)) \wedge (p_z \in getPms(r_y)) \wedge$$
$$(o_j = getObj(p_z)) \wedge (op_x = getOp(p_z))$$

In constraint of the Rule 3, user u_i can access object o_j with permission p_z successfully if the role of the u_i has a permission p_z, and p_z is accessing o_j with op_x.

4.2 Contracts Design

Different jobs are assigned to different contracts. First, SC acts as the entrance of the system on the blockchain, and maintains the identifier of *user* in a struct called *User*. It also stores the relationships between *user* and *role* which contains the address of a user and his role name. The relationships between *role* and RC are stored in a map called *rcIndex* which takes role name as the key and contract address as the value. Second, RC stores the relationships between *role* and *permissions* in two maps called *owned* and *managed*. They represent two operations: *write* and *read*. Each permission contains the name of its target *object* and the related DC address. RC manages the shared permissions among users in the same functional groups. Besides, DC maintains the identifier of *object*, it stores the file hashes from IPFS of the same categories in a map called *hashes*. This map contains the IDs and hashes of IPFS files. One SC, several RCs and DCs can make up an RBAC contracts system for permission control.

Figure 3 shows how these RBAC contracts are related on the blockchain. After the SC is first deployed, it deploys RCs and SCs on the demand of admin and stores their addresses in its lookup table. The rule of how the SC deploys RC and DC is that one RC for one role and one DC for one category of data. When a transaction wants to update a permission or record a file hash, the SC will search the address of the related contract first and send an invocation message.

4.3 Business Logic

When users in the system want to update permissions or file hashes, they must send a transaction to SC. Its input declares the operation they want to execute and provides the

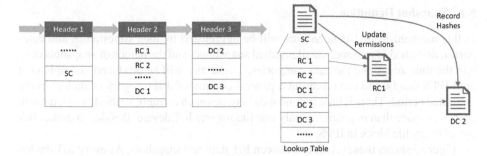

Fig. 3. Contract relations on blockchain

necessary parameters. SC will check their permissions first according to the data stored in SC and RCs, then invoke the functions of the corresponding contract. Figure 4 shows all the invocations that will happen in hash writing (a) and permission assignment (b) and their sequence.

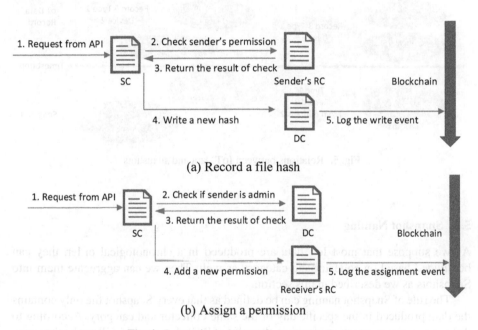

(a) Record a file hash

(b) Assign a permission

Fig. 4. Invocation sequence between contracts

5 Snapshot Mechanism

As we described in Sect. 2, in most cases, IoT data are produced in a chronological order (e.g. sensor data). They always contain a timestamp in data IDs, and are rarely changed. So, in this section, we design a simple mechanism to aggregate, store and query the IoT data records—the snapshot mechanism.

5.1 Snapshot Definition

In this mechanism, IoT data records will be aggregated by their timestamps and categories, and divided into specific files called snapshots. And the names of snapshots contain the time zones and the data categories. These files will be produced and uploaded onto IPFS finally, and can represent a general commit of this category of data of every separated period. There is little redundancy between each commit, so this file mechanism costs less space than maintaining only one file for one IoT device. Besides, it makes full use of every file block in IPFS.

Figure 5 shows these relations between IoT data and snapshots. As every IoT device is assigned a unique address on the blockchain as its identification, the producers of Snapshots are named by their addresses. And one snapshot can have several producers who have the same role and the same permissions (Doing the same job in the IoT network). But only the data records which have the same data category and are in the same time zone will be aggregated into the same snapshot.

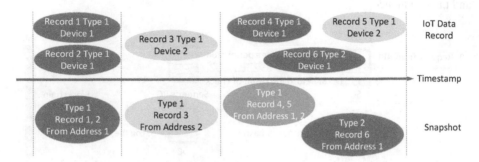

Fig. 5. Relations between IoT data and snapshots

5.2 Snapshot Naming

As we suppose that most IoT data are produced in a chronological order, they can be divided based on collector and category as well. Then we can aggregate them into Snapshots as we described in this section.

The rule of Snapshot naming can be defined as that every Snapshot file only contains the data produced in the specific day of the same collector and category. According to different requirements of aggregation, the rules of Snapshot naming will not be the same.

5.3 Iteration Rules

Even if the IoT data are mainly consists of read-only records, we may still have to update the Snapshot file in some cases (e.g. merging the data from different IoT devices with the same Snapshot name). In this kind of conditions, the solution is version control.

Figure 6 shows the whole process of Snapshot updating as follows.

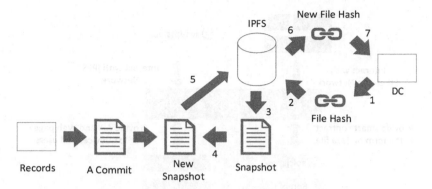

Fig. 6. The whole process of snapshot updating

1. Lock the file on the mission table and fetch the latest file hash from the DC.
2. Download the existed version of the snapshot file from IPFS.
3. Verify the file name with the rules in DC.
4. Merge this file with a new data commit, which contains some new records.
5. Upload the new version of snapshot file to IPFS.
6. Get a file hash as the receipt, which is different from the old one.
7. Sign and send a transaction to update the file hash in that DC.

Because of the features of IPFS, the hash of the snapshot file changes even if a byte of it is altered. Then, we are storing a new file onto IPFS while updating a snapshot and overwriting the file hash in DCs. The old one will be left in IPFS and its hash can be still found from a past transaction on the ledge of blockchain.

6 Prototype System

To verify our framework and evaluate its performance, we implement a prototype system for IoT data storage based on RBAC contracts and snapshot mechanism.

6.1 Overview

Figure 7 shows all the software and packages which were used in this system. To compare our framework with others, we took Ethereum as the blockchain base and developed a prototype system. Then we took Solidity and solcjs as the programing language for smart contracts and the compiler.

Also, we adopted Vue.js as the framework of Web UI, Spring Boot to develop the platform system. And we used web3j (i.e. the Ethereum Java API) and java-ipfs-api (i.e. the IPFS Java API) as the SDK to interact with the geth node and the IPFS network.

6.2 Implementation

RBAC Contracts. According to the contract design in Sect. 3, all three kinds of contracts are implemented into template contracts. And they can be easily deployed with some necessary information. Some events are defined in every contract that will produce logs in the transaction output and can be analyzed by Whisper in Web3j.

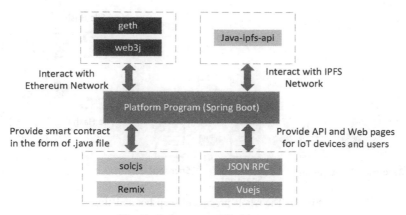

Fig. 7. Software used in this system

Snapshot Mechanism. Based on the design in Sect. 4 and the platform system, the snapshot mechanism is implemented in Java with asynchronous optimization. That means the response time of write requests will not be limited by the time cost of file uploading on both creating and updating.

Web UI. To display business logic in the system, we design and realize a Web UI as an extra component, of which Fig. 8 shows several transactions in our system.

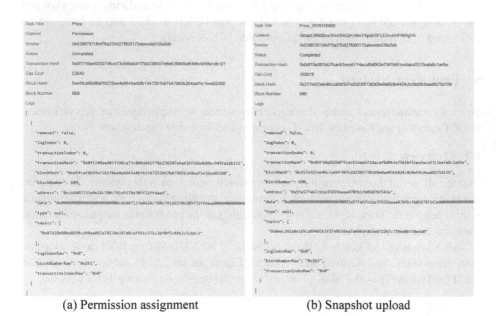

(a) Permission assignment   (b) Snapshot upload

Fig. 8. Screenshots of Web pages

Platform Program. To interact with the smart contract and IPFS, and provide reliable service to the Web UI, a platform program is essential. It includes the smart contracts files, SDKs and the services we developed. With Spring Boot and Web3j, this platform provides standard APIs in the format of JSON RPC.

6.3 Performance Evaluation

For the sake of comparing the performance of our framework which adopts the snapshot mechanism and IPFS with traditional DApps that store data on the blockchain directly, an experimental application was deployed. This application contained 1 SC, 10 RCs and 58 SCs for the case of supply chain, based on the architecture of an agri-food supply chain traceability system [18]. By sending concurrent requests to the platform program and calculating the average time cost and space cost, we made a comparison on multiple indicators.

This experiment was performed on a laptop with 8 cores and 16 GB memory. In the experiment, we simulated 8 nodes as IoT Device Nodes with 8 Ethereum accounts and 1 node as Data Hub Node in the network. We sent 10000 data records of 8 different categories continuously to each IoT Device Node. And we took the result of dividing the data record ID by 100 to divide the aggregation of snapshot files. The content of every record was a string with random content whose size is fixed 100 characters.

Finally, it cost 167 s in total for the whole network to store all the data to the IPFS and blockchain. 800 snapshot files were produced and 800 transactions succeeded. And the size of each snapshot file was about 12 KB. That meant it takes about 16.70 ms and 0.12 KB of space on average to store an IoT record in the form of a 100-character-long string on every node. The data processing capability of the whole network is 479.04 records per second.

To test the performance and scalability of the framework in a Unit Network (1 data hub with several IoT devices), we changed the amount of node and did some further experiments in the same environment, with the same naming rule and sent the same amount of records to each node. The results are displayed in Fig. 9, in which the average time cost (a) represents the average time interval between request and data be cached. And the transactions per second (TPS) represents (b) the number of records cached per second in the Unit Network.

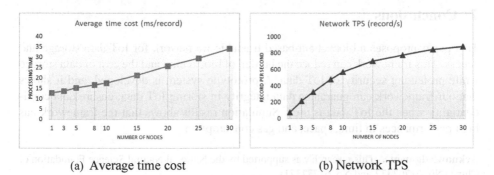

(a) Average time cost   (b) Network TPS

Fig. 9. Performance evaluation

As it is displayed in this chart, the average time cost on each node increased stably first due to the cost of network communication. The TPS of the unit network increases rapidly first and slowly last because of its inverse relationship with the average time cost. This result shows that every single unit should ha its top TPS limit because of the cost of network communication. And to balance the network TPS and the performance of each IoT Device Node, the number ratio of Data Hub Node to IoT Device Nodes should be well evaluated.

Compared with traditional DApps on Ethereum which wait for 15-20 s to confirm a block and save data in the contract storage, our system has a rapid processing speed which is not limited by the block time anymore. This experiment proved the performance and scalability of our IoT data system. By producing fewer transactions and lightening the traffic load on the blockchain network, our system makes it possible to realize a trans-organizational and scalable data sharing in IoT network. And it can connect several units or even different IoT networks with reliable access control.

We calculate all the transactions that happened in these experiments and list them in Table 1 with the corresponding results in SCBAC [12] and RBAC-SC [13]. Comparing with the results in SCBAC and RBAC-SC, the contracts in our RBAC have a lower consumption of gas on invocation.

Table 1. Gas cost of different operations

Operation	Gas used		
	Ours	SCBAC [12]	RBAC-SC [13]
Deploy SC	3,735,474	1,559,814	1,813,010
Deploy RC	493,380	–	–
Deploy SC	622,937	2,543,479	–
Register a new user	70,423	–	145,590
Assign a permission	54,630	90,000	153,531
Store a snapshot hash	103,210	–	–

7   Conclusions

This paper proposes a blockchain-based trustable framework for IoT data storage and access. This framework can reduce the burden of blockchain and the cost of data storage while protecting security of IoT data. A prototype system is developed, and it shows that our framework can guarantee data integrity in storing IoT data, ensure data confidentiality when the IoT data is used. Simulation results shows that the framework has high performances in time, space, and gas consumption.

Acknowledgments. This research was supported by the National Natural Science Foundation of China (No. 61702372 and No. 61772371).

References

1. Elijah, O., Rahman, T.A., Orikumhi, I., Leow, C.Y., Hindia, M.N.: An overview of internet of things (IoT) and data analytics in agriculture: benefits and challenges. IEEE Internet Things J. **5**(5), 3758–3773 (2018)
2. ur Rehman, M.H., Ahmed, E., Yaqoob, I., Hashem, I.A.T., Imran, M., Ahmad, S.: Big data analytics in industrial IoT using a concentric computing model. IEEE Commun. Mag. **56**(2), 37–43 (2018)
3. Yassine, A., Singh, S., Hossain, M.S., Muhammad, G.: IoT big data analytics for smart homes with fog and cloud computing. Future Gener. Comput. Syst. **91**, 563–573 (2019)
4. Lee, I., Lee, K.: The internet of things (IoT): applications, investments, and challenges for enterprises. Bus. Horiz. **58**(4), 431–440 (2015)
5. Zheng, Z., Xie, S., Dai, H., Chen, X., Wang, H.: An overview of blockchain technology: architecture, consensus, and future trends. In: 2017 IEEE International Congress on Big Data (BigData Congress), pp. 557–564. IEEE (2017)
6. Rifi, N., Rachkidi, E., Agoulmine, N., Taher, N.C.: Towards using blockchain technology for IoT data access protection. In: 2017 IEEE 17th International Conference on Ubiquitous Wireless Broadband (ICUWB), pp. 1–5. IEEE (2017)
7. Reyna, A., Martín, C., Chen, J., et al.: On blockchain and its integration with IoT. Challenges and opportunities. Future Gener. Comput. Syst. **88**, 173–190 (2018)
8. Xu, X., Rahman, F., Shakya, B., Vassilev, A., Forte, D., Tehranipoor, M.: Electronics supply chain integrity enabled by blockchain. ACM Trans. Des. Autom. Electron. Syst. (TODAES) **24**(3), 31 (2019)
9. Mondal, S., Wijewardena, K., Karuppuswami, S., Kriti, N., Kumar, D., Chahal, P.: Blockchain inspired RFID based information architecture for food supply chain. IEEE Internet Things J. (2019)
10. Ayoade, G., Karande, V., Khan, L., Hamlen, K.: Decentralized IoT data management using blockchain and trusted execution environment. In: 2018 IEEE International Conference on Information Reuse and Integration (IRI), pp. 15–22. IEEE (2018)
11. Ferraiolo, D., Cugini, J., Kuhn, D.R.: Role-based access control (RBAC): features and motivations. In: Proceedings of 11th Annual Computer Security Application Conference, pp. 241–48 (1995)
12. Zhang, Y., Kasahara, S., Shen, Y., Jiang, X., Wan, J.: Smart contract-based access control for the internet of things. IEEE Internet Things J. **6**(2), 1594–1605 (2018)
13. Cruz, J.P., Kaji, Y., Yanai, N.: RBAC-SC: role-based access control using smart contract. IEEE Access **6**, 12240–12251 (2018)
14. Benet, J.: IPFS-content addressed, versioned, P2P file system. arXiv preprint arXiv:1407. 3561 (2014)
15. Ali, M.S., Dolui, K., Antonelli, F.: IoT data privacy via blockchains and IPFS. In: Proceedings of the Seventh International Conference on the Internet of Things, p. 14. ACM (2017)
16. Wu, M., Wang, Y., Liao, Z.: A new clustering algorithm for sensor data streams in an agricultural IoT. In: 2013 IEEE 10th International Conference on High Performance Computing and Communications & 2013 IEEE International Conference on Embedded and Ubiquitous Computing, pp. 2373–2378. IEEE (2013)
17. Babar, M., Arif, F.: Smart urban planning using big data analytics to contend with the interoperability in internet of things. Future Gener. Comput. Syst. **77**, 65–76 (2017)
18. Tian, F.: An agri-food supply chain traceability system for china based on RFID & blockchain technology. In: 2016 13th International Conference on Service Systems and Service Management (ICSSSM), pp. 1–6. IEEE (2016)

A Hybrid Mutual Authentication Scheme Based on Blockchain Technology for WBANs

Jianbo Xu[1], Xiangwei Meng[1]([✉]), Wei Liang[1], Li Peng[1], Zisang Xu[2], and Kuan-Ching Li[3]

[1] School of Computer Science and Engineering, Hunan University of Science and Technology, Xiangtan 411201, Hunan, China
Xiangwei_Meng@126.com, {jbxu,wliang}@hnust.edu.cn, plpeng@hnu.edu.cn
[2] College of Computer Science and Electronic Engineering, Hunan University, Changsha 410082, Hunan, China
zisang_xu@hnu.edu.cn
[3] Department of Computer Science and Information Engineering, Providence University, Taichung 43301, Taiwan
kuancli@pu.edu.tw

Abstract. Wireless body area networks (WBANs) are important applications of the Internet of Things (IoT) in medical monitoring. WBANs are used to collect patients' physiological information and to achieve the forwarding of sensitive information between patients and medical service center. Carried out through a public channel, the transmission of sensitive information is susceptible to unpredictable attacks. Therefore, mutual authentication and key agreement between the sensors on patients and the hub node of the medical service center need to be performed before the message transmission to ensure the security of message transmission in the network. A lightweight anonymous mutual authentication and key agreement scheme for two-hop blockchain WBANs is proposed in this paper. This scheme satisfies both security and lightweight requirements, making it possible to implement a mutual authenticate and key agreement between sensor nodes on patients and different hub nodes across regions. In addition, the Automated Validation of Internet Security Protocols and Applications (AVISPA) is used to evaluate the security of the protocol. Finally, the computation cost and communication cost of the proposed protocol are compared with those of the related schemes, with the results showing that the proposed protocol shows a better energy consumption control.

Keywords: WBANs · Authentication · Blockchain · AVISPA

1 Introduction

Recently, the rapid development of blockchain technology and Internet of Things has received wide attention from researchers [1], both of which will play an important part in the future network. Blockchain technology, strong platform expansion and unsuccessful

© Springer Nature Singapore Pte Ltd. 2020
Z. Zheng et al. (Eds.): BlockSys 2019, CCIS 1156, pp. 350–362, 2020.
https://doi.org/10.1007/978-981-15-2777-7_28

modification of stored data [2–5], can prevent the paralysis of the entire network caused by the collapse of the primary node in a centralized network. The connection of each block in the blockchain depends on a one-way hash function. The block in the blockchain that is used by the Proof of Work (PoW) consensus mechanism consists of the block header, the data recorded in the block, and the nonce used to adjust the hash value of the block. The hash value of the previous block serves as an important part of the latter block header. The adversary maliciously tampering with data recorded in a certain block will change the hash value of the block, thus indirectly changing the value of the next block header. Generally, it is very computationally intensive for the server to find a suitable nonce, thus making it difficult for the adversary to tamper with the blockchain. It can be seen that the blockchain technology is very suitable for building a cloud service layer in the network.

With the rapid development of sensor technology and communication networks, the Internet of Things based on sensors and wireless networks has been widely applied [6–8]. The Internet of Things consists of plenty of sensors with data acquisition capabilities. The sensors are responsible for collecting data and sending them to server node in the network, and the same server node can also send messages to the sensor nodes, helping explain that the Internet of Things can be applied in plenty of fields such as smart home, intelligent transportation and healthcare. WBANs is a form of the Internet of Things, which can be applied to monitor the physical condition of patients in the medical system [9]. In WBANs, the sensor having a function of collecting human physiological data is attached to a patient or implanted in a patient. When abnormal physiological data are detected by the sensor, it will send the data to the medical service center in time. Medical service center will take appropriate treatment measures for patients according to the data. Therefore, WBANs have a promising future in the fields of physiological characteristics monitoring, family nursing monitoring and mobilization signs monitoring [10].

The message transmitted in WBANs is important information about the patient's physical condition, thus making it important to further ensure the security and privacy of message exchange in the network [11–13]. The sensor node and medical service center need to hold session for mutual authentication before message exchange to ensure that the other party is a legitimate node in the network. Furthermore, after confirming the identity of the other party, both parties of the session need to jointly generate a session key for encrypting the transmitted message. Considering that the sensor nodes in WBANs have resource constraints in terms of computing power and communication capabilities, with strong mobility, the mutual authentication and key agreement scheme should be lightweight and cross-regional.

1.1 Related Work

With the popularity of wireless sensors, the communication security of sensor networks has also been severely tested. Limited in size, wireless sensors cannot perform cryptographic calculations with large energy consumption, which is vulnerable to be attacked by the adversary. Therefore, how to design low-power mutual authentication and key agreement in sensor networks is an important issue in current research.

In 2012, Zhang et al. [14] proposed a scheme that data can be safely transmitted in body area network without key agreement. In 2014, Turkanović et al. [15] proposed a user authentication and key agreement scheme using XOR operation and cryptographic collision resistance one-way hash function in the Internet of Things. In 2016, Ibrahim et al. [16] proposed a secure protocol to realize anonymous authentication and confidential transmission for a star two-tier WBAN topology. Four cryptographic hash functions are used by this scheme to achieve authentication between sensor node and control node. In 2017, Li et al. [17] proposed a lightweight anonymous mutual authentication and key agreement scheme for centralized two-hop WBANs. The sensor node can complete the key agreement with hub node by using the hash function three times. However, Koya et al. [18] pointed out that Li et al.'s scheme is vulnerable to sensor node impersonation attacks. When the adversary gets the information in the memory of the sensor node, it will imitate the sensor node and authenticate with the hub node in the network. They proposed a mutual authentication and key agreement using physiological signals. However, this scheme has weaknesses in preventing eavesdropping attacks. In 2018, Li et al. [19] proposed a new anonymous mutual authentication scheme for three-tier mobile healthcare systems with wearable sensors. This scheme implements mutual authentication and key agreement among sensor nodes, control nodes and medical server. In 2019, Gupta et al. [20] introduced a lightweight anonymous user authentication and key-establishment protocol for wearable devices. However, it is not considered that when the session key is established, the adversary can imitate the user to destroy both sides of the session to achieve a unified session key.

1.2 Research Contributions

Researchers have proposed a number of WBANs mutual authentication and key agreement schemes, which, however, involve some shortcomings. This paper has remedied main defects involved in other agreements, with the specific details as follows:

This paper proposes a mutual authentication and key agreement scheme based on blockchain technology, which is anonymous as well as unlinkable and cross-region mutual authentication of the sensor node and the hub node can be achieved.

The patient's biometric identity is used as the identity password of the sensor node in this protocol [21, 22], which can effectively resist the attacker's sensor node capture attack. Thus, the adversary cannot pass the authentication of the hub node even obtaining the data in the memory of the sensor node.

Informal security analysis shows that the protocol is effective against common attacks. Finally, the Automated Validation of Internet Security Protocols and Applications (AVISPA) is used to evaluate the security of the protocol [23].

The protocol in this paper is compared with the related protocols in the computation cost and communication cost. The results show that the performance of this scheme is better than other schemes.

2   System Models

The system models in this paper are network model and adversary model, which are used in the scheme proposed in this paper.

2.1 Network Model

The network model is a two-hop blockchain network, including three nodes, namely, sensor node (N), super node (SN) and hub node (HN), with the network structure shown in the Fig. 1. Sensor nodes are attached to patients' body or implanted into their body to collect the patient's physiological data. The collected physiological data involve patients' privacy, which need to be encrypted before being sent to hub node through open channel. Sensor nodes have less storage space, energy reserve and communication capacity, making it necessary to forward data through super node before sending them to hub node. Super node, such as intelligent bracelet and phone and pad, is a large electronic device used by patients. Compared with sensor node, super node has more storage, computing, communication capabilities, which is mainly responsible for message forwarding between sensor node and hub node, and will not do other processing for forwarded message. Hub node collects and processes patient physiological data and provides them to the medical service center. The consortium blockchain network composed of many hub nodes serves as the cloud service layer of WBANs. The consortium blockchain network is securer than the centralized network. For example, the registration information of sensor node in hub node consortium blockchain will not be modified by the adversary. Even more, consortium blockchain network also has strong network extensibility and compatibility. Each sensor node can carry out mutual authentication and key agreement with different hub nodes across regions.

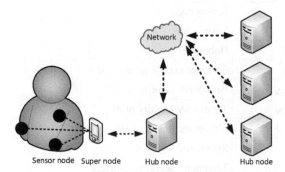

Sensor node   Super node   Hub node   Hub node

Fig. 1. Structure of a two-tiered blockchain WBANs.

2.2 Adversary Model

In order to better evaluate the security of the proposed scheme, we apply the widely-used Dolev-Yao (DY) threat model [24]. We define the adversary model as follows.

The system administrator (*SA*) is a fully trusted entity in the network.

The communication of any two nodes in the network is in the public channel, and the adversary can eavesdrop, tamper with and delete the messages transmitted in the public channel.

The adversary can capture any sensor node to steal information stored in its memory, and can impersonate the sensor node for mutual authentication and key agreement with the hub node.

The hub node over the cloud are treated as semi-trusted entities in the network. The adversary can steal sensor node registration information stored in blockchain form in hub node database, but cannot steal the master secret key k_{HN} of hub node stored in memory.

3   The Proposed Scheme

This section presents an anonymous mutual authentication and key agreement scheme based on blockchain technology. The scheme is divided into three phases: Initialization phase, registration phase and authentication phase. The initialization phase and the registration phase are performed over a secure channel. The authentication phase is performed over a public channel. It is assumed in WBANs that the sensor node and the hub node are synchronized with their clocks. The notations used in this paper are shown in Table 1.

Table 1. Notations used in this protocol.

Notation	Description
SA	System administrator
N	Sensor node
SN	Super node
HN	Hub node
id_N	Secret biometric identity of N
id_{SN}	Permanent identity of SN
tid_N	Temporary identity of N
k_{HN}	Master secret key of HN
k_N	Symmetric key of N
f_N, r_N	Temporary secret parameters
t_N	A timestamp generated by N
a_N, b_N	Authentication parameters stored in N's memory
x_N	Auxiliary parameter computed by N
η, α	Authentication parameters computed by HN

(*continued*)

Table 1. (*continued*)

Notation	Description
M_1, M_2, M_3	Data Packets transmitted in network
k_S	Session key between N and HN
$E_k(x)$	Symmetric encryption of x using key k

3.1 Initialization Phase

The system administrator (SA) initializes the hub node (HN) as follows.

Step A1: picks a HN's master secret key k_{HN}.
Step A2: Stores the k_{HN} into the HN's memory.

3.2 Registration Phase

The sensor node is bound to the patient by the patient's biometric information during the registration phase. SA registers a sensor node (N) and a super node (SN) as follows.

Step B1: Acquires the patient's secret biometric identity id_N.
Step B2: Picks a N's symmetric key k_N and generates the encryption $E_{k_N}(id_N)$.
Step B3: Picks a secret random parameter r_N for N.
Step B4: Computes $a_N = k_{HN} \oplus r_N$, $b_N = k_N \oplus h(r_N)$.
Step B5: Picks a unique identity id_{SN} for SN.
Step B6: Stores the tuple $<a_N, b_N>$ in N's memory.
Step B7: Stores the identity id_{SN} in SN's memory.
Step B8: Uses blockchain technology to store the tuple $<id_{SN}, E_{k_N}(id_N)>$ in each HN.

3.3 Authentication Phase

The sensor node performs anonymous mutual authentication and key agreement through the super node and the hub node. The authentication phase is shown in Fig. 2.

Step C1: $N \rightarrow SN$. N performs the following.

Acquires the patient's biometric secret identity id_N.
Picks a secret random parameter f_N.
Generates a timestamp t_N.
Computes $x_N = id_N \oplus f_N$.
Computes $tid_N = h(f_N, t_N)$.
Sends the message $M_1 = <a_N, b_N, x_N, t_N, tid_N>$.

Step C2: $SN \rightarrow HN$. SN performs the following.

Receives the message M_1 from sensor node.
Sends the tuple $<id_{SN}, M_1>$

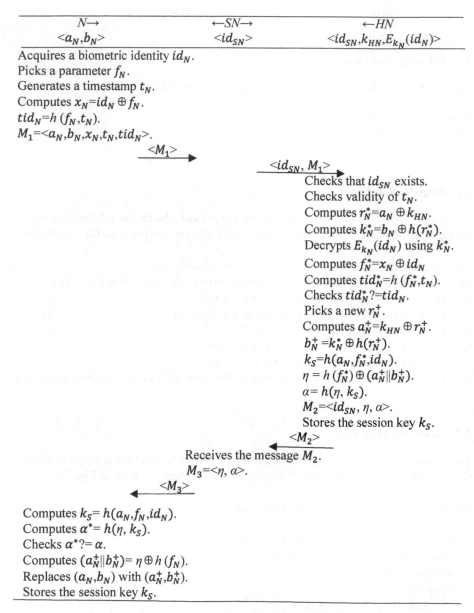

$N \rightarrow$	$\leftarrow SN \rightarrow$	$\leftarrow HN$
$<a_N, b_N>$	$<id_{SN}>$	$<id_{SN}, k_{HN}, E_{k_N}(id_N)>$

Acquires a biometric identity id_N.
Picks a parameter f_N.
Generates a timestamp t_N.
Computes $x_N = id_N \oplus f_N$.
$tid_N = h(f_N, t_N)$.
$M_1 = <a_N, b_N, x_N, t_N, tid_N>$.

$\xrightarrow{\quad <M_1> \quad}$

$\xrightarrow{\quad <id_{SN}, M_1> \quad}$

Checks that id_{SN} exists.
Checks validity of t_N.
Computes $r_N^* = a_N \oplus k_{HN}$.
Computes $k_N^* = b_N \oplus h(r_N^*)$.
Decrypts $E_{k_N}(id_N)$ using k_N^*.
Computes $f_N^* = x_N \oplus id_N$
Computes $tid_N^* = h(f_N^*, t_N)$.
Checks $tid_N^* ? = tid_N$.
Picks a new r_N^+.
Computes $a_N^+ = k_{HN} \oplus r_N^+$.
$b_N^+ = k_N^* \oplus h(r_N^+)$.
$k_S = h(a_N, f_N^*, id_N)$.
$\eta = h(f_N^*) \oplus (a_N^+ \| b_N^+)$.
$\alpha = h(\eta, k_S)$.
$M_2 = <id_{SN}, \eta, \alpha>$.
Stores the session key k_S.

$\xleftarrow{\quad <M_2> \quad}$

Receives the message M_2.
$M_3 = <\eta, \alpha>$.

$\xleftarrow{\quad <M_3> \quad}$

Computes $k_S = h(a_N, f_N, id_N)$.
Computes $\alpha^* = h(\eta, k_S)$.
Checks $\alpha^* ? = \alpha$.
Computes $(a_N^+ \| b_N^+) = \eta \oplus h(f_N)$.
Replaces (a_N, b_N) with (a_N^+, b_N^+).
Stores the session key k_S.

Fig. 2. Authentication and key agreement phase of our scheme.

Step C3: $HN \rightarrow SN$. HN performs the following.

Checks that id_{SN} is in its database. Aborts if the check fails.

Checks the transmission delay $\Delta t = t^* - t_N$, where t^* is the time when the tuple $<id_{SN}, M_1>$ was received. Aborts if the check fails.

Computes $r_N^* = a_N \oplus k_{HN}$.

Computes $k_N^* = b_N \oplus h(r_N^*)$.

Decrypts $E_{k_N}(id_N)$ using the symmetric key k_N^*.

Computes $f_N^* = x_N \oplus id_N$

Computes $tid_N^* = h(f_N^*, t_N)$.

Checks $tid_N^*? = tid_N$. Aborts if the check fails.

Picks a new secret random r_N^+.

Computes $a_N^+ = k_{HN} \oplus r_N^+$.

Computes $b_N^+ = k_N^* \oplus h(r_N^+)$.

Computes $k_S = h(a_N, f_N^*, id_N)$.

Computes $\eta = h(f_N^*) \oplus (a_N^+ || b_N^+)$.

Computes $\alpha = h(\eta, k_S)$.

Stores the session key k_S.

Sends the message $M_2 = <id_{SN}, \eta, \alpha>$.

Step C4: $SN \rightarrow N$. SN performs the following.

Receives the message M_2 from hub node.

Sends the message $M_3 = <\eta, \alpha>$.

Step C5: N receives the message M_3, and N performs the following.

Computes $k_S = h(a_N, f_N, id_N)$.

Computes $\alpha^* = h(\eta, k_S)$.

Checks $\alpha^*? = \alpha$. Aborts if the check fails.

Computes $(a_N^+ || b_N^+) = \eta \oplus h(f_N)$.

Stores the session key k_S.

Replaces the parameters (a_N, b_N) with the parameters (a_N^+, b_N^+) in its memory.

4 Security Analysis

In this section, informal security analysis is used to analyze the security of this protocol. And the protocol is evaluated using AVISPA.

4.1 Informal Security Analysis

In this section, informal security analysis is used to verify the protocol's ability to withstand common attacks.

Replay Attack. The replay attack means that the adversary sends authenticated information between N and HN to the network again. A common method of resisting replay attacks is to add a timestamp t_N to the transmitted information. If the adversary resends the messages that N sent to the HN without modification, the HN will verify whether the timestamp t_N expires after receiving the message. If the timestamp t_N expires, the mutual authentication will fail. Even if the adversary modifies the timestamp t_N, it cannot generate a $tid_N = h(f_N, t_N)$ that can be authenticated by HN.

Anonymous and Unlinkable Sessions. The purpose of this security function is to hide the true identity of any legitimate node and make a single node unlinkable between different sessions. N sends the newly generated message $M_1 = <a_N, b_N, x_N, t_N, tid_N>$ at each session establishment. The adversary cannot successfully link to the same N through this message. In addition, this scheme achieves unlinkable sessions by eliminating the relevancy between the same N and HN transmitting messages during different sessions. In order to prevent the tuple $<a_N^+, b_N^+>$ sent by HN to N from being linked with the tuple $<a_N^+, b_N^+>$ sent by H to HN in next session. HN encrypts the tuple $<a_N^+, b_N^+>$ using the hash function of the random parameter f_N. The adversary cannot get the session key k_S and the biometric identity id_N.

Forward/Backward Security. The forward/backward security of the protocol means that if the session key is leaked, it will not affect the security of past and future session key. The session key k_S of N and HN is generated by one-way hash function and is not transmitted over public channel. The tuple $<f_N, id_N>$ which constitutes the session key k_S is also unavailable to the adversary, who cannot get the session key k_S directly.

Hub Node Stolen Database Attack. The information stored in HN database is the registration information $E_{k_N}(id_N)$ of N. The patient's biometric identity id_N is encrypted by the symmetric key k_N of N. The adversary can capture N to get the parameter $b_N = k_N \oplus h(r_N)$ in its memory. But the parameter k_N is formed by the new random parameter r_N through XOR encryption in each round of conversation. The adversary cannot get tuple $<k_N, r_N>$.

Sensor Node Capture Attack. When N authenticates with HN, N will acquire the patient's biometric identity id_N and generate a new random number f_N for encrypting biometric identity id_N. The adversary can steal tuple $<a_N, b_N>$ stored in the memory of N by using the sensor node capture attack, but cannot get tuple $<id_N, f_N>$. That is to say, the adversary cannot generate the temporary identifier $tid_N = h(f_N, t_N)$ of N that can be authenticated by HN. Therefore, the proposed scheme still performs securely.

Jamming/Desynchronization Attacks. One authenticated party is destroyed by the adversary after updating the status, which makes another authenticated party unable to update the status synchronously. When the two states of authentication are not synchronized, the next round of authentication will not occur. The protocol in this paper only updates the status of N when authenticating, and the data in HN database will not make any changes. When the adversary intercepts the messages sent by HN to N, N sends the authentication request to HN again.

```
% OFMC
% Version of 2006/02/13
SUMMARY
  SAFE
DETAILS
  BOUNDED_NUMBER_OF_SESSIONS
PROTOCOL
  /home/span/span/testsuite/results/3.1.if
GOAL
  as_specified
BACKEND
  OFMC
COMMENTS
STATISTICS
  parseTime: 0.00s
  searchTime: 0.44s
  visitedNodes: 4 nodes
  depth: 2 plies
```

Fig. 3. OFMC report.

```
SUMMARY
  SAFE
DETAILS
  BOUNDED_NUMBER_OF_SESSIONS
  TYPED_MODEL
PROTOCOL
  /home/span/span/testsuite/results/3.1.if
GOAL
  As Specified
BACKEND
  CL-AtSe
STATISTICS
  Analysed  : 1 states
  Reachable : 1 states
  Translation: 8.16 seconds
  Computation: 0.00 seconds
```

Fig. 4. CL-AtSe report.

4.2 Simulation Based on AVISPA Tool

In this section uses AVISPA tool to verify the security of the protocol [23]. AVISPA (Automated Validation of Internet Security Protocols and Applications) is a security assessment tool for analyzing Internet security-sensitive protocols and applications. These four backends are described as follows: (1) On-the-Fly Model-Checker (OFMC). (2) Constraint-Logic-based Attack Searcher (CL-AtSe). (3) SAT based Model Checker (SATMC). (4) Tree Automata based on Automatic Approximations for the Analysis of Security Protocols (TA4SP). The results output by OFMC and CL-AtSe backend checkers can verify that the protocol is secure. The running results of OFMC and CL-AtSe backend checkers are shown in Figs. 3 and 4, respectively. The complete running process of the protocol is shown in Fig. 5 with the participation of adversary. The results show that the protocol meets the security requirements under specific security objectives.

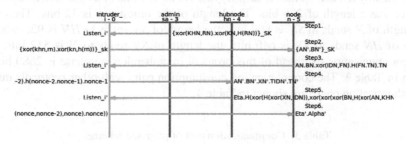

Fig. 5. Complete running process of the proposed protocol.

5 Efficiency Evaluation and Comparison

In this section, the performance of the proposed scheme in authentication phase is analyzed and compared with the related schemes in computation cost and communication cost.

5.1 Computation Cost

In order to facilitate the comparison of the calculated energy consumption of different protocols, T_h is used as the time unit of the encryption operation. Assume that the time of the symmetric encryption consumes T_{sym} and the time of the hash function is equal to the T_h. In the authentication phase, super node does not do any encryption operations and has no computational cost. The sensor node performs $4T_h + 2T_{XOR} = 4T_h$, and the hub node performs $6T_h + 6T_{XOR} + T_{sym} = 7T_h$. Table 2 is a summary of the consumption of different protocols in the authentication phase.

Table 2. Computation cost comparison.

Scheme	Sensor node	Super node	Hub node
Ibrahim et al. [16]	$5T_h + 2T_{XOR}$	–	$8T_h + 4T_{XOR}$
Li et al. [17]	$3T_h + 7T_{XOR}$	–	$4T_h + 12T_{XOR}$
Gupta et al. [20]	$4T_h + 4T_{XOR}$	$7T_h + 4T_{XOR}$	$5T_h + 3T_{XOR}$
Proposed scheme	$4T_h + 2T_{XOR}$	–	$6T_h + 6T_{XOR} + T_{sym}$

5.2 Communication Cost

In order to compare the consistency of communication cost of different protocols in the authentication phase, we are consistent with the assumption in [20]. Assume the random nonce, identity ID, and biometric identity id_N are all 128 bits in length. SHA3-256 hash function has a length of 256 bits. The length of the timestamp is 32 bits. Therefore, the length of N sends to SN is 800 bits, the length of SN sends to HN is 928 bits, the length of HN sends to SN is 640 bits, the length of SN sends to N is 512 bits. The total communication overhead of this protocol in authentication phase is 2880 bits as shown in Table 3. The communication consumption pairs with other protocols during the authentication phase are shown in Table 4.

Table 3. Communication cost of proposed scheme.

Communication between nodes	Communication cost
$N \rightarrow SN$	800 bits
$SN \rightarrow HN$	928 bits
$HN \rightarrow SN$	640 bits
$SN \rightarrow N$	512 bits

Table 4. Communication cost comparison.

Scheme	Communication cost
Ibrahim et al. [16]	2818 bits
Li et al. [17]	4672 bits
Gupta et al. [20]	3808 bits
Proposed scheme	2880 bits

6   Conclusions

In this paper, we proposed to implement anonymous mutual authentication and key agreement scheme for two-hop blockchain WBANs by using only a limited number of XOR operation and collision resistant one-way cryptographic hash function. Mutual authentication and key agreement between sensor nodes and hub nodes are performed across regions by using blockchain technology in cloud service layer. The informal security analysis proves that the proposed protocol is secure. Finally, the scheme is compared with the related schemes. The results show that the scheme, with lower computational cost and communication cost, can improve security. Therefore, the scheme is applicable to the practical application of WBANs.

Acknowledgments. This work was supported by the National Natural Science Foundation of China (Grant Nos. 61872138 & 61572188 & 61902125). Natural Science Foundation of Hunan province (Grant No. 2019JJ50187). Scientific Research Project of Hunan Education Department (Grant No. 18B209).

References

1. Islam, S.M.R., Kwak, D., Kabir, M.D.H., et al.: The Internet of Things for health care: a comprehensive survey. IEEE Access **3**, 678–708 (2015)
2. Liang, W., Tang, M., Long, J., et al.: A secure fabric blockchain-based data transmission technique for industrial Internet-of-Things. IEEE Trans. Industr. Inf. (2019)
3. Iansiti, M., Lakhani, K.R.: The truth about blockchain. Harvard Bus. Rev. **95**(1), 118–127 (2017)
4. Swan, M.: Blockchain: Blueprint for a New Economy. O'Reilly Media Inc., Sebastopol (2015)
5. Azaria, A., Ekblaw, A., Vieira, T., et al.: MedRec: using blockchain for medical data access and permission management. In: 2016 2nd International Conference on Open and Big Data (OBD), pp. 25–30. IEEE (2016)
6. Liang, W., Li, K.C., Long, J., et al.: An industrial network intrusion detection algorithm based on multi-characteristic data clustering optimization model. IEEE Trans. Industr. Inf. (2020)
7. Da Xu, L., He, W., Li, S.: Internet of Things in industries: a survey. IEEE Trans. Industr. Inf. **10**(4), 2233–2243 (2014)
8. Quan, W.W., Kumar, V.V., Sundaresan, S., et al.: Data streaming service for an Internet-of-Things platform. U.S. Patent Application 10/313,455, 4 June 2019
9. Tobón, D.P., Falk, T.H., Maier, M.: Context awareness in WBANs: a survey on medical and non-medical applications. IEEE Wirel. Commun. **20**(4), 30–37 (2013)

10. Varshney, U.: Pervasive healthcare: applications, challenges and wireless solutions. Commun. Assoc. Inf. Syst. **16**(1), 3 (2005)
11. Liang, W., Long, J., Chen, Z., et al.: A security situation prediction algorithm based on HMM in mobile network. Wirel. Commun. Mob. Comput. **2018** (2018)
12. Al Ameen, M., Liu, J., Kwak, K.: Security and privacy issues in wireless sensor networks for healthcare applications. J. Med. Syst. **36**(1), 93–101 (2012)
13. Al-Janabi, S., Al-Shourbaji, I., Shojafar, M., et al.: Survey of main challenges (security and privacy) in wireless body area networks for healthcare applications. Egypt. Inform. J. **18**(2), 113–122 (2017)
14. Zhang, Z., Wang, H., Vasilakos, A.V., et al.: ECG-cryptography and authentication in body area networks. IEEE Trans. Inf. Technol. Biomed. **16**(6), 1070–1078 (2012)
15. Turkanović, M., Brumen, B., Hölbl, M.: A novel user authentication and key agreement scheme for heterogeneous ad hoc wireless sensor networks, based on the Internet of Things notion. Ad Hoc Netw. **20**, 96–112 (2014)
16. Ibrahim, M.H., Kumari, S., Das, A.K., et al.: Secure anonymous mutual authentication for star two-tier wireless body area networks. Comput. Methods Programs Biomed. **135**, 37–50 (2016)
17. Li, X., Ibrahim, M.H., Kumari, S., et al.: Anonymous mutual authentication and key agreement scheme for wearable sensors in wireless body area networks. Comput. Netw. **129**, 429–443 (2017)
18. Koya, A.M., Deepthi, P.P.: Anonymous hybrid mutual authentication and key agreement scheme for wireless body area network. Comput. Netw. **140**, 138–151 (2018)
19. Li, X., Ibrahim, M.H., Kumari, S., et al.: Secure and efficient anonymous authentication scheme for three-tier mobile healthcare systems with wearable sensors. Telecommun. Syst. **67**(2), 323–348 (2018)
20. Gupta, A., Tripathi, M., Shaikh, T.J., et al.: A lightweight anonymous user authentication and key establishment scheme for wearable devices. Comput. Netw. **149**, 29–42 (2019)
21. Bao, S.D., Poon, C.C.Y., Zhang, Y.T., et al.: Using the timing information of heartbeats as an entity identifier to secure body sensor network. IEEE Trans. Inf. Technol. Biomed. **12**(6), 772–779 (2008)
22. Odelu, V., Das, A.K., Goswami, A.: A secure biometrics-based multi-server authentication protocol using smart cards. IEEE Trans. Inf. Forensics Secur. **10**(9), 1953–1966 (2015)
23. Burrows, M., Abadi, M., Needham, R.M.: A logic of authentication. Proc. R. Soc. Lond. A **426**(1871), 233–271 (1989)
24. Dolev, D., Yao, A.: On the security of public key protocols. IEEE Trans. Inf. Theory **29**(2), 198–208 (1983)

A Security Architecture for Internet of Things Based on Blockchain

Wei Yang[1(✉)], Hao Wang[1], Yadong Wan[2], Yuanlong Cao[1], Zhiming Zhang[1], and Shaolong Chen[1]

[1] School of Software, Jiangxi Normal University, Nanchang 330022, China
yw@jxnu.edu.cn
[2] School of Computer and Communication Engineering, University of Science and Technology Beijing, Beijing 100083, China

Abstract. Internet-of-Things (IoT) began to be widely used in smart city, smart agriculture, and smart factories. However, security issues have always threatened the development of the IoT. Blockchain is the current promising technologies, which uses several security mechanisms to protect system. In this paper, we propose a security architecture for IoT based on blockchain. Sensor data in IoT are collected by border-router, and is sent to blockchain network. The communication of IoT system is encrypted by AES algorithm. Smart contracts are used to build the access control mechanisms. Finally, theoretical analysis shows that the proposed architecture can secure against different attacks, as well as low latency.

Keywords: Blockchain · IoT security · Distributed network · Smart contract

1 Introduction

The era of Internet-of-Things (IoT) has arrived and will profoundly change the way of our work and life. It will be widely used in smart city, smart agriculture, and smart factories [1, 2]. Currently, there are many types of IoT standards and technologies. Narrowband IoT (NB-IoT), which is proposed by the 3rd Generation Partnership Project (3GPP), has been widely used in smart cities (such as water companies, power grid companies) [3]. LoRa IoT technologies, which is low cost and use unlicensed spectrum, is very popular in the field of smart agriculture [4]. The NB-IoT and LoRa belong to the low power wide area (LPWA) technologies. The IETF 6TiSCH working group is working on low-power, high-reliability short-range wireless communication technology for IoT [5]. It aiming to use in smart factories. The widespread use of the Internet of Things will greatly improve people's lives and travel and other aspects.

However, security events in the Internet of Things occur frequently and have serious consequences. In October 2016, the Mirai malware infection and control of IoT devices, launches distributed denial of service(DDoS) attacks against the DNS provider Dyn [6]. It causes many websites and online services to be inaccessible. RPL-based IoT have been widely used in smart cities and smart factories. It is vulnerable to routing attacks, which can greatly degrade network performance [7]. Currently, the Internet of Things

© Springer Nature Singapore Pte Ltd. 2020
Z. Zheng et al. (Eds.): BlockSys 2019, CCIS 1156, pp. 363–368, 2020.
https://doi.org/10.1007/978-981-15-2777-7_29

faces more serious security issues. Therefore, it is necessary to study the security of the Internet of Things.

Blockchain is the current promising technology, which uses cryptography to ensure the security of distributed ledgers. Blockchain technology is developing very fast. In 2008, Bitcoin is developed [8]. It opened the blockchain 1.0 era. It is the first generation of encrypted digital currency and is mainly used in finance. Ethereum, which is called blockchain 2.0, is developed [9] in 2013. Ethereum adopts smart contract technology, making it widely available in the financial, supply chain, reputation system, and IoT. And now, it has entered the era of blockchain 3.0, which is an inter-organizational mutual trust. Blockchain adopts several advanced technologies such as elliptic curve algorithm, hash algorithm, smart contract and distributed consensus mechanism. It has numerous advantages such as tamper resistance, traceability, anonymity and decentralization.

Current IoT system mostly adopts the cloud-based central management solution, which is vulnerable to single point of failure, privacy breaches and Denial-of-Service attacks. Blockchain, as a distributed network, can easily solve the above problems. Combining blockchain technology into the IoT is very promising and challenging. In the paper, we will propose our scheme based on the previous research.

The rest of this paper is organized as follows. Section 2 introduces the blockchain technology and reviews on the blockchain for the IoT. Section 3 proposes the security architecture for IoT based on Blockchain. Section 4 discusses the security of proposed scheme. Finally, Sect. 5 presents the conclusion.

2   Background and Related Work

2.1   Blockchain

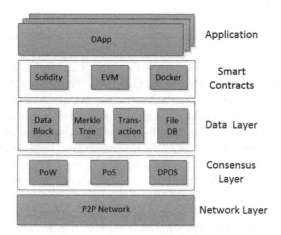

Fig. 1. The architecture of blockchain.

In these years, blockchain technology has developed very rapidly. From the earliest Bitcoin system to Ethereum, which introduced the concept of smart contracts. Currently,

HyperLedger Fabric is very popular. They are basically similar in the system architecture. The architecture of blockchain is shown in Fig. 1.

The blockchain is a distributed system, which adopt P2P protocol as transport protocol. It can tolerate single point of failure. In blockchain network, all nodes have the characteristics of equality, autonomy and distribution. The consensus layer is very important for the distributed blockchain system. Currently, there develop lots of consensus algorithm such as proof of work (PoW), proof of stake (PoS) and Delegated proof of stake (DPOS). PoW is a typical consensus algorithm, which is usually used in the Bitcoin system. In PoW, all nodes are competing to find random numbers, and this process is also known as mining. PoS is a different consensus algorithm. The choice of the next block is randomly selected according to the stake size and time in PoS. DPOS allows each node to choose delegates who can represent their own interests to generate a block.

The data layer mainly consists of the data block, Merkle tree, transaction and database. The data block is composed of the block header and the block body. The block header consists of block version, current hash, timestamp, previous hash, Merkle tree root and Nonce. Every transaction has a unique hash value. And the value of Merkle tree root is calculated based on all the hash value. A smart contract is a digital protocol that uses algorithms and programs to compile contract terms. Ethereum blockchain deploy lots of smart contracts.

2.2 Blockchain for the IoT

Yu et al. [10] provided an in-depth analysis of the security and privacy issues in IoT. They proposed a few blockchain-based solutions to security and privacy issues in IoT. Dai et al. [11] provided a survey of blockchain for IoT. They proposed a Blockchain of Things (BCoT) concept which represent synthesis of IoT and blockchain. It can improve the interoperability and security of IoT system.

Lo et al. [12] pointed out that the blockchain and IoT have many similar characteristic such as decentralization. They pointed out data and thing management is are two important research directions.

Huang et al. [13] proposed a security Industrial Internet of Things (IIoT) system based on the emerging blockchain technology. They proposed credit-based proof-of-work (PoW) mechanism for the low-power IIoT. Zheng et al. [14] given a survey on challenges and opportunities of blockchain technology. They pointed out the blockchain technology can be used in many applicants especially in IoT area.

3 Security Architecture for IoT Based on Blockchain

In this section, we propose a security architecture IoT for based on blockchain as shown in Fig. 2. Our design mainly focuses on IETF 6TiSCH IoT. But it also can apply to the other IoT (e.g. NB-IoT and LoRa). The security architecture consists of three parts: IoT System, Blockchain Network and Border Router.

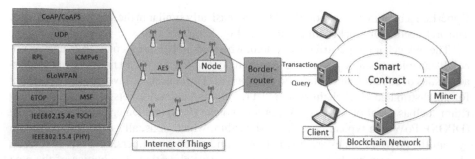

Fig. 2. The architecture of blockchain-based IoT system.

3.1 IoT System

The IoT system consist of hundreds of nodes. Each node is resource constrained (e.g. limited memory and power). And they are not belonging to blockchain network. The nodes in the network run a communication protocol stack. The bottom of protocol stack uses the IEEE802.15.4 standard, which is the typical short range physical layer standard. And IEEE802.15.4e, 6TOP and MSF are belonging to the medium access control (MAC) layer, which can achieve high reliable and low power network. The RPL, ICMPv6 and 6LoWPAN are belong to the router layer, which can form an Ipv6 network. The top of protocol stack adopts the CoAP standard, which is a tiny application protocol similar to HTTP. In IoT system, nodes adopt wireless communication ways. As wireless communication is easy to be eavesdropped, the communication messages should be encrypted by the AES algorithm.

3.2 Blockchain Network

The blockchain network mainly consist of many miners and clients. The border router periodically collects data uploaded by nodes in the IoT system and sends it to the blockchain network. The miners adopt the consensus algorithm (e.g. PoW, PoS) to choose one ledgers. The ledgers will package some transactions into data block. The other miners may accept the data block after authenticating successfully. Anyone want to modify the record data is almost impossible. The client can view the data at any time. Considering that most IoT systems may generate a large amount of sensor data, it is better to choose a faster blockchain such as private blockchain. The smart contract is an important part in the blockchain network, which allow transactions to be automated and do not require third parties. Here, the smart contract can be used to access management. Only the permission client can do relation operation. It can improve the security of the system.

3.3 Border Router

The border router plays an important role in the system. First, it can manage the resource-constrained nodes in the IoT system. Only the nodes, which successfully authenticate, can join the network. Second, it plays an intermediate role. It translates the sensor messages encoded by CoAP protocol into the JSON format acceptable by the blockchain nodes. Third, it can directly communication to the miners such as send transactions or query. It should be equipped with a high-performance processor and large memory, which is different from the nodes in the IoT system. The current Raspberry Pi can act as border router. It can run blockchain system such as Ethereum [9].

4 Security Analysis

In this section, we provide an in-depth security analysis for the proposed architecture. Our security architecture fully considers the advantage of blockchain technology. It can provide lots of security and private services for IoT system.

Compared to the cloud-based central system, blockchain network is a decentralization system which has an advantage in defending against certain specific attacks (e.g. DOS or DDOS attacks). And the blockchain network does worry about the problem of a single point of failure, which may happen in the cloud-based central system. The central system usually controls by a manager. If the attackers steal the account of manager, they can arbitrarily modify the system data. As we known, the data or translation in the blockchain network is tamper resistance.

Private protect is an important security service in the IoT system. In the cloud-based central system, user's data are stored arbitrarily and are easily exploited by hackers. The blockchain network can provide the autonomy service by public key cryptography mechanism. And the communication in the IoT system adopt the AES encryption algorithm, which is very adaptable to the resource-constrained IoT device. The access control is also important in the IoT system, the smart contract of the blockchain network can provide this security service.

5 Conclusion

The security and privacy issues have always hampered the development of IoT. Blockchain is considered a promising technology to improve system security. In this paper, we propose a security architecture for IoT based on blockchain. The resource constrained sensor node in IoT send the collected data to the border-router, and they are not belonging to blockchain network. The border-router can directly communication to the miners such as send transactions or query. Smart contracts are used to build the access control mechanisms. Security analysis shows that the proposed security architecture can defend against lots of IoT attack. In our future work, we will build a real blockchain system to verify the feasibility and effectiveness of the proposed security architecture.

Acknowledgments. This work is supported by the National Natural Science Foundation of China (No. 61741125) and Natural Science Foundation of Jiangxi Province (No. 20192BAB217007).

References

1. Lin, J., Yu, W., Zhang, N., et al.: A survey on internet of things: architecture, enabling technologies, security and privacy, and applications. IEEE Internet Things J. **4**(5), 1125–1142 (2017)
2. Yu, W., Liang, F., He, X., et al.: A survey on the edge computing for the Internet of Things. IEEE Access **6**(99), 6900–6919 (2018)
3. Chen, J., Ota, K., Wang, L., et al.: Guest editorial special issue on theories and applications of NB-IoT. IEEE Internet Things J. **5**(3), 1435 (2018)
4. Croce, D., Gucciardo, M., Mangione, S., et al.: Impact of LoRa imperfect orthogonality: analysis of link-level performance. IEEE Commun. Lett. **22**(4), 796–799 (2018)
5. Watteyne, T., Tuset-Peiro, P., Vilajosana, X., et al.: Teaching communication technologies and standards for the industrial IoT? use 6TiSCH! IEEE Commun. Mag. **55**(5), 132–137 (2017)
6. Sinanović, H., Mrdovic, S.: Analysis of mirai malicious software. In: 2017 25th International Conference on Software, Telecommunications and Computer Networks (SoftCOM), pp. 1–5. IEEE (2017)
7. Airehrour, D., Gutierrez, J.A., Ray, S.K.: SecTrust-RPL: A secure trust-aware RPL routing protocol for Internet of Things. Future Gener. Comput. Syst. **93**(5), 860–876 (2019)
8. Nakamoto, S.: Bitcoin: a peer-to-peer electronic cash system (2008). https://bitcoin.org/bitcoin.pdf
9. Ethereum: Blockchain APP Platforms (2019). https://www.ethereum.org/
10. Yu, Y., Li, Y., Tian, J., et al.: Blockchain-based solutions to security and privacy issues in the Internet of Things. IEEE Wirel. Commun. **25**(6), 12–18 (2018)
11. Dai, H., Zheng, Z., Zhang, Y., et al.: Blockchain for Internet of Things: a survey. IEEE Internet Things J. (2019, in Press)
12. Lo, S., Liu, Y., Chia, S., et al.: Analysis of blockchain solutions for IoT: a systematic literature review. IEEE Access **7**(6), 58822–58835 (2019)
13. Huang, J., Kong, L., Chen, G., et al.: Towards secure industrial IoT: blockchain system with credit-based consensus mechanism. IEEE Trans. Ind. Inform. **15**(6), 3680–3689 (2019)
14. Zheng, Z., Xie, S., Dai, H.N., et al.: Blockchain challenges and opportunities: a survey. Int. J. Web Grid Serv. **14**(4), 352–375 (2018)

Blockchain and Mobile Edge Computing

Redundant Virtual Machine Placement in Mobile Edge Computing

Siyi Gao, Ao Zhou$^{(\boxtimes)}$, Xican Chen, and Qibo Sun

State Key Laboratory of Networking and Switching Technology,
Beijing University of Posts and Telecommunications, Beijing, China
hellozhouao@gmail.com

Abstract. Mobile edge computing (MEC), as an extension of the cloud computing paradigm to edge networks, overcomes some obstacles of traditional mobile cloud computing by offering ultra-short latency and less core network traffic. The edge resources are virtualized to be shared among multiple mobile users. Consolidated server systems using server virtualization involves serious risks of hosting server failures. Redundant virtual machine placement can be an effective countermeasure. This problem has been well solved in cloud computing. However, it is a more nontrivial task to efficiently deploy virtual machines redundantly in MEC networks. To address this issue, a redundant virtual machine placement method in MEC is proposed. Firstly, this method estimates the minimum number of virtual machines required based on the performance requirements of the applications. Then, the redundant virtual machine placement problem is formulated as a combinatorial optimization formulation. Finally, a optimal placement strategy searching algorithm is proposed to determine the optimal location of the virtual machines. The strategy can preserve the minimum configuration in the event of failure of any k edge servers. The experiment results illustrates the effectiveness of our algorithm.

Keywords: Mobile edge computing · Virtual machine placement · Fault-tolerant · Redundant configuration · Combinatorial optimization

1 Introduction

Mobile edge computing (MEC), which extends the cloud computing paradigm to the edge networks, can provide proximity based services of various resource-intensive and time-critical applications to mobile users. The MEC Network is combined with a lot of cloudlets which can communicate with each other. Every cloudlet has several hosting servers where the virtual machines (VMs) can be placed. For many computation-intensive and time-sensitive mobile applications with advanced features, e.g., voice control, gesture and face recognition, as well as interactive online gaming, the requirement for response time is quite strict. One of the greatest benefits MEC brings to us is to reduce the response time and network resource consumption, as application requests from mobile users do not need to be propagated to the central cloud via long latency core links.

© Springer Nature Singapore Pte Ltd. 2020
Z. Zheng et al. (Eds.): BlockSys 2019, CCIS 1156, pp. 371–384, 2020.
https://doi.org/10.1007/978-981-15-2777-7_30

This paper presents a method to make a redundant configuration of VMs in anticipation of hosting server failures of MEC for various mobile applications. The fault-tolerance level of the mobile applications deployed in MEC can be measured by the sum acceptable number of simultaneous hosting server failures at cloudlets. In the area of the MEC, the services in case of any k components failures is called k-fault-tolerance [1]. The problem we need to figure out is to find a VM placement strategy that satisfies the required fault-tolerance level and the service level agreement (SLA) while minimizing the sum number of hosting servers at all cloudlets. Firstly, this method estimates the minimum number of virtual machines required based on the SLA of the applications. Then, we model the problem into a combinatorial optimization formulation. Finally, a optimal placement strategy searching algorithm is proposed to determine the optimal placement strategy.

The rest of the paper is organized as follows. Section 2 reviews some outstanding related works that have been dedicated to MEC, and VM placement. We depict the system model and define problem in Sect. 3. Formulation of the redundant virtual machine placement in MEC is expounded in Sect. 4. The redundant VM placement algorithm are elaborated and analyzed in Sect. 5. We present the simulation results in Sect. 6. Conclusion is drawn in Sect. 7.

2   Related Work

The combination of high-availability techniques and virtualization is a emerging issues. There are some existing resource allocation and provisioning methods mainly focus on optimization of performance and resource utilization in systems [2]. However, it is difficult to predict hosting servers failures which may result in terrible problems. The proposed method is categorized as a proactive approach and has an original advantage that keeps the minimum configuration of application service at any k hosting server failures. Loveland presented a simple redundant configuration method for VMs on multiple hosting servers is presented in [3]. And optimum method to solve the virtual machine placement problem with the condition of required fault-tolerance level [1]. However, all these solutions based on cloud computing which means only one server cloudlet (centre cloudlet) needed to be considered. We should take the transmission and the scheduling among the cloudlet into account in MEC Network [4].

In the research field of mobile edge computing, many works focused on the efficient resource management along the cloud-to-edge continuum. Such as service entity placement for social virtual application [5]. Hybrid method for minimizing service delay in edge cloud computing through VM migration and transmission power control [6].

In MEC architecture, response time consists of wireless delay from mobile users towards their nearby MEC servers, network delay among MEC servers, processing delay in MEC servers for supporting multiple applications and network delay to the central cloud of excess requests [7]. There are some excellent work which aim to figure out the problem how to place VMs [8,9] with the objective of minimizing the average response time with various requests demand and limited capacity of MEC servers in mobile edge networks [10,11].

The problem of virtual machine placement for minimizing the number of required hosting server is formulated as a bin packing problem [12,13]. The bin packing problem is known to an NP-hard problem which is difficult to solve completely in the realistic time, thus some heuristic algorithms are used to cope with this problem. The combinatorial optimization [14] has been studied for a long time. Methods like greedy graph colouring algorithm [15], convex optimization problem [16], simulated annealing algorithm (SA), genetic algorithm (GA), particle swarm optimization (PSO), artificial neural network (ANN) etc. is now applied to solve problems in all kinds of fields.

3 Background and System Model

3.1 Background

A large amount of cloudlet are deployed with base stations in MEC. Each cloudlet consists of a cluster of hosting servers. As Satyanarayanan proposed in his work [17], a failure of a hosting server becomes a serious problem in consolidated server systems using virtualization. When the hosting server goes down due to any failures of their components, all VMs on this server are unable to escape from service down. The method to make a redundant configuration of hosting server for multiple applications using VMs in cloud computing was presented in [1]. Different from cloud computing, the redundant VM placement in MEC is more complex because of the complex edge network environment and distribution of cloudlets. Therefore, the traditional method is not effective in MEC (Fig. 1).

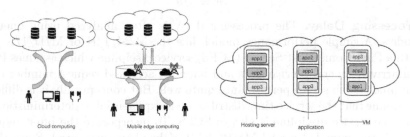

(a) Cloud computing network VS (b) Placement of virtual machines at
Mobile edge computing network   one cloudle

Fig. 1. Background

3.2   System Model

The MEC Network can be represented by a set of cloudlets $P = p_1, ..., p_N$ and Access Points (APs) interconnected by the Internet. Each cloudlet is co-located with a AP, and consists a large amount of hosting servers. Each hosting server can be virtualized into several VMs, and each VM can host one application instance. Because there are a large amount requests for a application, more than one application instances should be deployed. The proposed framework of MEC. AP (Access point) is usually nearest server cloudlet from user (Not always).

For application request processing, the service response time comprises: (1) the one hop wireless transmission delay for uploading requests of mobile users to their nearby MEC server. (2) The average processing delay of MEC Server, including the queuing time and the processing time. (3) Network delay between cloudlets. Sometimes the edge resources of a cloudlets cannot satisfy the needs of mobile users, the excess requests will be routed to the other cloudlets via the network.

- **Wireless Transmission Delay.** We will take one hop wireless transmission delay between mobile users and their nearby MEC server (AP) as w. According to [18], the wireless transmission rate is defined as θ which can be expressed as

$$\theta = B * log_2(1 + \frac{|h|^2 * P * d^{-\eta}}{\sigma^2})$$ (1)

where B and σ^2 denote the channel bandwidth and the variance of additive Gaussian noise, respectively; P is the pre-determined transmission power of mobile user; $|h|^2$ captures the Rayleigh fading effect and follows an exponential distribution with a unity mean; $d^{-\eta}$ signifies the path loss effect, where d specifies the distance from mobile user to the wireless access point and η is the path loss exponent. Therefore, the wireless transmission delay can be expressed as

$$w = d/\theta$$ (2)

- **Processing Delay.** The processing delay is often analyzed using queuing models. A simple performance model, like the M/M/1/K or M/D/1/K [19] with a First-Come-First-Served (FCFS) service discipline which assumes Poisson arrival, general service time and bounded accepted request number of K can predict web server performance quite well. But conceptually it is difficult to assume that the service time distribution is exponential or deterministic and that the service discipline is always FCFS. To incorporate the burst request arrival, the extended model MMPP/G/1/K has been presented. Since there is no general performance model that can apply various mobile applications, this paper introduce M/M/1 queue model as a basic example which assumes Poisson request arrival and exponential service time. The average response time r_i of application a_i from the server cloudlet p_j with a service rate μ_j^i and a request arrival rate λ_j^i is modeled as follows.

$$r_j^i = 1/(\mu_j^i - \lambda_j^i)$$ (3)

When the application gets c times larger computation power by using more VMs or virtual CPUs, the average response time is reduced a lot. Assuming the number of VM where application a placed at the server cloudlet AP is v_j^i.

$$r_j^i = 1/(\mu_j^i - \lambda_j^i/v_j^i) \tag{4}$$

Due to the limited computing capacity of the server, it may not be possible for a server to serve all the user task requests it received. If the workload of a server is too heavy, the queue time can become excessively long, potentially slowing down the mobile user's application. Thus, we assume that the maximum workload at each server is capped at an arrival rate of λ_{max}, and the remaining task requests will be offloaded to the other cloudlet. We determine the fraction ϕ_j of tasks the cloudlet processes as follows.

$$\phi_j = \begin{cases} 1 & if\ \lambda_{max} > \lambda(j) \\ \lambda_{max}/\lambda(j) & otherwise \end{cases} \tag{5}$$

$\lambda(j)$ is defined as the sum of the arrival rates at edge cloudlet p_j

$$\lambda(j) = \sum_{i=1}^{n} \lambda_j^i \tag{6}$$

- **Transmission Delay Between Cloudlets.** The user needs to relay its application task through the network. Assuming the offloaded task will be processed in the cloudlet located at AP p_j relayed to p_k. We assume that all offloaded tasks are of a uniform data packet size, and so delays incurred in transferring any task through the network between a pair of APs is identical. To model such a network delay matrix, denote by D the network delay matrix, where entry $D_{j,k}$ represents the communication delay in relaying a task between p_j and p_k.

The average response time for application a_i is

$$t_i = w + \sum_{j=1}^{N} \phi_j * r_j^i + (1 - \phi_j) * D_{j,k} \tag{7}$$

$$(1 \leq j \leq N, 1 \leq k \leq N)$$

According to the (2), (4), (7), required average response time for application a_i can be described as follows.

$$t_i = d/\theta + \sum_{j=1}^{N} \phi_j * (1/(\mu_j^i - \lambda_j^i/v_j^i)) + (1 - \phi_j) * D_{j,k} \tag{8}$$

$$(1 \leq j \leq N, 1 \leq k \leq N)$$

The total response time of all applications can be represented as follows.

$$t_{all} = \sum_{i=1}^{n} t_i (1 \leq i \leq n) \tag{9}$$

In order to get the minimum average response time, we formulated the problem as figuring out the shortest path from single source in a graph, which will be elaborated in Sect. 4.2.

4   Problem Formulation

4.1   Performance Requirements

According to the average response time constraint from (8) and the constraint of SLA, if any of the VMs report an SLA violation (e.g., high response time) perform dynamic re-allocation of VM from the hosting server to another hosting server such that the SLA is restored. Therefore we have a response time constraint for each mobile application which is described as

$$t_i \leq SLA \tag{10}$$

$$d/\theta + \sum_{j=1}^{N} \phi_j * (1/(\mu_j^i - \lambda_j^i/v_j^i)) + (1 - \phi_j) * D_{j,k} \leq SLA \tag{11}$$

$$(1 \leq j \leq N, 1 \leq k \leq N)$$

From the above formula, we can figure out the minimum number of VMs v_j^i for application a_i at server cloudlet p_j.

4.2   Quantity Bound of Hosting Server

The number of VMs allocated to an application a_i is limited by the performance requirements r_i. Assuming the minimum number of VMs for application a_i be v_i. Let the number of virtual machines for application a_i at server cloudlet p_j be v_j^i. Theoretically, it is possible to obtain a lower limit number m of hosting servers in redundant virtual machine placement problem by considering the number of VMs survived after k hosting server fails. Because of the quantity bound of hosting servers, the max number of VMs on a hosting server is CY. The number of surviving VMs at k hosting server failures out of m hosting servers is given by $(m - k) * CY$. Since these VMs must contain the minimum number of VMs v_i for all a_i, the following condition is obtained.

$$v_i = \sum_{j=1}^{N} v_j^i \qquad 1 \leq j \leq N \tag{12}$$

$$(m - k) * CY \geq \sum_{i=1}^{n} v_i \tag{13}$$

Because m is an integer value, the lower bound of m is given as follows.

$$m \geq 1/CY * \sum_{i=1}^{n} v_i + k \tag{14}$$

$$m \geq 1/CY * \sum_{i=1}^{n} \sum_{j=1}^{N} v_j^i + k \tag{15}$$

4.3   Reliability Requirements

k-redundancy is adopted for reliability enhancement. k-redundancy method allocates k redundant VMs to each application. To accomplish the k-fault-tolerance of the hosting server cloudlet, at least k redundant VMs for each application a_i are needed besides the minimum configurations estimated as v_i. In the conventional server cloudlet without virtualization, k-fault-tolerance is accomplished by preparing k redundant physical servers. The k-redundancy method is established on this conventional approach. The total number of redundant VMs for each application a_i, v_i' is expressed as follows.

$$v_i' = v_i + k \tag{16}$$

With the k-redundancy method, VMs that host the same application instances must not run on the same hosting server. Otherwise a failure of a single hosting server causes multiple downs of the same application instances and leads to SLA violations. Since the placement algorithm allocates VMs to the different hosting servers, this restriction is specified as the following constraint for m.

$$m \geq max(v_i') = max(v_i) + k \tag{17}$$

According to (15), another constraint for m is derived from the fact that the fact that the total number of required VMs n is not over the total available VMs on the m hosting servers. This restriction is expressed as follows and leads to another constraint condition for m.

$$m \geq 1/CY * (\sum_{i=1}^{n} v_i + k * n) \tag{18}$$

From constraints (15), (18), the minimum number of hosting servers m_{KR} by k-redundancy method is expressed as follows.

$$m_{KR} = max\{max(v_i) + k, \quad 1/CY * (\sum_{i=1}^{n} v_i + k * n)\}$$

$$= max\{max(\sum_{j=1}^{N} v_j^i) + k, \quad 1/CY * (\sum_{i=1}^{n} \sum_{j=1}^{N} v_j^i + k * n)\} \tag{19}$$

As the value of m_{KR} depends on the maximum value of v_i which varies within the following range.

$$1/n * \sum_{i=1}^{n} v_i \leq max(v_i) \leq \sum_{i=1}^{n} v_i - n + 1 \tag{20}$$

The minimum and the maximum required number of hosting servers by k-redundancy method are given as follows.

$$MIN = max\{1/n * \sum_{i=1}^{n}\sum_{j=1}^{N} v_j^i + k, \quad 1/CY * (\sum_{i=1}^{n}\sum_{j=1}^{N} v_j^i + k * n)\} \tag{21}$$

$$MAX = max\{\sum_{i=1}^{n}\sum_{j=1}^{N} v_j^i - n + 1 + k, 1/CY * (\sum_{i=1}^{n}\sum_{j=1}^{N} v_j^i + k * n)\} \tag{22}$$

4.4   Redundant Virtual Machine Placement Problem

The problem can be formulated as a combination optimization problem containing two constraints, one of them is average response time to ensure the performance requirements for an application, another is configuration for service provision stable. The optimization goal is to minimize the number of hosting servers. We can formulate the problem as

$$\min \quad \sum_{i}^{n} m_i$$

$$s.t. \quad \begin{aligned} t_i &\leq SLA, & 1 \leq i \leq n \\ v_j &\leq CY * m_j, & 1 \leq j \leq N. \\ v_i' &\geq v_i + k, & 1 \leq i \leq n \end{aligned} \tag{23}$$

5   Redundant Virtual Machine Placement Method

The problem we are supposed to solve is to minimize the number of hosting servers under the constraints of response time and k-fault-tolerance. This chapter can be divided into two parts. We provide a greedy enumeration-based placement method (OEPA) as a baseline in Sect. 4.1. On account of OEPA which costing too many time and resources is not efficient enough, we provide our algorithm in Sect. 4.2.

The second part depict the process of our algorithm, which is shown in Algorithm 2. The algorithm is aimed to figure out the number of VMs for each application at each edge cloudlet using shortest path from single source algorithm. Algorithm 3 aims to get the sum of number of the hosting servers at the entire edge networks by giving v_j^i from part one, the restriction of maximum number of VMs CY which can be placed on one hosting server, and the required fault-tolerance level k. Finally, as we has already known the set of VMs for all applications $v[]$ and number of hosting servers m at one edge server cloudlet, we can place the VMs at the appropriate position.

5.1   Optimal Enumeration Algorithm

We enumerate all possible placement cases of VRCs supporting n different applications in edge networks in this algorithm, and then compare the average response time, i.e., T_{avg} and the number of hosting servers m_{KR} among all placement cases to get the optimal placement case of VRCs with the minimal average response time and the minimal number of hosting servers. However, this problem can not be solved in a reasonable amount of time because of going through all the cases.

For each placement case, we consider assigning the mobile users' requests to MEC servers in a balanced manner which is implemented in the way described in [11]. After the assignment of overall requests to MEC servers, we calculate the average response time and the number of hosting servers. Compared with the current minimal values iteratively, we can get the minimum response time T_{min}, minimum number of hosting servers m_{min} as well as the VM placement method when the algorithm ends.

Algorithm 1. Optimal Enumeration Algorithm

Require: k, λ, μ, ω, ϕ
Ensure: T_{min}: Minimum average response time; m_{min}: Minimum number of hosting servers.
1: Initialize S denotes the set of all placement cases, $S \longleftarrow \emptyset$.
2: Enumerate all combinations for application i, i.e., $Q = \{Q_i, i \in n\}$, and record into set S
3: $T_{min} \longleftarrow \infty$; $m_{min} \longleftarrow \infty$
4: **for** $Q \subset S$ **do**
5:     Execute Procedure 1 of overall requests assignment based on placement case Q
6:     Evaluate the average response time T_{avg} for placement case Q; Evaluate the number hosting servers $m_K R$ for placement case Q;
7:     **if** $T_{avg} \leq T_{min}$ and $m_{KR} \leq m_{min}$ and satisfy k-redundancy **then**
8:         $T_{min} \longleftarrow T_{avg}$
9:         $m_{min} \longleftarrow m_{KR}$
10:    **end if**
11: **end for**
12: **return** T_{min}, m_{min}

5.2   Response Time Minimization Algorithm

– **Response Time Minimization Algorithm.** Although (8), (11) have given us a simple method to get the response time for applications, it's not a optimal way. We model it as getting the shortest path from single source problem. Assuming that request from application a is sent to the network, every edge server is able to deal with the request and return the response. Let us consider an example of p_1 respond to the request from a if there are 4 sever cloudlet altogether just like Fig. 2. All kinds of routing time is described in the table Path-Time. The simplest case is that p_1 receives the request and there are plenty of resources to deal with it as shown in row 1. If the queuing time is too long or lacking for resources, the request may be transported to the other cloudlet, finally be processed by either other cloudlet or not so busy p_1. Row 2–4 describe the latter. If the request is transported from p_i to p_j, the delay time at p_i is ignored. Now we need to figure out the response time from each cloudlet $p_1, p_2, p_3 ...$ and choose the minimum one. Therefore this problem can be defined as selecting the shortest path in a graph problem. The most commonly used and also most effective method to solve the shortest path from single source problem is Dijkstra algorithm. Our shortest path algorithm is more complex than Dijkstra because there is only weights on edge of graph, but also weight at each point which means queuing time and processing time.

Fig. 2. Routing graph

Path	Time
$a - p_1 - a$	$t_1 + 2 * w_1$
$a - p_i - p_1 - a$	$t_1 + w_1 + w_i + D_{1,i}$
$a - p_i - p_j - p_1 - a$	$t_1 + w_1 + w_i + D_{i,j} + D_{j,1}$
$a - p_i - p_j - p_k - p_1 - a$	$t_1 + w_1 + w_i + D_{i,j} + D_{j,k} + D_{k,1}$

$i, j, k = \{2, 3, 4\}, \quad i \neq j \neq k$

Routing between server cloudlet is caused by shortage of resources

Let G be a undirected graph. V(G) is all the points in this graph, consisting of two parts, users(s) and edge servers(v). Let $Dist$ be a shortest one among all paths. $Dist_{(}s, v)$ is the shortest path between starting point s and the ending point v. E is defined as the weights between points, which consists of two parts, w means the wireless transmission time between users and edge servers (dot lines in Fig. 2), D means the transmission delay between edge servers (solid lines in Fig. 2). At each server cloudlet, the cost of queuing and processing request is defined as t. The algorithm is described as Algorithm 1. $Transmission_i^j$ means that there are j times of transmissions before request came to p_i. From the shortest path algorithm, we can get response times from all kinds of request handlers for application i. Finally, we select the minimum one:

$$t_i = \min_{j}^{N} Dist_{(}s, v_j) \tag{24}$$

According to (11), (20), for one application a_i, we can get some relationships between response time t_i and number of VMs v_j^i.

- **Virtual Machine Placement Algorithm.** At each MEC cloudlet, in order to satisfy the k-fault-tolerance, the VMs that provide the same application service should be distributed to different hosting servers in case of hosting server failure. To satisfy the required fault-tolerance level, the more hosting servers can guarantee the quality of the web service. However we are supposed

---

Algorithm 2. Response Time Minimization Algorithm

Require: Q: A empty set.
  V: The set contains all points except starting point s.
  w, t, D: All kinds of time delays.
Ensure: $Dist_{(s}, v_i)$: Minimum distance from start point s to the other point v.
1: $Q = \{\}$, $V = sorted(\{v_1, v_2...\})$
2: $Dist_{(s}, v_i) = \infty$, i=0
3: **while** $|Q| < |V|$ **do**
4:     v_i = V[i], Dist=[]
5:     **for** j=0; j++; $j < V.length$ **do**
6:         Dist.add($\min_{transmission_i^j}$)
7:     **end for**
8:     $Dist_{(s}, v_i) = \min(Dist)$
9:     i++; $Q + v_i$
10: **end while**
11: **return** $Dist_{(s}, v_i)$

---

to reduce the number of hosting servers to save resources. The minimum number of hosting servers m_{KR} (19) is already formulated in Sect. 4.3.

The problem of virtual machine placement for minimizing the number of required hosting server is formulated as a bin packing problem [13]. The bin packing problem is known to an NP-hard problem which is difficult to solve completely in the realistic time. Our VMs placement algorithm is developed by the classical bin packing algorithm FFD (First-fit decrease). When we know v_i^j, the number of VMs of each application, and m_j, the number of hosting servers, we can get the heuristic algorithm to place the VMs on different hosting server just like FFD. The virtual machine placement algorithm is described as Algorithm 3.

Algorithm 3. Virtual Machine Placement Algorithm

Require: v[]: required number of VMs for each application at each cloudlet.
  m: number of hosting servers at each cloudlet.
Ensure: placement of VMs at hosting servers at each cloudlet.
1: $sorted_v[]$ = sort(v[]);
2: total = len($sorted_v[]$);
3: i=0,y=1;
4: **while** $i \leq total$ **do**
5:     **for** x = 1; x++; $x \leq m$ **do**
6:         placement[x,y] = $sorted_v[i]$;
7:         i++;
8:     **end for**
9:     y++;
10: **end while**
11: **return** placement[];

6   Performance Evaluation

6.1   Simulation Settings

To show the performance of our proposed minimum response time and redundant VMs algorithm, we developed a simulator python-based. We just simplify the problem as placing VMs for n = 10 applications at N = 4 edge cloudlets. Each application needs $v = 5$ VMs. The max number of VMs that a hosting server can afford is 4 (p = 4), the fault-tolerance level k = 3.

6.2   Comparison with Benchmark

– **Running Time Comparison.** Although OEPA is very simple and effective, it has a very high computational complexity because it has to enumerate all combinations of the placement cases for n applications so as to find the optimal placement leading to minimum average response time and the redundancy level. The comparison of running time and average response time is described as Fig. 3. According to the figure, algorithm OEPA's costs are much larger than FFD and our algorithm, so we don't take it into comparison below.

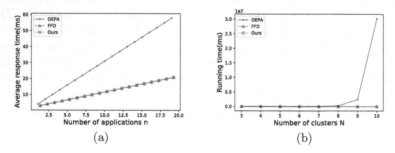

Fig. 3. Response time and running time comparison

– **Comparison with FFD.** First-Fit decrease (FFD) is a well known powerful heuristic approach to the bin packing problem [16]. The FFD is an effective solution to virtual machine placement where each application instance on the VM requires different size of resources. Let the required number of hosting servers for minimum configuration be m_{FFD}. Now we get inputs fixed, and compare the method between FFD and k-redundancy method. The required number of hosting servers are evaluated with the given parameters $p = 4$, and $1/n * \sum_{i=1}^{n} \sum_{j=1}^{N} v_j^i = 5$ (the average number of v_i). In order to observe the effects of the number of applications n, let $k = 3$ and comparison results is shown in Fig. 4(a). By observing it we found the phenomenon that our MIN approach is no advantage when n is small, but it requires minimum number of hosting servers and the growth thread is slow along with the increase of n. We can also observe the effects of the fault-tolerance level k by fixing the

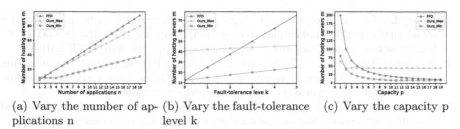

(a) Vary the number of applications n (b) Vary the fault-tolerance level k (c) Vary the capacity p

Fig. 4. Number of hosting servers varying from different variances

parameter $n = 10$ just like Fig. 4(b). The trend of number of required hosting servers is more stable in our MIN method than others. Figure 4(c) shows that With the increasing of the capacity, the number of hosting servers decreases a lot in all methods but our method has a minimum hosting server numbers.

7 Conclusion

In this paper, we have investigated the placement problem of VRCs for supporting multiple applications with the objective of minimizing the average response time with various requests demand, limited capacity and fault tolerance level of MEC servers in mobile edge networks. We first introduced a greedy algorithm as a benchmark, which can get the optimal result but the computational complexity is extremely high. To solve the problem more efficiently, we divide the problem into two parts. The first part focused to figure out the number of VMs for each application considering the response time constraint. The second part aimed to get the optimal placement method. Our approach is more efficiently than the common bin packing algorithm FFD.

Acknowledgments. This research is supported in part by the National Natural Science Foundation of China under Grant No. 61571066, No.61602054, (NSFC, 61571066, 61602054), and (BNSF, 4174100).

References

1. Machida, F., Kawato, M., Maeno, Y.: Redundant virtual machine placement for fault-tolerant consolidated server clusters. In: 2010 IEEE Network Operations and Management Symposium, NOMS 2010, pp. 32–39. IEEE (2010)
2. Attaoui, W., Sabir, E.: Multi-criteria virtual machine placement in cloud computing environments: a literature review. arXiv preprint arXiv:1802.05113 (2018)
3. Loveland, S., Dow, E.M., LeFevre, F., Beyer, D., Chan, P.F.: Leveraging virtualization to optimize high-availability system configurations. IBM Syst. J. **47**(4), 591–604 (2008)
4. Satyanarayanan, M.: The emergence of edge computing. Computer **50**(1), 30–39 (2017)

5. Wang, L., Jiao, L., He, T., Li, J., Mühlhäuser, M.: Service entity placement for social virtual reality applications in edge computing. In: IEEE INFOCOM 2018 - IEEE Conference on Computer Communications, pp. 468–476. IEEE (2018)
6. Rodrigues, T.G., Suto, K., Nishiyama, H., Kato, N.: Hybrid method for minimizing service delay in edge cloud computing through VM migration and transmission power control. IEEE Trans. Comput. **66**(5), 810–819 (2016)
7. Bisio, I., Delucchi, S., Lavagetto, F., Marchese, M.: Capacity bound of MOP-based allocation with packet loss and power metrics in satellite communications systems. In: 2012 IEEE Global Communications Conference (GLOBECOM), pp. 3311–3316. IEEE (2012)
8. Vmware. https://www.vmware.com/products/vsphere.html. Accessed 4 Apr 2019
9. Citrixxenserver. https://www.citrix.com/products/citrix-virtual-apps-and-desktops/. Accessed 4 Apr 2019
10. Zhao, L., Liu, J., Shi, Y., Sun, W., Guo, H.: Optimal placement of virtual machines in mobile edge computing. In: 2017 IEEE Global Communications Conference, GLOBECOM 2017, pp. 1–6. IEEE (2017)
11. Zhao, L., Liu, J.: Optimal placement of virtual machines for supporting multiple applications in mobile edge networks. IEEE Trans. Vehic. Technol. **67**(7), 6533–6545 (2018)
12. Jung, G., Joshi, K.R., Hiltunen, M.A., Schlichting, R.D., Pu, C.: Generating adaptation policies for multi-tier applications in consolidated server environments. In: 2008 International Conference on Autonomic Computing, pp. 23–32. IEEE (2008)
13. Bobroff, N., Kochut, A., Beaty, K.: Dynamic placement of virtual machines for managing SLA violations. In: 2007 10th IFIP/IEEE International Symposium on Integrated Network Management, pp. 119–128. IEEE (2007)
14. Korte, B., Vygen, J.: Combinatorial Optimization: Theory and Algorithms, 3rd edn. Springer, Heidelberg (2006). https://doi.org/10.1007/3-540-29297-7
15. Elsherif, A.R., Chen, W.-P., Ito, A., Ding, Z.: Design of dual-access-technology femtocells in enterprise environments. In: 2013 IEEE 24th Annual International Symposium on Personal, Indoor, and Mobile Radio Communications (PIMRC), pp. 2774–2779. IEEE (2013)
16. cvxbook. https://web.stanford.edu/~boyd/cvxbook/bv_cvxbook.pdf
17. Satyanarayanan, M., Bahl, V., Caceres, R., Davies, N.: The case for VM-based cloudlets in mobile computing. IEEE Pervasive Comput. (2009)
18. Yi, C., Cai, J., Su, Z.: A multi-user mobile computation offloading and transmission scheduling mechanism for delay-sensitive applications. IEEE Trans. Mob. Comput. **19**, 29–43 (2019)
19. Cao, J., Andersson, M., Nyberg, C., Kihl, M.: Web server performance modeling using an M/G/1/K*PS queue. In: 10th International Conference on Telecommunications, ICT 2003, vol. 2, pp. 1501–1506. IEEE (2003)

An Effective Resource Allocation Approach Based on Game Theory in Mobile Edge Computing

Bilian Wu[✉], Xin Chen, Ying Chen, and Zhuo Li

School of Computer Science, Beijing Information Science & Technology University, Beijing, China
wubilian1996@163.com, {chenxin,chenying,lizhuo}@bistu.edu.cn

Abstract. As a promising technology, mobile edge computing (MEC) can provide an IT service environment and cloud-computing capabilities at the edge of the mobile network, and also can reduce latency, improve user experience. In this paper, we have proposed a MEC system consisting of one privately service provider (SP) and multiple mobile users (MU). A game theory approach for resource allocation optimization is proposed to analyze the interaction between the leader SP and the followers MUs. We have introduced the congestion factor between different MUs. In addition, we prove the existence of the Nash equilibrium (NE) by game theory method and design an efficient the best response (BR) algorithm to solve this problem. An optimal equilibrium strategy can be obtained by the BR algorithm, and experiment results have demonstrated the efficiency and feasibility of the algorithm.

Keywords: Resource allocation · Game theory · Nash equilibrium · Mobile edge computing · Pricing

1 Introduction

With the continuous improvement and development of mobile multimedia applications, the demand for computation service resources are also growing. Moreover, mobile user (MU) has become an indispensable part of modern life in recent years. Especially short video applications have suddenly become popular, and the number of video has increased dramatically. Therefore, MUs are required to process large amounts of data. This is a great challenge for mobile users with limited computation ability [1]. To tackle the challenge, computing tasks can be offloaded from mobile terminals to edge cloud computing, which has powerful processing and computing capabilities. Hence, as a promising technology, mobile edge computing (MEC) is considered as a potential solution [2]. MEC can provide an IT service environment and cloud-computing capabilities at the edge of the mobile network, and can also reduce latency, improve user's experience.

The resource allocation issues of mobile device were analyzed in [3–5], but they only concerned the computation offloading problem. [6] only considered

© Springer Nature Singapore Pte Ltd. 2020
Z. Zheng et al. (Eds.): BlockSys 2019, CCIS 1156, pp. 385–396, 2020.
https://doi.org/10.1007/978-981-15-2777-7_31

the security defense problem and stable operation of the MEC network system. Although, there also had some works focused on the joint problem of network economics and resource allocation. A double auction mechanism with dynamic pricing was proposed by [7,8] and [15] focused on solving the problem of cost minimization to obtain the optimal dynamic pricing strategy effectively.

Instead, in our paper, we consider the joint problem of network economics and resource allocation with the form of pricing. A new effective resource allocation approach is formulated aiming at maximizing each user's utility in MEC scenario. We focus on the resource allocation in one service provider (SP) and multiple MUs as a non-cooperative game. The SP is a monopolist who sells a divisible limited resource with a fixed price to multiple MUs. We assume that each MU is independent of the others and makes its best strategy only based on its local information. Next, based on the price announced by the SP, all MUs make their strategy of purchasing computing service resources to maximizes their utilities. Furthermore, considering the existence of multiple MUs, different MUs will compete for the limited computing resource of SP. In addition, we introduce the congestion factor, which is related to the amount of resources purchased by other MUs. The main contributions of this paper are as follows.

- We consider the joint problem of network economics and resource allocation. Then, we propose a non-cooperative competition game model for one SP and multiple MUs in MEC scenario. The competing model in this paper can be extended to multi-SP scenarios.
- We take into channel gain and congestion cost. The aim of the game is to maximize the number of allocated computation resources users and their utilities with capacity constraints.
- We analyze the game model and prove that there exist a NE. A BR algorithm for finding the NE solution is proposed in the game. We analyze the performance of the algorithm theoretically and experimentally.

This paper is organized as follows: Sect. 2 introduces the problem formulation and puts forward the scenario about system model and game model. Equilibrium analysis and game solution will be given in detail in Sect. 3. Numerical experiment is proposed in Sect. 4. Section 5 analyzes related work in great detail and Sect. 6 gives a brief conclusion.

2 Problem Formulation

In this section, we will introduce a scenario in the mobile edge computing. We model the provider-user interaction as a leader-follower game. The leader, MEC service provider, gives a fixed price for per unit of resources. According to the price, followers, mobile users, purchase resources to maximize their profit, those resources which are provided by MEC SP. Then, the system model and the MUs competition model will be formulated as follows.

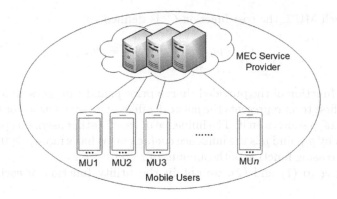

Fig. 1. An illustration of mobile edge computing scenario

2.1 System Model

As shown in Fig. 1, we consider a wireless network which consists of a SP and multi-users. The MEC SP is a monopolist who sells a divisible limited resource with a fixed price to multiple MUs. It can be regarded as a small data center for telecom operators deployed near network access nodes, and also can provide the services of expanding computing power and parallel processing tasks for the surrounding MUs.

Assume there is one MEC SP, denoted by $\mathcal{M}$, and Q is the number of units of divisible limited resources. The set of all MUs is defined by $\mathcal{I} = \{1, 2, ..., n\}$. The SP maximizes its payoff by selling the largest amount of resources to users. And user i maximizes its utility by purchasing resources from the supplier $\mathcal{M}$. The price announced by the provider (per unit resource) is denoted by p. We assume that each MU is independent of the others and makes its best strategy only based on its local information. Next, based on the price announced by the SP, all MUs make their strategy of purchasing computing service resources q_i to maximize their own profits. In the real network environment, every MU i has resource sharing or crowding relationship with other MUs. The congestion cost coefficient determined by the resource constrains of the wireless networks is denoted by κ_i, and $\kappa_i \geq 0$. Moreover, the congestion cost coefficient approximately follows a power law distribution, which is related to the amount of resources purchased by other MUs. And R_i will be a concave function. Therefore, the revenue function of every MU i can be computed as,

$$R_i = r_i q_i - \kappa_i q_i^2, \tag{1}$$

where r_i is the channel quality offset for the channel between user i and the MEC SP. The bandwidth of each sub-channel is w. Each user has a transmission power constraint P_i. We can define $r_i = w \log_2(1 + \alpha_i P_i)$, where $\alpha_i = h_i^2 / \sigma_i^2 w$, h_i is the channel gain and σ_i^2 is the Gaussian noise variance for the channel in [9]. Every MU has to pay for the computing service resource what they want to buy. For each MU i, the cost function C_i is defined as,

$$C_i = \mu q_i \sum_{j \in \{1,...,n\}} g_{ij} q_j + p q_i, \qquad (2)$$

here q_i is a function of the provided charge price p, and j denotes all MUs except MU i. The first term represents the network effect of its social group or the impact of other users' resources on it. The influence of user j (other users except i) on user i is denoted by g_{ij}, and μ is the influence coefficient. What's more $\mu \geq 0$. Thus, the C_i is an increasing function of the amount of resources q_i.

According to (1) and (2), we obtain the utility function of each MU i as follows,

$$U_i = R_i - C_i. \qquad (3)$$

Thus, it is obvious that U_i is a differentiable, increasing, and strictly concave utility function. When given the charging price of the SP, all MUs make a strategy to maximize their own utilities. Due to resource constraints Q, each MU can be considered as a competitor to compete for the limited resources. In the above competitive environment, and we regard the resource purchasing strategy as a non-cooperative game. The symbols used in this article are summarized in Table 1.

Table 1. List of notations

$\mathcal{M}$	The SP in MEC
Q	The number of unit computing service resources
$\mathcal{I} = \{1, 2, ..., n\}$	Set of MUs
p	The fixed price of per unit resource published by SP
q_i	The number of resources that MU i want to buy
R_i	The revenue of each MU i
r_i	The channel quality offset
κ_i	The congestion cost coefficient
μ	The influence coefficient of other users purchasing resources
C_i	The cost of each MU i
U_i	The utility of each MU i

2.2 Game Model

In this part, we formulate the purchasing resources game model $\mathcal{G}$ between MUs. The game model is denoted as $\mathcal{G} = \{\mathcal{I}, Q_i, U_i\}$. U_i is defined as the payoff function of MU i. The formulation of game model $\mathcal{G}$ is described as follows,

Players. Each MU is one participant and there are Q participants competing for computation service resources to maximize respective revenue.

Strategies. In order to maximize their revenues, each user makes a decision about the amount of computing service resources to be purchased based on the price announced by SP. The selection for MU i is $q_i \in Q_i$.

Payoffs. We denote $U_i(q_i, q_{-i})$ as the utility function for MU i, where $q_{-i} \in \coprod_{j \neq i} Q_j$ is the selection matrix consisting of all MUs except MU i.

Because of the limited computing services resources, the resources request quantities q_{-i} is a decreasing function. q_{-i} is defined as purchasing resources request quantities of all the other MUs except MU i, i.e.,

$$q_{-i} = [q_1, q_2, ..., q_{i-1}, q_{i+1}, ..., q_n], \qquad q_n \in [0, \infty). \tag{4}$$

In a competitive environment, each MU intends to maximize their own utilities, as shown in (5),

$$\max_{q_i \in [0, \infty)} U_i(q_i, q_{-i}) = r_i q_i - \kappa_i q_i^2 - \mu q_i \sum_{j \in \mathcal{I}} g_{ij} q_j - p q_i \tag{5}$$

$$s.t. \sum_{i=1}^{n} q_i \leq Q, \qquad \forall i \in \mathcal{I}, \tag{6}$$

$$q_i \geq 0, \qquad \forall i \in \mathcal{I}. \tag{7}$$

Every participant is selfish, since no player has any incentive to deviate from it in this game model unilaterally, the proposed game model is solved by Nash equilibrium (NE). From [10], the NE can be defined as indicated in below.

Definition 1. *A quantity profile* $q^* = (q_1^*, q_2^*, ..., q_m^*)$ *is a NE of the purchasing computing service resources requests game model* $\mathcal{G}$. *If at the equilibrium* q^*, *no player can further increase its profit by unilaterally altering its strategy, i.e.,*

$$U_i(q_i^*, q_{-i}^*) \geq U_i(q_i, q_{-i}^*), \qquad \forall i \in \mathcal{I}. \tag{8}$$

The NE has an obvious self-stabilizing property, enabling MUs at the equilibrium to achieve mutually satisfactory and comparatively optimal solutions without a biased incentive of users. This property is very important for non-cooperative computing resource allocation issues, because the MUs are selfish to act in their own interests and it can ensure our users' status be stable. Then we will prove that there is a unique NE in this game model $\mathcal{G}$ in the next section.

3 Equilibrium Analysis and Game Solution

In this section, we next study the existence of NE for the multi-user to purchase computing service resources. What'more, we give the solution method of the game model $\mathcal{G}$. Game theory is especially useful in finding out how these users interact and designing the best solution that no one wants to change their choice.

Each user makes a strategy about computing service resources based on the charge fixed price p announced by the SP to maximize their own incoming. By solving the following problems, the optimal q_i^* can be obtained as,

$$q_i^* = arg \max_{q_i \in [0,\infty)} U_i(q_i, q_{-i}, p). \tag{9}$$

Given the charge fixed price p announced by the SP, the MUs compete for the number of resources requests, which is a non-cooperative game. We will find the solution for this non-cooperative game in the following.

Proposition 1. (Best Response). *Given the charge fixed price p announced by the SP, the best response (BR) of each MU is the amount of purchase computing service resources requests, which is,*

$$q_i^{BR}(q_{-i}, p) = (\frac{r_i - p}{2\kappa_i} - \frac{\mu \sum_{j \in \mathcal{I}} g_{ij} q_j}{2\kappa_i})^+. \tag{10}$$

Proof. The best response of resources requests $q_i^{BR}(q_{-i}, p)$ can be obtained when the first derivative of U_i with respect to q_i is 0.

$$\frac{\partial U_i}{\partial q_i} = r_i - 2\kappa_i q_i - \mu \sum_{j \in \mathcal{I}} g_{ij} q_j - p = 0. \tag{11}$$

The second derivative of U_i with respect to q_i is,

$$\frac{\partial^2 U_i}{\partial q_i^2} = -2\kappa_i - \mu \sum_{j \in \mathcal{I}} g_{ij} < 0. \tag{12}$$

According to (12), we can know that every user's utility function is concave, since it can be guaranteed a global optimal of U_i. The optimal solution in this game as mentioned in (10). ∎

From the proposition above, it is observe that we can get the solution about resource allocation by the best response in (10). Next, we will prove that the strategy is in equilibrium state. In the meantime, the equilibrium strategy is unique and optimal.

Theorem 1. *Given the charge fixed price p announced by the SP, there is a NE of each MU in this competition game model $\mathcal{G}$.*

Proof. Let $q^* = \{q_1^*, q_2^*, ..., q_n^*\}$ be the equilibrium strategy of game $\mathcal{G}$, according to the (6), (7) and (10), there is,

$$\sum_{i=1}^n q_i^* \leq Q,$$
$$q_i^* = \frac{r_i - p}{2\kappa_i} - \frac{\mu \sum_{j \in \mathcal{I}} g_{ij} q_j}{2\kappa_i} \leq \frac{r_i - P}{2\kappa_i} < q_{max}.$$

Hence, through the above analysis, the strategy space is nonempty compact and convex. Besides, the players $\mathcal{I} = \{1, 2, ..., n\}$ also are a limited set in this game $\mathcal{G} = \{\mathcal{I}, Q_i, U_i\}$, so the game $\mathcal{G}$ has a NE in [11]. In summary, the computing service resources of purchasing game model has a NE for all MUs. ∎

Through the equilibrium analysis about the NE existence above, we prove that there is a NE in this game. It can be seen that given the charge fixed price p, there exists a NE of each MU in the proposed non-cooperative game. Then, how do we find this equilibrium solution? Primarily, we need to set the initial values, and represent the number of iterations by t. According to (10), we can get the best response strategy about utility of user. Finally, when ξ is small enough, the BR algorithm can achieve convergence of the state and get the game equilibrium solution. The details of equilibrium strategy q^* can be determined through Algorithm 1.

Algorithm 1. Equilibrium strategy algorithm based on Best Response

---

Input: The charge price p, the number of users n
Output: Optimal equilibrium strategy q^*
1: Initialize w, h_i, p_i, σ_i^2, k_i, μ, g_{ij}, ξ
2: Initializes the strategy of each MU i
3: **for** $t = 1 : T$ **do**
4:     **for** each MU $i \in \mathcal{I}$ **do**
5:         Calculate $U_i(q_i, q_{-i}), \forall q_i \in Q_i$, according to (3)
6:         $q_i^* = \underset{q_i \in Q_i}{argmax} U_i(q_i, q_{-i})$
7:         $q_i^t = (\frac{r_i - p}{2\kappa_i} - \frac{\mu \sum_{j \in \mathcal{I}} g_{ij} q_j}{2\kappa_i})^+$
8:         **if** $\| q^t - q^{t-1} \| > \xi$ **then**
9:             $t = t + 1$
10:         **end if**
11:     **end for**
12: **end for**

---

4   Numerical Experiment

To illustrate the results of the proposed game theory pricing problem, we simulate a scenario of one SP and multiple MUs with different parameters without losing generality. The simulation scenario is described in Fig. 1. We set the bandwidth of the provider to be $w = 10\,\text{MHz}$. The channel power gain of the MUs follows the Gaussian distribution in $CN(\mu_1, \sigma_1^2)$, where $\mu_1 = 10$, $\sigma_1^2 = 1$. And then, the thermal noise power of the MUs follows the Gaussian distribution $CN(\mu_2, \sigma_2^2)$, where $\mu_1 = 5$, $\sigma_1^2 = 1$.

In Fig. 2, we present a user-provider correlation with channel gain equalization, where the link thickness indicates the number of resources purchased, and shows the best response dynamic of the non-cooperative game for the three MUs case and the relationship between number of iteration and utility of users. From the figure, we can see that user's utility increases first, then slowly flattens and eventually would converge, and the convergence can be achieved quickly in non-cooperative game. What's more, the convergence rate has nothing to do with the initial value.

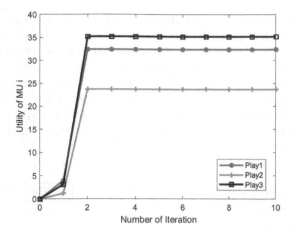

Fig. 2. Convergence of the best response for 3 MUs.

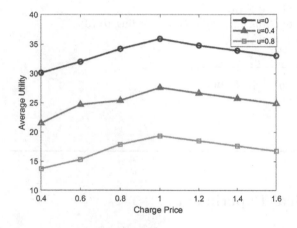

Fig. 3. The average utility with respect to the charge price.

Figure 3 shows the average utility between MUs with respect to the charge price. The value of μ can be set as 0, 0.4, 0.8, respectively. As we can see, for different parameter sets, the average utility of MUs always have an optimal charging price. We can find that with the price going up and the average utility increasing firstly but then decreasing affected by the influences coefficient μ. In addition, it can be observed that the value of the influence coefficient μ will affect the solution of the optimal price, and by adjusting the price p, the average utility can attain a state of optimal equilibrium. Besides, the higher the influence coefficient is, the lower the optimal price is. The reason is that the smaller μ is, the less cost each MU will pay. Then, they will obtain more utilities.

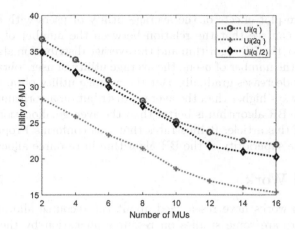

Fig. 4. The utility of MU i with respect to the number of MUs.

Figure 4 shows that when the strategy of purchasing computing service resources change, the utility of a single MU with respect to the total number of MUs. As the number of MUs increases, the utility of each user will be decreasing. But the utility curve of the strategy q^* is always higher than that of the double quantity $2q^*$ and half quantity $\frac{q^*}{2}$. This phenomena conforms Theorem 1 and Theorem 2. It can be observed that there exist only one NE in this game model. This is attributed to the influence of limited service resources. It can be seen that the q^* is the optimal equilibrium strategy which could make users maximize their utilities.

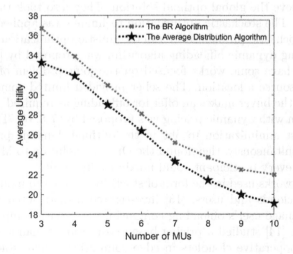

Fig. 5. The average utility of MUs with respect to the number of MUs.

In Fig. 5, we plot effects of the average utility of users with different algorithm, and we can see that the relation between the number of MUs and the average utility of the BR algorithm and the average distribution algorithm. With the increase of the number of users, the average utility of users obtained by these two algorithms decreases gradually. But the average utility obtained by the BR algorithm is always higher than the average distribution algorithm. This demonstrates that the BR algorithm is better than the average allocation algorithm in the scenario of this article. It illustrates that this conforms Proposition 1, and Fig. 5 shows the superiority of the BR algorithm in resource allocation.

5   Related Work

Many previous works have researched about the recourse allocation problem. And then, there are some studies on resource allocation by the computation offloading in MEC. [3] aimed at the energy-saving problem in cloud wireless access network, a non-convex energy minimization optimization problem was proposed. Next, they designed an iterative algorithm to solve the problem. [4] proposed the D2D-MEC technique to improve the computation capacity and integrated both techniques to focus joint computation offloading and resource allocation. [5] thought an Orthogonal Frequency-Division Multiplexing Access (OFDMA) based multi-users and multi-servers system. An energy efficient joint offloading and wireless resource allocation strategy were proposed.

A new resource allocation mechanism based on deterministic differential equation model was studied by [6,18]. They also considered the security defense problem and stable operation of the MEC network system. There is challenge that how to find the global optimal solution of recourse allocation. Therefore, [12] investigated a low-complex resource allocation algorithm based on game theory, which can achieve the global optimal solution. They also took the routing into considerations. The stochastic optimization technique was applied to transform the original stochastic problem into a deterministic optimization problem, and an energy-saving dynamic offloading algorithm was proposed by [2] and [17].

There also have some works focused on the joint problem of network economics and resource allocation. The seller provided limited computing service resources, and the buyer makes an offer for offloading as required. A double auction mechanism with dynamic pricing was proposed by [7,8,16]. They solved the problem of cost minimization to obtain the optimal dynamic pricing strategy effectively. Simultaneously, they found the Optimal Solution to Maximize Social Welfare which every participant could maximize its profit.

The others works used in the form of stackelberg game to model interactions between edge clouds and users. [13] investigated a distributed method based on price to manage user's offloading computing tasks with computation capacity constraints. [14] studied a pricing based cost-aware dynamic resource management for cooperative cloudlets in edge computing. Then, stackelberg game theory was used to describe the interaction between user and edge computing. Respectively, two algorithms were proposed for wait-time sensitive scenarios and computation-intensive scenarios.

[11] studied the cache incentive mechanism by using a stackelberg game approach with the consideration of congestion factors, and the interaction between two stages of stackelberg was analyzed. In addition, they also obtained the optimal pricing strategy and the cache strategy and designed of an optimal pricing algorithm. [10] focused on an incentive active caching mechanism in small cell networks. Particularly, they provided a closed-form expressions of the storage at the NE, and the optimal charging price was derived in a closed form.

Nevertheless, these works gave a few insights about resources allocation problem by the form of pricing in the MEC scenario. To deal with this issue, we focus on the resource allocation based on game theory for one service provider and multiple users in MEC system. Besides, an efficient resource allocation algorithm is proposed to achieve the maximum benefit of MUs.

6   Conclusion

In this paper, we consider the joint problem of network economics and resource allocation. We have proposed a MEC system consisting of one privately SP and multiple MUs. Next, a new effective resource allocation approach based on game theory in MEC scenario is proposed. In addition, we prove the existence of Nash equilibrium by game theory method and design an efficient the best response algorithm to solve this problem. The numerical experiment shows that our algorithm is effective.

Acknowledgments. This work is partly supported by the National Natural Science Foundation of China (Nos. 61872044, 61902029), the Key Research and Cultivation Projects at Beijing Information Science and Technology University (No. 5211910958), the Supplementary and Supportive Project for Teachers at Beijing Information Science and Technology University (No. 5111911128), Beijing Municipal Program for Top Talent Cultivation (CIT & TCD201804055) and Qinxin Talent Program of Beijing Information Science and Technology University.

References

1. Dinh, T.Q., Tang, J., La, Q.D., Quek, T.Q.: Offloading in mobile edge computing: task allocation and computational frequency scaling. IEEE Trans. Commun. **65**(8), 3571–3584 (2017)
2. Chen, Y., Zhang, N., Zhang, Y., Chen, X.: Dynamic computation offloading in edge computing for internet of things. IEEE Internet of Things J. **6**(3), 4242–4251 (2019)
3. Wang, K., Yang, K., Magurawalage, C.S.: Joint energy minimization and resource allocation in C-RAN with mobile cloud. IEEE Trans. Cloud Comput. (TCC) **6**(3), 760–770 (2017)
4. He, Y., Ren, J., Yu, G., Cai, Y.: Joint computation offloading and resource allocation in D2D enabled MEC networks. In: IEEE International Conference on Communications (ICC), pp. 1–6 (2019)

5. Cheng, K., Teng, Y., Sun, W., Liu, A., Wang, X.: Energy-efficient joint offloading and wireless resource allocation strategy in multi-MEC server systems. In: IEEE International Conference on Communications (ICC), pp. 1–6 (2018)
6. Hui, H., Zhou, C., An, X., Lin, F.: A new resource allocation mechanism for security of mobile edge computing system. IEEE Access **7**, 116886–116899 (2019)
7. Sun, W., Liu, J., Yue, Y., Zhang, H.: Double auction-based resource allocation for mobile edge computing in industrial internet of things. IEEE Trans. Industr. Inf. **14**(10), 4692–4701 (2018)
8. Han, D., Chen, W., Fang, Y.: A dynamic pricing strategy for vehicle assisted mobile edge computing systems. IEEE Wirel. Commun. Lett. **8**(2), 420–423 (2018)
9. Gajic, V., Huang, J., Rimoldi, B.: Competition of wireless providers for atomic users. IEEE/ACM Trans. Netw. **22**(2), 512–525 (2014)
10. Shen, F., Hamidouche, K., Bastug, E., Debbah, M.: A Stackelberg game for incentive proactive caching mechanisms in wireless networks. In: IEEE Global Communications Conference (GLOBECOM), pp. 1–6 (2016)
11. Zhao, K., Zhang, S., Zhang, N., Zhou, Y., Zhang, Y., Shen, X.: Incentive mechanism for cached-enabled small cell sharing: a Stackelberg game approach. In: IEEE Global Communications Conference (GLOBECOM), pp. 1–6 (2017)
12. Wu, B., Zeng, J., Ge, L., Tang, Y., Su, X.: A game-theoretical approach for energy-efficient resource allocation in MEC network. In: IEEE International Conference on Communications (ICC), pp. 1–6 (2019)
13. Liu, M., Liu, Y.: Price-based distributed offloading for mobile-edge computing with computation capacity constraints. IEEE Wirel. Commun. Lett. **7**(3), 420–423 (2017)
14. Wan, X., Yin, J., Guan, X., Bai, G., Choi, B.Y.: A pricing based cost-aware dynamic resource management for cooperative cloudlets in edge computing. In: IEEE International Conference on Computer Communication and Networks (ICCCN), pp. 1–6 (2018)
15. Yang, S., Pan, L., Wang, Q., Liu, S.: To sell or not to sell: trading your reserved instances in Amazon EC2 marketplace. In: 2018 IEEE 38th International Conference on Distributed Computing Systems (ICDCS), pp. 939–948 (2018)
16. Zhang, M., Huang, J.: Mechanism design for network utility maximization with private constraint information. In: IEEE INFOCOM 2019-IEEE Conference on Computer Communications, pp. 919–927 (2019)
17. Wang, C., Liang, C., Yu, F.R., Chen, Q., Tang, L.: Computation offloading and resource allocation in wireless cellular networks with mobile edge computing. IEEE Trans. Wireless Commun. **16**(8), 4924–4938 (2017)
18. Zhang, J., Xia, W., Yan, F., Shen, L.: Joint computation offloading and resource allocation optimization in heterogeneous networks with mobile edge computing. IEEE Access **6**, 19324–19337 (2018)

A Cloudlet Placement Method Based on Birch in Wireless Metropolitan Area Network

Kai Peng[1], Haodong Liang[2], Yiwen Zhang[3(✉)], Xingda Qian[1], and Hualong Huang[1]

[1] College of Engineering, Huaqiao University, Quanzhou, China
[2] Faculty of Electronic and Information Engineering, Xi'an Jiaotong University, Xi'an, China
[3] School of Computer Science and Technology, Anhui University, Hefei, China
zhangyiwen@ahu.edu.cn

Abstract. Mobile edge computing was proposed to push data centers towards network edges for reducing the network latency of delivering cloud services to mobile devices. Cloudlet is one type of edge servers which can provide abundant resources to mobile users. However, there are a large number of mobile users in Wireless Metropolitan Area Network (WMAN), and these users are always on the moving. Meanwhile, the number of cloudlets is limited. And therefore how to deploy cloudlets in WMAN is critical. In view of these challenges, a cloudlet placement method based on Balanced Iterative Reducing and Clustering Using Hierarchies is proposed in this paper. Compared to other methods, our proposed method not only can cover most of mobile devices, but also solve user mobility issues. In addition, a load balancing process is used in our proposed method which can balance each cluster better.

Keywords: Cloudlet placement · Mobile device · Birch · Load balancing

1 Introduction

With the development of newly computer network and big data, Mobile Cloud Computing (MCC) is becoming an effective method to extend capacity of mobile users by providing different types of services. However, it may cause delay by visiting the remote cloud [1–3]. Fortunately, Mobile Edge Computing (MEC) as a new technology was proposed to push data centers towards network edges for reducing the network latency of delivering cloud services to mobile devices [4]. Cloudlet is one type of edge servers which can provide abundant resources to mobile users [5,6]. Compared with remote cloud, cloudlet is deployed in a single-hop network location from mobile devices, and its physical proximity to mobile devices provides mobile devices with abundant computing resources and lower access latency.

Wireless Metropolitan Area Networks (WMAN) is a computer network that provides wireless Internet access to users in metropolitan areas. Placing cloudlet

© Springer Nature Singapore Pte Ltd. 2020
Z. Zheng et al. (Eds.): BlockSys 2019, CCIS 1156, pp. 397–409, 2020.
https://doi.org/10.1007/978-981-15-2777-7_32

in WMAN has a broad application prospect [7,8]. First, the metropolitan area has a high population density, which means that a large number of users will access the cloudlet, which can improve the quality of service (QoS) for users. As the utilization of cloudlet increases, the benefits of WMAN network service providers can be further improved.

However, there are a large number of mobile users in WMAN, and these users are always on the moving. Meanwhile, the number of cloudlets is limited. In Wireless Local Area Networks (WLAN), due to the small size of the network, the communication delay between the user and the cloudlet is negligible regardless of where the cloudlet is placed. And therefore how to deploy cloudlets in WMAN is critical. The reasonable placement of cloudlet helps to reduce the average access latency between mobile devices and cloudlets.

Although there are some studies focus on the cloudlet deployment in WMAN mainly assume that cloudlets and mobile devices are both fixed [9]. However, given the increasing of user size and the issues of user mobility in WMAN, fixedly placed cloudlets are not able to better handle response requests to mobile device application computing requirements. In addition, there are some studies that consider mobility [10], but do not consider the limitation of cloudlet resources and the load balancing of each cluster.

In view of these challenges, a cloudlet placement method based on Balanced Iterative Reducing and Clustering Using Hierarchies is proposed in this paper [13]. The main contributions can be summarized as follows:

(1) We proposed a cloudlet placement method named CPMB which not only can cover most of mobile devices, but also address user mobility.
(2) A load balancing strategy is used in both the initial cloudlet placement phase and the phase after the movement of mobile users.
(3) Compared to K-means, our proposed method CPMB is effective and efficient in terms of mobile device coverage and load balancing.

The remaining of this paper is recognized as follows. In Sect. 2, system model and problem formulation are introduced. Section 4 presents the comparison analysis and performance evaluation. Followed by the cloudlet placement method in Sect. 3. Section 5 summarizes the related work, and Sect. 6 concludes the paper and describes the future work. To simplify the discussion, key terms used in this paper are summarized in Table 1.

2   Preliminary

In this section, the system model and problem formulation are presented.

2.1   The System Mode

The framework of cloudlet based MEC is shown in Fig. 1. Different from the remote cloud, the cloudlet is near to the mobile users, which can provide low-latency service.

Table 1. Key terms and descriptions

Terms	Description
A	The set of points in mobile device activity area, $A = \{(x, y) \mid 0 \leq x \leq X, 0 \leq y \leq Y\}$
D	The set of mobile devices, $D = \{d_1, d_2, ..., d_i, ..., d_N\}$
d_i	The i_{th} $(1 \leq i \leq N)$ mobile device in D
$dp_i(t)$	The position of d_i at time t, $dp_i(t) = (dpx_i(t), dpy_i(t))$
CL	The set of cloudlets, $CL = \{cl_1, cl_2, ..., cl_j, ..., cl_M\}$
cl_j	The j_{th} $(1 \leq j \leq M)$ cloudlet in CL
AP	The set of AP, $AP = \{ap_1, ap_2, ..., ap_j, ..., ap_M\}$
$clp_j(t)$	The position of cl_j at time t, $cl_j = (clx_j(t), cly_j)$
$r(t)$	The coverage radius for cl_j at time t
$dc_j(t)$	The mobile device collection of $clp_j(t)$ at time

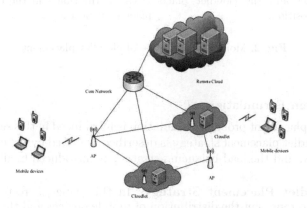

Fig. 1. The framework of cloudlet based MEC

Fig. 2 depicts an example with many mobile devices and a cloudlet. As shown in Fig. 2(a), the mobile devices are randomly distributed in a given area which represents the WMAN. It is assumed that the mobile devices are randomly distributed at time t as shown in Fig. 2(a). And location A is the best place to deploy a cloudlet equipped with an access point (AP) which evaluated by a certain placement method. More specifically, allowing the cloudlet to cover as many mobile devices as possible can reduce the average latency of users accessing the cloudlet. In addition, the host of a mobile devices is moving sometimes. And all the mobile devices run their own way. It is assumed that at time t', the mobile devices move to proximity to position B. The new distribution of mobile devices likes position B which is shown in Fig. 2(b). If the cloudlet is still deployed in location A at time t', the coverage rate of mobile devices is not high which may result in a low resource utilization of the cloudlet. In addition, these mobile devices cannot get better service. On the contrary, if the cloudlet can be moved to the location B shown in Fig. 2(b) according to the change of the mobile device distribution, the number of mobile devices in the cloudlet coverage will be greatly increased, and the resource utilization will be increased accordingly.

Therefore, it is significant to propose a feasible strategy to deploy the cloudlets reasonably and support the mobility of the mobile devices.

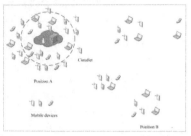 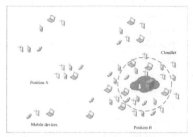

(a) The original mobile devices distribution and the cloudlet placement position.

(b) The after-moving mobile devices distribution and the cloudlet placement position.

Fig. 2. Motivation example of cloudlet placement.

2.2 Problem Formulation

The cloudlet placement problem formulation is introduced in this section. Firstly, the basic cloudlet placement strategy is described, followed by the cloudlet movement strategy, and the load balancing strategy is introduced finally.

Basic Cloudlet Placement Strategy. In this paper, a rectangular active area is used to represent the distribution of mobile devices and the placement of cloudlets. Other shaped areas can also be divided into rectangles of different sizes. It is assumed that the collection of mobile devices $clp_j(t)$ covered by cloudlet cl_j at time t is $dc_j(t)$. The $dc_j(t)$ is expressed as

$$dc_j(t) = \{d_i(t)|dis(dp_i(t), clp_j(t)) \leq r(t), 1 \leq i \leq N)\} \tag{1}$$

where $dis(dp_i(t), clp_j(t))$ indicates the distance between cloudlet cl_j and mobile device d_i. Then, $dis(dp_i(t), clp_j(t))$ is given as

$$
\begin{aligned}
&dis(dp_i(t), clp_j(t)) \\
&= \sqrt{(dpx_i(t) - clpx_j(y))^2 + (dpy_i(t) - clpy_j(y))^2}
\end{aligned} \tag{2}
$$

If cloudlet cl_j with the central position $P(x, y)$ is working to serve the mobile devices at time t, the number of mobile devices covered by cl_j at this time should satisfy the condition that $dc_j \geq L$. To choose the optimal placement of cloudlet and maximize the total number of covered mobile devices is decided by provided cloudlets, which is calculated by

$$TN(t) = |\bigcup_{j=1}^{M} dc_j(t)| \quad and \quad TN(t) \leq B \times L \tag{3}$$

where B represents the maximum number of sample nodes and L represents the maximum number of clusters.

Cloudlet Movement Strategy. The collection of mobile devices at $P(x, y)$ is denoted as $dc_{j,p}(t')$ after movement at time t'. Another position $P'(x', x')$ which is obtained by cloudlet placement algorithm meets the placement strategy and $dc_{j,p'}(t') \leq dc_{j,p}(t')$. In addition, there are no other cloudlets placing around P' at time t' within radius r. It is reasonable to move cl_j from P to P' [11].

By calculating the distance between the original location of the cloudlet and the potential target location, we can get the path graph of moving traces of mobile cloudlets at time $(t, t']$ which is denoted as $G = (E, V, W)$, where E represents the movable path of cloudlets, V represents the available positions for cloudlets and W represents the distance between any two positions.

Load Balancing Strategy. In a distributed system architecture environment, load balancing is an important part of ensuring efficient of the system. The objective of clustering algorithm itself is to maximize the number of users (mobile devices) in a single cluster and fails to pay attention to the balance of the number of sample nodes among the clusters. In another word, if the number of mobile devices covered by a certain cloudlet is too large, it will cause reduce the performance of this cloudlet, thereby reducing the quality of service for users. Meanwhile, another nearly by cloudlet that is idle may have low resource usage.

Above all, designing a load balancing strategy can balance the number of mobile devices in each cluster as much as possible.

3   A Cloudlet Placement Method Based on Birch (CPMB)

In this section, we mainly introduce the cloudlet placement method. Firstly the process of the proposed method is introduced, followed by the algorithm pseudocode.

3.1   The Process of Cloudlet Placement Method

The cloudlet placement method mainly consists of four steps. Namely, **Step 1: Decide the center points**, **Step 2: load balancing**, **Step 3: Movement**, and **Step 4: Load balancing**. Notice that load balancing optimization strategy is used in the two phases, namely, the initial phase and the phase after movement.

Step 1: Decide the center points
The Step 1 is based on Birch which mainly includes three phases [13, 14].
(1) Scan the collection of mobile devices, where each data point represents a mobile device. Establishing a clustering feature tree CF Tree with an initial structure similar to the balanced B+ tree in memory according to the given initial threshold T; (2) Reconstruct and compression the initial CF Tree by raising the threshold; (3) The reserved reclaim space is used to store potential outliers. After updating the threshold, try to insert into the CF. If these outliers still cannot be inserted, determine them as true outliers and delete them.

Based on the above operation, the final CF Tree is obtained. Additionally, determine the number of required cloudlets and the placement of the cloudlet based on the final CF Tree.

Notice that the initial threshold T is obtained by the following rules. For the mobile devices in the current region, the distance between any two mobile devices is calculated, and the mathematical expectation EX and the variance DX are obtained. After the weighting, the initial threshold T can be obtained by

$$T = p \times (EX + 0.25 \times DX) \tag{4}$$

where p is a pre-set percentage. If a memory overflow occurs in the subsequent process, we need to increase the CF Tree reconstruction. Moreover, the percentage should be increased appropriately.

Step 2: Load balancing process

After Birch clustering, the cloudlet center position is determined, and the number of mobile devices in each cluster, its average value, the distance between the center of the cloudlet and mobile devices as well as the distance between any two cloudlets are calculated respectively. If the following four conditions are met:

Condition 1: The absolute value of the number of mobile devices in the i_{th} cluster minus the average value is greater than half of the maximum value of the number minus the minimum value, that is, half of the range.

Condition 2: The distance from the j_{th} mobile device in the i_{th} cluster to the cloudlet center location is greater than the density threshold T.

Condition 3: The distance from the j_{th} mobile device to the k_{th} cloudlet center location is less than twice the density threshold T.

Condition 4: The distance between the i_{th} cloudlet to which the j_{th} mobile device belongs and the k_{th} cloudlet center location is smaller than the average distance between any two cloudlets.

If the following four conditions are met, the j_{th} mobile offload from the i_{th} cloudlet to the k_{th} mobile device.

The algorithm pseudocode is shown as follows.

Step 3: Movement process

We consider the same movement situation in [11,12]. This section designs a cloud service enhancement method for the cloudlet to provide support for applications in MEC environment. In step 2, the weight path map is provided, and the movement trajectory of each cloudlet is determined according to the weight path map.

We set the center of cloudlet before movement as the initial point, and form a directed graph with all the potential target points after movement. Based on the Dijkstra algorithm, we can find the shortest path of the cloudlet to the remaining potential target positions, and reduce the migration cost of the cloudlets.

The algorithm pseudocode is shown as follows.

Step 4: Load balancing process after movement

As the positions of cloudlets have changed, namely, the numbers of mobile devices will be changed accordingly. And therefore the load balancing needs to be considered again. The main process is the same as the step 2.

3.2 The Algorithm Pseudocode

The algorithm pseudocode is shown as follows.

Algorithm 1. A Cloudlet Placement Method Based on Birch

Input: Given Gaussian distribution dataset D, position of mobile devices $dp_i(t)$, density threshold T

Output: k(number of cluster), position of cloudlets $clp_j(t)$

1: $D \leftarrow$ loading()
2: **while** $i<N$ **do**
3:      $T \leftarrow$ Distance($dp_i(t)$)
4:      CFTreeCreate(D,T)
5:      Reserve recycling space $\leftarrow$ Store(potential outliers)
6:      $T' \leftarrow$ Increase(T)
7:      **while** Recycling space$\neq \emptyset$ **do**
8:          **if** CFTreeInsert(potential outlier)=False **then**
9:              True outlier $\leftarrow$ potential outlier
10:             Delete(True outlier)
11:         **else**
12:             CFTreeInsert(potential outlier)
13:             CFTreeAdjust(T')
14:         **end if**
15:     **end while**
16: **end while**
17: GlobalClustering()
18: ClusterRefine()
19: **Load balancing()**
20: When the condition is stasifed
21: **Movement()**
22: **Load balancing()**
23: **return** k,$clp_j(t)$

---

4   Experimental Evaluation and Discussion

In this section, comprehensive simulations and experiments are conducted to evaluate the performance of our proposed method. Firstly, the experimental setting is introduced in Sect. 4.1 and then the experimental result and discussion are described in Sect. 4.2.

4.1 Experimental Setting

It is assumed that each cloudlet is equipped with an AP and the mobile device accesses the network via Wi-Fi. Experiments are performed on randomly positional dataset which is generated based on Gaussian-distributed. The position dataset information is shown in Table 2, where μ, σ represents the mean and standard deviation respectively, and 500, 1000, and 1500 represent the number of mobile devices.

Table 2. The parameters of Gaussian distribution

Mobile devices	500 (μ, σ)	1000 (μ, σ)	1500 (μ, σ)
Moving devices of t	(700, 600), (1400, 500) (3200, 550), (2600, 560)	(800, 500), (1300, 520) (3000, 550), (2800, 540)	(700, 580), (1200, 520) (3100, 560), (2700, 540)
Moving devices of t′	(900, 560), (1200, 490) (3200, 550), (2600, 600)	(1000, 520), (1500, 540) (3300, 550), (2600, 560)	(900, 600), (1400, 540) (3300, 540), (2500, 560)

The shape of the mobile device active area A is set to a rectangle and the range of x-axis and y-axis range of this area are both in $[-1000\,\text{m}, 5000\,\text{m}]$. The location of the mobile device is randomly generated, the numbers of mobile devices distributed in area A are moderate values of $N \in \{500, 1000, 1500\}$, and the experimental period is set at 20 min. In this way, the ability of the CPMB algorithm to process dataset with different characteristics in different application scenarios is evaluated.

4.2 The Experimental Result and Discussion

In this section, the comparison of our proposed method CPMB and K-means in terms of coverage devices and load balancing is introduced.

Comparison of Coverage Devices. The comparison results of our proposed method CPMB and K-means in terms of covered devices are shown in this section. Generally speaking, the larger the covered devices, the better the placement results. Different scale of mobile devices (500, 1000, 1500) have been tested. The results are shown in Figs. 3, 4 and 5. More specifically, both the initial placement situation and the situation after the movement of mobile devices have been presented. We can conclude that the number of mobile devices covered by CPMB are larger than the number of mobile devices covered by the K-Means.

Additionally, the average coverage of mobile devices under the condition of different mobile devices is shown in Fig. 6. We can see that the coverage and average coverage of each cloudlet in different amounts of cloudlets obtained by CPMB are higher than K-Means. However, due to the certain number of mobile device active areas, as the number of mobile devices and cloudlets increases, the dense mobile device may be covered by multiple different locations of cloudlet and a discrete mobile device may also be overwritten by another cloudlet which

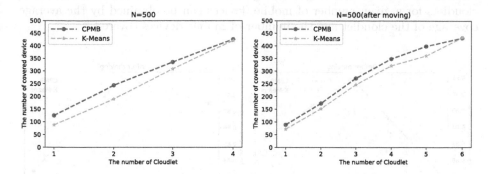

Fig. 3. $N = 500$ the number of covered mobile device before and after moving.

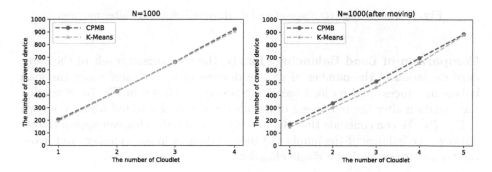

Fig. 4. $N = 1000$ the number of covered mobile device before and after moving.

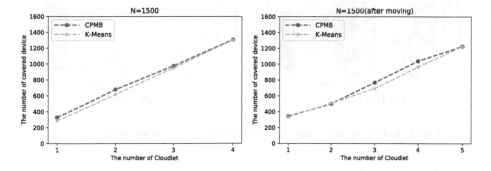

Fig. 5. $N = 1500$ the number of covered mobile device before and after moving.

leads to the decrease of average coverage. And therefore, a reasonable number of cloudlets for a given number of mobile devices can be obtained by the average coverage of the cloudlet and the number of mobile devices covered.

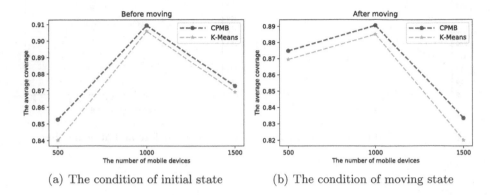

(a) The condition of initial state   (b) The condition of moving state

Fig. 6. The average coverage of mobile devices before and after moving.

Comparison of Load Balancing. Firstly, the comparison result of the standard deviation of the number of mobile devices in each cluster using the load balancing process and no load balancing process is shown in Fig. 7a. Secondly, the situation after the movement of mobile devices is also tested which is shown in Fig. 7b. We can conclude that the process of load balancing can appropriately improve the balance of the number of mobile devices in each cluster, and avoid the failure or overload of a single cloudlet.

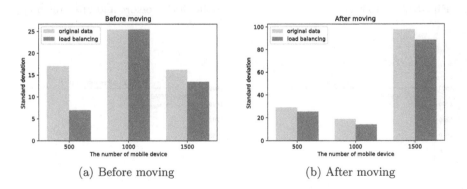

(a) Before moving   (b) After moving

Fig. 7. Initial and after load balancing optimization standard deviation.

However, considering load balancing, the number of mobile devices in the cluster may change, affecting the average coverage of mobile devices. Therefore, we additionally compare the average coverage of different amounts of mobile devices before and after load balancing. As shown in Fig. 8, we can see that the coverage that after using load balancing basically remains the same as before using this process. Therefore, it can be concluded that CPMB can balance the number of mobile devices in each cluster while keeping the average coverage.

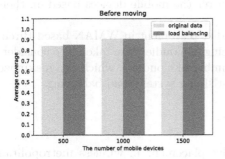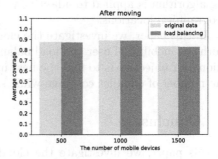

Fig. 8. The average coverage of mobile devices before and after load balancing.

5 Related Work

Wang et al. [6] studied the problem of edge server deployment in MEC environment. They used mixed integer programming (MIP) and assumed that each edge server has the same and limited computing resources to handle mobile user requests.

Jia et al. proposed two Cloudlet placement algorithms, namely, Heaviest-AP First method (HAF) and Density-Based Clustering (DBC) to determine the best placement of the Cloudlet [9]. The HAF algorithm sorts the access points according to the load of the access point, and then selects the highest access point of K from the sorting result as the placement position of the Cloudlet. The DBC algorithm calculates the density of the area user to determine where it is best to place the Cloudlet. However, like the HAF algorithm, their approach does not take into account the load balancing of the system.

The user in WMAN is mobile. If the user changes the location frequently, and the method of placing the cloudlet in a fixed manner may cause the user request to fail. Liang et al. [10] proposed a location-aware service deployment algorithm for cloudlet to reduce the network latency and the number of service instances that can accommodate tolerant network latency conditions. The algorithm divides the mobile user into multiple user clusters based on the user's geographic location, and then deploys the service instance to the nearest Cloudlet from the user cluster center. However, this algorithm also has certain deficiencies. When using the Kmeans algorithm, it is necessary to realize the size of the specified cluster, and there is no uniform standard to determine the optimal value.

Xiang et al. propose an adaptive cloudlet placement method for mobile applications over GPS big data [11]. The gathering regions of the mobile devices are identified based on K-means algorithm and the cloudlet destination locations are confirmed accordingly. Besides, the moving traces between the origin and destination locations of these mobile cloudlets are also technically achieved through our cloudlet movement principle. Zhang et al. propose an enhanced adaptive cloudlet placement approach for Mobile Application on Spark [12]. The covering algorithm is applied to adaptively cluster the mobile devices based on their geographical locations.

In this paper, we investigate the cloudlet placement in WMAN based Birch. Both the mobility of user and load balancing of cloudlets are taken into consideration, our objective is to find the best number of cloudlets, which can maximize the number of cloudlet coverage while satisfying system load balancing.

6   Conclusion

In this paper, we investigate the cloudlet placement in wireless metropolitan area network environment. To solve the problem, we introduce Birch clustering algorithm, which does not need to specify the K value in advance, to eliminate the interference of the initial center to the final clustering result. Experiments show that load balancing optimization is achieved without affecting the coverage of cloudlet mobile devices, reducing the average access latency between mobile devices and cloudlets serving mobile devices, and improving the resource utilization of cloudlets. In future work, we will use a real platform to verify the feasibility of the proposed methods and consider the assignment of mobile users to movable cloudlets.

Acknowledgments. This work is supported by the National Science Foundation of China (Grant No. 61902133), The Natural Science Foundation of Fujian Province (Grant No. 20-18J05106).

References

1. Quan, W., Cheng, N., Qin, M., Zhang, H., Chan, H.A., Shen, X.: Adaptive transmission control for software defined vehicular networks. IEEE Wirel. Commun. Lett. **8**, 653–656 (2018)
2. Zhang, Y., Cui, G., Deng, S., Chen, F., Wang, Y., He, Q.: Efficient query of quality correlation for service composition. IEEE Trans. Serv. Comput. (2018). https://doi.org/10.1109/TSC.2018.2830773
3. Xu, X., et al.: A computation offloading method over big data for IoT-enabled cloud-edge computing. Future Gener. Comput. Syst. https://doi.org/10.1016/j.future.2018.12.055. Accessed 24 Jan 2019
4. Peng, K., Leung, V., Xu, X., Zheng, L., Wang, J., Huang, Q.: A survey on mobile edge computing: focusing on service adoption and provision. Wirel. Commun. Mob. Comput. **2018** (2018). 16 pages, Article ID 8267838, https://doi.org/10.1155/2018/8267838
5. Satyanarayanan, M., Chen, Z., Ha, K., Hu, W., Richter, W., Pillai, P.: Cloudlets: at the leading edge of mobile-cloud convergence. In: International Conference on Mobile Computing. IEEE Computer Society (2014)

6. Wang, S., Zhao, Y., Xu, J., Yuan, J., Hsu, C.H.: Edge server placement in mobile edge computing. J. Parallel Distrib. Comput. **127**, 160–168 (2019). S0743731518304398

7. Xu, Z., Liang, W., Xu, W., Jia, M., Guo, S.: Capacitated cloudlet placements in wireless metropolitan area networks. In: 2015 IEEE 40th Conference on Local Computer Networks (LCN) (2015)

8. Xu, Z., Liang, W., Xu, W., Jia, M., Guo, S.: Efficient algorithms for capacitated cloudlet placements. IEEE Trans. Parallel Distrib. Syst. **27**(10), 2866–2880 (2016)

9. Jia, M., Cao, J., Liang, W.: Optimal cloudlet placement and user to cloudlet allocation in wireless metropolitan area networks. IEEE Trans. Cloud Comput. **5**(4), 725–737 (2015)

10. Liang, T.Y., Li, Y.J.: A location-aware service deployment algorithm based on k-means for cloudlets. Mob. Inf. Syst. **2017**, 1–10 (2017)

11. Xiang, H., et al.: An adaptive cloudlet placement method for mobile applications over GPS big data. In: GLOBECOM 2016–2016 IEEE Global Communications Conference. IEEE (2016)

12. Zhang, Y., Wang, K., Zhou, Y., He, Q.: Enhanced adaptive cloudlet placement approach for mobile application on spark. Secur. Commun. Netw. **2018**, 1–12 (2018)

13. Peng, K., Zheng, L., Xu, X., Lin, T., Leung, V.C.: Balanced iterative reducing and clustering using hierarchies with principal component analysis (PBirch) for intrusion detection over big data in mobile cloud environment. In: Proceedings of the 11th International Conference and Satellite Workshops, SpaCCS 2018, Melbourne, NSW, Australia, 11–13 December 2018 (2018)

14. Zhang, T., Ramakrishnan, R., Livny, M.: An efficient data clustering method for very large databases. In: Proceedings of the 1996 ACM SIGMOD International Conference on Management of Data (SIGMOD 1996), pp. 103–114. ACM, New York (1996)

Blockchain-Empowered Content Cache System for Vehicle Edge Computing Networks

Junjie Liu, Xuefei Zhang$^{(\boxtimes)}$, Yijing Li, Qimei Cui, and Xiaofeng Tao

National Engineering Lab for Mobile Network Technologies, Beijing University of Posts and Telecommunications, Beijing 100876, China
{JunjieLiu,zhangxuefei,liyijing,cuiqimei,taoxf}@bupt.edu.cn

Abstract. Content cache for Vehicle Edge Computing (VEC) Network is a promising service to reduce transmission delay and cost. Existing content cache system requires Road Side Units (RSUs) to participate in the content transmission process, however, RSUs are usually distributed along the road without strong security protection, which is vulnerable to being compromised by attackers. In this way, the cached content is vulnerable to tamper and the widespread dissemination of malicious content will bring a devastating blow to the trust mechanism of the caching system. In this paper, we propose a Blockchain-empowered content cache system, where the content index (containing the provider's address, the hash value of the content) is adopted to guarantee the validity of the content. The content index is deposited in the Blockchain system, the immutability and distributed architecture of Blockchain can effectively prevent the content index from being tampered. However, such tamper-resistance property comes at the cost of a long confirmation caused by the consensus process. A time-oriented Proof of Work (PoW) consensus algorithm is proposed to improve the Blockchain efficiency. And a local indexing set-based search mechanism is established to reduce the long search delay caused by the chain-based structure. Moreover, the simulation results also demonstrate that the Blockchain-empowered cache system can improve the hit ratio of servers by providing customized request information.

Keywords: Blockchain · Content cache · Consensus algorithm · VEC · Security

1 Introduction

In Vehicular Edge Computing Network (VECN), the application of content cache technique can effectively provide the QoS of users when requesting for some contents like videos. Caching and storing the content on Road Side Units (RSUs) and other wireless network edge infrastructures are regarded as a major cache technique which can reduce the information transmission distance as well as

Z. Zheng et al. (Eds.): BlockSys 2019, CCIS 1156, pp. 410–421, 2020.
https://doi.org/10.1007/978-981-15-2777-7_33

transmission delay [1]. Compared with the traditional centralized caching strategy, the distributed caching network has more nodes to provide content, and the distance between these nodes and users is shorter, which can further reduce backhaul traffic and data transmission delay [2,3]. For example, the authors in [4] proposed an interest item-based cache method, which improves the cache hit ratio and the transmission delay. In [5], the authors established a distributed cache resource allocation algorithm based on belief propagation. The algorithm achieves distributed content collaborative caching and transmission based on limited local information, which greatly reduces the average download delay.

Although the distributed cache strategy in VECN has those advantages, further development is hindered by security and privacy issues. In VECN, the limited security defend capability is not able to guarantee the validity of cache content where the cached content is vulnerable to tamper with [6–8]. Once the malicious cached content is sent to a vehicle, it will cause a great threat to the safety of drivers and passengers. However, researches of distributed cache system security mainly focus on security in the data transmission process. For example, [9] used random perturbation technology to interweave distributed storage data, realizing secure and fast encryption of sensitive data. Utilizing the characteristics of cached content, [10] proposed symbol-level and bit-level transport schemes to improve the physical layer security of the cache system. [11] investigated a dynamic fountain coding-based scheme for wireless access, combining with server selection strategy, the proposed scheme can effectively prevent the system from being eavesdropped. Although these methods can realize secure data transmission, they are unable to guarantee the security of content itself (such as inserting illegal information). And the widespread dissemination of malicious information will bring a devastating blow to the trust mechanism of the distributed caching system.

To solve these problems, this paper proposes a Blockchain-based content cache system for VECN. The immutability and distributed structure of Blockchain can effectively protect the security of cached content. However, the long confirmation delay caused by the consensus process is unbearable to vehicles, thus the consensus algorithm needs to be improved. Furthermore, the chain-based structure is another obstacle in terms of delay, the VEC server needs to traverse the entire Blockchain to find a desirable result, which means an efficient search method needs to be designed. The innovation of this paper can be summarized as follows:

1. A Blockchain-empowered content cache system is built to ensure the validity of cache content. By depositing the index (e.g., provider address, hash value, etc.) of the cached content in Blockchain, VEC servers and vehicles can verify the validity of the downloaded content, thus prevent the dissemination of malicious content.

2. A time-oriented Proof of Work (PoW) has been proposed to replace the traditional PoW. The newly proposed PoW can reduce the long confirmation delay caused by the consensus process. Meanwhile, the unique leader selection scheme guarantees the low occurrence probability of Blockchain fork, preventing the cache system from attacks like double-spending.

3. To accelerate the content searching process of Blockchain, we establish a local indexing mechanism. The index records in the newly generated block are sort by content identifier. The server address with the same content identifier is recorded in the local indexing set, so that the server can react to the content request with lower delay.
4. The hit ratio performance of the traditional cache replacement strategy is improved based on the cache records provided by the Blockchain. Instead of using local content request records, the proposed strategy can utilize the historical content request records of the current vehicles, thus improving the hit ratio of the cache replacement strategy.

2   System Model

As shown in Fig. 1, we consider a Vehicle Edge Computing (VEC) network, where K Road Side Units (RSUs) is uniformly distributed over the street. Each RSU is connected to a VEC server via high reliable cable, the VEC server can offer storage and computation capability to the VEC network. The kth VEC server in the system is denoted as V_k, $1 \leq k \leq K$. VEC is allocated with two major functions: one for caching the popular content of present district, another for executing current Blockchain-related operations (e.g., proof of work, execution of synchronization algorithms, etc.). Each RSU has a certain coverage area that vehicles in this area can only communicate with this RSU and apply to the corresponding VEC server with cache content information such as videos. When receiving the content request, VEC will search the content locally. If having this content in storage, it will return the content directly, otherwise, it will look for other servers with this content and download. In addition, all users in the system (VEC servers, vehicles, etc.) are assigned asymmetric key pairs for signature and authentication.

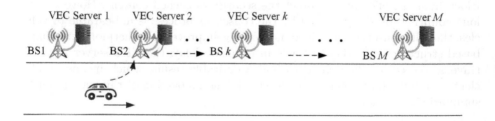

Fig. 1. Blockchain-empowered vehicle edge computing networks

2.1   Content Distribution Model

In the content cache system, the popularity of cache content is different, which means some types of content may be requested by vehicles for more time. ZipF is regarded as an effective way to represents the popularity difference [13], the popularity of content f can be denoted as

$$p_\alpha = \frac{1/f^\alpha}{\sum_{z=1}^{m} (1/z^\alpha)} \tag{1}$$

where α is the parameter of the Zipf distribution, m is the total number of the content and f is the ranking of the requested times of content.

3 Blockchain-Empowered Content Cache System

In this section, we provide a detailed description of the Blockchain-empowered content cache system. First, we provide an overview of the content cache process. Second, the generation and storage process of the content index is presented. Subsequently, we describe the Blockchain-based content cache strategy to show how the VEC server renews their storage space. In the end, the construction process of a local indexing set is described in detail.

3.1 Overall Flow of Blockchain-Empowered Content Caching

In this section, we give a detailed description of the Blockchain-based content cache process, the overall process is shown as Fig. 2. When a vehicle requests content from the VEC server, the VEC server retrieves the local indexing set according to the content identification. If the content is stored locally, the server returns the content directly to the vehicle. Otherwise, an optimal content source is selected from the indexing set according to the server's customized criteria, such as distance priority or cost priority. And the content cache strategy is carried out to renew the cache space. To download the desired content from the source, the VEC server needs to generate a content index firstly, which contains the address (public key) of the current server, the source address of the content, the timestamp of the index, and the hash value of the cached content. Subsequently, the VEC server attaches the digital signature to the index and broadcasts it to all VEC server for verification.

Having received the broadcast index, VEC servers verify the validity of the index, including the signature and the correctness of the hash value. After a period of time, VEC servers pack the verified index received during this period into a new block and begin the Proof of Work (PoW) process. After the PoW process, the new block will be added to the end of the Blockchain, which means the newly generated content index is successfully added to the Blockchain. Then, the current VEC server begins to download the content and transmit it to the vehicle.

After that, the VEC server renews the local indexing set according to the new block. The index records are sort by the content identification, the server request with the same content will be deposit in the same row of the indexing set. Meanwhile, the VEC server transmits the requested content to the vehicle. After the transmission, the vehicle will compare the hash value of the content, if it is the same with the hash value provided by the Blockchain, it means the content is authentic.

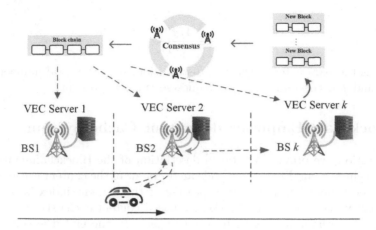

Fig. 2. The overall flow of the blockchain-based content cache system

3.2 The Process of Information Index Generation and Storage

In this section, the following two aspects are introduced in detail: one is the specific generation process of the content index, the other is the detailed steps of adding the index to the Blockchain.

When the VEC server decides to cache a new content, a content index $index_{id}$ is generated by VEC, where id is the identifier of the index automatically generated by the system. The format of the information index is shown in Table 1.

Table 1. The format of information index.

Identifier	Timestamp
Provider	Requestor
Filesize	Hash

$Identifier$ is the identification of the content, $FileSize$ is the size of cached files, $Provider$ is the address (usually represented by the server's public key) of the source VEC server, $Requestor$ is the address of request VEC server, $Timestamp$ is the generation time of the index, $Hash$ is the hash value of cached content.

Subsequently, the VEC server signs the newly generated index with its digital signature and broadcast it to all the VEC servers in the system. The format of the broadcasts information is as follows:

$$V_k \to V_{i \neq k} : message_{id} = (index_{id} \,\|\, Sig_{v_k}(index_{id})) \tag{2}$$

where Sig_{v_k} is the digital signature generated by the secret key of V_k

$$Sig_{v_k} = Sign_{SK_{v_k}}(index_{id}) \tag{3}$$

When the VEC servers receive the information, they verify the validity of the information and the hash value. After a period of time, each server packs the validated index received during that time into a new block *newblock*, the general form of *newblock* is as Table 2:

Table 2. The format of new block.

Index	Timestamp
Previous Hash	SelfHash
Transaction Data	

Subsequently, every server begins the Proof of Work (PoW) process. Different from the traditional PoW method, to reduce the confirmation delay of Blockchain and the occurrence probability of Blockchain fork (which may cause double spending attacks), a time-oriented PoW method is proposed in this paper:

$$Hash\,(\text{Prev Hash} + newBlock + nonce) < \text{Given value} \qquad (4)$$

$$leader = \{VEC_i\,|\text{minimum}\,(Hash\,(\text{Prev Hash} + newBlock + nonce_i))\} \qquad (5)$$

where *nonce* represents a random parameter, the only way to find a desirable nonce is to conduct a great number of attempts.

As shown in (5), traditional PoW schemes are replaced by the time-oriented PoW scheme. Each VEC server selects the minimum hash value received within the period as the leader. Compared with the traditional PoW, the time-oriented method avoids the Blockchain fork caused by the information inconsistent, thus reducing the occurrence probability of a double-spending attack. In addition, the proposed consensus process will be completed within the prescribed time, thus making the confirmation delay more controllable.

After the consensus process, each VEC server verifies the validity of *newblock* sent by *leader* and adds the block to the end of the Blockchain if the validity of *newblock* is confirmed.

3.3 The Update Process of Local Index Set

After *newblock* is added to the Blockchain successfully, each VEC server extract the information index in *newBlock* and update the local indexing set $\mathcal{D}$, the structure of $\mathcal{D}$ is as follows:

Identifier	$d_1, d_2, ..., d_i$

Where d_i is an address-time tuple $< Address, Timestamp >$, it is mainly used to record the server address containing the same content. When the Blockchain generates a new block, VEC server will extract the content index inside the block and generate a new tuple d_{i+1}. The renewed local indexing set is as follows:

Identifier	$d_1, d_2, ..., d_i, d_{i+1}$

4   Security Analysis and Numerical Results

4.1   Security Analysis

By implementing Blockchain-empowered content cache system, the security of the content in the vehicle edge computing networks has been guaranteed. The main advantages of the proposed system security is summarized as follows:

(1) *Verifiable and Traceable:* Since the information index (containing the hash value of the content) are recorded in the Blockchain system, vehicles can verify the validation of the content easily by inquiring any VEC server in the system. And the immutable feature of Blockchain guarantees that the information index is hard to tamper with. Moreover, once the vehicle finds the content has been modified, it can trace the previous records to find the source.

(2) *Request Response Delay:* Blockchain provides a more convenient way for servers to obtain their desirable content. For all content cache operation is recorded in the Blockchain system via information index, it is easy for servers to know the cached content in other servers. Therefore, instead of download from a single centralized server, VEC servers can obtain their desirable content through neighbour servers, which greatly reduce the response delay of the request.

4.2   Energy Consumption Model

Except for reducing the long confirmation delay, the newly proposed time-oriented consensus algorithm can also save energy in the hash computation process. Therefore, in this subsection, we will evaluate the energy consumption in different consensus algorithm.

It has been specified in [14] that the energy consumption of a CPU cycle is κf_m^2, thus the energy consumption during the hash calculation progress is

$$E_{hash} = \kappa K L_{CPU} f_m^2 \tag{6}$$

where κ is a constant value, f_m is the calculation frequency of a CPU, L_{CPU} is the expected number of CPU cycles during the calculation process. L_{CPU} can be denote as

$$L_{CPU} = f_m t \tag{7}$$

where t is the time consumption of the consensus algorithm. Combining (6) and (7), the energy consumption is as follows

$$E_{hash} = \kappa K t f_m^3 \tag{8}$$

4.3   Numerical Results

In this section, we evaluate the performance of the proposed Content cache system in terms of hit ratio and confirmation delay. Moreover, to verify the performance of our proposed algorithm, the classic Least Recently Used (LRU) and Least Frequently Used (LFU) are considered as the benchmark schemes [12]. LRU keeps the content which has been request recently, and when there is in sufficient storage, it replace the content with longest idle time. LFU stores the most frequently used content and content with lowest frequency will be evicted from the cache. The parameter settings is shown in Table 3.

Table 3. Parameter setting.

κ	10^{-27} W $\cdot$ s^3/cycles^3
M	100
m	500
f_m	3.5 GHz

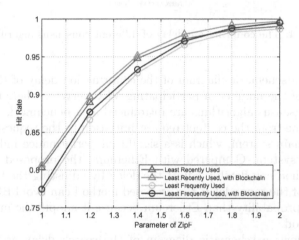

Fig. 3. Hit ratio with or without blockchain

Figure 3 is a diagram of system cache hit ratio versus ZipF distribution parameters. As you can see from the figure, the cache hit rate is rising as the ZipF parameter increases. Among the four caching strategies, the LRU-based caching strategy has a higher hit rate than the LFU-based caching strategy, because the LRU-based caching strategy can update more quickly, thus reflect the current needs of vehicles more accurately. At the same time, it is worth noting that the hit ratio of both methods has been improved by using the historical information of the current vehicle provided by the Blockchain. For the vehicles in the current coverage area, the Blockchain can provide the historical request information, while the traditional distributed cache decision can only provide the request information of the current area. The customized information provided by the Blockchain can help the cache strategy to predict the cache requirement of the vehicles more accurately, thus obtaining a higher cache hit ratio.

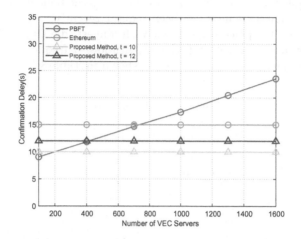

Fig. 4. The confirmation delay of different consensus algorithm

Figure 4 is a schematic diagram of the confirmation delay of the Blockchain as a function of the number of participating VEC servers, where the Ethereum and PBFT consensus algorithms are introduced as a benchmark. Confirmation delay is the time from the content request initiation to the request is confirmed by the Blockchain system, which is a significant performance indicator for the content cache system. Compared with Ethereum, the proposed time-oriented consensus method can flexibly adjust the delay by adjusting the time constrain t. In the case of the same delay, the proposed method can avoid Blockchain fork with a higher probability than Ethereum because it adopts the minimum value selection method.

Figure 5 shows a schematic diagram of the search delay as a function of Blockchain length. As can be seen from the figure, with the growth of Blockchain length, the delay of Blockchain-based or local indexing set-based search methods is increasing. However, it is obvious that the Blockchain-based search method takes more time to find a desirable result. When the vehicle sends a content request to the VEC server, the VEC server needs to traverse the whole Blockchain to find all the acceptable address, and select the appropriate one. However, the method based on the local indexing set only needs to search by content identification once to find all the required addresses, which greatly reduces the number of searches and the time delay.

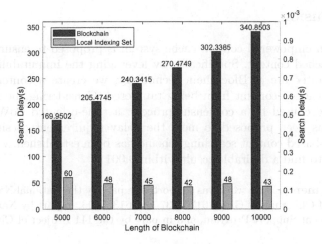

Fig. 5. The search delay comparison of blockchain and local indexing set

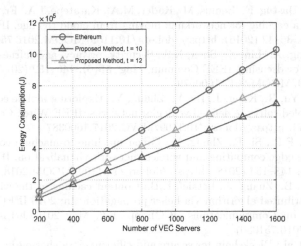

Fig. 6. The energy consumption in the consensus process

Figure 6 shows the energy consumption comparison between Ethereum and the proposed method. It is obvious that the scale of Blockchain results in more energy consumption for all the methods. Meanwhile, when the number of participating VEC servers is fixed, the energy consumption of the proposed scheme is smaller than Ethereum. The reason is that the proposed consensus algorithm has shorter confirmation delay, which means fewer attempts need to be conducted to getting a desirable result, thus saving the energy consumption in the consensus process.

5 Conclusion

A Blockchain-empowered content cache system is proposed to ensure the validity of the cached content. Specifically, by leveraging the immutability and distributed architecture of Blockchain technology, we create a content index to prevent the cached content from being tampered. Considering the long confirmation delay caused by a consensus process, a time-oriented PoW consensus algorithm has been proposed to meet the delay requirement. Besides, a local indexing set-based content searching scheme has been established, which enable VEC server to find a desirable result within 0.001 s.

Acknowledgments. This work was supported in part by the National Nature Science Foundation of China under Grant 61701037 and 61325006, in part by National Youth Top-notch Talent Support Program, and in part by the 111 Project of China B16006.

References

1. Zeydan, E., Bastug, E., Bennis, M., Kader, M.A., Karatepe, I.A., Er, A.S., Debbah, M.: Big data caching for networking: moving from cloud to edge. IEEE Commun. Mag. **54**(9), 36–42 (2016). https://doi.org/10.1109/MCOM.2016.7565185
2. Ni, J., Zhang, A., Lin, X., Shen, X.S.: Security, privacy, and fairness in fog-based vehicular crowdsensing. IEEE Commun. Mag. **55**(6), 146–152 (2017). https://doi.org/10.1109/MCOM.2017.1600679
3. Huang, X., Yu, R., Kang, J., He, Y., Zhang, Y.: Exploring mobile edge computing for 5G-enabled software defined vehicular networks. IEEE Wirel. Commun. **24**(6), 55–63 (2017). https://doi.org/10.1109/MWC.2017.1600387
4. Li, M., Yu, F.R., Si, P., Zhang, Y.: Green machine-to-machine communications with mobile edge computing and wireless network virtualization. IEEE Commun. Mag. **56**(5), 148–154 (2018). https://doi.org/10.1109/MCOM.2018.1601005
5. Liu, J., Bai, B., Zhang, J., Letaief, K.B.: Content caching at the wireless network edge: a distributed algorithm via belief propagation. In: 2016 IEEE International Conference on Communications (ICC), pp. 1–6, May 2016. https://doi.org/10.1109/ICC.2016.7510807
6. Kang, J., et al.: Blockchain for secure and efficient data sharing in vehicular edge computing and networks. IEEE Internet Things J. **6**(3), 4660–4670 (2019). https://doi.org/10.1109/JIOT.2018.2875542
7. Huang, D., Misra, S., Verma, M., Xue, G.: PACP: an efficient pseudonymous authentication-based conditional privacy protocol for VANETs. IEEE Trans. Intell. Transp. Syst. **12**(3), 736–746 (2011). https://doi.org/10.1109/TITS.2011.2156790
8. Yang, Z., Yang, K., Lei, L., Zheng, K., Leung, V.C.M.: Blockchain-based decentralized trust management in vehicular networks. IEEE Internet Things J. **6**(2), 1495–1505 (2019). https://doi.org/10.1109/JIOT.2018.2836144
9. Neagu, M., Miclea, L., Manich, S.: Interleaved scrambling technique: a novel low-power security layer for cache memories. In: 2014 19th IEEE European Test Symposium (ETS), pp. 1–2, May 2014. https://doi.org/10.1109/ETS.2014.6847844
10. Zhao, W., Chen, Z., Li, K., Liu, N., Xia, B., Luo, L.: Caching-aided physical layer security in wireless cache-enabled heterogeneous networks. IEEE Access **6**, 68920–68931 (2018). https://doi.org/10.1109/ACCESS.2018.2880339

11. Xu, Y., Du, Q., Song, H.: Security-enhanced wireless multicast via adaptive fountain codes over distributed caching network. In: 2018 IEEE SmartWorld, Ubiquitous Intelligence Computing, Advanced Trusted Computing, Scalable Computing Communications, Cloud Big Data Computing, Internet of People and Smart City Innovation (SmartWorld/SCALCOM/UIC/ATC/CBDCom/IOP/SCI), pp. 2089–2096, October 2018. https://doi.org/10.1109/SmartWorld.2018.00350

12. Goian, H.S., Al-Jarrah, O.Y., Muhaidat, S., Al-Hammadi, Y., Yoo, P., Dianati, M.: Popularity-based video caching techniques for cache-enabled networks: a survey. IEEE Access **7**, 27699–27719 (2019). https://doi.org/10.1109/ACCESS.2019.2898734

13. Su, Z., Hui, Y., Xu, Q., Yang, T., Liu, J., Jia, Y.: An edge caching scheme to distribute content in vehicular networks. IEEE Trans. Veh. Technol. **67**(6), 5346–5356 (2018). https://doi.org/10.1109/TVT.2018.2824345

14. Mao, Y., You, C., Zhang, J., Huang, K., Letaief, K.B.: A survey on mobile edge computing: the communication perspective. IEEE Commun. Surv. Tutorials **19**(4), 2322–2358 (2017). https://doi.org/10.1109/COMST.2017.2745201. Fourthquarter

Optimal Computation Resource Allocation in Vehicular Edge Computing

Shiyu Du[1], Qibo Sun[1(✉)], Jujuan Gu[2], and Yujiong Liu[1]

[1] Beijing University of Posts and Telecommunications, Beijing 100876, China
{dsy,qbsun,yjliu}@bupt.edu.cn
[2] The 54th Research Institute of CETC, Shijiazhuang 050000, China
gujujuan@163.com

Abstract. Vehicular edge computing is proposed as a new promising paradigm that provides cloud computation capabilities in close proximity to vehicles, which can augment the capabilities of vehicles. In this paper, we study the problem of computation resource allocation of edge servers for a vehicular edge computing system. We consider the constraint of limited computation resource of edge servers and vehicles can decide that vehicular applications are locally executed or offloaded to edge servers for execution to minimize the completion time of applications. We model the problem as a Stackelberg game and then prove the existence of Nash equilibrium of the game. Furthermore, we propose an algorithm to compute the Nash equilibrium effectively. Numerical simulation results demonstrate that our proposed algorithm can greatly reduce the average completion time for all applications and outperform the benchmark approaches.

Keywords: Local and Edge Equilibrium Computing · Computation resource allocation · Vehicular edge computing · Game theory · Nash equilibrium

1 Introduction

With the development of Internet of Things and wireless communication technology, vehicles can offer a variety of computation-intensive and delay-sensitive applications, which require massive computation resources. However, the resource-constrained vehicles are difficult to meet the computation resources requirements of applications. Vehicular edge computing (VEC) is proposed as a promising paradigm that provides cloud computation capabilities in close proximity to vehicles [1]. In VEC system, edge cloud resources are deployed on Road Side Units (RSUs). Each vehicle can offload its application to RSUs for execution [2,3].

There has been some research work on VEC. The authors in [4] proposed a contract-based computation resource allocation scheme to enhance the utilities of the mobile edge computing service providers. In [5], the authors proposed a distributed reputation management system, which can impact the resource allocation policy. In [6], the authors developed an energy-efficient computation offloading scheme, which jointly optimized computation offloading decisions. Existing

© Springer Nature Singapore Pte Ltd. 2020
Z. Zheng et al. (Eds.): BlockSys 2019, CCIS 1156, pp. 422–427, 2020.
https://doi.org/10.1007/978-981-15-2777-7_34

research generally consider that mobile edge computing servers on one RSU have infinite computation resources. However, the edge servers on one RSU always have limited computation resources, which is unable to meet the computation resource requirements of extensive vehicles.

To overcome the above problem, in this paper, we consider the constraints of limited computation resource of edge servers and the interaction between edge cloud resource providers and vehicles. Vehicles can decide that vehicular applications are locally executed or offloaded to edge servers on one RSU for execution to minimize the completion time of applications. We model the problem as a Stackelberg game which vehicles are leaders and the RSU is the follower. Under the vehicle-specific parameter of the optimal computation resource allocation strategy, the original game between vehicles can be transformed into a weighted congestion game. Next, we prove the existence of Nash equilibrium (NE) of the Stackelberg game, propose an algorithm to compute a NE. Finally, we show the numerical simulation results to prove that average completion time of all vehicular applications is greatly reduced using our proposed algorithm.

The rest of the paper is organized as follows. We describe system model and formulate the problem in Sect. 2. We prove the existence of NE of the Stackelberg game and propose an algorithm in Sect. 3. We present the numerical simulation results in Sect. 4. Finally, we conclude the paper in Sect. 5.

2   System Model and Problem Formulation

2.1   System Model

We consider that there are N RSUs located along a unidirectional road, the set of RSUs is denoted as $\mathcal{N} = \{1, 2, \cdots, N\}$. Each RSU is equipped with an edge server. The set of computation capabilities of RSUs can be denoted as $\{F^1, F^2, \cdots, F^N\}$. Based on the limited coverage range of each RSU, the road can be divided into N segments with length $\{L_1, L_2, \cdots, L_N\}$, respectively. The vehicles running within the nth segment can only access to RSU n.

There are M vehicles arriving at the start point of the road with a constant speed v. The set of vehicles is denoted as $\mathcal{M} = \{1, 2, \cdots, M\}$. Each vehicle m, $m \in \mathcal{M}$, has a computation-intensive and delay-sensitive application, which can be described as $T_m = \{x_m, b_m\}$, x_m is the size of input data of application T_m and b_m is the computation resources required to complete application T_m.

For the execution decision, we denote d_m, $d_m \in \{0, 1\}$, as the decision variable, i.e., $d_m = 1$ if vehicle m selects to offload its application T_m to RSU n for execution, and $d_m = 0$ if T_m is locally executed. Denote $\mathbf{d} = (d_m)_{m \in \mathcal{M}}$ as a computing offloading strategy profile of vehicles and denote $O_n(\mathbf{d}) \triangleq \{m | d_m = 1\}$ as the set of vehicles that offload their applications to RSU n.

We consider two computation approaches. For the local computing approach, one vehicle locally executes its application. The time cost of local computing is t_m^{local}. For the edge computing approach, the time cost of T_m by edge computing involves four parts: vehicle travel time, data transmission time, application computation time and result transmission time. Since the size of the computation result is often small, therefore, it can be neglected. Vehicle travel time of T_m is t_m^{travel}. Data transmission time of T_m is t_m^{send}. The computation time of T_m is t_m^{comp}. Thus, the time cost of edge computing is $t_m^{edge} = t_m^{travel} + t_m^{send} + t_m^{comp}$.

2.2 Problem Formulation

The objective is to identify the decision that minimizes the completion time of each application by executing locally or offloading to RSUs for execution. The time cost that application T_m is executed can be given as $C_m(\mathbf{d}, \mathbf{p}) = I_{0,d_m} t_m^{local} + I_{1,d_m} t_m^{edge}$, where $\mathbf{p}$ is the computation resource allocation of RSU and $I_{r,d_m} = 1$ if $d_m = r$, and $d_m \neq r$ otherwise. Finally, the time cost C of the system can be given as follows

$$C(\mathbf{d}, \mathbf{p}) = \sum_{m \in \mathcal{M}} C_m(\mathbf{d}, \mathbf{p}) \tag{1}$$

We can model the above optimization problem as a multiple-leader common-follower Stackelberg game problem and given as the Vehicular Edge Computation Offloading Game (VECOG). Vehicles are leaders and one RSU is the follower. Given a strategy profile $\mathbf{d}$, the objective of one RSU is to minimize the time cost of the system and denoted as $\min_{\mathbf{p} \geq \mathbf{0}} C(\mathbf{d}, \mathbf{p})$. The objective of each vehicle can be given as $\min_{d_m} C_m(d_m, d_{-m}, \mathcal{P}_n(d_m, d_{-m}))$, where $\mathcal{P}$ is the announced computation resource allocation policy of one RSU and d_{-m} is the strategies of all other vehicles except vehicle m. Furthermore, $\mathcal{P}^*$ is an optimal policy. In this paper, we address where there is a combination for the dynamic game that neither vehicles nor the RSU have an incentive to deviate, i.e., a subgame perfect equilibrium.

3 LEEC Algorithm

We observe that the optimal computation resource allocation policy $\mathcal{P}^*$ that RSU n allocates to $\mathbf{d}$ is a vehicle-specific parameter. Thus, vehicles has different weights of computation resource allocation, the interaction of vehicles can be modeled as a vehicular-specific weighted congestion game, which can be expressed as a tuple $\Gamma(\mathcal{P}) = < \mathcal{M}, (d_m)_{m \in \mathcal{M}}, (C_m)_{m \in \mathcal{M}} >$.

Theorem 1. *Under the optimal computation resource allocation policy $\mathcal{P}^*$ of RSU n, the strategic interaction of the vehicles can be modeled as a resource-dependent congestion game, which the resource-dependent weights are w_m^n. Thus, the time cost that application T_m is executed can be given as $\widetilde{C}_m(\mathbf{d}) = I_{0,d_m} t_m^{local} + I_{1,d_m} (w_m^n w(\mathbf{d}) + t_m^{travel} + t_m^{send})$, where $w(\mathbf{d}) = \sum_{i \in O_n(\mathbf{d})} w_i^n$.*

Proof. Depend on the optimal computation resource allocation policy, the computation time by edge computing is $\widetilde{C}_m^{edge}(\mathbf{d}) = \sqrt{\frac{b_m}{F^n}} \sum_{i \in O_n(\mathbf{d})} \sqrt{\frac{b_i}{F^n}}$. We define weight $w_m^n \triangleq \sqrt{\frac{b_m}{F^n}}$ for each tuple, and the time cost by edge computing in strategy profile $\mathbf{d}$ depends on the total weight $w(\mathbf{d})$. Thus, the strategic interaction of the vehicles can be modeled as a resource-dependent congestion game.

The objective of each vehicle is to minimize its time cost. We define the result strategic game $\Gamma(\mathcal{P}^*) =< \mathcal{M}, (d_m)_{m \in \mathcal{M}}, (\widetilde{C}_m)_{m \in \mathcal{M}} >$ as the Optimal Resource Allocation Computation Offloading Game (ORACOG). And if the $ORACOG$ has a pure strategy NE, then the $VECOG$ has an SPE. Furthermore, If there exists an exact potential function for the game, then the game has a pure NE.

Theorem 2. *The optimal resource allocation computation offloading game has an exact potential function defined as* $\phi(\boldsymbol{d}) = \sum_{m \in \mathcal{M}}(\phi_m^{local}(\boldsymbol{d}) + \phi_m^{edge}(\boldsymbol{d}))$, *where* $\phi_m^{edge}(\boldsymbol{d}) = I_{1,d_m}(w_m^n w_{\leq m}(\boldsymbol{d}) + t_m^{travel} + t_m^{send})$, $\phi_m^{local}(\boldsymbol{d}) = I_{0,d_m}t_m^{local}$.

Proof. First, we define two shorthand notations $w_{\leq m}(\mathbf{d}) = \sum_{j \in O_n(\mathbf{d}), j \leq m} w_j^n$ and $w_{>m}(\mathbf{d}) = \sum_{j \in O_n(\mathbf{d}), j > m} w_j^n$. Furthermore, we define $\phi_m = \phi_m^{local}(\mathbf{d}) + \phi_m^{edge}(\mathbf{d})$. Next, we consider strategy profiles $\mathbf{d} = (d_i, d_{-i})$ and $\mathbf{d}^\dagger = (d_i^\dagger, d_{-i})$, vehicle i changes its strategy between local computing and edge computing, i.e., vehicle i offloads T_i to one RSU in $\mathbf{d}$ and T_i is locally executed in $\mathbf{d}^\dagger$. Then, the difference of time cost between $\mathbf{d}$ and $\mathbf{d}^\dagger$ is $\widetilde{C}_i(\mathbf{d}) - \widetilde{C}_i(\mathbf{d}^\dagger) = w_i^n w(\mathbf{d}) + t_m^{travel} + t_m^{send} - t_i^{local}$, which is equal to the difference of potential function. Similarity, if vehicle i locally executes T_i in $\mathbf{d}$ and offloads T_i to one RSU in $\mathbf{d}^\dagger$, we can also show that $\phi(\mathbf{d}) - \phi(\mathbf{d}^\dagger) = \widetilde{C}_i(\mathbf{d}) - \widetilde{C}_i(\mathbf{d}^\dagger)$.

Thus, there exists an exact potential function for the game, and the $ORACOG$ has a pure NE. Then the $VECOG$ has an SPE. Next, we compute the NE of the $ORACOG$. We denote the proposed algorithms as Local and Edge Equilibrium Computing (LEEC) algorithm. We start the algorithm from the strategy profile that all vehicles decide to locally execute their applications. There are two phases to execute alternatingly in the algorithm. In the first phase, vehicle can offload to one RSU to decrease the completion time of application. In the second phase, vehicles can update their execution decision to find the best replies. Using the algorithm, we can compute the NE of the $ORACOG$ effectively.

4   Performance Evaluations

4.1   Simulation Setup

In this section, based on existing research works [4,7,8], we set various parameters for the numerical simulations. We consider that there is a 100-m road with one RSU, and computation capability of the RSU is assigned from 5 GHz to 10 GHz with a step value of 1 GHz. The number of vehicles is denoted from 5 to 30 with a step value of 5, and they run at the constant speed 120 km/hr. The computation capability of vehicle is assigned from the interval $[0.2, 0.4]$ GHz. The computation resource that each vehicle required is assigned from the interval $[1, 5]$ GHz. The size of input data of the vehicular application is assigned from the interval $[100, 300]$ KB.

To verify the performance of our proposed algorithm, we introduce three benchmark approaches. For *Local computing (LOCAL) algorithm*, all vehicles choose to execute their vehicular applications locally. For *Edge computing (EDGE) algorithm*, all vehicles choose to offload their applications to one RSU for execution. For *Random computing (RANDOM) algorithm*, vehicles randomly choose to locally execute their applications or offload the applications to one RSU for execution.

4.2 Comparison of Average Completion Time

(1) Impact of Number of Applications: Figure 1(a) shows the impact of the number of vehicular applications. We can observe that the average completion time of all applications is reduced by 60%, 43% and 25% comparing to LOCAL, EDGE and RANDOM. This is because our proposed algorithm considers the local and edge equilibrium computing. Furthermore, as the number of applications grows, the competition for computation resource of the RSU for the vehicles becomes greater. Thus, each vehicle can be allocated less computation resource when the vehicles offload their applications to the same RSU for execution, as a result, the average completion time of the applications is greatly increased.

(2) Impact of Computation Capability of One RSU: Figure 1(b) shows the impact of computation capability of one RSU on the average completion time of all applications. It can be observed that the average completion time of all applications significantly decreases when computation capability of the RSU increases using our proposed algorithm, this is because that there are more computation capability for the vehicles to compute their applications.

From Fig. 1(a) and (b), we can clearly observe that the average completion time of all applications using our proposed algorithm is less than benchmark approaches. Furthermore, the trend of numerical simulation result is much more stable using our proposed algorithm.

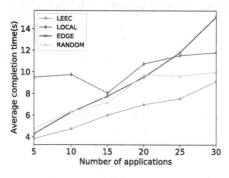

(a) Impact of number of applications

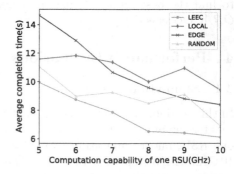

(b) Impact of computation capability

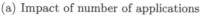

Fig. 1. Impact of the parameters.

5 Conclusion

In this paper, we study a computation resource allocation problem in a VEC system, which is under the constraint of limited computation resources of edge servers on one RSU. We formulate the computation resource allocation problem as an optimization problem and model the problem as a Stackelberg game which vehicles are leaders and the RSU is the follower. To solve the optimization problem, we propose an effective LEEC algorithm. Numerical simulation results demonstrate that compared with benchmark approaches, our proposed algorithm can greatly reduce the average completion time of all applications.

Acknowledgements. This research is supported by the National Natural Science Foundation of China under Grant 61571066.

References

1. Wang, S., Zhang, X., Zhang, Y., Wang, L., Yang, J., Wang, W.: A survey on mobile edge networks: convergence of computing, caching and communications. IEEE Access **5**, 6757–6779 (2017)
2. Dai, Y., Xu, D., Maharjan, S., Zhang, Y.: Joint load balancing and offloading in vehicular edge computing and networks. IEEE Internet Things J. **6**(3), 4377–4387 (2019)
3. Xiao, L., Zhuang, W., Zhou, S., Chen, C.: Learning while offloading: task offloading in vehicular edge computing network. Learning-based VANET Communication and Security Techniques. WN, pp. 49–77. Springer, Cham (2019). https://doi.org/10.1007/978-3-030-01731-6_3
4. Zhang, K., Mao, Y., Leng, S., Vinel, A., Zhang, Y.: Delay constrained offloading for mobile edge computing in cloud-enabled vehicular networks. In: 2016 8th International Workshop on Resilient Networks Design and Modeling (RNDM), Halmstad, pp. 288–294 (2016)
5. Huang, X., Yu, R., Kang, J., Zhang, Y.: Distributed reputation management for secure and efficient vehicular edge computing and networks. IEEE Access **5**, 25408–25420 (2017)
6. Guo, F., Zhang, H., Ji, H., Li, X., Leung, V.C.M.: An efficient computation offloading management scheme in the densely deployed small cell networks with mobile edge computing. IEEE/ACM Trans. Netw. **26**(6), 2651–2664 (2018)
7. Jošilo, S., Dán, G.: Wireless and computing resource allocation for selfish computation offloading in edge computing. In: IEEE INFOCOM 2019 - IEEE Conference on Computer Communications, Paris, France, pp. 2467–2475 (2019)
8. Zhang, K., Mao, Y., Leng, S., Maharjan, S., Zhang, Y.: Optimal delay constrained offloading for vehicular edge computing networks. In: 2017 IEEE International Conference on Communications (ICC), Paris, pp. 1–6 (2017)

Blockchain and Smart Contracts

Aplos: Smart Contracts Made Smart

Eranga Bandara[1], Wee Keong Ng[1(✉)], Nalin Ranasinghe[2],
and Kasun De Zoysa[2]

[1] School of Computer Science and Engineering,
Nanyang Technological University, Singapore, Singapore
{eranga,awkng}@ntu.edu.sg
[2] University of Colombo School of Computing, Colombo, Sri Lanka
{dnr,kasun}@ucsc.cmb.ac.lk

Abstract. Smart contract is a programming interface to interact with
the underlying blockchain storage models. It is a database abstraction
layer for blockchain. Existing smart contract platforms follow the imperative style programming model since states are shared. As a result, there is
no concurrency control mechanism when executing transactions, resulting
in considerable latency and hindering scalability. To address performance
and scalability issues of existing smart contract platforms, we design a
new smart contract platform called "Aplos" based on the Scala functional programming language and Akka actors. In Aplos, all blockchain-
related smart contract functions are implemented with Akka actors. The
Aplos platform is built over Mystiko—a highly scalable blockchain storage
for big data. Mystiko supports concurrent transactions, high transaction
throughput, data analytics and machine learning. With Aplos smart contracts over Mystiko, we have developed a blockchain for highly scalable
storage that aligns with big data requirements.

Keywords: Blockchain · Smart contract · Functional programming ·
Actor model · Big data · Scala · Akka

1 Introduction

1.1 Blockchian

Blockchain stores chronological sequence of transactions in a tamper-evident
manner. Each node in the blockchain has the exact same order of data. Since
blockchain is like a distributed storage, it uses a consensus algorithm to order
and maintain data consistency among nodes. Due to the decentralized trust
ecosystem in blockchain, various industries have adopted blockchain for their
applications.

Currently, there are various blockchain platforms in the market: Bitcoin [26],
Ethereum [7], Bigchaindb [24], Hyperledger [4] are some examples. Ethereum
and Hyperledger went beyond crypto-currencies to support different kind of asset
storage models that relate to various forms of business or e-commerce activities.
They introduced a new concept to blockchain called smart contracts.

© Springer Nature Singapore Pte Ltd. 2020
Z. Zheng et al. (Eds.): BlockSys 2019, CCIS 1156, pp. 431–445, 2020.
https://doi.org/10.1007/978-981-15-2777-7_35

432   E. Bandara et al.

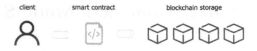

Fig. 1. Smart contract overview.

1.2   Smart Contract

Smart contract imposes an additional software layer between clients and blockchain storage (Fig. 1). Client requests are directed to scripts (smart contracts) that perform the logic needed to provide a complex service, such as managing state, enforcing governance, or checking credentials. Using smart contracts, users do not need to execute queries to save or retrieve data from blockchain storage. Instead smart contracts provide a programming interface to interact with the underlying blockchain storage models.

Smart contact is like a database abstraction layer for blockchain. It is similar to the Object Relational Mapping (ORM) tools in traditional programming frameworks. Unlike traditional ORMs, smart contract is capable of defining the business logic of an application. With smart contracts, business logic on the application layer can be moved to the blockchain layer. There are various smart contact platforms: Ethereum has the Solidity [34], Hyperledger fabric has the Chaincode [4], Kadena has Pact [29], RChain has Rholang [12], etc. Most of these platforms follow the imperative programming style with a shared memory model. There is no concurrency-control mechanism; they do not support concurrent execution of transactions. As a result, there is considerable latency and scalability suffers.

1.3   Aplos Smart Contract

To address issues on imperative style smart contract, we introduce the Aplos smart contract platform. This smart contract platform is built on the Mystiko blockchain, which is a highly Scalable blockchain targeted for big data [6]. Smart contract on the Aplos platform is written in the Scala functional programming [28,32] language based on Akka actors [2], so we have introduced this smart contract platform as a smart actor platform. The Actor model comes with message passing concurrency control [14,15]. We have introduced a functional programming model instead of an imperative programming. All transactions in Mystiko are executed using Akka actors. With Akka actors and functional programming-based concurrency control, the Aplos platform enables concurrent transaction execution, which leads to high transaction throughput for blockchain.

1.4 Paper Outline

The rest of the paper is organized as follows. Section 2 discusses the Mystiko blockchain, features, characteristics and architecture. Section 3 discusses the architecture of the Aplos smart actor platform on Mystiko blockchain. Section 4 discusses examples using the Aplos smart actors in a banking application built on top of Mystiko. Section 5 performs evaluation of the Aplos smart actor platform, in comparison to the Hyperledger fabric. Section 6 surveys related work. Section 7 concludes the Aplos platform with suggestions for future work.

2 Mystiko

2.1 Mystiko Overview

Mystiko is a highly Scalable blockchain system that utilizes the Apache Cassandra [20] distributed database (with Paxos consensus [21] as the underlying consensus platform). Mystiko uses the Apache Kafka and Akka streams [3] to handle back-pressure operations on big data. To facilitate full text search on blockchain data, Mystiko utilizes the Apache Lucene [22] based Elasticsearch [11]. It integrated with Apache Spark [25] based Mystiko-ML service to facilitate data analytics and machine learning. Mystiko addressed three main performance bottlenecks on existing blockchain platforms, namely, the Order-Execute architecture, full node data replication and imperative style smart contracts.

To address issues on the traditional Order-Execute blockchain architecture [4], Mystiko provides Validate-Execute-Group architecture [6]. This architecture allows one to validate and execute transactions whenever a client submits a transaction to the network. The client does not need to wait until a block has been created to commit the transaction. This new architecture provides high scalability and high transaction throughput.

All blocks, transactions, and asset information are stored in Cassandra database tables in Mystiko. Since it uses Cassandra for asset storage, Mystiko can stores larger data payloads with the assets. In Mystiko, every blockchain peer comes with a Cassandra node; these nodes are connected to one another in a ring cluster architecture. After executing a transaction, state update in a peer is distributed and replicated using sharding with Cassandra's Paxos consensus algorithm. In this way, Mystiko avoids the full node replication issue in conventional blockchains [35].

2.2 Mystiko Architecture

Most current blockchain systems are built as monolithic systems. A single program/service on the blockchain handles all the features in the blockchain. This includes handling consensus, maintaining the decentralized ledger, broadcasting transactions, checking double spends [26], etc. It is not an ideal design for a distributed system environment. In a monolithic system approach, one needs to build everything using a single programming language. When the codebase

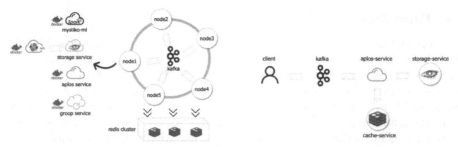

(a) Mystiko microservices architecture.   (b) Mystiko aplos service architecture.

Fig. 2. Mystiko blockchain architecture.

grows, it becomes unwieldy. Since only one service is available, it is not possible to scale. As such, Mystiko built using a microservice-based distributed architecture [31], solving all the aforementioned problems (Fig. 2(a)). In Mystiko, all the functionalities are implemented as small services (microservices). Different programming languages and enterprise-level distributed tools are used to build the services of Mystiko. These services are dockerized [10] and available for deployment using Kubernetes [18]. Figure 2(a) shows the architecture of Mystiko. It contains the following services/components:

1. Storage service (Cassandra-based block, transaction and asset storage)
2. Cache service (Redis [30] based cache service)
3. Aplos service (Smart actor service implemented using Scala and Akka)
4. Grooper service (Block creating service implemented using Scala and Akka)
5. Kafka (Message broker)
6. Mystiko-ML (Apache spark based machine learning service)

Storage is the place where the blocks, transactions and assets are stored in Mystiko. The order of the data will be decided by Cassandra's Paxos consensus algorithm. By default Cassandra does not provide serial consistency, it only provides eventual consistency. Cassandra introduced LWT [8] to achieve serial consistency, but it consumes lots of resources and time [19]. As an alternative to Cassandra LWT, Mystiko build a Redis cache-based system to achieve serial consistency. Aplos is the smart contract service on Mystiko blockchain. It is the core part that provides high scalability and transaction throughput for Mystiko blockchain. Grooper service is responsible for creating blocks. When creating a new block, it generates a block hash from the Merkle root hash and the previous block hash. Apache Kafka [17] is used as the message broker of the Mystiko blockchain. There are two main communication use cases of Kafka in Mystiko. First, by using Kafka for client-to-blockchain communication, Mystiko is able to handle back pressure operation in big data environments. It handles all the transaction messages that come to Kafka using Akka streams. Second, when generating blocks, Groopers communicates with one another to validate and approve the blocks. Each peer in the blockchain network has their own storage, Aplos and Grooper services.

Mystiko-ML is the Apache Spark based machine learning and analytic service on Mystiko blockchain. It supports to do analytic on both on-chain, off-chain storage and build the supervised or unsupervised machine learning models. These models can be used to do the predictions of real-time data.

3 Aplos Smart Actors

3.1 Overview

Aplos is the smart contract platform in Mystiko blockchain. All the peers in the network have their own Aplos service which run as a docker container. The business logic of blockchain applications (e.g., asset creation, validation, authorization) are written using the Scala functional programming based Akka actors. All transactions on the Mystiko blockchain executed using these smart actors. Actors consume messages. Based on the message they execute various business logic. By using Akka actors based smart contract, Mystiko supports concurrent transaction execution.

To create/update/search assets on the blockchain, clients needs to send transaction messages to the Aplos service with actor name, message type and the transaction attributes. Based on the actor name, the Aplos service finds the smart actor that needs to be invoked. It then passes the message to that actor. When transaction message arrives, the actor validates (check double spend and digital signature) and executes the transaction. Based on the execution outcome, it inserts transaction record into Mystiko storage transaction table and updates asset status in the corresponding asset table on Mystiko storage. The Aplos service interacts with Redis cache to validate the transaction and with Storage service to update asset status (Fig. 2(b)).

3.2 Transaction Messages

Aplos service consumes transaction messages from Apache Kafka (Fig. 2(b)). There is a Kafka topic which the service listens to. When submitting transaction to the Aplos service, the client publishes JSON encoded messages to the Kafka topic. Figure 6(b) shows an example of a transaction message in the following mentioned (Sect. 4) Promise application money transfer scenario. It defines the actor name, message type and other transaction attributes (account information, amount). When a message is received by the Aplos service, it creates a scala case class [28] based on the message type and delegates it to the corresponding actor. Based on transaction parameters, validation phase and execution phases are performed by the actor. Finally, the transaction response will be returned to the client.

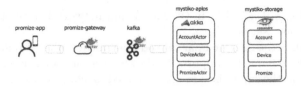

Fig. 3. Promize application architecture.

3.3   Concurrent Transactions

Smart actors communicate with one another using message passing. Since there is no shared state among actors, they are able to run concurrently. Akka actors come with two communication patterns `Ask` and `Tell` [2]. `Ask` is a blocking operation: When an actor A sends message to B actor by using `Ask`, actor A waits until actor B responds to the message. `Tell` is a non-blocking (fire and forget). When an actor A sends a `Tell` message to actor B, A does not need to wait until B responds to the message; actor A continues its future operations. In Aplos, we use the non-blocking `Tell` message pattern. When communicating between actors, they are message passing each other and doing the operations.

4   Promize Application

4.1   Promize Overview

We have built Promize, a peer-to-peer money transfer application for MBSL Bank, Sri Lanka [23] using the Mystiko blockchain with Aplos smart actor platform. We are introducing this application as an alternative to traditional ATMs (Mobile ATM [16]). With the Promize application, users may take money from registered authorities or their friends without going to an ATM. The architecture of the Promize service is described in Fig. 3. Users are given a Promize mobile application to do money transfer transactions. The mobile app sends requests to the smart actors on Mystiko blockchain when doing Promize transactions.

First, users register with the Promize service via the Promize mobile application. When a user registers, the mobile application sends a request to `AccountActor` (Fig. 5(a)) on Mystiko blockchain with credentials/account information. Upon account create request, `AccountActor` validates the user credential/account information and creates an account for the user in the Mystiko blockchain. Assume that two users (A and B) are registered on the Promize application. User A wants to take 1,000 rupees. User A asks User B (who already have Promize app installed on his phone) for 1,000 Rupees. User B starts the Promize app and chooses the transferring amount (Fig. 4(a)). This generates a QR code with embedding B's account number and transferring amount (Fig. 4(b)). This QR code will be scanned by user A and submit the Promize transaction (Fig. 4(c)).

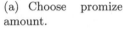

(a) Choose promize amount.

(b) Promize QR code.

(c) Scan promize QR code.

Fig. 4. Promize application.

When submitting the transaction, it sends Promize initializing request to `PromizeActor` (Fig. 5(b)) on the Mystiko blockchain, which checks the validity of the transaction and user accounts. If transaction is valid, a confirmation request with random number (transaction salt) will be sent to user B's Promize mobile application via push notification. Push notifications will be sent by `DeviceActor` on Mystiko blockchain. Then user B confirms this request in order to approve the Promize transaction. When confirming, Promize approve request will be sent with received random number to `PromizeActor` on the Mystiko blockchain, which checks the validity of the transaction parameters (transaction salt and accounts). If transaction parameters are valid, `PromizeActor` transfers requested money(Rs 1000) from user A's account to B's account. Finally transaction confirmation status will be sent to both User A and B. Then User B physically gives 1,000 rupees to user B.

The idea here is user A physically takes money from user B which the bank electronically transfers money from A's account to B's account via Promize transactions. The Promize service guarantees Non-repudiation, Confidentiality, Integrity, Authenticity and Availability of electronic transactions [16] using the blockchain.

4.2   Smart Actors

There are three main smart actors in this system: `AccountActor`, `PromizeActor`, and `DeviceActor`. The `AccountActor` corresponds to account creation and activation function. It consumes `Create` and `Activate` messages (Fig. 5(a)). The `DeviceActor` handles push notification sending functions. It consumes `Create` and `Notify` messages. The `PromizeActor` handles Promize transactions.

```
import akka.actor.{Actor, Props}
import com.score.aplos.paper.AccountActor.{Activate, Create}

object AccountActor {
  case class Create(messageType: String, execer: String, id: String,
                    accountId: String, accountPassword: String,
                    accountPhone: String, accountEmail: String,
                    deviceToken: String, deviceType: String)

  case class Activate(messageType: String, execer: String, id: String,
                      accountId: String, accountSalt: String)

  def props() = Props(new AccountActor)
}

class AccountActor extends Actor {
  override def receive: Receive = {
    case create: Create =>
      // verify digital signature
      // check double spend
      // create account on ledger

      // send message to device contract to create device
      val msg = DeviceActor.Create("create", create.execer, create.id,
        create.accountId, create.deviceToken, create.deviceType,
        create.accountId)
      context.actorOf(DeviceActor.props()) ! msg

      // send status back
    case Activate =>
      // verify digital signature
      // check double spend
      // update account on ledger
      // send status back
  }
}
```

(a) Account smart actor.

```
import akka.actor.{Actor, Props}
import com.score.aplos.paper.DeviceActor.Notify
import com.score.aplos.paper.PromizeContract.{Approve, Create}

object PromizeContract {
  case class Create(messageType: String, execer: String, id: String,
                    promizeId: String, promizeFrom: String,
                    promizeTo: String, promizeAmount: String)

  case class Approve(messageType: String, execer: String, id: String,
                     promizeId: String, promizeFrom: String,
                     promizeTo: String, promizeSalt: String)

  def props() = Props(new PromizeContract)
}

class PromizeContract extends Actor {
  override def receive: Receive = {
    case create: Create =>
      // verify digital signature
      // check double spend
      // create promize on ledger

      // send message to device contract to notify from account
      val salt = "<transaction salt>"
      val msg = Notify("notify", create.execer, create.id,
        create.promizeFrom, salt)
      context.actorOf(DeviceActor.props()) ! msg

      // send status back
    case Approve =>
      // verify digital signature
      // check double spend
      // update promize
      // send status back
  }
}
```

(b) Promize smart actor.

Fig. 5. Smart actors.

It consumes **Create** and **Approve** messages, corresponding to create and approve Promize transactions (Fig. 5(b)).

4.3   Transaction Messages

When performing transactions, a client sends transaction messages to smart actors on the Mystiko blockchain. The message contains JSON encoded string with smart actor name, message type and message parameters. Figure 6(a) shows the message sent by user when creating accounts. It contains account information. Figure 6(b) shows the message that corresponds to Promize transaction. It contains accounts and amount information.

When this messages arrives at the Aplos service, it first identifies the actor name and the message type. Then it creates a scala case class message with parameters and passes it to the corresponding actor. When actor receives this message, it validates the message (check and digital signature and message attributes) and performs the execute operation (e.g., create account and transfer money). When executing a message, it first checks for double spending. If there is no double spending, it creates a transaction and executes the transaction. When executing transaction, it create/update assets on the blockchain.

4.4   Concurrent Transaction

As mentioned earlier the Aplos platform supports concurrent transaction execution. All messages come to the Aplos service via Kafka. These messages are delegated to the corresponding actors in an asynchronous manner (non-blocking).

```
{
    "id": "<transaction id>",
    "execer": "<transaction executing user>",
    "messageType": "<message type>",
    "accountId": "<account id>",
    "accountPassword": "<account password>",
    "accountPhone": "<account phone no>",
    "accountEmail": "<account email>",
    "deviceToken": "<notification token>",
    "deviceType": "<mobile device type>",
    "digsig": "<digital signature>"
}
```

```
{
    "id": "<transaction id>",
    "execer": "<transaction executing user>",
    "messageType": "<message type>",
    "promizeId": "<promize id>",
    "promizeFrom": "<promize send account>",
    "promizeTo": "<promize receive account>",
    "promizeAmount": "<promize amount>",
    "digsig": "<digital signature>"
}
```

(a) Account create message.   (b) Promize create message.

Fig. 6. Smart actor messages.

Aplos smart actors communicate with one another via message passing. In account creation, when `Create` message comes to `AccountActor`, it first creates account by executing create function on Account actor. Then it pass a `Create` message to `DeviceActor` to create a device. `DeviceActor` executes that message and creates the device (Fig. 5(a)).

When Promize message is received by `PromizeActor`, it first creates Promize by executing `Create` on `PromizeActor`. Then it pass `Notify` message to `DeviceActor` to send push notification (Fig. 5(b)). `DeviceActor` executes `Notify` message and sends push notification to corresponding user.

5 Performance Evaluation

We have done a performance evaluation of the Mystiko Aplos smart actor platform. The evaluation results are obtained for the following metrics:

1. Invoke transaction throughput
2. Query transaction throughput
3. Transaction scalability
4. Transaction latency
5. Search performance

To obtain the results, we deployed multi-peer Mystiko cluster with Aplos smart actor service and Hyperledger Fabric cluster in separate AWS 2xlarge instances (16 GB RAM and 8 CPUs).

5.1 Invoke Transaction Throughput

For this evaluation, we recorded the number of invoke transactions that can be executed in each Mystiko blockchain peer. Invoke transaction creates transaction in the ledger and updates the status of the assets. We flooded invoke transactions for each blockchain peer and recorded the number of executed transactions. As shown in Fig. 7, we compared the transaction throughput of Mystiko with Hyperledger Fabric. Functional programming-based smart actor platform and Akka streams based back pressure handling of Aplos service provides the high invoke transaction throughput for Mystiko blockchain.

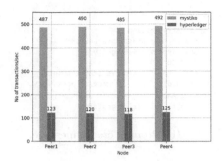

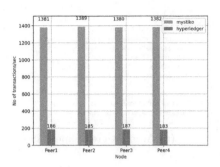

Fig. 7. Invoke transaction throughput of Mystiko and Hyperledger Fabric.

Fig. 8. Query transaction throughput of Mystiko and Hyperledger Fabric.

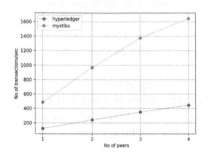

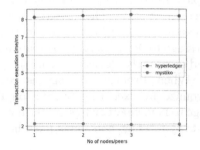

Fig. 9. Transaction scalability of Mystiko and Hyperledger Fabric.

Fig. 10. Transaction latency of Mystiko and Hyperledger Fabric.

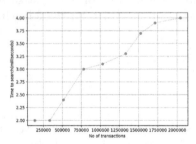

Fig. 11. Search performance of Mystiko.

5.2 Query Transaction Throughput

For this evaluation, we recorded the number of query transactions that can be executed in each Mystiko blockchain peer. Query transaction queries the status of the ledger. They neither create transaction in the ledger nor update the asset status. We flooded query transactions for each blockchain peer and recorded the number of completed transactions. As shown in Fig. 8, we compared the transaction throughput of Mystiko with Hyperledger Fabric. Since query transactions are not updating the ledger status, it has high throughput compared to invoke transactions. Likewise the query transaction throughput of Mystiko is higher than Hyperledger fabric. Functional programming-based smart actor platform, Akka streams based back pressure handling, Elasticsearch based search API are the main reasons for this result [6].

5.3 Transaction Scalability

For this evaluation, we recorded the number of invoke transactions (per second) over the number of blockchain peers in the network. We flooded concurrent transactions in each blockchain peer and recorded the number of executed transactions. Figure 9 shows transaction scalability comparison of Mystiko blockchain with the Hyperledger Fabric blockchain. The main reason for high scalability in Mystiko is the underlying Paxos-based Cassandra's master-less ring architecture [20]. In Cassandra, all blockchain nodes have write capability. So when adding a node to the cluster, it linearly increases the transaction throughput. The other reason is asynchronous and concurrent transaction handling on Aplos smart actor service.

5.4 Transaction Latency

Next, we evaluate transaction latency in Mystiko. We flooded concurrent transactions in each blockchain peer and calculated the average transaction latency. Figure 10 shows the transition latency comparison of the Mystiko blockchain with Hyperledger Fabric blockchain. Cassandra's high write throughput, Redis cache-based Validate-Execute-Group architecture and functional programming-based smart actors produce less transaction latency in Mystiko [6].

5.5 Search Performance

Mystiko allows one to search data in the transaction/block/asset tables using Elasticsearch. For this evaluation, we issued concurrent transaction search queries to Mystiko and compute the search time. As shown in Fig. 11, we achieved super fast search performance (few milliseconds time). The Apache Lucene index-based Elasticsearch storage and concurrent transaction execution of the Aplos service are the main reasons yielding super fast search in Mystiko.

Table 1. Smart contract platform comparison.

Platform	Blockchain	Public/Private	Turing complete	Loops	Functional	Concurrent transactions	Shared state	Communication contracts	Implemented language
Aplos	Mystiko	Private	Yes	Yes	Yes	Yes	No	Yes	Scala
Solidity	Ethereum	Both	Yes	Yes	No	No	Yes	Yes	C++/Solidity
Chaincode	Hyperledger	Private	Yes	Yes	No	No	Yes	Yes	Golang
Simplicity	Bitcoin	Public	No	No	Yes	No	Yes	No	Tcl/Haskell
Scilla	Zilliqa	Public	No	Recursion	No	No	Yes	Yes	OCaml
Pact	Kadena	Both	No	No	Yes	No	Yes	Yes	Haskell
Rholang	Rchain	Both	Yes	Yes	Yes	Yes	No	Yes	Java

6   Related Work

Much research has been conducted to improve the performance and address the issues of smart contracts [1,13]. Most of them followed imperative programming style and shared memory concurrency model. In this section, we outline the main features and architecture of these research projects.

Solidity (Ethereum) [34] is the most popular smart contract language today. It is a Turing complete language and resembles Javascript. As it supports Turing complete smart contracts, very complicated logic can be implemented in smart contracts, at the same opening it to vulnerabilities. To prevent infinite loops, execution is limited by a counter called "gas", which is paid for in Ethereum's unit of account, Ether, to the miner of the block containing the transaction. When a program runs out of gas, the transaction is nullified but the gas is still paid to the miner to ensure they are compensated for their computation efforts. Ethereum solidity smart contracts follows imperative style programming while Aplos contracts follows functional style. Also Solidity uses shared status and does not support concurrent transaction execution. But Aplos supports concurrent transaction executions without sharing status among Actors.

Chaincode (Hyperledger) [4] is the smart contract platform on Hyperledger Fabric which written in Golang. It defines assets on the blockchain as Golang Structs. The functions to create, update, get assets from the blockchain ledger are implemented as contract functions. Hyperledger Chaincode follows the imperative style programming model while Aplos follows the functional programming model. Both Aplos and Hyperledger Chaincode provides Turing complete smart contracts. They support loops and are vulnerable infinite looping. Both platforms not intended to be public blockchain, they are private blockchains. Smart contracts will not uploaded by any user. To prevent infinite loops and other vulnerabilities, developers and internal team must thoroughly test smart contracts before use.

Simplicity (Bitcoin) [27] is a typed, combinator-based, functional language. It is designed to work as Turing incomplete schematic without loops and recursion, to be used for crypto-currencies and blockchain applications. By using functional and Turing incomplete schematics it aims to improve upon existing crypto-currency languages, such as Bitcoin Script and Ethereum's Solidity. It avoids the shared global state, the transaction does not need to access any information outside the transaction. It also does not support communication contracts, that means contracts do not talk to each other. The functional programming model of Aplos is similar to the Simplicity model. However, Aplos used non shared status by using Actors. Due to this reason Aplos can talk with other smart contracts in the system.

Scilla (Zilliqa) [33], is an intermediate-level smart contract language for verified smart contracts. It has been designed as a principled language with smart contract safety in mind. Scilla manages read and write to a shared memory space and is designed for an account-based model, where contracts can communicate with each other. Scilla is not fully functional smart contract language as transactions affect the external state. Scilla supports looping constructs via well-founded recursive function definitions, so their termination can be proved statically. Both Aplos and Scilla contracts are capable of interacting with other contracts. But scilla use shared memory status while Aplos uses non shared actor based model.

Pact (Kadena) [29] is new programming language which mainly targeted for private blockchain. Pack follows Turing incomplete safety oriented design. Recursion in Pact is detected and causes an immediate failure at module load. Looping is only supported using map and fold on finite list structures. A benefit of this restriction is that Pact does not need to employ any kind of cost model like Ethereum's "gas" to limit computation. Pact follows the functional programming design, supports module definitions, imports and atomic transaction executions. Pact smart contract code is stored in an unmodified, human-readable form on the ledger. Both Aplos and Pact platforms support functional programming paradigm on their smart contracts. But Aplos with actor model support non shared statuses and concurrent transactions.

Rholang (RChain) [12] is designed to be used to implement protocols and smart contracts on a general-purpose blockchain. The compiled Rholang contract is executed in a Rho virtual machine (RhoVM). It admits unbounded recursion, behaviorally typed, Turing complete concurrent programming language, with a focus on message-passing and formally modeled by the pi-calculus. The language is concurrency-oriented, with a focus on message-passing through channels. When comparing Aplos and Rholnag, one can see their main concepts are similar. Both using concurrency oriented message passing and functional programming. But in Rholang transactions that do not interact must be able to complete at the same time.

The comparison summary of these smart contract platforms and Aplos platform is presented in Table 1. It compares running blockchain platform, blockchain type (public, private), Turing completeness, loop support, concurrent contract support, functional, concurrent execution, smart contract communication and implemented language details.

7   Conclusions and Future Work

With Aplos we introduced Scala functional programming and Akka actor based smart contract platform into Mystiko blockchain. By using Akka actors to build smart contract, Mystiko supports concurrent transaction execution. This results in high transaction throughput. With Aplos smart actors on Mystiko we have built a blockchain that has highly scalable storage aligned for big data requirements.

We have evaluated the scalability and transaction throughput with empirical evaluations. We have integrated Aplos smart actor platform with Mystiko blockchain into production grade applications in the banking and financial sectors. The deployments are votes of confidence for Aplos platform based Mystiko as an ideal blockchain system for big data and cloud storage.

Most recently we have released Mystiko version 2.0 with the Aplos actor platform. We follow the agile continuous delivery approach when building and releasing the product. The following features we will release in the future:

1. Secure multiparty computation [36] with Aplos framework.
2. Incorporate homomorphic encryption [5] to provide privacy and confidentiality features.
3. Integrate ETCD-based [9] distributed key/value pair storage to achieve fully decentralized caching.

References

1. Adrian, O.R.: The blockchain, today and tomorrow. In: 2018 20th International Symposium on Symbolic and Numeric Algorithms for Scientific Computing (SYNASC), pp. 458–462. IEEE (2018)
2. Akka: Akka documentation. https://doc.akka.io/docs/akka/2.5/actors.html
3. Akka: Akka streams documentation. https://doc.akka.io/docs/akka/2.5/stream/
4. Androulaki, E., et al.: Hyperledger fabric: a distributed operating system for permissioned blockchains. In: Proceedings of the Thirteenth EuroSys Conference, p. 30. ACM (2018)
5. Armknecht, F., et al.: A guide to fully homomorphic encryption. IACR Cryptol. ePrint Arch. **2015**, 1192 (2015)
6. Bandara, E., et al.: Mystiko - blockchain meets big data. In: IEEE International Conference on Big Data, Big Data 2018, Seattle, WA, USA, 10–13 December 2018, pp. 3024–3032 (2018)
7. Buterin, V., et al.: A next-generation smart contract and decentralized application platform. White paper (2014)
8. Cassandra: Cassandra LWT. https://docs.datastax.com/en/cassandra/3.0/cassandra/dml/dmlLtwtTransactions.html
9. Coreos: coreos/etcd, August 2018. https://github.com/coreos/etcd
10. Docker: Docker documentation, August 2018. https://docs.docker.com/
11. Elasticsearch: Elasticsearch documentation. https://www.elastic.co/guide/index.html
12. Eykholt, E., Meredith, G., Denman, J.: RChain architecture documentation (2017)
13. Harz, D., Knottenbelt, W.: Towards safer smart contracts: a survey of languages and verification methods, September 2018
14. Hewitt, C.: Actor model of computation: scalable robust information systems. arXiv preprint arXiv:1008.1459 (2010)
15. Hoare, C.A.R.: Communicating sequential processes. Commun. ACM **21**(8), 666–677 (1978)
16. Karunanayake, A., De Zoysa, K., Muftic, S.: Mobile ATM for developing countries, January 2008. https://doi.org/10.1145/1403007.1403014
17. Kreps, J., Narkhede, N., Rao, J., et al.: Kafka: a distributed messaging system for log processing. In: Proceedings of the NetDB, pp. 1–7 (2011)
18. Kubernetes: Kubernetes documentation. https://kubernetes.io/docs/home/?path=users&persona=app-developer&level=foundational
19. Kurath, A.: Analyzing serializability of cassandra applications. Ph.D. thesis, Master's thesis, ETH Zürich (2017)

20. Lakshman, A., Malik, P.: Cassandra: a decentralized structured storage system. ACM SIGOPS Oper. Syst. Rev. **44**(2), 35–40 (2010)
21. Lamport, L.: The part-time parliament. ACM Trans. Comput. Syst. (TOCS) **16**(2), 133–169 (1998)
22. Lucene: Apache lucene documentation. http://lucene.apache.org/
23. MBSL: MBSL bank. https://www.mbslbank.com
24. McConaghy, T., et al.: BigchainDB: a scalable blockchain database. White paper, BigChainDB (2016)
25. Meng, X., et al.: MLlib: machine learning in apache spark. J. Mach. Learn. Res. **17**(1), 1235–1241 (2016)
26. Nakamoto, S.: Bitcoin: a peer-to-peer electronic cash system (2008)
27. O'Connor, R.: Simplicity: a new language for blockchains, pp. 107–120, October 2017. https://doi.org/10.1145/3139337.3139340
28. Odersky, M., et al.: An overview of the scala programming language. Technical report (2004)
29. Popejoy, S.: The pact smart contract language, June 2017 (2016). http://kadena.io/docs/Kadena-PactWhitepaper.pdf
30. Redis: Redis documentation. https://redis.io/documentation
31. Richardson, C.: Microservices pattern. http://microservices.io/patterns/microservices.html
32. Scala: Scala documentation. https://docs.scala-lang.org/
33. Sergey, I., Kumar, A., Hobor, A.: Scilla: a smart contract intermediate-level language, January 2018
34. Solidity: Solidity documentation. https://solidity.readthedocs.io/en/develop/
35. Zamani, M., Movahedi, M., Raykova, M.: RapidChain: a fast blockchain protocol via full sharding. IACR Cryptol. ePrint Arch. **2018**, 460 (2018)
36. Zyskind, G., Nathan, O., Pentland, A.: Enigma: decentralized computation platform with guaranteed privacy. arXiv preprint arXiv:1506.03471 (2015)

A Trading Model Based on Legal Contracts Using Smart Contract Templates

Youqun Shi[✉], Zihao Lu, Ran Tao, Ying Liu, and Zhaohui Zhang

School of Computer Science and Technology,
Donghua University, Shanghai 201620, China
{yqshi,taoran,zhzhang}@dhu.edu.cn,
{2171739,2171779}@mail.dhu.edu.cn

Abstract. Smart contracts are often used to automate the execution of transactions so that the fairness, credibility and traceability can be ensured. Generally, for different trading events, different smart contracts are needed to be developed so as to meet the needs. This may lead to a reduction in efficiency, especially when large-scale transactions occur. In addition, trading contracts have complex life cycle and terms. Developing a smart contract based on the context of a contract is extremely difficult. These characteristics may do harm to the application of smart contracts in e-commerce. To this end, this paper proposes a trading model based on legal contracts using smart contract templates. The model can dynamically construct, store, and invoke smart contracts based on a smart contract template and the context of a trading contract, thereby improving the reusability of smart contracts and reducing the difficulty for use. Third-party information, like logistics information, is used as the triggering condition of smart contracts to enhance the reasonableness of execution. In this paper, the garment acquisition contract is token as an example to describe the construction method of a smart contract template. Finally, combined with the experiment and the life cycle of a legal contract, the validity and rationality of the model is discussed. The comparison with legal trading contracts in performance is also conducted.

Keywords: Blockchain · Smart contracts · E-commerce · Trading contracts

1 Introduction

A trading contract constrains the behavior of both parties from a legal perspective. However, some phenomena of dishonesty often occur, such as the buyer's default on the payment, the seller's default on the delivery and so on. These all seriously affect the normal order of trading and leave bad experience to participants.

In 2008, Nakamoto proposed blockchain as a trusted distributed ledger technology [1]. Due to the tamper-proof nature and the identity management method using public key cryptography, blockchain has been widely used to solve the trust problem [2, 3]. Proposed by Szabo [4] and implemented by Ethereum [5], smart contracts can be used to achieve high-level automation in blockchain system. That makes them able to the standardize the procedure in trading scenarios [6]. To develop suitable smart contracts,

© Springer Nature Singapore Pte Ltd. 2020
Z. Zheng et al. (Eds.): BlockSys 2019, CCIS 1156, pp. 446–460, 2020.
https://doi.org/10.1007/978-981-15-2777-7_36

the context of legal contracts is a good basis and reference. Such legal-contract-based smart contracts can further enhance the legal applicability [7].

The process of developing smart contracts based on contract text involves the regularization of contract texts [8], the modeling of contract semantics [9], the mapping from the semantics of legal contracts to the structure of smart contracts [10], and the deployment of smart contracts [11]. These are all technical in work, complex in process and heavy in workload. For large-scale transactions, if a separate smart contract is developed for each contract, not only the computing power and storage space of blockchain will be greatly occupied, but also the efficiency will be reduced. In addition, legal trading contracts generally have complex treaty conditions and life cycles [12]. It is difficult to develop smart contracts that meet all these requirements. Constructing smart contracts with smart contract templates can solve the above problems to some extent [13].

In order to solve the above problems, this paper proposes a trading model based on legal contracts using smart contract templates. In this model, smart contracts are stored, constructed and invoked dynamically, basing on smart contract templates and the legal contract. Third-party information (such as logistics information) are used as the triggering condition of smart contracts.

The rest of the text is organized as follows. Section 2 introduces related works. Section 3 presents the model we proposed, including the workflow, a smart contract triggering mechanism and a construction and invocation model of trading smart contracts. An example of the construction of the smart contract template is also described. Section 4 introduces the experiment and discusses the rationality and validity of the proposed model. Comparison with traditional legal contracts in performance is also conducted. Section 5 presents conclusion and discusses the limitation of this model.

2 Related Works

2.1 Smart Contracts for Trading

Smart contracts are designed to be Turing-complete when they are proposed [5]. Theoretically, smart contracts can implement any algorithm and logic function. Smart contracts have been used in a variety of trading scenarios.

Toyoda et al. proposed a method of using smart contracts for product ownership management and designed a corresponding POMS system [14]. In POMS, both parties in a trade need to actively invoke the smart contract to confirm the delivery and receipt of the product. Roman and Vu studied the application of blockchain in data trading and designed a corresponding process model [15]. They used smart contracts as the intermediary to receive the buyer's advance payment. When the smart contract is invoked by the buyer to confirm the receipt, it will automatically issue the advance payment to the seller. Lamberti et al. studied the application of blockchain in auto insurance claims [16]. They use IoT sensors to monitor and record the status of vehicles. When an accident occurs, the smart contract will determine the condition of the vehicle based on IoT data to match the applicable insurance contract terms. Hasan and Salah proposed a blockchain-based proof of delivery (PoD) method [17]. In their method, after the buyer has actively confirmed the receipt of the assets, the smart contract will combine the records provided by the logistics company with a special verification key. In this way, the status of the receipt and the authenticity of the goods can be verified, thus completing the trade.

Most of the above researches mainly focus on the trade itself, but not the reusability of smart contracts, the combination with legal contracts, or the objectivity of triggering conditions. Further research is needed.

2.2 Smart Contract Templates

A smart contract template is a public smart contract that is deployed in blockchain network and can be invoked by all relevant users [18]. When invoking a smart contract template, users can pass different parameters, so as to achieve the effect of invoking different smart contracts. For smart contracts with highly similar semantic structures, using smart contract templates can reduce the efforts of development and deployment of smart contracts, thus improving the reusability. However, there is currently few applications on smart contract templates for legal trading contracts. This requires further research.

The relationship between smart contracts template and smart contracts is shown in Fig. 1. In Fig. 1, the smart contract template (denoted as ST) has been deployed in the blockchain for relevant users to invoke. It consists of main logic (denoted as TL) and contract parameters (denoted as TP). TL describes the execution logic in a smart contract, while TP quantifies the execution process. When ST is invoked with different main logics (denoted as L_1 and L_2 respectively) and contract parameters (denoted as P_1 and P_2 respectively), the effect is equivalent to invoking two different smart contracts (denoted as SC_1 and SC_2 respectively).

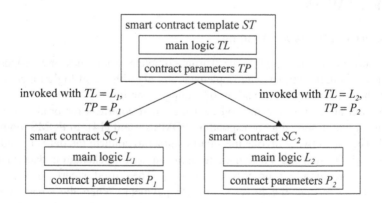

Fig. 1. Relationship between smart contract templates and smart contracts

2.3 Triggering Mechanism of Smart Contracts

In order to determine the status of the trade and thus match the applicable contract terms, two methods are usually adopted by most smart contracts. In one method, a smart contract is directly invoked by the participant of the trade for confirmation [19].

In the other, a smart contract monitors the status of the traded item in real time through IoT devices [20]. In the former method, since the confirmer of the trade is a direct stakeholder, the judgment on the execution effect of the trade may lack objectivity. In the latter, if the IoT information cannot upload to blockchain in time, the trigger of the smart contract will be doomed to fail. Therefore, the triggering conditions of smart contracts need to be optimized.

3 The Model

Using the model, smart contracts can be dynamically constructed based on contract text using smart contract templates. These smart contract templates are developed by professionals basing on the text of legal trading contract templates.

3.1 The Workflow

Buyers and sellers can trade through smart contracts on a blockchain platform. The workflow is as follows:

1. Registration: The buyer and seller get registration on the blockchain platform. The Certificate Authority (CA) of the Blockchain Platform will generate a set of public/private key pairs for each registered user for authentication.
2. Conclusion of The Legal Contract: The buyer and the seller select a contract template together and negotiate the details of the contract. They can also add additional terms as their need optionally.
3. Contract Confirmation: The blockchain platform generates a legal trading contract document based on the contract template selected, the details submitted and the additional terms. The document will be sent to both parties for confirmation. If the buyer and seller agree with the contract, they will use their own private key to generate a digital signature based on the document and upload it to the blockchain platform.
4. Contract Data Storage: According to the contract template selected by the two parties, the blockchain platform will search for the corresponding smart contract template deployed on blockchain. Meanwhile, a deposit block will be generated, which contains the detailed legal contract document, the digital signatures, signing dates. The deposit block will be stored into the blockchain.
5. Smart Contract Construction: Using the construction model of trading contracts based on smart contract templates, the blockchain platform creates the trading smart contract logically. This process is based on the selected smart contract template and the deposit block.
6. Trading Through Smart Contract: Using the invocation model of trading contracts based on smart contract templates, the buyer and seller invoke the constructed smart contract for trading.
7. Contract Revision: During the trade, the buyer and seller can always negotiate to amend the trading contract and modify the details in the contract. If the contract is amended, return to Contract Confirmation.

The workflow of the blockchain-based trading model is shown in Fig. 2.

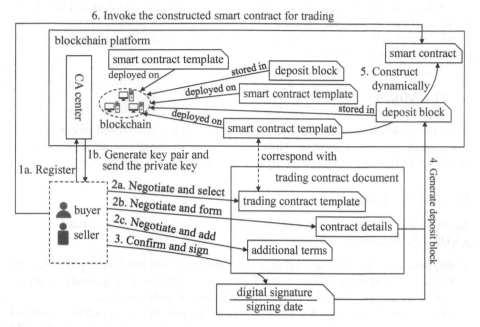

Fig. 2. The workflow of the blockchain-based trading model

3.2 A Smart Contract Triggering Mechanism Based on Third-Party Information

To make the triggering conditions of smart contracts more objective and reasonable, the model uses third-party information as the basis for judging the current state of a trade. Taking the buyer's confirmation of the receipt of the delivery as an example, the logistics receipt information of the goods can be used as the evidence of the buyer's receipt. That will automatically trigger the smart contract to execute the subsequent trading process. The process can be described by the pseudocode of *goodsSigned()*, as shown in Algorithm 1.

Algorithm 1 Pseudo-code of *goodsSigned()*
Triggering smart contract with logistics receipt information

Input: interface to query logistics information ($I_{logistics}$),
         traded goods ID (ID_{goods}),
         the buyer's ID (ID_{buyer})
         and the operation after buyer's receipt (O_{signed})
1: $info_{goods}$ ← qurey goods's logistics information by ID_{goods} through $I_{logistics}$
2: $state_{goods}$ ← the delivery state in $info_{goods}$ // a Boolean representing whether the goods has been signed for the delivery or not
3: $ID_{receiver}$ ← receiver's ID in $info_{goods}$
4: **if** $state_{goods} == True$ **and** $ID_{receiver} == ID_{buyer}$ **then**
5:     smart contract operates O_{signed}
6:     smart contract records the operation related information into blockchain
7: **end if**

3.3 A Construction and Invocation Model of Trading Smart Contracts Based on Smart Contract Templates

To ensure that the constructed smart contract is consistent with the trading contract in terms of performance logic, it is necessary to reasonably design the structure of the smart contract template, the storage method of contract data, and the invoking method of the constructed contract.

Structure of the Smart Contract Template
The smart contract template is mainly composed of template code, contract parameters, deposited content, and smart contract template ID. The specific design is as follows:

- Template code: It is developed by professionals and contains the basic logic of a legal trading contract. For example, when the buyer confirms the receipt, the seller will get the full payment.
- Contract parameters: It is generated from the details of a legal contract. The contract parameters will be used as runtime parameters for template code, including a clear quantification for triggering conditions and operations to take. For example, When the buyer (Alice) confirms the receipt (40 ordered sweatshirts), the seller (Bob) will get the full payment (RMB 8,000).
- Forensic content: The variable part of a smart contract, which corresponds to the signatures or official seals of the two parties and the signing dates. In the model, handwritten signatures are replaced with digital signatures, which generated by users' own private key on the trading contract documents. The signing date is recorded automatically when a digital signature is uploaded to blockchain.
- Smart contract template ID: The fixed parameter field of each smart contract template, which corresponds to the legal contract template ID, and can be used to find the specific smart contract template.

Contract Data Storage and Smart Contract Construction

This paper stores the contract parameters together with the forensic content in blockchain as a deposit block. The deposit block also includes smart contract template ID and trading contract ID, which describes the correspondence among the smart contract template, the deposit block, and the trading contract.

In this paper, the trading contract (including contract template, contract details, additional terms) is stored in the form of a text document in a trusted database of the blockchain platform. A unique contract ID is assigned to the document, corresponding to a single trade. The document is free for the parties to download. For judicial use, the digital signature stored in blockchain together with the contract document can also serves as a firm evidence.

Passing blockchain storage address of the deposit block to a smart contract template, the smart contract template will obtain the necessary parameters for specific smart contract construction. The contract data storage and trading smart contract construction method based on smart contract template is shown in Fig. 3.

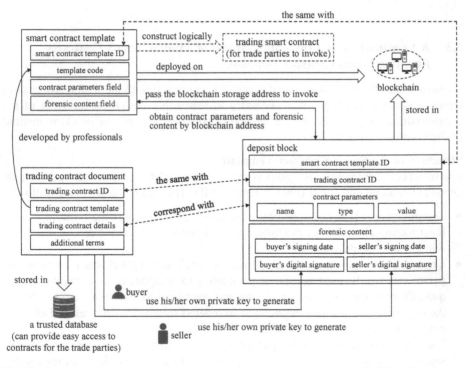

Fig. 3. Contract data storage and trading smart contract construction method based on smart contract template

Smart Contract Templates for Garments Trading

As a mature industry, pre-made contract templates are widely used for garment trade. Takes a common garment trading contract template as an example, this sub-section describes the construction method of a smart contract template. The usual content and terms are list as follows:

- Identity of the buyer (ID_{buyer}) and the seller (ID_{seller}) in the trade.
- The buyer must prepay a certain payment ($amt_{paymnet}$) to the intermediary account before the specified time limit ($T_{payment}$).
- The seller must deliver the designated garments (ID_{goods}) to the buyer through logistics before the specified time limit ($T_{delivery}$) after the buyer's prepayment. The contract also includes the description of the designated garments ($descr_{goods}$), such as quantity, size, and other specifications.
- When receiving the purchased garment, the buyer should issue the prepayment to the seller through the intermediary.
- If the buyer fails to pay the prepayment or the seller fails to deliver the goods within the time limit, the default terms ($terms_{default}$) need to be executed.
- The parties can add additional terms ($terms_{addl}$) optionally.
- The contract should be completed with the signatures or official seals of the parties and the signing dates.

Combined with the third-party information triggering mechanism, a specific smart contract template can be developed. So is the deposit block. This paper uses the account of the blockchain platform ($acct_{platform}$) as the intermediary account, an interface ($I_{logistics}$) to obtain logistics information of the traded garments, the parties' digital signatures (denoted as S_{buyer} and $Sseller$ respectively) on the contract as the handwritten signature or official seal. Buyer's signing date (DT_{buyer}) and seller's signing date (DT_{seller}) are recorded automatically.

In the process of generating a smart contract, the performance logic in the contract template, $acct_{platform}$, and $I_{logistics}$ are developed into the template code in the smart contract template by professionals. Including ID_{buyer}, ID_{seller}, $amt_{paymnet}$, $T_{payment}$, ID_{goods}, $T_{delivery}$, $descr_{goods}$, contract details are stored in the deposit block as contract parameters. S_{buyer}, S_{seller}, DT_{buyer}, S_{seller} are record as forensic content in the deposit block. $terms_{default}$ and $terms_{addl}$ are written as part of the trading contract document, which stored in a trusted database. The structure and execution process of the smart contract template can be described by $SCTemplate()$ in Algorithm 2.

Algorithm 2 Pseudo-code of *SCTemplate()*

Using deposit block to construct a trading smart contract

Input: the blockchain address of deposit block ($addr_{deposit}$)

1: $B_{deposit}$ ← get the deposit block in blockchain by $addr_{deposit}$

2: T_0 ← the later date between $B_{deposit}.DT_{buyer}$ and $B_{deposit}.DT_{seller}$

3: T_1 ← the date $B_{deposit}.ID_{buyer}$ pays $B_{deposit}.amt_{payment}$ to $acct_{platform}$

4: T_2 ← the date $B_{deposit}.ID_{seller}$ delivers $B_{deposit}.ID_{goods}$ to $B_{deposit}.ID_{seller}$

5: **if** (!T_1 and $T_1 < T_0 + T_{payment}$) **and** (!T_2 and $T_2 < T_0 + T_{payment} + T_{delivery}$) **then**

6:    O_{signed} ← the operation: $acct_{platform}$ issues $B_{deposit}.amt_{payment}$ to $B_{deposit}.ID_{seller}$

7:    $rec_{operation}$ ← query O_{signed} related operation records in blockchain

8:    **if** !$rec_{operation}$ **then**

9:      goodsSigned($I_{logistics}$, $B_{deposit}.ID_{goods}$, $B_{deposit}.ID_{buyer}$, O_{signed})

10:    **end if**

11: **else**

12:    interrupt the execution and record the violation on the blockchain

13: **end if**

Invoking Method of the Constructed Smart Contract

To ensure the correctness of the execution, it is critical to make sure that there is a correct correspondence among the smart contract template, deposit block and the transaction contract text. In addition, before passing the deposit block to the smart contract template, it is also essential to verify its validity and timeliness. That is, whether the deposit block represents the trading contract signed by the right trade parties and whether the deposit block represents the latest version of the contract.

In this paper, the validity of the deposit block is verified by checking digital signatures of both parties in the deposit data. This process can be described by the pseudocode of *isContValid()*, as is shown in Algorithm 3.

Algorithm 3 Pseudo-code of *isContractValid()*

Verifying the validity of the deposit block

Input: deposit block ($B_{deposit}$)

Output: a Boolean (True or False)

1: $cntrDoc$ ← get the trading contract document by trading contract ID ($ID_{contract}$) in $B_{deposit}$ from the database

2: $hash_{cntr}$ ← the hash of $cntrDoc$

3: PK_{buyer} ← get buyer's public key by $B_{deposit}.ID_{buyer}$

4: PK_{seller} ← get seller's public key by $B_{deposit}.ID_{seller}$

5: $hash_1$ ← decrypt $B_{deposit}.S_{buyer}$ with PK_{buyer}

6: $hash_2$ ← decrypt $B_{deposit}.S_{seller}$ with PK_{seller}

7: **if** $hash_1 == hash_{cntr}$ **and** $hash_2 == hash_{cntr}$ **then**

8:    **return** *Ture*

9: **else**

10:    **return** *False*

11: **end if**

Querying the latest valid deposit block with the same trading contract ID in blockchain and using its address as the input of the smart contract template, the timeliness of the deposit block can get guaranteed. Thus, even if a new deposit block is generated due to a contract revision, the smart contract template will only execute the latest contract terms. The process of the constructed smart contract invocation can be described by the pseudo-code of *invokeSC()*, as is shown in Algorithm 4.

Algorithm 4 Pseudo-code of *invokeSC()*

Invoking the constructed smart contract with contract ID

Input: trading contract ID ($ID_{contract}$)

1: $B_{deposit} \leftarrow$ query the latest deposit block in blockchain by $ID_{contract}$

2: $addr_{deposit} \leftarrow$ the address of $B_{deposit}$

3: **while** !*isContractValid($B_{deposit}$)*

4:     $B_{deposit} \leftarrow$ query the previous deposit block in blockchain with $ID_{contract}$

5:     $addr_{deposit} \leftarrow$ the blockchain address of $B_{deposit}$

6: **end while**

7: $tmpl_{SC} \leftarrow$ query the smart contract template by smart contract template ID in $B_{deposit}$

8: pass $addr_{deposit}$ to $tmpl_{SC}$

9: // for example, *SCTemplate($addr_{deposit}$)*

---

4   Implementation, Analysis and Comparison

4.1   Implementation

To make the proposed method work, all participants have to trade with their real identities. According to the research of Wüst and Gervais, this model is better to be implemented in the form of consortium blockchain [21].

By using Hyperledger Fabric, we have built an experimental system based on the proposed model. The results are show as follows (Figs. 4, 5 and 6).

Draft Trading Contracts

Fill Basic Information	Review, Confirm and Sign	Contract Drafted Successfully

You can draft a trading contract based on the agreement with the seller for **the ownership** of your interested works. In this process, a unique *Contract ID* will be generated, which you can give to the seller for further steps.

NOTE: In the trade, **only the ownership can be transfered**. The "designer" will never be changed.

Seller's Identity ID	310110198810011234	Work ID (to trade)	gw20416109c7f450a216dd3b8
Price	5000.00	Ownership Transfer	Buy Out

Cut off Date (GMT+0800):

· Buyer's Payment	2019-10-17	23:59:59	· Seller's Delivery	2019-10-18	15:59:59
· Buyer's Signing for Delivery	2019-10-20	13:59:59
Violations	Cancel the trade

Submit   Reset

Fig. 4. By using a template, the participant can draft a trading contract, in which the key points will be stored into deposit block and developed into a smart contract

Record ID   cr22ce3a85e69a1b4a16dd3e827ef

Record

```
{ "docType": "tradingContract",
  "msg": {
    "content": {
      "buyer": {
        "identityID": "310105000568310",
        "realName": "弈心服装有限公司"
      },
      "cutoffBP": "Thu Oct 17 2019 23:59:59 GMT+0800 ",
      "cutoffSD": "Fri Oct 18 2019 15:59:59 GMT+0800 ",
      "cutoffSfD": "Sun Oct 20 2019 13:59:59 GMT+0800 ",
      "draftTime": "Wed Oct 16 2019 17:09:31 GMT+0800 ",
      "price": "5000.00",
      "seller": {
        "identityID": "310110198810011234",
        "realName": "Tony Wang"
      },
      "workID": "qw20416109c7f450a216dd3b8deda"
    },
    "hash_contact": "a34d773dacd763bc1b46d5bb4a719ab653587aafdfda
```

Fig. 5. A deposit block generated according to the drafted contract

	2019.10.16 18:58:34	Prepayment Token: py0bc14a8ec575e318ede8e8e71ebbb3f1
Issue the Payment		Statement Tx Hash: 3621a9926f1ab123753c40af1ab72de40e0 683492266fc22f1920117ab5d3a75
	Tx Hash in Blockchian	54369d60711372228da2be6a4e31012a0b59892ce120e09ff18c 77500f6773ab

Fig. 6. During a transaction, related evidence is recorded in blockchain (such as the record of issuing the payment). Its Tx hash is available for the public to query and verify.

4.2 Effectiveness and Rationality

The life cycle of a contract can generally be divided into seven stages: negotiation and formation, storage and notarization, execution, monitoring and enforcement, modification, dispute resolution, and termination [12]. When a smart contract is used to realize a legal trading contract, its manifestation, rationality, and coverage in these stages are important criteria for judging whether the smart contract is effective. For these standards, the performance of the proposed model is as follows.

Negotiation and Formation

The buyer and seller negotiate together to select a legal trading contract template and fill the contract details.

Storage and Notarization

Asmart contract is not completely equivalent to a legal contract [22]. Besides deposit blocks in blockchain, legal contracts will also be stored on a trusted server. In that case, the digital signature, together with the off-chain contract text, can serve as a notarization for the contract. In addition, this mode can also greatly save the storage cost of blockchain and increase records' capacity of the block.

Execution

When basic operations of the contract have been done (such as the buyer's prepayment, the seller's delivery, etc.), using the construction and invocation model of trading smart contracts, smart contracts can be invoked to execute the subsequent trading procedure.

During the procedure, the execution log will be recorded in blockchain automatically by smart contracts, which provides good traceability. This facilitates the post-event supervision of the trade.

Monitoring and Enforcement
The trading smart contract supervises the whole procedure of the trade. If trading parties fail to finish the basic operations of the contract, the smart contract will be triggered to enter default process. Since there is no need for human intervention, it saves the efforts for manually checking the progress.

Modification
Trading parties may negotiate and modify the details of the contract any time they want. By trading contract ID, the revision history of a certain contract can also be queried and traced in blockchain.

Dispute Resolution
When dispute occurs, contract documents, together with digital signatures, can provide convincing evidence for resorting to relevant organization or the blockchain platform. Execution log recorded by the smart contract and historical deposit blocks can also serve as important evidence for liability determination and dispute resolution.

Termination
The termination of a contract can generally be divided into the following situations.

- Fulfilled Successfully: Since the execution log is recorded automatically by smart contracts, when a contract is fulfilled successfully, the smart contract can no longer perform any operations. Invoking smart contracts again can be used as a means of checking whether the contract has been terminated.
- Contract Default: When a contract default occurs, the smart contract will automatically enter the default procedure according to default terms in the trading contract.
- Termination by Negotiation: If trading parties agree to terminate the contract after negotiation, they can sign a blank contract by Modification, indicating the termination and the negotiation in the additional terms. At this point, the smart contract will be terminated successfully. Then they can use the Dispute Resolution to enter the follow-up procedure.

Through the analysis above, the proposed model can cover the entire life cycle of a trading contract. Relevant records in the blockchain can also provide credible evidence and traceability guarantees for the aftermath of the contract.

4.3 Comparison

Most of the existing smart contracts are more concerned with the trading logic itself [14–17]. This paper carries out further research on the reusability of smart contracts, the compatibility with the law, the method of dealing with contract defaults, and the objectivity of triggering conditions. What's more the proposed model also supports the modification of a contract. The comparison in these aspects is shown in Table 1.

As can be seen in Table 1, using this model used may help to improve trading efficiency, strengthen legal effect, and increase users' satisfaction to some extent.

Table 1. Comparison of the proposed model with other trading methods using smart contracts

Performance	Trading with smart contracts	
	Focus on trading logic only	The proposed model
Reusability	/	Through smart contract templates
Legal applicability	Passive forensics	Rights protection with legal contract
Contract default	Likely to cause logic errors in smart contracts	Terminate the smart contract and deal through legal methods
Objectivity	Actively triggered by the participant, or relying on IoT devices	Use third-party information as the reference
Modification	Not support	Support

5   Conclusion and Discussion

This paper proposes a trading model based on legal contracts using smart contract templates. In this model, smart contracts for trading are dynamically stored, constructed, and invoked based on the contract text. That improves the reusability of smart contracts. Another way to set triggering conditions of smart contracts is proposed. That is using third-party information, which can enhance the rationality of execution. Meanwhile, a garment trading contract is token as an example to illustrate the construction method of the smart contract template used. The paper also presents an experimental system and demonstrates the validity and rationality of the proposed model with the life cycle of legal contracts. Finally, a comparison with other existing smart contracts is conducted. The result shows that the model may enhance the performance of trading smart contracts to some extent.

The smart contract itself has the possibility of being attacked and illegally exploited. Once this happens, it will cause great harm to the proposed model. Therefore, the further work may study the safety measures of the model and the prevention measures against potential threats. In addition, due to some special characteristics, the proposed model may only work for trading contracts. It's meaningful to research further and extend the scenario to other popular areas of blockchain application, such as AI, IoT, and so on [23, 24].

Acknowledgments. This work was supported by Natural Science Foundation of Shanghai (No. 19 ZR1401900), Shanghai Science and Technology Innovation Action Plan Project (No. 1951 1101802), and National Natural Science Foundation of China (No. 61472004, 61602109).

References

1. Nakamoto, S.: Bitcoin: a peer-to-peer electronic cash system (2008). http://bitcoin.org/bitcoin.pdf
2. Jaoude, J.A., Saade, R.G.: Blockchain applications-usage in different domains. IEEE Access **7**, 45360–45381 (2019)
3. Diffie, W., Hellman, M.E.: New directions in cryptography. IEEE Trans. Inf. Theory **22**(6), 644–654 (1976)
4. Szabo, N.: Smart contracts (1994). http://szabo.best.vwh.net/smart.contracts.html
5. Buterin, V.: Ethereum: a next generation smart contract and decentralized application platform (2013). https://github.com/ethereum/wiki/wiki/White-Paper
6. Mohanta, B.K., Panda, S.S., Jena, D.: An overview of smart contract and use cases in blockchain technology. In: 2018 9th International Conference on Computing, Communication and Networking Technologies (ICCCNT), pp. 1–4. IEEE (2018)
7. Pereira, J.C.: The genesis of the revolution in Contract Law: Smart Legal Contracts. In: 12th International Conference on Theory and Practice of Electronic Governance, pp. 374–377 (2019)
8. Governatori, G.: Representing business contracts in RuleML. Int. J. Coop. Inf. Syst. **14**(2–3), 181–216 (2005)
9. Yu, L., Tsai, W., Hu, C., Li, B., Hu, J., Deng, E.: Modeling context-aware legal computing with bigraphs. In: 2017 IEEE Symposium on Service-Oriented System Engineering (SOSE), pp. 145–152 (2017)
10. Frantz, C.K., Nowostawski, M.: From institutions to code: towards automated generation of smart contracts. In: 2016 IEEE 1st International Workshops on Foundations and Applications of Self* Systems (FAS*W), pp. 210–215 (2016)
11. Wang, S., Ouyang, L., Yuan, Y., Ni, X., Han, X., Wang, F.: Blockchain-enabled smart contracts: architecture, applications, and future trends. IEEE Trans. Syst. Man Cybern. Syst. **49**, 2266–2277 (2019)
12. Governatori, G., Idelberger, F., Milosevic, Z., Riveret, R., Sartor, G., Xu, X.: On legal contracts, imperative and declarative smart contracts, and blockchain systems. Artif. Intell. Law **26**, 377–409 (2018)
13. Clack, C.D., Bakshi, V.A., Braine, L.: Smart contract templates: foundations, design landscape and research directions. CoRR abs/1608.00771 (2016)
14. Toyoda, K., Mathiopoulos, P.T., Sasase, I., Ohtsuki, T.: A novel blockchain-based product ownership management system (POMS) for anti-counterfeits in the post supply chain. IEEE Access **5**, 17465–17477 (2017)
15. Roman, D., Vu, K.: Enabling data markets using smart contracts and multi-party computation. In: Abramowicz, W., Paschke, A. (eds.) BIS 2018. LNBIP, vol. 339, pp. 258–263. Springer, Cham (2019). https://doi.org/10.1007/978-3-030-04849-5_23
16. Lamberti, F., Gatteschi, V., Demartini, C., Pelissier, M., Gomez, A., Santamaria, V.: Blockchains can work for car insurance: using smart contracts and sensors to provide on-demand coverage. IEEE Consum. Electron. Mag. **7**(4), 72–81 (2018)
17. Hasan, H.R., Salah, K.: Blockchain-based proof of delivery of physical assets with single and multiple transporters. IEEE Access **6**, 46781–46793 (2018)
18. Clack, C.D., Bakshi, V.A., Braine, L.: Smart contract templates: foundations, design landscape and research directions. arXiv preprint arXiv:1608.00771 (2016)
19. Yeh, K.H., Su, C., Hou, J.L., Chiu, W., Chen, C.M.: A robust mobile payment scheme with smart contract-based transaction repository. IEEE Access **6**, 59394–59404 (2018)

20. Gilcrest, J., Carvalho, A.: Smart contracts: legal considerations. In: 2018 IEEE International Conference on Big Data (Big Data), pp. 3277–3281 (2018)
21. Wüst, K., Gervais, A.: Do you need a blockchain? In: 2018 Crypto Valley Conference on Blockchain Technology (CVCBT), pp. 45–54 (2018)
22. Patel, D., Shah, K., Shanbhag, S., Mistry, V.: Towards legally enforceable smart contracts. In: Chen, S., Wang, H., Zhang, L.-J. (eds.) ICBC 2018. LNCS, vol. 10974, pp. 153–165. Springer, Cham (2018). https://doi.org/10.1007/978-3-319-94478-4_11
23. Salah, K., Rehman, M.H., Nizamuddin, N., Al-Fuqaha, A.: Blockchain for AI: review and open research challenges. IEEE Access 7, 10127–10149 (2019)
24. Almadhoun, R., Kadadha, M., Alhemeiri, M., Alshehhi, M., Salah, K.: A user authentication scheme of IoT devices using blockchain-enabled fog nodes. In: 2018 IEEE/ACS 15th International Conference on Computer Systems and Applications (AICCSA), pp. 1–8 (2018)

Would the Patch Be Quickly Merged?

Yuan Huang[1], Nan Jia[3], Xiaocong Zhou[1], Kai Hong[1], and Xiangping Chen[2(✉)]

[1] School of Data and Computer Science, Sun Yat-sen University,
Guangzhou 510006, China
[2] Guangdong Key Laboratory for Big Data Analysis and Simulation of Public
Opinion, School of Communication and Design, Sun Yat-sen University,
Guangzhou 510006, China
chenxp8@mail.sysu.edu.cn
[3] School of Management Science and Engineering, Hebei GEO University,
Shijiazhuang 050031, China

Abstract. Code review is one of the most time-consuming and costly activities in modern software development. For the code submissions that can not be accepted by reviewers, developers need to re-modify the code again. Developers desire to minimize the time-cost that spends in the code review process. In some cases, a submission might be submitted many times and still not be accepted. The number of review times has serious implications for defect repairs and the progress of development. Therefore, a few recent studies focused on discussing factors that effect submission acceptance, while these prior studies did not try to predict submission acceptance or the number of review times. In this paper, we propose a novel method to predict the time-cost in code review before a submission is accepted. Our approach uses a number of features, including review meta-features, code modifying features and code coupling features, to better reflect code changes and review process. To examine the benefits of our method, we perform experiments on two large open source projects, namely Eclipse and OpenDaylight. Our results show that the proposed approach in the problem of predicting submission acceptance achieves an accuracy of 79.72%, 80.03% for Eclipse and OpenDaylight, respectively. For the prediction of review times ranges, our method achieves an accuracy of 66.42% and 60.42% for Eclipse and OpenDaylight, respectively.

Keywords: Code review · Review time · Code patch · Feature engineering · Software maintenance

1 Introduction

Code review, an essential software engineering practice employed both in open source and industrial contexts, is normally recognized as the last step of software change [1–3]. After software change, a code change (or patch) is submitted by developer for review. Then, the code-reviewers will inspect the code and discuss

© Springer Nature Singapore Pte Ltd. 2020
Z. Zheng et al. (Eds.): BlockSys 2019, CCIS 1156, pp. 461–475, 2020.
https://doi.org/10.1007/978-981-15-2777-7_37

the change. Finally, they will accept the code change or suggest fixes. For software change, code review provides good value in identifying defects in code change before they are committed into the project's code base [4–6]. However, it is relatively expensive in terms of time and effort [7]. Especially, code change had been submitted many times and still not be accepted.

Existing research has found that many different factors in the process of review can influence acception. Baysal et al. [8] demonstrated that both of technical and non-technical can influence how long a code change's likelihood of being accepted. These factors include personal and organizational relationships, patch size, component, bug priority, reviewer/submitter experience, and reviewer load.

However, developer wonders if a patch can be accepted without delay. And from project manager's point of view they concern how many times have a patch needs to be reviewed. If a code change will cost an estimated too many review times, it will increase time cost and disrupt the schedule. To estimate review times can be a good way for developer and project manager to have a clear understanding of the code changes and make adjustments.

In this paper, we propose a novel method based on machine learning to help developer predict review times of their code change. We extracts review meta-information, structural coupling information and code modification information as discriminative features to measure the review times. Among them, review meta-information represents non-technical factors in review process, such as reviewers, submitter, project, etc. Structural coupling information represents relations between software entities which indicate the complexity of code change [9–11]. Code modification information represent the amount of code change via the number of modified methods, modified code lines, etc. [3,6]. We perform a case study of two large open source project, and we want to explore the following research questions in this paper:

RQ1: How effective is our method in predicting the acceptance of submissions?
RQ2: How effective is our method in predicting the review times of submissions?

The rest of the paper is organized as following. The data collection is presented in Sect. 2. Section 3 describes the methodology we used to extract discriminative features. The setups and results of experiment are discussed in Sect. 4. We discuss the related works in Sect. 5. Section 6 summarizes our approach and outlines directions of future work.

2   Data Collection

We extracted two open source review data automatically from the Gerrit[1] code review system. Gerrit is a widely used code review tool which can facilitates a traceable code review process for git-based software projects. Developers submit

---

[1] Gerrit, https://www.gerritcodereview.com/.

their collections of proposed changes to a Gerrit server before changes integrated to software code base. Reviewers in Gerrit are selected by three ways: invited by developers, or self-selected voluntarily by broadcasting a review request to the submission, or designated automatically owning to their acquaintance with the modified system components.

Figure 1 shows an example code review in Gerrit, we use this figure to illustrate the information in a review. In order to extract discriminative features that used to evaluate review times, our data collection is broken down into two portion:

(1) Review meta-data. We defined the non-technical factors in review process as review meta-data. During the review meta-data, we collected a variety of information about each review process including its submit time, the person who writes the patches, the project that patch belong to. We recorded all meta-data to evaluate the impact of non-technical factors to review times.

(2) Code change data. As an important part of review, the collection of code changes contains significant information of effecting the review times. Code change data recorded the information of change objective and change content. All this information reflect the degree of difficulty and operation capacity of the code change.

Fig. 1. An example Gerrit code review

3   Discriminative Features Extraction

This section introduces the step of discriminative feature extraction. Three types of features are extracted from review meta-data and code change data to predict the review times, they are: review meta-features, code coupling features, code modifying features. The detailed process of the feature extraction is described in the following.

Table 1. Review meta-features

Category	Feature	Descriptions
Review meta-features	MF_0	Owner of the review
	MF_1	Author of the code changes
	MF_2	Number of participations last month
	MF_3	Project of the code changes
	MF_4	Branch of the code changes
	MF_5	Time of submission

3.1 Review Meta-features

Review meta-features are extracted from review meta-data. There are many non-technical factors in the process of code review, which have a direct impact on the review approval. Review in practice is easily influenced by the factors, including the workload and expertise of reviewers, developers' experience, even be the submit time. To describe non-technical factors' impact on review, we extract 6 fine-gained meta-feature from review meta-data. All the features are presented in Table 1.

Feature MF_0 and feature MF_1 represent the owner and author of review respectively. In most time, owner and author are the same person. MF_0-MF_1 are used to described the influence of human factors in review. The familiarity to software projects for the developers can lead to large gaps in the review time [12]. We extracted feature MF_2 to describe familiarity of developers to the project. MF_2 is the number of the developers that participating in the patch submission of the project in past month.

Feature MF_3 and MF_4 represent the project and location of code changes. We use these two features to measure the diversity in code changes between different projects and different branches. Software entities in different projects and branches have different complexity and common modification goals, which will be reflected in the time needed for reviewers and developers to accomplish code changes.

Eyolfson et al. [13] studied the relationship between the submission time of modification and the correctness of submission code. They found that code submitted between late night and 4 a.m. was more prone to errors, while code submitted between 7 a.m. and noon was less prone to errors. Inspired by this conclusion, feature MF_5 is extracted to represent the submission time of code changes.

3.2 Code Modifying Features

Different from features MF_0 to MF_8, code modifying features use code information to describe the modify content and modification of code changes. Modification quantity and content are significant features in review process. Large modifications usually require the reviewers to spend more time reading and examine the code.

Complex modification objectives increase the difficulty of reviewers' work. Code modification can be divided into three types, insert, update and delete. From the perspective of software entities, modification of a class, a method or a attribute have different impacts on review. We count the number of modification from different types and software entities. All features are illustrate in Table 2.

Features TF_0-TF_2 represent the number of statements involving modification in the code changes, including statement insert, statement update and statement delete. Features TF_3-TF_6 describe the modification of classes and records the number of additional classes, changed classes, removed classes and class renaming. Class renaming will lead to a lot of change work so that we regard it as an independent feature. At method level, Features TF_7-TF_{10} are used to describe the number of method insert, method delete, method renaming and return type change. For parameters in method, there are some independent features to describe. Features $TF_{11}-TF_{14}$ are used to represent parameter type change, parameter renaming, parameter insert and parameter delete, respectively. Features $TF_{15}-TF_{16}$ represent the number of attribute renaming and attribute type change respectively. Moreover, Feature TF_{17} represents the type of condition expression change.

Table 2. Code modifying features

Category	Feature	Descriptions
Code modifying features	TF_0	Number of inserted statements
	TF_1	Number of update statements
	TF_2	Number of deleted statements
	TF_3	Number of additional classes
	TF_4	Number of changed classes
	TF_5	Number of removed classes
	TF_6	Number of renaming class
	TF_7	Number of inserted method
	TF_8	Number of deleted method
	TF_9	Number of renamed method
	TF_{10}	Number of changed return type
	TF_{11}	Number of changed parameter type
	TF_{12}	Number of renaming parameter
	TF_{13}	Number of inserted parameter
	TF_{14}	Number of deleted parameter
	TF_{15}	Number of renaming attribute
	TF_{16}	Number of changed attribute type
	TF_{17}	Number of changed condition expression

3.3   Code Coupling Features

With the evolution of software system, there are complex coupling relationships among software entities [3,14]. According to the code change propagation mechanism [15,16], code change tends to propagate from the initial node of change occurrence to the node that has coupling relationship with the initial node, and the coupling existing in the software entities makes the change logic more complex [17]. We try to describe the complexity of code changes via the structural coupling information between software entities. Code changes are divided into fine-gained software entities, including class, method and attribute. Specifically, at the code level, the input degree and output degree of a class are used to represent its structural coupling features. We summarize the common coupling rules at different granularities.

(1) Class-to-Class. In Java program syntax, *Inheritance* and *Implementing Interface* are the most common cases. For any classes C_i, we define subclasses of C_i as its output degree and supuerclasses as its input degree. As shown in Table 3, feature CF_0 represents the total input degrees of all classes in code changes and CF_1 represents the total output degrees. In addition, feature CF_2 and CF_3 represent the average number of classes' input degrees and output degrees in code changes, respectively.

(2) Method-to-Class. For class C_j and method M_i of C_i, if C_j emerges in M_i and not try define an attribute or invoke static attributes and methods, M_i and C_j satisfy the Method-to-Class coupling rule. The instance of rule including *Type-Casting(TC)*, *Instanceof (IO)* and *.class(DC)* et al. Feature CF_4 represents

Table 3. Code coupling features

Granularity	Feature	Descriptions
Class-to-Class	CF_0	Total input degrees of all classes
	CF_1	Total output degrees of all classes
	CF_2	Average input degrees of all classes
	CF_3	Average output degrees of all classes
Method-to-Class	CF_4	Total number of Method-to-Class coupling of all methods
	CF_5	Average number of Method-to-Class of all methods
Method-to-Attribute	CF_6	Total number of Method-to-Attribute coupling of all methods
	CF_7	Average number of Method-to-Attribute coupling of all methods
Method-to-Method	CF_8	Total number of Method-to-Method coupling of all methods
	CF_9	Average number of Method-to-Method coupling of all methods

the total number of Method-to-Class couplings of all methods in code changes. Feature CF_5 represents the average among methods.

(3) Method-to-Attribute. According to object-oriented programming mechanism, method-to-attribute coupling rule refers to a coupling relation between M_i contained in C_i and A_j contained in C_j. One of the most common is *Static Attribute Invoking*. Feature CF_6 is used to count the number of relations in code changes. Feature CF_7 represents the average among methods.

(4) Method-to-Method. This rule builds coupling relations at method level, which refers to a relation between M_i contained in C_i and M_j contained in C_j. The prime example are M_i invokes static method M_j of C_j(*Static Method Invoking*) and M_i invokes construction method M_j of C_j(*Construction Method Invoking*). In Table 3, feature CF_8 refers to the total number of this rule within methods of code changes. Feature CF_9 represents the average among methods.

4   Experiment

In this section, we present the performance of our approach on 2 open source projects. The goal of our study is to accurately predict if the submission can be accepted in current review and the review times of code changes.

4.1   Data Pre-processing

We choose 2 popular open source software's review data as our data set: Ecplise[2] and OpenDaylight[3]. Eclipse is an integrated development environment (IDE) used in computer programming, and is the most widely used Java IDE. Open-Daylight is a highly available, modular, extensible, scalable and multi-protocol controller infrastructure built for SDN deployments on modern heterogeneous multi-vendor networks. Table 4 details the selected projects including name, size and time span.

Table 4. The selected projects

Projects	Time span	No. of reviews
Eclipse	2016.1–2018.5	9455
OpenDaylight	2017.1–2018.8	6403

There was some noise in the data we collected from Gerrit. To that end we performed three pre-processing steps on the raw data:

(1) We focused only on the reviews that change files contain Java files, which are used to extract code coupling and code modifying information. This resulted in 743 reviews being excluded.

---

[2] https://www.eclipse.org/.

[3] https://www.opendaylight.org/.

(2) We also eliminated those data that had not been reviewed owning to the mission of label of review times. In addition, some submission in our dataset are clear outliers in terms of review times. For example, a submission took 150 times of review whereas the average review times of submissions are 5 times. To account for submission that were 'forgotten', we removed submissions in excess of 20 review times. Moreover, the proportion of these submission is less than 1%.

(3) To account for inactive developers in project we removed the least productive developers. Some developers wrote a small number of submissions. This might be because the developer are not the core maintainer of project. Ordering the developers by the number of their submission we excluded those developers submit less than 2 times. This resulted in the number of developers reduced from 612 to 488.

4.2 Research Question

Our study aims at addressing the following research questions:

- **RQ1: How effective is our method in predicting the acceptance of submissions?**
  Developers are primarily interested in getting their code change accepted as quickly as possible. We try to use features extracted from review information and code modifying information to help developers estimate if their submission can be accepted with only 1 review.
- **RQ2: How effective is our method in predicting the review times of submissions?**
  For most of submissions, it will take multiple reviews. Submissions requiring multiple reviews will consume a lot of labour and time. Predicting the review times required is helpful for managers to make reasonable arrangements. Therefore, we are more concerned about submissions that need review more than 10 times.

In order to evaluate the effectiveness of our method, we measured the *precision*, *recall* and F_1 of classification result. The *precision*, *recall*, F_1 are computed as following:

$$precision = \frac{TP}{TP + FP} \tag{1}$$

$$recall = \frac{TP}{TP + FN} \tag{2}$$

$$F_1 = 2 * \frac{precision * recall}{precision + recall} \tag{3}$$

$$accuracy = \frac{TP + FN}{TP + FN + TN + FP} \tag{4}$$

Where TP is the number of true positives(accepted reviews correctly categorized), FP is the number of false positives(accepted reviews incorrectly categorized), TN is the number of true negatives(not accepted reviews correctly categorized), and FN is the number of false negatives(not accepted reviews incorrectly categorized). Therefore, the *precision* is the percentage of positive instances identified by our classifier that are actually positive instances. The *recall* is the percentage of true positive instances that are successfully retrieved by our classifier. The F_1 is the weighted harmonic mean of the precision and the recall and can be used as a comprehensive indicator of the combined precision and recall values. *Accuracy* is also used as a statistical measure of how well a binary classification test correctly identifies or excludes a condition. That is, the *accuracy* is the proportion of true results (both true positives and true negatives) among the total number of cases examined. These four metrics are also suitable for negative instances.

4.3 Results

RQ1: How effective is our method in predicting the acceptance of submissions?
By default, the target of this research is to investigate how accurate our method can achieve in predicting the acceptance of submission. We used *XGBoost* [18] to train our model owing to its effectiveness. Additionally, the result is compared with others machine learning algorithms including *LR*, *SVM*, *RF* and *ANN*. Then 10-fold cross-validation approach is used to validate our classifier. According to 10-fold cross evaluation mechanism, the dataset was randomly partitioned into 10 subset. Of the 10 subset, a single subset was retained as the validation data for testing the model, and the remaining 9 subsets were used as training data. Based on the ten pairs of training and testing data, we trained and evaluated 10 models. The final results is gotten by average out the prediction for individual model.

For the research, we define submissions which got acceptance in 1 review as positive and submissions that needed to review more than once as negative. Table 5 shows the distribution of positive and negative data. We obtained 2,373 positive instances and 6,551 negative instances in project of Eclipse, 1,598 positive instances and 4,807 negative instances in project OpenDayLight.

Table 5. The positive and negative instances in the dataset

Projects	Positive	Negative
Eclipse	2905	6551
OpenDaylight	1598	4807

We applied our classifier in the dataset of Ecilpse and OpenDaylight respectively. As shown in Table 6, our result is compared with selected machine learning algorithms by means of *recall*, *precision*, F_1 and *accuracy*. The result of our model archived the best *accuracy* of 79.72% and 80.03% for two datasets. The *accuracy* of different machine learning models for the different datasets ranged from 73.34% to 80.03%, which indicates that the proposed features is effective in predicting submission acceptance. In project of Eclipse, with regard to negative instances that not be accepted in first review, the *precision*, *recall* and F_1 of our model were 82.16%, 90.56% and 86.16%. This considerable result indicates that the greatest part of negative instances could be correctly categorized. On the other hand, all models exhibited relatively poor performance on positive instances, and the values of *precision*, *recall* and F_1 of our model were 71.63%, 54.80% and 62.10%. A similar situation exists in OpenDaylight. The poor performance on the positive instances might be caused by the unbalanced positive and negative instances in datasets due to the number of negative instances were almost 2 times and 3 times higher than that of positive instances. According to a binary classification problem, the incorrectly categorized negative instances were doubled to lower the performance of positive instances.

Another thing worth noting is that, our model got lower *recall* on negative instances than other models. The values of *recall* of our model were 90.56% and 87.40%, while random forest archived 94.23% on dataset of Eclipse and artificial neural networks archived 96.71% on dataset of OpenDaylight. However, XGBoost outperforms other models in term of the *Accuracy*, which show that XGBoost are more suitable to handle the unbalanced dataset.

Table 6. Results of RQ1

Projects	Method	Positive instances			Negative instances			*Accuracy*
		Precision	*Recall*	F_1	*Precision*	*Recall*	F_1	
Eclipse	LR	69.39	33.72	45.38	74.84	92.98	82.93	73.99
	SVM	69.89	42.98	53.22	77.24	91.27	83.67	75.79
	RF	76.85	40.00	52.55	76.85	94.23	84.69	76.85
	ANN	63.21	49.42	55.47	78.37	86.44	82.21	74.58
	XGBoost	**71.63**	**54.80**	**62.10**	**82.16**	**90.56**	**86.16**	**79.72**
OpenDaylight	LR	60.47	33.66	43.24	78.36	78.36	84.66	74.86
	SVM	41.38	19.41	26.43	77.52	90.10	83.72	73.34
	RF	51.75	43.04	46.99	82.32	86.86	84.53	76.06
	ANN	49.18	9.71	16.22	76.59	96.71	85.49	75.26
	XGBoost	**50.39**	**50.78**	**50.58**	**87.57**	**87.40**	**87.49**	**80.03**

RQ2: How effective is our method in predicting the review times of submissions?

For review process in practice, the exact number of review times is not necessary for us, instead, we are concerned about the approximate times required for our submission. As shown in Fig. 2, we investigated 1000 reviews about the relevance between review times and average time. It is shown that when the review times is increased, days spent on review of a submission is increased. As we can observe, average time of submission that review under 2 times will not exceed one day. Submissions needed 2 to 6 review times take no more than a week. For submissions that needed morn than 6 times, the time required to review has increased dramatically. Submissions with 20 review times spent more than 60 days.

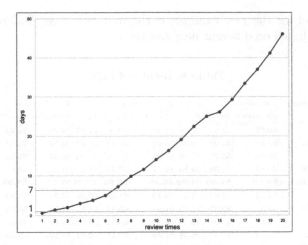

Fig. 2. Relevance between review times and average time

Accordingly, we firstly divide submissions into three categories according to their review times. Submissions in our datasets are 1 to 20 review times. Submissions with 1 review times is finished in a short time which we regard as a easy work and submissions within 2–6 review times may be regard as a normal work that it presumably needs more than a week. As for submissions within 7 to 20 review times, it might be a trouble for developers, which we regard as a hard work. Details of divided datasets is shown in Table 7.

Table 7. The distribution of the divided datasets

Projects	1 Reviews	2–6 Reviews	7–20 Reviews
Eclipse	2905	5203	1287
OpenDaylight	1598	3327	1338

As we can observed, both datasets consist of extremely unbalanced samples. We employed SMOTE algorithm [19] to resample minority class when training the model. SMOTE is a proposed oversampling approach in which the minority class is oversampled by creating "synthetic" examples rather than by oversampling with replacement. In order to avoid the over-fitting problem while expanding minority class regions SMOTE generates new instances by operating within the existing feature space. New instance values are derived from interpolation rather than extrapolation, so they still carry relevance to the underlying data set. To create a synthetic example, SMOTE searches for the nearest neighbors (having the same class label) of a minority-class example. A new synthetic example is then created at a random point on the line connecting the two genuine samples (this assumes that each dimension of feature space belongs forms a ratio scale), and class label for the new example is the minority class. Different synthetic examples are based on different neighbor pairs.

Table 8. Results of RQ2

Projects	Methods	1 Reviews			2–6 Reviews			7–20 Reviews			Accuracy
		Precision	Recall	F_1	Precision	Recall	F_1	precision	Recall	F_1	
Eclipse	LR	66.67	22.64	33.79	61.20	60.90	61.05	29.70	74.24	42.42	50.72
	SVM	64.04	43.92	52.10	64.07	57.18	60.04	33.57	71.21	45.63	54.98
	RF	60.00	54.73	57.24	64.96	72.14	68.36	46.31	35.61	40.26	61.52
	ANN	63.81	40.20	49.33	62.57	72.73	67.27	41.32	49.62	45.09	59.23
	XGBoost	**69.59**	**54.90**	**61.38**	**66.45**	**80.94**	**72.98**	**57.23**	35.99	44.19	**66.42**
OpenDaylight	LR	52.14	23.62	32.52	59.73	61.68	60.69	44.22	65.89	52.93	53.31
	SVM	44.48	23.95	31.03	57.58	65.11	61.11	47.08	55.96	51.13	52.75
	RF	48.57	44.01	46.18	59.10	69.31	63.80	54.09	39.40	45.59	55.87
	ANN	55.10	17.47	26.54	57.88	62.31	60.01	43.10	66.23	52.22	52.19
	XGBoost	**60.10**	37.54	**46.22**	**61.03**	**77.57**	**68.31**	**58.61**	47.35	**52.38**	**60.42**

We also trained multiple machine learning model via divided datasets and compared their effects with *XGBoost*. The result is shown in Table 8. The result of our model archived the best *accuracy* of 66.42% and 60.42% for two datasets. The *accuracy* of different machine learning models for the different datasets ranged from 50.72% to 66.42%, which indicates that out approach is effective in predicting review times. With regard to individual level reviews in Eclipse, the F_1 of our approach were 61.38%, 72.98% and 44.19% that correspond to 1 review, 2–6 reviews, 7–20 reviews, respectively. This result indicates that though we applied SMOTE algorithm to resample minority class, the problem of unbalanced data still has an effect on our results. As the result shown, all models present a poor score in minority class.

As we can observed, our approach exhibited relatively poor *recall* on 7–20 reviews for both projects than some models, even though our approach achived the best F_1. The values of *recall* of our approach were 35.99% and 47.35% for Eclipse and OpenDaylight, while logistic regression archived 74.24% for Eclipse and artificial neural networks archived 66.23% for OpenDaylight.

5   Related Work

A large body of work has qualitatively analyzed the modern code review process. Oleksii et al. [20] found that both personal metrics and participation metrics are associated with the quality of the code review process. Thongtanunam et al. [21] took a case study of 196,712 reviews spread across the Android, Qt, and OpenStack open source projects and found that the amount of review participation in the past is a significant indicator of patches that will suffer from poor review participation. Baysal et al. [8] found that non-technical factors can significantly impact code review, such as patch Size, priority and component. These research results inspired us to consider multiple influence factors in predict the time-cost in code review. In addition, Weissgerber et al. [22] conducted a quantitative analysis to investigate how long does it take for a patch to be accepted and found that smaller code changes are more likely to be accepted. Rigby et al. [23] found general principles of code review practives and the benefit of code review for knowledge sharing among developers.

Another of the practices focuses on the tool-based code review, which has been widely used in both industrial software and open-source software [24,25]. Microsoft uses CodeFlow to track the state (i.e., signed off, waiting, reviewing) of software participants (e.g., author or reviewer) in the development process; VMware [26] developed the open-source ReviewBoard, to reduce the human effort in peer code reviews. ReviewBoard uses multiple static analysis tools to automate the checks for coding standard violations and common defect patterns, and publish code review using the output from these tools. Facebook proposed a code review system, named Phabricator [27], which allows reviewers to take over a change and commit it themselves and provides hooks for automatic static analysis or continuous build/test integration. Besides, the open source Gerrit is a web-based code review tool [28]. Software developers in a team can review each other's modifications on their source code using Gerrit and approve or reject those changes.

6 Conclusion and Future Work

Code review is an essential and vital part of modern software development. Although studying the review process has a long research history, we are the first to present an model that predicts the submission acceptance and review times. To evaluate our approach, we used two datasets and more than 15,000 review data that we collected from Gerrit Code Review. Our experiment showed that our mining algorithm is effective and useful. The future research agenda mainly focus on the accuracy improvement of our approach. Firstly, taking more dimensions of features relating to code changes or review into consideration. Secondly, extracting inherent information from these features and combining features to attain discriminative information.

Acknowledgments. This research is supported by the National Natural Science Foundation of China (61902441, 61902105), China Postdoctoral Science Foundation (2018M640855).

References

1. McIntosh, S., Kamei, Y., Adams, B., Hassan, A.E.: An empirical study of the impact of modern code review practices on software quality. Empirical Softw. Eng. **21**(5), 2146–2189 (2016)
2. Huang, Y., Zheng, Q., Chen, X., Xiong, Y., Liu, Z., Luo, X.: Mining version control system for automatically generating commit comment. In: 2017 ACM/IEEE International Symposium on Empirical Software Engineering and Measurement (ESEM), pp. 414–423, November 2017

3. Huang, Y., Chen, X., Liu, Z., Luo, X., Zheng, Z.: Using discriminative feature in software entities for relevance identification of code changes. J. Softw.: Evol. Process **29**(7), e1859 (2017). e1859 smr.1859

4. Fagan, M.: Design and code inspections to reduce errors in program development. In: Broy, M., Denert, E. (eds.) Software Pioneers, pp. 575–607. Springer, Heidelberg (2002). https://doi.org/10.1007/978-3-642-59412-0_35

5. McIntosh, S., Kamei, Y., Adams, B., Hassan, A.E.: The impact of code review coverage and code review participation on software quality: a case study of the QT, VTK, and ITK projects. In: Proceedings of the 11th Working Conference on Mining Software Repositories, pp. 192–201. ACM (2014)

6. Huang, Y., Chen, X., Zou, Q., Luo, X.: A probabilistic neural network-based approach for related software changes detection. In: 2014 21st Asia-Pacific Software Engineering Conference, vol. 1, pp. 279–286, December 2014

7. Huang, Y., Jia, N., Chen, X., Hong, K., Zheng, Z.: Salient-class location: help developers understand code change in code review. In: Proceedings of the 2018 26th ACM Joint Meeting on European Software Engineering Conference and Symposium on the Foundations of Software Engineering, ser. ESEC/FSE 2018, pp. 770–774. ACM, New York (2018)

8. Baysal, O., Kononenko, O., Holmes, R., Godfrey, M.W.: The influence of non-technical factors on code review. In: 2013 20th Working Conference on Reverse Engineering (WCRE), pp. 122–131. IEEE (2013)

9. Chen, H., Huang, Y., Liu, Z., Chen, X., Zhou, F., Luo, X.: Automatically detecting the scopes of source code comments. J. Syst. Softw. **153**, 45–63 (2019)

10. Huang, Y., Kong, Q., Jia, N., Chen, X., Zheng, Z.: Recommending differentiated code to support smart contract update. In: 2019 IEEE/ACM 27th International Conference on Program Comprehension (ICPC), pp. 260–270, May 2019

11. Huang, Y., Hu, X., Jia, N., Chen, X., Xiong, Y., Zheng, Z.: Learning code context information to predict comment locations. IEEE Trans. Reliab. 1–18 (2019)

12. Thongtanunam, P., Tantithamthavorn, C., Kula, R.G., Yoshida, N., Iida, H., Matsumoto, K.-I.: Who should review my code? A file location-based code-reviewer recommendation approach for modern code review. In: 2015 IEEE 22nd International Conference on Software Analysis, Evolution and Reengineering (SANER), pp. 141–150. IEEE (2015)

13. Eyolfson, J., Tan, L., Lam, P.: Do time of day and developer experience affect commit bugginess? In: Proceedings of the 8th Working Conference on Mining Software Repositories, ser. MSR 2011, pp. 153–162. ACM, New York (2011)

14. Huang, Y., Jia, N., Zhou, Q., Chen, X., Yingfei, X., Luo, X.: Poster: guiding developers to make informative commenting decisions in source code. In: 2018 IEEE/ACM 40th International Conference on Software Engineering: Companion (ICSE-Companion), pp. 260–261, May 2018

15. Hassan, A.E., Holt, R.C.: Predicting change propagation in software systems. In: Proceedings of the 20th IEEE International Conference on Software Maintenance, pp. 284–293. IEEE (2004)

16. Malik, H., Hassan, A.E.: Supporting software evolution using adaptive change propagation heuristics. In: IEEE International Conference on Software Maintenance, ICSM 2008, pp. 177–186. IEEE 2008 (2008)

17. Ying, A.T., Murphy, G.C., Ng, R., Chu-Carroll, M.C.: Predicting source code changes by mining change history. IEEE Trans. Softw. Eng. **30**(9), 574–586 (2004)

18. Chen, T., Guestrin, C.: XGBoost: a scalable tree boosting system. In: Proceedings of the 22nd ACM SIGKDD International Conference on Knowledge Discovery and Data Mining, pp. 785–794. ACM (2016)

19. Chawla, N.V., Bowyer, K.W., Hall, L.O., Kegelmeyer, W.P.: SMOTE: synthetic minority over-sampling technique. J. Artif. Intell. Res. **16**, 321–357 (2002)
20. Kononenko, O., Baysal, O., Guerrouj, L., Cao, Y., Godfrey, M.W.: Investigating code review quality: do people and participation matter? In: 2015 IEEE International Conference on Software Maintenance and Evolution (ICSME), pp. 111–120. IEEE (2015)
21. Thongtanunam, P., McIntosh, S., Hassan, A.E., Iida, H.: Review participation in modern code review. Empirical Softw. Eng. **22**(2), 768–817 (2017)
22. Weißgerber, P., Neu, D., Diehl, S.: Small patches get in! In: Proceedings of the 2008 International Working Conference on Mining Software Repositories, pp. 67–76. ACM (2008)
23. Rigby, P.C., Bird, C.: Convergent contemporary software peer review practices. In: Proceedings of the 2013 9th Joint Meeting on Foundations of Software Engineering, pp. 202–212. ACM (2013)
24. Bosu, A., Carver, J.C., Bird, C., Orbeck, J., Chockley, C.: Process aspects and social dynamics of contemporary code review: insights from open source development and industrial practice at microsoft. IEEE Trans. Softw. Eng. **43**(1), 56–75 (2017)
25. Kononenko, O., Baysal, O., Godfrey, M.W.: Code review quality: how developers see it. In: 2016 IEEE/ACM 38th International Conference on Software Engineering (ICSE), pp. 1028–1038. IEEE (2016)
26. Balachandran, V.: Reducing human effort and improving quality in peer code reviews using automatic static analysis and reviewer recommendation. In: Proceedings of the 2013 International Conference on Software Engineering, pp. 931–940. IEEE Press (2013)
27. Tsotsis, A.: Meet Phabricator, the Witty Code Review Tool Built Inside Facebook (2006)
28. Gerrit. https://www.gerritcodereview.com/

Manual Audit for BitUnits Contracts

Siqi Lu[1,2], Haopeng Fan[1,2(✉)], Yongjuan Wang[1,2], Huizhe Mi[1], and Ling Qin[3]

[1] PLA Strategic Support Force Information Engineering University,
Zhengzhou 450000, People's Republic of China
fanhaopeng15gc@sina.com
[2] Henan Provincial Key Laboratory of Network Cryptography,
Zhengzhou 450000, People's Republic of China
[3] Hunan Agricultural University, Changsha 410128, People's Republic of China

Abstract. In the blockchain 2.0 era, smart contracts based on blockchain technology have been widely used in many fields such as sharing economy, digital payment, and financial asset disposal because of its dispersion, observability, verifiability and automatic execution. With the widespread application of smart contracts, the researchers gradually found many types of security problems, so the audit of smart contracts has become the vital way to ensure its security. This paper introduces the implementation mechanism of smart contract model, and summarizes 11 kinds of high frequency smart contract vulnerabilities, such as transaction order dependence, constructor out of control, denial of service, etc. Then, this paper selects the newly released BitUnits contract for auditing, find out its security hole and give the solution.

Keywords: Smart contracts · Manual audit · BitUnits contract · Vulnerability analysis · Contract security

1 Introduction

In 2008, Nakamoto proposed the concept of blockchain [3]. The combination of blockchain and smart contracts also made the development of blockchain technology into the 2.0 era [2]. Ethereum has developed a virtual machine that can execute Turing's complete scripting language for the development of smart contracts [4]. It provides a secure and credible execution environment for smart contracts and becomes the basic guarantee for the rapid development of smart contracts. Compared with traditional contracts, smart contracts have received wide attention due to their high efficiency, low cost and high degree of automation, but they also expose various security issues, such as The 'The DAO' project, 'Parity Wallet' and so on. According to statistics from the Token Club Research Institute on blockchain security incidents in recent years, the total number of attacks was 123, of which smart contracts accounted for 21%. To develop a complete smart contract, we need to start from the following points: Before the contract is developed, it is necessary to grasp the types of the related vulnerabilities and understand the latest security vulnerabilities to avoid security risks.

© Springer Nature Singapore Pte Ltd. 2020
Z. Zheng et al. (Eds.): BlockSys 2019, CCIS 1156, pp. 476–482, 2020.
https://doi.org/10.1007/978-981-15-2777-7_38

During the development process, developers need to pay attention to the warnings of the compiler tools. And make timely changes, the current mainstream compilation tools are Remix-IDE, truffle, etc. After the completion of the contract compilation, it is necessary to analyze the integrity of the contract function and the security of the contract to ensure that there are no security risks. Of the three steps, it is especially important to analyze the completed contract, which is the audit of the smart contract [1].

2   Basic Knowledge

2.1   Smart Contract Overview

Smart Contract [7] is a computer protocol designed to disseminate, verify or enforce contracts in an informational manner, essentially an executable computer program [6]. Figure 1 shows the smart contract model:

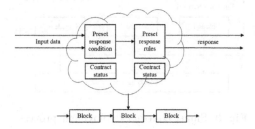

Fig. 1. Smart contract model

2.2   Smart Contract Execution Mechanism

Operating Environment
Each Ethereum node runs an Ethereum virtual machine (EVM). The EVM cannot access the network and file system and cannot communicate with other processes. Therefore, it can provide a secure and stable environment for the operation of smart contracts. Figure 2 shows the architecture of the EVM [5].

Deployment Process
The smart contract is deployed to the blockchain by sending a transaction. The deployment process is shown in Fig. 3 [9]. The contract is compiled into the EVM bytecode by the development tool, and then the bytecode is stored in the transaction data. Field, the transaction is sent to the Ethereum network via the RPC interface. After the other nodes on the network receive the transaction, they are executed through the EVM and reach a consensus and deployed to the blockchain.

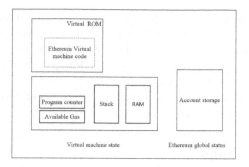

Fig. 2. EVM virtual machine architecture

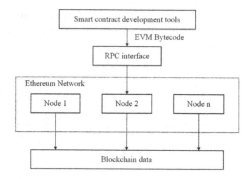

Fig. 3. Smart contract deployment process

Contract Call

Ethereum interacts with smart contracts deployed on the blockchain through the Application Binary Interface (ABI) in conjunction with the RPC interface [9]. First, the transaction is constructed. The SHA3 signature of the function to be called and other data to be passed in the parameters are passed to the Input field, and then the transaction is signed with the private key to Ethereum. After that, each node verifies and executes the transaction, and update the contract status information as soon as possible after transaction.

2.3   Smart Contract Common Vulnerabilities

At present, the vulnerabilities of smart contracts are mainly divided into three levels: Solidity, EVM and blockchain. The following article will refer to 11 vulnerabilities with high frequency of occurrence [8].

The integer overflow vulnerability

The Ethereum Virtual Machine (EVM) is an integer that specifies a fixed size data type. This means that an integer variable can only have a range of numerical representations. The integer overflow problem in the solidity language is divided into multiplication overflow, addition overflow, and subtraction overflow.

The denial of service vulnerability

The denial of service vulnerability, DOS, usually makes the original code logic inoperable, resulting in the consumption of Ethereum and Gas and the failure to provide services.

Time stamp dependence

A timestamp is a complete, verifiable data that can represent a piece of data that has been stored before a certain time, usually a sequence of characters that uniquely identifies a moment in time. In the blockchain, some smart contracts use the timestamp of the block as a trigger for certain operations.

The constructor is out of control

Constructors are special functions that are called only once when the contract is created and are used to initialize certain state variables. Prior to version 0.4.22, the constructor was defined as a function with the same name as the contract.

The default visibility (Visibility)

Functions in Solidity have visibility specifiers. For functions that are not qualified with the visibility specifier, the visibility defaults to public and can be called externally by the user.

Thort address/parameter attack

When parameters are passed to the smart contract, the parameters are encoded according to the ABI specification, and the EVM virtual machine relies on the specification to identify each field. When an attacker launches an attack, the last byte of the destination address sent by the token can be removed, and the destination address can be modified to modify the number of tokens sent.

Uninitialized storage pointer

The internal variable that is not initialized may point to other storage variables in the contract, resulting in a vulnerability.

tx.origin used for authentication

tx.origin is a global variable in Solidity that iterates through the entire stack and returns the address of the account that was originally sent (or exchanged). Using this variable to authenticate in a smart contract makes the contract vulnerable to attacks like web phishing.

The call of the delegate call

Solidity provides delegatecall function for implementing mutual calls and interactions between contracts. The illegal use of delegatecall is an important factor causing Parity Wallet security vulnerability.

Trading order dependence

In The DAO project, the splitDAO function that executes the split asset calls the Transfer event and the withdrawReward function, there is a phenomenon that the attacker has received funds but there is still a balance in the DAO record. That is a transaction order dependency vulnerability [10].

Re-enter

In TheDao project, the attacker has the opportunity to call the splitDAO function twice, so the purpose of multiple withdrawals is achieved. This type of vulnerability is a re-entry vulnerability.

3   Manual Audit for BitUnits Contracts

3.1   Contract Introduction

The BitUnits contract uses PoSToken as the token. PoSToken is the first Proof-of-Stake smart contract token on the Ethereum platform. It is based on the ERC20 token standard and implements all standard methods. BitUnits contracts implement bank-like functions, which provide users with the following functions: First, the revenue function, users will receive additional reward tokens when they hold PoSToken for more than a certain period of time; second, the transfer function, users can contract to other contracts or The address is sent to the token. Figure 4 shows the specific workflow of the contract:

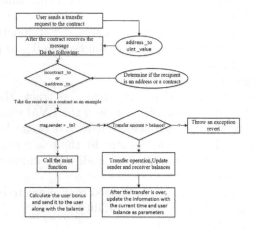

Fig. 4. Contract workflow

3.2   Contract Analysis

The overall development of the BitUnits contract is more rigorous, but there are still security risks. The problem code exists in getProinOfStakeReward(). The getCoinAge() function is called when the important parameter coinAge for calculating the reward value is obtained. In the code, when the contract calculates coinAge, it needs to take the user's previous currency record as a parameter. If the transferIns[address].length is too large when executing the for loop, the Gas value spent performing the operation exceeds the contract setting. The risk of Gas Limit causes the user to fail to properly withdraw assets.

In response to the above problem, if an illegal user has an intention to attack a user, the token can be continuously sent to the user, and the number of each transmission can be small. After a plurality of times, the transaction information recorded by the user address reaches a certain amount, and when the user sends When the message is taken out of the asset, the situation shown in Fig. 5 will appear:

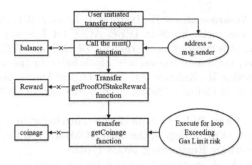

Fig. 5. Attack effect

Since the coinage parameter cannot be obtained, the getproofofStakeReward() function cannot calculate the reward. The mint function cannot update the balance for the user, and the user cannot get the bonus. Although the illegal users paid a higher price, they succeeded in achieving the goal of making the target users unable to retrieve the rewards in a short time, and the attack was completed.

4 Conclusions

This paper has carried out three aspects of work, one is to study the technology of smart contract, the related research on the smart contract work process, deployment process and calling process; the second is to summarize the existing high-frequency vulnerabilities; the third is to conduct a manual audit for the BitUnits contract. And found its vulnerability. From the current point of view, auditing is currently the main way to solve contract security problems, but its efficiency is low. If the rapid development of artificial intelligence technology is applied to the audit work, its combination with automation tools will combine the experience of manual auditing with the efficiency of tools, which will take the security of smart contracts to a new level.

References

1. He, H., Yan, A., Chen, Z.: Overview of intelligent contract technology and application based on blockchain. J. Comput. Res. Dev. **55**(11), 112–126 (2018)
2. Li, H., Sun, J., Yang, Y., et al.: A preliminary study on Ethereum based on blockchain 2.0. China Financ. Comput. **6**, 57–60 (2017)
3. Nakamoto, S.: Bitcoin: a peer-to-peer electronic cash system. Manubot (2019)
4. Fu, M., Wu, L., Hong, Z., Feng, W.: Research on intelligent contract security vulnerability mining technology [J/OL]. Comput. Appl. 1–8 (2019)
5. Huang, K., Zhang, S., Jin, S.: Research on block contract intelligent contract security. Inf. Secur. Res. **3**, 192–206 (2019)

6. Tikhomirov, S., Voskresenskaya, E., Ivanitskiy, I.: SmartCheck: static analysis of ethereum smart contracts. In: 2018 IEEE ACM 1st International Workshop on Emerging Trends in Software Engineering for Blockchain (WETSEB) (2018)
7. Bocek, T., Stiller, B.: Smart contracts – blockchains in the wings. In: Linnhoff-Popien, C., Schneider, R., Zaddach, M. (eds.) Digital Marketplaces Unleashed, pp. 169–184. Springer, Heidelberg (2018). https://doi.org/10.1007/978-3-662-49275-8_19
8. Jiang, B., Liu, Y., Chan, W.K.: ContractFuzzer: fuzzing smart contracts for vulnerability detection. In: Proceedings of the 33rd ACM/IEEE International Conference on Automated Software Engineering. ACM (2018)
9. Sergey, I., Hobor, A.: A concurrent perspective on smart contracts (2017)
10. Atzei, N., Bartoletti, M., Cimoli, T.: A survey of attacks on ethereum smart contracts (SoK). In: Maffei, M., Ryan, M. (eds.) POST 2017. LNCS, vol. 10204, pp. 164–186. Springer, Heidelberg (2017). https://doi.org/10.1007/978-3-662-54455-6_8

The Transformation from Traditional Application to Blockchain-Based Application

Zhanghui Liu[1,2], Zhihao Huang[1,2], Xing Chen[1,2(✉)], and Yan Chen[1,2]

[1] College of Mathematics and Computer Science, Fuzhou University,
Fuzhou 350108, China
`chenxing@fzu.edu.cn`
[2] Fujian Key Laboratory of Network Computing and Intelligent Information
Processing, Fuzhou 350108, China

Abstract. Traditional application uses centralized database and the data is managed and maintained by a single institution. Blockchain is a decentralized, non-tamperable, traceable, multi-party distributed database, which can greatly improve the security of data. It is crucial to transfer traditional application to blockchain-based application for many application scenarios. However, as a new field, most developers are not familiar with blockchain technology. Therefore we propose a method to transfer the traditional application to application based on Hyperledger Fabric. First, we finish the secondary development of Fabric-sdk-java and define a set of API mapping rules. Secondly, we compare the storage model between Mysql and CouchDB, and implement a SQL-Fabric transformation engine through the smart contract, which can parse SQL and automatically transform into read and write operations on the distributed ledger.

Keywords: Blockchain · Smart contract · Traditional application · Blockchain-based application · Transformation

1 Introduction

Traditional relational database and nosql database are managed and maintained by a single institution, which has absolute control over all data. Blockchain is a decentralized, tamper-proof, traceable multi-party distributed database, which can integrate many isolated databases unilaterally maintained by tradition and store them distributed on multiple nodes jointly maintained by many parties. Neither party can fully control these data and can only update them in accordance with strict rules and consensus, so as to realize information sharing and supervision among trusted parties, it is precisely because of the characteristics of blockchain, such as data is untamperable, decentralized and traceable, it is necessary to transfer the traditional application to blockchain-based application for many application scenarios, but this work is complicated and inefficient. In particular, blockchain is a new technology and few developers are familiar with

© Springer Nature Singapore Pte Ltd. 2020
Z. Zheng et al. (Eds.): BlockSys 2019, CCIS 1156, pp. 483–488, 2020.
https://doi.org/10.1007/978-981-15-2777-7_39

blockchain technology. To transfer an application to the blockchain-based application, developers need to be familiar with the operation method of middleware and the coding of smart contract, which virtually increases the costs learning and developing. Therefore we propose a method to transfer the traditional application to the application based on Hyperledger Fabric [1], which can improve the efficiency of application transplantation to a certain extent and reduce the cost of learning and development for developers. In our approach, firstly, we finish the secondary development of Fabric-sdk-java [2] and define a set of API mapping rules in application layer. Secondly, we use smart contract [3] to implement an SQL-fabric transformation engine, which can parse SQL and transfer to the data read-write operation on the distributed ledger.

2   Preliminary

Hyperledger Fabric is one of the Hyperledger projects sponsored by the Linux Foundation. Hyperledger Fabric is released version 1.0 in July 2017, and the latest version was released in August 2019. Unlike Bitcoin [4] and Ethereum [5], Hyperledger Fabric is not a running public blockchain network, but an open source framework for creating licensed blockchain networks. Hyperledger Fabric is the first blockchain framework to apply general-purpose programming language to implement smart contracts (referred as chaincode [6] in Hyperledger Fabric). The execution of smart contracts is within the scope of a channel. A channel is a logical grouping of a subset of participants. It securely tracks its execution history in an append-only replicated ledger data structure and has no cryptocurrency built in.

3   Approach

As shown in Fig. 1, the traditional application based on centralized database (taking Mysql as an example) can be structurally divided into three parts:

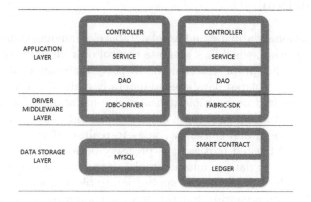

Fig. 1. Application architecture comparison

application layer, driver middleware layer and data storage layer. The difference between traditional application and blockchain-based application is that the underlying data of traditional application is stored in centralized database, while the data of the blockchain-based application is stored by all the joined nodes in the blockchain network, In our work, we proposes a method to transfer the traditional application to blockchain-based application based on the open source framework Hyperledger Fabric. Data is stored by the peer nodes. Each node accesses the underlying data ledger through the smart contract. Application layer interacts with blockchain network through Fabric-sdk. Our work can be divided into the following three parts.

3.1 Application Layer API Conversion

In traditional applications, application layer interact with the Mysql by invoking JDBC API. For application based on Hyperledger Fabric, Fabric-sdk-java API shall be invoked. To convert the traditional applications, the first is to convert related API in the application layer. Therefore, we developed a set of API similar with JDBC and defined the API mapping rules in the application layer. Users can convert the traditional methods of invoking and driving middleware just by revising codes according to the rules. As shown in Table 1, all the mapped API in the table are provided by the secondary development of driver middleware.

Table 1. API mapping rules

	Source API	Mapped API
(1)	Class.forName("com.mysql.jdbc");	Class.forName("com.FabricUtil");
(2)	Connection conn = DriverManager.getConnection(url, user, pw);	HFConnection conn = new HFConnection();
(3)	Statement stmt = conn.createStatement();	HFStatement stmt = conn.createHFStatement();
(4)	ResultSet rs = stmt.executeQuery(sql);	HFResultSet rs = stmt.executeQuery(sql);

3.2 Secondary Development of Driver Middleware

Driving middleware is an interactive tool between the application layer and the data storage layer, But the operation of Fabric-sdk provided by Hyperledger is very tedious, and the network configuration information is highly coupled with the code. We have finished the secondary development of Fabric-sdk-java and encapsulated the low-level interaction details between the middleware and the blockchain network, which has provided the application layer with a invocation API that is simple and easy to use. This tool decouples configuration information and code highly through the form of XML configuration file and passes SQL as a parameter to the smart contract and processes the returned data sets, including data type conversion, etc. Figure 2 shows the flow chart of the tool.

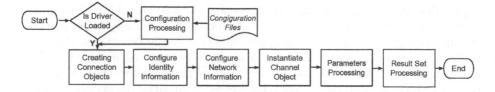

Fig. 2. Driver middleware

3.3   Data Storage Layer Conversion

In the application based on Hyperledger Fabric, smart contract receives parameters and triggers the specified method to realize the read-write operation on distributed ledger. The underlying data of Hyperledger Fabric can be stored in either file or database form on disk. CouchDB [7] is used as underlying state databases of Hyperledger Fabric. In our approach, we first compare Mysql with CouchDB storage model and unify a set of mapping specifications of storage structure. Then we implemented an SQL-Fabric transformation engine using smart contract, which can parse the SQL statements and automatically transfer to the data read-write operation of the distributed ledger.

Storage Structure Comparison. The storage structure of relational database is very different from that of CouchDB. In relational databases, data is stored in relational model, while CouchDB is a document-oriented key-value database, which does not conform to the normative standard and can store JSON directly, relational database consists of three hierarchical concept groups: database, table and record. CouchDB consists of two hierarchical concepts: database and document. Figure 3 shows a comparison of storage structures between the two database.

SQL-Fabric Transformation Engine. As shown in Fig. 4, the transformation engine is divided into SQL parsing layer, SQL-Fabric transformation layer and Fabric-chaincode API encapsulation layer. In addition, because CouchDB does not support joined query, the current transformation engine only supports single table query.

SQL Parse Layer. The SQL parsing layer includes SQL validity checking, SQL analysis, error handling and object encapsulation. The SQL parsing layer receives the SQL statements from SDK and preprocesses them. Firstly, the validity of different types of SQL is checked by parsing the SQL string. Secondly, the complex components of the SQL statement are simplified one by one, and the incompatible types of SQL are exceptionally handled.

SQL-Fabric Semantic Transformation Layer. The SQL-Fabric semantic transformation layer is mainly composed of parameter generation, API calling, and

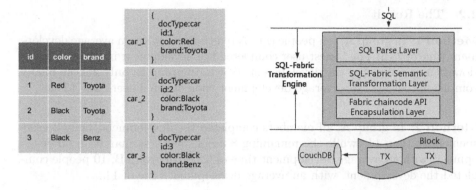

Fig. 3. Storage structure comparison   **Fig. 4.** SQL-Fabric transformation engine

error handling. It further analyzes the language objects generated by the upper layer, extracts the parameters corresponding to the various components of the SQL language object, and then converts them into a format type that conforms to the underlying read-write rules of the Fabric-chaincode. For example, when processing the select statement, we need to process the from clause, where clause, limit clause, etc., and convert it to CouchDB selector syntax.

Fabric-API Encapsulation Layer. Fabric API encapsulation layer is a simple encapsulation of underlying native API. For example, for the delete operation, only key values can be deleted in native API, which obviously cannot satisfy the complex no-key deletion request. Therefore, the encapsulation layer is compatible with different types of SQL statements by simply encapsulating existing native APIs.

4   Evaluation

4.1   The Setting

We adopted two methods to realize the transformation from traditional application to the application based on Hyperledger Fabric through investigation and evaluation experiments, and conducted two groups of experiments.

- Method 1: Use conventional way to modify the relevant code of the application layer and write smart contract code.
- Method 2: Use the transformation methods described in this paper.

We recruited 20 developers and assigned them the task of migrating the digital asset management system. The application contains 10 tables, the data access layer of the application contains 64 access requests. Ten of the developers had Hyperledger Fabric development experience and were divided into group A, while 10 in group B had no relevant development experience, every developer complete the task in two methods.

4.2 The Result

Method 1: In group A, ten people completed the task, with an average development time of 28 h. The fastest user completed the development in 24 h, while the slowest user completed the development in 36 h. In group B, only 2 users finally completed the task, the average development time of the 2 users was 120 h.

Method 2: In group A, all members completed the development. Only 2 users spent more than 1 h, while the remaining 8 users spent less than 0.7 h on development, with an average development time of 0.8 h. In group B, 10 people completed the development, with an average development time of 1 h.

5 Conclusion

This paper describes the necessity and problems of transfering traditional application to blockchain-based application. Therefore, we propose a method of transfering traditional application to blockchain-based application. And experiments have shown that the method described in this paper can improve the transformation efficiency of the application to a certain extent. In the future work, we will continue to improve our tools to support more complex SQL queries, especially join queries, and we hope that this method can be compatible with more blockchain platforms, such as Ethereum and EOS.

Acknowledgments. This paper is partly supported by the National Key R&D Program of China under Grant No. 2017YFB1002000, the Talent Program of Fujian Province for Distinguished Young Scholars in Higher Education, the Guiding Project of Fujian Province under Grant No. 2018H0017.

References

1. Hyperledger Fabric. https://www.hyperledger.org/projects/fabric. Accessed 5 May 2019
2. Java SDK for Fabric Client. https://github.com/hyperledger/fabric-sdk-java. Accessed 5 May 2019
3. Szabo, N.: Smart Contracts. Virtual School (1994)
4. Nakamoto, S.: Bitcoin: a peer-to-peer electronic cash system (2009). http://www.bitcoin.org/bitcoin.pdf
5. Ethereum Project. https://www.ethereum.org/. Accessed 20 May 2019
6. Hyperledger Fabric Chaincode. https://github.com/hyperledger/fabric-chaincode-java. Accessed 8 Apr 2019
7. CouchDB. http://couchdb.apache.org. Accessed 20 May 2019

Blockchain and Data Mining

A Survey on Blockchain Anomaly Detection Using Data Mining Techniques

Ji Li[1], Chunxiang Gu[1,2(✉)], Fushan Wei[1], and Xi Chen[1]

[1] State Key Laboratory of Mathematical Engineering and Advanced Computing,
Zhengzhou 450001, China
gcx5209@sohu.com
[2] Henan Key Laboratory of Network Cryptography Technology,
Zhengzhou 450001, China

Abstract. With the more and more extensive application of blockchain, blockchain security has been widely concerned by the society and deeply studied by scholars, of which anomaly detection is an important problem. Data mining techniques, including conventional machine learning, deep learning and graph learning, have been concentrated for anomaly detection in the last few years. This paper presents a systematic survey of the blockchain anomaly detection results using data mining techniques. The anomaly detection methods are classified into 2 main categories, namely universal detection methods and specific detection methods, which contain 8 subclasses. For each subclass, the corresponding research are listed and compared, presenting a systematic and categorized overview of the current perspectives for blockchain anomaly detection. In addition, this paper contributes in discussing the advantages and disadvantages for the data mining techniques employed, and suggesting future directions for anomaly detection methods. This survey helps researchers to have a general comprehension of the anomaly detection field and its application in blockchain data.

Keywords: Blockchain · Anomaly detection · Data mining · Graph analysis · Network security

1 Introduction

Blockchain is a distributed ledger system composed of P2P network proposed by Bitcoin [29]. In blockchain, sender and receiver can trade directly without trusted third party such as a bank, unlike existing online money transfer system. The most widely-used applications of blockchain are crypto currencies. They are used for international transactions because of low cost and fast transactions by the direct transactions. Blockchain has various features, such as fault tolerance, tamper resistance, and anonymity. Applications of the crypto currencies are conservation of assets utilizing fault tolerance and personal transactions that can protect personal information by anonymity. In addition, blockchain is used

© Springer Nature Singapore Pte Ltd. 2020
Z. Zheng et al. (Eds.): BlockSys 2019, CCIS 1156, pp. 491–504, 2020.
https://doi.org/10.1007/978-981-15-2777-7_40

for not only crypto currencies but also asset transactions other than currency, distributed application, document storage system, and registration of rand. The data structure of blockchain is a chain of hash values of blocks each of which contains a set of transactions. In this structure, an update of a transaction causes changes in all the blocks after the block containing the transaction. With this structure, update or delete of a blockchain transaction is extremely difficult by everyone including the creator of the transaction; thus tamper resistance is high. However, this feature becomes a problem in which blockchain system cannot modify fraudulent transactions made by miss operations or stolen secret keys. Because of this problem, once an illegal transaction, such as theft, occurs, the damage will expand. To suppress the damage, we need countermeasures, such as detecting illegal transaction at high speed and correcting the transaction before approval, or even predict suspicious users and abnormal events in advance, which leads to the problem of blockchain anomaly detection.

Although the anomaly detection technology has been greatly developed, the anomaly detection in the blockchain is not a trivial problem. On the one hand, the blockchain system is complex and diverse, meaning that there may be many kinds of abnormal situations, it is necessary to rationally select and apply the mechanisms of anomaly detection. On the other hand, anomaly detection technology is also constantly improving, and how to apply the novel anomaly detection technology flexibly to the blockchain data is also worthy of attention. In this paper, we focus on blockchain anomaly detection research using data mining techniques, summarizing the technological achievements that obtained from the perspective of data. The contributions of this paper are as follows:

(1) Providing a summary of the tools and systems related to blockchain anomaly detection.
(2) Presenting a categorized overview of the current research results on detecting blockchain anomaly.
(3) Giving suggestions on the selection and application of anomaly detection related data mining approaches by comparison.
(4) Discussing the future directions for blockchain anomaly detection.

The rest of this paper is organized as follows. In Sect. 2, we summarize the anomaly detection tools and systems developed for blockchain. In Sect. 3, we review the anomaly detection methods for blockchain data in detail. A following discussion on the advantages and disadvantages of the methods is presented in Sect. 4. In Sect. 5, we consider the open issues and show future directions on blockchain anomaly detection. Finally, we conclude this paper in Sect. 6.

2   Anomaly Detection Tools and Systems

In this section, some tools and systems related to blockchain anomaly detection will be introduced briefly.

Battista et al. [13] proposed a system for the visual analysis of Bitcoin flows in the transaction graphlaying foundation for high level analysis of it.

Bartoletti [3] et al. proposed a general framework supporting general purpose analytics on both Bitcoin and Ethereum, which was released as an open-source Scalalibrary. They illustrated the distinguishing features of their approach on a set of significant use cases. Kinkeldey et al. [21] developed a system named Bit-Conduite offering an entity-based access to the blockchain data and a visualization front end supporting high-level view on transactions over time. It strengthened the exploration of activity through filtering and clustering interactions. The work of [26] presented a systemic top-down visualization of Bitcoin transaction activity to explore dynamically generated patterns of algorithmic behavior. They exposed an effective force-directed graph visualization employed in their large-scale data observation facility to accelerate data exploration. The high-fidelity visualizations demonstrated allowed for collaborative discovery of unexpected high frequency transaction patterns, including automated laundering operations and programmatically generated spam transactions. They further discussed how the user community could develop coordinated defence against repeated denial of service attacks on the network from the data analytic perspective in their subsequent work [25].

The authors of [40] presented ADvISE, the first anomaly detection tool for blockchain systems which leveraged blockchain meta-data, named forks, in order to collect potentially malicious requests in the network/system while being resilient to eclipse attacks. ADvISE collected and analyzed malicious forks to build a threat database that enables detection and prevention of future attacks. They also proposed a Blockchain anomaly detection (BAD) solution [41] exploiting blockchain metadata to collect malicious activity. The idea is to collect the local attacks injected in the form of malicious transactions and resue them later to prevent similar attacks on the untainted nodes.

3   Blockchain Anomaly Detection Methods

In this section the anomaly detection methods for blockchain data will be introduced in detail along with related research results, and the categories of it is shown in Fig. 1.

3.1   Universal Detection Methods

The universal detection techniques are the anomaly detection techniques which are not designed for any specific type of anomaly, meaning that the techniques can detect different kinds anomalies at the same time or lay a firm foundation for it. Basicly, these techniques start from the user perspective or the transaction perspective or both, so they can be divided into 3 categories: entity portrait, transaction pattern recognition, and double angle detection model.

Entity Portrait. The main assignment of entity portrait is to restore users' activities and analyse types of these occurrences. A majority of the work on entity portrait is about deanonimization, especially in Bitcoin, which is based

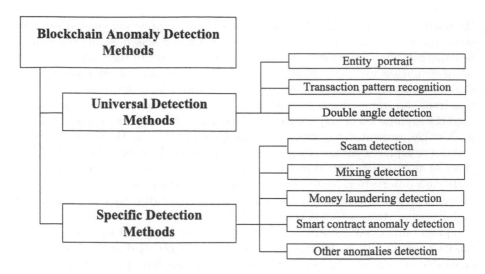

Fig. 1. The categories of Blockchain anomaly detection methods

on UTXO. To reduce the anonymity of the Bitcoin entities, Harlev [16] et al. used a labeled dataset of 434 entities with about 200 million transactions from the company Chainalysis as training dataset to built classifiers distinguishing among 10 categories, which included gambling, scam, Tor market and ransomware. They also used the SMOTE method [5] to deal with the class imbalance problem, and the best performance was achieved by the Gradient Boosting algorithm with an accuracy of 77% and F1-score of 75%. Another work using supervised machine learning to predict the type of yet-unidentified entities in Bitcoin is [50]. Which utilized a sample of 957 entities as training set data and built classifiers differentiating among 12 categories. Using the Gradient Boosting algorithm with default parameters. Some other researches exploited deep learning method to achieve address-user mapping. [39] developed a system that learned a mapping from address representations to a compact Euclidean space where distances directly corresponded to a measure of address similarity. They trained a deep neural network for address behavior embedding and optimization to finally obtain an address feature vector for each address. They also identified owners of addresses through address verification, recognition and clustering, where the implementation relied directly on the distance between address feature vectors. They set up an address-user pairing dataset with extensive collections and careful sanitation. In contrast to heuristic-based methods, their model showed great performance in Bitcoin user identification. More work on Bitcoin deanonimization was summed up and classified in [42], and [22] tried to apply existing deanonymisation methods for Bitcoin to Ethereum, including discovering IP addresses and clustering Bitcoin addresses. They found it difficult to apply these methods to Ethereum due to the differences between both networks. However, similar attacks are potentially feasible by exploiting some of the specifics of the Ethereum network. With the arouse of graph learning, an extremely powerful tool to extract the latent features of each vertex in a graph to fulfill various tasks, researchers are trying to exploit graph learning to deanonymizing cryptocurrencies, and the corresponding promises and challenges are discussed in [15].

Wile the deanonimization methods can assist anomaly detection indirectly, some other work try to characterize entities by their behavior patterns. In [18], the authors developed a mathematical model using a probabilistic approach to link Bitcoin addresses and transactions to the originator IP address. To utilize the model, they carried out experiments by installing more than a hundred modified Bitcoin clients distributed in the network to observe as many messages as possible. During a two-month observation period they were able to identify several thousand Bitcoin clients and bind their transactions to geographical locations. In [24], Maesa et al. investigated the presence of outliers in the indegree frequency distribution and the high diameter in the Bitcoin users graph. By manually analyzing the users graph they found out that these phenomena were generated by peculiar chains of transactions. They formally characterized such chains and automatically studied their impact on the dataset. Compared with the aforementioned heuristics methods, machine learning methods can take better advantage of the user's behavior information. Yin and Vatrapu [51] provided a first estimation of the portion of illicit activities in the bitcoin ecosystem with Bagging and Gradient Boosting. To improve the classification results, [17] investigated information revealed by the pattern of transactions in the neighborhood of a given entity transaction, and put forward new features for entity characterization from 5 aspects, including address, entity, temporal, centrality and motif. The effectiveness of the features were proved by subsequent experiments, in which they used decision tree to classify entities from a dataset consisted of 272 entities representing 5 categories involving gambling and darknet marketplace. Tang et al. [43] formally defined the problem of peer behavior classification in blockchain networks, and proposed a novel deep-learning-based method, termed PeerClassifier, to address the problem by extracting sequence data to represent peer behaviors.

Transaction Pattern Recognition. Transaction pattern recognition aims at determining the transaction type through machine learning methods. For example, [47] proposed a multiclass service identification scheme in Bitcoin based on novel transaction history summarization. The key idea was an elaborate way of pre-processing of transaction history and feature extraction, e.g. change in transactions is removed currency and digit conversion. For a given Bitcoin address, the features were generated from its transaction history and fed into a supervised classifier and the services operated by the addresses were identified among seven major services. Their scheme achieved 72% of classification accuracy with the Random Forests (RF) algorithm. Baek et al. [2] identified the suspicious transaction from Binance, another open-source cryptocurrency, through the means of defining and detecting the cryptocurrency wallets. By drawing the metadata of 38,526 wallets from etherscan.io, they investigated the transactions with discernible purpose. With features engineered from the clustering results generated by the EM algorithm for Gaussian Mixture Model and the k-means algorithm, they performed anomaly detection using RF, thus offering an insight into labeling the cryptocurrency wallets. While [2,47] both used supervised learning, transaction pattern recognition can also be achieved by unsupervised learning [1,32,38]. [1] analyzed blockchain transaction data with pairwise dominant set and central clustering approaches by testing and evaluating it with different measures and settings. It showed that the dominant set approach could achieve better clustering accuracy, and the in-depth information coming out of the approach can be useful for identifying anomalous transactions. Sayad et al. [38] proposed a model for anomaly detection over Bitcoin electronic transactions, inc which the One Class Support Vector Machines algorithm was used to detect outliers, and the k-means algorithm was used to group the similar outliers with the same type of anomalies. In [32] the author explored the use of k-means clustering on detecting patterns in the Ethereum transactional data. They evaluated the accuracy of the patterns formed and investigated whether or not anomalies occur.

Double Angle Detection. The entity portrait and transaction pattern recognition methods can locate abnormal users and transactions respectively, which are closely related actually. Double angle detection models try to find both of abnormal users and transactions (address). Pham et al. [34] used the dataset containing all Bitcoin transactions beginning from the networks creation until April 7th, 2013. Two graphs were generated by the Bitcoin transaction network: the user-as-node graph and the transaction-as-node graph. 12 features were extracted and k-means clustering, Mahalanobis distance, unsupervised SVM were leveraged to detect suspicious users and transactions. However, they found that the k-means clustering algorithm is not effective enough for anomaly detection. Thus they used local outlier factor (LOF) method proceeded by k-means clustering algorithm in their subsequent work [35], and detected one known case of theft out of the 30 known cases. The features have important effect on the results and therefore the improvement of features is an active research point. In [23], Lin et al. introduced new features as transaction history summary for Bitcoin address and entity classification. The transaction history summary was composed of basic statistics, extra statistics, and transaction moments, which made huge progress in terms of classification accuracy. To avoid the problem of heuristic feature extraction and more comprehensively represent the temporal and financial properties of dynamic transaction networks, Wu et al. [48] proposed a novel framework for Ethereum analysis via network embedding. They constructed a temporal weighted multidigraph to retain information as much as possible and presented a graph embedding method called T-EDGE which incorporated temporal and weighted information of financial transaction networks into node embeddings. They also implemented the proposed and two baseline embedding methods on realistic Ethereum network for two predictive tasks with practical relevance, namely, temporal link prediction and phishing/non-phishing node classification. Further anomaly detection of users and transactions can be conducted on their model.

3.2 Specific Detection Methods

The specific detection techniques are the anomaly detection techniques which are designed for certain anomalies.

Scam Detection. In early research, scam detection was usually conducted with heuristic feature extraction, and the detected scam had multiple types. Monamo et al. [27] investigated the use of trimmed k-means [12] on Bitcoin fraud detection, which assumed the existence of specific proportion of outlier within the user network. The algorithm successfully detected 5 of 30 known fraudsters with 14 currency and network features. In their subsequent work [35], Bitcoin fraud was described from both global (trimmed k-means) and local (kd-trees) perspectives. Another 3 binary classification algorithms, including maximum-likelihood based logistic regression, boosted logistic regression and RF, were employed to further explain the detected outliers. It showed that RF was the best performing classifier, and global outlier perspective surpassed the local viewpoint. Patil et al. [33] exploited cut k-means for unsupervised crime detection within the Bitcoin network and got results with improvements of detection rate.

Some other works focus on Ponzi schemes detection, one of the typical scams. Online Ponzi schemes are also referred as high-yield investment programs (HYIPs) [28], which promise outlandish interest rates on deposits but will eventually collapse. Bartoletti et al. [4] collected Bitcoin addresses used by Ponzi schemes and found Ponzi-related addresses by address clustering, thus constructing a dataset to train classifiers including RIPPER, Bayes network and RF. The experimental results showed that RF outperformed others, and they evaluated the importance of the features extracted by exploiting the feature selection functionality of Weka. Based on the individual inspection of HYIP activity in Bitcoin, [46] proposed a number of transaction-related features and the contributed features were evaluated based on gain values output by XGBoost classifier. In particular, a signed integer called *pattern* was assigned to each transaction and the frequency of each pattern was calculated as key features. However, although about 83% of HYIP addresses in the test dataset were correctly classified, the dataset was rather limited, some features related were not accurately calculated without considering the volatility of Bitcoin, and the approach was not feasible to process large transactions datasets. Consequently, they extended their work toward more solid and accurate HYIP owners Bitcoin addresses identification solutions in [45] by addressing the aforementioned issues. They proposed a novel dataset collection approach of scraping the HYIP-related topics in the Bitcoin forum, and a solid identification methodology consisting of several key ideas such as unit conversion and a sampling approach. However, both of [45, 46] analyzed the transaction history in a static manner, missing the time-variable information. Accordingly, they proposed an approach of time series analysis for Bitcoin transactions in [47], which could be used for anomaly detection. Given a (Bitcoin) address, their approach could extract several numerical features from transactions by sliding windows and anomaly scores calculation and calculate time series anomaly scores for its transaction history. The scheme was tested against the transaction history of Pirate@40s HYIP scheme.

Another scam that has been getting attention is *pump and dump* (P&D). [49] present the first detailed study of P&D schemes in cryptocurrency markets, which demonstrated that the persisting nature of P&D activities in the cryptomarket was the driving force of tens of millions of dollars of phony trading volumes each month. Using LASSO regularized GML and RF, they built various models that were predicated on the time and venue (exchange) of a P&D broadcast in a Telegram group. Chen et al. [8] took the leaked transaction history of Mt. Gox Bitcoin exchange as a sample, constructed the transaction history into three graphs and reshaped them as matrices. By using singular value decomposition (SVD) on the matrices, they identified many base networks which had a great correlation with the price fluctuation, and plenty of market manipulation patterns were found when further analyzing the most important accounts in the base networks, indicating that there was serious market manipulation in Mt. Gox exchange. In their subsequent work [9], they proposed an improved apriori algorithm to detect user groups which may involve in P&D schemes, and used the leaked transaction history of Mt. Gox Bitcoin exchange to verify the validity of the algorithm. In addition, many abnormal trading behaviors in the exchange were found by exploring some of the detected user groups. Different from the aforementioned works, [31] used deep learning to detect P&D in real-time, and presented a system named Limelight. They retrieved, prepared, labeled, and processed a dataset to train a model, which surpassed previously proposed models in the detection of P&D with high accuracy.

While, there are also some smart contract related scam detection techniques [10,44], which will be introduced in the fourth part of this subsection.

Mixing Detection. In [36], the authors proposed to model the Bitcoin network as a social network and to use community anomaly detection to discover mixing accounts. They presented the first technique for detecting Bitcoin accounts associated to money mixing, and demonstrate their proposal effectiveness on real data, using known mixing accounts. Eldefrawy [14] et al. conducted a longitudinal study to analyze the misuse of Bitcoin and obtained a quantitative estimate of the malicious activity that Bitcoin was associated with. To identify mixing transactions, they developed a new heuristic that extended previously known ones. They also found that Bitcoin addresses found on the dark web were significantly more active. Motivated by the success of graph embedding in social network analysis, Nan et al. [30] proposed a feature-based method to identify mixing services using deep autoencoder, testing their method on the real Bitcoin ledger. However, they used local outlier probabilities to evaluate the outlier node, which was slow for large databases. Besides, they could not properly define the mixing service transactions and further analyze their experiment results due to the lack of real data labels.

Money Laundering Detection. Ranshous et al. [37] introduced the idea of motifs in directed hypergraphs, considering a particular 2-motif as a potential laundering pattern. They identified distinct statistical properties of exchange addresses related to the acquisition and spending of bitcoin. Leveraging this to build classification models to learn a set of discriminating features, they could predict if an address is owned by an exchange. In [6], Chang et al. used heuristics based on transaction patterns to cluster nodes that were owned by the same entity. Instead of analyzing the Bitcoin network which contained almost 400 million edges, they used tables with much smaller sizes. The approach can be used for Anti-MoneyLaundering research.

Smart Contract Anomaly Detection. The smart contract anomaly only occurs in Ethereum. Chen et al. [7] conducted the first systematic study on Ethereum by leveraging graph analysis to characterize three major activities on Ethereum. Apart from getting new observations and insights from the graphs, they proposed new approaches based on cross-graph analysis to address two security issues in Ethereum, including attack forensics and anomaly detection. The anomaly detection algorithm was relatively simple, but their study was groundbreaking since it proved the power of graph analysis on anomaly detection. [10] proposed a machine learning method to detect smart Ponzi schemesin Ethereum. The ground truth data was obtained by manually checking the source code, and account features and code features were extracted to bulid an RF model, which was applied to identify latent smart Ponzi schemes. The proposed model had an advantage of evaluating any contract at the moment of its creation since the code features were extracted without source code. [44] investigated a new type of fraud in Ethereum: honeypots. They presented a taxonomy of honeypot techniques and introduced a methodology named HONEYBADGER that used symbolic execution and heuristics for the automated detection of honeypots. [20] proposed a system named ScanAT for characterizing bytecode-only smart contracts by automatically assigning multiple attribute tags. Using a deep learning approach, the ScanAT could extract attribute tags from the source code and metadata of known smart contracts and train their bytecode with the attribute tags. Then it could infer attribute tags from the bytecode of smart contracts alone, thus suitable for smart contract anomaly detection.

Other Anomalies Detection. The rest research on anomaly detection is mainly about identifying addresses related to illicit activities like *darknet markets* (DNM) and ransomware campaigns. Kanemura et al. [19] analyzed Bitcoin transactions and addresses related to darknet markets and proposed a voting based method which decided the labels of multiple addresses controlled by the same user based on the number of the majority label. Conti et al. [11] conducted a comprehensive study on ransomware and presented a lightweight framework to recognise and collect Bitcoin addresses managed by the same user or group of users (cybercriminals, in this case), including an approach for classifying a payment as ransom based on some statistical indicators.

4   Discussion

The anomaly detection methods mentioned in last section mainly exploit four kinds of data mining techniques: statistical (e.g. SVD), conventional machine learning (e.g. k-means and RF), deep learning (e.g. autoencoder) and graph learning (e.g. graph embedding). In this section we discuss the advantages and disadvantages of them.

The statistical-based approach is a relatively common method in the early days. It plays an important role in understanding the structure and nature of the blockchain network in the initial stage. At the same time, it has the characteristics of simple operation, easy understanding and convenient use. But its problem is also very obvious, that is, only some very basic conclusions can be obtained, and it is impossible to dig deep into the rich information contained in the blockchain data. In contrast, traditional machine learning-based methods can efficiently exploit anomalies in blockchain data and identify anomalous objects. The disadvantage is that it requires manual extraction of features, which is highly dependent on experience and requires a lot of work, and the effectiveness of the extracted features is not guaranteed. Deep learning is a choice that avoids feature extraction, and it can dig deeper into the information contained in the data than traditional machine learning. However, it should be noted that deep learning has certain requirements on the quantity and quality of training samples, and the interpretability of the results is relatively poor. Another technique that can deeply exploit blockchain data information is graph learning. Since its theoretical model is highly consistent with the research object, it has unique advantages in portraying the network structure of various activities in the blockchain, and the experiments have proved its effectiveness. Its shortcoming lies in the lack of theoretical support and the great impact of the modeling data into graphs process on the anomaly detection results.

Therefore, if the assignment is relatively simple or the dataset is not big enough, we should choose statistical techniques and conventional machine learning models; for complex assignments with enough data to explore, deep learning and graph learning models are better choices.

5   Future Directions

In this section we discuss the future directions of blockchain anomaly detection on the basis of existing methods.

(1) Further application of graph learning and deep learning. Since the main activities on the blockchain can be modeled as graphs/networks, and graph learning techniques are very good at handling such objects, graph learning techniques can be further applied to this problem. Other deep learning techniques and the combination of already existing algorithms are also worth attention.

(2) More reliable datasets. The lack of data is a major bottleneck restricting the development of blockchain anomaly detection technology. There are very few publicly-recognized data sets that have hampered experimental simulation. Therefore, it is necessary to collect more authentic and reliable tagged data sets.

(3) The consideration of chronological factors. Most of the current results only make abnormal findings from the business data of the blockchain itself, but ignore the value of time data. In fact, time series data is indispensable for activity characterization in blockchain, while anomaly detection methods with timing characteristics, such as time series analysis, recurrent neural networks, etc., can be part of the new technology.

(4) Dynamics and heterogeneity model. The majority of current methods tackle with static homogeneous models. On the one hand, graph structures are assumed to be fixed. On the other hand, nodes and edges from a graph are assumed to come from a single source. However, these two assumptions are not realistic in many scenarios. So the methods should be developed on dynamics and heterogeneity models.

6 Conclusion

This paper presented a survey of the blockchain anomaly detection approaches using data mining. The reviewed papers were investigated and classified into 2 main categories: universal detection methods and specific detection methods, which can be further divided into 8 classes. Tools and systems related to blockchain anomaly detection are also summarized. The strength and shortcomings of the data mining models are analysed through comparison, and the future directions of the problem are discussed from several aspects.

Acknowledgments. This work is supported by the National Natural Science Foundation of China (Nos. 61772548) and the Foundation of Science and Technology on Information Assurance Laboratory (No. KJ-17-001).

References

1. Awan, M.K., Cortesi, A.: Blockchain transaction analysis using dominant sets. In: Saeed, K., Homenda, W., Chaki, R. (eds.) CISIM 2017. LNCS, vol. 10244, pp. 229–239. Springer, Cham (2017). https://doi.org/10.1007/978-3-319-59105-6_20

2. Baek, H., Oh, J., Kim, C.Y., Lee, K.: A model for detecting cryptocurrency transactions with discernible purpose. In: Eleventh International Conference on Ubiquitous and Future Networks, ICUFN 2019, Zagreb, Croatia, 2–5 July 2019, pp. 713–717 (2019)

3. Bartoletti, M., Lande, S., Pompianu, L., Bracciali, A.: A general framework for blockchain analytics. In: Proceedings of the 1st Workshop on Scalable and Resilient Infrastructures for Distributed Ledgers, SERIAL@Middleware 2017, Las Vegas, NV, USA, 11–15 December 2017, pp. 7:1–7:6 (2017)

4. Bartoletti, M., Pes, B., Serusi, S.: Data mining for detecting bitcoin Ponzi schemes. In: Crypto Valley Conference on Blockchain Technology, CVCBT 2018, Zug, Switzerland, 20–22 June 2018, pp. 75–84 (2018)
5. Bowyer, K.W., Chawla, N.V., Hall, L.O., Kegelmeyer, W.P.: SMOTE: synthetic minority over-sampling technique. CoRR abs/1106.1813 (2011)
6. Chang, T.H., Svetinovic, D.: Improving bitcoin ownership identification using transaction patterns analysis. IEEE Trans. Syst. Man Cybern. Syst. (to be published). https://doi.org/10.1109/TSMC.2018.2867497
7. Chen, T., et al.: Understanding Ethereum via graph analysis. In: 2018 IEEE Conference on Computer Communications, INFOCOM 2018, Honolulu, HI, USA, 16–19 April 2018, pp. 1484–1492 (2018)
8. Chen, W., Wu, J., Zheng, Z., Chen, C., Zhou, Y.: Market manipulation of bitcoin: evidence from mining the MT. Gox transaction network. In: 2019 IEEE Conference on Computer Communications, INFOCOM 2019, Paris, France, 29 April–2 May 2019, pp. 964–972 (2019)
9. Chen, W., Xu, Y., Zheng, Z., Zhou, Y., Yang, E.J., Bian, J.: Detecting "pump & dump schemes" on cryptocurrency market using an improved Apriori algorithm. In: 13th IEEE International Conference on Service-Oriented System Engineering, SOSE 2019, San Francisco, CA, USA, 4–9 April 2019 (2019)
10. Chen, W., Zheng, Z., Ngai, E.C., Zheng, P., Zhou, Y.: Exploiting blockchain data to detect smart Ponzi schemes on Ethereum. IEEE Access **7**, 37575–37586 (2019)
11. Conti, M., Gangwal, A., Ruj, S.: On the economic significance of ransomware campaigns: a bitcoin transactions perspective. Comput. Secur. **79**, 162–189 (2018)
12. Cuesta-Albertos, J.A., Gordaliza, A., Matrán, C., et al.: Trimmed k-means: an attempt to robustify quantizers. Ann. Stat. **25**(2), 553–576 (1997)
13. Di Battista, G., Donato, V.D., Patrignani, M., Pizzonia, M., Roselli, V., Tamassia, R.: BitConeView: visualization of flows in the bitcoin transaction graph. In: 2015 IEEE Symposium on Visualization for Cyber Security, VizSec 2015, Chicago, IL, USA, 25 October 2015, pp. 1–8 (2015)
14. Eldefrawy, K., Gehani, A., Matton, A.: Longitudinal analysis of misuse of bitcoin. In: Deng, R.H., Gauthier-Umaña, V., Ochoa, M., Yung, M. (eds.) ACNS 2019. LNCS, vol. 11464, pp. 259–278. Springer, Cham (2019). https://doi.org/10.1007/978-3-030-21568-2_13
15. Gaihre, A., Pandey, S., Liu, H.: Deanonymizing cryptocurrency with graph learning: the promises and challenges. In: 7th IEEE Conference on Communications and Network Security, CNS 2019, Washington, DC, USA, 10–12 June 2019, pp. 1–3 (2019)
16. Harlev, M.A., Yin, H.S., Langenheldt, K.C., Mukkamala, R.R., Vatrapu, R.: Breaking bad: de-anonymising entity types on the bitcoin blockchain using supervised machine learning. In: 51st Hawaii International Conference on System Sciences, HICSS 2018, Hilton Waikoloa Village, Hawaii, USA, 3–6 January 2018, pp. 1–10 (2018)
17. Jourdan, M., Blandin, S., Wynter, L., Deshpande, P.: Characterizing entities in the bitcoin blockchain. In: 2018 IEEE International Conference on Data Mining Workshops, ICDM Workshops, Singapore, Singapore, 17–20 November 2018, pp. 55–62 (2018)
18. Juhász, P.L., Stéger, J., Kondor, D., Vattay, G.: A Bayesian approach to identify bitcoin users. PLoS ONE **13**(12), e0207000 (2018)
19. Kanemura, K., Toyoda, K., Ohtsuki, T.: Identification of darknet markets' bitcoin addresses by voting per-address classification results. In: IEEE International

Conference on Blockchain and Cryptocurrency, ICBC 2019, Seoul, Korea (South), 14–17 May 2019, pp. 154–158 (2019)

20. Kim, Y., Pak, D., Lee, J.: ScanAT: identification of bytecode-only smart contracts with multiple attribute tags. IEEE Access **7**, 98669–98683 (2019)

21. Kinkeldey, C., Fekete, J., Isenberg, P.: BitConduite: visualizing and analyzing activity on the bitcoin network. In: Eurographics Conference on Visualization, EuroVis 2017, Posters, Barcelona, Spain, 12–16 June 2017, pp. 25–27 (2017)

22. Klusman, R., Dijkhuizen, T.: Deanonymisation in Ethereum using existing methods for bitcoin (2018)

23. Lin, Y., Wu, P., Hsu, C., Tu, I., Liao, S.: An evaluation of bitcoin address classification based on transaction history summarization. In: IEEE International Conference on Blockchain and Cryptocurrency, ICBC 2019, Seoul, Korea (South), 14–17 May 2019, pp. 302–310 (2019)

24. Maesa, D.D.F., Marino, A., Ricci, L.: Detecting artificial behaviours in the bitcoin users graph. Online Soc. Netw. Media **3–4**, 63–74 (2017)

25. McGinn, D., McIlwraith, D., Guo, Y.: Towards open data blockchain analytics: a bitcoin perspective. R. Soc. Open Sci. **5**(8), 180298 (2018)

26. McGinn, D., Birch, D., Akroyd, D., Molina-Solana, M., Guo, Y., Knottenbelt, W.J.: Visualizing dynamic bitcoin transaction patterns. Big Data **4**(2), 109–119 (2016)

27. Monamo, P., Marivate, V.N., Twala, B.: Unsupervised learning for robust bitcoin fraud detection. In: 2016 Information Security for South Africa, ISSA 2016, Johannesburg, South Africa, 17–18 August 2016, pp. 129–134 (2016)

28. Moore, T., Han, J., Clayton, R.: The postmodern Ponzi scheme: empirical analysis of high-yield investment programs. In: Keromytis, A.D. (ed.) FC 2012. LNCS, vol. 7397, pp. 41–56. Springer, Heidelberg (2012). https://doi.org/10.1007/978-3-642-32946-3_4

29. Nakamoto, S., et al.: Bitcoin: a peer-to-peer electronic cash system (2008)

30. Nan, L., Tao, D.: Bitcoin mixing detection using deep autoencoder. In: Third IEEE International Conference on Data Science in Cyberspace, DSC 2018, Guangzhou, China, 18–21 June 2018, pp. 280–287 (2018)

31. Nilsen, A.I.: Limelight: real-time detection of pump-and-dump events on cryptocurrency exchanges using deep learning. Master's thesis, UiT Norges arktiske universitet (2019)

32. O'Kane, E.: Detecting patterns in the Ethereum transactional data using unsupervised learning. Master's thesis, UiT Norges arktiske universitet (2018)

33. Patil, V., Nikam, A., Pawar, J., Pardhi, M.: Bitcoin fraud detection using data mining approach. J. Inf. Technol. Sci. **4**(2), 1–6 (2018)

34. Pham, T., Lee, S.: Anomaly detection in bitcoin network using unsupervised learning methods. CoRR abs/1611.03941 (2016)

35. Pham, T., Lee, S.: Anomaly detection in the bitcoin system - a network perspective. CoRR abs/1611.03942 (2016)

36. Prado-Romero, M.A., Doerr, C., Gago-Alonso, A.: Discovering bitcoin mixing using anomaly detection. In: Mendoza, M., Velastín, S. (eds.) CIARP 2017. LNCS, vol. 10657, pp. 534–541. Springer, Cham (2018). https://doi.org/10.1007/978-3-319-75193-1_64

37. Ranshous, S., et al.: Exchange pattern mining in the bitcoin transaction directed hypergraph. In: Brenner, M., et al. (eds.) FC 2017. LNCS, vol. 10323, pp. 248–263. Springer, Cham (2017). https://doi.org/10.1007/978-3-319-70278-0_16

38. Sayadi, S., Rejeb, S.B., Choukair, Z.: Anomaly detection model over blockchain electronic transactions. In: 15th International Wireless Communications & Mobile Computing Conference, IWCMC 2019, Tangier, Morocco, 24–28 June 2019, pp. 895–900 (2019)
39. Shao, W., Li, H., Chen, M., Jia, C., Liu, C., Wang, Z.: Identifying bitcoin users using deep neural network. In: Algorithms and Architectures for Parallel Processing - 18th International Conference, ICA3PP 2018, Guangzhou, China, 15–17 November 2018, Proceedings, Part IV, pp. 178–192 (2018)
40. Signorini, M., Kanoun, W., Pietro, R.D.: Advise: anomaly detection tool for blockchain systems. In: 2018 IEEE World Congress on Services, SERVICES 2018, San Francisco, CA, USA, 2–7 July 2018, pp. 65–66 (2018)
41. Signorini, M., Pontecorvi, M., Kanoun, W., Di Pietro, R.: Bad: blockchain anomaly detection. arXiv preprint arXiv:1807.03833 (2018)
42. Avdoshin, S.M., Lazarenko, A.V.: Bitcoin users deanonimization methods. Trudy ISP RAN/Proc. ISP RAS 30(1), 89–102 (2018)
43. Tang, H., Jiao, Y., Huang, B., Lin, C., Goyal, S., Wang, B.: Learning to classify blockchain peers according to their behavior sequences. IEEE Access 6, 71208–71215 (2018)
44. Torres, C.F., Steichen, M., State, R.: The art of the scam: demystifying honeypots in Ethereum smart contracts. In: 28th USENIX Security Symposium, USENIX Security 2019, Santa Clara, CA, USA, 14–16 August 2019, pp. 1591–1607 (2019)
45. Toyoda, K., Mathiopoulos, P.T., Ohtsuki, T.: A novel methodology for HYIP operators' bitcoin addresses identification. IEEE Access 7, 74835–74848 (2019)
46. Toyoda, K., Ohtsuki, T., Mathiopoulos, P.T.: Identification of high yielding investment programs in bitcoin via transactions pattern analysis. In: 2017 IEEE Global Communications Conference, GLOBECOM 2017, Singapore, 4–8 December 2017, pp. 1–6 (2017)
47. Toyoda, K., Ohtsuki, T., Mathiopoulos, P.T.: Multi-class bitcoin-enabled service identification based on transaction history summarization. In: IEEE International Conference on Internet of Things (iThings) and IEEE Green Computing and Communications (GreenCom) and IEEE Cyber, Physical and Social Computing (CPSCom) and IEEE Smart Data (SmartData), iThings/GreenCom/CPSCom/SmartData 2018, Halifax, NS, Canada, 30 July–3 August 2018, pp. 1153–1160 (2018)
48. Wu, J., Lin, D., Zheng, Z., Yuan, Q.: T-EDGE: temporal weighted multidigraph embedding for Ethereum transaction network analysis. CoRR abs/1905.08038 (2019)
49. Xu, J., Livshits, B.: The anatomy of a cryptocurrency pump-and-dump scheme. In: 28th USENIX Security Symposium, USENIX Security 2019, Santa Clara, CA, USA, 14–16 August 2019, pp. 1609–1625 (2019)
50. Yin, H.S., Langenheldt, K.C., Harlev, M.A., Mukkamala, R.R., Vatrapu, R.: Regulating cryptocurrencies: a supervised machine learning approach to de-anonymizing the bitcoin blockchain. J. Manag. Inf. Syst. 36(1), 37–73 (2019)
51. Yin, H.S., Vatrapu, R.: A first estimation of the proportion of cybercriminal entities in the bitcoin ecosystem using supervised machine learning. In: 2017 IEEE International Conference on Big Data, BigData 2017, Boston, MA, USA, 1–14 December 2017, pp. 3690–3699 (2017)

Understanding Out of Gas Exceptions on Ethereum

Chao Liu$^{(\boxtimes)}$, Jianbo Gao, Yue Li, and Zhong Chen

School of Electronics Engineering and Computer Science, Peking University,
Beijing 100871, China
{liuchao_cs,gaojianbo,liyue_cs,zhongchen}@pku.edu.cn

Abstract. Ethereum is by far the most popular smart contract platform
in the public blockchain category. In Ethereum, special programs named
smart contracts codify the "self-governed accounts". By design, users
can send transactions to smart contracts, which will automatically lead
to code execution and state modification. Unlike regular programs, smart
contracts are restricted in execution by gas limit, *i.e.*, a form of runtime
resource. If a transaction uses up all available gas, an out of gas (OG)
exception will trigger, reverting state until right before the transaction. In
this work, we empirically studied the OG exceptions on Ethereum for the
very first time. In particular, we collected exception transactions using an
instrumented Ethereum client. By investigating OG exceptions, we found
OG stand out in terms of both occurrences and damages. Moreover, we
focused on individual contracts and transactions, aiming at discovering
and identifying common causing factors triggering these exceptions. At
last, we also investigate existing tools in preventing OG exceptions. The
results call for further research and study in this direction.

Keywords: Blockchain · Ethereum · Runtime exception · Out of gas ·
Empirical study

1 Introduction

In recent years, the interest for blockchain technology has grown higher, both
in academia [8,15–17,19] as well as in industry [4,9,13,21]. Generally speaking,
blockchain is a new paradigm for distributed system with its prominent empha-
sises on trust and decentralization. In particular, it can be seen as a replicated
append-only log built upon chain of blocks, where each block contains an ordered
list of transactions. Through ingenious integration of consensus protocol, cryptographic algorithms, and economic mechanism, blockchain proves a transparent,
tamper-free, yet decentralized way of data sharing. For example, in Bitcoin, the
blockchain is used as a publicly available shared ledger among network peers (*aka*
miners, clients, or nodes), which effectively facilitates a decentralized payment
system without the need for a trusted third-party (TTP).

© Springer Nature Singapore Pte Ltd. 2020
Z. Zheng et al. (Eds.): BlockSys 2019, CCIS 1156, pp. 505–519, 2020.
https://doi.org/10.1007/978-981-15-2777-7_41

By design, Bitcoin adopts programmable transaction scripts (*i.e.* smart contracts) to achieve flexible processing logic [20]. This allows developers to realize non-trivial settlement logic, with examples like escrow service, micropayment channel, and private transaction. However, lack of Turing-complete capability as well as its UTXO account model has limited Bitcoin's application in broader areas [5]. Hence, Ethereum [21] was proposed to address the issues, and later become the first public decentralized computing platform. Unlike Bitcoin, Ethereum adopts the explicit account model. In particular, every account in Ethereum resides directly on the blockchain and has its own state persisted by so-called state database [21]. An account consists of four fields: (1) `nonce` used to prevent replay attack; (2) `balance` standing for account's holding of Ether (or `ETH`), Ethereum's native cryptocurrency; (3) `storageRoot` representing account-owned storage data (structured as a Merkle tree); and (4) `codeHash` referring to self-governance code. Here, the last two fields (*i.e.*, `storageRoot` and `codeHash`) are key for smart contracts, which in turn set them apart from ordinary accounts.

```solidity
1  pragma solidity >=0.4.22 <0.7.0;
2  contract EtherBank {
3      mapping (address => uint256) public balances;
4      function deposit() external payable {
5          require(balances[msg.sender] + msg.value >= balances[
               msg.sender]);
6          balances[msg.sender] += msg.value;
7      }
8      function withdraw(uint256 amount) external {
9          require(amount <= balances[msg.sender]);
10         balances[msg.sender] -= amount;
11         msg.sender.transfer(amount);
12     }
13 }
```

Fig. 1. `EtherBank`: an example smart contract written in Solidity.

Smart contracts, in essence, are special programs running on the blockchain. When received transactions from other accounts, contracts will be automatically loaded and executed according to their predefined logic (as specified by `codeHash`). In Fig. 1, we show an example contract named `EtherBank` written in Solidity. Solidity is a statically typed object-oriented high-level programming language dedicated to smart contract programming, and by far the most popular and widely used in Ethereum. It supports features like native big integer (`uint256/int256`) type, dynamic array, user-defined `struct`, multiple inheritance, and important blockchain primitives (*e.g.*, `msg.sender`, `block.number`).

In Ethereum, smart contracts are always first compiled into bytecode, then deployed and executed in EVM (Ethereum Virtual Machine) along with the transaction processing mechanism. Here, every instruction thus executed will be charged a fee to compensate for the resources spent, as well as prevent potential

DoS attacks. More specifically, the fee is always pre-paid by the sender on a transaction basis, and are further factorized into two related parameters around the concept of gas, *i.e.*, `tx.gasLimit` and `tx.gasPrice`. Here, `tx.gasLimit` specifies maximal amount of gas available to the transaction, whereas `tx.gasPrice` converts gas units into ETH value (the exact fee paid by transaction sender). If, after transaction execution, there are unused gas left, the remaining part will be refunded back to transaction sender in ETH in the same rate as `tx.gasPrice`.

During execution, there are cases where a transaction uses up all available gas limit, *e.g.*, it runs into an infinite loop. When that happens, EVM will force the transaction to an immediate stop, reverting all intermediate states modified since transaction execution. In this case, we say the transaction has encountered an *out of gas (OG) exception* [21], or in short, gas exception.

Out of gas exceptions are problematic in at least three aspects. First of all, it causes money loss for transaction sender. As of August 30th, 2019, typical market value for this kind of loss spans from several cents towards several tens of cents US dollars per transaction. In addition, these exceptions also mean a kind of resource waste for the entire system as a whole. Instead of choosing and processing transactions that are doomed to fail, miners could have spent scarce resources on other normal transactions, which are more "meaningful" for the network. Last but not least, previous literature [14] has also revealed direct link between out of gas exceptions and severe contract vulnerabilities, putting billions of US dollars under threat according to the study.

While there are previous works concerning the gas mechanism of Ethereum [7,10–12,14,18,22], none of them are either complete or explicitly towards out of gas exceptions in a general form. Besides, there also lacks a comprehensive and empirical treatment on these exceptions, or any other types. In this work, we present a *first systematic and empirical analysis* on out of gas exceptions. In particular, we aim to answer the following research questions (RQs):

- **RQ1.** How do out of gas exceptions exist in Ethereum? To what extent does it affect external users, network peers, as well as the blockchain as a whole?
- **RQ2.** What are the main factors or reasons for out of gas exceptions? Are there lessons developers, researchers, and users can learn from?
- **RQ3.** How effectively do existing tools or methods can help in preventing out of gas exceptions? What are the limitations?

In summary, the main contributions of our work are:

- We give a comprehensive taxonomy of EVM runtime exceptions, and find that the two most commonly seen exception types are out of gas and explicit revert, which combinedly account for around 95% of all exception instances, *w.r.t.* both external transactions as well as internal message calls.
- To the best of our knowledge, we are the first to conduct large scale empirical analysis on out of gas exceptions in Ethereum blockchain. Our study shows that this kind of exceptions is very prevalence in the world of smart contracts, and has already caused significant amount of losses in the past.

- We investigate reasons behind out of gas exceptions. In particular, we identify four possible factors, *i.e.*, misunderstanding of transaction mechanism, conservative gas limit, compiler derived bug, and unbounded mass operation.
- We study existing tools and methods in use of preventing out of gas exceptions. The result suggests room for further research and investigations.

2 Background

2.1 Smart Contract and EVM

In Ethereum, all the miners (*i.e.*, clients, or network nodes) join in the same peer-to-peer network, combinedly maintaining a single view of the so-called world state, where the world state can be seen as an enumeration of accounts, which are further divided into EOAs (externally owned users) and smart contracts. By design, an EOA can send transactions to other accounts. These transactions may specify ETH to transfer as well as optional input data. If the transaction target (denoted by tx.to) is another EOA, nothing special will happen (other than ETH transfer). However, if tx.to points to an existing smart contract, Ethereum will load contract's code as well as transaction input data, and send them to EVM (Ethereum Virtual Machine) for further execution. As long as no exception occurs during execution, the result will be persisted and synchronized across the whole network. Besides interacting with an existing smart contract, users can also deploy new contracts by leaving tx.to to empty, and filling in the transaction input (*i.e.*, tx.input) with appropriately encoded init code [3].

During transaction execution, contracts can interact with each other by calling respective public functions. Since EVM is designed as a single-threaded machine, this kind of internal message call will immediately trigger a new execution frame, and change context to it for further execution. After the call returns (whether normally or exceptionally), execution will resume to where it left before and continue thereafter. In the bytecode level, this internal call is realized by a set of CALL instructions, *i.e.*, CALL, CALLCODE, DELEGATECALL, and STATICCALL. They both expect parameters like ETH value to transfer, message call data, return data position, as well as gas limit for the internal call. Sometime, these contract-generated message calls are also known as internal transactions, as opposite to external transactions fired directly by EOAs. As far as EVM concerns, internal and external transactions are of little difference, since both are processed and executed in exactly the same way. However, for analysis purpose, the internal transactions are much more difficult to capture than external ones since they may only reside during runtime execution.

Like regular programs, contracts in execution may trigger unexpected behaviours, or runtime exceptions, *e.g.*, divide a number by zero, lack necessary instruction parameters, and not enough gas available. In the bytecode level, EVM provides very little support towards handling exceptions. Besides, right until the latest version of Solidity (*i.e.*, v0.5.11 released in August 13th, 2019), it is still impossible for smart contracts to conduct common try/catch operations *w.r.t.* runtime exceptions. Thus, the only safe and possible way for exception handling is to fully revert current call, as well as all its sub-calls. In default, runtime exceptions will automatically "bubble up" or be re-thrown, causing the whole external transaction to revert. A few exceptions are message calls triggered by low-level functions like `call`, `delegatecall`, and `staticcall` of the target contract.

2.2   The Gas Mechanism of Ethereum

To circumvent around the inevitable halting problem stemming from Turing-completeness, as well as to provide economic incentive to external users and blockchain miners, Ethereum defines a systematic expenditure metering mechanism around the concept of gas. In general, gas measures the amount of processing resources that are allowed for or has already been consumed by a specific transaction (*aka* gas cost). In Ethereum, every transaction must specify a finite number of gas limit, *i.e.*, `tx.gasLimit`, which restricts the maximal amount of gas that can be used by the transaction. Besides, every valid block also has to set its own gas limit, *i.e.*, `block.gasLimit`, which corresponds to the maximal accumulated gas cost that are allowed for all the transactions in that block.

Definition 1 (Transaction Gas Cost). *The gas cost for a specific transaction (denoted by* `tx`*) consists of three parts: (1) intrinsic gas cost; (2) execution gas cost; and (3) deploy gas cost.*

$$C(\texttt{tx}) = C_{intrinsic}(\texttt{tx}) + C_{execution}(\texttt{tx}) + C_{deploy}(\texttt{tx}) \tag{1}$$

Note, the Eq. 1 does not include a potential gas refund, since the latter happens after finishing execution and has nothing to do with an out of gas or otherwise exceptional transaction.

While intrinsic cost and deploy cost are straightforward to calculate [21], the execution gas cost is rather complicated. In fact, EVM charges execution cost in a just-in-time manner, before each instruction execution, until whether it goes to a normal halt or encounters any kind of runtime exception. Particularly, if available gas is not enough to pay for an additional instruction, EVM will trigger out of gas exception, halt execution immediately, and revert intermediate state.

One important rationale and design target for Ethereum gas mechanism is to ensure every transaction as well as instruction uses a "comparable" amount of gas *w.r.t.* resources it spent during execution. Failing to achieve this goal has proven to be dangerous by previous DoS attacks [1,2,6,11,22]. To this end, the execution cost of each instruction can be dividend into three parts *w.r.t.* three different critical resources, *i.e.*, computation, runtime memory, and storage. A complete gas schedule for all EVM instructions can be seen in [21].

3   Methodology

Our study consists of three phases (Fig. 2): (1) data collection; (2) empirical analysis; and (3) tool evaluation. First of all, we collect data by deploying two full-synced Ethereum clients (*i.e.*, `Geth` and `Parity` with different settings), and

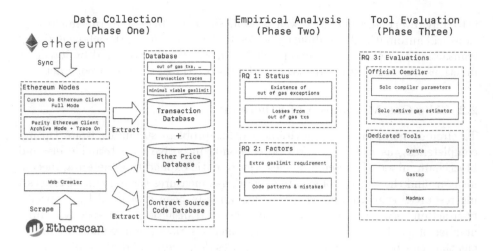

Fig. 2. An overview of our methodology.

scraping from blockchain explorer like Etherscan. The collected data are stored into a dedicated offline database for further analysis. Secondly, we use automatic script and manual inspection to investigate the overall status of out of gas exceptions, with a focus on their causing factors or behind reasons (***RQ1*** and ***RQ2***). At last, we investigate the effectiveness of existing tools in helping prevent out of gas exceptions (***RQ3***) using historical transactions as reference.

In particular, we deployed two Ethereum full nodes on the Mainnet, *i.e.*, one `Geth` client and one `Parity` client. Both nodes are set to sync to the latest block height, *i.e.*, $8,547,396$ as of September 14th, 2019. We instrumented the `Geth` by adding code to identify and extract transactions triggering at least one instance of any runtime exceptions (including out of gas). The `Geth` node is running in `full` syncmode with state pruning `on` for about one month, on a machine with 2 Intel(R) Xeon(R) E5-2680 v4 CPUs (28 cores, 56 threads), 378 GB RAM, and 2 TB SSD. Besides, we also maintain a `Parity` node in `archive` pruning mode with tracing `on`. Archive nodes are special as they also provide the unmatched ability to replay past transactions, retrieve execution traces, as well as send simulated transactions at any point of time in history, which normal full nodes (with state pruning `on`) cannot offer. The `Parity` node we use in this work is based on QuikNode's dedicated Ethereum node service, which exposes standard Web3 JSON-RPC APIs through both HTTP and WebSocket protocols. It takes about 2 days for this node to fully synchronize.

4   Results

4.1   *RQ1*: Status Quo

Exception Taxonomy. We first look at different runtime exceptions in EVM. In particular, we are interested in comparing out of gas with other exception types. In summary, we identify a number of 16 different exception types in EVM, and further group them into six major categories. In Table 1, we show this taxonomy, as well as the absolute occurrences and relative scales of each type.

Table 1. Comparing out of gas exception with other exception types in EVM.

Exception	Occurrence			Percentage	
	All	External	Ratio	All	External
(1) *Explicit Revert*					
REQUIRE-STYLE REVERT (RR)	14, 000, 856	**11, 456, 103**	1.22	8.12%	**64.91%**
ASSERT-STYLE REVERT (AR)	990, 183	925, 701	1.07	0.57%	5.24%
(2) *Out of Gas*					
DEPLOY OUT OF GAS (DOG)	10, 963	10, 963	1	0%	0.06%
EXECUTE OUT OF GAS (EOG)	**155, 373, 273**	4, 281, 071	**36.29**	**90.09%**	24.25%
(3) *Stack Overflow/Underflow*					
CALL-STACK OVERFLOW (CSO)	10, 032	1, 113	9.01	0%	0.01%
DATA-STACK UNDERFLOW (DSU)	153, 445	53, 501	2.87	0.09%	0.30%
DATA-STACK OVERFLOW (DSO)	152	152	1	0%	0.001%
(4) *Illegal Instruction*					
INVALID JUMP DESTINATION (IJD)	1, 341, 130	1, 306, 785	1.03	0.78%	7.40%
INVALID OPCODE (IO)	232, 226	189, 518	1.23	0.13%	1.07%
(5) *Not Enough Ether*					
INSUFFICIENT BALANCE (IB)	359, 822	356, 517	1.01	0.21%	2.02%
(6) *Miscellanea*					
CLIENT DECISION, ILLEGAL WRITE, *etc.*	1, 693	1, 692	1.00	0%	0.01%
◇ *Summary*					
Out of Gas (DOG + EOG)	**155, 384, 236**	4, 291, 945	**36.20**	**90.09%**	24.32%
Explicit Revert (RR + AR)	14, 991, 039	**12, 137, 417**	1.24	8.69%	**68.77%**
Other Exception Types	2, 098, 500	1, 684, 217	1.25	1.22%	9.54%
◇ *Summery (excluding DoS attacks)*					
Out of Gas (DOG + EOG)	4, 666, 508	4, 233, 428	1.10	21.86%	24.10%
Explicit Revert (RR + AR)	**14, 987, 686**	**12, 134, 192**	**1.24**	**70.20%**	**69.07%**
Other Exception Types	1, 696, 017	1, 654, 643	1.03	7.94%	9.42%

The data shown in Table 1 are presented by analyzing all the transactions from genesis block (*i.e.*, block #0) towards block #8, 547, 396 (*i.e.*, as of September 14th, 2019). In the **Occurrence** column, we show values for three related concepts: (1) number of exception instances, including external and internal transactions; (2) number of external transactions; and (3) average number of exception instances per external transaction. And in the **Percentage** column, we show numbers for the instances and the external transactions. We have the following observations:

- (1) out of gas and explicit revert are two most commonly seen types of exception in Ethereum, which combinedly account for more than 90% of the occurrence in terms of both exception instances (*i.e.*, external transactions plus internal message calls) as well as external transactions.

- (2) When considering all the transactions, out of gas alone accounts for more than 90% of all exceptions, with explicit revert only takes another 8%. However, after excluding the notorious DoS attacks [1,2] by eliminating transactions from block #2, 250, 000 till #2, 750, 000 (both inclusive), the situation swaps, where out of gas now occupies slightly more than 20%, whereas explicit revert takes up another 70%. In fact, only 58, 517 external transactions in the above interval contribute to a total of 150, 717, 728 exception instances, or nearly 2, 576 instances per transaction. This suggests the gigantic influence of these DoS attacks on our study. Hence, in the rest of this work, we will always exclude transactions from block #2, 250, 000 to #2, 750, 000, in order to minimize the unfavourable effects of the DoS attacks.
- (3) On average, all the exception types in Table 1 take place more than once in a single external transaction. In other words, there are at least an external transaction that has witnessed more than one exception. Or, some contracts tend to ignore or not fully revert in case of deep runtime exceptions. Besides, transactions may also trigger more than one type of exceptions. This can be checked by adding all the relative percentage of external transactions for each exception type, which yields around 105%, exceeding the normal 100%.

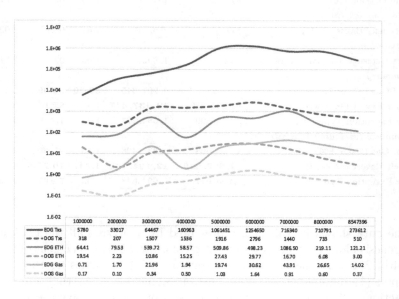

Fig. 3. Transactions, gas units, and ETH values affected by out of gas exceptions.

Accumulative Losses. In Fig. 3, we show the accumulative losses of both EOG (in full lines) and DOG (in dashed lines) exceptions. The numbers are divided into three groups: (1) affected external transactions (shown as Txs); (2) accumulated gas (shown as Gas in units of 10^9 gas); and (3) ETH values (shown as ETH). The data shown in Fig. 3 are gathered and summarized in intervals of $1,000,000$ blocks, from block #0 to #8,547,396. Note, as for loss of gas (and deriving ETH), we show the accumulated gas limit of all exception instances (*i.e.*, counting the sum of proposed gas limit for each exception transaction). While this does not trivially equal to total loss of gas (and corresponding ETH), it is the best proxy we can get and there are evidences showing these two values do not differ significantly (*i.e.*, in orders of magnitude). And the ETH shown is calculated by counting each transaction individually considering each individual tx.gasPrice. We have the following observations:

- (1) The losses result from out of gas exceptions are enormous, with as large as several hundred thousand transactions involved every one million blocks (or slightly less than 1 transaction per block), causing a total amount of some hundreds of ETH wasted (or tens of thousands of US dollars with a fairly low exchange rate of \$150/ETH). While inside out of gas exception itself, EOG dominates DOG in terms of resulted transaction, gas, and ETH losses.
- (2) Both exceptions, EOG and DOG, experience a similar trend for the three shown indexes (*i.e.*, external transactions, gas units, and wasted ETH). For example, consider the external transactions involved in each exception type, *i.e.*, EOG txs and DOG txs, both start at a very small volume, then quickly climb to reach their maxima, and at last stay steady. In particular, both EOG txs and DOG txs get their maximal value between block #5,000,000 and #6,000,000 (the blockchain hype), *i.e.*, 1,254,650 for EOG and 2,796 for DOG.
- (3) The lines of wasted gas and ETH for each exception type match very well, suggesting a relatively stable gas price across large interval of blocks.

Individual Accounts. To further understand out of gas exception, we group the exception instances according to their sender and receiver addresses. In other words, we want to find those accounts sending and receiving the most out of gas exceptions (both EOG and DOG) whether by transactions or message calls.

In Table 2, we show top 10 accounts sending and receiving most out of gas exceptions, respectively, from among a total number of 1,101,591 and 148,940 such accounts, respectively. We also estimate the real value of ETH loss with an exchange rate of \$150/ETH. We have the following observations:

- (1) All the accounts in both lists see a large number of out of gas exceptions during their existence, with the top accounts involved in more than one million instances for both EOG and DOG. However, the accounts causing the most wasted gas as well as ETH (*i.e.*, 0x0601~266d and 0xd0a6~7ccf) are not these seen the most exceptions. In particular, the underlined account 0xd0a6~7ccf (EOSSale) has caused more than 164 ETH loss in only 44,721 function calls, far behind the 0x04 contract with 1,412,148 instead.
- (2) The accounts in the second list (*i.e.*, receiving the most exceptions) has caused far more losses than in the first list (*i.e.*, sending the most exceptions).

Table 2. A list of top 10 accounts sending and receiving most out of gas exceptions.

Account address	Instance	Gas	Ether	
(1) *Accounts Sending Most Out of Gas Transactions*				
0x60bf91ac87fEE5A78c28F7b67701FBCFA79C18EC	**1, 213, 760**	9, 917, 594	0.17	($24.88)
0x4B9e0d224DABCC96191cacE2D367A8d8B75C9C81	68, 957	209, 168	0.002	($0.34)
0x68C769478002B2E2Db64fE3Be55C943fE4Fbd6b1	57, 257	242, 976	0.003	($0.45)
0xE4c94d45f7Aef7018a5D66f44aF780ec6023378e	56, 388	6, 134, 966	0.12	($18.26)
0x0000000000085d4780B73119b644AE5ecd22b376	25, 079	497, 667, 177	4.60	($689.86)
0x06012c8cf97BEaD5deAe237070F9587f8E7A266d	22, 847	**1, 486, 219, 348**	**40.37**	**($6055.3)**
0x7c5Cb1220Bd293Ff9cf903915732e51a71292038	15, 024	639, 357, 019	8.29	($1243.74)
0x0000000000013949F288172bD7E36837bDdC7211	11, 212	108, 082, 558	0.31	($46.91)
0xd0a6E6C54DbC68Db5db3A091B171A77407Ff7ccf	10, 298	96, 311, 375	2.49	($373.67)
0x414FBf684A6426cf6012623f51170a5A86161d52	10, 041	55, 541	0.0006	($0.09)
(2) *Accounts Receiving Most Out of Gas Transactions*				
0x0000000000000000000000000000000000000004	**1, 412, 148**	4, 236, 441	0.06	($9.30)
0x744d70FDBE2Ba4CF95131626614a1763DF805B9E	81, 830	3, 826, 605, 402	49.93	($7489.45)
0xd0a6E6C54DbC68Db5db3A091B171A77407Ff7ccf	44, 721	**7, 658, 554, 274**	**164.20**	**($24630.2)**
0x06012c8cf97BEaD5deAe237070F9587f8E7A266d	38, 118	792, 031, 653	24.70	($3704.29)
0x8d12A197cB00D4747a1fe03395095ce2A5CC6819	35, 300	975, 469, 855	23.99	($3598.60)
0xb1690C08E213a35Ed9bAb7B318DE14420FB57d8C	33, 486	1, 286, 027, 958	37.60	($5639.40)
0x419D0d8BdD9aF5e606Ae2232ed285Aff190E711b	30, 622	578, 076, 676	5.94	($890.97)
0xba7435A4b4C747E0101780073eedA872a69Bdcd4	30, 483	1, 590, 815, 838	9.99	($1498.03)
0x86Fa049857E0209aa7D9e616F7eb3b3B78ECfdb0	26, 523	320, 330, 157	11.43	($1715.05)
0x5EdC1a266E8b2c5E8086d373725dF0690af7e3Ea	23, 943	1, 437, 343, 328	13.30	($1995.45)

Since the amount of losses (both gas and ETH) are always equal regardless of the calling directing, this may suggests an asymmetry between transaction senders and their receivers, *i.e.*, large number of ordinary accounts (whether EOAs or smart contracts) tend to send transactions a small group of popular contracts (mostly smart contracts), *e.g.*, those well-known ERC-20 tokens.

- (3) The precompiled contract 0x04 ranks first as the most out of gas exception receiver, whereas it only acts as an identity function for input data (*i.e.*, returning what it gets). This is more surprising considering the huge amount of exceptions versus a negligible wasted gas. In fact, all these exceptions stem from some internal message calls, and all but one calls have set a gas limit of 3 units. Even more, the Parity seems not identifying these internal calls. After carefully inspecting relevant traces, we finally confirm the existence of these transactions, as well as the exceptions.
- (4) There are two accounts appearing in both lists as sending and receiving most out of gas exceptions, *i.e.*, the underlined 0xd0a6∼7ccf (EOSSale) and the tilded 0x0601∼266d (KittyCore), which happens belong to two popular token standards, ERC-20, ERC-721.

4.2 *RQ2*: Causing Factor

Common Causing Factors. By manually inspecting exceptional transactions, their execution traces, as well as related contracts, we have found some common causing factors for out of gas exceptions, as summarized below:

- (1) *Misunderstanding Transaction Mechanism.* This is a commonly seen and most trivial causing factor for out of gas exceptions, especially *w.r.t.* to external transactions. In particular, according to the transaction processing mechanism, if the transaction target/destination (`tx.to`) is a smart contract, Ethereum will load that contract's code and starting running along with transaction input (`tx.input`) in EVM. Note, this process is automatically triggered by Ethereum without user intervention. Thus if the user overlooks or ignores the aforementioned contract execution mechanism, and sets transaction gas limit to its minimal viable value (*i.e.*, the very basic intrinsic gas cost for a valid external transaction, 21, 000 for normal transfer and 53, 000 for contract creation), there will always be out of gas exception since not a single gas unit is available for further contract execution. In our data set, we have found a total number of 542, 193 external transactions having this kind of problem, accounting for nearly one fifths of such transactions. Besides, the problem does not see a clearly decreasing in terms of transaction numbers as time passes by. In particular, we have found 41, 820 external transactions suffering from the problem from block #8, 000, 000 to #8, 547, 396, whereas the highest number per one million blocks is just 175, 204 for interval #4, 000, 000 to #5, 000, 000.
- (2) *Conservative Gas Limit.* This kind of problem stems from the fact that the transactions can terminate without any exception but are otherwise set with a lower gas limit than needed. For example, the transaction 0xf31d~9557 in block #8, 547, 387 happens to run out of gas with a relative small gas limit 30, 000. By setting a much higher gas limit, we find the actual gas needed for the transaction is only 37, 112, or 7, 112 more units compared to original gas limit. In other words, the user could have saved a gas loss of 30, 000 units by merely paying 7, 112 units more, that's a 22, 888 units net earning.
- (3) *Compiler Derived Bug.* Sometimes, the problem for out of gas exception may stem from hidden bugs or flaws of the contract compiler (in most cases the `solc` Solidity compiler.) An example of this kind is the under-gas call to precompiled identity contract 0x04 [21], where the message call only gets 3 units of gas for execution. This accounts for about 2% of all the exception instances found in our data set. According to [21], the gas cost for identity contract is 15 units plus 3 per input word. In other words, the cost is always large or equal to 15, where a gas limit of 3 is doomed out of gas. In fact, we have seen a large number of such instances during our investigation. While we do not know the cause of this problem, and it may not be a big problem for users, it at least reflects the fact that Solidity compilers are not mature right now, and should be carefully checked in production environment.
- (4) *Unbounded Mass Operation.* The authors of [14] have revealed several gas-related contract vulnerabilities which may trigger unexpected behaviours, *e.g.*, locking specific functions forever, or running into a doomed out of gas loop. This phenomenon is confirmed in our investigation by transaction 0x448b49f72d23ecdb281bf1a92d94ab63ef3efc58937d80f51fa2dadd02591bdb, where two contracts mutually call each other recursive, lead to out of gas.

4.3   *RQ3*: Tool Evaluation

Gas Estimator. Gas estimators are tools or services that can output an estimated gas cost for proposed transactions. Depending on required input and perform timing, gas estimators can be divided into two classes: (1) offline estimators that only need contract code as input, and can be run for once, then use any number of times later; (2) online estimators that utilize Ethereum client's capability to run transactions on top of specific world states without writing back, which need both contract code as well as transaction to function, and have to be run any time a new transaction or world state is presented.

In this section, we investigate the potential benefits of using offline gas estimators. In particular, we test the `solc` native gas estimator (`--gas`) on a small set of 5 contracts. We leave other tools, *e.g.*, the `GASTAP` proposed by Albert *et al.* in [7], to further studies.

Table 3. `solc` native gas estimator in use of preventing out of gas exceptions.

Address	Contract	Function			Instance		
		All	*Solve*	*Ratio*	*All*	*Solve*	*Ratio*
0xd0a6E6C54DbC68Db5db3A091B171A77407Ff7ccf	EOSSale	30	17	57%	44,651	0	0%
0x8d12A197cB00D4747a1fe03395095ce2A5CC6819	EtherDelta	27	18	67%	33,738	6,402	19%
0xb1690C08E213a35Ed9bAb7B318DE14420FB57d8C	SaleAuction	18	12	67%	33,041	0	0%
0x86Fa049857E0209aa7D9e616F7eb3b3B78ECfdb0	DSToken	21	9	43%	26,011	24	0.1%
0x1F0480a66883De97d2b054929252aaE8F664c15c	NePay	22	12	55%	16,333	0	0%

In Table 3, the results are shown in two groups: (1) with respect to public functions (*Function*); and (2) with respect to message calls (*Instance*). For each group, from left to right, the values are read: (1) number of instances in our data set; (2) number of instances `solc` helps to prevent; (3) the extent `solc` can help. In this experiment, we use a `v0.4.25` version `solc` compiler since both contracts in Table 3 only accepts compiler version `v0.4.x`. We have the following observations:

- (1) As for public functions, `solc` can help in preventing nearly half of the gas exceptions. In other words, considering an average contract, `solc` gives meaningful estimations for about half of the public functions. Note, the `solc` gas estimator is so conservative that it rejects any function with any kind of loops (*e.g.*, reading from a dynamic array) or unbounded calls. Thus the results it returns should be always exact upper bound for a public function.
- (2) When considering transaction distribution, `solc` seems do not have any applaudable effects. In particular, as shown by contract `0xd0a6~7ccf`, not a single of the exception instance can be saved with help `solc`. The reason for this is these instances all calls to functions that are not covered by `solc` (so it cannot give any useful information *w.r.t.* gas cost). Note, the test instances are all collected from our previously found out of gas transactions, so the result shown here is skewed towards hard cases where loops and unbounded

calls exist, and may not be fair to `solc`. However, what is clear is that if we want to solve those real-world out of gas problems, `solc` estimator alone is far from helpful, and we need more powerful tools for this purpose.

5 Related Work

Chen *et al.* [10] studied the use of Solidity language in writing smart contract. They identified seven gas-costly source code level patterns where the official Solidity compiler (`solc`) failed to optimize. They then built a tool called `GASPER` which can find three of these seven patterns using contract bytecode. In [12], the same author reported 24 bytecode level anti-patterns, and then built a contract optimizer named `GasReducer` baed on these anti-patterns.

Grech *et al.* [14] studied three smart contract vulnerabilities that are directly related to Ethereum gas mechanism. In particular, all these three vulnerabilities can be exploited by hackers to lock a target contract down, effectively making it unusable forever. The authors then devised a static analysis tool named `MadMax` to help find these gas-related vulnerabilities.

Albert *et al.* [7] proposed a gas analyzer for smart contracts named `GASTAP`, which can infer an upper bound for each function's gas cost. At the same time, Marescotti *et al.* [18] proposed a worst-case gas consumption estimation technique inspired by bounded model-checking techniques. Their method was built on top of the so-called gas consumption paths (GCPs), then they used SMT solver and EVM's gas consumption capabilities to retrieve concrete gas limits. However, since [18] lacks a tool implementation as well as subsequent experiments, we do not know its effectiveness on real world smart contracts.

There is a gas cost alignment problem in Ethereum, which states that if the gas mechanism assigns much less gas cost for a certain instruction, then hackers could utilize the instruction to launch a DoS attack against the Ethereum network. Both Chen *et al.* [11] and Yang *et al.* [22] concluded that Ethereum's current gas mechanism, despite been changed many times, still left considerable rooms for misuse and DoS attacks. Besides, [11] also proposed an adaptive gas cost mechanism aiming at defending these potential DoS attacks.

6 Conclusion

In this work, we investigate the out of gas exceptions on Ethereum blockchain. By using instrumented Ethereum client, we collect a large data set of exception transactions as well as their execution traces. We then start by looking at the prevalence of different exceptions, where out of gas stood out with a large number of occurrences as well as money losses. Moreover, we summarize common causing factors for out of gas exceptions, with an emphasis on misunderstanding of transaction mechanism, conservative gas limit, and compiler derived bugs. At last, we investigate the effectiveness of existing tools in helping prevent out of gas exceptions. The results suggest further research and study on this topic.

Acknowledgments. This work is supported by National Natural Science Foundation of China under the grant No.: 61672060.

References

1. Ethereum continues to suffer from DDoS attacks (2016). https://www.ethnews.com/ethereum-continues-to-suffer-from-ddos-attacks
2. Transaction spam attack: next steps (2016). https://blog.ethereum.org/2016/09/22/transaction-spam-attack-next-steps/
3. Contracts - solidity 0.5.11 documentation: creating contracts (2019). https://solidity.readthedocs.io/en/v0.5.11/contracts.html#creating-contracts
4. Home - enterprise ethereum alliance (2019). https://entethalliance.org
5. A next-generation smart contract and decentralized application platform, ethereum white paper (2019). https://github.com/ethereum/wiki/wiki/White-Paper
6. Security alert: Ethereum constantinople postponement (2019). https://blog.ethereum.org/2019/01/15/security-alert-ethereum-constantinople-postponement/
7. Albert, E., Gordillo, P., Rubio, A., Sergey, I.: GASTAP: a gas analyzer for smart contracts. arXiv preprint arXiv:1811.10403 (2018)
8. Alharby, M., Aldweesh, A., van Moorsel, A.: Blockchain-based smart contracts: a systematic mapping study of academic research (2018). In: Proceedings of the 2018 International Conference on Cloud Computing, Big Data and Blockchain (2018)
9. Androulaki, E., et al.: Hyperledger fabric: a distributed operating system for permissioned blockchains. In: Proceedings of the Thirteenth EuroSys Conference, p. 30. ACM (2018)
10. Chen, T., Li, X., Luo, X., Zhang, X.: Under-optimized smart contracts devour your money. In: 2017 IEEE 24th International Conference on Software Analysis, Evolution and Reengineering (SANER), pp. 442–446. IEEE (2017)
11. Chen, T., et al.: An adaptive gas cost mechanism for ethereum to defend against under-priced DoS attacks. In: Liu, J.K., Samarati, P. (eds.) ISPEC 2017. LNCS, vol. 10701, pp. 3–24. Springer, Cham (2017). https://doi.org/10.1007/978-3-319-72359-4_1
12. Chen, T., et al.: Towards saving money in using smart contracts. In: 2018 IEEE/ACM 40th International Conference on Software Engineering: New Ideas and Emerging Technologies Results (ICSE-NIER), pp. 81–84. IEEE (2018)
13. Cheng, R., et al.: Ekiden: a platform for confidentiality-preserving, trustworthy, and performant smart contracts. In: 2019 IEEE European Symposium on Security and Privacy (EuroS&P), pp. 185–200. IEEE (2019)
14. Grech, N., Kong, M., Jurisevic, A., Brent, L., Scholz, B., Smaragdakis, Y.: MadMax: surviving out-of-gas conditions in Ethereum smart contracts. Proc. ACM Program. Lang. 2(OOPSLA), 116 (2018)
15. Kosba, A., Miller, A., Shi, E., Wen, Z., Papamanthou, C.: Hawk: the blockchain model of cryptography and privacy-preserving smart contracts. In: 2016 IEEE Symposium on Security and Privacy (SP), pp. 839–858. IEEE (2016)
16. Kumaresan, R., Bentov, I.: How to use bitcoin to incentivize correct computations. In: Proceedings of the 2014 ACM SIGSAC Conference on Computer and Communications Security, pp. 30–41. ACM (2014)
17. Luu, L., Chu, D.H., Olickel, H., Saxena, P., Hobor, A.: Making smart contracts smarter. In: Proceedings of the 2016 ACM SIGSAC Conference on Computer and Communications Security, pp. 254–269. ACM (2016)

18. Marescotti, M., Blicha, M., Hyvärinen, A.E.J., Asadi, S., Sharygina, N.: Computing exact worst-case gas consumption for smart contracts. In: Margaria, T., Steffen, B. (eds.) ISoLA 2018. LNCS, vol. 11247, pp. 450–465. Springer, Cham (2018). https://doi.org/10.1007/978-3-030-03427-6_33

19. Miers, I., Garman, C., Green, M., Rubin, A.D.: Zerocoin: anonymous distributed e-cash from Bitcoin. In: 2013 IEEE Symposium on Security and Privacy, pp. 397–411. IEEE (2013)

20. Nakamoto, S., et al.: Bitcoin: a peer-to-peer electronic cash system (2008)

21. Wood, G., et al.: Ethereum: a secure decentralised generalised transaction ledger. Ethereum Proj. Yellow Pap. **151**(2014), 1–32 (2014)

22. Yang, R., Murray, T., Rimba, P., Parampalli, U.: Empirically analyzing ethereum's gas mechanism. arXiv preprint arXiv:1905.00553 (2019)

Toward Detecting Illegal Transactions on Bitcoin Using Machine-Learning Methods

Chaehyeon Lee[(⊠)], Sajan Maharjan, Kyungchan Ko, and James Won-Ki Hong

Department of Computer Science and Engineering, POSTECH,
Pohang 37673, Korea
{chlee0211,thesajan,kkc90,jwkhong}@postech.ac.kr

Abstract. As an emergent electronic payment system, Bitcoin has attracted attention for its desirable features such as disintermediation, decentralization, and tamper-proof recording of data. The Bitcoin network also employs public key cryptography to prevent the disclosure of information related to participating users. Although the public key cryptography ensures the privacy and hides the true identity of users in the Bitcoin network, it has recently been abused for illegal activities that have tarnished the charm of this novel technology. Detecting the illegal transactions associated with illicit activities in Bitcoin is therefore imperative. This paper proposes a machine-learning based approach that classifies Bitcoin transactions as illegal or legal. The detected illegal transactions can be excluded from the subsequent block, promoting user acceptance and adoption of the Bitcoin technology.

Keywords: Bitcoin · Illegal transaction detection · Classification · Bitcoin transaction analysis · Transaction feature extraction

1 Introduction

Bitcoin [1] is a fully-distributed, peer-to-peer network in which all network participants maintain identical copies of the data without third-party intervention. The disintermediation from a third-party has allowed the cross-border transfer of values between buyers and sellers with low transaction fees and little processing. Blocks of data in the Bitcoin network are recorded sequentially in order of their occurrence; this technique is known as the blockchain technology [2]. As a cryptocurrency, Bitcoin is advantaged by data integrity, data invariance, and privacy guarantee through address anonymity. However, the pseudo-anonymity of the network participants has exposed Bitcoin to illegal transactions in the black market.

Various darknets have abused blockchain technology for illegal use [3]. According to statistical records, the total dollar value of Bitcoin in the darknet market has been steadily increasing since 2011 (see Fig. 1) [4]. In 2017, when the trading value reached its maximum, bitcoins worth $770 million were traded

© Springer Nature Singapore Pte Ltd. 2020
Z. Zheng et al. (Eds.): BlockSys 2019, CCIS 1156, pp. 520–533, 2020.
https://doi.org/10.1007/978-981-15-2777-7_42

through darknets. Silk Road, the Amazon of the darknet market, has sold prohibited drugs such as hemp, cocaine, and heroin, and illegal commodities such as child pornography, stolen goods, malicious codes, and weapons. Silk Road was built on the Tor network and is accessible only through the Tor browser. By July of 2013, nearly a million users had purchased various illicit items through bitcoins.

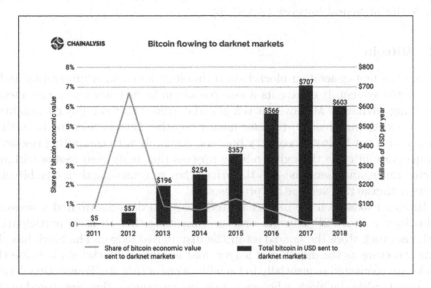

Fig. 1. Bitcoin values (in USD) sent to darknet markets from 2011 to 2018. Orange line graph shows the proportion of darknet Bitcoin transactions over all Bitcoin transactions (Source: Chainalysis [4]) (Color figure online)

The enactment of cryptocurrency laws in hindered not only by transactions involving illegal goods, but also by money laundering and scamming activities. Therefore, the detection of illegal transactions in blockchains is imperative.

Our research focuses on Bitcoin, the most commonly used cryptocurrency in illegal transactions. We first extract the transaction features from Bitcoin data, and classify the transactions as legal or illegal. We then collect the distinguishing features of the legal and illegal transactions. We build machine-learning models and train them on the extracted features, which are labeled as legal or illegal. To verify the effectiveness of the training, we finally check the classifications of the machine-learning models on the test set.

The remainder of this paper is organized as follows. Section 2 explains the background and related work. Section 3 describes the classification process and implementations of the proposed detection system. The experimental results and discussion are presented in Sects. 4 and 5, respectively. Section 6 concludes the paper and suggests improvements and future work.

2   Background and Related Work

This section introduces the blockchain technology underlying this paper and the machine-learning technology used in developing the detection system. We first explain what Bitcoin is, and describe the structure and characteristics of a Bitcoin transaction. We also introduce the two machine-learning algorithms implemented in our detection system, namely, the random forest classifier [5] and Artificial Neural Network (ANN) [6].

2.1   Bitcoin

Bitcoin is a first-generation blockchain technology based on cryptography and a distributed system. It represents a new paradigm in currency and a new means of making payments. Moreover, it is a global currency that can buy commodities such as existing currencies, transfer money to other Bitcoin users or to institutions, and is not limited to country borders. Anybody with computing resources can generate bitcoins through a mining process that finds hash results within a specific range, and users who own the private key can consume their own bitcoins through transaction verification processes.

Bitcoin is based on the blockchain technology, a data-distributed processing technology with a P2P network structure, meaning that all users participating in the network store the same data in the distributed ledger. The block has the same structure as the distributed ledger, and is called a blockchain because the blocks are connected sequentially in time like a chain (Fig. 2). Transaction details are stored inside the block, whereas in existing currencies, they are stored in the central server (typically a bank).

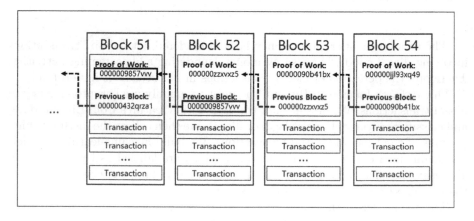

Fig. 2. Example of a blockchain structure

2.2 Transactions

A transaction is a data structure encoding the behavior of the value transmitted among the Bitcoin network participants. Each transaction is recorded in the distributed ledger of the participants. Transactions are of different types with different numbers of input and output values. Figure 3(a) demonstrates the most common form of transaction: one output of bitcoin remittance from one input value, and another output that returns the remaining balance to the original owner. As Bitcoin lacks a mechanism that automatically returns the remaining bitcoin to its original owner, the owner must generate the output that performs his function. The transaction in Fig. 3(b) sends multiple inputs to one address, and that in Fig. 3(c) allows multiple output values in one transaction for distributing and sending bitcoins to multiple addresses. The sum of the input values should be greater than or equal to the sum of the output values, and the difference between the two sums is a transaction fee. The transaction fee rewards the miner who has included that transaction in the block, and the higher the transaction fee, the faster it is included into a block.

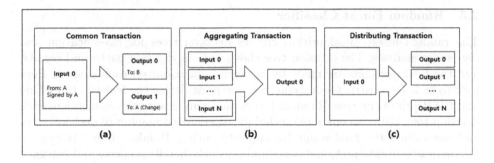

Fig. 3. The three types of Bitcoin transactions

Bitcoin does not operate with balances. It considers only the unconsumed transaction output (UTXO) scattered in the blockchain, which is locked by certain owners. In other words, the input value of the transaction is the UTXO consumed by the transaction, and the output is the UTXO newly generated by the transaction. The UTXO, which is a transaction output resulting from a transaction, is a Bitcoin lump that is unconsumed at present but will likely be consumed by the owner in future. As a UTXO cannot be split into smaller units when used as a transaction input, it is wholly (not partially) consumed, and the remaining difference is constructed as a new UTXO.

As shown in Fig. 4, the hash of the first transaction and the index of the output value provide the input value of the next transaction. That is, the output of the previous transaction is the input value of a new transaction. The value between Bitcoin addresses moves with the creation of the ownership chain of UTXOs. A transaction is connected to the chain structure simultaneously with the block, so the flow of the bitcoin can be traced through the transaction chain.

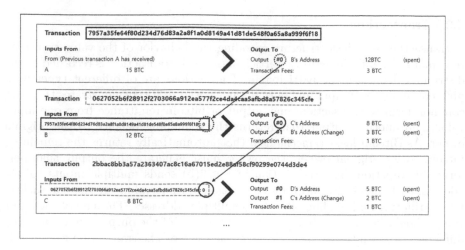

Fig. 4. A transaction chain

2.3 Random Forest Classifier

The random forest [5] algorithm creates decision trees for classification and regression analysis. The decision tree shows various decision paths and results, and the final decisions are made by answering questions on each element from root to leaf. To construct a decision tree, one must decide the features to include and the depth of the tree. Random forest randomly selects the elements of each decision tree. Using an ensemble technique, it creates a number of decision trees and determines the final result by majority voting. Random forest is easy to understand and interpret, and can simultaneously handle numeric and category data. In this paper, we implemented a classification model using the random forest algorithm to determine the illegal/legal categories.

2.4 Artificial Neural Network (ANN)

An ANN [6] mimics the nervous system of a living organism. The artificial neurons (nodes) in an ANN are abstractions of nerve cells (neurons). As a learning algorithm, it mimics human intelligence by replicating the behaviors of neurons that receive stimulus signals and convey them to another neuron. The nodes in an ANN are interconnected through several layers. The data to be learned are inserted through the input layer, processed in one or more hidden layers, and output as the final result through the output layer.

2.5 Related Work

Zambre and Shah [7] proposed a machine-learning-based system that determines the characteristics of users related to bitcoin thefts, and identifies users performing similar actions. To detect bitcoin thefts and fraudulent activity, they extracted the associated bitcoin transaction information and classified the extracted characteristics by a k-means [8] clustering algorithm.

Toyoda et al. [9] analyzed the transaction patterns of users collecting bitcoin addresses related to the high-yielding investment program (HYIP). They extracted the characteristics of these patterns, such as the number of transactions associated with the bitcoin address and the number of blocks mined, and labeled the bitcoin address with HYIP or non-HYIP for classifying the cybercrime groups through supervised learning.

Although the bitcoin addresses and clusters associated with Bitcoin crimes have been identified and classified in many researches, the classification of transactions from the transaction features alone appears not to be reported. Therefore, the present paper considers the common characteristics of crime-related bitcoin transactions.

3   Classification Process and Implementation

To classify bitcoin transactions as illegal or legal, we employed a four-step procedure commonly used in classification algorithms. The four steps are transaction collection, feature extraction and labeling, training by a machine-learning model, and testing (Fig. 5). The collected dataset contains both illegal and legal transactions obtained from a verified source (forum sites: Blockchain Explorer [10], WalletExplorer [11]) as hash values only. To extract the relevant features of such transactions from a Bitcoin node, we wrote a Python script invoking JSON-RPC calls. As classification algorithms require a labeled dataset, we manually assigned a label to each transaction (legal = 1; illegal = 0). The dataset consisting of different features was trained by machine-learning classification algorithms and the learning performance was evaluated by the F1-score measured on the test set. The following subsections describe each step in detail.

3.1   Transaction Collection

Before implementing the machine-learning model, we collected hash lists of the illegal and legal transactions from an explorer site and a forum site, which are publicly available. The blockchain data search site Blockchain Explorer [10] has released some of the transaction hashes associated with Silk Road. Specifically, it provides a hash list of all transactions indicating activities involving a proven Silk Road address that had received bitcoins from another address. Meanwhile, the forum site WalletExplorer [11] discloses the categories of data used in specific groups, such as exchanges, memory pools, gambling, and darknets. The illegal transaction list in this study was compiled from the Silk Road category, and the legal transaction list was compiled from transaction lists traded through exchanges (the Silk Road Seized Coins Address is 1F1tAaz5x1HUXrCNLbtMDqcw6o5GNn4xqX [12]).

We built a simple web crawler in Python using the Beautiful Soup library [13] to obtain the list of hash values of the above transactions. This list contains 956 K

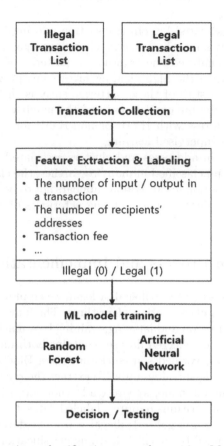

Fig. 5. Bitcoin transactions classification procedure using Machine Learning Algorithms

illegal transactions and 800 K legal transactions. Note that experimental dataset contained more illegal than legal transactions, which does not necessarily reflect the proportions of illegal and legal transactions in the network. The collected data constitute only a fraction of transactions in the entire Bitcoin network, and only a portion of the collected data was learned by the machine-learning model to alleviate the data imbalance.

3.2   Feature Extraction and Labeling

3.2.1   Feature Extraction

After extracting the transaction list, we extracted the key features for training the machine-learning models. Illegal transactions may exhibit common characteristics such as high transaction fees that are quickly included in blocks, multiple identical outputs inside one transaction (indicating money laundering), or bitcoins distributed to multiple addresses. To identify the common patterns associated with illegal transactions, we extracted nine characteristics from the transaction details (Table 1).

Table 1. List of the extracted transaction features for distinguishing legal and illegal transactions

Name	Transaction features to be extracted
vin	Number of inputs
vout	Number of outputs
vin_value	Value of input
vout_value	Value of output
fee	Transaction fee
in_addr	Number of transmission addresses owning the UTXOs to transmit
out_addr	Number of receiver addresses that will own new UTXOs after the transaction
size	Transaction size
value	Transaction amount

The Python script returns the transaction details of a given transaction hash through the JSON-RPC calls available in Bitcoin Core [14,15]. The Python script handles the JSON response from a Bitcoin full-node and extracts the relevant features, namely, the number of inputs and outputs included in the transaction, the input and output values (i.e., the amounts of bitcoin transmitted by the sender address and received by the recipient address), the transaction fee, the number of real owners of the UTXO included in the input (i.e., the number of sender addresses possessing the UTXO), the number of receiving addresses owning the new UTXO after the transaction output, the transaction size, and the amount of bitcoin traded through the transaction. The dataset containing these features was stored in a CSV file.

3.2.2 Labeling
When training a classification algorithm, the training data must be labeled. Therefore, after extracting the features of each transaction, we manually labeled each transaction as either legal (1) or illegal (0) (see Figs. 6 and 7).

3.2.3 Data Set Configuration
Although our dataset contained more illegal transactions than legal ones (956 K versus 800 K), we randomly selected only portions of the dataset during our experiments, varying the dataset size and distribution ratio of legal-to-illegal transactions (Fig. 8). Before training the machine-learning models, we must define the sizes of the training and test sets. The training-test split was set to 60:40 of each experimental dataset.

txid	vin	vout	vin_value	vout_value	fee	in_addr	out_addr	size	value	legal
ae018d96(	1	2	0.007559	0.007522	3.66E-05	1	2	373	0.007522	0
26641f6eb	1	2	0.007727	0.007691	3.66E-05	1	2	373	0.007691	0
66d9e2d0:	1	2	0.007896	0.007859	3.66E-05	1	2	373	0.007859	0
45059044t	1	2	0.00847	0.008433	3.65E-05	1	2	369	0.008433	0
cfc2e5716(	1	2	0.008664	0.008628	3.65E-05	1	2	372	0.008628	0
c105f56b0	2	2	0.010104	0.010036	6.74E-05	1	2	670	0.010036	0
804623f3e	1	2	0.00063	0.000594	3.64E-05	1	2	369	0.000594	0
d8d6927e(	1	2	0.012415	0.012396	1.89E-05	1	2	372	0.012396	0
53d3021c:	1	2	0.089659	0.089587	0.000072	1	2	372	0.089587	0
6e97d9c24	1	17	1.006517	1.006334	0.000183	1	17	729	1.006334	0
efd57f85a(	2	151	20.5324	20.53106	0.001344	2	151	5372	20.53106	0
915e3a2a:	1	750	0.00013	3E-05	0.0001	1	750	25691	3E-05	0
6b774ad1(	1	750	0.00013	3E-05	0.0001	1	750	25691	3E-05	0
cd4c7a30t	1	750	0.00013	3E-05	0.0001	1	750	25691	3E-05	0
81b3593f7	1	750	0.00013	3E-05	0.0001	1	750	25691	3E-05	0
730e2d30f	1	750	0.00013	3E-05	0.0001	1	750	25691	3E-05	0
79b80066:	1	750	0.00013	3E-05	0.0001	1	750	25691	3E-05	0
b6433b02:	1	749	0.000107	7.49E-06	0.0001	1	749	25658	7.49E-06	0
1c80ad7c(	1	749	0.000107	7.49E-06	0.0001	1	749	25657	7.49E-06	0
ab052c7a:	1	749	0.000107	7.49E-06	0.0001	1	749	25657	7.49E-06	0
5f4feab6ft	1	749	0.000107	7.49E-06	0.0001	1	749	25657	7.49E-06	0
bcd5c9eff:	1	749	0.000107	7.49E-06	0.0001	1	749	25657	7.49E-06	0
b29ffb7e3	1	749	0.000107	7.49E-06	0.0001	1	749	25657	7.49E-06	0
4debeeb5'	1	750	0.00013	3E-05	0.0001	1	750	25691	3E-05	0

Fig. 6. Part of the features of the collected illegal transactions

txid	vin	vout	vin_value	vout_value	fee	in_addr	out_addr	size	value	legal
a96ffb520	1	2	7.64508	7.645065	1.45E-05	1	2	225	7.645065	1
83147fd30	1	2	0.007208	0.007197	1.13E-05	1	2	226	0.007197	1
35c1b6c0a	2	1	0.128235	0.128213	2.24E-05	2	1	339	0.128213	1
655386ad:	1	2	0.002576	0.001564	0.001013	1	2	225	0.001564	1
bc243976(	2	2	0.009532	0.008406	0.001126	2	2	372	0.008406	1
698da853(	2	31	1.13794	1.130844	0.007096	2	31	1352	1.130844	1
27fd48662	5	5	1.440317	1.437517	0.0028	5	5	918	1.437517	1
8c897bab(	21	8	60.63592	60.62092	0.015	21	8	6486	60.62092	1
ba73d042(	2	2	0.023513	0.022881	0.000632	2	2	374	0.022881	1
d51fcaaa8	1	2	0.119195	0.118103	0.001091	1	2	474	0.118103	1
7bc2f2126	1	21	654.7712	654.7691	0.002005	1	21	895	654.7691	1
a55295fe5	1	2	0.254216	0.25387	0.000346	1	2	336	0.25387	1
c918c5eec	2	2	0.033389	0.032889	0.0005	2	2	373	0.032889	1
3368b041:	1	2	0.198	0.198	0.00E+00	1	2	225	0.198	1
bfd3dead(	1	2	0.025254	0.025254	0.00E+00	1	2	225	0.025254	1
11d8afcd3	1	2	0.019251	0.019251	0.00E+00	1	2	226	0.019251	1
3c4aeaa9f	3	2	0.02418	0.02418	0.00E+00	1	2	521	0.02418	1
a3ad42b6:	5	2	0.035254	0.035254	0.00E+00	3	2	815	0.035254	1
7c7487544	1	2	0.092598	0.092598	0.00E+00	1	2	226	0.092598	1
cf89ab402	1	2	0.0745	0.0745	0.00E+00	1	2	226	0.0745	1
87a47b78:	1	2	0.084901	0.084901	0.00E+00	1	2	224	0.084901	1
5150d1e0!	1	2	0.076567	0.076567	0.00E+00	1	2	226	0.076567	1
a324254d(	1	2	0.0299	0.0299	0.00E+00	1	2	225	0.0299	1
75afbb62(	1	2	0.042106	0.042106	0.00E+00	1	2	225	0.042106	1

Fig. 7. Part of the features of the collected legal transactions

3.3 Training of the Machine-Learning Models

After extracting the relevant transaction features, we trained our supervised-learning classification algorithms based on the assigned labels. The transactions were classified as legal or illegal by the random forest classifier and ANN. The random forest and ANN models were implemented on the application programming interface provided by sklearn [16] and Tensorflow library [17]. The implemented ANN model consists of one input layer with nine features, two hidden layers (one with five nodes, the other with tree nodes), and one output layer.

```
df_legal= df_legal.sample(n=15000, random_state=42)

df_illegal = df_illegal.sample(n=15000, random_state=42)

total_dataset = pd.concat([df_legal, df_illegal])
total_dataset = total_dataset.sample(frac=1, random_state=20) #shuffling the rows
total_dataset.head()
```

	vin	vout	vin_value	vout_value	fee	vin_addr	vout_addr	size	value	legal
167561	2	13	58.849709	58.849034	0.000676	1	13	742	58.849034	1
166937	1	2	0.061290	0.061199	0.000090	1	2	225	0.061199	1
285581	1	3	0.644528	0.644128	0.000400	1	3	405	0.644128	1
226110	6	2	2.441035	2.440835	0.000200	6	2	1157	2.440835	0
220417	1	2	109.420700	109.420700	0.000000	1	2	225	109.420700	0

Fig. 8. A dataset configuration example (The number of selected legal and illegal transactions: 15000)

3.4 Testing of the Machine-Learning Models

After the training phase, the model has learned a classifier that distinguishes between the features of legal and illegal transactions. In the test phase, the classifier predicts the labels of the list of transactions in the test set. To evaluate the accuracy of our model, we compared the labels predicted by the models with the initial labels (indicated by the columns "predicted" and "legal" respectively in Fig. 9).

	vin	vout	vin_value	vout_value	fee	vin_addr	vout_addr	size	value	legal	predicted
105434	1	2	9.947201	9.947059	0.000142	1	2	225	9.947059	1	1
778620	2	2	10.380195	10.380195	0.000000	1	2	437	10.380195	0	0
81045	1	2	0.054972	0.054769	0.000203	1	2	369	0.054769	1	1
161583	2	2	0.230636	0.230509	0.000127	2	2	373	0.230509	1	1
145809	1	10	21.225073	21.224720	0.000353	1	10	497	21.224720	1	1
795216	1	2	37.000000	36.999500	0.000500	1	2	258	36.999500	0	0
41669	2	2	0.036420	0.036121	0.000299	2	2	373	0.036121	1	1
919183	2	2	6.972490	6.971990	0.000500	2	2	375	6.971990	0	0
769965	4	2	4.012682	4.012182	0.000500	4	2	668	4.012182	0	0
330165	2	2	0.050182	0.050082	0.000100	1	2	373	0.050082	1	1
176961	1	2	0.129450	0.129337	0.000113	1	2	226	0.129337	1	1
477081	1	2	2.498500	2.498400	0.000100	1	2	258	2.498400	0	0
708818	1	2	124.267277	124.267277	0.000000	1	2	259	124.267277	0	0
230629	1	5	34.034622	34.034387	0.000234	1	5	325	34.034387	1	1
485605	1	2	6.220000	6.220000	0.000000	1	2	258	6.220000	0	0
594489	2	2	130.485053	130.485053	0.000000	2	2	440	130.485053	0	0
245285	1	2	0.096262	0.096149	0.000113	1	2	226	0.096149	1	1
850423	1	2	16.177256	16.177256	0.000000	1	2	258	16.177256	0	0

Fig. 9. Prediction results of the test set

4   Results

The random forest classifier and ANN classified the transactions as legal or illegal. We conducted several experiments with different dataset sizes and distribution ratios of legal-to-illegal transactions. When the class distribution is distorted, the accuracy cannot properly measure the efficiency of the classifier, so we instead evaluated the F1 scores [18] of the classification algorithm. The results of each classifier are listed below.

4.1   Random Forest Classifier

The F1 score of the random forest classifier ranged from 0.93 to 0.98, depending on the distribution ratio and volume of the data. The F1 score increased as more data were included in the model learning. The legal-to-illegal transaction ratios were varied as 1:1, 5:1, and 1:5, and the best results were obtained at a ratio of 1:1 (Table 2).

Table 2. F1 Score of the random forest classifier

# of legal txns	# of illegal txns	F1-score
1500	1500	0.9419
4000	4000	0.9533
15000	15000	0.9668
30000	30000	0.9735
20000	4000	0.9868
4000	20000	0.9324

4.2   ANN Model

The F1 score of our ANN classifier varied from 0.82 to 0.89, depending on the values of the hyper-parameters such as batch size, sample distribution and number of iterations. Like the random forest model, the ANN classifier was evaluated on datasets with different sizes and distribution ratios. When the distribution of the sample data was skewed, our algorithm did not accurately predict the label of the class containing fewer samples (Table 3).

Table 3. F1 scores of the ANN classifier

# of legal txns	# of ilegal txns	Iteration	Batch size	F1-score
5000	5000	10000	100	0.8227
15000	15000	10000	100	0.8330
30000	30000	10000	100	0.8344
5000	1000	10000	100	0.8854
30000	6000	10000	100	0.8730
1000	5000	10000	100	0.8712
6000	30000	10000	100	0.8670

5   Discussion

Our proposed system based on machine-learning identified and classified the possibly illegal transactions in a Bitcoin network. The proposed ANN model delivered a low F1 score when the class distribution was skewed. This limitation could be overcome by adopting a machine-learning based technique that handles skewed class distributions.

Most of the features in our experimental dataset had similar ranges of values. Therefore, no normalization and regularization techniques [19] were incorporated in the proposed neural network architecture. Nonetheless, we expect that these techniques would improve the performance of the classification model. A neural network model is commonly regularized by the dropout [20] method.

Second, the transaction data obtained from the forum site referenced during the transaction collection had already been labeled at the forum site using similar set of features. The test dataset in our experiments was not exposed during the model learning, but might have been previously trained by similar algorithms; in other words, the test dataset might have been exposed to a similar model. Because we obtained the test set in the same way as the training set, the test set may have been overfitted. Therefore, if we test the model on incoming/live transactions from the Bitcoin network, the measured F1 score may be lower than the experimental values reported here.

According to the Bitcoin literature, bitcoin address clustering might identify addresses that likely belong to the same person. Extracting a group of bitcoin addresses that frequently generate illegal transactions would assist in identifying those and other illegal transactions, but our implementation lacks information on bitcoin address clustering.

6   Conclusion

The detection and classification of illegal transactions in the Bitcoin network is essential for recognizing and blocking users wishing to exploit Bitcoin for illegal activities. In this paper, we implemented and verified a system that detects illegal transactions using machine-learning techniques. The system based on random forest and ANN algorithms achieved relatively high F1 scores, but several improvements are needed. In future work, we will re-verify the proposed model on arbitrary transaction sets in the Bitcoin network. We also expect that the model performance will increase after incorporating the improvements in the Discussion section. Once illegal transactions on the Bitcoin network are successfully detected, we intend to expand our analysis to Ethereum hacking cases and the detection of illegal transactions on Ethereum.

Acknowledgments. This work was supported by the ICT R&D program of MSIT/IITP. [No. 2018-0-00539, Development of Blockchain Transaction Monitoring and Analysis Technology] This work was also supported by the ICT R&D program of MSIT/IITP. [No. 2018-0-00749, Development of virtual network management technology based on artificial intelligence].

This research was supported by the MSIT (Ministry of Science and ICT), Korea, under the ITRC (Information Technology Research Center) support program (IITP-2017-2017- 0-01633) supervised by the IITP (Institute for Information & communications Technology Promotion).

References

1. Nakamoto, S.: Bitcoin: a peer-to-peer electronic cash system (2008)
2. Swan, M.: Blockchain: Blueprint for a New Economy. O'Reilly Media Inc., Sebastopol (2015)
3. Harvey, C.R.: Bitcoin myths and facts (2014)
4. https://www.chainalysis.com/
5. Pal, M.: Random forest classifier for remote sensing classification. Int. J. Remote. Sens. **26**(1), 217–222 (2005)
6. Zurada, J.M.: Introduction to Artificial Neural Systems, vol. 8. West Publishing Company, St. Paul (1992)
7. Zambre, D., Shah, A.: Analysis of Bitcoin network dataset for fraud. Unpublished Report (2013)
8. Hartigan, J.A., Wong, M.A.: Algorithm AS 136: a k-means clustering algorithm. J. R. Stat. Soc. Ser. C (Appl. Stat.) **28**(1), 100–108 (1979)
9. Toyoda, K., Ohtsuki, T., Mathiopoulos, P.T.: Identification of high yielding investment programs in Bitcoin via transactions pattern analysis. In: 2017 IEEE Global Communications Conference, GLOBECOM 2017, Singapore, pp. 1–6 (2017)
10. https://www.blockchain.com/ko/explorer
11. https://www.walletexplorer.com/
12. https://www.blockchain.com/btc/address/1F1tAaz5x1HUXrCNLbtMDqcw6o5G Nn4xqX?offset=0&filter=6
13. https://www.crummy.com/software/BeautifulSoup/bs4/doc/
14. Bitcoin core. https://bitcoin.org/en/bitcoin-core
15. Btcoin core json apis. http://chainquery.com/bitcoin-api
16. https://scikit-learn.org/stable/
17. https://www.tensorflow.org/?hl=en
18. Goutte, C., Gaussier, E.: A probabilistic interpretation of precision, recall and F-score, with implication for evaluation. In: Losada, D.E., Fernández-Luna, J.M. (eds.) ECIR 2005. LNCS, vol. 3408, pp. 345–359. Springer, Heidelberg (2005). https://doi.org/10.1007/978-3-540-31865-1_25

19. Zou, H., Hastie, T.: Regularization and variable selection via the elastic net. J. R. Stat. Soc. Ser. B (Stat. Methodol.) **67**(2), 301–320 (2005)
20. Srivastava, N., et al.: Dropout: a simple way to prevent neural networks from overfitting. J. Mach. Learn. Res. **15**(1), 1929–1958 (2014)

RETRACTED CHAPTER: Urban Jobs-Housing Zone Division Based on Mobile Phone Data

Xiaoming Liu[1]([✉]), Luxi Dong[1], Meijie Jia[2], and Jiyuan Tan[1]

[1] Beijing Key Lab of Urban Intelligent Traffic Control Technology,
North China University of Technology, Beijing 100144, China
wangyixdncut@163.com
[2] Capital Aerospace Machinery Corporation Limited, Beijing 100076, China

Abstract. Most of the existing researches were divided jobs-housing zones based on temporal activity variation, which were lack of mining spatio-temporal interaction characteristics. With the trend of big data and artificial intelligence, mobile phone data is provided an emerging source for urban research. This paper is proposed traffic semantic concept to extract commuters' origins and destinations. According to extracted data, four characteristic indexes (including the volumes of user, aggregation, dissipation and new increment) are analyzed traffic semantic attribute. Combining with the geographic information of base stations and traffic semantic, an unsupervised k-means clustering algorithm based on weighted Mahalanobis distance function is used to divide 200 jobs-housing zones in Shenzhen. Moreover, the commuting index is calculated to measure tendency of jobs-housing zones. Compared with the actual land use data, the results are verified reliability of method. All these findings can be helpful to analyze travel behaviors and make urban planning.

Keywords: Big data · Mobile phone data · Traffic semantic · Jobs-housing zone · Commuting index

1 Introduction

Land use is the basis and premise of urban planning. From a historical perspective, the land use classification framework was established by using planning linguistic measures and semantic structure [1, 2].

The traditional travel survey methods were difficult to obtain the real-time information of jobs-housing zone due to high cost, long period and the small sizes of survey sample data, etc. [3]. Urban jobs-housing zones and travel behaviors were closely intertwined. Many traffic models were established by analyzing travel behaviors based on residents' trajectories [4]. On one hand, the residents' trajectories were provided opportunities to understand travel behaviors. Human dynamic mobility could present certain temporal population variations in places; on the other, the interaction between human

---

The original version of this chapter was retracted: The retraction note to this chapter is available at https://doi.org/10.1007/978-981-15-2777-7_67

dynamic mobility and land use occurred at any moment. People moved to different jobs-housing zones and participated in social activities. Therefore, the complex travel behaviors were shown in different jobs-housing zones.

The mobile phone detail records were presented as samples of temporal activity variation. Researchers started to identify types of jobs-housing zone and analyze commute origins and destinations. Demissie et al. [5] estimated the dynamic OD matrices and developed two approaches to analyze commuting trips between workspace and residence. Oshin et al. [6] presented a novel accelerometer framework based on a probabilistic algorithm, it was identified human mobility state in real-time with 2 s. Jiang et al. [7] analyzed meaningful spatial human mobility patterns from raw mobile phone data for urban planning.

Inspired by these exploratory researches, temporal activity variations were widely used to classify jobs-housing zones. Soto and Frías-Martínez [8] constructed eigenvectors based on the covered area of base stations. A clustering method was used to identify different types of jobs-housing zone. Frias-Martinez et al. [9] used a similar method to analyze urban interest places in Manhattan based on the twitter data. Pei et al. [10] proposed a 'Densi-Graph' method based on the contour map of the kernel density of POIs (point of interest) to identify jobs-housing zones. Temporal activity variations were also applied to describe relationships between jobs-housing zone and human mobility [11].

However, simply adding more characteristics of temporal activity variations for jobs-housing zone division was not a remedy. The ignorance of spatial interaction information was made related research encounter a bottleneck on improving classification accuracy. The above researches were considered human mobility to be homogeneous, but human mobility was predecessor and successor activities with different spatio-temporal characteristics. That is, the movement between two consecutive activities were treated as a travel. Independent homogeneous activities were happened in these places. On the contrary, considering commute origins and destinations, the activities were treated as heterogeneous [12]. Therefore, the urban discrete places were incorporated spatial interactions into jobs-housing zone division. Yan et al. [13] analyzed the influence degree between jobs-housing zone and commuting time cost based on smartphone data. A method was clustered two type of curves (multi-scale index curve and probability density curve) and obtained eight joint-patterns as well as spatial divisions. Jia et al. [14] adopted a support vector machine to classify the remote sensing imagery (RSI) and mobile phone positioning data (MPPD). The two classification results were used a decision fusion strategy to generate the jobs-housing map.

Up to now, research on extracting information from mobile phone data for urban planning are slow. Different from all previous studies, four contributions of this paper would be summarized as follows:

(1) The comparison of every 10-min human mobility in different locations are extract four types of traffic semantic based on mobile phone data.
(2) A novel unsupervised clustering algorithm is used to identify jobs-housing zones based on the characteristics of human mobility with spatial interaction.
(3) As an experiment, all base stations are divided into 200 jobs-housing zones in Shenzhen based on traffic semantic attributes, geographic location coordinates and temporal characteristics of human mobility.
(4) A commuting index is proposed and measured tendency of jobs-housing zones. In general, this paper is provided a valuable new extraction method for big-data driven traffic planning.

The rest of paper is arranged as follows: mobile phone records are used in Sects. 2 and 3, including data description and data preprocessing. Then, an unsupervised k-means clustering algorithm is applied to identify traffic semantic attribute based on every 10-min four characteristic indexes. As a preliminary test, all jobs-housing zones of Shenzhen are divided. A commuting index is calculated to measure tendency of jobs-housing zones. The result is presented in Sect. 4. Finally, the conclusion is given in Sect. 5.

2 Data and Characteristic Selection

2.1 Data Description and Preprocessing

In this paper, mobile phone data is used to divide jobs-housing zones in Shenzhen. Communications Corporation is built 14393 base stations. The average coverage radiuses of base stations are 500 m. When a mobile phone user received or sent voice call or a message or an Internet service, the location register system is recorded data in base station. The average mobile phone records are produced by per person per day is 32.5. For privacy protection, personal information is not obtained from mobile phone data. Each user assigns with a matching number ID in dataset. Each record contains user ID, timestamp that a call was took, base station ID (set cell ID) and event type (voice call, message, surfing the Internet or passive communication), etc.

To improve system efficiency and performance of the query function, data preprocessing is carried out as follows:

Step1: The flag ID is presented the covered range of base stations. Zero means base station is within the range of Shenzhen. One means base station is out of range. The flag ID is equal to one that will be removed.
Step2: Several successive data are recorded in the same position and deleted intermediate data.
Step3: Time difference Δt_n in adjacent records is calculated. If Δt_n is less time threshold (set 60 s), the following step will be processed.
Step4: Voronoi diagram is established urban space model based on base stations [15]. The repeat number of vertex coordinates are equal to 2 in adjacent Voronoi diagram, which is ping-pong data. The ping-pong data will be deleted.

2.2 Traffic Semantic Framework

In this study, one of the purposes is to evaluate the use of mobile phone data on commuters' jobs-housing zone division. Mobile phone data are unstructured until they are converted into traffic semantic. In order to study commuting behaviors, traffic semantics are used to divide study area into four types of land use, including CBD, workspace, residence and mixed area. Four types of land use are defined as follow:

(1) CBD is classified as Central Business District.
(2) Workspace is classified as industrial areas, office buildings, education and administrative areas.

(3) Residence is equipped with commerce, entertainment, culture, markets, greenbelts and public facilities.
(4) Mixed area is classified as nightlife areas, airports, scenic spots, express roads, main roads and collector roads.

2.3 Characteristic Selection for Jobs-Housing Zones

The coverage areas of base station are matched with the scales of jobs-housing zone. A specific type land use or traffic semantic attribute could be characterized by extracting coverage area of base stations. The four types of land use are classified as CBD, workspace, residence and mixed area. Traffic semantic attributes are identified based on four characteristics, which are defined as the volumes of user, the volumes of aggregation, the volumes of dissipation and the volumes of new increment.

In general, traffic semantic is matched with jobs-housing zone, which is an unsupervised pattern recognition problem. The eigenvectors of traffic semantic are constructed for each base station, which contain 581 temporal characteristics, $x_j = \left\{ x_j^1, \cdots, x_j^{581} \right\}$. $X = \left\{ x_1, \cdots, x_j, \cdots, x_n \right\}$ is used to represent the whole characteristics of traffic semantic dataset. The eigenvectors contain primary semantic, secondary semantic and characteristic of optimization. As previous discussed, the primary semantic contains four traffic semantic. The volumes of user contain 144 secondary semantics. Each of the other three primary semantics contain 143 secondary semantics. Moreover, the eight characteristics of optimization are added to analyze traffic sematic. The 581 temporal characteristics are shown in Table 1.

Table 1. The temporal characteristics are selected for traffic semantic

Characteristic	Quantity	Effect
Primary semantic		
The volume of user	144	Distinguish the duration trend of volume of user for each base station in every 10 min
The volume of aggregation	143	Distinguish the duration trend of volume of aggregation for each base station in every 10 min
The volume of dissipation	143	Distinguish the duration trend of volume of dissipation for each base station in every 10 min
The new increment	143	Distinguish the duration trend of volume of new increment for each base station in every 10 min

(*continued*)

Table 1. (*continued*)

Characteristic	Quantity	Effect
Characteristic of optimization		
The peak and valley value of volume of user	2	Distinguish the peak and valley values of volume of user for each base station in every 10 min
The peak and valley value of volume aggregation	2	Distinguish the peak and valley values of volume of aggregation for each base station in every 10 min
The peak and valley value of volume dissipation	2	Distinguish the peak and valley values of volume of dissipation for each base station in every 10 min
The peak and valley value of new increment	2	Distinguish the peak and valley values of volume of new increment for each base station in every 10 min

The division of jobs-housing zone depends on traffic semantic and spatial geographical location. The three spatio-temporal characteristic indexes (latitude and longitude, traffic semantic and the difference of the new increments) are selected to apply in a novel unsupervised clustering algorithm in Table 2. To eliminate the effect of different magnitudes, normalization is applied to each characteristic. The temporal variation of the primary semantic is made prominent in clustering method, which is set to either 0 or 1. Normalization is calculated as follows:

$$y = \frac{x - x_{min}}{x_{max} - x_{min}} \tag{1}$$

In Eq. (1) x_{max} is represented row maximum in characteristic matrix. x_{min} is represented row minimum in characteristic matrix.

Table 2. The spatio-temporal characteristics of jobs-housing zone

Characteristic	Definition	Effect
Latitude Longitude	The location of base stations	The geographical location of the base stations
Traffic semantic	The types of traffic semantic	Characterizations of the jobs-housing zone as workspace or residence reflection
The difference of the volumes of new increment	The difference between morning peak (valley) and evening valley (peak) of every 10-min the volumes of new increment	Distinguish the traffic flow in each base station between morning peak (valley) and evening valley (peak)

3 Methodology

3.1 The Temporal Characteristic of Human Mobility for Traffic Semantic

To study trend of four traffic semantic attributes in each base station, the number of mobile phone data is recorded and analyzed over a given period. The characteristics of traffic semantic attribute are associated to each base station, which could be represented as a two-dimensional matrix $x_n(T, t)$. Each element $x_n(T, t)$ contains the characteristics of traffic semantic attribute during 10-min time interval t of each day T, where $n \in \{1, \cdots, 14393\}$ is represented the number of base stations, $T \in \alpha = \{1, \cdots, 7\}$ represented each day and $t \in \{1, \cdots, 144\}$ is represented 10-min time interval. With the total number of records in 24-h period, the characteristic x_n of each base station is defined by information of traffic semantic attribute in $x_n(T, t)$. Each element $x_n(t)$ contains the average value of records during 10-min time interval t throughout all days T. Thus, the characteristic $x_n(t)$ is calculated as:

$$x_n(t) = \frac{1}{\|\alpha\|} \sum_{T \in \alpha} x_n(T, t) \tag{2}$$

The traffic semantic attribute is different between weekdays and weekends. The differences are reflected mobile phone use. The records of each time interval t is studied in two types of days, including weekdays (Monday to Friday, defined β_1) and weekends (Saturday and Sunday, defined β_2). The traffic semantic attribute is defined as ($++$ represent as concatenation of weekdays and weekends):

$$x_{n,\beta_i}(t) = \frac{1}{\|\beta_i\|} \sum_{T \in \beta_i} x_n(T, t) \tag{3}$$

$$x_n = x_{n,\beta_1} + + x_{n,\beta_2} \tag{4}$$

where $\beta_1 \cap \beta_2 = \varnothing$ and $\beta_1 \cup \beta_2 = \alpha$.

Location register system is not updated events in time. Thus, mobile phone records could not be reflected the real-time but the relative number of users in each base station. To analyze every 10-min human mobility in different locations, the relative number of users of per base station is zero at 3:00 a.m. The calculating rule is carried out as follow:

Step1: If the users are new which have not been previously recorded, the relative number of users of the corresponding base station is added one.

Step2: If the users have been previously recorded, then recorded users are judged whether they move into the base station or stay in the base station. The following condition will be judged.

Step3: If they move into, the number of users of the former base station is subtracted one. If they stay in, the number of users of the base station remains the same.

3.2 Method for Jobs-Housing Zone Division

In this paper, traffic semantic, geographical location of base station and unsupervised k-means clustering algorithm is applied to divide jobs-housing zone with homogeneous characteristics. To accurately divide jobs-housing zones, a clustering algorithm based on weighted Mahalanobis distance function is applied to calculated similarity of characteristics. Although Mahalanobis distance is eliminated the effect of different magnitudes, two problems are still solved as follow:

(1) The different importance of characteristic is influenced on clustering analysis.
(2) The high dimensional characteristic matrix is influenced on clustering efficiency.

To solve above problems, A and B are extracted as samples from the n dimensional total samples (all base stations with three indexes) based on the mean μ and covariance matrix C. $Q = diag(\sqrt{q_1}, \cdots, \sqrt{q_n})$ is represented the weight vectors of n characteristic based on diagonal matrix of individual components, where q_n is represented weight coefficient and $\sum\limits_{l=1}^{n} q_l = 1$. The Mahalanobis distance between A and B is defined as:

$$d(A, B) = \sqrt{(A - B)^T Q^T C^{-1} Q(A - B)} \tag{5}$$

where C is represented $n \times n$ covariance matrix. C^{-1} is data standardization that can be reduced dimension of characteristic matrix.

Step1: The characteristic indexes in Table 2 are selected to construct characteristic matrix.
Step2: The mean μ and covariance matrix C is calculated as follow:

$$cov(A, B) = \frac{\sum\limits_{i,j=1}^{n} (A_i - \bar{A})(B_j - \bar{B})}{n - 1} \tag{6}$$

$$C = \begin{bmatrix} c_{11} & \cdots & c_{1n} \\ \vdots & \ddots & \vdots \\ c_{n1} & \cdots & c_{nn} \end{bmatrix} \tag{7}$$

where $\bar{A}$ and $\bar{B}$ is represented the mean of samples A and B separately. $cov(A, B)$ is represented the value of covariance for samples A and B. C contains the total $cov(A^i, B^j)$.
Step3: The Mahalanobis distance between each sample is calculated.
Step4: $K(K = 4)$ base stations are selected from n base stations as the initial clustering centers. The remaining base stations are classified based on similarity (distance) of sample clustering centers. Euclidean distance is used to measure similarity. The c_q is defined the center of qth class. The Euclidean distance ($d(x_j, c_q) = \sum\limits_{p=1}^{4} \omega_p \left| x_j^p - c_q^p \right|$, where ω_p is represented weighted function) and similarity ($s(x_j, c_q)$) is calculated by an unsupervised k-means clustering algorithm.

3.3 Calculation of Commuting Index

To analyze spatial distribution of jobs-housing zones, the commuting index is calculated to measure tendency of jobs-housing zones to be workspace or residence. The value of commuting index (set CI_k) is between -1 and 1. The calculating rule is carried out as follow:

$$CI_k = \begin{cases} \frac{vol_{mk}-vol_{ek}}{\max(vol_{mk}-vol_{ek})}, & if\ vol_{mk} > vol_{ek} \\ \frac{vol_{ek}-vol_{mk}}{\min(vol_{mk}-vol_{ek})}, & if\ vol_{mk} < vol_{ek} \end{cases} \tag{8}$$

In Eq. (8) vol_{mk} is represented average hourly incremental flow in rush hours (7 a.m. to 10 a.m.). vol_{ek} is represented average hourly incremental flow in rush hours (5 p.m. to 8 p.m.).

Step1: If the value of commuting index is close to -1 for four continuous days in five weekdays, the jobs-housing zone is classified as residence.
Step2: If the value of commuting index is close to 1 for four continuous days in five weekdays, the jobs-housing zone is classified as workspace.
Step3: If the value of commuting index is close to 0 for four continuous days in five weekdays, the jobs-housing zone is classified as mixed area.

4 Result

4.1 The Results of Human Mobility Distribution

According to the above calculating rule, the 10-min relative number of users of per base station is obtained. The distribution of every 10-min human mobility is reflected travel

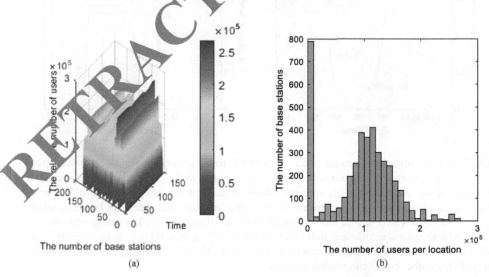

Fig. 1. (a) The results of every 10-min population density in different locations. (b) The distribution of human mobility.

demand in different locations, which is shown in Fig. 1. Due to the different geographical locations of base station, the number of aggregations are also different during different time periods. The daily average cumulative number of users are less than 5000 in urban outskirts. The daily average cumulative number of users are more than 200000 in urban center, which is shown in Fig. 1(a) and (b) separately.

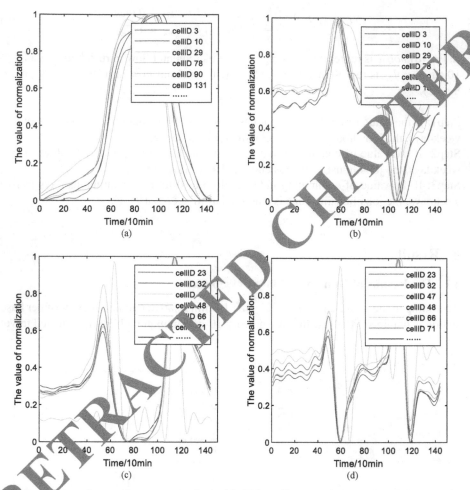

Fig. 2. (a) The volumes of user are matched with CBD traffic semantic in results of cluster 1. (b) The new increments are matched with CBD traffic semantic in the results of cluster 1. (c) The volumes of user are matched with workspace traffic semantic in results of cluster 2. (d) The new increments are matched with workspace traffic semantic in results of cluster 2. (e) The volumes of user are matched with residence traffic semantic in results of cluster 3. (f) The new increments are matched with residence traffic semantic in results of cluster 3. (g) The volumes of user are matched with mixed area traffic semantic in results of cluster 4. (h) The new increments are matched with mixed area traffic semantic in results of cluster 4.

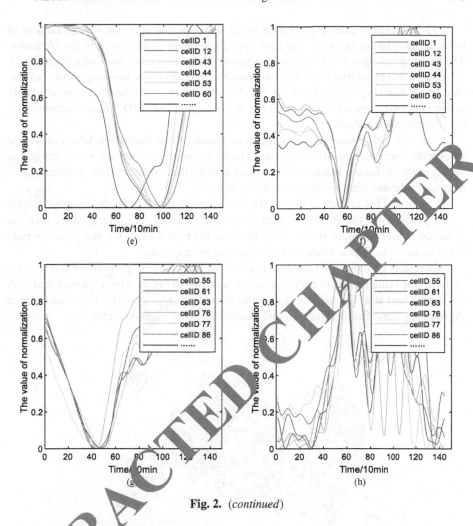

Fig. 2. (*continued*)

4.2 The Results of Traffic Semantic

The normalization characteristics of traffic semantic is matched with land use. The four typical types of land use (Huaqiang North Commercial Area, Nanshan Science and Technology Park, Xiangmi Lake Residential Area and Lotus Hill Park) are selected the initial clustering centers. The k-means clustering method is applied to process temporal characteristics of the remaining base station. The convergence threshold is set as the portion of less than 5%. Additionally, the k-means clustering method is run 50 times. The results of cluster are recorded with the minimum within-cluster sum of squares criterion in each iteration. The four typical traffic semantic attribute is shown in Fig. 2. The clusters are carried out as follows:

Cluster 1: This cluster is shown the behavior happens in weekdays. Rapid inflow of users happens in the morning. The peak appears at the noon and drops in the afternoon. The lowest point shows up in the early morning. These characteristics indicate the CBD.

Cluster 2: This cluster is shown two same height peaks in the morning and afternoon. The lowest point is presented at noon. So, the curve represented that users gathered only in working time. However, users can't outflow at noon in the CBD. These characteristics are described workspace.

Cluster 3: This cluster is shown the same characteristic during weekdays as well as weekends. Users outflow in the morning. The lowest point presents at noon. Users gather slowly in the afternoon. These characteristics indicate the residence where residents leave to work in the morning and return in the evening.

Cluster 4: This cluster is shown the lowest point presents in the morning. Users gather gradually in the afternoon, then the peak appears in the evening. After that, the volumes of user decrease slowly. Nevertheless, the mixed behavior phenomenon only happens in urban. These characteristics indicate mixed areas.

All results of cluster 1 to 4 are matched with cell ID in geographic information system. The visualization of traffic semantic is shown in Fig. 3, which is consistent with the actual land use. Figure 3 is shown the Shenzhen citizen center, Nanshan Science Technology Park, Baishizhou area and Shenzhen World's Window etc.

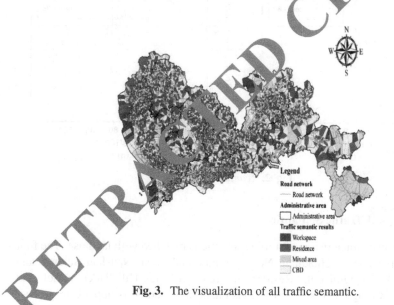

Fig. 3. The visualization of all traffic semantic.

To evaluate the accuracy of identification results, the proportions of functional area classification is regarded as an index, which is shown in Table 3. As shown in Table 3, The method is better than FCM, BP neural network and Random forests.

Table 3. Accuracy of identification results

Method	Residence	CBD	Temporary workspace	Mixed areas	The overall accuracy
Our method	88.13%	91.02%	78.64%	73.09%	82.72%
FCM	76.00%	83.69%	70.76%	66.13%	74.15%
BP neural network	80.22%	85.81%	73.44%	68.94%	77.10%
Random forests	78.90%	83.00%%	72.81%	66.90%	75.40%

4.3   The Results of Jobs-Housing Division

To determine the optimal number of jobs-housing zones, the 20 jobs-housing zones are divided based on geographical locations in Shenzhen. The boundary of jobs-housing zones is clipped and refined based on geographic information system. The division result is shown in Fig. 4.

Fig. 4. The result of jobs-housing zones in Shenzhen.

As the method mentioned in this paper, all normalization characteristics of new increment is calculated as vol_{mk} and vol_{ek}. Each value CI_k of base stations are calculated and marked in jobs-housing zone ID. Figure 5 is shown the temporal variation of commuting index separately. Figure 5(a) is indicated commuters enter workspace in the morning and move out in the evening. Figure 5(b) is indicated a completely different travel behavior in the residence. Figure 5(c) is indicated mixed area without commuting characteristics.

Figure 6 is shown the values of commuting index for each base station in geographic information system. The red is represented workspace attributes. The blue is represented residence attributes. The deeper red is represented stronger workspace attributes. The deeper blue is represented stronger residence attributes. The high value of commuting index (e.g., 1, 0.78 and 0.81) is typical workspace, such as the center of Baoan District,

Huaqiang North Commercial Area and Nanshan Science and Technology Park. The low value of commuting index (e.g., -1, -0.73 and -0.89) is typical residence, such as Xiangmi Lake Residential Area, Shekou Residential Area and Gangxia Residential Area. The value of commuting index for mixed area without commuting characteristics is close to zero.

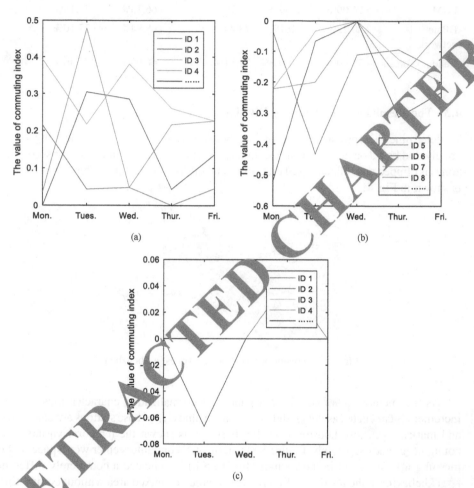

Fig. 5. (a) The temporal variation of commuting index in workspace. (b) The temporal variation of commuting index in residence. (c) The temporal variation of commuting index in mixed area with both workspace and residence.

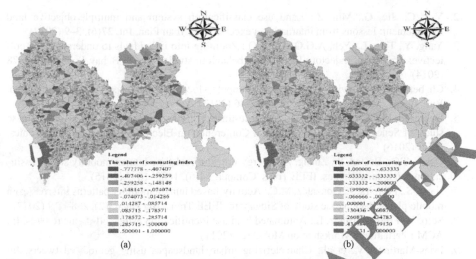

Fig. 6. (a) The values of commuting index on Monday. (b) The value of commuting index on Tuesday. (Color figure online)

5 Conclusion

In this paper, the traffic semantic concept is proposed to extract commuters' origins and destinations based on mobile phone data. First, the four characteristic indexes (including the volumes of user, aggregation, dissipation and new increment) are calculated based on extracted data. An unsupervised k-means clustering algorithm is applied to identify traffic semantic based on four characteristic indexes. The four typical traffic semantic are classified as CBD, workspace, residence and mixed area. Second, combining with the geographic information of base stations and traffic semantics, A novel unsupervised clustering algorithm based on weighted Mahalanobis distance function is applied to divide 200 jobs-housing zones in Shenzhen. Moreover, the commuting index is calculated to measure tendency of jobs-housing zones to be workspace or residence. Third, compared with the actual land use data, the result is associated with the traffic semantic to improve the model computational efficiency and division accuracy. All these findings could be helpful to the government for urban planning in the future.

Acknowledgment. This article is partially supported by the Beijing Natural Science Foundation (No. 8172018) and National Key Research and Development Program of China (No. 2018YFB1601003) and the China Postdoctoral Science Foundation (No. 2017M620673) and the Beijing Municipal Natural Science Foundation (No. 8184070). The authors gratefully thank anonymous referees for their useful comments and editors for their work.

References

1. Jie, G.: The characteristics and enlightenment of the land classification system in the UK. Urban Plan. Int. **27**(6), 16–21 (2012)

2. Yao, C., Jie, G., Min, Z.: Land use classification system and multiple-objective land management: lessons from international experience. Urban Plan. Int. **27**(6), 3–9 (2012)
3. Yang, Y., Tian, L., Yeh, A.G.O., Li, Q.Q.: Zooming into individuals to understand the collective: a review of trajectory-based travel behaviour studies. Travel Behav. Soc. **1**(2), 69–78 (2014)
4. Chaberko, T., Kretowicz, P.: Geographical input to local public transport planning in Poland. Bull. Geogr. Socio Econ. Ser. **22**(22), 35–46 (2013)
5. Demissie, M.G., et al.: Inferring origin-destination flows using mobile phone data: a case study of Senegal. In: 13th International Conference on Electrical Engineering/Electronics IEEE (2016)
6. Oshin, T.O., Poslad, S., Zhang, Z.: Energy-efficient real-time human mobility state classification using smartphones. IEEE Trans. Comput. **64**(6), 1680–1693 (2015)
7. Jiang, S., Ferreira, J., Gonzalez, M.C.: Activity-based human mobility patterns inferred from mobile phone data: a case study of Singapore. IEEE Trans. Big Data **3**(2), 208–219 (2017)
8. Soto, V., Frías-Martínez, E.: Automated land use identification using cell phone records. In: ACM International Workshop on MobiArch (2011)
9. Frias-Martinez, V., et al.: Characterizing urban landscapes using geolocated tweets. In: Privacy, Security, Risk & Trust, pp. 239–248. IEEE (2013)
10. Pei, T., et al.: A new insight into land use classification based on aggregated mobile phone data. Int. J. Geogr. Inf. Sci. **28**(9), 1988–2007 (2014)
11. Zhang, T., Sun, L., Yao, L., Rong, J.: Impact analysis of land use on traffic congestion using real-time traffic and POI. J. Adv. Transp. **1**, 1–8 (2017)
12. Wu, L., et al.: Intra-urban human mobility and activity transition: evidence from social media check-in data. PLoS ONE **9**(5), e97010 (2014)
13. Yan, L., et al.: Evaluating the multi-scale patterns of jobs-residence balance and commuting time–cost using cellular signaling data: a case study in Shanghai. Transportation **46**, 777–792 (2018)
14. Jia, Y., et al.: Urban land use mapping combining remote sensing imagery and mobile phone positioning data. Remote Sens. **10**(3), 1–21 (2018)
15. Okabe, A., Boots, B., Sugihara, K.: Spatial tessellations: concepts and applications of Voronoi diagrams. Coll. Math. J. **4**(1), 1–14 (2000)

Quantitative Analysis of Bitcoin Transferred in Bitcoin Exchange

Yang Li[1,2]([⊠]), Zilu Liu[1,2], and Zibin Zheng[1,2]

[1] School of Data and Computer Science, Sun Yat-sen University,
Guangzhou 510275, China
{liyang99,liuzl9}@mail2.sysu.edu.cn
[2] National Engineering Research Center of Digital Life, Sun Yat-sen University,
Guangzhou, China
zhzibin@mail.sysu.edu.cn

Abstract. In this paper, a new Bitcoin address clustering algorithm is proposed for Bitcoin exchanges. The proposed algorithm aims to classify the cold wallets, hot wallets and user wallets in the Bitcoin exchanges, which are verified by off-chain information from the Internet. By analyzing the structures of different Bitcoin exchanges, we find that most Bitcoin exchanges exist weakness in managing the reasonable amounts of bitcoins kept in hot wallets. A large amount of Bitcoins stored in hot wallets can meet the users' withdrawal demands but may increase the risk of attack. However, a small amount of bitcoins in hot wallet may be inconvenient to frequently transfer for cold wallet. The problem then is modeled as a Bitcoin withdrawal prediction problem for hot wallets. We adopt traditional and classific supervised learning methods to solve the problems. Numerical experiments show that the proposed approach provides reasonable prediction results. Furthermore, we simulate two processes to analyze our results. The first process shows that Facebook-prophet outperforms other methods if there is no transaction occurred from cold wallets to hot wallet. The second process shows that the more transactions from cold wallets to hot wallets, the smaller Bitcoins required for hot wallets. Overall, our work is valuable and useful for the Bitcoin exchanges' business.

Keywords: Bitcoin exchanges · Bitcoin wallet · Clustering · Time series · Prediction

1 Introduction

Bitcoin is the first and widest spread cryptocurrency which was proposed in 2008 and released in 2009 as an open-source software [1]. It has attracted significant attention with the capital market up to 320 billion dollars in 2017 (coinmarketcap.com). Unlike traditional currencies, Bitcoin is decentralized and public. Everyone can take part in it on the peer-to-peer Bitcoin blockchain network. The value of Bitcoin is not based on any tangible asset, but instead, it is based on the security of a consensus algorithm [2].

© Springer Nature Singapore Pte Ltd. 2020
Z. Zheng et al. (Eds.): BlockSys 2019, CCIS 1156, pp. 549–562, 2020.
https://doi.org/10.1007/978-981-15-2777-7_44

Bitcoin is transferred through transactions using common cryptographic primitives (i.e., digital signatures, hash functions) to provide authentication securities and capabilities. All transactions are included in a public log available distributed ledger called blockchain. The blockchain is the core mechanism for the Bitcoin [3,4]. The process that the transactions are verified and agreed by all the nodes in the Bitcoin network called mining [5]. The process used to reach agreement among the untrustworthy nodes called consensus algorithms. Currently, the secure blockchain is serving as a digital assets infrastructure and system.

Bitcoin has emerged as a popular medium of exchange and has a rich and extensive ecosystem. The members in Bitcoin ecosystems include miners, traders, merchants, hoarders who believe that each Bitcoin is going to be worth millions in one day and consumers who simply spend Bitcoin to buy goods or services. They play important roles in ecosystems. The applications in Bitcoin ecosystems include Bitcoin exchanges that provide a marketplace for traders, pools, services that contain wallet services and mixer Bitcoin [6], gambling and others.

The most popular application in the Bitcoin ecosystem is Bitcoin exchange which own approximately 40% Bitcoin addresses in the whole Bitcoin network (walletexplorer.com, 2019). A Bitcoin exchange is a digital marketplace where traders can buy and sell Bitcoins using different traditional currencies or other virtual currencies [7]. It is an online centralized platform and in charge of users' Bitcoins. Therefore, it always suffers from a lot of attacks which are highly-rewarding activities for attackers. It is estimated that Bitcoin exchanges lose $2.7 million every day on average, and this figure is set to increase in the future. Specifically, Mt. Gox once enjoyed the status of being a monopolist as it dominated an estimated 80–90% of the Bitcoin-Dollar trading volume. However, it fell in early 2014 and is reported in losing 754,000 of its customers' Bitcoins [2]. Many reports analyze the price behaviors in Mt. Gox with it's leaked data. For example, [8] detected a number of short-lived bubbles. [9] found the market manipulation of Bitcoin from mining the Mt. Gox transaction network. Recently, cryptocurrency exchange Binance has confirmed a large scale data breach, in which hackers stole more than $40 million (approximately 7,000 Bitcoins) from it. The influence of the attacks and steals is harsh for the whole ecosystem, especially for the users.

The main safeguard procedures in Bitcoin exchanges used to avoid the attacks can be summarized into two aspects. Firstly, the basic infrastructure is provided for users, which is capable of withstanding attacks including hacking and denial-of-service attacks. It includes a valid https used to certificate, the secure and complex password needed to ensure that no one can brute force it, two-factor authentication acquired to protect user accounts, and so on. Secondly, the techniques of cold storage and hot storage are applied and the risk control system is carefully designed in the internal of Bitcoin exchanges.

For Bitcoin exchanges, most Bitcoins stored in the cold wallets which don't access the internet are safe. However, there is a risk of attack for the hot wallets which must access the internet frequently in order to meet the users' withdrawal demands. The effective method to deal with this problem except the safeguard procedures is that the hot wallets keep the minimum Bitcoins, the loss will be small once the bitcoins are stolen by hackers. However, a smaller amount of bitcoins will be inconvenient for the cold wallets to transfer Bitcoins frequently to the hot wallets due to the complicated procedures. In address the aforementioned concerns, we convert it to a prediction problem, which predicts the number of bitcoins the hot wallets should keep. In this paper, we first present an automatic Bitcoin exchange address clustering method, which can automatically classify the Bitcoin addresses into the hot wallets, cold wallets, and user wallets. Then we analyze the structures of the different Bitcoin exchanges. Lastly, we apply some supervised learning methods to predict the number of Bitcoin withdrawn from hot wallets and evidence that the problem defined and methods proposed are effective and valuable.

The remaining parts of this paper are organized as follows. In Sect. 2, we provide a method of how to automate Bitcoin exchange address clustering. Section 3 describes our analysis of structures in different Bitcoin exchanges through hot wallet, cold wallet and fees. Section 4 provides our proposed model for the prediction of the number of bitcoins withdrawn from hot wallets in Bitcoin exchanges and shows our experiments, settings, results, and quantitative analysis. Section 5 concludes this paper and discusses possible future extension and analysis.

2 Automatic Bitcoin Exchange Address Clustering

2.1 Bitcoin Address

A Bitcoin address is an identifier of 26–35 alphanumeric characters, beginning with the number 1, 3 or bc1. Bitcoin addresses can be obtained by one-way encryption hashing of public keys which can be done without an internet or registration with Bitcoin network. The hash algorithm is a function that converts a data string into a numeric string output of fixed length.

To transfer Bitcoins from one address to another is operated through transactions. A transaction contains one or more input addresses, and one or more output addresses. For each input address, it must refer to an unspent output address in previous transaction. For each output address, it can only be spent once. The outputs of all transactions included in the blockchain can be categorized as either unspent transaction outputs (UTXOs) or spent transaction outputs. UTXOs are origin from coinbase transactions which is the first transaction in a block created by a miner. Besides, a transaction must be signed by the private key associated with each input address in order to be verified. After a completion of a transaction, UTXOs referenced by its inputs are removed from the UTXO set maintained by every Bitcoin node, and its outputs are added into the UTXO set. Ignoring coinbase transactions, if the value of a transaction's outputs exceeds its inputs, the transaction will be rejected, otherwise, any difference in value may be claimed as a transaction fee offered to the Bitcoin miner who creates the block containing this transaction.

2.2   Bitcoin Wallet

Definition 1 (Wallet [10]**).** *A collection of addresses with the same security policy together with a software program or protocol that allows spending from those addresses in accordance with that policy.*

A Bitcoin wallet is a software abstraction which manages multiple addresses and keeps a secret piece of data called a private key or seed. It's convenient to generate new addresses and transfer Bitcoin to other addresses. For a transaction, the wallet software will automatically choose the input addresses to construct it. Besides, the Bitcoin wallet provides mathematical proof that they have come from the owner of the wallet and can sign the transaction. After that, all transactions can be broadcast to the network through the Bitcoin wallet.

Storing Bitcoin in a safe and secure manner is more important than ever before. Multiple solutions are available to users to achieve this goal. Hot wallets and cold wallets are the common solutions that distinguish between internal and external threats.

Definition 2 (Hot wallet/Cold wallet [10]**).** *A hot wallet is a wallet from which Bitcoins can be spent without accessing cold storage. Conversely, a cold wallet is a wallet from which Bitcoins cannot be spent without accessing cold storage.*

A hot wallet refers to a Bitcoin wallet that is not kept in cold storage and can connect to the Internet in some way. Connecting to the internet means the potential risk, because most computer systems have hidden vulnerabilities that can eventually be used by hackers or malware to break into the system and steal the Bitcoins.

A cold wallet refers to a Bitcoin wallet that is kept in cold storage and can not connect to the Internet. It is safe and reliable but inconvenient for users to transfer Bitcoins compared to the hot wallet.

2.3   Bitcoin Exchange

Figure 1 shows a simple structure of Bitcoin exchange. Users can deposit Bitcoins to Bitcoin exchange by the address given by Bitcoin exchange. Thus, the user wallet is created by Bitcoin exchange and the private key of the address is held by the Bitcoin exchange.

The main functions of the cold wallet described previously include two aspects. Firstly, it is used to store a large number of Bitcoins which received from hot wallets or other cold wallets due to the consideration of safety. Besides, the cold wallet may adopt the multiple signatures and other technologies in the Bitcoin exchange. Secondly, it is used to send the Bitcoins to hot wallets in order to keep sufficient balances and to cold wallets to ensure the security of the Bitcoins.

The main function of the hot wallet is to maintain a Bitcoin pool for the user's withdrawal demand. It receives the Bitcoins from the user wallet and the extra Bitcoins will be transferred to cold wallets to save. Besides, it needs to withdraw Bitcoins from cold wallets if the number of Bitcoins is insufficient.

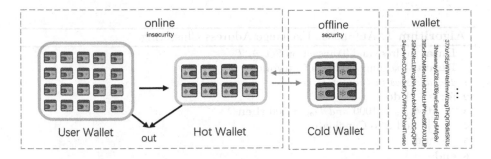

Fig. 1. The structure of Bitcoin exchange

2.4 Automatic Bitcoin Address Clustering

We make a detailed definition of addresses in the cold wallet (c-addresses), addresses in the hot wallet (h-addresses) and addresses in the user wallet (u-addresses) as follows. Specifically, the parameters are selected here through analysis and statistic, and the value of parameters is relatively reasonable.

Definition 3. *The address A satisfies the following conditions called address in the cold wallet of Bitcoin exchange.*

(1) The total received Bitcoins of A is bigger than 1000.
(2) The number of transactions between h-addresses and c-addresses occupies at least 60% of the total transactions.
(3) The total transactions of A and transaction rate computed as (total transactions/period) is low. But, the number of mean transactions computed as (total Bitcoins/number of transactions) is high. Especially, there exists a lot of transactions with a large amount.

Definition 4. *The address A satisfies the following conditions called address in the hot wallet of Bitcoin exchange.*

(1) The total received Bitcoin of A is bigger than 1000.
(2) There exist the patterns (1, 2, 3, 4, 5)-to-many or many-to-(1, 2, 3, 4, 5) which represents the withdrawal or deposits operated by users.
(3) The total transactions of A and transaction rate is high. But, the number of mean transactions is low. Especially, there exist a lot of transactions with little amount.

Definition 5. *The address A is related to h-addresses, but not c-addresses called address in the user wallet of Bitcoin exchange.*

The process of the automatic exchange address clustering is shown in Algorithm 1. The $a - conn$ represents all addresses which have transactions with a. a_{count} represents the total number of transactions, a_{rate} represents the transaction rate. $a_{cold}, a_{hot}, a_{user}$ represents the address a in cold wallet, hot wallet, user wallet respectively. $b_{cold}, b_{hot}, b_{user}$ represents the address b in cold wallet, hot wallet, user wallet respectively.

Algorithm 1. Automatic Exchange Address Clustering

Data: Address and Transaction Set A, T
Result: Exchange Address Categories
1 *1. Addresses in Candidate;*
2 **for** $a \in A$ **do**
3 | **if** $A_{recv} > 1000$ *and* $T_{top} > 500$ **then**
4 | | add a to Candidate
5 | **end**
6 **end**
7 *2. Addresses in cold wallet;*
8 **for** $a \in Candidate$ **do**
9 | **for** $b \in a - conn$ **do**
10 | | compute the number of transaction bn, and the rate of transaction br
11 | | **if** $bn > 300$ *and* $br > 10$ **then**
12 | | | $a - conn$ tags as $h(a - conn)$;
13 | | **end**
14 | **end**
15 | **if** $len(h(conn\text{-}hot)) \: / \: len(a\text{-}conn) > 0.6$ **then**
16 | | add a to cold wallet
17 | **end**
18 | **if** $T_{rate} < 20$ *and* $T_{mean} > 400$ **then**
19 | | add a to cold wallet
20 | **end**
21 **end**
22 *3. Addresses in hot wallet;*
23 **for** $a \in Candidate$ **do**
24 | **if** $c - address \in a - conn$ *and* $a.count > 300$ *and* $a.rate > 10$ **then**
25 | | add a to hot wallet
26 | **end**
27 **end**
28 *4. Addresses in hot wallet;*
29 **for** $a \in A$ **do**
30 | **if** $a \notin Candidate$ *and* $a - conn \in h - address$ **then**
31 | | add a to user wallet
32 | **end**
33 **end**
34 *5. Cluster addresses;*
35 **if** a_{cold} *has transactions with* b_{cold} **then**
36 | a_{cold} and b_{cold} in the same cluster
37 **end**
38 **if** a_{hot} *and* b_{hot} *have transactions with same c-address* **then**
39 | a_{hot} and b_{hot} in the same cluster
40 **end**
41 **if** a_{user} *and* b_{user} *have transactions with same h-address* **then**
42 | a_{user} and b_{user} in the same cluster
43 **end**

---

3   Analysis of Structure in Bitcoin Exchange

3.1   Data Set

The h-addresses and c-addresses in Bitcoin exchanges always contain a large number of Bitcoins. We collect the first 100,00 addresses in bitinfocharts.com on 2019/08/20 as the seeds to explore the whole addresses. The transactions of these addresses are collected from a Bitcoin block explorer service called blockchain.info. The service provides data on Bitcoin transactions. A transaction includes transaction hash, summary, inputs and outputs. The summary contains the size, weight, received time, included in blocks, confirmations and the visualize. The Inputs and outputs contain input addresses, output addresses, inputs and outputs, total input, total output, fees, fee per byte, fee per weight unit, estimated BTC transacted and the scripts.

We first apply the cluster algorithm to these addresses and extend them to relevant addresses. Then, the c-addresses, h-addresses, and u-addresses are aggregated into different exchanges. The detail is described in Algorithm 1. We verify our results compared with bitinfocharts.com which tags some addresses with Bitcoin exchange wallet. Besides, we collect some open addresses in public forums (i.e., Twitter, Reddit) and Bitcoin exchanges. The Bitcoin exchanges may announce some addresses publicly which are the most reliable information. As a result, the collected addresses with tags have 94% accuracy with our algorithm's findings and the findings are larger than the collected addresses. Besides, we have some interest findings.

Finding 1. The h-addresses in different exchanges transferred to each other sometimes.

Finding 2. The c-addresses in different exchanges transferred to each other through some specific addresses sometimes, the specific addresses are tagged as the services which provided the wallet service to exchanges.

Finding 3. The c-addresses transferred to u-addresses sometimes, but the number of this is little.

Next, we cluster the Bitcoin exchange addresses into h-addresses, c-addresses, and u-addresses. And select the typical exchange addresses to analyze.

3.2   Hot Wallet Address Analysis

Different exchanges have different structures on how to manage the Bitcoins with hot wallet addresses. We divide them into three categories. The first is that there only exists one hot wallet address at one time which illustrates that the Bitcoin exchange owns one hot wallet (OO). The second is that there exists more than one hot wallet addresses (OM), the third is that there exist more than one hot wallet addresses at different time (MM) which illustrates that the Bitcoin exchange may update their addresses to avoid the trace sometimes. The result is shown in Table 1.

We selected two typical Bitcoin exchanges (Binance, Huobi) to make further analysis. The number of transactions and the balance of Bitcoins everyday are

Table 1. Three categories of hot wallet addresses

Exchanges	OO	OM	MM
Binance	Y	N	N
Huobi	N	Y	Y
Bittrex	Y	N	N
Bitstamp	N	Y	N
Bitfinex	Y	N	N
Coincheck	N	Y	Y
Poloniex	N	Y	Y
Kraken	N	Y	Y

shown in Fig. 2. It demonstrates that Binance only has one h-address and keep approximately 6000 Bitcoins every day. But Huobi has different h-addresses at different time and the balance of Bitcoins is changing every day which is not same as Binance.

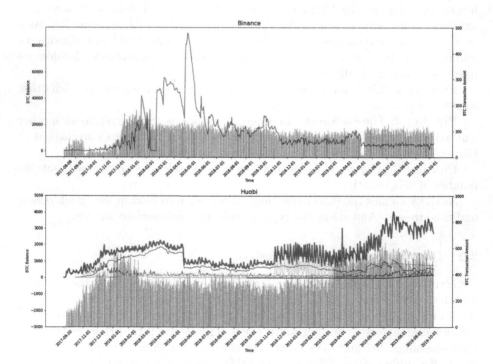

Fig. 2. The behaviors of hot wallet addresses in Binance and Huobi

3.3 Cold Wallet Address Analysis

The c-addresses are the most important since most of Bitcoins are stored in them in the Bitcoin exchanges, it's not convenient to make a lot of transactions due to the isolation from the internet. We divide them into two categories. The first is the number of daily transactions (TN). The second is that if there exist one or more cold wallets at a different time (OM). The result is shown in Table 2. At the same time, we select some typical Bitcoin exchanges (Binance, Huobi, Bitfinex) to make a further analysis, which is shown in Fig. 3. It demonstrates that Huobi only has one cold wallet address, but Binance has different cold wallet addresses at a different time. Besides, Binance and Huobi have little transactions associated with cold wallets, but Bifinex has unstable and relatively large transactions associated with cold wallets.

Table 2. Two categories of cold wallet addresses

Exchanges	TN	OM
Binance	2.5	N
Huobi	1.7	Y
Bittrex	1.6	N
Bitstamp	1.1	Y
Bitfinex	8.2	N
Coincheck	8.4	Y
Poloniex	3.1	Y
Kraken	1.7	Y

3.4 Fee Analysis

The h-addresses generate a lot of transactions every day in order to meet the demands of users' withdrawal. They also transferred the Bitcoins from user wallet to hot wallet occasionally. The daily transaction fees are different in each exchange, which is shown in Fig. 4. Figure 4 demonstrates that some exchanges manage the transferring due to the degree of crowdedness in the Bitcoin network, the less crowded of the bitcoin network can decrease the total fees. However, Poloniex provides high and stable transaction fees in order to make the transaction wrapped in the blockchain as soon as possible.

4 Supervised Learning for Prediction

In this section, we convert the previous proposed problem to a prediction problem. The previous proposed problem can be described as how much amount

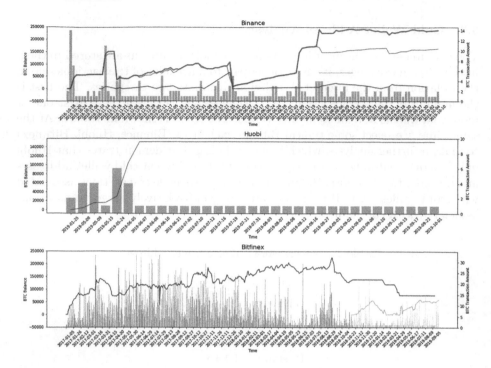

Fig. 3. The cold wallet addresses in the selected Bitcoin exchanges

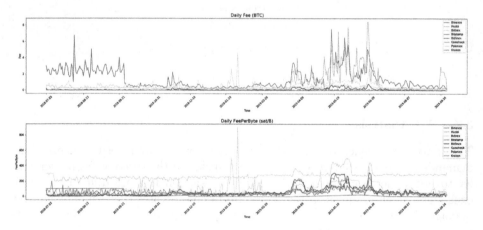

Fig. 4. The average fee in the different Bitcoin exchanges

of Bitcoins should be kept in the hot wallet. On one side, a large amount of Bitcoins stored in hot wallets can assure the demands of users' withdrawal but may increase the risk of attack. On the other side, a small amount of bitcoins make it more safe but may be inconvenient to transfer Bitcoins frequently to the hot wallets due to the complicated procedures (i.e., multiple signatures, internal audit) for cold wallet. The prediction problem can be described as that the prediction of the number of Bitcoins withdrawn from hot wallet address. Besides, we neglect to minimize fees according to the crowdedness of Bitcoin networks since the policy is different in Bitcoin exchanges described previously.

The number of Bitcoins withdrawn from hot wallets is collected from hot wallets' transactions. We choose 1-h as a interval to aggregate the transactions to a time series. The interval of 1-h is a relatively modest value. The main reason of 1-h is that the average interval of transactions is under 1-h in hot wallets of Bitcoin exchanges.

We predict the 1-h time series using the traditional method, Arima [11] and several classic model, Support Vector Machine with RBF kernel (SVM) [12], and XGBoost (XGB) [13]. Besides, we adopt the Long Short Term Memory (LSTM) [14] which is suit for predicting the time series and use the facebook-prophet [15] which is a procedure for forecasting time series data based on an additive model. Here, we adopt the root mean square error (RMSE) as our measurement. The RMSE is computed as $RMSE = \sqrt{\frac{\sum_{t=1}^{T}(\hat{y}_t - y_t)^2}{T}}$, where $\hat{y}_t$, y_t is the predicted values and true value for times t respectively.

We choose two typical Bitcoin exchanges (Binance and Huobi) as our examples to make a further analysis. Binance only owns one hot wallet address and Huobi owns many hot wallet addresses. The results are shown in Table 3, which demonstrates that these models perform similarly with RMSE.

Table 3. RMSE of models in Binance and Huobi

Model	Binance	Huobi
ARIMA	98.954	100.541
SVM	131.53	111.68
XGB	101.63	112.37
LSTM	147.69	102.89
Facebook-prophet	124.89	105.59

To better measure the results, we simulate the process of deposits and withdrawal in Bitcoin exchanges. The biggest amount of Bitcoins the hot wallet should maintain is x, which represents that the hot wallets do not acquire the withdrawn from cold wallets. The process to find x is described as follows. We first define a series that begins in a deposit from user wallet to hot wallet and ends in the next deposit from user wallet to hot wallet. The intermediate-range does not include the transactions associated with cold wallets. Then, for each model, we sum all the positive value (deposits) and all the negative values (withdrawal, predicted by each model in Table 3) in the series to a number saved in the list A. The largest required Bitcoins is equal to the absolute value of the minimum common subsequence in A. The result is shown in Table 4.

Table 4. The required amount of bitcoins in Binance and Huobi

Model	Binance-balance	Huobi-balance
ARIMA	3000	9650
SVM	550	550
XGB	6800	10950
LSTM	550	1200
Facebook-prophet	3200	6600
Best	3850	6250

The best model in Table 4 is that we apply the real withdrawal records to compute, which means that we know the future withdrawn from users. As a result, Facebook-prophet performs better compared to other models, which have a minimum difference with the Best model. Furthermore, we discuss the number of transactions between cold wallets and hot wallets. The current average retain of the Bitcoin in Binance and Huobi is 6200 and 4200 respectively and the number of transactions between cold wallet addresses and hot wallet addresses is 2.0. In address the aforementioned problem, we define a new process to simulate this situation as follows. We first define that the largest require Bitcoins is *upper*, the largest amount of withdrawal in past records is 1000 set as *lower*. Then, when the remaining Bitcoins in hot wallets is below than *lower*, the cold wallet will transfer some Bitcoins to hot wallet until the total amount is $\frac{upper+lower}{2}$ and the transaction count plus 1. When the remaining Bitcoin in hot wallets is larger than *upper*, the hot wallet will transfer the redundant Bitcoins to cold wallets, and keep the total amount *upper*. The results of the relationship between

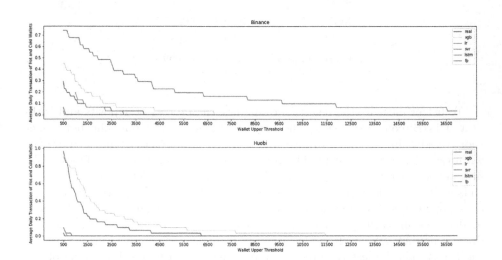

Fig. 5. The relationship between transaction and wallet upper threshold

the times between hot wallet and cold wallet and upper are shown in Fig. 5. The results show that the more transactions from cold wallets to hot wallets, the smaller Bitcoins required for hot wallets. The number of transactions also performs better compared to Fig. 3.

5 Conclusions and Future Works

In this paper, we propose a new Bitcoin address clustering algorithm for classifying the cold wallet, hot wallet and user wallet in the Bitcoin exchanges. At the same time, we aggregate and verify them in exists exchanges (Binance, Huobi, Bittrex, Bitstamp, Bitfinex, Coincheck, poloniex, kraken) by off-chain information from the Internet. Various structures are adopted by different Bitcoin exchanges and we define a general problem of predicting the Bitcoin withdrawn from hot wallets, which is not related to the type of exchanges' structures. The traditional and classific supervised learning methods are adopted to solve the prediction problem. Furthermore, we simulate two processes to analyze our results. The results show that the more transactions from cold wallets to hot wallets, the smaller Bitcoins required for hot wallets. In the future, we will extract more accurate and integrated Bitcoin exchange addresses. Furthermore, we will monitor all the user wallet addresses and design a more reasonable and accurate framework for Bitcoin exchanges.

Acknowledgments. The work described in this paper was supported by the National Key Research and Development Program (2016YFB1000101), the National Natural Science Foundation of China (U1811461, 61722214) and the Guangdong Province Universities and Colleges Pearl River Scholar Funded Scheme (2016).

References

1. Nakamoto, S., et al.: Bitcoin: a peer-to-peer electronic cash system (2008)
2. Corbet, S., Lucey, B., Urquhart, A., Yarovaya, L.: Cryptocurrencies as a financial asset: a systematic analysis. Int. Rev. Financ. Anal. **62**, 182–199 (2019)
3. Zheng, Z., Xie, S., Dai, H., Chen, X., Wang, H.: An overview of blockchain technology: architecture, consensus, and future trends. In: 2017 IEEE International Congress on Big Data (BigData Congress), pp. 557–564. IEEE (2017)
4. Zheng, Z., Xie, S., Dai, H.-N., Chen, X., Wang, H.: Blockchain challenges and opportunities: a survey. Int. J. Web Grid Serv. **14**(4), 352–375 (2018)
5. Eyal, I., Sirer, E.G.: Majority is not enough: Bitcoin mining is vulnerable. Commun. ACM **61**(7), 95–102 (2018)
6. Tran, M., Luu, L., Kang, M.S., Bentov, I., Saxena, P.: Obscuro: a Bitcoin mixer using trusted execution environments. In: Proceedings of the 34th Annual Computer Security Applications Conference, pp. 692–701. ACM (2018)
7. Böhme, R., Christin, N., Edelman, B., Moore, T.: Bitcoin: economics, technology, and governance. J. Econ. Perspect. **29**(2), 213–38 (2015)
8. Cheung, A., Roca, E., Su, J.-J.: Crypto-currency bubbles: an application of the phillips-shi-yu (2013) methodology on Mt. Gox Bitcoin prices. Appl. Econ. **47**(23), 2348–2358 (2015)

9. Chen, W., Wu, J., Zheng, Z., Chen, C., Zhou, Y.: Market manipulation of bitcoin: evidence from mining the Mt. Gox transaction network. In: IEEE INFOCOM 2019-IEEE Conference on Computer Communications, pp. 964–972. IEEE (2019)
10. Gennaro, R., Goldfeder, S., Narayanan, A.: Threshold-optimal DSA/ECDSA signatures and an application to Bitcoin wallet security. In: Manulis, M., Sadeghi, A.-R., Schneider, S. (eds.) ACNS 2016. LNCS, vol. 9696, pp. 156–174. Springer, Cham (2016). https://doi.org/10.1007/978-3-319-39555-5_9
11. Contreras, J., Espinola, R., Nogales, F.J., Conejo, A.J.: ARIMA models to predict next-day electricity prices. IEEE Trans. Power Syst. **18**(3), 1014–1020 (2003)
12. Suykens, J.A.K., Vandewalle, J.: Least squares support vector machine classifiers. Neural Process. Lett. **9**(3), 293–300 (1999)
13. Chen, T., Guestrin, C.: XGBoost: a scalable tree boosting system. In: Proceedings of the 22nd ACM SIGKDD International Conference on Knowledge Discovery and Data Mining, pp. 785–794. ACM (2016)
14. Hochreiter, S., Schmidhuber, J.: Long short-term memory. Neural Comput. **9**(8), 1735–1780 (1997)
15. Taylor, S.J., Letham, B.: Forecasting at scale. Am. Stat. **72**(1), 37–45 (2018)

Image Clustering Based on Graph Regularized Robust Principal Component Analysis

Yan Jiang[1], Wei Liang[2(✉)], Mingdong Tang[3], Yong Xie[2], and Jintian Tang[1]

[1] Key Laboratory of Particle and Radiation Imaging, Ministry of Education, Tsinghua University, Beijing 100084, China
{yanjiangthu,tangjt}@tsinghua.edu.cn
[2] College of Software Engineering, Xiamen University of Technology, Xiamen 361024, China
{wliang,yongxie}@xmut.edu.cn
[3] School of Information Science and Technology, Guangdong University of Foreign Studies, Guangzhou 510420, China
mdtang@gdufs.edu.cn

Abstract. Image clustering has become one of the most popular themes in web based recommendation system. In this study, we propose a novel image clustering algorithm referred as graph regularized robust principal component analysis (GRPCA). Unlike existing spectral rotation or k-means method, no discretization step is required in our proposed method by imposing nonnegative constraint explicitly. Besides, in GRPCA an affinity graph is constructed to encode the locality manifold information, and the global graph structure is respected by applying matrix factorization. The proposed method is robust to model selection that is more appealing for real unsupervised applications. Extensive experiments on three publicly available image datasets demonstrate the effectiveness of our algorithm.

Keywords: Clustering · Machine learning · Computer vision · Data mining

1 Introduction

Clustering plays an important role in modern web service, such as recommendation system, image indexing and annotation. Many algorithms have been successfully used for image clustering, thus the data in the same group are similar while the data points in different groups are dissimilar. In web service based applications one can access recommendation system by HyperText Transfer Protocol as illustrated in Fig. 1.

Many works [11,12,17] have demonstrated that feature engineering can improve performances of content based image retrieval [5]. Convolutional neural networks (CNN) have been widely used in computer vision community, CNN

© Springer Nature Singapore Pte Ltd. 2020
Z. Zheng et al. (Eds.): BlockSys 2019, CCIS 1156, pp. 563–573, 2020.
https://doi.org/10.1007/978-981-15-2777-7_45

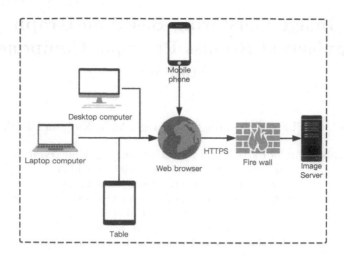

Fig. 1. Architecture of modern webservice based image search system.

extracts image feature at different scales automatically [2] and learns superior feature representation. However, training deep neural networks heavily depends on tuning parameters [6,10]. In document clustering, Non-negative Matrix Factorization (NMF) aims to learn the parts of objects by finding two non-negative matrices [13]. In [1] and [17] sparse coding is utilized for face recognition and clustering. Subspace learning and cluster indicator matrix are learned by a unified objective function in [15]. K-means has been widely used in clustering for its simplicity, Diskmeans [20] incorporates discriminative information in cluster indicator estimation that provide new insight into clustering methods. Besides, manifold structure [8] of data is a crucial property in clustering, NCut [18] and its extension show promising performances in image segmentation. Researches suggested that simultaneously perform matrix factorization and structured sparsity enable parts-based representation more accurately [4,9,12]. In [3,19] utilize both locality manifold structure and global discriminant information for image clustering.

In this paper, we propose a new clustering algorithm, namely Graph Regularized Robust Principal Component Analysis (GRPCA). We explicitly impose nonnegative constraint to make the estimated cluster indicator matrix more accurate. Additionally, the geometrical information of data is encoded by constructing a nearest neighbor graph in GRPCA objective function. In our method, the locality manifold information and nonnegative matrix factorization techniques are incorporated in an optimization framework to avoid overfitting and make the results robust. Finally, this study presents a theoretical justification about our algorithm.

The rest of this paper is organized as follows: Notations are introduced in Sect. 2. Theoretical justifications about our GRPCA algorithm are detailed in Sect. 3. Experiments are given in Sect. 4. The conclusions are presented in Sect. 5.

2 Notations and Definitions

We use $X = \{x_1, x_2, \ldots, x_m\} \in \mathbb{R}^{n \times m}$ to denote image data set in this study, where n stands for the number of features and m denotes the number of images. The jth image sample in data set is denoted as $x_j = [x_{1j}, x_{2,j}, \ldots, x_{nj}]^T \in \mathbb{R}^n$, which is an n-dimensional column vector. Matrix trace operator is denoted as $trace(\cdot)$. The Frobenius norm of matrix $X \in \mathbb{R}^{n \times m}$ is defined as Eq. (1). The ℓ_1-norm of a matrix is defined as Eq. (2) which leads to sparsity solution in multi-task learning [14].

$$\|M\|_F = \sqrt{\sum_{i=1}^{n} \sum_{j=1}^{m} m_{ij}^2} = \sqrt{\sum_{j=1}^{m} \|m_j\|_2^2} \tag{1}$$

$$\|M\|_1 = \sum_{i=1}^{n} \sum_{j=1}^{m} |m_{ij}|_1 = \sum_{j=1}^{m} \|m_j\|_1 \tag{2}$$

3 Graph Regularized Robust Principal Component Analysis

Essentially, Principal Component Analysis (PCA) aims to find two matrices that best approximate the given data matrix in the sense of ℓ_2 distance [16]. Suppose the means of X is subtracted in each feature dimension. PCA can be rewritten as Eq. (3)

$$\min_{U,V} \|X - UV^T\|_F^2 \tag{3}$$
$$s.t. \quad V^T V = I$$

where $U \in \mathbb{R}^{n \times c}, V \in \mathbb{R}^{m \times c}$, identity matrix is denoted as I. Based on manifold learning theory that high-dimensional data reside on a low-dimensional submanifold embedded in ambient space. Suppose two samples that are approximate in ℓ_2 distance should be closer after mapping from the original space. To ensure that mapping one can minimize Eq. (5), where $L = D - W$ and L is defined as Laplacian matrix [8], D is a diagonal matrix with $D_{ii} = \sum_{j=1}^{m} w_{ij}$. Heat kernel is taken to measure the affinity between samples as defined in Eq. (4).

$$A_{i,j} = \begin{cases} e^{-\frac{\|\mathbf{x}_i - \mathbf{x}_j\|^2}{t^2}} & \text{if } \mathbf{x}_i \in \mathcal{N}(\mathbf{x}_j) \text{ or } \mathbf{x}_j \in \mathcal{N}(\mathbf{x}_i). \\ 0 & \text{otherwise.} \end{cases} \tag{4}$$

$\mathcal{N}(x_j)$ denotes a set of samples that closest in distance to x_j, which depicts data locality information by a k-nearest neighbor graph as Eq. 5.

$$\min_{V} \sum_{i,j=1}^{m} \|v_i - v_j\|^2 W_{ij} = trace(V^T L V) \tag{5}$$
$$s.t. \quad V^T V = I$$

Intuitively, in our proposed GRPCA objective function Eq. (6) is composed of three parts. The global reconstruction error is measured by minimizing ℓ_2 norm; the second part considers local manifold structure; ℓ_1-norm can guarantee sparsity of matrix V. Moreover, it is hard to recover the cluster labels from spectral rotation or k-means methods, due to mixed signs by using generalized eigenvalue decomposition. The proposed GRPCA guarantees a more accurate relaxation by the nonnegative constraint.

$$\min_{U,V} \ \left\| X - UV^T \right\|_F^2 + \lambda_1 trace(V^T LV) + \lambda_2 \|V\|_1$$
$$s.t. \ V^T V = I, V \geq 0 \tag{6}$$

3.1   Optimization Method

The objective function of GRPCA defined in Eq. (6) is not convex in both U and V together, it is unrealistic to find the global minima. However, an iterative based optimization algorithm is proposed in our study that monotonously decrease the objective function in each iteration and converge to a local minima eventually. When V is fixed, we arrive at Eq. (7)

$$\mathcal{J}(U) = \min_{U} \ \left\| X - UV^T \right\|_F^2 \tag{7}$$

Taking the derivative of $\mathcal{J}(U)$ w.r.t U, and setting the derivative to zero, we have Eq. (8)

$$\frac{\partial \mathcal{J}}{\partial U} = -2XV + 2U = 0 \tag{8}$$

We arrive at $U = XV$ and substitute it into Eq. (6), we have Eq. (9) where E is a matrix with all elements equal to one.

$$\min_{V} \ \left\| X - XVV^T \right\|_F^2 + \lambda_1 trace(V^T LV) + \lambda_2 trace(V^T E)$$
$$s.t. \ \begin{cases} V^T V = I \\ V \geq 0 \end{cases} \tag{9}$$

or equivalently

$$\min_{V} \ trace(V^T(-X^T X + \lambda_1 L)V + \lambda_2 V^T E)$$
$$s.t. \ \begin{cases} V^T V = I \\ V \geq 0 \end{cases} \tag{10}$$

The Lagrangian function of minimization problem with equal constraint in Eq. (10) is as follows.

$$\min_{V} \ trace(V^T(-X^T X + \lambda_1 L)V + \lambda_2 V^T E) + \tfrac{\xi}{2} \left\| V^T V - I \right\|_F^2$$
$$s.t. \ V \geq 0 \tag{11}$$

Let ξ be the Lagrange multiplier for the orthogonality constraint in Eq. (11) and ϕ_{jk} be the Lagrange multiple for constraint $v_{jk} \geq 0$ respectively. To insure the orthogonality satisfied ξ should be large enough, in our experimental setting we fix it as 10^6. Let $M = (-X^T X + \lambda_1 L)$ we arrive at the following formulation

$$\mathcal{L} = trace(V^T(-X^T X + \lambda_1 L)V + \lambda_2 V^T E) + \frac{\xi}{2} \left\| V^T V - I \right\|_F^2 + trace(V^T \Phi)$$

Let derivatives of $\mathcal{L}$ equal to zero

$$2MV + \lambda_2 E + 2\xi V(V^T V - I) + \Phi = 0 \tag{12}$$

Using the Karush–Kuhn–Tucker conditions [7] which lead to the following updating rules.

$$V_{ij} \leftarrow \frac{(2\xi V)_{ij}}{(2MV + \lambda_2 E + 2\xi V V^T V)_{ij}} V_{ij} \tag{13}$$

The procedure of GRPCA is summarized in Algorithm 1 and the iteration begins with a random matrix V_0.

Algorithm 1. Clustering based on Graph Regularized Robust Principal Component Analysis

---

Require: Data matrix $X \in \mathbb{R}^{n \times m}$, λ_1, λ_2, c, k, $t = 1$, V_0;
Ensure: Clustering assignment matrix V^*;
1: **repeat**
2:     Compute $V_{ij}^{(t+1)} \leftarrow \frac{(2\xi V^{(t)})_{ij}}{(2MV^{(t)} + \lambda_2 E + 2\xi V^{(t)} V^{(t)T} V^{(t)})_{ij}} V_{ij}^{(t)}$;
3:     Normalize V such that $(V^T V)_{ii} = 1$ for $i = 1, ..., c$;
4:     $t = t + 1$;
5: **until** convergence
6: **return** Sparsity matrix V;

3.2   Convergence Analysis

Definition 1. $G(f, f')$ *is an auxiliary function of* $h(f)$ *when the following two conditions are satisfied*

$$1. \ G(f, f') \geq h(f)$$
$$2. \ G(f, f) \ = \ h(f)$$

Based on the auxiliary function mentioned above, we have the following lemma.

Lemma 1. *If* G *is auxiliary function of* h *the* h *is non-increasing under the update rule*

$$f^{(t+1)} = \arg\min_f G(f, f^t) \tag{14}$$

Proof.

$$h(f^{t+1}) = G(f^{t+1}, f^{t+1}) \le G(f^{t+1}, f^t) \le G(f^t, f^t) = h(f^t)$$

□

Theorem 1. *The objective value of Eq. (11) is non-increasing using the proposed Algorithm 1.*

Proof. Let us define

$$G(V_{ij}, V_{ij}^t) = h_{ij}(V_{ij}^t) + h'_{ij}(V_{ij}^t)(V_{ij} - V_{ij}^t) + \frac{(MV^t + 0.5\lambda_2 E + \xi V^t V^{tT} V^t)_{ij}}{V_{ij}^t}(V_{ij} - V_{ij}^t)^2$$

By setting $\frac{\partial G(V_{ij}, V_{ij}^T)}{\partial V_{ij}} = 0$, we have

$$h'_{ij}(V_{ij}^t) + 2\frac{(MV^t + 0.5\lambda_2 E + \xi V^t V^{tT} V^t)_{ij}}{V_{ij}^t}(V_{ij} - V_{ij}^t) = 0$$

Then we have

$$V_{ij} = V_{ij}^t - \frac{V_{ij}^t h'_{ij}(V_{ij}^t)}{(2MV^t + \lambda_2 E + 2\xi V^t V^{tT} V^t)_{ij}}$$

$$h'_{ij}(V_{ij}) = \frac{\partial h(F)}{\partial V_{ij}} = (2MV + \lambda_2 E + 2\xi V(V^T V - I))_{ij}$$

Let us define

$$V_{ij} = V_{ij}^t - \frac{V_{ij}^t (2MV + \lambda_2 E + 2\xi V(V^T V - I))_{ij}}{(2MV^t + \lambda_2 E + 2\xi V^t V^{tT} V^t)_{ij}}$$

Obviously

$$V_{ij} = \frac{V_{ij}^t (2\xi V)_{ij}}{(2MV^t + \lambda_2 E + 2\xi V^t V^{tT} V^t)_{ij}}$$

According to Lemma 1, we can see the objective function monotonically nonincreasing updating rule

$$V_{ij}^{t+1} = V_{ij} = \frac{V_{ij}^t (2\xi V)_{ij}}{(2MV^t + \lambda_2 E + 2\xi V^t V^{tT} V^t)_{ij}}$$

□

4   Experiments

In order to validate the clustering performance of our method, we applied our method on three publicly available image datasets and compared with several state-of-the-art clustering methods, such as k-means [20], Ncut [18], RGNMF [9] and self-tuning spectral clustering (SC) with heat kernel [21].

Table 1. Data sets descriptions

Datasets	Samples	Subclass number	Number of features
PIE	41368	68	1024
MNIST	70000	10	784
COIL-20	1440	20	1024

4.1 Data Sets Descriptions

Extensive empirical studies have been performed on image data sets[1]. Table 1 provides more details, which includes one face image dataset PIE, one object image dataset COIL-20, one hand written digital image dataset MNIST.

4.2 Experimental Setup and Evaluation Metrics

To obtain a fairly experimental evaluation, we use clustering accuracy (ACC) and normalized mutual information (NMI) for performance evaluation in our experiments defined in Eqs. (15) and (16).

In Eq. (15), we define $\delta(x, y) = 1$ if $x = y$; $\delta(x, y) = 0$ otherwise. $map(q_i)$ is mapping function that uses Kuhn-Munkres algorithm to obtain the best match between ground truth labels and permutation labels. A larger ACC indicates better performance.

$$Accuracy = \frac{\sum_{i=1}^{m} \delta(s_i, map(r_i))}{m} \qquad (15)$$

NMI is another widely used measurement for evaluating the clustering results. Given two arbitrary variables C and C' the mutual information between those variables are $MI(C, C')$. Moreover, $H(C)$ and $H(C')$ denote the entropies of C and C', respectively. Obviously, a larger NMI indicates better clustering results, $NMI(C, C') = 1$ if C is identical with C'.

$$NMI = \frac{MI(C, C')}{\max(H(C), H(C'))} \qquad (16)$$

In all experiments we specified the size of neighborhood $k = 5$ for our GRPCA and its competitors. Two parameters λ_1 and λ_2 have to be initialized in the proposed clustering method, we tune them from $\{10^{-3}, 10^{-2}, 10-1, 1, 10, 100, 1000\}$ and report the best result in the following subsections.

4.3 Performance Comparison

To ensure a fair comparison, we randomize the experiments and conduct the evaluations with different cluster number c, ten test runs are conducted on each c and the mean error of the performance are reported.

---

[1] http://www.cad.zju.edu.cn/home/dengcai/Data/data.html.

Table 2. Clustering performance on PIE dataset.

#c	Accuracy (%)					NMI (%)				
	kmeans	NCut	SC	RGNMF	GRPCA	kmeans	NCut	SC	RGNMF	GRPCA
4	47.5	93.6	**100**	99.4	**100**	33.1	97.0	98.4	**99.0**	**99.0**
12	43.1	87.0	97.1	97.5	**97.6**	51.7	92.3	97.5	97.6	**98.6**
20	38.2	82.7	87.9	88.2	**95.5**	55.8	87.6	92.5	95.8	**96.5**
28	34.4	77.3	84.1	86	**91.0**	59.8	88.9	90.1	92.1	**93.2**
36	34.8	77.6	78.0	88.2	**89.3**	57.2	89.7	85.3	**97.5**	97.4
44	34.1	75.8	73.1	87.1	**87.5**	60.2	87.5	86.4	94.3	**96.9**
52	33.1	76.2	70.3	82.3	**85.2**	63.3	88.3	84.9	92.6	**95.8**
60	32.4	72.6	68.7	77.9	**84.2**	64.2	87.1	84.2	90.7	**93.5**
68	31.3	68.2	80.5	76.2	**85.7**	61.1	91.5	92.7	90.0	**92.8**

Table 3. Clustering performance on COIL20 dataset.

#c	Accuracy (%)					NMI (%)				
	kmeans	NCut	SC	RGNMF	GRPCA	kmeans	NCut	SC	RGNMF	GRPCA
4	82.1	88.3	69.9	**90.2**	89.5	65.1	50.4	68.8	**90.0**	87.6
6	75.4	85.0	71.4	95.4	**97.3**	78.6	51.3	60.3	92.8	**95.7**
8	61.2	79.7	57.7	90.1	**90.5**	75.8	48.6	54.4	**93.8**	91.1
10	67.8	77.4	56.3	**86.7**	**86.7**	73.4	47.1	55.1	87.1	**87.8**
12	70.1	77.6	51.2	82.9	**89.3**	73.0	45.4	58.6	84.9	**89.1**
14	68.4	71.1	52.1	86.1	**87.2**	76.9	47.8	55.7	**90.5**	89.4
16	60.9	72.2	49.8	**82.3**	82.2	74.3	45.9	58.1	**88.6**	85.7
18	63.0	65.6	50.7	77.7	**82.7**	74.2	47.3	56.5	**88.1**	84.1
20	67.3	68.2	47.5	**81.7**	80.0	73.8	42.6	54.9	**89.5**	86.8

Tables 2, 3 and 4 illustrate the clustering results of different algorithm over three datasets. We investigate the influences of two essential parameters λ_1 and λ_2 on our GRPCA. The parameter λ_1 controls the penalty term of manifold regularizer and λ_2 controls the sparsity of V, which plays a very important role in cluster indicator matrix estimation. As it can be seen from Figs. 2 and 3 that the GRPCA is stable w.r.t. different parameters when clustering *Accuracy* or *nmi* metric as a function of the two parameters. Especially, the proposed algorithm remains stable over a large range. GRPCA achieves consistently good performance even when λ_1 becomes extremely large and λ_2 becomes extremely small. As we have described that GRPCA is insensitive in terms of parameters optimization and the model selection part can be avoid, which makes our method more applicable in unsupervised learning.

Table 4. Clustering performance on MNIST dataset.

#c	Accuracy (%)					NMI (%)				
	kmeans	NCut	SC	RGNMF	GRPCA	kmeans	NCut	SC	RGNMF	GRPCA
2	92.5	93.6	94.1	**99.4**	**99.4**	70.1	70.4	74.5	92.5	**95.0**
3	86.3	87.8	88.6	96.2	**97.6**	71.3	71.5	71.3	91.6	**91.7**
4	79.2	72.7	77.9	80.2	**85.5**	61.4	61.6	61.1	**82.3**	81.4
5	65.8	65.8	68.5	**72.6**	72.4	57.2	57.2	58.9	**75.3**	75.3
6	65.4	65.3	67.4	**77.3**	74.6	56.3	53.7	56.2	**75.0**	75.0
7	64.2	58.2	64.1	65.2	**74.5**	56.2	56.5	57.3	77.3	**77.4**
8	59.2	58.7	52.9	65.3	**68.4**	53.3	56.3	53.1	**72.8**	72.8
9	59.2	55.4	59.7	64.9	**69.2**	56.1	55.4	53.5	**67.0**	67.0
10	56.1	56.2	55.2	63.4	**72**	53.6	53.2	53.7	**66.9**	66.8

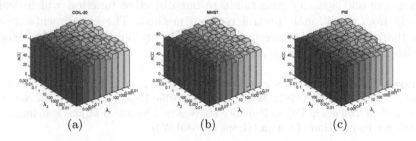

Fig. 2. Clustering accuracy with respect to different parameters λ_1 and λ_2 on image datasets. (a) COIL-20, (b) MNIST, (c) PIE.

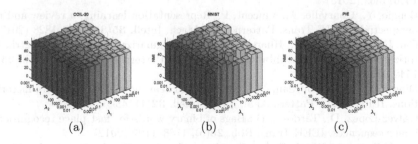

Fig. 3. Clustering NMI index with respect to different parameters λ_1 and λ_2 on image datasets. (a) COIL-20, (b) MNIST, (c) PIE.

From the evaluations we have the following observations:

1. GRPCA outperforms SC and RGNMF because it incorporates global and manifold information into a joint framework. The sparsity constraint makes cluster indicator matrix estimation more faithful.
2. GNMF [3,8] outperforms NCut and SC in Tables 2 and 4, a possible reason is that simultaneously utilizing global and local data information is more discriminative than considering those two factors separately.
3. Ncut outperforms k-means demonstrating that data manifold structure is beneficial for clustering [1].

5   Conclusions

In this study, we propose a new clustering algorithm GRPCA as well as the efficient solution framework. Most of the existing spectral clustering algorithm utilize only local data information, while K-means mainly focus on global data structures. We additionally take global information and locality manifold structure in a unified objective function. To obtain cluster indicator matrix, we impose nonnegative and sparsity constraints to our objective function which deviate severely from traditional spectral rotation method. The experimental results show that our proposed clustering method not only outperforms other existing algorithms but also robust to model selection.

Acknowledgments. This work was supported by the National Natural Science Foundation of China (NSFC) (81670090) and the Scientific Research Program of New Century Excellent Talents in Fujian Province University, China and Fujian Provincial Natural Science Foundation of China (Grant 2018J01570).

References

1. Bao, C., Ji, H., Quan, Y., Shen, Z.: Dictionary learning for sparse coding: algorithms and convergence analysis. IEEE Trans. Pattern Anal. Mach. Intell. **38**(7), 1356–1369 (2015)
2. Bengio, Y., Courville, A., Vincent, P.: Representation learning: a review and new perspectives. IEEE Trans. Pattern Anal. Mach. Intell. **35**(8), 1798–1828 (2013)
3. Cai, D., He, X., Han, J., Huang, T.S.: Graph regularized nonnegative matrix factorization for data representation. IEEE Trans. Pattern Anal. Mach. Intell. **33**(8), 1548–1560 (2010)
4. Ding, C.H., Li, T., Jordan, M.I.: Convex and semi-nonnegative matrix factorizations. IEEE Trans. Pattern Anal. Mach. Intell. **32**(1), 45–55 (2008)
5. Gálvez-López, D., Tardos, J.D.: Bags of binary words for fast place recognition in image sequences. IEEE Trans. Rob. **28**(5), 1188–1197 (2012)
6. Goodfellow, I.J., Warde-Farley, D., Mirza, M., Courville, A., Bengio, Y.: Maxout networks. arXiv preprint arXiv:1302.4389 (2013)
7. Gordon, G., Tibshirani, R.: Karush-kuhn-tucker conditions. Optimization **10**(725/36), 725 (2012)

8. He, X., Niyogi, P.: Locality preserving projections. In: Advances in Neural Information Processing Systems, pp. 153–160 (2004)
9. Huang, S., Wang, H., Li, T., Li, T., Xu, Z.: Robust graph regularized nonnegative matrix factorization for clustering. Data Min. Knowl. Disc. **32**(2), 483–503 (2018)
10. Ioffe, S., Szegedy, C.: Batch normalization: accelerating deep network training by reducing internal covariate shift. arXiv preprint arXiv:1502.03167 (2015)
11. Jiang, B., Ding, C., Tang, J.: Graph-Laplacian PCA: closed-form solution and robustness. In: Proceedings of the IEEE Conference on Computer Vision and Pattern Recognition, pp. 3492–3498 (2013)
12. Kong, D., Ding, C., Huang, H.: Robust nonnegative matrix factorization using L21-norm. In: Proceedings of the 20th ACM International Conference on Information and Knowledge Management, pp. 673–682. ACM (2011)
13. Lee, D.D., Seung, H.S.: Algorithms for non-negative matrix factorization. In: Advances in Neural Information Processing Systems, pp. 556–562 (2001)
14. Nie, F., Huang, H., Cai, X., Ding, C.H.: Efficient and robust feature selection via joint 2, 1-norms minimization. In: Advances in Neural Information Processing Systems, pp. 1813–1821 (2010)
15. Nie, F., Wang, X., Huang, H.: Clustering and projected clustering with adaptive neighbors. In: Proceedings of the 20th ACM SIGKDD International Conference on Knowledge Discovery and Data Mining, pp. 977–986. ACM (2014)
16. Nie, F., Yuan, J., Huang, H.: Optimal mean robust principal component analysis. In: International Conference on Machine Learning, pp. 1062–1070 (2014)
17. Saha, B., Pham, D.S., Phung, D., Venkatesh, S.: Sparse subspace clustering via group sparse coding. In: Proceedings of the 2013 SIAM International Conference on Data Mining, pp. 130–138. SIAM (2013)
18. Shi, J., Malik, J.: Normalized cuts and image segmentation. Departmental Papers (CIS), p. 107 (2000)
19. Yang, Y., Xu, D., Nie, F., Yan, S., Zhuang, Y.: Image clustering using local discriminant models and global integration. IEEE Trans. Image Process. **19**(10), 2761–2773 (2010)
20. Ye, J., Zhao, Z., Wu, M.: Discriminative k-means for clustering. In: Advances in Neural Information Processing Systems, pp. 1649–1656 (2008)
21. Zelnik-Manor, L., Perona, P.: Self-tuning spectral clustering. In: Advances in Neural Information Processing Systems, pp. 1601–1608 (2005)

Research on Marketing Data Analysis Based on Contour Curve in Blockchain

Yanjie Wang[✉] and Jianping Li

College of Information Engineering, Quzhou College of Technology, Quzhou 324000, Zhejiang, China
wangyjqz@163.com

Abstract. In-depth analysis of corporate marketing data is conducive to companies making sound marketing decisions in blockchain. This paper proposed a marketing data analysis method based on contour curve for the deep analysis of marketing data. Firstly, the analysis of marketing data contour, standard deviation, frequency and monotonicity is given. Then, based on the above parameter analysis, the total, mean, kurtosis and skewness of the marketing data contour are given. And the concentration degree was analyzed. Finally, the kurtosis, skewness and concentration of the marketing data were analyzed experimentally through simulation experiments. The analysis of the three abstract scales can play a more positive effect on the formulation of the sales strategy.

Keywords: Marketing data · Blockchain · Contour curve · Kurtosis · Skewness

1 Introduction

The development of informatization has driven the transformation of enterprises. A reasonable analysis of enterprise sales data through scientific data analysis methods can effectively improve the marketing decision-making level of enterprises. The current corporate marketing has gradually changed from extensive marketing to refined marketing, and massive marketing data provides data support for refined marketing. Through scientific and reasonable analysis of huge marketing data, data analysis to guide corporate marketing will become the main direction of corporate marketing development.

Research on data analysis has yielded some good research results. The paper [1] provided an in-depth analysis of the status quo, problems and countermeasures of big data analysis research. The paper [2] summarized the computational intelligence methods in big data analysis, and combined the characteristics of big data to discuss the problems and further research directions of computational intelligence research in big data analysis. Literature [3] analyzes media sentiment through social events, political campaigns, and corporate strategy data and implements active learning through algorithms. The paper [4] proposed a kernel entropy manifold learning algorithm, which uses information metrics to measure the relationship between two financial data points and generate a reasonable low-dimensional representation of high-dimensional financial data. The paper [5] used predictive analysis algorithms in the Hadoop/Map Reduce environment to predict the prevalence of diabetes. The paper [6] studied human-to-human

© Springer Nature Singapore Pte Ltd. 2020
Z. Zheng et al. (Eds.): BlockSys 2019, CCIS 1156, pp. 574–581, 2020.
https://doi.org/10.1007/978-981-15-2777-7_46

recommendations through collaborative filtering and compares this method to baseline profile matching methods. The paper [7] analyzed the use of qualitative data analysis software by researchers and conducted data analysis on this basis. The paper [8] used statistical learning theory to effectively construct extreme learning machines and is used in large-scale social data analysis. The paper [9] proposed an infinite depth neural network method for big data analysis. In addition, the paper [10–13] highlighted the in-depth analysis of various data.

Although the above research on data analysis had achieved some good results, the in-depth analysis of sales data has not been involved. Therefore, this paper proposed a marketing data analysis method based on contour curve, and analyzed the attributes of the contour by establishing the outline of the marketing data.

The specific organizational structure of the rest of the paper are as follows: Sect. 2 gives the analysis of marketing data based on the contour curve; Sect. 3 gives the experimental analysis; finally, the work summary of this paper is given.

2 The Analysis of Marketing Data Based on Contour Curve

2.1 The Analysis of Marketing Data

The marketing data profile can holistically show the overall level of marketing of the target product during the cycle. For example, for a contour curve of profit, the length of the curve represents the average period of profit, and the point on the curve represents the average value of the profit.

For the marketing parameter S of the target product X, in the statistical period T, the total number of statistics is N, and the statistical time of the i-th time is T_i, then the total length of the data contour corresponding to the marketing parameter S is defined as $T = \min(T_i, T_2, \cdots T_N)$, and the marketing data contour value of point j is:

$$Y_j = \frac{X_{1j} + X_{2j} + \cdots + X_{Nj}}{N} \tag{1}$$

Where X_{ij} represents the value of the marketing parameter of the target product X at the jth point of the statistical time i.

For profit, this parameter is the value of the total profit cycle Pro_All; for the sales revenue structure, the scattered sales income Sal_retail and the overall sales income Sal_whole need to calculate the contour curve.

The marketing data standard deviation is used to collectively represent the marketing fluctuations of the target product at various time points. For a certain time node, when the standard deviation of the contour corresponding to the time point is large, it indicates that the marketing of the product at that time point is discretely distributed, which may be due to the change of the marketing strategy and the instability of the sales link.

For the marketing parameter S of the target product X, in the statistical period T, the total number of statistics is N, and the statistical time of the i-th time is T_i, then the total length of the data contour corresponding to the marketing parameter S is defined as $T = \min(T_i, T_2, \cdots T_N)$, and the standard deviation of the marketing data profile of point j is:

$$D_j = D(X_{1j}, X_{2j}, \cdots, X_{Nj}) \tag{2}$$

Where X_{ij} represents the value of the marketing parameter of the target product X at the *j*th point of the statistical time *i*. $D_j = D(X_{1j}, X_{2j}, \cdots, X_{Nj})$ indicates the standard deviation of the data.

The frequency of marketing data is based on the outline of marketing data, and analyzes the fluctuation pattern of the contour curve of marketing data. By frequency domain analysis of the contour curve of marketing data, the fluctuation amplitude and phase of the contour curve of marketing data can be obtained at each frequency. When the fluctuation curve of the marketing data is small at all frequencies, it indicates that the target product has a stable trend throughout the sales period, that is, there is a relatively fixed sales amount; when the fluctuation amplitude is much larger than the other frequencies at a certain frequency, indicating that the target product sales are in an unstable state.

For the target product X, if the marketing data contour curve of a corresponding marketing parameter S is Y, the frequency of the parameter S is $rFFT(Y)$, where $rFFT$ is a real sequence fast Fourier transform.

The monotonic curve of marketing data is similar to the standard deviation of marketing data profiles, and can also be used to measure the marketing status of a target product at a certain point in time. Each point on the monotonic curve indicates whether the target product sale presents a monotonous trend at that point in time. In theory, under different marketing modes, sales at each time point are discretely distributed and do not have obvious monotonicity. When the marketing data on a certain time node shows obvious monotony, it indicates that the product sales strategy has a big problem.

For the marketing parameter S of the target product X, in the statistical period T, the total number of statistics is N, and the statistical time of the *i*-th time is T_i, then the total length of the data contour corresponding to the marketing parameter S is defined as $T = \min(T_i, T_2, \cdots T_N)$, and the value of the marketing data monotonic curve at point j is:

$$M_j = MK(X_{1j}, X_{2j}, \cdots, X_{Nj}) \tag{3}$$

Where X_{ij} represents the value of the marketing parameter of the target product X at the jth point of the statistical time *i*. $MK(X, Y, ...)$ represents the monotonic trend of the discrete sequences calculated by the Mann-Kendall algorithm.

The Mann-Kendall algorithm process is as follows.

(1) For the time series, calculate the statistics of the test.

$$S(\mathbf{X}) = \sum_{k=1}^{n-1} \sum_{j=k+1}^{n} \operatorname{sgn}(x_j - x_k) \tag{4}$$

Where $\operatorname{sgn}(x) = \begin{cases} 1, & x > 0 \\ 0, & x = 0 \\ -1, & x < 0 \end{cases}$.

(2) When n is large enough, it can be proved to follow a normal distribution with a mean of 0 and a variance of $\text{var}(S) = n(n-1)(2n-5)/18$. When n > 10, the standard normal system variables are calculated by the following formula.

$$z = \begin{cases} \frac{S-1}{\sqrt{\text{var}(S)}}, & S > 0 \\ 0, & S = 0 \\ \frac{S+1}{\sqrt{\text{var}(S)}}, & S < 0 \end{cases} \tag{5}$$

The positive or negative of z indicates that the original time series is in a monotonous increasing trend or a monotonous decreasing trend; the size of $|z|$ represents the credibility of the monotonic trend.

When $|z| \geq 0.84$, it shows the 80% confidence of the monotonic trend of the original time series. At this time, the original data is considered to be monotonous.

2.2 Marketing Data Type Profiling

The marketing data type profile is a further statistical analysis based on the marketing data profile curve and is an overview. For each type of data, the calculated statistical characteristics include the total amount of data, mean, peak, etc., and specific statistical characteristics, such as skewness and concentration, for specific marketing data. The general statistical characteristics of marketing data are analyzed as follows.

(1) Total marketing data
   For the outline C of a certain marketing data, the total amount of marketing data W is $W = SUM(x_1, x_2, \cdots, x_n)$.
(2) Marketing data mean
   For the outline C of a certain marketing data, the marketing data mean E is $E = AVE(x_1, x_2, \cdots, x_n)$, and AVE is the *mean* function.
(3) Marketing data *kurtosis*
   The kurtosis, also known as the kurtosis coefficient, characterizes the number of features of the probability density distribution curve at the peak value. If the marketing data profile is regarded as a distribution in probability space, with the normal distribution as the reference, the kurtosis can represent the concentration of the marketing data distribution in a short time; then the *kurtosis* coefficient is larger under the same standard deviation. The distribution has more extreme values, then the rest of the values are more concentrated around the mode, and the distribution is steeper, that is, there is a higher marketing data in a shorter period of time.

For a certain marketing data profile C, the data *kurtosis* is as follows.

$$k = \frac{\frac{1}{n}\sum_{i=1}^{n}(x_i - \mu)^4}{(\frac{1}{n}\sum_{i=1}^{n}(x_i - \mu)^2)^2} \tag{6}$$

Where μ represents the marketing data mean and n represents the marketing data profile C length.

(4) Marketing data skewness

The skewness coefficient is a feature number that describes the degree to which the distribution deviates from the symmetry. The marketing data contour is regarded as a distribution on the probability space, with the normal distribution as the reference. When the distribution is bilaterally symmetric, the skewness coefficient is 0. When the skewness coefficient is greater than 0, the distribution is right-biased. When the skewness coefficient is less than 0, the distribution is left-biased. Intuitively, when the skewness coefficient is less than 0, it indicates that the overall marketing data is presented in a rapid and slow distribution pattern. When the skewness is greater than 0, the overall marketing data is presented in a slightly slower and more urgent distribution pattern.

For a certain marketing data profile C, the data skewness is as follows.

$$W = \frac{1}{n} \sum_{i=1}^{n} (\frac{x_i - \mu}{\sigma})^3 \tag{7}$$

Where μ represents the mean value of the marketing data, σ represents the standard deviation of the marketing data, and n represents the length of the marketing data profile C.

(5) Marketing data concentration

The concentration of marketing data indicates the proportion of marketing data sets in the overall time.

The concentration of marketing data is as follows.

$$C = \frac{1}{n} \sum_{i=1}^{n} I\{x_i \geq Th\} \tag{8}$$

Where n represents the length of the marketing data and $I\{\bullet\}$ represents the symbol function as follows.

$$I\{f\} = \begin{cases} 1 , f = True \\ 0 , f = False \end{cases} \tag{9}$$

Th represents the threshold. When the marketing data is above the threshold, it is considered that the marketing data is concentrated at this time. On the contrary, the marketing data is not concentrated. In general, the value of the threshold Th can be set to correspond to different time concentrations.

3   Experiment Analysis

The method proposed in this paper is mainly for the analysis and research of marketing data, and through the analysis and research of marketing data to further guide the improvement of sales strategy. Therefore, the analysis of various indicators for marketing data was conducted in the experiment.

The experiment implemented the proposed algorithm on the Visual Studio 6.0 platform. The PC configuration in the simulation environment is: CPU Core i7-4790 3.60 GHz, RAM = 8 GB, Windows 10 Professional.

The experimental data is the sales data of Suzhou Pinzheng Machinery Co., Ltd. from 2016 to 2018.

The experiment analyzes the three indicators of kurtosis, skewness and concentration of marketing data.

3.1 Marketing Data Kurtosis Analysis

The kurtosis analysis of sales data from 2016 to 2018 is shown in Fig. 1.

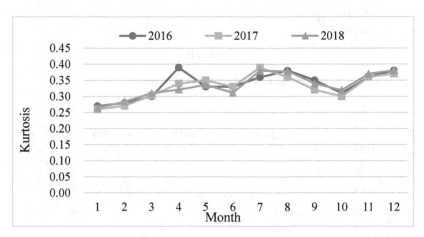

Fig. 1. Marketing data kurtosis.

Figure 1 shows the sales data kurtosis from 2016 to 2018. In the first three months, the marketing data kurtosis is low, indicating that the marketing data did not show a high peak during the three months.

3.2 Marketing Data Skewness Analysis

The marketing data skewness analysis from 2016 to 2018 is shown in Fig. 2.

Figure 2 shows the marketing data skewness from 2016 to 2018. Generally speaking, in the first half of the year, the marketing data skewed to the left, and the marketing data showed a pattern of rapid and slow distribution. In the second half of the year, the marketing data skewed to the right, and the marketing data showed a mode of distribution.

3.3 Analysis of Marketing Data Concentration

The marketing data concentration analysis of 2016–2018 is shown in Fig. 3.

Figure 3 shows the marketing data concentration in 2016–2018. The sales data concentration of the whole year is relatively stable, indicating that the proportion of marketing data concentration is relatively uniform in the overall time.

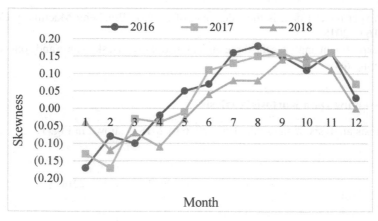

Fig. 2. Marketing data skewness.

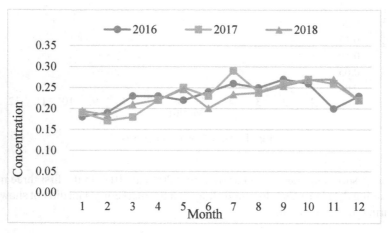

Fig. 3. Marketing data concentration.

4 Conclusions

This paper proposed a marketing data analysis method based on contour curve for the deep analysis of marketing data. The total, mean, kurtosis, skewness and concentration of marketing data contours are based on the above parameters analysis. The degree was analyzed. Finally, the kurtosis, skewness and concentration of the marketing data were analyzed experimentally through simulation experiments. The analysis of the three abstract scales can play a more positive effect on the formulation of the sales strategy.

Acknowledgment. This work was supported by Guiding Project of Quzhou Science and Technology Plan in 2018 (2018004).

References

1. Guan, S., Meng, X., Li, Z., et al.: Big data study on the current situation, problems and countermeasures. J. Intell. **34**(5), 98–104 (2015)
2. Guo, P., Wang, K., Luo, A., et al.: Computational intelligence for big data analysis: current status and future prospect. J. Softw. **26**(11), 3010–3025 (2015)
3. Cambria, E., Wang, H., White, B.: Guest editorial: big social data analysis. Knowl.-Based Syst. **69**, 1–2 (2014)
4. Huang, Y., Kou, G.: A kernel entropy manifold learning approach for financial data analysis. Decis. Support Syst. **64**, 31–42 (2014)
5. Kumar, N.M.S., Eswari, T., Sampath, P., et al.: Predictive methodology for diabetic data analysis in big data. Procedia Comput. Sci. **50**, 203–208 (2015)
6. Krzywicki, A., Wobcke, W., Kim, Y.S., et al.: Collaborative Filtering for people-to-people recommendation in online dating: data analysis and user trial. Int. J. Hum. – Comput. Stud. **76**(C), 50–66 (2015)
7. Woods, M., Paulus, T., Atkins, D.P., et al.: Advancing qualitative research using qualitative data analysis software (QDAS) reviewing potential versus practice in published studies using ATLAS.ti and NVivo, 1994–2013. Soc. Sci. Comput. Rev. **34**(5), 597–617 (2016)
8. Oneto, L., Bisio, F., Cambria, E., et al.: Statistical learning theory and ELM for big social data analysis. IEEE Comput. Intell. Mag. **11**(3), 45–55 (2016)
9. Zhang, L., Zhang, Y.: Big data analysis by infinite deep neural networks. J. Comput. Res. Dev. **53**(1), 68–79 (2016)
10. Roda, F., Musulin, E.: An ontology-based framework to support intelligent data analysis of sensor measurements. Expert Syst. Appl. **41**(17), 7914–7926 (2014)
11. Thorp, K.R., et al.: Proximal hyperspectral sensing and data analysis approaches for field-based plant phenomics. Comput. Electron. Agric. **118**(C), 225–236 (2015)
12. Bock, H.H., Gaul, W., Okada, A., et al.: Advances in data analysis and classification. Data Anal. Mach. Learn. Knowl. Discovery **5**(4), 356–364 (2015)
13. Jain, A., Bhatnagar, V.: Crime data analysis using pig with hadoop. Procedia Comput. Sci. **78**, 571–578 (2016)

Knowledge Mapping and Scientometric Overview on Global Blockchain Research

Peng-Hui Lyu[1][✉], Ran Tong[2], and Rui Yuan Wei[2]

[1] School of Management, Hefei University of Technology, Hefei, People's Republic of China
Sibiling@mail.ustc.edu.cn
[2] Institute of Computer Network Systems,
Hefei University of Technology, Hefei, People's Republic of China

Abstract. In the past few years, block-chain research literatures have increased rapidly, but there have been fewer attempts and efforts to map global research in block-chain related research. The main purpose of this study is to assess global progress and explore the current trends in block-chain studies. Scientific quantitative measurement methods were utilized targeting the Science Citation Index Extension (SCI-E) and Social Science Citation Index (SSCI) from the WoS database until 2018. The block-chain related literatures were investigated as a whole in this paper. This paper adopts the literature measurement method and knowledge visualization technology to clarify the status of authoritative publications in global block-chain documents. The CiteSpace software was used to conduct a research on the subject categories, author cooperation networks, national cooperation networks as well as the institutional cooperation networks. The authors of the literature and the cited references were thoroughly examined, highlighting the main aspects and providing research frontier for block-chain research.

Keywords: Lock chain research · Scientometric · Research cooperation · Web of science · Knowledge mapping

1 Introduction

The blockchain is not the first - and certainly not the last network boom we will experience [1]. As a disruptive technology, block-chain technology and distributed ledgers have drawn tremendous attention and triggered multiple projects in different industries [2]. A ground breaking paper "Bitcoin: A Peer-to-Peer E-Cash System" published by a scholar named "Satoshi Nakamoto" in the scholastic mailing group, originated block-chain technology in 2008 [3]. The name of the founder of Satoshi Nakamoto's Bitcoin began from 2007, to explore the use of a series of technologies to create a new currency, Bitcoin. On October 31, 2008, the Bitcoin White Paper was released. On January 3, 2009, the currency system starts running. The main technologies supporting the Bitcoin system include hash functions, distributed ledgers, block-chains, asymmetric encryption, and proof of work, which were employed to form the initial version of the block-chain. From 2007 to the end of 2009, Bitcoin was in its stage of technological experiment in which a

© Springer Nature Singapore Pte Ltd. 2020
Z. Zheng et al. (Eds.): BlockSys 2019, CCIS 1156, pp. 582–590, 2020.
https://doi.org/10.1007/978-981-15-2777-7_47

very small number of people participated, and related business activities have not been launched yet. The first bitcoin exchange was born on February 6, 2010. On May 22 in the same year, someone bought 2 pizzas with 10,000 bitcoins. On July 17, the famous bitcoin exchange Mt.gox platform was established, which marked that Bitcoin really entered the market. Despite the complexities associated with bitcoin technology, it is possible to understand Bitcoin and enter the market to participate in the trading process of bitcoin. Many discussion topics related to bitcoin can be found in Bitcointalk.org forum, e.g. mining bitcoin on their own computers, and buying and selling bitcoin on Mt.gox.

Christidis K believes that with the right block-chain, applications that previously could only run through trusted middlemen can now run in a decentralized manner without the need for central authority and with the same certainty to achieve the same functionality [4]. This is based on the following characteristics of the block-chain:

With the rapid development of block-chain research, block-chain technology is becoming widely used in various industries: finance [5], corporate governance [6], medical insurance [7], smart transportation [8], construction industry [9], chemical industry [10], Internet of Things security etc. [11], and sharing economy [12], etc. In order to understand the development status of block-chain and predict the development trend of block-chain in the future, this paper uses CiteSpace software to analyze the authoritative literature on block-chain in WoS database, and analyze the current status of the block-chain global issue, subject classification, and the research Cooperation networks (author, country and institution). Finally, we analyzed the key words of the authors and the references, to analyze the research hotspots and research frontiers of the block-chain research. The process of the rise and development of the block-chain is presented in a timeline map.

2 Data and Methods

2.1 Data Sources

The Web of Science (WoS) database is the most authoritative database for researching specific topics, it has indexed journals which considered to constitute the world's most important (influential) journals [13]. In addition, the Science Citation Index (SCI) from Web of Science (WoS) is the most widely accepted and frequently used database for scientific analytical publications [14]. Therefore, all the literature on block-chain research in this paper was collected from the online version of Science Citation Index Extension (SCI-E) and Social Science Citation Index (SSCI) published by Clarivate Analytics [15]. Block-chain-related research terms including but not limited to "blockchain", "block chain" and "block-chain", can be retrieved to the maximum extent possible of the search terms as hoped with this paper. The irrelevant records are minimized, so the search strategy is arranged as TS = ("block*chain*"), the time span is 1990–2018, and the search time is January 31, 2019. Based on this search strategy 1,056 articles were found in the SCI-E and SSCI databases. All our research is based on the dataset of these articles retrieved from key databases as mentioned above.

2.2 Methodologies

This paper uses the bibliometrics method to mainly investigate the research trends. Schneider and Borlund (2004) believed that research and analysis conducted by bibliometric method can be used to understand and evaluate the completed work and the content needs to be investigated [16]. Bibliometric studies can also analyze the trends in international cooperation networks and the impact of multilateral scientific networks, and joint publications with three or more countries as indicators for the outcomes of international research [17]. According to Narin et al. the basic principle of bibliometric analysis is to quantify scientific publications by determining productivity through technical performance parameters [18]. In recent years, bibliometric research has become an objective method for assessing individual's contribution to the advancement of knowledge [19].

Social network analysis methods are used to identify the relationships of local, national and international partnerships [20]. In order to explore the cooperation situation of global block-chain publishing, this paper uses CiteSpace software to analyze the individual, institutional and national characteristics of 1,056 documents, draw the cooperative networks on block-chain literatures and analyze the distribution of their producers. The weight of the contribution of the issuing agencies or countries in the block-chain research field was further explored either, clarifying the cooperative relationship and laying the foundation which can be used for the in-depth study of the block-chain domains.

3 Results and Discussion

3.1 Global Publication Trend

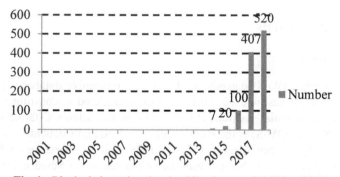

Fig. 1. Block chain topic-related publication trend (1990 to 2018)

The publication trends of annual papers in block chain research from 1990 to 2018 were shown in Fig. 2. It can be seen from Fig. 1 that the block-chain research was almost in blank before 2013. The first literature on the block-chain appeared in 2013. Hence, it can be stated that the real initiation of block-chain literature research was in 2013. The number of block-chain publications has exploded after 2015. Which indicated that, as an emerging research topic, the block-chain research is not only a new field, but also a hot research field in recent years.

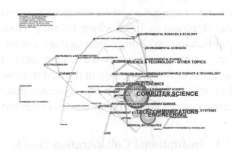

Fig. 2. Subject categories for block-chain research

Fig. 3. National cooperation network of block-chain research

3.2 Subject Categories of Papers

Through the use of CiteSpace tool the 63 disciplines which belong to block-chain literatures from 2013 to 2018 were mapped as shown in Fig. 2. It can be seen from Fig. 2 that Computer science is the largest group in the network, followed by Engineering, which means that Computer science and Engineering are the most involved disciplines in the block-chain research diagram. The thick purple circles around these two nodes, indicates that they have a high degree of centrality, Computer science (0.35), and Engineering (0.2). Accordingly, they are the key nodes constituted the subject categories network here. The block-chain is primarily concerned with computer science disciplines, including theory and methods, information systems, software, hardware and artificial intelligence, and interdisciplinary applications; followed by engineering disciplines, it focuses on electronics and electrical engineering and communications. In addition, the block-chain is also related on business, economic, financial and other disciplines. With the continuous development of block-chain technology, the research is expected to expand into further disciplines, gradually shifting from theoretical research to application realization.

3.3 National Collaboration Trends

The country cooperation network in Fig. 3 shows the publication map in the block-chain research from 2013 to 2018. China has published 260 articles in the block-chain research, ranking first among all countries, USA 255, ranked second, England 81, third. Followed by Italy (60), Germany (60), South Korea (46), Australia (45), France (41), India (41), Japan (40). P.R. China takes the ratio 25% in all of the block-chain publications, USA 24% and England 8%. These three countries published over 50% of the block-chain papers in the world and they are the main countries dedicated to the block-chain research. Among the top 10 countries, only P.R. China and India are developing countries, and the rest are developed countries. Among them, the nodes represented by USA, Italy, England, Australia, Scotland, Wales, Netherlands have a purple aperture around them. The thicker the purple aperture, the higher their intermediate degree, which indicates the importance of a node with several publications in the network diagram. China is in close contact with other nodes, as to connect the entire corporation network [21].

At the same time, it also means that these top productive countries have mastered most of the resources of block-chain technology and played a vital role in promoting the development of block-chain research. Some countries have a large proportion of the publications with high intermediary center, such as USA, England and Italy; they are key countries to promote the development of block-chain research. Some countries such as India or Spain are among the best in production, however, their mediation center still low within the network. This indicates that these countries have not yet formed enough close contact with other countries in the block-chain research.

3.4 Institutional Collaboration Trends

According to the node size of Fig. 4, it can be seen Beijing University of Posts and Telecommunications from P.R. China is the organization with the most publications. In 2013–2018, 20 related block-chain papers were published by them. The second rank goes to Chinese Academy of Sciences with a publication count of 15. Peking University and Beijing University of Aeronautics and Astronautics published 14 papers, ranking third. Among all of them, there are 7 institutions from the P.R. China, published 96 block-chain literatures. There is 1 institution from the USA and another from Australian, both with a total of 10 articles. There is 1 institution from Canada with 9 articles. Most of the high-yield global institutions on block-chain papers are mainly colleges and universities. In addition, a few research institutes are also high-yield institutions such as CSIRO.

To understand the research links between agencies, Fig. 4 shows all the partnerships in the world based on blockchain research. Beijing University of Posts and Telecommunications, Peking University, Beijing University of Aeronautics and Astronautics, University of British Columbia, Guangdong University of Technology, University of Hong Kong, Chinese Academy of Sciences and other research institutes all have purple apertures in the network, which means high centrality. These institutions are research cooperation. The institutional cooperation network can be broadly divided into five cooperative sub-networks: the first is a cooperation group centered on MIT; the second is a cooperative group based on Cornell Univ and Cornell Tech; the third is Nanyang Technol. Univ, CSIRO and Univ Sydney are the core sub-networks; the fourth is a sub-network with Beijing Univ Posts & Telecommun, Univ Texas San Antonio and Temple Univ as the main nodes, the last one being Peking Univ, Chinese Acad A subnetwork of key nodes of Sci and Beihang Univ.

3.5 Keywords and Co-words Networks

Author's keywords analysis is beneficial to grasp the research hotspot of the block-chain publication and to identify the knowledge structure in the block-chain domain. Figure 5 shows the clustering result of co-words network of the papers. According to Jie Li et al.'s description of CiteSpace's many functions: Modularity is an index to evaluate the degree of network clustering. The Q value is in the interval [0,1]. In general, $Q > 0.3$ means that the obtained network community structure is significant; when $S > 0.5$ clustering is reasonable [22]. In Fig. 5 their $Q = 0.6383$, the structure is proved to be significant; their $S = 0.6987$, which proves that the clustering community structure is significant and reasonable.

Fig. 4. Institutional collaboration network   **Fig. 5.** Co-words networks map of block-chain publications

The top ten high frequency labels and keywords are grouped and explained as blow, virtual currency research is mostly about the bitcoin research, similar situation is to Ethereum. Bitcoin is a well-known, peer-to-peer, decentralized electronic money system that moves funds by generating any number of aliases (or addresses), allowing all users to benefit from pseudonyms [23]. Kiviat, Trevor I introduces block-chain technology on its most well-known applications: currency transfer and payment with bitcoin, explaining how block-chain trading happens, and why this technology is highly innovative for exploring bitcoin, the economic characteristics of the currency, and putting bitcoin in the long-term evolution of currency technology, especially in the field of bitcoin chain trading regulation [24]. Harald Vranken discusses the basic operation of Bitcoin and explores the development in hardware for bitcoin mining. Bitcoin mining is highly competitive, and their applications are also competitive. Mining hardware benefit from the lower cost of electricity [25]. Tschorsch F and Scheuermann B conducted a survey of digital currencies, and provided an overall technical perspective on the distributed currency, pointing out many research opportunities [26].

In terms of smart contracts, the focus is to improve its reliability, providing a pass called Town Crier (TC). Validated data feed systems provide a powerful and practical way to hinder Ethernet evolution [27]. Luu L studied the security of running Ethereum smart contracts in an open distributed network like cryptocurrency and formalizing the semantics of Ethereum smart contracts and make recommendations as a solution for recorded errors.

In the aspect of Internet of Things (IoT), the main research is to construct the IoT electronic business model, and propose the IoT e-commerce model; Building an IoT system; IoT security etc.

The block-chain research hotspots are mainly divided into 9 clusters, in which the largest 4 clusters are summarized: block-chain technology (e.g. performance; power; transaction; clustering; effectiveness; supply chain integration; buyer; purchasing and supply management; value creation eco-system); cloud computing (e.g. data provenance; edge computing; permissioned block-chain; fog computing); scalability; proof of stake (pos)); challenge (e.g. economics; radio frequency identification; risk; liquidity; safety); p2p (smart contract; cryptography; smart grid; data; ethereum; hash; merkle tree; app; javascript; web; merkledag; file system).

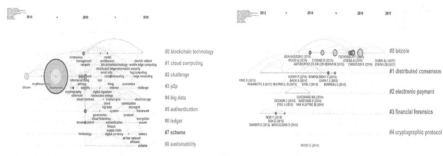

Fig. 6. Timeline view of author keywords   **Fig. 7.** Timeline view of cited references

In order to sort out the emergent and development process of the block-chain from 2013 to 2018, this paper clusters the author keywords and draws a timeline view, as shown in Fig. 6. In 2014, the term "bitcoin" appeared as the author's keyword for the first time in the block-chain literatures in the WoS database. In 2015, the "block-chain" appeared as the author's keyword and "cryptocurrency" emerged. After 2015, the number of author's keywords increased year by year, predicting that future research on block-chain will increase sharply.

3.6 Co-citation Network of References

Figure 7 shows the references cited in the block-chain literatures from 2012 to 2016. All the references in the clusters refer to the key literatures with higher frequency and centrality. Based on their content, the highly cited literature can be divided into 3 classes: the first class is Cluster #0, labeled as bitcoin by LLR, including electronic payment; e-commerce; technology acceptance model; technology adoption; perceived ease; cryptocurrency; internet. The second class is Cluster #1 focused on distributed consensus, including lightning network; duplex micropayment channel; service; proof of irretrievability; off chain transaction; trade off; tutorial; proofs of work. The third class is Cluster #4 focused on cryptographic protocol, such as trusted hardware; logic; programming paradigm; distributed information system; electronic medical record; authenticated data feed; semantic web; trust layer.

4   Conclusions

This paper carried out bibliometric analysis of 1,056 block-chain documents from the WoS database. The research results show that the block-chain is an emerging field, starting from 2013. Block-chain mainly involves computer science disciplines, including theory and methods, information systems, software, hardware and artificial intelligence. In engineering disciplines, it mainly focuses on electrical and electronic, energy, etc., and there are many subfields under the field of electronic communication. The outer layer of block-chain research is also applied to business and economics, finance and other disciplines. Computer science is the earliest discipline the block-chain research originated from. Later, with the continuous development of block-chain technology, it continues to extend to other disciplines, transitioning gradually from theoretical research to application realization as time went by. The analysis of the author's cooperation network shows that scholars in the field of block-chain have general research cooperation. Research cooperation exists in the form of small groups in the current stage of block-chain research. Each group usually has several core authors and other less important group members. Most of the authors in this small group are geographically similar or have the same nationality. The analysis of the national cooperation network shows that the block-chain literature published by USA, P.R. China and England overpass 50% of the world total literature in this area. They are the main countries dedicated to the research and global development in block-chain. Institutional cooperation network shows that, most of the global high-yield institutions of block-chain papers are mainly colleges and universities. In addition, a few research institutes are also high-yield institutions, and there is no close relationship between the institutions. The cooperation mechanism between them is also geographically centered, and there is not yet a large and frequent cross-regional cooperation network. Statistical and cluster analysis of author keywords shows that the research on block-chain is mainly focused on digital currency, smart contracts and the Internet of Things.

Through the quantitative analysis of blockchain literature, some suggestions for better development of blockchain are proposed: expanding the application of blockchain technology in various disciplines; strengthening the exchange of inter-blockchain technology; strengthening the research institutions of various institutions. In cooperation, they should actively seek scientific research institutions with complementary technologies. They can make full use of the advantages of universities and actively establish a technology R&D cooperation mechanism combining production, study and research.

Acknowledgements. This research was supported in part by grants from the Humanities and Social Sciences project of the Chinese Ministry of Education (19YGC630116) and the Hong Kong Scholars Program (XJ-2016064). The authors are grateful for the constructive comment of the referees on the earlier version of this paper for their helpful discussion.

References

1. Marsal-Llacuna, M.-L.: Future living framework: is blockchain the next enabling network? Technol. Forecasting Soc. Change **128**, 226–234 (2018)
2. Nofer, M., Gomber, P., Hinz, O., Schiereck, D.: Blockchain. Bus. Inf. Syst. Eng. **59**(3), 183–187 (2017)
3. Sidhu, J.: Syscoin: a peer-to-peer electronic cash system with blockchain-based services for E-business. In: 2017 26th International Conference on Computer Communication and Networks (ICCCN), pp. 1–6. IEEE (2017)
4. Christidis, K., Devetsikiotis, M.: Blockchains and smart contracts for the internet of things. IEEE Access **4**, 2292–2303 (2016)
5. Peters, G.W., Panayi, E.: Understanding modern banking ledgers through blockchain technologies: future of transaction processing and smart contracts on the internet of money. In: Tasca, P., Aste, T., Pelizzon, L., Perony, N. (eds.) Banking Beyond Banks and Money. NEW, pp. 239–278. Springer, Cham (2016). https://doi.org/10.1007/978-3-319-42448-4_13
6. Yermack, D.: Corporate governance and blockchains. Rev. Finance **21**(1), 7–31 (2015)

7. Qi, X., Sifah, E.B., Asamoah, K.O., Gao, J., Du, X., Guizani, M.: MeDShare: trust-less medical data sharing among cloud service providers via blockchain. IEEE Access **5**(99), 14757–14767 (2017)

8. Yuan, Y., Wang, F.Y.: Towards blockchain-based intelligent transportation systems. In: IEEE International Conference on Intelligent Transportation Systems. IEEE (2016)

9. Xu, S., Weber, I., Zhu, L., et al.: A taxonomy of blockchain-based systems for architecture design. In: IEEE International Conference on Software Architecture. IEEE (2017)

10. Sikorski, J., Kraft, M.: Blockchain technology in the chemical industry: machine-to-machine electricity market. Appl. Energy **195**, 234–246 (2017)

11. Kshetri, N.: Blockchain's roles in strengthening cybersecurity and protecting privacy. Telecommun. Policy **41**, 1027–1038 (2017). S0308596117302483

12. Pazaitis, A., Filippi, P.D., Kostakis, V.: Blockchain and value systems in the sharing economy: the illustrative case of Backfeed. Technol. Forecasting Soc. Change **125**, 105–115 (2017)

13. Boyack, K.W., Klavans, R., Börner, K.: Mapping the backbone of science. Scientometrics **64**(3), 351–374 (2005)

14. Braun, T., Schubert, A.P., Kostoff, R.N.: Growth and trends of fullerene research as reflected in its journal literature. Chem. Rev. **100**, 23–38 (2000). Published on the web dec 10, 1999. Chem. Rev. **31**(13), 23–38 (2000)

15. Chen, W., Chen, S., Qi, D.C., Gao, X.Y., Wee, A.T.: Surface transfer p-type doping of epitaxial graphene. J. Am. Chem. Soc. **129**(34), 10418–10422 (2007)

16. Schneider, J.W., Borlund, P.: Introduction to bibliometrics for construction and maintenance of thesauri: methodical considerations. J. Documentation **60**(5), 524–549 (2004)

17. Gómez, I., Fernández, M.T., Sebastián, J.: Analysis of the structure of international scientific cooperation networks through bibliometric indicators. Scientometrics **44**(3), 441–457 (1999)

18. Narin, F., Olivastro, D., Stevens, K.A.: Bibliometrics: theory, practice and problems. Eval. Rev. **18**(1), 65–76 (1994)

19. Yi, H., Xi, Z.: Trends of DDT research during the period of 1991 to 2005. Scientometrics **75**(1), 111–122 (2008)

20. Anderson, G., Ge, Y.: The size distribution of Chinese cities. Regional Sci. Urban Econ. **35**(6), 756–776 (2005)

21. Chaomei, C., Zhigang, H., Shengbo, L., Hung, T.: Emerging trends in regenerative medicine: a scientometric analysis in CiteSpace. Expert Opin. Biol. Ther. **12**(5), 593–608 (2012)

22. Mizuno, T., Takayasu, M., Takayasu, H.: The mean-field approximation model of company's income growth. Phys. A Stat. Mech. Appl. **332**(C), 403–411 (2012)

23. Spagnuolo, M., Maggi, F., Zanero, S.: BitIodine: extracting intelligence from the bitcoin network. In: Christin, N., Safavi-Naini, R. (eds.) FC 2014. LNCS, vol. 8437, pp. 457–468. Springer, Heidelberg (2014). https://doi.org/10.1007/978-3-662-45472-5_29

24. Simkin, M.V., Roychowdhury, V.P.: Stochastic modeling of citation slips. Scientometrics **62**(3), 367–384 (2005)

25. Rousseau, R.: Robert Fairthorne and the empirical power laws. J. Documentation **61**(2), 194–202 (2005)

26. Tschorsch, F., Scheuermann, B.: Bitcoin and beyond: a technical survey on decentralized digital currencies. IEEE Commun. Surv. Tutorials **18**(3), 2084–2123 (2016)

27. Fan, Z., Cecchetti, E., Croman, K., et al.: Town crier: an authenticated data feed for smart contracts. In: ACM Conference on Computer & Communications Security (2016)

Prediction of Bitcoin Transactions Included in the Next Block

Kyungchan Ko(✉), Taeyeol Jeong, Sajan Maharjan, Chaehyeon Lee,
and James Won-Ki Hong

Department of Computer Science and Engineering, POSTECH, Pohang 37673, Korea
{kkc90,dreamerty,thesajan,chlee0211,jwkhong}@postech.ac.kr

Abstract. This paper proposes a method to predict transactions that
are likely to be included in the next block from the mempool of unconfirmed transactions in the Bitcoin network. To implement the proposed
method, we applied machine learning to the transactions data collected
from the Bitcoin network and divided our implementation into the following three objects: Data Collector; Data Preprocessor; and Analyzer.
We used the random forest classifier algorithm because the problem of
predicting the likelihood of a transaction to be included in the next block
is a binary classification problem. We evaluated the performance of our
model by comparing transactions in the mempool against transaction
published in the next two blocks mined at the time of our experiments.
For both blocks, our model has a prediction accuracy of more than 80%
and a minimal false negative error. The analysis of transaction inclusion
in the next block is fundamental as it could drive the price of Bitcoin or
signify the properties of a given transaction such as illegal or legal.

Keywords: Bitcoin · Blockchain · Transaction prediction ·
Transaction selection policy · Machine learning

1 Introduction

Bitcoin [1], the world's first cryptocurrency gave rise to the blockchain [2,3]
technology and is operated in a distributed peer-to-peer (P2P) environment. Its
network consists of "nodes" that maintain their own copy of the blockchain and
transmit and verify new "transactions", which indicates the transfer of Bitcoin
between addresses. Transactions are collected and grouped together into a single
unit called a 'block' in a blockchain. Bitcoin establishes consensus among its distributed nodes through a mechanism called the Proof-of-Work (PoW) [4] consensus which determines the creation of next block and requires miners to perform
a computationally intensive task for block generation. In Bitcoin, miners need
the motivation to benefit themselves via mining because it requires extensive
use of computing resources, time, and electric power [5]. To incentivize miners,
the success of mining in Bitcoin is rewarded with new Bitcoins (BTCs) and fees
for all the transactions included by the miner in the block. Thus, while mining

© Springer Nature Singapore Pte Ltd. 2020
Z. Zheng et al. (Eds.): BlockSys 2019, CCIS 1156, pp. 591–597, 2020.
https://doi.org/10.1007/978-981-15-2777-7_48

new blocks, miners make selective choices on which transactions to include in the next block and focus on transactions that have high fees to maximize their revenue.

Transaction fee is an important factor that determines the transaction confirmation in the blockchain. Transactions with a very high amount of Bitcoins sent to "exchange addresses" can be interpreted as being traded through the exchanges. Thus, if a transaction is included in the block and transferred to the address of an actual exchange, it affects the price of Bitcoin. This paper suggests a method to predict which of the transactions currently in the mempool are included in the next block by collecting Bitcoin transactions and analyzing them through a machine learning algorithm. We perform our study in the belief that in-depth analysis of Bitcoin transactions inclusion into next block could reveal insights regarding the nature and behaviour of the Bitcoin network such as price volatility and legality of transactions.

The remainder of this paper is organized as follows: Sect. 2 describes existing related work, Sect. 3 presents details on our proposed method, Sect. 4 presents experimental setup and results from the proposed method and Sect. 5 presents the conclusion with contributions and our future work.

2   Related Work

Al-Shehabi [6] introduced an approach that used the mempool state with a weight vector to predict the necessary 'feerate' that is capable of confirming a transaction in the intended time frame. The author used the perceptron machine learning algorithm to generate weight vectors for different block target ranges with historical mempool snapshots. The author analyzed the relationship between 'feerate', confirmation time, and miner preference in snapshots. This study indicated whether a transaction is confirmed within the next four blocks with an accuracy of 90.72%. Fiz et al. [7] created a model of the selection process wherein mining pools perform on the set of unconfirmed transactions. The authors view the prediction of whether an unconfirmed transaction will be part of the next block as a supervised classification problem. The authors do not collect real-time unconfirmed transaction in mempool and simply reconstruct a mempool state using historical transactions in the blockchain via the API from blockchain.info [8]. Therefore, a few transactions that were in the mempool at that time may no longer exist. Pontiveros, Norvill and State [9] also proposed a method to detect changes to the transaction policy of mining pools. The authors treat the transaction selection policy as a classification problem. Subsequently, this study demonstrates how changes in the policy by a mining pool can be detected based on their own scenario.

3   Proposed Method

The purpose of this work is to predict whether or not a transaction from the mempool will be included in the next block in the Bitcoin blockchain. Given that the current height of blockchain is block 101, our work involves the prediction of which transactions from the mempool is likely to be mined into the next block, block 102, into the blockchain. Figure 1 shows our prediction framework that is designed to achieve the aforementioned objectives. The framework consists of - Bitcoin Core client [10], Data Collector, Preprocessor and Analyzer.

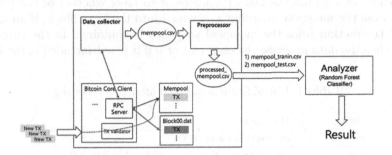

Fig. 1. Proposed framework for predicting transactions to be mined in the next block

The Bitcoin Core client stores historical blocks as well as real-time transactions occurring in the network and stores them in the mempool. The client also facilitates an RPC server that allows retrieval of unconfirmed transactions and historical blocks through RPC requests. The Data Collector stores snapshots of the mempool state before receiving the newly created block. In Fig. 1, the Data Collector collects data from the client using RPC request/response and stores them in a CSV file. The Preprocessor reads the CSV file and organizes the features used for the machine learning model of the Analyzer and performs labelling. Due to large volume of transactions in mempool, we do not store entire details of transactions. We further split the CSV file into training and testing whereby the training CSV file is used for learning the random forest classifier and testing CSV file is used to evaluate the model. Our proposed method is divided into three steps through the framework described above as follows: Data Collection; Data Processing; and Data Analysis.

A. Data Collection. The Data Collector collects two types of data via RPC functions: unconfirmed transactions which are collected by using the RPC function 'getrawmempool' and; block data corresponding to the current highest block by using the RPC functions - 'getbestblockhash' and 'getblock'. Additionally, in Bitcoin, abnormal blocks (empty blocks and blocks with very small size) are occasionally generated. We consider these types of blocks as outliers, and we skip the collection of the blocks if their block size is smaller than the criteria size. Since the timing of snapshot of the mempool state is important, the Data Collector actively monitors for new blocks and saves the mempool state immediately before a block is received. This allows collection of unconfirmed transactions prior to block generation.

B. Data Processing. Due to short interval between successive blocks generation, we are unable to collect entire features of unconfirmed transactions. Table 1 shows the list of features we have collected as well as configurations applied to those features from the data processing step. The Data Preprocessor is used to sort transactions according to 'feerate' and 'txchainFeerate' in descending order from the mempool. Since, we store immediate snapshot of mempool before block generation, we also use the Data Preprocessor to label whether or not a transaction from the mempool snapshot was mined into the next block. If an unconfirmed transaction from the mempool snapshot is contained in the successive block, then the data processor labels it as 1 or 0 if it is not included in the block.

Table 1. List of features collected after preprocessing

Data	Description
fee	transaction fee in BTC
size	virtual transaction size as defined in BIP 141
feerate	fee/size
txchainCnt	number of related (connected) transactions in mempool
txchainFee	sum of fees of related (connected) transactions in mempool
txchainSize	sum of sizes of related (connected) transactions in mempool
txchainFeerate	txchainFee/txchainSize
timepast	past time after a transaction enters in mempool
num-inputs	number of inputs in a transaction
num-outputs	number of outputs in a transaction
sum-inputs	sum of input values in a transaction
sum-outputs	sum of output values in a transaction
tps	transaction per second
mpsize	mempool size
prebs	size of previous block
avg-feerate	feerate on average in mempool
pos-feerate	position of feerate in mempool (in descending order)
c-avg-feerate	sum of feerates of related transactions on an average in the mempool
c-pos-feerate	position of the sum of feerates of related transactions in mempool (in descending order)
next-height	height of the next block
label	Included in the next block(1) or not(0)

C. Data Analysis. During the Data Analysis stage, the analysis is performed by considering the refined data as a feature created by the preprocessor. We implemented the random forest classifier [11] because we considered it as a binary classification problem as to whether or not unconfirmed transactions are included in the next block. Thus, the Analyzer learns the model using train.csv and verifies the performance of the model by using test.csv.

4 Experiment

4.1 Experiment Setup

In-mempool transactions used for learning were collected from 2019-08-13 to 2019-08-15 corresponding to transactions from block heights 589823 to 590115 (approx. 300 blocks). Abnormal blocks, block size less than 1MB, were not collected. A total of 3,154,728 transactions were collected for training the random forest classifier, and the performance of the model was evaluated with data corresponding to block heights 590919 and 590920.

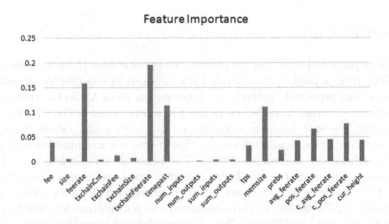

Fig. 2. Feature importance of transaction features

4.2 Feature Importance

Figure 2 shows the impact of each feature on whether or not a transactions from mempool will be included in the next block. Our findings suggest that the features - 'txchainFeereate', 'feerate', 'timepast', and 'mpsize' exhibit high feature importance among the features used in learning as seen by their values. Existing studies did not explore the feature 'txchainFeereate' although we added it because this would be the highest consideration to maximize profits and showed that the feature exhibits the highest feature importance.

4.3   Results

Table 2 shows the performance of the random forest classifier on the test dataset. We used Accuracy, Precision, Recall, and F1-score as evaluation metrics. Accuracy exceeded 80% for both blocks. Additionally, the learned model exhibits a very high recall, which is the ratio of transactions that the model predicts will be included in the block to the transactions actually contained in the next block. This implies that there is little or no false negative error.

Table 2. Performance results on test dataset

Block number	Accuracy	Precision	Recall	f1-score
590919	0.81	0.81	1.00	0.90
590920	0.80	0.81	0.98	0.89

5   Conclusion

This paper proposed a method to predict the transactions to be included in the next block from a pool of unconfirmed transactions in the Bitcoin network. To implement the proposed method, we developed a Data Collector that collects transactions occurring in real-time in the Bitcoin network; a Data Preprocessor to construct features that are utilized in the analysis and labels them using historical information; and an Analyzer that includes a machine learning model that learns from the preprocessed data. The problem is considered as a binary classification, and thus random forest classifier was used as the Analyzer. As a result of the experiment, our classifier was trained with the data collected from 2019-08-13 to 2019-08-15, and we evaluated the learned model with blocks at block heights 590919 and 590920. Both blocks exhibited more than 80% accuracy. Our results indicated that there was little or no false negative error.

A future study involves validating the proposed method with a number of classification algorithms other than the random forest. Additionally, we plan to add more refined features and systemize the proposed methods such that transactions can be collected and analyzed in real-time and automatically updated.

Acknowledgments. This work was supported by the ICT R&D program of MSIT/IITP [No. 2018-000539, Development of Blockchain Transaction Monitoring and Analysis Technology] in Republic of Korea.

References

1. Nakamoto, S.: Bitcoin: A peer-to-peer electronic cash system (2008)
2. Swan, M.: Blockchain: Blueprint for a New Economy. O'Reilly Media, Inc., Sebastopol (2015)

3. Crosby, M., et al.: Blockchain technology: beyond bitcoin. Appl. Innov. **2**(6–10), 71 (2016)
4. Bitcoin Wiki - Proof of work. https://en.bitcoin.it/wiki/Proof_of_work. Accessed 20 Sept 2019
5. O'Dwyer, K.J., David, M.: Bitcoin mining and its energy footprint, pp. 280–285 (2014)
6. Al-Shehabi, A.: Bitcoin transaction fee estimation using mempool state and linear perceptron machine learning algorithm (2018)
7. Fiz, B., Hommes, S.: Confirmation delay prediction of transactions in the bitcoin network. In: Park, J., Loia, V., Yi, G., Sung, Y. (eds.) CUTE 2017, CSA 2017. LNEE, vol. 474, pp. 534–539. Springer, Heidelberg (2017). https://doi.org/10.1007/978-981-10-7605-3_88
8. blockchain.info Explorer. https://www.blockchain.com/explorer. Accessed 15 Sept 2019
9. Pontiveros, B.B.F., Norvill, R., State, R.: Monitoring the transaction selection policy of Bitcoin mining pools. In: NOMS 2018–2018 IEEE/IFIP Network Operations and Management Symposium. IEEE (2018)
10. Bitcoin Core v0.17.1 Released. https://bitcoin.org/en/release/v0.17.1. Accessed 20 Sept 2019
11. Liaw, A., Wiener, M.: Classification and regression by randomForest. R news **2**(3), 18–22 (2002)

Knowledge Distillation Based on Pruned Model

Cailing Liu$^{(\boxtimes)}$, Hongyi Zhang$^{(\boxtimes)}$, and Deyi Chen

School of Optoelectronics and Communication Engineering,
Xiamen University of Technology, Xiamen 361000, China
1044120864@qq.com, zhanghongyi@xmut.edu.cn, 972275518@qq.com

Abstract. The high computational complexity of deep neural networks makes them challenging to deploy in practical applications. Recent efforts mainly involve pruning and compression the weights of layers to reduce these costs, and use randomly initializing weights to fine-tune the pruned model. However, these approaches always lose important weights, resulting in the compressed model performing that is even worse than the original model. To address this problem, we propose a novel method replaced the traditional fine-tuning method with the knowledge distillation algorithm in this paper. Meanwhile, With the Resnet152 model, our method obtained the accuracy of 73.83% on CIFAR100 data and 22x compression, respectively, ResNet110 SVHN achieve 49x compression with 98.23% accuracy and all of which are preferable to the state-of-the-art.

Keywords: Deep neural networks · Model compression · Pruning · Knowledge distillation · Accelerate

1 Introduction

Faced with the main three challenges of optimizing includes model size, runtime memory, number of computing operations. Within the realm of compression network modeling technology, several representative methods for parameter pruning/sharing [4,12], low-rank approximation [14], knowledge distillation [11], quantization and binarization [6], structure sparse [8], and efficient framework such as SqueezeNet [9], Xception [1], MobileNet [7] and so on are designed. However, most of these methods can only address one or two challenges mentioned above. Moreover, some of the techniques require specially designed software/hardware accelerators for execution speedup [2].

2 Related Work

This paper will explore relevant aspects of model compression by quantization or pruning and so on of primitive neural operations.

© Springer Nature Singapore Pte Ltd. 2020
Z. Zheng et al. (Eds.): BlockSys 2019, CCIS 1156, pp. 598–603, 2020.
https://doi.org/10.1007/978-981-15-2777-7_49

Paper [2,10] by quantifying weights of real values into binary/ternary weights, weights values are limited to f$(-1, 1)$ or f$(-1, 0, 1)$. Although the model size can be significantly reduced, and significant speedup is achieved in a specific computing library. However, this low-order approximation of the quantized form causes a partial loss of precision.

A low-rank matrix technique such as singular value decomposition (SVD) is used to approximate the weights matrix in the neural network [3]. This method is applicable to the fully-connected layers, which can deduct 3x the size of the model, but it still has no notable advantage in acceleration. Since DNN is like resnet/densenet them the calculation operations in mainly come from the convolution layer.

Network pruning is a versatile method that was originally used to compress deep networks, but the method did not reduce the model storage. To tackle the problem, papers [4,12,13] achieve effective compression of the model, but do not speed up in time. Therefore, this paper improves the algorithm proposed in [12], removing the filtering and corresponding feature maps, and combining the knowledge distillation to change the traditional random initialization weights.

3   A Method of Combining Pruning and Distillation

The main focus of this paper is to find a way to optimize the pruned model, so that the method can reduce the size of the model storage and speed up the convergence.

3.1   Pruning

Pruning neurons have proven to be effective for deep convolutional neural networks with limited learning resources. The pruning process determines how many neurons and channels are removed from each layer.

We use the method of L_1-norm based neuron pruning, which proposed by Li et al. [12]. Quantitatively, let C_i be the number of input channels in the i-th convolutional layer, h_i/w_i means the *height/width* of the input feature maps, $X_i(X_i \in \mathbb{R}^{C_i \times h_i \times w_i})$ denotes the input feature map while X_{i+1} be the output feature map, which is the input feature map of the next convolutional layer. $N_{i,j}$ $(N_{i,j} \in \mathbb{R}^{C_i \times k \times k})$ be the j-th neuron of the i-th convolutional layer. The parameters of the convolutional layer are $C_{i+1}C_i k^2 H_{i+1}W_{i+1}$. As is showed in Fig. 1, when a neuron $N_{i,j}$ is pruned, its corresponding feature map $X_{i+1,j}$ is removed, which reduces $C_i k^2 H_{i+1}W_{i+1}$ operations. The kernels that apply on the removed feature maps from the neurons of the next convolutional layer are also removed, which saves additional $C_{i+2}k^2 H_{i+2}W_{i+2}$ operations. Assuming that c and the i+1-th layer. The function Eq. 1:

$$L_1\left(X_{i,j}\right) = \frac{1}{N} \sum_{n=1}^{N} \left\|\mathbf{X}_{i,j}^n\right\|_1 \tag{1}$$

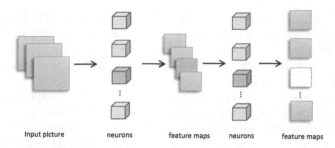

Fig. 1. Yellow cubes represent the pruned neuron, and the yellow squares represent their corresponding feature maps. (Color figure online)

3.2 Knowledge Disstillation

Hinton [5] points that training a teacher model before training students with the knowledge distillation (KD) method. This procedure is shown in Fig. 2.

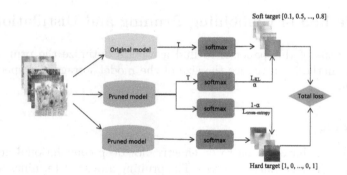

Fig. 2. Original model as teacher model, pruned model as student model.

The distillation process is to transfer knowledge to the distillation model by training knowledge on the transfer set and using soft target distribution for each situation in the transfer set. After training, the temperature was set 1. Cross-entropy loss function is modified as Eq. 2.

$$L_{cross-entropy}\left(y_{true}\|Q_s\right) = \sum_{i\in\{1,2\}} y_{true} \log \frac{1}{Q_s} \tag{2}$$

$$D\left(Q_T\|Q_s\right) = H\left(Q_T, Q_s\right) - H\left(Q_T\right) = \sum_{x} Q_T(x) \log \frac{Q_T(x)}{Q_s(x)} \tag{3}$$

Where y_{true} represents the out of the real ground output, and Q_s is the output of the student model. Optimizing the loss function is equivalent to minimize the

Kullback-Leibler (KL) divergence in Eq. 3 between the original model output and the student model. Softmax non-linearity is modified as follows Eq. 4:

$$q_i = \frac{\exp\left(z_i/T\right)}{\sum \exp\left(z_j/T\right)} \tag{4}$$

Where z_j is summed input of class j in the output layer. T is the temperature. q_i is the output of class j. Temperature is used both in teacher and student model. Secondly, it is beneficial to use the ground truth labels. By interpolating the ground truth labels into the training process, better performance can be maintained. Thus we can get the following loss function Eq. 5:

$$L_{KD}\left(W_{student}\right) = \alpha T^2 * L_{KL}\left(Q_S^\tau, Q_T^\tau\right) + (1-\alpha) * L_{cross-entropy}\left(Q_s, y_{true}\right) \tag{5}$$

At the same temperature (T > 1), Q_s^τ and Q_T^τ correspond to the soft target of students and teachers, respectively. α as a hyperparameter to adjust the weights average of the two components of loss. First component of the L_{KD} makes the optimization towards of the student to the similar softened softmax distribution of the teacher, while the second component of the L_{KD} makes the optimization towards approximating the ground truth labels. Use the knowledge of distillation to train a label-free student network when α is set to 1.

4   Experiments

We evaluate our approach on standard datasets with popular DNN. We pruned and distilled using the benchmark data CIFAR10/CIFAR100/SVHN on ResNet, which are different from VGG networks on CIFAR10 used in other model compression methods. The model parameters of VGG are mainly concentrated in the fully connected layer, while ResNet parameters concentrated in the convolution layer. Therefore, pruning and distillation our chosen network is more challenging. We implemented all networks and model training procedures in Pytorch and python3. For all datasets, we adopted the same experimental setting. We used every network to train an original model with 150 echoes, lr sets to 0.1 and weights sets to $1e - 4$. We used the SGD to Nesterov momentum and set momentum to 0.9, while we drop the learning rate by 0.1 at (70, 90) epochs. For retraining models, we used 40 echoes and 0.001 lr. The consequences are as follows Table 1.

The result is shown below in Tables 1 and 2. The accuracy of the model test for knowledge distillation has been higher than that of the original model and the randomly initialized pruned model. At the same time, it can be noted that the test time is also reduced.

Table 1. Test time of a single image comparison on benchmark datasets. Time1 is random initialization pruned model test time for each image. Time2 is knowledge distillation pruned model test time for each image.

Model	Time1	Time2
VGG16	0.4356 ms	0.2243 ms
ResNet18	0.3429 ms	0.2626 ms
ResNet56	0.3588 ms	0.2997 ms
ResNet152	0.4323 ms	0.3865 ms
ResNet50	0.2687 ms	0.2301 ms
ResNet110	0.2346 ms	0.1953 ms

Table 2. VGG16 and ResNet18 on CIFAR10, ResNet56/152 on CIFAR100, ResNet50/110 on SVHN. VGG16, ResNet18, ResNet56, ResNet152, ResNet50, ResNet110 are original models. VGG16-pruned-1, ResNet18-pruned-1, ResNet56-pruned-1, ResNet152-pruned-1, ResNet50-pruned-1, ResNet110-pruned-1 represent retraining model with random initialization fine-tuning method. VGG16-pruned-2, ResNet18-pruned-2, ResNet56-pruned-2, ResNet152-pruned-2 represent retraining model with the distillation method.

Dataset	Model	Error(%)	Parameters	Pruned(%)	FLOPs	Pruned(%)
CIFAR10	VGG16	6.39	14.29M		30.21M	
	VGG16-pruned-1	6.52	4.58M	68.02	22.34M	29.34
	VGG16-pruned-2	**6.03**				
	ResNet18	6.51	0.66M		9.74M	
	ResNet18-pruned-1	6.54	0.52M	21.21	8.48M	12.93
	ResNet18-pruned-2	**6.21**				
CIFAR100	ResNet56	29.57	0.82M		36.89M	
	ResNet56-pruned-1	29.34	0.68M	16.55	30.62M	15.53
	ResNet56-pruned-2	**28.98**				
	ResNet152	26.45	2.30M		99.89M	
	ResNet152-pruned-1	26.40	1.79M	22.26	81.63M	18.27
	ResNet152-pruned-2	**26.17**				
SVHN	ResNet50	3.71	0.72M		32.77M	
	ResNet50-pruned-1	3.42	0.48M	33.01	22.99M	29.84
	ResNet50-pruned-2	**2.82**				
	ResNet110	2.45	1.65M		72.15M	
	ResNet110-pruned-1	2.51	0.84M	49.01	46.98M	34.89
	ResNet110-pruned-2	**1.77**				

5   Conclusions

This paper proposes a method to introduce a combination of regularized neuron pruning and knowledge distillation to reduce the computational cost. This is useful for further understanding and improving the structure. In the future work, we hope to explore training network methods that are not only less complex but also have fewer neurons per layer, and we will experiment on Imagenet or larger datasets to improve the efficiency of the model.

References

1. Chollet, F.: Xception: deep learning with depthwise separable convolutions. In: Proceedings of the IEEE Conference on Computer Vision and Pattern Recognition, pp. 1251–1258 (2017)
2. Courbariaux, M., Hubara, I., Soudry, D., El-Yaniv, R., Bengio, Y.: Binarized neural networks: Training deep neural networks with weights and activations constrained to +1 or −1. arXiv preprint arXiv:1602.02830 (2016)
3. Denton, E.L., Zaremba, W., Bruna, J., LeCun, Y., Fergus, R.: Exploiting linear structure within convolutional networks for efficient evaluation. In: Advances in Neural Information Processing Systems, pp. 1269–1277 (2014)
4. Guo, Y., Yao, A., Chen, Y.: Dynamic network surgery for efficient DNNs. In: Advances in Neural Information Processing Systems, pp. 1379–1387 (2016)
5. Hinton, G., Vinyals, O., Dean, J.: Distilling the knowledge in a neural network. arXiv preprint arXiv:1503.02531 (2015)
6. Hou, L., Yao, Q., Kwok, J.T.: Loss-aware binarization of deep networks. arXiv preprint arXiv:1611.01600 (2016)
7. Howard, A.G., et al.: Mobilenets: Efficient convolutional neural networks for mobile vision applications. arXiv preprint arXiv:1704.04861 (2017)
8. Huang, Z., Wang, N.: Data-driven sparse structure selection for deep neural networks. In: Ferrari, V., Hebert, M., Sminchisescu, C., Weiss, Y. (eds.) ECCV 2018. LNCS, vol. 11220, pp. 317–334. Springer, Cham (2018). https://doi.org/10.1007/978-3-030-01270-0_19
9. Iandola, F.N., Han, S., Moskewicz, M.W., Ashraf, K., Dally, W.J., Keutzer, K.: Squeezenet: Alexnet-level accuracy with 50x fewer parameters and <0.5 mb model size. arXiv preprint arXiv:1602.07360 (2016)
10. Jacob, B., et al.: Quantization and training of neural networks for efficient integer-arithmetic-only inference. In: Proceedings of the IEEE Conference on Computer Vision and Pattern Recognition, pp. 2704–2713 (2018)
11. Lan, X., Zhu, X., Gong, S.: Knowledge distillation by on-the-fly native ensemble. In: Proceedings of the 32nd International Conference on Neural Information Processing Systems, pp. 7528–7538. Curran Associates Inc. (2018)
12. Li, H., Kadav, A., Durdanovic, I., Samet, H., Graf, H.P.: Pruning filters for efficient convnets. arXiv preprint arXiv:1608.08710 (2016)
13. Zagoruyko, S., Komodakis, N.: Paying more attention to attention: Improving the performance of convolutional neural networks via attention transfer. arXiv preprint arXiv:1612.03928 (2016)
14. Zhang, X., Zou, J., Ming, X., He, K., Sun, J.: Efficient and accurate approximations of nonlinear convolutional networks. In: Proceedings of the IEEE Conference on Computer Vision and Pattern Recognition, pp. 1984–1992 (2015)

Blockchain Applications and Services

BTS-PD: A Blockchain Based Traceability System for P2P Distribution

Xuecong Li[1,3], Qian He[1,2(✉)], Bingcheng Jiang[1], Xing Qin[1,2], and Kuangyu Qin[2]

[1] State and Local Joint Engineering Research Center for Satellite Navigation and Location Service, Guilin University of Electronic Technology, Guilin 541004, China
137933082@qq.com, heqian@guet.edu.cn, jiangbc1990@126.com, 985422187@qq.com
[2] Guangxi Key Laboratory of Cryptography and Information Security, Guilin University of Electronic Technology, Guilin 541004, China
122669@qq.com
[3] CETC Key Laboratory of Aerospace Information Applications, Shijiazhuang 050081, China

Abstract. The application of peer to peer (P2P) technology has brought convenience to people, however, it has caused some social problems such as copyright infringement and the spread of Trojans and viruses. In order to effectively monitor malicious activities and security violations, it is essential to build a data traceability framework, with which each data object in the P2P environment can be tracked and recorded. Blockchain technology provides a promising mechanism for establishing a file distribution traceability system due to the natures, such as openness, decentralization and anti-tampering. In this article, we propose BTS-PD, a blockchain based traceability system for P2P distribution. The related information of P2P seed file is stored in the blockchain to ensure the credibility of the traceability information. InterPlanetary File System (IPFS) is used to store the P2P seed to expand the storage of the fabric blockchain. Based on BTS-PD, it becomes more credible and convenient for tracking security of P2P distribution. Implemented based on the Hyperledger Fabric, the experiment results show that BTS-PD can work well and support normal P2P distribution.

Keywords: Blockchain · Traceability · P2P · Data distribution · IPFS

1 Introduction

With the rapid development of information technology, the network has profoundly affected people's lives and has become one of the most important modes of communication in modern society. The application of P2P technology represented by BT download changes the traditional way of disseminating information resources, realizes the sharing of computing resources and services between users, and makes the way for users to obtain network resources more convenient, which greatly meet the needs of users for file sharing.

However, while P2P technology brings new development opportunities to information dissemination, it also faces severe data security challenges [1, 2]. Anyone can join

© Springer Nature Singapore Pte Ltd. 2020
Z. Zheng et al. (Eds.): BlockSys 2019, CCIS 1156, pp. 607–620, 2020.
https://doi.org/10.1007/978-981-15-2777-7_50

the P2P network to provide content and services to others, while also finding and requesting the resources he needs from the network. On the one hand, since the uploading and downloading of files are performed between users, the traceability of the business and even the search of the file provenance are almost impossible to achieve. On the other hand, as long as one node is infected with a virus in the P2P network, the virus can be spread to neighbor nodes through internal sharing and communication mechanisms, which can result in the theft of confidential information, and even the paralysis of the whole network in a short time. Therefore, an effective technique is needed to trace the source of document distribution and ensure the credibility of distribution traceability information.

With the stable operation and development of Bitcoin network for many years, its underlying technology blockchain has gradually attracted widespread attention from all walks of life. Blockchain is a decentralized, non-tampering, traceable and multi-party maintained distributed database [3, 4]. Therefore, the establishment of a traceability system based on blockchain can provide a new solution to the regulatory problems of P2P file distribution. However, there is a storage bottleneck in the blockchain. IPFS has gained much popularity because its content-addressable and non-tamperable can help expand the storage capacity of blockchain.

In this paper, we design BTS-PD, A Blockchain based Traceability System for P2P Distribution. Through the proposed system, users can be aware of the download source of the P2P file and avoid downloading to the fake seed file. The main contributions of this paper can be summarized as follows:

1. Aiming at the problem caused by the lack of traceability mechanism in the P2P distribution network, the information and distribution paths of the seeds are stored on the blockchain to ensure the credibility of the P2P seed traceability information, and to facilitate the tracking and querying of the traceability information more conveniently.
2. Private IPFS cluster is used to store the original P2P seed file and blockchain information. The smart contract deployed on the blockchain stores such information as seed ID, IP and hash value to solve the storage shortboard problem of Fabric blockchain. Based on these stored data, the traceability system can be implemented, and then realize the protection, verification and recovery of each distributed file in the P2P system.
3. BTS-PD is implemented, and the function and performance are tested in real experiments. Through BTS-PD, users can trace the P2P distribution path information including file, IP of the P2P file contributor, and judge the authenticity of the seed, and obtain the real seed file.

The remainder of the paper is organized as follows. Section 2 discusses the related work. Section 3 presents the proposed BTS-PD and its workflow. In Sect. 4, we describe the system implementation process, and Sect. 5 gives test results. Finally, the conclusions and possible optimization directions are presented in the Sect. 6.

2   Related Work

P2P technology has become a hot research topic since its emergence. In the white paper "Controlling Peer to Peer Bandwidth Consumption" [5], it is mentioned that P2P networks provide a shared infrastructure that is difficult to trace and prevent, and provide cover for criminal activities.

In order to measure behaviors of the peer to determine whether there is a case of user damage, many efforts have been made to deploy trust management mechanisms in P2P networks. Different trust models have been built in [6, 7] to help peers contribute their sources to other entities. Cai [8] et al. introduce a secret sharing based trust protocols for structured P2P trust management [9] and trust decision making [10].

[11] explains the security issues, the risks and vulnerabilities of P2P technology, including risks that relate to data security, spyware, viruses, adware, copyright infringement and unwanted pornography. The authors also present a method in P2P file sharing that could help minimize and counter these problems in P2P file sharing. However, since the proposed tool is a just sharing in two clients, it has not other functions like searching, halting downloads and previewing the content.

Although some improvements have been made, none of these solutions can solve the security problem of P2P from the root. Blockchain technology provides new technical ideas and methods for data sharing and data trace. In [12], the idea of applying blockchain technology to food supply chain was proposed, but it has not been put into practice. [13] proposes a food safety traceability system based on the blockchain and the EPC Information Services, but the test results show that the amount of data is one of the key factors limiting the system performance, and the P2P network model still needs to be optimized. The proposed double-chain structure [14] of the blockchain satisfied the needs of data privacy protection and data sharing with large traffic and fast response. However, this scheme cannot detect data leakage sources, and lacks theoretical support for data block segmentation.

3   System Framework

3.1   Overview

BTS-PD consists of two modules: the P2P based resources distribution platform (PRDP) and consumer traceability platform (CTP). The design of resources distribution platform is based on the P2P based massive scalable remote sensing data distribution system proposed in the previous work of our group [15, 16], which is used to provide users with fast resources distribution services. The consumer traceability platform not only can help the user to identify the authenticity of the required seeds, but also can trace the information of the seeds. The system architecture is shown in Fig. 1.

The functions of each sub module of PRDP are described in detail as follows.

(1) **The shared distribution platform website:** Resources providers upload and add details of resources such as type, keywords, creation time, usage, etc. to the shared distribution platform website. Users can quickly find the required resources through this platform.

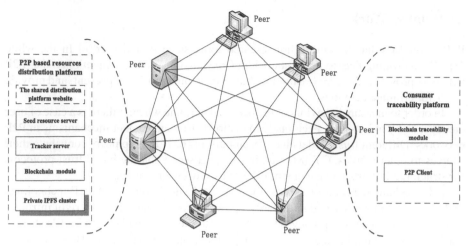

Fig. 1. The architecture of BTS-PD.

(2) **Seed resource server:** This module is responsible for parsing commands, generating seed files of relevant resources, and providing downloadable resources for resource distribution. At the same time, send a message to Tracker to update the seed list. As a permanent seed server, it also automatically stores the relevant information on the blockchain after generating the P2P seed file.

(3) **Tracker server:** The Tracker server is responsible for tracking the status information and resource distribution information of nodes in P2P network. When a new node connects to a Tracker server to request resources, Tracker returns a list of Peers that can provide downloadable resources to the new node based on statistics. That is to say, it can provide traceability information for users i.e. information of multiple contributors when downloading P2P files.

(4) **Private IPFS cluster:** IPFS nodes must be authorized to join the IPFS cluster, which has strong privacy protection features. This privatized storage network has two functions. One is to solve the storage shortboard problem of blockchain. The P2P seed file is stored on the IPFS cluster to implement distributed storage. Only the returned hash value is stored on the blockchain to reduce the storage pressure. The other is that the user can download the real file directly through IPFS when judging that the obtained seed is false.

(5) **Blockchain module:** The main function of the blockchain module is the data interaction including the upload of the initial seed information and the traceability information on blockchain, the request of on-chain information.

The CTP consists of two sub modules.

(1) **Blockchain traceability:** Users connect to the P2P based data distribution platform through this module, which mainly has the following functions: (1) Implementing user management, including registration, login and deletion of user identity, query of user account information and historical operation records, etc. (2) requesting seed

information on blockchain and verifying the authenticity of seeds; (3) querying for traceability information of P2P seed files by seed ID or name.

(2) **P2P Client:** By comparing the SHA256 value of the seed calculated by the SHA256 algorithm with the SHA256 value obtained by querying from the blockchain to confirm that the seed is true, the client directly starts the download of the P2P file.

3.2 Workflow of the Main Information Exchange

The flow of the main information exchange, including uploading seed information to the blockchain, validating seeds, and the interaction traceability information is shown in Fig. 2. The process of uploading the initial information of the seed is as follows:

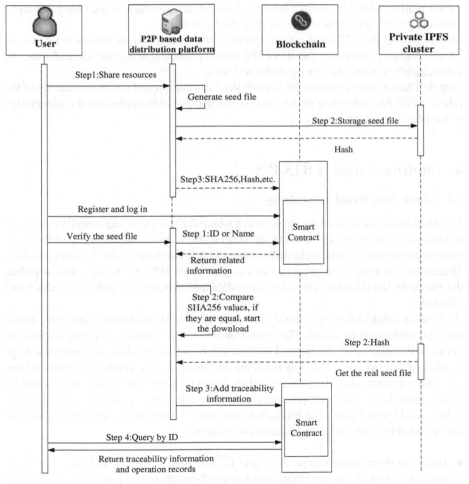

Fig. 2. The flow of BTS-PD.

Step 1: The data owner uploads the data to be shared to the P2P based data distribution platform, and generates the P2P seed file by the seed resource server.

Step 2: The seed file is then stored to IPFS, and IPFS returns a hash value.

Step 3: The SHA256 value, hash value, seed's name, user name and IP address are stored in the blockchain system.

After the user queries and obtains the required seed file through the shared distribution platform website, the authenticity of the seed can be verified through our system. The process is as follows:

Step 1: Query and get the SHA256 value of the seed from the blockchain according to the ID or name.

Step 2: The system compares the SHA256 value of the seed file calculated by SHA256 algorithm with the value obtained in step 1. If the two are equal, the client of the distribution platform directly initiates the download, otherwise, the real seed file is obtained from the private IPFS cluster according to the hash value.

Step 3: During the P2P file download process, the traceability information, i.e., the IP address of the contributor, the ID of the user who downloaded the file and time are automatically uploaded to the blockchain system.

Step 4: The system can return the traceability information and operation records of the relevant P2P files according to the needs of the user, so as to implement the supervision of the file distribution process.

4   Implementation of BTS-PD

4.1   Blockchain Based Traceability

The blockchain is a chained data structure in which the blocks are sequentially connected in chronological order. The amount of data on the block is increasing, and there are storage performance bottlenecks that are not suitable for storing a large number of files. Therefore, our system adopts a model that combines IPFS to manage data together, the major design decision is to select what data and computation to keep on-chain and off-chain.

Consortium blockchain is jointly initiated by several institutions, and some nodes must be authorized to access. The confirmation of the transaction is only carried out between the alliance or the internal staff of the organization, does not involve a large number of external users with low trust, the consensus cost is significantly reduced and it is easier to supervise. Hyperledger Fabric is a typical implementation of consortium blockchains. It takes security, privacy, supervision and other requirements into full consideration. Figure 3 shows our blockchain traceability subsystem architecture based on fabric and IPFS with three organizations as examples.

- There are three organizations A, B and C. The peer 1, peer 2, and peer 3 of these organizations join the same fabric consortium blockchain and join the same channel. Each node maintains a ledger with the same data. The authorized node can quickly access the P2P seed file traceability information.

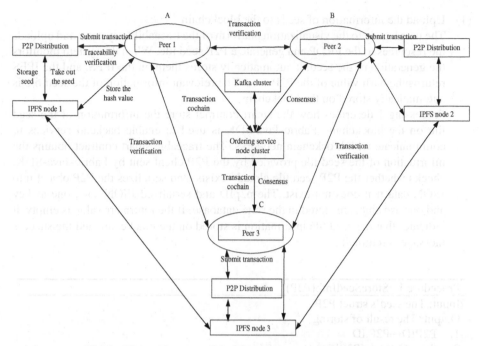

Fig. 3. The architecture of the blockchain traceability subsystem.

- The IPFS storage node 1, node 2, and node 3 form a private distributed storage cluster to expand the storage of the fabric blockchain. The P2P seed file is stored on the distributed IPFS nodes.
- The Kafka-based consensus ordering service node cluster consists of an ordering service node cluster, a Kafka cluster, and a Zookeeper cluster. This will prevent single point failures and increase the throughput of the blockchain system. The function of the ordering service node cluster is to sort the transactions sent by each blockchain node. In the concurrent scenario, the order of transaction of each blockchain node needs to be determined and reaching consensus by orderer. The orderer generates blocks and sends them to the peer. Once transaction validation is passed, the generated blocks are added to the blockchain.

4.2 On-chain Module

Considering that the key information and traceability information of the seed file must be immutable, the data is on-chain and most of the data interaction takes place on the blockchain. We implement some of the business logic on-chain by smart contracts. So the design of the smart contract affects the operation of the whole system. Here we describe it in detail.

The Traceable smart contract can store the P2P seed information and traceability information on the blockchain. The contract also provides methods for querying the traceability information and the historical operation record for users.

(1) Upload the information of seeds to the blockchain

The user logs in to the visualization platform of the traceability system, and uploads the resources to the PRDP and generate a P2P seed file. When the system monitors the generation of the seed, it automatically stores them on the IPFS, and the IPFS returns the hash value of the P2P seed. The relevant information of the seed file is automatically stored on the blockchain.

Processing 1 describes how the smart contract store the information of the seed file on the blockchain. Fabric-Java-SDK is used to enable backend services to communicate with blockchain networks. The traceable smart contract obtains the information of the seed file provided by the P2P client sent by Fabric-Java-SDK, checks whether the P2P seed file already exists, and serializes the P2P object into JSON data if it does not exist. The p2pID and serialized JSON data, one as key and one as value, are stored in the state database. If the return err value is empty, it indicates that the seed file information is stored on the blockchain and the success message is returned.

Procedure 1   StoreSeedInfo(P2P)

Input: The seed's struct P2P
Output: The result of storing
1.   P2PID←P2P.ID
2.   tbs←GetState(P2PID)
3.   if tbs=true
4.   return P2P Seed has exist
5.   else bs←Marshal(P2P)
6.   err←PutState(P2PID, bs)
7.   if err != null
8.   return Error
9.   else return Success

---

(2) Retrieval and Verification of Seed Files

After the user obtains the seed file, log in the proposed BTS-PD to verify the authenticity of the seed. Call lookup method of smart contract to get key information of seed from blockchain according to ID or name. The retrieval processing is shown below.

The P2P client uses the SHA256 algorithm to calculate the SHA256 value of the seed file. At the same time, the SHA256 value of the P2P seed is queried from the IPFS and Fabric based blockchain traceability subsystem and compared with the value calculated by the client. If the SHA256 value is the same, the seed is true, and the P2P download is performed directly. The comparison is different, that is, the seed is false, the real seed is obtained from the IPFS private network cluster, and the P2P distribution network platform client download is started.

Procedure 2   QuerySeedInfo(P2P)
Input: Input: The seed's struct P2P
Output: The result of querying
1.   P2PID←P2P.ID
2.   PBytes←GetState(P2PID)
3.   if PBytes == null
4.   return P2P seed does not exist
5.   else p2p_onchain ← Unmarshal(Pbytes，& P2P)
6.   SHA256← SHA256(P2P)
7.   if p2p_onchain.SHA256 equal SHA256
8.   return the seed is ture
9.   else return the seed is fake

(3) Add traceability information

During the process of downloading a P2P file, the P2P client automatically obtains the IP address of the contributor, the IP address of the downloader, the download time, and records the information on the blockchain. The points of the user who added the traceability information are also automatically increased.

The process of adding traceability information is shown in Processing 3. The value of this p2pID in the state database is queried first, and if so, it is deserialized into P2P. Get the IP address of the contributor, the ID of the user who downloaded the file and the current, and append this information to the traceability information of P2P. P2P is serialized into JSON data and stored in the state database.

Procedure 3 AddTraceInfo(P2P,trace)
Input: The struct of P2P seed and trace
Output: The result of adding traceability information
1.   P2PID←P2P.ID
2.   trace.DownloadID←downloadID
3.   trace.Time←currentTime.String()
4.   trace.IP←ip
5.   P2P.Traces ←add(P2P.Traces,trace)
6.   bs←Marshal(P2P)
7.   err←PutState(P2PID，bs)
8.   if err != null
9.   return Error
10.   else return Success

4.3 Off-chain Module

IPFS is a globally interconnected distributed file system which integrates the advantages of distributed hash table, version control system and self-certification system. It has the features of content-addressable, non-tampering, and decentralization. When a file is stored in an IPFS service node, IPFS calculates a unique encrypted hash based on the file content. Private IPFS clusters are restricted to use within a group or organization. Nodes with the same swarm-key can participate in the network.

No matter what type of data, it can be shared on the IPFS storage network. After successfully uploading the data, the data is encrypted and saved permanently. Fabric blockchain is not suitable for storing large text, images or videos. Combined with IPFS and blockchain technology, we store the seed file in the IPFS network. The fabric only stores the hash value returned by the IPFS and other key information, so the seed file is off-chain, whereas its hash is on-chain. The storage scheme is shown in Fig. 4.

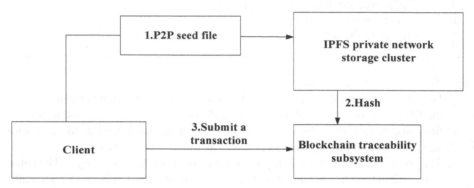

Fig. 4. The storage scheme of IPFS.

5   Experimental Evaluation

The experimental environment consists of four HP Z220 workstations and one laptop with the same configuration. One workstation is equipped with seed server and tracking server, the other three workstations and a notebook are downloaded clients. The P2P download client joins the blockchain traceability subsystem and requests download from the seed resources server to form a P2P distribution network. The specific hardware parameters are shown in Table 1.

Table 1. Hardware parameters.

Configuration	Parameters
Seed resource server, tracker server	CPU: Intel Xeon E3, memory:16G
Download client (HP workstations)	CPU: Intel Xeon E3, memory:16G
Download client (laptop)	CPU: Intel i7 4710MQ, memory:16 G
Switch	H3C S5024P-EI

5.1 File Distribution Performance Comparison

We upload a 10 MB file named test.txt to the P2P based resources distribution platform, and generate a P2P seed named test.txt.torrent. Then the seed is stored in the private network IPFS. The SHA256 value, the Hash value returned by IPFS, and other information of the seed are stored on blockchain together. We copy test.txt.torrent and tamper it as a fake seed. Finally, the genuine and fake seeds are introduced into the BTS-PD for verification.

We measure the distribution time of 10 MB data in three cases:

I: Distribution data through Original P2P distribution system
II: Distribution data through BTS-PD when seed is genuine
III: Distribution data through BTS-PD when seed is fake

Figure 5 show that BTS-PD can correctly verify the authenticity of the seed, and can obtain genuine seeds from the IPFS cluster when encountering fake seeds. In case I, it does not need to verify the authenticity of the seed and obtain the real seed, so the distribution time is slightly faster than BTS-PD (298 ms–346 ms). In case III, When a fake seed is encountered, it needs to obtain a real seed from IPFS, so the distribution time overhead is slightly larger than the first two cases. When using the 1 GB large file for the same distribution experiment, it was found that the data graphs of the three cases were almost identical, indicating that the time required to verify the seed with the SHA256 value and obtain the real seed from the IPFS was negligible during the distribution process. Therefore, adding the blockchain traceability and verification functions to the original P2P distribution network platform has little impact on the download performance.

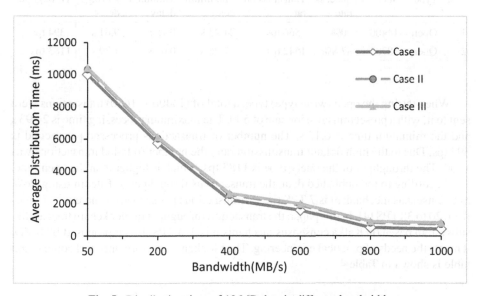

Fig. 5. Distribution time of 10 MB data in different bandwidth.

5.2 Blockchain Traceability Performance Evaluation

The blockchain traceability subsystem consists of three Ordering sorting service nodes, three Peer nodes, four Kafka service nodes, three Zookeeper service nodes and three IPFS nodes. It is deployed in workstations configured with 4-core CPU and 8-G memory by server type serial number. The configuration version used is shown in Table 2.

Table 2. Configuration version.

Configuration	Version
Fabric	Fabric 1.2
Go	go1.9.4 linux/amd64
Docker-compose	1.22.0 build f46880fe
Hyperledger Caliper	Master

The system performance is measured by throughput, delay, and success rate. Among them, throughput is the number of transactions submitted to the ledger per second (tps), delay is the blockchain response time, and success rate is the P2P download success rate. We test the performance of open (write) and query (read) respectively. The results are shown in Table 3.

Table 3. Experimental results.

Test	Type	Success	Success rate	Transmission rate	Maximum delay	Minimum delay	Average delay	Throughput
1	Open	14400	90%	566 tps	24.93 s	0.15 s	9.61 s	394 tps
2	Query	8783	87.8%	1542 tps	7.96 s	0.01 s	1.79 s	1183 tps

When testing the open (write type) type, a total of $(14400 + 1600)$ transactions were sent to it, with a preset transmission rate of 500. The maximum processing time is 24.93 s and the minimum time is 0.15 s. The number of transactions processed per second is 394 tps. Due to the high default transmission rate, the number of failed transactions was 1600. The throughput of the query type is 1183 tps, which is higher than the open type.

According to the published data, the transactions throughput of Bitcoin using PoW as a consensus mechanism is 7 TPS (i.e., 7 transactions per second). Ethereum's ranges from 20 to 30 TPS [4]. In this paper, the transaction throughput of blockchain traceability subsystem based on Kafka consensus mechanism is 394 TPS. In our proposed BTS-PD, it meets the needs of practical engineering. The blockchain performance test comparison table is shown in Table 4.

Table 4. Blockchain performance test.

Type	Consensus mechanism	Transactions throughput
Bitcoin	Pow	7
Ethereum	Pow	20–30
Fabric	Kafka	394 (test results of the proposed solution)

6 Conclusions

In order to realize credible distribution of the P2P system, a blockchain based traceability system for P2P distribution is proposed. BTS-PD consists of resource distribution and consumer traceability, which provides protection, verification and recovery of seeds with its decentralization and data tampering prevention of blockchain. On the basis of not affecting file download performance, smart contract is used to filter false seeds and automatically add traceability information. At the same time, the problem of storage shorts in the blockchain is compensated by IPFS technology. Generally speaking, this system provides some useful inspiration for ensuring the security of data, and can provide more secure and reliable distribution services for users.

Here are also some future works to optimize the traceability system: (1) Enhance the blockchain's gossip protocol to improve the synchronization efficiency of blocks and messages; (2) Improve the throughput performance of blockchains through an optimized reasonable overlay networking protocol.

Acknowledgments. This work is supported in part by the National Natural Science Foundation of China (61661015,61967005), Guangxi Innovation-Driven Development Project (AA17202024), Guangxi Key Laboratory of cryptography and information security Found (GCIS201701), Guangxi Collaborative Innovation Center of Cloud Computing and Big Data Found (YD1901), CETC Key Laboratory of Aerospace Information Applications Found, Young and middle-aged backbone teacher of Guangxi colleges and universities Found and High Level of Innovation Team of Colleges and Universities in Guangxi Outstanding Scholars Program Funding.

References

1. Pouwelse, J., Garbacki, P., Epema, D., Sips, H.: The bittorrent P2P file-sharing system: measurements and analysis. In: Castro, M., van Renesse, R. (eds.) IPTPS 2005. LNCS, vol. 3640, pp. 205–216. Springer, Heidelberg (2005). https://doi.org/10.1007/11558989_19
2. Qureshi, B., Min, G., Kouvatsos, D.: MTrust: a trust management scheme for mobile P2P neworks. In: IEEE/IFIP International Conference on Embedded and Ubiquitous Computing (2011)
3. Srikanta, P., Tripathy, S., Sukumar, N.: Blockchain based security framework for P2P filesharing system. In: 2018 IEEE International Conference on Advanced Networks and Telecommunications System (ANTS), pp. 1–6 (2018)
4. Andoni, M., et al.: Blockchain technology in the energy sector: a systematic review of challenges and opportunities. Renew. Sustain. Energy Rev. **100**, 143–174 (2019)

5. P-Cube Technology (Whitepaper): Controlling Peer to Peer Bandwidth Consumption (2013)
6. Jia, M., Wang, H., Ye, B., et al.: A dynamic grouping based trust model for mobile P2P networks. In: IEEE International Conference on Services Computing, pp. 848–851 (2016)
7. Liu, Y., Zhang, G., He, J., et al.: MP2P high capacity and security resource node selection strategy based on Bayesian game. J. Commun. **37**(1), 110–115 (2016)
8. Biao, C., Zhishu, L., Zhen, L.: Threshold secret sharing based trust security in structured P2P network. In: 2010 Third International Symposium on Intelligent Information Technology and Security Informatics (IITSI). IEEE Computer Society (2010)
9. Cai, B., Li, Z., Fu, D., Cheng, L., Luo, S.: Structured topology for trust in P2P network. In: Second International Workshop on Knowledge Discovery and Data Mining. IEEE Computer Society (2009)
10. Robles, R., Choi, M., Cho, E.: A paradigm solution to P2P security issues. In: International E-Conference on Advanced Science and Technology. IEEE (2009)
11. Biao, C., Liangying, C.: Trust decision making in structured P2P network. In: International Conference on Communication Software and Networks. IEEE Computer Society (2009)
12. Tse, D., Zhang, B., Yang, Y., Cheng, C., Mu, H.: Blockchain application in food supply information security. In: Proceedings of IEEE IEEM, pp. 1357–1361, December 2017
13. Lin, Q., Wang, H., Pei, X., Wang, J.: Food safety traceability system based on blockchain and EPCIS. IEEE Access **7**, 20698–20707 (2019)
14. Wang, Z., Tian, Y., Zhu, J.: Data sharing and tracing scheme based on blockchain. In: 8th International Conference on Logistics, Informatics and Service Sciences (LISS), pp. 1–6, Toronto (2018)
15. Xinlei, Y., Qian, H., Li, C.: P2P based massive scalable remote sensing data distribution with access control. Comput. Sci. **44**(11), 274–278 (2017)
16. Chen, Z., He, Q., Jiang, B., Cao, L., Li, F.: Hypds: enabling a hybrid file transfer protocol and peer to peer content distribution system for remote sensing data. In: 2019 IEEE 25th International Conference on Parallel and Distributed Systems (ICPADS), pp. 1–6, December 2019

Blockchain-Based Credible and Privacy-Preserving QoS-Aware Web Service Recommendation

Xiaoli Li[1], Erxin Du[1], Chuan Chen[1,2(✉)], Zibin Zheng[1,2], Ting Cai[1], and Qiang Yan[3]

[1] School of Data and Computer Science, Sun Yat-sen University, Guangzhou, China
chenchuan@mail.sysu.edu.cn
[2] National Engineering Research Center of Digital Life,
Sun Yat-sen University, Guangzhou, China
[3] WeBank Co. Ltd., Shenzhen, China

Abstract. With a growing number of alternative Web services that provide the same functionality, QoS-aware Web service recommendation is becoming increasingly important. However, collecting users' observed QoS values is a challenging task for a recommender system. First, users don't want to supply their observed QoS values due to privacy. Second, some user-contributed QoS values may be untrustworthy. There have been some centralized works on credible QoS prediction or privacy-preserving QoS Prediction. However, no research has been done to solve both the two problems simultaneously. Also, it's difficult to guarantee the fairness and independence of the central server. In this paper, we propose a Blockchain-based Credible and Privacy-Preserving QoS-Aware Web service Recommendation framework. We first separate the traditional Matrix Factorization model into two disjoint parts: private factors and public factors, and train public factors collaboratively while keeping private factors secret. Then, we use blockchain, which based on the peer-to-peer network, to implement our proposed model. Through blockchain, users who don't trust each other can reach a consensus without a central server. We conduct a series of experiments on a realworld dataset and analyze the proposed scheme in terms of accuracy, privacy, security, and complexity.

Keywords: Blockchain · Credible · Privacy-preserving · QoS

1 Introduction

A Web service is a kind of self-describing programmable application, which is implemented in a standard language or a specific protocol to achieve interoperability in network environments [1]. *Programmableweb.com* reports that there is a total of 20,525 public Web services available on the Web. Beyond that, a lot of private Web services provided by companies or individuals, and can be accessed via the Internet. And, the rapid adoption of cloud computing and mobile computing further accelerates the increase of available Web services

© Springer Nature Singapore Pte Ltd. 2020
Z. Zheng et al. (Eds.): BlockSys 2019, CCIS 1156, pp. 621–635, 2020.
https://doi.org/10.1007/978-981-15-2777-7_51

on the Internet [2]. Among these massive Web services, lots of them provide similar functions. Quality of Service (QoS) is usually employed to describe the nonfunctional characteristics of Web services [3]. The purpose of QoS-aware Web service recommendation is to recommend the services with superior QoS values from a large number of functionally equivalent Web services to service users.

In general, the QoS of Web services has some properties, including price, popularity, response time, throughput, reliability, availability, etc. And several of QoS properties (e.g., reliability, response time, throughput, availability, etc.) are user-dependent and closely related to the unpredictable Internet connections and the heterogeneous user environments, they vary seriously from user to user. For example, because web services operate over the Internet and likely serve different users spanning worldwide, the user-perceived reliability and response-time may differ from user to user due to different user locations, and vary from time to time due to dynamic service workloads and network conditions. In such setting, Web service evaluation at the client side can obtain more accurate QoS values on the demanded Web services.

However, collecting QoS values at client side is a challenging task. First, there is currently no policy to protect users from privacy issues. Malicious recommender systems may abuse the data and infer private information from the data. So users may do not want to supply their observed QoS values. Second, some user-contributed QoS values on services may be untrustworthy. Malicious users may give high QoS values to their services and bad mouthing their competitors' services' QoS values.

Consequently, it is desired to design a credible and privacy-preserving QoS prediction approach. Collaborative Filtering (CF), which can make personalized QoS values prediction based on the users' observed QoS values in the past, is a widely used prediction technique. There have been many works on credible CF QoS prediction or privacy-preserving CF QoS prediction. However, no research has been done to solve both the two problems simultaneously. In addition, the works conducted so far are centralized, in which all the QoS values are stored in a central server. However, it's difficult to guarantee the fairness and independence of the central server, and users may hesitate to provide their QoS values to the server. Designing decentralized QoS prediction methods using a peer-to-peer (P2P) network is an exciting challenge. In such setting, users can control their own QoS data. Using a P2P schema, we can break the control of a central server and prevent it from learning users' data. Also, we can divide the computation load among each peer, and each peer computes its part. In this way, the efficiency of CF algorithms might improve.

The solutions of P2P system can be used with blockchain which uses a P2P network to achieve decentralized data operation and preservation. Blockchain naturally overcomes all kinds of drawbacks of centralized system, and at the same time avoids the problem of man-made evils or unexpected loss of data. Blockchain has unique advantages in Web Service recommendation: (1) Message delivery and broadcasting are performed, allowing each node to connect and exchange messages with each other. (2) The data of each transaction are collectively identified and maintained by some participants of the exchange, which solves the problem of mutual trust among multiple participants. (3) Blockchain is a write-once, read-many system. All users share this system to which they can all write and read, and one party's data cannot be erased or changed by anyone. (4) Incentive mechanism can ensures benefits to the honest users, and the payment is agreed and pledged according to the use of QoS values data and the work of calculation.

In this paper, we propose a Blockchain-based Credible and Privacy-Preserving QoS-Aware Web service Recommendation framework. We first design a Privacy-Preserving Federated Matrix Factorization (PPFMF) model, which separates the traditional Matrix Factorization model into two disjoint parts: private factors and public factors. Private factors are users' latent factors while public factors are services' latent factors. Then, Federated Gradient descent optimization method is used to train the PPFMF model. In each iteration, each user generates his/her local users' gradients and local services' gradients. They train their users' latent factors based on their local users' gradients, and contribute their local services' gradients to generate a global services' gradient matrix. After that, they use the global services' gradient matrix to train their services' latent factors. In order to generate a consensus among the users who do not trust each other, we use blockchain, which based on P2P network, to implement our proposed model. To the best of our knowledge, this is the first work that designs a credible and privacy-preserving QoS prediction framework, particularly using blockchain and smart contract technologies. The detailed contributions of this paper include:

- We propose a PPFMF model to predict Web service QoS. Users maintain their QoS values and train their users' latent factors independently and locally. This implies that no users' personal information will be transmitted to other users.
- We propose a Federated Gradient Descent algorithm to solve the optimization problem. We extend federated learning to cover MF scenarios. The Federated Gradient Descent algorithm aggregates the local services' gradients contributed from users to generate a global services' gradient matrix shared by all users. Then, all users use global services' gradients instead of their local services' gradients to update the services' latent factors.
- We use blockchain, which based on P2P network, to generate credible global services' gradients. In our framework, users are network nodes, and each node can play either one of, or a combination of three roles, being Data Provider, Requester, and Miner. Through blockchain, users who don't trust each other can reach a consensus and generate global services' gradients without a central server. Users who contribute trust local services' gradients and compute useful work will be rewarded.

The rest of this paper is organized as follows. Section 2 presents an overview of our framework. Section 3 introduces the Privacy-Preserving Federated Matrix Factorization model. Section 4 introduces how blockchain generates credible global services' gradients. Section 5 shows how a requester generates recommendation from global services' gradients. Section 6 analyzes and discusses the experimental results. Section 7 introduces some related works. Section 8 concludes the paper and gives some future directions.

2 An Overview of Our Framework

Figure 1 describes the main framework of blockchain-based credible and privacy-preserving QoS-Aware Web service recommendation. As the basic property of public chain, the thing on chain including ledger, transaction, smart contract is transparent. Thus, sensitive data should not be recorded on chain. And, the framework is divided into onchain and offchain sectors.

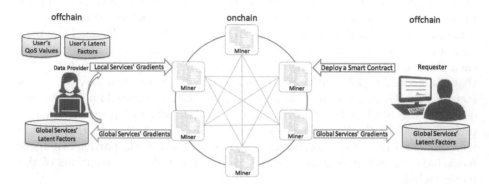

Fig. 1. The main framework of Blockchain-based Credible and Privacy-Preserving QoS-Aware Web Service Recommendation.

Offchain. Users maintain their QoS values and generate their own users' gradients and local services' gradients in each iteration. Then they update their users' latent factors based on their local users' gradients independently and locally and contribute their local services' gradients to the blockchain. This implies that only the gradients of the services are transmitted from users to the blockchain. Thus, the attackers cannot recover original QoS values nor users' personal information. After blockchain generates global services' gradients, users use the global services' gradients instead of their local services' gradients to update global services' latent factors.

Onchain. The chain mainly performs the calculation of global services' gradients and distribution of rewards. The framework consists of three common entities, as follows:

- Requester. A requester sends a query for the recommendation on some specific services. He/She deploys a smart contract and writes requests. Also, He/She should deposit transaction fees in the blockchain transactions to pay back data providers and miners.

- Data Provider. A user who decides to respond and contributes his/her local services' gradients is a data provider. Some of the data providers may be selfish and strategic; only the contributions of the honest data providers should be accepted and rewarded.
- Miner. A user may choose to be a miner to contribute computation work. All the miners work cooperatively to validate and record transactions. In return, the blockchain will pay back miners for their work. Once a transaction is done, the miners can get the transaction fee immediately.

3   Privacy-Preserving Federated Matrix Factorization

We describe the PPFMF model as a two-phase process. Phase 1, Objective Function Construction. The prediction problem is modeled as an optimization problem of an objective function. Phase 2, Federated Gradient Descent. The concept of Federated Learning is combined with Gradient Descent to solve the optimization problem. Federated Learning is proposed by Google recently [4]. In Federated Learning framework, a single user updates the model parameters locally and uploads the parameters to a central parameter server, thus jointly training the centralized model together with other data owners. Recent works of Federated Learning all focus on on-device machine learning. To our best knowledge, we are the first to extend federated learning to cover Matrix Factorization scenarios. The notations of PPFMF are summarized in Table 1.

Table 1. Notations of Privacy-Preserving Federated Matrix Factorization

n	The number of services
P	The number of users
l	The number of factors
R^M	$R^M \in \mathbb{R}^{1 \times n}$, the user-service matrix of user M
r_j^M	An entry in R^M, QoS value of service j observed by user M
I_j^M	Equal to 1 if the value r_j^M is available and equal to 0 otherwise
U^M	$U^M \in \mathbb{R}^{1 \times l}$, the users' latent factor matrix of user M
S^M	$S^M \in \mathbb{R}^{l \times n}$, the local services' latent factor matrix of matrix
S	$S \in \mathbb{R}^{l \times n}$, the global services' latent factor matrix
S_j^M	The j-th column of S^M, representing the factor vector for service j
$\|\bullet\|_F^2$	The Frobenius norm
u_l^M	The l-th factor of user M in the matrix U^M
s_{lj}^M	The l-th factor of service j in the matrix S^M
s_{lj}	The l-th factor of service j in the matrix S
G	$G \in \mathbb{R}^{l \times n}$, the global services' gradient matrix
g_{lj}	The lth gradient of service j in the matrix G
γ	A rarameter for renalizing large values in the matrices U^M and S^M
α	Learning rate, which controls the sreed of gradient descent iteration

Phase 1: Objective Function Construction. In this paper, we construct an objective function for every user. Take one of the user M as an example:

$$\min_{U^M, S^M} \mathcal{L}^M \left(U^M, S^M \right) = \frac{1}{2} \sum_{j=1}^{n} I_j^M \left(r_j^M - U^M S_j{}^M \right)^2 + \frac{\gamma}{2} \| U^M \|_F^2 + \frac{\gamma}{2} \| S^M \|_F^2 \quad (1)$$

Phase 2: Federated Gradient Descent. Every user performs gradient descent to find a local minimum of its objective function. The gradient descent algorithm loops through all available values in the user-service matrix and train the l factors one by one. One gradient step intends to decrease the square of prediction error of only one value. Similarly, we take user M as an example:

Local Training for Users' Latnet Factor Matrix. User M initializes its users' latent factor matrix with small random numbers independently. At the each iteration, user M generates its users' gradients as following:

$$\frac{\partial \mathcal{L}^M}{\partial u_l^M} = \gamma u_l^M - \sum_{j=1}^{n} I_j^M \left(r_j^M - U^M S_j^M \right) s_{lj}^M \quad (2)$$

Then user M iteratively updates the matrices U^M by a magnitude proportional to α in the opposite direction of the gradient.

$$u_l^{M,t+1} = u_l^{M,t} - \alpha \frac{\partial \mathcal{L}^M}{\partial u_l^M} \quad (3)$$

where t means the t-th iteration. During the local training, the users does not need to exchange the data with others. This distributed mechanism naturally prevents the leakages of QoS values and the users' latent factors.

Local Services' Gradients Generation. The requester initialize a shared services' latnet factors matrix with small random numbers. Then, user M generates its local services' gradients at the each iteration as following:

$$\frac{\partial \mathcal{L}^M}{\partial s_{lj}^M} = \gamma s_{lj}^M - I_j^M \left(r_j^M - U^M S_j^M \right) u_l^M \quad (4)$$

Global Training for Services' Latent Factor Matrix. The basic idea of generating global services' gradients is to take the average of all local services' gradients:

$$g_{lj} = \sum_{i=1}^{P} \frac{\partial L^{(i)}}{\partial s_{lj}^{(i)}} \quad (5)$$

Users and requester use global services' gradients instead of their own local services' gradients to update global services' latent factors. The latent factor s_{lj} move iteratively by a small step of the global gradients, where the step size is controlled by a learning rate α.

$$s_{lj}^{t+1} = s_{lj}^t - \alpha g_{lj} \quad (6)$$

4   Blockchain-Based Credible Recommendation

The chain mainly performs the calculation of global services' gradients and distribution of rewards. Blockchain aggregates local services' gradients contributed from users to generate global services' gradients. Through blockchain, users who don't trust each other can reach a consensus and generate global services' gradients without a central server. And the users who contribute trust gradients and computation can get paid. In this section, we first introduce how to generate global services' gradients based on Practical Byzantine Fault Tolerance (PBFT) [5], and then describe the detailed process of Web Service Recommendation based on blockchain.

4.1   PBFT Consensus Process

After a specific period or a specific number of users finish their local services' gradients, blockchain should compute global services' gradients based on these local services' gradients. However, some users may be untruthful. As shown in Fig. 2(a), untrust gradient vector can force the barycenter of all the vectors farther from the "correct area". In additional, malicious gradients may easily prevent the convergence of the federated gradient descent algorithm.

In this paper, we utilize PBFT [5] as consensus mechanism for our scheme. PBFT works on the assumption that less than one-third of the miners are faulty (f), which means that there should have at least $n = 3f + 1$ miners to tolerate f faulty miners. Thus $f = \lfloor b(n-1)/3 \rfloor$. To tolerate f faulty miners, we define a robust choice function to select trust gradients as Krum aggregation rule in [6]. But there is some difference between our function and Krum. First, we are computing the matrix of gradients instead of a single gradient vector. Second, we are choosing a set of trust gradients, not an optimal one. As shown in Fig. 2(b), we introduce our function as follow. Let $\|D_i - D_j\|^2$ respects the squared distances of the local services' gradient matrics of $data\ provider\_i$ and $data\ provider\_j$. For any $i \neq j$, we denote by $i \to j$ the fact that $data\ provider\_j$ belongs to the $n - f - 2$ closest providers to $data\ provider\_i$. Then, we define the score $s(i) = \sum_{i \to j} \|D_i - D_j\|^2$ for each $data\ provider\_i$. The gradient matrix which minimizes the score for all providers is selected as the barycenter. If two or more providers have the minimal score, we choose the one with the smallest identifier. Finally, we select the $n - f - 2$ closest providers to the barycenter as the set of trust providers. Their gradients can be accepted, and then the global gradients are generated by averaging these accepted local gradients.

$$r \times g \leq g \times g \tag{7}$$

For $data\ provider\_i$, if $data\ provider\_j$ belongs to the $n - f - 2$ closest users to $data\ provider\_i$, the miner in charge of $data\ provider\_i$ voted for $data\ provider\_j$. If at least $2f + 1$ miners agree on $data\ provider\_j$, it will be accept as a trustful data provider. Blockchain assigns a miner to each data provider, and the miner is responsible for verifying whether the gradients matrics of other data providers are too far from the gradients matrix of the data provider. We define a robust choise function to tolerate f faulty providers. As shown in Fig. 2, g represents the gradient vector of *data provider_M*, r_1 and r_2 are the two furthest vectors from g.

$$\frac{2\alpha}{\arccos \frac{r_1 \times r_2}{|r_1| \times |r_2|}} = \frac{2f+1}{3f+1} \tag{8}$$

We use g to represent the gradient vector of *data provider_M*. The amount of influence *data provider_M* has over the objective function can be bounded by the sum of the squares of the elements of g. As shown in Fig. 2, g is bounded below by $\|g \times g\|$.

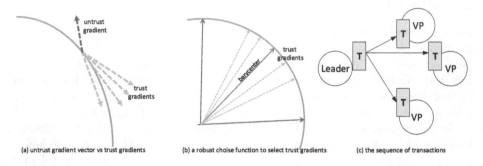

(a) untrust gradient vector vs trust gradients   (b) a robust choise function to select trust gradients   (c) the sequence of transactions

Fig. 2. PBFT consensus process for credible web service recommendation

The PBFT consensus process is carried out by all miners. The requester computes the proposed choice function and sends the calculated trust gradients to blockchain. Figure 2(c) shows the sequence of transactions of PBFT consensus process. The transaction in this scene is a request to verify the validity of the requester's calculated trust gradients. Each miner is a Validating Peer (VP). The first miner to verify the transaction is chosen as leader, then it broadcasts the transaction to other miners for verification and audit. The VP validates the transaction and broadcasts it to other VPs. After a few seconds (defined as batch timeout) or after a set number of pending transactions (defined as batch size), the leader creates a block of the pending transactions, maintaining order by timestamp. Then it broadcasts this candidate block to other VPs to obtain a consensus on the block using PBFT. If $2f + 1$ peers agree, then each VP executes all the transactions and appends the block as the next block on their private ledger. Each block is hashed with the value of the previous block, creating a chain of blocks.

4.2   Key Operations of Blockchain-Based Recommendation

In the proposed blockchain for Web Service Recommendation, we adopt the Boneh–Franklin digital signature scheme for system initialization. After registration on a trusted authority, each user is regarded as a legitimate entity in the blockchain network.

Before introducing the detailed process, we briefly introduce the cryptographic primitives that are utilized in the design of our proposed protocol. To prevent users from cheating by copying gradients from other users, the users need a tool to hide their gradients temporarily, yet with the ability to reveal them later. This task can be easily fulfilled by a cryptographic primitive known as commitments schemes. Pedersen commitment scheme [7] has strong security properties (e.g., information-theoretic hiding). It provides two security properties, namely, hiding and binding. The hiding property implies that it is infeasible for other users to learn the true value of gradients given by the commitment user; Likewise, the binding property implies that it is infeasible for the commitment user to reveal with different gradients that produce the same commitment.

The detailed process of the Web Service Recommendation based on blockchain is depicted in Fig. 3 and can be described as follows:

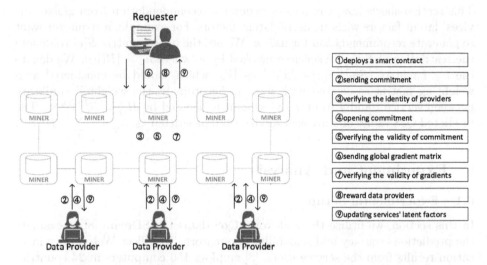

Fig. 3. The key operations of blockchain-based Web Service Recommendation

Step 1: A requester deploys a smart contract (SC), and writes his query for a recommendation on some specific services into this SC. In addition, he deposits transaction fees, initializes global services' latent factor matrix with small random numbers, and set the number of iterations. This SC will be propagated to other nodes, i.e., the other nodes can run the copies of this SC. Step 2: The data providers read the requester's requests from (the copies of) this SC and decide to respond. They generate their local services' gradients and use the Pedersen commitment scheme to hide their gradients. Subsequently, they write their responses (the commitments of their local services' gradients) into (the copies of) this SC. Step 3: The miners of blockchain verify the identities of data providers based on PBFT consensus mechanism as Fig. 2(c). The transaction in this scene is a request to verify the identity of the data provider. Step 4: After a specific period or a specific number of data providers written their local services' gradients, data providers open their commitments. Step 5: Miners verify if these commitments are valid by PBFT Consensus Process. Step 6: The requester computes the proposed choice function and sends the calculated trust gradients to blockchain. Step 7: The miners utilize PBFT to verify the validity of the requester's calculated trust gradients. Step 8: The data providers whose gradients be accepted can receive the reward from the requester. And the operations of blockchain will inevitability create block awards that can be split among the miners as their rewards. Step 9: Every node running the copies of this SC can get the global gradients. Requester and data providers can use the global services' gradients to update the services' latent factors.

5   Recommendation Generation

This section shows how a requester generates recommendation from global services' latent factors without users' latent factors. For example, a requester want to generate recommendation for user u. We use the $n_u \times f$ matrix $S[u]$ to denote the restriction of S to the services invoked by u, where $n_u = |R(u)|$. We denote the $l \times l$ matrix $(S[u]^T S[u] + \lambda I)^{-1}$ as W_u, which should be considered as a weighting matrix associated with user u. Accordingly, the weighted similarity between service i and j from u's viewpoint is denoted by $H_{ij}^u = S_i^T W^u S_j$. The predicted QoS values of u invoked service i can be written as: $r_{ui} = \sum\limits_{j \in R(u)} H_{ij}^u r_{uj}$.

6   Experiment and Analysis

6.1   Experimental Setup

In this section, we utilize the real-world QoS dataset WSDream [8] to evaluate the prediction accuracy and scalability of our work. To collect Web service invocation results from the service users, [8] employs 150 computers in 24 countries from PlanetLab and uses Axis2 to generate client-side Web service invocation codes and test cases automatically. We use the throughput matrix (TPMatrix), which records the historical invocation QoS data from 339 users on 5825 web services. We randomly removed entries from the TPMatrix and employed different prediction approaches to predict the missing QoS values in the matrix. The removed QoS values are used as ground truth to evaluate the prediction accuracy. Matrix density refers to the percentage of unremoved entries in the user-item matrix.

Mean Absolute Error (MAE) and Root Mean Square Error (RMSE) metrics are used to measure the prediction quality of our method in comparison with other collaborative filtering methods. MAE is defined as

$$MAE = \frac{\sum i,j(r_{ij} - \hat{r}_{ij})}{K} \qquad (9)$$

and RMSE is defined as

$$RMSE = \sqrt{\frac{\sum i, j(r_{ij} - \hat{r}_{ij})^2}{K}} \tag{10}$$

where $\hat{r}_{ij}$ is the predicted QoS value, and K is the number of predicted values.

To study the prediction performance, we compare our approach (named as FMF) with other well-known approaches: user-mean (UMEAN), item-mean (IMEAN), user-based prediction algorithm using PCC (UPCC) [9], item-based algorithm using PCC (IPCC) [10], and hybrid CF approach which combines the user-based CF and service-based CF (UIPCC) [11].

6.2 Results and Analysis

Table 2 shows the MAE and RMSE results of different prediction methods on TPMatrix (total 339 users) under different density condition. To study the impact of the number of users, we vary the number of training users as 64, 128, 256 and 339. Figure 4 shows the convergence performances of FMF with different number of users. IPCC, the baseline method for comparison, is a widely studied privacy-preserving CF method, which uses all 339 users' QoS values for recommendation.

Table 2. MAE and RMSE comparison with basic approaches (a smaller MAE or RMSE value means better prediction accuracy).

Methods	MAE						RMSE					
	5%	10%	15%	20%	25%	30%	5%	10%	15%	20%	25%	30%
UMEAN	53.875	53.834	53.815	53.800	53.803	53.799	110.369	110.380	110.381	110.382	110.374	110.392
IMEAN	27.288	26.859	26.715	26.641	26.593	26.571	66.101	64.808	64.386	64.177	64.042	63.963
UPCC	27.218	22.612	20.471	19.261	18.2583	17.462	61.018	54.553	51.014	48.858	47.167	45.873
IPCC	27.018	26.194	25.557	23.972	22.575	21.565	63.001	60.398	57.761	54.8811	52.666	51.021
UIPCC	26.756	22.370	20.219	18.927	17.891	17.079	60.798	54.456	50.704	48.295	46.453	45.059
FMF	**26.502**	**21.213**	**18.609**	**17.319**	**16.705**	**15.542**	**59.870**	**50.434**	**45.831**	**44.020**	**42.901**	**41.028**

Privacy. Our model separates traditional Matrix Factorization into private factors and public factors. Users maintain their QoS values and train their users' latent factors independently and locally. They only send their local services' gradients to Blockchain. The attackers cannot recover original QoS values nor users' latent factors.

Security. The security of our work is based on PBFT, which requires that less than one-third of the miners are faulty. This is possible because we adopt a trusted authority to register all users. And all transactions are recorded on the blockchain and traceability can be used to query transaction information. A user who frequently send untruthful gradients will be removed by the trusted authority.

Accuracy. The experimental results of Table 2 shows that: Under all experimental settings, our method obtains smaller MAE and RMSE values consistently, which indicates better prediction accuracy. As shown in Fig. 4, the accuracy of prediction increases as the total number of users increases. If the user sets are enlarged, the recommendation will be more accurate. Through incentive mechanism, we can motivate more participants to collaborate.

7 Related Work

To the best of our knowledge, this is the first work that designs a P2P based credible and privacy-preserving QoS prediction framework. The work of this paper is mainly related to three aspects: credible CF QoS prediction, privacy-Preserving CF QoS Prediction, and distributed recommendation. Several studies referred to these areas will be introduced in the following.

To resolve the trustworthiness of QoS, [12] and [13] proposed reputation mechanism, in which the QoS values contributed by low reputed users is excluded, and the missing QoS values are predicted using the purified QoS data. They calculate the reputation of each user based on the difference of their contributed QoS values and the weighted average of other users' QoS values and takes the users with low reputation values as untrustworthy users. [14] presented a feedback-based trust model, which collects the feedback of similar neighbors to the prediction results, and then uses the feedback to evaluate the user's trust.

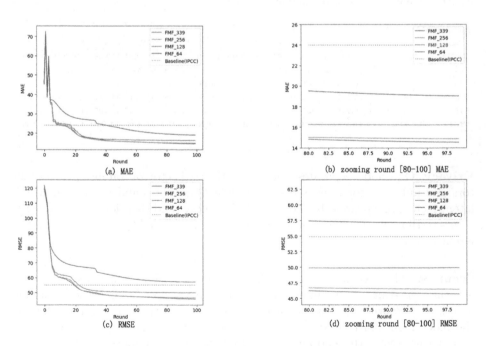

Fig. 4. Impact of the number of training users

Neither trying to calculate users' reputation precisely nor collecting QoS feedback, [15] simply employs the unsupervised clustering algorithm to identify the untrustworthy users based on clustering information.

In order to protect user privacy, [16] presented a randomized perturbation based privacy-preserving QoS prediction framework. In which, the observed QoS values of each user undergo a data obfuscation process. This method trades off between privacy and accuracy. Moreover, [17] questioned the security of randomized perturbation technology. [18] proposed a privacy-preserving QoS prediction framework via Yao's garbled circuit and homomorphic encryption, which can produce the same prediction results as non-private methods without revealing any private information. [19] proposed a privacy-preserving solution via differential privacy, which ensures that the prediction result is insensitive to the removal or addition of any QoS record by adding noise according to Laplace mechanism.

The works above are centralized, it's difficult to guarantee the fairness and independence of the central server. Eliminating the use of a centralized server, some researchers proposed solutions based on the idea that users possess their data over the past decades. [20] proposed a obfuscation based approach to distributed recommendation. A user sends his/her ratings and a query for recommendation on a specific item. Other users decide to respond and send their information to the requester. This approach requires transferring the users' profiles over the network, thus posing privacy issues. Moreover, attackers may act as active users in multiple scenarios. They can easily figure out the differences between similarities computed successively. Based on such differences, it can find out the ratings of the item for which the rating was manipulated. [21] adapts ElGamal Scheme of homomorphic encryption to calculates the Pearson Correlation Similarity between two-parties without revealing the raw customer preferences to each other. This method makes the assumption that all vendors are semi-honest and do not collude. Canny proposes two peer-to-peer (P2P) systems [22] in which, recommendations are generated by applying iterative addition of user rating vectors based on conjugate gradient algorithm so that privacy can be protected by homomorphic encryption technology. Considering peers are untrusted, this paper checks for both the original data (via ZKPs) and the sums computed from it (via a sample majority). However, ZKP and homomorphic encryption incur communicational overhead. Also, this P2P method assumes a write-once, read-many, or WORM storage system (a blackboard). Generally, WORM services are commercial implementations and charged, and it is not clear whether they can be extended to thousands or even hundreds of sites.

8   Conclusion and Future Work

This paper investigated how to design a credible and privacy-preserving QoS Prediction approach. First, we explained the main framework by dividing it into two parts: offchain and onchain. Then, the privacy-preserving federated MF model was introduced in detail and how blockchain generates trust global services' gradients was demonstrated. In addition, we showed how a requester generates recommendation from global services' gradients without users' latent factors. A real-data-based experiment was conducted to evaluate the overall performance of our scheme. Then we analyzed our schemes in terms of accuracy, privacy, security and complexity.

The proposed scheme will solve the problem of user privacy and untruthfulness, which make a significant contribution to the development of Web service. However, there is still much room for improvement. In the future, we will study how to reduce the iteration rounds in order to minimize the communication delay. We will also combine incentive mechanism and reputation mechanism to encourage more people to participate, and improve the Federated Gradient Descent algorithm and choice function to further reduce the computing costs.

Acknowledgments. The work described in this paper was supported by the National Key Research and Development Program (2016YFB1000101), the National Natural Science Foundation of China (11801595, 61722214), the Natural Science Foundation of Guangdong (2018A030310076), the Guangdong Basic and Applied Basic Research Foundation (2019A1515011043) and the CCF-Tencent Open Fund WeBank Special Funding.

References

1. McIlraith, S.A., Son, T.C., Zeng, H.: Semantic web services. IEEE Intell. Syst. **16**(2), 46–53 (2001)
2. Duan, Q., Yan, Y., Vasilakos, A.V.: A survey on service-oriented network virtualization toward convergence of networking and cloud computing. IEEE Trans. Netw. Serv. Manag. **9**(4), 373–392 (2012)
3. Zeng, L., Benatallah, B., Ngu, A.H., Dumas, M., Kalagnanam, J., Chang, H.: QoS-aware middleware for web services composition. IEEE Trans. Softw. Eng. **30**(5), 311–327 (2004)
4. Konecný, J., McMahan, H.B., Ramage, D., Richtárik, P.: Federated optimization: distributed machine learning for on-device intelligence. CoRR **161002527**(5), 1–38 (2016)
5. Castro, M., Liskov, B.: Practical Byzantine fault tolerance and proactive recovery. ACM Trans. Comput. Syst. (TOCS) **20**(4), 398–461 (2018)
6. Blanchard, P., Guerraoui, R., Stainer, J.: Machine learning with adversaries: Byzantine tolerant gradient descent. In: Annual Conference on Neural Information Processing Systems 2017, pp. 119–129 (2017)
7. Pedersen, T.P.: Non-interactive and information-theoretic secure verifiable secret sharing. In: Feigenbaum, J. (ed.) CRYPTO 1991. LNCS, vol. 576, pp. 129–140. Springer, Heidelberg (1992). https://doi.org/10.1007/3-540-46766-1_9
8. Zheng, Z., Zhang, Y., Lyu, M.R.: Distributed QoS evaluation for real-world web services. In: ICWS 2010 Proceedings of the 2010 IEEE International Conference on Web Services, pp. 83–90. IEEE (2010)
9. Breese, J.S., Heckerman, D., Kadie, C.M.: Empirical analysis of predictive algorithms for collaborative filtering. In: 14th Proceedings of Conference on Uncertainty in Artificial Intelligence, pp. 43–52. Morgan Kaufmann (1998)
10. Sarwar, B.M., Karypis, G., Konstan, J.A., et al.: Item-based collaborative filtering recommendation algorithms. In 10th Proceedings of the International Conference on World Wide Web, pp. 285–295. ACM (2001)

11. Zheng, Z., Ma, H., Lyu, M.R., King, I.: QoS-aware web service recommendation by collaborative filtering. IEEE Trans. Serv. Comput. **4**(2), 140–152 (2011)
12. Qiu, W., Zheng, Z., Wang, X., Yang, X., Lyu, M.R.: Reputation-aware QoS value prediction of web services. In: SCC 2013 Proceedings of the 2013 IEEE International Conference on Services Computing, pp. 41–48. IEEE (2013)
13. Xu, J., Zheng, Z., Lyu, M.R.: Web service personalized quality of service prediction via reputation-based matrix factorization. IEEE Trans. Reliab. **65**(1), 28–37 (2016)
14. Chen, L., Feng, Y., Wu, J.: Collaborative QoS prediction via feedback-based trust model. In: Proceedings of the 6th IEEE International Conference on Service-Oriented Computing and Applications (SOCA), pp. 206–213. IEEE (2013)
15. Wu, C., Qiu, W., Zheng, Z., Wang, X., Yang, X.: Qos prediction of web services based on two-phase k-means clustering. In: Proceedings of the 2015 IEEE International Conference on Web Services (ICWS), pp. 161–168. IEEE (2015)
16. Zhu, J., He, P., Zheng, Z., Lyu, M.R.: A privacy-preserving QoS prediction framework for web service recommendation. In: Proceedings of the 2015 IEEE International Conference on Web Services (ICWS), pp. 241–248. IEEE (2015)
17. Kargupta, H., Datta, S., Wang, Q., Sivakumar, K.: Random-data perturbation techniques and privacy-preserving data mining. Knowl. Inf. Syst. **7**(4), 387–414 (2005)
18. Badsha, S., Yi, X., Khalil, I., Liu, D., Nepal, S., Bertino, E.: Privacy preserving location recommendations. In: Bouguettaya, A., et al. (eds.) WISE 2017. LNCS, vol. 10570, pp. 502–516. Springer, Cham (2017). https://doi.org/10.1007/978-3-319-68786-5_40
19. Liu, X., et al.: When differential privacy meets randomized perturbation: a hybrid approach for privacy-preserving recommender system. In: Candan, S., Chen, L., Pedersen, T.B., Chang, L., Hua, W. (eds.) DASFAA 2017. LNCS, vol. 10177, pp. 576–591. Springer, Cham (2017). https://doi.org/10.1007/978-3-319-55753-3_36
20. Polat, H., Du, W.: Privacy-preserving top-n recommendation on horizontally partitioned data. In: The 2005 IEEE/WIC/ACM International Conference on Web Intelligence (WI 2005), pp. 725–731. IEEE (2005)
21. Zhan, J., Hsieh, C.-L., Wang, I.-C., Hsu, T.-S., Liau, C.-J., Wang, D.-W.: Privacy-preserving collaborative recommender systems. IEEE Trans. Syst. Man Cybern. **40**(4), 472–476 (2010)
22. Canny, J.: Collaborative filtering with privacy. In: Proceedings 2002 IEEE Symposium on Security and Privacy, pp. 45–57. IEEE (2002)

A Blockchain-Based Data-Sharing Architecture

Yongkai Fan[1,2(✉)], Jinghan Wang[1], Zhenting Hong[2], Xia Lei[1], Fanglue Xia[1],
Junjie Ma[1], Cong Peng[1], and Xiaofeng Sun[1]

[1] Department of Computer Science and Technology, China University of Petroleum,
Beijing 102200, China
fanyongkai@gmail.com
[2] TUS College of Digit, Guangxi University of Science and Technology, Liuzhou 545006, China

Abstract. In the new global economy, data has become an important resource.
Sharing data can bring their value into full play. Before the process of data sharing,
due to the limitations of personal storage resources, data owners usually upload
data to a public cloud server for storage. However, the method of storing data to
the cloud cannot guarantee that stored data has not be accessed when its owner is
unknown, and such unauthorized access behavior often results in a loss of interest
to the data owner. To solve this problem, in this paper, a blockchain-based data
sharing architecture is proposed. The architecture uses the way to store meta-data
in isolation from raw data to avoid the possibility of user data being stolen and
to ensure information security in the process of data sharing. At the same time,
it describes a blockchain network model for data sharing to ensure that there is
no association between unrelated entities. On the other hand, it also provides a
way for data owners to distribute fine-grained access control permissions based
on specific scenarios.

Keywords: Data sharing · Blockchain · Access control · Hyperledger fabric ·
Data management

1 Introduction

Data has become an important resource in human society. The huge demand for real
data in various industries has led to an explosive growth of information. However, there
are some data security risks when data brings high productivity. To be detailed, small
companies or individual users cannot retain all data at the same time due to the limitations
of data storage resources. In order to reduce the cost of data storage and data protection,
they chose cloud services to store some data. In this case, when the cloud service usage
rights that the user purchased expires or the user replaces the storage service provider.
There is no guarantee that the data stored on the cloud has been completely removed,
so it may bring the risk of privacy leakage to users. In the data storage access process,
the storage service provider's commitment is the only thing to ensure data security and
the user cannot guarantee the confidentiality and integrity of data when they put their
personal data on the cloud. The data owner always has no right to gain full control of
the data [1]. In other words, it seems passive for the data owners to decide to store data

© Springer Nature Singapore Pte Ltd. 2020
Z. Zheng et al. (Eds.): BlockSys 2019, CCIS 1156, pp. 636–647, 2020.
https://doi.org/10.1007/978-981-15-2777-7_52

in a third party. Meanwhile, the current centralized storage architecture will also result in the inability of data stored on the cloud to circulate and cause serious problems such as data silos.

In recent years, with the joint promotion of the government and various fields, blockchain technology has developed rapidly and has gradually gained attention from all walks of life. With the continuous maturity of blockchain technology, academia and industry have begun to explore the innovative application of blockchain in finance [2], health care [3] and even games [4]. In the blockchain system, the non-tampering and non-repudiation are the most prominent property of the blockchain. The data is verified by nodes on the blockchain network and finally written to the blockchain. It cannot be tampered with and any legal node can access the data on the blockchain at any time. Meanwhile, it can trace the historical data to establish its integrity. The blockchain also makes use of symmetric-key algorithms of cryptography to protect the confidentiality of data. As the core of the blockchain technology, the consensus mechanism ensures that the nodes on the blockchain network can reach an effective consensus on the newly added data and synchronize the node information of the whole network. The mentioned properties of the blockchain can compensate for the shortcomings of existing data sharing methods in a large part.

Compared with centralized data storage method, distributed decentralized storage can better protect the confidentiality and integrity of data. By combining with providing fine-grained access control methods to data owners, the benefits of data owners have been further ensured. Blockchain technology can guarantee the data's integrity and safeguard data cannot be tampered with. It also ensure the synchronization and effectiveness of the entire network data in each period. In this paper, a data-sharing architecture based on blockchain technology is proposed. By combining the research of related work, we choose to combine consortium blockchain and distributed storage system to construct an extensible data sharing architecture under the fine-grained access control that could improve access to track data and trace the historical information of data access.

The remainder of this paper is organized as follows. Section 2 reviews the related works and introduces the knowledge of blockchain. Then, Sect. 3 describes the storage method of shared data and the main process of data sharing. The data-sharing scheme implementation is been shown in Sect. 4. Section 5 tests the proposed model and analyzes its feasibility. Finally, Sect. 6 concludes the paper and introduces our future works.

2 Related Work and Background

2.1 Data Sharing Architecture

In previous data sharing related research work, Sundareswaran et al. [5] propose a method of automatic recording of access to data stored in the cloud, which allows owners of data in the cloud to review content and enforce protection measures when threatened. Liang et al. [6] propose a distributed and trusted data source architecture based on blockchain technology to prevent tampering with data source records. Xia et al. [7] propose a system that uses blockchain technology to audit shared data in cloud storage, which effectively reduces the risk of malicious attacks on shared data. Ferdous et al. [8] propose a distributed operation monitoring architecture based on blockchain technology, which deploys logging and data on the blockchain to ensure that malicious users cannot destroy or tamper with logs while reducing the cost of system monitoring. Hammi et al. [9] propose an original distributed system called bubble of trust, which ensures the identification and authentication of devices in the system and ensures the integrity and availability of data in the system. It meets the security requirements on the Internet of Things. Almutairi et al. [10] propose a distributed access control architecture for multi-user virtualized environments based on security management and software engineering principles, with detailed specifications to meet the access control needs of cloud storage users.

The main contribution in this paper is to store metadata and data in isolation while using a combination of access control and smart contracts to ensure the security of shared data, so that data can only be accessed by entities authorized by the data owner. Based on this, we propose a blockchain-based data-sharing architecture, which ensures shared data cannot be leaked and the data access records are traceable, so as to realize to share private data between individuals or organizations.

2.2 Blockchain

The concept of blockchain was from the bitcoin open source project proposed by Japanese scholar Nakamoto in [11]. Even to this day, with the gradual development of blockchain technology, people gradually realize that the value of blockchain for society is far more than bitcoin. The architecture of decentralized distributed provides a good idea for solving a series of data security problems brought by traditional centralized database systems that need to introduce third-party authorities to ensure data security. Blockchain technology is no longer limited to digital currencies. It has emerged in many fields such as finance, health care, the Internet of Things, credit reporting and so on.

The essence of a blockchain is a distributed database. Blockchain technology is a solution to reach an effective consensus among multiple nodes. Each node in the blockchain network achieves consistency in transaction results through a consensus mechanism. In order to solve the data processing anomaly for the Byzantine problem, the Bitcoin blockchain network uses the Proof of Work (PoW) [12] to protect the security of the network and it is designed to achieving protection by increasing the cost of malicious nodes. The same method is also used in the Proof of Stake (POS) consensus mechanism of Ethereum and Delegated Proof of Stake (DPoS) consensus mechanism of EOS. The other method is represented by the Byzantine Fault Tolerant Algorithm (PBFT) [13], which allows an effective consensus to be reached between nodes with a small number of malicious nodes failing. The design of the consensus mechanism as mentioned above detached the blockchain system from the dependence on third-party entities and become an efficient new decentralized system architecture.

The data in the blockchain is sequentially stored in the ledger in the order of generation time. The essence of the ledger is a decentralized distributed database. All data in it is maintained by the full node in the blockchain system. For blockchain, the block is the basic unit of the blockchain. A block consists of a block header and a block body. The data contained in the block header includes the hash value, timestamp, random number and version number of the previous block, and the block body, as the main body of the storage of transaction data, stores the private key, transaction information and digital

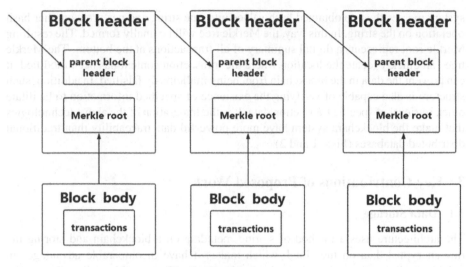

Fig. 1. Blockchain structure

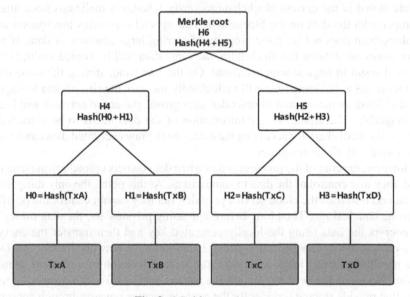

Fig. 2. Merkle tree structure

signature of both parties to the transaction. The blockchain relies on digital summaries to ensure traceability and resistant to modification of data in the system. It maps all the block data generated in a specific time into a fixed-length binary string through hash and stores it in the header of the next block. All the blocks rely on this rule to connect in sequence to form a blockchain. Such a structure allows any changes of data in the blockchain system will change the hash value of the subsequent block. At the same time, it is also necessary to calculate the hash value of each transaction data. Then the system merges the two obtained hash values into one string and performs another hash operation on the string. In this way, the Merkle tree will be finally formed. The resulting Merkle root represents a digital summary of all transactions at the bottom. The Merkle tree can quickly locate the location where the transaction content has been modified, it can prevent the data in the blockchain from being maliciously falsified. In addition, such structure is also capable of verifying the existence of specified information to facilitate quick retrieval of specific transaction data. It is the integration of the above technologies that make the blockchain system have more powerful data traceability than traditional distributed databases (Figs. 1 and 2).

3   Key Contributions of Proposed Work

3.1   Data Storage

The architecture uses a method of storing metadata on a blockchain and storing the raw encrypted data on the cloud, which makes it have incomparable advantages in quickly finding information about data and ensuring data confidentiality. Due to the consensus approach in the blockchain, all nodes on the blockchain network need to store all data stored in the current blockchain to verify whether a malicious node attempts to tamper with the data on the blockchain. This special consensus mechanism makes the blockchain does not have the property of storing large amounts of data. If a data owner stores the data on the blockchain, the same data will be copied multiple times. This will result in huge storage overhead. On the one hand, storing the same data in multiple nodes at the same time will undoubtedly increase the risk of data leakage. On the other hand, as the amount of uploaded data grows, the entire network will become unmanageable. Therefore, the key information of the data needs to be extracted and stored in the blockchain for accessing the data, and the raw encrypted data can be stored in the cloud with richer resources.

However, the crux of the problem is that when data owners upload private data to the cloud, they lose control of the data to some extent. At this point, the only thing that the user can do is to trust the cloud service provider, but they cannot control the possibility of private data leakage. Therefore, before uploading private data, the data owner must first encrypt the data using the locally generated key and then transfer the encrypted data over a secure channel to a designated location on the network for storage. Due to some unreliable factors in cloud storage, the storage location of ciphertext should be random. Nodes on the network provide the storage services for data owners. In return, nodes that provide storage services for the network receive rewards through appropriate reward mechanisms (Fig. 3).

In terms of data encryption, the encryption strength and encryption efficiency of the symmetric encryption algorithm are very high, and it is more suitable for personal devices with relatively weak computing power and relatively small storage space. The data owner encrypts the data using a symmetric key, and then packs the key, the hash value of the data, and the storage location of the data in the network into metadata for uploading to the blockchain network. By isolating the metadata from the raw encrypted data, even if the ciphertext stored by the data owner in the cloud is stolen, the stolen ciphertext will not bring any available information to the malicious attacker. Thus, it

Fig. 3. The node registers on the blockchain network to provide storage services for the blockchain network. When a user submits a data storage service request, the blockchain network randomly assigns a data storage node to provide the service.

can protect the data information from being leaked and guarantee that the interests of the data owner are not violated. The way metadata is stored in isolation from the raw encrypted data is as shown in the following Fig. 4.

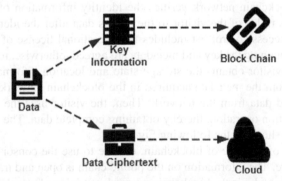

Fig. 4. The system architecture of blockchain-based stores metadata and raw encrypted data in isolation. In this architecture, we store the key information of the data in a blockchain and stores the raw data on the cloud.

3.2 Data Access Method

Based on the storage method as mentioned above that achieves the separation of metadata and raw encrypted data, the way of data access is mainly performed by the following method: At first, the data owner generates a symmetric key locally and uses the key to encrypt the data. Then transfer the ciphertext to the cloud through a secure channel for storage and store the key in a personal account on the blockchain.

The process of accessing data is as follows: The data visitor first sends a data access request to the data owner. If the request is allowed, the data owner issues a proof of identity

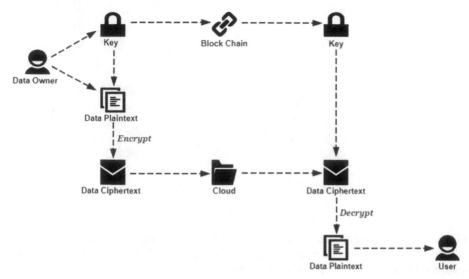

Fig. 5. The main process of data sharing

to the data visitor and assigns him access to the corresponding data on the blockchain, otherwise, the access request is rejected. The data visitor then uses the identity certificate issued by the data owner to apply for obtaining the key and the metadata to the blockchain network. The blockchain network verifies the identity information of the visitor and checks the access rights of the visitor to the access data after the identity verification succeeds. If the access control list includes the operational license of the request, the application for obtaining the key and metadata are agreed, otherwise, reject the request. Finally, the data visitor obtains the storage state and location information of the raw encrypted data from the metadata acquired in the blockchain network and downloads the raw encrypted data from the network. Then, the visitor uses the obtained key to perform a decryption operation, thereby obtaining complete data. The main process of data sharing is as shown in the following Fig. 5.

In the choice of the type of blockchain, choose to use the consortium blockchain in this architecture. The information on the public chain is open and transparent. In the public blockchain, nodes in the blockchain network can join or leave the network at will and are allowed to view the information data in the blockchain network at any time. Full freedom can be potentially harmful to the data stored on the blockchain network, contrary to the system's privacy guarantee requirements for keys in this architecture. Any data only be accessed by a specific entity, and the process of accessing does not need to be verified by all nodes in the blockchain network. The information provided by this part of the data and the historical access information generated during data sharing only need to be shared in a small number of entities. Due to the protection of data owners for their private data and their personal interests, this architecture abandoned the public blockchain and chose to implement it on the consortium blockchain. Different from the public blockchain, nodes in the consortium blockchain cannot join the blockchain network arbitrarily, and nodes added to the blockchain network cannot access all the data on the blockchain at will. The maintenance of the consortium blockchain also only needs to be completed by part of nodes.

4 Data Sharing Scheme Implementation

In this architecture, we use access control mechanisms to effectively tracking data usage records. Among them, the access control mechanism checks whether the identity of the data visitor entity is legal. After that, it judges the operation request based on the grant status of the access resource permission previously set by the data owner. If the data owner does not authorize the visitor, refusing to provide resource access service, otherwise provide the corresponding service. If a data visitor is detected to perform an illegal act, the request will be denied and the original access rights of this visitor will be revoked. According to the user's reasonable setting of access control rights, it provide data owners with a more flexible way to share data. Data owners can give different data visitor different operational privileges. The fine-grained access control method makes the whole data sharing architecture have nice scalability, which is consistent with the increased scalability of the system to the network as the access network node increases. The use of access control mechanisms enables auditing of data sources and usage, reducing the risk of data leakage while sharing data.

4.1 Data Sharing Network Model

The architecture chose to use the Hyperledger Fabric open-source project initiated by the Linux Foundation as a consortium blockchain. Fabric has good scalability while supporting membership in the blockchain. In a consortium blockchain network, the identity of all participants is known and the membership information is true and valid. Prior to joining the blockchain network, members of the blockchain have been authenticated

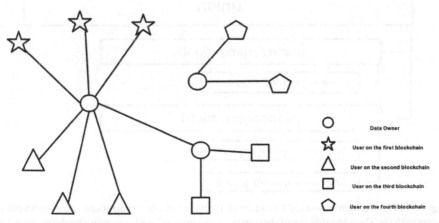

Fig. 6. The data-sharing network model. The circle represents the owner of the data. The remaining points of different shapes represent data visitors in different blockchain. Nodes on different blockchain cannot exchange information.

and licensed to access the network. After the real identity authentication is successful, each data owner can create consortium blockchain on the network for data sharing with specific members, and the same data owner can create multiple consortium blockchain at the same time. Communication between different consortium blockchain held by the same data owner is not possible, and the data on the blockchain and the configuration and operation information of the consortium blockchain cannot be shared. The data between the consortium blockchain is isolated from each other. Entities on the network can share their data as a data owner and act as a data visitor at the same time. If data visitor also wants to share his own data, he needs to create a consortium chain of its own. The data between this newly created blockchain and the one it just visited is also isolated. That is to say, there is only one entity for data sharing on a blockchain, and the entity is also the creator of this consortium blockchain. Other entities on this chain are connected to the consortium blockchain as visitors of the data. The data-sharing network model is as shown in the following Fig. 6.

4.2 Data Sharing

Data owners in the consortium blockchain can further fine-grain the access control rights of the shared data. In a consortium blockchain, data owners can create multiple organizations. The members of each organization are different from each other and they have one manager of the organization. The shared data content in different organizations is not the same, but it allows intersections between data sets. Organization managers can continue to assign permissions to further generate new organizations. The organization deployed in this way has a hierarchical relationship. The upper-level organization can view the authority assignment status of the organization existing under the organization and the underlying organization, and the lower-level organization cannot view the

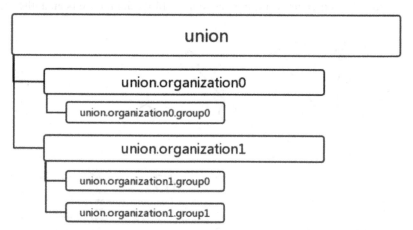

Fig. 7. In a blockchain network, data owners can create multiple organizations and assign administrators to them. The administrator of the organization can continue to create under the organization. A node cannot see the organization's creation of the upper layer and other organizations in the same layer.

authority assignment status of the upper-level organization. The hierarchical access control design approach gives data owners a flexible means of deploying permissions. The data owner partitions the data and groups the visitors according to the specific needs that appear in the actual scenario. The current permission allocation status is allowed to be modified at any time during the entire data sharing process. The permission assignment hierarchy is as shown in the following Fig. 7.

5 Application Analysis

The performance of blockchain has always been one of the most important factors constraining its large-scale application. However, with the continuous deepening and vigorous promotion of blockchain research, the blockchain platform will usher in a bright future [14]. This article chose to use Hyperledger Caliper [15] is a test tool for the experiment.

Hyperledger Caliper is a test tool for evaluating the performance of blockchains. Users can test blockchains by setting a specific set of parameters. The performance metrics currently supported by Caliper include the success rate of transaction delivery, the throughput of transactions, the latency of receiving transactions, and the consumption of network and CPU. These indicators will be returned to the user as test results.

A variety of roles are defined in the schema of this article, such as the owner of the data and the visitors to the data. Visitors to the data will also have different access levels depending on the organization they belong to. Therefore, the performance and required resources of different roles may be different, but the difference is not great. Tables 1 and 2 give the experimental test report. The performance indicators of the blockchain shown in Table 1 will vary with the experimental equipment, while the resource consumption of the nodes shown in Table 2 will not be excessively fluctuated due to different equipment. The experimental test data shows that the architecture proposed in this paper can work correctly in a real network environment.

Table 1. Blockchain performance metrics

Succ	Fail	Send rate	Max latency	Min latency	Avg latency	Throughput
500	0	71.0 tps	1.78 s	0.01 s	0.55 s	70.9 tps
500	0	84.7 tps	6.26 s	0.02 s	2.90 s	72.1 tps
500	0	97.0 tps	10.32 s	0.01 s	4.18 s	73.6 tps
500	0	101.6 tps	11.67 s	0.01 s	4.73 s	71.0 tps

Table 2. Resource consumption of blockchain nodes

Name	Memory	CPU %	Traffic in	Traffic out
peer0.org0.example.com	25.02 mb	6.81%	146 kb	139 kb
peer1.org0.example.com	23.21 mb	6.90%	143 kb	143 kb
peer0.org1.example.com	23.23 mb	6.48%	145 kb	142 kb

6   Conclusion and Future Works

Informatization represents an important productive force in the development of the modern era. With the advent of social informatization, we are doing data producers all the time, and on the other hand, we cannot do without the services that data brings to us. As a new type of technology, blockchain can trace data naturally and guarantee data integrity and irreversibility. The use of this property of blockchain combined with access control technology can effectively ensure the security and reliability of data in the sharing process.

In this paper, we propose a data-sharing architecture based on blockchain. It is used to solve the problem of stealing data information without the permission of the data owner. This architecture isolates metadata from the content of the data. It relies on the combination of blockchain and cloud storage to protect data privacy. Besides, we have designed a method to implement access control on the blockchain to further elaborate on the mechanism of data sharing.

For future works, we plan (1) to use the trusted execution environment to generate membership information in the blockchain to ensure the authenticity of the identity from the source; (2) to combine smart contracts so that data owners can define their data assets in contracts, and provide visitors with grants such as query and modification; (3) to design a consensus algorithm that tolerates errors and does not consume a lot of resources.

Acknowledgment. This work is supported by CERNET Innovation Project (No. GII20180406), Guangxi Higher Education Undergraduate Teaching Reform Project (No. 2017JGZ135), Beijing Higher Education Young Elite Teacher Project (No. YETP0683), and Beijing Higher Education Teacher Project (No. 00001149).

References

1. Henze, M., Hummen, R., Matzutt, R., et al.: Maintaining user control while storing and processing sensor data in the cloud. Int. J. Grid High Perform. Comput. **5**(4), 97–112 (2013)
2. Hofmann, E., Strewe, U.M., Bosia, N.: Discussion—how does the full potential of blockchain technology in supply chain finance look like? In: Hofmann, E., Strewe, U.M., Bosia, N. (eds.) Supply Chain Finance and Blockchain Technology. SF, pp. 77–87. Springer, Cham (2018). https://doi.org/10.1007/978-3-319-62371-9_6
3. Azaria, A., Ekblaw, A., Vieira, T., et al.: MedRec: using blockchain for medical data access and permission management. In: International Conference on Open & Big Data (2016)

4. Cryptokitties [EB/OL]. http://www.cryptokitties.co/

5. Sundareswaran, S., Squicciarini, A., Lin, D.: Ensuring distributed accountability for data sharing in the cloud. IEEE Trans. Dependable Secure Comput. **9**(4), 556–568 (2012)

6. Liang, X., Shetty, S., Tosh, D., et al.: ProvChain: a blockchain-based data provenance architecture in cloud environment with enhanced privacy and availability. In: Proceedings of the 17th IEEE/ACM International Symposium on Cluster, Cloud and Grid Computing, pp. 468–477 (2017)

7. Xia, Q., Sifah, E.B., Asamoah, K.O., et al.: MeDShare: trust-less medical data sharing among cloud service providers via blockchain. IEEE Access **5**, 14757–14767 (2017)

8. Ferdous, M.S., Margheri, A., Paci, F., et al.: Decentralised runtime monitoring for access control systems in cloud federations. In: 2017 IEEE 37th International Conference on Distributed Computing Systems (ICDCS), pp. 2632–2633 (2017)

9. Hammi, M.T., Hammi, B., Bellot, P., et al.: Bubbles of Trust: a decentralized blockchain-based authentication system for IoT. Comput. Secur. **78**, 126–142 (2018)

10. Almutairi, A., Sarfraz, M., Basalamah, S., et al.: A distributed access control architecture for cloud computing. IEEE Softw. **29**(2), 36–44 (2011)

11. Nakamoto, S.: Bitcoin: a peer-to-peer electronic cash system (2008)

12. Gervais, A., Karame, G.O., Wüst, K., et al.: On the security and performance of proof of work blockchains. In: Proceedings of the 2016 ACM SIGSAC Conference on Computer and Communications Security, pp. 3–16 (2016)

13. Castro, M., Liskov, B.: Practical Byzantine fault tolerance. In: OSDI, pp. 173–186 (1999)

14. Rouhani, S., Deters, R.: Performance analysis of Ethereum transactions in private blockchain. In: 2017 8th IEEE International Conference on Software Engineering and Service Science (ICSESS), pp. 70–74 (2017)

15. Hyperledger Caliper [EB/OL]. https://github.com/hyperledger/caliper/

Hyper-FTT: A Food Supply-Chain Trading and Traceability System Based on Hyperledger Fabric

Kui Gao, Yang Liu(✉), Heyang Xu, and Tingting Han

College of Information Science and Engineering, Henan University of Technology,
Zhengzhou 450000, China
liu_yang@haut.edu.cn

Abstract. Building a food traceability system provides an effective way solving the problems arousing in the food safety domain. Blockchain is preferred to construct a commodity traceability system due to its innate immutability and consistency of stored data, maintained through cryptographic means and consensus mechanism. While current blockchain based traceability system just collects and stores verified commodity information in the chain, which is composed of a decentralized ledger architecture. But the information is less accurate or intact which cannot trace the real food source along the food supply-chain. We propose to establish a Hyperledger-based Food Trading and Traceability system called Hyper-FTT, by aggregating all the providers including food warehousing enterprises, food processing enterprises and food retails to reach agreements and conclude business transactions on the chain, then an unbroken food supply-chain can be formed to provide trusted food tracing. Implementation and experiments are conducted to evaluate the performance of the proposed demonstration system.

Keywords: Food traceability · Food trading · Food supply-chain · Blockchain · Hyperledger fabric

1 Introduction

With the improvement of living standards, people pay more and more attention to food safety and quality. However, food safety incidents frequently happen in recent years. For example, Europe explored "horsemeat scandal" in 2013 [1]. In China, reports of "trench oil" happened from time to time [2]. These food safety issues not only endanger human health but also bring food panic. The food supply chain is an integrated functional network structure model, which is including food production, processing, warehousing, transportation, and retail [3]. All suppliers involved in food supply chain are autonomous with their own profit demands, and there is a game relation of them. At the same time, there is also a game relation between suppliers and regulatory authorities in the food supply chain. How to accurate find the source of the food crises and the perpetrators belongs to food traceability, which is a complex and challenging problem [4].

© Springer Nature Singapore Pte Ltd. 2020
Z. Zheng et al. (Eds.): BlockSys 2019, CCIS 1156, pp. 648–661, 2020.
https://doi.org/10.1007/978-981-15-2777-7_53

Traditional technologies, such as database, cloud computing and big data, can achieve information sharing and collaboration in game relation of subjects. However, the technologies will cause many other problems. For example, it is difficult to transport data between multiple centralized data centers. Blockchain technology is a transparent and verifiable system, which is seen as a new way to provide trusted service [5]. Some popular blockchain platform, such as Hyperledger Fabric [6] and Ethereum [7], are widely used in. When a transaction occurs between two participants, the network will automatically execute the invoked smart contract (SC) to complete the transaction [8]. Recently, blockchain technology is frequently adopted to resolve the problem of commodity traceability. For example, Watanabe et al. [9] developed a decentralized rights management system, in which to management the copyrights of videos. Tian et al. [10] proposed an agri-food supply chain traceability system by blockchain and RFID technologies. The proposed system can gather all the information in agri-food circulation and record it in blockchain to guarantee food safety. Toyoda et al. [11] developed a product ownership management system to anti-counterfeits in the supply chain. Caro et al. [12] proposed an agricultural food supply chain traceability management approach and implemented it under two blockchain platforms, i.e. Ethereum and Hyperledger Sawtooth. Lin et al. [4] constructed a food safety traceability system based on blockchain and EPC information services (EPCIS), and proposed two data management architectures with on-chain and off-chain ways to solve the issue of data explosion caused by the application of the blockchain for Internet of Things.

Food traceability is different from other traceability sources, not only in the aspect of food circulation, but also in the changes of food's properties and states. Although many researchers have explored food traceability, using blockchain technology to solve this issue, which is a new field and still exists some following challenges. First, most traceability systems only accentuate the information traceability instead of guarding against the information falsification in food circulation and processing, and so the information authenticity is difficulty to guarantee [13]. Second, existing traceability systems ignore the supply chain manufacturers or just intercept a small supply chain information [11], which are incomplete and difficulty to trace the source. Third, existing systems are lack of transparency and often produce some information islands. The enterprise resource planning (ERP) systems between enterprises in the same supply chain are not interoperable, and the enterprise autonomous ERP system cannot be connected to the traceability system.

In this paper, we propose a hyperledger-based food supply-chain trading and traceability system called Hyper-FTT. The system can aggregate all the food warehousing enterprises, food processing enterprises and food retails to trade on the blockchain. The supply chain is complete, food circulation and processing can be regulated, in which all information is traceable. At the same time, Hyper-FTT provides an interface for the autonomous ERP of each trader to interface with the blockchain and thus can break the information island. There the proposed system can form a "complete chain, complete cycle, and complete coverage" of the food supply chain to achieve accurate and reliable traceability. Finally, we implement Hyper-FTT on the base of Hyperledger Fabric v1.1 and the system performance and throughput are evaluated under different operating modes and system configurations.

The rest of this paper is organized as follows. Section 2 explains the scenario of Hyper-FTT. Section 3 describes the Hyper-FTT system architecture. The block data structure and smart contract are given in Sect. 4. The implementation and experimental analysis are presented in Sect. 5. Finally, we conclude this paper in Sect. 6.

2 Hyper-FTT Application Scenario

The Hyper-FTT application scenario is shown in Fig. 1, in which traders represent all suppliers and manufacturers in the food supply-chain, administration of traders and administration of quality to represent the administrations.

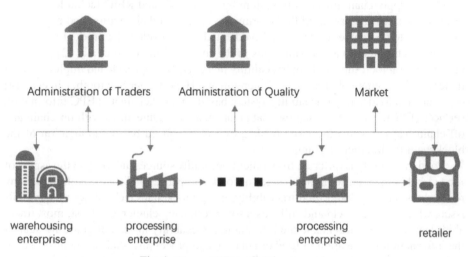

Fig. 1. Hyper-FTT application scenario.

Traders: All suppliers and manufacturers (food warehousing enterprises, food processing enterprises and food retails, etc.) of food supply chain. Traders must submit qualification certificates to administration of traders. Only those who pass the qualification examination can participate in the food supply chain. They are autonomous entities and can make deals on the blockchain.

Administration of Traders: Who is responsible for examining and verifying the qualification certificates submitted by traders and then issuing a certificate ID to the approved trader. The administration of traders also undertakes the verification of the assets in the real world before uploading the information onto the blockchain network. It means that you can transform real-word assets into blockchain assets at this organization and vice versa. The role of this part can be undertaken by the bureau of industry and commerce.

Administration of Quality: This organization examining and verifying quality of all kinds of foods and storing the approved food information on the blockchain ledger. The stored information includes raw information of food, processing and circulations of food information. It can establish the relationship of food information associations in the supply chain. The role of this part of the system can be undertaken by the quality and technology supervision bureau.

Market: This organization collecting food information owned by each food manufacturer and providing a decentralized trading platform. A trader can view all foods information on blockchain ledger and select the food that they want to trade. We create a secondary index of food information in the market, which can help to search and analyze food information.

The processes for a trader to join Hyper-FTT and start a transaction are as follows.

Step 1: The trader submits a qualification certificate to administration of traders. If approved, then it will get a certificate ID; otherwise, it will be rejected.
Step 2: Administration of quality verifies the food information submitted by traders and records it in the blockchain ledger.
Step 3: The admitted traders can view the food information and negotiate the transaction with other traders in the market. And then, a transaction can be concluded.

3 Hyper-FTT System Architecture

The system architecture of Hyper-FTT is illustrated in Fig. 2, which can be divided into two parts: one is the configuration of blockchain network, the other is the client application.

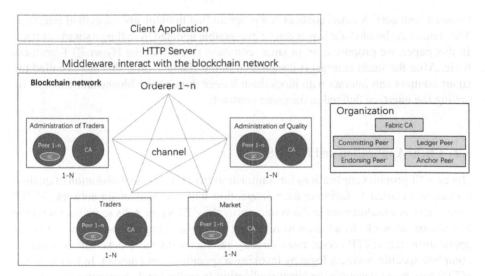

Fig. 2. Hyper-FTT system architecture.

3.1 Blockchain Network

The blockchain network of Hyper-FTT contains following features, namely distributed and chained storage of transaction records, fine-grained access control based on identity authentication, hot-pluggable consensus protocol in Orderer cluster and rich smart contracts to support blockchain network business logic. Besides, the system uses CouchDB database, which supports rich query instructions, to store blockchain ledger data. The functions of each component are described as follows.

Orderer: This component is responsible to receive all the transaction requests in the blockchain network on the specified channel, sort these transaction requests by consensus protocol, then package the verified transaction requests into blocks and finally broadcast them to the blockchain network through gossip communication.

Organization: Hyperledger fabric is managed by all organizations. Administration of traders, administration of quality, traders and market are embedded in the blockchain network as organizations. In the hyperledger fabric, an organization can have a local fabric CA as well as a set of nodes, which have multiple roles, such as committing peer, endorsing peer, ledger peer and anchor peer. Local fabric CA can manage certificates of all nodes in an organization. Only the node that the administrator has authenticated through the fabric CA can install the smart contract. A node can install multiple smart contracts and the operations completed by calling SC will be irreversible stored in the blockchain ledger.

Channel: A channel provides a dedicated bridge for a set of specific organizations. In Hyper-FTT, the channel maintains communication between administration of traders, administration of quality, traders and market.

Smart Contract: A smart contract is a program that implements a specified interface. The state of the blockchain ledger can be irreversible updated by calling a smart contract. In this paper, we propose a set of smart contracts to achieve the Hyper-FTT business logic. After the smart contract is instantiated in the channel, all nodes that installed the smart contract can interact with blockchain ledger through the blockchain network by calling the interface defined in the smart contract.

3.2 Client Application and HTTP Server

Hyper-FTT provides applications for administration of traders, administration of quality, traders and market to facilitate them interaction with the blockchain network. HTTP server acts as a middleware in the system, providing RESTful APIs to interact with the blockchain network. In addition to receiving and processing requests from the client application, the HTTP server must directly interact with the blockchain network to complete specific business logic by invoking a specific smart contract. In this way, the HTTP server can decouple the client application from the blockchain network.

4 Design and Implementation of Hyper-FTT

4.1 Blockchain Ledger Data Structure

As mentioned above, a trader should first submit qualification certificates to administration of traders. Then after passing the qualification examine, the trader can participate in the food supply chain. Administration of traders will issue a certificate ID and a blockchain certificate to the trader, then irreversibly stores the trader information as a key-value pair on the blockchain ledger and provides asset interaction under the blockchain. The data structure for storing trader information is shown in Table 1.

Table 1. The data structure of trader.

Prefix	Trader
Key	Certificate ID

Value	{
	Id: Certificate ID,
	Identity_Information: Trader's location, corporation, etc,
	Business_LicenceNumber: Trader in industry and commerce bureau registration code,
	Asset: Trader's assets on blockchain network
	}

After traders pass the qualification examine and record in the blockchain ledger, they can submit food information that they have to administration of quality. The data structure for storing food information is shown in Table 2. Each machine has a universally unique identifier, denoted by UUID, which should be guaranteed that the UUIDs are unique for all machines in the same space-time and at the same time, UUIDs generated by the same machine at different time are different.

Table 2. The data structure of food.

Prefix	Food
Key	Composite(Owner, Id)

Value	{
	Id: UUID,
	Owner: Certificate ID,
	Food_Name: Food name,
	Date: Food date of manufacture,
	Characters: Food color, smell, size, etc,
	Previous_Key: Key of the previous food,
	Transaction_State: untrading/trading/traded
	}

According to the attribute of the previous key in the data struct of food, we can trace the food previous information. A food's transaction state attributes have three values, which are untrading, trading and traded. When a raw food is stored in the blockchain ledger, the value of Previous_Key is null and the Transaction_State is set as untrading. When the food is trade between traders, the Transaction_State is changed to trading. When a trade is finished, the food Transaction_State is set to traded. Then the new owner anew records the food with Previous_Key and sets the new food Transaction_State as untrading. Figure 3 shows the changing food information of food processing. Figure 4 shows the information changing in food transaction.

When a food transaction occurs, both sides of the transaction need to submit the necessary information to trigger the execution of trading smart contract. The data structure for stored transaction information is shown in Table 3. When a transaction is initiated, the State value is purchasing and when the transaction is finished, the State value becomes purchased.

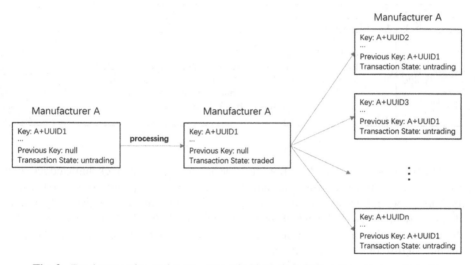

Fig. 3. Food processing and renew record in blockchain ledger at same manufacturer.

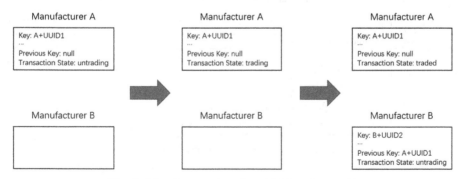

Fig. 4. Manufacturer A trades with Manufacturer B.

Table 3. The data structure of transaction.

Prefix	Transaction
Key	Composite(Seller,Buyer,TxId)

Value	{
	    Seller: Seller.ID,
	    Buyer: Buyer.ID,
	    UnitPrice: Unit price of food,
	    Foods: The key value of the foods to be traded,
	    Transacted_Foods: Successfully transacted food,
	    Asset: Total assets required for this transaction,
	    Transacted_Asset: Actual realized trading assets,
	    State: purchasing/purchased
	}

4.2 Smart Contract Design

In this paper, we design a variety of smart contracts to implement the business logic of Hyper-FTT. According to their functions, they can be divided into three categories.

A. Storage Smart Contract

The storage smart contract can be divided into two categories. One is used to store raw information (such as traders information and raw food information), which can be stored directly after being authenticated. The other is used to store processing food information, which requires that its raw food information should first pass the examination of administration of quality. The process of the later is described in Algorithm 1. First, read raw food information through RFK (line 1 Algorithm 1), if raw food exists in blockchain ledger, then update raw food Transaction_State to traded (line 2–5, Algorithm 1). Base data structure of food, RFK, pname and nCharacters set new foods information (line 6–8, Algorithm 1), then according to processing foods number create new foods and update blockchain ledger (line 9–14, Algorithm 1).

Algorithm 1 Restorage processing food

Inputs:
Key values of raw food (RFK), name of the processing food (pname), characters of the processing foods (nCharacters), number of the processing foods (number).
Outputs:
```
1     rf = GetState(RFK);
2     if rf != null
3         nf = rf;
4         rf.Transaction_State = traded;
5         PutState(RFK,rf);
6         nf.Transaction_State = untrading;
7         nf.Previous_Key = RFK;
8         update nf's Food_Name and Characters use pname and nCharacters;
9         while number != 0
10            uuid = CreateUUID();
11            nf.Id = uuid;
12            PutState(Composite(nf.Owner, uuid), nf);
13            number--;
14        end while
15    endif
```

B. Trading Smart Contract (TSC)

A transaction mainly involves two entities, i.e., a seller and a buyer. In order to make a transaction, the buyer first needs to get all food information from the market, selects the needed food and submits the required quantity and the acceptable price. After the seller receiving the buyer's information, they will negotiate the final quantity. Finally, involved foods will be transported from seller to buyer in the real world: the buyer purchases the involved foods, confirms their information and returns the other foods that not pass qualification examination. The execution of TSC contains two steps. First, both parties initiate a transaction. Second, involved foods are transported from the seller to the buyer in the real world. Then a transaction is completed.

In the first step of TSC buyers and sellers need to submit identity information, such as the keys of the foods to be trade, which can be described in Algorithm 2. Initially, the transaction state of all the traded foods will be set as trading (line 1–5, Algorithm 2), temporarily deduct all costs of the transaction from buyer's assets (line 6–7, Algorithm 2). Finally, base data structure of transaction, seller identity, buyer identity, etc., create transaction information and update blockchain ledger (line 8–12, Algorithm 2).

Algorithm 2 Trading smart contract part 1

Inputs:
Seller.ID (STID), Buyer.ID (BTID), key of the foods to be trade (FoodsKey), unit price of food (UnitPrice), number of transaction foods (FoodsQuantity).
Outputs:

```
1     for FK in FoodsKey
2        fk = GetState(FK);
3        fk.Transaction_State = trading;
4        PutState(FK, fk);
5     endfor
6     buyer = GetState(BTID);
7     buyer.Asset -= UnitPrice*FoodsQuantity;
8     nt = new Transaction;
9     update nt's Seller, Buyer, UnitPrice, Foods and Asset use STID, BTID, UnitPrice,
      FoodsKey, UnitPrice*FoodsQuantity;
10    nt.State = purchasing;
11    PutState(BTID, buyer);
12    PutState(Composite(STID,BTID,TxId), nt);
```

When the involved foods are transported from the seller to the buyer in the real world, it will trigger the second step of the TSC. The process of this step is described in Algorithm 3. In this step, the buyer needs to submit the transaction key and the verified foods keys to TSC. First, read transaction information, seller information and buyer information through the key value of transaction (line 1–3, Algorithm 3). Then the verified foods will change the owner and other foods will return back to the seller with their corresponding assets back to the buyer (line 4–19, Algorithm 3). Finally, update the blockchain ledger (line 20–23, Algorithm 3).

Algorithm 4 Trace part

Inputs:
The food key (TFK)
Outputs:
```
1   tf = GetState(TFY);
2   push(TraceInformation, tf);
3   while tf.Previous_Key != null
4       TFK = tf.Previous_Key;
5       tf = GetState(TFY);
6       push(TraceInformation, tf);
7   endwhile
8   return TraceInformation;
```

C. Traceable Smart Contract

Hyper-FTT supports a verify of traditional query methods, including block number query, certificate ID query, HASH query, etc. In addition, it also provides a function of convenient traceability searching. A transaction can be quickly queried based on the designed transaction structure. Via the Previous_Key in the date structure of food, we can trace the source of food at any point in the food supply chain. The trace process of food source is shown in Algorithm 4.

Algorithm 3 Trading smart contract part 2

Inputs:
Key value of transaction (TS), key of verified foods (VerFoods), quantity of verified foods (VerQuantity).
Outputs:
```
1    ts = GetState(TS);
2    BTID = ts.Buyer;  btid = GetState(BTID);
3    STID = ts.Seller;   stid = GetState(STID);
4    for TF in ts.Foods
5        tf = GetState(TF);
6        if TF in VerFoods
7            tf.Transaction_ID = traded;
8            nf = tf;
9            nf.Owner = BTID;
10           nf.Id = CreateUUID();
11           nf.Transcation_State = untrading;
12           PutState(Composite(nf.Owner, nf.Id), nf);
13           stid.Asset += ts.UnitPrice;
14       else
15           tf.Transaction_State = trading;
16           btid.Asset += ts.UnitPrice;
17       endif
18       PutState(TF, tf);
19   endfor
20   PutState(BTID, btid);
21   PutState(STID, stid);
22   upadate  ts's  Transacted_Foods,  Transacted_Asset  use  VerFoods,  VerQuanti-
         ty*ts.UnitPrice and set the State is purchased;
23   PutState(Ts, ts);
```

---

5 Experimental Configurations and Result Analyses

5.1 System Configuration

System throughput is generally used to evaluate the performance of all kinds of blockchain systems [14–16]. In order to achieve accurate results, all submitted food information used in the experiment is authentic. In the experiment, the system has two traders, each trader contains one peer. The designed smart contract is installed on the peer to complete the business logic in the food supply chain. At the same time, this system uses the CouchDB database to store transaction data. The Orderer peer uses solo consensus protocol. All nodes (peer, order, fabric ca) run as containers. A series of experiments are performed on CentOS 7 with core i3-7100 processors and 4G RAM. The throughput of Hyper-FTT is evaluated by requests per second (RPS), the rate at which requests are completely processed. We use the locust [17], a load-based open source test framework for evaluating system throughput under increasing request arrival rates. We conduct two experiments to test the system transaction read and write.

5.2 Result Analyses

A. Reading Test

The system throughput is related to the real-time performance of the machine, so the system throughput will fluctuate when testing on different times. In this paper, we take the mean value of the results of three independent experiments to smooth the system throughput fluctuation caused by the machine performance. Figure 5 shows the results of the Hyper-FTT reading test. The figure shows the relationship between the throughput of the query operation and the median of response time. In the case of a low request arrival rate, the throughput of the system increases linearly with the increase of request arrival rate. After the request arrival rate reaches 35, as the request arrival rate increases, the throughput of the system grows slowly and the median of response time increases rapidly. When the request rate reaches 90, the throughput of the system decreases with the number of requests increase. This shows that when the request rate reaches a certain level, the performance of the server becomes the bottleneck of system throughput growth.

B. Write Test

The blockchain ledger records the transaction data in the form of block, so the storage of the transaction data is related to the configurations of blocks. In Hyper-FTT blockchain network, each block includes three parameters, which are batch time, max message count and block size. Once the transactions in blockchain network satisfies any of these three conditions, then the blockchain network will produce a new block. The write test can be divided into two parts, the part I is to test the impact of change max message count on system throughput and the part II is change block size. The write test block configurations are shown in Table 4.

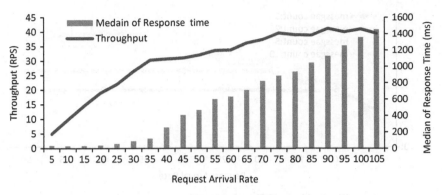

Fig. 5. Hyper-FTT reading test.

Table 4. Hyper-FTT write test block configuration.

Part	Consensus protocol	Batch timeout(s)	Max message count	Block size (KB)
I	Solo	2	1, 2, 5, 10	512
II	Solo	2	30	8, 16, 32

The result of the test part I is shown in Fig. 6. It can be seen that when the block size is constant, the throughput of write operation increases with the increasing of the number of recorded transactions. When the request arrival rate is too small, it cannot meet the max message count or block size of the block configuration when it reaches batch timeout, the throughput of the system is determined by batch time. when the request arrival rate is small, smaller configurations (max message count, block size) make it easier to publish new blocks. While with the increasing of request arrival rate, the throughput of the system is determined by max message count. Also, the throughput of the system increases with the max message count increasing, but when the max message count reaches 5, the throughput of the system reaches a limit of 13 RPS. When the number of max message count is 1, 2, 5, as the request arrival rate increase, a write failure may occur during the writing process. Therefore, we can conclude that, before the optimal max message count is reached, the throughput of the system increases with the increasing of the max message count and then the performance of the Orderer becomes the bottleneck of system throughput growth.

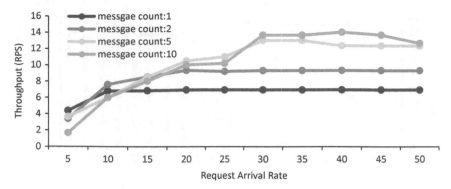

Fig. 6. Hyper-FTT write test with messages variation.

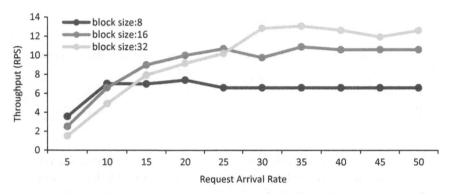

Fig. 7. Hyper-FTT write test with block size variation

Figure 7 shows the results of the throughputs under different block sizes. It can be seen that the system throughput under changing block sizes has the same trend with the changing max message counts. When the block size reaches 16 k, the throughput of the system becoming steady.

6 Conclusion

In this paper, we propose a food trading and traceability system that can provide services for government, enterprises and consumers. The system can support trading among autonomous enterprises to build into the Market which can associate the relationship of food variation throughout the food circulation. So the system can form the "complete chain, complete cycle, and complete coverage" of the food supply chain to obtain accurate and reliable food traceability. Extensive experiments have been conducted to evaluate the system performance. The experimental results show that Orderer service has a great influence on the system throughput under different configurations. In the future work, the index in the market will be optimized to support more efficient query and search for food products in the consumer perspective.

Acknowledgments. This paper is partially supported by the National Natural and Science Foundation of China (61702162), Program for Innovative Research Team (in Science and Technology) in University of Henan Province (17IRTSTHN011), Plan for Scientific Innovation Talent of Henan University of Technology (2018RCJH07), Natural Science Project of the Education Department of Henan Province (No. 19A520021), Plan for Nature Science Fundamental Research of Henan University of Technology (No. 2018QNJH26) and the Research Foundation for Advanced Talents of Henan University of Technology (2017BS016).

References

1. Boyaci, I.H., Temiz, H.T., et al.: A novel method for discrimination of beef and horsemeat using Raman spectroscopy. Food Chem. **148**, 37–41 (2014)
2. Jing, X., Ziyu, L., Beiwei, L.: Research on a food supply chain traceability management system based on RFID. Agric. Mech. Res. **34**(2), 181–184 (2012)
3. Lin, Q., Wang, H., et al.: Food safety traceability system based on blockchain and EPCIS. IEEE Access **7**, 20698–20707 (2019)
4. Creydt, M., Fischer, M.: Blockchain and more - algorithm driven food traceability. Food Control **105**, 45–51 (2019)
5. Yuan, Y., Wang, F.: Blockchain: the state of the art and future trends. Acta Automatica Sinica **42**(4), 481–494 (2016)
6. Cachin, C.: Architecture of the hyperledger blockchain fabric. In: Workshop on Distributed Cryptocurrencies and Consensus Ledgers, vol. 310 (2016)
7. Wood, G.: Ethereum: a secure decentralised generalised transaction ledger. Ethereum Proj. Yellow Pap. **151**, 1–32 (2014)
8. Clack, C., Bakshi, V., Braine, L.: Smart Contract Templates: essential requirements and design options. arXiv preprint arXiv:1612.04496 (2016)
9. Watanabe, H., Fujimura, S., Nakadaira, A.: BRIGHT: a concept for a decentralized rights management system based on blockchain. In: IEEE 5th International Conference on Consumer Electronics, ICCE-Berlin, Berlin, pp. 345–346 (2015)
10. Tian, F.: An agri-food supply chain traceability system for China based on RFID & blockchain technology. In: 13th International Conference on Service Systems and Service, ICSSSM, pp. 1–6 (2016)
11. Toyoda, K., Mathiopoulos, P.T., Sasase, I., Ohtsuki, T.: A novel blockchain-based product ownership management system (POMS) for anti-counterfeits in the post supply chain. IEEE Access **5**, 17465–17477 (2017)
12. Caro, M.P., Ali, M.S., Vecchio, M., Giaffreda, R.: Blockchain-based traceability in agri-food supply chain management: a practical implementation. In: IoT Vertical and Topical Summit on Agriculture - Tuscany, IOT Tuscany, pp. 1–4 (2018)
13. Liu, P., Liu, W., et al.: Study on application of the fast digital signature algorithm in food traceability system. Digit. Content Tech. Appl. **6**(23), 172–178 (2012)
14. Raikwar, M., Mazumdar, S., Ruj, S., Sen Gupta, S., Chattopadhyay, A., Lam, K.: A blockchain framework for insurance processes. In: 2018 9th IFIP International Conference on New Technologies, Mobility and Security, NTMS, Paris, pp. 1–4 (2018)
15. Yang, Z., Yang, K., et al.: Blockchain-based decentralized trust management in vehicular networks. IEEE Internet Things **6**(2), 1495–1505 (2018)
16. Yuan, P., Xiong, X., et al.: Design and implementation on hyperledger-based emission trading system. IEEE Access **7**, 6109–6116 (2018)
17. Locust. https://www.locust.io/. Accessed 27 Aug 2019

BBCPS: A Blockchain Based Open Source Contribution Protection System

Qiubing Zeng, Xunhui Zhang, Tao Wang$^{(\boxtimes)}$, Peichang Shi, Xiang Fu, and Chenhui Feng

College of Computer, National University of Defense Technology,
Changsha 410073, China
{zengqiubing18,zhangxunhui,pcshi,fuxiang13,fengchenhui18}@nudt.edu.cn,
taowang.2005@outlook.com

Abstract. In the current open source ecosystem, developers rely on internal factors, such as ideology, interesting, and other external factors, such as reputation, learning, to participate in the contribution of open source software. However these things are not enough to support their continuous contribution. Meanwhile, for social coding communities, for example Github, collaborative developers, especially peripheral contributors, they do not receive any intellectual property after participating in the contribution. The lack of effective intellectual property protection and reasonable material incentives restrict developers' participation in open source contributions to a certain extent, which therefore hinders the development of open source ecology. In this paper, we combine the Trustie open source community with blockchain technology by recording developers' contributions and corresponding tokens on blockchain. We design and implement a blockchain based open source contribution protection system, and enhance the enthusiasm of contributors to continuously participate through the transformation of property rights to potential material incentives.

Keywords: Blockchain · Open source · Social coding · Intellectual property protection · Material incentives

1 Introduction

With the development of the open source ecosystem, more and more open source projects have emerged, and more and more developers are participating in the open source contribution. The crowd intelligent development mode in the open source world leads to the rapid iteration of software and the quick bug fix process. Many open source software, such as Mysql, Spark, Tensorflow benefit from the crowd contribution and become successful in the end.

However, there are still some problems with the current open source ecosystem. **Firstly, developers lack of intellectual properties.** In the current open source communities, for example Github, the repository creators in the community have all the management rights. For other contributors, especially the peripheral contributors, even though their contributions are recorded in the platform, they cannot gain any corresponding rights in addition to the role modification, which means that the current open source community does not take individual's intellectual property into consideration. **Secondly, developers especially peripheral developers do not continuously contribute to open source projects.** Relevant research [1] shows that there are many kinds of motivations for developers to contribute to open source software, including internal factors such as ideology, interesting, internalized extrinsic factors such as reputation, learning, and external factors such as career and pay. Among these factors, Har et al. [2] thought that getting paid is the main factor that keeps developers engaged in continuous contributions. However, as of 2019, there lacks of material incentive mechanism in Github[1] that promotes the continuous contribution of contributors. By focusing on the turnover of developers in Github communities, Foucault et al. [3] found that for many popular open source projects, although there was always a large number of external contributors participated in the project contribution, the newly added peripheral contributors tend to stop contributing after a period of time. That is to say, the current open source community is difficult to maintain the continuous activity of new developers to a certain extent.

In order to stimulate developers to contribute continuously, enhance the enthusiasm of developers, promote the emergence of wisdom, Github sets up the sponsor mechanism[2]. Through this mechanism, some contributors can involve in the community's activities by continuously sponsored by others. Although this approach allows developers to continuously participate in the open source project on the basis of material incentives, it does not combine the contributions of developers with open source projects, which means that the sponsors can only sponsor a person rather than sponsor their related activities towards an open source project. And at the same time, this mechanism does not consider the intellectual property protection problem of various kinds of contributors.

Based on the above analysis, we consider combining the collaborative development behavior of developers in the open source ecosystem with intellectual property protection. By recording the contribution of developers in a more secure and tamper-proof manner on blockchain, developers' intellectual properties can be well protected. And by creating the user account and recording users' property right proportion according to different open source projects, the potential material incentives can be formed, which will promote the enthusiasm of developers and enhance their contributions.

The contributions of this paper include the following: (1) we propose a blockchain based open source contribution protection system, called *BBCPS*[3]. (2) we realize the converting of developers' contributions to intellectual properties and record their cumulative interests in the form of account balance. (3) we

---

[1] https://github.com.

[2] https://help.github.com/en/articles/about-github-sponsors.

[3] http://git.trustie.net/qiubing/chain_creator_nodejs_trustie_fabric2.git.

realize the non-perceived combination of traditional development behavior and blockchain network interaction.

The rest of this paper is organized as follows: Sect. 2 provides the review of the related work. The architecture of *BBCPS* is proposed in Sect. 3. Section 4 describes the core workflows of *BBCPS*. The discussion is introduced in Sect. 5. Finally in Sect. 6, we present the conclusion and future work.

2   Related Work

2.1   Trustie

Trustie[4] is an open source community, which integrates crowd collaboration, resource sharing, runtime monitoring, and trustworthiness analysis into an unified framework [4]. Trustie is mainly designed for university teachers and students and is based on an idea of grouped practice teaching, focusing on reading and maintaining high quality open source software. The Trustie platform supports open source code reading and evaluation, analysis and sharing of open source resources, and collaborative development of practical projects. Trustie can provide goal planning, milestone setting to control the progress of the project work in order to ensure the realization of the target plan. It also provides projects' progress statistics, analysis, notifications, and other mechanisms to ensure consistency and integrity of the code modified between collaboration teams [5].

There are nearly 1,000 teachers and students from more than 150 universities in China who join the Trustie community, as well as researchers from about 25 research institutes and innovation laboratories, including the Beidou open source lab, the first robotic operating system team in China called Micros, the international top robot racing team Nubot and the Guangzhou Supercomputing Center. In addition, more than 200 free software enthusiasts have contributed their own code, development experience and documents to Trustie projects.

2.2   Hyperledger Fabric

Bitcoin is a digital cryptocurrency, which was introduced in 2009 by Nakamoto [6]. The blockchain is its main core technology. Blockchain can be thought of as a public ledger, which is connected by hashes of individual blocks, each of which stores several transaction records [7]. Its core technologies include: encrypted hash, digital signature and consensus protocol. It has the advantages of security, transparency and high anonymity.

Hyperledger fabric is a secure enterprise-level alliance blockchain that supports node management and authentication. Each user can connect to each other through a certificate. Data can be managed securely. Fabric is an implementation of a distributed ledger platform that leverages familiar and proven technologies to run chaincode with a modular architecture that allows for pluggable implementation of various functions [8]. The fabric distributed ledger protocol runs on

---

[4] https://www.trustie.net/.

peer nodes. The role of peer nodes are divided into two types. one is a validating peer, which is used to reach consensus [9]. The other is a non-validating peer, used to endorse transactions, store blocks, and so on.

2.3 Blockchain in Intellectual Property Protection

In recent years, intellectual property protection issues have received increasing public attention because counterfeit products and trademarks will cost hundreds of billions of dollars a year [10,11]. O'Dair et al. [12] considered about the combination of the music industry and blockchain technology, which can use the blockchain technology to protect the intellectual property of musical works. The Soundchain[5] platform is one of the representatives, which is widely used in Russia to undertake property right protection activities in the music industry.

In the "Industrie 4.0", 3D printing technology is a revolutionary innovation [13]. Researchers think that its manufacturing process is a commodity [14,15] and is vulnerable to copyright issues. Holland et al. [16] combined blockchain technology to commercialize the entire process chains, which effectively prevented intellectual property theft. Once there is any risk on the way, it can be identified and the corresponding solution is provided. The program is currently being developed by a project called SAMPL.

Similar to the music and 3D printing industry, the copyright problem of artwork is also hard to deal with because its rapid spread on the Internet will cause serious negative impact to the creators and the entire industry [17,18]. Zhaofeng et al. [19] proposed a digital copyright management scheme for artworks based on watermark and blockchain, which is highly robust and secure. When the suspicious image data is abused and spread on the network without authorization, the system can be used to track the thief's responsibility.

CKshare is a trusted mold redesign knowledge sharing platform based on private cloud and blockchain technology. It uses the raw data of a private cloud storage mold to record mold data and use a blockchain network to ensure data security and reliability [20]. The platform can be extended to other similar application scenarios.

There are many areas for intellectual property protection using blockchain technology, including electronic media data such as music, images, video, 3D printing, and various product supply chains. However, there is few application focusing on the intellectual property protection of open source contributions.

2.4 Blockchain in Open Innovation

Blockchain technology was originally designed to support cryptocurrency. However it is now increasingly proven to be suitable for many other cases. The definition of open innovation is described as a distributed and reliable solution supported by blockchain technology and derivatives [21].

---

[5] https://vc.ru/25112-soundchain-ico.

Gitcoin is a distributed application based on the Ethereum blockchain. It is designed to reward people for their contributions to open source and wants to build a world where everyone is far from financial troubles to work. It provides opportunities for developers to work for and get paid from open source projects. Thus the corresponding open source project can attract a large number of excellent developers to participate. Rewarders write the reward rule into the smart contract. Anyone who implements a related function can reward a number of Ethercoins or Bitcoins. After a developer publishes the solution to the task, and the rewarder approves the solution, the smart contract can automatically complete the transaction[6].

One drawback of Gitcoin is that the rewarder needs to manually confirm that the solution submitted by the developer meets the requirements, which not only wastes time, but also leads to non-objective judgments. In order to solve this problem, Król et al. [22] proposed ChainSoft, which refined the process flow by using Travis CI tools and Oracles technology [23]. Then the verification process becomes automatic, and the rewarder does not need to verify the code manually. After the verification is completed, the smart contract will complete the remaining transactions. However, this method requires the rewarder to write a number of test cases in advance, which is difficult to implement.

de la Rosa et al. [24] aims at providing Small and Medium Enterprises (SMEs) with the right open innovation intellectual property protection. A Networked Innovation Room (NIR) was developed using blockchain and smart contract technology. This will reduce the concerns of SMEs about intellectual property.

Blockchain has a large number of applications in open source innovation. We can learn and reference excellent development techniques and ideas, and apply them to open source contribution protection.

3   The Architecture of *BBCPS*

In order to better protect the contribution of collaborative developers in the open source ecosystem and increase their enthusiasm of participating, we propose *BBCPS*. As shown in Fig. 1, it consists of three parts: Client, Trustie, and Fabric Network. Next, we will describe each part in detail.

3.1   Chain Tool

There are a large number of open source projects in the open source world. Developers can participate in the open source projects in a variety of ways, such as: issues, pull request, push, and comment. However the way developers want to modify the code directly can only be done by push or pull request. This involves two identities for developers: core developers and peripheral developers. The core developer can directly push the latest code that has been modified to the repository, and can review and determine whether to merge pull requests,

---

[6] https://gitcoin.co.

which are sent by peripheral developers. Peripheral developers can only modify the code by sending a pull request, after it is accepted by the core developers and merged into the repository, the code changes will take effect.

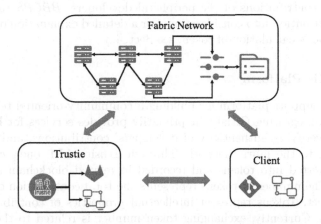

Fig. 1. The architecture of *BBCPS*

In this chapter, we use Chain Tool, also known as Client, to record core information of the push and pull request operations in the block, permanently store all data, and ensure data's authenticity by characteristics of the blockchain. In addition, in order to better stimulate developers to continuously contribute to open source projects, *BBCPS* has designed the token mechanism. Developers can get token rewards for any changes made to a project source code, for example adding a line of code to reward a token. The token value is stored in the world state of the Fabric Network, and modification to state of the world is permanently recorded in block by the blockchain. To this end, the system has designed different token calculation processing mechanisms for core and peripheral developers.

Core Developer. Core developers are the main contributors to open source projects. In a traditional distributed collaboration environment, core developer can directly push code changes to remote repository after editing locally, and other members can synchronize latest code version through the pull operation. The workflow for core developers in *BBCPS* is different from traditional process because it needs to record key information of code push and update related token value in the blockchain. For a detailed explanation of the core developer's calculation of token, see Sect. 4.2.

Peripheral Developer. There are a large number of peripheral developers in the open source world. They participate in contribution of the open source projects through issues, comments, and pull requests. Although peripheral developers are different from core developers and do not have actual administrative rights to a project, they often provide very innovative ideas and solve difficult problems in the open source projects. It is necessary to record, preserve and reward contributions of the peripheral developers. *BBCPS* takes the pull request contribution into consideration. For a detailed explanation of the peripheral developer's calculation of token, see Sect. 4.3.

3.2   Trustie Platform

Trustie is a support platform for building a community-oriented teaching practice [4]. By integrating Gitlab[7], it primarily provides services for hosting code repository, verifying authenticity of developers' contributions, and distributing transactions to the fabric network. Through Trusite API, one's contributions can be converted into tokens and recorded in related blockchain account permanently. The number of tokens represents the total contribution of developers to the project. Tokens represent intellectual properties of contributors to target projects. Currently, exchanging token number is related to the number of modified code lines while committing.

3.3   Fabric Network

BBCPS uses the Hyperledger Fabric[8] to build a blockchain network. Fabric supports pluggable consensus mechanisms and membership service components. The well-known consensus mechanism are kafka and raft, which have much higher tps than Bitcoin and Ethereum. fabric supports multi-channel, high performance and scalability.

Figure 2 shows the architectural diagram of the Fabric blockchain, divided into three parts. The left side A_1 stands for client application, which is used to interact with the fabric network. Fabric officially supports and provides a large number of SDKs for calling components in the network. The middle part is the core of Fabric network, which consists of channels and certification authorities. Among them, CA_1 and CA_2 are responsible for providing authentication for all members of the entire network. $Channel_1, Channel_2, \cdots, Channel_n$ can be regarded as different chains, which can be created infinitely for each project in the actual development process. The channel internally contains CC and O_1. CC refers to the alliance, and each time a channel is created, a new alliance is created. O_1 is a orderer node, responsible for reaching consensus in the network and acting as a mining block. The right module refers to the component relationship diagram inside $channel_2$. R_1 and R_2 represent two different organizations, and the open source community Trustie can act as one of the organizations, and R_1 and R_2 together form the alliance CC_2. P_1 and P_2 are nodes in two organizations, which can be used to install chain codes, transaction endorsements, storage

---

[7] https://about.gitlab.com/.

[8] https://www.hyperledger.org/projects/fabric.

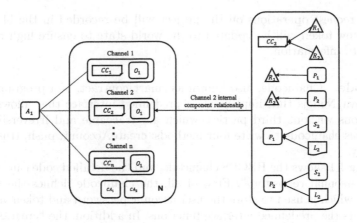

Fig. 2. The architecture of *BBCPS*'s blockchain network

books, etc., including S_2 and L_2 components. S_2 refers to the smart contract, which supports account creation, Token query, Chain push, Chain trustiePush, etc. Each smart contract is instantiated in each channel. L_2 refers to the ledger information, and two nodes P_1 and P_2 store ledger information for each channel, including the block and world state data of the respective projects.

Listing 1.1. *BBCPS* Chaincode

```
package main
var trustieLogger = shim.NewLogger("trustieContract")
type TrustieChaincode struct {}
type Account struct {
Password string
Token     int
}
func (t *TrustieChaincode) Init(stub shim.
   ChaincodeStubInterface) pb.Response {}
func (t *TrustieChaincode) Invoke(stub shim.
   ChaincodeStubInterface) pb.Response {}
func (t *TrustieChaincode) createAccount(stub shim.
   ChaincodeStubInterface, args [] string) pb.Response {}
func (t *TrustieChaincode) push(stub shim.
   ChaincodeStubInterface, args [] string) pb.Response {}
func (t *TrustieChaincode) trustiePush(stub shim.
   ChaincodeStubInterface, args [] string) pb.Response {}
func (t *TrustieChaincode) query(stub shim.
   ChaincodeStubInterface, args [] string) pb.Response {}
func main() {}
```

When a developer creates a new git project, the platform can generate a channel for it, and the channel corresponds to the built project. The developer's push and pull request operations on the project will be recorded in the blockchain, and the new token will be updated to the world state to ensure high reliability of the data information.

Chaincode.   Chaincode, also known as smart contract, is a program written in Go/Java/Nodejs that implements a predefined interface that allows trusted transactions without third parties, which are traceable and irreversible. This article uses chaincode to write four methods: createAccount, push, trustiePush, and query.

Listing 1.1 shows the BBCPS chaincode, and the detailed code can be viewed on the personnal repository[9]. First of all, the chaincode defines the structure Account, which is used to store the user account password and token value, and implements the predefined interface functions. In addition, the "createAccount" function is used to create an account, and the"query" function is used to query the token value owned by the user. The "push" function is used to record the push data of core developer into the blockchain and update the user's token value in the world state based on the contribution size. The "trustiePush" function is for peripheral developers, it can also record pull request data and update the user's token value.

4   The Workflows of *BBCPS*

There are mainly three workflows in *BBCPS*, namely project creation workflow, code push workflow and pull request workflow.

4.1   Project Creation Workflow

Based on the characteristics of Trustie and Hyperledger Fabric, each time we use the chain tool to create a project, we will create the corresponding repository on Trustie, and generate the related channel in the Fabric Network.

Figure 3 shows the project creation workflow of *BBCPS*. The developer uses the Chain Tool to create the project. Firstly, the user calls the "Chain CreateProject" function by entering the project name to send a http post request to Trustie. Secondly, Trustie gets the request through the Restful API and judges the project name. If it exists, Trustie creates an empty repository for the project, otherwise the project creation fails. Thirdly, Trustie returns the Res. Fourthly, when getting the Res, Chain Tool estimates Res.state. If it indicates success, Chain Tool clones the empty repository automatically, otherwise Chain Tool stops rest operation. Fifthly, Chain Tool executes the "CreateChannel" function using curl command, which can send a request to the Fabric Network for creating a new channel. Finally, the "CreateChannel" function modifies the channel configuration file, instantiates the existing chaincode on the new channel, add organizations to the new channel and returns success, which means that the repository and its related channel are created successfully.

---

[9] http://git.trustie.net/qiubing/bbcpschaincode.git.

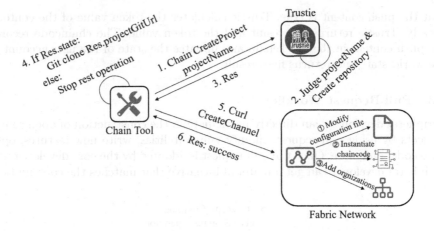

Fig. 3. Project creation workflow of *BBCPS*

4.2 Code Push Workflow

Push is one of the core functions of the platform. It is the basis for the core developers in the open source project to update the local code to the repository in real time, and also records the updated content and corresponding contribution value in the blockchain.

Figure 4 shows the code push workflow of *BBCPS*. The developer uses the Chain Tool to push the latest content. Firstly, the user calls the "Chain Push" function to upload the latest commit information from the local repo to Trustie. Secondly, Trustie updates the repository information and returns result. Thirdly, Chain Tool executes the "Push" function using curl command, which can send a request to the Fabric Network for saving push data. Fourthly, the Fabric Network calls the chaincode to send a request to the Trustie to determine whether the push content actually exists, rather than artificial falsification. Fifthly, after verifying

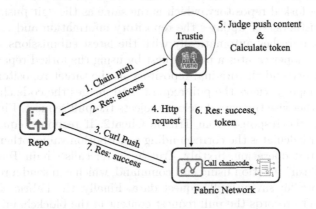

Fig. 4. Code push workflow of *BBCPS*

that the push content is true, Trustie calculates the token value of the content. Finally, Trustie returns the result and the token value. The chaincode records the push content in the blockchain and updates the state of the user account in the world state and returns final result.

4.3 Pull Request Workflow

Peripheral developers can directly participate in the construction of open source projects by using pull request, modify vulnerabilities, write new features, optimize code, and more. Once the pull request is adopted by the core developer, the peripheral developer can get a material incentive that matches the contribution.

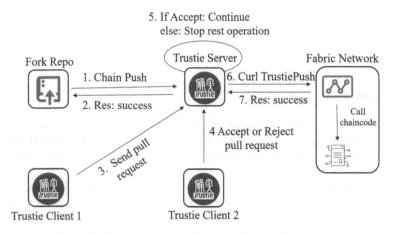

Fig. 5. Pull request workflow of *BBCPS*

Figure 5 shows the pull request workflow of *BBCPS*. The developer uses the Chain Tool and Trustie webpage to send pull request. Firstly, the peripheral developer calls the "Chain Push" function to upload the latest commit information to the forked repository, which is the same as the "git push" command. Secondly, Trustie Server updates the repository information and returns result. The webpage refreshes automatically with the latest submissions. Thirdly, the peripheral developer creates a pull request by using the forked repository as the source repository and the original repository as the target repository. Fourthly, the core developer reviews the pull request, and merges the code changes if it is acceptable, otherwise the core developer rejects the pull request. Fifthly, Trustie Server judges the response from Trustie Client2. If response equals 'Accept', Trustie Server calculates the corresponding contribution value, otherwise Trustie Server stops rest operation. Sixthly, Trustie Server calls Chain Tool to execute the "TrustiePush" function using curl command, which can send a request to the Fabric Network for saving pull request data. Finally, the Fabric Network calls the chaincode to records the pull request content in the blockchain, updates the value of the user account in the world state and returns the process result.

5 Discussion

To theoretically analyze the effectiveness of the Fabric Network, we obtain Trustie's latest pull request and commit data, about 7 times per second. We also use GHTorrent's mysql dump on September 1, 2018 to count the same data from July 25, 2018 to August 25, 2018. The results show that August 14, 2018, the largest amount of data, about 314 times per second. In addition, Fabric's official data indicates that its TPS can reach 3,500 [25]. So, we believe that BBCPS can support the real open source community scenario.

Our work is based on the open source ecosystem. Although we can't ensure that developers commit indiscriminately, if the developer commits maliciously, it will actually hinder the development of the project. Under the open source ecological mechanism, it will lead to a large loss of core and peripheral developers, which will eventually lead to project failure. We can design a visual monitoring mechanism to enhance and improve the supervision of the developer's contribution.

6 Conclusion and Future Work

In this paper, we present a distributed, secure, and trusted platform called *BBCPS* for permanently recording the contributions of developers on blockchain and assigning corresponding potential material incentives. *BBCPS* consists of three parts, Client, Trustie and Fabric Network. By integrating the git tool and fabric SDK operations, the Client can execute the git command without perceiving the fabric network process. Meanwhile, the Trustie integrates the client when merging codes through pull request. For developers, the pull request operation habit is the same as Github. The Fabric Network, which is used to store developers' contributions and property right proportion can protect the intellectual property of open source contributors and motivate developers to contribute continuously. In the future, the work can be extended to address the following issues:

(1) Optimize the material incentive mechanism. Now *BBCPS* only considers the repository changing behaviors, including the "push" and "pull request" operations. It does not take other software process products into consideration, such as issues, comments, code reviews and so on. In addition, the evaluation of code change contributions is too simple, which is judged only by the increase and decrease of the code.
(2) Replace the appropriate consensus mechanism. Currently, the consensus mechanisms "raft" and "kafka" supported by Hyperleger Fabric are non-BPFT. Once there are evil nodes in the network, the system will be paralyzed. In this regard, we will find or design a consensus mechanism that is suitable for the open source ecosystem in the future.

Acknowledgments. The research is supported by the National Natural Science Foundation of China (Grant No. 61772030) and the GF Innovative Research Program.

References

1. von Krogh, G., Haefliger, S., Spaeth, S., Wallin, M.W.: Carrots and rainbows: motivation and social practice in open source software development. MIS Q. **36**(2), 649–676 (2012)
2. Hars, A., Ou, S.: Working for free? Motivations for participating in open-source projects. Int. J. Electron. Commer. **6**(3), 25–39 (2002)
3. Foucault, M., Palyart, M., Blanc, X., Murphy, G.C., Falleri, J.-R.: Impact of developer turnover on quality in open-source software. In: Proceedings of the 2015 10th Joint Meeting on Foundations of Software Engineering, pp. 829–841. ACM (2015)
4. Wang, H., Yin, G., Li, X., Li, X.: TRUSTIE: a software development platform for crowdsourcing. In: Li, W., Huhns, M.N., Tsai, W.-T., Wu, W. (eds.) Crowdsourcing. PI, pp. 165–190. Springer, Heidelberg (2015). https://doi.org/10.1007/978-3-662-47011-4_10
5. Wang, H.: TRUSTIE: towards software production based on crowd wisdom. In: Proceedings of the 20th International Systems and Software Product Line Conference, pp. 22–23. ACM (2016)
6. Crosby, M., Pattanayak, P., Verma, S., Kalyanaraman, V., et al.: Blockchain technology: beyond bitcoin. Appl. Innov. **2**(6–10), 71 (2016)
7. Zheng, Z., Xie, S., Dai, H., Chen, X., Wang, H.: An overview of blockchain technology: architecture, consensus, and future trends. In: 2017 IEEE International Congress on Big Data (BigData Congress), pp. 557–564. IEEE (2017)
8. Cachin, C.: Architecture of the hyperledger blockchain fabric. In: Workshop on Distributed Cryptocurrencies and Consensus Ledgers, vol. 310, p. 4 (2016)
9. Thakkar, P., Nathan, S., Viswanathan, B.: Performance benchmarking and optimizing hyperledger fabric blockchain platform. In: 2018 IEEE 26th International Symposium on Modeling, Analysis, and Simulation of Computer and Telecommunication Systems (MASCOTS), pp. 264–276. IEEE (2018)
10. Simpson, T.W., Williams, C.B., Hripko, M.: Preparing industry for additive manufacturing and its applications: summary & recommendations from a national science foundation workshop. Addit. Manuf. **13**, 166–178 (2017)
11. Chow, D.C.K.: International Business Transactions: Problems, Cases, and Materials. Wolters Kluwer Law & Business, Alphen aan den Rijn (2015)
12. O'Dair, M., et al.: Music on the blockchain: blockchain for creative industries research cluster. Middlesex University Report 1, pp. 4–24 (2016)
13. Holland, M., Stjepandić, J., Nigischer, C.: Intellectual property protection of 3D print supply chain with blockchain technology. In: 2018 IEEE International Conference on Engineering, Technology and Innovation (ICE/ITMC), pp. 1–8. IEEE (2018)
14. Yang, S., Tang, Y., Zhao, Y.F.: A new part consolidation method to embrace the design freedom of additive manufacturing. J. Manuf. Process. **20**, 444–449 (2015)
15. Kim, D.B., Witherell, P., Lipman, R., Feng, S.C.: Streamlining the additive manufacturing digital spectrum: a systems approach. Additive manufacturing **5**, 20–30 (2015)
16. Holland, M., Nigischer, C., Stjepandić, J., Chen, C.H.: Copyright protection in additive manufacturing with blockchain approach. Transdiscipl. Eng.: Parad. Shift **5**, 914–921 (2017)
17. Zeng, J., Zuo, C., Zhang, F., Li, C., Zheng, L.: A solution to digital image copyright registration based on consortium blockchain. In: Wang, Y., Jiang, Z., Peng, Y. (eds.) IGTA 2018. CCIS, vol. 875, pp. 228–237. Springer, Singapore (2018). https://doi.org/10.1007/978-981-13-1702-6_23

18. Jnoub, N., Klas, W.: Detection of tampered images using blockchain technology (2019)
19. Zhaofeng, M., Weihua, H., Hongmin, G.: A new blockchain-based trusted drm scheme for built-in content protection. EURASIP J. Image Video Process. **2018**(1), 91 (2018)
20. Li, Z., Liu, X., Wang, W.M., Vatankhah Barenji, A., Huang, G.Q.: CKshare: secured cloud-based knowledge-sharing blockchain for injection mold redesign. Enterp. Inf. Syst. **13**(1), 1–33 (2019)
21. Rosa, J., et al.: A survey of blockchain technologies for open innovation, November 2017
22. Król, M., Reñé, S., Ascigil, O., Psaras, I.: ChainSoft: collaborative software development using smart contracts. In: CRYBLOCK 2018-Proceedings of the 1st Workshop on Cryptocurrencies and Blockchains for Distributed Systems, Part of MobiSys 2018, pp. 1–6. ACM (2018)
23. Zhang, F., Cecchetti, E., Croman, K., Juels, A., Shi, E.: Town crier: an authenticated data feed for smart contracts. In: Proceedings of the 2016 ACM SIGSAC Conference on Computer and Communications Security, pp. 270–282. ACM (2016)
24. de la Rosa, J.L., et al.: On intellectual property in online open innovation for SME by means of blockchain and smart contracts. In: 3rd Annual World Open Innovation Conference WOIC (20160
25. Androulaki, E., et al.: Hyperledger fabric: a distributed operating system for permissioned blockchains. In: Proceedings of the Thirteenth EuroSys Conference, p. 30. ACM (2018)

BCSolid: A Blockchain-Based Decentralized Data Storage and Authentication Scheme for Solid

Ting Cai[1,2], Wuhui Chen[1(✉)], and Yang Yu[1]

[1] School of Data and Computer Science, Sun Yat-sen University,
Guangzhou 510006, China
cait9@mail2.sysu.edu.cn, chenwuh@mail.sysu.edu.cn
[2] College of Mobile Telecommunications,
Chongqing University of Posts and Telecommunications, Chongqing 401520, China

Abstract. Solid (Social Linked Data) aims to radically change the way web applications work today, giving users true data ownership and improved privacy. However, it is facing two challenges, one is that data in centralized repositories needs to be separated from social web applications that force users to share their information. In addition, a decentralized authentication that guarantees who can operate on user's data with a secure privacy protection is another significant issue. In this paper, we address these challenges by proposing a blockchain-based decentralized data storage and authentication scheme for Solid, termed BCSolid, in which a user's data can be independent of multiple web applications and can switch data storage service easily without relying on a trusted third party. Meanwhile, our scheme gurantees data ownership and user's privacy by leveraging the blockchain miners to perform authentication with the help of certificateless cryptography. Additionally, we present a possible instantiation to illustrate how "transactions" in BCSolid are processed. To our knowledge this is the first work to promote the Solid project using blockchain. The evaluation results show that our scheme can gurantee a low latency network and is a promising solution to Solid.

Keywords: Solid · Blockchain · Storage · Authentication · Certificateless cryptography

1 Introduction

Solid (Social Linked Data) is a web re-decentralization project led by Tim Berners-Lee, the inventor of the World Wide Web [1]. It aims to deprive of its control over users' private data from large internet companies and return it to users themselves. By controlling their own data, users can choose how to use it for profit. This may respond to fears of a series of data leaks event as illustrated by the Facebook scandal, where Cambridge Analytica illegally acquires the Facebook information of up to 87 million users at the last count of March

Z. Zheng et al. (Eds.): BlockSys 2019, CCIS 1156, pp. 676–689, 2020.
https://doi.org/10.1007/978-981-15-2777-7_55

2018. The overuse of user data by internet giants such as Google, Facebook, Amazon brings lots of challenges in data security [3]. Therefore, the trend of serious centralization of the internet is an urgent need to be contained, and the devotion to promote Solid project is of great significance.

Emerging web applications such as MeWe and open source project DTP, just like a Solid project, are intended to break the highly monopolized internet landscape formed by tech giants of the central services [2]. Centralization refers to the fact that today's network largely run on a centralized repositories structure, and each application based on one social network platform can collect and control all the data, which brings security issues and privacy disclosure. Generally, a Solid project has to face two challenges: (1) how to separate data from applications that force users to share their information, and thus make a user can choose where to store data and authorize other users or applications to access the data; (2) how to achieve an authentication that ensures data only belongs to user himself while other entities without the knowledge of the user's real identity. To do so, a decentralized structure will properly handle these issues: release data from centralized repositories, implement distributed control, and return them to users.

Blockchain offers a convenient platform for Solid data storage and protection. However, incorporating the blockchain may bring high cost of data storage and computation to Solid [6,7]. Fortunately, the IPFS (Interplanetary File System) is one way to solve this problem. It can act as an advanced peer-to-peer network technology and implement the interconnection of each node in a decentralized scenario. With such a design, the Solid data can be stored on the IPFS while a pointer to the storage address will be stored on blockchain. When a Solid user sponsoring data access requests from the IPFS, the blockchain will determine whether to authorize or refuse, which depends on the authentication of the sponsor worked by the distributed blockchain miners instead of a trusted centralized server.

Authentication is another challenge to promote the Solid project. The most prominent problem is how to ensure if the data belongs to a Solid user in the case where the user's identity remains private [2]. With a blockchain, the miners can make authentication when a Solid user requests for a data access without any knowledge about his certificate of identity. Therefore, a secure and efficient authentication policy is essential. Traditional Public Key Infrastructure (PKI) [4] uses a certificate to realize public key authentication through confirmation of identity between public key and private key, in which introduces too much redundancy. As an alternative, Identity Based Authentication (IBE) [5] reduces complexity in certificate management whereas key escrow is an unavoidable problem for it to authenticate a user. This is where Certificateless cryptography [8] steps in. Meanwhile, to achieve the above functions with a low network latency is a challenging work. As such, we propose to apply the certificateless cryptography into a blockchain-based Solid system, in which we can use the identity of a Solid user (e.g., WebID) to generate keys efficiently, and employ efficient Elliptic

Curve Cryptography (ECC) algorithm to construct the public key cryptosystem. In this work, our specific contributions are in the following:

- We propose a scheme for Solid data storage and authentication. It separates data from applications and prevents users from being forced to share information with various applications that may deliberately leak a user's privacy data. Moreover, it implements user authentication to enable a data owner has both ownership and control of the data by letting the blockchain miners work together.
- We design a storage scheme with a combination of on-chain and off-chain. In addition, the off-line storage layer introduces the secure multiparty computation into the IPFS, which can decrypt the online encrypted solid data in a secure way.
- We propose to employ the certificateless cryptography in a blockchain-based Solid system. It offers an effective way to authenticate Solid users, in turn, the blockchain provides a convenient way to broadcast a Solid user's public key. In addition, we discuss to use a light-weight ECC algorithm to perform keys generation, signature and verification, which can reduce computational overhead and bring with a low latency for Solid networks.
- Discuss how the blockchain works in a Solid system via a study case. To our best knowledge, this is the first paper contribute to Solid and we believe that our work can be used as a reference to the Solid project promoters.

The paper is organized as follows. Section 2 presents the system model of BCSolid. In Sect. 3, we discuss storage architecture and how authentication is done in our scheme. Section 4 discusses how to achieve a secure and efficient authentication with the certificateless cryptography. In Sect. 5, a concrete use case are given to describe the process of transactions in the proposed system. Section 6 concludes the paper.

2   System Model

In this section, we present the system model and the relevant functional descriptions for our scheme. In our system, the involved participants include Solid User, POD Server, Off-chain Repository and Miner, as shown in Fig. 1.

Solid Users, identified by $U = \{U_1, ..., U_i, ..., U_n\}$, are the person or organization who own data and request for services (e.g., store files, access and trade, etc.) from system. When these users wish to ask for a request, they need to post a transaction to the blockchain network. In our system, a registered user has a unique Solid Web Identity and Discover (WebID), which can be used to provide universal usernames or IDs for various Solid applications, and to bind to a unique entity as identifiers containing related social information.

POD Servers, identified by $S = \{S_1, ..., S_j, ..., S_m\}$, served as a medium for providing Solid services with users, are not controlled by any third party. S can be from the free providers of commercial entity established by the Solid founding team or the users whose personal computers are installed and run as

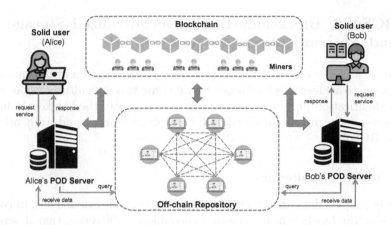

Fig. 1. The system model of BCSolid.

a node-solid server on network. In this way, a Solid user can be easy to decide where the data is stored, local or online.

Miners mainly verify an unconfirmed transaction and, if valid, add it into a block so that the activities such as store, access to data, modify, etc. in our system are traceable and accountable. That is, the security of the underlying blockchain is built on these miners. Note that U and S can also be miners if they join in the blockchain network and contribute their computing resources. Likewise, a certain amount of rewards perhaps a token are required to motivate the miners to participate in mining.

Off-chain Repository, served as an additional storage to blockchain, is a fully-distributed peer-to-peer architecture where the Solid data is actually stored. It is the key point to Solid storage in that the blockchain has proved to be inefficient and expensive to store data. In our design, any Solid data (e.g., web page, PDF file, photo, video, etc.) can be transferred and stored on an off-chain repository that may be a user's own computer. For simplicity, we denote it as IPFS in paper.

In our scheme, we require that U send a request to S to get registered before obtaining services from the proposed system, i.e., $U_i = \{WebID_{U_i}, K_{U_i}^P, K_{U_i}^S\}$, where $K_{U_i}^S$ is saved by U_i. Then, U_i can request a service $action$ by utilizing POD Server to send a transaction T_{U_i} to the blockchain. There are many category of services which are pre-defined as $action$ by system, where $action = \{store, access, setACL\}$. An authenticated user whose T_{U_i} is validated by Miner can be serviced, for example, a verified user U_i who requests access to a data store in system can obtain an address value $Addr$ related to a storage location on IPFS. Upon the work of Miners in blockchain, U can take ownership of his own data and improve privacy in $action$ with S.

3   BCSolid: Blockchain-Based Decentralized Storage and Authentication Scheme for Solid

Solid is an active response to the current severe centralization of the internet [2]. At present, to achieve this goal needs to overcome two difficulties such as storage and authentication [9]. To tackle these issues, we apply the blockchain in Solid to propose a decentralized scheme for Solid data storage and authentication, termed BCSolid.

3.1   Storage Architecture

A tightly coupled data and applications leads to centralization. Thus, in BCSolid we employ the blockchain to achieve a decoupled architecture that it separates web applications from the user data, allows a user to control his storage and usage, and ensures effective authentication and privacy protection. More explicitly, the architecture of BCSolid includes three layers: the off-chain storage layer, blockchain layer and application layer.

Application Layer. The application layer is the BCSolid Client that provides users with entrance to interact with Solid POD servers. After successfully registered, a user can get a Solid POD that acts as the BCSolid Client. Without depending on any central server, the Solid POD can run locally on a user's personal computer, or on an online Solid POD provider of your choice. BCSolid Client supports all operations for Solid actions, such as registration, storage, access, data trading, and etc. More importantly, it allows a Solid user to interact with the underlying blockchain.

Blockchain Layer. The blockchain layer serves as a "trusted third party" working in the following ways: (a) Before a POD server forwarding data to IPFS, it promotes a transaction that announces clearly whose data will be stored where on IPFS to the blockchain. If the transaction is validated by miners, blockchain will record the Solid user's WebID and the storage address on IPFS. In this way, blockchain *helps manage data storage*; and (b) When a Solid user requests data from IPFS, it promotes a transaction on the chain, where the blockchain plays a role as an authenticator to the user. If the transaction is validated by miners, it will be written into a block and the data will be sent from the IPFS nodes to the requester. Hence, in our scheme *authentication is performed through the blockchain* instead of a trusted server. Here are also additional descriptions of the blockchain layer as follows:

Blockchain Transaction: A "transaction" in a BCSolid system is a *request for services* (e.g., data storage or access) from a Solid user. We define a transaction as the form: $T_{U_i} = (WebID_{U_i}, Timestamp, action)$, where *action* is simple denoted. For example, $action \rightarrow store||Addr$ is to store data in a certain address *Addr*.

Consensus Protocol: A novel mechanism called Proof-of-Useful-Work (PoUW) [12], as an alternative approach to PoW, is a suitable consensus mechanism for our scheme. As such, any miner in a BCSolid system can work for a Solid provider (e.g., Inrupt) and be rewarded with blocks under a proof of their work by a similar trusted hardware to the Intel SGX.

Miners Awards: There are three ways to incentive miners to work for BCSolid. First, a traditional service fee from the centralized server can be transferred to miners. Second, a Solid provider such as Inrupt will pay miners reward for their computing useful work. Last, create block awards is a reward of blockchain itself, in return, it can be sent to miners as their rewards.

Off-Chain Storage Layer. The off-chain storage layer utilize IPFS to store the actual data values, whereas the blockchain only stores metadata such as pointer, hash value, signature, etc. To protect sensitive Solid data, we suggest to make necessary encryption when an online storage is performed. We use a combination of IPFS and Secure Multi-Party Computing (SMPC) [13] as the off-chain storage layer for BCSolid. A Solid user can be stored with encryption by his own public key. More importantly, a data owner does not need to worry about the disclosure of decryption keys when sharing data with another entity. As depicted by Fig. 2, the specific approach is to divide the encryption key mathematically into shares (also known as secret sharing [14]) and store each share on an IPFS node. With a designed SMPC protocol, these nodes can jointly decrypt or perform proxy re-encryption [15] to enable data sharing. In this way, a Solid storage provider cannot learn anything about user's raw data because it is encrypted with keys solely mastered by the users. Moreover, a Solid user is able to control his data and authorize other users or applications in a BCSolid system to access it.

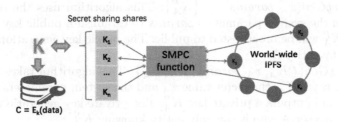

Fig. 2. Decryption on IPFS with SMPC.

Here, an off-chain storage layer has three functions: (*a*) *encrypting data* delivered by registered Solid users with the encryption keys generated by system; (*b*) *storing* users' data and the secret sharing keys; and (*c*) jointly performing *decryption or proxy re-encryption.*

3.2   Authentication of Blockchain Transactions in BCSolid

As discussed in Sect. 3.1, a BCSolid provides an effective data storage scheme to cope with the internet's decentralization. Next, we focus on another issue existing in the Solid project, that is, how to make secure and efficient authentication for a Solid user. Fortunately, in BCSolid a user can be easily verified on the blockchain. For example, a user A will get a $WebID_A$ and a pair of keys (K_A^P, K_A^S) after registration, then he can post a transaction T_A signed with his private key K_A^S to the blockchain. To be verified, a miner is to check whether: (1) T_A is indeed signed by user's private key K_A^S, and (2) K_A^P does belong to the user A associated with $WebID_A$.

The certificateless cryptography scheme is able to achieve the above function, which can be seen as a public key cryptosystem between the traditional PKI and IBE [10]. In certificateless cryptography, a KGC provides a master key and generates a partial private key for a user based on his identity, and then the user is to use his own secret value and the partial private key to create a private key. This way, both KGC and user participate in private key generation, thus avoiding the key escrow problem in IBE. Next, we will illustrate how to create keys K_A^P and K_A^S for a Solid user A.

(1) $Setup(1^\lambda) \rightarrow \{K_S^M, params\}$: This algorithm takes the security parameter 1^λ as input, outputs the system public parameters $params$ and a secret master key K_S^M. The set up algorithm is run by KGC.
(2) $PKeyGen(WebID_A, K_S^M, params) \rightarrow \{PK_A^S\}$: This algorithm takes the identity $WebID_A$ of user A, the secret master key K_S^M and the system parameters $params$, and outputs a partial private key PK_A^S to entity A.
(3) $SetSVal(WebID_A, params) \rightarrow \{x_A\}$: This algorithm uses the identity $WebID_A$ of user A and the system parameters $params$ to generate a secret value x_A. This set secret value algorithm is run by entity A.
(4) $PubKeyGen(x_A, params) \rightarrow \{K_A^P\}$: This algorithm uses the secret value x_A and the system parameters $params$ to establish a public key K_A^P. After that, K_A^P will be broadcasted to public. The public key generation algorithm is run by entity A.
(5) $PriKeyGen(PK_A^S, x_A, params) \rightarrow \{K_A^S\}$: This algorithm takes the partial private key PK_A^S, the secret value x_A and the system parameters $params$ as input, and outputs a private key K_A^S. The private key generation algorithm is run by user A who is the only entity knowing K_A^S.

Based on the above steps we further define functions such as $Encrypt()$, $Decrypt()$, $Sign()$ and $Ver()$ in the following.

– $Encrypt\ (M \in \mathcal{M}, WebID_A, K_A^P, params) \rightarrow C \in \mathcal{C} \vee \perp$, this encryption algorithm takes a message M, user's identity $WebID_A$ and public key K_A^P, and the system parameters $params$ as input, and returns a ciphertext C or $Error$. Where, the plaintext space $\mathcal{M}$ and the ciphertext space $\mathcal{C}$ are determined by $params$ and $WebID_A$.

- $Decrypt\,(C \in \mathcal{C}, K_A^S, params) \rightarrow M \in \mathcal{M} \vee \bot$, this decryption algorithm takes as input a ciphertext C, user's private key K_A^S and system parameters $params$, and returns a plaintext M or $Error$.
- $Sign(M \in \mathcal{M}, K_A^S, params) \rightarrow \sigma_A$, this signature algorithm inputs message M, user's private key K_A^S and system parameters $params$, and outputs a signature σ_A of entity A.
- $Ver(M \in \mathcal{M}, \sigma_A, WebID_A, K_A^P, params) \rightarrow Valid \vee Invalid \vee \bot$, this verify algorithm takes a message M, a signature σ_A, user's ID $WebID_A$, user's public key K_A^P, and system parameters $params$, and returns a result of $Valid$ or $Invalid$ to check if the verification passed or not.

From the formal definition, given above, of algorithms that allows the certificateless cryptography to be applied in a BCSolid system. Since there are many ways to achieve it, we do not give the concrete construction steps of the cipher scheme here. The more discussion about constructing the certificateless public key cryptosystem refers to Sect. 4, in which we devote to realize a more lightweight encrypting and signing outcome in BCSolid. We also define an algorithm $VerID()$ to check whether a public key K_A^P belongs to an identity $WebID_A$ or not. And, the formal notation is: $VerID(WebID_A, K_A^P, params) \rightarrow Valid \vee Invalid \vee \bot$.

4   Discussions

There are several algorithms to achieve the proposed cryptography, and what is their impact on performance? Can BCSolid provide a secure authentication with a low network latency? To answer these questions, we propose to use ECC to construct the certificateless public key cryptosystem in a BCSolid system and perform the following testing and evaluation.

(1) Make a comparison of security and key-length between ECC and other asymmetric encryption algorithms.
(2) With regard to performance measurement in signature generation and verification, we tested it with a built-in speed command in OpenSSL. Specifically, all cryptographic algorithms are conducted on 16.0 GB Intel Core i7-7700 CPU @ 3.60 GHz of 64 bit Windows 10 machine.
(3) To evaluate the difference in performance of two authentication algorithms (i.e., ECC and RSA) though a SSL handshake. We leverage Amazon EC2 Linux instantiate to simulate an environment and model for our test. Apache 2.4.3 was deployed on CentOS 6.5 is running as the web server. Furthermore, OpenSSL is an enabler of SSL communication for the apache web server and provides HTTP services and certificate configuration for running tests. On the other hand, we use Apache JMeter 2.8 as a client application to test the performance of web server at different loads, and it was configured to allow access to different sizes of resources (HTTP GET) and 68% session reuse. TLS 1.2 is the version of SSL in test.

We compare ECC with other asymmetric encryption algorithms and the results are shown in Table 1. The key lengths using current encryption methods like RSA, DSA and DH increase exponentially with the increase of security levels, while the key length of ECC increases linearly. For example, a 128-bit security level requires a 256-bit ECC key, but a 3,072-bit RSA key. Increasing to a 256-bit security level requires a 512-bit ECC key, but a 15,306-bit RSA key. Obviously, *ECC has a favorable security per bit ratio and is able to provide the same security level with a shorter key length.* Compared to a 2048-bit RSA key, ECC 256-bit keys are 64,000 times harder to crack.

Table 1. Security comparison of ECC and RSA/DSA/DH

Time to break key (MIPS years)	Security strength (Bits)	Key size (Bits)		
		ECC	RSA/DSA/DH	The ratio
10^{12}	80	160	1024	1:6
10^{24}	112	224	2048	1:9
10^{28}	128	256	3072	1:12
10^{47}	192	384	7680	1:20
10^{66}	256	512	15360	1:30

Table 2. Signature generation and verification test

Algorithm	Size (bits)	Sign (s)	Verify (s)	Sign (/s)	Verify (/s)
RSA/DSA	2048	0.0028925	0.000091	345.8	10978.2
ECC	256	0.0002	0.00055	4574.25	1811.15
ECC	384	0.0004	0.0021	2305.3	479.05

Table 2 demarcates the signature generation and verification performance for RSA 2048 bits, DSA 2048 bits, ECC 256 bits and ECC 384 bits. The results show that *ECC is more efficient than RSA in signature generation.* Compared to a 2048 RSA sign operation, ECC 256-bit sign operation is almost 13 times faster. However, ECC-256 is about 5 times slower than RSA-2048 for a verify operation. Overall, the cost for signature generation and verification in ECC is almost the same, whereas verification in RSA is much more efficient than generating a signature.

Figure 3(a) is the server performance metrics tested on the cloud host. We can see that *ECC-256 performs well than RSA-2048 and RSA-3072 at different file sizes.* On the other hand, in order to evaluate the differences between ECC and RSA in the process of authentication, we set three files of different sizes (i.e., 0k, 200k and 1200k) to be retrieved in the tests. We apply these to design our four experimental scenarios, and compare the performance metrics like throughout

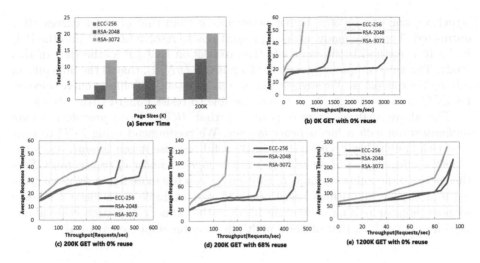

Fig. 3. Comparison of authentication algorithms (ECC 256, RSA 2048, RSA 3072).

and response time. Note that a 0k file does not imply an empty payload because there still transfers the HTTP headers in the process.

As shown (b), (c), (d) and (e) in Fig. 3, they illustrate the response time versus throughput metrics run by the above mentioned four tests under different file sizes and session reuse. The X axis denotes throughput at the client and the Y axis denotes latency (response time) at the client. Specifically, Fig. 3(b) shows the results for 0k GET with 0% reuse. We have found that there is limits of CPU saturation on test servers because each handshake is set to a full handshake in this scenario. The details are as follows: RSA 3072-bit and RSA 2048-bit are up to approximately 500 requests/sec and 1200 requests/sec respectively, and for ECC 256-bit is proved to be highly adaptable before 2600 requests/sec. *Most important, ECC-256 has the ability to process a much higher number of transactions.* Figure 3(c) illustrates the results of 200k GET with 0% reuse that follows the same trend as Fig. 3(b). In Fig. 3(d), a 68% reuse means that 2/3 handshakes are abbreviated from TLS. Therefore, the average response time decreases compared to the preceding test. Meanwhile, we can see the gap between them on CPU saturation is narrowing as the throughput increases. Figure 3(e) shows the results for 1200k GET with 0% reuse. We observe that ECC 256-bit and RSA 2048-bit are tend to reach the network saturation state, but RSA 3072-bit has reached the CPU usage limit. Note that, 256 bit ECC is as secure as 3072 bit RSA, whereas ECC 256-bit shows much more efficient than RSA 3072-bit.

As for the security of authentication in a BCSolid system, it largely depends on the adopted digital signature. In BCSolid, the security of digital signature is based on the Elliptic Curve Discrete Log Problem (ECDLP). Security of ECDLP requires us to select a proper parameters of elliptic curves so that the quadratic twist has a large enough prime divisor ρ. Secp256k1 is an elliptic curve based on the finite field Fp. It is considered to be safe enough due to its special construction, and can be 30% higher performance than that of other curves after optimized. There are many attacking algorithms to resolve ECDLP, and the Pollard's Rho method is the most effective attacks on ECDLP at the time of this study. The time complexity for Pollard's p is $O(\sqrt{\pi N/2})$, that is the difficulty in solving is exponential. We suggest that the parameter N of elliptic curve selected for ECC is large enough ($\geq 2^{191}$), are feasible to resist Pollard's Rho attack.

The above analysis answers positively that *BCSolid can provide a secure authentication with a low network latency*. We recommend using ECC to construct the public key cryptosystem in BCSolid because it *can improve the sign-cryption efficiency and help scale to a much higher number of transactions*. Furthermore, in the follow-up implementation we can use more lightweight encrypting and signing algorithms based on ECC. For example, to achieve a scheme without bilinear pairing computing because the bilinear operation costs about 20 times as much as that of point multiplication on elliptic curves [11].

5 Case Study

In this section, we use one case to describe how transactions are processed in a BCSolid system. Note that, transactions in our scheme refer to storing, accessing and sharing data instead of strictly financial. Assume that Alice is a Solid user, Bob is of a friend on the social network. Alice is willing to upload and share a group of photos with Bob. As illustrated in Algorithm 1, we show a detailed step-by-step overview of related procedures and functions.

User Registration. Procedure UserRegist in Algorithm 1 illustrates the process of Alice's registration. More specifically, first, Alice is to communicate with a POD server to get a POD and $WebID_A$. Then, a KGC initializes the key center to create the system parameters *params* and a secret master key K_S^M. In setup, the KGC is to broadcast *params* to the blockchain. As such, every user in system (e.g., Alice and Bob) has a knowledge of *params*, and meanwhile, Alice creates a secret value x_A by her own to prepare for the next key generation. To be registered on the blockchain, Alice needs to send a request to the KGC appending with her identity $WebID_A$. After receiving the message, the KGC will generate and send back a partial private key PK_A^S to Alice, together with a $Sign_{K_K^S}(WebID_A)$ signed by its own private key K_K^S. Here, we denote the two steps by functions $SendRequest()$ and $RecvRequest()$. After that, Alice will check if the message comes from the KGC, and if succeeds, she is able to utilize *params*, PK_A^S and x_A to create the key pairs of (K_A^P, K_A^S).

Note that, only Alice can create the keys because she is the only entity who knows x_A. In addition, K_A^P will be broadcasted to the public, while K_A^S is only kept by her own.

Storage Transaction. After successfully registered to the blockchain, Alice is able to store her photos on the POD. We assume that Alice stores photos at an address *Addr* on IPFS. To do that, Alice will request a storage transaction on blockchain, which is defined as $T_{A_1} = (WebID_A, Timestamp, store\|Addr)$.

Algorithm 1. BCSolid Storage Access Algorithm

1: **procedure** STOREACCESS
2:    $WebID, POD \leftarrow http\ URI$
3:    $Addr \leftarrow hash(data)$
4:    $u_{Alice} \leftarrow WebID_A, T_{A_1}, T_{A_2}, \sigma_{A_1}, \sigma_{A_2}, K_A^P, K_A^S, ACL$
5:    $u_{Bob} \leftarrow WebID_B, T_B, \sigma_B, K_B^P, K_B^S$
6:    **procedure** USERREGIST(1^λ)
7:       $u_{Alice} \leftarrow POD\ URL, WebID_A$
8:       $Setup(1^\lambda) \Rightarrow params, K_S^M$
9:       $x_A \leftarrow SetSVal(WebID_A, params)$
10:       SendRequest($WebID_A$)
11:       RecvRequest($PK_A^S, Sign_{K_K^S}(WebID_A)$)
12:       **if** $Ver(WebID_A, Sign_{K_K^S}(WebID_A), K_K^P, params)$ **then**
13:          $PubKeyGen(x_A, params) \Rightarrow K_A^P$
14:          $PriKeyGen(PK_A^S, x_A, params) \Rightarrow K_A^S$
15:       **end if**
16:    **end procedure**
17:    **procedure** STOREDATA($Addr$)
18:       $T_{A_1} = (WebID_A, Timestamp, store||Addr)$
19:       $\sigma_{A_1} \leftarrow Sign_{K_A^S}(T_{A_1})$
20:       Broadcast(T_{A_1}, σ_{A_1})
21:       **if** $VerID(WebID_A, K_A^P, params)$ && $Ver(T_{A_1}, \sigma_{A_1}, WebID_A, K_A^P, params)$
    then
22:          T_{A_1} is to write into a block;
23:       **else** Abort;
24:       **end if**
25:    **end procedure**
26:    **procedure** SETACL($WebID_B, ACL$)
27:       $ACL \leftarrow AddACL(WebID_B)$
28:       $T_{A_2} = (WebID_A, Timestamp, ACL||Addr)$
29:       $\sigma_{A_2} \leftarrow Sign_{K_A^S}(T_{A_2})$
30:       Broadcast(T_{A_2}, σ_{A_2})
31:       **if** $Ver(T_{A_2}, \sigma_{A_2}, WebID_A, K_A^P, params)$ && $VerID(WebID_A, K_A^P, params)$
    then
32:          T_{A_2} is to write into a block;
33:       **else** Abort;
34:       **end if**
35:    **end procedure**
36:    **procedure** ACCESSDATA($WebID_B, WebID_A||Addr$)
37:       $T_B = (WebID_B, Timestamp, access||WebID_A||Addr)$
38:       $\sigma_B \leftarrow Sign_{K_B^S}(T_B)$
39:       Broadcast(T_B, σ_B)
40:       **if** $(VerID(WebID_B, K_B^P, params))$ && $Ver(T_B, \sigma_B, WebID_B, K_B^P, params)$
    then
41:             **if** $WebID_B \in ACL$ **then**
42:                T_B is to write into a block;
43:             **else** Abort
44:             **end if**
45:          **else** Abort
46:       **end if**
47:    **end procedure**
48: **end procedure**

Along with a signature σ_{A_1}, T_{A_1} will be broadcasted to all participants in network. Then, the miners will check T_{A_1} against some validation rules that set by creators of the specific BCSolid system.

In our design, the validation rules that a miner follows to obey are as follows: (1) check whether Alice's public key K_A^P matches the identity $WebID_A$ as included in a transaction T_{A_1}; and (2) validate the transaction signature σ_{A_1} with Alice's public key K_A^P. To sum up, if T_{A_1} is verified, it will be stored into a block and become part of the blockchain.

Access Control Transaction. Alice is to create an access control list (ACL) that specifies who can access her photos. When Alice is willing to share her photos with Bob, she needs to add Bob's $WebID_B$ into the ACL. Similarly, Alice will create a transaction as $T_{A_2} = (WebID_A, Timestamp, ACL\|Addr)$, where $ACL\|Addr$ simply represents an action of renewing the ACL at an IPFS address $Addr$. With a signature σ_{A_2}, Alice posts T_{A_2} on the blockchain. Once the miners receiving T_{A_2}, they are responsible to verify it with the system's validation rules. If passes, T_{A_2} will be written into a block.

When Bob wants to access Alice's photos, he can create a trade transaction T_B (see line 37, Algorithm 1) including Alice's identity $WebID_A$ and the storage address $Addr$ he is required. And, sign T_B with his private key K_B^S and post them on the blockchain. In such a process, the miners need to first check if T_B is vccce's ACL. Only after all requirements are met, T_B is to write into a block, and the photos will be send to Bob from a storing IPFS node.

To sum up, any user like Alice can easily store and share her data with Bob or someone else in a BCSolid system using her own unique WebID$_A$ and POD.

6   Conclusion

In this paper, we present BCSolid, a decentralized scheme for Solid data storage and authentication based on the blockchain. More specifically, the IPFS is leveraged as an off-chain storage repository to help store and encrypt the actual data values. The certificateless cryptography is employed to achieve a convenient authentication in BCSolid. In addition, we study a cases and provide the detailed algorithm to describe how to process transactions and how to achieve authentication in a BCSolid system. The evaluation results suggest that the ECC can be employed to construct the public key cryptography, since it performs considerably reducing the network delay time. In the future, we plan to consider the proposed scheme under more real application senarios (e.g., data trading), develope and test our secure protocols in authentication on a protosystem.

Acknowledgments. The work described in this paper was supported by the National Key Research and Development Plan (2018YFB1003800), the National Natural Science Foundation of China (61802450), the Natural Science Foundation of Guangdong (2018A030313005), the Program for Guangdong Introducing Innovative and Entrepreneurial Teams (2017ZT07X355) and the Science and Technology Research Program of Chongqing Municipal Education Commission (KJZD-K201802401).

References

1. Sambra, A., Guy, A., Capadisli, S., Greco, N.: Building decentralized applications for the social Web. In: Proceedings of the 25th International Conference Companion on World Wide Web, pp. 1033–1034. International World Wide Web Conferences Steering Committee. ACM (2016)
2. Mansour, E., et al.: A demonstration of the solid platform for social web applications. In: Proceedings of the 25th International Conference Companion on World Wide Web, pp. 223–226. International World Wide Web Conferences Steering Committee. ACM (2016)
3. Zheng, Z., Xie, S., Dai, H.N., Chen, X., Wang, H.: Blockchain challenges and opportunities: a survey. Int. J. Web Grid Serv. **14**(4), 352–375 (2018)
4. Thompson, M.R., Essiari, A., Mudumbai, S.: Certificate-based authorization policy in a PKI environment. ACM Trans. Inf. Syst. Secur. (TISSEC) **6**(4), 566–588 (2003)
5. Boneh, D., Franklin, M.: Identity-based encryption from the Weil pairing. SIAM J. Comput. **32**(3), 586–615 (2003)
6. Chen, W., et al.: Cooperative and distributed computation offloading for blockchain-empowered industrial internet of things. IEEE Internet Things J. **6**(5), 8433–8446 (2019)
7. Qiu, X., Liu, L., Chen, W., Hong, Z., Zheng, Z.: Online deep reinforcement learning for computation offloading in blockchain-empowered mobile edge computing. IEEE Trans. Veh. Technol. **68**(8), 8050–8062 (2019)
8. Zhang, Y., Deng, R., Zheng, D., Li, J., Wu, P., Cao, J.: Efficient and robust certificateless signature for data crowdsensing in cloud-assisted industrial IoT. IEEE Trans. Ind. Inform. **15**(9), 5099–5108 (2019)
9. Rafiq, Y., Dickens, L., Russo, A., Bandara, A.K., Yang, M., Stuart, A.: Learning to share: engineering adaptive decision-support for online social networks. In: Proceedings of the 32nd IEEE/ACM International Conference on Automated Software Engineering, pp. 280–285. IEEE (2017)
10. Aitzhan, N.Z., Svetinovic, D.: Security and privacy in decentralized energy trading through multi-signatures, blockchain and anonymous messaging streams. IEEE Trans. Dependable Secur. Comput. **15**(5), 840–852 (2018)
11. Gayathri, N.B., Thumbur, G., Kumar, P.R., Rahman, M.Z.U., Reddy, P.V.: Efficient and secure pairing-free certificateless aggregate signature scheme for healthcare wireless medical sensor networks. IEEE Internet Things J. **6**(5), 9064–9075 (2019)
12. Zhang, F., Eyal, I., Escriva, R., Juels, A., Van Renesse, R.: {REM}: resource-efficient mining for blockchains. In: 26th {USENIX} Security Symposium ({USENIX} Security 2017), pp. 1427–1444. ACM (2017)
13. Halevi, S., Hazay, C., Polychroniadou, A., Venkitasubramaniam, M.: Round-optimal secure multi-party computation. In: Shacham, H., Boldyreva, A. (eds.) CRYPTO 2018. LNCS, vol. 10992, pp. 488–520. Springer, Cham (2018). https://doi.org/10.1007/978-3-319-96881-0_17
14. Zou, S., Liang, Y., Lai, L., Shamai, S.: An information theoretic approach to secret sharing. IEEE Trans. Inf. Theory **61**(6), 3121–3136 (2015)
15. Chen, W.H., Fan, C.I., Tseng, Y.F.: Efficient key-aggregate proxy re-encryption for secure data sharing in clouds. In: 2018 IEEE Conference on Dependable and Secure Computing (DSC), pp. 1–4. IEEE (2018)

Research on Enterprise DNS Security Scheme Based on Blockchain Technology

Jichuan Zhang[1], Jianhong Zhai[1(✉)], Ru Yang[2], and Shuyan Liu[1]

[1] School of Computer Science and Technology,
Harbin Institute of Technology, Harbin 150001, China
zhaijh@hit.edu.cn
[2] School of Computer Science and Technology, Heilongjiang Institute of Engineering,
Harbin 150006, China

Abstract. Almost every activity on the Internet starts with a DNS query, and 80% of the query requests will hit on the local DNS cache server. As an important network infrastructure, the local DNS solves the DNS request query problem of the intranet users, but also faces many serious threats, such as single point of failure, DNS pollution, and vulnerability to DDoS attacks. In this paper, we propose an enterprise-level DNS service scheme based on blockchain technology. A distributed structure is formed by installing the blockchain service (Ethereum) on multiple servers. Multiple block nodes provide DNS resolution service at the same time, which can effectively solve the problem of single point of failure. Each block node has the domain name verification function. When the domain name information is updated, multiple nodes implement the voting verification through smart contract, which can effectively reduce the DNS pollution. In the case of DDoS attack, multiple nodes can effectively decompose the attack traffic through load balancing algorithm. In addition, blockchain nodes can run consensus algorithm, which means that even if a node is attacked, the DNS service can still run normally.

Keywords: Blockchain · Smart contract · Ethereum · DNS · Load balancing

1 Introduction

Almost every activity on the Internet starts with a DNS request, and 80% of requests will hit on the local DNS cache server. As an important network infrastructure, the local DNS solves the problem of DNS request query of intranet users, but it also faces many serious threats [1], such as single point failure [2], DNS pollution [3] and vulnerability to DDoS attacks [4, 5]. The current part mainly introduces the blockchain technology used to solve those security problems, and safety analysis will be discussed in the next section.

© Springer Nature Singapore Pte Ltd. 2020
Z. Zheng et al. (Eds.): BlockSys 2019, CCIS 1156, pp. 690–701, 2020.
https://doi.org/10.1007/978-981-15-2777-7_56

1.1 Blockchain

Block Chain technology [6, 7] is a decentralized distributed storage scheme, which includes point-to-point transmission [8], consensus mechanism [9], cryptographic algorithm and other technologies [10]. It has the characteristics of decentralization, sequential data, collective maintenance, programmability, security and trustworthiness [11, 12].

In 2013, the development team led by Daniel Kraft launched Namecoin [13] with the help of blockchain technology [14]. Daniel Kraft builds Namecoin on the blockchain of Bitcoin by expanding the contract protocol on the Bitcoin network. Namecoin is the first product of the combination of domain name system and blockchain technology. Namecoin writes the domain name ".bit" into the block chain, which is beyond anyone's control and ensures that the website can publish information freely. However, due to the fact that ".bit" cannot be censored, it facilitates illegal behavior, and the default browser does not support resolving ".bit" domain name, so plug-ins need to be installed. This bottleneck leads to Namecoin cannot be popularized on a large scale [15].

1.2 Ethereum

Ethereum [16] is a programmable blockchain that, instead of giving users a set of actions, allows them to customize the process of implementing features. Ethereum Virtual Machine (EVM) in a narrow sense refers to the protocol that defines the decentralized application platform. The function of EVM is to compile intelligent contract code into machine code that can be executed on Ethereum and provide the operating environment of intelligent contract. In addition, EVM is Turing-complete and provides a good programming interface that allows developers to write programs that run on EVM using the JavaScript-like language.

1.3 Smart Contract

Smart Contract [17, 18] is script code that runs on the blockchain and can be customized by the user to set rules and deploy them on the blockchain, automatically running when external conditions meet the trigger rules. In terms of security, intelligent contracts guarantee security through public-private key encryption between multiple accounts. In terms of resource consumption, the blockchain service deployed on Ethernet workshop only needs to consume virtual currency when transactions occur, and virtual currency can be supplemented in real time through the test environment on the private chain [19]. Therefore, the resource consumption of intelligent contract mainly comes from the consumption of underlying infrastructure, such as electricity fee and server maintenance fee.

Organization. The structure of the paper is as follows. Firstly, the key technologies on which the system is based are introduced in the first chapter. In the second chapter, how to deal with single point of failure, DNS pollution and DDoS attack is analyzed in detail. The third chapter introduces the system architecture, load balancing, DNS query and other core functions. The fourth chapter analyzes the experimental results and feasibility. In the last chapter, the future research direction is introduced.

2   Safety Analysis and Scheme Design

This part mainly analyzes the security problems existing in enterprise DNS, and then designs a feasible solution to solve the above problems based on the blockchain technology [20, 21].

2.1   Analysis of Enterprise DNS Security Threats

Data Spoofing. Data spoofing attacks usually tamper with DNS data in some way to gain the analytical control of domain names in order to deceive recipients, including cache poisoning, DNS hijacking and so on.

Cache Poisoning. The attacker inserts the "pollution" cache record into the cache record of the normal DNS name server. The polluted cache record [3] means that the IP address corresponding to the domain name in the DNS resolution server is not the real address, but the address tampered by the attacker. These addresses usually correspond to the server controlled by the attacker.

DNS Hijacking. In terms of the attack results, DNS hijacking (redirection) is very similar to cache poisoning. The purpose of the attack is to control the resolution record of a specific domain name, causing the IP address corresponding to the domain name to be tampered with as a fake site controlled by the attacker. Attackers usually initiate DNS hijacking in two ways. One is to directly attack the domain name registrar or the domain name site to obtain the account password to control the domain name, which can modify the IP address corresponding to the domain name. Another is to attack the authoritative name server and directly modify the resource records in the regional file.

DDoS. Since the DNS uses a tree structure, the resolution of the DNS depends on the root. Therefore, the DNS server is easily attacked due to too much concurrent traffic, that is, a DDoS attack occurs. DDoS attacks [4, 5] is a kind of attack method that makes enterprise network unable to provide services normally. In enterprises, the most important thing is the recursive DNS server. If there is no appropriate load balancing strategy, the recursive DNS server may temporarily be offline because of the high concurrent traffic query load.

Single-Point Failure. The traditional enterprise network architecture diagram is shown in Fig. 1. The primary domain name server in the local area network is deployed in a single point. The PCs in the enterprise rely on the server to complete the domain name query. Once the DNS server is down, the entire local area network cannot operate normally [2].

2.2   Security Scheme Based on Blockchain Technology

Defense Against Data Spoofing Attacks. This paper analyzes the attack process of cache poisoning and DNS hijacking, and then finds that there are two main ways of attack. One is that the DNS response message is maliciously exchanged by the attacker before returning, and the other is that the resource record in the upper DNS server zone file is modified. Based on the above analysis, this paper proposes to store DNS records and multi-node voting mechanism on the blockchain to prevent DNS spoofing.

Storing DNS on the Chain. By using the tamper-proof feature of blockchain, the DNS records that are absolutely correct after verification are stored on the blockchain, so as to prevent the attacker from modifying the resource records and resist the cache poisoning attack.

Multi-node Voting to Ensure Record Accuracy. When domain name data is updated, voting mechanism is implemented. Multiple nodes initiate DNS query at the same time and vote on the results. According to the principle of more votes and higher credibility, DNS records with absolute majority of votes are saved on blockchain.

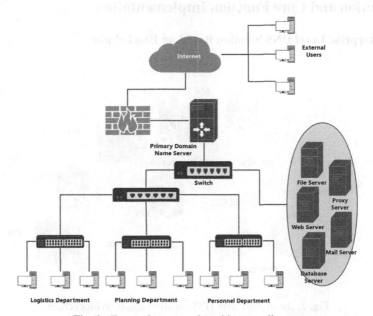

Fig. 1. Enterprise network architecture diagram

Defense Against DDoS Attacks. For the DDoS attack, this paper proposes to transform the load balancing strategy to offload the DNS server and improve the server load capacity.

New Load Balancing Strategy. Commonly used load balancing strategies are Round Robin, Least Connections, and Hash algorithms. The paper is based on the minimal connection algorithm. Multiple nodes send heartbeat packets to the load balancer to characterize the survival state and attach the load information of the nodes to the heartbeat packets. The load balancer sorts the processing priority of nodes according to the received load information, and the DNS query traffic is forwarded to the nodes with smaller load for processing.

Solution to Single Point Fault. To solve the single point failure problem, this paper proposes a distributed architecture to reduce the risk of single point failure.

Distributed DNS Architecture. Blockchain is a native distributed architecture. This paper transforms the servers with lower utilization rate such as file server, mail server and proxy server in Fig. 1 into blockchain node by installing blockchain service on each node. And then each node installs the DNS service, each pair of nodes is a primary and secondary server, and multiple block nodes can provide DNS resolution services at the same time. When a node server is crashes, other nodes can still provide domain name resolution, thus avoiding the single point of failure of traditional DNS services.

3 Solution and Core Function Implementation

3.1 Enterprise-Level DNS Solution Based on Blockchain

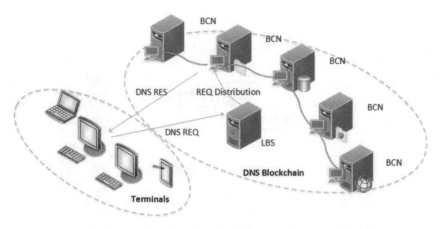

Fig. 2. Enterprise-level DNS solution based on blockchain

Based on the above analysis, this paper presents an enterprise-level DNS solution based on blockchain technology, as shown in Fig. 2.

In the solution, the DNS service system is composed of a load balancing server LBS (Load Balancing Server) [22] and a group of block nodes (BCN). Block nodes can be either independent dedicated machines or servers with low utilization in local area networks, such as FTP servers, file servers, etc. These block nodes are equipped with BIND services and private blocks of Ethereum to build a private chain for DNS services.

LBS Node. The main task of the LBS is to receive the DNS request sent by the terminal user and forward it to the corresponding BCN. The domain node resolves the domain name and sends the analysis result directly to the terminal user. The LBS distribution DNS request depends on the Block Chain Resource Queue (BCRQ). The priority of the BCRQ is determined by the Resource Free Rate (RFR) of each BCN.

BCN Node. The BCN node includes three functions: load status feedback, DNS query, and update block DNS record.

Load Status Feedback. Each BCN periodically sends a heartbeat packet to the load LBS node. The heartbeat packet contains the current physical CPU utilization as RCPU, memory usage as RRAM, and bandwidth usage as RNET.

DNS Query. Receiving a forwarding DNS request from the BCN node, querying whether the domain name has been hit in the blockchain, and if there is no hit, initiating a query request to a different upper-level DNS server, and returning the result to the client.

Update Block DNS Record. If the user's DNS query does not hit the local private chain, the DNS record needs to be updated in the blockchain. The BCN first initiates a record-update-voting-contract, and the five BCN servers query the IP of the specified domain name, and the returned result is used as a candidate record. If there is the highest score candidate record, save the (domain name, IP) binary record to the blockchain, otherwise randomly select the nearest IP address for reverse query, if it is correct, save it in the blockchain. Otherwise, this vote is over.

3.2 Load Balancing

The LBS receives resource heartbeat packets from each BCN node, including three parameters of RCPU, RRAM, and RNET, and then uses Eq. 1 to obtain the resource idle rate RFR of each BCN. The LBS maintains a resource queue BCRQ, dynamically updates the BCRQ whenever a resource heartbeat packet is received, and selects the node with the highest resource idle rate from the BCRQ to process the DNS request from the client.

$$RFR = 1 - (RCPU * 50\% + RRAM * 25\% + RNET * 25\%) \tag{1}$$

BCRQ priority update algorithm is shown in Table 1.

Table 1. The BCRQ priority update algorithm

Algorithm 1: The BCRQ priority update algorithm
Input: Heartbeat package returned by BCN
Output: Priority query

- Step1: Receive heartbeat packets from BCNi; Read RCPU, RRAM and RNET;

- Step2: Calculate the new RFRi of BCNi according to formula 1;

- Step3: If the new RFRi > the original RFRi, according to the size of the new RFRi, insert the BCNi into the corresponding position, go to Step5;

- Step4: Insert BCNi into the end of BCRQ;

- Step5: Waiting for a new heartbeat package.

To prevent a large number of queries in the same cycle are sent to the same block, in the first half of the BCRQ queue during distribution, take a BCN as the target and forward the DNS query information to it. If the query information record exists in the blockchain, the domain name resolution information that is queried is directly returned to the terminal user. If the domain name information record does not exist in the blockchain, the block initiates an iterative query to the upper-level DNS server, and the block returns the result of the query to the terminal user. It is worth noting that the record is not stored in the blockchain. The writing of the new domain name information requires multiple blocks to query different upper-level DNS servers, and the result is asynchronously voted, and the voting can be written into the blockchain.

When configuring the DNS service for the end user, first add the IP address of the LBS as the preferred DNS in the DNS server configuration list and add several BCN IP addresses as the backup DNS to prevent single point of failure.

3.3   Resource Update Voting Contract

The main application scenario of the voting contract [23, 24] is when a BCN initiates a domain name resolution information update request, and the BCN sends the update information and the data signature to the voting contract after being encrypted by the private key. After the voting contract verifies the authenticity of the received information, it broadcasts a voting request to initiate a vote, and decides whether to update the DNS record according to the voting result.

When the domain name information searched by BCNi is not hit in the blockchain resource record, BCNi queries the designated upper-level domain name server to query the IP corresponding to a DNS domain name. In order to prevent attackers from implementing DNS spoofs, methods of asynchronous concurrent verification and voting to update resources are adopted. It is assumed that when each BCN conducts DNS information verification, attackers cannot attack most BCN, and real DNS resolution records can be generated after voting. Each BCN is assigned a different parent DNS server in the scheme.

Some well-known websites in the Internet may have a large number of mirror sites, so the DNS resolution records obtained by each BCN may be different. Two rounds of DNS reverse resolution and forward resolution are adopted for verification in the scheme. The Resource update strategy is described in Table 2.

Table 2. Resource update strategy

Algorithm 2: Resource update strategy
Input: BCNi block initiates an update request
Output: Validation results

- Step1: BCNi initiates an update request and broadcasts the update message;

- Step2: After each BCN receives the update message, start verification;

- Step3: According to the domain name information recorded by DNS resources, the BCN nodes initiate forward resolution request to the superior DNS;

- Step4: Receive a DNS reply from the parent and participate in a round of voting

- Step5: IF the round of voting is successful, start the domain name file contract, goto Step9; Else goto Step 6;

- Step6: According to the IP information recorded by DNS resources, select the IP address with the minimum number of hops, and launch the reverse resolution request to the superior DNS;

- Step7: Receive the DNS reply from the superior, participate in the second round of Voting

- Step8: IF the second round of voting (DNS reverse resolution) is successful, start the domain name file contract;

- Step9: End

3.4 Domain Name File Contract

When the local DNS server updates the resource record, it needs to call the domain name file contract to complete the writing to the blockchain. DNS resource records (RR) are stored in the blockchain database. There are six types of RR: A, SOA, NS, PTR, CNAME and Other. Therefore, the meanings of different types of RR files should be written in the intelligent contract to help the subsequent analysis to be carried out smoothly. Figure 3 shows the structure definition and access scripts for DNS records.

```
pragma solidity ^0.4.0;
contract DNS {
    mapping(string => Record) dns_records;
    // dns_record fields definition
    struct Record {
        string name;
        uint ttl;
        string class;
        string d_type;
        string value;
    }
    // add a dns record to blockchain
    function addRecordToBlock(string memory name,uint ttl,string memory class,string memory d_type,string memory value) public {
        Record memory record = Record(name,ttl,class,d_type,value);
        dns_records[name] = record;
    }
    // search a dns record by domain name
    function searchRecord(string memory name)view public returns(string memory,uint,string memory,string memory,string memory){
        Record memory record = dns_records[name];
        return(record.name,record.ttl,record.class,record.d_type,record.value);
    }
}
```

Fig. 3. DNS record smart contract script

4   Experiment and Discussion

4.1   Experimental Environment

The experiment adopts OpenStack virtual technology and uses two dawning servers as computing nodes and control nodes, where computing nodes are used to provide virtual resources and control nodes are used to control communication and resource allocation between virtual machines. Through OpenStack technology, six virtual servers are used as LBS and five BCN.

The configuration of two Dawning servers and six virtual machines is as follows (Table 3):

Table 3. Configuration of physical host and virtual machine

Name	Type	CPU	Memory	Storage	System
Control node	Physics machine	8cores, 2.13 Hz	32G	500G	Ubuntu 16.04.5 LTS
Compute node	Physics machine	8cores, 2.13 Hz	8G	500G	Ubuntu 16.04.5 LTS
LBS	Virtual machine	2cores, 2.13 Hz	4G	40G	Ubuntu 18.04.2 LTS
BCN	Virtual machine	2cores, 2.13 Hz	4G	40G	Ubuntu 18.04.2 LTS

4.2   DNS Query Service Experiment

DNS query results can be divided into two cases, cache hits and cache misses.

In the case of hits, compare the query time on the blockchain with the query time of the native DNS. The result is shown in Table 4.

Table 4. Cache hits

Domain Name	Time spent on DNS service in blockchain (s)	Time spent on DNS service (s)
baidu.com	0.012249	0.004193
douban.com	0.012253	0.060361
csdn.com	0.508864	0.124433
sogou.com	0.012241	0.004169
youku.com	0.012255	0.124427
github.com	0.012249	0.004192
pptv.com	0.012254	0.124443
jianshu.com	0.012237	0.004187
nba.hupu.com	0.012244	0.124406
……		

Excluding special cases such as network congestion and other problems, about 5000 pieces of data were tested in the case of hitting on the chain, and the average response time of DNS request in the two ways was 0.012 s and 0.064 s, respectively. Therefore, the block DNS server processed requests much faster than the native DNS server.

In the case of a miss, compare the query time on the blockchain with the query time of the native DNS. The result is shown in Table 5.

Table 5. Cache miss

Domain name	Time spent on DNS service in blockchain (s)	Time spent on DNS service (s)
people.com.cn	0.508841	0.004196
xinhuanet.com	0.508845	0.028299
cctv.com	0.508850	0.027573
qstheory.cn	0.124482	0.060364
ifeng.com	0.508846	0.028301
chsi.com.cn	0.124449	0.028307
hrb.ganji.com	0.252581	0.124433
tianya.cn	0.508860	0.252584
tieba.baidu.com	0.508854	0.004180
......		

In the case of missing on the chain, about 5000 pieces of data were tested and the average DNS request response time of the two ways was 0.39 s and 0.062 s, respectively. The processing speed of the request was significantly different between the block DNS server and the native DNS server, but within the acceptable range.

5 Future Work

The purpose of this research is to ensure the security and availability of enterprise DNS server. Experimental results show that enterprise-level DNS server combined with blockchain has great advantages in the case of hit on the chain. The main reason is that the main DNS server is configured with load balancing algorithm, which is conducive to more efficient processing of user DNS query requests. However, there are still some problems to be further studied in the aspect of out-of-chain lookup. On the one hand, although blockchain can guarantee the single point failure of DNS server, DDOS attack, cache spoofing and other problems, the cost of query is still considerable. On the other hand, if the size of data processing is different, there may be some variables in the running time. These problems need to be further optimized and further studied.

Acknowledgments. This study is part of the Heilongjiang Natural Science Fund Joint Guidance Project. The project number is JJ2019LH0412.

References

1. Marrison, C.: Understanding the threats to DNS and how to secure it. Netw. Secur. **2015**(10), 8–10 (2015)
2. Giggins, T.: Single point of failure and availability. In: Institution of Engineers, Australia (1994)
3. Castro, S., Zhang, M., John, W., Wessels, D., Claffy, K.: Understanding and preparing for DNS evolution. In: Ricciato, F., Mellia, M., Biersack, E. (eds.) TMA 2010. LNCS, vol. 6003, pp. 1–16. Springer, Heidelberg (2010). https://doi.org/10.1007/978-3-642-12365-8_1
4. Alieyan, K., Kadhum, M.M., Anbar, M., et al.: An overview of DDoS attacks based on DNS. In: International Conference on Information & Communication Technology Convergence. IEEE (2016)
5. Zargar, S.T., Joshi, J., Tipper, D.: A survey of defense mechanisms against distributed denial of service (DDoS) flooding attacks. IEEE Commun. Surv. Tutor. **15**(4), 2046–2069 (2013)
6. Halpin, H., Piekarska, M.: Introduction to security and privacy on the blockchain. In: 2017 IEEE European Symposium on Security and Privacy Workshops (EuroS&PW), pp. 1–3. IEEE (2017)
7. Crosby, M., Pattanayak, P., Verma, S., et al.: Blockchain technology: beyond bitcoin. Appl. Innov. **2**(6–10), 71 (2016)
8. Khacef, K., Pujolle, G.: Secure peer-to-peer communication based on blockchain. In: Barolli, L., Takizawa, M., Xhafa, F., Enokido, T. (eds.) WAINA 2019. AISC, vol. 927, pp. 662–672. Springer, Cham (2019). https://doi.org/10.1007/978-3-030-15035-8_64
9. Zoican, S., et al.: Blockchain and consensus algorithms in internet of things. In: 2018 International Symposium on Electronics and Telecommunications (ISETC). IEEE (2018)
10. Li, X., Jiang, P., Chen, T., et al.: A survey on the security of blockchain systems. Future Gener. Comput. Syst., S0167739X17318332 (2017). https://doi.org/10.1016/j.future.2017.08.020
11. Shao, Q.F., Jin, C.Q., Zhang, Z., et al.: Blockchain: architecture and research progress. Chin. J. Comput. **41**(5), 969–988 (2018)
12. Pilkington, M.: Chapter 11: blockchain technology: principles and applications. In: Research Handbook on Digital Transformations, p. 225 (2016)
13. Shao, Q., Jin, C., Zhang, Z., Qian, W., Zhou, A.: Blockchain technology: architecture and progress. Chin. J. Comput. **41**(05), 969–988 (2018). (in Chinese)
14. Ikpeazu, J., Okoro, B.: On P2P electronic transaction networks: a reaction to bitcoin and namecoin (2013)
15. Ramachandran, A., Kantarcioglu, M.: SmartProvenance: a distributed, blockchain based dataprovenance system, pp. 35–42 (2018). https://doi.org/10.1145/3176258.3176333
16. Hu, N., Deng, W., Yao, S.: Research status and challenges of internet DNS security. Chin. J. Netw. Inf. Secur. **3**(03), 13–21 (2017). (in Chinese)
17. Wright, C., Serguieva, A.: Sustainable blockchain-enabled services: smart contracts. In: 2017 IEEE International Conference on Big Data (Big Data), pp. 4255–4264. IEEE (2017)
18. Zhou, E., Hua, S., Pi, B., et al.: Security assurance for smart contract. In: 2018 9th IFIP International Conference on New Technologies, Mobility and Security (NTMS). IEEE (2018)
19. Wang, S., Yuan, Y., Wang, X., et al.: An overview of smart contract: architecture, applications, and future trends. In: 2018 IEEE Intelligent Vehicles Symposium (IV), pp. 108–113. IEEE (2018)
20. He, Y., Hong, L., Cheng, X., et al.: A blockchain based truthful incentive mechanism for distributed P2P applications. IEEE Access **PP**(99), 1 (2018)
21. Ehmke, C., Wessling, F., Friedrich, C.M.: Proof-of-property: a lightweight and scalable blockchain protocol. In: Proceedings of the 1st International Workshop on Emerging Trends in Software Engineering for Blockchain. ACM (2018)

22. Xiong, Z., Yan, P., Wang, J.: A self-adjusting size-based load balance policy for web server cluster. In: The Fifth International Conference on Computer and Information Technology (CIT 2005), pp. 368–374. IEEE (2005)
23. Denktas, B., Pekdemir, S., Soykan, G.: Peer to peer business model approach for renewable energy cooperatives. In: 2018 7th International Conference on Renewable Energy Research and Applications (ICRERA). IEEE (2018)
24. Atzei, N., Bartoletti, M., Cimoli, T.: A survey of attacks on ethereum smart contracts (SoK). In: Maffei, M., Ryan, M. (eds.) POST 2017. LNCS, vol. 10204, pp. 164–186. Springer, Heidelberg (2017). https://doi.org/10.1007/978-3-662-54455-6_8

A Dual-Chain Digital Copyright Registration and Transaction System Based on Blockchain Technology

Wei Liang[1,4], Xia Lei[2(✉)], Kuan-Ching Li[3], Yongkai Fan[2], and Jiahong Cai[5]

[1] The College of Computer Science and Electronic Engineering, Hunan University,
Changsha 410082, Hunan, China
[2] The Department of Computer Science and Technology, China University of Petroleum,
Beijing 102249, China
Leixia2008530059@163.com
[3] The Department of Computer Science and Information Engineering, Providence University,
Taichung City, Taiwan
[4] The School of Opto-Electronic and Communication Engineering,
Xiamen University of Technology, Xiamen 361024, Fujian, China
[5] The School of Software, Xiamen University of Technology, Xiamen 361024, Fujian, China

Abstract. The increasing demand for digital copyright transactions in the big data era causes the emergence of piracy and infringement incidents. The traditional centralized digital copyright protection system based on centralized authority management of authoritative organizations has high registration cost. Blockchain, as a decentralized protocol, has the characteristics of decentralization, anonymity, auditability, security and persistency, which provide a solution to the current problems in the field of digital copyright. Combining with blockchain technology, this paper proposes a digital copyright registration and transaction system with double chain architecture. The blockchain based on digital copyright registration and management chain (RMC) and digital copyright transaction and subscription chain (TSC) can prevent information disclosure and improve the privacy protection by segregating account information and transaction information. Meanwhile, transforming the previous one-chain architecture into multiple chains in parallel on the RMC and TSC can reduce the redundant amount of computation, the consensus efficiency and improve the throughput rate. Experimental analysis shows that the system has the advantages of short registration time, high throughput and good scalability.

Keywords: Digital copyright · Blockchain · TSC/RMC · Consensus mechanism

1 Introduction

With the rapid development of digital publishing industry [1–3], piracy and infringement incidents emerge in endlessly. At present, digital copyright protection is mainly based on centralized authority management of authoritative institutions, but this pattern has some problems: (1) The centralized authorization management increases the trust cost and

© Springer Nature Singapore Pte Ltd. 2020
Z. Zheng et al. (Eds.): BlockSys 2019, CCIS 1156, pp. 702–714, 2020.
https://doi.org/10.1007/978-981-15-2777-7_57

accounting cost with the tedious process and the transaction efficiency is anomalously low [4–6]; (2) The centralized copyright control mechanism is vulnerable to be attacked and tampered, which results in low security of data storage; (3) In addition to official publications, a large number of videos, pictures, and online articles have copyright protection requirements for the purpose of protecting their originality. However, the current centralized copyright protection scheme has clearly failed to meet the requirements of digital copyright protection [7, 8]. For these reasons, many digital works creators are unwilling to apply for digital copyright protection.

Blockchain is a distributed ledger that can safely store transaction information and other data [9, 10]. Therefore, the advantages of blockchain technology such as decentralization, anonymity, auditability, security and persistency are conducive to solve the existing problems in the digital copyright registration and transaction system [11, 12]. Blockchain technology has begun to expand in digital copyright protection in recent years, and the research mainly focuses on blockchain-based digital rights management and the related application platforms [13].

In order to integrate blockchain technology with digital copyright registration and transaction system efficiently, this paper proposes a digital copyright registration and transaction system based on permissioned blockchain. The whole network consists of RMC and TSC, in which RMC only stores and queries account information, digital copyright information and post-transaction information, but does not execute transactions, and TSC only stores information useful for transactions such as digital copyright transfer and subscription and performs related transactions. It not only protects the sensitive information in the digital copyright system, but also guarantees the public's right to supervise the transaction.

2 Blockchain

In 2008, blockchain was first proposed by Satoshi Nakamoto in Bitcoin: A Peer-to-Peer Electronic Cash System [14]. The blockchain is a continuous sequence of blocks which consists of the cryptographic hash values of the previous block, timestamps and transaction data, and all the blocks are guaranteed by encryption mechanisms and consensus mechanisms that cannot be tampered or falsified. In particular, more complicated functions in the blockchain such as auto-pay and digital rights management can be achieved by smart contracts [15–17].

According to the characteristics of different application scenario, different types of blockchains can be selected, which include public blockchain and permissioned blockchain.

(1) Public Blockchain: A completely decentralized blockchain. Any node can participate in voting, accounting, building blocks, and also need an incentive mining mechanism. But because all nodes need to participate in voting, the transaction speed is anomalously slow. Bitcoin is a typical representative of the public chain.

(2) Permissioned Blockchain [18]: A partially decentralized blockchain that includes all non-public chains such as private chains and alliance chains. Only permissioned nodes can participate in voting, accounting and building blocks. Since the information stored in the digital copyright registration and transaction system is mostly

privacy information, and does not require large-scale public nodes participation, the permissioned blockchain is applied as the basic structure in this paper.

The blockchain infrastructure is composed of six layers, including data layer, network layer, consensus layer, incentive layer, contract layer, and application layer [9]. Each layer cooperates to achieve a decentralized trust mechanism. A block is a basic structural unit of a blockchain, and it is composed of a block header containing metadata and a block body containing transaction data (Fig. 1).

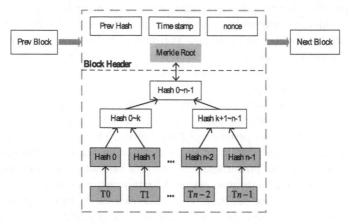

Fig. 1. The structure of blocks

2.1 Consensus Mechanism

Early Bitcoin blockchains used the Proof of Work (PoW) [14] to ensure the consistency of distributed ledger in Bitcoin networks. With the development of blockchain technology, researchers have proposed a variety of mechanisms that can reach consensus without relying on calculation, such as the Proof of Stake (PoS) [19] mechanism and the Delegated Proof of Stake (DPOS) mechanism.

In order to solve the Byzantine General's Problem [20], Practical Byzantine Fault Tolerance (PBFT) [21] is proposed by Miguel Castro and Barbara Liskov at the OSD199 Conference in 1999 as the first widely used Byzantine fault tolerance algorithm. The algorithm reduces the complexity of the original Byzantine fault-tolerant algorithm and improves the efficiency. But there are still some shortcomings in the application environment of copyright protection. The static network structure in the PBFT algorithm results that it cannot dynamically join and delete nodes. Anomalously, the public chain mainly uses the mechanism of POW and POS, while the permissioned chain mainly uses PBFT and an improved PBFT algorithm—Concurrent Byzantine Fault Tolerance (CBFT) [18]. Therefore, this paper chooses CBFT as a consensus algorithm for the digital copyright registration and transaction system which can join and delete nodes dynamically and improve efficiency by carrying out voting and transactions in parallel.

2.2 Smart Contract

In 1993, the cryptographer Nick Szabo first proposed the smart contract, which was defined as a series of computerized protocols, a set of programmed rules corresponding to presupposition conditions [22]. In blockchain, smart contracts are expressed as specific computer languages. Once the pre-set conditions in the contracts are met, the corresponding operations will be triggered automatically. This is also called "chain code". Smart contracts deployed on blockchains in this paper includes copyright registration contract, copyright inquiry contract, copyright transaction contract and copyright subscription contract.

2.3 IPFS

IPFS [23] is a distributed storage mode that cares about neither the location of the central server nor the file name and path, but what may appear in the file. After placing any file on IPFS, the encrypted hash value is calculated based on the content of the file. When IPFS is required to provide a file, it uses a distributed hash table to find the node where the file is located, and then retrieves the file and verifies it.

3 Data Interaction and Storage Model for Digital Copyright Protection with Double Chain Structure

3.1 Double Chain Architecture

At present, accounts and transactions are all placed on one blockchain in traditional copyright protection system, this architecture results in a large number of different data on the system. With the increase of services and nodes, the latency of transactions will be higher and higher. Moreover, this design has poor privacy and scalability, and low throughput.

In order to solve the above problems, a dual blockchain architecture which includes digital copyright registration and management blockchain (RMC) and digital copyright transfer and subscription blockchain (TSC) is proposed. The specific assignment of the double blockchain is respectively as follows:

(1) RMC: Store and query account information, digital copyright information and post-transaction information only, but do not execute transactions. Only the internal node can join the blockchain. When one node joins, it is required to verify its digital certificate and meets the requirements of the chain. RMC stores all processing information, including personal information of application, operation information of salesman, copyright information after transfer and account balance information. Sensitive information can only be broadcasted and recorded on this channel to ensure the applicant's privacy and the security of the sensitive data in system.

(2) TSC: Store only useful information such as digital copyright transfer and subscription and execute related transactions, but not the account information. Everyone can join the TSC chain which is only used as a channel for transaction and settlement. The data stored in TSC is encrypted so that only the participants can see the data.

Moreover, TSC can be divided into two categories: internal TSC chains and TSC chains across RMC. Internal TSC chain refers to the rapid completion of transactions within the same RMC chain by rapidly communicating with one RMC chain. TSC chains across RMC need to communicate with multiple RMC chains to complete transactions across RMC chains. When the TSC chain completes the transaction and returns the post-transaction information to the RMC chain, the RMC chain modifies its account information and account balance and preserves these changes to the blockchain. The CBFT algorithm is applied in the scheme to ensure consistency and prevent tampering.

By the RMC and TSC chains architecture, different nodes can belong to the same blockchain or different blockchains. Only when information needs to be traded can it be shared on the chain of trading blocks. When creating a new RMC chain, the access conditions of the chain can be determined according to its use. When new nodes join the chain, they must meet the access conditions. The dual blockchain network can ensure the transparency of information on the same blockchain and the confidentiality of information between different blockchains. The whole network can make nodes join different blockchains and access different privileges information according to different business requirements. The multi-channel mechanism avoids the contradiction between information disclosure and privacy protection in the same blockchain network, and improves the utilization of the network.

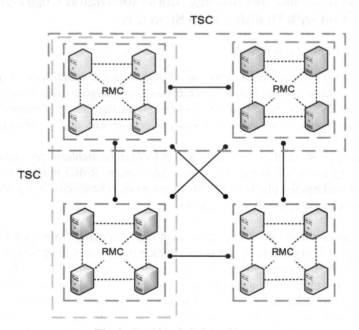

Fig. 2. Dual blockchain architecture

3.2 Analysis of Computational Capability of Copyright Transaction System with Double Chain Structure

First, a mathematical model for copyright transaction system is established based on dual blockchain, assuming that:

(1) n authoritative copyright management institutions: It could manage the accounts of creators and subscribers, and issue new contracts or abolish old ones;
(2) m creators: The original creators of digital works;
(3) l subscribers: The most common users can subscribe to a digital work on the chain.

Suppose the total number of transactions per day is L including copyright registration, copyright transfer and subscription transactions, the working time of the management institution per day is T hours, the building time of a block is Δt seconds, and the communication times for each block voting of each node is K. Thus, the analysis of the required computational capability of dealing with transactions by the one blockchain architecture which is composed of n authoritative copyright management institutions as n nodes in the chain is as the following.

(1) Each node stores m accounts, so the total number of accounts stored by all nodes is mn.
(2) Each node should exchange messages Kn^2 times for a block voting each time. In addition, in order to ensure the security and privacy of copyright information, every message has to be signed and unsigned, encrypted and decrypted, that each message needs 4 times calculations. Therefore, every block construction needs $4Kn^2$ block encryption calculations. Besides, because the number of blocks per day is $3600T/\Delta t$, each node needs to exchange messages $3600T Kn^2/\Delta t$ times per day and $14400T Kn^2/\Delta t$ blocks ciphers. Therefore, each node demands $Kn^2/\Delta t$ exchanges of messages and $4Kn^2/\Delta t$ block ciphers per second.
(3) The average number of transactions to be processed per second is $L/3600T$. Each node has to deal with each transaction, and each transaction has to be signed and unsigned, encrypted and decrypted, Therefore, it should deal with $L/3600T$ transactions per second and compute $L/900T$ transactions.
(4) Because the number of transactions per day is L, each node needs m queries per transaction, and each node needs mL queries per day, so the average number of queries per node is $mL/3600T$ per second.

In summary, when dealing with transactions with conventional single-chain architecture, any node needs to exchange $Kn^2/\Delta t$ messages per second on average, and implement $4Kn^2/\Delta t$ block encryption calculation, $L/900T$ transactions encryption calculation and $mL/3600T$ times query calculation. On the other hand, the number of transactions that one block needs to process is at least:

$$\frac{L}{\frac{3600T}{\Delta t}} = \frac{L\Delta t}{3600T}. \tag{1}$$

Assuming that the capacity of a block is C M, that is, $1.05 \times 10^6 C$ bytes, and the capacity of one transaction is about q bytes, it is necessary to satisfy formula (2). Otherwise, the saturation of the block exceeds the capacity limit, so that all transactions cannot be completed.

$$\frac{L\Delta t}{3600T} \leq \frac{1.05 \times 10^6 C}{q} \tag{2}$$

In addition, the block building time of a block mainly depends on the consensus time. Let's assume that it takes T_1 seconds for each message to be exchanged and T_2 seconds for each encryption calculation, then:

$$\Delta t = Kn^2 T_1 + 4Kn^2 T_2 \tag{3}$$

By formulas (2) and (3),

$$\frac{KL(T_1 + 4KT_2)}{3600T} n^2 \leq \frac{1.05 \times 10^6 C}{q}. \tag{4}$$

Thus

$$n \leq \sqrt{\frac{3.78 \times 10^9 CT}{qKL(T_1 + 4KT_2)}} \tag{5}$$

It's obvious that when the number of nodes in the blockchain network is large, the communication traffic will be anomalously large and the performance will be worse by single blockchain architecture. In addition, this architecture has poor scalability and requires a large amount of computational power with slow calculation and consensus, which leads to low throughput. Therefore, we consider constructing a blockchain by n RMC chains, in which each RMC chain is a blockchain consisting of n_0 nodes, where

$$n_0 = \min\left(\sqrt{\frac{3.78 \times 10^9 CT}{qKL(T_1 + 4KT_2)}}, \sqrt{n}\right) \tag{6}$$

Each copyright authority is an RMC chain composed of n_0 nodes, which uses CBFT algorithm to ensure consistency and prevent tampering. Formula (5) demonstrates that appropriate values of n_0 can ensure the security and reliability of data and improve the efficiency of consensus, thus resulting in higher throughput. Moreover, the analysis of the required computational capability of dealing with transactions by n RMC chains is shown as follows.

(1) The average number of accounts to be stored per node is m/n, so the total number of accounts to be stored by all nodes is mn_0.
(2) Each node needs to exchange messages Kn_0^2 times for a block voting each time. In addition, in order to ensure the security and privacy of copyright information, each message needs to be signed and unsigned, encrypted and decrypted. Therefore, $4Kn_0^2$ times calculations are required for a block voting.

(3) Each transaction involves at least two accounts. Assuming that there are more accounts in complex situations, such as four accounts, and all transactions are averagely divided into n RMC chains. The average number of transactions to be processed per second is $L/900nT$. Therefore, the average number of transactions per second that required to be processed by each node is $L/900nT$ and encrypted by each transaction is $L/225nT$.

(4) Since each node in each RMC chain processes $L/900nT$ transactions per second on average, each node needs $mL/900n^2T$ transaction query calculations per second, and all nodes in each RMC chain process $mn_0L/900n^2T$ transaction query calculations per second in total.

Comparing with the computing capability required by single-chain architecture, the memory required is significantly reduced, and the speed of consensus is significantly increased by using n RMC chains to process transactions in parallel. The workload of all nodes in one RMC chain is far less than that of in single-chain architecture. Therefore, the parallel processing architecture of n RMC chains greatly reduces computational power and improves throughput.

Account information is maintained through RMC chain, and TSC chain is also responsible for executing transactions and maintaining transaction data. Each RMC chain can be traded internally without the involvement of unrelated organizations. Each RMC chain participates in several TSC chains, but does not need to participate in all TSC chains. Therefore, the number of TSC chains and accounts can be changed. Normally, no more than 10 organizations participate in each transaction, so the number of TSC chains needed and the number of nodes contained in each TSC chain are much smaller than n. Thus, the workload of each node in each TSC chain is far less than that of in the single chain architecture. On the other hand, TSC chains do not store the account information of the transaction, but only obtain account information from RMC chains when needed. When the transaction is completed, TSC chains delete account information, so each node of the TSC chain needs to store account much less than m. Thus, the transaction query workload of each TSC chain is much less than that of in single-chain architecture.

4   Digital Copyright Registration and Transaction System with Double Chain Structure

4.1   System Structure Design

The most important feature of the digital copyright protection system based on blockchain technology is that the traditional data storage structure is replaced by blockchain distributed storage structure. It has the advantages of decentralization, security, traceability and tamper-proof. In order to improve the efficiency of the system, this paper designs a new digital copyright registration and transaction system based on dual blockchain architecture. The system structure is shown in Fig. 3.

The entities involved in the system are mainly shown as follows:

(1) Creator: The original creator of digital works can fill in the form with the DCI code of the digital copyright he applied for, and then the chain code of copyright

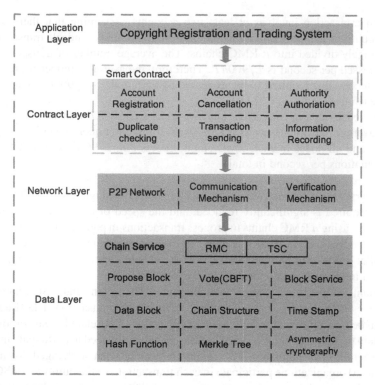

Fig. 3. Copyright registration and transaction system architecture

registration is executed. The information of the digital works, including the digital works, DCI, author, type of works, creation time, is stored on the chain.

(2) Administrators: Administrators can manage the accounts of creators and subscribers, publish new contracts to the chain, or abolish old contracts on the chain.

(3) Subscribers: Subscribers can subscribe a digital work on the chain and execute the copyright subscription chain code to obtain the right to read the digital works on the chain.

4.2   Data Interaction and Storage Mechanism for Digital Copyright Protection

The data layer in this paper adopts the blockchain bottom-layer facility composed of the CBFT consensus algorithm and the digital copyright registration data interaction and storage model based on dual blockchain. The data interaction and storage system network architecture of the digital copyright registration and transaction system based on dual blockchain is shown in Fig. 2.

When the creators should register the copyright in this system, it can initiate the transaction of digital copyright registration by logging in the system and filling in DCI and other information of digital works. When the creators want to transfer the digital copyright, it can initiate the copyright transfer transaction by inputting the new copyright owner and the digital copyright that needs to be transferred. Subsequently, the system calls the intelligent contract, deducts the copyright fee from the balance of the new copyright owner according to the pre-set copyright transfer fee, increases the copyright fee from the balance of the creator, and completes the copyright transfer transaction. In addition, other users can subscribe the digital rights and initiate copyright subscription transactions by using the relevant information filled in during copyright registration.

The main steps of digital copyright registration (or query) on RMC chain are as follows:

(1) Registration: Every user who visits RMC should first obtain an identity certificate through registration. The user's registered copyright account is generated by the public key of the user's certificate.
(2) Storage: Users log into the system and upload digital works to IPFS. If uploaded successfully, IPFS will generate unique hash values for works. Users can access digital works stored in IPFS through the hash values of works.
(3) Creation of copyright registration (or query) proposals: Users initiate copyright registration (or query) proposals through the client in which the proposal header contains the name and version of the contract. Signature is generated by the user's private key to ensure that the proposal data is not tampered with, and the proposal data is composed of the function name and parameters of the contract which are the user's input information. Different types of proposals contain different function names and transfer different function parameters. The function parameters of copyright registration proposal are composed of hash digest of digital works, access control list and user's information. Moreover, the copyright query proposal consists of hash abstract and user's identity information.
(4) Verification proposals: The client sends proposals to all nodes of an RMC chain and calls the copyright registration (or query) chain code deployed on the RMC chain. These nodes need to verify whether the proposal format is correct, whether there is a replay attack, and whether the proposal signature is valid. After the above verification, the node will simulate the execution of the copyright contract. The node needs to sign the execution result and package the proposal and execution result back to the client.
(5) Consensus confirmation: The client collects enough proposal responses, verifies the signature and execution results of the node, and submits the proposal responses to the RMC chain. All nodes will sort proposals, pack blocks and broadcast them to other nodes, and use CBFT consensus mechanism to initiate the confirmation of consensus for the generation of blocks.
(6) Block synchronization: In each RMC chain, each node randomly sends current snapshots of local accounts, such as the block height, the block hash value, the state tree hash value and other summary information of the accounts, and receives snapshots of accounts sent from other nodes, which are processed by snapshots between nodes. Account comparison and block requests ultimately make all the nodes of the network achieve a consistent state of accounts in a relatively short period of time.

The main steps of digital rights transfer (or subscription) transactions on RMC and TSC chains are as follows:

(1) Registration: Digital works creators log into the system, register their identity and obtain registration certificates and transaction certificates.
(2) Creation transaction proposals: The user successfully logs on to the client, creates a copyright transfer transaction proposal, calls relevant account information from the RMC chain, and sends the transaction proposal to each node in the TSC chain.
(3) Verification proposal: The nodes in TSC chain execute copyright transfer (or subscription) chain code. These nodes need to verify whether the proposal format is correct, check the structure of the transaction message, the integrity of the signature, whether duplicate, whether the version of the read-write collection matches, and return the proposal result to the client.
(4) Consensus confirmation: After the client collects enough nodes support, the transaction is encapsulated in the block, which is then sent to other nodes in the TSC chain, and CBFT consensus mechanism is used to initiate the consensus.
(5) Executing and recording transactions: If consensus checks are passed, TSC chain executes legal transactions and writes down the transactions. It updates metadata in blocks, records the legitimacy of transactions and other information, and modifies account information and account balance on RMC chain accordingly.

5 Experimental Results and Analysis

Throughput is a measure of a system's ability to process requests per unit time. The throughput is expressed by the number of transactions per second, which includes copyright registration, copyright transfer and subscription transactions. The throughput can be expressed as:

$$v = \frac{L_{\Delta t}}{\Delta t} \tag{7}$$

Where Δt is the consensus interval, and $L_{\Delta t}$ is the number of transactions contained in a block.

According to the algorithm proposed in this paper, we implement the algorithm in Java language. Based on the copyright registration data, the blockchain network is constructed, and the throughput is used as the evaluation index to compare with multiple blockchain platforms. Figure 4 shows that the system has the characteristics of high throughput than others.

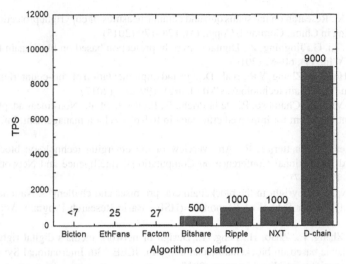

Fig. 4. Throughput comparison between the proposed algorithm and other blockchain platforms

6 Conclusion

At present, many digital copyright protection systems based on centralized copyright management mechanism have high maintenance cost, ease of privacy disclosure, data tampering and vulnerability to attack. This paper analyses the pain points of current digital copyright protection and proposes a digital copyright registration and transaction system based on dual blockchain to separate account information from transaction information. In the future, we can continue to improve the system in terms of how to meet users' demand more safely and efficiently.

Acknowledgements. This research was funded by the Fujian Provincial Natural Science Foundation of China (Grant 2018J01570) and the CERNET Innovation Project (Grant NGII20170411).

References

1. Park, H., Yoon, H., Hwang, J.: Prospect of the next-generation digital content industry: three perspective approach to the user acceptance of the realistic content technology. In: 18th International Conference on Advanced Communication Technology (ICACT), pp. 675–680. IEEE (2016)
2. Ma, Z.: Digital rights management: model, technology and application. China Commun. **14**(6), 156–167 (2017)
3. Baratè, A., Haus, G., Ludovico, L.A., Perlasca, P.: Managing intellectual property in a music fruition environment. IEEE MultiMed. **23**(2), 84–94 (2016)
4. Yuan, Y., Wang, F.Y.: Current status and prospects of Blockchain technology development. J. Autom. **42**(4), 481–494 (2016)
5. Fan, K.F., Mo, W., Cao, S., et al.: Progress in digital rights management technology and application. Chin. J. Electron. **35**(6), 1139–1147 (2007)

6. Zhai, Y.X.: Research on the status quo and countermeasures of copyright protection in digital publishing in China. Commun. Copyr. (3), 178–179 (2015)
7. Jian, W., Li, G., Jingning, Z.: Digital copyright protection based on blockchain technology. Radio TV Inf. (7), 60–62 (2016)
8. An, R., He, D.B., Zhang, Y.R., et al.: Design and implementation of anti-counterfeiting system based on Blockchain technology. CMD J. 4(2), 199–208 (2017)
9. Casado-Vara, R., Chamoso, P., De la Prieta, F., Prieto, J., et al.: Non-linear adaptive closed-loop control system for improved efficiency in IoT-blockchain management. Inf. Fusion 49, 227–239 (2019)
10. Chatterjee, R., Chatterjee, R.: An overview of the emerging technology: blockchain. In: 2017 3rd International Conference on Computational Intelligence and Networks (CINE), pp. 126–127 (2017)
11. Savelyev, A.: Copyright in the blockchain era: promises and challenges. National Research University Higher School of Economics (HSE), Basic Research Program Working Paper (2017)
12. Xu, R., Zhang, L., Zhao, H., Peng, Y.: Design of network media's digital rights management scheme based on blockchain technology. In: IEEE 13th International Symposium on Autonomous Decentralized Systems (2017)
13. Meng, Z., Morizumi, T., Miyata, S., et al.: Design scheme of copyright management system based on digital watermarking and blockchain. In: 2018 IEEE 42nd Annual Computer Software and Applications Conference (COMPSAC), vol. 2, pp. 359–364. IEEE Computer Society (2018)
14. Nakamoto, S.: Bitcoin: A peer-to-peer electronic cash system. Consulted (2008)
15. Nguyen, Q.K.: Blockchain-a financial technology for future sustainable development. In: 2016 3rd International Conference on Green Technology and Sustainable Development (GTSD), pp. 51–54 (2016)
16. Bradbury, D.: Blockchain's big deal. Eng. Technol. 11(10), 44–47 (2016)
17. Swan, M.: Blockchain: Blueprint for a New Economy. O'Reilly Media Inc., Newton (2015)
18. Tsai, W.T., Yu, L., Wang, R., Liu, N., Deng, E.Y.: Blockchain application development techniques. J. Softw. 28(6), 1474–1487 (2017)
19. King, S., Nadal, S.: PPCoin: Peer-to-Peer Crypto-Currency with Proof-of-Stake (2012)
20. Lamport, L., Shostak, R., Pease, M.: The Byzantine generals problem. ACM Trans. Program. Lang. Syst. (TOPLAS) 4(3), 382–401 (1982)
21. Castro, M., Liskov, B.: Practical Byzantine fault tolerance. In: Proceedings of the USENIX Association, pp. 173–186 (1999)
22. Kosba, A., Miller, A., Shi, E., et al.: Hawk: the blockchain model of cryptography and privacy-preserving smart contracts. In: 2016 IEEE Symposium on Security and Privacy (SP), pp. 839–858. IEEE (2016)
23. Sicilia, M.-A., Sánchez-Alonso, S., García-Barriocanal, E.: Sharing linked open data over peer-to-peer distributed file systems: the case of IPFS. In: Garoufallou, E., Subirats Coll, I., Stellato, A., Greenberg, J. (eds.) MTSR 2016. CCIS, vol. 672, pp. 3–14. Springer, Cham (2016). https://doi.org/10.1007/978-3-319-49157-8_1

Nebula: A Blockchain Based Decentralized Sharing Computing Platform

Bin Yan, Pengfei Chen$^{(\boxtimes)}$, Xiaoyun Li, and Yongfeng Wang

School of Data Science and Computing, Sun Yat-sen University, Guangzhou, China
{yanb25,chenpf7,lixy223,wangyf226}@mail2.sysu.edu.cn

Abstract. Nowadays, there is a considerable amount of idle computers whose computing resources are partially wasted. On the other hand, the demand of resources is rapidly growing, since the explosion of data and the complexity of algorithms. To settle the contradictions, we develop Nebula, a decentralized platform based on blockchain for sharing computing resources. Nebula leverages blockchain to gather the scattered computing resources and provide a secure and vibrant computation trading market. Compared to traditional cloud platform, Nebula guarantees extra security because all transactions in this platform are validated by smart contracts. No one can tamper the transaction orders which are recorded by a widely distributed ledger. In Nebula, the resource consumer can order resources from resource providers with a very simple declarative script. When a deal is done, consumers can submit jobs to suppliers with a docker instance. Moreover, we model the order matching procedure of users' requests into a global maximum matching problem in a bipartite graph. We adopt the Hungarian algorithm to find an order matching policy, bringing an 10% increase to the matching rate in our best case. Moreover, we leverage the Proof of Authority (PoA) consensus algorithm called Clique, rather than Proof of Work (PoW) to increase the efficiency of Nebula, which provides nearly no less security but requires negligible computation on reaching consensus. To our best knowledge, we are the first to propose a general blockchain based platform for sharing computing resources, which fully utilizes the features of blockchain to achieve the scalability, the optimal order matching and a high performance.

Keywords: Blockchain · Cloud computing · Smart contract · Ethereum · Resource sharing

1 Introduction

Last decade has witnessed the growing demand of computational resources, as researchers have to deal with larger data and more complex algorithms. Especially with the advent of Big Data and Artificial Intelligence (AI), massive computation resources are needed including CPU and GPU. On the contrary, a considerable amount of devices, such as PC and servers in the data center are always running under low utilization [5,6,14]. For example, as stated by [5], 80% of servers

© Springer Nature Singapore Pte Ltd. 2020
Z. Zheng et al. (Eds.): BlockSys 2019, CCIS 1156, pp. 715–731, 2020.
https://doi.org/10.1007/978-981-15-2777-7_58

in Google's data center are running under 20% utilization. These computers show a great potential to fill the requirement gap but fail to gather together and being scheduled. Highly distributed devices around the world currently are not reliably connected and arranged to meet the requirement of the users.

As for organizing the public computing resource, some systems such as BOINC [1], SETI [18] are successful pioneers. However, the computing resources are joined in a volunteer way which makes them are unstable. Moreover, they are designed for some specific jobs especially for science computing. People need a long-time learning curve to run their jobs in such a platform. Recently, the blockchain technology has been proposed and widely studied in both of academic world and industry world [2–4,12,15,16,21,22]. From one survey [23], we can see there are many fields where Blockchain can be applied.

Due to the tamper-resistant, security, and token based ecology of Blockchain, it has been widely used in many fields such as food tracking, currency exchange and so on. Recently, a novel kind of cloud computing named decentralized cloud computing driven by Blockchain emerges such as Golem [10], iEXEC [11], SONM [19], UChain [20]. Although they are capable to run decentralized applications on their chains, they are not sufficient to support general computing. SONM [19] is the most similar to our paper. However, it does not provide an global optimal order matching policy, which leads to a low efficiency. To integrate the idle resources and overcome the drawbacks of existing systems, we develop Nebula, a decentralized platform based on Ethereum [7] for computational resources sharing.

Two main problems should be resolved for any sharing platform like Nebula. The first one is security. In our implementation, smart contract, as a validator, ensures every attempt to modify the system (e.g. a user's request) is legal and all the data accepted by the system is consistent. The blockchain technique itself further makes sure that data is unmodified and trusty.

The second one is stimulation. Nebula, like an ecosystem of *Sharing Economy*, should fairly reward suppliers and charge consumers. Nebula leverages a cryptocurrency called Nebula Token as a payment of computational resources. Nebula Token is free to transfer to/from Ether (i.e., Ethereum Token) [7] and for every transaction an indicative price will be proposed, which both reduce the fluctuation of its value.

Nebula has a specially designed architecture. It fully utilizes the feature of blockchain technique. All the business logic functions of the system are written in smart contracts [13], which are mainly deployed in our customized blockchain, the *sidechain*. The sidechain connects with Ethereum, or the *mainchain*, by a smart contract called *channel*. Other peripheral components including Data Cache (DC), NAT-service (Network Address Transformation service), etc, provide extra features or support to the system, as described in detail in Sect. 3.

In the matching step between suppliers and customers' orders, we model orders into a bipartite graph and apply Hungarian algorithm to promote the matching rate. After the optimization, the matching procedure costs nearly the same time but gets an increase of 10% matching rate in our case.

The contributions of this paper are summarized as follows. **First**, we introduce Nebula, the blockchain based decentralized platform for sharing computing resources. We present the components, their functions and the utilization of the blockchain technique in detail. **Second**, we show the optimization of the order matching procedure and the performance gain by experiments.

The rest of the paper is organized as follows. In Sect. 2 we discuss the motivation and show the overview. In Sects. 3 and 4, we talk about the detailed implementation of the system. Then we evaluate our system in Sect. 5, including the cost of matching procedure and the throughput of the system. At last, we conclude the paper in Sect. 6.

2 Motivation and System Overview

Our motivation is around the contradictions between current requirements of computing and the idle computing resources. In recent years, data has been growing explosively fast and the algorithm has become much more complex. They bring great challenges to researcher's available computing resources. It is not practical for individuals or organizations to purchase machines infinitely to come up with the demand.

On the other hand, a considerable amount of devices around the world are idle, indicating great potential to fill the requirement gap. The solution to the contradiction is a platform which gathers and schedules idle devices, regardless of their locations, types and performance. Next, we introduce Nebula in a nutshell, a decentralized platform based on Ethereum [7] for sharing computing resources.

2.1 Decentralization

Decentralization is an important feature of Blockchain. It allows trading between peers without centralized organizations. The decentralization presents in two ways. (i) **The backend**. Nebula sits on Ethereum, a distributed peer-to-peer platform. It provides a high availability and reliability and maintains the validity of data. (ii) **The resources**. Nebula is more of an agency than a provider because the resource Nebula provided is owned by end users from all over the world. Some of users, called suppliers, contribute their devices into the system with Nebula Token as a reward, while other users, called customers, pay for the usage of devices with Nebula Token.

2.2 Ethereum Based System

As a Ethereum-backed system, Nebula fully utilizes the feature of Ethereum, such as the smart contract technique, the digital currency and its immutability of data.

Smart Contract. The smart contract is a major component of Ethereum, intended to digitally enforce the performance of codes. It is deployed to the blockchain by the administrator after the initialization of the blockchain. The deployed contract is stored as a transaction in the system, hence it is immutable and transparent. In Nebula, the smart contract implements almost all the business logic. *The Market contract* especially accepts users' orders and validates requests. Other contracts support, for example, the persistent storage of orders, the validation of deals and a channel for token circulation as described in Sect. 3, etc.

Digital Currency. Ether is a fundamental token for the operation of Ethereum. Based on Ether, Nebula introduces *Nebula Token* as a payment for transactions between buyers (i.e., customers) and sellers (i.e.,suppliers). Nebula proposes an indicative price for every transaction and fix the exchange rate between Ether and Nebula Token to avoid fluctuation. The indicative price is given by a regression model based on our history transaction prices. We leave it as a future work to build a more sophisticated and accurate model. Nebula Token will be the main stimulation for device owners to join the system.

Immutability. All transactions on the Ethereum blockchain are immutable. Any manipulated transaction invalidates the PoW (Proof of Work) and thus will be rejected. Nebula utilizes this kind of immutability and stores all the transaction data in the blockchain.

3   Detailed Design of Nebula

In this section, we demonstrate the design of the system in detail. We show the architecture of the system and introduce important smart contracts, especially the *market* and *channel* contracts. Then, we describe the workflow of token circulation. Lastly, we show the optimization of the order matching procedure and then describe and analyze the Hungarian algorithm.

```
time: 2h              ------------------------- the order duration
price: 0.1 RMB/h      ------------------------- the price of this order
resources:            ------------------------- define the buy/sell resources
   network:           ------------------------- network resource
      bandwidth: 2 Mbits/s
   cpu:               ------------------------- the number of cpu cores
      cores: 1
   memory:            ------------------------- the volume of memory
      size: 1GB
   gpu:               ------------------------- the number of GPU
      num: 1
```

Fig. 1. An example of declarative script for resource demand.

3.1   Architecture

We describe how the user interacts with the system before introducing the step to launch the system and the function of peripheral services.

Usage. Here we introduce the typical workflow of users. Firstly, (a) the customer should describe his demand of resources with a declarative script. The script expresses as a YAML file shown in Fig. 1. After scripts being parsed by the *client*, the order is placed to the system with the help of the *node service*, which hides the complex interaction. Then, (b) the supplier can join his machine by running the *worker service*, which benchmarks the device and establishes a connection to Nebula. The supplier is required to explicitly confirm his devices, and sends his request of provision the same way as the customer does. Finally, if the supplier's provision is satisfactory to the customer's demand, a deal is done and each side will be notified. Then the customer can submit tasks to the supplier's worker machine with a docker instance.

Launch of Nebula. Launching Nebula includes building the blockchains, deploying the contracts and starting the significant services.

Nebula is built on top of two blockchains, a *mainchain* and a *sidechain*. The mainchain essentially is the Ethereum. The sidechain is a Nebula-specific blockchain where our contracts are deployed. A separated sidechain isolates a stable and controllable environment to operate and maintain the system. To allow token to circulate between blockchains, a channel contract is deployed onto both blockchains as a connector. Other indispensable *peripheral services* serve differently as described below in detail.

Figure 2 shows the main architecture of Nebula. To launch Nebula, (1) we firstly build the sidechain and deploy the smart contracts in the sidechain. Particularly, the channel contract is also deployed and the circulation between the mainchain and the sidechain is thus established. Then, (2) the *DC (Data Cache)* service and (3) the *NAT-service* are launched in sequence and the system is now ready to response to users' request.

Peripheral Services. Here we introduce other building bricks of Nebula, DC and the NAT-service. Every peer in the sidechain is required to maintain a cache service called DC (Data Cache), in order to reduce the response delay. DC is essentially a server with a database, which caches and tracks the state of the sidechain, responses the query from users and asynchronously sends requests to the sidechain on behalf of the users.

Nebula also contains NAT-service for users across different subnets to connect with each other. The service also allows the supplier to control their worker machines in a different subnet.

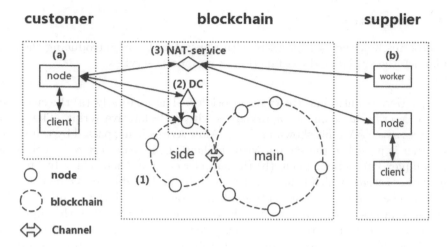

Fig. 2. Nebula architecture. Mainchain stands for Ethereum. Sidechain is a Nebula-specific blockchain where contracts are deployed. Two blockchains are interacted by a channel.

3.2 Networking

In practice, the customer and the supplier may not locate in the same subnet. Even worse, the machine owner and his cluster are likely to be separated in the network, which prevents the owner from managing his devices. To support the cross-network communication, Nebula provides an *NAT-service* to establish a tunnel, by which the real-time communication can be performed.

3.3 Consensus Algorithm

We leverage PoA rather than the traditional PoW algorithm to achieve consensus in the sidechain, achieving a much less mining delay and reducing the waste of resources. We choose the *Clique PoA* algorithm as it is used stably for years in the famous Rinkeby testnet [17].

In Clique, a block is authored if it is signed by a peer from the list of authorized signers. The cost of signing is negligible compared to the PoW computation. Every signer is only allowed to sign one out of *SIGNER-LIMIT* consecutive blocks to protect the network from being damaged by the malicious user. The authorized user list is set in the genesis block, and changes as users being voted in or out.

3.4 Smart Contract

Computation Market. The smart contract *Market* implements the market of the system, where orders are accepted, validated, stored and finally matched one-to-one. Various functions are defined in the Market contract that handle the creation, cancelation and modification of the orders, as well as the joining and exiting of devices.

Listing 1.1. Pseudocode Code of function PlaceOrder

```
contract Market {
    ...
    function PlaceOrder(
        UserType userType,
        uint duration,
        uint price,
        uint[] benchmarks
    ) returns (uint) {
        /* omit validation codes here */
        if (userType == UserType.CUSTOMER) {
            uint lockedSum = calculate payment for an hour;
            if (fail to transfer lockedSum token to msg.sender) {
                error("failed to prepay a unit of token");
            }
        }

        ordersAmount = ordersAmount + 1;
        uint orderId = ordersAmount;
        orders[orderId] = Order(
            userType, msg.sender,
            duration, price, benchmarks,
        );
        emit OrderPlaced(orderId);
        return orderId;
    }
}
```

Listing 1.1 shows the function *PlaceOrder* as an example, the handler for the creation of orders. The function accepts parameters like a user type (one of supplier or customer), the duration of the task, the bid price and a set of benchmarks specifying the amount of resources. After the place-order request is sent to the system, the validation will be performed at the earliest (omitted in the listing codes). Then a unit of token is prepaid to the intermediate account as an advance fee (Line 10–14). Otherwise the request will be rejected if the transfer fails. Next, the order is persistently stored into the system (Line 18–24). Lastly, the function call succeeds, as an event is emitted and the index of the order (*orderId*) is returned.

Channel and Nebula Token. A special method named channel is applied to allow token circulation between mainchain (Ethereum) and our sidechain. A token circulation from Ethereum to the sidechain takes the following steps, as illustrated by Fig. 3.

- The user transfers his Ether to the channel account on Ethereum.
- The Nebula administrator(a privileged daemon) notifies the channel on the sidechain.

– The sidechain channel, with a nearly infinite amount of Nebula Token obtained on deployment, finally transfers the equivalent Nebula Token to the user.

The user is free to get his Ether back to Ethereum in the opposite way, or exchange between Nebula Token and Ether on the sidechain.

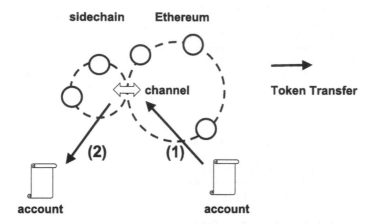

Fig. 3. Demonstration of token circulation between Ethereum and our sidechain.

3.5 Order Description

Users can buy or sell the resources by sending an *order* to the system. An order consists of a plenty of fields including the user type, the duration, the bid price and the specification of the resources, such as the number of CPU cores, the capacity of the memory and the storage device, etc. We generally embed the order into a vector in the order assigning procedure (see Sect. 3.6), with the user type discarded.

3.6 Order Assigning

Order assigning is the procedure to assign a satisfactory supplier's order to a customer's one. We say a supplier's order is *satisfactory*, if the duration and the resources offered by the supplier is no less than what the customer requests. Moreover, the price from the supplier is lower than that from the customer.

The orders arrive in the system continuously. To simplify the design of the matching step, orders are buffered before issued to the matching algorithm batch by batch. The order which fails to find his counterpart by the algorithm will be recalled to the buffer and wait for the next try.

To obtain the maximum matching rate, we transform the batch of orders into a bipartite graph and adopt the Hungarian algorithm to find the perfect (maximum) matching.

Order Embedding and Graph Construction. A customer's or supplier's order is turned into a vector $V_C \in \mathbb{R}^n (V_S \in \mathbb{R}^n)$, with the duration, the bid price and the resources included.

Our ultimate goal is to match orders between two groups of users, namely customers and suppliers. It is equivalent to find a maximum matching of a bipartite graph between two vertex sets, the customer's vector set and the supplier's vector set.

Here we show Algorithm 1 to construct the bipartite graph. Initiate the graph with empty edge and vertex (line 1). For each vector provided as input, add a corresponding vertex to the graph representing the vector (line 2–7). For each vertex pair (V_C^i, V_S^j) from customer's vertex set and supplier's vertex set, we examine whether V_S^j is satisfactory to V_C^i, i.e. $V_C^i \prec V_S^j$. The *partial order* is defined over the vector as Definition 1. The returned result by Algorithm 1 is a bipartite graph.

Definition 1. *For any two vectors $V, U \in \mathbb{R}^n$, we define $V \prec U \iff \forall i \in \mathbb{Z}$, $V_i < U_i, 0 \le i < n$*

Algorithm 1. Graph Construction

Data: customer's order embedding matrix $M_C = [V_C^1 \cdots V_C^n]$ and supplier's one
$\quad\quad M_S = [V_S^1 \cdots V_S^m]$
Result: a constructed bipartite graph
1 $G \leftarrow (V, E)$;   // G is an empty Graph denoted by empty vertex V and edge E
2 **for** V_C^i in M_C **do**
3 $\quad\mid$ $V.add(V_C^i)$;
4 **end**
5 **for** V_S^i in M_S **do**
6 $\quad\mid$ $V.add(V_S^i)$;
7 **end**
8 **for** V_C^i in M_C **do**
9 $\quad\mid$ **for** V_S^i in M_S **do**
10 $\quad\mid\quad\mid$ **if** $V_C^i \prec V_S^j$ **then**
11 $\quad\mid\quad\mid\quad\mid$ $E.add((V_C^i, V_S^j))$;
12 $\quad\mid\quad\mid$ **end**
13 $\quad\mid$ **end**
14 **end**
15 **return** G

Hungarian Algorithm. Finally, we adopt Hungarian algorithm (Algorithm 2) to find the maximum matching. Figure 4 shows a tiny example for the algorithm. The idea behind it is simple. For every vertex in a part, we try to find its

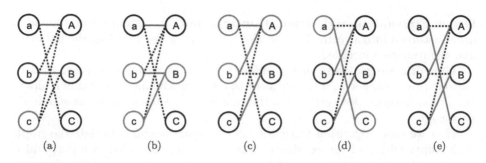

Fig. 4. Hungarian algorithm example. (a) Initially "a" matches "A", "b" matches "B". "c" is left over and to be matched. (b) There is no available counterpart for "c", so "c" preempts "b" and gets its counterpart "B". (c) There is no available counterpart for "b", so "b" preempts "a" and gets its counterpart "A". (d) "a" has another available counterpart "C", so "C" is assigned to "a". (e) The final result of the matching.

counterpart in the other part. If there are available counterparts, assign one of them to the vertex. If all of its candidate counterparts have been assigned, we "grab" one of the unavailable counterpart and recursively try to find a new counterpart for the unlucky grabbed one. Figure 4(b)–(d) illustrates the process in detail.

Algorithm 2. Hungarian algorithm

Data: adjacency matrix of a bipartite graph $G \in \{\text{True}, \text{False}\}^{n \times n}$
Result: a counterpart array $C \in \mathbb{Z}^n$
1 $C \leftarrow [-1 \cdots -1];$ // -1 means counterpart not found
2 $V \leftarrow [\text{False} \cdots \text{False}];$ // V[i] represents whether the i-th node has been visited
3 $i \leftarrow 0;$
4 **while** $i < n$ **do**
5 | $V \leftarrow [\text{False} \cdots \text{False}];$
6 | $Find(i);$
7 | $i \leftarrow i + 1;$
8 **end**
9 **return** C

Here we calculate the time complexity of the matching step. The graph construction step compares every pair of orders from two sets, thus it costs $O((\frac{n}{2})^2) = O(n^2)$, where n is the total number of orders. It is easy to show that the complexity of the Hungarian algorithm is $O(V \cdot E)$, noting that for every vertex in the graph, *Find* costs no more than $O(E)$ and *Find* is invoked for every vertex. Thus the overall complexity of the matching is $O(V^2 + VE)$, where $O(n) = O(V)$.

The complexity of the matching step is almost the same as the naive First Fit algorithm, especially when the number of order is under a couple of thousands. However, the Hungarian algorithm raises the matching rate by 10% in the best case, as shown in Sect. 5.

Deal Opening. When two orders are matched, a corresponding *deal* is opened to record the matching relationship of the orders. Listing 1.2 shows the implementation of function *OpenDeal*, which handles the validating and recording of the deal. The function firstly checks the consistency of the opening deal, such as the user types, the constraint of price, duration and the benchmarks (Line 7–13). The constraint of the numeric fields should be trivially satisfied, since the order assigning procedure only matches satisfactory ones. After passing all the requirement check, the deal is recorded on the blockchain and an event is emitted to mark the success.

3.7 Delivery of Computing Resources

The computing resources are delivered by means of running the customer's task on the supplier's working machine. To get his working machine ready, the supplier (1) binds the address of the working machine with his personal account, and (2) places a selling request to the system. After the orders are matched between the customer and supplier, both users are able to query their counterpart and the status of the order from the command line.

To assign a task to the working machine, the customer (1) builds a docker image which contains the code and its corresponding data, and (2) uploads the image to a public image repository like Docker Hub. Then, the customer (3)

Algorithm 3. Find

Data: index $i \in \mathbb{Z}^+$ of a node to look for its counterpart
Result: True if succeed, False otherwise

1 **for** $t \leftarrow 0$; $t < n$; $t \leftarrow t + 1$ **do**
2 $\quad$ **if** $G[i][t]$ *and* $!V[t]$ **then**
3 $\quad\quad$ $V[t] \leftarrow$ True;
4 $\quad\quad$ **if** $C[t] == -1$ *or* $Find(C[t])$ **then**
5 $\quad\quad\quad$ $C[i] = t$;
6 $\quad\quad\quad$ $C[t] = i$;
7 $\quad\quad\quad$ return True
8 $\quad\quad$ **end**
9 $\quad$ **end**
10 **end**
11 return False

---

informs the working machine to run the task by providing the image repository and the image tag. Notified by the request, a piece of script in the working machine pulls and runs the image and sends the execution log back to the customer.

The following reasons make us choose docker to deliver tasks. **First**, docker provides stable operation. A docker image packs up the code with the supportive environment, which conceals the uncertainty of the counterpart machine. **Second**, docker has negligible run-time overhead compared to the virtual machine. The containers share the machine's OS system kernel and therefore do not require an OS per application. **Third**, the cgroups technique allows controllable delivery of resources. cgroups is a Linux kernel feature that limits and isolates the resource usage of a collection of processes. Every task launched by Nebula is limited to what written in the supplier's provision order.

3.8 Payment Strategy

The payment strategy mainly focuses on credibility and fairness. Credibility is obviously realized, since Nebula is built upon Ethereum and mainly implements its business logic in smart contracts. We will talk about achieving fairness in detail. Here we define fairness as nobody is able to earn an extra benefits (token or computing resources) by any means.

When a customer places an order to the system, an advance charge will be paid to an intermediary address. If the prepay fails, the transaction will be reverted by the sidechain and thus the request is rejected. After the task begins, tokens will be continuously transferred from the customer to the supplier with the intermediary address as an agent. Only after the working machine finishes his round, the token will be transferred to the supplier's account. If the order is illegally canceled, the prepaid token will be sent to his counterpart as a compensation. Because of this prepaying strategy, a dishonest user is not able to steal tokens/resources by any means.

4   Implementation of Nebula

Nebula is a complicated system. The implementation of Nebula involves various programming languages like Go and Python and open source tools. The components are interacting by gRPC, a language-neutral framework with high performance to perform remote procedure calls. The number of code has exceeded 50 thousands of lines.

Listing 1.2. Pseudocode Code of function OpenDeal

```
contract Market {
    ...
    function OpenDeal(uint buyID, uint sellID) {
        Order buy = orders[buyID];
        Order sell = orders[sellID];

        require(buy.userType == UserType.COSTUMER);
        require(sell.userType == UserType.SUPPLIER);
        require(sell.price <= buy.price);
        require(sell.duration >= buy.duration);
        for (i = 0; i < sup.benchmarks.length; i++) {
            require(sell.benchmarks[i] >= buy.benchmarks[i]);
        }

        dealAmount = dealAmount + 1;
        deals[dealAmount] = Deal(
            sell.benchmarks, _sellID, _buyID, buy.duration, sell.price
        );
        emit DealOpened(dealAmount);
    }
}
```

4.1 Services

Most components in Nebula are designed as services to make it accessible by the third-part software. For example, the node service, the DC service and the worker service are shown in Sect. 3. All services in Nebula are implemented in Golang. The reason we prefer it to other languages like C++, Java is that it is efficient and it naturally supports multi-threading, which is convenient for asynchronous communication. Golang proves to be a good language to implement a service in practice.

4.2 Smart Contract

The smart contracts are written in solidity [7] with version ^0.4.20. In the production environment, we use Geth [9] to build a blockchain and use Truffle to compile and deploy the contract.

We choose a mature solution called Truffle Suite, a group of open-source tools for the blockchain developer. Included in Truffle Suite, Ganache [8] is used to build the mock blockchain, Truffle is used to compile, deploy and debug the contracts, and Dizzle is used to develop the frontend of the web interface.

4.3 Web Interfaces

Nebula provides a GUI interface based on web to help non-programmers to interact with Nebula. The backend for the website is essentially some of the services or components mentioned in Sect. 3, such as DC and sidechain.

5   Experimental Validations

5.1   Throughput of Sending Orders

The major delay of sending an order comes from mining in the blockchain. Besides, other factors affect the delay, including the state of the network, the performance of the machine and so on. To avoid the influence and reveal the standard performance of Nebula, we instead show the relationship between the block interval and the average delay of placing an order.

We build the blockchain using Ganache with the parameter *blockTime* set ascendingly from 0 s to 16 s, which simulates the various mining delay in practice. As a comparison, the mining delay is 10 s–20 s in the Rinkeby testnet.

We sequentially place orders and record the average response time. To test the throughput, we concurrently send orders to the system and record the average delay. Figure 5 shows the experiment result. It is obvious that the response time approximates to the block interval, since a request is acknowledged only after the corresponding block has been signed. The throughput is much higher than the serial case, with an increase of 43% in the best case.

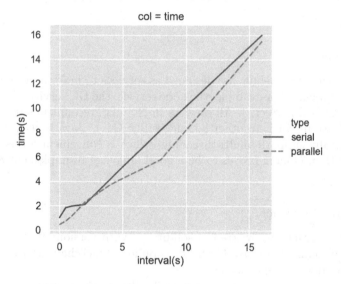

Fig. 5. Throughput of Nebula.

5.2   Matching Rate of Hungarian Algorithm

We design experiments to compare the successful matching rate of Hungarian algorithm against two benchmarks, the First Fit algorithm and Best Fit algorithm.

We firstly show the implementation of the benchmarks. The First Fit algorithm assigns the *first* satisfactory supplier's order to the customer's one. The Best Fit algorithm assigns the *closest* order among the satisfactory ones to the customer. The distance between orders is measured by the euclidean distance between two corresponding embedded vectors.

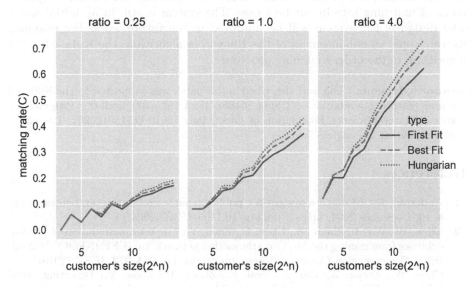

Fig. 6. Matching rate of the customers' order. ratio = number of suppliers/number of customers

Figure 6 shows the matching rate of customers' order under the variety of the number of supplier's order. The matching rate of the Hungarian algorithm is always the highest among any other algorithms, as it is capable to find the maximum matching.

When the number of customer's orders is about four times than the supplier's, the matching rate (for the supplier's order) among the algorithms is nearly the same, since its counterpart's number is adequate and the naive algorithm could perform just as well. However, when the number of supplier's orders exceeds the customer's, the Hungarian algorithm shows huge performance improvement compared to the naive algorithms. Inspired by the result, Nebula will automatically choose between the Hungarian algorithm and Best Fit algorithm, according to the ratio of the orders. A higher matching rate avoids the rematch of the orders and thus can highly speed up the matching step.

6 Conclusion

This paper introduces Nebula, a blockchain based decentralized platform for sharing computing resources. To our best knowledge, Nebula is the first platform that fully utilizes the features of blockchain and avoids the weakness by peripheral services, such as data cache and the NAT-service. We emphasize on the novel architecture with two blockchains, i.e., the Ethereum and the sidechain. We also show how other peripheral services are deployed upon the sidechain. Lastly, we examine the throughput of placing orders and shows the average delay. We also present the adoption of the famous Hungarian algorithm and the 10% improvement of matching rate in our best case. The system is still in an initial stage. The design of the system will be improved in the future work. For example, we can apply an enhancement of the Hungarian algorithm, the Kuhn-Munkres algorithm, to the order matching procedure.

Acknowledgments. The work described in this paper was supported by the National Natural Science Foundation of China (61802448, U1811462) and the Program for National Natural Science Foundation of Guangdong (2019A1515012229). The corresponding author is Pengfei Chen.

References

1. Anderson, D.: BOINC: a system for public-resource computing and storage, pp. 4–10, December 2004. https://doi.org/10.1109/GRID.2004.14
2. Chen, W., Wu, J., Zheng, Z., Chen, C., Zhou, Y.: Market manipulation of bitcoin: evidence from mining the Mt. Gox transaction network. In: IEEE INFOCOM 2019-IEEE Conference on Computer Communications, pp. 964–972. IEEE (2019)
3. Chen, W., Zheng, Z., Cui, J., Ngai, E., Zheng, P., Zhou, Y.: Detecting Ponzi Schemes on Ethereum: towards healthier blockchain technology. In: Proceedings of the 2018 World Wide Web Conference, pp. 1409–1418 (2018)
4. Dai, H., Zheng, Z., Zhang, Y.: Blockchain for Internet of Things: a survey. CoRR abs/1906.00245 (2019). http://arxiv.org/abs/1906.00245
5. Delimitrou, C., Kozyrakis, C.: Quasar: resource-efficient and QoS-aware cluster management. In: 19th International Conference on Architectural Support for Programming Languages and Operating Systems (ASPLOS) (2014)
6. Delimitrou, C., Kozyrakis, C.: Paragon: QoS-aware scheduling for heterogeneous datacenters, vol. 41, pp. 77–88, May 2013. https://doi.org/10.1145/2490301.2451125
7. Ethereum. https://www.ethereum.org/
8. Ganache. https://www.trufflesuite.com/ganache
9. Geth website. https://github.com/ethereum/go-ethereum/wiki/Geth
10. Golem. https://golem.network/
11. Iexec. https://iex.ec/
12. Li, Z., Kang, J., Yu, R., Ye, D., Deng, Q., Zhang, Y.: Consortium blockchain for secure energy trading in industrial Internet of Things. IEEE Trans. Industr. Inf. **14**(8), 3690–3700 (2017)
13. Luu, L., Chu, D.H., Olickel, H., Saxena, P., Hobor, A.: Making smart contracts smarter. In: Proceedings of the 2016 ACM SIGSAC Conference on Computer and Communications Security, CCS 2016, pp. 254–269. ACM, New York (2016). https://doi.org/10.1145/2976749.2978309
14. Mars, J., Tang, L., Skadron, K., Soffa, M.L., Hundt, R.: Increasing utilization in modern warehouse-scale computers using bubble-up. IEEE Micro **32**(3), 88–99 (2012). https://doi.org/10.1109/MM.2012.22

15. Nakamoto, S., et al.: Bitcoin: a peer-to-peer electronic cash system (2008)
16. Qiu, X., Liu, L., Chen, W., Hong, Z., Zheng, Z.: Online deep reinforcement learning for computation offloading in blockchain-empowered mobile edge computing. IEEE Trans. Veh. Technol. **68**(8), 8050–8062 (2019)
17. Rinkeby testnet. https://www.rinkeby.io/#stats
18. Seti@home. https://setiathome.ssl.berkeley.edu/
19. Sonm. https://sonm.com/
20. Uchain. https://uchain.world/
21. Wang, J., Wang, H.: Monoxide: scale out blockchains with asynchronous consensus zones. In: 16th {USENIX} Symposium on Networked Systems Design and Implementation ({NSDI} 19), pp. 95–112 (2019)
22. Zheng, P., Zheng, Z., Luo, X., Chen, X., Liu, X.: A detailed and real-time performance monitoring framework for blockchain systems. In: 2018 IEEE/ACM 40th International Conference on Software Engineering: Software Engineering in Practice Track (ICSE-SEIP), pp. 134–143. IEEE (2018)
23. Zheng, Z., Xie, S., Dai, H.N., Chen, X., Wang, H.: Blockchain challenges and opportunities: a survey. Int. J. Web Grid Serv. **14**(4), 352–375 (2018)

A Novel Vehicle Blockchain Model Based on Hyperledger Fabric for Vehicle Supply Chain Management

Kun Wang, Mingzhe Liu(✉), Xin Jiang, Chen Yang, and Hong Zhang

State Key Laboratory of Geohazard Prevention and Geoenvironment Protection,
Chengdu University of Technology, Chengdu 610059, China
liumz@cdut.edu.cn

Abstract. Counterfeit vehicle parts bring about huge economic losses to the legitimate parts industry and serious injury to users. It is difficult to identify counterfeits since very few participants have end-to-end visibility of products across their supply chain. This paper aims to explore the potential of blockchain in solving complex supply chain processes. We provide a blockchain-based vehicle supply chain management to replace rigid supply chains, resulting in more efficient and secure service for all participants. To verify the feasibility of proposed management, we simulated vehicle supply chain in Hyperledger Fabric. We use Hyperledger Caliper to conduct the performance of proposed system in terms of transactions per second and transaction latency. The simulation results show the proposed model could be used for vehicle supply chain in a real environment.

Keywords: Counterfeit · Vehicle · Supply chain · Blockchain · Hyperledger Fabric

1 Introduction

With the emergence of information and communication technology, economic globalization makes the global trade become possible, and a growing number of companies depend on multiple suppliers to provide parts and ingredients. The ever-present problems, such as a lack of transparency, accountability across supply chains, counterfeit products reduce the efficiency and reliability that exist between business participants.

Counterfeit vehicle parts are a $ 45 billion-dollar problem in the global market. And Ford is recalling 782,384 Ford, Lincoln, and Mercury vehicles to have their passenger-side front airbag inflators replaced [1]. Very few vehicle manufacturers have end-to-end visibility of products across their supply chain. When they recall counterfeit or defective products, there is no way to track the products upstream and no way to know exactly which vehicles were affected.

Blockchain has become a hot technology because of its advantages such as transparent, verifiable and tamper-proof trading history, and these characteristics can protect against any party's mistakes [2]. Many organizations [3–7]

© Springer Nature Singapore Pte Ltd. 2020
Z. Zheng et al. (Eds.): BlockSys 2019, CCIS 1156, pp. 732–739, 2020.
https://doi.org/10.1007/978-981-15-2777-7_59

explore the potential of distributed ledger technology, even though this is a young technology that faces multiple challenges [2, 8].

In this paper, we design a blockchain-based vehicle supply chain system to replace rigid supply chains, resulting in more efficient and reliable service for users. We simulate multi-channel vehicle supply chain in Hyperledger Fabric. And we use Hyperledger Caliper as a benchmarking tool to conduct the performance of the proposed model in terms of transactions per second and transaction latency.

The rest of this paper is organized as follows: Sect. 2 explains the blockchain-based applications for the vehicle industry, blockchain platform, and related research works; Sect. 3 describes the scenario of vehicle supply chain, the detailed system architecture and sample network; Sect. 4 presents the performances of the proposed system, and Sect. 5 concludes the paper.

2 Related Work

Blockchain could be segregated into three categories, i.e., public blockchain, private blockchain, and permissioned blockchain [9]. In a public blockchain, anyone can participate without a specific identity. Permissioned blockchains, on the other hand, run a blockchain among a set of known, identified participants. The decentralized distributed ledger ensures the accuracy of a document, tracking, verifying ownership, and transferring property deeds [10]. Although ledgers in blockchain are transparent, the transaction data is encrypted. This cryptography algorithm protects data from theft and also maintains the integrity of data [11]. Many industrial blockchain companies (i.e., Provenance, Fluent, Skuchain and Blockverify) use blockchain to improve supply chain networks [12, 13].

MOBI [14] is a nonprofit organization that aims to make mobility services more efficient and safer, and less congested by promoting standards and accelerating the adoption of blockchain, distributed ledger, and related technologies in the mobility industry. They have formed an alliance with partners such as GE, BMW, Ford and Bosch, and supply chain company such as Chronicled, and NGOs. Hyperledger Fabric, an open-source [15] blockchain platform, is one of the projects of Hyperledger [16] under the auspices of the Linux Foundation [17]. Augur is a decentralized prediction market platform. The Augur Project's goal is to revolutionize prediction markets, and, in doing so, change the way that people receive and verify authenticity [18]. According to IBM, 66% of banks around the world will expect to have blockchain in commercial production at scale by the end of 2020 [19]. Wang et al. [20] identified that blockchain technology can be used for the purpose of keeping records of transparency and provenance-tracking.

To the best of our knowledge, many blockchain companies focus on the financial industry and few companies are open-source. It is difficult to modify blockchain network for their own supply chain. Furthermore, most of the systems focused on some part of the product life cycle in the vehicle industry. Therefore, we designed a vehicle blockchain system based on Hyperledger Fabric to provide the entire life cycle and customized services in vehicle industry.

3 System Architecture of Vehicle Supply Chain Management

3.1 Scenario of Vehicle Supply Chain Management

The scenario of proposed vehicle supply chain management is shown in Fig. 1. The scenario of vehicle supply chain management includes six organizations: regulators, manufacturers, suppliers, retailers, consumers, and recyclers. Initially, regulators create vehicle templates (i.e., brand, model) that are allowed to enter the market; Then, Manufacturers get templates from regulators and record information in the production process of the product; Suppliers then get vehicle and parts from manufacturers and record information about the distribution of vehicles and their parts to the market; Finally, Retailer, consumers, and recyclers record information related to themselves.

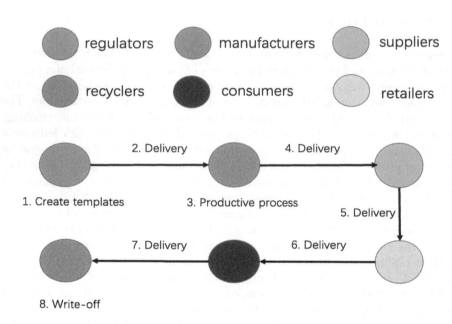

Fig. 1. Scenario of vehicle supply chain management.

3.2 System Architecture

The proposed blockchain-based structure of vehicle supply chain management is shown in Fig. 2. We build the network layer of the vehicle supply chain management based on the Hyperledger Fabric and build the front-end web service based on Node.JS. The proposed system is permissioned that distinguishes it from other blockchain-based systems. This feature allows only the valid participant to participate and enroll in the blockchain network through a user identity manager. The user identity manager in Hyperledger Fabric provides certificates for user enrollment and user authentication. Users send HTTP requests to call APIs, which are used to get services, e.g., user identity management, smart contracts, and consent management.

In order to keep the consistency of every ledger, the same smart contracts have been deployed to all nodes. Transactions are sent by users (i.e., regulators, manufacturers, suppliers, retailers, consumers, and recyclers.) through many APIs to call backend services (create, read, update, and delete), provided by the deployed smart contracts.

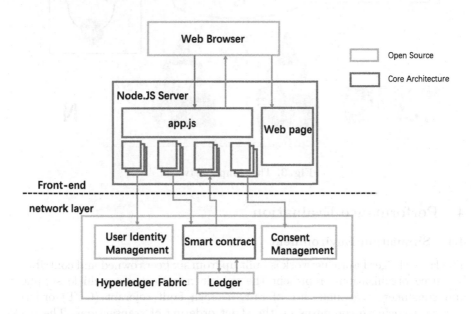

Fig. 2. System architecture of the proposed vehicle supply chain management.

3.3 Sample Network

Hyperledger Fabric allows an organization to simultaneously participate in multiple, separate blockchain networks (N) via channels. We will start with one as shown in Fig. 3. Three organizations, R_1, R_2, and R_3 have a need for a private communication so they set up channel C_1, which is governed according to the policy rules specified in channel configuration CC_2 created by R_1, R_2, and R_3. We can see channel C_1 has been connected to the ordering service, which is administrated according to the policy rules specified in network configuration NC_1 created by R_1, R_2, and R_3. We are going to use three certificate authorities (CA_1, CA_2, and CA_3) to issue certificates to administrators and network nodes in our network; one of for each organization. Peer nodes are the network components where copies of the Ledger are hosted. As mentioned in 3.4, we also define and deploy a smart contract S_1 to C_1. Every organization has a client application that can perform business transactions within C_1.

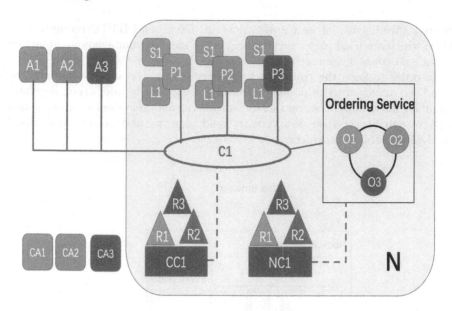

Fig. 3. The sample network.

4 Performance Evaluation

4.1 Simulation Environment

The Hyperledger Fabric network is built up from six peers owned and contributed by three organizations, represent the vehicle manufacturer, vehicle suppliers, and consumers. We make use of raft, a crash fault tolerant (CFT) ordering service, to achieve consensus on the strict ordering of transactions. The backend implementation for vehicle supply chain management is described in Table 1.

We use Hyperledger Caliper as a benchmarking tool to conduct the performance of the designed system in terms of transactions per second and transaction latency. Hyperledger Caliper environmental setup is presented in Table 2.

4.2 Simulation Results

In order to evaluate transaction per second (TPS) of query process, we provide a comparison between three different user categories—100 users, 200 users, and 500 users. As shown in Fig. 4, every group of users query the system at the same time and each category was tested five times. The group with 100 users has an average TPS about 100. When increasing the number of users querying the system at the same time, TPS increases and is nearly as same as the number of users.

We also use the same number of user groups in order to evaluate the latency of query process. Figure 5 shows that the latency of 100 users, 200 users are stabilized at around 10 ms. When the number of users increase to 500, the response time of the system climbs to about 11 ms.

Table 1. The back-end development environment

Component	Description
Hyperledger Fabric	V1.4
Node	V8.15.0
Docker-compose	Version 1.21.0
Docker engine	Version 18.09.7
Python	V2.7.15
CPU	Intel(R) Core(TM) i5-8500 CPU@ 3.00 GHz *6
Memory	8 GB
Operating systems	Ubuntu Linux 18.10

Table 2. Hyperledger Caliper environmental setup

Component	Description
Node	V8.11.4
CLI tool	Node-gyp
Docker-compose	Version 1.13.0
Docker engine	Version 18.09.7

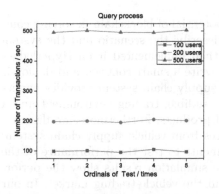

Fig. 4. TPS of query process.   **Fig. 5.** The latency of query process.

As illustrated in Fig. 6, we investigate the transaction per second (TPS) of invoke process (i.e., create, update, and delete). The user-group with 100 users has an average of 22 tps, for 200 users, it is about 35 tps, and for 500 user, it is about 43 tps. The TPS is higher as the number of users requesting simultaneously increases.

Figure 7 describes the latency of invoke process is higher than that of query process. Because additional time is required to perform endorsement and ensures all the peers in the network keep their ledgers consistent with each other. The latency of group with 100 users is around 1000 ms and it increases as the number of users requesting at the same time.

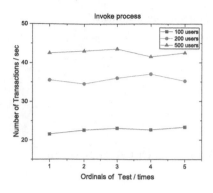

Fig. 6. TPS of invoke process.

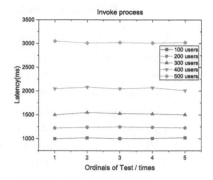

Fig. 7. The latency of invoke process.

According to the China Association of Automobile Manufactures (CAAM), 2.8 million cars sold in the Chinese market in January with the largest number of cars sold in 2019 [21]. The TPS of invoke process is high enough to meet the market requirements.

5   Conclusions

The aim of our research is to explore the potential of blockchain in solving complex vehicle supply chain processes. We describe the scenario and the system architecture of vehicle supply chain and then implemented it on Hyperledger Fabric. In order to effect transactions, we write a smart contract and deploy it to sample network. Our proposed vehicle supply chain system provides participants with a flexible, secure, anonymous, audible, trading environment and a credible ledger to quickly track individual products. Furthermore, we design a web application for users to get the services from vehicle supply chain system. Finally, we carry out a number of experiments to test the performance of the proposed vehicle supply chain model. The simulation results show the performance of proposed model could be used in the vehicle-trading market. In our future work, we will test the reliability and stability of the model in real vehicle supply chain environment.

References

1. Atiyeh, C., Blackwell, R.: Massive Takata airbag recall: everything you need to know, including full list of affected vehicles. Car & Driver (2016)
2. Bonneau, J., Miller, A., Clark, J., Narayanan, A., Kroll, J.A., Felten, E.W.: SoK: research perspectives and challenges for bitcoin and cryptocurrencies. In: 2015 IEEE Symposium on Security and Privacy, pp. 104–121. IEEE (2015)
3. Bishop, G.: Illinois begins pilot project to put birth certificates on digital ledger technology (2017)

4. Browne, R.: IBM partners with Nestle, Unilever and other food giants to trace food contamination with blockchain. CNBC, 22 August 2017

5. Iansiti, M., Lakhani, K.R.: The truth about blockchain. Harv. Bus. Rev. **95**(1), 118–127 (2017)

6. Simonsen, S.: Reasons the UN is jumping on the blockchain bandwagon (2017)

7. Jiang, X., Liu, M., Yang, C., Liu, Y., Wang, R.: A blockchain-based authentication protocol for WLAN mesh security access. CMC-Comput. Mater. Contin. **58**(1), 45–59 (2019)

8. Croman, K., et al.: On scaling decentralized blockchains. In: Clark, J., Meiklejohn, S., Ryan, P.Y.A., Wallach, D., Brenner, M., Rohloff, K. (eds.) FC 2016. LNCS, vol. 9604, pp. 106–125. Springer, Heidelberg (2016). https://doi.org/10.1007/978-3-662-53357-4_8

9. Pilkington, M.: Chapter 11: blockchain technology: principles and applications. In: Research Handbook on Digital Transformations, p. 225 (2016)

10. Spielman, A.: Blockchain: digitally rebuilding the real estate industry. Ph.D. thesis, Massachusetts Institute of Technology (2016)

11. Singh, S., Singh, N.: Blockchain: future of financial and cyber security. In: 2016 2nd International Conference on Contemporary Computing and Informatics (IC3I), pp. 463–467. IEEE (2016)

12. Allison, I.: Skuchain: here's how blockchain will save global trade a trillion dollars. International Business Times, 8 February 2016

13. Abeyratne, S.A., Monfared, R.P.: Blockchain ready manufacturing supply chain using distributed ledger (2016)

14. MOBI: mobility open blockchain initiative. https://dlt.mobi

15. Androulaki, E., et al.: Hyperledger fabric: a distributed operating system for permissioned blockchains. In: Proceedings of the Thirteenth EuroSys Conference, p. 30. ACM (2018)

16. Hyperledger. https://www.hyperledger.org

17. TL Foundation. https://www.linuxfoundation.org

18. Peterson, J., Krug, J.: Augur: a decentralized, open-source platform for prediction markets. arXiv preprint arXiv:1501.01042 (2015)

19. Guo, Y., Liang, C.: Blockchain application and outlook in the banking industry. Financ. Innov. **2**(1), 24 (2016)

20. Wang, J., Wu, P., Wang, X., Shou, W.: The outlook of blockchain technology for construction engineering management. Front. Eng. Manag. **4**(1), 67–75 (2017)

21. CAAM. http://www.caam.org.cn/

A Novel Exploration for Blockchain in Distributed File Storage

Zuoting Ning[1]([⊠]), Lu Li[2], Wei Liang[3], Yifeng Zhao[4], Qi Fu[4], and Hongjun Chen[5]

[1] Department of Information Technology, Hunan Police Academy,
Changsha 410138, China
b12100023@hnu.edu.cn

[2] Chinese GreatWall Technology group Co. LTD., Changsha 410205, China

[3] School of Opto-Electronic and Communication Engineering,
Xiamen University of Technology, Xiamen 361005, China
wliang@xmut.edu.cn

[4] School of Computer Science and Engineering,
Hunan University of Science and Technology, Xiangtan 411201, China

[5] Hunan Institute of Traffic Engineering, Hengyang 421001, China
hongjunkm2010@hotmail.com

Abstract. Distributed file storage provides reliable access to data through redundancy spread on distributed nodes. Various application scenarios emerge, such as include data centers, storage in wireless networks and peer-to-peer storage systems. Storing data by using code, such as an erasure code, calls for less redundancy compared with simple replication in terms of reliability. Nevertheless, since data fragments are periodically replaced when some nodes fail, a key acute question is how to generate encoded data fragments in a distributed way when transferring as little data as possible over the network. For a coded system, a new node to repair from a node failure is to download subsets of data from some surviving nodes, reconstructs some lost coded blocks by using the downloaded fragments, and stores them at the new node. This procedure is not optimal. In this paper, we introduce blockchain to protect distributed data in terms of node failure and etc. We show that blockchain can significantly improve the integrity and credibility in distributed file storage systems. Furthermore, we harvest theory discovery of blockchain in distributed file storage system.

Keywords: Blockchain · Privacy · Distributed file storage

1 Introduction

Distributed file storage aims to store data reliably over long periods of time by distributed storage nodes which may be unreliable. Applications involve storage in large data centers and peer-to-peer storage systems such as OceanStore [1,3], Total Recall [2,4], and DHash++ [3,5], that use nodes across the Internet for

© Springer Nature Singapore Pte Ltd. 2020
Z. Zheng et al. (Eds.): BlockSys 2019, CCIS 1156, pp. 740–746, 2020.
https://doi.org/10.1007/978-981-15-2777-7_60

distributed file storage. In wireless sensor networks, obtaining reliable storage over unreliable motes might be desirable for robust data recovery [4,6], especially in catastrophic scenarios [5,7].

In all above scenarios, guaranteeing data reliability requires the introduction of redundancy. Replication is the simplest form of redundancy, which is explored and adopted in practical storage systems. As a generalization of replication, erasure coding harvests better performance in terms of storage efficiency. For example, we firstly segment a file of size F into m parts, that is, each of size F/m, and then code them into n encoded pieces by using an (n, m) maximum distance separable (MDS) code, finally, store all coded pieces at n nodes. Then, the source file can be recovered from any set of m coded fragments. The result is optimal in terms of the redundancy and incredibility tradeoff, because m fragments, provide the minimum divided data for restoring the original file, which is size F. Some research [2–6,8] explores erasure codes instead of replication. For some special cases, erasure coding harvests orders of magnitude higher reliability compared with replication, e.g., [7]. By using network coding, **Alexandros** (network coding for distributed storage system) put forward the notion of regenerating codes, which allow a new node to recover data from the surviving nodes.

However, once there is malicious attack towards any set of m pieces, the source file can not be recovered. To conquer this challenge, Gkantsidis and Rodrigues [8,9] put forward the scheme that probabilistically check data blocks to decrease computation costs. Krohn et al. [11] proposed a scheme to provide in-network detection, which is based on the homomorphic signature. Jaggi et al. [10,11] proposed a polynomial-time algorithm for protecting multi-cast networks against pollution attacks. Ho et al. [9,10] presented a pollution attacks scheme in multi-cast networks by carrying out a polynomial hashing computation.

In this research, We explore blockchain for data integrity and incredibility in distributed file storage system.

2   Problem Statement

Throughout this paper, we address the integrity and credibility concerns users face when using distributed file storage. We focus specifically on blockchain for distributed file storage platforms. These platforms continuously collect personal data, while the users have no knowledge or control of these actions. In this paper, we assume that the services follow the specified protocol. It is noteworthy that the same system might be used for collecting other personal data, for example, users share their personal data for specific concerns (such as scientific research). On the basis of this, our research protects against common issues as follows:

Data Belonging. Our research mainly pays close attention to guaranteeing that authorized users have full control of their personal data. As well, the system recognizes the users as the owners of the data and regards the services as guests with corresponding authorized permissions.

Data Transparency and Incredibility. Each user on the platform has complete transparency over data trace, such as what data is being collected and how they are accessed.

Access Permission. One major concern with applications is that users are required to grant access permissions upon logon. These permissions are granted indefinitely and the only way to alter the agreement is by opting out. On the contrary, in our research, the users can freely alter the permissions and revoke access to all visited data. What's more, all the corresponding access-control policies and protocols are stored on a blockchain by a secure way, in which only the delegated users have permission to change them.

3   Proposed Solution

We have an overview of our decentralized system. As illustrated in Fig. 1, the main three entities which comprise the system are users, services, and nodes, the users focus on storing, downloading and using distributed files; the services provide such applications who require processing distributed files for operational or business related reasons (e.g., personalized service); while the nodes store file fragments and are entrusted with the blockchain and a distributed private key-value. As the users in the system are commonly anonymous, we can store file profiles and verify their identity on the blockchain.

The system is mainly designed as the following: The blockchain accepts two new types of transactions: T_{access}, used for access control management; and T_{data}, for data storage and retrieval. These operations could be easily deployed to a software development kit (SDK), which services can utilize through development process.

For detailed illustration, consider the following scenarios: a user installs an application that uses our platform for storing files. Once the users sign up for the first time, a total new shared identity for each user is created and sent to the blockchain in a T_{access} transaction, along with the corresponding permissions. Files are segmented into fragments and stored at nodes by a distributed way, all fragments are encrypted by using a shared encryption key and sent to the blockchain in a T_{data} transaction, which subsequently routes them to an off-blockchain key-value pool, only maintaining a pointer to the data on the blockchain. Moreover, the pointer is the SHA-256 hash value of the segmented data.

The users can query the data by using a T_{data} transaction with the associated pointer. Then, the blockchain verifies whether the digital signature belongs to the user or not. Finally, the user can modify the permissions at any time by issuing a T_{access} transaction with new permissions. Developing a web-based dashboard, which allows an overview of one's file data as well as the ability to modify permissions, is fairly trivial and is similar to developing centralized-wallets.

The off-blockchain key-value store is an implementation of Kademilia [23], a distributed hash table (D-HT), with added persistence using Level DB^2 and an interface to the blockchain. The D-HT is maintained by a series of nodes in the

network that are possibly disjoint from the blockchain network, which perform
approved read or write transactions. Files are randomized over the nodes and
replicated to guarantee high availability. Alternative off-blockchain solutions are
considered for storage. For instance, a centralized cloud might store the data.
However, this calls for an authorized and credible third-party, and this has some
advantages in the aspect of scalability and deployment.

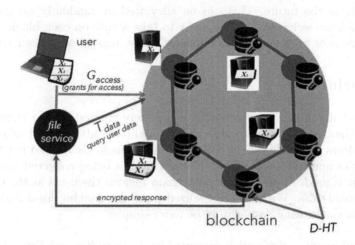

Fig. 1. Blockchain-based distributed file storage system.

4   Discussion

In general, blockchain assumes all nodes are equally untrusted and their proportion in the collective decision-making process is just based on their computational
resources (known as the Proof-of-work algorithm) [27]. In other words, as to node
n, trust n resources(n) (probabilistically) determines its weight in voting. This
leads to inverse effects, namely, most notably vulnerability to excessive energy
consumption and high-latency.

Commonly, Proof-of-Work argues that nodes pouring significant data into the
system are less likely to deceive. Similarly, we might define a new dynamic rule
of trust based on node behavior, so that good action agreeing with the protocol
are responded. Particularly, as to every node, we set the trust value which is
regarded as the expected value of their behavior. Equivalently, considering what
we are dealing with is a binary random variable, we define the expected value as
the probability p. A simple and effective way to approach this probability is to
make statistic of good and bad actions that a node carries out, then, squash it
into a probability by using the sigmoid function. In practice, as to every block
b, we evaluate the trust score of each node as C

$$rely\_t_n^{(b)} = \frac{1}{1 + e^{(-\alpha)(\#legal - \#illegal)}} \tag{1}$$

in which α is the step size.

According to this equation, the network can endow more weight to the on-chain nodes and compute data blocks more efficiently. As it takes time to gain trust in the system, it is immune to forge attacks. This mechanism might attract other types of attacks, such as nodes increasing their reputation to behaving maliciously in the future. This can be alleviated by randomly selecting some nodes which are weighted by their trust to take a vote on each block. This can avoid single user from having too much influence, regardless of their trust-level.

5 Conclusion

Distributed file storage shouldn't be completely trusted in the third-parties, in which they are inevitably vulnerable to malicious attacks and misuse. This paper explores to enable this by utilizing a blockchain. Users need not trust any third-parties and are master over the data that is being collected about them and how it is used. Moreover, the blockchain regards the users as the owners of their personal data. With a decentralized platform, making legal and credible decisions about storing data should be more simpler.

Acknowledgments. This work is supported by the Open Research Fund of Key Laboratory of Network Crime Investigation of Hunan Provincial Colleges under granted No. 2017W-LZC005, and the Science and Technology Projects of Hunan Province of China under granted No. 2017SK1040.

References

1. Rhea, S., et al.: Maintenance-free global data storage. IEEE Internet Comput. **5**, 40–49 (2001)
2. Bhagwan, R., Tati, K., Cheng, Y.-C., Savage, S., Voelker, G.M.: Total recall: system support for automated availability management. In: NSDI (2004)
3. Dabek, F., Li, J., Sit, E., Robertson, J., Kaashoek, M., Morris, R.: Designing a DHT for low latency and high throughput (2004)
4. Dimakis, A.G., Prabhakaran, V., Ramchandran, K.: Decentralized erasure codes for distributed networked storage. IEEE Trans. Inf. Theory **52**(6), 2809–2816 (2006)
5. Kamra, A., Feldman, J., Misra, V., Rubenstein, D.: Growth codes: maximizing sensor network data persistence. In: ACM SIGCOMM (2006)
6. Rhea, S., Eaton, P., Geels, D., Weatherspoon, H., Zhao, B., Kubiatowicz, J.: Pond: the OceanStore prototype. In: Proceedings of USENIX File and Storage Technologies (FAST) (2003)
7. Weatherspoon, H., Kubiatowicz, J.D.: Erasure coding vs. replication: a quantitative comparison. In: Proceedings of IPTPS (2002)
8. Gkantsidis, C., Rodriguez, P.: Cooperative security for network coding file distribution. In: IEEE INFOCOM (2006)

9. Ho, T., Leong, B., Koetter, R., Meard, M., Effros, M., Karger, D.: Byzantine modification detection in multicast networks using randomized network coding. In: ISIT (2004)
10. Jaggi, S., Langberg, M., Katti, S., Ho, T., Katabi, D., Meard, M.: Resilient network coding in the presence of Byzantine adversaries. In: IEEE INFOCOM (2007)
11. Krohn, M.N., Freedman, M.J., Mazieres, D.: On-the-fly verification of rateless erasure codes for efficient content distribution. In: Proceedings of the IEEE Symposium on Security and Privacy, Berkeley, CA, USA, 9–12 May 2004, pp. 226–240 (2004)
12. Bolosky, W.J., Douceur, J.R., Ely, D., Theimer, M.: Feasibility of a serverless distributed file system deployed on an existing set of desktop PCs. In: Proceedings of SIGMETRICS (2000)
13. Dabek, F., Kaashoek, F., Karger, D., Morris, R., Stoica, I.: Wide-area cooperative storage with CFS. In: Proceedings of ACM SOSP (2001)
14. Rowstron, A., Druschel, P.: Storage management and caching in past, a large-scale, persistent peer-to-peer storage utility. In: Proceedings of ACM SOSP (2001)
15. Weatherspoon, H., Chun, B.-G., So, C.W., Kubiatowicz, J.: Long-term data maintenance in wide-area storage systems: a quantitative approach, Technical report, UC Berkeley, UCB/CSD-05-1404, July 2005
16. Blake, C., Rodrigues, R.: High availability, scalable storage, dynamic peer networks: pick two. In: Proceedings of HOTOS (2003)
17. Chun, B.-G., et al.: Efficient replica maintenance for distributed storage systems. In: NSDI (2006)
18. Tati, K., Voelker, G.M.: On object maintenance in peer-to-peer systems. In: Proceedings of IPTPS (2006)
19. Godfrey, P.B., Shenker, S., Stoica, I.: Minimizing churn in distributed systems. In: Proceedings of ACM SIGCOMM (2006)
20. Swan, M.: Blockchain: Blueprint for a New Economy. O'Reilly Media Inc., Newton (2015)
21. Bitcoin, N.S.: A peer-to-peer electronic cash system. Consulted 1(2012), 28 (2008)
22. Kondor, D., Pósfai, M., Csabai, I., Vattay, G.: Do the rich get richer? An empirical analysis of the Bitcoin transaction network. PloS One 9(2), e86197 (2014). https://doi.org/10.1371/journal.pone.0086197. PMID: 24505257
23. Maymounkov, P., Mazières, D.: Kademlia: a peer-to-peer information system based on the XOR metric. In: Druschel, P., Kaashoek, F., Rowstron, A. (eds.) IPTPS 2002. LNCS, vol. 2429, pp. 53–65. Springer, Heidelberg (2002). https://doi.org/10.1007/3-540-45748-8_5
24. Vickrey, W.: Counterspeculation, auctions, and competitive sealed tenders. J. Finance 16, 8–37 (1961)
25. Wood, G.: Ethereum: a secure decentralized transaction ledger. http://gavwood.com/paper.pdf
26. Ben-Sasson, E., et al.: Zerocash: decentralized anonymous payments from Bitcoin. In: S&P (2014)
27. Nakamoto, S.: Bitcoin: a peer-to-peer electronic cash system. Consulted 1(2012), 28 (2008)
28. Cleve, R.: Limits on the security of coin flips when half the processors are faulty. In: STOC (1986)
29. Asharov, G., Beimel, A., Makriyannis, N., Omri, E.: Complete characterization of fairness in secure two-party computation of boolean functions. In: Dodis, Y., Nielsen, J.B. (eds.) TCC 2015. LNCS, vol. 9014, pp. 199–228. Springer, Heidelberg (2015). https://doi.org/10.1007/978-3-662-46494-6_10

30. Bentov, I., Kumaresan, R.: How to use bitcoin to design fair protocols. In: Garay, J.A., Gennaro, R. (eds.) CRYPTO 2014. LNCS, vol. 8617, pp. 421–439. Springer, Heidelberg (2014). https://doi.org/10.1007/978-3-662-44381-1_24
31. Kumaresan, R., Bentov, I.: How to use bitcoin to incentivize correct computations. In: CCS (2014)

Insurance Block: A Blockchain Credit Transaction Authentication Scheme Based on Homomorphic Encryption

Lijun Xiao[1]($\boxtimes$), Han Deng[1], Minfu Tan[1], and Weidong Xiao[2]

[1] The Department of Accounting, Guangzhou College of Technology and Business, Guangzhou 510850, Guangdong, China
ljxiaoxy@126.com

[2] The School of Software Engineering, Xiamen University of Technology, Xiamen 361024, Fujian, China

Abstract. The data transaction in insurance has problems in terms of low security, high management cost and difficulty in supervision. This paper proposes a trustable blockchain based transaction authentication scheme based on homomorphic encryption. By considering the features of distributed authority management in insurance business, a shared insurance account book is realized as well as the data consensus, smart contracts and special chained storage structures. The experimental results show that the proposed scheme has high security and effectiveness.

Keywords: Insurance blockchain · Data consensus · Smart contract · Authority management

1 Introduction

As a new emerged financial technology, insurance data blockchain is widely concerned by researchers. In the existing insurance data trading systems, a third-party organization is required for certification. In the insurance business, the user's credit information is sensitive, which cannot be leaked. Most insurance companies are not willing to share the data that is benefit for the whole industry development. The secure data sharing and data transaction are critical in this field. The establishment of the decentralized consensus management mechanism and the credit evaluation model system will have great significance for the healthy and rapid development of insurance data blockchain technology [1–3].

The research and application of blockchain in foreign countries show the characteristics of alliance, financial level and overall layout. Large stock exchanges in several countries claim to use blockchain technology to increase efficiency and speed up liquidation. Blockchain technology is improving and many research institutes have proposed some new consensus mechanisms, including proof of state, delegated proof of state, ripple, tendermint, etc. Blockchain uses asymmetric encryption, which avoids the leakage

© Springer Nature Singapore Pte Ltd. 2020
Z. Zheng et al. (Eds.): BlockSys 2019, CCIS 1156, pp. 747–751, 2020.
https://doi.org/10.1007/978-981-15-2777-7_61

of user information. But other users can still observe the trading information of the current user. Many algorithms are proposed to solve these problems. The zero-knowledge proof algorithm proposed by zero-coin can avoid the leakage of user transaction information but can verify whether the transaction is valid. At the same time, many papers studied mining without permission and proposed corresponding solutions [4–7].

This work primarily establishes blockchain and big data in the use of insurance, including data encryption and privacy protection, user credit model establishment, insurance enterprise reputation model establishment, consensus mechanism and chain expansion technology, etc. It can address the credit bottleneck of the insurance industry.

2 Homomorphic Encryption Based Insurance Blockchain

A new homomorphic encryption domain transaction authentication algorithm is proposed by considering the Paillier homomorphic public key encryption system. This algorithm realizes the data transaction among encrypted ciphertext data in Paillier homomorphic public key encryption system [8, 9]. In addition, the algorithm can extract watermark without decryption or decryption, and can effectively verify the insurance data information, so as to realize the accuracy of the insurance data identity investigation algorithm in the homomorphic encryption domain. The verifier can use homomorphic encryption in insurance data transactions to prevent replay attacks. The concrete steps of trading model are described as follows:

(1) Key generation $KeyGen_\varepsilon(\lambda)$: randomly select two large prime numbers p and q, remember $W = p \cdot q, \lambda = lcm(p - 1, q - 1)$. Here, $lcm(\cdot)$ denotes the least common multiple. An integer $r \in \mathbb{Z}^*_{W^2}$ is randomly selected, which satisfying formula (1).

$$\gcd\left(L\left(r^\lambda \bmod W^2\right), W\right) = 1 \tag{1}$$

where $\mathbb{Z}_{W^2}$ represents the set of all integers less than W^2. $\mathbb{Z}^*_{W^2}$ represents the set of all integers in $\mathbb{Z}_{W^2}$ that are mutually prime with W^2. $\gcd(\cdot)$ represents the maximum common factor, $L(x) = \frac{x-1}{W}$. Therefore, (W, r) and λ which can be obtained are respectively used as a public key for encryption and a private key for decryption.

(2) Encryption process $Encrypt_\varepsilon((W, r), M)$: For any plain text $M \in \mathbb{Z}_W$, an integer $t \in \mathbb{Z}^*_W$ is randomly selected. The public key (W, r) and the random encryption parameter t are used to calculate the corresponding cipher text $\in \mathbb{Z}^*_{W^2}$ with the following formula:

$$C = E(M) = r^M \cdot t^W \bmod W^2. \tag{2}$$

Because t is randomly selected in the encryption process, different cipher text C can be obtained for the same plain text M. But the different cipher text C can be decrypted into the same plain text M. This is the probabilistic property of a Paillier encryption system.

(3) Decryption process $Decrypt_\varepsilon(\lambda, C)$: The private key λ is used to calculate the corresponding plain text for cipher text C.

$$M = D(C) = \frac{L(C^\lambda \bmod W^2)}{L(r^\lambda \bmod W^2)} \bmod W, \tag{3}$$

$L(x) = \frac{x-1}{W}$. It is easy to know that the above Paillier encryption system has the homomorphic properties of addition and multiplication, and also satisfies the following properties: for $\forall m_1, m_2 \in \mathbb{Z}_W, k \in \mathbb{N}$,

$$D\Big(E(m_1) \cdot E(m_2) \bmod W^2\Big) = (m_1 + m_2) \bmod W;$$

$$D\Big(E(m)^k \bmod W^2\Big) = km \bmod W.$$

In the transaction data, we constitute the insurance data as the matrix form of $m \times n$, and set it as $P = (p_{ij})_{m \times n}$, satisfying

$$P = \begin{pmatrix} 1 & 2 & \cdots & n \\ n+1 & n+2 & \cdots & 2n \\ \vdots & \vdots & \ddots & \vdots \\ (m-1)n+1 & (m-1)n+2 & \cdots & mn \end{pmatrix}. \tag{4}$$

Then, according to the encryption process of Paillier homomorphic public key encryption system, an integer $t_{ij} \in \mathbb{Z}_W^*$ is randomly selected, public key (W, r) and random encryption parameter t_{ij} are used, and corresponding ciphertext $c_{ij} \in \mathbb{Z}_{W^2}^*$ is calculated according to the following formula:

$$c_{ij} = E(p_{ij}) = r^{p_{ij}} \cdot t_{ij}^W \bmod W^2 \tag{5}$$

where $1 \le i \le m, 1 \le j \le n$. Record the position coordinate matrix of the encrypted cipher text core as $C = (c_{ij})_{m \times n}$,

$$C = \begin{pmatrix} c_{11} & c_{12} & \cdots & c_{1n} \\ c_{21} & c_{22} & \cdots & c_{2n} \\ \vdots & \vdots & \ddots & \vdots \\ c_{m1} & c_{m2} & \cdots & c_{mn} \end{pmatrix} \tag{6}$$

3 Experimental Results and Analysis

A. Ability against Removal Attack

In this section, several random data removal experiments in insurance business are conducted, and the result is compared with other two methods [10, 11]. The result is shown in Table 1. With the increase of the removal attack intensity, our scheme has a higher anti-attack index than the other two schemes, which shows a higher anti-removal attack ability. Therefore, the scheme in this paper is effective in anti-removal attack against transaction data during insurance trading, so it can be considered that the algorithm has a better effect on these removal attacks.

Table 1. Analysis of ability against removal attack

Experiment	Attack	Literature [10]	Literature [11]	Ours
1	Remove 1% entities	1	1	1
2	Remove 5% entities	1	0.99	0.97
3	Remove 20% entities	0.85	0.87	0.89
4	Remove 50% entities	0.61	0.64	0.76

B. **Ability against Passive Attack**

The anti-combination attack capability of the algorithm refers to the attack of the IP layout after embedding watermark information by using any two or more attack methods, and the ability of the algorithm to correctly extract the watermark information in the processed IP layout. Since the algorithm is robust to various passive attacks, any combination of these types of attacks can be effectively resisted. For a type of attack in which these attacks are combined with a graphics removal attack, the ability of the algorithm to resist combined attacks depends mainly on the ability to resist graphics erasure attacks. This is also reflected in the experimental results in Table 2.

Table 2. Comparison of security metrics

Security metrics	UMAP protocol	Literature [10]	Literature [11]	Ours
Anti-nonsynchronous attack	N	N	N	Y
Anti-replay attack	N	N	N	Y
Anonymity	Y	Y	Y	Y
Frontier security	Y	Y	Y	Y
Anti-heuristic attack	N	Y	Y	Y

4 Conclusion

In view of the difficulties in trust authentication of insurance data transactions in insurance business, This paper designs a blockchain transaction authentication method based on homomorphic encryption. The method utilizes insurance data transaction security mechanism ans sets up the insurance data transaction type. When the registration and authentication of member management node are finished, the configuration file of node is modified and the broadcast module of blockchain is reconfigured. It realizes the real-time data authentication of insurance blockchain. Although the authentication has a challenge, insurance blockchain has been widely concerned. All the issues in application of blockchain will be addressed gradually.

References

1. Karame, G.O., Androulaki, E., Capkun, S.: Double-spending fast payments in bitcoin. In: Proceedings of the 2012 ACM Conference on Computer and Communications Security, pp. 906–917. ACM (2012)
2. Liang, W., Tang, M., Long, J., et al.: A secure fabric blockchain-based data transmission technique for industrial Internet-of-Things. IEEE Trans. Ind. Inf. **15**(6), 3582–3592 (2019)
3. Melanie, S.: Blockchain: Blueprint for a New Economy. O'Reilly Media Inc., USA (2015). https://docs.com/nikolaou/1336/swan-2015-blockchain-blueprint-for-a-new-economy
4. Conti, M., Kumar, E.S., Lal, C.: A survey on security and privacy issues of bitcoin. IEEE Commun. Surv. Tutor. **20**(4), 3416–3452 (2018)
5. Eyal, I., Sirer, E.G.: Majority is not enough: bitcoin mining is vulnerable. Commun. ACM **61**(7), 95–102 (2018)
6. van den Hooff, J., Kaashoek, M.F., Zeldovich, N.: VerSum: verifiable computations over large public logs. In: Proceedings of the 2014 ACM SIGSAC Conference on Computer and Communications Security, pp. 1304–1316. ACM (2014)
7. Atzei, N., Bartoletti, M., Cimoli, T.: A survey of attacks on Ethereum smart contracts (SoK). In: Maffei, M., Ryan, M. (eds.) POST 2017. LNCS, vol. 10204, pp. 164–186. Springer, Heidelberg (2017). https://doi.org/10.1007/978-3-662-54455-6_8
8. Di Francesco, M.D., Marino, A., Ricci, L.: An analysis of the bitcoin users graph: inferring unusual behaviours. In: Cherifi, H., Gaito, S., Quattrociocchi, W., Sala, A. (eds.) Complex Networks & Their Applications V. COMPLEX NETWORKS 2016 2016. Studies in Computational Intelligence, vol 693. Springer, Cham (2017). https://doi.org/10.1007/978-3-319-50901-3_59
9. Maesa, D.D.F., Marino, A., Ricci, L.: Data-driven analysis of bitcoin properties: exploiting the users graph. Int. J. Data Sci. Anal. **6**(1), 63–80 (2018)
10. Mazieres, D.: The stellar consensus protocol: a federated model for internet-level consensus. Stellar Development Foundation (2015)
11. Chepurnoy, A., Larangeira. M., Ojiganov, A.: A prunable blockchain consensus protocol based on non-interactive proofs of past states retrievability. arXiv preprint arXiv:1603.07926 (2016)

Blockchain Electronic Voting System for Preventing One Vote and Multiple Investment

Jianquan Ouyang(✉), Yifan Deng, and Huanrong Tang

College of Information Engineering, Xiangtan University, Xiangtan, China
27894827@qq.com, 201821562139@smail.xtu.edu.cn,
tanghuanrong@126.com

Abstract. An anonymous online voting system based on blockchain is proposed for the problem that the voting process details are not public, citizens do not trust, and the results cannot be verified. Using the characteristics of blockchain cryptography and distributed networks, it is possible to perfectly solve the problem of voting data security and server single point of failure. Recording by the id of the account for data verification in the future. The pricing mechanism of the Ethereum system can effectively prevent the situation of one vote and more investment, and truly realizes the openness and transparency of the voting process technically, and realizes the anonymity of the voter identity to a certain extent. In the long term, it is planned to study IPFS distributed storage in depth and distribute the voting data of the uplink to different nodes to achieve higher security and transparency.

Keywords: Data security · Blockchain · Smart contracts · Single point of failure · Anonymous voting

1 Introduction

For many years, voting has been seen as the primary method by which individuals share opinions on controversial issues. It is widely used in candidate elections, party and government and daily life resolutions. This is a democratic approach that allows people to formally and boldly express their views on the issue of voting. Since ancient times, there has been a pottery exile method, and today there is a voting software APP. But no matter which way can't escape the single point of failure attack, the integrity and reliability of the data is even controlled by a completely unknown third party. The anonymity of the vote makes it impossible to disclose the data, which greatly weakens the credibility of the voting event.

On the other hand, blockchain is an emerging technology that provides network-distributed, single-point-free services that ensure data reliability through cryptographic functions and consensus algorithms. Ethereum [1] is an open source distributed computing platform with a Turing-complete scripting language in which software engineers can deploy decentralized applications (DApps) and benefit from distributed features inherited from blockchain technology. Therefore, blockchain technology can perfectly solve the current pain point in the voting industry - the issue of trust.

© Springer Nature Singapore Pte Ltd. 2020
Z. Zheng et al. (Eds.): BlockSys 2019, CCIS 1156, pp. 752–757, 2020.
https://doi.org/10.1007/978-981-15-2777-7_62

Based on the current privacy and security issues of the voting industry, based on the blockchain technology foundation, I have done the following work:

1. Build a private chain for voting and deploy two nodes for voting test;
2. A smart contract for recording the results of the account voting is proposed. When there is a case of multiple votes, the agreement can detect and record the already voted account and terminate the transaction;
3. The safety of the gas mechanism of the Ethereum platform was tested by experimental tests, and the results of the analysis were compared for the reasons for the failure.

2 Related Work

2.1 Blockchain

On October 31, 2008, a researcher named "Zhong Ben Cong" published a ground-breaking paper on Bitcoin in the cryptography mail group "Bitcoin: A Peer-to-Peer Electronic Cash System [2]". The blockchain has the characteristics of decentralization, non-tamperability, and rule transparency [3], which is the fourth milestone in the evolutionary history of human credit following blood credit, precious metal credit, and central banknote credit [4].

2.2 Smart Contract

The smart contract, the 2.0 version of the blockchain, was introduced in 1995 by Szabo [5], who pointed out that "smart contracts promote the execution of contracts by using protocols and user interfaces." The smart contract based on blockchain technology [6] includes Hyperledger [7], Ethereum [8] and so on. Based on the above platform, it can support multiple blockchain application scenarios.

2.3 Blockchain Electronic Voting System

In view of the mistrust of the electronic voting system, some scholars have begun to study: Ko [9] and others in the "Towards secure e-voting using ethereum blockchain" studied the relying on Android devices Ethereum wallet, based on blockchain Secure, transparent electronic voting system. Tarasov [10] and others in the "The future of e-voting" scheme in addition to the use of blockchain to meet transparency, privacy and integrity, also proposed a registration phase for verifying user identity, and track user votes. Meeser [11] et al. proposed a system suitable for medium-sized elections based on Ethereum, using threshold keys and linkable ring signatures in decentralized, transparent, trustless voting on the ethereum blockchain. Japanese scholar FUJIOKA [12] and others in the "A practical secret voting scheme for large scale elections", for the scene that requires anonymity, proposed a combination of blind signature and electronic voting.

Based on the above existing work, there are many problems in the voting system industry that need to be solved urgently, such as: the decentralization and privacy protection are not fully realized, and the design of the mobile terminal has not been applied yet, and the tracking problem of voting data has not been applied. In order to better protect user privacy and guarantee the credibility of voting data, this paper proposes an anonymous online voting system based on blockchain. On the basis of the realization of voting, it is also possible to detect the id of the input account and trace the voting data. Based on the Ethereum system, it is possible to prevent the phenomenon of one vote and more investment. The use of blockchain wallets to save and apply for public and private keys can guarantee the privacy of voters. In the future, it is planned to study IPFS distributed storage in depth and distribute the voting data of the uplink to different nodes to achieve higher security and distribution.

3   Experimental Design

3.1   Summary of the Experimental Process Design

The voting scheme implementation method proposed in this paper is based on the Ethereum smart contract. The corresponding method of deploying the smart contract on the blockchain is invoked through the JavaScript API interface of the Web3.js library, and the whole voting process is realized. For smart contract development, use the most widely used programming language, the Solidity language. In addition, the React front-end framework based on Nodejs was designed to develop a DApp for the voting system to show the interaction process of the entire voting system. Figure 1 is a diagram of the voting system architecture.

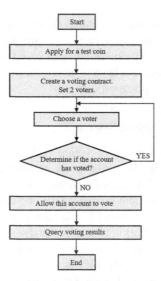

Fig. 1. Diagram of the voting system architecture.

The flow chart of the intelligent contract voting system, the specific operation steps are described as follows: (1) test coin application: apply for test coins from the water pipe, only for testing use, this experiment is based on the Kovan test network; (2) Create a candidate for the contract, citizens can vote for the corresponding candidate after deploying the contract on their own client; (3) The citizen chooses a voter, If the ticket has already been voted, the transaction cannot be carried out.

After the vote is over, the system can announce all account voting. Since the user information citizen corresponding to each account cannot be known, the blockchain-based voting system can ensure the identity of the participant in the case of public disclosure.

3.2 Experimental Detailed Design

Based on the theory of blockchain and smart contract, this paper builds an Ethereum private chain experimental environment and implements a voting contract. The experimental environment is: CPU is Inter®CoreTMi7-1536 M, the frequency is 3.30 GHz, the memory is 16 GB, the operating system is MACOS, the browser is Remix (kernel version 4.4.0), the wallet is MetaMask, and the programming language is Solidity. The voting contract established a private chain experimental environment through the Ethereum client Go-Ethereum. The supporting software required for this environment is shown in Table 1.

Table 1. Experimental environment required by the system.

Software	Description
Solc	Solidity Language Compiler
Remix	Provides an IDE to compile and debug smart contracts
Testrpc	Ethereum's local test environment
Truffle	Ethereum's smart contract development framework can quickly compile and deploy smart contracts locally
Web3.js	A JavaScript library that establishes communication with the Ethereum node
Node.js	JavaScript runtime environment

The voting smart contract in this article is based on the Solidity language and uses EVM as the operating environment. The compilation results are shown in Fig. 2.

Compiling with Browser-Solidity verifies that the smart contract is correct. After voting for the id = 1 candidate, the number of votes for user 1 can be displayed. The ethercan can view the transaction details. Contracts that are successfully compiled and deployed will be automatically uploaded to the blockchain and connected in the form of hashes to prevent third parties from tampering with the voting results and to ensure the integrity and correctness of the voting data.

When the same account is voted for the same person, the contract can be detected, causing the transaction to fail. With the newly registered account 2 for voting, a successful transaction can be executed and recorded in the voter tag array. And shown in Fig. 3.

Analyze the reason for the transaction failure and find that when the account initiates the first transaction, the system sets the gas limit unit to the unit that has used the natural gas quantity. After that, the account does not have the right to use the natural gas quantity. Ethereum system definition can no longer initiate transactions. The transaction comparison experiment proves as shown in Fig. 4.

Fig. 2. The result of the compilation.

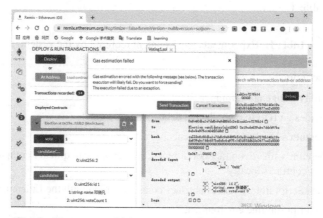

Fig. 3. One-vote multi-investment transaction prompt failure.

Fig. 4. Successful transaction and failed transaction gas comparison.

4 Summary

Based on the intelligent contract theory and the Ethereum experimental environment, this paper develops a blockchain-based electronic voting system, which solves the problem of mistrust in the voting industry by taking advantage of the underlying technology of the blockchain. While technically ensuring the security of voting data, through the study of the Ethereum platform, the situation of one vote and multiple investment was prevented, and the voting data was recorded for future inquiry. The feasibility of the project has been verified, and the next step will continue to improve the system functions and enhance the usability and robustness of the system.

After completing the functional requirements, the authors think about further research on true anonymity, mobility, throughput, and distributed storage.

Acknowledgment. This article is supported by CERNET's next-generation Internet technology innovation project: Research on blockchain source tracing technology to e-commerce under ipv6 (NGII20180902).

References

1. Buterin, V., et al.: A next-generation smart contract and decentralized application platform, white paper (2014)
2. Nakamoto, S.: Bitcoin: A Peer-to-Peer Electronic Cash System. Manubot (2019)
3. Yong, Y., Feiyue, W.: Current status and prospects of blockchain technology development. Autom. Chem. **42**(4), 481–494 (2016)
4. Swan, M.: Blockchain: Blueprint for a New Economy. O'Reilly Media Inc., Sebastopol (2015)
5. Szabo, N.: Formalizing and securing relationships on public networks. First Monday **2**(9) (1997)
6. Qifeng, S., Cheqing, J., Zhao, Z., et al.: Blockchain technology: architecture and progress. Chin. J. Comput. **41**(5), 969–988 (2018)
7. Buterin, V.: A next-generation smart contract and decentralized application platform [EB/OL]. Accessed 01 May 2018. https://github.com/ethereum/wiki/wiki/. White-Paper
8. https://ethereum.org/en/
9. Yavuz, E., Koc, A.K., Çabuk, U.C., et al.: Towards secure e-voting using ethereum blockchain. In: 2018 6th International Symposium on Digital Forensic and Security (ISDFS), pp. 1–7. IEEE (2018)
10. Tarasov, P., Tewari, H.: The future of e-voting. IADIS Int. J. Comput. Sci. Inf. Syst. **12**(2), (2017)
11. Meeser, F.L.: Decentralized, transparent, trustless voting on the ethereum blockchain (2017)
12. McCorry, P., Toreini, E., Mehrnezhad, M.: Removing trusted tallying authorities, Technical report, Newcastle University (2016). Cited on, Technical report (2016)

Trustworthy System Development

An Authority Management Framework Based on Fabric and IPFS in Traceability Systems

Jiangfeng Li, Yifan Yu, Shili Hu, and Chenxi Zhang[✉]

School of Software Engineering, Tongji University, Shanghai 201804, China
{lijf,1452736,1931530,xzhang2000}@tongji.edu.cn

Abstract. The traceability system is significant to consumers because it can protect the health of consumers and the stability of society. With the development of blockchain technology, it is concerned by researchers of the traceability system because of its immutability and consensus mechanism. For guaranteeing the confidentiality of core data, it is necessary to control data permissions in the supply chain. However, the existing blockchain authority management frameworks mostly concentrate on the medical field and the Internet of Things (IoT). They have to take a long time to reach consensus and store lots of data in the chain. The most important is that the number of transactions submitted per second has always been a bottleneck. In this paper, we proposed an authority management framework used to control the authority of different roles in the traceability system. It pays attention to store small amounts of data on the chain, optimize the consensus rate, and increase the number of transactions per second (TPS). We design a simple experiment to contrast the performance of our framework and the MedRec [1] framework, and the results show that our framework's consensus rate and TPS are better than the MedRec [1].

Keywords: Blockchain · Authorization · TPS · IPFS · Traceability system

1 Introduction

In recent years, consumers all over the world have encountered many product safety issues. Frequent accidents such as listeria infection [10], poisonous milk [14], and trench oil [14] have caused consumers to lose trust in product safety. In this grim situation, the traceability system is useful for rebuilding consumer confidence by tracking the position of the product in the supply chain. With the development of blockchain, its traceability and consensus mechanism perfect matching traceability system has attracted the attention of researchers. Due to the traceability and non-modifiability of the blockchain, it can record every step

© Springer Nature Singapore Pte Ltd. 2020
Z. Zheng et al. (Eds.): BlockSys 2019, CCIS 1156, pp. 761–773, 2020.
https://doi.org/10.1007/978-981-15-2777-7_63

about the product transfer in the supply chain, and there is no fear that the participants in the supply chain will tamper with the data during future reviews. The consensus mechanism ensures that each participant approves the data uploading to the blockchain, and avoids forged data uploading. Many researchers have proposed some chains about traceability system based on these characteristics [2,13–15].

Although blockchain guarantees the reliability of data in the traceability system, public data has the potential to reveal corporate trade secrets. In order to solve this problem and ensure the traceability requirement of products in blockchain, adding authority management to the traceability system is a suitable solution. There are currently many authority management models based on blockchain. One of the solutions is to create and transfer permission through transactions [5,8]. The permissions in this scheme are particular blockchain transactions. Another solution is to control the permissions through smart contracts [1,6,9]. By combining the smart contracts with the traditional authority management model [12], we can get an authority management framework running on the blockchain. In general, the smart contract-based authority management model is more widely because of its simple implementation.

Although there are many authority management frameworks based on blockchain, there are still some problems in these frameworks. First of all, the authority management frameworks in [1,3,5–9,11] mostly adopt the consensus algorithm of Proof-of-Work (PoW), which has large calculation overhead and low consensus efficiency. Secondly, the privacy requirements of the company's confidential data in the traceability system require protection of the data on the blockchain. The authority management frameworks in [5–9] mostly store original data directly on the blockchain, and this way destroys the privacy of the data and puts pressure on the data store. Finally, most of the authority management frameworks concentrate on e-health [1,3,11] and the Internet of Things (IoT) [7–9]. They need to be modified to fit the traceability scenario.

In order to solve the above problems, we propose a new Hyperledger Fabric-based authority management framework for traceability systems. For improving the efficiency of calculation, the speed of consensus, and increasing the transactions per second (TPS), we abandoned Ethereum as our platform for development and switched to Hyperledger Fabric. Our framework selects the more suitable Kafka algorithm as the consensus algorithm and gives up traditional consensus algorithms that require a lot of computation and time, such as PoW and Proof-of-Stake (PoS), which helps us save much time for block consensus. On the other hand, our framework is a coalition chain, and the necessary entry barriers increase the security of blockchain data. Besides, storing indexes on the blockchain instead of original data further increases data security. Meanwhile, for ensuring that the traceability system can utilize the non-modifiability of the blockchain, we use IPFS to store the original data and obtain the index according to the original data. Finally, we got a four-tiered authority management framework.

To test the performance of our framework, we reconstructed a MedRec [1] framework for the traceability system as a baseline based on the principles in [1]. Then we designed two sets of simulation experiments to test the performance of these two frameworks, which are the stand-alone test with batch upload to IPFS and the multi-machine test with batch upload to IPFS. The experimental results show that our framework's execution time of the same operation sequence is shorter than the MedRec [1] framework, regardless of the overall execution time or the execution time of crucial operations.

The paper is structured as follows. Section 2 describes the related work in authority management of the traceability system. Section 3 describes the structures of our framework, the vital smart contracts, and operations. Section 4 describes our experimental design and analyzes the experimental results. Section 5 concludes the paper.

2   Related Works

With the frequent occurrence of product safety issues and the increasing emphasis on product traceability, coupled with the convergence of blockchain technology and traceability requirements, many researchers have begun to introduce blockchain in traceability scenarios to ensure that product traceability information will not tamper [2,13–15]. Tian [13] proposed a blockchain-based traceability system for the Chinese agri-food supply chain. Tse et al. [15] also turned their attention to the Chinese food industry and proposed a decentralized food authentication model with blockchain. Moreover, they compared this model with the traditional food management model. Aside from the food industry, Biswas et al. [2] created a wine traceability system based on blockchain.

In order to ensure that the traceability system does not disclose the company's confidential data and consumers can use the traceability of the blockchain to ensure product security, it is necessary to add appropriate authority management functions to the blockchain. Ouaddah et al. [8] and Maesa et al. [5] focus on combining authority management with the blockchain transaction, and then they will create and transfer permission as a particular transaction on the blockchain. On the other hand, Azaria et al. [1], Neisse et al. [6] and Outchakoucht et al. [9] pay attention to utilizing the smart contract to complete authority management. Azaria et al. [1] and Neisse et al. [6] implemented an authority management framework directly with smart contracts on the Ethereum, and Outchakoucht et al. [9] improved the authority management function by adding smart contracts to FairAccess [8]. From the perspective of business scenarios, Azaria et al. [1], Rifi et al. [11] and Dagher et al. [3] mainly focus on e-health, while Ouaddah et al. [8], Outchakoucht et al. [9] and Novo [7] focuses on the IoT field. These two research fields occupy the vast majority of the relevant literature in our research, and there are few kinds of research about the authority management of blockchain in the traceability system except Neisse et al. [6].

Many researchers have done some research on the privacy protection of blockchain data. Kosba et al. [4] developed a platform based on cryptography for developing smart contracts. Developers can develop directly on the platform without considering the privacy of the data. When one program calls the contract, the transaction data can be automatically encrypted by some encryption protocols to avoid data leakage. However, most researchers solve this problem by storing original data off-chain. Zyskind et al. [16] proposed a DHT-based blockchain framework. In this framework, data is stored off-chain by DHT, then the index of these data is stored on the blockchain. This solution not only ensures the security of private data but also uses blockchain to guarantee that the data stored off-chain can not tamper. At the same time, storing indexes rather than original data on blockchain also reduces the storage pressure on the machine. Azaria et al. [1] also reduce the amount of data stored on blockchain by storing original data in the database.

3 Hyperledger Fabric and IPFS-based Authority Management Framework

Although many researchers are researching the authority management framework of the blockchain, there are still some problems [1,3,5–9,11]. Most of these researches utilize the consensus algorithm of PoW or PoS, and the block generation is slower, which significantly drags down TPS. Additionally, there is a danger of data leakage in these research results [5–9]. Therefore the public data on the blockchain is not friendly to the enterprises. How to protect enterprise privacy while ensuring data traceability is also an enormous problem. Since many researchers' research fields are e-health [1,3,11] and IoT [7–9], how to study a suitable blockchain authority management framework for traceability scenarios is also worth considering.

In order to solve these problems, we propose a new Hyperledger Fabric and IPFS-based authority management framework for traceability systems. By using the Hyperledger Fabric to develop a coalition chain, the framework sets barriers to entry, which reduces the possibility of data leakage. The Kafka algorithm is used to replace the PoW and PoS that required a lot of computation and time, which speeds up the block generation and improves the TPS of the blockchain. For protecting the data privacy, the framework introduces IPFS for storing original data. At the same time, the hash value of the original data generated by IPFS is stored on the blockchain to ensure that the original data has not tampered. Finally, we got a blockchain authority management framework. This framework contains two essential types of smart contracts, one for authority management of roles in the traceability system and the other for querying and modifying traceability data. At the same time, the framework provides five crucial operations. This paper will describe these in detail later.

3.1 Architecture

Our authority management framework has four main layers: business layer, authority layer, contract layer, and data layer (see Fig. 1). The business layer is responsible for providing API interfaces to users. The authority layer is used to determine the identity of users and the operation to be performed and then invoke the corresponding smart contract from the contract layer. The contract layer is mainly to store smart contracts and interact with the data layer. The data layer is designed to store traceability data.

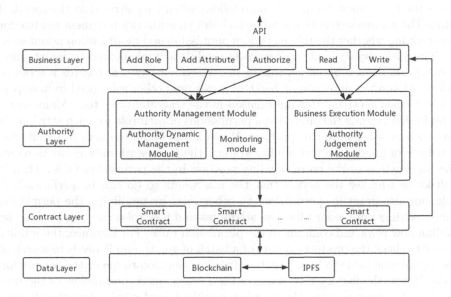

Fig. 1. Authority management framework architecture

Business Layer. This layer is mainly used to provide users with the API interfaces of the traceability system. It divides these API interfaces into two categories. One is traceability information query, information modification, and authority grant designed for ordinary users. The other is for administrators of the traceability system. The traceability system administrators can add new roles and attributes to the traceability system through specific API interfaces. These API interfaces are implemented on the Fabric SDK. The user's request is processed as the input of the interface. Then the framework will store the traceability information in the blockchain, and the result of this operation is used as the output.

Authority Layer. The primary function of the authority layer is to control the permission of the functions mentioned in the business layer, including determining whether the role has the corresponding operation permission when querying information, modifying information and authorizing other roles, and completing permission creation when adding new roles or new attributes. The authority layer mainly has two modules, namely the authority management module and the business execution module. The authority management module mainly consists of two sub-modules, which are the authority dynamic management module and monitoring module. The authority dynamic management module is mainly to complete permissions creation and assignment when adding new roles or new attributes. It also can grant permission to other roles. The monitoring module is used to recover temporary permissions when they arrived at the specified time. The business execution module includes an authority judgment module for determining whether the role has query permission and modification permission.

The authority dynamic management module is implemented by maintaining a role permission table. Each role in the traceability system records a series of information when processing a batch of goods, and other roles need to have permission when accessing this information in the traceability system. Maintaining a table that records the operational permissions of each role for each attribute is an excellent solution to this problem. When a role wants to query or modify the attribute of goods in a traceability system, the framework only needs to query the information of the corresponding position in the permission table. Then it will know whether the action that the role wants to do can be performed. A role can also grant its permissions to other roles by modifying the permission table. Adding permissions for new attributes and new roles can also be done by adding new rows and columns to the permission table. For instance, the retailer wants to check the production date of a batch of goods, and it needs to search in the permission table to know whether it has permission to query the production date. If not, the factory role can give the retailer query permission to the production date by modifying the permission table. In order to achieve the function of the monitoring module, it only needs to change the value of the corresponding position in the permission table to unavailable after the role's operational permissions for an attribute expires. The implementation of the business execution module requires two steps. The first step is to query whether the permissions in the permission table are available, and the second step is to obtain traceability information.

Contract Layer. The contract layer is mainly used to store the smart contract information of the blockchain network so that the authority layer can directly find the required smart contract from this layer. There are two types of smart contracts in this layer. One is the role permission list contract, and the other is the business execution contract. The role permission list contract can be used to obtain all the permissions that a role has and to determine whether the role has access to the corresponding attribute. It stores permissions in the form of attribute names, access methods, and expiration dates. The role can find out whether it has legal permission by the attribute name and the corresponding access method. When the permission already has exceeded the expiration date, the contract will tell the role that it does not have the corresponding access rights. When the role gains new permissions, the contract writes the corresponding permissions to the blockchain so that the role can use it later. The business execution contract provides query and modification for a specific attribute. Each attribute in the traceability system has a corresponding contract. After the roles obtained the access rights from the role permission list contract, they can query and modify the data through the API interfaces provided by the contract. When the role queries data, it will obtain the hash of the file stored on the IPFS from the blockchain according to the data ID provided by the role. When the role modified data, it stores the original data on the IPFS and stores the obtained hash on the blockchain.

Data Layer. The data layer is mainly utilized to complete the storage of information. It contains two modules, which are blockchain and IPFS. The blockchain stores shared information, including small-scale information and hashes of large files on IPFS. IPFS is an auxiliary module for reducing the amount of data stored on the blockchain. For example, if the information to be stored contains video, it can be stored on IPFS. Then the IPFS can provide a hash calculated by a hash function according to the original data. This hash can be stored on the blockchain to ensure irreparable modification and privacy of the data.

Blockchain is the storage core of the entire framework. The technical points that are considered in this paper are ledger technology, smart contract, and consensus mechanism. The ledger is the sequenced, tamper-resistant record of all state transitions in the Fabric, and there is a state database to maintain the current Fabric state. In the scenario of this paper, the control of the permissions need to record the current state, and the transfer process of the permissions and the change of the traceability information can also be recorded through the ledger for review, so Fabric's ledger technology is very suitable. This article selects the default state database LevelDB, which does not require additional management costs. And it performs better than CouchDB in the authority management scenario. This scenario does not require rich text queries, and LevelDB is more suitable for the Orderer node. The use of smart contracts has been mentioned in the contract layer. The choice of consensus algorithm is also the key to this module. The traditional blockchain consensus mechanisms, such as PoW and PoS, mostly require a lot of computing power, which makes the block generation extremely slow. The framework in this paper sorts the messages through Kafka, coordinates the nodes by Zookeeper, and finally makes the Orderer node complete the consensus and quickly generate the blocks. The purpose of IPFS is to ensure the privacy of traceability information and reduce the size of the blockchain. If the information is stored directly on the ledger's ledger, all information will be disclosed once the ledger is revealed. If the hash value of the IPFS is stored in the blockchain, the leakage of the ledger will only lead to the leakage of the hash value, and the specific information cannot be directly obtained, which ensures the privacy of the data to some extent. Storing the hash value also relieves the storage pressure of the blockchain.

3.2 Operation

The framework provides five crucial operations: adding new roles, adding new attributes, authorizing, querying information, and modifying information. Adding a new role means that a new business node appears in the traceability system, and the system needs to integrate the new role into it. Adding a new attribute means that the traceability system needs to record a new type of traceability information. Authorizing means granting permission the role had to another. Querying or modifying information means querying or modifying the specific content of an attribute.

Add Role. When the traceability system adds a new role generally with a new set of attributes, this framework will add a new role permission list contract and some new business execution contracts to the blockchain for this new role. The role permission list contract records the initial permission information of this new role, and these business execution contracts provide read and write interfaces for new attributes. Next, other roles can authorize the new role by modifying the role permission list contract of the new role. The new role can also modify the role permission list contracts of other roles to authorize other roles.

Add Attributes. When the role wants to add a new attribute to the traceability system, the framework will create a new business execution contract for this attribute. Through this contract, a role with access rights can query and modify this attribute. Next, the role can authorize other roles so that they can query and modify the attribute.

Authorize. This operation means that a role modifies the role permission list contract of another role, thereby copying the attribute access rights the role had to another role so that another role can perform the same operation on the attribute.

Read. By calling the read interface written in the business execution contract of an attribute, the role can obtain the hash that refers to the specific content stored in the IPFS about this attribute. Through this hash, the role can query the corresponding file from IPFS to get the original data.

Write. By calling the write interface written in the business execution contract of an attribute, the role can write the hash that refers to the specific content stored in the IPFS about this attribute into the blockchain. For obtaining this hash, the role can upload the original data to IPFS.

4 Experiment

To evaluate the performance of our framework, we reconstructed a MedRec [1] framework for the traceability system as a baseline based on the principles in [1]. For improving the accuracy of the experiment, we use the same sequence of operations to test the execution time of the two frameworks. Also, to avoid the contingency of the experiment, we test the execution time of the two frameworks under different CPU utilization and average the execution time of multiple experiments. Then we designed two types of simulation experiments to test the performance of these two frameworks, which are the stand-alone test with batch upload to IPFS and the multi-machine test with batch upload to IPFS. The experimental results show that our framework's execution time using the same operation sequence is shorter than the MedRec [1] framework.

4.1 Experimental Design

In this experiment, we selected two physical machines and built a virtual machine on one physical machine as our experimental environment. The configuration of one physical machine as follows: Intel Core i5-7300HQ CPU, 16 GB RAM, Windows10 64-bit operating system. The configuration of another physical machine is as follows: Intel Core i7-3700HQ CPU, 4 GB RAM, CentOS7 64-bit operating system. The configuration of the virtual machine is as follows: 2-core 2-thread CPU, 6 GB memory, Ubuntu 18.04 64-bit operating system.

In order to compare the performance of the two frameworks, we chose the same sequence of operations. This sequence of operations contains all five crucial operations described above, and the initial state of the two authority management frameworks remains the same. The specific steps of this sequence of operations are as follows:

(1) Add a role called Factory with an attribute named FactoryOperator;
(2) Add two FactoryOperator records to the blockchain. The record content is ID 1 with FactoryOperator operator1 and ID 2 with FactoryOperator operator2;
(3) Factory queries which FactoryOperator operated the ID 1 and ID 2 products;
(4) Add a role called Retailer with an attribute named RetailerOperator;
(5) Add an attribute called RetailerSellingPrice for Retailer;
(6) Retailer queries which FactoryOperator operated the ID 1 and ID 2 products;
(7) Factory assigns the read permission of the FactoryOperator to Retailer;
(8) Retailer queries which FactoryOperator operated the ID 1 and ID 2 products.

The two test environments in this experiment are the stand-alone test with batch upload to IPFS and the multi-machine test with batch upload to IPFS. The stand-alone test with batch upload to IPFS means that the two frameworks only run on a virtual machine without communicating with other machines and use IPFS to store original data. The multi-machine test with batch upload to IPFS means that the two frameworks run on a virtual machine and a physical machine, and use IPFS to store original data. In the above two test environments, we tested the execution time of each operation in the operation sequence under the condition that the CPU utilization was 30%, 50%, and 80%. We repeated the test five times in each test environment and averaged the execution time of each operation.

4.2   Experimental Results and Analysis

After testing in two test environments, we obtained the average execution time of each operation of the two frameworks under the same operation sequence. After analyzing the results of the experiment, we can see that our framework is better than the MedRec [1] framework based on Ethereum.

Table 1. The execution time of operations in the stand-alone test environment

CPU utilization	Framework	Add role(s)	Write(s)	Read(s)	Add role(s)	Add attribute(s)	Read(s)	Authorize(s)	Read(s)
30%	Fabric framework	65.676	6.744	0.128	51.548	30.198	0.054	2.106	0.124
	Fabric framework with IPFS	52.648	6.824	0.168	53.678	32.046	0.096	2.13	0.17
	MedRec framework	75.598	30.228	0.092	75.546	45.292	0.04	15.22	0.168
50%	Fabric framework	50.612	6.622	0.132	51.078	30.826	0.062	2.094	0.136
	Fabric framework with IPFS	51.134	6.694	0.144	54.11	31.326	0.062	2.126	0.204
	MedRec framework	75.604	30.264	0.116	75.572	45.296	0.056	15.232	0.154
80%	Fabric framework	53.964	6.7	0.168	56.318	32.102	0.064	2.12	0.136
	Fabric framework with IPFS	56.488	6.814	0.172	59.234	32.244	0.06	2.104	0.196
	MedRec framework	78.68	30.224	0.108	84.608	45.324	0.038	15.236	0.16

Stand-Alone Test Environment. In the stand-alone test environment, we got the results shown in the following table (see Table 1). At the same time, in order to test the changes in our framework after using IPFS, we also tested the execution time of not using IPFS. From the experimental results obtained, we have reached the following conclusions:

(1) In the case of Kafka consensus, adding roles, adding attributes, writing information, and authorizing of the Fabric framework have visible performance improvement. Moreover, the execution time of reading information is similar to the MedRec [1] framework;

(2) According to the experiment, since the MedRec [1] framework needs to calculate when generating the block, the CPU utilization in this process is significantly higher than our framework, even if this tow framework has the same CPU utilization at the beginning. In the case of 50% CPU utilization at the beginning, the MedRec [1] framework's CPU utilization is near full load, and our framework is far from full load; In the case of 80% CPU utilization at the beginning, Fabric framework is close to full load, and the MedRec [1] framework is still full load;

(3) The performance of the Fabric framework is similar when the CPU utilization is around 30% and 50%. The performance reduces significantly when the CPU utilization reaches 80%, but it is still better than the MedRec [1] framework;

(4) When using IPFS as a tool for specific traceability information storage, the performance of the Fabric framework will slightly reduce. However, in order to improve the privacy of the data, these losses are acceptable;

(5) The MedRec [1] framework sometimes needs more time when it generates blocks, which causes the execution time of some operations slower than other iterations under the same conditions.

(6) The Fabric framework with IPFS is faster than the Fabric framework under the condition of 30% CPU utilization. The reason is that the operation is temporarily suspended when starting the network, and the operation is performed after completing this process.

Table 2. The execution time of operations in the multi-machine test environment

CPU utilization	Framework	Add role(s)	Write(s)	Read(s)	Add role(s)	Add attribute(s)	Read(s)	Authorize(s)	Read(s)
30%	Fabric framework	52.366	6.722	0.144	51.408	31.112	0.084	2.11	0.148
	Fabric framework with IPFS	53.456	6.886	0.192	55.97	32.864	0.126	2.044	0.184
	MedRec framework	75.638	30.294	0.092	75.666	45.364	0.068	15.232	0.174
50%	Fabric framework	51.086	6.668	0.228	51.238	30.622	0.056	2.124	0.134
	Fabric framework with IPFS	58.04	6.938	0.16	61.9	35.088	0.124	2.104	0.24
	MedRec framework	78.644	30.226	0.102	75.57	48.302	0.046	15.224	0.146
80%	Fabric framework	54.054	6.756	0.164	57.87	32.098	0.078	2.098	0.178
	Fabric framework with IPFS	58.948	6.952	0.178	60.362	33.998	0.08	2.096	0.488
	MedRec framework	78.608	30.228	0.096	78.56	48.378	0.056	15.236	0.146

Multi-machine Test Environment. In the multi-machine test environment, we got the results shown in the following table (see Table 2). At the same time, in order to test the changes in our framework after using IPFS, we also tested the execution time of not using IPFS. From the experimental results obtained, we have reached the following conclusions:

(1) The execution time of most operations in the multi-machine environment is slightly lower than the stand-alone environment, but it is still better than the MedRec [1] framework;
(2) Other conclusions are roughly consistent with the conclusions in the stand-alone environment.

5   Conclusion

With the frequent occurrence of product safety issues, product traceability has gradually attracted people's attention. The combination of blockchain technology and traceability system has led many researchers to research the traceability system based on blockchain [2,13–15]. Nevertheless, for the protection of corporate data, researchers are beginning to focus on how to control permissions on the blockchain [1,5,6,8,9]. Nonetheless, there are many problems with these blockchain-based authority management models. The authority management models in [1,3,5–9,11] adopt the PoW or PoS, which need much time to generate a block. Secondly, the authority management models in [5–9] store original data directly on the blockchain and destroy the privacy of the data. Finally, most of the authority management models focus on the fields of e-health [1,3,11] and IoT [7–9]. In order to solve these problems, we propose an authority management framework based on Hyperledger Fabric and IPFS. This four-layer framework uses the Kafka algorithm as the consensus algorithm to speed the block generation and utilizes IPFS to store original data to protect data privacy. Through experiments, we also confirmed that the execution time of our framework is shorter than the MedRec-based framework in the same operation sequence. This paper still needs improvement due to time and article length. In this paper, only the execution time of the framework under a sequence of operations is used to reflect its efficiency, and other feasible parameters need to be considered. At the same time, only one framework was selected for comparison, so the next step is to enrich the structure of the control group. In the future, we can also try to design more efficient consensus algorithms to enhance the framework of this paper.

Acknowledgments. This study was funded by the National Natural Science Foundation of China (Grant No. 61702372).

References

1. Azaria, A., Ekblaw, A., Vieira, T., Lippman, A.: MedRec: using blockchain for medical data access and permission management. In: 2016 2nd International Conference on Open and Big Data (OBD), pp. 25–30. IEEE (2016)

2. Biswas, K., Muthukkumarasamy, V., Tan, W.L.: Blockchain based wine supply chain traceability system. In: Future Technologies Conference, pp. 1–7 (2017)

3. Dagher, G.G., Mohler, J., Milojkovic, M., Marella, P.B.: Ancile: privacy-preserving framework for access control and interoperability of electronic health records using blockchain technology. Sustain. Cities Soc. **39**, 283–297 (2018)

4. Kosba, A., Miller, A., Shi, E., Wen, Z., Papamanthou, C.: Hawk: the blockchain model of cryptography and privacy-preserving smart contracts. In: 2016 IEEE Symposium on Security and Privacy (SP), pp. 839–858. IEEE (2016)

5. Maesa, D.D.F., Mori, P., Ricci, L.: Blockchain based access control. In: Chen, L.Y., Reiser, H.P. (eds.) DAIS 2017. LNCS, vol. 10320, pp. 206–220. Springer, Cham (2017). https://doi.org/10.1007/978-3-319-59665-5_15

6. Neisse, R., Steri, G., Nai-Fovino, I.: A blockchain-based approach for data accountability and provenance tracking. In: Proceedings of the 12th International Conference on Availability, Reliability and Security, p. 14. ACM (2017)

7. Novo, O.: Blockchain meets IoT: an architecture for scalable access management in IoT. IEEE Internet of Things J. **5**(2), 1184–1195 (2018)

8. Ouaddah, A., Abou Elkalam, A., Ait Ouahman, A.: FairAccess: a new Blockchain-based access control framework for the Internet of Things. Secur. Commun. Netw. **9**(18), 5943–5964 (2016)

9. Outchakoucht, A., Hamza, E., Leroy, J.P.: Dynamic access control policy based on blockchain and machine learning for the Internet of Things. Int. J. Adv. Comput. Sci. Appl. **8**(7), 417–424 (2017)

10. Pouillot, R., et al.: Infectious dose of Listeria monocytogenes in outbreak linked to ice cream, United States, 2015. Emerg. Infect. Dis. **22**(12), 2113 (2016)

11. Rifi, N., Rachkidi, E., Agoulmine, N., Taher, N.C.: Towards using blockchain technology for eHealth data access management. In: 2017 Fourth International Conference on Advances in Biomedical Engineering (ICABME), pp. 1–4. IEEE (2017)

12. Sandhu, R.: Rationale for the RBAC96 family of access control models (1997)

13. Tian, F.: An agri-food supply chain traceability system for China based on RFID and blockchain technology. In: 2016 13th International Conference on Service Systems and Service Management (ICSSSM), pp. 1–6. IEEE (2016)

14. Tian, F.: A supply chain traceability system for food safety based on HACCP, blockchain and Internet of things. In: 2017 International Conference on Service Systems and Service Management, pp. 1–6. IEEE (2017)

15. Tse, D., Zhang, B., Yang, Y., Cheng, C., Mu, H.: Blockchain application in food supply information security. In: 2017 IEEE International Conference on Industrial Engineering and Engineering Management (IEEM), pp. 1357–1361. IEEE (2017)

16. Zyskind, G., Nathan, O., Pentland, A.: Enigma: decentralized computation platform with guaranteed privacy. arXiv preprint arXiv:1506.03471 (2015)

Deep Learning Based Dynamic Uplink Power Control for NOMA Ultra-Dense Network System

Xu Liu[1(✉)], Xin Chen[2], Ying Chen[2], and Zhuo Li[2]

[1] School of Automation, Beijing Information Science and Technology University, Beijing, China
lxmmdm96@163.com
[2] School of Computer Science, Beijing Information Science and Technology University, Beijing, China
{chenxin,chenying,lizhuo}@bistu.edu.cn

Abstract. As the development of blockchain and 5G, all kinds of intelligent devices have increasingly higher requirements on data rate and computing power, a large number of base stations are used, optimizing service cost and equipment energy consumption have become new challenges. It is certain that blockchain will be an important technology for the successful development of 5G network. As a new research direction, non-orthogonal multiple access technology (NOMA) combined with ultra-dense network (UDN) can effectively improve system capacity and reduce service cost. In this paper, we study a dynamic energy efficiency (EE) optimization problem under uplink NOMA communication in UDN. In order to ensure the real-time requirement of user equipment, a markov decision process (MDP) model is constructed by quantifying resources in access points (APs) and user equipments (UEs). On this basis, we propose a Deep Q-Network (DQN) based dynamic uplink power control algorithm to maximize the EE. According to different uplink channel gains in different base stations, UE transmission power is controlled through the center node. Through emulation and comparison with traditional Q-learning algorithm, experimental results show that DQN algorithm can effectively improve the EE of the system.

Keywords: Non-orthogonal multiple access (NOMA) · Ultra-dense network (UDN) · Markov decision process (MDP) · Energy efficiency (EE) · Deep Q-Network (DQN)

1 Introduction

With the development of IoT technology, the number of smart devices such as mobile phones, computers, tablets, smart bracelets increases dramatically, making the combination of blockchain and 5G possible [1,19]. According to Ericsson mobility report in June 2019 [2], there are 7.9 billion people using mobile phones

© Springer Nature Singapore Pte Ltd. 2020
Z. Zheng et al. (Eds.): BlockSys 2019, CCIS 1156, pp. 774–786, 2020.
https://doi.org/10.1007/978-981-15-2777-7_64

globally, and this number will continue to grow in the 5G era. Meanwhile, with the developement of 5G, more and more computation-intensive applications with high energy consumption and low time delay, such as virtual reality, augmented reality and interactive games, are becoming available [16]. Due to the limited battery capacity and computing ability of intelligent devices, current wireless network cannot meet the needs of ultra-reliable low latency communications. In order to increase network capacity improve quality of service, mobile edge computing (MEC) become a promising technology in 5G system. The combination of ultra-dense network (UDN) and MEC has become an important technology for 5G [3]. In [4] and [5], UDN is composed of a macro base station (BS) and a number of small BSs. The macro BS is responsible for the basic coverage and collaborative management of resources. The small BSs with low power are densely deployed within the scope of macro BS coverage, and mainly used to transfer user data. According to [6], with the increase in the number of base stations, overall energy consumption of UDN system also rises dramatically, thus reducing the system energy consumption while ensuring the quality of service has became an important direction of current 5G research.

In order to solve the interference control and resource management problem in UDN, we introduce non-orthogonal multiple access (NOMA) technique. Unlike orthogonal multiple access (OMA), NOMA allocates multiple users in the same channel, and uses a complex receiver design to improve spectrum efficiency. [7,17,18] do not consider the NOMA uplink scheduling problem, reducing transmission latency and signaling overhead, which leads to a grant-free uplink transmission. According to [8,9] and [10], the combination of UDN and NOMA, as an important research field, faces many challenges, such as user pairing, transmission distortion, interference effect, resource allocation, power control, interruption probability analysis, etc.

Compared with 4G, UDN deploys more base stations with more complex structure and higher energy consumption. In order to reduce energy consumption of whole communication system, and improve energy efficiency (EE), many researches have been carried out in this field. In order to improve energy efficiency, [11] formulated the power allocation (PA) problem as a mixed integer nonlinear programming (MINP) problem, and a algorithm called QPSO was introduced to obtain a solution with lower complexity. [12] formulated the EE resource allocation problem as a mixed integer non-convex optimization problem. By using convex relaxation and dual decomposition techniques, they solved the problem of EE optimization of heterogeneous UDN downlink channel to optimize sub-channel allocation and power allocation. [13] introduced NOMA in UDN, and proposed a matching algorithm to allocate appropriate AP and resource blocks (RBs) for multiple users. They aimed at improving the throughput in UDN. [15] studied the subcarrier assignment in NOMA, and a local optimal subcarrier assignment algorithm is proposed based on many-to-many matching theory.

Different from these studies, we mainly study the transmission power control problem of the uplink channel. This paper transforms the optimal EE problem into a dynamic power control (PC) problem by establishing a MDP model. This paper proposes a DQN-based NOMA ultra-dense network uplink PC algorithm. In this method, NOMA technology is adopted to transmit user data and improve channel utilization, which could largely improve the network throughput. For the dynamic power control problem in actual situations, DQN is applied to conduct the power control to improve energy efficiency. The main contributions of this paper are as follows:

- Unlike other papers that only considered how to maximize throughput, we consider the equilibrium problem between throughput maximization and energy consumption reduction. To tackle the uplink channel resource shortage in the UDN and improve system capacity, we incorporate NOMA in the UDN scenario and apply the uniform channel gain difference pairing method to perform user pairing.
- The actual power control problem in the 5G UDN scenario is formulated as a MDP based stochastic optimization problem, whose aim is to maximize EE. Then, DQN algorithm is introduced to solve the optimal solution of this dynamic real-time PA problem.
- We conduct a series of experiments to evaluate the performance of the proposed algorithm, and the results show that as the number of users and BSs increases, the interference becomes stronger. In addition, the EE obtained by the DQN algorithm is still better than other algorithms.

The rest of this paper is organized as follows. We introduce the NOMA UDN model and describe the problem in Sect. 2. Section 3 formulates the optimization problem and the DQN-based framework. Section 4 gives the experiment results and analysis. In Sect. 5, we conclude the whole paper.

2 System Model

2.1 Ultra-Dense Nework Model

In this paper, we construct an ultra-dense network (UDN) system with NOMA, which consists of a CAP and K BSs. As shown in Fig. 1, the CAP is located in the center of the whole system, which is used to control K BSs distributed around it. The indices for the AP is defined as $k \in \{1, 2, \cdots, K\}$. Due to technical limitations, it is assumed that each BS can serve Q users.

Unlike traditional OMA uplink (UL) transmissions, in the NOMA uplink, user data from multiple user equipments (UE) is transmitted to the base station through the same subcarrier [14]. Each UE emits power independently of the other, but signals received at the BS end interfere with each other. In this system, multiple users of the same BS transmit data to BS through the same subcarrier with transmitting power $p_{m,n}^k \leq P_{max}$, which P_{max} is the biggest transmitted power of each UE. According to the NOMA protocol, each BS has N subchannels and each subchannel can support M UEs, which $m \in \{1, 2, \cdots, M\}$ and $n \in \{1, 2, \cdots, N\}$. Definiting the channel gain of M UEs in subchannel in descending

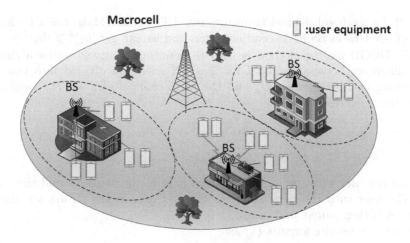

Fig. 1. A NOMA ultra-dense network model

order, and we can get $|h_1|^2 \geqslant |h_2|^2 \geqslant \cdots \geqslant |h_M|^2$. M UEs send signals to BS through N subchannels. Define the bandwidth resource of each BS as B, the bandwidth of each subchannel is $B_n = \frac{B}{N}$.

We assume that CAP can collect complete instantaneous channel quality information (CQI) and resource state of BSs in the coverage area. CAP then selects the appropriate BSs for UE and allocates available subchannel resources according to the proposed scheme.

2.2 Computation Model

In UDN, the AP and UEs in each small cell apply NOMA, which means that users in the same cell can multiplex on the same subchannel. Considering the ideal successive interference cancellation situation, we denote $p_{i,j}^{k,t}$ as the transmitting power of signal transmitted by the i-th user to the k-th BSs through the j-th subchannel at time slot t. Then the signal-to-interference-plus-noise ratios (SINR) in uplink between UE i and BS k at the t-th time solt can be expressed as:

$$\gamma_{i,j}^{k,t} = \frac{|h_{i,j}^{k,t}|^2 p_{i,j}^{k,t}}{\sum_{m=i+1}^{M} |h_{m,j}^{k,t}|^2 p_{m,j}^{k,t} + I^{k,t} + \sigma_Z^2} \tag{1}$$

where

$$I^{k,t} = \sum_{n=1,n\neq j}^{N} \sum_{m=1}^{M} p_{m,n}^{k,t} |h_{m,n}^{k,t}|^2 \tag{2}$$

$I^{k,t}$ represents interference from other UEs occupied in different sub-channels within the same BS, and the $\sum_{l=i+1}^{M} |h_{l,j}|^2 p_{l,j}^t$ is the interuser interference. σ_Z^2 is the additive white Gaussian noise (AWGN) in subchannal.

In order to reduce system complexity and the amount of computation, we use uniform channel gain difference (UCGD) pairing method and assume that

$m = 2$, i.e. each subchannel transmits two UE signals. Make the UL channel gain of 2N UEs in BS in descending order, and we can get $|h_1|^2 \geqslant |h_2|^2 \geqslant \cdots \geqslant |h_{2N}|^2$. UCGD pairing method is used to maintain relatively uniform channel gain difference between paired UEs. The 2N users are divided into two sets, the strong channel gain set H_s and the weak channel gain set H_w, which are respectively expressed as:

$$H_s = |h_1|^2, |h_2|^2, \cdots, |h_N|^2 \tag{3}$$

$$H_w = |h_{N+1}|^2, |h_{N+2}|^2, \cdots, |h_{2N}|^2 \tag{4}$$

Pair the user with the highest channel gain in the weak set and the strong set. The user with the second highest channel gain in the strong set and the weak set is then paired, and so on.

So we can rewrite formula (1) as:

$$\gamma_{1,j}^{k,t} = \frac{|h_{1,j}^{k,t}|^2 p_{1,j}^{k,t}}{|h_{2,j}^{k,t}|^2 p_{2,j}^{k,t} + I^{k,t'} + \sigma_Z^2} \tag{5}$$

$$\gamma_{2,j}^{k,t} = \frac{|h_{2,j}^{k,t}|^2 p_{2,j}^{k,t}}{I^{k,t'} + \sigma_Z^2} \tag{6}$$

where

$$I^{k,t'} = \sum_{n=1, n \neq j}^{N} \sum_{m=1}^{2} p_{m,n}^{k,t} |h_{m,n}^{k,t}|^2 \tag{7}$$

According to the Shannons capacity formula, the data rate from UE i to BS k at time solt t in uplink can be expressed as:

$$R_{1,j}^{k,t} = B_n \log_2(1 + \gamma_{1,j}^{k,t}) \tag{8}$$

$$R_{2,j}^{k,t} = B_n \log_2(1 + \gamma_{2,j}^{k,t}) \tag{9}$$

Therefore, the total sum rate of all the BSs is:

$$R_{sum}^t = \sum_{k=1}^{K} \sum_{j=1}^{N} R_{1,j}^{k,t} + \sum_{k=1}^{K} \sum_{j=1}^{N} R_{2,j}^{k,t} \tag{10}$$

The total transmit power consumption of UL at time solt t is:

$$P_{sum}^t = \sum_{j=1}^{K} \sum_{i=1}^{N} p_{i,j}^{k,t} \tag{11}$$

As the energy consumption and throughput are modeled, according to (11), the EE at time instant t is defined as:

$$\max_{p^t} EE = \frac{R_{sum}^t}{P_{sum}^t + P^c} \tag{12}$$

As mentioned in the analysis above, the energy-saving power control problem of uplink NOMA UDN system can be expressed as follows:

$$\max_{\boldsymbol{P}^t} \quad EE \tag{13}$$

$$\text{s.t. } C1 : P_{sum}^t \leq P_{\max}^K \tag{13a}$$

$$C2 : p_{k,n}^t \geq 0, \forall k, n \tag{13b}$$

$$C3 : p_{k,n}^t \leq p_{\max}, \forall k, n \tag{13c}$$

$$C4 : R_{k,n}^t \geq R_{\min}, \forall k, n \tag{13d}$$

$$C5 : I^{k,t} \leq I_{\max} \tag{13e}$$

where R_{min} represents the minimum UL transfer rate. C1 is the transmission power limit of all UEs; C2 and C3 is the transmission power limit of each UEs; C4 represents that the data rate of each user is greater than the minimum UE data rate R_{min}; C5 represents interference limits between UEs.

From (13), due to the offline options require the future information of stochastic various such as channel gain h and interference I. However, lose information is hard to obtain, thus, offline solution is a challenging task.

3 Problem Formulation

Due to the lack of channel state information (CSI) priori knowledge, traditional optimization algorithms are difficult to solve such problems. To maximize EE, 5G UDN power control with NOMA technology is expressed as a Markov decision process (MDP). We adopt a model-free deep learning framework DQN to solve the MDP problem without prior knowledge. This section is main about DQN.

3.1 Background

We present the dynamic power control problem as an infinitely continuous MDP. As a sequential decision-making mathematical model, MDP is built on the basis of two objects, which are environment and agent. The advantage is that no prior knowledge of any environmental dynamics is required. The elements include state, action, strategy, and reward.

DQN is one of the most popular reinforcement learning (RL) methods to solve MDP problems. As a kind of RL, DQN is improved on Q-learning algorithm and convolutional neural network. For the machine learning framework in this paper, we define a tuple $\langle S, A, R \rangle$, representing state space, action space and reward function respectively. The details are as follows.

- **State space:** The network state of each time slot t contains the real-time CSI of all BSs, which can be expressed as $S_t = \left\{ R_{n,k}^t, P_{n,k}^t \right\}$. In other words, the agent can get the data rate and transmission power of the system through the state space.

Algorithm 1. DQN based dynamic power control algorithm

Input:
    List of actions to be taken by UEs, Maximum noise limit $I_{\max}$, Minimum transfer rate limit $R_{\min}$.

Output:
    The Q network parameter

1: Initialize replay memory D to capacity N
2: Initialize the state-action value network $Q^*(s_t, a_t; \theta)$ and the traget network $Q^*(s_t', a_t'; \theta^-)$
3: **for** episode= 1,M **do**
4:     Initialize the NOMA UDN communication system and the state s_1
5:     **for** t=1,T **do**
6:         Apply with the ε-greedy algorithm to select a random action a_t from the current Q value output,otherwise a_t=arg max$Q(s_t, a_t)$
7:         execute a_t, get the reward r_t and new state s_{t+1}
8:         Store transition (s_t, a_t, r_t, s_{t+1}) in D
9:         **if** the replay memory D is full **then**
10:            Sample a random batch of samples transitions (s_i, a_i, r_i, s_{i+1}) from D
11:            **if** s_{i+1} is s_T **then**
12:                $y_i = r_i$
13:            **else**
14:                $y_i = r_i + \gamma \max Q'(s_{i+1}, a_{i+1} \mid \theta^-)$
15:            **end if**
16:            Update the parameter of DNN θ by minimizing the loss: $L = E[(y_t - Q^*(s_t, a_t; \theta))^2]$
17:            Update target network parameter update $\theta_- = \theta$ every C step
18:         **end if**
19:     **end for**
20: **end for**

- **Action space:** The transmission power of each user's uplink channel is determined by agent. Therefore, the action at time slot t is defined as a_t, and the action space is A, where $a_t \in A$. So the action is $a_t = \left\{ p_{1,n}^{k,t}, p_{2,n}^{k,t}, \cdots, p_{m,n}^{k,t} \right\}$, and each action corresponds to a state.
- **Reward function:** In some manuscripts, reward functions are carefully designed to increase the transmission rate of agents and reduce interference. Inspired by these previous works, EE is used directly as a reward function and is shared by all agents, which the reward function is

$$r_t = \frac{R_{sum}^t}{P_{sum}^t + P^{c,t}} \tag{14}$$

The final ultimate goal of the optimization problem is to find the appropriate transmission power and maximize the EE of the system. So, the expected function $Q_\pi(s_t, a_t)$ based on the initial state can be conducted as

$$Q_\pi(s_t, a_t) = \mathbb{E}_\pi \left[\sum_{t=1}^{T} \gamma^t EE(t \mid s_t = s, a_t = a) \right] \tag{15}$$

where $\mathbb{E}$ is the expectation, γ^t represents the discount factor mapping from future rewards to the current state, and $0 < \gamma^t \leq 1$. Therefore, the power control strategy to maximize energy efficiency can be expressed by

$$\Phi^*(s_t) = \arg \max Q(s_t, a_t) \tag{16}$$

3.2 Deep Q-Network Method

In order to deal with the huge status-action space, Deep Neural Network (DNN) is used to deal with a large amount of training data to obtain the optimal Q value function. Through bellman optimality equation, the optimal state-action value function can be expressed as

$$Q(s_t, a_t) = (1 - \alpha)Q(s_t, a_t) + \alpha[r_t + \gamma \max Q(s_{t+1}, a_{t+1})] \tag{17}$$

where α is the learning rate that affects the learning speed and effect.

The most important update weight in DNN is updated by minimizing the loss function $L(\theta)$, where $L(\theta)$ can be expressed as

$$L(\theta) = E[(y_t - Q^*(s_t, a_t; \theta))^2] \tag{18}$$

where $y_t = r_t + \gamma \max Q(s_{t+1}, a_{t+1}; \theta^-)$. The weight θ and θ^- are the current and future update parameter in DNN, respectively. Then, the dynamic power control process in ultra-dense system is represented by Algorithm 1.

4   Emulation

This section presents the emulation settings and results of the dynamic power control framework based on DQN. In terms of the emulation environment, we consider an area of $1\,\text{km} * 1\,\text{km}^2$. CAP is deployed in the center of this area, with multiple small cells around it. Firstly, we make a comparison and determine the learning rate. Secondly, we compare the DQN algorithm with Q-learning algorithm, maximum power distribution method, and random power distribution. Finally, the performance of DQN algorithm and q-learning algorithm is compared and analyzed. Emulation results show that compared with Q-learning algorithm, the EE of DQN algorithm is significantly improved. As the number of UEs increase, the effect of DQN is still better than q-learning.

4.1   Emulation Environment

To evaluate the performance of our proposed solution, we use Python for emulation and analysis. The DNN used in the model contains two complete hidden layers of parameters. The more neurons, the better the experiment and the slower the program. There are 128 neurons in the first layer and 64 neurons in the second. Memory size is the size of the Memory bank. Batch size is the number of samples taken from the memory bank each time. Memory size and

Table 1. Hyper-parameters setup of DQN training

Parameter	Value
Number of T per episode	100
Observe episode number	100
Explore episode number	9900
Train interval	10
Initial η	10^{-3}
Initial ϵ	0.2
Final η	10^{-4}
Final ϵ	10^{-4}
Memory size	50000
Batch size	256
Number of BS(K)	$2, 4, 6, 8, 10, 12, 14$
Number of users in each BS(M)	$8, 10, 14, 18$

Batch size can control the accuracy and learning rate of DQN. It is implemented using Tensorflow 1.13. Table 1 lists the system settings. We set emulation parameters conforming to 5G specifications and standards. We assume system radius is 500 m. The system has one acer station and five small base stations. The number of BSs and UEs will be specified in the comparative experiment.

4.2   Learning Rate

Due to DQN algorithm is composed of Q-Learning and within DNN, and the learning rate is the most key parameters, adjusting the depth of the neural network training can influence the performance of the algorithm. When the learning rate is set too low, the agent can't get the last iteration of feedback, which may affect the long-term feedback situation, cause a long time of iteration to get the optimal strategy of convergence. On the contrary, if the learning rate is too high, it is difficult to converge to the optimal strategy. This is a defect of gradient descent in deep learning networks. Therefore, in this paper, the learning rate of 0.01, 0.001 and 0.0001 is respectively set, and the number of iterations is 10000, and the comparison is shown in Fig. 2. It can be seen from Fig. 2 that when the learning rate $\gamma = 0.01$, it converges to the 3000th iteration with a faster convergence rate and higher energy efficiency. Therefore, we choose the learning rate $\gamma = 0.01$ for our emulation.

4.3   Algorithm Comparison

In this subsection, we compared the algorithm from three aspects: time slot, number of UEs and number of BSs. As shown in Fig. 3, the emulation adopts DQN

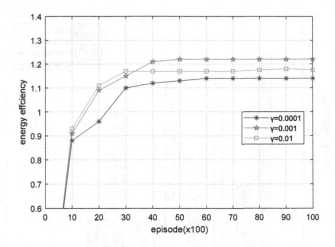

Fig. 2. Comparisons of different learning rate

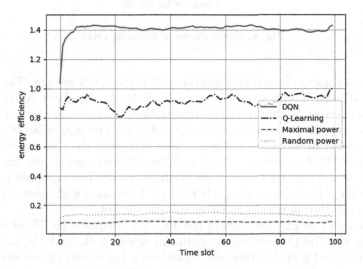

Fig. 3. Comparisons of all power allocation schemes

algorithm with learning rate of 0.01, Q-learning algorithm, maximum power distribution and random power distribution for com parison. With the change of time slot t, the UE task scale and channel gain keep changing, plus large-scale fading according to the change of distance, the emulation result EE fluctuates. According to the emulation results, maximum power and random power distribution is relatively stable but EE is too low, while Q-learning is relatively high but fluctuates a lot. Only DQN is smoother and have highest EE in these methods. In the real UDN environment, user density and location change with time, so DQN algorithm must have good generalization ability.

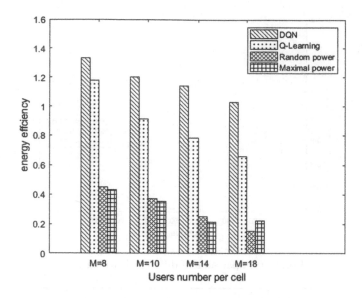

Fig. 4. Comparisons of different users

Figure 4 depicts the EE of a multi-user NOMA UDN system. The number of users M in each base station is set to be 8, 10, 14, 18. After 50 repetitions, the average result is obtained. The results show that as the number of users increases, the EE of DQN is greater than Q-Learning and other algorithms. As the number of users in the base station increases, the user interference in the uplink NOMA system increases, and the EE decreases as the interference increases. When the number of users per base station has increased to 18, the EE of the DQN has been significantly reduced. Compared with other algorithms, DQN has a flattering trend and EE is still the highest.

The number of BSs also affects the EE. We compare the EE of the DQN algorithm and the Q-Learning algorithm in different BS and UE numbers in Fig. 5. Since the EE of the other two algorithms is lower, only the results of DQN and Q-Learning are shown here. The number of BSs $K = 2, 4, 6, 8, 10, 12, 14$ and two kinds of UE density $M = 8, 10$ were used for the test. As the number of BS increases, the total energy consumption of the system increases, while the total uplink rate of the system remains unchanged. Therefore, as the number of BS increases, EE continues to decrease. DQN get a higher EE than Q-Learning in the test scenarios. From Fig. 5, the $M = 8$ scheme is better than the $M = 10$ scheme. When the $BS = 14$, the system with $M = 8$ can achieve almost 37% more energy efficiency than the system with $M = 10$ by DQN optimization. Under the resource limit of the same number of base stations, the DQN can obtain higher EE, which means users can get higher data rates and better service.

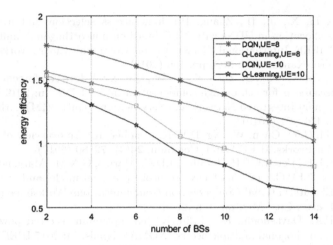

Fig. 5. Comparisons of different BSs and UEs

5   Conclusion

This paper studies the power control of uplink UDN multiuser devices based on NOMA. An efficient multi-user power control scheme based on DQN is proposed to solve the problem of user density and user equipment transmitting power control. In this scheme, NOMA technology and DQN algorithm are used to improve the capacity of users and the overall system, so as to obtain the optimal resource allocation scheme to improve energy efficiency. Emulation results show that EE is significantly improved compared with the traditional resource allocation algorithm. In future work, we will consider the resource allocation problem of mobile edge computing in UDN and deduce the optimal solution to this problem.

Acknowledgments. This work is partly supported by the National Natural Science Foundation of China (Nos. 61872044, 61902029), the Key Research and Cultivation Projects at Beijing Information Science and Technology University (No.5211910958), the Supplementary and Supportive Project for Teachers at Beijing Information Science and Technology University (No. 5111911128), Beijing Municipal Program for Top Talent Cultivation (CIT & TCD201804055) and Qinxin Talent Program of Beijing Information Science and Technology University.

References

1. Luong, N.C., Xiong, Z., Wang, P., Niyato, D.: Optimal auction for edge computing resource management in mobile blockchain networks: a deep learning approach. In: 2018 IEEE International Conference on Communications (ICC), Kansas City, MO, pp. 1–6 (2018)
2. Ericsson Mobility Report. https://www.ericsson.com/49d1d9/assets/local/mobility-report/documents/2019/ericsson-mobility-report-june-2019.pdf. Accessed 1 Oct 2019

3. Seng, S., Li, X., Ji, H., Zhang, H.: Joint access selection and heterogeneous resources allocation in UDNs with MEC based on non-orthogonal multiple access. In: 2018 IEEE International Conference on Communications Workshops (ICC Workshops), Kansas City, MO, pp. 1–6 (2018)
4. Yang, X., Yu, P., Feng, L., Zhou, F., Li, W., Qiu, X.: A deep reinforcement learning based mechanism for cell outage compensation in 5G UDN. In: 2019 IFIP/IEEE Symposium on Integrated Network and Service Management (IM), Arlington, VA, USA, pp. 476–481 (2019)
5. Wu, Q., Li, G.Y., Chen, W., Ng, D.W.K., Schober, R.: An overview of sustainable green 5G networks. IEEE Wirel. Commun. 24(4), 72–80 (2017)
6. de Souza, L.L., Pereira, P.H.M., Silva, J.D.C., Marins, C.N.M., Marcondes, G.A.B., Rodrigues, J.J.P.C..: IoT 5G-UDN protocols: practical model and evaluation. In: 2018 IEEE International Conference on Communications Workshops (ICC Workshops), Kansas City, MO, pp. 1–6 (2018)
7. Rabee, F.A., Davaslioglu, K., Gitlin, R.: The optimum received power levels of uplink non-orthogonal multiple access (NOMA) signals. In: 2017 IEEE 18th Wireless and Microwave Technology Conference (WAMICON), Cocoa Beach, FL, pp. 1–4 (2017)
8. Yin, Y., Peng, Y., Liu, M., Yang, J., Gui, G.: Dynamic user grouping-based NOMA over Rayleigh fading channels. IEEE Access 7, 110964–110971 (2019)
9. Sun, Y., Ding, Z., Dai, X., Dobre, O.A.: On the performance of network NOMA in uplink CoMP systems: a stochastic geometry approach. IEEE Trans. Commun. 67(7), 5084–5098 (2019)
10. Zeng, J., et al.: Investigation on evolving single-carrier NOMA into multi-carrier NOMA in 5G. IEEE Access 6, 48268–48288 (2018)
11. Fang, F., Cheng, J., Ding, Z.: Joint energy efficient subchannel and power optimization for a downlink NOMA heterogeneous network. IEEE Trans. Veh. Technol. 68(2), 1351–1364 (2019)
12. Liu, Y., Li, X., Ji, H., Zhang, H.: A multi-user access scheme for throughput enhancement in UDN with NOMA. In: 2017 IEEE International Conference on Communications Workshops (ICC Workshops), Paris, pp. 1364–1369 (2017)
13. Zhang, J., Xu, W., Chen, W., Gao, H., Lin, J.: Joint subcarrier assignment and downlink-uplink time-power allocation for wireless powered OFDM-NOMA systems. In: 2018 10th International Conference on Wireless Communications and Signal Processing (WCSP), Hangzhou, pp. 1–7 (2018)
14. Zhang, N., Wang, J., Kang, G., Liu, Y.: Uplink nonorthogonal multiple access in 5G systems. IEEE Commun. Lett. 20(3), 458–461 (2016)
15. Shahab, M.B., Irfan, M., Fazlul Kader, Md., Shin, S.Y.: User pairing schemes for capacity maximization in non-orthogonal multiple access systems. Wirel. Commun. Mob. Comput. 16, 2884–2894 (2016)
16. Shafi, M., et al.: 5G: a tutorial overview of standards trials challenges deployment and practice. IEEE JSAC 35(6), 1201–1221 (2017)
17. Fu, Y., Wen, W., Zhao, Z., Quek, T.Q.S., Jin, S., Zheng, F.: Dynamic power control for NOMA transmissions in wireless caching networks. IEEE Wirel. Commun. Lett. 8, 1485–1488 (2019)
18. Sun, Y., Wang, Y., Jiao, J., Wu, S., Zhang, Q.: Deep learning-based long-term power allocation scheme for NOMA downlink system in S-IoT. IEEE Access 7, 86288–86296 (2019)
19. Dai, Y., Xu, D., Maharjan, S., Chen, Z., He, Q., Zhang, Y.: Blockchain and deep reinforcement learning empowered intelligent 5G beyond. IEEE Netw. 33(3), 10–17 (2019)

Cooperative Traffic Signal Control Based on Multi-agent Reinforcement Learning

Ruowen Gao[(✉)], Zhihan Liu, Jinglin Li, and Quan Yuan

Beijing University of Posts and Telecommunications, Beijing 100876, China
{gaoruowen,zhihan,jlli,yuanquan}@bupt.edu.cn

Abstract. This paper proposes a traffic signal cooperative control algorithm based on multi-agent reinforcement learning (MARL), and design a framework of edge computing under traffic signal control scene. By introducing edge computing into the scene of traffic signal cooperative control, it will bring minimal response time and reduce network load. We abstracted the traffic signal control problem into the Markov decision process (MDP). The traffic state is discretized by feature extraction to avoid the curse of dimensionality. We propose a fusion of multi-agent reinforcement learning and coordination mechanisms through collaborative Q-values. The action selection strategy of an intersection depends not only on its own local reward, but also on the impact of other intersections. Different from considering only adjacent intersections, algorithm combines the static distance and dynamic traffic flow, and considers the cooperative relationship between neighbor and non-neighbor nodes. Finally, we show through simulation experiments on SUMO that our algorithm can effectively control traffic signal.

Keywords: Edge computing · Traffic signal control · Multi-agent reinforcement learning · Coordination mechanism · Fuzzy control

1 Introduction

Traffic signal control has become the common form of traffic management. There are many intelligent algorithms used in traffic signal control, such as fuzzy logic, genetic algorithms and so on. Reinforcement learning has also been applied by many scholars because of its no-model and self-study. El-Tantawy et al. [1], Arel et al. [2] applied reinforcement learning in traffic signal control, but they adopt full state representation.

The traffic flow at intersection is influential, then a few scholars such as Kok et al. [3] considered the coordination mechanism in traffic signal control. Medina et al. [4] used Max-plus algorithm to implement coordination, but utilized a model-based reinforcement learning that adds complexity to model-free methods such as Q-learning.

Because traffic signals control has the characteristics of real-time, it is difficult to deploy calculation and control process in the cloud. Edge computing has an irreplaceable role in real-time, short-period data, local strategy and other scenes. Therefore, traffic signal control can be better accomplished through edge computing, which has the advantages of mitigating network load and reducing response time. However, the application of edge computing in the field of traffic signal control has not received attention.

© Springer Nature Singapore Pte Ltd. 2020
Z. Zheng et al. (Eds.): BlockSys 2019, CCIS 1156, pp. 787–793, 2020.
https://doi.org/10.1007/978-981-15-2777-7_65

We propose a traffic signal cooperative control algorithm and design a framework of edge computing to solve these problems. The main contributions are as follows:

(1) An edge computing architecture under the traffic signal cooperative control scene is proposed, and various cooperation modes between the remote cloud server and various edge nodes are considered.
(2) A traffic signal control scheme based on MARL is proposed. We define the edge and non-edge intersections, and consider the different optimization targets. In addition, the traffic state is discretized by feature extraction.
(3) We integrate MARL and coordination mechanisms through collaborative Q-value. The action selection strategy of intersection depends not only on its own local returns, but also on the impact of other intersections.

2   System Model and Problem Formulation

2.1   The Framework of Edge-Assisted Traffic Signal Control

A three-tier framework for edge computing in traffic signal cooperative control scene is designed as shown in Fig. 1, which mainly includes edge computing nodes, coordinator nodes, and remote cloud server terminals.

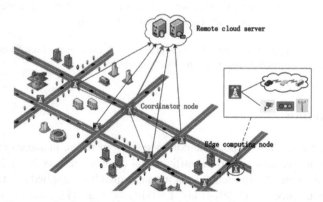

Fig. 1. Framework of traffic signal cooperative control based on edge computing.

A roadside unit is selected as edge computing node at each intersection, and is mainly used to sense traffic data of intersection. In order to reduce the pressure of storing massive data, edge computing node performs targeted data preprocessing work, such as data cleaning, data integration. On the premise that each edge computing node completes data collection and preprocessing, the remote cloud server performs certain processing according to the valid information transmitted by edge computing nodes as the central control. When coordinated control is performed on a large-scale road network, the remote cloud server first divides the network into different sub-areas and chooses the coordinator node in each sub-area. The remote cloud server broadcasts the division and selection results to the coordinator nodes of each sub-area, and coordinator nodes broadcast the partition attribution information to all edge computing nodes in the sub-area. The coordinator node is mainly used to collect useful information from edge computing nodes in the sub-area, and design a reasonable sub-area traffic signal control scheme, and send the scheme to each edge computing node. Then the edge computing node manages the traffic signal of the intersection according to the control results.

2.2 Building MDP

The traffic signal control problem can be modeled as MDP. The MDP framework requires a description of states, actions, and rewards. For multi-intersection cooperative control, rewards will be defined in the next section.

States: For intersection i, we define its state s^i as a vector of length P, $s^i = (d_1^i, d_2^i, \cdots, d_P^i)$, where P is the number of phases of the intersection and d_j^i is the traffic demand of phase j in intersection i. We discretize the traffic state by feature extraction, considering the two factors of traffic density and the waiting time of the lead vehicle.

We divide the variables into different fuzzy sets. The defined fuzzy sets for traffic density are $\{VS, S, M, B, VB\}$. $\bar{w}_j^i$ represents the level of traffic density, and is the maximum value of traffic density level of all lanes in the phase, $\bar{w}_j^i = \max\left(\bar{w}_{j_1}^i, \ldots, \bar{w}_{j_L}^i\right)$. We select trapezoidal and triangular membership functions, and define the membership functions of traffic density $w_{j_l}^i$ and traffic density levels $\bar{w}_{j_l}^i$ depicted in Fig. 2(a). Similarly, the waiting time of lead vehicle is discretized into: $\{VL, L, M, H, VH\}$. $\bar{q}_j^i$ represents the level of the waiting time of lead vehicle, $\bar{q}_j^i = \max\left(\bar{q}_{j_1}^i, \cdots, \bar{q}_{j_L}^i\right)$. The membership functions of waiting time $q_{j_l}^i$ and waiting time levels $\bar{q}_{j_l}^i$ is depicted in Fig. 2(b).

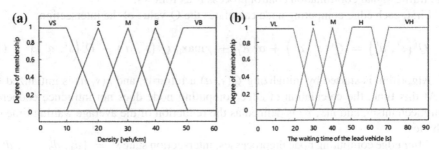

Fig. 2. (a) Traffic density membership functions. (b) Waiting time membership functions.

Traffic demand of phase d_j^i is based on the fuzzy control rules, and discretized into $\{VL, L, M, H, VH\}$. The discrete value is used to indicate the demand level. The higher the value, the higher the demand for the phase. We define 25 fuzzy control rules based on experience, as shown in Table 1. Therefore, for intersection i, the traffic demand $(d_1^i, d_2^i, \cdots, d_P^i)$ of all phases constitutes the state space s^i of the intersection.

Table 1. The fuzzy control rules.

d^i_{jl}		$\bar{w}^i_{jl}$				
		VS	S	M	B	VB
$\bar{q}^i_{jl}$	VL	VL	VL	L	M	H
	L	VL	VL	L	M	H
	M	VL	L	M	H	VH
	H	L	L	M	H	VH
	VH	L	M	H	VH	VH

Actions: For intersection i, the action is the phase of the next pass, $a^i = p^i_j$. Action affects the phase sequence and the phase duration. Consider these situations: P^i_{act} is the calculated target green phase and P^i_{cur} is the current green phase. If P^i_{act} is the same as P^i_{cur} direction, extend the green time of P^i_{cur} to maximum green duration MAX_{gre}. If directions are different, consider two cases: (a) If the P^i_{cur} duration is less than MIN_{gre}, first set the green duration of P^i_{cur} to MIN_{gre}. After waiting for the minimum green duration, set the next green phase to P^i_{act}; (b) If the P^i_{cur} duration is greater than MIN_{gre}, the green phase directly goes to P^i_{cur}, but still needs to go through the yellow light stage.

3   Proposed Algorithm

We use MARL to solve MDP to obtain traffic signal control strategy. The Q-learning algorithm [5] is an off-policy temporal difference learning algorithm. It uses the Q-value to represent the maximum discounted sum of long-term rewards by the optimal policy. The traffic signal coordination control process is as follows:

First, each edge computing node calculates the Q-value of the intersection:

$$Q^i\left(s^i, a^i\right) = Q^i\left(s^i, a^i\right) + \alpha\left[R^i_L + \gamma\max_{a'} Q^i\left(s', a'\right) - Q^i\left(s^i, a^i\right)\right] \quad (1)$$

Algorithm is started by initializing $Q(s, a)$ arbitrarily, and $r(s, a)$ is initialized to 0. At this time, the calculation of edge computing node does not introduce cooperation mechanism, and $r(s, a)$ is defined as the reduction of the average waiting time of vehicles.

After edge computing node preprocesses, intersection state $s^i = \left(d^i_1, d^i_2, \cdots, d^i_p\right)$ and the corresponding phase set $M^i = \{(n^i_1, p^i_1), (n^i_2, p^i_2) \ldots (n^i_N, p^i_P)\}$ are sent to the coordinator node. P indicates the number of phases of the intersection, N indicates the number of neighbors of the intersection, (n^i_1, p^i_1) indicates that the phase of the signal associated with the lane associated with the neighbor node n^i_1 of the intersection i is p^i_1.

The coordinator node calculates the influence factor based on the physical spacing and the actual traffic flow. We define $f(i, j)$ as the influence factor of the intersections j after the intersection i takes an action. Considering the following three situations: (a) The intersection i and j are adjacent, and the lane corresponding to the green phase after the action of i leads to the j. At this time, the action of i will increase the additional traffic demand at j. The definition of the influence factor is as follows:

$$f(i, j) = \frac{1}{g_{ij}}\left(d^{j}_{desP} + \Delta d_{ij}\right) \tag{2}$$

d^{j}_{desP} represents the traffic demand of intersection j, and g_{ij} represents the physical distance between the intersections. Δd_{ij} represents the increased traffic demand. (b) The intersection i is adjacent to j, but the lane corresponding to the green phase after the intersection i takes an action does not lead to the j. We define the influence factor as d^{j}_{desP}/g_{ij}. (c) Intersection i and j are not adjacent. At this time, only the influence of the physical distance between the intersections is considered, that is, $1/g_{ij}$.

Then, the instant reward of the intersection is updated as follows:

$$R^{i} = \sigma_1 R^{i}_{L} + \sigma_2 R^{i}_{N}, \sigma_1 + \sigma_2 = 1 \tag{3}$$

R^{i}_{L} indicates the local returns and is defined as the reduced average waiting time of the vehicles of intersection. R^{i}_{N} indicates the impact on the other intersections after the intersection takes an action. M represents the number of intersections in the sub-area:

$$R^{i}_{N_i} = \frac{f(i, 1) * Q^1(s^1, a^1) + f(i, 2) * Q^2(s^2, a^2) + \ldots + f(i, M) * Q^M(s^M, a^M)}{f(i, 1) + f(i, 2) + \ldots + f(i, M)} \tag{4}$$

In order to maximize traffic flow away from the saturated area, we consider the different optimization targets, and define the boundary of saturated and unsaturated regions as edge intersections, and the other internal intersections are non-edge intersections. Edge intersection is the breakthrough of saturated area, and it emphasizes that it can quickly reduce the saturation, so $\sigma_1 > \sigma_2$. For non-edge intersections, it emphasizes reducing the average saturation in the area and weakening its own return, so $\sigma_1 < \sigma_2$.

4 Evaluation

SUMO [6] simulation software is used to evaluate the algorithm. We experiment in simulation road network in which 4*4 intersections are arranged unevenly. We considered two scenes for different traffic flows. In scene 1, road network is a light traffic flow. In scene 2, the center four intersections are defined as non-edge intersections, that is, the relevant area is saturated, and the other outer intersections are edge intersections. Webster Algorithm and non-cooperative algorithm are used to compare with our algorithm. The non-cooperative algorithm abstracts the traffic signal control problem into the MDP of Sect. 3 without cooperation mechanism. We calculated the average waiting time of the vehicles passing through at least 4 intersections. The results as follows (Table 2):

Table 2. The average waiting time of the vehicle.

Method	Cooperative	Non-cooperative	Webster
Scene 1	19.6 s/veh	24.5 s/veh	31.3 s/veh
Scene 2	51.8 s/veh	76.6 s/veh	89.0 s/veh

In scene 2, we selected several representative intersections to further reflect the control effect, the results are shown in Fig. 3. The abscissa represents the intersection id. The ordinate is the average waiting time of the intersection, which represents the average waiting time for a single vehicle at a single intersection.

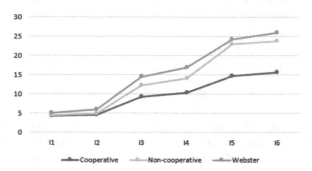

Fig. 3. The average waiting time of the intersection.

The experimental results show that under the light traffic flow and saturated traffic flow, the designed algorithm can achieve effective traffic signals control, and the control effect is more significant at saturated intersections. This is because the algorithm we designed can interact with the environment to adaptively adjust the signal control strategy, and introduces a coordination mechanism between intersections. Under the saturated traffic flow, multi-objective optimization is also applied to the edge intersections and non-edge intersections, and the vehicle dissipated in the saturated region is gradually realized. In addition, we have tried five iterations of 500 rounds for the designed algorithm. The experimental results have the characteristics of co-frequency oscillation, which shows that the algorithm has certain stability.

5 Conclusion and Future Works

This paper designs a framework of edge computing under traffic signal control scene, which effectively reduces response time and reduces network load. We also propose a traffic signal control algorithm based on MARL and coordination mechanisms.

In this paper, the traffic network is regarded as a distributed multi-agent system. The sharing knowledge such as Q-table between the intersections needs to be supported by the communication mechanism, then improving the efficiency of message transmission is worthy studying. In addition, we also can use the deep neural network to approximate the Q-value function in future work.

Acknowledgments. This work was supported in part by the Natural Science Foundation of China under Grant 61876023 and Grant 61902035, and in part by the Natural Science Foundation of Beijing under Grant 4181002.

References

1. El-Tantawy, S., Abdulhai, B.: An agent-based learning towards decentralized and coordinated traffic signal control. In: 2010 13th International IEEE Conference on Intelligent Transportation Systems (ITSC). IEEE (2010)
2. Arel, I., Liu, C., Urbanik, T., et al.: Reinforcement learning-based multi-agent system for network traffic signal control. IET Intell. Transp. Syst. **4**(2), 128 (2010)
3. Kok, J.R., Vlassis, N.: Using the max-plus algorithm for multiagent decision making in coordination graphs. In: Bredenfeld, A., Jacoff, A., Noda, I., Takahashi, Y. (eds.) RoboCup 2005. LNCS (LNAI), vol. 4020, pp. 1–12. Springer, Heidelberg (2006). https://doi.org/10.1007/11780519_1
4. Medina, J.C., Benekohal, R.F.: Traffic signal control using reinforcement learning and the max-plus algorithm as a coordinating strategy. In: 2012 15th International IEEE Conference on Intelligent Transportation Systems (ITSC), pp. 596–601. IEEE (2012)
5. Watkins, C.J.C.H., Dayan, P.: Q-learning. Mach. Learn. **8**(3–4), 279–292 (1992)
6. Krajzewicz, D., Hertkorn, G., Rossel, C.: SUMO (simulation of urban mobility). In: Proceedings of the 4th middle East Symposium on Simulation and Modelling, pp. 183–187 (2002)

A Trustworthiness-Based Time-Efficient V2I Authentication Scheme for VANETs

Chen Wang[1,2], Jian Shen[1,2], Jin-Feng Lai[3], and Jianwei Liu[4(✉)]

[1] School of Computer and Software,
Nanjing University of Information Science and Technology, Nanjing 210044, China
wangchennuist@126.com, s_shenjian@126.com
[2] Cyberspace Security Research Center, Peng Cheng Laboratory,
Shenzhen 518000, China
[3] School of Information and Communication Engineering,
University of Electronic Science and Technology of China, Chengdu, China
lcf2018@uestc.edu.cn
[4] School of Cyber Science and Technology, Beihang University, Beijing 100191, China
liujianwei@buaa.edu.cn

Abstract. Many researchers have conducted many researches on secure communication in VANETs, which have focused on secure V2V or V2I communications. However, current security schemes often require complex identity re-authentication when vehicles enter a new infrastructure coverage, which will greatly reduce the efficiency of the entire network. The proposed trustworthiness-based time-efficient vehicle to infrastructure authentication scheme in this paper achieves rapid re-authentication of vehicles through secure ownership transfer between infrastructures.

Keywords: Trustworthiness evaluation · V2I authentication · VANET · Time-efficient · Handover

1 Introduction

The development of the next generation networks and cloud computing push the researches of intelligent transportation [1,8,9]. Vehicular ad hoc networks (VANETs) are the most considered network model for an intelligent transportation system. Vehicles in the network can communicate with each other, which is referred to as the vehicle-to-vehicle (V2V) communication [2,5]. Additionally, roadside infrastructure also communicates with vehicles, known as the vehicle-to-infrastructure (V2I) communication. Secure V2I communication can provide a channel for uploading vehicle attribute parameters and their surrounding road condition information. At the same time, the release of the traffic summary information from the remote server can also be guaranteed.

1.1 Motivation

However, most schemes nowadays designed for V2I communication require the vehicles to re-authenticate with every RSU when they join in the ranges of

© Springer Nature Singapore Pte Ltd. 2020
Z. Zheng et al. (Eds.): BlockSys 2019, CCIS 1156, pp. 794–799, 2020.
https://doi.org/10.1007/978-981-15-2777-7_66

different RSUs. Although this authentication method can authenticate the identity of the vehicle every time, it also brings about problems such as large communication overhead and redundant operation.

Our Contributions. In this paper, a possible solution to the above problem is presented. The novel scheme is named as a trustworthiness-based time-efficient V2I authentication scheme. The contributions can be described as follows:

An Efficient V2I Authentication Phase is Proposed for a Newcomer. For the new vehicles entering the network, this paper gives a detailed handover authentication process. Operations are simplified by the protocol when a vehicle is already authenticated by an RSU in the network.

Trustworthiness Evaluation is Utilized to Strengthen the Authentication Process. The trustworthiness of a vehicle is evaluated by the cloud and help the RSUs to authenticate and accept the vehicle.

1.2 Related Work

Many researches have been made to achieve high-efficient authentication in VANETs. Hao et al. [4] proposed security protocols to detect compromised RSUs and their colluding malicious vehicles. They established a distributed key management framework to revoke the rights of malicious vehicles. The key distribution protocol presented in their paper was claimed to be able to prevent RSUs from misbehaving. Chen et al. [3] proposed a beacon-based trust management system to resist internal attacks from sending false messages in VANETs. Additionally, the system enhances the location privacy of VANETs. Qu et al. [7] provided background information of VANETs and classify security issues in VANETs. They present the general secure process and point out corresponding authentication methods. They also review privacy preserving methods and discuss the tradeoff between security and privacy. To achieve safety message authentication in VANETs, Oulhaci et al. [6] proposed a secure and distributed certification system architecture. This architecture is claimed to be able to resist against false public-key certification. The simulation results in their paper show the robustness of their new design. However, their paper also points out that the scheme needs to be further strengthened in terms of privacy.

1.3 Organization

The remainder of this paper is organized as follows. Section 2 presents some preliminaries of this paper, including bilinear pairing and the method of trustworthiness evaluation. Section 3 presents the proposed scheme. Section 4 provides the performance analysis. Finally, the conclusion is drawn in Sect. 5.

2 Preliminaries

In this section, some necessary preliminaries utilized in this paper are listed, including bilinear pairing and the method of trustworthiness evaluation.

2.1   Bilinear Pairing

Let $\mathbb{G}_1$ and $\mathbb{G}_2$ be two groups of the same prime order q. Let $\mathbb{G}_1$ be an additively written group, and let $\mathbb{G}_2$ be a multiplicatively written group. Given a mapping e, a bilinear pairing on $(\mathbb{G}_1, \mathbb{G}_2)$: $\mathbb{G}_1^2 \to \mathbb{G}_2$ satisfying the following properties is called a cryptographic bilinear map.

Bilinearity. $e(aP, bQ) = e(P, Q)^{ab}$ for all $P, Q \in \mathbb{G}_1$ and $a, b \in Z_q^*$. This can be expressed in the following manner. For $P, Q, R \in \mathbb{G}_1$, $e(P + Q, R) = e(P, R)e(Q, R)$ and $e(P, Q + R) = e(P, Q)e(P, R)$.

Non-degeneracy. If P is a generator of $\mathbb{G}_1$, then $e(P, P)$ is a generator of $\mathbb{G}_2$. In other words, $e(P, P) \neq 1$.

Computability. e can be efficiently computed.

2.2   Trustworthiness Evaluation

The definition of trustworthiness can ba found in [10]. The vehicle trustworthiness $\mathfrak{T}$ of a vehicle is calculated by cloud server according to the attributes of this vehicle.

3   Our Proposed Scheme

In this section, the proposed time-efficient V2I authentication scheme is detailedly described.

3.1   Overview of Our Scheme

In view of the problem of secure handover of vehicles between two adjacent RSUs, we propose a trustworthiness-based time-efficient V2I authentication scheme. Figure 1 depicts the application scenario of the proposed scheme. The general process of the scheme is as follows. First, based on the current trustworthiness level of the vehicle, the RSU and the vehicle complete the authentication and generate a initial session key. Then, when the RSU communication range to which the vehicle belongs changes, the previous RSU sends a handover certificate (OC) to the next RSU and the vehicle, and the latter RSU sends a token to the vehicle. Finally, the vehicle resumes communication with the roadside infrastructure after the vehicle and the latter RSU simultaneously calculate the corresponding session key.

3.2   Setup Phase

The setup phase aims to generate public and private key pairs for vehicles and roadside infrastructures. The key generation center (KGC) generates a bilinear paring $\hat{e} : G \times G \to G_T$, where G and G_T are two cyclic groups with order p satisfying the mapping relation. Hash functions $H1, H_2, H_3$ are chosen as: $H_1 : G \to \{0,1\}^*$, $H_2, H_3 : \{0,1\}^* \to Z_p^*$ Besides, g and h are two different generators in the group G. $a_i, a_{i+1}, \cdots$ are randomly chosen from non-zero integer group Z_p^* with prime order p for roadside infrastructure $RSU_i, RSU_{i+1}, \cdots$.

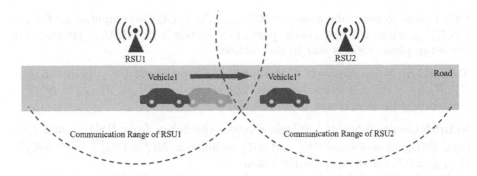

Fig. 1. Description of the proposed scheme

3.3 V2I-Initial Authentication Phase

The second phase of the proposed scheme is named as V2I-initial authentication phase. This phase aims to help a RSU authenticate a vehicle's identity when the vehicle participate in the network under the signal coverage of the RSU and generate a session key for the RSU and this vehicle. This phase is composed of three phases: **PreKeyGen**, **VehiSKGen** and **RSUSKGen**.

PreKeyGen: The RSU and the vehicle generate a Diffie-Hellman secret key with each other's public key, respectively. RSU_i calculates $SK_1 = (PK_{v,1})^{a_i}$ and the vehicle calculates $SK_1 = (PKI_{i,1})^u$, where a_i and u are the private key of RSU_i and the vehicle. Then, RSU_i chooses $r_i \in Z_p^*$. $R_{i,1} = g^{r_i}$ is calculated and kept secret by RSU_i. $R_{i,2} = h^{r_i}$ is then calculated and sent to the vehicle together with a timestamp T_1 recored before sending the message.

VehiSKGen: In this algorithm, the vehicle check the timestamp T_i from RSU_i. Then, the vehicle calculates SK_2: $SK_2 = R_{i,2} \cdot PKI_{i,2}^{uH_2(ID\|T_1\|H_1(SK_1))}$,
Finally, the vehicle computes the session key SK: $SK = \hat{e}(SK_2, g)$.

RSUSKGen: RSU_i calculates SK_3: $SK_3 = R_{i,1} \cdot SK_1^{H_2(ID\|T_1\|H_1(SK_1))}$.
Finally, RSU_i computes the session key SK: $SK = \hat{e}(h, SK_3)$.

3.4 V2I-Handover Authentication Phase

The third phase of the proposed scheme is named as the V2I-handover authentication phase. When a vehicle exits the signal coverage of the previous RSU and enters the coverage of the next RSU, the system performs this phase to hand over the communication between the vehicle and the infrastructure to the next RSU.

OCGen: This algorithm is performed by RSU_i to generate handover certificate (OC) to RSU_{i+1} and the vehicle. RSU_i chooses a random number $r \in Z_p^*$. OC_1 is computed as: $OC_1 = SK_1^{rH_3(SK)}$, where SK_1 is calculated in the algorithm PreKeyGen and SK is the session key generated in the algorithm RSUSKGen.

OC_1 is sent to next infrastructure RSU$_{i+1}$. Then, OC_2 is computed as: $OC_2 = PKI_{i+1,2}^{a_i r}$, where $PKI_{i+1,2}$ is the part of the public key of RSU$_{i+1}$ generated in the setup phase. OC_2 is sent to the vehicle.

TokenGen: When received OC_1 from RSU$_i$, a random value r_{i+1} is chosen from Z_p^*. $R_{i+1,1} = g^{r_i+1}$ is calculated and kept secret by RSU$_{i+1}$. $R_{i+1,2} = h^{r_i+1}$ is treated as a token and sent to the vehicle.

VehiSKGen2: When the vehicle receives the token from RSU$_{i+1}$ and OC_2 from RSU$_i$, he computes SK_1^* and SK_2^* as follows: $SK_1^* = OC_2^{uH_3(SK)}$, $SK_2^* = R_{i+1,2} \cdot SK_1^*$, where $R_{i+1,2}$ is the token.
   Finally, SK^* of the vehicle is calculated as: $SK^* = \hat{e}(SK_2^*, g)$.

RSUSKGen2: RSU_{i+1} also computes SK_1^* and SK_3^* as follows: $SK_1^* = OC_1^{a_{i+1}}$, $SK_3^* = R_{i+1,1} \cdot SK_1^*$.
   Finally, SK^* of RSU_{i+1} is calculated as: $SK^* = \hat{e}(h, SK_3^*)$.

4   Performance Analysis

The proposed scheme is simulated on GNU Multiple Precision Arithmetic (GMP) library and Pairing-Based Cryptography (PBC) library[1] to show its efficiency. C language is utilized on a Linux system with Ubuntu 16.04 TLS, a 2.60 GHz Intel(R) Xeon(R) CPU E5-2650 v2, and 8 GB of RAM. The results are shown in Fig. 2. The time cost on the designed handover authentication phase is reduced by half compared to the time required for the initial authentication phase.

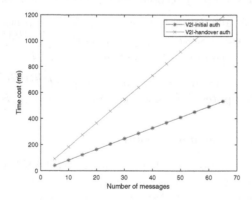

Fig. 2. The overhead comparison of a vehicle in different phases in the proposed scheme

---

[1] https://crypto.stanford.edu/pbc/.

5   Conclusion

To reduce the time cost of re-authentication for a vehicle who has been already authenticated by an infrastructure in the network when it enters a new infrastructure coverage, a novel trustworthiness-based time-efficient V2I authentication scheme is proposed in this paper. The scheme is composed of two phases: V2I-initial authentication phase and V2I-handover authentication. Handover phase reduce the time cost of authentication phase.

Acknowledgment. This work is supported by the National Natural Science Foundation of China under Grant No. 61922045, No. 61672295, No. U1836115, the Peng Cheng Laboratory Project of Guangdong Province PCL2018KP004, the State Key Laboratory of Cryptology under Grant No. MMKFKT201830, the 2015 Project of Six Personnel in Jiangsu Province under Grant No. R2015L06, the CICAEET fund, and the PAPD fund.

References

1. Chen, X., Huang, X., Jin, L., Ma, J., Lou, W., Wong, D.S.: New algorithms for secure outsourcing of large-scale systems of linear equations. IEEE Trans. Inf. Forensics Secur. **10**(1), 69–78 (2014)
2. Chen, X., Li, J., Weng, J., Ma, J., Lou, W.: Verifiable computation over large database with incremental updates. IEEE Trans. Comput. **65**(10), 3184–3195 (2016)
3. Chen, Y.M., Wei, Y.C.: A beacon-based trust management system for enhancing user centric location privacy in VANETs. J. Commun. Netw. **15**(2), 153–163 (2013)
4. Hao, Y., Cheng, Y., Zhou, C., Song, W.: A distributed key management framework with cooperative message authentication in VANETs. IEEE J. Sel. Areas Commun. **29**(3), 616–629 (2011)
5. Jiang, T., Chen, X., Ma, J.: Public integrity auditing for shared dynamic cloud data with group user revocation. IEEE Trans. Comput. **65**(8), 2363–2373 (2016)
6. Oulhaci, T., Omar, M., Harzine, F., Harfi, I.: Secure and distributed certification system architecture for safety message authentication in VANET. Telecommun. Syst. **64**, 1–16 (2017)
7. Qu, F., Wu, Z., Wang, F.Y., Cho, W.: A security and privacy review of VANETs. IEEE Trans. Intell. Transp. Syst. **16**(6), 2985–2996 (2015)
8. Shen, J., Liu, D., Lai, C.F., Ren, Y., Sun, X.: A secure identity-based dynamic group data sharing scheme for cloud computing. J. Internet Technol. **18**(4), 833–842 (2017)
9. Wang, C., Shen, J., Liu, Q., Ren, Y., Li, T.: A novel security scheme based on instant encrypted transmission for internet of things. Secur. Commun. Netw. (2018). https://doi.org/10.1155/2018/3680851
10. Wang, C., Xiao, L., Shen, J., Huang, R.: Neighborhood trustworthiness-based vehicle-to-vehicle authentication scheme for vehicular ad hoc networks. Concurrency Comput.: Practice Exp. (2018). https://doi.org/10.1002/cpe4643

Retraction Note to: Urban Jobs-Housing Zone Division Based on Mobile Phone Data

Xiaoming Liu, Luxi Dong, Meijie Jia, and Jiyuan Tan

Retraction Note to:
Chapter "Urban Jobs-Housing Zone Division Based on Mobile
Phone Data" in: Z. Zheng et al. (Eds.): *Blockchain*
and Trustworthy Systems, **CCIS 1156,**
https://doi.org/10.1007/978-981-15-2777-7_43

This conference paper is retracted on request of co-author Luxi Dong. After publication, Luxi Dong informed the publisher that he submitted the manuscript and signed the copyright transfer form on behalf of all co-authors without informing them and provided a false email address of the corresponding author to the publisher. The other co-authors confirmed that they were not aware of publication of this conference paper. All authors agree to this retraction.

The retracted version of this chapter can be found at
https://doi.org/10.1007/978-981-15-2777-7_43

Author Index

Bai, Xiaoying 267
Bandara, Eranga 431
Barati, Masoud 322

Cai, Jiahong 702
Cai, Ting 621, 676
Cao, Yuanlong 363
Chen, Chuan 621
Chen, Deyi 598
Chen, Gongliang 33
Chen, Hongjun 740
Chen, Lin 226
Chen, Pengfei 715
Chen, Shaolong 363
Chen, Wuhui 676
Chen, Xi 491
Chen, Xiangping 461
Chen, Xican 371
Chen, Xin 385, 774
Chen, Xing 483
Chen, Xingren 123
Chen, Xuehong 60
Chen, Yan 483
Chen, Ying 385, 774
Chen, Zhong 505
Cheng, Tong 47
Cheng, Xiaohui 101
Cui, Qimei 410

De Zoysa, Kasun 431
Deng, Han 747
Deng, Yifan 752
Doan, Kimberly 226
Dong, Luxi 534
Du, Erxin 621
Du, Shiyu 422

Fan, Haopeng 476
Fan, Lei 33
Fan, Xing 137
Fan, Xinxin 226
Fan, Yongkai 636, 702
Feng, Chenhui 662

Fu, Jinhua 92
Fu, Qi 740
Fu, Xiang 662

Gao, Jianbo 505
Gao, Kui 648
Gao, Ruowen 787
Gao, Siyi 371
Gao, Zhen 150
Gao, Zhimin 226
Gu, Chunxiang 491
Gu, Jujuan 422
Gui, Qiong 101
Guo, Zhaohui 150

Han, Tingting 648
He, Qian 607
He, Yun-Hua 288
Hong, James Won-Ki 520, 591
Hong, Kai 461
Hong, Zhenting 636
Hu, Cheng 275
Hu, Shili 336, 761
Hu, Yan 288
Huang, Hualong 397
Huang, Yongzhong 92
Huang, Yuan 461
Huang, Zhihao 483

Jeong, Taeyeol 591
Jia, Meijie 534
Jia, Nan 461
Jiang, Bingcheng 607
Jiang, Xin 732
Jiang, Yan 563

Ko, Kyungchan 520, 591

Lai, Jin-Feng 794
Lee, Chaehyeon 520, 591
Lei, Xia 636, 702
Li, Bin 92
Li, Fengying 185

Li, Hong   288
Li, Ji   491
Li, Jiangfeng   336, 761
Li, Jianping   574
Li, Jinglin   787
Li, Kuan-Ching   350, 702
Li, Lu   740
Li, Peng   137
Li, Xiaoli   621
Li, Xiaoyun   715
Li, Xuecong   607
Li, Yang   549
Li, Yijing   410
Li, Yue   505
Li, Zhuo   385, 774
Li, Zujian   175
Liang, Haodong   397
Liang, Wei   350, 563, 702, 740
Liu, Cailing   598
Liu, Chao   505
Liu, Jiaheng   92
Liu, Jianwei   794
Liu, Ji-Yao   288
Liu, Junjie   410
Liu, Mingzhe   732
Liu, Shuyan   690
Liu, Xiaoming   534
Liu, Xu   774
Liu, Yang   648
Liu, Ying   446
Liu, Yuan   123
Liu, Yujiong   422
Liu, Zhanghui   483
Liu, Zhihan   787
Liu, Zhongxing   185
Liu, Zilu   549
Lu, Siqi   476
Lu, Zihao   446
Luo, Peiran   3
Lyu, Peng-Hui   582

Ma, Junjie   636
Ma, Zhaohui   161
Maharjan, Sajan   520, 591
Meng, Xiangwei   350
Mi, Huizhe   476

Ng, Wee Keong   196, 431
Ning, Zuoting   740

Niu, Baoning   137
Niu, Tong   101

Ouyang, Jianquan   109, 752

Pan, Heng   240
Peng, Cong   636
Peng, Kai   397
Peng, Li   350

Qian, Xingda   397
Qin, Kuangyu   607
Qin, Ling   476
Qin, Panke   15
Qin, Xing   607

Rana, Omer   322
Ranasinghe, Nalin   431

Sharma, Shantanu   196
Shen, Jian   794
Shi, Peichang   662
Shi, Weidong   226
Shi, Yang   336
Shi, Youqun   446
Si, Xueming   92, 240
Song, Zhe   47
Su, Yinxue   3
Sun, Li-Min   288
Sun, Qibo   371, 422
Sun, Xiaofeng   636
Sun, Yuxiang   109

Tan, Jiyuan   534
Tan, Minfu   747
Tang, Huanrong   752
Tang, Jintian   563
Tang, Mingdong   275, 563
Tang, Yongli   15
Tao, Ran   446
Tao, Xiaofeng   410
Tian, Haibo   3
Tong, Nian   81
Tong, Ran   582

Wan, Yadong   363
Wang, Chao   288
Wang, Chen   794
Wang, Hao   363

Wang, Jie 60
Wang, Jing 212
Wang, Jinghan 636
Wang, Jinhai 212
Wang, Kun 732
Wang, Lingfu 212
Wang, Tao 662
Wang, Wenbo 15
Wang, Yanjie 574
Wang, Yong 47
Wang, Yongfeng 715
Wang, Yongjuan 92, 476
Wang, Yujue 81
Wei, Fushan 491
Wei, Rui Yuan 582
Wu, Bilian 385
Wu, Xiaonian 81

Xia, Fanglue 636
Xiao, Lijun 747
Xiao, Weidong 747
Xie, Chunmei 305
Xie, Songyou 305
Xie, Yong 563
Xu, Hai-Chuan 71
Xu, Heyang 648
Xu, Jianbo 350
Xu, Lei 226
Xu, Maozhi 60
Xu, Shouhuai 226
Xu, Shumei 258
Xu, Zisang 350

Yan, Bin 715
Yan, Qiang 621
Yan, Xixi 15
Yang, Chen 732
Yang, Guoyu 185
Yang, Jinsheng 150
Yang, Ningbin 258
Yang, Ru 690

Yang, Wei 363
Yang, Yan 161
Yao, Zhongyuan 240
Ye, Qing 15
Ye, Zhibo 81
Yeh, Wei-Chang 212
Yin, Jiajun 109
Yu, Jianjian 33
Yu, Xinying 185
Yu, Yang 676
Yu, Yifan 761
Yuan, Quan 787

Zan, Chao 71
Zeng, Qiubing 662
Zhai, Jianhong 690
Zhang, Ao 267
Zhang, Chenxi 336, 761
Zhang, Hong 732
Zhang, Hongyi 598
Zhang, Jichuan 690
Zhang, Jing 15
Zhang, Meng 60
Zhang, Shuangfeng 123
Zhang, Xuefei 410
Zhang, Xunhui 662
Zhang, Yiwen 397
Zhang, Zhaohui 446
Zhang, Zhihong 175
Zhang, Zhiming 363
Zhao, Yifeng 740
Zhao, Yulong 137
Zhao, Zongqu 15
Zheng, Xiaodong 305
Zheng, Zibin 549, 621
Zhou, Ao 371
Zhou, Quan 258
Zhou, Xiaocong 461
Zhu, Wei 305
Zhu, Weihua 240

Printed in the United States
by Baker & Taylor Publisher Services